THE GREAT

CONTEMPORARY

ISSUES

POPULAR CULTURE

THE GREAT CONTEMPORARY ISSUES

OTHER BOOKS IN THE SERIES

DRUGS
Introduction by J. Anthony Lukas

THE MASS MEDIA AND POLITICS
Introduction by Walter Cronkite

CHINA
O. Edmund Clubb, *Advisory Editor*

LABOR AND MANAGEMENT
Richard B. Morris, *Advisory Editor*

WOMEN: THEIR CHANGING ROLES
Elizabeth Janeway, *Advisory Editor*

BLACK AFRICA
Hollis R. Lynch, *Advisory Editor*

EDUCATION, U.S.A.
James Cass, *Advisory Editor*

VALUES AMERICANS LIVE BY
Garry Wills, *Advisory Editor*

CRIME AND JUSTICE
Ramsey Clark, *Advisory Editor*

JAPAN
Edwin O. Reischauer, *Advisory Editor*

1975 PUBLICATIONS

THE PRESIDENCY
George E. Reedy, *Advisory Editor*

U. S. AND WORLD ECONOMY
Leonard Silk, *Advisory Editor*

FOOD AND WORLD POPULATION
Sen. George McGovern, *Advisory Editor*

SCIENCE IN THE TWENTIETH CENTURY
Walter Sullivan, *Advisory Editor*

THE GREAT CONTEMPORARY ISSUES

POPULAR CULTURE

The New York Times

ARNO PRESS

NEW YORK/1975

DAVID MANNING WHITE

Advisory Editor

Library of Congress Cataloging in Publication Data
Main entry under title:
Popular culture.
(The Great contemporary issues)
"A Hudson group book."
Collection of articles from the New York Times.
Bibliography: p.
Includes index.
1. United States—Popular culture—Addresses, essays, lectures. I. White, David Manning. II. New York Times. III Series.
E169.1.P598 973 75-7816
ISBN 0-405-06649-X

Manufactured in the United States of America by Arno Press Inc.

The editors express special thanks to The Associated Press, United Press International, and Reuters for permission to include in this series of books a number of dispatches originally distributed by those news services.

A HUDSON GROUP BOOK
Produced by Morningside Associates. Edited by Joanne Soderman

Contents

Publisher's Note About the Series

It would take even an accomplished speed-reader, moving at full throttle, some three and a half solid hours a day to work his way through all the news The New York Times prints. The sad irony, of course, is that even such indefatigable devotion to life's carnival would scarcely assure a decent understanding of what it was really all about. For even the most dutiful reader might easily overlook an occasional long-range trend of importance, or perhaps some of the fragile, elusive relationships between events that sometimes turn out to be more significant than the events themselves.

This is why "The Great Contemporary Issues" was created—to help make sense out of some of the major forces and counterforces at large in today's world. The philosophical conviction behind the series is a simple one: that the past not only can illuminate the present but must. ("Continuity with the past," declared Oliver Wendell Holmes, "is a necessity, not a duty.") Each book in the series, therefore, has as its subject some central issue of our time that needs to be viewed in the context of its antecedents if it is to be fully understood. By showing, through a substantial selection of contemporary accounts from The New York Times, the evolution of a subject and its significance, each book in the series offers a perspective that is available in no other way. For while most books on contemporary affairs specialize, for excellent reasons, in predigested facts and neatly drawn conclusions, the books in this series allow the reader to draw his own conclusions on the basis of the facts as they appeared at virtually the moment of their occurrence. This is not to argue that there is no place for events recollected in tranquility; it is simply to say that when fresh, raw truths are allowed to speak for themselves, some quite distinct values often emerge.

For this reason, most of the articles in "The Great Contemporary Issues" are reprinted in their entirety, even in those cases where portions are not central to a given book's theme. Editing has been done only rarely, and in all such cases it is clearly indicated. (Such an excision occasionally occurs, for example, in the case of a Presidential State of the Union Message, where only brief portions are germane to a particular volume, and in the case of some names, where for legal reasons or reasons of taste it is preferable not to republish specific identifications.) Similarly, typographical errors, where they occur, have been allowed to stand as originally printed.

"The Great Contemporary Issues" inevitably encompasses a substantial amount of history. In order to explore their subjects fully, some of the books go back a century or more. Yet their fundamental theme is not the past but the present. In this series the past is of significance insofar as it suggests how we got where we are today. These books, therefore, do not always treat a subject in a purely chronological way. Rather, their material is arranged to point up trends and interrelationships that the editors believe are more illuminating than a chronological listing would be.

"The Great Contemporary Issues" series will ultimately constitute an encyclopedic library of today's major issues. Long before editorial work on the first volume had even begun, some fifty specific titles had already been either scheduled for definite publication or listed as candidates. Since then, events have prompted the inclusion of a number of additional titles, and the editors are, moreover, alert not only for new issues as they emerge but also for issues whose development may call for the publication of sequel volumes. We will, of course, also welcome readers' suggestions for future topics.

Introduction

It was 1883, and the average work week in the United States was about 70 hours. That year, Richard Jefferies, a self-taught novelist and naturalist, wrote what must have seemed a science-fiction fantasy to our weary but pragmatic great-grandfathers: "I hope that succeeding generations will be able to be idle. I hope that nine-tenths of their time will be leisure time; that they may enjoy their days, and the earth, and the beauty of this beautiful world; that they may rest by the sea and dream; that they may dance and sing, and eat and drink."

Jefferies' idyll hasn't quite come to pass, although with automation proceeding rapidly (For at my back I always hear Time's winged computers hurrying near) it is not errant speculation to foresee a 30-hour or even a 25-hour work week before the end of the century. If only one-seventh of our time will be spent on the job, how will we utilize/enjoy/pass or kill the remaining hours? The pattern is already suggested if we consider how most Americans spend the weekday hours between 5:30 P.M. and 7:30 the following morning—a reasonable chunk of leisure. Or, during the 62 consecutive hours from Friday afternoon until Monday morning, even subtracting 24 hours for sleeping and another 12 for taking showers, eating and other necessities, most of us have more than 25 hours of weekend leisure time.

If we were to take an instant audit of what any American over 21 was doing during a leisure hour we would find a broad spectrum of activity, from the sublime to the kinky, from the epitome of banality to a rare *apercu* of the nature of our very existence. We might find 250,000 of us reading the plastic, mechanico-eroticism of Harold Robbins, whose art is, generously put, neo-pithecanthropoid and whose work epitomizes what we mean when we refer to popular culture as a *product.* Perhaps another 300,000 of us are building a canoe, a grandfather's or a digital clock or a prefabricated harpsichord. A great many of us are playing tennis or fishing or maybe just walking in the countryside. Most of us, however, are sitting in front of our television sets with a can of beer or cola, a bowl of munchies and a passive challenge to the tube to entertain us.

This volume gives a wide-ranging overview of how the popular arts have developed during the past century. *The New York Times* with its tenacious curiosity about virtually every aspect of American life could no more neglect the ever-changing mass culture in America than it could political or economic stories. You will learn quite a bit about the early history of motion pictures, radio and television, since *Times* reporters and special writers were on hand at the beginning days of these media. In the genre of popular literature you will find out that the term "best seller" was an epithet coined by Harry Thurston Peck, editor of *The Bookman*, in 1896, or ponder how an unsuccessful dentist by the name of Zane Grey authored books that sold more than 17 million copies by the time he died in 1939 at age 64. Or Grace Metalious, whose *Peyton Place* had sold 300,000 hard cover and nearly 10 million paperback copies by 1964 when she died at age 39. Incidentally, *Peyton Place* is a perfect example of the kind of popular work that makes critics gag, if not retch, but is loved by the G.A.P., the Great American Public. They not only read it, they watched it by the millions on television and later on the motion picture screen.

Another favorite of the G.A.P. was General Lew Wallace's *Ben Hur*, although the book seemed at first a dismal flop. Within a year of its publication in 1880, it began to move and has since sold more than five million copies. Its stage version ran for 33 years, and we read in *The New York Times* for April 2, 1907, that 2,500 consecutive performances were given at New York's Academy of Music. Made into one of the earliest film spectacles before World War I, *Ben Hur* was to become a great box-office success twice again, with Ramon Navarro and Charlton Heston achieving their zenith popularity in the title role.

Buffalo Bill was the hero of hundreds of dime novels in the 1880's, but Colonel Cody's Wild West Show was equally a part of our popular culture. A *Times* reporter covering Col. Cody's show on March 30, 1899, expressed his delight with the "chief item on the program, a presentation of the battle of San Juan Hill." All this and Annie Oakley, too. But, as E. E. Cummings so aptly put it, Buffalo Bill's defunct, and there were hundreds of thousands who'd exclaimed, Jesus, he was a handsome man!

There are those who look back on the "good, old days" when the air was filled with fewer decibels, when New York's Eighth Avenue didn't flaunt marquees advertising a "12-hour porno-thon" for $2.00 and when our popular culture was less blatant. On March 7, 1875, America's centennial year, New Yorkers had their choice of going to Booth's Theatre to see a production of *Henry V*, or to Wallace's to see Dion Boucicault (in person) acting in his own play *The Shaughran*, or to the Union Square to see *Two Orphans*. If the theater wasn't their dish, there was a Walking Match between Messrs. E. P. Weston and J. H. Judd at Barnum's Hippodrome, a minstrel show with "negro delineation" at Bryant's Opera House or a concert at the 14th Street Armory by Gilmore and the 22nd Regiment Band.

Today, with the advent of motion pictures, radio and the ubiquitous television, the choices are multiplied, but whether or not the cultural level in the aggregate is higher is a much debated issue. Elitist critics, who wrap the mantle of *haute culture* around them tighter than Linus's blanket, decry the odious kitsch which apparently satisfies the Great Audience. The media managers too often help fulfill the elitists' prophecy of mass taste; they tumble over each other in trying to prove H. L. Mencken was right when he said, "No one ever went broke underestimating the taste of the American people."

What is important, it seems to me, is whether we have sufficient choices about the mode and manner in which we spend our leisure hours; whether, indeed, we have a cultural democracy. Despite the Cassandra wails of those who equate mass culture with one of the seven plagues that Moses invoked against the Egyptians, I see no evidence that a Gresham's Law of Culture exists in this country. Whether I spend my life going to art museums (and there are more than I physically could visit in my lifetime), in reading or seeing or hearing the "classics" or whether I choose to watch all of television's cops and robbers series from *Peter Gunn* to *Kojak* is my personal choice. It really is no mortal wound to my sensibility if my neighbor prefers a re-run of *Bonanza* at 7 P.M., while I decide to go to the Biograph Theater in Richmond, Virginia, to see Fellini's *Amarcord*. Undoubtedly, I may consider myself as possessing a superior value system or critical judgment by preferring Fellini to the Cartwright clan, but if my neighbor derives enjoyment and surcease from his workaday anxieties by watching it, I have no more reason to look down my nose at him than he has to enter my art theater and yell "Culture Vulture!"

I would have the right to protest vehemently if somehow my tastes could not be fulfilled because there are not as many of me as there are of him. For those who worry excessively that the Jacqueline Susanns, the John Waynes or whomever the archtype popular communicator on their current *kitsch*-list will drive out Good Art, here is a point to remember. It doesn't take a very large percentage of the available American audience to make a viable market. That is why we have some specialized magazines that are both stimulating to readers and profitable to publishers, albeit with fewer than 50 thousand subscribers (or about *one* out of every 4,000 people in the United States). It also explains why we now have thousands of paperback book titles to choose from. Granted that *Jaws* or a tour-de-force chiller such as *The Taking of Pelham 123* sells millions, it is also economically feasible to publish paperback editions of less spectacular sellers like David Riesman's *Lonely Crowd* or Hesse's *Siddartha*.

Popular culture will continue to be discussed, debated, excoriated and overpraised, and its devotees won't object to that. Love it or hate it, they reason, so long as Americans are not apathetic about Frank Sinatra, Dr. Stillman and his diets or Jackie Onassis. We should realize that 99 per cent of the television programs and perhaps 98 per cent of today's novels, films, and popular music from Victor Herbert to Simon and Garfunkel probably will be forgotten or a matter of bewilderment or laughter to our grandchildren.

Still, can we be sure that just because a song, a movie, a novel is very popular it will not endure? Robert Burns's poems and songs belonged to the people of his day long before the litterateurs in Edinburgh lionized and eventually ruined the unfortunate man. John Huston's *Treasure of Sierra Madre*, like von Stroheim's masterful *Greed* before it, makes the point of Chaucer's *Pardoner's Tale*, that the root of evil is greed. It wouldn't surprise me if 100 years from now our descendants will acknowledge all three of these works as concise, powerful statements of the human condition. Will it matter then that von Stroheim's or Huston's works came out of Hollywood while Chaucer's came from medieval England?

Say what you will about popular culture—that there is too much gratuitous violence in television and motion pictures, or that much of it is utterly banal and even dehumanizing. Your argument has considerable relevance. But recognize that it reflects what the Great Public wants to read or view. When in history did the Great Public invariably seek the Rational or Beauty? The average Roman who frequented Nero's *circus maximus* nearly 2000 years ago couldn't blame television, Mickey Spillane or Bernarr McFadden's *True Stories* for his predilection for seeing lions tear apart winsome Christian virgins.

The New York Times has covered the saga of popular culture without fear or favor, as you will see in the following pages, but nowhere in the thousands of stories and articles and editorials was it carried with a truer perspective and heart than in an editorial of April 10, 1941. When Earle H. Graser was killed in an automobile accident, the *Times* editorialized: "Earle H. Graser was killed in an automobile wreck early Tuesday morning, but the rumor that the Lone Ranger is dead is unfounded. It was a man who died—a man with a silver voice, a modest, pleasant personality, several college degrees, and, it was said, an ambition to act Hamlet. But he didn't take the Lone Ranger with him. The Lone Ranger doesn't die, and Silver, his horse, will never get broken-winded.

The Lone Ranger under that name, came into being in this generation for a radio public, but under various names he has been alive for many centuries. He was Ulysses, William Tell and Robin Hood; he was Kit Carson, Daniel Boone, and Davy Crockett; he was honest, truthful and brave, and so he remains.

In the simple hearts of children, and possibly of adults who were willing to take a vacation from what unhappily has to be printed in the front pages of newspapers, he was as real as the policeman on the corner. He still is, and his trusty steed waits to carry him on his errands across the face of the wondrous West, where the air is crystal and virtue never lacks for reward."

Yes, Virginia, there is a popular culture.

David Manning White

"Unsurpassed in American fiction!

"A book of uncommon quality, a superb piece of story telling which nobody who finds pleasure in the art of fiction can afford to neglect.

"Miss Mitchell can do more than tell a story. She can people it with characters who live, grow older and change under our eyes, as do our friends.

"In narrative power, in sheer readability, surpassed by nothing in American fiction!" —**J. DONALD ADAMS, N. Y. Times Book Review**

MARGARET MITCHELL'S

GONE WITH THE WIND

"Fascinating and unforgettable! A remarkable book, a spectacular book, a book which is certain to be a sensation, *a book that will not be forgotten!*

"The characters have intense individuality; the 'spirit' of the period is recorded, as it should be recorded, not from the standpoint of the historian, but from that of the contemporary participating . . . in a vast, detailed panorama; the background is magnificent in its assembling of details." —**FANNY BUTCHER, Chicago Tribune**

"Not many books leave the reader so breathless! It is not too much to say that it is among the most powerful and original novels in American literature . . . a book to own and re-read and remember forever!" —**SAMUEL TUPPER, Jr., Atlanta Journal**

"If we are not misled by an enthusiasm that shakes us to the very marrow of our bones, this is one of *the finest American novels of this century!"* —**LOS ANGELES SATURDAY NIGHT**

AT ALL BOOKSTORES • 1037 PAGES • $3.00

Sixth Large Printing— 140th Thousand!

"THE BEST . . .

It seems to me the best novel that has ever come out of the South. In fact, I believe it is unsurpassed in the whole of American writing."

—JULIA PETERKIN

"VIVID . . .

I never read anything, in fiction or history, which gave such a vivid, true picture . . . so penetrating, objective, complete!"

—DOROTHY CANFIELD FISHER

"MATURE . . .

A maturely conceived, splendidly written, significant contribution to Southern literature."

—UNIVERSITY NEWS

"WILL LIVE . . .

One of those too rare novels which a discriminating reader will desire to own and keep close at hand."

—ATLANTA AMERICAN

"MODERN . . .

A very modern story. Thousands of women have lived it since 1929."

—CONSTANCE LINDSAY SKINNER

"ASTOUNDS . . .

Ten hundred pages of narrative that astounds, with characters that charm. Bound to be a sensation."

—SCRIPT

"IMPRESSIVE . . .

What Thomas Nelson Page and Mary Johnston have done in part, Miss Mitchell gives her readers with impressive thoroughness."

—PHILA. INQUIRER

"THROBBING . . .

A broad canvas, throbbing with life and with color. There is never a moment's letdown; material for twenty motion pictures!"

—N. Y. AMERICAN

"ABSORBING . . .

It will be hailed as The Great American Novel and it will deserve all the praise that it receives."

—BOSTON HERALD

"A MIRACLE . . .

From first page to last, a book of action . . . nothing short of a miracle in these days."

—N. Y. WORLD-TELEGRAM

"EXCITING . . .

Peopled with real characters, filled with the drama of conflict, I can not see how anyone can fail to find it tremendously exciting."

—PHILADELPHIA RECORD

"THRILLING . . .

The story tumbles down upon us with the onrush of a mountain torrent. It leaves little time to catch our breath."

—HARPER'S MAGAZINE

"POWERFUL . . .

The most satisfactory, most convincing, most powerful presentation of the period that has ever been put into fiction!"

—LOS ANGELES TIMES

"BREATH-TAKING . . .

Sherman's march and the fate of Atlanta crashes straight through the center of the book and leaves you quite breathless."

—N. Y. HERALD TRIBUNE

THE MACMILLAN COMPANY

NEW YORK • CHICAGO • BOSTON • ATLANTA • DALLAS • SAN FRANCISCO

CHAPTER 1

Nothing Like a Good Book

Advertisement for Margaret Mitchell's Gone With the Wind
The New Book Times Book Review, *July 19, 1936*

Courtesy The Macmillan Company

Sixpenny Novels and Paper Covers

To The New York Times's Saturday Review:

A London dispatch in THE NEW YORK TIMES of Jan. 28 says that Messrs. Methuen & Co. are about to issue sixpenny novels, but have no intention of undermining the sale of the books in their more expensive form. No one is warranted in disputing the word of a respectable firm, but any bookseller of moderate experience, much more any bookseller well acquainted with the course of trade, knows that the sale of the more costly editions will be diminished by the appearance of the cheap editions.

The sum of 5s. 6d., or, allowing for the discount on the six-shilling price, the sum of 4s., is a temptation to many a reader of cheap novels, and when eight books are offered to him for the cost of one, he will take the eight and leave the one. There is an excellent American house which publishes "cloth" and "paper" editions almost simultaneously, charging a dollar for one and half a dollar for the other. Allowing for discounts, the purchaser of the paper edition saves 40 cents, or enough to buy a second novel, and in this town to pay the admission fee to a free fight in the "subway," and most buyers prefer the economical course.

There are a few persons who dislike paper covers, but their number diminishes yearly, and there are many who make a merit of buying paper editions, saying, austerely, "It does not seem right to waste 75 cents on a cloth-bound book until you know whether or not it is worth keeping. So I buy the paper covers first, and—" The rest is silence, for they do not return to buy the cloth-covered edition. What is more, they want paper-covered editions of everything, from the classics down to the newest copyrighted novel. The following conversations are not manufactured; they are transcribed from notes made in an excellent shop:

I.

Customer—Have you "Isabel Carnaby"?

Salesman—"Concerning Isabel Carnaby"? Yes, Madam. Seventy-five cents.

C.—Oh! I don't—want—that! Doesn't it come in paper?

S.—Yes, Madam; there it is.

C.—I suppose it's just the same as the other? (Suspiciously.) Is it just the same? Do you know that it is just the same?

S.—Yes, Madam.

C.—Then why is it cheaper? But I'll take it. I'm not going to pay 75 cents for a book! (Exit with the air of one who teaches valuable lessons to young men.)

II.

(Time, early in 1897.)

Customer—Have you "Quo Vadis" in paper covers?

Salesman—No, Sir.

C.—Great mistake! Book ought to be within reach of everybody. What is the price of the cheap edition?

S.—There is no cheap edition.

C.—No cheap edition! (Exit, speechless.)

III.

Customer (wearing the best of English clothes and worth, watch and jewelry included, at least $800 as he stands. He addresses the salesman confidentially)—Er—when is Lord Roberts's book going to appear in paper. Ten dollars is too much for one book!

Salesman (not confidentially, but cheerfully, being young and fancying that he is doing a favor)—There is a cheap edition now, $2.50; cost you $1.88.

Customer—Can't waste money, you know! I'll wait for the paper!

(Departs to join the band waiting for paper "Bismarcks," "Forbidden Lands," and "Ave Romas."

IV.

Charitable Dame—Is this the Prayer Book and Hymnal counter?

Salesman—Yes, Madam. (He surveys an array of about two hundred styles, and wonders what counter she thought it was.)

C.—Well, you see, I have a class of po-oo-or boys in Sunday school. (Pauses.)

S.—Yes, Madam.

C.—It's a ve-ry poor class!

S.—Yes, Madam. Er-very-er-kind of you!

C. (rapidly)—And I thought as I shall want a large quantity—there are five of the boys—you might give me a special discount on the paper covered editions. It's for charity you know and Christmas and at this blessed season we all want to do something.

S.—Yes, Madam. Delighted, if we could, Madam, but we don't carry paper-covered Prayer Books and Hymnals, Madam. Might try—&—'s. They have 'em—if any one does! (Customer goes.) Charity!

V.

Young woman, perfectly dressed and equipped with chewing gum, a tremendous capacity for dragging her feet as she tries to walk, and a voice.—"Miss Amecca." Ow! Isn't that puffickly deah!Ow, I do just adoah Gibson! You can always tell a Gibson gell anywhe'e! Emm-mm! "Afve Rome"—"Afve Rome"—Why don't they have English titles? Is that Mr. C'awfohds ve'y last novel?

Salesman—It isn't a novel, Madam. It describes Rome and the Romans. (Tips the two volumes out of the box.) Pictures of churches—and temples—and ruins, and—

Young Woman—Is the'e a pohtwait of Luchezia Bawger in it? No, I don't want it. Mummer gave me a list—oh, here it is! "P'isoners of Hope," "Checkee Hills," "Pewtans," "Hel—Hel—Helbeck of Ban-Bannister," and "Eaveline Inz." That's all! And she wants 'em all in paper that you've got in paper. Have you got 'em down? Well, there's the list. I do think those Gibsons in "Miss Amecca" are puffickly deah! (Pulls down a pile of Gen. Wheeler's "Santiago" and goes, leaving it on the floor and wasting no time in apologies.)

Salesman—Well!

There is no denying that the number of books sold, counting by titles, has increased immensely both here and in Great Britain, but the average price and the average profit were never so small as now, and both grow smaller. There are still readers who value books more than money, and pay for them willingly; there are still superbly honest, honorable publishers who resist all temptations to descend to the newest devices for obtaining the thirty pieces of silver without seeming to betray and abandon all Christian teaching, but nobody encourages either the honest reader or the honest publisher. The dishonest reader calls the first a fool and the second a miser; the dishonest publisher hates the first and does his best to ruin the second. The evil of which both are victims has its sources beyond and below literature, and the trade in literary products. Its name is avarice.

SECOND AVENUE.

Boston, Jan. 28, 1899.

February 4, 1899

"MOVIES" IMPROVE OUR FICTION

Rex Beach Says They Have Made Authors More Careful Regarding Actuality and Vividness

By Joyce Kilmer.

EVEN the most prejudiced opponent of the moving pictures will admit that they are becoming more intellectually respectable. Crude farce and melodrama are being replaced by versions of classic plays and novels; literature is elevating the motion picture. And Mr. Rex Beach believes that the motion picture is benefiting literature.

This author of widely read novels had been talking to me about the departments of literature—the novel, the short story, and the rest—and among them he named the moving picture. I asked him if he believed that moving pictures were dangerous for novelists, leading them to fill their books with action, with a view to the profits of cinematographic reproduction. He said:

"Well, authors are human beings, of course. They like to make money and to have their work reach as large an audience as possible. I suppose that the great majority of them keep their eyes on the screen, because they know how profitable the moving picture is and because they want their work seen by more people than would read their novels."

"Do you think that this harms their work?" I asked.

"It might if the novelists overdid it," he answered. "It would harm their work if they became nothing but scenario

writers. But so far the result has been good.

"The tendency of the moving picture has been to make authors visualize more clearly than ever before their characters and scenes that they are writing about. Their work has become more realistic. I do not mean realistic in the sense in which this word is used of some French writers; I do not mean erotic or morbid. I mean actual, convincing, clearly visualized.

"Literature has elevated the moving picture, keeping it out, to a great extent, of melodrama and slap-stick comedy. And in return, the moving picture has done a service to fiction, making the authors give more attention to exact visualization."

"Has American fiction been lacking in visualization?" I asked.

"No," said Mr. Beach. "American novelists visualize more clearly today than they did four or five years ago, before the moving picture had become so important, but they always were strong in visualization. This sort of realism is America's chief contribution to fiction."

"Then you believe that there is a distinctively American literature?" I asked. "You do not agree with the critic who said that American literature was 'a condition of English literature'?"

"I do not agree with him," Mr. Beach replied. "American writers use the English language, so I suppose that what they write belongs to English literature. But there is a distinctively American literature; Americans talk in their own manner, think in their own manner, and handle business propositions in their own manner, and naturally they write in their own manner. American literature is different from other kinds of literature just as American business methods are different from those of Europe.

"Fiction written in America must necessarily be tinged with American thought and American action. I have no patience with people who say that America has no literature. They say that nothing we are writing today will live. Well, what if that is true? It's true not only of literature but of everything else.

"Our roads won't last forever; they're built in a hurry to be used in a hurry. But they're better roads to drive and motor over than those old Roman roads of Europe. Our office buildings won't last as long as the Pyramids, but they're better for business purposes.

"Personally, I've never been enthusiastic over things that have no virtues but age and ugliness. I'd rather have a good strong serviceable piece of Grand Rapids furniture than any ramshackle, moth-eaten antique."

"But don't you think," I asked, "that the permanence of a book's appeal is a proof of its greatness?"

"I don't see how we can tell anything definite about the permanence of the appeal of books written in our time. And I don't mean by literature writings that necessarily endure through the ages. I believe that literature is the expression of the mind, the sentiment, the intellectual attitude of the people who live at the time it is written. I admit that our literature is ephemeral—like everything else about us—but I believe that it is good."

Mr. Rex Beach was not pacing his floor nervously; he was crossing the room with the practical intention of procuring a cigarette. Nevertheless his firm tread lent emphasis to his remarks.

"There is a sort of literary snobbery," he said, "noticeable among people who condemn contemporaneous literature just because it is contemporaneous. The strongest proof that there is something good in the literature of the day is that it reaches a great audience. There must be something in it or people wouldn't read it.

"The people are the final judges; it is to them that authors must appeal. Take any big question of public importance—after it has been discussed by politicians and newspapers, it is the people who at last decide it.

"A man may have devoted his life to

some tremendous achievement, and have left it as a monument to his fame. But it is to public opinion that we must look for the verdict on the value of his life's work.

"Take Carnegie, for example; when he dies, you bet people will have his number! His ideas are a tremendous menace, and the people who believe as he does about peace will find themselves generally execrated one of these days.

"It may seem to you that this has nothing to do with literature. But it has a good deal to do with it. I know that many things have been said about the effect on literature of the war. But I want to say that the war will have, I hope, one admirable effect on American writers—it will make them stir up the American conscience to a sense of the necessity for national defensive preparation. The writers must educate the people in world politics and show them the necessity for defensive action. Americans have a sort of mental inertia in regard to public questions, and the writers must overcome this inertia.

"The writers must stir up the politicians and the people. There's been a whole lot of mush written about peace. There always will be war. We can't reform the world.

"The pacifists say that it is useless to arm because war cannot be prevented by armaments. The obvious answer to that is that neither can the failure to arm prevent war. And the verdict after the war will be better if we are prepared for it. The writers must call our attention to the folly of leaving ourselves open to attack.

"It's hard to reach the conscience of the American people on any big issue. We are too independent, too indifferent, too ready to slump back. That's one of the penalties of democracy, I suppose; the national sense of patriotism becomes atrophied. It needs some whaling big jolt to wake it up. Every American writer can help to do this.

"The trouble is that we have too many men with feminine minds, too many of these delicate fellows with handkerchiefs up their sleeves. I can't imagine any women with ideas more feminine than those of Bryan—could any woman evolve anything more feminine than his peace-at-any-price idea?"

Mr. Beach smiled. "I suppose I should not be talking about world politics," he said. "There are so many men who have specialized in that subject and are therefore competent to talk about it. I am only a specialist in writing."

"Do you think," I asked, "that writers should be specialists in writing? Some people believe that the best fiction, for example, is produced by men who do some other work for a living."

"I certainly believe that a writer should devote himself to writing," said Mr. Beach. "This is an age of specialization, and literature is no exception to the general rule. Literature is like everything else; you must specialize in it to be successful."

"This has not always been the case, has it?" I asked. "Has literature been produced by people who made writing only an avocation?"

"Surely," said Mr. Beach. "It is only within the last few years that writers have been able to write for a living and make enough to keep the fringe off their cuffs."

I asked what had caused this change.

"It has been caused chiefly by the magazines. The modern magazines have done two important things for fiction—they have brought it within everyone's reach, and they have increased the prices paid to the authors, thus enabling them to make a living by devoting themselves exclusively to writing.

"But it has been said," I ventured, "that a writer, no matter how talented he may be, cannot make a comfortable living out of writing fiction unless he is most extraordinarily gifted with ideas, and that therefore a writer takes a tremendous risk if he throws himself upon literature for support."

"How is a writer going to get ideas for stories," asked Mr. Beach in turn, "unless he uses ideas? The more ideas a man uses, the more ideas will come to him.

"The imaginative quality in a man is like any other quality; the more it is functioned, the better it is functioned. If you fail to use any organ of your body, nature will in time let that organ go out of commission.

"It is just the same with imagination as with any organ of the body. If a writer waits for ideas to come to him, and ceases to exercise his imagination, his imagination will become atrophied. But if he uses his imagination, it will grow stronger and ideas will come to him with increasing frequency."

Mr. Beach is an enthusiastic advocate of the moving picture. In the course of his discussion of it he advanced an interesting theory as to the next stage of its development.

"The next use of the moving picture," he said, "will be the editorial use. We have had the moving picture used as a comic device, as a device to spread news, and as an interpreter of fiction. But as yet no one has endeavored to use it as a means to mold public opinion in great vital issues of the day.

"Of course, it has been used educationally, and as part of various propaganda schemes. But it will be used in connection with great political problems. It will become the most powerful of all influences for directing public opinion in politics and in everything else.

"It will play a mighty part in the thought of the country and of the world.

"I have seen men and women coming from a great moving-picture show almost hysterical with emotion. I have heard them shout and stamp and whistle at what they saw flashed before them on a white sheet as they never did in any theatre.

"What a strong argument 'The Birth of a Nation' presents! Now, suppose that same art and that same equipment were used to present arguments about some political issue of our own time, instead of one of our fathers' time. What a force that would be!"

July 11, 1915

The Continued Story

By HENRY IRVING DODGE

MILLIGAN threw down the magazine in disgust. "Hang it all, I didn't know that was a continued story or I never would have begun it. I hate 'em. I just got to where he took her in his arms and now I've got to wait a whole month to see what he's going to do next."

The editor of the Morning Clarion pondered a bit, then: "Milligan, you and the other fellows that are always damning the continued story make me laugh—you're so inconsistent."

"I don't see how."

The editor blew several whiffs of cigar smoke through his nose and said, as if he'd shifted to another topic: "What papers have you got there?"

"All; TIMES, Sun, Post, Mail, Globe, Journal, World, Telegram. Which'll you have?"

"I only wanted to know why you have so many. Doesn't any one of them give you all the news?"

"Practically. But in a different way. I'm particularly interested in the case of that young ruffian that assaulted the old man up at 125th Street and Seventh Avenue two or three days ago. They had him up before the Magistrate day before yesterday. His case was adjourned over till today. I've been following it."

The editor picked up one of the papers and glanced at the item referred to. "It's the continued story," he observed. "Has the principal earmark—brief synopsis of foregoing circumstances for the fellow who sees it today for the first time. Take any one of your papers there and see how many items it contains that do not refer to a beginning that was in yesterday's paper or the paper of the day before. You'll find precious few."

Milligan ran through the bundle quickly, then looked up with amazed surprise. "I'm blest if you aren't right."

"The newspapers live on the continued story," the editor went on, "just as the magazines do. It's necessary to their very existence. There aren't enough new things occurring every day to fill our columns, even if we should play them up to the limit. So we must string the interesting things that happened yesterday and the day before or last week along through today and into tomorrow or into next week if possible.

"Life itself is a continued story, laid down at night and taken up in the morning. The newspapers simply print the report of the continuous performance, serve it to the public hot off the griddle, as they say. Almost every day starts a serial with some new sensation: curious murders, conceived and executed by erratic persons with unaccountable motives; divorces of persons who have always been esteemed paragons of social virtue; or the eccentric cropping out in the most unexpected way of some real-life story that has disappeared suddenly, like an underground river, and run along only to come to the surface again, cause a sensation, then drop out of sight, while the whole public tries to figure out its devious subterranean windings and just when and where it'll reappear and what it'll bring to the surface with it—and buys papers.

"Take the Elwell case—a sensation for days, rife with speculation, both vain and sane, then silence. Everybody asks what is being done. Then a few more developments. Then the river drops again into the depths of mystery—'to be continued' in the near future—possibly.

"Some of these real-life continued stories last a few days, others weeks or even months, principally because of their sensational, gripping quality. Others, again, not necessarily sensational, are absorbing because of the strong, picturesque, famous characters they carry along—Pershing, Clemenceau, the Tiger of France, a title gripping enough to hold any one.

"At the present writing we have two intensely interesting continued stories involving antithetically different characters—namely, Caruso and Monk Eastman. Everybody wants to know the circumstances attending the killing of the notorious gunman. Eastman was a thug, yet a man who seemed to have at least one redeeming quality—personal courage. His career was a lurid one, involving State's prison and winding up with a military funeral. It lent itself peculiarly to dramatic exploitation. Also, everybody—opera-goer and non-operagoer—scans the papers for news of the condition of Caruso.

"You see, Milligan, you and others who affect to hate the continued story in the magazines read daily instalments of many such for two or three months, stories which aggregate hundreds of thousands of words, and which no magazine could possibly publish inside of five years.

"The magazine continued story is usually well constructed up to a dramatic, an artistic, a satisfactory finish. But your newspaper continued story is not always so satisfactory. It often apparently comes to an end but is only—and most exasperatingly—suspended. Take the case of Dorothy Arnold. The girl disappeared some years ago, a search was kept up for months, the whole public hanging upon each new development as recorded in the newspapers, then the search was abandoned and the girl became nothing but a fading memory. Several years elapsed and the drama was resumed. A convict in a Rhode Island State Prison confessed that he was one of a trio of miscreants who had taken the body of a girl—whom he had reason to believe was Dorothy Arnold—and buried it somewhere near West Point. Instantly public interest was revived—but not the same quality of interest that was felt when it was believed that the girl was still alive, an interest of the brain rather than of the heart, an interest in the story rather than in the girl.

"We learned one day that Inspector Faurot was to dig for the body in the concrete cellar of a certain abandoned and ghostly mansion near West Point. From day to day we bought newspapers—all of them—for we felt that each reporter would describe the occurrence from his own viewpoint, that he would supply details or atmosphere that the others might omit. Well, Faurot dug. No result. The story was suspended again for a few days—then we read that the convict was to be taken to the alleged place of burial to point out the exact spot, and we hung with bated breath upon what the next development might be, and again bought all the newspapers. Everybody bought them, from clergymen to bartenders.

"The whole thing was like the revival of an old melodrama, with the importance of the characters shifted. The last protagonist was the Rhode Island convict. Every eye was on him. Again they dug. No result. The story—'to be continued.' Neither Poe, De Maupassant or Kipling ever schemed out a more weird tale.

"The success of the magazine and of the newspaper continued story as well is almost wholly due to man's love of the dramatic. One almost never sees a humorous serial. And the dramatic quality of the newspaper continued story is naturally enhanced from day to day, as circumstances and facts are dug up. That's what makes it a great story. The reporter has everything but his own skill furnished him. But the fiction writer must dig up his facts, create his characters out of his own consciousness. That's why his job is so much more difficult than that of the journalist. In still another way he is handicapped in the race with his reportorial brother. Truth, which is always stranger than fiction, is forever supplying the reporter with unbelievable sensations. To beat these and yet keep far within the limit of human credulity is a task that taxes the most ingenious fiction-writing brain. But it must be done, for the public, grown used to "strong medicine" in fact, must have even stronger medicine in fiction.

* * * * *

"The reporter has the advantage of the romance writer in this, that he has a very severe critic in the editor, whose scissors are kept forever sharpened by a well-balanced, alert appreciation of the value of space and just what the public demands, and an everlasting pride in apt phrases and fine diction, whereas the romancer has few besides flatterers to turn to.

"The public cares for the story more than for the news. Suppose the papers should give but the bare facts of a crime, undecorated or 'played up' by the skillful dramatists of the reportorial staffs. Public interest would be small. Why, do you ask, do we devote thousands of dollars' worth of space—column after column—to to the literal report of a single trial? Simply because there is nothing more dramatic than words uttered on the witness stand. They most always have a portentous bearing. And so thoroughly does the editor appreciate this that he always sends his best men to report big cases and often employs famous fiction writers to play up local color and scenic effect.

" 'Now, then, madam, tell us what you have done, how you have lived, since your marriage to B.—only such things as relate to this case'!

"Isn't that a great line with which to end the day's instalment of a divorce case?

"Or in a murder case: 'Jane Williams, take the stand, please.' The oath is administered. 'On a certain night, what time did you retire?'

" 'Nine, sir.'

"That seems simple, but it may be corroborative evidence of the most vital quality.

"'That's all,' says the counsel for the defense. The time for adjournment has arrived. The Judge nods to the clerk of the court. Jane is about to step down, when: 'One moment, please,' exclaims the prosecuting attorney. And the adroit reporter winds up with the suggestion that Jane has let herself in for a grueling cross-examination — tomorrow morning. The editor truned to Milligan: 'Don't you think you'd have a bunch of tomorrow's evening papers?'

"Nor are the editors and the reporters the only dramatizers of the game of reporting facts. Counsel for both sides do their best to make the continued story of their activities sensational. How dramatic is the position of the counsel for the defense, how heroic. No matinee idol ever had half the chance that he has. Nor is that gentleman the only one interested in playing up a great criminal trial. The District Attorney must make capital out of it, political capital. Alone, austere, isolated from public sympathy, he stands there, the defender of the people—that's his pose. The continued story, with Whitman and Becker playing the leading parts, ran from day to day, long enough to put the District Attorney in the Gubernatorial chair and Becker in the electric chair.

"Among newspaper continued stories Bryan and Roosevelt were for a long time best sellers. For years and years they appeared every day in almost every paper of the country, and often two or three times in each issue. It would have been impossible to keep up public interest in these men unless they themselves had furnished enough material of dramatic quality to make good copy. Each lived an absorbingly interesting continued story, the big scenes of which occurred with each political campaign. In between they kept up a continuous performance, holding us by force of personality, dazzling us by brilliant versatility.

"Roosevelt dropped out of politics and went big game shooting in Africa. Then we saw him in a new rôle, plaintiff in a libel case. Next we see him in South America, expressing his restless, wonderfully adventurous and—to the public—fascinating spirit in hazardous exploration of untraveled lands and rivers. Then the doughty soldier, offering all for the country he loved above all things, and then—CURTAIN!

"The other headliner looms up on the dim horizon of memory like a horseman coming over the rim of the prairie and approaching—the boy orator of the Platte—holding aloft his cross of gold. Then candidate ad infinitum. Then—we jump to the recent past—Secretary of State, entertainer on the 'big grape juice time,' valiant knight of peace. What next? we wonder, and keep our pens alert and our presses ready.

"The newspaper continued story has a civic value in that it often checks crime and promotes beneficence. The recital of court procedure, the ever-flowing spring of supply and inspiration, the editor's best friend, has a repressive influence by keeping the penalty of crime always before the weak, would-be criminal element of the community. On the other hand, it is claimed by some criminologists that it encourages crime among the weak and the vain by exploiting it.

"If a man in whose case we are interested is arrested on Sunday or late at night, say, and is to be brought up in court next day, we all wait and watch and buy papers to see what is done to him. Our indignation at certain things makes us go out of our way to buy the paper and read the sequel. For that reason the street car toughs that are arrested on Sundays and tried on Mondays are the means of selling many evening papers, because we all love to see justice meted out to those we hate.

"Now for the humane influence: A poor family is evicted. We notice the fact and perhaps throw the paper aside. But tomorrow we read again of the same case. Some person has sent a little money to the unfortunate family and by suggestion we do likewise, and so it goes. Or the heart interest: Let a little girl lose her yellow dog and tens of thousands of persons will indulge in evening papers for days to see whether she found it or not.

"Everybody knows that the newspaper continued detective story is without a peer as a best seller. Few are more absorbing or more brilliantly told then was that of Commissioner George Dougherty's pursuit of the Rosenthal gunmen. From day to day the public followed the detectives up into New York State, down on Long Island, over to New Jersey, then across to Massachusetts and finally over to Williamsburg, where the gunmen were caught.

"So you see, Milligan, you fellows who kick at continued stories in the magazines spend ten times as much money buying continued stories in the newspapers. And not for the news half so much as for the continued stories."

January 30, 1921

CANDY OUTSELLS BOOKS.

Almost 7 Pounds of Sweets Bought for Each Book, Survey Reveals.

The average American requires six and nine-tenths pounds of candy to get through one volume of reading matter, according to statistics compiled by the American Booksellers' Association. The comparison is based on the per capita consumption of books and of candy, but does not take into consideration the fact that more than one person may read each book, a situation which is not paralleled in the field of candy.

In the matter of cost, the figures disclose that twice as much money is spent for candy as for books throughout the United States. A further observation mournfully revealed by the association is that Germany, with one-third the population, publishes three times the number of new titles per year. New titles here totaled 4,263 for the first half of this year.

August 6, 1928

"Book of the Month" Scheme Adopted for Merchandise

With the idea of "a book a month" launched successfully, the scheme apparently has suggested itself to manufacturers in other lines as too good to be confined to the booksellers. A hosiery manufacturer, for instance, is now featuring "a color a month," while a silk manufacturer styles his conception "Fabric of the Month Club."

The aim, of course, is to promote sales by the centring of attention on carefully selected, quick-moving merchandise, by giving it special distinction as a monthly feature.

September 9, 1928

RETAILERS ATTACK BOOK CLUB SYSTEM

Arthur Brentano Jr. Says the Monthly Groups Played Large Part in Depression Last Year.

URGES PUBLISHERS TO ACT

New Yorker Speaks at Convention in Boston—Baltimorean Calls Organizations "Intellectual Sham."

From a Staff Correspondent of The New York Times.

BOSTON, May 13.—War was declared on the monthly book clubs today at the opening session of the twenty-ninth annual convention of the American Booksellers' Association. Arthur Brentano Jr., president of the organization, sounded the keynote of the meeting when he blamed the book club system of distribution for playing a large part in the depression which he said the booksellers had suffered in the last year.

Mr. Brentano was followed by Frank L. Magel of Baltimore, chairman of the association's board of trade, who proposed a resolution branding such organizations as the Literary Guild and the Book-of-the-Month Club as "intellectual shams" and protesting against their "methods of marketing a limited number of so-called best books of the month through self-styled guilds or clubs conducted for profit," as detrimental to author, publisher and bookseller alike.

Sees Trade Restraint Tendency.

The resolution, which was referred to a committee for action at Thursday's session, read, in part, as follows:

"Resolved, that the American Booksellers' Association hereby emphatically protests against the method of marketing a limited number of so-called 'best' books of the month through self-styled 'clubs' or 'guilds' conducted for profit on the following grounds:

"1. There is no 'best' book of the month. The word 'best' implies a selection from things that are comparable. There are hundreds of books published every month which are of general interest. * * * Even within these several fields there is no 'best' book. There are many superb books published in each month and in each field each having its own intellectual or emotional appeal. The attempt to choose a 'best' book from this mass of varied excellence and interest is an absurdity. It is an intellectual sham.

"2. It is beyond the physical powers of any limited committee of six or seven professional writers to cover the whole field. Furthermore, with all due respect to such committees, it is beyond their intellectual qualifications.

"3. The self-styled 'clubs' and 'guilds' are commercial organizations and are run for profit. They are not colleges, or universities, or national academies, or royal societies, or even meistersingers. The judgments of their paid committees, however honest the committeemen may endeavor to be, are expected to produce a commercial result.

Holds Other Books Are Hurt.

"4. The books that are sold by these 'clubs' or 'guilds' receive an amount of concentrated and factitious advertising which is detrimental to the sale of scores of other books in the same field of an equal or superior order of merit.

"5. The influence of these 'clubs' and 'guilds' tends to the acceptance of books on 'authority' and to the making of moguls out of otherwise excellent committeemen. It tends to discourage the reading of book reviews and browsing in book stores and prevents the discovery of the fact that the limit of intellectual effort is greater than six minds can compass.

"6. The methods of marketing books through these 'clubs' and 'guilds' is detrimental to the interests of authors, of publishers and of booksellers through whom, if at all, the cultural needs of the people at large must be supplied.

"7. The practice of permitting the officers or employes of these 'clubs' and 'guilds' to inspect manuscripts or proofs in advance of publication in order that their committeemen may be presented with a narrow choice out of a field which they could not by any possibility consider in its entirety is the root of a parasitical growth which is infesting the whole field of authorship, publication and bookselling. We charge that it tends toward a restraint of trade which is beyond the protection and scope of the copyright laws and out of harmony with the idea of free competition in an open field."

Attempt to Combat Clubs Failed.

An unsuccessful attempt by the booksellers to combat the book clubs on their own ground was disclosed in the report of Stanley Remington of Baltimore, treasurer of the Booksellers' Association. He disclosed that the "book selection department," created last year with the idea that booksellers, aided by volunteer boards of eminent critics, could select their own best books of the month and boost sales by intensive advertising campaigns, failed for lack of support.

The venture, he reported, suffered a loss of $7,193 from May 10, 1928, to April 30, 1929. Profits from other departments offset this deficit so that the association was able to report an operating loss of only $6,685 for the year.

A statement replying to the criticisms against the book clubs was issued by Harold Guinzburg, president of the Literary Guild.

"The book clubs," he said, "are a legitimate, fair business enterprise, which are succeeding only because the public wishes them to succeed. If the public ever wishes to purchase books in another manner it will do so. The charge that we are a combination in restraint of trade is absolutely false. If there were anything to that phase of their complaint, the booksellers long ago would have taken their case to court.

"As a matter of fact, book clubs have been functioning in Germany for ten years. In that period the number of book titles, the number of book stores and the amount of book sales have increased. It is a little too early perhaps to judge the results in this country, but, in my opinion, the clubs have created a new interest in books, have increased sales and have exercised a wholesome influence upon the book publishing business.

"As for myself, I would welcome the formation of more book clubs, and that is my answer to the attack of the booksellers' convention, which, by the way, is nothing new. They attacked the low-priced reprint edition, the growth of circulating libraries—in fact, every development which forced them to better methods of merchandising and sale."

Delegates to the convention were welcomed this afternoon by Mayor Malcolm E. Nichols, who said he appeared to deliver an "uncensored address."

Mr. Brentano said in part:

It is no secret that, generally speaking and with but few exceptions, the retail book trade of the country has not had a prosperous year, has not even had the normal increase that any healthy industry should have in a prosperous period as indicated by the reports of banks, department stores and other retail organizations.

"It is, of course, rather difficult for any individual to place his finger on the weakened pulse of the book trade. It is my personal opinion, however, that the book clubs and their methods of publicity, advertising and distribution have played an important part in this depression.

"In setting up a committee of critical authority to select the outstanding book of the month for their subscribers, the book clubs have usurped the inalienable right of every book buyer and book reader to think for himself and to select his own literary diet, thereby removing one of the incentives for visiting bookstores.

When you have 100,000 or more book buyers sitting tight in the smug satisfaction of getting the so-called best book each month that some one else has chosen for them, you are undermining the book browsing habit; you are taking sales away from many many titles that are of equal value to the prescribed diet.

May 14, 1929

CLUB REPLIES TO BRENTANO

Scherman Suggests Official of Firm Has Changed Attitude.

In reply to the recent announcement by Brentano's that it had severed relations with book clubs and would submit no more manuscripts to the Book-of-the-Month Club, Literary Guild and similar organizations, Harry Scherman, vice-president of the Book-of-the-Month Club, Inc., issued a statement yesterday in which he said:

"Brentano's say that book clubs are 'menaces' to the booksellers. Yet about a year ago, before our judges chose the last book by Bernard Shaw, Lowell Brentano, head of the publishing branch of the firm, told us that Shaw originally did not want his book submitted to us, because Shaw felt that his distinction entitled him to special terms.

"Mr. Brentano, however, he himself told us, persuaded Shaw to allow him to sell the book to us, and not only that, but Brentano actually reduced the contemplated retail price of the book upon our insistence, making the first edition a $3 instead of a $4 book; then, after our edition, raising the retail price to $4.

"Now, if we are 'menaces,' if our activities are so injurious to booksellers and publishers, why was Brentano's so keen to sell the Shaw book to us, over Mr. Shaw's first reluctance, when that author learned that we could not, even for him, change our uniform buying system?"

May 22, 1929

Book Clubs Wield Vast Influence in Publishing Industry

By ERIC PACE

Fans of Nathaniel Hawthorne's novel "The Scarlet Letter" know that a big red "A" used to stand for a kind of sin. But nowadays, in the hushed inner sanctums of the Book-of-the-Month Club, the same symbol may mean fame and power and hundreds of thousands of dollars for a writer.

The club sticks labels bearing its version of the scarlet letter on books that are prime candidates for its judges to pick as books-of-the-month at their regular closed-door meetings. And being chosen by the club, or by its arch-rival, the Literary Guild, or by others of the nation's 200 book clubs is particularly important for an author because the clubs have come to wield vast influence in the shaky book-publishing industry.

Many hardcover books reach more readers through clubs than book stores. Dee Brown's "Bury My Heart at Wounded Knee," for example, has sold 275,000 copies through stores and 315,000 through the Book-of-the-Month Club. The Literary Guild has sold more than 325,000 copies of Frederick Forsyth's "The Odessa File," while store sales have totaled about 195,000.

The million-member Literary Guild has long been thought of as the more popularly inclined of the two big clubs, but the staid Book-of-the-Month has been broadening its appeal lately with zesty new choices. For the month of August, its 1.25 million members will be offered "Marilyn," Norman Mailer's new book about Marilyn Monroe. It is illustrated with 100 photographs, several of which show her in the nude.

"Things have changed," the club's imperturbable president, Axel G. Rosin, observed the other day. Its executive vice president, Warren Lynch, added, "The cheering thing is that our judges are keeping up with the times." And its advertising manager, David Soskin, declared, "We've become tastefully aggressive."

Yet Jacqueline Susann, the best-selling novelist, said recently that "the Book-of-the-Month Club is still wearing corsets, they're still strait Laced in terms of their selections; but the Literary Guild is wearing pantyhose—they're modern."

Miss Susann's strong views may reflect the fact that her current best-seller, "Once Is Not Enough," and an earlier one, were picked by the Literary Guild, while none of her books has been an "A" choice at the Book-of-the-Month Club, much less a selection.

But they also reflect the importance of book-club selection in an industry where book-club payments make up a solid percentage of hard-cover trade publishers' profits. Book-club sales have more than doubled in the last 10 years, and being picked by a club often gives an author more publicity and more power in getting his book sold to a paperback house. It can also provide him with masses of money. The Book-of-the-Month Club's standard guarantee against royalties is $85,000, which is generally split 50-50 between the author and his hardcover publisher. This was the case, for instance, with the $85,000 guarantee agreed to for the club's June selection, Arthur Rubinstein's autobiographical "My Young Years," which was brought out earlier by Knopf.

But the Book-of-the-Month pays much larger sums for books that it wants to make sure it gets — $325,000 for Svetlana Alliyuyeva's memoirs, for instance. The club, which is actually a commercial corporation, pays royalties of 10 per cent of the price it charges for its main offerings. Terms vary among the other clubs—and some books are chosen by several clubs, on one basis or another.

Book clubs also vary widely in size and scope. Reader's Digest Condensed Books has more than a million subscribers, and it sends them a succession of volumes, each of which contains several—generally five—condensed books.

Smaller clubs include the Anti-Communist Book Club, as well as the Little Kid's Soft Cover Book Club, and one called the Circle of the Mystic & Occult Arts.

Most clubs follow essentially the same system: they pick books and send them, under a variety of arrangements, to those members who want them. Many of the books are sent automatically to members unless they say no to a specific book. This practice, known as negative option, has attracted controversy in recent years.

The clubs use various methods to pick the books they send out. At Book-of-the-Month, executives say that the four-man panel of judges makes selections on the basis of literary merit, and Mr. Rosin said recently, "The judges don't have the responsibility of trying to tell us what will sell."

Who Are the Judges?

The judges, mostly in their 60's, are literary figures: Gilbert Highet, John K. Hutchens, Clifton Fadiman and Wilfrid Sheed. Another judge, Paul Horgan, stepped down from the panel last year and became a nonvoting associate judge. Such is the judges' dignity that Mr. Sheed, whose friends call him Bill, is referred to around the club's subdued Park Avenue headquarters as Wilfred.

Club executives like to emphasize the importance of the judges, who meet in an elegant office conference room, over lunches sent in from the Dallas Cowboy restaurant.

Despite the grandeur of the judicial proceedings, however, the judges only pick what the club calls its "full selections"—one or two books for each month, and a couple of others in the course of a year, for a total of 17, for example, in 1972.

A far larger—and growing—number of other books is offered to the membership, on one basis or another, after being picked by the club's staff, which keeps careful track of how well books sell.

The staff also sifts through the hundreds of books that are sent in each month and labels a few of them "A" books, which means that they are to be read by all the judges and discussed, as the "A" labels stipulate, "at the next meeting." Each of the judges also has the right to declare a work an "A" book on his own.

The original red "A" in American literary history was the embroidered symbol that Hester Prynne, the 17th-century heroine of Hawthorne's 1850 novel, was condemned to wear on her breast as punishment for having committed adultery.

But notions of sin have changed along with literary fashions, Mr. Rosin noted, "and as one of our judges said, Hester would barely get a 'C'—today."

Mr. Rosin recalled the days, 20 years ago, when members even objected to J. D. Salinger's novel about adolescent torment, "Catcher in the Rye," saying "our son is not like that," and when one judge objected to Robert Ruark's novel "Something of Value" because it had gory atrocity scenes.

But things *have* changed, and the club management recently took an option on the book that the British novelist Piers Paul Read is writing about the Uruguayan rugby players who survived an Andean plane crash by turning to cannibalism.

Another sign of change was the recent selection of Alan Lelchuk's steamy novel of campus sex and violence, "American Mischief." The club's staff bought it to use as an alternate selection, but when the judges later promoted it to a full selection, Mr. Rosin recalled, "I was floored."

More Open-Minded

Roger W. Straus Jr., the president of Farrar, Straus & Giroux, which published the Lelchuk book, said later that "the Book-of-the-Month Club is getting to be more open-minded in terms of the kind of literature they're prepared to offer their members."

And some publishing executives, going further, suggest privately that the club's management, in line with its "tasteful aggressiveness" policy, has encouraged the judges to pick not merely good books, but good books that are expected to sell well.

Yet Mr. Lynch insisted that "we didn't go to our judges and say, 'let's get a little more vivacious; it's just that publishers are coming through" with books like the Mailer work.

And club executives maintain that Mr. Mailer's "Marilyn" was chosen because of the quality of the writing.

Vivacious or not, the club's net sales for the nine months ending with March were a resounding $39,920,890 — up from $37,469,844 for the same period a year before.

Such sales figures are sufficient to provide the main executives with handsome salaries.

The club's stock is largely held by Mr. Rosin, the son-in-law of its late founder, Harry Scherman, and by Mr. Scherman's widow. It was selling at $21 a share last week, down from a high of 31¾ for the year. Net income a share was $1.45 for the nine months ended in March, up from $1.38 for the same period a year ago.

The Literary Guild's staff members make all their own choices of books, which they consider an advantage since they do not have to postpone some decisions until a judges' meeting, as the Book-of-the Month Club does.

In point of fact, though, when the Book-of-the-Month judges do meet, they usually make their pick fairly quickly. But the session at which the Marilyn Monroe book was chosen went on unusually late into the day.

Robert Markel, a vice president at Grosset & Dunlap, the book's publishers, said later that he had provided a set of the photographs for the occasion, and he observed, "With all those pictures of Marilyn to look at, no wonder the judges took so long."

May 29, 1973

PULP WRITERS FIND MARKET DWINDLING

Only 33 Magazines Left in Lower-Price Field—Word Rate Reduced by Half.

Facts about writing for the all-fiction or "pulp paper" magazines and tales of the working habits of some of the world's most prolific writers were told yesterday following the regular Friday meeting of the American Fiction Guild.

The guild, organized eighteen months ago, has a membership of 200 writers, most of them regular contributors to the pulp magazines. The largest chapter is here in New York. Arthur J. Burks is the national president.

Three years ago some seventy-three pulp paper magazines were published. The average rate paid for stories was 2 cents a word and writers whose names had appeared often on covers were paid considerably more. The best rate was 10 cents a word, the minimum about one-half a cent. Now there are only about thirty-three such magazines and pay has been cut approximately in half.

There are a few of the regulars who average 100,000 words a month. There are some who maintain "fiction factories," staffs of assistants organized after the manner of the staff of the elder Dumas and who thus have a hand in the production of an even greater total. Others write fast without help. Arthur Burks wrote his 80,000-word novel, "Rivers Into Wilderness," published last year by Mohawk and to be reissued this year by Dodd, Mead, in ten days.

Wallace R. Bamber said that Henry Bedford-Jones, one of the best known of the pulp-paper writers, starts work each morning in his home in Hollywood with a repeating phonograph blaring the same record over and over and five stacks of manuscripts on his worktable.

He starts writing on one story, keeps at it until he hits an impasse, then shifts to a second. He thus ranges rapidly through his manuscripts, solving a difficult situation only when as much of the fast, smooth going work as possible has been done.

Two of the pulp writers, Albert Richard Wetjen, who also sells many of his stories to the large national weeklies, and Philip Richards, write by touch system in dark rooms. Why Mr. Richards likes to write in the dark was not known, but Mr. Wetjen once explained that he started writing while living alone in a shack near Salem, Ore. He worked outdoors every day and his only illumination in the shack was a smoky oil lamp. His imagination seems to work best, he said, in semi-darkness.

There is strong competition now in the pulp paper market. Writers accustomed to the higher pay of the "smooth paper" magazines have found decreasing markets for the last few years and many have entered the lower price field.

In the pulp market plot must dominate rather than character, and action must be fast and melodramatic. There must be a clear separation of virtue and vice. Romantic interest must be played down, a major reason, it was agreed yesterday, why motion picture companies draw only lightly from the pulp paper field.

The meeting was held in Rosoff's restaurant in West Forty-third Street.

May 13, 1933

The Favorite Books Of Americans

A Gallup Survey Indicates How Hollywood Has Influenced the Public's Reading

The Reading Room.

From a Line Engraving by Stanley Anderson. From "Fine Prints of the Year: 1931." (Minton, Balch & Co.)

By GEORGE GALLUP
Director, American Institute of Public Opinion

TO the average American book publisher, sitting behind a shiny desk somewhere in Manhattan, there are really two publics in the United States. The first is the small and important one, centering in the urban areas of the country, which has acquired the habit of buying books. The other is the plain American public which works, sleeps, votes and pays taxes but seldom digs into its pocket for book money.

While best-seller lists and other statistics show what the book public is reading, little is known about the reading preferences of the millions of ordinary Americans, most of whom live on the far side of the Hudson River on farms and in small towns and cities of the forty-eight States. Which books hold the greatest interest for them? What would they say if you asked them: "What is the most interesting book you have ever read?"

During the past two years the American Institute of Public Opinion has made soundings among men and women in all parts of the country and in all walks of life, asking just this question. Some of the institute's findings might have been guessed at. The Bible, for instance, has been the best-selling book in the United States for generations, and no one will be surprised at the number of Americans who consider it "the most interesting book I ever read."

One fact that is scored and underscored in these studies is the tremendous influence of Hollywood on reading tastes. Another is the overwhelming preference for historical and romantic fiction. In all, these ordinary Americans picked more than a thousand different book titles.

But the lists add up to something. Nearly one voter in every five named the Bible, making it the leading choice. The Bible has probably occupied some such position for decades, but how long it will retain its place with Americans is problematical, for it is much less popular with young people, we found, than with their parents and grandparents. The following table shows how the interest in the Bible declines with younger persons in the 1938 survey:

Age.	**Naming Bible Per Cent.**
Fifty and over	**37**
Forty-nine to thirty	**17**
Under thirty	**6**

* * *

Of the nineteen books that ranked next in order of interest this year, eight were published in the last few years. The rest, with only one exception, were all published before 1900. This leaves a puzzling gap between 1900 and 1930. What has happened to the best-sellers of those years—to "Main Street," to "The Story of Philosophy," to "So Big" and "Elmer Gantry" and to "The Private Life of Helen of Troy"?

The institute's surveys show how a new wave of best sellers has taken their places. Leading the list is Margaret Mitchell's story of the Civil War, "Gone With the Wind," the only book

which approaches the Bible in the number of mentions. With women it is actually named more often than the Bible, and it also leads the Bible in New England and other Eastern States. Probably the book would have ranked first in the South too had not Southern voters given an exceptionally large first-place vote to the Bible. Where Miss Mitchell's book will rank next year or the year after that is a question nobody can answer, but it is apparently as popular with the public this year as it was last year. Twelve per cent of those having opinions mention it in both the 1937 and 1938 surveys.

After "Gone With the Wind" none of the books receives more than 5 per cent of the mentions, but the books most often named are:

"Anthony Adverse," by Hervey Allen.

"The Citadel," by A. J. Cronin.

"How to Win Friends and Influence People," by Dale Carnegie.

"The Good Earth," by Pearl Buck.

Then, with only one or two exceptions, comes a parade of popular classics. The complete list of twenty books is as follows:

1938 SURVEY

1. The Bible.
2. Gone With the Wind.
3. Anthony Adverse.
4. The Citadel.
5. How to Win Friends and Influence People.
6. The Good Earth.
7. Ben-Hur.
8. Northwest Passage.
9. Little Women.
10. A Tale of Two Cities.
11. Les Misérables.
12. Magnificent Obsession.
13. Adventures of Tom Sawyer.
14. Treasure Island.
15. Count of Monte Cristo.
16. Robinson Crusoe.
17. Ivanhoe.
18. The Green Light.
19. David Copperfield.
20. Call of the Wild.

* * *

One thing comes immediately to mind about the leading books in the list. Nearly all of them have been seized upon by Hollywood as motion-picture material. Even the Bible has been screened in part, and "Gone With the Wind" has been in casting pains for more than two years.

"Anthony Adverse" was brought to the screen and became one of the leading "money" films of 1935. "The Citadel," "The Good Earth," "Little Women" and "A Tale of Two Cities" have recently been turned into outstanding pictures. Hollywood is preparing to produce a film version of Kenneth Roberts's "Northwest Passage" and has even scooped up the title rights to Dale Carnegie's personality handbook, "How to Win Friends and Influence People." "Ben-Hur," seventh on the list, is not among the books filmed recently but it was one of the greatest box-office pictures of all time.

What film treatment may mean to the life of a book is indicated by the fact that merely to break even a good picture has to show to about 15,000,000 persons. A book, on the other hand, can become a best seller if it sells a few thousand copies. Hollywood did not create the original popularity of these books, but in giving them film treatment and a far greater audience the movies have unquestionably added to the circulation and endurance of the books themselves.

The influence of the movies on reading is familiar to every public librarian. When the film of "David Copperfield" was advertised in Cleveland two years ago, Cleveland public library authorities ordered more than a hundred and twenty-five extra copies of the Dickens story to meet the demand they knew would follow. They were right. Although the additional books brought the total of available copies to more than five hundred, Cleveland readers kept the library shelves bare of "Copperfield" both during and immediately after the run of the film, and the rush extended to other Dickens books as well.

The effect of the movies on reading is far from one-way, of course. In the light of its record-breaking popularity as a novel, movie producers expect "Gone With the Wind" to become one of the greatest box-office pictures in history. (It is partially this conviction that has made the search for an actress to play the part of Scarlett O'Hara such an agonizingly earnest business for the producers.) So Hollywood is probably more careful than ever nowadays to examine new books that seem to interest the public.

For reasons best known to itself, however, Hollywood has not yet produced Walter Edmonds's story of early New York State, "Drums Along the Mohawk," although it ranks just below the first twenty in the institute's test and was higher last year. Other high-ranking books which have not found their way to the screen are "An American Doctor's Odyssey" and "The Life of Madame Curie." In spite of their non-fictional basis, both are rich in picture material and may yet find their way to the screen.

* * *

Fiction leads non-fiction in public interest in all sections of the country—whether in Boston, Los Angeles or elsewhere. In their study of "Middletown in Transition," Robert and Helen Lynd point out that the reading of non-fiction increased during the early part of the depression, but has since fallen off, according to library records in Middletown. The Lynds trace the temporary interest in "heavy" books to a suddenly felt need to understand the problems of depression. Today, however, the public is inclined to overlook the serious thinkers. Fiction is the favorite, and the first hint of history of economics is H. G. Wells's "Outline of History," thirtieth on the list and a best-seller long before the depression.

Even in fiction the novel of "social significance" is less likely to rank high in popular interest than the romantic kind. Sinclair Lewis's publishers advertised that "It Can't Happen Here" was of special importance because of its timely dissection of fascism, and so it undoubtedly proved; but "It Can't Happen Here" ranked lower than Lewis's earlier books, "Main Street" and "Arrowsmith," with the public. In spite of its impressive sales, John Gunther's "Inside Europe" is mentioned as "most interesting book" by only a few.

These patterns hold good for the Institute's 1937 survey as well. Last year's lists show the same predominance of fiction over non-fiction, the same balance of recent books and popular classics, and the same influence of Hollywood. Certain individual books were higher last year than today:

1937 SURVEY.

1. The Bible.
2. Gone With the Wind.
3. Anthony Adverse.
4. The Good Earth.
5. Magnificent Obsession.
6. A Tale of Two Cities.
7. The Green Light.
8. Les Misérables.
9. Ben Hur.
10. David Copperfield.
11. Count of Monte Cristo.
12. Little Women.
13. Drums Along the Mohawk.
14. American Doctor's Odyssey.
15. Treasure Island.
16. How to Win Friends and Influence People.
17. Uncle Tom's Cabin.
18. All Quiet on the Western Front.
19. The Virginian.
20. Adventures of Tom Sawyer.

* * *

Two books which have dropped most sharply in the year's time are the Lloyd C. Douglas romances, "Magnificent Obsession" and "The Green Light," books which probably owed part of their 1937 popularity to the movies. On the other hand, the "Adventures of Tom Sawyer" is more popular this year than last year, very possibly because of the showing of the technicolor picture "Tom Sawyer" in the meantime.

Most of the books in the two surveys are equally popular with young people and older people, but there are interesting differences. Older persons mention the Bible, "Robinson Crusoe," "Uncle Tom's Cabin," "Ben Hur" and "Pilgrim's Progress" much more often than young people do. Young people, however, explain most of the popularity of "Northwest Passage," "Magnificent Obsession" and "All Quiet on the Western Front."

* * *

Finally, it is interesting to note that although "Gone With the Wind" is more popular with women than with men, "How to Win Friends and Influence People" is decidedly more popular with men. The leading choices of men and women in the 1938 study are:

MEN.

1. The Bible.
2. Gone With the Wind.
3. Anthony Adverse.
4. How to Win Friends and Influence People.
5. Adventures of Tom Sawyer.
6. The Citadel.
7. Ben Hur.
8. Treasure Island.
9. Count of Monte Cristo.
10. A Tale of Two Cities.

WOMEN.

1. Gone With the Wind.
2. The Bible.
3. Anthony Adverse.
4. The Citadel.
5. Little Women.
6. The Good Earth.
7. Magnificent Obsession.
8. Northwest Passage.
9. Les Misérables.
10. Lantern in Her Hand.

The surveys themselves followed identical patterns in 1937 and 1938. Those who were questioned represented a cross-section of the country at large, from New England to California, and they included among others professors and share-croppers, housewives and telephone girls, business men, farmers and persons on the WPA.

"What is the most interesting book you have ever read?" they were asked. They answered what came into their minds, without the aid of lists or suggestions. Sometimes they were stumped. But throughout the country six persons in every ten singled out some book as their favorite, while the others declared that "no special book occurred" to them or that they did little reading at all. Women had less trouble in making up their minds than men, and professional people and white-collar workers showed more ease than others.

It is a long road to knowing the complete story of the public's reading preferences, and the Institute's surveys leave many interesting questions unanswered. Have Americans always given such a forward place in their reading to romantic and heroic materials as they do today? What would the public's choices have been ten, twenty or fifty years ago? Unfortunately there are no records of the public's likes that are comparable, and it is impossible to say where a book like "Uncle Tom's Cabin" would have ranked eighty years ago, on the eve of the Civil War, or how the Bible itself has fared from decade to decade.

The surveys do indicate which books are in the center stream of popularity today and which books of the past enjoy the stoutest life. Perhaps they give us a new glimpse of ourselves, as well.

January 15, 1939

The "Best Seller" Lists--and How They Grew

By ALICE P. HACKETT

THE first best seller lists in America, published just a little over fifty years ago, were the idea of Harry Thurston Peck, then editor of the literary magazine, The Bookman. At first these lists were uncorrelated, simply published in the magazine as they came from a dozen or so stores throughout this country and from a few in Canada. As the lists grew in popularity they were enlarged to include more and more stores, eventually were consolidated into a single list of "six best sellers," and by the early Nineteen Hundreds the term was part of the American language.

It is so thoroughly accepted today that almost any book is apt to be referred to as a "best seller." This is not always a misusage. There are best sellers and best sellers. Many newspapers publish their local best-seller lists; the trade papers and book review sections print national lists based on countrywide canvass; even individual bookstores publicize their own best sellers. A local author in a small town may be the best seller in his own community and never even approach a metropolitan list. Reports, gathered nationally from bookstores, do, however, give a generally accurate picture of what the nation is reading.

The titles in the box on Page 2 of this issue are from The Bookman, from 1896 to 1912, and thereafter from Publishers' Weekly, magazine of the American book trade, which in 1912 began to publish its own best-seller lists according to The Bookman's original plan.

In the early years no attempt was made to make separate fiction and nonfiction lists. It happened that fiction rose to the top—the first two titles in fiction are, therefore, given for the years up to 1917. During the First World War the general public apparently began to be more interested in nonfiction than ever before, just as in World War II books about the war were often read more eagerly than novels. From 1917 on, the top fiction and top nonfiction titles of each year were separately collected and can be given in those two classifications.

Increased production figures do not mean that publishers can "make" best sellers. Best sellerdom is still achieved through public approval. Attention once gained, spectacular success can be built up through clever publicity, widespread advertising and expert merchandising methods, but it is as true today as it ever was that it is only the books that have something to offer which the public wants or needs that can be pushed to the big best-seller class. Whether that something the public wants is meritorious is another question. Readers may want information, vicarious excitement, or inspiration. If a book does not offer something welcomed by its readers, it will not sell in large quantities no matter what pressure methods may be used upon them by its salesmen.

Frequently the whole theory of best sellers and best-seller lists is attacked as overemphasis of a few popular books. It is implied that they are unworthy while much better books never reach the many readers whom they would benefit. But I think it futile either to attack or to defend best sellers. They exist. The large number of copies a book has sold is too attractive a fact both to the seller and the casual book buyer to be ignored by either.

AND when the record of best sellers, kept over a fifty-year period, such as this, is studied with discernment, it offers a fascinating survey for the social historian. These books are what Americans bought and read during the past half century. They may not be the books they *should* have bought and read. But by whatever chance or circumstance they were persuaded to do so, these were the books most widely purchased and read.

For the reader who is not a historian but who has always been and always will be a reader, a glance back over the titles of ten, thirty or fifty years evokes memories not only of the books themselves but of the circumstances in which he read them.

Many of the best sellers of the Eighties and Nineties and early Nineteen Hundreds are forgotten today. But a surprising number of them persist and are read by new generations. "Pollyanna" and "Seventeen" are sold and read today and of course such solid classics as "The Education of Henry Adams" and "The Outline of History." It is the middle-aged person to whom "A Lady of Quality," "When Knighthood Was in Flower" and "To Have and to Hold" will bring a nostalgic twinge.

Going further down the list one comes upon authors, living fresh in memory, authors such as Ellen Glasgow, whose "The Deliverance" was second only to Winston Churchill's "The Crossing" on the list of best-selling novels of 1904; to Rex Beach with "The Barrier" in 1908; Jeffery Farnol's "The Broad Highway" in 1909; and to the late Booth Tarkington's "The Turmoil" in 1915. Then came the topical books and novels of World War I, by Ian Hay, H. G. Wells, Ambassador Gerard and Blasco Ibañez. Post-war years marked the first appearances of the familiar moderns, who brought a new tone into our fiction—Sinclair Lewis, Edna Ferber, John

Charles Dana Gibson.

Erskine, Thornton Wilder, Pearl S. Buck. In the Thirties and Forties are titles which have become household words—"Anthony Adverse," "Gone With the Wind," "How to Win Friends and Influence People," "The Grapes of Wrath," "The Robe," "Strange Fruit," "Forever Amber."

To run over the best sellers of fifty years quickly is to evoke a lightning panorama of history, from Victorian morals to western expansion, then to war, postwar changes in our manners, gathering political tension, economic depression, war again. If we knew the titles of the books that will be best sellers in the Nineteen Fifties, Nineteen Sixties and Nineteen Seventies, we would gain a pretty good hint as to what our future will be.

Alice P. Hackett, a staff member of Publishers' Weekly, is the author of "50 Years of Best Sellers: 1895-1945."

October 6, 1946

FIFTY YEARS OF BEST SELLERS

1896

"Tom Grogan," by F. Hopkinson Smith.
"A Lady of Quality," by Frances Hodgson Burnett.

1897

"Quo Vadis," by Henry Sienkiewicz.
"The Choir Invisible," by James Lane Allen.

1898

"Caleb West," by F. Hopkinson Smith.
"Hugh Wynne," by S. Weir Mitchell.

1899

"David Harum," by Edward Noyes Westcott.
"When Knighthood Was in Flower," by Charles Major.

1900

"To Have and To Hold," by Mary Johnston.
"Red Pottage," by Mary Cholmondeley.

1901

"The Crisis," by Winston Churchill.
"Alice of Old Vincennes," by Maurice Thompson.

1902

"The Virginian," by Owen Wister.
"Mrs. Wiggs of the Cabbage Patch," by Alice Hegan Rice.

1903

"Lady Rose's Daughter," by Mrs. Humphry Ward.
"Gordon Keith," by Thomas Nelson Page.

1904

"The Crossing," by Winston Churchill.
"The Deliverance," by Ellen Glasgow.

1905

"The Marriage of William Ashe," by Mrs. Humphry Ward.
"Sandy," by Alice Hegan Rice.

1906

"Coniston," by Winston Churchill.
"Lady Baltimore," by Owen Wister.

1907

"The Lady of the Decoration," by Frances Little.
"The Weavers," by Gilbert Parker.

1908

"Mr. Crewe's Career," by Winston Churchill.
"The Barrier," by Rex Beach.

1909

"The Inner Shrine." Anonymous (Basil King).
"Katrine," by Elinor Macartney Lane.

1910

"The Rosary," by Florence Barclay.
"A Modern Chronicle," by Winston Churchill.

1911

"The Broad Highway," by Jeffery Farnol.
"The Prodigal Judge," by Vaughan Kester.

1912

"The Harvester," by Gene Stratton Porter.
"The Street Called Straight," by Basil King.

1913

"The Inside of the Cup," by Winston Churchill.
"V. V.'s Eyes," by Henry Sydnor Harrison.

1914

"The Eyes of the World," by Harold Bell Wright.
"Pollyanna," by Eleanor H. Porter.

1915

"The Turmoil," by Booth Tarkington.
"A Far Country," by Winston Churchill.

1916

"Seventeen," by Booth Tarkington.
"When a Man's a Man," by Harold Bell Wright.

1917

"Mr. Britling Sees It Through," by H. G. Wells.
"The First Hundred Thousand," by Ian Hay.

1918

"The U. P. Trail," by Zane Grey.
"My Four Years in Germany," by James W. Gerard.

1919

"The Four Horsemen of the Apocalypse," by V. Blasco Ibanez.
"The Education of Henry Adams," by Henry Adams.

1920

"The Man of the Forest," by Zane Grey.
"Now It Can Be Told," by Philip Gibbs.

1921

"Main Street," by Sinclair Lewis.
"The Outline of History," by H. G. Wells.

1922

"If Winter Comes," by A. S. M. Hutchinson.
"The Outline of History," by H. G. Wells.

1923

"Black Oxen," by Gertrude Atherton.
"Etiquette," by Emily Post.

1924

"So Big," by Edna Ferber.
"Diet and Health," by Lulu Hunt Peters.

1925

"Soundings," by A. Hamilton Gibbs.
"Diet and Health," by Lulu Hunt Peters.

1926

"The Private Life of Helen of Troy," by John Erskine.
"The Man Nobody Knows," by Bruce Barton.

1927

"Elmer Gantry," by Sinclair Lewis.
"The Story of Philosophy," by Will Durant.

1928

"The Bridge of San Luis Rey," by Thornton Wilder.
"Disraeli," by Andre Maurois.

1929

"All Quiet on the Western Front," by Erich Maria Remarque.
"The Art of Thinking," by Ernest Dimnet.

1930

"Cimarron," by Edna Ferber.
"The Story of San Michele," by Axel Munthe.

1931

"The Good Earth," by Pearl S. Buck.
"Education of a Princess," by Grand Duchess Marie.

1932

"The Good Earth," by Pearl S. Buck.
"The Epic of America," by James Truslow Adams.

1933

"Anthony Adverse," by Hervey Allen.
"Life Begins at Forty," by Walter B. Pitkin.

1934

"Anthony Adverse," by Hervey Allen.
"While Rome Burns," by Alexander Woollcott.

1935

"Green Light," by Lloyd C. Douglas.
"North to the Orient," by Anne Morrow Lindbergh.

1936

"Gone With the Wind," by Margaret Mitchell.
"Man the Unknown," by Alexis Carrel.

1937

"Gone With the Wind," by Margaret Mitchell.
"How to Win Friends and Influence People," by Dale Carnegie.

1938

"The Yearling," by Marjorie Kinnan Rawlings.
"The Importance of Living," by Lin Yutang.

1939

"The Grapes of Wrath," by John Steinbeck.
"Days of Our Years," by Pierre Van Paassen.

1940

"How Green Was My Valley," by Richard Llewellyn.
"I Married Adventure," by Osa Johnson.

1941

"The Keys of the Kingdom," by A. J. Cronin.
"Berlin Diary," by William L. Shirer.

1942

"The Song of Bernadette," by Franz Werfel.
"See Here, Private Hargrove," by Marion Hargrove.

1943

"The Robe," by Lloyd C. Douglas.
"Under Cover," by John Roy Carlson.

1944

"Strange Fruit," by Lillian Smith.
"I Never Left Home," by Bob Hope.

1945

"Forever Amber," by Kathleen Winsor.
"Brave Men," by Ernie Pyle.

October 6, 1946

MARK TWAIN.

Living Now in Riverdale—His Old Home in Hartford and the Life He Lived There.

OULD the gods of merriment and laughter be imagined as dwelling not only in the man in whom they have incarnated themselves, but also in his immediate neighborhood, the picturesque community of Riverdale on the Hudson must be now peopled with the jolliest crew of imps and sprites that ever joked together since fun began. For the most famous humorist of America, and of the world, has set up there a shrine for his much traveled household gods. Indeed, an account of Mark Twain in his various homes would be a theme rich enough for a whole volume of absorbing interest. It would be a miniature panorama of American scenery, cities, and communities, North and South, East and West, at one extreme pioneering and frontier life, at the other the most cultivated society in America: a comprehensive exhibit of American character, life, manners, and customs, such as no American author but Mark Twain possibly has known.

Born in 1835 in Missouri, working at his trade of printing in St. Louis, Cincinnati, Philadelphia, and New York, a pilot on Mississippi River steamboats, a silver miner and an editor in Nevada, a reporter, gold miner, and reporter again in California; a correspondent in the Hawaiian Islands, an editor living in Buffalo, then finally committed to authorship, a resident of Hartford, where he had two homes, with a Summer residence at Elmira and another in the Adirondacks; a great traveler beyond his own country in lands old and new—he would seem to be a cosmopolitan, at home in all places, exemplifying throughout his life the characteristic ability of the frontiersman to land anywhere on his feet. A near kinsman quotes him as saying that he can be contented anywhere if he does not have to move, while a friend of many years, Mark Twain, says he has lived more and in more places than any one he ever knew. In a letter this friend writes: "You can never picture the mining camp structures of the dear fellow or the hardships of his Pacific Coast life."

In "Roughing It" Mark Twain has described one of these mining camp homes, a small, rude cabin built in the side of the crevice of a cañon and roofed with canvas, a corner being left open "to serve as a chimney, through which the cattle used to tumble occasionally at night, and mash our furniture and interrupt one's sleep."

In striking contrast with this mining cabin was the beautiful house in Buffalo, given as a wedding present to Mr. and Mrs. Clemens by the bride's father, Mr. Jervis Langdon. It had all been kept a secret from Mark Twain, who was shown through the brilliantly lighted house, mysteriously filled with kinsmen and friends, till finally the young wife broke out, "It's ours—yours and mine—a gift from father!" With all eyes turned curiously upon him, his own eyes wet with tears, his voice choking with emotion, he replied, his thoughts spontaneously expressing themselves even here in the form of humor: "Mr. Langdon, whenever you are in Buffalo, if it's twice a year, come right up here, and bring your bag with you. You may stay over night, if you want to. It sha'n't cost you a cent." In this reply one feels the secret of that carrying force which has given Mark Twain his high place in American letters. The form of his perception is humorous, he instinctively clothes a thought or feeling in humorous guise, but he sees more than that aspect of things, and, paradoxical as it may sound, exercises a high degree of restraint in the very act of exaggeration.

When he finally relinquished journalism for authorship and went to Hartford, he lived in the house of Mrs. Isabel Beecher Hooker until he built his own house. This beautiful and costly residence, designed by Edward Tuckerman Potter, stands on a picturesque slope on Farmington Avenue near the Park River, which runs through Mr. Clemens's grounds, making a loop so near the house that from the windows one almost fancies the land on the further side an island. In the spacious library there is a fine old oak mantel over the fireplace, which Mr. Clemens brought from a house in Scotland. Over the fireplace is an inscription in brass, which in a measure explains why this house and the library in particular became a notable centre of hospitality. The inscription reads: "The ornament of a house is the friends who frequent it." This room achieved a distinction for sociability and hospitality, which still elicits eloquent appreciation from the neighbors of Mr. and Mrs. Clemens, though it is now a decade since they have occupied their Hartford house. In the evenings they gave themselves and their time to entertaining their friends, and being agreeable to a degree which was exceptional for literary people. They had many distinguished visitors, authors and actors, whom they shared generously with their friends, not in evening soirées, but at dinner parties, to which enough were invited to make a large gathering. Mr. Clemens, with his inexhaustible fund of stories and his inimitable way of telling them, entertained his guests for hours, and there were no moments of lagging or dullness.

The machinery for all this entertaining, according to one of Mr. Clemens's neighbors familiar to the house, was managed by Mrs. Clemens. She had a great faculty for carrying on the household and family. The house was very charming, and the entertainments agreeable to everybody. Mrs. Clemens had the faculty of giving the dinner party, and Mr. Clemens embroidered it.

After the children were grown they used to have plays, neighborhood dramas, in which Mr. Clemens took a part. They acted some of Shakespeare's plays and brought out 'The Prince and the Pauper' with great elaboration. Mr. Clemens appeared in it. They had a regular stage improvised, and scenery.

On the evenings of holidays they had the custom of having large parties, in which every one took part in charades. Mr. Clemens was the principal promoter of these.

One never saw him smile in telling a story. He always preserves a look of seriousness. It may be said that his house was one where a great many people with wants called. The neighbors' impression was that these wants were all pretty carefully investigated and responded to generously and conscientiously. The family wanted to be liberal and just and do everything they possibly could do for every one.

Mr. Clemens was a most domestic man. Certainly he was the most domestic man in Hartford or anywhere else. He went out very little. He was almost always exclusively at home. He played billiards a good deal. Through the day he would play alone; in the evenings with his friends.

Probably it is no news that he smoked more than twenty-four hours in the day. He went regularly to church every Sunday with his wife. Coming out from church he would sometimes light his cigar before he out of the church porch.

His mother visited him here some years ago. She was a very old-fashioned person and he was careful not to say or do anything which he thought would shock the strict religious convictions he knew her to have in previous years. One day she said to him, 'Samuel, don't be so careful. My sentiments are the same as yours,' at which he was thunderstruck. She had the same drawl in her speech which he has. He came honestly by it.

He was very kind and sympathetic in the neighborhood. He visited informally among the people, and was always welcome and exceedingly entertaining. When out walking he would improvise poetry when moved by some sight—the trees, for instance. Once he was walking when there had been an ice storm, and the trees were glittering with ice. He broke out into a magnificent improvisation. There was a long exordium. It was very impressive.

One Winter he read the works of Browning to a class of ladies. It proved him to be a great reader. They saw Browning as they could not have done without his dramatic interpretation. It was very powerful. It cannot be said that he missed his vocation by being an author, but he would have been a great actor. He would have had just as much success on the stage. His secret is force. He strikes a tremendous blow. It can't be avoided.

The feeling in the community for the Clemens family is one of warmth. Generally new-comers have to wait a long time for social recognition. It was not so in their case. They were at once taken into everything, and with the greatest cordiality. There is a very general regret at their absence. If they should come back, their house would become again a centre of hospitality, and Mr. Clemens's appearance here in any public capacity, a dinner, or the like, would be the signal for great pleasure. They are a pair, Mr. and Mrs. Clemens; they work together.

In the billiard room at the top of the house, where Mark Twain did much of his writing, is a small writing desk, a few bookshelves filled with miscellaneous books, works of history, and the French book of our old friend Ollendorf. On the walls hang a few prints, one of Gutenberg, and some illustrations by Remington. In a little window behind a photograph of an autograph-covered programme of a complimentary dinner given to Salvini at the Brunswick, New York, in 1883, I found framed with an old-fashioned postage stamp inclosed for reply, a letter requesting Mr. Clemens to write an article on housekeeping a hundred years hence. A world of readers would be only too glad to have him live to comply with that request. On the wall near the door, in a frame, hung the original checks paid to Mrs. Grant for General Grant's Memoirs. The first read:

No. 313. New York, Feb. 27, 1886.
NEW YORK NATIONAL BANK.
Pay to the order of Mrs. Julia D. Grant, Two Hundred Thousand Dollars.
$200,000. C. L. WEBSTER & CO.

Beneath it the second read:

No. 169. New York, Oct. 1, 1886.
MT. MORRIS BANK.
Pay to the order of Mrs. Julia D. Grant, One Hundred and Fifty Thousand Dollars.
$150,000. C. L. WEBSTER & CO.

On the opposite wall hung a water-color representative of Mark Twain's favorite study, the den in the rocks at Quarry Farm, Elmira. This study, designed by Alfred H. Thorp, Mr. Clemens occupied in the Summer, which his family often spent at the Langdon place. His intimate friend, the Rev. Joseph H. Twichell, has put me in possession of a description of this vine-covered study in Mark Twain's own language:

It is the loveliest study you ever saw. It is octagonal, with a peaked roof, each face filled with a spacious window, and it sits perched in complete isolation on top of an elevation that commands leagues of valley and city and retreating ranges of distant blue hills. It is a cozy nest, with just room in it for a sofa and a table and three or four chairs; and when the storms sweep down the remote valley, and the lightning flashes above the hills beyond, and the rain beats upon the roof over my head—imagine the luxury of it!

Here the "Tramp Abroad," begun at Heidelberg and continued at Munich, was completed or rewritten, for he was so dissatisfied with the first draft of the book that he was inclined to abandon it altogether.

During his sojourn in Hartford Mark Twain often ran down to New York. A pretty tale is told of his return home one afternoon with a young lady who was then taking a course of study at Smith College. On leaving the Grand Central Station Mr. Clemens had a seat in the parlor car between her, whom he did not then know, and an elderly woman. The latter presently desired the window opened. Mr. Clemens came to her assistance. On reaching the Park Avenue tunnel she wished it closed. Again he assisted her. When the train entered the Harlem lowlands she wished it open, and again Mr. Clemens was polite. After entering the open country beyond the Bronx a strong wind came into the car, and she asked to have the window closed, which Mr. Clemens promptly had done. Meanwhile the Smith College girl, turning in her chair, had been unable to suppress a smile. Mr. Clemens observing this, remarked in a low voice: "I've traveled all over the world, and have met this woman before."

From that time until New Haven was reached Mr. Clemens entertained the under graduate with characteristic sallies of wit. After the train slowed up at that station he and she emerged from the car for sandwiches, but lingered at the counter until the train had started without their knowing it. Seizing her hand, Mr. Clemens at his best pace ran after the train with mademoiselle, and with much effort leaped to the steps, assisting her to rise ahead of him. Once on the train, he told her who he was, she having already suspected, but not knowing for a certainty. Many years have passed without another meeting. The two are now near neighbors on the Hudson. They not infrequently come to town by the same train.

For reasons of which he is the only proper judge, Mr. Clemens has a rule with regard to being interviewed, which has made necessary the writing of this article, mainly from such incidents as his friends and associates have felt at liberty to tell. These have responded with a courtesy and an enthusiasm which have made its preparation an enjoyable experience, while Mr. Clemens's own kindness and hospitality have made obvious the reason for the loyalty and enthusiasm of his friends. "Make all the charges you want to against me," said Mr. Clemens in his fun-provoking drawl. "That's all right. Anybody has a right to his opinion of me, but don't say I said anything."

CHARLES TILDEN SEMPERS.

December 7, 1901

Will Rogers in Minnesota Sends Advice to Coolidge

To the Editor of The New York Times:

MINNEAPOLIS, Minn., April 9.—Just been over today and addressed the Legislature of the great State of Minnesota. A fellow named Johnson interpreted for me. I didn't go to Norway, Sweden and Denmark last year. I didn't think there was any use as I knew I was going to play here this year.

They are still hollering for farmers' relief and are trying to throw out Senator Shaw, who is in the United State Senate, and bring back Magnus Johnson, the best milker that ever hit Capitol Hill.

Mr. Coolidge has been invited here to this State, but if I were him I would be afraid to come.

Yours, WILL.

April 10, 1927

Will Rogers in Chicago Discusses Politics and Crime

To the Editor of The New York Times:

CHICAGO, April 10.—Bill Thompson is a fast worker. Elected two days ago, he decided he would like to start Mayoring about tomorrow. No lame duck Mayors in this burg. When the votes are counted your hat is waiting. Congress and the Senate ought to do that. Why give 'em six months to repent on salary? This is the Rogers and Dawes plan. Yours,

WILL.

P. S.—Buried a bandit here yesterday. Had thirty-five thousand dollars' worth of flowers. It's the florist that's backing this crime wave. Undertakers advertise their high-priced coffins: "Fit for a bandit." Glorified crime.

April 11, 1927

Novel Prohibition Debate Proposed by Will Rogers

To the Editor of The New York Times:

VINCENNES, Ind., April 12.—It's all the rage now to hold a debate on prohibition, if you can find a crowd drunk enough to pay to hear it.

I hereby challenge Billy Sunday on the subject: "Resolved, That the talk and arguments used for and against prohibition are worse on the public's morals than the drinking." Billy can take either side, affirmative, negative, progressive or farmers' relief.

At the finish we will split 50-50. He can take the decision and I will take the gate receipts.

Yours for getting this settled by the right people,

MR. ROGERS.

P. S.: Let me hear from this, Billy, over in Aurora, right away. If you don't take me, why, Aimee will.

April 13, 1927

Will Rogers Reveals a Sure Drawing Card for Lectures

To the Editor of The New York Times:

ONEONTA, N. Y., May 16.—When I am playing in a town and it looks like there is not going to be much of a house, I announce through the papers that that night I will read passages from "Elmer Gantry," the Baptist sheik, and the house will be packed with Methodist and Presbyterian women. Old Elmer sure had It.

Yours,

WILL.

May 17, 1927

Rogers Knows How It Feels To Have Your Radio Go Bad

To the Editor of The New York Times:

LOS ANGELES, Cal., July 1.—Wasn't it great about Commander Byrd and his gang landing safe?

Don't tell Mrs. Byrd, but my nurse says he is better looking than Lindbergh. I can imagine how humiliated he was when his radio went on the bum. Mine went fluey during the ninth inning of a tied world series game, and I wished I had had an ocean to drop it into. Yours,

WILL.

P. S.—Lost my last tube today and have no interior mechanical connection with the outside world. In fact I've lost my outside aerial.

July 2, 1927

Will Rogers Finds Washington Better With Congress Away

To the Editor of The New York Times:

WASHINGTON, Aug. 26.—Tourists, you are missing something if you don't visit Washington while the politicians are not here. You have no idea the difference it makes. The bootleggers have followed their constituents back home. The embassy bars are closed; even Washington's national pest, the lobbyists, have gone home to take up another collection. Why, if they could get this Capitol moved away from here this would be one of the best towns in America. I think there are people in this city smart enough to vote. Yours,

Boosting for a town that's not to blame for its shortcomings,

WILL ROGERS.

August 27, 1927

"Quo Vadis" as History.

Written for THE NEW YORK TIMES by
Harry Thurston Peck,
Professor of Latin in Columbia University, Editor of "Harper's Classical Dictionary."

"Quo Vadis" has been the most extensively circulated book of the year that has just ended. It heads all the booksellers' lists as the work that was oftenest called for, and the gap between it and the next most popular novel is an enormous one. It was not only first, but there was practically no second. Now there are two kinds of popular novels, of which "Trilby" and "Beside the Bonnie Brier Bush" may be taken as respective types. One is always not only bought and circulated and read by every one, but it is also widely talked about. It is the subject of newspaper jokes. It is parodied. It is taken as a text by sensational clergymen. It is a theme for village reading clubs and literary societies. Its success is, in fact, a noisy one. The other kind of book is also bought and circulated and read by every one, but it is not so very much discussed. "Quo Vadis" belongs to the second rather than to the first of these two classes of popular books. All intelligent readers know of it. Most of them have bought it or borrowed it, and have perused it. But they do not say a great deal about it. It has not been burlesqued on the stage. The professional funny man has not taken it up. No enterprising manufacturer, so far as I am aware, has yet brought out a Quo Vadis shirt-collar or a Sienkiewicz necktie.

The principal reason for this is found in the fact that it is essentially a serious book. It is, indeed, less a novel than a picture of manners, a study of social, intellectual, and political conditions. It is an attempt to embody in the form of a story a bit of the Roman "Culturgeschichte." Consequently such discussion as it has so far excited springs from the very natural and interesting questions: "As a social picture, is it in reality a true one?" and "Is the author in its pages buttressed by historic fact, or is he simply drawing on a powerful and exuberant imagination?" These questions have been asked of me again and again, and it is from this point of view that a few words may be appropriately written here of what is undeniably the most widely read novel of the day.

There are three points as to which one should consider the book in estimating its historical value. These are, first, the purely archaeological question as to its mise en scene, the accuracy of its details, and the glimpses which it gives of Roman usage and custom in the imperial age; second, the personal, relating to its representation of historical characters; and, third, its general fidelity to truth in the impression that it gives of the spirit of the time, and of the thought and feeling of the Roman people during the reign of Nero.

On the archaeological side it may be said that "Quo Vadis" is in the main accurate and reliable. Its author has evidently read much of classical literature and of those works that deal with ancient life and manners. A thousand little touches make this certain, and they show its author to possess an innate historical instinct and an admirable sense of proportion. Some of his bits of description are really fine, and glow with color. Such is his picture of the great Forum Romanum through which Lygia was carried by the slaves of Aulus Plautius. The forest of glittering columns, the white fronts of the temples, the maze of porticos, the din of the money changers, the strange cosmopolitan throng swarming amid the countless arches and colonnades, the mountebanks and sharpers—all these are drawn with a vigor and vivacity that bring them sharply before us and make us see with our own eyes one of the most wonderful sights that the world has ever known. Equally good is the vivid picture of the palace of Nero and of the midnight orgy at which roses dropped from the vaulted ceiling upon the panting, sweating, wine-inflamed banqueters, who clashed their goblets of gold as the shameless dancing girls mingled with the throng, while Emperor and guests alike all wallowed in a license that knew no bounds. And no less forceful and true is the account of the scene in the amphitheatre where the Christians were destroyed after shameful tortures, torn apart by horses, hurled from a height to fall in bloody pulp upon the arena, crucified, or rent by savage beasts.

But Sienkiewicz is not an archaeologist, and his wide reading, his careful study, and his glowing imagination have not given him that absolute command of detail which can belong only to the specialist in any subject. There are slips to be detected here and there, a few of which may be indicated as illustrative of all. Thus, on the very first page and elsewhere, Petronius, the rich and splendid patrician, is housed in an "insula." Now an "insula" was a building apart from any neighboring houses, and occupying a "block" by itself, like some of the great hotels of modern cities. There is nothing absolutely impossible in the ascription of such an abode to Petronius, for in the smaller towns like Pompeii "insulae" were sometimes the dwellings of the rich and great. Yet at Rome the word is properly to be understood of a tenement house let out in flats, while the home of the wealthy was styled "domus." There is an anachronism involved in the introduction, at the end of the ninth chapter, of a freedman, with "his face marked with smallpox"; for no mention of smallpox in Europe is found until four hundred years after the period described in "Quo Vadis," and no Roman author ever speaks of such a disease. A literary blunder occurs in relation to the writings of Petronius. In the second chapter he is described as purchasing at a book shop a copy of his own work, the "Satyricon," (better "Satira";) while in the eleventh chapter he is said to be still at work upon his "Feast of Trimalchio." But the "Feast of Trimalchio" is not, as the author appears to think, a work separate from the "Satyricon," but is merely one of the episodes contained in that curious book, the best remaining specimen of the ancient novel. A famous saying which has been often misquoted in modern times is ascribed to Petronius in the misquoted form. This is "ne sutor ultra crepidam"—properly "ne sutor supra crepidam." The proper names are often incorrectly given, as Vitelius for Vitellius, Caius for Gaius, and the author prefers Capiton to Capito, Trimalchion to Trimalchio, and so with other names. These things and others like them are none of them important, but are merely little flaws in a really fine and impressive piece of work by no means affecting its genuine fidelity to fact.

As to the delineation of historical characters, high praise must also be given here. Petronius, the glass of fashion at Nero's court—soldier, administrator, athlete, poet, novelist, cynic, refined debauchee, sublimated man of the world as such men were at Rome—is a picture filled out with plausibility and skill from the slight sketch preserved in Tacitus. Vitellius, the glutton; Poppaea, the sweet-faced wanton, who bathed herself in asses' milk and set human blood flowing in the gutters; Acte, the freedwoman of Nero, once his mistress and now neglected by him, but still loving him—these and others are true to the ancient authorities who have preserved their personal histories. If one may take exception to any of our author's portraiture, this should be done, perhaps, regarding the view he gives of Nero. This moral monster is set before us with intense vividness—a strange compound of monkey, drunkard, and buffoon, blinking his corpse-like eyes, leering malignantly, and with a ghastly face tinged by the bluish color of his tunic. As he sits at his feast, peering through the emerald that serves him as a lens, he is a hideous and appalling figure. But while, in the main, the Nero of "Quo Vadis" is the Nero of Suetonius, there is an exaggeration of his vanity and of his morbid greed for flattery that passes almost into the region of caricature. And this rather mars the artistic effect of the delineation as a whole.

As to the impression given in the book of the spirit and the tendencies of the Neronian age, it may be said that in this also Sienkiewicz is accurate and trustworthy, if we understand his description to refer strictly to the City of Rome and not to the Roman Empire as a whole. For between the Roman City and the Roman State a great difference existed. It is often asked how a political organization could be held together when such things as Tacitus and Suetonius narrate were possible—the capital of the State a seething mass of physical and moral corruption, an Emperor alternating between the moods of a tiger and the tricks of an ape, a society rotten to the very core. But as a matter of fact, the Roman city was, as an eminent modern historian has described her, the lightning-rod that drew upon itself all the bolts of horror and destruction, to leave the rest of the empire blessed with smiling peace and political contentment in its role of tributary and purveyor to the capital. For it is not true that the provinces in the first century were tainted and terrorized as was the seat of Government, and hence the folly is egregious of those who talk so glibly about the corruption of the Roman people as the cause of the empire's ultimate dismemberment. These persons are, in fact, the same unsuspecting and guileless souls who think that the defeat of France in the Franco-Prussian War was due to moral causes and was a tribute to the superior virtue of the Germans—a pleasing tenet impossible to any one familiar with the darker phases of modern German life.

Rome itself, however, was just the Rome that "Quo Vadis" reveals to us. Its ablest men had long before laid by the old religion in everything except the picturesque and stately forms that still were vaguely reminiscent of the days of national virility; and they had begun to weary of the cold and shadowy philosophy that had for a time usurped the place of faith. And all through the lower strata of society a new belief was germinating with a vitality which, apart from a supernatural origin, laid an unshakable grasp upon the human heart, because it taught what neither the theology nor the philosophy of paganism had ever really cared to teach—the universal brotherhood of man.

HARRY THURSTON PECK.

January 29, 1898

A NOTABLE NOVEL.*

Churchill's "Richard Carvel"—An Event of Importance in American Fiction.

Reviewed for THE NEW YORK TIMES SATURDAY REVIEW by Hamilton W. Mabie.

The appearance of Mr. Winston Churchill's novel of manners and of adventure, "Richard Carvel," promises to be an event of importance in the history of American fiction. Mr. Churchill is a new writer, and the advent of a fresh talent is always interesting. Every novelist of any real gift has his own point of view, and gives us a picture of life from a new angle: imagination, insight, skill, and character conspire, in a novel combination, to open a vista hitherto closed. The advent of a true maker of fiction means, therefore, an addition to the resources of literature and of life.

Mr. Churchill's field is, moreover, essentially an untrodden one; he had its earliest bloom and harvest of impression, sentiment, and fact. Other men have touched its outskirts, but no one has traversed it before. The Annapolis of the late pre-Revolutionary period has not been painted before on such a scale and from a knowledge so intimate and so alive with intelligence and sympathy. The London of Charles James Fox and of David Garrick has found many delineators, but it has not been approached before from the standpoint of an American colonist, who could feel its charm at the very moment when his heart was aflame with indignation at its dull indifference or active hostility to the rights of Englishmen beyond the sea.

There were promising qualities in Mr. Churchill's earlier story, "The Celebrity," but one could hardly have found in that slight and somewhat loosely constructed sketch the prophecy of a piece of fiction so mature, so thoroughly made in the technical sense, so large in outline, and yet so rich in significant detail, as "Richard Carvel." For this novel is the most extensive piece of semi-historical fiction which has yet come from an American hand; it is on a larger scale than any of its predecessors, and the skill with which the materials have been handled justifies the largeness of the plan.

American fiction began with the publication of "The Spy," a story which owes its interest to its theme and to Cooper's easy way of handling his materials, rather than to any deep insight into character or any notable charm of style. There have been a number of fairly successful attempts in the field of semi-historical fiction, but none of them made any real impression until the appearance of Dr. Mitchell's "Hugh Wynne," a novel of distinct quality and full of a delightful atmosphere. The material in American history for semi-historical fiction is almost inexhaustible, but it has hardly been explored as yet.

*RICHARD CARVEL By Winston Churchill, 12mo. New York: The Macmillan Company. $1.50

There are indications, however, that it is beginning to touch the imagination of the country; a result due in large measure to the new spirit in which the later historians have approached their themes and dealt with them. In "The Virginians" Thackeray occasionally makes us aware that he is not entirely at home on this side the ocean, but his sensitiveness to social conditions gave him a true insight into old Virginia life. It is to this picturesque and dignified life in the tidewater country that Mr. Churchill returns in "Richard Carvel." Cooper portrayed conditions on the outskirts of old New York, Dr. Mitchell made his Revolutionary sketch with Philadelphia as a background, Mr. Paul Ford has chosen another part of the same field, Mr. Churchill goes back to the seaboard life on the Chesapeake, the Potomac, and the James. In "Prisoners of Hope" Miss Johnston gave us a very sympathetic and interesting study of this life at an earlier period and with special reference to social conditions; in "Richard Carvel" we have a study of manners at the very moment when the old order was changing and the rising tide of democracy in the new world was about to destroy much of the old-time stateliness and elegance. Mr. Churchill has drawn the Colonial aristocracy with a free hand; he has made us see its habits of life, its elaborate dress and equally elaborate manners, its assemblies and routs, its easy tolerance of the social vices, and its somewhat fiery defense of its own dignity. In contrast with this old-time society, preserving the old-world tradition of personal elegance in the simplicity of new-world conditions and following implicitly the lead and fashion of that old world, he shows us the rising lawyer and landowner, the dissolute parson, the brave figures of the ardent young leaders who were soon to surrender ease of life for arduous service in the field.

As a companion picture, by a series of rapid and picturesque incidents, we are transported to London and introduced to the brilliant and dissolute society the splendor and the vices of which were reproduced in fainter colors at Annapolis. That society was rich in men of strong personality; but Charles James Fox was still in the full tide of his early dissipations, and the splendid chapter of his heroic opposition to a stubborn King and to a succession of servile or corrupt Ministers was still to be written. The show and brilliancy of that irresponsible, gambling, prodigal, and witty period Mr. Churchill has thrown upon his spacious canvas with a steady and skillful hand, holding a happy balance between individual character and fortune and the rich and varied social background. In the perilous task of introducing historic personages, Mr. Churchill has not failed to show his intimate knowledge of the men of the time and his power to realize them in his imagination. If he has not made us see all of Fox, he has made all of Fox comprehensible to us.

The charm and value of this reproduction of contemporary English society on both sides of the Atlantic at a critical moment in the history of both branches of the English-speaking race can be appreciated only when one becomes aware, by the impression left in his own mind, of the clearness with which the opposing forces of progress and conservatism on both sides of the sea are shown in terms of social and political action. After reading "Richard Carvel" one understands why the King was permitted to pursue a course the sheer folly of which Sir George Trevelyan has recently pointed out with cogency and wealth of illustration.

Something ought to be said of Mr. Churchill's novel from the side of incident and adventure, for it has uncommon narrative interest; but it is as a story of manners that "Richard Carvel" must be judged, and from this standpoint there is good ground for believing that it has come to take its place as a piece of enduring literature.

HAMILTON W. MABIE.

July 1, 1899

Mr. Churchill on Historical Fiction.

In an interview published in a recent number of The Critic, Mr. Winston Churchill expresses some views concerning historical fiction which seem to me worthy of comment. Whatever may be said of the quality of his writing, Mr. Churchill has become one of the most popular authors of historical novels in this country. His books influence thousands of readers, among them a large number of young people. So, anything he says on the subject of historical fiction in general has considerable importance. Asked if, in taking Daniel Webster for a character in a novel, he would represent Webster as he was, with his defects, Mr. Churchill replied: "I should consider it wrong to expose the weaknesses of a man like Webster, because he is a historical ideal that should not be shattered. The same is true in regard to Hamilton; whereas, with a man like Aaron Burr, I should not hesitate to portray him exactly as he was, as that would mean no loss to historical ideals." It seems pitiful that such a view should be expressed by a mature man who has sufficient intelligence and energy to write novels so ambitious as "Richard Carvel" and "The Crisis." Reduced to bald terms, it means, of course, that the historical novelist need have no conscience in dealing with men of the past, no justice, no duty to tell his readers the truth. As an acquaintance of mine remarked on reading the reference in the interview to Burr, Mr. Churchill apparently advocates the doctrine that when a great figure is down, it is perfectly fair to hit him.

I wonder if the time will come when we shall appreciate the childish folly and the dishonesty of dealing with history as Mr. Churchill would deal with it in fiction! From generation to generation, lies about great men are passed down by people who take credit to themselves for their misrepresentation. The evil finds its widest scope and does its most pernicious work in our public schools, by means of the ridiculously partisan books which the children are given to study. What grown man who thinks at all does not look back either with amusement and contempt or with indignation at the misleading teaching given at school in the spirit of patriotism? A good deal of the information, it is true, is honestly offered by writers and teachers whose prejudices lead them astray, but the consequences are none the less deplorable. It is not often that a writer comes out openly like Mr. Churchill and advocates dishonesty.

JOHN D. BARRY.

April 12, 1902

Gen. Wallace and Ben Hur

By STEWART HOLBROOK

MOST literate Americans have read or at least heard of Gen. Lew Wallace's tremendously popular "Ben Hur: A Tale of the Christ" which appeared with little noise in 1880. The book seemed at first a dismal flop, but within a year its sale started to pick up and it has never ceased. Thirty-three years after its publication, a Chicago mail-order house purchased an edition of 1,000,000 copies—"each book covered with a jacket showing a gorgeous reproduction of the Chariot Race"—and sold them with little effort. "Ben Hur" was translated into almost every language and was also one of the first novels to be put into "raised letters," as Braille used to be known.

What makes "Ben Hur" historically important, however, is neither its wide popularity nor its theme. It is an epochal book because it was the first American novel to break through the rustic and village opposition to popular fiction. "Ben Hur" rode that gilded chariot right through the front door to enter the homes of Hard-Shell Baptists and Methodists and other non-novel-reading sects, and to an eager welcome. Thousands of back-country Americans first learned the charms of fiction from "Ben Hur." "Uncle Tom's Cabin" doesn't count because it was not considered a novel at all but a Christian tract dictated by a Northern Congregational god.

The man who wrote "Ben Hur" was as remarkable as his book, but all else about him, save this one volume, has largely been forgotten. He was born Lewis Wallace at Brookville, Ind., in 1827, the son of a distinguished father. Young Wallace was a restless youth who liked to hunt, to fish, play soldier, and also to write and paint. Before he left home to serve as an officer in the Mexican War he had finished a novel, "The Man at Arms: A Tale of the Tenth Century." It was never published. He also started another story titled "The Fair God," of which more later.

DURING the Eighteen Fifties Wallace practiced law, was elected to the United States Senate, and moved his home to Crawfordsville, Ind., where he devoted much time to drilling a militia company. At the outbreak of war in 1861 he was made adjutant general of the State and did a bang-up job recruiting Hoosiers and drilling them. He went to war himself and made a fine record, serving ably at Fort Donelson, at Shiloh, stopped the Confederate General Kirby-Smith in

General Lew Wallace.

his attempt on Cincinnati, and held the formidable Jubal Early at bay in 1864 when the raider seemed about to take Washington.

Full of military honors, Wallace returned to Indiana after the war and completed the novel he had started many years before. "The Fair God" (1873) was quite a success, and its author at once began work on his magnum opus. It has often been related that Wallace was inspired to write "Ben Hur" as a reply to the heretical utterances of Col. Robert Ingersoll, the noted agnostic. This story was doubtless manufactured as publicity pap to please those readers to whom the amiable Ingersoll was a horned devil. Wallace himself said his inspiration came from a passage in the New Testament: "Now, when Jesus was born in Bethlehem of Judea, in the days of Herod, the King, behold there came three wise men from the East to worship him."

He began writing "Ben Hur" in 1875, with the idea of serial publication in a magazine. He put an immense amount of work into the background—studying and checking books of travels and travelers, comparing them with detailed maps, delving into geology and ethnology—writing slowly and constantly. He wrote as often as he could in the beech grove around his Crawfordsville home; but his law practice called for some attention, and he wrote at his book in his office, in courtrooms, in hotels. He composed Tirza's song, "Wait Not," on a belated train between Indianapolis and Crawfordsville. He worked best, he believed, beneath a favorite old beech tree.

How often, when its thick branches have protected me with their cooling shadows, has it been the only witness to my struggles; and how often, too, has it maintained great dignity when it might have laughed at my discomfiture. The soft twittering of birds, the hum of bees, the lowing of the kine, all made this spot dear to me.

BUT he didn't finish the book under the beeches. Instead, the last chapter was done in "a vile old chamber" in the fort at Santa Fe, a "gloomy den indeed," where he found himself by grace of having been appointed Territorial Governor of New Mexico in 1878. Here he could not devote all his time to writing. Hell was popping. He had a feuding cattle war on his hands, and he also had William Bonney, worse known as Billy the Kid, a buck-toothed, adenoidal hoodlum who killed for the hell of it and is the hero of several dismal ballads.

"Ben Hur" appeared in mid-1880. Very slowly it worked into a best-seller. In thirteen years it had sold 600,000 copies. It reached the 1,000,000-copy mark about 1911. The House of Harper informs me that at least 2,500,000 copies have been sold. The exact figure cannot be known.

"BEN HUR" made Wallace a national character, and in 1881 President Garfield appointed him Minister to Turkey, telling him: "General, I shall expect another book out of you," and added, "Your official duties will not be too numerous to allow you to write. Locate it in Constantinople." Thus did a President give an assignment to write a book. And the United States Government subsidized Wallace with a well-paid sabbatical that lasted four years. Wallace followed Garfield's suggestion, writing "The Prince of India," a rather tiresome and long-winded tale with the Wandering Jew as a principal character. The book appeared in 1893 and did very well, though it never achieved the popularity of "Ben Hur."

Throughout his long life Wallace remained simple and democratic. Tall, erect and urbane, and fluent as well, he was a favorite, second only to Ingersoll, on the lecture platform. An interviewer wrote that Wallace was most generous of his time in encouraging young writers. Will D. Howe, now at work on what is certain to be a charming autobiography, thinks that Wallace's interviewer was possibly overly enthusiastic. Mr. Howe recalls Wallace, whom he knew, as a man who kept his eye pretty much on the ball, who was not prone to giving much time or thought to young writers of the day.

In spite of "Ben Hur's" theme, Wallace was never a member of any church. He died in 1905, aged 78, a typical relic of the old school, still wearing his Custer-like mustaches, plus a beard in the Benjamin Harrison tradition.

There can be little doubt as to "Ben Hur's" influence. Carl Van Doren, who was reared in a region where popular novels, in spite of the pure and prissy fiction of E. P. Roe and J. G. Holland, had never really been accepted, hands the palm to "Ben Hur" and to "Ben Hur" almost alone for breaking down the barriers of Hard-Shell Calvinism and letting American fiction into the homes of the pious pioneers of the Middle and Far West.

"'Ben Hur,'" says Mr. Van Doren, "positively won the ultimate victory over village opposition. It was read by thousands who had read no other novel except perhaps 'Uncle Tom's Cabin,' and they hardly thought of either book as a novel. Still more thousands learned to know the geography, ethnology and customs of first-century Judea and Antioch as through no other source." Mr. Van Doren also thinks that "Ben Hur" contains "a vitality which has a touch of genius."

MANY American missionaries and colporteurs were inspired to their work by "Ben Hur." One of the best of them, the bluff and able Albert L. Shelton, who spent so many years in China and Tibet, said flatly that the idea of becoming a missionary had never entered his head until his first reading of Wallace's book. Other missionaries translated "Ben Hur" into Oriental languages.

The play, which William Young adapted from the book, increased "Ben Hur's" fame and sales. On April 2, 1907, the stage version gave its 2,500th consecutive performance at New York's Academy of Music; and "Ben Hur" road companies played every American city that could offer a theatre with a stage large enough for the treadmill needed for "The Stupendous Chariot Race—Real Horses, Real Charioteers."

August 6, 1944

A FINE NOVEL OF THE CIVIL WAR

Miss Mitchell's "Gone With the Wind" Is an Absorbing Narrative

GONE WITH THE WIND. *By Margaret Mitchell.* 1,037 pp. *New York: The Macmillan Company.* $3.

By J. DONALD ADAMS

THIS is beyond a doubt one of the most remarkable first novels produced by an American writer. It is also one of the best. I would go so far as to say that although it is not the equal in style or in artistic conception of such a first novel as Miss Roberts's "The Time of Man," it is, in narrative power, in sheer readability, surpassed by nothing in American fiction. "Gone With the Wind" is by no means a great novel, in the sense that "War and Peace" is, or even "Henry Esmond," to name only novels which dealt, like this one, with past periods of time. But it is a long while since the American reading public has been offered such a bounteous feast of excellent story telling. If this tale of the Civil War and the Reconstruction days which followed does not attract to itself more readers than even "Anthony Adverse" I shall be more than mildly surprised.

Miss Mitchell's performance is remarkable on several counts. She spent, we are told, seven years in writing this book. One can readily believe that, and as heartily wish that more young novelists would follow her example. Even so, that a first book should display a narrative sense so sure, so unwaveringly sustained through more than a thousand pages, is little short of amazing. But Miss Mitchell can do more than tell a story. She can people it with characters who are not merely described, but who live, grow older and change under our eyes, as do our friends. At least four of the people in this book achieve a quality of life as vivid as may be caught on the printed page.

"Gone With the Wind" seems to me the best Civil War novel that has yet been written. It is an extraordinary blending of romantic and realistic treatment, as any worthwhile re-creation in fiction of those years should be. I am not forgetting Mary Johnston's "The Long Roll" and "Cease Firing," nor Miss Glasgow's "The Battleground," of which the first two contained the most vivid battle scenes of the Civil War that have been done in fiction, and the last, though by no means on the level of Miss Glasgow's maturer work, a vivid picture of what the war meant to non-combatants in the South. Nor am I forgetting a more recent book, Stark Young's "So Red the Rose." But that novel, looked at now in retrospect, was more a personal statement, a memorial wreath laid before a cherished tradition and way of life, than it was a work of the creative imagination.

Miss Mitchell's book is more objective in its approach, more in the mood, let us say, of McKinlay Kantor's "Long Remember." It is, however, much wider in scope and filled with a greater vitality. Miss Mitchell, like Mr. Kantor, paints no battle scenes; like him, she chooses a focal point about which swirls the war itself. Many things happen in her book; it is full of movement, but the guns are off-stage. So too are the great figures which the war produced; they are only spoken names, and the things which happened to Scarlett O'Hara and to Ashley Wilkes, to his wife Melanie and to Rhett Butler, are the things which happened to many other lives in that time and place.

The story opens in the plantation country of Northern Georgia, immediately before the war. Most of the action takes place in and about Atlanta, the sprawling new city of the South, a crossroads planted in the red mud and soon a hustling town, rising as the railroads come and cross it east and west and north and south. That choice of Atlanta (Miss Mitchell's native city) as the focal point of her novel was a happy one. It has not been done before in the fiction of the period, and it brings to her book a freshness and vitality of background.

Atlanta, once the war was begun, was much more the nerve center of the lower South than Charleston, where it was born, or the other older cities, like Savannah and Augusta, which looked pridefully

Margaret Mitchell.

askance at the blustering and arrogant newcomer. There were army headquarters and feverishly busy hospitals, and much of what industrial activity the South could then muster. There too, when the war was over, the brutal and crushing force of Reconstruction closed in most ominously. Miss Mitchell has brought those scenes vigorously before us; the anxious and the bedeviled city leaps to life before our eyes. This is background done with a skill more practiced hands might envy.

But Miss Mitchell's real triumph is Scarlett O'Hara, a heroine lacking in many virtues—in nearly all, one might say, but courage. She is a vital creature, this Scarlett, alive in every inch of her, selfish, unprincipled, ruthless, greedy and dominating, but with a backbone of supple, springing steel. Daughter of an immigrant Irishman who by force of character and personal charm fought his way into the ranks of the plantation nabobs and married a belle of aristocratic family, she was earthily Irish, with but little trace of her mother's gentle strain, and a complete rebel against the standards and taboos of the society in which she was reared. She is a memorable figure in American fiction, a compound of Becky Sharp and of a much better woman, Dorinda of Miss Glasgow's "Barren Ground." But she lives in her own right, completely, and will, I suspect, for a long time to come.

An almost equally vital figure is Rhett Butler, scapegrace son of a Charleston family, cynical and hard-bitten realist (but no more realist than Scarlett herself), who saw the hopelessness of the South's position from the first, and who, as a daring blockade runner, lined his pockets during the war. The remarkable thing about Miss Mitchell's portrait of him is that she has taken a stock figure of melodrama and romance, even to the black mustache, the piercing eyes and the irresistible way with women, and made him credible and alive.

The battle of wills between these two, set against the cross-current of Scarlett's self-deceiving love for Ashley Wilkes, makes an uncommonly absorbing love story, and one that Miss Mitchell manages to tell with rarely a false note, and which she carries to a logical and unforced conclusion. It is an ending entirely in key with Scarlett's character; if there is any weakness, any lingering doubt in one's mind as to the validity of the final scene between Rhett and Scarlett, it must lie in the motivation of Rhett. One wonders whether a man as deeply in love with a woman as we are told he was with Scarlett could have made her believe that he wanted only her body.

Melanie, whom Ashley Wilkes married, and Ashley himself, are foils for these two. Ashley was the man of honor and the romantic idealist, swept from his bearings and left purposeless when the life he loved and into which he fitted was swept away; he cannot adjust himself to the new time and to the made-over world, as Rhett could, and Scarlett, with her fighting salvage of her father's plantation and her shrewdly managed but unprincipled handling of her lumber business in Atlanta. And Melanie—she is all that Scarlett is not, outwardly Amelia of "Vanity Fair" to Scarlett's Becky, but underneath the shyness, the sweetness, the generous loving heart, a core of courage and determined will which save her from flatness and the milk and water of negative goodness.

These are only Miss Mitchell's most fully drawn characters, the central figures of her story. She has a host of others, excellently if sketchily done. She draws on the whole social fabric of the ante-bellum, war time and Reconstruction South for her people. They are all there, from the field hand and the Georgia Cracker to the Yankee carpetbagger, and she interests us in them all. Her dialogue is good (though I doubt the authenticity of her rendering of Negro speech—it would not, I think, meet with Joel Chandler Harris's approval) and her telling of such events as Scarlett's flight from Atlanta to Tara (her plantation) with Melanie and her new-born child, through the war-swept countryside, is excellent narration. Her style is not distinguished, but if it seldom touches beauty it is a good instrument and serves her purpose well.

Let me end by saying that although this is not a great novel, not one with any profound reading of life, it is nevertheless a book of uncommon quality, a superb piece of story-telling which nobody who finds pleasure in the art of fiction can afford to neglect. He would be a rash critic who would make any prophecies as to Miss Mitchell's future. She has set herself a hard mark to match with a second book, and I hope only that she will not set too soon about it.

July 5, 1936

NOVEL IS THE FIRST BY MISS MITCHELL

'Gone With the Wind' Also Her Last, She Says—Earnings of Book Put at $500,000

Margaret Mitchell

Margaret Mitchell, her friends said, was more surprised than any one else at the phenomenal sale of her first—and she says, last—novel "Gone With the Wind." She's that kind of person.

She isn't very big, just over five feet and 100 pounds; she isn't very old, just past 30. She's a former newspaper woman, a reporter for six years on The Atlanta Journal, and she's married to the advertising manager of the Georgia Power Company, John R. Marsh. They have no children.

She lives in an ordinary apartment in Atlanta from which she flees to the mountains or the seashore occasionally to escape the constant telephone calls, the importunates ringing her doorbell asking her to buy this, endorse that, or accept honorary membership in some society.

Many things contributed to the background from which came Scarlett O'Hara, who may turn out to be one of the immortals of fiction, Rhett Butler, Ashley, Melanie and the others who people her 1,037-page book of which 1,350,000 copies already have been printed and the end not yet in sight.

She was born of a Southern family; her father, Eugene Mitchell, is an Atlanta lawyer. The family was, as President Roosevelt jokingly characterized Senator Carter Glass, "unreconstructed rebels." Margaret Mitchell said she was 10 years old before she learned Robert E. Lee was defeated.

As a child she read everything in the family library, especially history, and an accident that put her on crutches for three years gave opportunity for further reading during her teens.

In 1926 she began writing "Gone With the Wind." Some of it she typed, a lot of it she scribbled with pen or pencil on anything handy. Manuscript piled up in the closets, desk drawers, on table tops.

In June, 1935, she and Mrs. Medora Perkerson were having luncheon in Atlanta with H. S. Latham, who had been sent South by the Macmillan Company to scout for new authors. They were busy scanning the list of their friends, suggesting prospects to Mr. Latham.

"Peggy has written a book," Mrs. Perkerson finally remarked. Mr. Latham politely said he'd like to see it.

That night, as he was preparing to leave town, Margaret Mitchell and her "manuscript" arrived. Mr. Latham took one look and went out and bought another suitcase. A few days later a telegram came to her saying the book had been accepted, subject to some rewriting. Six months of back-breaking labor at the typewriter writing, revising, typing, completed the task. Just a year from the Latham-Mitchell-Perkerson luncheon saw its first printing.

Then came the deluge. Macmillan's reported day's sales of as high as 50,000 copies. It became a fad, then almost a religion. Numerous persons around Atlanta make a living guiding tourists to what they say was the O'Hara homestead, although Miss Mitchell insists the whole book was imaginary, with no definite house or persons in mind.

Harassed almost beyond endurance, Miss Mitchell was quoted last Fall as saying: "I hope I never write another thing as long as I live."

Her profits from the book—reprints, movies, foreign rights, &c.—are estimated at more than half a million dollars.

May 4, 1937

FICTION WITH A HOLD ON HISTORY

The Historical Novel, Says Mr. Guthrie, Gives Us a Richer Sense of the Present

By A. B. GUTHRIE JR.

I STOOD with my son one afternoon on top of Independence Rock in eastern Wyoming. It had been a great landmark for early emigrants to Oregon and California who made us a continental nation. There they had stopped to rest and clean up and repair equipment and refresh their draft animals. There, on the granite slopes and levels of the upthrust, they had inscribed their names with chisels and nails and plain paint, asserting personality, as Bernard De Voto happily said, against the vast impersonality of the desert.

A great many of those old names remain today, names inscribed with the dates of lost afternoons, of long-broken camps on the green of the Sweetwater River. Reading them, while the western wind sweeps at you and space flows endlessly all about, you live in that other time—if you know about it. A sort of awe and a sort of hunger enter you, and you think America, America, thinking not of flags and martial music and orations but of dust-gray wagon covers and screeching axles and the gees and haws of drivers and the graves along the way.

While my son and I stood silent in the wind and sun, a new and shiny car pulled up to the foot of the rock, and a man got out. After a while we climbed down, and I said "Hello" to the man. He said, "What is this overgrown boulder, anyhow?"

I tried to tell him, but the question had been a mere courtesy. He didn't want to hear of ox trains and forerunners and the hard, brave journey to the Columbia. He wanted to tell me about his new automobile.

He knew a lot about it.

He didn't know about our history, and it made me think about my own job, since I write novels that make use of history. How should history be handled in fiction? Why should it be handled at all?

Mr. Guthrie has written best-selling historical novels of the American West, "The Big Sky," and the Pulitzer prize-winning "The Way West."

I SHAN'T try to give all the answers here, or to speak as an authority except as every man is his own. It's all right with me that other historical novelists will have other rules and other reasons, though probably I'll continue to think mine are best.

The first question facing the historical novelist is this: Shall he deal with the actual figures of history and the actual events, or shall he go outside them? If he goes outside, what shall be his limits? If he employs the record, what violence, if any, may he do it? May he invent words for the mouths of skeletons, may he have dead limbs acting as live limbs never did, may he amend the facts, extend the annals?

My answer is that I don't like to tinker with the facts. I don't like to assume, no matter if counter-evidence is waiting, that an actual mouth said something or that an actual body did something that has no support in the record. Liberties like these tend to muddy history, as the little story of George Washington and the cherry tree has muddied history. And they seem to me to be almost acts of disrespect, like disfigurements of headstones. If the record is used, let the user be the prisoner of it!

The position poses another and difficult question. Things don't happen in the shape of novels. They happen haphazardly or anti-climactically or coincidentally, in disregard of literary form. Fiction isn't fact; it is the representation of fact and as representation requires authorial management of the facts.

So what? So the historical novelist with scruples against invention and distortion may parallel but not employ the record. He may make up his own properties, his own adventures and his own cast, using the real paraphernalia as models, the real adventures as suggestions, the real characters as background figures, held within the limits of what is known of them. As background, the people of history help to establish time, place, atmosphere, general situation. Besides, they can hardly be ignored. A story of the fur trade without at least mention of men like Jed Smith and Jim Bridger would have little hold on history.

It may not need to be said that even this method of paralleling the record involves commitments to fact. The author has to be true to his period and his place. His people must talk as people did. The concerns of real people have to be the concerns of his cast. The big events, the big questions, the big conflicts of the times can't be ignored; they must be reflected in the degree that they would have been had his characters been sure-enough persons.

THIS field is freer, nevertheless, and I think the novelist working in it may discover profits more important than mere convenience. I think he may find his novel is a better novel, a more illuminating novel, a novel really truer to times and people than the one he might have written starring actual event and individual. Even the writer without too great a respect for facts may find that to be true. There are limits even to the violences that may be inflicted on history. The writer in this freer field can point up theme by the manipulation of the details in which theme is lost. He can underscore significances because he is the master and not the servant of his materials.

Still, it isn't easy, even with invented crews and circumstances to avoid the amendment or enlargement of fact. Somewhere the imagined man may collide with the man of history. Somewhere the make-believe situation may mix with the real. The man of fact has to speak; the real situation has to be dealt with. What then? Well, I do the best I can, telling myself that unavoidable deviations from my rules don't invalidate the rule. I get the real man off the stage with as little clatter as possible, meantime keeping him at least true to character. I fight shy of violence, if not always of addition, to situation. Above all, I work to escape the pass at which even these small liberties must be taken with the record.

I suppose

it may be asked—at least it has been asked of me—why historical novels should be written at all, aside from the strictly personal and mercenary considerations of the author. The facts of history are there, in histories, for anyone who wants to learn them. We know the issues and events, or we can find them out. And by their recorded actions and utterances we know the kind of men who lived in a given time and place just as we know a tree by its fruits.

No single answer answers. I'll say, first, that not enough history is being taught, not enough is popularly known. The historical novel, if not a defensible substitute for history, still is better than nothing.

And even if students were taught enough history, and if adults knew enough, the historical novel, it seems to me, could be justified if only because the good ones clothe the bones of history with flesh and recreate for us the people, problems, passions, conflicts and social directions that, in non-fiction treatment, remain dust for too many of us. Men aren't known by their actions, or at any rate they don't live and breathe and acquire dimension through a knowledge of them alone. Men are known through the whys of action, too. Understand a man thoroughly and you can predict how he'll act. The best of the historical novelists seek to do that—to understand men and to acquaint you with them. Thus their actions become, not accidental or inexplicable, as many actions appear to be, but of a piece with the men themselves. Men and actions both grow real, both persuasive, and together illuminative of the record.

If the historical novel needs a further, and moral, justification, the justification can be found, and in it also a support for the position that not enough history is taught or known. I'm speaking particularly but by no means exclusively of the American historical novel. I believe all of us become better citizens, richer and better-directed human beings, through a knowledge of the dreams and deeds of the men and women who went before. In America I think we cannot appreciate freedom, opportunity, progress, convenience, obligation, without an appreciation of spent hope and sweat and blood and treasure. And most of us, I'm afraid, don't have it.

December 3, 1950

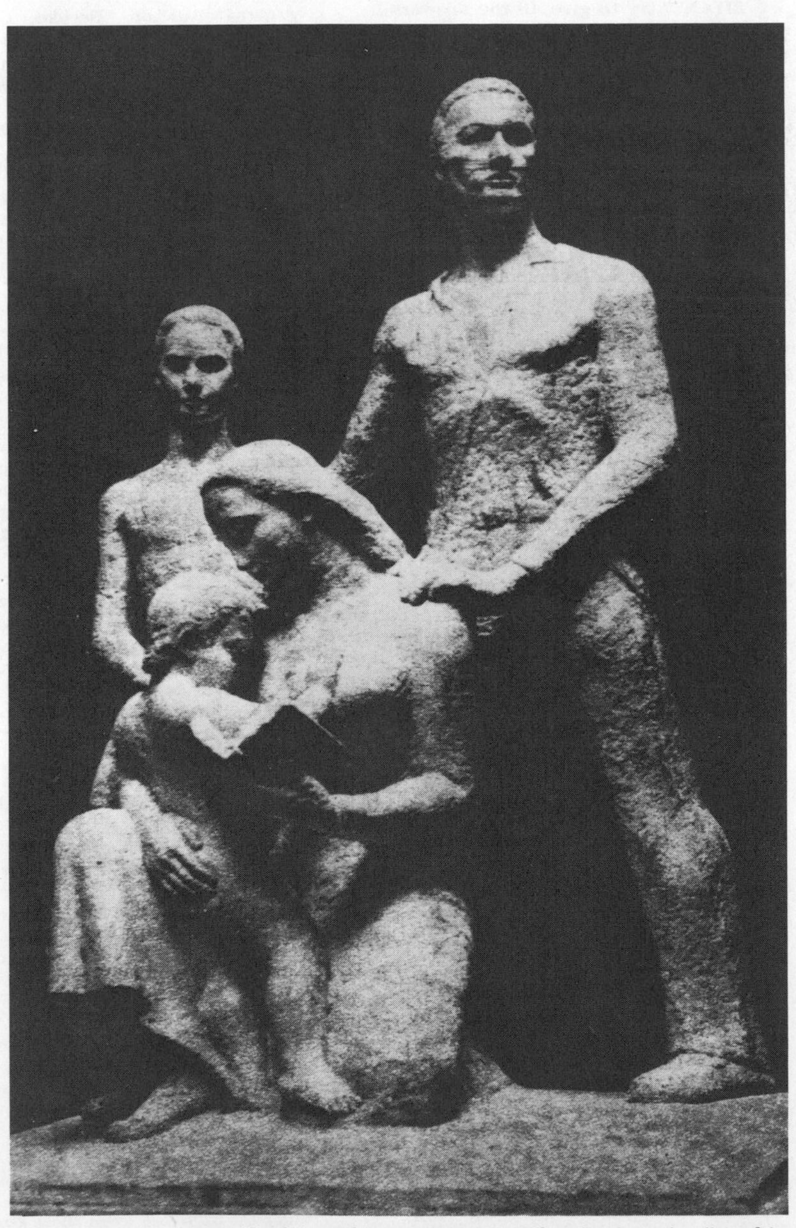

"Pioneer Family," model for a monument by William Zorach, courtesy the sculptor.

"We need to know the dreams and deeds of the men and women who went before."

IRVING STONE CRITICIZES

Some Writers of Historical Novels 'Run Wild,' He Says

Special to The New York Times.

WASHINGTON, Jan. 7—Irving Stone hurled a few literary rocks tonight at some historians and writers of historical novels.

Mr. Stone, author of biographical fiction, opened a Library of Congress lecture series on the novel.

He quoted Prof. Carl Bode of the University of Maryland as having said that "the biographical novel still goes its bosomy way, its flimsy clothing tattered and torn in exactly the wrong places."

Mr. Stone said that Professor Bode must have meant such books of "historical" fiction as "Forever Amber" or "Kitty," whose "writers took the license of combining sensational material from a hundred different sources" and who let "their fictional fancies run wild."

"Forever Amber" was written by Kathleen Winsor and "Kitty" by Rosamond Marshall.

As for truth in history, he said that "the number of lies and part truths still resting comfortably and respectably in history is a constant source of astonishment to me."

January 8, 1957

"THE VIRGINIAN."

Owen Wister's Stirring Novel of Western Life.

Owen Wister has come pretty near to writing the American novel. He has come as near to it as any man can well come, and at the same time has beautifully demonstrated the futility of the expectation that the typical novel of American life will ever be written. Mr. Wister has set forth a phase of life which is to be found only in the United States, and he has pictured it with graphic delineative force, with picturesqueness, and with brilliant narrative power. "The Virginian" ought to live as an artistic embodiment of a species of man fast passing into a remembrance. The Western cowboy has generally been depicted chiefly in the comic papers, where he has been caricatured to make fun for those utterly ignorant of his real nature. Mr. Wister pleads for him that he is a man, and a pretty good man at that. He makes his plea by going out into the cowboy country, living with the cowboy, studying him at close range, getting under the thickness of his suspicion of the Eastern "dude," becoming his friend, and then summing up the results of his observation in a tale which deftly combines realism with fancy. "The Virginian" is, therefore, in the broad sense, a historical novel. It is a study of men and times. It rings true, and we believe is to be a faithful study.

Certainly the book is absorbingly interesting. It contains humor, pathos, poetic description, introspective thought, sentiment, and even tragedy. Its level is admirably sustained, and the development of the characters is masterly. Perhaps there never was just such a cowboy as this transplanted Virginian, whose name is never told in the story. Perhaps there was. The great West is a good deal like the ocean. All sorts of things and persons happen there, and no one has a right to say that any creation of the novelist's fancy exceeds possibility. It will probably be conceded that this particular cowboy is not exactly typical. Yet he possesses traits which one instinctly feels are real. The quick, penetrative wit, the readiness of tongue, the self-control—these are qualities which cannot be rare among the strenuous, venturesome, hardy spirits of the West.

The poetic feeling of the man appears to be natural, and it is probably one of the truest touches in the novel. Simple men who live near to nature usually have poetic sensibility. Primitive peoples have it. Clarke Russell and other litterateurs of the sea have found plenty of it among sailors. Those of us who see only the outward aspects of these men do not become acquainted with their intimate thoughts. Mr. Wister shows us plainly that he was long in penetrating below the surface of his hero. Even those men whom we meet every day sometimes uncover to us unsuspected depths.

The heroine of the story is lovable. She is a most desirable woman, and the author has depicted with genuine skill her long combat with herself before she is ready to yield to her love for the cowboy, and to face the disapproval of Eastern conventionalities as embodied in her relatives. She is an admirable character study. But she and the hero are not the only ones in the book. "Shorty," the weakling, whose tragic fate was inevitable, is another. So is Trampas, the evil personage of the tale. Cleverly drawn contrasts, though mere sketches, are the pompous minister and the adorable Bishop. The book is full of real people.

In incident and episode the story is rich. The victory of the Virginian over Trampas in the gentle art of drawing the long bow is delightful, and fiction does not contain anything more deliciously humorous than the Virginian's story of Delmonico and the frogs. It is worthy of Mark Twain at his best. The climax of the story is reached when the Virginian shoots Trampas, who has insulted him and given him till sundown to leave town. The struggle between the Virginian's love and his Western sense of honor is admirably depicted. The woman tells him that if he shoots Trampas she will not be his wife, and he endeavors to show her how it would be impossible for him to continue to live in his own land if he ran away. This chapter is written with splendid power.

This story will undoubtedly be read very widely. It will appeal to both men and women, for both will take into their affection the hero. The illustrations are excellent, and the book is handsomely made.

June 21, 1902

TALE OF THE WEST

THE LIGHT OF WESTERN STARS. By Zane Grey. Harper & Bros. $1.35 net.

Enter iron-jawed, desperate-but-lots-of-good-in-him cowboy, over six feet, darkly handsome. Languid, beautiful, rich, society-weary heroine, who has never yet been made to feel. Enter also simple, straight-forward Western woman, many other cowboys, mere children, big, strong men as they are, wicked Mexicans, scoundrelly Sheriff. Backdrop of blue mountains, looking nearer than they are; foreground of desert, cactus, gray bunch grass, coyotes and jack-rabbits.

There you have it. A Western romance with all the proper ingredients, familiar and beloved.

Bing! bang! in the very first chapter, when the desperate cowboy-with-lots-of-good-in-him forces the frightened, mumbling padre to marry him to the languid, rich society belle, though something occurs to break off the ceremony before it is finished. Or, stay, are we sure? Perhaps it was finished. Perhaps the society belle and the reckless iron-jaw were married. Well, we don't know. Time must tell.

Madeleine, or Majesty, as she is cleverly called, buys a ranch and by spending more or less money and five months turns it into a bower of bloom and alfalfa, with golf links for the cowboys and patent bread-mixers for the same favored creatures. Meanwhile the desperate hero is in Mexico, fighting with the rebels or against them. But he returns, drunker than ever, so that Majesty has the opportunity to make a stirring, scornful, all-womanly-tender speech to him, thereby redeeming him from rum and the devil, even as she has redeemed the desert from dust and the Mexicans from dirt.

Yet, despite all these familiar properties, Mr. Grey's book holds a lot of fascination. It is easy to perceive that he loves the wild and beautiful land of which he writes. There are descriptions of singular charm, and in places he succeeds in communicating the actual feel of his own enthusiasm. The scene in which Stewart conquers Majesty's cold self-sufficiency has an element of true passion that atones for a great deal of melodrama, and there is melodrama in much of the story between the two. If the obsession that a Western novel must be composed of certain time-honored ingredients could only be dissipated, and many pages of stock in trade cleared away, the book would appeal to people who really care for the West, and who think the romance and life that actually exist there are sufficient for a writer's purpose.

As to Mr. Grey's competence in telling a story in which incident crowds incident, escapes, rescue, sudden death, mad devotion, and shameless perfidy follow page on page, there can be no doubt. The book is probably exactly the kind of book it was meant to be; and will be breathlessly read by people who want the colors laid on thick, and are not bothered because the composition as a whole is out of drawing.

January 25, 1914

ZANE GREY, 64, DIES SUDDENLY ON COAST

Wrote More Than 50 Novels, Most of Them Dealing With Western Adventure

17,000,000 COPIES SOLD

Noted for His Catches of Game Fish—Once a Dentist, Won Fame After Hardships

ALTADENA, Calif., Oct 23 (AP)—Zane Grey, whose prolific pen converted a romantic picture of the old West into colorful reality for millions of readers, died here early today at the age of 64. The author who wrote more than fifty novels—all of them in longhand—suffered a sudden heart attack at his home.

His family said that, although he was under treatment for a heart ailment, he had appeared in excellent spirits. He suffered a slight attack of indigestion yesterday, but said it was "nothing to worry about." Death was attributed to coronary thrombosis.

Surviving are his widow, two sons, Romer Zane Grey and Loren Grey, and a daughter, Mrs. Robert W. Carney.

Wrote 100,000 Words a Month

Mr. Grey, who deserted dentistry after four years of unsuccessful practice in New York, wrote at the amazing rate of 100,000 words a month, never revising his manuscripts after the first draft. Mrs. Grey attended to all revisions.

The writer, whose most spectacularly successful book, "Riders of the Purple Sage," appeared in 1912, still was producing fiction regularly thirty-five years after publication of his first novel, "Betty Zane," in 1904.

His death coincided with the appearance of his newest work, "Western Union," a tale of the development of the nation's telegraphic system.

Private funeral services will be held at a Pasadena mortuary Wednesday afternoon, after which the body will be cremated.

PASADENA, Calif., Oct. 23 (UP)—Zane Grey's more popular works were made into movies and most of them were extremely profitable for the producers. More than 17,000,000 copies of his novels have been sold.

Went Hungry in Early Days

Zane Grey was a literary phenomenon. Judged by any accepted literary standard, the more than fifty novels he wrote were bad. But one of them, at least, sold a million and a half copies and Mr. Grey, who went pretty hungry in the early days of his authorship, spent the latter years of his life rewriting it (under a variety of titles) when not seeking tuna and marlin in his yacht that was equipped with $100,000 worth of deep-sea fishing tackle or wandering about the various estates he maintained.

Like most authors, Mr. Grey began writing because of an irresistible urge for self-expression. He gave up the career of a dentist in order to put words on paper. He developed into a master salesman of words when, after five years of failure, he all but bludgeoned Harper & Brothers into publishing his first novel. No reliable statistics are available as to the exact number of words he wrote or the exact number of dollars he made between 1905—when "The Spirit of the Border" was published—and his death, but each would be staggering if they were.

Harper's readers wanted to turn down his successful novel, "The Heritage of the Desert," because, in the words of one of them, it was "too bludgy." Years later T. K. Whipple, writing in The Saturday Review of Literature, trying to explain the writing of Grey, said: "His art is archaic, with all the traits of archaic art. His style * * * has the stiffness that comes from an imperfect mastery of the medium. It lacks fluency or facility; behind it always we feel a pressure toward expression, a striving for a freer and easier utterance."

Of a Pioneer Family

Zane Grey had every right to go to the West for his inspiration. His great-great-grandfather was Colonel Ebenezer Zane, an exile from Denmark who came to America with William Penn and who, for twenty years, held Fort Henry against the Indians and British. Descendants of Colonel Zane founded Zanesville, Ohio, where Zane Grey was born on Jan. 31, 1875, the son of Lewis M. and Alice Josephine Zane Grey. His mother had Indian blood in her heritage. His father was a backwoods man, farmer, preacher and finally a doctor.

Mr. Grey's first literary effort was made when he was a boy—a penciled tale of shooting and sudden death called "Jim of the Cave," remuneration for which was burning of the manuscript (it was written on strips of wall paper) and paternal tanning of the author's hide. After that he confined his authorship to essays for the English class of the Zanesville High School until he started out to fulfill his father's ambition by learning dentistry at the University of Pennsylvania. After graduation, in 1896, he started practice in New York, having an office on Thirty-first Street.

Played Baseball in College

Before going to college, Mr. Grey had been a semi-professional ballplayer, and had organized a team at Jacktown, Ohio. A "scout" for the University of Pennsylvania saw him pitch a game against a Baltimore team, and talked him into choosing the University of Pennsylvania as his college. He did, and was a member of the Varsity ball team for four years. A poor student, whose mind wandered continually to the fields and woods, he made a good reputation as a ballplayer, and his athletic prowess made him many friends.

An avid reader as well as nature lover, he found the confinement of a New York dental office distasteful. During vacations he went fishing and canoeing, and wrote articles about his ventures for several outdoor magazines. Then he felt the urge to write a book, and recalled a story his mother had told him about Betty Zane, the Colonel's sister, who had run through a gantlet of fire with an apronful of gunpowder when Fort Henry was besieged on Sept. 11, 1782.

At that time he lived in a dingy flat. He wrote the book under a flickering gas lamp in a tiny kitchen, spending an entire Winter on the task. The first publisher to see it sent it back with a printed rejection slip; the next damned it with faint praise, and Ripley Hitchcock, editor for Harper's, took the trouble to tell the young dentist to stick to his drill. Mr. Grey liked the book he had written so well, however, that he borrowed money and published it himself. It received good reviews, but, because the printer lacked a publisher's outlets, it sold poorly—one of the few Zane Grey books in that category.

Quit Dentistry in 1904

That was in 1904. Mr. Grey quit dentistry that year and went with his mother, brother and sister to live in the country. He was determined to be a writer. Soon afterwards, Nov. 21, 1905, he married Miss Nina Elizabeth Roth of New York. They went to live in a cottage at Lackawaxen, Pa.

Mr. Grey finally used up all his savings, having earned nothing from his writings. He wanted to quit, but his wife would not listen to the idea. They lived on her savings, and, when these were about gone, the first of their three children, Romer Zane Grey, was born. Just about this time Mr. Grey met Colonel C. J. (Buffalo) Jones, who was lecturing in New York on his efforts to hybridize the disappearing buffalo with black Galway cattle. He talked the old plainsman into letting him go West with him (at his own expense) to write of the colonel's exploits and prove to a skeptical public that the old-timer actually roped wild animals as he said in his lectures.

The two went to Arizona. They left Flagstaff with a caravan of Mormons, crossed the Painted Desert and the head of Grand Canyon, Lee's Ferry, and kept on to House Rock Valley, where Jones kept his buffalo. He lived with Texas Rangers and wild-horse hunters of Utah during these months. When he returned to New York after chasing mountain lions, lassoing them, and bringing them alive to camp, Harper's encouraged him to write "The Last of the Plainsmen."

But when it was done, Mr. Hitchcock of Harper's handed it back to him, saying:

"I don't see anything in this to convince me that you can write either narrative or fiction."

Success at Last

Mr. Grey wrote later how he staggered from the office in Franklin Square literally blinded with disappointments but determined to show the editor how wrong he was. He spent a cold, almost snow-bound Winter at Lackawaxen, writing his first Western romance, "The Heritage of the Desert." This time the editor did not reject his work. Instead he handed the young author a contract. Harper & Brothers has been his publisher ever since.

Mr. Grey's struggles to be a successful writer did not end with the acceptance of "The Heritage of the Desert," which was a success from the sales point of view. He could get no magazine editor to serialize his next book, "Riders of the Purple Sage." He went into the publishing office and talked Mr. Duneka, the vice president, into publishing it. That was the book which, by 1934, had sold a million and a half copies. It started the great popularity which brought to his twenty-five published works of fiction an estimated 56,141,905 readers in the first twenty years of his literary career.

ZANE GREY

Fame and wealth came to Mr. Grey after "Riders of the Purple Sage" became a best-seller in 1912. Since then such books as "The Lone Star Ranger," "The Mysterious Rider," "The Thundering Herd," "To the Last Man," "The U. P. Trail," "The Vanishing American" and "Wild Horse Mesa" added to his prosperity. Many of them were turned into moving pictures that were great successes.

His Exploits in Fishing

Mr. Grey never lost his love for sports. He wrote many tales based on his adventures as fisherman, being internationally famous for his exploits with game fish of all kinds. Whenever he broke a record—as he did on more than one occasion—he would wire THE NEW YORK TIMES and other papers from the nearest port, telling the size of his catch.

Among his books on this subject were "Tales of Fishes," "Tales of Fishing Virgin Seas," "Tales of the Angler's Eldorado" and "An American Angler in Australia." He also wrote many books for young people, such as "Ken Ward in the Jungle," "The Short Stop," "The Young Pitcher," "The Young Forester" and "The Young Lion-Hunter."

Last Friday his latest romance was published. It was his fifty-fourth book, a historical novel of the stretching of the strand of wire across the continent which became the Western Union, that gives title to the book. Within the last two weeks Mr. Grey had written Harper & Brothers that he had three more manuscripts ready. They will be published posthumously as "$30,000 on the Hoof," "The Young George Washington" and "The Frontier Wife."

October 24, 1939

The Galloping Westerns

By HOFFMAN BIRNEY

NEARLY half a century ago —in 1902 to be exact—a staid and humorless Philadelphian wrote a best-selling novel. Almost overnight it elevated Western fiction from the dime-novel category to the exalted status of buckram bindings, complete respectability, and two-dollar prices. That book was Owen Wister's "The Virginian," contributor to Americana of the immortal line: "When you call me that, *smile!*"

True, American boys continued to buy and read "Buffalo Bill," "Young Wild West," "Diamond Dick," and other lurid weeklies, but the dime novel (it seldom cost more than a nickel, by the way) was on its way out when B. M. Bower, whose initials concealed the fact that the author was a woman, wrote "Chip of the Flying U," in 1904. It had vanished completely when Zane Grey's first Western novel, "Heritage of the Desert," appeared in 1910. During the forty years since that debut, Westerns have been gaudy perennials on publishers' lists. About two hundred are printed yearly and are classed as sell-outs in first printings of four or five thousand. Among those issued since the first of this year—to take a few titles at random — are: "Two-Bit Rancher" by Charles N. Heckelmann (Doubleday), "Valley of Gold" by Earle E. Perrenot (Phoenix), "Single Jack" by Max Brand (Dodd, Mead), "Draw or Drag" by Wayne D. Overholser (Macmillan), "Gunman Gunman" by Nelson C. Nye (Sage) and "Ranger's Luck" by William McLeod Raine (Houghton Mifflin.)

Records show that Western novels sell best in the cattle country itself. The bulk of first printings go to rental libraries, to Army and Navy installations, and to veterans' hospitals. This writer has supervision of a small library at Fort Bliss, Tex., and here Westerns are far and away the most popular form of fiction. A recent donation of fifteen new Westerns was shelved on Wednesday and all had been withdrawn by Friday.

Many of those first-edition Westerns will probably be reissued within a year or two in 25-cent pocket-size editions. In this form they may sell from 300,000 to 500,000 copies—no insignificant income to author and original publisher.

There remain the motion pictures, radio and television, all of which have seen the hard-riding and straight-shooting cowboy advance from a melancholy Class B standing to top billing. Television, of course, was not even a scientist's dream when Clarence E. Mulford created "Hopalong Cassidy" — and look at Hopalong today!

THE widely discussed revival of interest in Western themes on the screen and the air would seem to be less a renaissance than a relentless and evenly paced development. Better scripts have made their contribution and the bonanza of color photography has been tremendous. But there are no real breaks in the trail from "Diamond Dick's Revenge" to "The Virginian" and "Riders of the Purple Sage." Such screen heroes as Bronco Billy Anderson, grim William S. Hart, and flashy Tom Mix were prototypes of such current idols as Gene Autry, Roy Rogers, and The Lone Ranger. Our interest in the West, our demand for more and yet more Western novels, more and better Western movies, is not strange. It typifies a historic heritage, for the history of this nation is the history of its western frontier. By the time America had reached the farthest West, the majestic movement toward it was stamped indelibly upon our national thought. It was inevitable that the factual heroes and villains of that movement be followed by a thousand fictional descendants.

THE word "typical" is inescapable in any consideration of today's—and yesterday's—Western fiction. Plot, scene, action and characters have become classically stylized. One hero—or villain—is permitted a maximum of two revolvers. Or (under extreme circumstances and at extreme ranges), a rifle. Strangulation may enter only in the form of capital punishment for such low-down varmints as hoss thieves. Feminine characters may seek employment only as schoolteachers or "biscuit shooters," with an occasional dance hall gal whose heart must be 24-carat, unalloyed—and not in her work.

On the male side, a survey of some forty titles shows cowboy heroes overwhelmingly outnumbering rangers, soldiers, fighting sheriffs, and other vocations. Thirty-two of the forty books have a ranch as principal locus. Every one of the forty includes a gunfight, a series of gunfights, or a climactic pitched battle in which from six to a dozen outlaws bite the alkali.

Proficiency with a six-shooter is an absolute requirement for the hero but his formal education should not have advanced beyond the three R's: Rifle, Rope and Running-iron. Only one of forty heroes was a college graduate—an archeologist who hired out to guide the heroine across the Sonoran desert, but he tactfully concealed his erudition for more than two hundred pages.

A PUBLISHER who was consulted in connection with this article remarked that "readers of Westerns are a loyal group." After one has read thirty or forty typical Westerns, one reaches the conclusion that those loyalists are also singularly uncritical. The geography and history of the West, its mountains, deserts and rivers; its towns, its fauna and flora and where they may be found, the distribution of Indian tribes, the manifold intricacies of the cattle business—all these call for a highly specialized knowledge which very few writers of typical Westerns possess. There are exceptions, of course, and notable ones, but as a class Western novels include more glaring errors than any other type of book. Many writers seem to have adopted the attitude that if the readers don't worry about exaggerations and inaccuracies, why should the writer?

A few examples might be cited:

Item: A uniformed company of Texas Rangers, its captain wearing a sword. The Rangers never wore any distinctive uniform; no Ranger officer ever wore a sword.

Scene: Southern Arizona, where a herd of 20,000 cattle was pastured on twenty sections of land. To graze more than twenty-five cows to a section (640 acres) is perilously close to overstocking. Sagebrush in southern Arizona, in the Tularosa Basin of New Mexico—there is none.

From Jacket Design by Paul Laune for "Draw or Drag."

Item: "He carried a seven-shot Colt .45 low on his thigh." Colt never made a seven-shot revolver in any caliber.

Item: "I sneaked him out a mess of cartridges for his old thutty-thutty rimfire." This statement was dated more than ten years before the introduction of the .30-.30 cartridge, which was centerfire.

Item: "There's wild steers runnin' them mountains that ain't ever even seen a man!" Which would warrant the question of how the critters happened to become steers.

THE list could be continued indefinitely, but to what end? The typical Western is a quantity-production job, hastily written and abounding with errors, but readers love 'em and clamor for more. Who cares if Sioux Indians are placed in New Mexico or giant cactus in Nevada or Texas? Westerns aren't written for ethnologists or botanists but for the average American male who neither knows nor cares when the divided skirt supplanted the riding habit.

Today barbed-wire fences checkerboard the once open ranges. One can drive from coast to coast and from border to border and never leave hard-surfaced roads. The cowboy has become a farmhand who rides a pickup truck as often as he does a horse. The Last Chance and the Bucket of Blood now dispense soda-pop or possibly 3.2 beer as sidelines to gasoline and oil. But the West of the trail herds, of Billy the Kid and Henry Plummer; of John Wesley Hardin and Wyatt Earp, will never die. It is our history and our heritage and its immortality is assured in the classic Western—two hundred of them yearly.

Mr. Birney, author of "Vigilantes," "Roads to Roam," and other books on the West, is currently technical editor for the Ordnance Department Research and Development, Sub-office ROCKET, Fort Bliss, Tex.

March 12, 1950

ENTERTAINING MYSTERY.

IN "The Circular Staircase" (Bobbs-Merrill) Mary Roberts Rhinehart has given the jading reading public a tale of mystery with a new piquancy. It might be possible, though it would be difficult, to contrive a more involved network of circumstances and a create a more hopeless mystification. But it would not be possible to invent a more pleasantly diverting character than the lady (it would be a pleasure to call her young, but she confesses to gray hairs) who is at the centre of the myste.y an' who herself narrates it. Written in any old style, "The Circular Staircase" would be the sort of thing people sit up nights to finish; written in the delightfully humorous vein which makes it stand out so much above the ordinary detective story, it is bound to be, with more than usual deserts, a popular success.

It is all about an old house with an unsuspected secret chamber, a bank President who loots his own institution in order to hoard the spoil where he can feel it his own; a doctor who buries a pauper's corpse for the body of the bank President; an unruly son; two Nemesi in the forms of women; a matter of three or four murders; two unhappy love affairs and one tragic one; an automobile and a freight car, and a gentlemanly detective who ought to have married the lady who was no longer young—and who will do so yet if an entertaining author will be so good as to write another book.

August 22, 1908

VERSE GAVE START TO MRS. RINEHART

Mystery Story Writer Got $22 for Poetry Composed While in Hospital.

BEGINS HER BOOKS AT END

Tries to Meet Criticisms of Her Readers—New Tale of Crime Is Published Today.

At the start of her writing career Mary Roberts Rinehart made profit out of poetry. She had contracted diphtheria from her eldest son, Stanley M. Rinehart, now, as president of the firm of Farrar & Rinehart, her senior publisher. While she was convalescing she wrote some verse. Fumigated manuscripts sent from her hospital room were accepted and she received $22.

She wrote much verse in the next few months, then short stories, plays and novels. All of her recent books have been best sellers. Ordinarily a mystery novel by her can be counted on to sell 100,000 copies, at least. Many have sold far more. Her latest mystery, "The Album," was published yesterday by Farrar & Rinehart.

Ten years ago, with a capitalization of $500,000 she incorporated —"Mary Roberts Rinehart, Inc., producing and writing books. The corporation has since been dissolved but the stock could still pay dividends.

Writes in Longhand.

When she works--and she works daily from 10 to 4, and sometimes, under pressure, much longer— her writing desk looks something like a sewing table covered with a patchwork quilt in progress. She writes in longhand, and uses pins to keep batches of manuscript together. When she has finished a full-length novel, she has written it at least three times and there is enough manuscript to fill a good sized bureau drawer.

For a detective novel she writes an "undercover" and a surface story. Such books, of course, begin with the ending. Above the foundation of the crime itself and its result she sketches in characters, further crimes and incidents for suspense. She makes a careful list of each time the foundation story projects up into the tale of the action, furnishing real clues.

She becomes "very tired and very nervous" while writing a mystery story, but finds humor even harder to write. The most difficult book she ever wrote, according to her son, was "My Story," her autobiography.

When one of her magazine serials is running she receives hundreds of letters and goes through them and tries to make replies. Many who wrote to her objected that she had used unfair devices in her book "The Door," which sold 120,000 copies. She worries over such charges and has made every effort to make such criticism of "The Album" entirely unreasonable.

Makes Notes at Night.

She says that she "detests the word inspiration," but says that if it ever does come to her it is just after she has gone to bed at night. Then she puts down notes, sentences, paragraphs. Her first glance in the morning is at her bedside table to make sure the notes are still there.

She writes about one novel a year and enough short stories and articles to fill about two-third of another book. Sometimes she likes to talk about the work she is doing. At other times the topic is banned. Sometimes her publishers have been surprised by the receipt of a manuscript of which she has told them nothing.

May 30, 1933

A WRITER OF THRILLERS TALKS OF CRIME

By S. J. WOOLF

SINCE the days when Poe solved an actual New York murder by deduction, and, transferring the scene of the crime from this city to Paris, made a story out of it, the thriller has always had its devotees, not only here but abroad. Gaboriau and Doyle followed his methods. For years the youth of our nation read Nick Carter and Old Cap Collier.

But though Sherlock Holmes was accepted in the best society, and every now and then a detective tale became a best seller, it was not until a number of prominent persons, including President Wilson, confessed their pleasure in this type of story that the old-time hair-raising thriller again came into its own.

Undoubtedly the most popular author in London today, if popularity is to be judged by sales, is Edgar Wallace. In the last ten years he has written 140 novels, most of them detective stories, of which about 5,000,000 copies are sold each year. The ragamuffin in the East End and the King recovering from an almost fatal illness find relaxation in his books. The buses as they crawl through the crowded Strand are plastered with advertisements bearing Wallace's name. At one time six theatres in London were producing his melodramas, and many moving-picture houses were flashing his scenarios on their silver screens.

But Wallace does not stop with novels and plays. This man with an infinite capacity for work finds time to contribute to the newspapers each day a column of dramatic criticism and an article on racing. Now he is in this country to get atmosphere. I saw him a couple of days after his arrival, and in the short time that he had been in one of New York's smartest hotels he had turned a Louis XVI drawing room into a workshop. But this was entirely fitting. He no more belongs in a rococo room than does Henry Ford, who likewise is a genius of mass production.

It was early when I went to see him. When he opened the door to me he was wearing a silk dressing gown over his flannel pajamas. But despite the

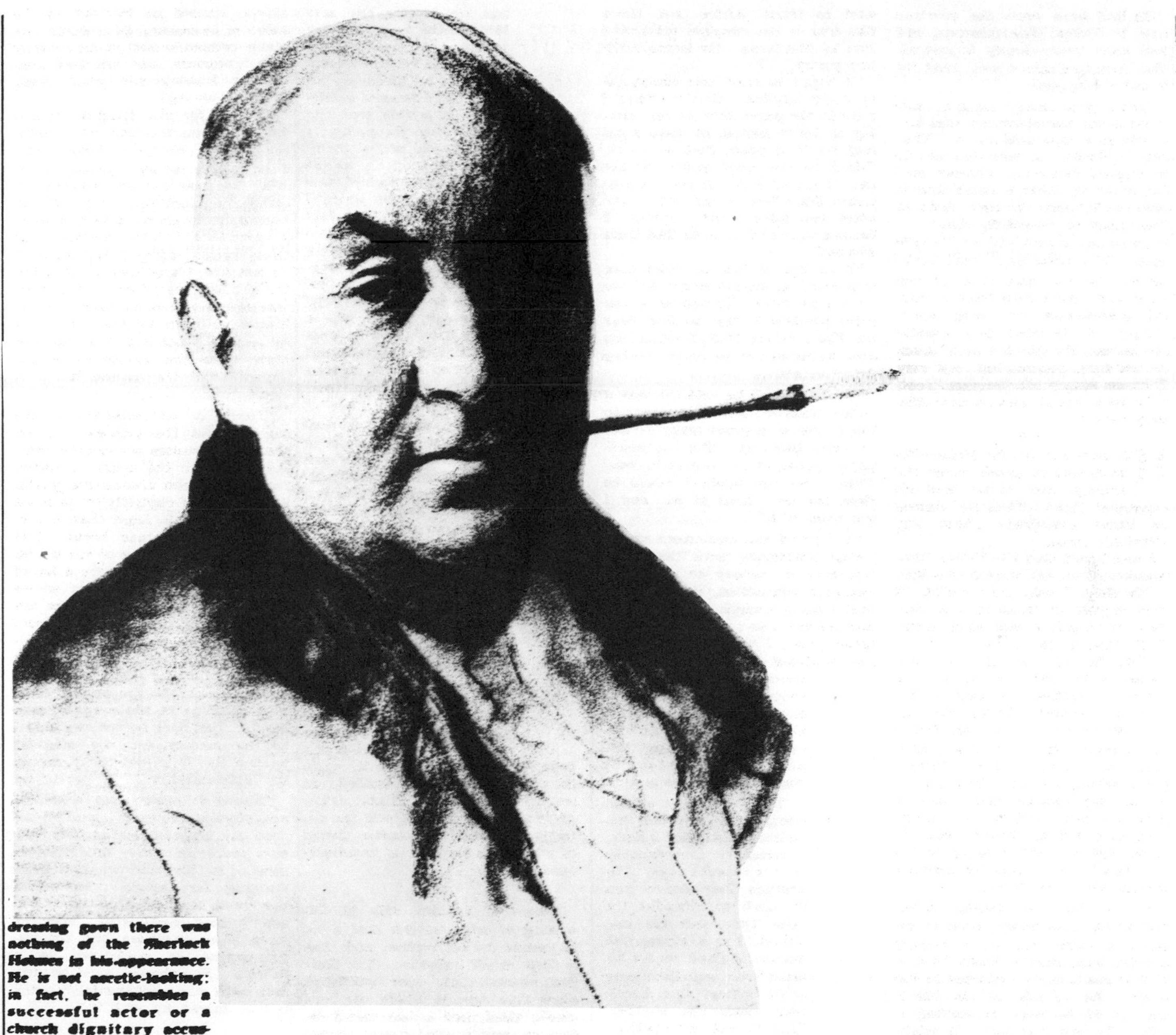

Edgar Wallace.
Drawn From Life by S. J. Woolf.

dressing gown there was nothing of the Sherlock Holmes in his appearance. He is not ascetic-looking: in fact, he resembles a successful actor or a church dignitary accustomed to good living.

He is a big man and he is heavy. He does not look like a hard worker. His eyes do not sparkle and his mouth normally turns down at the corners. His hair, which is gray, is thinning on top. A forehead that bulges above the eyes is thus made to seem higher. His face is round. One would say that he is a man who has force and energy, but who is physically inactive. I was not surprised that he dictates his books. He has several typists.

Wallace carries an extraordinary cigarette holder. It is long and black and polished. It never leaves his hands, apparently, and it causes him no end of trouble. When he first puts a cigarette into it, it seems invariably to fall out and, when the cigarette is finished, he always has trouble in removing the butt.

Edgar Wallace, Mass Producer of Detective Tales, Thinks There Is a Tendency to Sentimentalize the Criminal

It was with a wave of the holder, as if it were a wand, that he ushered me into the transformed room; but it was Wallace and not the wand that had changed it. The furniture was covered with piles of newspapers. A table upon which a plume pen would have been in place was littered with ginger ale bottles, empty cigarette packages, letters and, what was most strange, a book on the Renaissance by Walter Pater. Near by stood a dictaphone, while several steel cabinets holding wax cylinders were standing against the walls.

It seemed impossible that so many things could have been accumulated in such a short time; what appeared there looked like the collection of a year rather than of a couple of days. But before I had had time to look around he wanted to know what American paper published English racing news; for just as a pastime he runs a racing stable, and spends a great part of his leisure there and at the tracks.

Though the room was dark I found a place to work close to one of the windows. Mr. Wallace seated himself in a comfortable chair and lighted a second cigarette. By the time he got to the fourth or fifth I stopped counting. He began to talk. He is one of those people who give an interviewer no trouble. He is interested in almost everything and nothing "gets by" him. He likes to talk. The result is that one subject naturally leads to another.

He had been down the previous day to Police Headquarters, and had been tremendously impressed. The detective school was what interested him most.

"It's a great thing," he said, "and there is but one other city that has anything comparable to it. That city is Berlin. A detective has to be trained just as a reporter does for, after all, there is much that is common between the two. Both of them must be essentially observers. A reporter is sent out an assignment. The better he is, the clearer picture he will give of what has happened. He draws from a careful observation of many small things. A detective does exactly the same. He forms a conclusion, not from generalities, but very often from seemingly inconsequential details that would escape the ordinary man."

***

HE reverted to the Police Department to speak about the line-up and other methods employed there. Then he wanted to know something about Mr. Whalen's career.

I mentioned that the Police Commissioner had sold papers as a boy.

"So did I," said the novelist. "I sold papers in front of the very club of which I was later president; that is, the Press Club."

Then he went on to tell something of his life. In itself it is quite as exciting as any of his stories. He was adopted when he was nine years old, as his father and mother were both dead, by a fish porter who lived in Billingsgate, whom he described as "a stocky big-featured man, with a powerful nose and a chin beard such as Abraham Lincoln wore. He never did a crooked thing in his life, and his wife was the gentlest mother that ever lived."

At 11 he was selling newspapers on Fleet Street, then he became a cabin boy on a fishing trawler and, finally, when he was still in his teens, he enlisted in the army. As he told of his life it was as if he were recounting a tale. He was detached. It might have been some one else he was talking about. In the army he was sent to South Africa, and there the wife of the chaplain interested him in literature. He began writing poetry.

"I began to read new books, especially Kipling. One morning I read in the paper that he was coming to South Africa, so down I sat and wrote a poem that was published in the local paper on the day of his arrival. It made a hit. I met the editor of the paper, and what was more, I met Kipling. I became a contributor to The Cape Times."

When his period of enlistment was over, he drifted naturally into newspaper work. He became a war correspondent during the Boer War for The Evening Mail. I asked him how he happened to begin writing detective stories.

"For a time," he said, "I was a police reporter, and I was sent to the scenes of a great many crimes to write them up. But the newspaper game is an uncertain one. Every now and again I would be fired for no reason at all, and I got tired of it.

"I enjoyed the excitement of arriving practically with the police wherever a robbery or a murder had been committed, but I decided that I knew enough about them to concoct my own crimes, for which, incidentally, I would be paid and not punished. I got a lot of fun writing them. Perhaps to write them is almost as exciting as to be present at an actual crime. To read them is exciting, too, and that explains the vogue for detective stories.

"The ordinary human being lives a rather restricted life. Most people, of necessity, are creatures of circumstances. The average Englishman gets up each morning at the same time, has his tub, shaves, has a kipper and marmalade and tea for his breakfast, and then gets to his office. One day is very much like another. This is not altogether natural.

"Even the grubbiest clerk has his dreams and sees himself the hero of some romance or adventure. We all want to get away from ourselves at times, we all crave some form of excitement. It is this that the detective story supplies. It takes people out of themselves and often keeps them out of mischief. One of the things of which I am proudest is the fact that in a census, taken in a number of nursing homes, of the kind of reading that sick people do, my novels led by a large percentage. There was a great satisfaction in that for me, for it showed that I could so interest them as to make them forget their pains.

"Of course," he continued, "the first object of a detective story is to convey the impression of reality. If the reader does not accept the tale as he would a newspaper account it immediately loses some of its interest. That is the reason why I do not believe in the amateur detective in fiction. We all of us have had friends who regarded themselves as detectives, and we know how often they were off the track in the simplest things. These smart amateurs who happen in on the scene of a crime and then go ahead and solve it, while the professionals are baffled, do not exist in real life. Today crime detection is a science, and the detective of today has studied things of which the amateur is hopelessly ignorant.

"There is another side to the writing of crime stories that a lot of people do not realize, and that is their moral influence. The Raffles stories that were published some time ago, in which the hero was a thief, had a bad moral influence, and a good many crimes could be traced directly to them. Why even the Sherlock Holmes stories caused an increase in the sale of cocaine. Of course we study criminals now in an entirely new manner, and we are constantly looking for what made them go wrong.

"Now I for one disagree with a lot of prison wardens who maintain that criminals differ little from people outside prison walls. Why because a man commits an offense against society should he be taught to grow roses and have a pet bird? The trouble with these prison workers is that they do not know anything about criminals. How can they? The man who opens oysters at an oyster bar knows no more of the life of an oyster and what it does in its wild state than the keeper of a zoo knows about the natural life of a tiger.

"There is an analogy in the warden and the prisoner, except that the prisoners are craftier than the oysters or the tigers. I know, for I have been around the world. A criminal in captivity is no more like one that is loose than a tortoise is like a race horse. The trouble with so many of our prison reformers is that they see a lot of men behind bars, some of whom are cowed and some of whom are sly, and they are fooled by them. We have a lot of that in England—old ladies who are trying to make life brighter for the wrongdoer, and wardens who are putting their own children in the care of murderers. This does no one any good—neither society nor the offender against it. It is just cheap, maudlin sentimentality.

"Above all else, most criminals are physical cowards, and it has been my experience that they fear pain more than they do imprisonment. In England we still have flogging for certain crimes, and the result has been that the crimes are seldom committed. Why, I have seen prisoners beg for imprisonment in preference to a lashing. Punishment must be sure and swift and sentimentality must not be mixed up with it."

November 10, 1929

CREATING CHARLIE CHAN

CHARLIE CHAN, the Chinese detective who figures so prominently in the mystery yarns of Earl Derr Biggers, has interested sufficient readers to warrant an inquiry into his origins. Now, with the latest of the series, "Charlie Chan Carries On," on view at the Roxy Theatre as a talking picture, Mr. Biggers tells the interesting history of his character.

"Charlie was born in a rather roundabout way," explained Mr. Biggers. "In 1919 I had a couple of plays in rehearsal at the same moment on Broadway and when that job was finished I found myself with a blood pressure that was trying for the altitude record. In the following Spring I was sitting one evening on a lanai on the water's edge at Waikiki Beach, Honolulu, carrying out the doctor's orders for a long rest. I had not thought particularly about what I would write next.

An Idea for a Murder.

"Suddenly there in the twilight I thought of an excellent way of murdering a man—the swimming ashore from a ship in the harbor trick, that later was to be the backbone of 'The House Without a Key.' When I got back to the mainland, however, I devoted myself to short stories for the 'Post' for a long time and it was four years after my return that I decided to do the Honolulu mystery story.

"I arranged to spend the Summer in the Berkshires, but before going up there I went to the New York Public Library and glanced through a huge bunch of Honolulu papers in order to refresh my memory about the islands. In one of the dailies I came across a small, unimportant item to the effect that Chang Apana and Lee Fook, Chinese detectives on the Honolulu force, had arrested one of their countrymen for being too friendly with opium.

Chinese Sleuths.

"If I had known before that there were Chinese on the police force over there, I had forgotten it. But I decided at once that, for added local color, a Chinese detective would be a good idea in 'The House Without a Key.' Sinister and wicked Chinese were old stuff in mystery stories, but an amiable Chinese acting on the side of law and order had never been used up to that time.

"So Charlie appeared in the Honolulu mystery, starting as a minor and unimportant character. As the story progressed, however, he modestly pushed his way forward, and toward the end he had the lion's share of the spotlight. Scarcely had the story stopped running in the 'Post' when I began to hear from people all over the country who wanted another Charlie Chan story. The idea had never occurred to me to write a series, but the possibilities looked good. So I wrote 'The Chinese Parrot,' still one of the most popular of the Chan stories. Then 'Behind That Curtain,' 'The Black Camel' and 'Charlie Chan Carries On.'

The Original Chan.

"Meanwhile, in Honolulu, practically all the characters in 'The House Without a Key' had been connected with real people—quite without reason—and Chang Apana, an old Chinese who had been on the force more than thirty years, was designated as the original of Charlie Chan. But I never met Chang until I had written three of the Chan stories, and when I did I found none of Charlie's charactertistics noticeable. The character of Charlie Chan, for better or worse, is entirely fictitious."

Warner Oland enacts the title rôle in the Fox picture, "Charlie Chan Carries On." It is, incidentally, the first sympathetic rôle of his film career. The cast includes John Garrick, Marguerite Churchill, Warren Hymer, Marjorie White, William Holden, C. Henry Gordon, Jason Robards, Peter Gawthorne, John T. Murray and many other favorites. It was directed by Hamilton MacFadden.

March 22, 1931

SAYS MRS. CHRISTIE STILL LACKS MEMORY

Husband of Novelist Asserts She Has Only Faint Idea of Her Identity.

SPECIALISTS ARE SKEPTICAL

Question Is Raised as to Who Is to Pay for Search Costing Thousands of Pounds.

Special Cable to THE NEW YORK TIMES.

LONDON, Dec. 15.—Mrs. Agatha Christie was recuperating today from her eleven-day disappearance at the home of her sister near Manchester. She is being kept in the strictest seclusion.

"My wife is far too ill to be worried," said her husband, Colonel Archibald Christie, today. "How she got to Harrogate she doesn't know, except that she got there by train. She has a faint idea that she is Mrs. Christie and that I am not her brother, as she first thought, but her husband."

Although her husband states she is suffering from loss of memory, reports of the life of the missing writer of detective novels at the fashionable Harrogate hotel where she was found indicate that she got along beautifully without it. She sang, danced, chatted and generally acted like the average patron. She registered under the name of Mrs. Tressa Neele of South Africa.

Demand for Her Books Jumps.

What Mrs. Christie has suffered in loss of memory has been her gain financially. At least two newspapers are publishing her novels in serial form and book publishers have been rushing her old works to meet the demand caused by her sensational disappearance and the equally sensational search for her.

Hundreds of amateur detectives were today putting away their lynx eyes, gum shoes and Sherlock Holmes peajackets and resting from their weary trampings over the Surrey Downs. The non-detective portion of the public is enjoying a laugh at their expense because they, as well as the "regulars," did not think it worth their while to follow the obvious clue which would have led them to their quarry, since Mrs. Christie left a note wherein she said she was going to a "Yorkshire spa." She went to the best known of the Yorkshire spas.

Had Gay Time at Hotel.

While every other patron in her hotel was interested in her disappearance she herself did not recognize the numerous photographs of herself in the newspapers at the hotel, although her interest in such mysteries had been life-long.

After her husband, Colonel Christie, had met his wife in the lobby and had been welcomed by her with a "stony stare," the police examined the room, finding a score of detective novels and a bottle which they confiscated.

Thousands of people gathered at the railway stations along the Harrogate-to-London line to catch a glimpse of Mrs. Christie. At Harrogate her husband hurried her into a private compartment. He refused to permit any one to speak to her. It was noticed that she appeared to be in good humor, while her husband seemed very worried.

The Christies fooled the crowd of people waiting at the London station by changing cars at Leeds and proceeding to Manchester, where they went to the home of Mrs. Christie's sister at Cheadle.

Newspapers and medical men show reluctance to accept the case as one of lost memory. Two leading mental specialists consulted by The Westminster Gazette were agreed, says that paper, "that whatever may have been the cause of Mrs. Christie's extraordinary behavior, it was not loss of memory."

One specialist, who has an international reputation is quoted as saying, "a person who has lost his or her memory may lose all recollection of identity without losing memory of things like music but he or she would be in such a state of distress that it would be apparent to everybody and they would not calmly manufacture a new identity, as Mrs. Christie did with such completeness."

Another authority whose contributions to the pathology of the mind have earned knighthood for him gave it as his firm conviction that a person suffering from loss of memory could not act in a normal manner nor mix with the public without arousing suspicions of insanity.

Meanwhile the question is being asked, "Who is going to refund to the rate payers the cost of the extensive police search for Mrs. Christie and who is going to pay for the damage done by the searchers in the neighborhood of Newlands corner?"

December 16, 1926

BARS REAL MURDER IN MURDER STORIES

Ellery Queen Agrees With Van Dine They Are Puzzles to Be Played With, "Not Read."

DIVORCED FROM REALITY

Author Puts in Four Months at Office Hours to Build Mystery Novel Like a House.

Ellery Queen, a pseudonymous writer of detective stories, who really hides his true identity behind his pseudonym, gave his own recipe for the manufacture of detective novels in an interview yesterday. In full agreement with S. S. Van Dine, who said last week that detective stories are primarily puzzles rather than novels, he said that they should be written not to be read but to be played with.

There is no relationship, he said, between a real murder and a murder story. The story, he emphasized, is a puzzle divorced from all reality, with more clues than probably would exist in reality and wholly artificial barriers. Some of the most interesting detective novels, he said, have been based on official theories concerning a crime —which solved the story but not the real case.

"In 1930 there were 850 detective novels published," he said. "Surely most of them were pounded out to make money, and it is just as sure that most of them did not make money. The average sale even in that happier time was somewhere between 3,000 and 3,500 for each title.

"One reason so many did not sell is that they did not fit definitely into any particular class of reading. They were supposed to be mysteries, but they mixed a dash of mystery with watered romance or high adventure.

"The pure puzzle story is far less likely to fail. A good puzzle always has a market. But to make up one you must put your real energy, not into characterization or atmosphere, but into a mathematically logical plot."

To each of his own books—the last one was "The Egyptian Cross Mystery," and the next, to be published in April by Stokes, will be "The American Gun Mystery"—he gives about four months. He keeps office hours from 9 to 5 in an office some miles away from his home.

Most of the first month is ordinarily necessary to find a fundamental situation, the foundation problem on which the book must rest, and to the decision of which character involved in this situation shall be the criminal.

"The next month," the author said, "is given to building the story. You have your crime and your criminal—a foundation and a roof. Then you build up and down—fitting in clues like doors and windows, and draw your characters and their traits as carefully as an architect draws floor plans. You have certain points to make, supplementary situations to conceive, and your choice of characters and locale must be thoroughly selected to at once deepen the mystery and provide for thorough plausibility.

"Then for two months you write and rewrite, smoothing and finishing. The last chapter and a complete, thoroughly detailed outline should be written first. When I have finished my synopsis I can tell, practically to the page, exactly where in the finished book any given incident will occur and what will be said about it."

In this manner Ellery Queen writes about two books a year, with four months free from writing. His books have sold fairly well, he said, although none has been published serially in a magazine and none has been made into a motion picture. He came into the field about four years ago.

January 16, 1933

Mystery Reviews

THE BIG SLEEP. ***By Raymond Chandler.*** ***277 pp.*** ***New York: Alfred A. Knopf.*** **$2.**

Most of the characters in this story are tough, many of them are nasty and some of them are both. Philip Marlowe, the private detective who is both the narrator and the chief character, is hard; he has to be hard to cope with the slimy racketeers who are preying on the Sternwood family. Nor do the Sternwoods themselves, particularly the two daughters, respond to gentle treatment. Spoiled is much too mild a term to describe these two young women. Marlowe is working for $25 a day and expenses and he earns every cent of it. Indeed, because of his loyalty to his employer, he passes up golden opportunities to make much more. Before the story is done Marlowe just misses being an eyewitness to two murders and by an even narrower margin misses being a victim. The language used in this book is often vile—at times so filthy that the publishers have been compelled to resort to the dash, a device seldom employed in these unsqueamish days. As a study in depravity, the story is excellent, with Marlowe standing out as almost the only fundamentally decent person in it.

February 12, 1939

THE MALTESE FALCON. ***By Dashiell Hammett.*** **267 pp.** ***New York: Alfred A. Knopf.*** **$2.**

If the locution "hard-boiled" had not already been coined it would be necessary to coin it now to describe the characters of Dashiell Hammett's latest detective story. All of the persons of the book are of that description, and the hardest boiled one of the lot is Sam Spade, the private detective, who gives the impression that he is on the side of the law only when it suits his book. If Spade had a weakness it would be women, but appreciative as he is of their charms, never, even in his most intimate relations with them, does he forget to look out for the interests of Samuel Spade. And it is as well that he does, for the criminals, men and women, with whom he comes in contact in this story are almost as hard-boiled as he. Mr. Hammett, we understand, was once a Pinkerton operative, and he probably knows that there is very little romance about the detective business. There is none of it in his book, but there is plenty of excitement.

February 23, 1930

By BRUCE RAE

THE GLASS KEY. *By Dashiell Hammett.* 282 pp. *New York: Alfred A. Knopf.* $2.

THERE can be no doubt of Mr. Hammett's gifts in this special field, and there can be no question of the success of his latest book. Municipal politics at its lowest is his theme and he has done the subject justice with a score of convincing underworld characters and their satellites. Senator Ralph Bancroft Henry is up for re-election, with the backing of the unsavory Paul Madvig, when the Senator's son, Taylor Henry, is murdered. Ned Beaumont, Madvig's lieutenant, apparently knows something about the crime, and so do half a dozen others, including a gambler's girl and a couple of gunmen. The Senator has a daughter, of course, and Beaumont, who strikes one as a cheap honky-tonker, falls in love. Plenty of authentic and coarse dialogue gives realism to the story. Mr. Hammett's new book is bound to find favor, although probably not as much as was accorded his earlier work, "The Maltese Falcon."

May 3, 1931

Dashiell Hammett, Author, Dies; Created Hard-Boiled Detectives

Originator of 'Thin Man' and Sam Spade of 'Maltese Falcon' —Jailed for Aiding Reds

Dashiell Hammett, the dean of the so-called "hard-boiled" school of detective fiction and author of "The Maltese Falcon," died yesterday morning at the Lenox Hill Hospital. He was 66 years old.

Mr. Hammett had been ill several times in the last four years with a lung ailment. He contracted tuberculosis while serving overseas in World War I but recovered after a long convalescence.

Mr. Hammett won his fame as an author in the late Nineteen Twenties and early Thirties. He put his name to a series of detective novels whose characters were, by modest estimate, at one remove from the stuffy, formal sleuths who moved through the mystery fiction of the day, disdaining evil. Before him paragons had trapped scoundrels in the dark lair of their own duplicity.

Mr. Hammett brought the form a step closer to reality. His detectives were tough or urbane or both, but they were by no means inaccessible to the common temptations of man. They were drawn in part from the writer's eight years of experience as a Pinkerton agent.

Associated Press

Dashiell Hammett

Created Sam Spade

Probably his most famous creation was the detective, Sam Spade, from "The Maltese Falcon," a man whose name was eloquent of his rough-cut, get-to-the-core-of-things style.

His novels included "The Glass Key," "The Dain Curse," "Red Harvest" and the famous "The Thin Man."

After 1935 he produced little to match his first works, though he long continued to enjoy the accessory benefits of having his writing adapted to virtually every form of entertainment—radio, motion pictures, television, magazine serialization, even cartoon strips.

Mr. Hammett's association with various left-wing causes from about the time of World War II led finally to a conviction for contempt of court in 1951.

He had been a trustee of the bail fund of the Civil Rights Congress, an organization that was designated by the Attorney General as a Communist front. The fund had posted bond for four top Communist leaders who jumped bail. Mr. Hammett and three other trustees were sentenced for refusing to name persons who contributed to the fund. The author served six months at the Federal Correctional Institute near Ashland, Ky.

Invoked Fifth Amendment

Called before the Senate Permanent Subcommittee on Investigations, headed by the late Senator Joseph R. McCarthy of Wisconsin, Mr. Hammett invoked the Fifth Amendment when asked if he was then or had been at any time a member of the Communist party. He told the committee that he was "sincerely afraid" he might incriminate himself.

Mr. Hammett's prose style invited such descriptive words as "lean, driving, hard." His work was several times likened to that of Ernest Hemingway by qualified critics and, in one case at least, it was Hemingway, not Hammett, who was the beneficiary of the comparison. Another writer said that Mr. Hammett's work was not fiction but "life magnified."

In 1953, Mr. Hammett's novels were plucked from the shelves of seventy-three of 189 American libraries overseas as a result of a volley of State Department confidential directives, based largely on testimony before the McCarthy committee.

Ten memorandums went out to the libraries, listing Mr. Hammett and fifteen others as undesirable authors. While the eleventh memorandum was being prepared, President Eisenhower told a news conference that he thought "someone got frightened." He said that he would not himself have removed Mr. Hammett's books. Soon thereafter a new directive went out, authorizing the return of Mr. Hammett's books from storage to circulation.

Mr. Hammett was always placing distraction in the way of his heroes, usually in the persons of young women. It was typical enough of his detectives to spend a lavish evening in the company of one, neglecting no favor, and then to ransack her purse for the ultimate clue.

In a newspaper interview Mr. Hammett once described his view of a character this way:

"I see in him a little man going forward day after day through mud and blood and death and deceit — as callous and brutal and cynical as necessary—towards a dim goal, with nothing to push or pull him

towards it except he's been hired to reach it."

Native of Maryland

This indifference to ordinary morality joined to devoted pursuit of a private code was a frequent trait of Hammett characters. It was written of Nick Charles, "The Thin Man" hero, that he "devoted himself to an intensive study of the liquor problem from the consumer's standpoint."

Mr. Hammett was born on Maryland's Eastern Shore and put in three years at the Baltimore Polytechnic Institute, which he left at the age of 13. He worked as a newsboy, freight clerk, railroad laborer, advertising man as well as Pinkerton detective. He once caught a man who had stolen a Ferris wheel.

Mr. Hammett, a slender 6-foot-tall man with a crest of gray hair, was a painstaking craftsman who worked and reworked his stories until he was satisfied he could do no better. He was a night worker, and sometimes, if pressed, worked on a book or motion picture thirty-six hours at a stretch.

In keeping with his request, arrangements have been made for Mr. Hammett to be buried Friday in the Arlington National Cemetery. Mr. Hammett served as a sergeant with the Motor Ambulance Corps in the First World War. In World War II, at the age of 48, he enlisted in the Army and served for two years in the Aleutian Islands.

Mr. Hammett's latest residence was at 63 East Eighty-second Street as the house guest of Lillian Hellman, the playwright. Miss Hellman will speak at the funeral service at 4 P. M. Thursday at the Frank E. Campbell Funeral Church, Madison Avenue at Eighty-first Street.

Mr. Hammett's marriage in 1920 to Josephine Annas Dolan of Anaconda, Mont., ended in divorce. Surviving are two daughters, Mrs. Mary Miller and Mrs. Josephine Marshall, and four grandchildren.

January 11, 1961

An Interview With Mister Rex Stout

The Author of the Nero Wolfe Detective Stories Discusses His Work and the War

By ROBERT van GELDER

WITH Rex Stout you have one certainty: that whatever you are you won't be misunderstood. The author of the Nero Wolfe detective stories is more articulate than are most writers and has more free energy. One has the impression that he has lived more and worked less than the majority of his peers. His beard is not a particularly good beard: it has rather the sparse look of barberry bushes that have been trampled by the house painters. The beard's purpose, probably, is to ambush one's attention from the eyes above it, which are not cataloguing eyes and seem to reflect open judgments, but are intent and observing to a rare degree.

Mr. Stout said that he writes detective stories because they pay well. Before turning to Nero Wolfe he wrote four novels; two had very good notices here and were even better received in England and in France.

"But I know of only three reasons why a man should write serious fiction. One, if you love words and want to put them together in a way that pleases you—that was my reason for writing the four novels. The second reason, if you're burning to tell other people what you think is wrong, that is, if you're the preacher type. Some of the best writers now are fundamentally preachers. Johnny Steinbeck, I think, is one. The third reason to write serious fiction is if you are a great writer. There are damn few great writers and I'm not one of them. While I could afford to I played with words. When I could no longer afford that I wrote for money."

Born in Kansas, the son of a superintendent of schools, Mr. Stout left the University of Kansas while in his freshman year and enlisted in the Navy. "I wanted to see the ocean." That was in 1906 and the term of his enlistment was four years. He was made yeoman paymaster on President Theodore Roosevelt's yacht. "As it happened there were only seven men in the wardroom and that left them one short for two tables of whist. So they fixed it up to make me a warrant officer, which would give me the freedom of the wardroom and would fill out the second table. After a time I got tired of whist and, as a warrant officer can resign, I resigned."

Then a succession of jobs, including clerking in a cigar store. Mr. Stout heard that an uptown New York hotel needed a manager. He bought some striped pants and a cutaway and applied. The costume clinched the job and the elevator man and the telephone girl—old hands in the hotel business—tutored him so that he could keep it. He left this post to write for a living.

"But if I was paid $18 for a short story, and it was Summer, I went to baseball games until I was broke again. If I got $3,000 for a 90,000-word story that Bob

Pirie MacDonald.

Rex Stout.

Davis had bought, and it was Winter, I went to the opera until I was broke again. Never even got my laundry out. I decided, hell, that life wasn't getting me anywhere. And the stories weren't any good. I made up my mind to go into business until I had $150,000 or was 40 years old. I was three months short of 40 when I had the $150,000. I wrote my novels, but in the depression I lost my money."

"What was the business?"

"I invented a system of accounting that I sold to banks."

"Had you ever worked in a bank?"

"No."

"Were you an accountant?"

"No." A pause. "You see, I have a—a sort of a trick mind for figures. When I was a kid, 9, 10, 11, along in there, I toured Kansas as a sort of exhibit. I'd stand in a schoolroom with my back to the blackboard, or blindfolded, and rows of figures—eleven or twelve across and eleven deep—were written on the board. I'd look at this block of figures for, well, six seconds, then turn my back again and give the total, the sum that they added up to.

"My father didn't like it. You see, it made me a freak. I realized that too, and I didn't like it. No, I've lost the trick. I think I consciously lost it. But even now I find it impossible to make a mistake in addition.

"I turned to words instead of figures. I'd always loved words—had read the Bible through when I was 3½, read Macaulay when I was 3, and so on. But with words I wasn't a freak."

He said that until the war started he had thoroughly enjoyed writing stories about Nero Wolfe.

"I never worked more than three months a year. Not quite three months. Thirty-nine or forty days on each novel, and I'd do two a year.

"No, there's nothing much to planning them. Of course, I was lucky on having hit on the name —Nero Wolfe. Simple but odd, people remember it. And Wolfe was born; he wasn't synthetic. I didn't have to sit down and decide: 'What color will his eyes be? Well, they'll be blue. How much will he weigh? How will he walk? What expressions will he use?' He was born.

"I tried another detective later, Tecumseh Fox—because the Saturday Evening Post editors wanted a fresh detective—and he never was born. He was put together piece by piece and wasn't worth a damn.

"As for the story, you take a setting that interests you, think of what might happen in that setting, choose the most entertaining happenings, and then ask yourself: 'Well, why would a man want to buy that champion bull? Why would some one murder a man because of a bull?' The answers come right along. You have your plot. You write it.

"It was pure pleasure—a game.

"Then Munich gave me my first belly-ache. I'd always been healthy; I became dyspeptic. That's true. I had pains most of the time after Munich, a nervous stomach.

"I started making speeches, debating these America First fellows, going on the radio to answer them, doing all I could to wake people up to the danger.

"Listen, if we get in now, right now, 200,000 American lives and fifty billion dollars probably will be the cost of beating Hitler. If we listen to the isolationists and wait until Hitler is ready for us, until we are next on his timetable, we'll spend five million American lives and two or three hundred billion dollars. What in God's name is the sense of that?

"I'm not dyspeptic any more. The nervousness is all going out, you see, in these speeches. But Nero Wolfe gets smaller. Can't keep my mind on him."

Mr. Stout led the way onto the sunny roof of his house. The Stout place is called High Meadows. It is near the crest of one of the long slopes to the south of the Berkshires. Straight ahead a ten-mile view of meadows, trees and hills. Mr. Stout gestured toward Pawling.

"Quite a colony of the subversive element over there." He named a number of prominent isolationists. "With a 75-millimeter gun placed right here, I'll bet I could pot them."

September 21, 1941

Erle Stanley Gardner, Author of the Perry Mason Mystery Novels

'The Fiction Factory'

By ALBIN KREBS

As the best-selling American author of the century, Erle Stanley Gardner often insisted that he was "not really a writer at all," and to be sure, there were many critics who enthusiastically agreed with him.

But millions of readers who have bought more than 170 million copies of his books in American editions alone, looked upon Mr. Gardner, creator of the redoubtable defense lawyer Perry Mason, as a master storyteller.

Gardner fans did not, in fact, expect his fast-paced detective stories to be literary gems, which they were not. They turned to his novels for entertainment, knowing that each would be crisply written in a no-nonsense style, intricately plotted, with a satisfying happy ending.

Thus, over a period that spanned more than 35 years, there existed a constant market for the lawyer-turned-writer's books. The incredibly prolific Mr. Gardner, who enjoyed being referred to as "the fiction factory" and "the Henry Ford of detective novelists," worked furiously to keep his reading market satiated.

Statistics on the sales of his books, which change daily with speedometer relentlessness, are staggering. His paperback publishers alone, in the mid-1960's, were selling 2,000 Gardner books an hour, eight hours a day, 365 days a year. Translated into 30 languages and dialects, Gardner novels sold at a rate of about 20,000 a day abroad.

By late 1969, Mr. Gardner had produced more than 140 books, of which 80 were Perry Mason tales and 15 works of nonfiction. At the age of 80, he was still turning out four or five volumes a year with machinelike regularity.

Enslaved by Success

Mr. Gardner turned to writing because he sought more time to go exploring and camping, and for what he called "the opportunity to search for more color in life." But his success — in the popular, if perhaps not the critical, sense — in many ways enslaved him.

"I have become chained to my fiction factory because my audience can't get enough of my stories, no matter how fast I write them," he once said.

A burly man of average height who dressed in cowboy clothes and boots and presented the wide-open, hearty demeanor of the stereotypical Westerner, Mr. Gardner was described by an old friend as "restless, romantic, adventurous, generous, impulsive, idealistic, hospitable and both sophisticated and unsophisticated."

His idealism and generosity led him to found "The Court of Last Resort," a private organization dedicated to helping men thought to have been imprisoned unjustly.

He brought to his writing a deep admiration for, and devotion to, the law, and so diligently did he research the presentation of his fictional cases that among his fans were several law school deans, who praised his accuracy in portraying courtroom scenes, and the soundness of his heroes' legal maneuvers. The only known legal slip he made was a simple and, to him, inexplicable one: He let a beneficiary to a will be also a witness to it.

The author was born in Malden, Mass., on July 17, 1889. His mother was the former Grace Adelma Waugh, his father Charles Walter Gardner, a mining engineer whose occupation gave Erle a much-traveled childhood in Massachusetts, Oregon, Alaska and California. He finished high school in Palo Alto, Calif., then briefly attended Valparaiso University in Indiana. "I was kicked out for slugging a professor," he said.

While still in his teens, Mr. Gardner was arrested for promoting an illegal boxing match. In the process of wriggling out of his legal difficulties, he became fascinated with the law and obtained a job, at $20 a month, as a typist for a law firm in Oxnard, Calif. At the age of 21, after he had read law for an average of 50 hours a week over a three-year period, he was admitted to the California bar.

From 1911 to 1916 Mr. Gardner practiced law in Oxnard. In defending poor Chinese and Mexicans there, he developed an intense sympathy for the penniless and the friendless who ran into legal troubles, and for those he considered unjustly accused.

In such clients' behalf, he tirelessly nosed about in forgotten statutes and cases to find just the right precedents to fit his needs. At the proper moment, he would spring the precedent on the judge and jury—much as his lawyer hero, Perry Mason, would do in dozens of novels in the years to come.

A Hectic Existence

"It got so he won all his cases," a former law partner of Mr. Gardner's told an interviewer some years ago. "In the courtroom Erle radiated self-confidence at all times. His voice was resonant and carried well. He was big, stocky, plain-looking.

"Erle didn't try for the dapper, slick-lawyer look. The jurors probably considered him as ordinary as themselves, which suited him just fine.

"His way with a hostile witness was plain wizardry. He could coax the fellow along, right into telling outright lies, or into confusion so complete the fellow would end up babbling and no jury could possibly take his testimony seriously." Much, again, in the manner of Perry Mason.

Despite his local celebrity as a defender of the underdog, Mr. Gardner felt compelled to make money, and he abandoned law in 1918 to work as a tire salesman. He did well, but missed the courtroom, and so in 1921 he joined a law firm in Ventura, Calif. He also started writing stories for the pulp magazines that were popular at the time.

It was a hectic existence, Mr. Gardner said years later. "I still have vivid recollections," he said, "of putting in day after day trying a case in front of a jury, which is one of the most exhausting activities I know about, dashing up to the law library after court had adjourned to spend three or four hours looking up law points with which I could trap my adversary the next day, then going home, grabbing a glass of milk with an egg in it, dashing upstairs to my study, ripping the cover off my typewriter, noticing it was 11:30 P.M., and settling down with grim determination to get a plot for a story.

Erle Stanley Gardner

"Along about 3 in the morning I would have completed my daily stint of a 4,000-word minimum and would crawl into bed.

The self-discipline, the ability to use his energies to the utmost, the single-mindedness of purpose Mr. Gardner developed during the 1920's were to stay with him for the rest of his life.

By 1930 Mr. Gardner, who had reached a point where he was attacking the typewriter with such ferocity that his fingers often bled, was dictating all his fiction. In 1932 he turned out 224,000 words while still working two days a week at his law practice.

Rejected Several Times

That output included two full-length novels, one of which was "The Case of the Velvet Claws." It was turned down by several publishers before it reached the desk of Thayer Hobson, then president of William Morrow & Co.

Mr. Hobson saw in "The Case of the Velvet Claws," which Mr. Gardner had dictated in less than four days, the germ for a series of books. He suggested that Mr. Gardner specialize in a single main character rather than try to invent new characters in new locales for each of his detective novels.

Mr. Gardner agreed to standardize the bulk of his forthcoming work with one character, the brilliant lawyer, Perry Mason, hero of "The Case of the Velvet Claws," a best-seller in 1933. The Mason novels that followed also had standardized titles, all beginning with "The Case of the . . ." and many including alliterations.

Over the years there appeared "The Case of the Waylaid Wolf," "Sulky Girl," "Duplicate Daughter," "Spurious Spinster," "Bigamous Spouse," "Darling Divorcee," "Amorous Aunt," "Worried Waitress," "Beautiful Beggar," "Fabulous Fake" and many more Mason mysteries.

Mr. Gardner fashioned another detective series around the character of Doug Selby, a virtuous, hard-hitting, rather smug young district attorney. The Selby books also had stock titles, all beginning with "The D.A. . . ." Among them were "The D. A. Calls It Murder," "Goes to Trial," "Cooks a Goose" and "Breaks an Egg."

A third series of detective stories, written under the pseudonym of A. A. Fair, centered on the exploits of Bertha Cool, a fat, middle-aged private detective, and Donald Lam, a guileful, self-styled genius. Among the Lam-Cool books were "Widows Wear Weeds" and "Cut Thin to Win." The last book in the series, "All Grass Isn't Green," will be published March 27.

With the success of his first three books, Mr. Gardner gave up his law practice altogether. For five years he did his writing in house trailers parked in lonely desert spots. Before long, however, he began buying odds and ends of real estate along the length of the West Coast, on which he built about a dozen hideouts where he could go to write and avoid people.

The nucleus of the "Gardner fiction factory" was the writer's 1,000-acre Rancho del Paisano, at Temecula, Calif., which he bought in 1938. Situated on a desert benchland 100 miles southeast of Los Angeles, Rancho del Paisano consists of a hodgepodge of buildings—10 guest cottages, a dozen garages, fireproof manuscript vaults and several house trailers.

One building housed Mr. Gardner's office, law library, extensive gun collection and sleeping quarters. In another rambling structure, six secretaries worked fulltime transcribing Mr. Gardner's booming voice from tapes.

Rose at Dawn

Mr. Gardner was up daily at dawn. After three hours of dictation, he would stroll down to the ranch's main house, taken up largely by a huge living-dining room, to have breakfast with his staff of some 20 retainers (all of whom called him "Uncle Erle") and usually a half dozen guests.

The rest of his working day was devoted to more dictation, then pencil revisions of typescripts. In his prime, he could have a novel ready for his publishers within six weeks from the time he started it.

For nine years, Mr. Gardner devoted several hours a week to the supervision and criticism of scripts for the popular Perry Mason television show, seen weekly on the Columbia Broadcasting System network through the season of 1966. The series quickly gobbled up all his own Mason stories, and a staff had to be hired to write fresh scripts.

The television series continued to be seen in syndication after it went off C.B.S., and each episode was dubbed or subtitled into 16 languages for showings abroad. Since Mr. Gardner was the majority stockholder in Paisano Productions, which packaged the series, over a decade he was said to have earned about $15-million from the Mason show. The sale of his books and a radio series that preceded the TV shows had already made him a multimillionaire, however.

Dollar Volume 'Gigantic'

"The dollar volume of my one-man fiction factory is gigantic," he told an interviewer. "The profits are enormous, and the taxes are astronomical. I don't mind if the government gets more than anybody else of what I earn, and it wouldn't do me any good if I did."

Wayne Miller—Magnum

At his ranch in 1963, Erle Stanley Gardner placed his latest book atop a collection of his works. The number of titles increased steadily until his death.

A man of many interests, Mr. Gardner was widely read in psychology, archeology, criminology, penology and geology. He was an excellent photographer. Although he was a crack shot with either rifle or pistol, he gave up hunting with firearms more than 20 years ago, when he decided the odds were too strongly against the animals. Instead, he learned to hunt with bow and arrow.

Mr. Gardner's consuming love for the outdoors provided him with material for his nonfiction books, among them "Mexico's Magic Square," "Hunting Lost Mines by Helicopter," "Hunting the Desert Whale" and "The Desert Is Yours."

On his camping trips, Mr. Gardner like to take along the comforts of civilization, which included a small refrigerator truck, air-conditioned camper vehicles, a cook, his executive secretary, Jean Bethell, and at least one more dictationist, in case he felt the urge to write.

In 1912 Mr. Gardner married the former Natalie Talbert, and they had a daughter, Grace, now Mrs. Alan R. McKittrick. The couple were separated in the early 1930's.

Mrs. Gardner died in 1968, and soon afterward Mr. Gardner married Mrs. Bethell, a divorcee who had been his secretary since 1930. (In the Mason stories, Della Street was modeled after Jean Bethell and her two sisters, Peggy and Ruth, who also served as Gardner secretaries. All the sisters lived at Rancho del Paisano.)

Praised and Dismissed

Book critics who specialized in crime stories, such as Anthony Boucher, writing in The New York Times Book Review, consistently praised Mr. Gardner for his intricate plotting and his simple narrative style. Other critics, however, dismissed his novels as "mere entertainments" or "pap."

None of which bothered Mr. Gardner in the least.

"I write to make money, and I write to give the reader sheer fun," he said. "People derive a moral satisfaction from reading a story in which the innocent victim of fate triumphs over evil. They enjoy the stimulation of an exciting detective story.

"Most readers are beset with a lot of problems they can't solve. When they try to relax, their minds keep gnawing over these problems and there is no solution. They pick up a mystery story, become completely absorbed in the problem, see the problem worked out to a final and just conclusion, turn out the light and go to sleep. If I have given millions that sort of relaxation, it is reward enough."

March 12, 1970

Mysterious Fun for Millions of Innocent Escapists

By MARGERY ALLINGHAM

AT the end of World War I, Agatha Mary Clarissa Christie was working as a dispenser in a Red Cross hospital. She "thought it would be fun" to write a detective story. The result has been, indeed, no end of fun for some tens of millions of innocent escapists in one of the most harrowing quarter centuries in history. In the school of detective fiction, Agatha Christie is today the undisputed Head Girl. Her fiftieth whodunit, "A Murder Is Announced," (see below) will be published simultaneously nearly all over the world tomorrow.

The first Christie, "The Mysterious Affair at Styles," took two years to find a publisher and, although it introduced the now famous Belgian detective Hercule Poirot, it was not outstandingly successful. Then in 1926 Agatha Christie wrote "The Murder of Roger Ackroyd." This book sold well, and the dramatic version, in which Charles Laughton had one of the first of his London triumphs, went even better. From that moment, with a steady output of two books a year, she has become one of the two main pillars of the most essentially modern (if, also, one of the most odd) form of literature the language has yet produced.

With her brilliant contemporary, Miss Dorothy Sayers, she has helped to mold a somewhat loose art form into a concrete shape and to give it both life and a tradition. If Miss Sayers has presented the detective story with literary distinction, Agatha Christie has kept its hair short and its feet on the ground, and of the two writers she is probably, in the purest sense of the term, the more intellectual.

As it emerges today the detective story proper is a form of entertainment almost entirely cerebral, since it aims to provide a means of escape for those who do not wish for some excellent private reason to take their emotions for a ride with the novelists. In its never-never land where Death is merely a cipher for the most important happening, and the puzzle is the thing, it is perhaps not at all surprising that a charming, shrewd and essentially civilized matron should be high priestess of the cult.

Agatha Christie's 50th

Agatha Christie

Agatha Christie
Regatta Mystery

Agatha Christie
Crooked House

The Murder of Roger Ackroyd
by Agatha Christie

THE lady herself is good-looking and possesses what our fathers used to call so admiringly "a presence." She has a sensitive yet very strong face, which, in photographs, is apt to appear uncharacteristically wistful. Her smile is ready and broad and her movements are vigorous and oddly schoolgirlish. She is kindly, very feminine, large, unaffected, almost alarmingly efficient and not one-tenth as simple as a casual observer might suppose.

At first glance one might take her for the matron of a great hospital, or a prima donna, or the Queen Mother of Some-

Miss Allingham's own mysteries ("Death of a Ghost," "More Work for the Undertaker," etc.) have tingled many a spine in her native England and in America, too.

where, yet out of a roomful of intelligent people it is she whom the stranger would select to entrust with the keys of the safe, the baby, or even his "copy" for the mail. She looks not only kind but capable.

She has been married twice; first to a young army officer, Archibald Christie, from whom she obtained a divorce in 1928, and second, in 1930, to Max Mallowan, the distinguished Professor of Archaeology at London University, whom she met at Ur of the Chaldees in Iraq where he was digging with Leonard Woolley. Ever since then she has been tremendously interested in her husband's work and has traveled again and again to the Middle East, where much of it is done. She likes the desert and the sea far better than the cities, and is allergic to noise. The talkies and radio depress her and London sees her rarely.

She lives in Devonshire, where she was born. She has a grown daughter, a sister who criticizes her work and a sensible dog who dislikes the typewriter. Collecting and decorating houses are a vice with her, she says, for she never has time to live in them. This last is hardly remarkable, for her energy must be something of a taskmaster. During the war she decided to take up higher mathematics as a relaxation and then, not exhausted by this or her two mysteries a year, threw off a novel or so of a more emotional kind under the pseudonym of Mary Westmacott.

HER tales sell in every form in every language, including Japanese. In Turkey she is the best-selling English writer, and only recently the world-wide sales of her books, as estimated by her American publisher, reached the 75,000,000 mark, 35,000,000 of them in the United States.

Her appeal is made directly to the honest human curiosity in all of us. The invitation she gives her readers is to listen to the details surrounding the perfectly horrid screams from the apartment next door. Her characters, slapped in with an easy charm which has grown surer with the years, are the people we each know best. They are the nice or nasty everyday folk who sit at our tables and borrow our lawn mowers or scowl at us mysteriously (and unfairly) in trains. They are Gluyas Williams models, every one of them, and the adventures which befall them and the mysteries in their lives which M. Poirot's "little gray cells" uncover, or Miss Marple's uncanny wits disclose, are not so utterly fantastic that they may not, just possibly, be true. After all, one never really knows one's neighbors, does one? Not quite. What about the fellow who is reading this article over your shoulder now?

There is no other reality in her tales, nor does the genuine detective story permit any. Grief is out of place here, so is horror, so is fear. These are too near home for the escaping reader in this age of peril. The rest is puzzle and first-class puzzle, too. To be convincing, the man who says he always guesses an Agatha Christie mystery should also be able to forecast election results and the winners of horse races.

In her own sphere there is no one to touch her, and her millions of readers are going to buy her new story, "A Murder Is Announced," and like it.

THE impression she leaves is that she is a woman of extraordinary ability who could have done anything she chose to do. What she has done is to entertain more people for more hours at a time than almost any other writer of her generation. Taking it by and large, in this day and age it is difficult to think of any work which could possibly have been more useful.

When her hundredth book is published (on present form this should take place in the fall of '75) she will doubtless receive the "family canonization" of other minor saints and take her place between Florence Nightingale and Grace Darling.

June 4, 1950

Agatha Christie: "High priestess of the cult."

New Mystery

A COFFIN FOR DIMITRIOS. By Eric Ambler. 281 pp. New York: Alfred A. Knopf. $2.

The Turkish police dossier on the man called Dimitrios, fragmentary as it is, credits him with just about all the crimes on the calendar, and Charles Latimer, an English writer of detective stories, feels an irresistible desire to learn more about the man. His adventures in search of this information begin in Istanbul and end in Paris, with several stops along the way, and they are such as to give Latimer more excitement than he has bargained for and to convince him that writing about crime is much easier and infinitely safer than mixing in the affairs of criminals. This is the third of Mr. Ambler's mystery-adventure thrillers to be published in this country, and it affords additional proof of his genuine talent for that type of fiction.

October 22, 1939

Color of the East

PASSAGE OF ARMS. By Eric Ambler. 246 pp. New York: Alfred A. Knopf. $3.95.

By JAMES M. CAIN

AS an old hand at intrigue, violence, and Asia, Mr. Ambler kicks this tale off with his usual skill. Girija Krishnan, an Indian employed in Malaya, is ordered, as a rubber plantation's clerk, to arrange burial for eight Chinese who have been ambushed by a British patrol in the guerrilla fighting of some years back. He gets the job done in a few pages which brilliantly evoke the countryside. Then he notices things the British have missed. From them he deduces that these Chinese, instead of being ordinary terrorists, must have formed a guard, probably for an arms cache, tucked away in some ravine. If he can only find these guns, store them safe from the weather and sell them without paying the prescribed penalty (which is death), he can gain the capital he will need to start a bus line for that part of the peninsula.

It takes Girija three years to cook up his plans. A buyer is found, the agent for Indonesian revolutionaries. Shipment, however, needs certain signatures on customs papers, and as the patsy to furnish these, an American is baited in, a middle-aged manufacturer named Olsen, on an around-the-world tour with his wife. The rest, once Olsen puts his name on the dotted line, is the disaster his naïveté leads to. He gets in deeper and deeper, winding up in a Sumatran jail, where he, the wife, and a Eurasian lady are caught in a shooting raid and mauled up by guards, Communists, insects and disillusionment.

The start, as I have said, tingles. The detail throughout is superb, especially the glimpses the author gives us into various Asian minds. And yet, for one reader at least, things began to sag, early on. I would say the trouble was too much integrity, not too little: Mr. Ambler apparently set out to master his background, and wound up with its mastering him.

Seeking a plausible antagonist, he passed up the hackneyed adventurer, and hit on the middle-aged Olsen—perhaps, I must add, with some idea of doing another Quiet American, (the Greene book is mentioned once, in an oddly arresting way). If so, this American is not only quiet but dull. And the trap the background has furnished is so fiendishly perfect that not even Casanova could get out of it by his own wits alone. So Olsen is saved by others, and totes up, first to last, a straw man.

Getting back to first principles, we see once again the importance of a love story, as the armature on which all else is built. I found myself wishing, I confess, that someone, somewhere, in this book, would find a girl to seduce, or want to. No such thing happens. No love of any kind, whether sexy, noble or renunciatory, reareth its ugly head, unless Olsen's devotion to his wife, occasionally remembered, counts as such.

In short, for a picture of Southeast Asia, in all its color and the savagery of its current turmoil, this is tops, and gets down to bedrock. For poetics, it's a little skimpy.

Mr. Cain is the author of "Serenade," "Mildred Pierce" and other novels.

Eric Ambler.
"Passage of Arms."

March 6, 1960

On Assignment With James Bond

ON HER MAJESTY'S SECRET SERVICE. By Ian Fleming. 299 pp. New York: New American Library. $4.50.

By ANTHONY BOUCHER

YOU can't argue with success. Nothing this review can say is going to keep a few million American readers (including our President) from reading the latest adventure of James Bond, 007, C. M. G. But simply *pro forma*, I must set down my opinion that this is a silly and tedious novel. Even Bond fans generally agree that his creator reached an unprecedented low with his last book, "The Spy That Loved Me." This new one must rank quite a bit above that nadir; but it is still a lazy and inadequate story—the mixture as in Fleming's major successes, but with noticeably inferior ingredients.

Once more Bond challenges the sinister mastermind of a powerful secret organization; but the mastermind isn't very sinister, the organization isn't very powerful, and Bond, about as effectual as Nayland Smith in his endless duels with Fu Manchu, fails in his one major objective and leaves the mastermind at large.

Incidentally to all this, Bond gets married. Since the girls whom he beds with even casually died in previous novels, you may imagine the fate of his bride. Most astonishing, even the gambling (about which Fleming can write brilliantly) is absurd here: Bond meets his bride in a fantastic game of chemin-de-fer in which he wins 46,000 New Francs, loses 400,000 and breaks even.

My complaint is not that the adventures of James Bond are bad literature (an impression heightened this time by a girlish rash of exclamation points — a mannerism which Fleming's previous publisher presumably deleted), but that they aren't good bad literature. Far too little happens for the inordinate amount of words, and even that little is far too simple. (Bond, for instance, keeps escaping death through no skills of his own but simply through the phenomenal bad marksmanship of all his enemies; Col. Sebastian Moran would have finished him in one chapter.)

One thinks longingly, not so much of writers like Eric Ambler and Geoffrey Household, who have elevated the thriller to the status of art, as of the really good colporteurs—the Sax Rohmers and the Edgar Wallaces and even, God help me, the E. Phillips Oppenheims, who at least knew how to keep a story filled with inventive incident rather than a swank succession of snobbish brand names.

They just aren't writing bad books like they used to.

Mr. Boucher is the veteran appraiser of whodunits for The Times Book Review.

August 25, 1963

Ian Fleming Created James Bond

Special to The New York Times

In little more than a decade James Bond became the world's best known secret agent.

Countless readers avidly followed his undercover war against Soviet master spies and terrorists and later against a mysterious international crime syndicate.

Mr. Fleming equipped his hero with an impeccable social background, good looks, bravery, toughness and a disillusioned sort of patriotism.

More important, the double-O identification number, carried by only three men in the British Secret Service, authorized him to kill in the line of duty. It was a privilege Bond exercised frequently and sometimes reluctantly, most often with a .25-caliber Beretta automatic that he carried in a chamois shoulder holster.

President Kennedy and Allen Dulles, while he was the head of the Central Intelligence Agency, said that they enjoyed Mr. Fleming's books. In fact, it was probably the President's praise in 1961 that was largely responsible for their enormous popularity here. In Britain, Prince Philip led the cheering section.

Mr. Fleming wrote 12 books, all but two about Bond, and was working on the 13th when he died. All told, they sold more than 18 million copies, mostly in paperback editions, and were translated into 10 languages.

Two highly profitable films, "Doctor No" and "From Russia With Love," were made from his novels, a third, "Goldfinger," was recently completed and is awaiting release and others are planned.

Mr. Fleming had made $2.8 million from his books, according to his agent, Peter Janson-Smith. In March, in a complex transaction for tax purposes, he sold a 51 per cent interest in his future income to a British holding company for $280,000.

Critics on Both Sides

Critics differed on the merits of his works. Some said he was an aristocratic Mickey Spillane, pandering to the public's taste for sadism and sex. A critic in London's New Statesman called "Doctor No," which tells of how Bond destroys a missile-sabotage center in the Caribbean, "the nastiest book" he had ever read.

"There are three basic ingredients in 'Doctor No,'" he said, "all unhealthy, all thoroughly English: the sadism of a schoolboy bully, the mechanical, two-dimensional sex-longings of a frustrated adolescent, and the crude snob-cravings of a suburban adult.

"Mr. Fleming has no literary skill. But the three ingredients are manufactured and blended with deliberate, professional precision."

On the other hand, the contemporary novelist Kingsley Amis, in a 40,000-word study, described Bond as tender rather than sadistic, classless rather than snobbish and a moderate Tory rather than a Fascist.

On the whole, American critics did not take Mr. Fleming quite so seriously, regarding his books as thrillers that had tended to become less thrilling in recent years.

Mr. Fleming said he thought of them as entertainment of no special significance. He attributed their popularity to a hunger for larger-than-life heroes that was left unsatisfied by most contemporary fiction.

At the same time Bond's adventures slaked a public thirst for information about espionage that had been whetted by such events as the trial of Dr. Klaus Fuchs, the Burgess-McLean case, the U-2 incident and the growing awareness of the work of the C.I.A.

The first of the novels, "Casino Royale," published in London without fanfare in 1953, described Bond's destruction of Le Chiffre, the head of the French branch of Smersh, the Soviet espionage and terror ring, Bond's nearly fatal torture and his discovery that the woman he had fallen in love with was a Soviet agent.

Mr. Fleming later said he wrote the book because he needed to keep his mind off his impending marriage, marking the end of his bachelor days.

"Writing about 2,000 words in three hours every morning, he said, "'Casino Royale' dutifully produced itself. I wrote nothing and made no corrections until the book was finished. If I had looked back at what I had written the day before I might have despaired."

Hewed to the Contemporary

Other novels followed rapidly. In "Goldfinger" Bond foils a plot to rob Fort Knox; in "Moonraker" he prevents the firing of a missile into the heart of London; in "Live and Let Die" he destroys Smersh's chief agent in the United States, a Negro dabbler in voodoo and racketeering known as Mr. Big.

In "From Russia With Love," Bond escapes from Smersh's plot to destroy him but appears to be dying of poison as the book ends. Concern over his fate mounted among the public. His publishers finally stated, "After a period of anxiety the condition of No. 007 shows definite improvement."

Mr. Fleming liked to point out that Smersh, although often thought to be a fictional organization, existed as a Soviet counterespionage organization during and after World War II Its name is the combined form of the Russian words "smyert spionam," meaning death to spies.

When Smersh was disbanded, Mr. Fleming set up SPECTRE, as Bond's opponent. It was unquestionably fictional, the word being formed from the initials of Special Executive for Counter-intelligence Terror, Revenge and Extortion.

Under the leadership of Ernest Stavro Blofeld, whose career began as a double or triple agent in prewar Warsaw, SPECTRE has enlisted the services of former Gestapo agents, disenchanted Smersh operatives, members of the Mafia, the Red Lightning Tong and other master criminals.

In "Thunderball" Bond balks the organization's plot to extort millions of dollars from the United States with a stolen nuclear bomb. He continues his pursuit of Blofedl in "On His Majesty's Secret Service" and appears to have destroyed him in his most recent adventure, "You Only Live Twice," both of which were serialized in the magazine Playboy.

Mr. Fleming was often accused of making Bond a thinly disguised projection of himself. In their love of fast cars, golf, gambling and gourmet cooking, in their skill with firearms and cards, the two men were indeed similar, but Mr. Fleming once said, "Apart from the fact that he wears the same clothes that I wear, he and I really have little in common. I do rather envy him his blondes and his efficiency, but I can't say I much like the chap."

Mr. Fleming said he had conceived Bond as "a hero without any characteristics who was simply the blunt instrument in the hands of his government."

However, as with most authors, Fleming's experiences largely shaped those of his creation.

Father in Parliament

Mr. Fleming was born on May 28, 1908. His father, Major Valentine Fleming, at one time a Conservative member of Parliament, was killed while fighting on the Somme in 1916. His obituary in The Times of London was written by Winston Churchill.

The boy was educated at Eton, Britain's most exclusive school, and Sandhurst, the military academy. While there he was a member of the rifle team and competed in a match against the United States Military Academy.

He earned a commission, but resigned before beginning active service in the largely inactive British Army of the 1920's. He also said later that he regarded tanks and trucks as a step downward from horses and sabers.

Planning to enter the diplomatic service, he learned excellent French and German at the Universities of Munich and Geneva. He stood seventh on the service's entrance examinations, but since there were only five vacancies he decided to try journalism.

Worked for Reuters

He joined Reuters, the international news agency, and in 1929 was appointed its Moscow correspondent.

"Reuters was great fun in those days," he said. "The training there gives you a good straightforward style. Above all, I have to thank Reuters for getting my facts right."

Keystone

Ian Fleming

There was a difference of opinion about this among Bond fans. They delighted in finding errors in the novels, such as the sending of a woman gang leader to Sing Sing, a men's prison.

After four years he was offered the post of assistant general manager of Reuters in the Far East, but feeling the need for money, he decided to join a private bank in London. In 1935 he became a stockbroker and remained one until the outbreak of war in 1939.

Mr. Fleming was commissioned in the Royal Navy and became in time personal assistant to Rear Admiral J. H. Godfrey, director of naval intelligence. The admiral was the prototype of "M," the retired seadog who heads Bond's secret service.

More important, it was Mr. Fleming's wartime service, from which he emerged as a commander, that provided the insights into the technique and practice of intelligence work that his readers found enthralling.

After the war, he became foreign manager of The Sunday Times of London. His contract provided for two months of vacation a year, which he spent at Goldeneye, his home near Oracabessa in Jamaica. Mr. Fleming did most of his writing there and the island provided the background for many of his novels.

Like Bond, Mr. Fleming was tall (6-foot-1) and slender (168 pounds). His curly hair was graying, his complexion was ruddy and his nose had been broken.

The novelist was a collector of first editions and rare books and published The Book Collector, the bibliophilic magazine.

August 13, 1964

It's Not a Case of Whodunit But How It Will All End

By DAPHNE DU MAURIER

WHAT is a suspense novel? The term is a loose one today, covering any story from a whodunit to a frivolity turning on which dark stranger gets the blonde. People in doubt, people mystified, people groping their way from one situation to another, from childhood to middle age, from joy to sorrow—these are the figures in the true suspense novel. They are traveling along a road of uncertainty toward an unseen goal. The suspense novel succeeds if the reader says to himself at the final page, "Yes—it couldn't happen any other way." In its end (to paraphrase Mary, Queen of Scots) is its beginning.

I had my first suspense story read to me at the age of 3 or 4. It was about a kitten, Tom, who, left alone in a kitchen, crawled up the chimney and lost himself in the flues. He wandered, bewildered, from one dark hole to another, and seeing at last a chink of light fell through it to an attic. In the corner a rat was sitting, dressed in a purple coat, his yellow teeth, like fangs, bared in a grin. The rat muttered, "Get him." And out of the shadows scurried a little woman rat, in a blue apron, who, seizing the kitten in a net, laid him down, a prey, before her lord and master. She then covered him with flour and rolled him with a rolling pin. I can see the picture now. Tom, on his back, helpless, and the male rat, in his purple jacket, watching from the corner, motionless.

The fact that Tom was rescued in the end by a friendly terrier did not reassure me. The rat and his mate lived to pursue their evil ends. The last picture showed them hurrying with bundles over their shoulders to another hiding place, where they might lure other kittens, although Tom had tea back in the safe kitchen with the dog who had saved him, yet . . . . From that moment, maybe, dates this particular reader's, and writer's, preoccupation with suspense.

Miss du Maurier is the well-known author of such suspenseful best sellers as "Rebecca," "My Cousin Rachel" and "The Scapegoat."

HOW many characters took the place of poor Tom in after years! The Princess who must never walk in the woods by night because of goblins, and whose safety line, like Ariadne's in the labryinth, was a white thread. Jim Hawkins, crouching with his mother in a ditch, while blind Pew tapped the road calling out in his high singsong voice, "Where's that boy?" Jane Eyre, walking in anguish, hearing the fiendish chuckle of a madwoman.

Looking back over twenty-five years of writing, I can see now, with greater clarity than I did once, the influences that molded certain stories of my own. Long John Silver peers through the eyes of Joss Merlyn, landlord of "Jamaica Inn." The second Mrs. de Winter in "Rebecca" walked with more timidity than did Jane Eyre, but as Kipling had it in his poem they are sisters under their skins.

The reading of youth, the burning of the midnight candle, lights a similar flame in the imagination of other authors. And each one of us brings his own small brand to the fire. The inner problem, unknown to the conscious self, comes to the surface as a book or poem, and somebody, beset with troubles, sets forth on the uncertain journey. In what shape he reaches his destination, whether triumphant or downcast, or indeed whether he comes to journey's end at all, is not just a matter of technique or craftsmanship; it depends upon the progress of the writer's inner man.

The first short story I wrote was about two people meeting in a London fog by the river, each determined on suicide. My choice of subject can be explained by my age. I was just 14. The characters, a man and woman, were both middle-aged. Each had a sorry tale to tell. The man of drunkenness, loose living, deserting his wife, leaving her to poverty. The woman of infidelity, prostitution, loneliness and, so, despair. The two strangers clung to each other, in their misery, finding some sort of comfort.

"If only," said the man, "I could find the one I lost. If only I could find the road back." The woman, as far as I remember, did not answer. Because the story ended with the next line: "The fog suddenly lifted."

This, my first attempt at suspense, was a gloomy affair. But, dimly, I believe I know what I was trying to say.

My last novel, "The Scapegoat," has been called a suspense novel both in Great Britain and in the United States. The suggestion being that because the narrator of the story has a double, a Frenchman, and for just under a week takes his double's place and deceives his double's family, the suspense must, for the reader, lie in whether the narrator is found out. This, to my mind, is missing the target. When I was writing the story, I was not concerned for one moment about unmasking the narrator. I wanted to discover, for myself, what happened to a man who was no longer himself. Would he, assuming the identity of another, shed his own? Would he take on the sins and the burdens and the emotions of the man he had replaced, or would his own hidden secret self become released in the other's image and so take charge?

THE suspense, therefore, to the writer writing the book was not whether John the narrator would reveal himself but what he would become. Everything he said, everything he did, would have some effect upon his family not his own and so, in some way, change their lives. Would it be for good or for evil? Could he help or mar? Heal or destroy? No one forced him to any decision. He blundered—as every one of us blunders who uses his own carefully built-up known personality as a mask or double. He blundered until the moment of crisis came when the child in the story, believing him to be the father whom she passionately loved, went down by night into the well of broken glass, thinking, by so doing, she could atone for her father's crime.

When she did this, something happened to the narrator John. He no longer blundered. He knew he must heal, and not destroy. The child, in innocence and ignorance, had shown him the way. The suspense, from then onward, lies in wondering what John will do to try and mend the broken lives of this family where he is an intruder. He seems to be on the point of succeeding when the real John—Jean—returns. The suspense now shifts its angle. And the writer says, as she writes, "What will happen now?"

It is not a case of "The fog suddenly lifted." At 50 the answer comes more slowly than it did at 14. Sinners cannot become saints overnight. The world remains the world. Men and women go on making the same mistakes, over and over again. Even after they have suffered and gone down to the depths—to the well—pain and realization of pain is useless unless the source is found. Why are we unhappy? Why are we hungry? What are we looking for?

If the writer had known the answer to these questions she would not have written a suspense novel but would be carrying a banner and leading a new crusade. As it is, she can only feel with the reader who has read to the end of the story that Jean, the Frenchman, must surely grow in perception and understanding when he finds that his family now expect these qualities from him; and that John, the scapegoat, having discovered love, need not wander in the wilderness like his legendary prototype, or fling himself from a pinnacle like the Greek pharmakos, but live with love in his heart, mind and soul.

There are always loose threads in every suspense story. Incidents that appear unrelated. Phrases unexplained. Characters who fade away. My greatest problem in "The Scapegoat" was why I had to let the sick wife Françoise die. It seemed to me wrong. It was turning her into a martyr. For days I worried and fretted, pondering on how to keep her within the framework of the story, and so in the family circle. It seemed to me, if she died, then evil had triumphed. She had become a scapegoat in her turn.

Then something clicked, and I knew why she died. She died trying to save the only thing that mattered to her, the miniature of her husband as he had once been. A false image. She

was clinging to something that did not exist. She had not the courage to know him as he really was. She could not face up to truth. She was sick. She had to die. When I realized this, the relief was amazing. I no longer felt sorry for Françoise. She had killed herself. I had not killed her.

IT will be seen, therefore, that the writing of a suspense story is not easy. There is no trick way of solving difficulties. The writer does not sit before a typewriter, tongue in cheek, thinking, "Here's a good way out. This will fox 'em." It means sweat and blood and tears. And very often a temperature as well.

One of the nicest compliments ever paid to me was by one of my daughters early this year. She said, after reading a much-praised novel by a contemporary, not, I may say, a suspense novel, "Oh, I'm bored with this, it's nothing but talk, talk, talk. If only somewhere, at some point, there could be a chapter ending like one of your books would, with, 'The door suddenly opened.'"

I was back again in the schoolroom, writing my story. "The fog suddenly lifted." Thirty-six years ago. If the answers meantime have become more elusive, the style has not altered. I wonder now if my next novel might not be about a man—not a kitten—called Tom, who, wandering one day in the attic of an old house, loses himself, and finds, staring at him from a corner, wearing a purple coat, someone who.... A pity to give away the plot. Good against evil, as usual. But perhaps this time a solution to the problem at last?

December 22, 1957

Heathcliff Doesn't Smoke L & M's

By ***GARY JENNINGS***

Like most other growing boys, I have always aspired to grow up to be the kind of man that women would admire and adore. But, for the longest time, despite a rabid reading of boy-into-man-type books, I never could learn much more than to keep my fingernails clean and always run around the car to open the door on her side. As it turned out, I was reading the wrong books. Not until just now have I finally discovered the women's perfect man, what he should be, delineated for me in detail.

He would have a strong mouth with a full lower lip betokening temper and sensuality, hands that were used to controlling a horse or a willful child—or a woman. He would be impatient of foreigners, arrogant, sure of himself, but contrarily kind and gentle. He would be an ardent lover....

That quotation comes from one volume of what I've found to be a whole vast literature on the women's man. I was introduced to it quite by accident. After residing for a while in a wee village abroad, I had become impatient with foreigners, arrogant, long in the lip and, worse, devoid of anything to read—until I found that this town boasts a small English-language library, and its fiction shelf consists of exactly 21 novels of the kind known in the trade as "Gothic romances."

Every one of these books was written by a woman or by a man under a female pen name. Every one claims to be a "national best-seller!"—so we must conclude that countless other women agree with the authoresses' ideas of perfect manliness and that they pant and palpitate at *the easy way he moved in his dark, well-cut suit, the resolute tilt of his head, the fair hair tumbling over his brow, the slight tenseness about the mouth that was his control over a sense of humor always too ready to laugh at life and himself.*

All of these italicized quotations are, I swear, the actual words of one or another of the lady authors. I have excerpted them because, while I feel that every man may profit by reading and heeding them, I doubt that any man with any better way to kill time is going to indulge in a 21-volume reading orgy like mine. And so, before I get on with the profile of the typical gemlike women's man, let me say a few words about the setting in which we find this jewel—the Gothic romance itself.

To begin with, the adjective "Gothic" derives from the architecture of the ancient, crumbling manor, mansion or castle in which the action takes place. For the nonarchitect, however, a Gothic romance is more easily identifiable by its heavy dependence on words of two o's—moonlight moors, gloomy tombs, looming doom.

The two-o books all have moody, broody titles like "Secret of Ravencroft," "The Keys of Kilraven" and "Castle of Ravenbourne." They vary in locale and period from the Cornwall coast to the Deep South bayous, and from the 1800's to the present day. Every single one of them is ballyhooed by the jacket blurb as a new "Jane Eyre" or "Wuthering Heights." The blurbs lie. The only thing these novels resemble is each other. Whether set in two-o moor or o-u bayou, the plots, characters, incidents and dialogue are easily interchangeable.

The heroine, either a bride, a young widow or a governess, arrives chez Ravensgrave either newly wed to the Master of the manor, or to claim her inheritance of the estate, or to tutor the Master's motherless children. The place is seething with sinisterness because, say, the Master's first wife has earlier fallen off a Cornish cliff under suspicious circumstances. (Though why "suspicious," I don't know. According to these novels, there are always so many women mooning along the Cornwall cliffs it should be no surprise that a few fall off.)

For the bulk of the book nothing at all happens except a lot of threats, feints, bluffs and lurkings. The housekeeper, Mrs. Gargoyle, hisses dark hints. Painted portraits eerily shift their gaze. Unaccountable bloodstains drip from the rafters. Karloff laughter—*mm-bwa-hahaaa*—echoes from a locked turret room.

One thing that bothers the male reader—evidently it doesn't faze the female fan—is that these stories are usually told in the first person; that is, by the beleaguered heroine herself. It's obvious from the start that, for all the *mm-bwa-hahaaa,* the spooks and bogies didn't get her. This tends to vitiate the "heartstopping suspense" that every jacket promises.

Another stylistic peculiarity of all these novels is that whenever something happens—or doesn't happen, which is oftener—the narrative pauses while the nodding reader gets

Mr. Jennings is a freelance writer now living in Mexico.

nudged with a reminder of The Story Thus Far. This always takes the form of the heroine's settling herself in her room for a solo recap, contorted of syntax, curly with question marks.

I contemplated the history of the Leland females who so often died before they reached one and twenty years. Was I to be one of them? Was the attempt to smother me with a pillow an actual intended murder? Had the milk been heavily drugged that night so if Edward had not been here and had not quickly obtained the services of a village doctor and also brought Dr. Newman to my side promptly, I would have surely died?

However, our intent in examining these novels is not to pick nits but to pick the lady authors' brains for their notions of the man magnificent. Assume, then, that you want to pattern your future self after one of the women's men who figure in the Gothic romances. Heroes and villains aside, the male population in these novels includes uncles, plantation overseers, old family retainers and peasants. The first thing is to ask yourself: which of these stalwarts shall I emulate? Uncles are easy.

Uncle James broke the tension with a gentle laugh.

Uncle Timothy gave a throaty chuckle.

Uncle Edgar gave his deep amused chuckle.

The peasant's usual role is merely to mill about at critical junctures and mutter rebelliously.

Everything was changing in the village. Disaster was threatening; forelocks were pulled with a sullen gesture.

But you'll also have to gabble a cleft-palate dialect and dispense folk wisdom and timely warnings to *de young mist'is.*

"You don't expect things that happen to they ordinary folk to happen to 'ee, do 'ee?"

"I've got my drop of Welsh blood. And all the Welsh have what we call a 'knowingness'. . . ."

"There be things in this house. . . ."

Still, it's the hero who ought to grab us, so let's examine him—and the ways in which we might remake ourselves in his image. We should start at birth, since, ideally, the hero is born either illegitimately or under a curse. That would also enable our getting ourselves christened with an heroic name. The men's monickers in these books range from Anglo-Biblical (Jon, John, Jonathan) and Ruritanian (Rupert, Max, Rudolf) to names that sound like the trademark of a cheap piano — Saint Clair Le-Grand is one I came across. In the 21 volumes I studied, the most popular hero-name, by far, is Jonathan. Robin and Noël run neck and neck in second place.

Your attempts to emulate the hero may be a bit delayed until you determine which of the main male protagonists *is* the hero and which the villain. Throughout the book, the heroine is equally attracted to both of them, right up until the denouement on the very-next-to-last page, when that nutty bimbo in the turret room is revealed to be old Grandsire LeGrand, the original Master of Le-Raven-sur-Bayou and—as the secret lover of Mrs. Gargoyle, who was his half-sister all along—the father of the true heir, LeRoi, who has been piskie-mazed by Maum Jemima's voodoo, so that LeGume, *her* bastard son (by the ne'er-do-well cousin LeGree), has passed as the imposter claimant to the estate. . . .

Well, never mind. After a dozen or so of these Gothic romances, you'll find that sorting out the hero and the villain is a cinch. The one named Jonathan, who's been snarling, nasty and insufferable since page 2, is the hero. The jolly pink giant — like Ritchie, for instance *(bright blue eyes, laughing. The thick shock of hair, not red red, more of an auburn)*—inevitably turns out to be a murderer, an imposter, a ravisher of helpless slave girls and a smoker of cigarettes.

The smoke from his cigarette curled out toward me. I opened the window on my side; even so, my clothes would reek of tobacco for days. . . .

In distributing habits and manners among her characters, the lady novelist gives the villains and weaklings all the loathsome addictions—homicide, perversion, hot toddies, L & M's—while the hero is made a sandwich man for everything the authoress admires. He advertises her favorite haberdashery; . . . *his Sulka smoking jacket, his Jäger bathrobe. . . .* He drives her favorite car: . . . *a grey Rolls-Royce and very beautiful. . . .*

The lady authors are equally specific about a myriad physical features of the hero *sans-pareil.* Take him from the top.

He ran a hand over his thick hair . . . always awry.

A tall, slender man with . . . unruly hair that always seemed in need of a barber's shears.

He had straight black hair that sprang up from his high forehead as if it had a life of its own. . . .

Presumably these fellows have been permanently tousled by the hair-raising horrors at Ravensnest. That effect, at least, is easy enough to imitate. The next is not.

The nose was strong and faintly crooked, with a marked hump of bone at the bridge. . . .

. . . the broken nose, the traces of plastic surgery. . . .

Only the hatchet nose, self-important and big for the face, saved him from being too handsome, too romantic.

In the 21 books I endured, the hawk-hooked or bent-prow hero is almost ubiquitous. Another favored sign of masculinity is to be gimped for good.

. . . he limped, noticeably, and used a stick. . . .

"He is — well — a cripple. His legs are completely paralyzed."

His limp always softened me toward him. . . .

The hobbling hero is so much the desideratum, in fact, that a heroine encountering a normally ambulatory male may be downright revolted:

And now that I knew he was not crippled, not confined to his wheel chair, I found his physical beauty almost . . . infuriating.

However, the hero's physical eccentricities — his tangled topknot, sidewise snout and sidehill gait — don't count for nearly so much as his equally skewed behavior. For one thing, the hero has to do most of the Gothic novel's two-o-ing: he is perpetually moody, aloof and brooding.

He sighed . . . a shuddering sigh as he added, "And I am so very . . . very tired."

His face was ashen, tortured.

He slumped down on a chair, and looked up at me, his eyes pleading for understanding.

Okay. Now you've declared your demons, and the heroine has helped you exorcise them. The next thing is to declare your devotion and desire for her. Let us count the ways.

Speak up. *"I cannot remain quiet. From the moment I saw you sitting so solemn and still in the cemetery, I must confess I was deeply stirred."*

Talk tough. *"Hester — Hester," he murmured, "do you think I'm giving you up? . . . Never for a moment—*

remember, I am a LeGrand too. Nothing shall hold me from what is mine."

Talk foolish. *"I could catch life from you. Like the measles."*

Promise her anything. *"We will live at Darkwater if you wish. It is very lovely. And plenty of lively children about will banish its ghosts, or make them happier ones. . . ."*

It's all right for uncles to chuckle and ghosts to guffaw, but if ever a hero were to approach lovemaking with a light heart it would repel the heroines as would a sudden bad smell. No, you must remember that love is a sober, solemn, even somber business.

Tell her so. *"When the whim moves me, I may very well deal you a blow that seems ruthless. You will be wise never to expect kindness from me for long."*

She'll get the picture. *And so this then was all there was to love—this hurting, this ache?*

The more spirited heroes accompany their surly declarations of love with an occasional physical contact. For best results, I gather, this is done clumsily: *. . . pressing her tightly to him in a clumsy comforting gesture which she found unexpectedly moving.* And what moves her, it seems, is a kind of electricity innate in heroes, as in certain eels.

. . . his fingers closed over mine. There was a strange instant in which I sensed through his clasp something of the stormy force of this man. . . .

When he stepped toward me suddenly and put his thin, strong hands upon my shoulders, I gasped. I could feel their warmth and strength through the goods of my dress.

Now, it would be nice if the lady novelist would pause at that point and tell us ordinary men how to achieve that calorific effect right through a girl's dress-goods. Does one pat the thin, strong hands on her shoulders? Squeeze? Knead? We'll never know. The authoress may pause, yes, but only to give us a rundown on the goods of that damned dress: *a cornflower blue foulard printed with half moons. The fullness of the bodice was drawn in at the waist and descended in a double box plait to the hem.*

But skip the laying-on-of-hands technique. According to all 21 of my Gothic romances, what first and forever impresses a female is one particular organ of the masculine anatomy. All the other heroic qualities of lopsided physique, half-asinine intellect and mesmeric forces pale to nothing beside this one outstanding fixture of the human male. Give up?

Those eyes. You looked at those eyes and suddenly you forgot the pain in your back or the draught from the open door or a thousand and one other tiresome things. . . .

Those were Jonathan Towers's eyes. These are Jonathan Merrill's:

Large and brilliant, they were beautiful eyes, the sort of eyes that saw everything, but with kindness and a clarity that would see through to a truth that would surely be a good truth, as the deep truth is always good.

The hero's eyes radiate light: *He came toward her, his eyes twinkling maddeningly.* And heat: *Johnny was watching me with smoldering eyes.* Or quench it: *The chill in his gray eyes cut through my every defense.* They collapse: *His eyes crinkled wickedly.* And congeal: *Daniel's eyes had hardened.*

You might expect that in a healthy male a lot of the abilities and effects attributed to the eyes—smoldering, prodding, penetrating, etc.—would better be located anatomically somewhat farther south. But actually, in these novels, nothing ever happens below the belt except an occasional twitching of the trusty riding crop against the polished boots.

Though the hero's X-ray eyes occasionally make the heroine feel peeled to the buff, there is seldom anything, from the first page to the next-to-last, more sexy than a chaste kiss. On the *last* page, after all the mysteries have been resolved, after the ghost has been laid and the burdens of secrecy are lifted, the hero and heroine are at last free to go into a passionate clinch.

And then what happens? What does the hero win in reward for all his physical and mental misery, his incessant brooding and insensate eye-rolling? I'll tell you. The guy and gal fling themselves into each other's arms. Then there's a gap of white space on the page. Then there's a new paragraph that begins: *Afterward....*

Afterward, though it seemed to me I was possessed by a wild kind of joy, still I found I was crying uncontrollably, and as he tried to soothe me I ran from him, down to the edge of the water, holding my clothes awkwardly around me. . . .

You may well wonder, is it worth it? That expensive nose job, the crutched-up extremities, all that ogling and agony, for a consummation that's no more memorable than a half-inch of white paper?

Well, I'll let you know. There's this cute little librarian, see, who runs the library in this village and who checked-out all those 21 Gothic romances for me to read. She admires and adores me, but not for any heroic qualities. She's got the notion that we share the same taste in literature. ■

LEWIS NICHOLS

July 27, 1969

Take a Rocket to the Moon . . .

By VILLIERS GERSON

THOSE "suspect" literary forms designed solely to entertain—the thriller, the detective mystery and the Western—have, as every schoolboy knows by now, a new rival in science fiction. Though the number of science fiction volumes is small when compared to mysteries, more science fiction novels and anthologies will be published this fall alone than in any previous full year.

What, then, are these tales of science fiction? They are stories of adventure, thought-provoking tales freed from the everyday environment. And yet they are more. Science fiction must be placed in the sense of writing we call fantasy, that compendium of "ghouls, and ghosties, and things that go boomp i' the night" which has always had appeal, but only for a limited audience. More recently, science fiction seems to have had an appeal that mounts with each day's news.

Although the genre has been growing to maturity in America since 1923, it was not until Aug. 6, 1945, that the full implication of science fiction struck the general public. On that day, of course, the atomic bomb fell on Hiroshima. No longer did science belong to the few. It became everybody's business.

In a scientific age such as ours, the lessons of science apply not only to reality, but to fiction as well. Unlike fantasy, science fiction depends upon "fact"—the essence of science. An example: prior to 1945, the writers of science fiction were well aware of the possibility of atomic power. They acted upon the assumption that it would ultimately be discovered, wrote stories about the effect of atomic power on our world — and saw those stories come true.

FANTASY UNLIMITED

From jacket designs by Leo Manso, Edward R. Collins and Joseph Trautwein

TODAY the SF writers (as the devotees call them) are writing about interplanetary travel, about the rockets which will flash from the earth to the stars. Few doubt that, in a generation or two, fact will catch up with fancy. Here is one of the sources of the pleasure science fiction gives to its readers. Who would not have a glimpse into the future, when that future is predicated upon scientific fact?

Because of this basis of fact, the SF writer, in contradistinction to the fantasist, has certain duties. Where the latter may people Mars with werewolves, if he will, the SF writer must take into account the planet's geography, temperature, air pressure, chemistry, and probable ecology before he can invent a Martian. In other words, the imagination of the pure fantasy writer is bound by little or no restriction; that of the author of science fiction is delimited. This is not a hindrance, but an asset. The believability, the reality of the story is enhanced; and the prophecy made that much stronger. The reader of fantasy may shudder, but he is assured by the reflection that such things cannot happen; the reader of science fiction may also shudder, but he has no such assurance. Science fiction *may* happen! This is not to proclaim that all science fiction is horrific. Some stories are—some are not, depending on the inclination of the writer.

Newcomers to science fiction may feel that all such stories are merely extensions of Wells' "War of the Worlds," but this is not the case. There are many main types of science fiction, for example: tales of interplanetary travel; time travel into the future, the past, etc; microcosmos and macrocosmos, stories of travel into the infinitely small and the infinitely large; the lost continent story, Mu, Atlantis, Subterra.

No SF story, of course, abides by these categories. A story may fall into two, three or more types. It is variability that endears science fiction to its readers, and why, in the hands of good writers, the stories are forever new and unhackneyed.

Yet it takes more than a good idea to make good science fiction. Most SF stories written during the Twenties and Thirties were of the blood-and-galactic-thunder type. Scientifically they were excellent; as writing they left much to be desired. When faced with an apparently insoluble problem the earlier writer had his protagonist bring out a ray-gun: Zap! Zap! It was the exceptional writer—such as Murray Leinster, considered the "dean" of SF authors; Don A. Stuart, the pseudonym of the astute John W. Campbell, Jr., editor of "Astounding Science Fiction"; Stanley G. Weinbaum, whose death in 1935 was a real loss, and a few others—who laid the foundation for the more mature and thought-provoking stories published today.

Due credit for this rise in quality must be given to the editors of the SF magazines,

Mr. Gerson is a science fiction writer and has collected science fiction since 1923.

who raised their standards and forced the writer to raise his. Because of these editors authors such as Ray Bradbury, A. E. Van Vogt, Robert A. Heinlein, John D. MacDonald, L. Ron Hubbard, Wilmar H. Shiras, Frederic Brown, Theodore Sturgeon, Edmond Hamilton, Eric Frank Russell, and a few others—the outstanding science fiction writers of today—had the chance to develop their skills, their imaginations, and their audiences.

The future of science fiction seems assured. New readers are being lured daily to the new medium, and once attracted they become devotees. In this, history repeats itself, for the same experience was true of the detective mystery. Many unbiased observers believe the detective story has reached a point of stasis. Psychologically, the science fiction story offers a sublimation as potent as that of the detective mystery. Where the latter captured and transformed the aggression characteristic of our times, the former offers the reader a painless method of capturing science—of making it familiar, less fearful, a part of his life experience.

September 24, 1950

Fact Catches Up With Fiction

Yesterday's fantasies of space flight, nuclear bombs and so on are today's realities. Where do the authors go from here?

By ISAAC ASIMOV

TWENTY-FIVE years ago, space flight was virtually the exclusive property of a small group of young men, most of them in their teens, who wrote and read science fiction. The outside world was largely unaware that these men, or science fiction, or even the concept of space flight, existed. Among those who did know of this field of literary endeavor, reaction varied from amused tolerance to annoyed contempt. "Escapism," they said.

Yes, it was escapism. It was escape from the problems of the Nineteen Thirties, the threat of fascism and of war, the thought of what aerial bombardment might do to cities. But it was escape into the harder world of the Nineteen Sixties. The young authors wrote—and a few people read—of the danger of nuclear warfare and of the struggle to achieve space flight. If the authors were escaping from one horrid reality, they were doing so by facing future hazard without blinkers. That is not classical escapism. It might even be called foresight.

Now the world has entered the age into which science-fiction authors "escaped" a generation ago. The front pages of the newspapers read like some of the highly imaginative stories of the Thirties. The President of the United States can call for a concerted effort to place a man on the moon and be greeted with a soberly enthusiastic response.

But science fiction suffers a malady no other branch of literature does. Each year sees possible plots destroyed.

NOTHING the world can do will ever destroy the blazing six-shooter of the Western hero, or the efficacy of strychnine in the soup, or the palpitations of the virtuous working girl. But as soon as a man makes a successful lunar flight, no science-fiction writer can ever sit down to compose an epic dealing with the first flight to the moon (as I once did back in 1939). Another basic plot will have been killed.

This has been happening ever since science began its drive to remake the world, and remake it, and remake it. Edgar Allan Poe knew the balloon only as a means of lifting man from the ground, so he sent a balloon to the moon. That's dead now. We know the limitations of balloons. Other writers sent their heroes to unknown portions of the earth's surface and found Lilliput in the South Seas, King Solomon's mines in Africa, isolated remnants of the Inca civilization in the Amazon and Shangri-La in Tibet.

All dead. We know the surface of the earth too well now. There are no mysterious civilizations. Even the poles have been ransacked.

Fictional expeditions were sent to the center of the earth and to the bottom of the oceans. But the earth has no such convenient holes in it, we are quite sure, and the bottom of the ocean has been reached. All gone.

The first half of the twentieth century saw stories about the mysterious power of the atom and, increasingly, stories about space flight. The atom bomb, by exploding, destroyed a vast array of plots that used atom bombs as the science-fictional gimmick. And now we are on the verge of killing stories dealing with at least the beginning of space flight. Whatever is there left to write about? Only everything, that's all.

IT is important to realize a few things about science fiction. The obvious motivation for writing is to earn an honest living, and the obvious motivation for reading it is to be entertained. But the same holds true for the other "specialty literatures"—the mystery, the Western, the romance, the adventure.

The fact is that above and beyond this interplay of earning a living and of being entertained, science fiction differs from its cousins in having much more to give. This fact is obscured by the ridiculous travesties miscalled "science fiction" that are produced in Hollywood, and by the nonsense miscalled "science fiction" that is to be found in comic books. Unfortunately, it is these low-level products that the average man thinks of when he thinks of science fiction.

Too bad, for there are thoughtful science-fiction stories produced (admittedly for money and admittedly to entertain) which soberly consider the interaction of man on society and society on man.

In this, science fiction at its most thoughtful resembles the main-stream novel at its most thoughtful. But science fiction goes beyond even the main stream in one respect—it does not deal with society as it exists, but with societies that may exist in the future.

This turning to the future is *not*

ISAAC ASIMOV, an Associate Professor of Biochemistry at the Boston University School of Medicine, is well-known as a writer of science fact as well as of science fiction.

FREE FLIGHT — Back in 1928, a science-fictioneer envisioned a propulsion belt—a working reality in 1961.

escapism, but has its own peculiar importance. If that was not evident in the Thirties, it is certainly evident now. Society will not long exist if its leaders do not more or less accurately consider the future and make appropriate provision therefor. The successful science-fiction story—of the type I consider truly important—poses a social problem and suggests a possible outcome (though not neces sarily a "solution").

Thus, a number of years ago, Robert A. Heinlein wrote a novelette dealing with the development of atomic weapons. In it the United States set up a vast project for the purpose, calling its scientists together to work on the problem. The weapon was developed and used to end a war.

CONSIDERING that the story was written in 1941, this was pretty good, but not in itself unusually remarkable. Many science-fiction writers were busily developing one form or another of the atom bomb. In that same year of 1941, I wrote a story in which uranium fission was accurately, though briefly, described. Another writer described the atom bomb so precisely, in 1944, that the F. B. I. was called in to check on possible information leaks. (There weren't any. It was just logical forethought.)

But it is not the real function of science fiction to predict the next gadget. This is comparatively easy to do. It is more difficult to predict the *consequences* of that gadget upon man and society. It is this that Heinlein goes on to do—correctly.

For, in his story, when the weapon was used and the war ended, people were faced with the problem of controlling the deadly atomic menace that had been developed. One person suggested that the United States simply keep control and enforce a world order to its liking. But the hero of the story responded:

"* * * I wish it were that easy. But it won't remain our secret; you can count on that. It doesn't matter how successfully we guard it; all that anyone needs is the hint given by [the weapon] itself and then it is just a matter of time until some other nation develops a technique to produce it * * *.

"* * * Once the secret is out * * * the whole world will be comparable to a room full of men, each armed with a loaded .45. They can't get out of the room and each one is dependent on the goodwill of every other one to stay alive. All offense and no defense * * *."

How's that for 1941?

IN my opinion, it was more important to have foreseen the nuclear stalemate that now exists, than to have predicted any number of gadgets. If, twenty years ago, more statesmen had seen the future as clearly as this science-fiction writer had, we might not be in the deadly situation that now exists.

Robert Heinlein had posed a social problem: how could one prevent disaster, once a weapon capable of destroying the human race was in the hands of opposing forces in a world riddled with national rivalries and suspicion? His suggested outcome was that mankind might find no way of preventing disaster. The title of his story was: "Solution Unsatisfactory." And Heinlein's plot is now among those that are dead.

WHAT more can we write about? Can we write about space flight in these days of satellites and astronauts? Of course. There may be no point in discussing satellites and astronauts themselves, but what about the future effects upon ourselves of the consequences of these developments?

ON THE WAY—In 1927 a prophet in fiction foresaw an atomic-powered rocket (left). It doesn't exist yet, but the Thor does.

TOMORROW?—*In a contemporary prognosis, there is this concept of "The Delegate From Venus," with Khrushchev on hand.*

Suppose there is a going colony on Mars. Getting the colonists out there is not very important for story purposes; in fact, it is scarcely science fictional. But they're there. and they need water, in which Mars is poor. They get their water supplies from the earth, but, as a matter of fact, we are having our own problems with the supply of fresh water even now, and it will be worse in the time of the Martian colony.

You can easily imagine that there will be strong pressure to put an end to water exports to Mars, and that could mean the end of the Mars colony. But the colonists on Mars may well be in their second or third generation and they might not wish to return to earth. So they organize a flight to Saturn, where they pick up the necessary water in Saturn's rings (which are, it is believed on excellent evidence, made up of ice particles).

THE flight takes months, and earthmen—for psychological reasons—are unable to coop themselves up in a spaceship for so extended a trip. Martian colonists, accustomed to living under domes with artificial light, heat, air and gravitation, find space flight only more of the same and can make trips of any duration.

The story (which I wrote once) is naturally filled with conflict and excitement and can be read, I hope, for purposes of sheer entertainment. However, it also poses a social problem: would new conflicts arise among mankind after the establishment of colonies on other planets? And if so, what might be the result?

My suggested outcome: conflicts might indeed result and this might be good, for it could be that the colonists, rather than earthmen themselves, might be equipped to explore space further—and it would be the conflict that would send them out there.

It is easy enough to think up problems that deal not with space flight itself but with the consequences. Such problems can be far more important than any number of engineering trivialities; and it is those problems that are the most legitimate concern of the science-fiction writer.

In establishing colonies on the moon, what will happen to sexual mores if only a few women can be sent out there? Suppose an intelligent race of extraterrestrials is discovered? How can contact best be made? How certain can we be that relations will be peaceful? What measures must be taken to ensure safety?

What will be the role of religion in a world in which space flight is a reality? What effect on the usual beliefs will result from the discovery of other intelligent beings? Or, more subtly, consider the Biblical drama in which sin and salvation form the all-embracing conflict involving God and man, with the rest of the universe only a backdrop. How can the importance of that struggle be maintained in a society in which the penetration of space reveals earth—more and more realistically—to be an inconsiderable speck of dust?

Or—let's make an about-face. Suppose it turns out that the radiation belts surrounding earth make any hope of space flight, beyond a quick circling of the earth a la Gagarin, impractical. How will mankind adjust to the situation, at this late date, of finding itself without the opportunity for space flight after all?

THERE are also any number of legitimate social problems that do not involve space flight but that concern the thoughtful science-fiction writer just as deeply as Mars does. In fact, the species of plot that has replaced space flight as the chief problem with which the science-fiction writer must deal involves the consequences of the population explosion. Story after story is written about societies in which crowding has reached unbearable proportions.

THE results are invariably grisly. The worst I can think of appeared in an extremely effective story written by Frederik Pohl (who has often dealt with the population explosion). In this story, further population increase was prevented by a simple expedient. When the decennial census was taken, every eleventh person, or every twenty-third or every twenty-ninth (depending on the state of the population at the time) was executed. Pure chance made the decision, and the conflict in the story rested on the wild attempts people made to influence the purity of the chance—in their own favor, of course. This outcome was not advocated as desirable, but it was pointed out as one necessity that might arise.

It is as easy to foresee an overcrowded world now as it was to foresee nuclear weapons in the Thirties. It is just as important now, as it was then, to foresee the consequences as well as the fact, and to take measures early. Otherwise, once again, the consequences will overtake us, find us unprepared, and leave us no reasonable countermeasures.

THERE are other serious problems here on earth, too. We need not venture out into space to find them.

There is increasing specialization in science; an increasing difficulty in communicating between one specialty and another, an increasing difficulty in training enough scientists broadly enough. Carried to its extreme, will the system break down of its own weight? How do we conserve brainpower? How do we safeguard the rare minds that can cut across the specialties?

How will mankind be affected by the further development of automation? With machines to do the routine working and thinking, what will happen to the vast majority of men who are capable of no more than routine? Will education be drastically revised? Or will boredom be the deadly epidemic of the future?

Is telepathy possible? If it is, what kind of a world would we live in if telepathy could be amplified and made a common means of communication? What would happen to privacy? Would there be a telepathic élite and, a nontelepathic mass and, if so, what would the relation be between the two groups?

How might fallout affect the future of the race? How might the use of artificial organs affect it? How might —— ?

Well, what have we got to write about?

Everything.

Astounding Story! About a Science Fiction Writer!

By GODFREY SMITH

The Clarke space calendar: by 1980, landings on other planets; by 2000, colonization of other planets; by 2030, human contact with extraterrestrials; by 2060, the creation of artificial life; by 2090, immortality.

LONDON.

ARTHUR C. CLARKE, doyen of science-fiction writers and first man to predict that communications satellites like Early Bird and Telstar would circuit the earth, came to the door himself. He wore plum-colored carpet slippers and a comfortable cardigan. Baldish and bespectacled, he looked like a middle-grade civil servant—which he once was. Since those days, however, he has written nearly 40 books, which have sold five million copies in 30 languages. He has twice been chairman of the British Interplanetary Society. He has won the $2,800 Kalinga Prize award by UNESCO for the popularization of science and the Stuart Ballantine Medal of the Franklin Institute for pioneering the concept of communications satellites.

He said we could drink Scotch, beer or coffee; we chose coffee, and his mother, a lady with those russet cheeks which only a lifetime in the English countryside can give, brought it in with a plate of piping hot sausage rolls and some macaroons. Clarke settled in his chair, began to eat a roll with his customary deliberation, and talked about his life.

He was born on Dec. 16, 1917, at Minehead in Somerset, where his father was a farmer. The exhilarating flow of his ideas about the unfathomable future which science offers mankind still comes through in a pleasing West Country accent. He said he was first converted to science fiction by the March, 1930, issue of an American pulp magazine called Astounding Stories: "They were shipped across the Atlantic as ballast and sold in Woolworth's for 3d. each. I used to haunt Woolworth's in my youth to pick up issues that I had missed. I had a complete collection of S.F. magazines — Astounding, Amazing and Wonder. They are all gone now. But those old pulps were wonderful in their day."

He made his first telescope from a lens and cardboard tube as a schoolboy and mapped the moon: "I used to know my way around it very well." He modified an old bicycle torch to transmit speech along its light beam: "That's coming in now with lasers in a big way." He left school at 19, because it was not so easy in those days to get to college without money, and went into the Government Exchequer as an auditor. There he might well have remained to this day if it had not been for the Second World War.

FOR Clarke, the beauty of the job was the short hours and long holidays, which gave him plenty of time to exploit his obsession with space. He joined a dozen other enthusiasts in the British Interplanetary Society, founded in 1933 by P. E. Cleator, a civil engineer. They used to meet in London pubs where they were treated as amiable lunatics. Time has put that right: the journal of the B.I.S., which they once mimeographed, is now a major technical publication.

A. V. Cleaver, now chief engineer of the rocket department at Rolls Royce (which makes the propulsion system for the Blue Streak missile), was one of the original eccentric dozen and is still one of Clarke's closest friends. Even when the B.I.S. resumed its work after the war, he recalls, "it would not be a big-headed exaggeration to say that we carried the torch for space flight. There was still a bit of a tendency in the corresponding American Rocket Society to regard space flight as a bit far out. They tended to concentrate on more immediate applications like guided missiles."

No one, for example, took any notice when, in October, 1945, Clarke, then a young Royal Air Force flight lieutenant specializing in radar, wrote an article in Wireless World entitled, "Extra-Terrestrial Relays." In it he exactly predicted a system by which three satellite stations could insure complete radio and TV coverage of the globe. Each satellite would have to be 22,000 miles high; its plane would have to coincide with the equator and it would revolve with the earth so that for all practical purposes it was stationary above our planet. It took two decades for him to be proved right. But by then he was famous, anyway.

After the war Clarke went to King's College, London, on an ex-serviceman's grant and won a first-class honors degree in physics and mathematics in two years. He had completed only one term of a graduate course in applied astronomy and advanced mathematics when his dean put him up for the associate editorship of a physics journal called Science Abstracts, published by the Institute of Electrical Engineers: "It was certainly a fascinating job. Every science journal in the world arrived on my desk in all languages. It was a job which suited me perfectly, but in two years my first books and articles had started to sell. My part-time income was higher than my full-time. I just resigned and that was it. A year later, in 1952, my book 'The Exploration of Space' was taken up by the Book-of-the-Month Club and, of course, I was sitting pretty."

TODAY Clarke is probably the highest-paid science-fiction and science writer in the world. But his tastes are modest. Customarily he spends most of the year in Colombo, Ceylon. "I started living there 10 years ago," he said. "It happened quite accidentally. I stayed there one afternoon on the way to Australia and the Great Barrier Reef to do my first underwater book. I talked to some of the Ceylon skin divers, particularly the assistant director of the Colombo Zoo. And I just decided to settle down there. I like the sun and I could live anywhere and that was it. My partner, Mike Wilson [a film producer who works with him on his other ob-

---

GODFREY SMITH is editor of the magazine section of The Sunday Times, London.

INSPIRATION—Clarke was converted to science fiction, he says, by the March, 1930, issue of Astounding Stories. This copy, though tattered and taped, is now an S.F. collector's item.

session, underwater exploration], married one of the beauties of the island. I now have as many friends in Ceylon as I have in England or America."

He lives in a bungalow in Cinnamon Gardens, a fashionable section of Colombo. He used to live nearer the sea but salt corrosion drove him a mile inland. "There's one long room of about 30 to 40 feet and other rooms off that. There are servants' quarters, a small garage and a little garden. I call it the most expensive dog kennel in the world, because I have left my Aleutian there. I've been back there for only one month in the last two years."

The reason for this long exile is his collaboration with producer Stanley Kubrick on the script for their science-fiction film, "2001: A Space Odyssey." The collaboration began from a chance conversation at lunch between Roger Caras, then head of Columbia Pictures' sales department, and Kubrick, who remarked that he had been researching an idea for an S.F. film to end them all. It seemed to him that the only man who could logically help him with a project as ambitious as this was Clarke, all of whose books Kubrick had devoured. But, mused Kubrick, Clarke was a hard man to reach. "Not at all," said Caras, "I have his address in my pocket." Caras and Clarke had met at a skin-diving convention in Boston some eight years before.

Kubrick at once wrote to Clarke, saying he had heard that Clarke was coming to America to write a book for Time, Inc., and inviting Clarke to visit him. Soon the two men were locked together in travail on "2001." "I cast around through my published material for what would make a good film," said Clarke, "and I picked out a story called 'The Sentinel,' about the discovery on the moon of the first extraterrestrial artifact. I read the draft to Stanley, which was terrible, but it was the germ of a film."

"Stanley and Arthur are two really intellectual people," Caras says. "They threw the most incredibly stimulating conversational darts at each other. They are like a couple of seers sitting there deciding when the next flood or catastrophe will come. It is definitely a cerebral marriage and something startling is bound to come of it."

THE film has been conceived in epic proportions. Six months before the cameras first turned last December, 36 technical designers from 12 countries began work on the sets and props. More than 40 top industrial and scientific firms in the United States and Europe were consulted and NASA experts worked with Kubrick to insure scientific accuracy. The film is scheduled for release in early 1967 (screenplay by Kubrick and Clarke); the book of the film (by Clarke and Kubrick) is due out late this year.

"You can say," says Clarke, "of '2001' that it's been a wonderful experience streaked with agony."

He thinks he will go on to make other space films: "No, not with Stanley. I am sure he will never do a space film again. He never repeats himself. But I am quite sure this will start interest in some of my other stories. A few of my things have been on TV, but one reason nothing has been sold in the last two years is that I have blocked all sales of all my properties. This was just to get it all back into my control." He is reticent about his earnings: "Let's just say I am not starving."

I SAID that I understood his marriage—to a Jacksonville, Fla., girl in June, 1953—had broken up. "Exploded would probably be a better term," he said. "I have been married just the once. We lived together occasionally at various times—in Miami, in London, in this house, in fact, for a period." (Our conversation took place in the modest North London home of his brother Fred, a heating engineer; a third brother runs the family farm in Somerset.) "No, I won't marry again. That's very definite."

I asked him if he thought sex would play any part in the infinite futures he has charted with such idiosyncratic skill. "I imagine people will still get around to it," Clarke said. "I mean, where the hell can it go from where it is now? My imagination balks at any further possibilities."

This is a rare defeat for Clarke's vaulting imagination. Open any of his books at random and in half a dozen paragraphs you are likely to find your mind lifted out of its terrestrial anchorage and sent soaring into infinite space. He writes clear, workmanlike prose which draws its solidity and confidence from his formal scientific training but is occasionally laced with passages of something like poetry. In "Childhood's End," for instance, generally acclaimed

UNDER WATER—Not confining himself to the mysteries of outer space, Arthur Clarke also has a passion for underwater exploration. Here he makes his way along the Great Barrier Reef off Australia.

as his finest novel, the earth's first spacecraft, Columbus, is soon to be launched on its maiden voyage.

One starlit night at the launching site something makes Reinhold Hoffman, architect of the Columbus, glance upwards and he knows that he has lost his race—"not by the few weeks or months that he had feared, but by millennia. The huge and silent shadows driving across the stars, more miles above his head than he dared to guess, were as far beyond his little Columbus as it surpassed the log canoes of paleolithic man. For a moment that seemed to last forever Reinhold watched, as all the world was watching, while the great ships descended in their overwhelming majesty—until at last he could hear the faint scream of their passage through the thin air of the stratosphere. He felt no regrets as the work of a lifetime was swept away. He had labored to take men to the stars, and in the moment of success the stars—the aloof, indifferent stars—had come to him. This was the moment when history held its breath, and the present sheered asunder from the past as an iceberg splits from its frozen, parent cliffs, and goes sailing out to sea in lonely pride. All that the past ages had achieved was as nothing now: only one thought echoed and re-echoed through Reinhold's brain:

"The human race was no longer alone."

CLARKE is equally at home as a polemical essayist. In his "Profiles of the Future," for instance, he opens with a chapter entitled "Hazards of prophesy: the failure of nerve." In it he takes the reader at a fast clip through the depressing annals of the many eminent scientists who have denied the possibility of every great scientific breakthrough that is now commonplace.

The great American astronomer, Simon Newcomb, he observes, wrote a celebrated essay proving that men would never fly. The distinguished Canadian astronomer, Prof. J. W. Campbell, estimated in 1938 that it would take 1 million tons of take-off weight to carry 1 pound of payload on a round trip to the moon. The correct figure, says Clarke, for today's primitive fuels and technologies is roughly 1 ton per pound—"a depressing ratio but hardly as bad as that calculated by the professor."

"Some of my best friends are astronomers," says Clarke, "and I'm sorry to keep throwing stones at them—but they do seem to have an appalling record as prophets." Even *after* President Eisenhower had announced the United States satellite program, the new British Astronomer-Royal, Dr. Richard van der Riet Woolley, was not impressed. "Space travel," he snorted, "is utter bilge." Sputnik went into orbit the next year.

The Americans, Clarke maintains, have not been noticeably more progressive. The greatest failure of nerve in all history, he claims, one which changed the future of the world, was the Pentagon's decision virtually to abandon long-range rockets for almost half a decade: "The Russians had no such inhibitions. Faced with the need for a 200-ton rocket they went right ahead and built it. By the time it was perfected it was no longer required for military purposes, for Soviet physicists had bypassed the United States' billion-dollar tritium bomb and gone straight to the smaller, lighter and cheaper lithium bomb. Having backed the wrong horse in rocketry, the Russians then entered it for a much more important event — and won the race into space."

He concludes: "Of the many lessons to be drawn from this slice of recent history, the one that I wish to emphasize is this. Anything that is theoretically possible will be achieved in practice, no matter what the technical difficulties, if it is desired greatly enough."

To this sweeping principle he appends a corollary which he calls Clarke's Law. "When a distinguished but elderly scientist states that something is possible, he is almost certainly right. When he states that something is impossible, he is very probably wrong."

Then, in case his opponents still have any wind left in them, he adds a final uppercut: "Perhaps the adjective 'elderly' requires definition. In physics, mathematics and astronautics, it means over 30; in the other disciplines, senile decay is sometimes postponed to the forties."

In a time chart at the end of "Profiles of the Future," Clarke lists the great scientific advances from 1800 to the present, then extrapolates developments from now until the year 2100. By 1970 he predicts space laboratories and nuclear rockets; by 1980 landings on other planets; by 2000 the colonization of planets and creation of artificial intelligence; by 2030 human contact with extraterrestrials; and by 2060 the creation of artificial life. By 2080 he predicates that machine intelligence will overtake man's; by 2090 he thinks we shall have achieved immortality.

He plans to go to the moon himself, when it is a scheduled flight in about 1980. He has a £5 bet that man will make his first round trip there in 1969.

CLARKE has few unfulfilled goals. He would like to see the first proof that life exists beyond the earth and thinks we may get it in the next few years through information from the moon and perhaps Mars. Beyond that, and much more unlikely, the first proof of *intelligent* life. "It is statistically almost certain," he says. "They are much more likely to find us than we are them. We are obviously too young and have only had civilization of sorts for a very short period of time. The universe is of the order of 10 billion years old. Any other civilization could be at least a thousand times older than ours."

But he is unwilling to speculate about the nature of alien races: "It would be completely futile since we have not a single fact to base it on. But as there may be thousands of times as many cultures in the galaxy today as in the entire history of the earth, all terrestrial forms of society, including man, bees, termites, automatic telephone exchanges and other presently unimaginable forms, may be repeated countless times."

IN "Childhood's End," however, he makes members of the master race extremely reluctant to leave their spaceships and show themselves to mankind. When they eventually do their reason becomes clear: they are made in the image of the devil with horns and tails. Despite their unpromising externals they are benign rulers, though something of a strain at cocktail parties where they are likely to sit in a corner reading a book at the rate of a page a second.

He finds himself unable to take sides in the great controversy about the creation of the universe: "I just don't feel any emotional preference for the steady-state or the big-bang theory. I go for the steady bang, if anything."

Clarke does not resent criticism from serious and intelligent writers. His fellow science-fiction novelist, Brian Aldiss, has said that some of Clarke's reminiscences in "Voices From the Sky" were rather vain. "He is quite right," Clarke admits. "But if you don't blow your own trumpet, who will? My nickname before the war used to be Ego. But now that I've got over my self-conceit, I'm one of the nicest guys I know.".

He regards his own work as primarily entertainment with some educational value. He thinks that the age of great individual scientists seems over but he has been deeply influenced by Jacques Cousteau, the undersea explorer, and Dr. Louis Leakey, the anthropologist, whose work on man-apes will be reflected in "2001."

It is sometimes said that Clarke is not good at human relationships. But as his friend A. V. Cleaver explains, "He's very friendly and generous, but his head—it's in the clouds, or I should say it's really in outer space or even probably underwater." (Eleven of Clarke's books are about underwater exploration.)

He gets a lot of mail from fans all over the world and answers every letter, however briefly. The Russians are among his most avid readers. Nowadays he no longer contributes to S.F. magazines, because they can't pay enough, but confines his output to magazines like Playboy and Life. He has given up lecturing, which he used to enjoy, since an undiagnosed illness which may have been polio paralyzed him for two months and left his chest muscles impaired, though this isn't noticeable when he talks.

He still reads other people's space fiction for pleasure. He regards H. G. Wells as far and away the greatest S.F. writer of all time, criticizing him only for propagating the idea that life alien to the earth was likely to be horrible. He thinks that so far science fiction has produced only two pieces of literature — Swift's "Gulliver's Travels" and Wells's "The Time Machine."

He considers the late Prof. J. B. S. Haldane the greatest man he has ever known. Haldane once said that Clarke was the only man who had written anything new about religion (in "The Nine Billion

Names of God") for the last 2,000 years. Clarke says that he has no religion ("All metaphysical speculations are centuries premature — we must learn something about the real universe first.") but is deeply interested in it. "I sometimes say I am a crypto-Buddhist because I am sympathetic to the Buddhist and Schweitzer attitude of reverence for life. I hope that higher forms of civilization will reciprocate."

He thinks that communication with the dead is very unlikely but telepathic communication between the living very probable. He believes immortality is inevitable, "either as a by-product of current work on the genetic code or through electronic personality storage." He is not, however, keen on this development. "It will result," he says, "in a society more static than the classical Chinese and will mean the end of social and cultural evolution. The real enemy is not death but pain and grief, and their conquest is more worthwhile."

CLARKE had an afterthought: "I have one ambition—to have a dolphin for a friend. I nearly said 'to own one,' but it is a question of who owns who.

"They say that happiness is a childhood wish achieved in adult life. I always wanted the biggest Meccano set. When I am completely senile all I shall want is a large room with a soft carpet and the largest set. Then I shall happily revert to childhood. They've stopped making the No. 10 sets, so I must try to get one of them quickly before it's too late."

But Clarke will not have to wait till his dotage to receive world recognition. He has demonstrated, with exemplary brilliance, the truth of the epigram of his hero, Haldane: "The universe is not only queerer than we imagine—it is queerer than we *can* imagine."

March 6, 1966

The Early Asimov

Edited by L. P. A. Shmead.
540 pp. New York: Doubleday & Co. $10.

Building Blocks of the Universe

By Isaac Asimov.
287 pp. New York: Lancer. Paper, $1.25.

Of Time and Space and Other Things

By Isaac Asimov.
222 pp. New York: Lancer. Paper, $1.25.

Where Do We Go From Here?

Edited by Isaac Asimov.
384 pp. New York: Fawcett. Paper, $1.25.

Beyond Control

Seven Stories of Science Fiction.
Edited by Robert Silverberg.
208 pp. New York: Thomas Nelson. $5.95.

The Gods Themselves

By Isaac Asimov.
288 pp. New York: Doubleday & Co. $5.95.

New Dimensions II

Edited by Robert Silverberg.
229 pp. New York: Doubleday & Co. $5.95.

The Astounding-Analog Reader

Edited by Harry Harrison and Brian W. Aldiss.
530 pp. New York: Doubleday & Co. $7.95.

By THEODORE STURGEON

When reviewing science fiction (or science writing, or speculative writing about science or about science fiction), it becomes necessary from time to time to organize an Isaac Asimov festival. So prolific is this extraordinary man — on his 50th birthday he celebrated the publication of his 100th book — and so illustrious that it is easy to set his efforts aside with the feeling that everyone will find out about the book anyway, and besides he'll have another one out in a few minutes.

Asimov has achieved a unique status, for not only is he admired and, by many, loved for his work in s.f. and for his engrossing regular science column in The Magazine of Fantasy and Science Fiction, but he is equally respected by professionals in some 20-odd scientific disciplines. He has become the most perfect and the most inclusive interface between hard science (including math) and the layman, for he has a genius for bringing the obscure into the light. His writing career began in the so-called "Golden Age" of s.f., under the aegis of the late John W. Campbell Jr. (though according to his generous notes in "The Early Asimov," his first story was bought by Frederik Pohl).

"The Early Asimov" contains all his science fictions from 1940, when he was a teen-age college student, through 1948; and they are fascinating to read. They are chronologically arranged, and the rubrics carry a wealth of anecdote, so that the development of this towering young mind becomes as engrossing as the stories themselves. Asimov came slowly to the fullness of the characterizations that marks his later fiction, but rapidly indeed to his knack of reordering facts and to his clear logic, even where logic led him to the wildest speculation.

There are 27 works in this big 540-page volume, together with an introduction, preliminary notes for each story, and a bibliography of the 60 stories written in what he calls "the Campbell Years." (Special mention must be made of one of the most remarkable pieces ever written — a tiny article called "The Endochronic Properties of Resublimated Thiotimiline," which Campbell ran as a "non-fact article" and which caused quite a jolt among physical chemists.) This is a book which can be read for the enjoyment of the stories or for its many levels of speculation — sociological as well as scientific — or as the amusing, affecting, sometimes poignant, sometimes hurtfully honest documentation of the development of a writer.

Another early Asimov comes to us in paperback: the Abelard "Building Blocks of the Universe," reissued by Lancer. It is a guided tour through the periodic table, an anecdotal introduction to each of 102 elements — what they are, where and how they are extracted or purified, how they were discovered and by whom. Like almost all of Asimov, joyfully readable, the book gives one a fine hold on surrounding reality; the next time you read "calcium carbonate" or "fluoride" on a label, you'll know something about calcium and carbon and fluorine that you never imagined: perhaps that, if your cooking gas is of a low enough grade, you are burning the substance of diamonds, and you are baking heart of pearl into your muffins, and that you could keep fluorine quite safely in a wax bottle while it would gobble holes in glass. The book is indexed.

Even more enriching — because the subject matter is not restricted even by so wide parameters as all-the-elements-

there-are — are the articles Asimov writes for The Magazine of Fantasy and Science Fiction, now collected in a number of paperbacks, one of which is "Of Time and Space and Other Things." Some of these are hard-science explications of astronomy, chemistry, physics and other disciplines. Some are speculative, and some are opinion. All are readable, sensible and often jovial.

Then there is the editor-anthologist Asimov. One might expect from Asimov more than just another "I like these stories because" book; it must surely be an anthology-plus, and that is precisely the nature of "Where Do We Go From Here?" It contains some of the most amusing and thought-igniting stories ever written: Heinlein's "—And He Built a Crooked House" and Arthur Clarke's "The Deep Range," for example, and others as good. So, if all you want is excellent yarns, you have your guarantee.

But Asimov goes further and, after each story, adds a few hundred words of commentary and some questions. Wonderful questions, some directing the reader to further elucidation of the scientific aspects of the story he has just read, some challenging the reader's own thought processes. As if that were not enough, he adds an appendix of suggested reading — two book titles for each of the stories.

Then of course there's the Asimov who shows up in anthologies, such as the excellent "Beyond Control," edited by Robert Silverberg (who is rapidly qualifying, by the way, for this kind of festival himself). It's an ingeniously conceived "subject" anthology, turning upon man's ability to advance technologically a little faster than commonsensically. Silverberg shows a nice balance in his selection of Alfred Bester, James Blish, Terry Carr, Philip K. Dick and William Tenn, and includes one of his own. The Tenn is amusing, the Bester gruesomely dramatic, and Asimov's yarn (1956) is cautionary, not only about the writing and rewriting of history but about the nature of research, research grants and researchers. A good writer writes well when he knows what he is writing about. Asimov knows about everything, but he knows research granting particularly, sardonically, delightfully well.

And to demonstrate that the Asimov story machine has not been abandoned or outgrown (with such things as his Bible book and his Shakespeare book and his Dirty Old Man book, which I bypass) he has a recent novel, "The Gods Themselves" (his first in 15 years) and an appearance in New Dimensions II, again a Silverberg selection, this time of original stories.

The novel is in three parts, the first and third a more or less continuous narrative, and the middle one an effort to respond to a Campbellian challenge: "Write me a story about a creature which thinks as well as a human but not like a human." In this Asimov does not completely succeed — who could, really? — but all the same, he has created an extraordinary alien species. The villain of the piece is stupidity in its many aspects, and here he gives us a view in depth of the kind of infighting and ego maximation that goes on in the scientific fraternity.

His New Dimensions II story is a sturdily-constructed outer space tale in which a most Asimovian character saves the ship by parallel expertises in science and psychology. It is pleasant to see it carrying itself so well in the company of such explosive new writers as Gardner Dozois, James Tiptree Jr. and R. A. Lafferty. A real bonus is the inclusion of not one, but two of Barry M. Malzberg's sour astonishments.

Harry Harrison and Brian W. Aldiss are compiling a landmark monument to John Campbell. The first (I think) of two big volumes has now appeared, packaging some of the high points in Campbell's prestigious magazine: "The Astounding-Analog Reader." The earliest entry (1932) is Campbell's own, and the most recent (1946) is the late Fredric Brown's "Placet Is a Crazy Place." Between these are some of the finest hardcore s.f. stories ever written — Heinlein, Bester, Simak, Murray Leinster and others, every one soaked in the very essence of Campbell. Among them is "Nightfall," by Asimov, surely one of the most memorable of all s.f. concepts and the story which, in 1941, put him in the very front ranks. It is not included in "The Early Asimov," by the way, and it is good to have it within reach again.

Any assessment of Isaac Asimov turns into a monument to John W. Campbell Jr. One may well envy the recent reader of s.f. the discovery and excitement, provocation and learning, new perspective and sheer wonder, that Campbell and Campbell's stable gave and give. ■

January 28, 1973

MR. TARKINGTON'S TALE OF A SMALL TOWN

THE MAGNIFICENT AMBERSONS. By Booth Tarkington. Illustrated. Doubleday, Page & Co.

IT is often interesting, and sometimes rather painful, to watch an author struggling with the conclusion of his book. Again and again do we see the same thing; plot and characters developing up to a given place, developing by growth instead of manufacture, and then being suddenly seized upon by their creator and forced to behave in a way which will bring about the desired result—that result usually being "a happy ending." Mr. Booth Tarkington's new novel, "The Magnificent Ambersons," is a case in point. Until the last few pages are reached the book develops in a thoroughly natural and intensely interesting way. Characters and environment, acting and reacting upon one another, make the plot; it all seems absolutely real, the story one of flesh-and-blood people, the town whose changes have such an effect upon these people as much an actual place as any city on the map of the United States. And then suddenly the novel is seized upon, and a happy ending tacked on to it perforce.

The scene is laid in a midland town—a small, clean, pretty delightful little town when the story opens, which is some time in the eighties. The first chapter describes, and that in the most delightfully amusing way imaginable, the simple "homespun" quality of this place which was such a perfect background for the "magnificence" of the Ambersons, its richest and most aristocratic family, whose house was known as the "Amberson Mansion," and stood in the very best and most desirable part of the "Amberson Addition"—the tract of land which Major Amberson had bought and cut up into building lots with such notable success. The Ambersons were the town's royalty, their "mansion" its palace. Major Amberson had two sons and a daughter, but only one grandchild, George Amberson Minafer, the son of his lovely daughter Isabel, and it is this George Amberson Minafer, heir to all the magnificence of the Ambersons, who is the central character in the book. He is a boy of about 8 when we first meet him, already quite conscious of his inheritance, and prone to regard all the other inhabitants of the town as "riff-raff." These early years, however, are quickly passed over, and most of the action of the book takes place while George is in his late 'teens and early twenties, a good-looking, gallant, high-spirited, charming, and intensely arrogant youth, with a tendency toward the dramatic—not to say theatrical. Long before this, however, his behavior had given many excellent people cause to desire, and to desire fervently, that he might some day "get his come-upance," which was the word they used instead of deserts. And the main theme of the story is how their wish was fulfilled, and George "got his come-upance" through the action of forces none of them could control.

When George returned from college for the Christmas holidays of his sophomore year, his manners had become more polite, but no less insufferable; "M. le Duc had returned from the gay life of the capital to show himself for a week to the loyal peasants belonging to the old château." His adoring mother gave a ball in his honor, and it was at this ball that George first met his mother's old friend, Eugene Morgan, and that "little beauty" who was Morgan's only daughter, Lucy. Those who have read "Seventeen" will not need to be told how dexterously, with what perfect understanding and delicious, chucklesome humor Mr. Tarkington describes a boy of this age and his love affairs. That letter from George to Lucy, in which he tells her about his "theory of life," is as amusing as any bit in "Seventeen." But Willy Baxter had plenty of wholesome discipline, and George Amberson Minafer none at all. From the very first he was not merely permitted but encouraged to regard himself as a young prince, whose prerogative it was to ride rough-shod over everybody. His weak, charming young mother, married to a man she did not and could not love, literally worshipped her son. All his life she thought everything he did was "noble and perfect." Thereby she planted the seeds of her own tragedy—and of his.

For while there is a great deal of humor in "The Magnificent Ambersons" there is a good deal of pathos, too. When George at last got his come-upance he "got it three times filled and running over. The city had rolled over his heart," and all the magnificence of the Ambersons was a thing of the past. The little town seems to change, in fact, before our very eyes, to change into a city smoke-begrimed and dingy and prosperous, with factories and yet more factories breaking out all over it. And as the town of which they and their belongings were the pride changed beyond recognition, so, too, did the fortunes of the Ambersons change.

One cannot help feeling sorry for gay, unlucky, irresponsible George Amberson the elder, who has been so delightful a companion through many chapters; and for poor old Fanny Minafer, too, who had her day of passion and of heart-break, who did so much unintentional mischief, and then subsided into a gossiping, bridge-playing middle age; and for weak, pretty Isabel, with her last pathetic plaint, and for proud, sensitive George, who smarted at the bare thought of "talk," and who believed himself so heroic and so noble while, with the cocksure ruthlessness of arrogant youth, he laid strong hands upon two lives and stripped them of the joy he could not understand.

In writing of a story like this one, where the characters bring about the drama and the one depends altogether upon the other, it is manifestly unfair to give more than a slight hint either as to the development of the characters or the course of the plot. "The Magnificent Ambersons" is a small-town story; and who among American writers can reproduce the small-town atmosphere better than Booth Tarkington? It tells of a boy in his teens, the period of which Mr. Tarkington has long since proved himself past master. And it contains, too, a tenderly drawn picture of a middle-aged romance and of a love that never died. In his solemnity and his arrogance and his way of taking himself with the most intense seriousness, George Amberson Minafer is as irresistibly funny as our old friend Willy Baxter. Only George had his own way, and not until it was too late did he realize what he had done. The book is long, but it does not drag; exasperating as George often is, he fascinates and interests the reader exactly as he fascinated and interested the people about him. He might be detestable, but he was never dull, and so it is easy to sympathize with Lucy, that "independent, masterful, self-reliant little American" who fell in love with George and was never "able to climb out." It is scarcely necessary to say that the book is well written; it is an admirable study of character and of American life—but we do wish Mr. Tarkington had not tacked on those last two chapters.

October 20, 1918

Review of Books

ANOTHER MINERVY-ANN

MIRANDY. By Dorothy Dix. With Illustrations by E. W. Kemble. Hearst's International Library Company.

THIS remark from Sir Conan Doyle comes forcibly to mind as we read Dorothy Dix's altogether delightful "Mirandy":

> We talk so much about art that we tend to forget what this art was ever invented for. It was to amuse mankind—to help the sick and the dull and the weary.

Very "sick, dull and weary" must be the reader whom it does not lure into forgetfulness of his troubles, and to whom it does not administer the frequently repeated tonic of a hearty laugh. Never since Mr. Harris's inimitable "Minervy-Ann" has there been such a fascinating lady of color as "Sis Mirandy"; but whereas Minervy-Ann is the illuminating interpreter of "a day that is dead," Mirandy brings shrewd and searching philosophy to bear upon the problems of modern life: "Revising the Ten Commandments," "Women's Clubs," "Why Men Don't Marry," "Women Popping the Question," "Worrying," "Why Women Can't Vote," "Matrimony," "Creeds," "Being Good," &c. In the dialect of her race she discourses most amusingly upon every topic of which she treats, and there is not a chapter that does not contain goodly chunks of solid wisdom wrapped up in the fun. The philosopher of Archey Road himself does not go more directly to the heart of things than does the old washerwoman with her keen and humorous outlook upon life. Over and over, in the midst of our laughter, do we exclaim "Rem acu tetigisti!" We commend to maidens her solution—and we believe it is the true one—of the much-discussed problem, "Why men don't marry." Equally clear and pungent is she upon all matrimonial experiences, upon "the woman question" in its various phases, upon the rewards of self-sacrifice, and upon sundry theological topics. "The Advantages of Invalidism" should be published and distributed as a tract among a certain type of sufferers from "dis new-fangled ailment dat dey calls de nervous prosperity":

> Hit lets you in for doin' all dat you wants to do, an' lets you out of doin' all de things dat you don't want to do. All dat you got to do is to call yo' temper nerves, an' you can say whut you likes to folks, an' instid of battin' you over de head lak you deserves, dey has got to sympathize wid you, an' take hit becaze you say you're sick.

But it is dangerous to "put in one's thumb and pull out a plum," so full of tempting plums is every chapter. Many books of greater pretension are far less richly freighted with wisdom, while as for enjoyment pure and simple, few will be found to furnish as much.

The illustrations are clever and characteristic, though why the artist should at times portray Mirandy with her self-confessed figure of a feather-bed, and again present her with as straight a front as the girls at whom her Ike was given to casting sheep's eyes, is a puzzle.

For "the sick, the dull, and the weary" we prescribe "Mirandy," and not less for happy souls on the lookout for a good laugh, and for the many who would be the better for having a brisk breeze of common-sense blow the cobwebs from minds bemused by too much modernity.

July 5, 1914

SATURDAY'S CHILD

SATURDAY'S CHILD. By Kathleen Norris. With frontispiece. The Macmillan Company. $1.50 net.

A VERY pretty and pleasant though somewhat long-winded story is this new one by Mrs. Norris. "Saturday's Child," so the old rhyme tells us, must work for a living, and that is just what Susan Brown does, first as bookkeeper in a downtown office, later as companion to a rich, spoiled semi-invalid girl, Emily Saunders, and finally as wife and mother. She has more than one love affair in the meanwhile, and although the reader discovers the identity of her destined mate in the opening chapters, it takes Susan over 450 closely printed pages to find him, during which she escapes "throwing her cap over the windmills" only by accident and the narrowest possible margin.

The scheme of the story enables the author to present plenty of strong contrasts, and she makes full use of the opportunity. However, the first few chapters with their picture of the shabby boarding house run by Susan's gentle, kindly, unbusinesslike aunt, where "a lost pair of overshoes * * * was a real tragedy" and "every door in the dark hallways shut in its own little story of suffering and privation" are decidedly the most interesting. There is verisimilitude, too, in the account of the office and Susan's companions therein, and although this, like all the rest of the book, suffers from a lack of pruning, the fault makes less for weariness here than is sometimes the case further on. They are real people, the office force and the inmates of the boarding house, people such as one encounters every day, well and sympathetically portrayed, while Susan herself is a genuine girl with plenty of small failings, a cheerful disposition, and a charm which makes her transference from the boarding house to the Saunders's luxurious home seem quite plausible. The scene of the tale is San Francisco, and life as it is lived there by the very rich is Susan's next experience. It is not pictured in a very alluring way, and indigestion, both mental and physical, reigns there as it did in the shabby "Front Office," but Susan, not being a saint but a very normal girl, fond of gayety and pretty things, finds it fascinating for a time and nearly becomes a willing victim to its ease and comfort. She is reserved, however, for an entirely different fate, and when we leave her declares herself the most fortunate of women.

The novel reads much like a rather embellished account of actual happenings; we feel as if we really knew many of the characters, from the Miss Lords and Billy Oliver of the boarding house to the poor but estimable Carrolls and the rich but not at all estimable Saunders, who provide an excellent foil for the others' virtues. Like so many novels of the present day, this book preaches the gospel of work and service, emphasizing the old truism that an idle life is never a happy one. It is a more ambitious piece of work than any Mrs. Norris has before attempted, and it has the same qualities of sincerity and humor which have helped to make her former stories popular. It is, on the whole, smoothly and pleasantly written, and the dialogue is easy and natural. True, the description of the strike lacks vividness, and one is inclined to be skeptical over the account of Anna's wistful glances at Susan doing housework, yet this very skepticism is a tribute to the humanness of the characters. "Saturday's Child," in short, is a simple, cheerful, wholesome story, telling of everyday people and everyday lives in an agreeable manner, with abundant common sense, a manly hero, and a heroine who, always attractive, develops into a fine, strong woman. Mrs. Norris's admirers will find this new book greatly to their liking.

August 30, 1914

PERSONALITY PLUS

PERSONALITY PLUS. By Edna Ferber. Illustrated. Frederick A. Stokes Company. $1 net.

ALL those who know and love Emma McChesney—to know her and to love her being one and the same thing—will be interested in the career of the son Jock whose "yellow streak," inherited from a worthless father, caused his plucky mother so many anxious moments. In the five stories gathered together in this volume under the title of one of them, "Personality Plus," Miss Ferber tells us what happened to Jock—and his mother—when that self-confident young man graduated from college and went into the advertising business. Jock has his ups and downs, his failures and successes, but always that sunniest and bravest of women, Mrs. McChesney, secretary of the T. A. Buck Featherloom Petticoat Company, stands behind him, as big hearted and shrewd as in the days when we first met her "representing T. A. Buck." In truth, Jock's various haps and mishaps are of interest to us principally as they affect that splendid example of the modern business woman, his mother.

As in all Miss Ferber's work there is a certain fine, human quality in these stories which makes a swift and irresistible appeal. They are all so real, so instinct with the life of "that great, big, solid, safe, spot-cash mass known as the middle-class"—the class Emma McChesney belonged to and understood so well that even though there came a time when the very up-to-date advertising company declared her methods "old fashioned" and a letter "Dictated But Not Read" took some of the sparkle from her eyes and some of the buoyancy from her carriage, she was justified in the end and saved the Featherloom Company "real money—and large chunks of it," to quote T. A. Buck, once junior, who reappears in this new volume, as does Fat Ed Myers, Mrs McChesney's former rival.

There is in the concluding story a hint that the author intends that it shall be our farewell to Emma McChesney, but if this is so we trust that she will reconsider and change her mind. For amid all the more or less excited talk in praise and dispraise of the modern woman it is good to have before us so fine a representative of the type as this Mrs. McChesney, who was "as motherly as she was modern," and could help and understand her son all the better because of her own personal experiences. No wonder Jock felt that one of the biggest things he could do was "Making Good with Mother."

September 30, 1914

ANOTHER COUNTER-REVOLUTION.

Strange and ominous ideas are stirring in literary and publishing circles. In London the other day two ladies, both novelists, both, of course, the highest kind of authority on "sex," publicly debated the question, "Is "There Any Alternative to the Sex "Novel?" This is almost a confession that many readers are crying out for such an alternative. Miss SHEILA KAYE-SMITH did not hold out much hope for them. But this was because she identified the sex novel with the love story. The latter, she believes, will last as long as fiction is written at all. She admits, for our comfort, that there is now a pronounced drift away from the sex novel produced by those who do not look into their hearts and write, but look into Professor FREUD and speculate.

On the other hand, Miss REBECCA WEST did not conceive that the sex novel, as such, could be considered a work of art at all. Human nature cannot be classified according to instinct, especially when we undertake to explain everything by a single instinct; and if we are going to develop the novel and maintain its position in literature we must widely extend its theme. Yet Miss WEST rather perversely contended that novels are made much too easy to read, and favored refining their style until they become subjects of profound analytic study. On this point, Mr. J. C. SQUIRE, who acted as second for the lady duelists, declared that if people had to take two months to read a novel and then felt it a duty to read it ten times over in order to find out what was its precise artistic merit, it might possibly be good for the reader, but it would certainly "knock the bottom out of the fiction market."

Other signs of a revolt against the revolters in fiction and in poetry are discernible to the close observer. It is even said that there is an impending lurch back to Victorianism, or at least to that somewhat less dreadful thing, "post-Victorianism." Young ladies are actually seen reading Tennyson. Moreover, some of them have left off thinking of their fathers and mothers as tyrannical obscurantists. This does not mean that parental ways of looking at life are approved of, but at any rate they are tolerantly thought of as interesting because so "quaint." One bold English critic describes the counter-revolution as having reached the point where "the "wicked parent is acquiring a halo "of benevolence." Then he makes the audacious prediction: "Very "soon revolutionary young women of "the fashionable sort will put away "their Oriental divans, and, leaning "their heads against antique anti-"macassars, will read the 'Idylls of "the King.'" This is a horrifying prospect.

June 28, 1923

Mrs. Stratton-Porter's Last Work

THE KEEPER OF THE BEES. By Gene Stratton-Porter. 505 pp. Illustrated. Garden City: Doubleday, Page & Co. $2.

GENE STRATTON-PORTER'S last book, "The Keeper of the Bees," full as it is of her particular method and mannerisms, will stand as typical of the school of fiction she fostered. It is the finished product of one who, through constant practice, had come to aim with an almost uncanny accuracy at the heart of the million. Mrs. Stratton-Porter knew and understood that prosperous multitude who have every reason to find satisfaction in the comfortable philosophy of Pippa and Pollyanna; she knew their likes and their pet aversions, their prides and their prejudices, as few writers have known them. As a result, "Freckles," "The Girl of the Limberlost," "The Harvester," "Laddie" and the rest of the glorious company of her apostles simply couldn't help being best sellers. Her last book will slip easily into that enviable category.

As its name suggests to all who know Mrs. Stratton-Porter's way, "The Keeper of the Bees" has its horticultural interludes aplenty. Along with these, very naturally enough, runs much informative material on the bee industry. The author's long association with women's magazines and their features makes the mention of vitamines inevitable. But her happy sense of humor serves amply to "garnish" even the pages devoted solely to dietetics. That humor of hers, springing as it did from a native sense of fun, has a buoyancy about it, a spontaneity, that can ill be spared from American popular fiction. It sparkles throughout this yarn in refreshing contrast to the self-consciously sophisticated "wise cracks" which mar so much of present-day writing.

But quite apart from the philosophy and the manner of it all, "The Keeper of the Bees" stands on its own feet as a story. Mrs. Stratton-Porter never joined the ranks of those who believed that a tale consisted in a catalogue of mental processes. She saw to it in all her books that people did things. In "The Keeper of the Bees" she made no exception to this rule. Action followed on action's heels. Even the garden declines to stay static.

The narrative concerns itself chiefly with one James Lewis Macfarlane, an American war hero, who retains sufficient Scotch from his parents to burr, according to the author, even through a verse of Scripture that didn't boast a single "r." Macfarlane's wounds had not healed in the army hospitals. Their poison permeated his whole system, and even weakened his mental resistance. But at the decision to send him to a tuberculosis camp to die he resolutely balked. Being in the army, it was not his to reason why. But he left—decamped from the army sanitarium without so much as a kit bag for his troubles. Through the series of incidents that finally lead him to a bee farm in California, we need not dally. There the chief scenes of the story take place. The narrative thread, of course, winds on through his fight for health and happiness. He starts up the sunshine route of open air, right food, right thoughts. With Mrs. Stratton-Porter as the guide, the reader follows along it by the young soldier's side with ever-increasing interest. The author lays great stress on the purifying effect of tomato juice, but the part of his daily regimen that means the most to the tale comes in his association with the sea. In and on the shores of the salty, sanitary Pacific, Jamie not only gets health by easy instalments but gets married. This marriage to a veiled woman, whose very name he does not know, and who leaves him at the conclusion of the ceremony, smacks more of Charlotte Brontë's Yorkshire than Mrs. Stratton-Porter's Main Street. But "it all comes out right in the end."

The Late Gene Stratton-Porter.

A Drawing by James Montgomery Flagg.

The book presents its quota of likable personalities. There is Margaret Cameron, a woman "who might well have been typical of a universal mother, and exactly the right kind of mother at that." There is the Bee Master himself, and, most original and distinctive of all, the Little Scout. This character one must put under the head of ambisextrous. The author has used the Little Scout to supply a goodly part of the story's fun and mischief. Despite the coolly calculated appeal of "The Keeper of the Bees," a sense of sincerity shines out through its pages. Mrs. Stratton-Porter wrote as she did because she felt what she was saying and believed in it thoroughly. She has packed it full of her cheery optimism, her homely wisdom, her love of fields and flowers, and her own abundant and abiding faith. The publishers have given the volume on its posthumous publication a colorful and attractive form. Lee Thayer has decorated it gaily and Gordon Grant has furnished the full-page illustrations. A motion-picture version of "The Keeper of the Bees" has already been made. Gene Stratton-Porter's last message to the younger generation can hardly fail of a large public. F. FRASER BOND.

August 16, 1925

A TITANIC NOVEL OF ADVENTURE

Allen's "Anthony Adverse" Is Rich in Picaresque Romance

ANTHONY ADVERSE. By Hervey Allen. 1,224 pp. New York: Farrar & Rinehart. $3.

By PETER MONRO JACK

ANTHONY ADVERSE" is America's most original contribution, certainly its longest, perhaps indeed its only contribution to the great tradition of the picaresque novel. It has the humors, gusto, gayety, variety of episode and character and more than the range that mark "Gil Blas" and "Roderick Random." Prodigious enough as an achievement at a time when fiction is in a lean and querulous distemper with our present discontent, it will readily be taken by those who wish for it to portend the return of the long jolly discursive novel. But exuberance in fiction flourishes generally in flourishing times. At the moment "Anthony Adverse" is an anomaly rather than an anticipation, though we may say so with regret, a monstrous deviation to confound our sociological critics for a time, a delightful, unexpected windfall of ripe and abundant romance; but if it is a rare experience in our time its success will be the more welcome.

Taking its title and general tenor from the picaresque romance, its half-philosophical nature, however, goes deeper. What "Jean-Christophe" did for the turn of 1900 it does, with considerably more entertainment and less pretentiousness, for the turn of 1800. It also bridges two eras with the personal fortunes of a hero of distinction. It hinges the last flamboyancy of eighteenth-century aristocracy with the first seriousness of nineteenth-century individualism in industry, banking, empire building, and the like.

Beginning in the authentic picaresque manner with * * * "the loud crack of a whip, the shouts of a postilion, and the heads of two horses made their appearance prick-eared against the sky" on the hill of Gergovia, in French Auvergne—beginning, in 1775, with the beguiling reassurance of pure narrative, it ends, circa 1825, thousands of miles away in style and personality and mores, in a new world and another language, with a pioneer party from Missouri in search of the promised land (it is now called New Mexico) coming upon the little madonna that had ridden in the coach fifty years ago: "Why, swan to 'man, if hit h'aint a heathen idol!" and it is set up for a mark at 350 yards.

In these fifty years Anthony, whose Christian name came from the saint and the other from the untoward circumstances of his birth, had been brought up by a Jesuit father and apprenticed to the mercantile interests of the British at Leghorn. He had seen Napoleon bring liberty to Leghorn in the course of his Italian campaign, ruin its trade and mulct its citizens. He had set out for the West Indies to collect a debt that the Spanish policy of disallowing trade with her colonies made too intricate for correspondence. In Havana he had found the money sunk in the slave trade and had recouped his firm by commandeering a slaver, crossing to the Grain Coast of Africa to make an earthly paradise for himself of the Gallego establishment on the Rio Pongo near Bangalang, supervising the man-hunts and slave cargoes for the Carolina rice plantations and Virginia cotton and tobacco fields, salving the general conscience (just beginning to be pricked by certain English reformers) with healthier slaves and cleaner ships; making, thereby, a sounder profit.

With rather more than three years of that soul-destroying business he had returned to Leghorn a rich man, not only with the spoils of the African trade but with the inherited fortune of his foster-father, whose grandson, though illegitimately, in point of fact he was. He had again seen Napoleon—by this time First Consul—in Paris, while the Treaty of Amiens was being arranged, and he had found Ouvrard the banker being squeezed of millions to provide for the new army that was to conquer England from Boulogne. Ouvrard, the English Barings, and the mysterious Continental Rothschilds—"men," as his friend the banker from Leghorn put it, "of a new cast of mind, men whose mental and financial speculations leap across old national boundaries to embrace the affairs of the whole world in a planetary economy"—were engaged in a scheme of extraordinary ramifications, certainly leaping across all national policies, treaties, and wars, to mulct the Spanish Mexican colonies of their gold. Anthony had become the bankers' representative in New Orleans—which was under the Spanish, French and American flags in a succession of months—working with an English agent in New York, and there he had helped to build up the fortunes of the Southern States by enabling the French to fight against the English and the English to fight against the French and the Spanish to pay for the excitement of being ravaged by both.

Anthony's further adventures—for the picaresque novel is stopped only by the mortality of man, to delay which with increasing ingenuity is its first talent—include a long wandering in the uncharted land of bear and wild Indian, incarceration in San Lazaro of Mexico City by the Marquis whose coach had galloped over the hills of Auvergne (containing his mother who had died of her unfaithfulness to the Marquis, leaving behind Anthony and the madonna), and rescue by the Dolores whom he had serenaded in Havana. With Dolores he had settled for a comparatively uneventful ten years in the village of La Luz to the north of El Paso, and there, after his death, in the ruins of the church, had been found the little madonna which had followed him from the convent-orphanage of Leghorn to Cuba and Africa and Paris and the Mexican wilds, symbol of the continuity of life, or of the continuing virtues of life—faith and fortitude.

This necessary outline of a book of half a million words, a volume really of three books bound together, as the publishers put it irresistibly, "for the convenience and comfort of the public," may be properly ignored except in so far as it establishes the stamina as well as the range of the novel, which the word picaresque might misrepresent. Its cohesive principle is more subtle, bound up with recurrent symbols and motivations. Anthony is ideally the centre and prolocutor of these events, a suspensive character, peculiarly susceptible to the quality of places and persons and things as these come to mean something directive to him. So Mr. Allen settles, as by so many anchors, the wayward flotilla of events. The madonna is such a symbol, the bronze boy is another, Castor or Pollux, Christ or John, the sign of the uncompleted self, the immortal twin that Anthony discovers when the bronze melts in the furnace of West Africa. Even the playing of "Malbrouck s'en va-t-en guerre" is more than it seems, held in the memory against the dramatic moment.

And the characters in the book contrive to act in the same way, urging the action forward while being very special creations in themselves. The merchant Bonnyfeather (in secret the Jacobite Marquis of Aberfoyle) is as sound as a portrait by Raeburn, and he and his chief clerk Sandy McNab have a Scotch between them as powerful as John Galt's and probably as unintelligible to outsiders. At his casa in Leghorn we meet Captain Bittern, whose voice was "like a constant gale keening through taut rigging * * * tilting a plate of soup into his transverse cavern at one fell motion * * * the captain's eyes looking out over the horizon of the bowl as if in search of distant icebergs"—and if this reminds one too readily of Tom Pipes one may as well admit that the comparison is a good one.

The Captain Jorham and his wife (a Putnam *once* from Bosting, and still with an overpowering air of virtue and dignity on board ship) is a welcome incorporation into the picaresque. And so, too, is that other captain, of the slaver, with his surprising degeneracies, a character perfectly in the old style, but with how dexterous a twist of the modern clinical knife! Florence, Faith, Dolores, Angela (whom Anthony shared with the First Consul), Cheecha and Neleta the reader must discover for himself.

The Marquis is the only character badly managed, our best memory of him being that he read Rabelais in bed at night; after that we do not take his villainies seriously. There are episodes like Captain Jorham's miracle with the bottle of red wine, Captain Bittern's cabin chair consecrated to the shocking loves of "that Peleologus girl" and later the disputed throne of the Prophetess Johanna Heathcote's Muggletonians, the ride over the Alps in the berlin with Aristide at the reins, which are already almost classical.

Mr. Allen himself is not obtrusive. "Anthony Adverse" is essentially a story and a very great story, but it gathers up so much wit and wisdom by the way that Mr. Allen is revealed on every page as that rare thing nowadays, a creative humanist; and we suspect it is he, and not his Marquis, who reads Rabelais at night. We should not be surprised and we could not be anything but pleased if his "Anthony Adverse" became the best-loved book of our time.

Utopia in Tibet

LOST HORIZON. By James Hilton. 277 pp. New York: William Morrow & Co. $2.50.

JAMES HILTON, whose "And Now Good-Bye" brought him flattering attention from the critical world, contrives in his third novel a mixture of Wellsian fantasy, Eastern mysticism and an adventure yarn. It is engagingly written for the most part, it is often effective, but it seems to be little more than an intellectual tour de force.

One suspects Mr. Hilton of not having arrived at the age where the pangs of growing old are genuinely felt, of not having himself yet experienced the painful, unreasoning clutch at the kind of security which means only not to die. Instead, he seems to have speculated about the human craving for imperishability. And there is a synthetic quality about this story of an intellectually ripe Englishman in his late thirties who is precipitated into a Tibetan monastery whose lamas have learned to prolong their lives for several centuries.

By means of a somewhat inept prologue, we learn that in Baskul a native made off with a luxurious plane intended to carry its four passengers from that spot of uprisings to a safe Indian city. The plane disappeared. Then the novelist present tells the neurologist that their old school friend Glory Conway was the English consul among the missing passengers. More, he discovered Conway some time later, a victim of amnesia, in China, where the latter on regaining his memory tells part of his adventures and then disappears.

Conway, the American, the woman missionary and the young vice consul found themselves stranded in the wilds of Tibet with their inexplicable pilot dead. They are led to Shangri-La, the exquisite, unaccountable lamasery with American bathtubs. Conway, the only one who shows himself truly appreciative of this fabulously beautiful hidden world, learns from the Head Lama that the four of them are to be kept there forever. And forever is indeed a long word from the lips of the Head Lama, who is now over 250 years old. As Conway learns of the history of the lamasery, its project to retain this fragment of the world intact from the doom overhanging the rest of the universe, its secret of timelessness and how it was bestowed on its rare visitors who never went back, he is completely beguiled.

Of the four new visitors, only the young vice consul is impatient to leave. It is his frenzy and his love affair with a Manchu princess there (a lovely young girl around 90) that bring about the dénouement. But this is a climax merely so far as excitement and action are concerned; it resolves nothing. Nor does the epilogue, which, as inadroit as the prologue, tells merely of the novelist's unsuccessful search for Conway. So doing, Mr. Hilton may be obliquely warning us that Conway dreamed this. Perhaps he is saying that Conway experienced what de Soto and Great-grandfather, drowsing in the sun, and the human race dreams of. If this was his intention, he has not matched it with his execution.

What remains in the memory of the reader is a delicately imaginative picture of the lamasery and its ideals. The characters in the book were too vaguely realized and their problems were too evasive to matter then or now.

October 15, 1933

A Memorable Character

GOOD-BYE, MR. CHIPS. By James Hilton. 126 pp. Boston: Little, Brown & Co. $1.25.

THIS unclassifiable little story lies, as Mr. Woollcott says, somewhere in that "untrodden domain between the short story and the novel." One might, perhaps, call it a novelette, except that it has nothing at all of that machine-made briskness one ordinarily associates with novelettes, which too often in the proof turn out to be neither flesh nor fowl nor good red herring. Still less does it deserve to be ranked with the plotless inanities that fall under the general, if rather vague, heading of "character sketch."

In its way, "Good-Bye, Mr. Chips," is a minor miracle—one of those rare and living pieces of writing which transcend classification, which require no precedent and are certain to have no successful imitators. To convey the precise flavor of this piece by attempting to describe it would be impossible. It is written with such economy and exactness that the substance of a 600-page chronicle and a shrewd commentary on life have been compressed into a few thousand words—yet one is not conscious, while reading it, of any undue condensation. It has tenderness and humor, and smoothly avoids the pitfalls of sentimentality and bathos. Above all, it creates in Mr. Chips himself a memorable and living character.

Mr. Chipping—his boys call him Chips—came to Brookfield as a junior master at the age of 22. Brookfield was an old foundation, established as a grammar school in the reign of Elizabeth, and it might with better luck have become as famous as Harrow. But the luck had not been very good, and Brookfield had its ups and downs, never sinking altogether into nonexistence, never becoming quite illustrious. It remained a good school of the second rank; the sort of school which, when mentioned, would sometimes make snobbish people confess that they rather thought they had heard of it.

In his early twenties, Chips had been ambitious. He had dreamed of a headship, or at any rate a senior mastership, in a first-class school. It was only gradually, after repeated trials and failures, that he came to realize the inadequacy of his qualifications. By that time he had been at Brookfield more than a decade, and the possibility of staying where he was had begun to fill a comfortable niche in his mind. At 40 he was rooted, settled, and quite happy. At 50 he was the doyen of the staff. At 60, under a new and youthful head, he *was* Brookfield, the guest of honor at Old Brookfieldian dinners, the court of appeals in all matters affecting Brookfield history and tradition.

The reticent story of Chips's life—of his tragically brief marriage, his clash with innovation in the person of a new headmaster and his victory (for, whatever the headmaster thought, Brookfield by now couldn't get on without Chips), his retirement at the age of 65, and his emergence from that retirement during the war to assume the active headship—forms an unexpectedly touching chronicle. How Chips, a shy fellow with no particularly marked traits of personality, came through the mellowness of time to represent an embodiment of beloved tradition, forms an unexpectedly acute and interesting commentary on the ways of the world. Mr. Chips himself, with his jokes, familiar to three generations of school boys, with the eccentricities and liberties he permitted himself as his years advanced, with his crusty but deeply rooted loyalties—to the classics, to Brookfield, and to England—is a figure to cherish in one's memory.

June 17, 1934

A Missionary Heritage

Writer Is Said to Have Felt It a Duty To Search Out and Defend Humanity

By THOMAS LASK

Pearl Buck was the daughter of a missionary family and that fact colored her entire life: the books she wrote, the causes she took up, the audience she sought and ultimately her position as a writer. She was herself a missionary in the fundamental meaning of the word.

An Appraisal

Less concerned with theological orthodoxy (she resigned from the Presbyterian Board of Foreign Missions after a controversy), she felt it her duty in life to search out and defend the humanity common to all men: Orientals and Westerners, black Americans and children of mixed blood, the mentally retarded and the powerless. Her humanitarianism took many forms and some commentators felt that the energy and resources she put into these projects should have gone into the writing of her books, which became, after she won the Nobel prize in 1938, facile, slack, undistinguished.

It is a questionable point though. Her literary defects were the other side of her virtues. She wanted a broad-based, popular audience. "One cannot dismiss lightly a magazine bought and read by three million people," she said at one point—a sentiment that for many critics sounds the death knell of significant writing. But there is little evidence to show that a more aloof, more disciplined approach to the writing of fiction would have resulted in different work. Neither in her attitude to mankind nor in her literary gifts was she a James Joyce.

Yet it was her missionary heritage that was responsible for whatever distinction her career does have. Had she not lived her early and formative years in China (Chinese was her first language) and got to know the people in a way impossible for anyone only passing through, she would not have been able to write her best work, "The Good Earth." And out of the China experience came also the two books on her parents. Forgotten among her many best sellers, they may turn out to be the more enduring. For they are not only a serious analysis of the missionary personality but a record of what it meant to be part of a religious ministry in China in those years. That such American efforts did not always show this country in its best light can be gathered from the severe criticisms she leveled at some members of the brotherhood in her article, "Is There a Case for Foreign Missions?"

"The Good Earth," the book most closely connected with her name, was, as the reviewer in this newspaper noted, "less a comment on life in China than upon the meaning and tragedy of life as it is lived in any age." But the novel also made visible a side of China, earthy, unromantic, timeless, that was new to the American reader used to more exotic China fare. In it she was able to achieve a union of the regional and universal, one that she was never quite able to duplicate, though she went on to write more than 85 books and hundreds of short stories, articles and other nonfiction pieces. She had no standing among literary critics. But her books have been translated into a dozen other languages and the list of her works in print takes up more than a column of fine type in the catalogue. What the critics disdain, her multitude of readers embrace. It's an arrangement she would have approved of.

March 7, 1973

A Modern Saint Is the Hero of A. J. Cronin's Novel

***THE KEYS OF THE KINGDOM.* By A. J. Cronin. 344 pp. Boston: Little, Brown & Co. $2.50.**

By KATHERINE WOODS

THE new novel by the author of "The Citadel" is a magnificent story of the great adventure of individual goodness. And yet it is an essential trait of its hero's character that he could not have thought of the word "magnificent" as in any sense applied to his achievements, or the word "great" to his life. He saw himself as a man of puny strivings, and humility was in the very sinew of his saintliness, along with courage and brotherliness and truth. Just so, innately, was Francis Chisholm a man of great adventure. And the novel with a modern saint as hero sharpens a mercilessly perceptive wit in the portrayal of a sinner also, and stabs us to the examination of universal values, in an engrossingly dramatic story about a Roman Catholic priest who went to China as a missionary.

As a fisherman's son in the Scottish Border town of Tweedside, the lad Francis Chisholm never thought of going into the priesthood. He was brought up in his father's church, but his mother was the daughter of a non-conformist mystic, and tolerance lay at the very base of happiness in their home. Yet when catastrophe had made him an orphan shipyard worker, at 12, he had already learned to shrink from "religion" as a word that held hate. He had always shrunk, too, from unreticent piety, such as seemed to cast an aura about his playmate Anselm Mealy. But if he was outspoken, often rebellious, and naturally solitary, he loved and suffered for his fellow-men no less sincerely; and in all his sense of "desperate reserve toward God" he loved God with the deeper need. In a devastating sorrow of his young manhood he saw a guidepost to his own destiny. To serve God and man, he took his fervent spirit and his unharnessed mind into the church's organization, where his ardor and honesty seemed to win him more failure than success.

Through the first third of its progress, "The Keys of the Kingdom" sustains an excellent pace as a better-than-average novel which offers a sincere and skillful, though not extraordinary, development of a difficult but not especially unusual theme. The saint moves along a trying way, harassed by others' rigidities and his own self-doubt. The sinner's feet have begun their sure climb upward. A wretched complication of domestic tragedy has been handled with delicacy and daring. And A. J. Cronin is supplying, in short, an acceptable successor to his widely read book of four years ago. Then suddenly the reader is caught and held in the excitement of tense incident. And "The Citadel" is forgotten. What cannot be forgotten, now, is the whole strange close-knit episode of the false miracle. From that first climax "The Keys of the Kingdom" steps to a road apart. It runs its course, now, in unflagging, mounting interest and in far-reaching significance, with the subtlety that conceals subtlety piercing to fundamental question through gripping event. Three times after that, the life of Francis Chisholm is to pass through breathless crisis, with many other moments of excitement scattered through his always straightforward and completely individual career.

It is after the mordant yet compassionate searching of the false miracle that Father Chisholm is sent to China by the unconventional Scottish Bishop who is one of the most likable of the well-drawn minor characters. And there the rest of the main action takes place, through thirty years. Such action—and such years! Their intensity culminates, perhaps, in the epidemic of plague. Or perhaps their highest point is the bandit attack which sweeps the priest in savage necessity from his "pretty gospel of peace" and forces the sacrifice of his dearest principle for his people's sake. Their greatest hour of physical peril—not without its martyrdom—follows the capture by brigands in the hills. But from the first the remote inland mission that had sounded like a hopeful post seems to hold out only stuff for despair, and Francis Chisholm inches a toilsome and resolute way from one struggle to another.

© Bachrach.

A. J. Cronin.

The "400 communicants" so happily listed by Canon Anselm Mealy are found at once to have been "rice Christians" only; storm has destroyed the mission buildings; the congregation has melted away; refusal to pay native catechists to collect conversions turns local indifference to abuse. But this missionary will not give up. Neither will he baptize the "heathen" through bribery or duress. His zeal, like Dr. Livingstone's, is for better lives, not results by numbers. With some knowledge of medicine he opens a dispensary. But when personal gratitude moves the town's richest merchant to polite readiness for conversion, the priest blazes out in wrath: "You have neither inclination nor belief. Now please go."

In just such ways, however, mutual respect grows and strengthens between the people of Pai-tan and this man of a different faith. With little aid, Francis Chisholm works for children, the hill folk, the poor. When missionaries of another Christian sect come with their church and clinic, the leading citizens would willingly have driven them away, for their priest-friend's comfort; but to Father Chisholm the newcomers are associates, not rivals. And they are standing together, singing their common hymn "joyful and triumphant" in torture, in the scene which rings down the curtain on this part of the drama. It is to rise again on an old man, lame and scarred and enfeebled, succeeded by two young go-getters as he starts back home. No one who has read Dr. Cronin's earlier work needs to be told with what compact dramatic skill event has followed event and idea has been held safely back from the edge of symbolism. But "The Keys of the Kingdom" is a better book than "The Citadel," as its greater human warmth and vitality touch a broader significance with more profundity and finesse.

When Father Chisholm's atheist friend sacrifices his life untheatrically for his fellow-men it never occurs to the priest to urge a deathbed conversion, or to fear the closing of heaven's doors against a soul of Dr. Tulloch's nobility. "I still can't believe in God," says the dying man in grim honesty; and the priest, as honestly, answers, "Does that matter now? He believes in you." To all-knowing and all-loving Divinity, what is formal creed, variation, even denial, from striving and struggling men? But goodness—goodness is what matters; and what is that?

Underlying the whole course of this novel is the difference between good and evil in ordinary men. There is almost nothing here of what the world calls vice. And the book's outstanding sinner is very ordinary indeed. The Anselm Mealy pricelessly portrayed in this story is a successful career man in his church: he would have been equally successful in any business, profession, or office where roseate self-confidence, extrovert geniality, facile enthusiasm and shrewd executive ability moved within the spiritual closed-circle of material satisfaction and untroubled self-approval, to assure their happy possessor's popularity and gain. Anselm's unctuous piety is as sincere, and as inevitable, as his clichés; his gross self-seeking is as unconscious as his lack of sympathy: he is simply incapable of sympathy, or of anything else that requires sensitiveness, spiritual understanding, or naked lonely thought. It will be unfortunate if "The Keys of the Kingdom" is read as "attacking the church" (any church) and discussed from that point of view primarily. Certainly Dr. Cronin is attacking worldliness and bigotry and over-organization, and the claim of man-made standards or establishments to stand between man and his God. But the breadth of his attack is against the ancient deadly evil of intolerance and greed and arrogant complacency, wherever they may be: in church, class, nation; in you and me. And he is telling us too how the sure values without which there can be no real brotherliness grow in loneliness and question from the soil of humility to true spiritual power.

A second reading of "The Keys of the Kingdom" has left this reviewer even more absorbed and impressed than the first. It is not a flawless book: it has perhaps some redundancy of disaster, some overemphasis. But its human force grows in retrospect. And especially, reading the eventful story again, one is struck by the subtlety of thought which slowly gathers its thrust and polishes its steel. In today's black twilight of tawdry false gods, the terror of a world confused and weakened by insidious petty evil, we look here at simple individual goodness—or religion, if you like—suffering yet triumphant, in a kind of morning freshness and strength. It is never goodness that is dull, unimaginative, self-satisfied, domineering. These are components of evil, wherever they are found. To these, goodness is antithesis, even if in doubt. If the worldly reward is ironic, what does it matter? In goodness is the shining adventure, not without hope.

July 20, 1941

Jumbo Romance of Restoration London

FOREVER AMBER. By Kathleen Winsor. 972 pp. New York: The Macmillan Company. $3.

By WILLIAM DU BOIS

BALZAC (and only a Frenchman would have dared) once said that woman's virtue is man's greatest invention. Anglo-Saxon moralists have denied this hotly, as an insult to both sexes; and yet Anglo-Saxon booksellers, if they are honest, will confess that few characters in fiction are more beloved by female readers than the successful harlot. With this well-documented truism in mind, we approach Kathleen Winsor's first novel with a confident prediction: "Forever Amber" is a booksellers' natural, destined for a brilliant performance on the main aisle at Brentano's. For Miss Winsor's heroine, reduced to her essence, is a happy harlot, and nothing more; and the décor which her author has re-created for her (the "gay, bawdy, stinking, brilliant, dirty city of London" under Charles II) is the perfect background for a heroine of her habits.

Early along in the action the partner in Amber's first affair remarks that she possesses "the world's most marketable commodity—enough for ten women." Amber's career in the next decade more than justifies an apparent hyperbole. It includes such assorted lovers as a highwayman, an aging earl, a lawyer's clerk, a captain in the Horse Guards, the Duke of Buckingham, a merchant prince, and (of course) the King, in person. It produces several offspring—one of royal blood. It takes in balls at Whitehall, brawls in Whitefriars and mixed bathing in the Thames. There is pimping and poisoning and the wild clash of swords at dawn; incessant lechery in odd corners of Newgate Prison, city inns and noble antechambers. There are glimpses, now and again, of such figures as Clarendon and Barbara Palmer, Nell Gwynne and Minette, and the sad Portuguese princess who became such an embarrassed English Queen. For heaping measure, there is a spine-chilling murder while the Great Fire rages across London—and a whole section devoted

to the Great Plague, sickening and wonderfully real in its profusion of grisly detail.

Miss Winsor's heroine, it seems, is the epitome of her times: as such, she fulfills her creator's purpose admirably. Whether she is flouncing through the Royal Exchange in search of a husband to give her first child a name—or learning the art of housebreaking under expert tutelage, after a sojourn in debtors' prison—or making her first really profitable liaison as a putative actress—or calmly committing bigamy with a rich invalid at Tunbridge Wells—or nursing a lover through the plague—or languishing in her third husband's country house while she waits for him to try out a new Italian poison on her . . . in all these crises, and others too numerous to mention, Amber St. Clare conducts herself shrewdly, courageously, and quite amorally.

Throughout, she remains faithful—in spirit, if not in practice—to her first capable seducer. Bruce, Lord Carlton, leaves her promptly enough for a career in America, but turns up in London now and again—often enough, in fact, to father most of her children. Eventually, he marries a perfect lady back in Virginia, and brings her to court. Amber's head-on collision with this worthy female does not belong among the book's happier moments, though it does serve to put an end to Carlton's left-handed honeymoons—at least, for a time. When Miss Winsor's imagination pants itself out at last, Amber is sailing for Virginia to surprise Bruce with yet another child, confident that she can capture him all over again.

Kathleen Winsor.

THIS jumbo product, as most readers will know by now, is not only Kathleen Winsor's first novel but virtually her first writing as well. A Berkeley graduate, class of '38, married to an all-American football ace of the Mid-Thirties, she first discovered Amber's background while helping her husband on a history theme; her only previously published writing was a series of articles on football (from the woman's angle) published in a California paper. Since then the young author has delved long and hard in the rakish history of the era—and poured out her research with a prodigal hand. Despite the urge of that final chapter, she vows and swears she'll write no more for a time.

Her book is thrown together with a fine disregard for repetition or pattern. Its style is a wonderful, wide-eyed parroting of the gadzooks school. History is blended recklessly with fiction, to include all the angles of seventeenth-century England that Miss Winsor feels an urge to examine. England's most unworthy sovereign is presented as a cross between a periwigged marionette and a pre-war Gable, retaining the best features of each. . . . But even the most hardened reviewer must bow his head before this glittering mélange, and admit that Macmillan has a hit on its hands, perhaps second only to "Gone With the Wind." For Miss Winsor is a born storyteller, for all her turgid amateur writing, her incredible sentiment and her hot-house appraisal of history. She knows how to keep that story moving—even when, as one often suspects, she hasn't the slightest idea where it is taking her, or why.

October 15, 1944

Bells, Bells, Bells, Bells

THE MIRACLE OF THE BELLS. By Russell Janney. 497 pp. New York: Prentice-Hall. $3.

By WILLIAM DU BOIS

RUSSELL JANNEY will be remembered fondly for his production of "The Vagabond King." Now, just turned 60, he has sat down determinedly and proved once more that a showman can also write a novel. If his "Miracle of the Bells" seems a bit like an actress who has ventured into Forty-Fifth Street at high noon with her make-up on, put that down to the occupational hazards of a busy lifetime in the theatre. There's no escaping the fact that the author's heart is in the right place, even when his characters are hamming most outrageously to make their points.

Mr. Janney's story comes straight from the Miracle-Man catalogue, and he milks it astutely with both ears turned to the groundlings. His hero is one Bill Dunnigan, Broadway press-agent de luxe; his girl is one Olga Trocki, a Pennsylvania Pole straight from Coaltown, her lungs marked by the black doom of the Breaker, even as she zooms to stardom in Hollywood. Dunnigan is bringing her body back to Coaltown as the story opens: Olga's next-to-last request was that she be buried among her beloved hills; her last, and most important, wish was that the bells of her parish church be rung just before her burial. * * * At the moment Bill is a press agent in disgrace and down to his last hundred. Even in these dire straits (with no job in prospect, his heart twisted with unuttered love) he cannot resist spending his last dollar to have *all* the church bells in Coaltown rung in Olga's honor—starting at sunset four days before the funeral.

NO student of dramaturgy need be told what happens after Mr. Janney steps briskly away from that act-one curtain. The precise reason for the miracle that follows this orgy of bell-ringing is his secret, so far as the reviewer is concerned. Suffice it to say that Coaltown is a better place after Bill Dunnigan has left it. A purse-proud priest has seen the error of his ways—and his grundyish sister has made a national hook-up with her recipe for beaten biscuits. A pearl-diver in a local beanery has opened his own dog-wagon and christened a sandwich the St. Michael Special in honor of Olga's patron saint. An atheistic union leader has seen the error of his ways and brought his men to early mass with their head-lamps burning in the dawn. Even the harpy who owns the mines has succumbed to Bill's charm and helped him to give Olga's open-air funeral exactly the chromatic touch to make a wow finish.

If this report seems to err on the gaudy side we can only offer the evidence of Mr. Janney's own prose. Each page is constructed on the declamatory pattern, sown ankle-deep with exclamation points and blocked into many a set speech of the type that once made the rafters ring when the theatre was not ashamed to be theatrical. But it cannot be said too often that the author's evangelism is beyond reproach—or that the story he tells will be enjoyed mightily by many readers. Miracles *do* happen—even nowadays, even in the unhappy heart of man. Mr. Janney deserves an audience for that earnest hope, and we've no doubt they'll come in droves.

Russell Janney.

September 8, 1946

People Who Read and Write

By JOHN K. HUTCHENS

The Doctor's Busy

Up from the bayous of Northern Florida the other day came Dr. Frank G. Slaughter, and before you could say "In a Dark Garden" a roving member of this department had tracked him down. "In a Dark Garden" is Dr. Slaughter's sixth novel in as many years (it is reviewed on Page 4 of this issue), and already it seems headed for a large audience, what with a Dollar Book Club distribution, an Armed Services edition now on the press, and an advance trade printing that is respectable even in this boom season. The doctor, being a craftsman, has already put the book out of his mind and is at work on a seventh. It will be another jumbo-romantic adventure special, dealing with pioneer Florida in the last days of the Spanish rule, circa 1818.

Dr. Slaughter, fresh from research on the above, admitted he liked the preparation for one of these tasks. Getting ready for "Dark Garden," he shipped two bookbags of reference works before he sailed for Manila as chief surgeon aboard the hospital ship Emily M. Weder; in Florida he relived some of the exploits of his forthcoming doctor-protagonist. He even likes the writing, which proceeds at a lively tempo of 4,000 words a day.

The first Slaughter novel, "That None Should Die," appeared in 1941. A modest success here, it was a best seller in the Scandinavian countries and one of the last American translations to roll off the Copenhagen presses before the Nazis moved in. Royalty statements, scrupulously kept by the underground, and paid in full last year, enabled him to give up his practice in Jacksonville and write on a full-time basis. In the interval five other novels had emerged from his typewriter, each with a doctor-hero and written in a variety of places. For instance, "Dark Garden," to the best of his knowledge, is the first Civil War novel to be composed aboard a hospital ship in mid-Pacific.

And the doctor himself is probably the busiest auctorial M. D. of the day, his schedule calling for a novel annually, a factual book on medicine each year (he is the author of the recently published "New Science of Surgery" and has just delivered a book on psychosomatic medicine to his publisher) and lecture tours and popular medical biographies. But he cheerfully expects to meet every deadline. He lives deep in the Florida pine-barrens, with the nearest operating room in Jacksonville, and no telephone.

September 29, 1946

Talk With Mrs. Keyes

By HARVEY BREIT

In recent writing experience, perhaps no author has had such phenomenal success as Frances Parkinson Keyes (rhymes with sighs): She has just come out with "Joy Street," which, from all legible signs, looks like it will do better than "Dinner at Antoine's" (1948), which did better than "Came a Cavalier" (1947), which in turn did better than "The River Road" (1945)—each of which, by the way, successively cracked the million-copy mark. The golden touch, you'd say, and you'd be right.

And yet Mrs. Keyes doesn't know how to write a best seller. "Perhaps a clever author," she says, "much cleverer than I am, could deliberately set out to write a best seller and do it. He may be able to do it once, but I don't think he could go on doing it." And, for evidence, she cites her past three novels, saying: "If you were writing in a pattern I don't think you could be that successful all three, and maybe four, times."

Not only does Mrs. Keyes not know how to write a best seller, she isn't primarily interested in the phenomenon. She is more pleased by the fact that she was chosen the outstanding Catholic woman in the United States for 1946. And, as for writing, she says, perhaps startlingly: "I have always been much more interested in being a woman of letters than a best seller author. I want still to turn out the kind of work I have always been interested in turning out—biography and travel sketches and verse."

Mrs. Keyes was born in 1885 at the University of Virginia. When she was 19, she married Henry Wilder Keyes, the former Governor of New Hampshire and a United States Senator. Before Mr. Keyes died in 1938, his wife was already well on her way to becoming more famous than her husband.

When recently Mrs. Keyes' visitor entered her rooms, she rose from her chair with slight but nevertheless visible effort. "I am sensitive neither to age nor weight," she said. "I was not ever thus. I was for twenty-five years done up in an iron frame because of a minor spinal difficulty—a fall that was never X-rayed. I explain it to you, but I neither apologize nor do I wish to emphasize it. If you watch me get up or sit down you will see that I do it with my hands."

So considerately did Mrs. Keyes get her visitor over any difficulties he may have felt. The pursuit of information, nevertheless, was still on the agenda. How did Mrs. Keyes get started on a book? Had, for instance, "Dinner at Antoine's" gotten crystallized by some incident at a dinner party?

"Yes, it did," Mrs. Keyes said. "But it is impossible to generalize. Sometimes it is an impression, very often it is a real experience. Sometimes I pull various things together. An anecdote here, an experience there, an environment remembered — many things having nothing to do with each other begin to assemble and fall together. I begin to write and the people come alive and do what they please."

Didn't Mrs. Keyes think she ought to exercise more control? "If they don't come alive for me," Mrs. Keyes replied, "they won't come alive for someone else. As a matter of fact, it gets quite extreme. I have had cases where someone insists on staying alive even though I had planned his death."

But didn't Mrs. Keyes believe in enforced interment? "No," Mrs. Keyes replied. "I wouldn't change it. I think it would be dishonest writing if I'd do otherwise."

The author considered the entire question of honesty and best sellers.

"You know," she said after a while, "I am not a reviewer's author. I rarely get a good press. But I think you have to have a renewed feeling of reality each time you write, and the people must seem real to you, and you must put into each book the best you are capable of doing. If you don't, people are going to know it."

Technically, how did Mrs. Keyes make certain she was putting into each book the best of herself? "It's an extraordinary experience for me," Mrs. Keyes said. "I draft everything in longhand and read it aloud, making changes along the way. This version gets into triple space manuscript, and that's changed about forty times, and finally it gets into double space and I hope that's the end."

Frances Parkinson Keyes.

That seemed a fair enough safeguard. Was there any other test Mrs. Keyes applied to her effort to be honest? Mrs. Keyes nodded. "A solemn pledge I made to myself," she said, "that I'd never let anything leave my hands that didn't represent the most sincere and earnest effort of which I am capable. At that time," she added.

"At that time," Mrs. Keyes continued, "because I look back at the early things I did and I wonder how they got published."

December 10, 1950

THAT 'TREE' KEEPS GROWING

New Musical Is Based on Work That Was Play, Novel and Movie

By BETTY SMITH

Author of the novel, "A Tree Grows in Brooklyn," on which is based the musical of the same name, opening Thursday, at the Alvin Theatre.

IN 1930, while a student at the University of Michigan, I wrote my first full-length play. It was about poor people who lived in Brooklyn. It was very social conscious, as was the style back in 1930. Its title was "Francie Nolan." It won the Avery Hopwood Award in Drama, was never produced and eventually got lost.

In 1010, after I had had pub lished seventy-five one-act plays I had written (a few in collaboration), I decided to write a novel. I did not know how to write a novel so I wrote it as a play—all dialogue and stage directions. It was in scenes and acts and amounted to practically a cycle of eight full-length plays. It took two years to convert 800 pages of play script into 400 pages of novel. It was a novel about poor people who lived in Brooklyn. I called it "A Tree Grows in Brooklyn." It was published. It was a success.

In 1945, it was made into a movie. I did not work on it. I had had enough trouble mastering the medium of the play and then that of the novel. I didn't feel up to tackling a new medium.

Broken Resolution

In late 1949, George Abbott and Robert Fryer acquired the novel, planning to make a musical of it. I was very pleased. But I made it very plain to Helen Strauss, my agent, that I wouldn't work on the play under any circumstances. I came to New York and, accompanied by my agent, went to meet Mr. Abbott. Outside his office door I again told her very firmly that I wouldn't work on the play.

Mr. Abbott and I started discussing the form the musical would take. I began making suggestions. Miss Strauss broke in to say: "It is understood that Miss Smith does not wish to work on the play." I looked at her blankly and said: "But I *am* working on it." So we began collaborating ten minutes after we met. It was days later that an embarrassing thought came to me. Mr. Abbott had not asked me to work on the script with him! I had just started working with him!

I think it was one of the most amiable collaborations in dramatic history. We never disagreed on script. With no elaborate plan of procedure, we went to work on the play. Sometimes I wrote the first draft of a scene and turned it over to George. He worked on it, then turned it back to me. I worked on it. This happened three or four times and then we sat down and worked on it together. Sometimes George made the first draft. It was about fifty-fifty. We had one trait in common. Both of us were avid cutters. With something like delight, I cut his lines. In a matter-of-fact way he cut my lines. By accident I cut many of my own lines. With ruthlessness, he cut his own scenes and lines.

After the fourth draft, we could no longer say, "My lines," or "Your lines." They were our lines. George got on to the way of doing my dialogue. I learned a little of his incisiveness in writing. Now a line can be taken at random from the play and half of the words are his, half mine. But in all honesty, I must say that the technique of the play belongs to George. It will take me a long time to know half as much about dramatic technique as he does.

Well, afte ten months, we had what we called a working script. It was a thin little thing of ninety-four typed pages. All of a sudden the slight script became the center of intense activity. Arthur Schwartz and Dorothy Fields came in to do the music and lyrics. Jo Mielziner produced sketches of the sets. Irene Sharaff made sketches of the costumes. Herbert Ross explained his scenario for the ballet. The backers came in and suddenly almost a quarter of a million dollars backed up those ninety-four pages.

A whole intricate organization was put into motion to service the script. Directly or indirectly, probably 2,000 people were involved in it. I had a moment of sheer terror when I realized that so much depended, so much was set in motion by those typed words bound in a red cover.

Rehearsals, leading into tryouts started. For two months I left the world. I had no other life than that involved in the production. I ate with the people of the play, walked with them, talked to them. We talked always of the play and its production. I answered no mail, resented outside phone calls. I ate sandwiches and coffee, mostly, and slept when I had a chance. I had no time for a manicure or to buy a new dress. To be dramatic, I lived only for the script.

Then we opened in Philadelphia. I stayed up that night waiting for the papers. To quote "Variety" of April 4, "* * * 'Tree' opened at the Forest last Tuesday (27) to two rave notices and one very good one." It's all over, I thought, and fetched up a deep sigh of relief. I took my shoes off and crawled into bed. I had no other plans than to sleep for three days and nights. I was settling into the first deep sleep when the phone rang. It was George. "The notices are good," I said. "Yes," he said. "Come right over to the theatre." Astonished, I asked why. He told me that we had some re-writing to do. So I put my shoes back on and it all started again.

We took out a charming Biergarten scene and with it my favorite song of the play, "Tuscaloosa." This, to strengthen the story line. A lovely ballad, "The Bride Wore Something Old," was pulled out with a wrench and a rhythm song substituted. The dances were shortened, lengthened or discarded or re-created. Mr. Schwartz and Miss Fields wrote two new songs. Miss Fields wrote new lyrics or pointed up old ones. Scenes were merged, rewritten or new ones put in. The actors rehearsed new lines and business. New costumes came in. The orchestration was polished. Lines were shortened, cut or polished. New lines were written.

All of a sudden it was over. The play was "frozen" and a great silence seemed to fall on the world. I went back to the hotel with my script, now worn and ragged and dog-eared. I put the shabby little thing away in my trunk with a feeling of elation and sorrow. It was as if, after bringing up a child from infancy and trying to make a good boy out of him, all of a sudden he went out into the world on his own. You were happy that he was going out to live his own life —what kind the New York critics will decide on Thursday—but saddened because he was no longer around to bring up.

April 15, 1951

Talk With Frank Yerby

By HARVEY BREIT

EVERY once in a while—not often, mind you—there appears on the literary horizon an author who, for one reason or another, can't help but produce best-selling novels. Frances Parkinson Keyes is one such. Frank Yerby is another. Now, take Frank Yerby: at the ripe age of not quite 35, he has come up with his sixth novel, "A Woman Called Fancy," and the chances are very good (as good, say, as Ray Robinson beating Jake LaMotta in a rematch) that it will be a thumping best seller, as were the five novels before it. Each of the five were book-club selections and each had a distribution of at least a million copies. "The Foxes of Harrow," Mr. Yerby's first, went to over two million.

The phenomenal Mr. Yerby was born in Augusta, Ga., a town he lived in pretty steadily for his first twenty years. He went to school in Augusta's Paine College, to Fisk, to the University of Chicago. "I was a fairly dreadful kind of student," Mr. Yerby says. "Non-athletic, very studious, took scholastic honors, what the boys today would call a grind. I had my master's at 21, could have had my doctorate at 23 if I hadn't run out of money. Which," Mr. Yerby sagely addended, "is all to the good."

How did Mr. Yerby write a novel? "I've done a novel every year for six years," Mr. Yerby said. That meant, then, quite a tight regimen, didn't it? Mr. Yerby nodded. "I frequently write right around the clock," he said. "I work as much as eighteen hours a day. Not only that; I rewrite. I rewrote 'Fancy' three times. And not only that: I do a lot of research. I read, read, read for my preliminary work. I've been spending as much as six hours a day in the library on background material for my new novel."

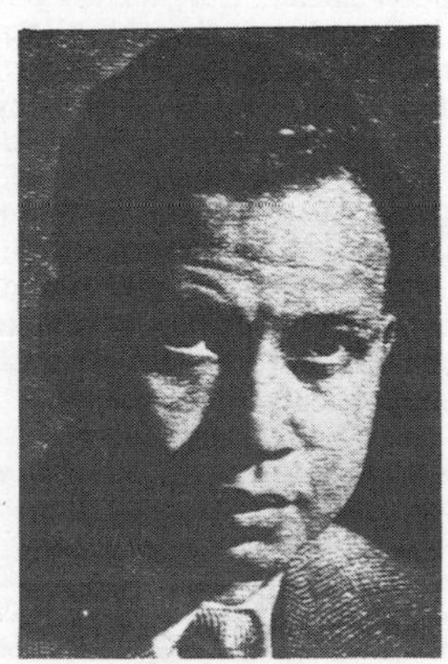

Frank Yerby.

MR. YERBY didn't exactly hesitate. He said, "My notes for a novel always outweigh in bulk the novel itself. Sometimes it's three times over." Well, this data struck an observer as all to the good; at least, one could feel, Mr. Yerby's novels weren't "quickies." It turned out that Mr. Yerby had pretty strong feelings on the entire matter of the relationship between writer and reader.

"I think the novelist," Mr. Yerby said, "has a professional obligation to please his reading public." At the age of 20, when Mr. Yerby was writing poetry for the little magazines, was he writing for any other reason than that he had to? Or wasn't that it? Of course that was it. "Because a writer has a duty to his reader," Mr. Yerby said with honest passion, "it doesn't mean in any way that he has the right to write *down* to his reader. All the brows, high, middle and low, should be able to read his book, but for different reasons. The novelist has no right whatsoever to insult his public."

If one took a hypothetical situation in which Mr. Yerby found his work lacked any corresponding response in the reading public, would he go on writing? "I would have to," Mr. Yerby said. "I write because I have to. What I get out of it financially doesn't come under consideration at all. I write exactly what I feel and think I want to do, but within that framework I try to give pleasure to the reading public. Take it from the other angle: the novelist hasn't any right to inflict on the public his private ideas on politics, religion or race. If he wants to preach he should go on the pulpit. I mean this from a professional, artistic point of view."

There would be many instances of accepted great novels that Mr. Yerby would have to combat. Mr. Yerby knew it. "Now, for example," he said, "when I read 'Anna Karenina,' I find myself skipping the political, peasant-in-relation-to-the-land parts. I really feel Tolstoy was getting that sort of thing out of his system. That sort of thing just isn't the novelist's job."

WHAT if you were a novelist interested in contemporary political life? "It's important to know," Mr. Yerby countered, "your character's emotional life, his emotional reaction to political ideas, but what the political ideas themselves are is a matter of indifference to the novelist. I hate above all things the heavy hand of the author offstage creaking the on-stage machinery. The novelist must try to write with a universality of appeal so that it hits all segments of the people. To do that, a novel must have characters that are alive and a story that is interesting. It is my contention that a really great novel is made with a knife and not a pen. A novelist must have the intestinal fortitude to cut out even the most brilliant passage so long as it doesn't advance the story."

Did Mr. Yerby feel he had the intestinal fortitude? "I do," he said, "but not enough. The spirit is willing but the flesh is weak. I have learned though. My danger has always been a too great fluency. I used to be adjective-happy. Now I cut them with so much severity that I find I have to put a few adjectives back."

May 13, 1951

Talk With Mr. Costain

By LEWIS NICHOLS

HAVING worked out the 930 pages of "The Tontine" (see page 5), Thomas B. Costain might be pardoned if he wished to sit down for a year and glance off into space. This is not his way, however, for such glances have a tendency to make him nervous. What also tends to make him nervous, in a rueful sort of way, is that try as he may, all Costain stories seem to end up at 200,000 words or better. This has gone on so long it is more or less habit, like that of not loafing. Could be that someone, somewhere, might envy him.

He went into these and other matters the other day, as a small pile of typewritten pages near by represented the start of another book. Thus far the pile is just a few inches high, not the towering column it will become if his second anxiety again proves not unfounded.

"The family thinks I should take a long rest after each book, but I started late and have a lot of ideas," he said. "After 'The Tontine' I did take a month, but it was a month filled entirely with fear.

"You see, so many writers just stop writing. There's a change in temperament or metabolism or something, and they just stop. I'm afraid that if I quit for any length of time, I'd never begin again. Of course, there's a change in metabolism—or whatever it is—which comes at some stage in every book. You can tell it when you realize something is wrong and have to go back. But that's temporary.

"I work every morning, all seven of them, then go out to lunch, to a show, the movies, a ball game (Giants) — or just read. The point is I work every day, and you don't have to do a great deal each time before it mounts up. Everyone wants to loaf, sure, but when that hits you—work anyway. The first half-hour will be chaff, but after that everything will be all right.

"ONE personal burden is that I can't seem to conceive any story that can be written in a short form. 'The Tontine' is about 350,000 words. If I hadn't started the characters at 16, but had entered them in the tontine older, it would have been far shorter. But once they were in at 16, there was nothing to do but go on."

Of his various stories, which was the shortest, the novelette, as it were, among them? Mr. Costain thought a moment, then guessed "Son of a Hundred Kings." He got up, crossed the room, pulled down a copy from the shelf and then, with the automatic gesture of every book owner, blew dust from the top—whether there or not. "Four hundred and sixty-five pages," he announced in a tone of morbid surprise. "Not so short. Must be fairly close to 200,000 words after all."

All of this even flow of work goes on at a Carleton House desk (1790), for which Mr. Costain happily negotiated over a period of several years. An anachronism on its polished top is a pile of yellow paper, without which no former newspaper man (Guelph, Ont., Daily Mercury) and editor (MacLean's Magazine, Saturday Evening Post) ever feels comfortable. Mr. Costain starts off with a pencil, then for first revision shifts to a typewriter. Reverse this or change it, and the whole system probably would break down. There might even be just short shorts, between long years of loafing.

"There were a great many revisions of 'The Tontine' and thank heaven I could make them. It was revised by books and by chapters. I'm afraid I was pretty free and easy and there were a good many mistakes, which other people fortunately found.

"I've wondered many times how Dickens worked. He had to send his stories off chapter by chapter. You couldn't be in a worse fix than that—each chapter finished, gone and unrecallable.

"Luckily I have a pretty fair memory for my work—not for anything else. I can go into the next room looking for something and forget what it was by the time I get there. On the other hand, I can remember where any minor note of research may be in a pile of papers. I also can remember the relationship between characters and events and places. That helps."

Since all stories come from somewhere, what was the initial idea, the acorn, for "The Tontine"? "That's one of the things I can't remember," Mr. Costain said. "Maybe I first heard of a tontine because Balzac's father was in one. At any rate, I didn't think of it seriously until I was writing 'The White and the Gold.' Henri Tonti—the son of the tontine's inventor—was with LaSalle, and as I did research I thought there's a story for me."

Now fractionally beyond 70, Mr. Costain deplores only the inevitable passage of time. "I wish I were starting out now," he said. "There are dozens of stories I'd like to write, great new fields I'd like to know all about. But one at a time, though—now that I've had my month off."

September 25, 1955

Small Town Peep Show

PEYTON PLACE. By Grace Metalious. 372 pp. New York: Julian Messner. $3.95.

By CARLOS BAKER

THIS is the earthy novel of small-town life in New Hampshire which sprang into the news some weeks ago when the Gilmanton School Board dismissed young George Metalious from his position as principal of the local grammar school. "They told me it was because of my wife," said Mr. Metalious. "They don't like her book." Later, the school board said they had dismissed the young teacher for reasons of their own, which had no bearing on the novel. The author herself still insisted that word had got around Gilmanton that "Peyton Place" was a real shocker: "People suddenly decided that George is not the type to teach their sweet innocent children."

Whatever the merits of the Metalious case, the novel lives up very fully to its advance billing. It opens on a warm autumn day in the Thirties with a comparison between Indian summer and a woman ("Ripe, hotly passionate, but fickle, she comes and goes as she pleases"). What follows is a carefully calculated exposé of the comings and goings of a large cast of typical characters in a small New England town until another Indian summer some ten years later.

We learn that life behind the scenes in New Hampshire is not widely different, fictionally speaking, from life in Winesburg, Ohio, Hecate County, Conn., or Gibbsville, Pa. It is only (if that is possible) a little "riper," a little more "hotly passionate," a little more frankly detailed—and, perhaps, a little more widely inclusive than the small-town chronicles of Messrs. Sherwood Anderson, Edmund Wilson and John O'Hara. The late Sinclair Lewis would no doubt have hailed Grace Metalious as a sister-in-arms against the false fronts and bourgeois pretensions of allegedly respectable communities, and certified her as a public accountant of what goes on in the basements, bedrooms and back porches of a "typical American town."

Mrs. Metalious, who is a pretty fair writer for a first novelist, comes and goes with the Indian Summer air of an emancipated modern authoress who knows the earthy words and rarely stints to use them. Samples of the adventures in store for readers of "Peyton Place" would include the following: Successive violations of a 14-year-old girl by her stepfather, leading to an abortion sadly performed by the town's admirable doctor. A murder in a "shacker's" hut with secret burial of the remains in a sheep pen. A suicide in a bedroom closet. A carnival accident which amputates a young girl's arm. A high-school seduction in which the girl is bought off by the boy's rich and corrupt father. The seduction of the local dress-shop proprietress by the village schoolmaster. The deflowering of her nubile novelist-daughter by an erotically expert New York literary agent. A lengthy hard-cider binge in a locked cellar involving among others the town handyman who imbibes as a protest against his wife's multiple adulteries. The strangling of a pet tomcat at the feet of a dead spinster by a neurotic boy who has retchingly peered through a backyard hedge at the amorous activities of a neighbor couple.

If Mrs. Metalious can turn her emancipated talents to less lurid purposes, her future as novelist is a good bet. Another good bet is that the citizens of Gilmanton, N. H., can look forward to a busy Indian summer of open or surreptitious reading.

Mr. Baker is chairman of the Department of English at Princeton.

September 23, 1956

Grace Metalious Is Dead at 39; Author of 'Peyton Place' Novel

Writer Shocked the Nation With Story of Lurid Life in New England Town

Catapulted to Success

With one book, Mrs. Metalious shocked the nation. Her novel described lurid sex life in what is often thought of as rock-ribbed New England society.

The book lifted her from a desperately poor obscurity as a teacher's wife and mother of three children to glamorous success.

"I don't go along with all the claptrap about poverty being good for the soul, and trouble and struggle being great strengtheners of character," she wrote later, when, in contrast to her early hungry years, her pleasant open face took on a modest plumpness.

"Peyton Place" was published in 1956. It sold 300,000 hardcover copies and more than 8 million in paperback, clinging to the best-seller list for more than a year. Mrs. Metalious received $125,000 for the film rights. The movie earned $11 million for 20th Century-Fox.

The book caused an immediate stir in Gilmanton, N. H. where her husband's contract as teacher and principal of the Gilmanton Corner School was not renewed even before the novel was in print. The school board denied that the book had anything to do with its decision, but Mrs. Metalious insisted: "They didn't want him in Gilmanton. Not him, and not his nutty wife."

Some critics described "Peyton Place" as a worthy literary effort for a first novel, although they deprecated its lust and violence. Mrs. Metalious was commended for exposing the double life of a community; one critic observed that she would have won the praise of Sinclair Lewis for tearing the top off small-town smugness.

However, it is debatable whether literary merit alone sold so many copies or made it one of the most talked-about novels in the United States.

The townspeople of Gilmanton at first were incensed at what they took as a personal exposure of their society. "Their attitude is that 'we know these things happen but you're not supposed to write about it in a book so everyone else knows, too,'" Mrs. Metalious said.

Was Married at 17

Grace de Repentigny Metalious was born in Manchester, N. H., of French ancestry. Her parents separated when she was 11 years old. She was married to George Metalious in 1942 when both were 17 years old.

Mr. Metalious was then working as a mill hand but the couple decided that he should study for a teacher's license. He taught at several schools before going to Gilmanton in 1955, while Mrs. Metalious was finishing "Peyton Place."

"When did I begin to write?" she once asked. "I have been writing for as long as I can remember."

In the fourth grade, a teacher criticized her for making up a story about a fictitious brother. In the seventh grade, she wrote a detective story. But it was not until she sent the manuscript of "Peyton Place" to an agent, Jacques Chambrun, that she finally reached the printed page.

Her sudden success helped the family buy a 178-year old house in Gilmanton, moving out of one called "a shack glorified with asbestos siding and inside of which nothing worked."

In 1959, Mrs. Metalious wrote "Return to Peyton Place," which sold more than four million copies in paperback. "The Tight White Collar," in 1960, sold two million copies. Her last novel "No Adam in Eden" was published in September.

All of the novels were in a setting familiar to her, the small

Associated Press

Grace Metalious

towns of New England and they all had an inquiring, iconoclastic attitude.

Wrote of Hard Life

Although she was elated by her success, Mrs. Metalious was always shy of public appearances. She wrote freely about her life, a hard-working one that apparently bore little resemblance to the stormy lives she created in her books.

But she was shy when it came to speaking. New Yorkers once saw her fingers steal the show from her words during an intensive television interview several years ago. As she spoke, her words were upstaged by the constant movement of her fingers as they braided and ran through her long brown hair.

The friction that "Peyton Place" caused with her neighbors has now faded and Mrs. Metalious was a familiar figure in the neighborhood of Gilmanton and Laconia.

In 1958, the Metaliouses were divorced. Mrs. Metalious was married to T. J. Martin, a disk jockey, but divorced him after two years and was remarried to Mr. Metalious.

The couple bought a motel colony on the shores of Paugus Bay in Laconia. They called it Peyton Place. Last October, Mr. Metalious announced that they were again separating.

Mrs. Metalious is survived by her husband, now guidance director of the Ludlow High School, Ludlow, Vt.; a married daughter, Marsha, a son, Christopher, an another daughter, Cynthia.

February 26, 1964

Books of The Times

Just a Hint of the Plot

"Valley of the Dolls" is another story. In fact, it is a life story, or as near to it as a writer with careful lawyers can get. One shouldn't give it all away, but here's a hint: Did you ever see "A Star is Born"? This book is that film (plus snippets of "Stage Door" and "All About Eve") as it might have been "recreated" in print-form by a slightly bashful fan of Harold Robbins.

Jacqueline Susann, whose first (nonfiction) book was about a poodle, has added to this mélange of the penalties of theatrical success the problems of excessive mammalian development and the ravages of sedatives, which are apparently known as "dolls" out Hollywood way (if you take one you enter the "valley," presumably of Despond). Anyway, there's a great deal of suffering in this novel—what rising to the "hill" of stardom, or even such lesser peaks as being a successful agent's wife, entails—which, the characters all tell each other, only Seconal can relieve. Unfortunately, for them and us, it doesn't.

So: derivative novels, good, middling and ridiculous, and none of them up to the original. The recommendation here seems obvious. Don't bother with "The Tenant" or "The Firedrake" or "Valley of the Dolls." Instead, look up "The Trial" or any other Kafka; read, oh, Winston Churchill; go see Judy Garland—Ooops!

February 4, 1966

Raven-haired, deeply tanned and radiant

Jackie Susann picks up the marbles

By Martin Kasindorf

She dropped to the sand, and he took her in his arms. When their lips met it was everything she knew it would be. And when he took her, she knew it had been the moment she had waited for all her life. His caress was gentle yet firm. She reached out for him and held him close . . . closer . . . until they were united like the sand that joins the wave that draws it back into the sea.

"Please don't ever leave me," she whispered.

And he held her close and promised he would never let her go again.

—JACQUELINE SUSANN,
"Once Is Not Enough" (1973).

One night during the annual American Booksellers Association convention in early June, a chartered bus ferried a load of bookstore owners from a party at Irving Wallace's house to the palmy entrance of the Beverly Hills Hotel, a celebrity establishment which any Jacqueline Susann reader learns to describe down to the hallway broom closets. The free ride to Jackie Susann's cocktail bash was a good-natured gesture by Simon & Schuster. The company had published her previous novel, "The Love Machine," but refused to meet the stiff financial and marketing terms of the author and her husband-manager-promoter, Irving Mansfield, and lost the rights to the latest Susann book, "Once Is Not Enough," to Wm. Morrow & Co.

At the door of the Maisonette Room off the hotel's lobby, Morrow crowed over its catch with

Martin Kasindorf is Newsweek's deputy bureau chief in Los Angeles.

a five-foot-high cardboard reprint of a full-page newspaper advertisement: "May 6, 1973. Jacqueline Susann makes publishing history." On that date, six weeks after publication, the new work was listed as number one fiction best seller by The New York Times Book Review. "You could say that hundreds of novelists have done the same," the ad burbled, "but only one, man or woman, has ever had three No. 1 best sellers in a row."

In 1966 her first pills-and-sex novel, "Valley of the Dolls," appeared. In 1969 came the more male-oriented "The Love Machine." And now there is her tale of "mental and spiritual incest" among the miserable rich—carefully crafted linear soap opera about a strong father and his confused young daughter, named January. It is set, partly autobiographically, in the usual glamorous and strangely unappealing worlds of Susann books—the international jet set, Broadway, publishing, cafe society, Hollywood, big-time magazine journalism.

Suddenly the visiting bookmen were face to face with the story-telling phenomenon herself. An ageless pop-culture queen, she was raven-haired, deeply tanned and radiant, as if she would go on writing one best seller after another as long as the Supreme Court would let her. She stayed seated on a stool just inside the door. She was, in fact, suffering from a mild flareup of the double lobar pneumonia, brought on by years of overwork, which nearly killed her in New York last winter.

But Jackie wasn't missing her party for anything. The author fixed each arriving guest with intelligent brown eyes and a firm handshake. She sang out a greeting in a deep, mature alto. "Hi! How are you? Good to see you. The bar is in there --food, everything."

Off in a corner, critic Eliot Fremonth-Smith recalled his review of the blockbusting "Valley of the Dolls," which, at 14,800,000 copies, will go into the next edition of the Guinness Book of World Records as the most popular novel of all time, ahead of "Peyton Place." He remembered writing, "It's Hedy Lamarr's kind of book. Why should Jacqueline Susann pick up all the marbles?" Now he had an answer. "Her formula is action, movement. Her books just zip along. They're terrible, but they go. Others try the same formula, but their stories don't go anywhere. And she's a total professional. Everything she does is calculated. Look at her over there. She's not drinking. She's working."

After slamming through as many as 29 television talk shows and newspaper interviews a week to flog her earlier books, the novelist has been forced down to two appearances a day in the aftermath of her illness. To her astonishment, her new book approached first place while she was in a hospital bed.

Even before publication, she could have relaxed. She had earned $1.2-million in advances from Morrow, foreign publishers, book clubs and Bantam Books, which will bring out the paperback edition next summer. Yet she misses her grueling old tour circuit. In her $100-a-day terrace suite at the Beverly Hills Hotel a few days before the party, she worried, "Even a good book can die on the vine if it's not promoted." (Later, while she and Irving were in Britain and France introducing the overseas editions, "Once Is Not Enough" dropped to number two on The Times list after nine weeks. "Watergate has knocked off everything," she mournfully explains the slower sales rate of her current book compared to past figures. "When women get home at night they want to turn on the television set and watch the hearings on replay, not read novels.")

A driving philosophy, aided by the public relations innovations of the 62-year-old Mansfield, a former television producer, has brought the only child of well-to-do Philadelphia portrait painter Robert Susann world fame and more than $5-million. Her books have sold a total of 885,000 in hardback and 20,300,000 in paperback. She enjoys the best table at Sardi's and the conversation-stopping adulation of directors and stars at her beloved, pink and green Polo Lounge in the Beverly Hills Hotel. Best of all, her relationship of more than 28 years with Mansfield is one of the most mutually devoted in the annals of the famous.

The only blemish on her happiness is most book reviewers. They have ganged up in packs to accuse her of tailoring her work to discontented middle-aged females, and one has summed up her career's product as "sensationalist, sex-obsessed, superficial garbage you should be ashamed to read." She has even been accused of employing a ghost writer.

Far from laughing all the way to the bank, writer Susann becomes so unnerved by such articles that Mansfield knows better than to show them to her. Resolved to find something favorable in mentions of her works, she took it as a compliment that Kurt Vonnegut Jr., whose "Breakfast of Champions" has seized the number one spot from her, satirically equipped his "Slaughterhouse-Five" hero with a copy of "Valley of the Dolls" to allay the isolation of a mindless life of hedonism on the planet Tralfamadore.

Embattled, Susann carries on with a profound belief in her own worth. "A good writer," she insists, "is one who produces books that people read —who communicates. So if I'm selling millions, I'm good. If you think critics have vilified me, you should see what they did to Zola. They called him a yellow journalist. And Dickens . . . oh, they murdered him in his time. It's like chocolate ice cream. You're not supposed to like it because it's common."

Rather like beautiful young January Wayne, Jacqueline Susann is somewhat motivated by the desire to be worthy of her own father, who died 16 years ago. "When I was 8 years old," she remembers, "my father said, 'There will be no one to carry on the name of Susann.' I said, 'I'll cary it on, Daddy. I'm going to be an actress.' And he smiled and said, 'Well, if you're going to be an actress, be a good actress. Be a people-watcher.' That advice didn't stand me in good stead as an actress, because I got cast as what I looked like—a glamorous divorcée who gets stabbed or strangled. But as a writer, I can do what I want."

Jackie grew up in upper-middle-class comfort near Philadelphia's Rittenhouse Square. Robert Susann, of Dutch-Jewish ancestry, would get $5,000 for a portrait of a society *doyenne* or a merchant prince. Her mother, now retired, was a public-school teacher. Jackie's I.Q. was tested at 140, and a fifth-grade English teacher told her mother, "Jackie should be a writer. She breaks all the rules, but it works."

After a childhood spent at Saturday tryout matinees with her father, she decided on a Broadway career. At 16, she says, her parents presented her with a one-way train ticket to New York, and wished her well. It is hard to know how literally to take this account, for, again like her latest heroine, she lives in an uncomfortable gap between two generations. Her conversation is delightfully earthy in the contemporary mode, and she will uncork a startlingly intimate bedroom story at a solemn dinner party. Yet she obscures her age in mist. She admits to 46, looks 42 most of the time, and is more probably in her early 50's. "I have a cult," she smiles. "It's best for me to be ageless to my readers." In two of her novels, the condition of existence of a mentally retarded child, understandingly portrayed, is kept a closely guarded family secret. The Mansfields have a 20-year-old son they seldom talk about.

She had a moderately lucrative acting career, typecast as a murderess or murderee. She co-wrote a play, "Lovely Me," which ran for all of four weeks on Broadway in 1946. Thereafter her writing was a hobby confined to hotel rooms on tour. Nowadays, this Early Susann, long locked away in a trunk, is worth more than the autographs of some Founding Fathers. Family Circle paid $3,500 for the tale of Gwendolyn, a pigeon who watched Busby Berkeley movies on television.

When Jacqueline realized that her acting career was on the Plateau of the Dolls, she decided to start writing in earnest. "Write what you know," the saying goes. Aside from Irving, she happened to be best acquainted with her overweight poodle, Josephine. The longest extant work of Susann nonfiction, *"Every Night, Josephine!,"* 240 bright pages of poodle lore, was snapped up by Bernard Geis. It sold 35,000 hardback copies, reaching number eight briefly on one bestseller list. Since then it has sold 1,700,000 paperbacks. Most of the elements of her storytelling acumen were in place—short, punchy sentences, a lot of dialogue and plenty of creative name-dropping.

Geis urged Jacqueline to write an immediate sequel based on Josephine's life as a doggie celebrity after the book's publication in November, 1963. The author thought the idea premature. Besides, by that time she was into her second draft of "Valley of the Dolls," which she "wrote out of anger" because so many of her show-biz friends were hooked on upper and downer pills. She kept going, handed in her fifth and final draft only 18 months after beginning, and instantly started on "The Love Machine."

"Valley of the Dolls" provided the first example of what is sometimes termed the Susann "formula." The serviceable, onrushing prose describes glittering professions Susann is more or less familiar with. She daubs her rough-hewn but always fascinating *roman à clef* characters with traits and backgrounds which make their models as obvious as neon signs. An example of how she does it, from "Once Is Not Enough," in which producer Mike Wayne is telling his daughter about a novelist named Tom Colt:

"Look, babe, remember about six years ago when all the newspapers carried the story of how he had a dogfight with a shark? . . . He also fought a bull in Spain. Knocked out a professional fighter in a bar. When his plane crashed, he walked a mile into town with a broken leg. He can also drink any man under the table and he can knock out Muhammad Ali with one hand tied behind him." Hemingmail? Mailerway?

A list of the well-known to whom Susann-book resemblances have been noted includes Judy Garland, Ethel Merman, Marilyn Monroe, Jackie Gleason, Mike Todd, Grace Kelly, Marlene Dietrich, Greta Garbo, Gloria Steinem and entertainment executive James T. Aubrey Jr.

SUSANN parades her creations through eye-popping but soft-core passages of kinky sex which titillate the reader into wondering how much she *really knows* about "these people." At life's top, there is disease, neurosis, disaster. A 17-year-old beauty is rendered a near-vegetable for three years by a horrible motorcycle crash. A movie star develops breast cancer on the eve of a promising marriage to a breast fetishist; naturally, she commits suicide. Middle-aged Palm Beach matrons are just as desperate about keeping their looks, and older men their prostates, as any aging couple in Duluth. Most Susann marriages are scarred by infidelity. A satisfying sex life is generally possible only under the influence of drink or deadly Dr. Feelgood "speed" shots.

The marvel of "Valley of the Dolls" was that through clever plotting Jackie Susann grasped a *clichéd* theme, the tawdriness behind the glitter of show business, and breathed new life into it. In an atmosphere of Chekhovian gloom, she followed three women from 1945 to 1963, tracing their interrelated careers and love affairs. One, Anne Welles, was a reserved New England brunette who became a top demonstrator of cosmetics in television commercials. The second was Neely O'Hara, an evocatively hoydenish, talented singer who reaches the heights of idolatry only to turn into a suicidal, self-indulgent, nasty, overweight frump who nearly steals Anne's hard-won English husband. Most appealing was a busty blond movie sex symbol, Jennifer North. Starting out as ambitious friends, these dolls have one depressing encounter after another with bitchy old theatrical lionesses, spoiled scions, unfaithful or mentally defective husbands, and exploitative European film directors, until all fall prey to the dangerous pills the author calls "dolls." The sex symbol commits suicide. (In a tragic coincidence, Jennifer North was played in the movie version by Sharon Tate, later murdered.) The three stories are skillfully interleaved so that a riveting episode involving one of the women doesn't end until a new episode about one of the others has been well launched. Thus the pages keep turning.

"The Love Machine" was "an attempt to get into men's ids," as Susann puts it. Paralleling the rise and fall of one character, Robin Stone, an outwardly emotionless climber in the power-crazy world of network television's executive suites, is the man's personal metamorphosis from a hung-up sex machine, who shouts "Mother!" at his drunken climaxes, to a human being able at last to fuse sex with love.

"Once Is Not Enough," whose melodramatic title is based on a quote by the late comedian Joe E. Lewis about his unwillingness to accept the loss of the good life, adds the ingredient of ruthless power and Lesbian lust in the aging Jet Set to the usual mix of show-biz personnel. The plot is Susann's most complex, and twisting surprises are sprung with newly demonstrated skill.

It is all gut-level, powerful stuff. There is little waiting around for the principals to define themselves by their actions. They are quickly etched by their own dialogue or in the speeches of others. "You watch," Anne Welles is laboriously told by a secretary, speaking of the man she will later wed. "Lyon Burke will own this town one day. . . . Lyon just walks in with the English charm and the movie-star looks, and wham! he comes off with everything he wants. But after a while you realize you don't know what he's really like—and what he thinks of you, or of anyone. . . . But whatever you think about him, you still wind up adoring him."

Susann spells out her main points unmistakably, as when Neely is lying unhappily in bed after seeing her husband frolicking with a naked wench in the backyard swimming pool: "Tears ran down her face. God, all her life she had dreamed about something like this. A big house, a guy you loved, kids. She had them all . . . only there was no time to enjoy it."

There are occasional anachronisms. For example, Robin Stone talks of his occupational "bag" in 1960. A particularly irritating expression the writer keeps using is "in the kip," for "in the sack." Has *anyone* ever described anyone else as good or bad in the kip? It is likely, though, that these minor quibbles are overlooked by most readers racing through the sudden revelation of a Lesbian affair or rooting for pure January Wayne to keep her virtue in a confrontation with a crude, pawing Roman.

Whatever the similarities in all the novels, the author heatedly denies that she writes to a formula. "If I had a formula, and knew that I wrote women well, I would stick to that, like writers of Gothic novels," she says. To Susann, her work is not so much formula as familiarity. "John O'Hara," she ventures, "wrote about certain types of people. So did Colette. In 'Valley of the Dolls,' for example, I was telling a story that could have fit into Washington or medicine, but I stick to the worlds I know."

Roman à clef? "Oh, well," she shrugs, "they can keep calling it that. It'll only make my books sell, I don't care. When Somerset Maugham wrote a book, everyone would say, 'Oh, God, who is Willie writing about now?' When Flaubert wrote 'Emma Bovary,' 20 women in town said they were Emma. I start writing with a theme in my mind. Then I start asking, what kind of a personality? And because I have a good ear, I unconsciously pick up certain people. But that doesn't mean those people have led that life. Going back to Shakespeare's time, there was a Hamlet, but not such as he wrote it."

Why must everyone who climbs to the peak of Mt. Everest in her books tumble into the Valley of the Dolls? "You don't think Jackie Onassis or Howard Hughes are happy, do you?" Susann asks. "The mesage I've always tried to get across is, we're all trying for the top of Mt. Everest, but, boy, when you're up there, you get rocks thrown at you."

Jacqueline Susann is a surprisingly committed moralist, for all the four-letter words and the sex, grown more graphic since one reviewer twitted her for euphemizing the male sex organ as "Charlie." She uses her latest novel for some mournful jeremiads on the state of American theater and films. Through her square young heroine, she objects to frontal nudity, musicals like "Hair," and "those dreary motorcycle pictures." A fan of Sinatra and Ella Fitzgerald, she recently sighed, "Nineteen sixty-seven was the last year everything was all right."

Paradoxically, her writing displays an unending tolerance toward homosexuality. The young Italian, Sergio, who befriends Robin in "The Love Machine," has done as much as Lance Loud to upgrade the gay image.

The professed influences on her writing are solid enough —Eugene O'Neill, James T. Farrell, Sinclair Lewis, Theodore Dreiser and Nietzsche (the part about it being a sin to have talent and not use it). She respects many contemporary authors at a distance, especially Mailer, Roth, Updike and Mary McCarthy. She realizes that they freeze her out of "literary" circles. "Too many of them want to be Jacqueline Susann and won't admit it," she argues. "They get together in little groups and ask, how does she do it, why does she sell? And then they're all reviewed by their friends. But the only people I don't admire are the people who try to imitate me. And there are so many of them."

Indeed, the sales explosion of "Valley of the Dolls" spawned an entire subindustry of Susannia. For example, several staffers of Newsday wrote "Naked Came the Stranger," a spoof by "Penelope Ashe." Upcoming is "The Greek," by Frenchman Pierre Rey, about a shipping magnate. Bernard Geis "kept hiring others to write Jacqueline Susann books," she complains. She paid him $400,000 to buy her way out of a further two-book commitment. "When a studio has a Marilyn Monroe," she explains, "every other studio is hiring Jayne Mansfield and Mamie Van Doren. But when your *own* studio does the hiring . . . !"

Most of her copiers have proven to have feet of *clef*. "Jackie has imitators, but not rivals," intones Simon & Schuster editor-in-chief Michael Korda. With an air of condescension, most imitators are content to whip up a thin ragout of disguised celebrities and trot them through their seamy sexual paces, taking little time for motivation. Susann is not cynical. She genuinely believes in her mission and her characters, feels so close to them that she will point out to friends a certain table at "21" where Mike Wayne "sat" at a key point in the book. Despite some badly-motivated love entanglements, she at least attempts to explain aberrant behavior in psychologically oriented flashbacks. "No one is born with a black hat," she says. Karla, a reclusive old movie queen in "Once is Not Enough," isn't simply labeled a bisexual. Instead, there is a long account of her spiritless childhood on a rocky Polish farm, in which the first beautiful thing she sees is a nun who initiates her into ballet.

THE Mansfields do not ostentatiously display their connection with the famous. They own neither a yacht nor an out-of-town home. If Jacqueline drops as many names in conversation as she does in her books, it's because most, if not all, of those she lists as friends of the couple have become close to them. "Barbara Walters of course," Jackie muses with pride. "Doris [Day]. Joan Crawford—we like to have lunch upstairs at '21.' Harriet Ames, Walter Annenberg's sister. Sammy Cahn. Our lawyer, Arthur Hershkowitz." After a moment she adds brightly, "*Merv's* a friend."

She cannot account for her success. "If I knew," she asks, "do you think I'd be worried about my next book? First of all I'd get a Jackie Doll to send on the road, and I'd grind one out every year."

The appeal of her books is not hard to explain, actually. It starts with the graphic, grabbing cover designs. Much like a well-designed television series or a mass-appeal movie like "Airport," a Susann novel includes characters attractive to every generation among potential readers. There is the added voyeuristic feeling of sharing ostensible low-down insider gossip about idols. Along with sex for practically everybody, and a little psychoanalysis and medical reporting for those so inclined, she includes violent action of a type more expectable in books by men like Harold Robbins. The latest Susann novel includes a flashback gang-rape of a convent full of Polish nuns by occupying Russian troops, and an up-to-date break-in, knifepoint robbery and fatal fistfight in the Hamptons.

As Bantam Books president Oscar Dystel puts it, "She has an absolute gift for making you turn the page. It's her climactic tempo. You come to a point, and then it explodes, and then it goes on and there is another explosion. There must be six or seven apexes in a book."

Who reads these primal-force novels? "She's primarily a woman's writer," Jay Allen recognizes. "Her readers are the people who love to watch soap operas." Executives at bookstores have told Jacqueline, "Once you get over 100,000 hard-cover books, you are dealing with people who have never bought a book in their lives." Her past novels have gone over 300,000, and "Once is Not Enough" is already halfway there.

By and large, the yearning women who vicariously live in Susann's worlds through her stories are cold to women's liberation. At their most rebellious, therefore, most of the women in Susann's pages greet their subservient, male-manipulated lot in life with a hard-eyed acceptance. In "The Love Machine," a dumpy girl snaps, "I've got an I.Q. of 136, but I'd trade it in for half a brain and a pretty face." Susann women may be the last in modern fiction to go wild over men who call them "toots" and "baby."

Starting a novel with a broad theme in mind and no outline, she pads purposefully into the study at the rear of her airy, 24th-floor condominium apartment on Central Park South. She pulls a swivel chair up to a light blue office model Royal and starts typing. She types with two fingers on the right hand, one finger on the left. The drapes stay closed to ward off distractions, but to little avail: As a gift, Mansfield redecorated the study's walls in pink patent leather, and the drapes are Pucci prints.

She forges ahead for up to 30 pages at a sitting during the first draft. As she goes, she constructs elaborate wall charts indicating the action at a glance. The second draft, on pink paper, may include some of the original yellow pages which "seem to work." The third draft is blue, with scatterings of pink and perhaps yellow. The fourth is green, and the fifth—ah!—mostly white.

When the final pressure is on, she wakes at 9:30 A.M., drinks a stalling cup of coffee and takes Joseph Ian for a walk. Joe is the male poodle successor to Josephine, who died in 1970. The dog's urned ashes hold an honored place in the kitchen. At 11, Jacqueline enters the study and works until 3 P.M. She eats a banana and returns to the typewriter until 6. Irving has been at the Fifth Avenue office of their Sujac Corporation all day, handling the countless details of the Susann business.

He negotiates the American and European contracts with publishers and book clubs. He squabbles over the couple's right to approve foreign book jackets. He huddles with publicists on plans for introductory parties. He chivvies publishers for the latest sales accountings and for bigger promotional budgets. He intuitively approves or disapproves the requests of reporters for interviews with his wife.

Until the last four months of a project, the couple goes out to dinner. Toward the end, Jackie walks alone to a neighborhood restaurant. She works again from 9 P.M. until 1 A.M.

Jacqueline allows neither Mansfield nor her eager publisher of the moment to peek at the book until the fifth draft is done. "It's not out of vanity," she says. "If they're thinking something is in and they say I've got to put it back in, it's too many cooks."

AT last comes publication and a round of high-budget promotion along merchandising lines invented by the brilliant team of Mansfield and Susann. From the day they tossed a celebrity bring-your-own-poodle party to help launch "Josephine," they have steadily advanced the science of teaching stodgy publishers how to sell books. For "Valley of the Dolls," they placed newspaper ads in the entertainment pages, not just the literary pages. Irving conceived the idea of screen-testing book covers so the title will show up well in both color and black-and-white reception when Jackie holds up a copy on talk shows.

Expert performances on the talk shows are all part of the effort. "In the Green Room on the Johnny Carson show a few weeks ago," Jay Allen relates, "Jackie was watching a kinky-haired young actress on the monitor. When she went onstage she turned to the girl and said, 'You remind me so much of January and you'd be great for it.' Suddenly she had the girl on her side—and she immediately switched the focus from this girl to the subject of her book."

Jackie says gratefully, "Irving was one of the hottest producers there was, but when he read 'Valley of the Dolls,' he said, 'It's your turn now.' And he turned down every show and subjugated his career to mine." The well-meshed couple has had unbounded success except when it comes to the motion picture versions of Susann novels. Twentieth Century-Fox picked up "Valley of the Dolls" at the manuscript stage for a bargain $200,000. The lurid picture grossed $28-million. Jackie is still suing Fox for later releasing a tawdry and unrelated sexploitation picture called "Beyond the Valley of the Dolls." Next, she received $1.5-million from Columbia Pictures for "The Love Machine," but the bowdlerized film was a box-office dud. On her latest book, she yearned to write the screenplay. She won neither that right nor any advance payment at all, given the changed economics of the movie industry. But she says she is content with Paramount's deal for a flat 10 per cent of gross earnings.

At least these movies let Jackie keep her hand in at acting. She always makes a cameo appearance playing a newspaper reporter, which is what she always tells newspaper reporters she wouldn't mind being.

Plagued with the image of a hard-shelled, unfeeling commercialist, Jackie has at least one unfailing sentimental spot —animals, of course. She regularly feeds a family of cats who live in the well-clipped hedges at the Beverly Hills Hotel. To help Doris Day at a giant Actors and Others for Animals charity bazaar held on a Burbank studio back lot recently, Jackie donated 750 paperback copies of *"Every Night Josephine!,"* then, despite her shaky health that weekend, sat patiently for hours autographing them for excited spectators who paid $1 apiece for what is still her favorite work.

Jacqueline Susann will soon start writing "Good Night, Sweet Princess," the long-delayed sequel to the Josephine book. After that, she will begin work on "The Comedy Twins," in which the taller member of a vaudeville team falls by the wayside in later life, while the undersized brother two-fists his way to success. One imagines it is a *roman à clef* about Napoleon.

Her writing shows no hint of flagging, but there are signs that she wants to slow her life to a pace nearly reduced enough for the critics to catch up with her. "I used to think I had to hawk a book to make it number one, and I almost died of pneumonia," she said a few weeks ago, comfortably crossing one tanned, white-slacked leg over the other in her hotel living room. "I watched this book come out. When it hit number two I had just got out of the hospital, and I thought I would like it to stay two a long time because it's such a comfortable feeling. You're way up there, but you've got a place to go up to. When you're number one, you have no place to go but down. And it's such a big drop from one to two." ■

August 12, 1973

Books of The Times

By CHARLES POORE

THE great game of politics is played in Allen Drury's "Advise and Consent"* for the ultimate stakes of life and death. This is the best novel about Washington I have ever read. It is set in the future. But every page crackles or murmurs with overtones and undertones of events in our own time.

At the heart of Mr. Drury's story is a Senate battle over a President's nomination for Secretary of State. The man is, in the cant phrase, a controversial figure. And so are all the other leading figures—the Senators, the Ambassadors, the Justice of the Supreme Court, the Vice President, who is, as usual, alternately snubbed and exalted, the dutifully glittering hostesses who stand, predictably, as arbiters of Washingtonian elegance, particularly the elegance of electoral politics, which is so often the triumph of the protocolic over the bucolic.

Once the fight over the nomination is well and fiercely joined, its clamor stirs the world. But since Washington—that center of stately homes of uncertain tenure—considers itself the world, Mr. Drury is able to concentrate his drama there. He misses no gesture of significant action, from the White House to the Capitol, no decibel of significant sound from the droning of a politician's obligatory speech to the sardonic moaning at the Press Club bar.

Chief Demagogue in Action

We have, in this country, an office not named in the Constitution or any statute. It is the office of Chief Demagogue, and it has been filled by some peculiar and dangerous characters down the years. In "Advise and Consent," it is occupied by a venomous charlatan in the Senate who rises to a position of lethal eminence on the tide of a national movement called COMFORT—Committee on Making Further Offers for a Russian Truce. "As for me," he says, "I had rather crawl on my knees to Moscow than die under the atom bomb!"

In this phase of the book you may recall the days just after World War II when howling mass meetings were being told that it was a warmongering crime to get tough with the Bolshies. Then came the rape of Czechoslovakia. And Hungary. And, most recently, Tibet. To mention a few.

Now, in Mr. Drury's story, it seems that the Muscovites are about to establish an armed Kremlin exurbia on the moon. And this country, which has never ceased to be assailed for lack of complacency in being first with the atomic bomb, is assailed in reverse (as it was over the sputniks) for being overcomplacently slow about a moon landing.

The controversial nominee for Secretary of State is known to be inclined to favor patting the Russian tiger. The Senate committee looking into his qualifications is disturbed by that. It is even more disturbed when he tells lies about his past membership in a cell formed by dreary Marxists. Nevertheless, his nomination might have gone through if an idealistic young Senator who was guilty of a faraway moral lapse had not also had the past rise up and confront him fatally.

This is the moment for ultimate command decisions. Neither the tremendous forces commanded by the White House nor the forces commanded by the Senate will yield with any willingness. There are, however, infinitudes of maneuvers open to both—and it is in showing how savagely they are carried out that Mr. Drury, a member of the Washington bureau of The Times, shows us the inner turmoils of Washington with incomparable clarity.

He proves here, if proof is needed, that the novel is the best of all ways to interpret modern life. A dozen books on Washington politics written in what we may indulgently call completely nonfiction form can't match "Advise and Consent" in telling us how our politicians and statesmen—the patricians, you might say, of the servant classes—live and think and work and affect mankind's destiny.

Reality on the Potomac

It has taken me about three weeks, off and on, while other books were occupying my reviewing time, to read "Advise and Consent," and I'm glad I read it so slowly. That way, the lives of the main persons concerned have unfolded page by page—so much so that Washington, an extraordinarily implausible place when I lived there, has at last taken on for me the reality of human life. But the disadvantage of this leisurely system of reading, of course, is that you are able to guess how almost everything in the book is going to come out, so prodigally has Mr. Drury strewn his pages with clues to the future.

Clues to the future of his story, with its lengthy life histories of everyone, its jubilantly frank view of the politician's—and the newspaper man's—modus of vivending along the unquiet Potomac. And also clues to the future of America about which we may, paradoxically, show, with prudence, every concern and no concern. For this country is so great that it survives both those who would save it and those who would destroy it. With or without advice or consent from various quarters.

These are the great abstractions. But Mr. Drury has primarily written a book about human beings. And I don't think anyone who reads it will remember anything in the book longer than the scene where one of the men about to die says good-by to his small, impudent daughter, Pidge.

*ADVISE AND CONSENT. By Allen Drury. 616 pages. Doubleday. $5.75.

March 11, 1959

The Gaudy Career of Jonas Cord Jr.

THE CARPETBAGGERS. By Harold Robbins. 679 pp. New York: Simon & Schuster. $5.95.

By MURRAY SCHUMACH

IT was not quite proper to have printed "The Carpetbaggers" between covers of a book. It should have been inscribed on the walls of a public lavatory. Ostensibly Harold Robbins' long novel is about the men and women in Hollywood, aviation, high finance. Actually it is an excuse for a collection of monotonous episodes about normal and abnormal sex—and violence ranging from simple battery to gruesome varieties of murder. What is intended as grim realism by the man who wrote "The Dream Merchants" and "A Stone for Danny Fisher" becomes boring for the simplest of reason: the author's caricatures, as presented here, are non-human.

The hero of this novel—if the word is permissible in such a book—is Jonas Cord Jr. (Anyone familiar with either the movie or aviation industries will quickly guess the name of the man whose career inspired Mr. Robbins.) Another major character is the expensive Hollywood call girl who becomes a great star and then a Sister of Mercy. Then there is Nevada Smith, an Indian half-breed, who (after committing a few murders and a number of bank robberies) becomes a sort of male nurse for Cord during childhood. Cord later acquires a wife (another more or less inevitable bit of type casting in this kind of novel), who floats in and out of the book between his sexual exploits in coast-to-coast harems.

The author has no problem disposing of characters when he no longer needs them. He just has them die. Sometimes he is content with natural causes—but he prefers death by violence (there is one with a bull whip.) If Mr. Robbins had no more talent than a verbose pulp-writer, it would be of no importance that his book is aimed so low. In the sections in which he avoids the lurid, he writes graphically and touchingly; on these pages, his dialogue is moving and his people have the warmth of life. It does not happen often in "The Carpetbaggers."

Mr. Schumach is Hollywood correspondent for The Times.

June 25, 1961

Criminals At Large

Arthur Hailey's **IN HIGH PLACES (Doubleday, $4.95)** (winner of the 1961 Doubleday Canadian Prize Novel Award) extrapolates the global conflict to a phase in which the Soviet Union, having tucked away India and Japan, is now ready to liberate North America by atomic fission. This is the view of a Canadian Prime Minister named James Howden whose sense of urgency and destiny ("there is no one else; no one else with my own stature, with intellect and foresight to make the great decisions to come.") leads him to plump for an "Act of Union" that would unite Canada and the United States. Howden's reasons are strategic and logistical, and while it won't do to reveal them here, let it be said that they are big, very big. It's still hard to believe in a novel in which a remark like "In my opinion, international tension at this moment is more serious and dangerous than at any time since 1939" stuns an audience of Cabinet ministers.

January 21, 1962

There's a lot more than snow precipitated during the blizzard that descends on Arthur Hailey's **AIRPORT** (Doubleday, $5.95). The General Manager of Lincoln International Airport is about to go pfft with his wife; his brother, a traffic controller, may be preparing to crack up at the worst possible moment; his brother-in-law, a trouble-maker from the pilots' union, is hoping to land a fractured aircraft on a landing strip occupied by a stalled Boeing 707. (While the injured are being given first aid, he meditates on the troubles he has with *his* wife.) A mob of disgruntled homeowners, led by a local pettifogger, is holding a protest meeting over noise abatement. And a truck loaded with airline dinners is contributing to physical fitness by being lost in the storm. Mr. Hailey is a plodding sort of writer, but he has just the talent to suggest the crashing ennui of airport routine, where only a mortal disaster can provide color. ■

April 7, 1968

The Irving Wallace Phenomenon

By MICHAEL LYDON

THE MAN & THE MACHINE—Writer Wallace and his Underwood, his faithful companion since his 13th birthday 39 years ago, in the paneled office of his home in Brentwood, Calif. Together, they earn close to $325 an hour, turning out a string of best sellers (next: "The Seven Minutes," about an obscenity trial, due in September) that have brought him some $4-million in book sales, plus $3-million in movie rights.

"IRVING WALLACE sat musing and quite still in the scarred old wooden swivel chair. His good briar pipe had been cold minutes before he noticed it. When he did, he diverted his attention to a small round tin of tobacco. He lifted off the lid, pushing back the crimped, off-white paper with the stubby fingers on the meaty hands on the surprisingly thin arms that protruded from his bulky frame. He took a pinch of the cured weed which Sir Walter Raleigh had introduced into England in the reign of Elizabeth I and put it in his pipe, lighting it with a paper match he took from a book, closing, according to directions, the cover before striking.

"Through the curling, pungent blue smoke, Wallace looked at his typewriter, the battered gray and black Underwood with its oversized and dented platen. He had had the machine for 39 years; it had been his parents' present on his 13th birthday. He was never Bar Mitzvahed; that typewriter made him a man. It was, he knew, almost half as old as typewriters themselves. He remembered that Henry Mill had been granted a patent by Queen Anne in 1714 to make a writing machine, but that an American, Christopher Latham Sholes, had made the first practical one in 1867. Remington marketed it in 1874, and it was Mark Twain, old Sam Clemens, who wrote the first book on one.

"He had written a book or two on his, Wallace thought, puffing out a small belch of gray smoke. Thirteen, in fact; twelve published, one just finished. How many unpublished and unfinished ones he couldn't remember. Not to count hundreds of magazine articles. Or the plays, short stories, movie and TV scripts; plus outlines, drafts, revisions, letters and research notes. Maybe even a poem or two.

"He could almost see the millions—billions—of letters, numbers, and punctuation marks that had flowed like a vast smudgy river unceasingly from the ungainly machine. Over the years the Underwood had been re-

MICHAEL LYDON is a San Francisco-based freelance writer.

paired countless times to bear the cumulative strain of all those hunt and peck tappety-tap-taps that had been his life work.

"Millions of letters, he thought; millions of dollars, too. Not as many dollars as letters, but enough. Few in all history had made more from writing than he. That tide of letters had been a fertile Nile to Irving Wallace, he reflected. His silver-blue S3 Bentley with the small bars built into the doors, the graciously sprawling house, the framed autographs of Freud, Shelley, Dickens and Gauguin on the walls, not to include the Giacommettis, Bonnards, Matisses and Modiglianis (though nothing flashy); the replica of the Plaza's Oak Bar in his den, the exquisite chairs from the Flea Market and the little enamel snuffboxes, the videotape machine, the maid, the Japanese gardener—all these and more the Underwood's rush of unbroken tappings, each a distinct act of his own will, had bestowed upon him.

"Funny, he mused on, but the Underwood had never said a word. It had suffered him all these years, seen him writhe with indecision, shout with joy, write on steadily, muse for hours as he was doing now. What secrets did it know? 'No one, not even a wife, knows the person deep inside, behind all the defenses,' he murmured. But did the typewriter know, and had its silence in those tappings, spoken? And what had it said? His pipe was again cold and he slowly knocked the ashes into the cut-glass ashtray. . . ."

THE clumsy parody must cease. Irving Wallace, the best-selling author's best-selling author, deserves more than a bad imitation of his own style. Simply as a phenomenon, Wallace and his colossal success demand a certain deference, if not awe.

About 30,000 new books are published in America each year; 3,000 of them are novels. The average novel sells 1,500 to 2,000 copies. If 15,000 copies are sold quickly the book is a best seller. If it sells 25,000 copies the author is a "property" to be feted and cosseted by his publishers. If the author can hit 25,000 twice, do well on the paperback, and sell the book to the movies, he is a "major property."

Wallace makes midgets of these giants. A conservative estimate of the sales of his books in all editions to date is 20 million copies; the true figure is probably closer to 30 million. They are still selling and he is still producing. His first best seller, "The Chapman Report," published in 1960, has sold three million paperback copies in America alone; his second, "The Prize," will eventually catch and probably pass "Chapman."

"The Man," his story about the first Negro President, is his hardback record holder: 105,000 sales. His most recent book, "The Plot," sold 90,000 hardback copies, and 1.5 million paperbacks have already been snatched up by loyal Wallaceites at $1.25 a copy.

IT is safe to say that Walace has earned $4-million from book sales, but that's only half the story; the sale of film rights has brought almost $3-million. "The Chapman Report," starring Efrem Zimbalist Jr. and numerous attractive women, was a box-office bonanza for Warner Bros., and Wallace owns 5 per cent of it. Paul Newman was the hero in M-G-M's "The Prize"; Sammy Davis Jr. heads a group that bought the rights to "The Man" for $250,000; and Indie-Branco Productions paid the same for "The Three Sirens." Fox is now scouting European locations for a finished script of "The Plot," and has already paid Wallace $1.5-million for the rights to that and two other novels, one of which is his just completed book, "The Seven Minutes," and the other still only an idea and notes.

Fox's huge advance against 5 per cent of the gross—a deal inked in 1965, more than three years before the shooting of the first foot of film and based on a half-dozen pages of outlines for the three novels—is just one of Wallace's record-making contracts. Fox was just copying Wallace's precedent-making deal with Simon and Schuster and Pocket Books: another $1.5-million advance

THE MAN, THE PAD, THE CAR—Novelist Irving Wallace at home with his silver-blue S3 Bentley. The car has individualized bars built into the doors. The house has framed autographs of Freud, Shelley, Dickens and Gauguin, as well as a collection of art works by Giacommetti, Bonnard, Matisse and Modigliani. It also has a replica of the Plaza's Oak Bar, a videotape machine, a Japanese gardener and a maid.

HIS first three books—one novel, "The Sins of Philip Fleming," and two non-fiction collections — were mild successes but hadn't freed him from being a Hollywood scriptwriter. In 1959, desperate to be writing books full time, he gambled. Meeting New American Library's Victor Weybright in Beverly Hills, he talked for ten minutes about two proposed books, "Chapman" and "The Twenty-Seventh Wife," the story of Mormon leader Brigham Young's last wife, and asked for a $25,000 advance. Weybright, a paperback pioneer, said yes on the spot. Freedom money in hand, Wallace bid farewell to the studios and started writing. "I lost millions on that deal," he recalls now. 'Chapman' is one of the 85 biggest books ever and I get 3 per cent—one fifth of my present royalty. But it was worth it. It started the whole thing rolling."

Indeed, it did. Eleven years later Wallace is a pre-eminent member of a small group that Richard Schickel in Life called "the big money writers." In these years he has had five consecutive smashes, each one a fat book thick with not-so-graphic sex, intrigue, power politics and personal crises. Baroque contractual complexities, plus the secrecy and puffery of the publishing and movie worlds, make picking the world's richest writer as hard as picking the world's richest man. Paul Nathan, columnist for Publisher's Weekly, guesses that Harold Robbins ("The Carpetbaggers," "The Adventurers"), who just sold "The Inheritors" to Joseph E. Levine's Avco-Embassy Films, may now be ahead of Wallace. Or, he says, James Michener ("Hawaii," "The Source") might top both of them. Ian Fleming was right up there; so is Morris West, so is John O'Hara, and Jacqueline Susann and David Slavitt/Henry Sutton are coming on strong.

The rewards of such élite membership are great, but inclusion has a great if less tangible cost: the unbridled derision of critics who feel themselves members of that more amorphous group, the literary establishment. Reviewers in the high-middle- to low-highbrow range (the highbrows ignore him completely), see Wallace novels as cannibals see missionaries: plump offerings for satisfyingly bloody rendering. Their attacks, which are as integral to the "major novel" ritual as the sales, and which are less reviews than assaults on the money-writer phenomenon, betray a fear and incomprehension of that phenomenon. " i know there're some people terrified of the bomb," wrote Bob Dylan, "but there are other people terrified to be seen carrying a modern screen magazine." He might have said an Irving Wallace novel.

Newsweek said of "The Prize": "For the connoisseur who deliberately seeks out the worst movie of the year or the most tasteless pop song, this novel is full of rewards." Time, which dubbed "Chapman" "melo-traumatic," asked about "The Plot": "Can a book that is obviously destined to be a best seller be all bad? Answer: "Yes." Many reviewers mention Wallace's wealth slurringly, but Herbert Kubly in the Saturday

Review gave clearest vent to the critical fury:

"Ideas are sprung over breakfast Bloody Marys in Hollywood's Beverly Hills Hotel or over Scotch-on-the-rocks in New York's Toots Shor's"—Mr. Kubly's distaste makes a few drinks sound like Babylonian license—"or on a long-distance phone between the two. A publisher makes a deal with a film producer who promises an advertising snow job and a seven-star cinematic production. Among such Hollywood-inspired best sellers are works by . . . Irving Wallace. . . . Such trashy books purveyed as literature with a high price can hardly stimulate long-range buying and reading of fiction."

WALLACE, as the cynical and sybaritic pasha of the potboilers and gloating owner of a secret formula to sap the Western literary tradition for his own enrichment, is a straw man. The real Irving Wallace, who, far from being cynical, possesses a boundlessly optimistic naiveté, suffers (albeit patiently) from the abuse heaped upon his effigy.

Formula? "If I had a formula, I'd be ten times richer than I am today." Hollywood double agent? "They don't know my neuroses about Hollywood. Since I quit movies I've been back to the studios maybe four times, and I have nothing to do with making my novels films." Money-hungry bargainer? "I feel I should be paid for my work, but I let my two agents and my lawyer do the bargaining. I take what they get me." (Paul R. Reynolds is his New York agent handling books; Evarts Ziegler handles movies on the Coast. Both have been with him about 20 years, and both are assisted by Paul Gitlin, a New York literary lawyer.) Writing at poolside in the Southern California sun? "I don't even have a pool!"

"It's partly my fault," he said, typically self-effacing. "When my novels did well, I felt honored. The culture says money is good, so I was proud. I talked about it. 'Wallace is always talking about money'—right away I was tagged. When I complained about the treatment, 'Crying all the way to the bank' was the attitude I got back. I've quit fighting it, quit complaining. Critics make their judgments, readers make theirs I'm glad the readers make theirs for me."

He'd love to be taken seriously in Partisan Review, but he knows all about "the professors." "Professors like to say the hungry writer, like the hungry fighter, is the best.

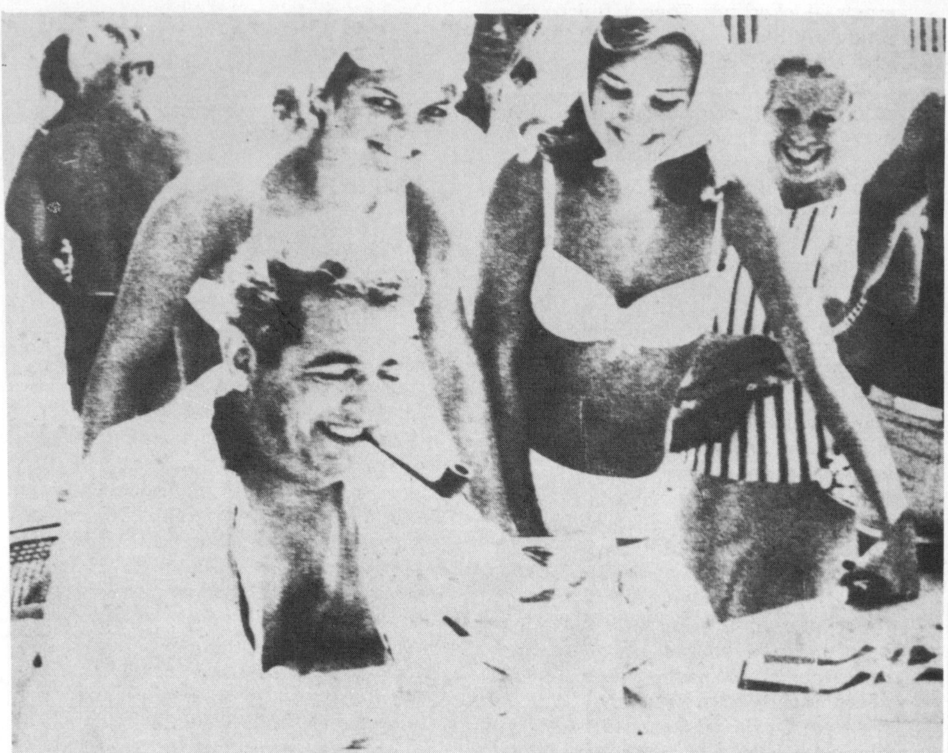

THE CELEBRITY—Wallace autographs the French edition of his novel "The Man" at Juan-les-Pins. His comment on critics: "More of the literati should be interested in what makes three million people read a book."

But hungry writers can be bought. When you're financially free you can write as you please. I'm more independent now than I ever was. I resent the idea that I'm catering; I'm not, unless maybe it's a subconscious desire to please. The critics just won't believe that I write about what interests *me*, and that I write as best as I know how."

Wallace does desire to please, but he does write seriously and the novels are the best he can do. Each one is a lonely labor that starts years before writing with a flashed idea. In voluminous notes built from research done intermittently over a period of months and years he works out characters and outlines plots that look like micro-circuitry. Then comes writing, months of six-day weeks, eight-to-ten-hour days, at the Underwood in his office.

It is all earnest business and, as in any business, records are kept—the paneled office has a whole wall of deep files. An inveterate saver, Wallace has neatly stuffed in them manuscripts, rejection slips, daily journals, research notes, correspondence and just about every piece of paper on which he has ever written anything. Unlike many compulsive savers, Wallace uses his material; he often dips into work he did decades earlier for information he can use now. Included are work records; in "The Writing of One Novel," his latest book, which tells how he wrote "The Prize," he is able to report:

	Working Days	Man Hours
General Research	260	857
Fictional Story Notes	36	288
First Complete Writing	94	752
Rewriting First Draft	84	672
Writing Final Draft	82	328
Checking Copy Editor's Queries	6	54
Legal Revisions	3	14
Correcting Galleys and Page Proofs	17	136
	582	3,101

(Should he make $1-million from the book and film, however, he will have been paid almost $325 an hour.)

He also reveals his daily progress chart. He began writing "The Prize" Oct. 19, 1960, and wrote steadily until Feb. 24, 1961. He wrote the most (33 pages) on the last day, but averaged about ten pages a day. Some days he got nowhere at all.

His life is ruled by the demanding business of writing. "I go in regular cycles. When the writing becomes more real than real life, that's great. Then I can't turn it off. I'm like a monk—locked up. Then I finish, I've produced, made something; no guilts, and I feel good. For a few months I goof off, relax, go to Europe. I stop making schedules for myself every day. Then comes the rough time, months of the niggling feeling that I should be working again. I lose interest in relaxing, but I'm scared of the head-cracking work of getting into the new book. But one day it starts and I'm all excited again."

THE effigy Wallace is disliked, envied and mocked; the hard-working man inspires no such emotions. He is a simple and generous person who wishes no one harm. Without being egocentric, he likes himself and his life. Strikingly handsome when young, at 52 he is still good-looking in a slightly florid, heavy way—though he's heavier than he'd like to be and diets intermittently. He's been married to his charming and delicately pretty wife, Sylvia, for 28 years, and is a proud father of two children: David, a 21-year-old bearded film-maker at San Francisco State College, and Amy, an independent 13-year-old who is already set on being a writer.

Like millions of men in the executive class, he is careful to exercise, taking long walks and runs every morning; he also plays boule and shoots an occasional game of snooker on the battered pool table in his office. A self-dubbed ambivert, half extro-, half intro-, he enjoys his social life of cocktail parties and small dinners with his writer-film executive friends, and has favorite restaurants without being a gourmet.

One of his very few authorial indulgences is collecting bartenders. He knows it's imitation Hemingway, but that's half the fun. "They read all my books, then fight with me about them," he said, "and they're invaluable for research!" Harry Cipriano of Venice's Harry's Bar is a good friend; Harry is sending him ashtrays with "Irving's Bar Brentwood" stamped in where "Harry's Bar Venezia" is on the originals. Wallace is tickled pink.

Little has changed radically since he was a well-paid screenwriter, but not a millionaire. He lives in the same 11-room house in discreetly wealthy Brentwood, west of Beverly Hills, though it has been recently renovated to the height of ivory wall-to-wall hushed elegance. Never a fastidious dresser, he buys a ready-made suit or two every year in one trip to his favorite store. He travels more than he used to, and stays at the best hotels—the Plaza, London's Dorchester, Le Crillon or Le George V in Paris, and the Danieli in Venice, his favorite city — and always in suites, but he has always traveled beyond his means. He'll never be a jet-setter because he's afraid to fly. His passion for things—autographs, objets d'art, and exotic knick knacks—goes back to childhood; he now just has more money and time to acquire them.

Wallace's life is, in fact, all of a piece. Writing is all he has ever done; his earliest memory is drawing stories on wrapping paper in his father's dry-goods store in Kenosha, Wis. His parents, though not well-educated, had brought a respect for writers and literature from Russia, and they encouraged their only son s ambition. Unlike those he calls "New York writers," Wallace never suffered any anti-Semitism in the small town, nor any conflicts about being a kid who devoured library books. He also played football, saxophone in the school band, and was a nationally-ranked high-school debater.

His urge to write, however, was never just the artist's need to express; for Wallace the joy was writing itself. From the first, writing was less a means to the end of expression and more a means of support and an end in itself. At 13 he submitted his first story, about a family trip to Pike's Peak, and shortly thereafter discovered "Writers' Yearbook" in a drugstore. "I was overwhelmed to see that *markets* were listed, and I suddenly realized that this thing I liked to do, I might be able to make a living at it."

HE never looked back. He sold his first article, about race horses and their winnings, to Horse and Jockey for $5 when he was 15; at 17 he sold his first short story. One day, he recalls, he had 50 stories out to magazines and got 12 rejection slips in the mail. He turned a post-graduation trip to Central America, paid for by features done along the way, into his first book, "My Adventure Trail," and before his 18th birthday also wrote a biography of Defoe; neither was published.

Berkeley, California's tiny, unaccredited Williams Institute was his college choice because of its intense writing program, but he quit after two terms to move to Los Angeles and start his career. There, from 1935 until he joined the Army in 1942, he wrote everything: ghost-written stories for celebrities like W. C. Fields (who passed out during the interview), a half-dozen plays (two were commercially produced), short stories and political exposés. They were adventuresome days for a boy barely 20, and he recalls the high points with pride: his 1940 interview with Japan's foreign minister, who talked belligerently of war; the terror of flying through a typhoon into Shanghai; and his and Sylvia's 1941 work honeymoon in Mexico where he met Diego Rivera. He still has Rivera's engraved calling card.

The war was spent writing training and propaganda films for the Army, working with John Huston and Frank Capa. His main effort, "Know Your Enemy Japan," wasn't finished until after the war. Back at freelancing, he was, by 1948, writing for top magazines like The Saturday Evening Post and Reader's Digest, making up to $20,000 a year. "When I was at the top I wanted to quit," he says now and, like many before him, succumbed to the lure of Hollywood. "I was getting $750 an article, working weeks on each one; the studios offered $750 every Friday. So I did it. After working alone so long, I liked the gregariousness, but I hated conference writing and having dumb actors tear my words apart."

BY the mid-fifties his undistinguished movie career (his best-known credit is "The West Point Story," with James Cagney) was a galling burden. Wallace knew he had books to write, books about people and what they were like in their private worlds. Journalism had put limits on his fascination with the action behind the walls of institutional respectability. His love of detail had made him a prodigious researcher; he wanted to use his imagination, which was always asking, "What if . . .?"

His first two efforts, done at night and on weekends, were modest nonfiction collections, one about the real people who inspired famous fictional characters ("The Fabulous Originals," 1955), the other ("The Square Pegs," 1957), capsule stories of well-known eccentrics. Like his life of P. T. Barnum ("The Fabulous Showman," 1959), they were competent and interesting, but still journalistic.

His first (and shortest and best) novel was "The Sins of Philip Fleming" (1959). The story of an unhappily married and professionally stagnated screenwriter who finds himself impotent in his first affair, it had a comfortably small scale and was at times sensitive. Its fatal flaw—in his later novels there are many fatal flaws—was the absurdly happy ending: the hero finally makes love, fixes up his marriage, relates to his son and gets a great idea for a movie, all in 24 hours. Unfortunately, despite its being as or more sexually frank than any of his later works, "Fleming" did not sell, and in 1959 Wallace made the New American Library deal for "The Chapman Report." (Incidentally, Wallace the Sexy Novelist is also a myth. His treatment of sex, surprisingly for a man so literal-minded, is much less graphic than is his discussion of menus or architecture.)

THE rest, as recounted above, is history. "Chapman" in 1960; "The Prize" in 1962; "The Three Sirens" (the least successful of the big five) in 1963; "The Man" in 1964; and "The Plot" in early 1967. "The Seven Minutes," which, from his editors', agents', and Fox's executives' reactions, should also be big business, will be out this September. The uniformity of their titles, their critical and public receptions and their eventual transference onto the screen are mirrored within the novels themselves. What is not true of Agnew slums is true of Wallace novels: read one and you've read 'em all.

Yes, "Chapman" is about a sex survey of the rich young women in the Briars (in fact, Wallace's own Brentwood); "The Prize" is the Nobel Prize; "Sirens" is the adventures of an anthropological team in a South Pacific paradise; the sudden elevation of quiet Senator Douglass Dilman, a Negro, to the Presidency is what made "The Man" "explosive! . . . controversial!"; and "The Plot" is high-level personal and political intrigue around a Paris summit conference.

"The Seven Minutes" will tell of the prosecution of a book for obscenity. Wallace novels, like Cook's tours, take you everywhere (and with such attention to microscopic detail that they could be guidebooks), but always the same way. A bad and boring way it is.

The critics are right about that. Wallace novels are, sadly, atrocious. All depend on mechanical variations of the "Grand Hotel" device: a dramatic event suddenly brings a half-dozen, if not more, diverse and troubled characters together. The characters, most ready-made to standard clichés (the drinking writer, the over-the-hill reporter, the neurotic scientist), or barely changed from real people (the Eisenhowerish ex-President, the Christine Keelerish call girl), submit whatever individuality they do have to the demands of the involute plots.

Each novel's lure is the appeal to voyeurism—Richard Schickel quotes (movie producer Jerry) Wald's Law: "Show the audience the inner workings of something they are curious about, but don't know much about." So each event and setting is real or almost real, and Wallace indulges his love of researched fact until story lines get bogged down by vast gobs of data, much of which is dropped into the characters' casual conversation. "The Prize's" protagonists are prone to page-long discussions of esoteric information about former Nobel laureates, and "The Plot's" Jay Doyle—referring to himself in the third person—is made to muse as follows on why his Kennedy assassination book will be accepted in Europe:

"Yes, the British publishers possessed the historical conditioning to accept his book, just as their European neighbors (whose heritage included the conspiratorial liquidations of Henri IV, King Alexander, Foreign Minister Barthou, Archduke Francis Ferdinand, Chancellor Dolfuss, Trotsky, and whose knowledge included a familiarity with Balkan murder societies like the IMRO and the Black Hand society and the Croatian Ustasa, and political cabals as varied as the Soviet MKVD and KGB and Nazi Gestapo, all their roots going deep into ancient times to the Ides of March) would accept his evidence and book."

Wallace calls his novels "novels of commitment," and each poses and answers, he believes, great moral questions for our times. Can Americans live in a sexual Utopia? Can universal disarmament be achieved? How would the country react to a black President? Is the Nobel Prize sacrosanct or is it, along with all worldly honors, tainted by human baseness?

But just as the ideas grown out of his exposé-voyeurism, however well grounded on "fact," are essentially clichés (i.e., sex surveyors measure love with numbers), his moral affirmations are grounded on nothing more firm than a sort of swinger's Boy Scout code (i.e, true love and its inevitable companion, good sex, can conquer all neuroses). The first three-fourths of every book depict the heroes in the throes of all the lower emotions (though nothing too perverse) which are, in the last fourth, sometimes in the last ten pages, put to rout by Hope and Goodness. Either the exposé stance or the moral stance would make the novels consistent; their combination allows Wallace and the reader to indulge their taste for sneaking suspicions of men and institutions without ever having to follow these suspicions through. The Nobel Prize, concludes "The Prize" after 600-plus pages of scandal, is still A Shining Symbol, even though, heh-heh, *we* know all about it.

With true earnestness Wallace disagrees. On the one hand, he is modest about his writing. "I am no philosopher," he said at one point during three afternoons of talk. "I like to think, but I'm not deep. I'd like to write better, to do more sensory writing, better description. I try to write stylistically, but I'll sacrifice a good sentence for a good paragraph." Yet he also defends himself vigorously. Without pretending to comparison, he sees himself in a long line of novelist-story tellers: Balzac, Dickens, Defoe, Maugham and Romain Rolland. Tolstoy is his favorite writer.

Wallace believes he writes better than Harriet Beecher Stowe or Upton Sinclair, but he admires their strong stands. "They took the world by the neck and shook it. A novel can do that; I hope mine do. My novels have to be about something that is important to me on this earth because writing is my life statement; and they have to be stories because I love stories.

"My son tries to tell me that novels are dying and are irrelevant. I say No! The novel is still part of the scene. Some things have never changed, like avarice and love and lives and emotions. That is what the novel deals with, the great emotions and the issues of the day."

NOVELS are his own favorite reading. He still dips into his childhood favorites—"Of Human Bondage" and "Robinson Crusoe"; Styron, O'Hara, Graham Greene and Arthur Koestler are his contemporary favorites. His nonfiction reading runs to good literary biography and detailed accounts of real crimes. Politically an emotional liberal—he was fervently behind Eugene McCarthy and wore a peace symbol on a thong around his neck long before it was fashionable—he loved the power of Eldridge Cleaver's "Soul on Ice," and the linguistic brilliance of Norman Mailer's "The Armies of the Night" and "Miami and the Siege of Chicago."

Wallace appreciates experimental writing, but has a mild scorn for what he calls "contemplating-their-navel-writers" and for books "that seem like the last 20 pages were left off." He knows the value of Ulysses, "the effort to tell the whole secret jungle of a person's mind," but adds, "There was so much dullness in it. I think young people are hoaxed by the professors and cultists into seeing more than there is in books like that." His talents, which he values, are, he said, "narrative drive, good ideas, good plotting and the ability to present many points of view."

They are talents, and they do raise Wallace's work above the hundreds of books published each year in the same genre that do not sell. The plot does have a kind of cumulative tension that could be called "gripping"; the others create, at minimum, a sluggish hold on one's attention, like that of a long evening of television. And the razzle-dazzle acrobatics of the interplay of characters can be awesome.

Wallace novels also violate no taboos, threaten no one, introduce no shocking ideas, and move at a pace as comfortable as that of a bar car lounger; they are so intrinsically good-hearted that they must deeply satisfy the convinced reader's desire to be right. Each novel's affirmative ending after the journey through scandal brings a self-satisfied feeling of goodness, like finding out after a trip that there's no place like home.

His final defense is his popularity. "I have ideas that interest people. I tell stories and readers are hungry for stories. What a lovely thing it is to sit down for three nights and be carried away by a book! People have such limited lives; they want to be taken to new places, meet new people. I think it's wonderful that I can reach out and touch them. Readers share my interests; they want the imagination of fiction, but they also want things to learn. I am where the action is; my readers look over my shoulder at the action. I don't think there is anything wrong with popularity; I think more of the literati should be interested in what makes three million people read a book. There has to be value in it."

There is, for in one way Wallace is not a writer. A man whose mind has an inbred instinct for the popular, he is a creator of a popular entertainment. Like other such creators and merchandisers of leisure pleasure, he is a businessman, and has a businessman's ethics. "[Writing] was a respectable job to be done," he wrote in the introduction to "The Sunday Gentleman," a 1965 collection of his best magazine work. "It was an accommodation to a mature necessity of life, a way to survive and seek security for one's self and one's dependents. I still remember the legend on a glass paperweight, an insurance company gift that my father used to have on his desk when I was a boy. It read, 'The world owes no man a living.'"

THAT his form of entertainment, made for the public's enjoyment and his livelihood, comes in book form is on one level an unfortunate confusion. His novels should not be judged just with other books, but with bingo, television, professional sports, amusement parks and the movies. There "Do they like it?" is an acceptable if frankly commercial criterion of worth. There is no reason to pick Wallace out of the mass of those who deal in pleasurable if idle fantasies for profit. It is not a matter of conspiracy or travesty that his books become movies; it is as natural an exchange between entertainment media as turning live football into televised football into non-fiction-book football. Wallace made the point directly while discussing paperback books: "Paperback fiction is a big reason for the slimming number of magazines, and I bet it will become an increasing challenge to TV."

But because his creation is in part "literary," Wallace suffers disadvantages that similar titans of entertainment would not stand for. He does not, for one thing, make their kind of money; he is not as rich as Hugh Hefner, Frank Sinatra or the network and movie magnates. Wallace has, it must be remembered, made more for Simon and Schuster and 20th Century-Fox than he has for himself. His earnings, unlike those of a corporation head are, no matter how ingeniously spread, taxed as income. Wallace's income varies, but it is generally in the 60 per cent to 70 per cent bracket. He is, moreover, subject to the fierce rage that critics would never dream of visiting on the owner of a vast and profitable chain of bowling alleys.

Yet, even Wallace books are books and not bowling alleys. Unfortunately for him, the day of the great popular novel is gone; while an excellent novel can be popular from time to time, the Dickenses of today, who, while following public whim, can still avoid debasing their creations, are making movies or rock 'n' roll. Wallace is aware of his uneasy straddling of the fence between attempted art and the entertainment business. In the same introduction quoted above he wrote of his "ambivalent feeling toward my work ... I believed in this responsibility of the writer to his art as much as I believed that he had other responsibilities ..." (i.e., to making a living). But, ultimately, he does call himself an artist, and his uneasy criticism of himself as an artist is more devastating than that of his critics.

AT the end of the long interview he was trying to explain the sudden affirmative ending of his novels. He knew, he said, that single crises well resolved could not change a lifetime of unhappy habits and, yes, his novels consistently portrayed his characters being thus cured. "Well," he said, pacing deliberately, "I do believe that passing a crisis can help, that some people beat their hangups. Look at me. Have I ended up ambiguously? I'm not complacent about myself, but I would not say I have come to 52 with nothing accomplished, with myself in the gray area between black and white."

He paused. "But there *is* more to it than that. You see, I just can't stand to have my important characters end up badly. I've put so much time, so much of myself into them, that I just can't let them go.

"Maybe all my endings are wish-fulfillment. Maybe it's an anti-death thing. If I let the characters be tragic, dead, or without hope, then I'd die, too. I feel sometimes when I'm writing that, well, I always turn my face at the moment of truth. I guess I do that. A friend of mine once told me that I'll only be a critical darling when I write a book that is completely drawn out of myself and ends on a note that doesn't let you know what the hell will happen. Well, I can't write that book to please the critics, but I could to please myself. No, I haven't done it yet."

He took his pipe from his lips and spread his arms wide, a slightly worried look on his face. "Maybe some day I will. I just don't know." ■

March 23, 1969

NEW PUBLICATIONS.

THE ADVENTURES OF TOM SAWYER. By MARK TWAIN. Illustrated. The American Publishing Company. 1876.

Shades of the venerable Mr. Day, of the instructive Mrs. Barbauld, of the persuasive Miss Edgeworth! Had you the power of sitting to-day beside the reviewer's desk, and were called upon to pass judgment on the books written and printed for the boys and girls of to-day, would you not have groaned and moaned over their perusal? If such superlatively good children as Harry and Lucy could have existed, or even such nondescript prigs as Sandford and Merton had abnormal being, this other question presents itself to our mind: "How would these precious children have enjoyed Mark Twain's *Tom Sawyer?*" In all books written for the amusement of children there are two distinct phases of appreciation. What the parent thinks of the book is one thing; what the child thinks of it is another. It is fortunate when both parent and child agree in their conclusions. Such double appreciation may, in most instances, simply be one in regard to the fitness of the book on the part of the parent. A course of reading entirely devoted to juvenile works must be to an adult a tax on time and patience. It is only once in many years that such a charming book as *Little Alice in Wonderland* is produced, which old and young could read with thorough enjoyment. If, thirty years ago, *Tom Sawyer* had been placed in a careful father's hands to read, the probabilities would have been that he would have hesitated before giving the book to his boy—not that Mr. Clemens' book is exceptional in character, or differs in the least, save in its cleverness, from a host of similar books on like topics which are universally read by children to-day. It is the judgment of the book-givers which has undoubtedly undergone a change, while youthful minds, being free from warp, twist, or dogma, have remained ever the same. Returning then to these purely intellectual monstrosities, mostly the pen-and-ink offspring of authors and authoresses who never had any real flesh and blood creations of their own, there can be no doubt that had Sandford or Merton ever for a single moment dipped inside of *Tom Sawyer's* pages, astronomy and physics, with all the musty old farrago of Greek and Latin history, would have been thrown to the dogs. Despite tasseled caps, starched collars, and all the proprieties, these children would have laughed uproariously over *Tom Sawyer's* "cat and the pain-killer," and certain new ideas might have had birth in their brains. Perhaps, had these children actually lived in our times, Sandford might have been a Western steam-boat captain, or Merton a fillibuster. *Tom Sawyer* is likely to inculcate the idea that there are certain lofty aspirations which Plutarch never ascribed to his more prosaic heroes. Books for children in former bygone periods were mostly constructed in one monotonous key. A child was supposed to be a vessel which was to be constantly filled up. Facts and morals had to be taken like bitter draughts or acrid pills. In order that they should be absorbed like medicines it was perhaps a kindly thinker who disguised these facts and morals. The real education swallowed in those doses by the children we are inclined to think was in small proportion to the quantity administered. Was it not good old Peter Parley who in this country first broke loose from conventional trammels, and made American children truly happy? We have certainly gone far beyond Mr. Goodrich's manner. There has come an amount of ugly realism into children's story-books, the advantages of which we are very much in doubt about. We draw our pictures, utterly indifferent as to the subjects. Now, it is perfectly true that many boys do not adopt drawing-room manners. Perhaps it is better that little paragons—pocket Crichtons—are so rare. Still, courage, frankness, truthfulness, and self-reliance are to be inculcated in our lads. Since association is everything, it is not desirable that in real life we should familiarize our children with those of their age who are lawless or dare-devils. Granting that the natural is the true, and the true is the best, and that we may describe things as they are for adult readers, it is proper that we should discriminate a great deal more as to the choice of subjects in books intended for children. To-day a majority of the heroes in such books have longings to be pirates, want to run away with vessels, and millions of our American boys read and delight in such stories. In olden times the *Pirate's Own Book* with its death's-head and cross-bones on the back, had no concealment about it. It is true, edition after edition was sold. There it was. You saw it palpably. There was no disguise about it. If a father or mother objected to their child's reading the *Pirate's Own Book*, a pair of tongs and a convenient fireplace ended the whole matter. To-day the trouble is this: That there is a decidedly sanguinary tendency in juvenile books. No matter how innocent, quiet, or tame may be the title of a child's book, there is no guarantee that the volume your curly-headed little boy may be devouring may not contain a series of adventures recalling Capt. Kidd's horrors. In the short preface of *Tom Sawyer*, Mr. Clemens writes, "Although my book is intended mainly for the entertainment of boys and girls, I hope it will not be shunned by men and women on that account." We have before expressed the idea that a truly clever child's book is one in which both the man and the boy can find pleasure. No child's book can be perfectly acceptable otherwise. Is *Tom Sawyer* amusing? It is incomparably so. It is the story of a Western boy, born and bred on the banks of one of the big rivers, and there is exactly that wild village life which has schooled many a man to self-reliance and energy. Mr. Clemens has a remarkable memory for those peculiarities of American boy-talk which the grown man may have forgotten, but which return to him not unpleasantly when once the proper key is sounded. There is one scene of a quarrel, with a dialogue, between Tom and a city boy which is perfect of its kind. Certain chapters in Tom's life, where his love for the school-girls is told, make us believe that for an urchin who had just lost his milk-teeth the affections out West have an awakening even earlier than in Oriental climes. In fact, Tom is a preternaturally precocious urchin. One admirable character in the book, and touched with the hand of a master, is that of Huckleberry Finn. There is a reality about this boy which is striking. An honest old aunt, who adores her scapegrace nephew, is a homely picture worked with exceeding grace. Mr. Clemens must have had just such a lovable old aunt. An ugly murder in the book, overminutely described and too fully illustrated, which Tom and Huck. see, of course, in a graveyard, leads, somehow or other, to the discovery of a cave, in which treasures are concealed, and to which Tom and Huck. fall heirs. There is no cant about Mr. Clemens. A description of a Sunday-school in *Tom Sawyer* is true to the letter. Matters are not told as they are fancied to be, but as they actually are. Mr. Walters is the Superintendent of the village Sunday-school, and this is Mr. Clemens' idea about him and his actions:

"When a Sunday-school Superintendent makes his customary speech, a hymn-book in the hand is as necessary as the inevitable sheet of music in the hands of a singer, who stands forward on the platform and sings a solo at a concert, though why is a mystery, for neither the hymn nor the sheet of music is ever referred to by the sufferer. This Superintendent was a slim creature of 35, with a sandy goatee, and short, sandy hair; he wore a stiff standing collar, whose upper edge almost reached his ears, and whose sharp points curved forward abreast the corners of his mouth—a fence that compelled a straight look out ahead, and a turning of the whole body when a side view was required; his chin was propped on his spreading cravat, which was as broad and as long as a bank-note, and had fringed ends; his boots were turned sharply up, in the fashion of the day, like sleigh-runners—an effect patiently and laboriously produced by the young men by sitting with their toes pressed against a wall for hours together. Mr. Walters was very earnest of mien and very sincere and earnest at heart, and held sacred things and places in such reverence and so separated them from wordly matters that unconsciously to himself his Sunday-school voice had acquired a peculiar intonation which was wholly absent on week days."

Have any readers ever seen a Sunday-school "show off"? If they have, it was done exactly as Mr. Clemens tells it:

"Mr. Walters fell to 'showing off,' with all sorts of official bristlings and activities, giving orders, delivering judgments, discharging directions here, there, everywhere that he could find a target. The librarian 'showed off,' running hither and thither with his arms full of books, and making a deal of the splutter and fuss that insect authority delights in. The young lady teachers 'showed off,' bending sweetly over pupils that were lately being boxed, lifting pretty, warning fingers, at bad little boys, and patting good ones lovingly. The young gentlemen teachers 'showed off,' with small scoldings and other little displays of authority, and fine attention to discipline—and most of the teachers, of both sexes, found business up at the library, by the pulpit; and it was business that frequently was to be done over again, two or three times, (with much seeming vexation.) The little girls 'showed off' in various ways, and the little boys 'showed off' with such diligence that the air was thick with paper wads and the murmur of scufflings; and, above it all the great man sat, and beamed a majestic judicial smile upon all the house, and warmed himself in the sun of his own grandeur—for he was 'showing off' too."

Tom, like all boys, gets good and bad by fits and starts, and becomes a member of the order of the Cadets of Temperance, "being attracted by the showy character of their regalia." Tom swears to abstain from smoking, chewing, and profanity, in order to wear the uniform of the Cadets of Temperance on the occasion of the expected death of a rural Judge, when the regalia is to be sported at his funeral. But as the Judge don't die soon enough, Tom, disgusted with waiting, throws off his regalia and relapses again.

"He handed in his resignation at once, and that night the Judge suffered a relapse and died. Tom resolved that he would never trust a man like that again. The funeral was a fine thing. The cadets paraded in a style calculated to kill the late member with envy. Tom was a free boy again, however; there was something in that. He could drink and swear now, but found, to his surprise, that he did not want to. The simple fact that he could, took the desire away and the charm of it."

If Mr. Clemens has been wanting in continuity in his longer sketches, and that sustained inventive power necessary in dovetailing incidents, *Tom*, as a story, though slightly disjointed, has this defect less apparent. As a humorist, Mr. Clemens has a great deal of fun in him, of the true American kind, which crops out all over the book. Mr. Clemens has an audience both here and in England, and doubtless his friends across the water will re-echo the hearty laughs which the reading of *Tom Sawyer* will cause on this side of the world. We are rather inclined to treat books intended for boys and girls, written by men of accredited talent and reputation, in a serious manner. Early impressions are the lasting ones. It is exactly such a clever book as *Tom Sawyer* which is sure to leave its stamp on younger minds. We like, then, the true boyish fun of Tom and Huck., and have a foible for the mischief these children engage in. We have not the least objection that rough boys be the heroes of a story-book. Restless spirits of energy only require judicious training in order to bring them into proper use. "If your son wants to be a pirate," says Mr. Emerson somewhere, "send him to sea. The boy may make a good sailor, a mate, maybe a Captain." Without advocating the utter suppression of that wild disposition which is natural in many a fine lad, we think our American boys require no extra promptings. Both East and West our little people are getting to be men and women before their time. In the books to be placed, then, into children's hands for purposes of recreation, we have a preference for those of a milder type than *Tom Sawyer*. Excitements derived from reading should be administered with a certain degree of circumspection. A sprinkling of salt in mental food is both natural and wholesome; any cravings for the contents of the castors, the cayenne and the mustard, by children, should not be gratified. With less, then, of Injun Joe and "revenge," and "slitting women's ears," and the shadow of the gallows, which throws an unnecessarily sinister tinge over the story, (if the book really is intended for boys and girls,) we should have liked *Tom Sawyer* better.

January 13, 1877

Mark Twain on "Huck Finn."

It will be recalled that not long ago the Omaha public library barred out Mark Twain's "Huckleberry Finn" on the ground that its influence upon the youthful mind was pernicious. The Omaha World-Herald sent him a telegram, which called forth the following characteristic letter:

York Beach, Me., Aug. 23.—Dear Sir: Your telegram has arrived, but as I have already said all I want to say concerning Huck Finn's new adventures, there is no need to say it over again. I am making this remark by mail instead of telegram in order to secure speed; your courtesy requires this promptness of me. Lately it has twice taken a telegraphic dispatch four hours and a quarter to reach me here from Boston, a distance of forty or fifty miles; therefore, if I should answer you by that vehicle I estimate that it would be upward of eight days on the wire, whereas I can get it to you by mail in two.

I am tearfully afraid this noise is doing much harm. It has started a number of hitherto spotless people to reading Huck Finn, out of a natural human curiosity to learn what this is all about—people who had not heard of him before; people whose morals will go to wreck and ruin now.

The publishers are glad, but it makes me want to borrow a handkerchief and cry. I should be sorry to think it was the publishers themselves that got up this entire little flutter to enable them to unload a book that was taking too much room in their cellars, but you never can tell what a publisher will do. I have been one myself.

MARK TWAIN.

September 6, 1902

LAD

LAD: A DOG. By Albert Payson Terhune. With frontispiece. New York: E. P. Dutton & Co.

LAD is no imaginary creation, but the portrait of a real dog, the wisest, bravest, most faithful and most lovable of collies. It is to his memory that this book which relates fragments of his biography is dedicated, and having read it, no one will wonder that when at last he died "a heart-sick gloom hung over The Place"—the home he had guarded so loyally and so well. Told in the form of short stories, these adventures of his at dog shows and in encounters with thieves and various other more or less objectionable persons will surely appeal not only to all lovers and masters of dogs, but to many who have never owned any and who have no general and indiscriminate liking for them.

They are, moreover, interesting stories in themselves. The rivalry between dignified Lad and the more showy Knave for the affections of dainty, temperamental, white and gold Lady is both comic and pathetic; and who can read without something of a choke the tale called "Quiet," which tells how, when his adored "Mistress," the human goddess he devoutly worshipped, was desperately ill, Lad lay outside her door, never barking, perfectly silent, but obstinately refusing to go away, or fail to sympathize with him when, after the danger was over and he had felt her dear hand on his head once more he went wild with delight and indulged in a perfect orgy of puppet-like mischief—who was usually of a benign dignity! The book contains twelve stories, and Lad is the hero of all but one of them. This single exception, "Wolf," tells of the son of Lad and Lady. Although of course a collie of the very bluest of blue blood, he was physically a "throwback to some forgotten ancestor whose points were all defective." There seemed no hope whatever that Wolf would ever add to the string of cups and of ribbons which were among the cherished trophies of "The Place"; yet the time came when he won a very special cup all his own.

No one who has ever watched a working collie control a flock of sheep will have any doubts as to the general intelligence of the breed, but few are as wise and dear as Lad, who was indeed what his master called him—"a super-dog." These chronicles of his life, from its early gayeties to that "Day of Battle" when he, an old dog, was treacherously attacked by two young ones, and bravely and desperately fought for the life he so nearly lost, are a most welcome addition to dog-literature. They are delightfully written; so much better done indeed than any other of Mr. Terhune's work which has ever come to our attention that comparison is quite out of the question. To read the book is to find a new and dear friend in "Lad: A Dog."

August 10, 1919

REBECCA OF SUNNYBROOK

How Kate Douglas Wiggin Was Induced to Turn Her Enormously Popular Books Into a Play

ONCE AN AMATEUR ACTRESS

Her First Effort a Child's Story Written for St. Nicholas

By EMILY M. BURBANK

THE coming to New York of "Rebecca," after a season of great success in Boston and throughout New England, brings to mind many interesting facts relative to the play and its maker, Kate Douglas Wiggin.

To begin with, it was no longer ago than the Spring of 1908 that Mrs. Wiggin first submitted "Rebecca" to Messrs. Klaw & Erlanger, and received from them, in due course, several friendly and facetious responses, which ran much as follows: "Several of us have read 'Rebecca,' your play, and we don't really know whether it is a play or only a delightful evening's entertainment. We don't know how much or how little money there may be in it, but there is something fascinating about it; it's too good to let go by, and so we accept it."

The following summer and autumn, managers and playwrights bent their best efforts to the selecting of a cast, and early in the winter of 1909, "Rebecca" was put in rehearsal—that is to say, was laid on the table of that uncompromising clinic, Managerial Dissection.

The playwright's own description of this ordeal is most amusing. And it is of interest, too, as coming from one who has won many laurels in another literary field, is the recipient of the degree of Doctor of Letters, and is much in demand as a platform lecturer and responder to after-dinner toasts on both sides of the Atlantic. "I discovered at once that playwrights are of no importance whatever when it comes to rehearsals; they are merely necessary evils! Why, they cut out—very courteously, I confess—my most cherished scene of pathos, and clamored for 'fourteen laughs' in its place—or something to that effect!" she added, with a quick glance of

merriment directed toward her listeners. "It would make a better story if the change had not improved the play; but that I am sure was only an accident!"

Here, however, as well as at every crisis in her career, Mrs. Wiggin's native cleverness and adaptability served her well; for with her, it amounts to a positive gift, the ability to seize and assimilate the other person's point of view, while gently but relentlessly imposing her own convictions upon her associates. In an incredibly short time she had acquired that extra "sense" which enables the playwright to project himself across the footlights and into the dollar seats, while deftly taking the pulse of the box-office! Feats, both of them, believe me, performed by Ibsen, Rostand and William Shakespeare! It must be done, or theatres close.

The ultimate outcome of an amicable compromise, always within the limits of art, was the "Rebecca" play, as produced for the first time in Springfield, Mass., on November 15, 1909; a monument to a great intelligence, willing to adapt its art instincts and creative impulse, trained in one school to a superior knowledge of stage-craft gained in quite another.

This adjusting of a play after it is put in rehearsal is, of course, customary. The late Clyde Fitch—most successful of American playwrights—virtually rewrote his plays in rehearsal, elaborating some parts and curtailing others, according to the abilities and requirements of the actors cast for them. One could almost state that a play not rehearsed by Clyde Fitch was a play not written by him, so necessary was it for him to see his work in action, before developing and completing it.

Kate Douglas Wiggin's personality and her work are amazingly alike, and must be the despair of her biographers, who, armed with butterfly-net and sensitive plate, pursue her darting, flashing, vibrant spirit, forgetting, however, in the breathless chase to do more than admire, until lo, she is gone! And yet, as with all shimmering, gossamer expressions of nature, the virtue and power of this author and her work lie in just this subtle evasiveness, this persistent, darting flash, this gentle afterglow of fading mauve and gold.

It may be said of "Rebecca" and her author that they are not gay, nor sad, pathetic, dramatic, witty, nor wise, but all these—and more!

The play, like the books, is what the casual observer would describe as "simply a photograph of life in an old New England village," and it is quite true that we have all seen, and some of us known, folk like Rebecca's Mr. Simpson, Uncle Jerry, Miss Miranda, and Miss Jane. (These two always live together; it is necessary in order to produce the types.) But how much art is required to write out and then to stage such naive types few can realize. In its line "Rebecca" is a masterpiece. Though their setting is flowering uplands and meadows of sweet-mown hay, patches of phlox and borders of myrtle, it will be found that Mrs. Wiggin's New England characters have as poignant problems, as ardent loves and hates, as animate a fevered city. From beginning to end, and without one note of exaggeration, she has kept the whole play quivering with life; touching the imagination, kindling enthusiasm; breaking the heart with pathos, and mending it with mirth; until, long before the curtain falls on the happy ending, the characters and their story have become a part of our very being. To accomplish this, to master her medium, as Mrs. Wiggin has, allowing the thought to lift its voice clear and firm above the words, is to be an artist.

Apropos of the difference between written and spoken language, I recall something which Mark Twain said. It was in Vienna, and he was preparing to give a "reading" from his own works, in English. "Preparing," he emphasized this: "for I, nor no one else, can successsfully speak anything written for print. I have to change my written sentences into spoken sentences; altogether a different art." This from so "natural" a writer as Mark Twain!

To return to "Rebecca": it is now eleven years that she has been known in book form, to a large and enthusiastic public; her fame has crossed the Atlantic, and soon she is to be translated into French. But in all this vast number of "Rebecca" enthusiasts, not one has loved the merry, pathetic, adorable child, who grows into fair womanhood, and meets her Prince Charming, nor pities the poor Simpsons, "always a-movin' on," more than does the author of their being.

A cherished memory is that of Mrs. Wiggin reading from manuscript, as soon as the ink was dry, one of the "New Chronicles of Rebecca." It was in August, 1907, and the author was entertaining a house party at Quillcote-on-Saco, her Maine home, where, in a large and beautiful house, more than a hundred years old, (furnished in the period of its prime, and shaded by stately elms), she passes a part of each Summer, writing and welcoming her friends. Mrs. Wiggin always prefers to do her writing in the country, and one has but to see Quillcote to know that its mistress and nature are on the very best of terms; that is to say, each knows—and keeps—her place! The fields and all green growing things, are allowed to advance intimately to the doorstep; the author knowing from long experience that they will never intrude upon her their ingratiating personalities, nor the details of their daily lives.

At Quillcote work and play alternate serenely to an obligato furnished by the Saco's rapids, whose pulsing energy has cut a deep bed for the river, forming a picturesque gorge some miles in length. There was a time when the study was the shade of an apple tree, but now a great desk, always in commission, stands in the paneled window niche of a low-studded room on the ground floor of a wing, to the right of the front door. It was not there, however, that we gathered to hear certain chapters from "Rebecca," but in the barn—and such a barn! It had been recently cleared and smoothly floored for village dances, and great, sturdy benches of old, weathered timber, placed against the walls. From the rafters hung huge wrought-iron lanterns for lighting at night, and on the small stage, occupying the space opposite the large double doors, a piano had been placed, at which Mrs. Wiggin has composed some of her charming songs. That afternoon the doors were thrown wide open, showing a lovely view of sunny, fragrant meadow, rolling, crescendowise, to the cool rim of a neighboring wood—Nature's drop-curtain! There, in Rebecca's own country, author and friends laughed and wept together over our heroine's finding a wedding ring for Mrs. Simpson, who, unlike all the other Riverboro ladies, had never had any!

Judging from her own statements, made from time to time, I should say that Mrs. Wiggin's stories grew quite naturally when the central idea has once taken definite shape. In the case of "Rebecca," the other characters were sketched in as the entourage of her vivid little personality. Later the possibilities of each type seized the imagination of the author and were developed afterward into the constellation of stars that furnish the "New Chronicles of Rebecca." This is why the play calls for an "all-star" cast; each character is "important," every line is, in all truth, "worth hearing"; there is no "padding," because there is literally no room for it.

Should you ask, "Did it all really happen in Maine?" I would answer, "It might have." I once put a similar question to Mrs. Wiggin concerning her "Tom o' the Blueberry Plains" in the village watch-tower collection. Her answer was, "Yes, there was a little witless lad who mended chairs and—that's his hut you see in the pasture off there," (we were driving at the time); "I used him as my theme, and then elaborated it."

It was in the same Summer (1907) that Mrs. Wiggin told us of Miss Charlotte Thompson's suggesting that there was a play in her "Rebecca" books. "I cannot see it myself," I remember her saying at the time, and it was rather under protest that she agreed to try it in collaboration. As Miss Thompson had had extensive experience in the dramatizing of books, it was her part to block out the play, arranging acts and scenes in accordance with the established rules of play building. Mrs. Wiggin's part was the actual writing of the play, for Rebecca, the play, was written as such; it is not merely the two books dramatized. By condensing the story and adapting it to the stage Mrs. Wiggin has emphasized its comedy and tragedy and brought into relief, as stated earlier, a rustic idyll—as notable a contribution to national drama as is Smetana's "Bartered Bride," Charpentier's "Louise," or "The Old Homestead." In point of strength "Rebecca" the play is much superior to "Rebecca" the book.

The desire to write a play had long possessed Mrs. Wiggin. It was merely the idea that there was a play in the "Rebecca" books that surprised her. Once mistress of the outline, she worked with ease and inspiration, aided by her natural love of the drama, long familiarity with it as a keen observer and sympathetic friend of actors and playwrights, and some practical experience gained as an amateur actress, when a younger woman. In fact, no less an actor-manager than Dion Boucicault, seeing her play in San Francisco, where she was then living, made her flattering offers to go on the professional stage. But it was as creator, not as interpreter, that Kate Douglas Wiggin was to charm, and in so doing help the world. And if motherhood in the ordinary sense of the term has been denied her, surely no one has given birth to more original, more bewitching, children of the brain and the heart than hers.

Mrs. Wiggin's knowledge of and practical experience with little children was gained when, as a young woman, she taught in a California kindergarten. She was in the habit of returning to the East to study during vacations, and on one of these occasions the school funds were at a very low ebb, and to reimburse them Mrs. Wiggin, then Miss Kate Douglas Smith, wrote "The Birds' Christmas Carol" and "The Story of Patsy." The first edition of each was sold at the kindergarten and had a great success. Later on Mrs. Wiggin, then a widow, happened to be in New York, when some one suggested her offering the printed stories to a regular publisher. Houghton Mifflin & Co. chanced to be the house selected, and they have published her books ever since.

Her literary debut, however, antedates "Patsy" and "The Ruggleses," even the kindergarten incident, and when described by the author, is unforgettable.

It seems that her stepfather died, leaving a considerable amount of property. "But," as Mrs. Wiggin exclaims, "the town grew in the wrong and the unexpected direction. The property vanished and we needed money for the butcher and baker, so I decided to write a story for children and try St. Nicholas. I sent it off, and after a reasonable length of time began to watch mails from the East; my family watching them, too, which was much more nerve wracking! Finally my daily trip to the Post Office was rewarded. I was handed a letter bearing the stamp of the St. Nicholas editorial rooms. I opened it, my heart beating so that I could scarcely see or hear. There was the check; my story had been accepted! That was enough, and I flew home, delirious with the fever of first authorship. But the sight of home calmed me somewhat and reminded me that the family would be interested in the amount of the check. I could not remember quite, in my agitation, but it had looked like a dollar and a half. That was modest, but I did not seem to care much; for you see I was an author! However, I stopped and took it out of the envelope again, when—only fancy!—it was for a hundred and fifty dollars! And then I did a very human thing; I crumpled the check back into the envelope, with the formal letter of acceptance, smoothed the smiles out of my face, and entered the house. My mother spoke first: 'Of course, you didn't hear from St. Nicholas!' Then my sister: 'If you did, of course they didn't pay you anthing!' Their patience was losing its sweetness. 'Guess how much?' I asked, holding the letter up triumphantly. They guessed incredulously up to fifty dollars. But I kept on saying, 'Still more.' My sister burst in with the exclamation: 'We ought not to pay a single vulgar, sordid bill; we ought to use the money to raise a monument to Kate in the back yard!'"

That was the beginning, and to-day Kate Douglas Wiggin can claim an audience of half a million, and is translated into six languages.

Since in "Rebecca" the tides and undercurrents of human emotions of old and young are those that are common to all mankind, there would seem to be every probability of its invading not only England, but France and Germany, as Mr. Fitch's plays have done. We know that Mark Twain's humor and wisdom in dialect have made all the world laugh, and Mr. Dunne once told the writer of this article that "Mr. Dooley" had been translated into Russian. Hence, the translating of "Rebecca" for a foreign stage would seem easy, and those of us who have seen Rebecca alight from the stage on her arrival from Sunnybrook Farm, and lived with her in the quaint old village day by day, till Prince Charming wooed and won her, refuse to believe that any tongue, known or unknown, could even veil her charms.

Knowing Mrs. Wiggin's unusual conversational powers, and her brilliant repartee, which give her pre-eminence at any festal board she graces, it is always surprising to hear her assert that she can never think except through the medium of a pen or pencil. With truth she might add that, granted the pen or pencil, she cannot help thinking in literary form, as the following stories prove.

It was in 1898. We happened to be in London at the same time, and had arranged to meet for luncheon or tea. Mrs. Wiggin was leaving town the next day with her sister, and some one asked, "Where do you go?" "To a chicken farm down in Kent," she answered. "I am off for a rest, and I am telling no one my address, for the London season has quite worn me out." Did she rest? In her way, she did, no doubt, but on emerging from that chicken farm, after a short stay, she confessed to the completed manuscript of a new story, "The Diary of a Goose-Girl," for which a magazine paid her a thousand dollars down, and the book royalties from it are still coming in.

Again, when the round of social duties in New York had exhausted her, Mrs. Wiggin went to a sanitarium for a rest cure. All work was forbidden, and this in her case would seem to mean writing, of course. But soon a fever set in which baffled her doctors till the patient confessed in the following manner: "Doctor, which would you prefer, to have me write a little, or allow the last chapters of 'Rebecca of Sunnybrook Farm' to remain coiled up in my brain in their present highly inflamed condition?" "Write it out at once, Madam; by all means get rid of it!" said her greatly relieved physician.

To gratify some of the playwrights, New York friends and admirers who had expressed regret that "Rebecca" was not to be given in their city until its second season, Mrs. Wiggin planned a theatre party last May for a matinée performance during its week in Bridgeport, Conn. Twenty-five of us made the trip from New York in a private car, were entertained at luncheon by our hostess, and guided by her to the theatre. At 2 o'clock not a seat was empty, and a tremor of unusual excitement agitated the house, for news had gone out that the author of "Rebecca of Sunnybrook Farm," the "Penelope" books, "Timothy's Quest," "The Old Peabody Pew," "The Birds' Christmas Carol," and all the other enchanting stories, was to be present. There were some who immediately recognized the features, the winsome smile, and youthful and modish appearance of the author; and these directed the attention of the audience to her box, where, in response to insistent applause, she rose after the third act and made a graceful speech. As she resumed her seat hundreds of handkerchiefs, large and small, fluttered like birds on the wing—"carriers," in fact, of delighted recognition, grateful joy and salutation!

October 22, 1910

Elsie, and Other Fragile Heroines

By G. B. STERN

LONDON.

MOST of us, when we have formally declared our favorite reading to be Shakespeare, Montaigne's Essays, Gibbon's "Decline and Fall," and James Joyce's "Ulysses," will own, perhaps, to a feebler self which cherishes—and conceals—some low yearning for a form of literature which alone can satisfy certain more private moods; for shockers, let us say, or for detective yarns, or incredible sagas of cowboys and sheriffs in the Wild West. It may be that your affections are for that cheap line of cretonne-window-curtain story, of earnest young husband and pretty young wife, and a rose-pink silk jumper which the young husband cannot afford to buy for the young wife. And there are tales of passion in some throbbing and wholly fanciful tropic that is not of Capricorn nor yet of Cancer. * * *

My own special freak in taste is for the style of juvenile story-book given by our grandmothers and our great-aunts to our parents when at a tender age. These specimens of high ethics and bad prose have a fascination for me that may be morbid, but which, nevertheless, I have made no attempt to conquer. Many of the choicest and the most exaggerated come from America—the whole "Elsie" Series, in fact; thirty-two of them. And "Queechy"; and "The Wide Wide World." Over here we can produce in competition the works of Mrs. Sherwood and Miss Edgeworth, Grace Aguilar and Emma Marshall and Dean Farrar, and the unknown author of "Anna Lee, the Maiden, the Wife and the Mother"—which, with really noble self-control, I did not steal from the dusty ground behind the bookshelf of the parlor of the old sawmill, where I found it.

Let me quote you a sample taken at random from "Mildred and Elsie"—which is, roughly, about the eleventh of the "Elsie" books—that you may roll it upon your tongue and get the true luscious flavor of it. Elsie is now 8 years old. ("Christmas With Granma Elsie" is about seventeen books on, and she is still going strong!)

Listen to Elsie and her father, about to pay a visit to some cousins:

"Please tell me, papa, * * * are Cousin Milly's father and mother my uncle and aunt?"

"You may say Uncle Stuart and Aunt Marcia to them, though they are really your cousins. Well, what is it?" seeing a doubtful, troubled look in the eyes lifted to his.

"Please, papa, don't be vexed with me," she murmured, dropping her eyes and blushing deeply, "but would it—be quite—quite true and right to call them so when they are not really?"

He drew her closer and, softly kissing the glowing cheek, "I should prefer to have you call them aunt and uncle," he said, "and I cannot see anything wrong or untrue in doing so; but if it is a question of conscience with you, my darling, I shall not insist."

"Thank you, dear papa," she said, looking up gratefully and drawing a long sigh of relief; "but I want to do as you wish. Please tell me why you do not think it wrong."

"They may adopt you as their niece, you them as your uncle and aunt," he answered, smiling down at the grave, earnest little face.

"What a nice idea, papa!" she exclaimed with a low, musical laugh, her face growing bright and glad; "that makes it all right, I think."

Such ethical discussions occur frequently in all these books. If you share my singular twist of mind, you will gradually find them passionately, absorbingly interesting; more so, indeed, than that more modern but very similar fashion of introspective psychology in fiction which hails from Russia. * * * I should like to put up Elsie Dinsmore against a Dostoievsky hero in an argument. Is the difference in their textures as great as our scornful intellectuals would probably like to make out? I trow not. But Elsie is the sounder on her basic principles, and would win.

Indeed, the children of these special realms of story are nearly always heavy with religion; the pages of their little worn Bibles are "well thumbed," and their powers of extensive quotation from the well-thumbed pages must have been most disconcerting to the more worldly of their elders, who possibly regretted, now and then, having raised these small Frankensteins, these implacable critics of every hairbreadth swerve from what they considered "right." "Victoria," by the same author as the celebrated "Fairchild Family," tells of the terrific conflict between a nine-year-old, who decided, on certain points of theological dogman, that she would discard the Protestant for the Roman Catholic Church, and her outraged parents, grandparents, aunts and uncles, in-laws and visiting ministers. The bratling won, * * * but she had the luck bestowed upon all such bratlings, of calling down upon herself a severe illness, exactly when most required; the sort of illness that makes you flushed but not spotty, frail but not skinny, breathing with difficulty but not through the nose. Elsie Dinsmore was able to function in the same way, after more than a year's colossal struggle with Authority (to whom she had refused to read aloud from a book that was not the Bible, on a Sunday), involving punishments that would have been considered brutal in the Black Star criminal battalion of the Foreign Legion.

Ellen Montgomery of "The Wide Wide World" and Fleda, the less well-known heroine of "Queechy," mainly excelled in the gift of ready tears. They burst into sobs, they wept bitterly, the big drops hung on their eyelashes or stole softly down their cheeks, their lips quivered, their slight forms heaved and shook, their eyes were moist, they cried silently and they cried passionately, and they cried at least three times to a page. Accurate statistics prove that Fleda cried 911 times to Ellen's 872, but Ellen probably was the better stayer of the two, and cried for longer at a time.

Both these children had, like Elsie, their religious preoccupations and their rather too simply made converts. Mr. Carleton was a hardened, cynical atheist; his reputation confirmed him as proof against all attack. One day he was leaning against a ship's rail at sunset:

"What makes you believe in God, Fleda?" he questioned, curiously. She pointed to the red ball of fire on the horizon: "Who made that, Mr. Carleton?" It was only a little child's answer, but it sufficed. Henceforth he never doubted. * * *

Later on she married him, but for many years he was still Mr. Carleton to her, and she blushed when he came near her. Ellen Montgomery had the same difficulty in familiarizing Mr. John into plain John—but that portion of Ellen's history which lingers in my memory was when her mamma sent her forth, all by herself, to buy merinos at the big drapery store. It was a thrilling adventure. A horrid shopman was rude to her and tossed her pattern on to the floor, and she was rescued by old Mr. Snellbody himself, who treated her to a nice warm hood and escorted her home, plus merinos, to her mamma. What a thrill this incident lent to all one's own juvenile shopping expeditions! At any moment * * * But Ellen was luckier than I, who never found a tradesman to "crack a bottle of fish sauce or stand a man a cheese!"

"Home Influence" and its sequel, "A Mother's Recompense," were given to me in a set with "The Swiss Family Robinson" and "Mansfield Park." Why that irrelevant quartet were chosen to be linked by the bonds of mutual green cloth and gold lettering I cannot tell, but even now Jane Austen has eccentric associations for me.

"Home Influence" and "A Mother's Recompense" tell us about an English family, the Hamiltons—Mr. Hamilton, whose eyes sometimes flash with a noble indignation; Mrs. Hamilton, who is a presence of virtue and mildness that—again mark the affinity!—is only found nowadays in the "divine idiot" of Russian fiction; and their four children—my haughty Caroline, my willful, headstrong Percy, my sainted Herbert and my gleeful Emmeline. The adjectives, hung round the neck of each, are at no time detachable. A pair of orphan cousins come to live with the Hamiltons—my timid Ellen and my handsome Edward. Edward breaks a vase, and the Hamiltons think that Ellen did. That is the plot of the two books. The amount of punishment that Noble Indignation and Mild Goodness can inflict when they really set themselves to it, makes one shudder to believe that in this respect, at least, the portrait of mid-Victorian family life is a faithful one. At the age of 22, or thereabouts, Ellen is still—though of her own free will, now—sitting up most of the night secretly doing fine needlework to pay for the vase; and still getting misunderstood all over the place, and from every angle, because she refuses to go to parties with my dark and haughty Caroline (who jilts an Earl and elopes with a wicked Lord), and my gleeful Emmeline (with glossy ringlets), who dances like a fairy. As for my headstrong Percy—I only remember this passage about him: He was mixed up in some unkind prank against an unpopular master; smitten by conscience, he apologized to the victim, and then—

With tossed curls and glowing cheeks, he bounded into the room and cast himself impetuously at Mrs. Hamilton's feet. "Now I am indeed forgiven, now I am indeed your own Percy!" he cried. * * *

He was, at the time of this episode, supposed to be a normal and high-spirited schoolboy of about 15.

Well, but in what spirit was this curious goblin race of youngsters created? "The Elsie Books," "Home Influence," "The Wide, Wide World," "Queechy," "The Fairchild Family," "Anna Lee," "St. Winifred's," "The Crofton Cousins"—were they romance or realism? Surely not such a wide gulf can have yawned between children then and children now! Surely no boy of 15 can ever have said to his mother, "Now I am indeed your own Percy!" and not only have said it, but felt it. Allowing for all changes of manners, customs and education, there is yet some human element akin to all ages and all nations, which apparently had to be soaked out of nineteenth century juvenile fiction before it was allowed to be served up. It would be interesting to know the psychology of the authors, and whether behind the stilted sentiments and staid behavior lay genuine idealism—an incredible but sincere invocation to the mid-Victorian young to take these horrible puppets for models.

A reaction was inevitable, of course. And nowadays there is almost a touch of eager propitiation in the tone of books written for children, as though the author could not sufficiently acquit himself of any possible charge of priggishness. To write absolutely from the child's point of view; to introduce human naughtiness, not patronizingly condoning it, but as a matter of course; to present grown-ups with tolerance, or else to burlesque their grotesque stupidity; to understand all fanciful dreams, all riotous nonsense; to assume certain rights of the child kingdom, to send preaching to the devil and moral principles thrice to the devil—is this attitude our twentieth-century apology to children for the Puritan humbug of the nineteenth century?

Yes—the grown-ups are afraid! They are afraid of the scornful words, "priggish muck"! Time's revenges!—little Lucy, little Marmaduke, little Adelaide, would not have dared to exclaim "Priggish muck!" at the gift of, say, "Constancy Rewarded"!

Let us reconstruct, in the language of 1850, such an occasion:

"Here, my dear little daughter," said Mr. Dinsmore, fondly stroking the glossy ringlets that clustered so profusely on his Elsie's fair neck, "here is a story book that I trust you will find as instructive in its precepts as it is entertaining to your more leisure hours."

"Oh, thank you, dear kind papa," and Elsie's eyes swam with tears and her cheeks glowed; "I am sure I do not deserve half your generosity. But—" She faltered and cast herself sobbing at his feet. "Would it be right, would it not be selfish, for me to accept it, when so many more unfortunate little girls have not even a hymnbook?"

So much for the outward decorum of their behavior. What disdain, what weariness, what rebellion was repressed in the childish reader of these tales will, alas, never be laid starkly before us. We can only imagine how the real child, smothered under the artificialities of good conduct and exemplary sentiments, must surely have despised its meek little prototype in fiction; must have longed for laughter flashing down the page, for incident without the eternal sermon tagged on, like the clattering tin kettle to the tail of a dog.

And yet these books were, after all, the first attempts at exclusive literature for children. Before the nineteenth century I can find not even the first faint forerunners of Our Christmas List of Attractive Juvenile Fiction. Not in England. Fairy tales existed—Andersen and Grimm and Perrault and "The Arabian Nights" and some of these may have drifted the way of the English child. Otherwise they must have read their Bibles, poetry and ballads, perhaps history and travel, and the same stories as were provided for grown-ups. Jane Austen was still in her early teens when she skimmed mischievously Mrs. Radcliffe's dark and thrilling mysteries.

The period of the Elsie books and "The Fairchild Family" must also have been, for the grown-ups, the period of Bulwer Lytton, equally stilted and artificial and long-winded; but little Marmaduke and Adelaide could not possibly be allowed to read "Night and Morning" or "Ernest Maltravers"—both, I believe, looked upon as extremely daring tales. And, rather later, Ouida! Just supposing little Addie should pick up "Moths." * * * I remember picking it up myself, at the age of about 8, and wondering why the Russian Count made all that silly fuss about Vere and the silver-throated Correze. * * * But Ouida was for the worldly minded. The sentimental browsed over Mrs. Hungerford and Rhoda Broughton—"Molly Bawn," "Red as a Rose Is She," "Not Wisely but Too Well," "Cometh Up as a Flower"—the titles recall the sweetly cloying, pathetic atmosphere of heroines like snowdrops, who wilted and died because of misunderstandings with gentlemen who had long, long yellow mustaches. Such effects are not achieved with tongue in the cheek * * * and there can be little doubt of the equal sincerity of the writer of that moving tale in which the lighthouse keeper's little daughter is subjected to the fearful problem of conscience as to whether or

"Listen to Elsie and her father."

not she ought to stand upon the big family Bible, in order to reach the lamp and light it, during a storm.

We may smile at such episodes, but not scoff at them—for they are too sad, in an opposite direction from the sadness intended by the author. For me—and for you, if they attract you—such a collection of books is no more than—well, a collection, funny and pompous and old-fashioned, their very absurdities giving rise to affection. For me, and for you, and for the happy and enlightened children of today, whose bookshelves are stuffed with treasure. But they inspire, also, the vision of a quaint little figure with prim lips and serious eyes, hair smoothed back with a round comb; and behind her the shadowy ranks of Victorian children. * * * "Sir" to their fathers and "Madam" to their mothers; the formal barriers of convention separating them from all sympathy, from all but the most ruled and perfunctory kindness. Little Lucy, and little Adelaide, and little Marmaduke, Harriet and Edwin and Charlotte * * * joyless, thwarted victims of the most horrible age that ever flattened the small human soul in an attempt to improve it.

"All that is ended!" In the reaction the twentieth-century child may be enjoying too tender a handling of its psychology, too sturdy an independence, too precocious a personality. Yet when, helped by such story books as I have described, our imaginations grope backward and re-live a period in which brains as well as sofas were stuffed with horsehair, and when naturally romping children suffered and were cramped and cowed, we cannot but admit that such a reaction is from heaven.

June 17, 1923

WHEN THE LITTLE ANGELS REVOLTED

Louisa Alcott Led the Revolution Which Has Changed the World of Children's Literature

By MILDRED ADAMS

IT is fifty years since Louisa May Alcott wiped her last pen on the voluminous skirt of her scribbling suit, took off for the last time the famous cap whose angle used to tell her family how fiercely genius was burning, and bade farewell to her two worlds.

The adult world of post-Civil War days, in which she was a nervous and overburdened spinster, had given her fame and fortune, but not much happiness. The juvenile world for which and about which she wrote the books that have lasted all these years was much more to her liking. There she had scope for her energy and her ideas. There she was the tomboy Jo March, or the active and beloved Aunt Jo to a host of nieces and nephews and waifs and strays. There she could handle aches and pains and sorrows and put them in their proper places as the muted strains that made her harmonies all the richer for their minor melody.

In the minds of every new crop of children who each year make a fresh discovery of the little green books, she is still writing for children. It was only a few years ago that a modern girls' magazine, which prides itself on the quality of its current stories, asked its readers what was their favorite book. "Little Women" led all the rest. And when the movie of the same name recently charmed America, one heard frequently repeated the alleged remark of one youthful cinema fan to another, "I hear they've already got the book out. Ain't it wonderful how fast they can write!"

IT is easy enough for an Alcott addict to explain how it is that the simple annals of the March family have continued to charm generations of children from the end of the Civil War to the second decade after the World War, and why it is that their fame seems in no danger of waning. One speaks of the author's fresh style, of the vigor of her prose and the energy of her opinions. Another avers that she was a rebel in her own day, that her books were "advanced" when they first appeared, and that the world of feminine education is just beginning to catch up to the ideas embodied in them. Another murmurs "universal appeal," and "the pull of homely sentiment."

But look at the turbulent half century and more that separates 1938 from 1868, when "Little Women" was first published. Look at the difference between the America for which she wrote and the America in which we live. Look at the free young modern in shorts or ski pants, and then at the shawled, bonneted and heavily petticoated young person who was in fashion then. Either there must have been the stuff of greatness in her books to leap the chasm between them and still hold popularity—a thesis which Alcott critics from Henry James down have refused to recognize—or else the difference in surfaces is less important than it looks.

THE world of the Sixties and the Seventies was a mixture of the stuffy and the adventurous. President Grant was followed by Hayes, by Arthur and by Garfield. Geographically, it was a world in which most of the population still lived east of the Appalachians and the West was a synonym for endless opportunity and exciting adventure. The public traveled in trains lit with kerosene lamps, on horseback, in carriages or covered wagons. It made the Grand Tour through Europe, and its ships brought all the riches of the Orient back to Boston and New York. At home it surrounded itself with an architecture which was a mingling of the massive and the jigsaw. Decoration was rampant. Furniture was carved black walnut heavily upholstered in horsehair, and the favorite wall color was brown. Little boys went to church dressed in velvet suits with white lace collars and little girls were puffed, ringleted and rosebudded within an inch of their precious lives.

It is hard to tell from this distance, and with all the material and mechanical changes that have come over the world, what those little boys and girls were actually like. If you ask their grown-up selves—the modern grandmother and grandfather—you are likely to be told that their favorite grandchild is the image of them at the same age. But this is obviously prejudiced testimony.

If you look at those so-called mirrors of reality—the books that were written for, and presumably about, children, you will find contrasts so startling that the boys and girls of that period seem almost to have belonged to a species totally different from that of the boys and girls of today. There is, for instance, the matter of the more than human goodness that was assumed to be the child's ideal. The Rollo books began in 1837, and moved onto the market and into the minds of their youthful readers as smoothly as molasses candy into buttered pans. The Lucy books were their feminine counterpart, and if Rollo was a good boy, Lucy was an even better girl. In 1851 appeared that extraordinarily moral tale, "The Wide, Wide World," whose virtuous heroine dissolved into tears on every other page. In 1852 came "Uncle Tom's Cabin," hot with indignation and sweet with a pink and gold heroine who died piously and was borne to heaven on spun sugar-candy clouds. In 1853 Charlotte Yonge produced "The Heir of Radcliffe," over which Jo March (and Louisa Alcott) wept in the garret.

And in 1867 there appeared the first of the Elsie books, whose unbearably moral heroine still turns up on the shelves of Sunday-school libraries.

If little boys were gentlemen in those books, little girls were ladies of angelic sweetness. They never slapped their baby brothers, never muddied their pinafores, never mussed their golden curls. Their favorite attitude was standing at mother's knee, or wistful at a window with the neck curved and the eye fixed on eternity. Their innate goodness was potent to curb a headstrong brother or redeem a sinful father from his erring ways.

They were tidy needlewomen, embroidering samplers with pious mottoes at an early

The little women of post-Civil War days have one thing in common with the girls of today: With both generations Louisa May Alcott was—and is—a favorite. But in almost every other respect what differences the years have wrought!

Photograph courtesy Jane Bland

age. They learned to tinkle sweet melodies on the piano in the parlor, they took baskets to the sick and dropped a tear over the sins of their erring neighbors. In fact, dropping a tear was their favorite indoor and outdoor sport, and it is only after a good dose of the ordinary girls' books of the period that one understands just why Lewis Carroll, a decade later, set Alice to swimming in a whole sea of tears.

COMPENSATION for such excessive goodness lay in the then prevailing obsession with graves and horror stories. A homemade collection of poems for a little girl aged 6 were all concerned with graves and worms and early dying. A gift book of the period—"The American Book of Beauty, or Friendship's Token"—had as its pièce de résistance a tale of ghouls and grave robbing which would make even a modern permanent wave straighten out and stand on end.

In this super-saccharine or overly melodramatic world the Alcott books must have fizzed like clear cold water from a soda spring. Written by the tomboy daughter of a progressive educator, full of vigor, enthusiasm and indignation against what she considered unhealthy tendencies in the lives of the children of her day, they had about them a kind of homely humanity that rendered them instantly popular.

Louisa Alcott opened all the windows with a bang and let the cold outside air rush into stuffy parlors and stuffier heads. Her children were no curled and ruffled darlings but human boys and girls whose tempers were uncertain, whose faults were manifest and acknowledged. They played games, got into mischief, ran away from home and came penitently back again, cried and fought and made up and began all over again, like normal human beings. If they had more freedom than most children of that period it was a freedom which was intentional, for Louisa Alcott was her father's daughter, and her father was an educator who believed in freeing children's minds and children's bodies.

That the children responded to this new naturalism was proved by the success of "Little Women" and the insatiable appetite of the "little tyrants" for more. How it struck some of their elders may be inferred from a curious review of "Eight Cousins" which Henry James wrote, and which Katharine Anthony quotes in her fascinating new book about Miss Alcott.

"Miss Alcott," said he, "is the novelist of children. She deals with the social questions of the child world, and, like Thackeray and Trollope, she is a satirist. * * * Miss Alcott seems to have a private understanding with the youngsters she depicts, at the expense of their pastors and masters; and her idea of friendliness to the infant generation seems to be, at the same time, to initiate them into the humorous view of them taken by their elders when the children are out of the room. * * * All this is both poor entertainment and poor instruction. What children want is the objective, as the philosophers say; it is good for them to feel that the people and things around them that appeal to their respect are beautiful and powerful specimens of what they seem to be. * * * What has become of the 'Rollo' books of our infancy and the delightful 'Franconia' tales?"

One forbears from commenting on the literary taste of a great novelist who preferred the syrupy Rollo books to the fresh vigor of "Eight Cousins," but it may be noted that the manner in which Henry James telescoped "what children want" with what "is good for them" was typical of his day. The resulting confusion has not disappeared from modern thinking, but the emphasis has shifted. Current opinion in the Sixties took it for granted that what was good for children was thereby what they wanted. Certain educators in the Nineteen Thirties proceed on the opposite theory that what they want is thereby good for them.

THAT shift in emphasis is only one of the changes that have come about both in the real world and the world of children's books. The West, which was so romantic then, is chiefly famous now as a dust bowl. Boston's cultural glory has been obscured from the man in the street by the sound and fury of her politicians. The automobile, the autobus and the airplane have supplemented the slow train of the Eighteen Sixties. The telephone, which appeared in "Jo's Boys," is—like the radio which was not yet invented—a commonplace which affects the lives of the great majority of American children.

No longer do they trudge along a dusty road to school; they are driven in the family car or the community bus. Their radius of amusement has widened with the speeding up of transportation and the new means of communication. Where the Alcott girls wrote and staged their own plays, the modern children see their favorite fairy stories projected on moving-picture screens, and hear from a wooden box tales in which bandits, mysteries and sudden death are offered as the preludes to a peaceful night.

The games that girls play have grown more strenuous as their skirts have shortened. Their tennis has speeded up, their swimming has grown more professional. In addition to the sled and the skates of the Sixties they now have skis, with all the added speed and danger that go with those picturesque implements. They still ride horses—but as a fashionable sport rather than a fast means of getting about the countryside. They still make the lives of celebrities miserable with their rage for autographs as they did when the girls of Vassar pursued Miss Alcott, but nowadays it is likely to be the movie star rather than the writer of girls' books who is most hounded.

Of the corresponding changes that have come to the story children, perhaps the shift in ideals is the most marked and significant. In the middle of the last century it was sung of little Kate that

Because she was so good a girl,
The little girls and boys
Presented her a Christmas box
Brimful of pretty toys.

Nowadays the first line would have to read "Because she was so good an all-around athlete," or a cultivator of personality plus. The modern story-book girl wants to be a good hockey player. She wants to win swimming races, to play championship tennis. No longer does she smooth the pillows of the sick or take pretty baskets to the poor—changes in grown-up attitudes lead her rather to want to be the head of a hospital or a social agency. Instead of tinkling sweet tunes in the parlor she longs to be a concert pianist or a radio singer. She sees herself as a movie star, as a war correspondent, as running a tea room or leading a revolution. Or she wants simply to marry and live happily ever after—the young love story for growing girls is said to be on the increase.

The literature made for the growing girl of today is much richer in variety than that which came to her grandmother's hand. Look, for instance, at the new books for children—a book about Hungary, a book about Russia, a whole group of books about Egypt. A book about a Jacques Cartier, another about Lewis and Clark.

These and their fellows are not limited to moral tales, or to the "objectives" which Henry James's philosophers regarded so highly. They move with equal ease through history, science and modern school life. They employ photographs to heighten the sense of reality on the one hand, and on the other they range about the worlds of fancy and fantasy.

Yet always, to balance the modern girl's ration, there are reprints of the best her grandmother knew, the best her mother read, beautifully illustrated and dressed in a format that would have seemed worth a fairy prince's ransom compared with the drab little volumes of the General Grant era.

These books are needed as balance. However children's literature has changed, it takes only a brief submersion in the modern variety to make one realize that as a mirror of reality it, too, leaves something to be desired. If the ideal of 1868 was an unpleasant and inhuman angel, the ideal of 1938 frequently comes close to being an unpleasant and inhuman brat. Or so capable in emergency that one trembles for the fate of this untidy world when they grow up. Modern story-book heroines who are athletic and capable are also to be described as somewhat hard and brittle. Where Jo and Beth, Meg and Amy met obstacles and recognized them as John Bunyanish ogres that must be met—and conquered if possible—the modern story-book child can never admit even the possibility of defeat. She assumes that heroism is expected of her, and she is as stoic as a glass eye.

Louisa May Alcott wrote just when the tide was turning toward these newer virtues, and she managed to combine the old and the new. Her Jo wanted to be a famous author, her Rose wanted to be a healthy, active and popular girl, her Beth simply wanted to be good. Perhaps the very fact that she rounded the picture and took in the gentle, the tender and the sentimental, as well as the ambitious and the athletic, is one reason for the continuing popularity of the very human March girls, whose author knew exactly how it felt to fall down. Or perhaps their popularity proves that under a frighteningly assured surface the girls of 1938 are not so very different from those of 1868 and 1888 after all.

March 6, 1938

CHILDREN MAKE OWN BOOK LIST

Little Folk Have a Say at Last Regarding What They Like in Fiction—New Kind of Guide for Librarians

In William Dean Howells's beloved "Christmas Every Day in the Year" the father began, "Well, once there was a little pig—" But the little girl put her hand over his mouth. She said she had heard little-pig stories until she was perfectly sick of them. It was decided then to have a story about Christmas, though "Papa" protested that he had told about Christmas as often as about little pigs. "But Christmas is lots more interesting than pigs," the little girl explained.

If she had been a present-day young woman between the ages of 8 and 14, with a "Daddy" instead of an old-fashioned "Papa," she might have indexed her taste in fiction so strongly beforehand, with a damning mark against pigs and a note of praise for Christmas, that the father's error in judgment would have been impossible. That is what thousands of young readers have done this year, at the suggestion of interested and resourceful grown-ups, with the result soon to be published, "The Winnetka Graded Book List," which will be a manual of youthful taste.

Three hundred schools of thirty-four cities in seventeen States have cooperated in placing in the hands of the ingenious director of this work, Superintendent Carleton Washburne of the Winnetka public schools, and Miss Mabel Vogel, his research assistant, the material they have compiled.

Little Critics.

Representing the literary reactions of more than 36,000 children, this unique book list, the cost of compiling which has been borne by the Carnegie Institute, will be published by the American Library Association, already the publisher of graded book lists that have appeared at intervals since 1915 to indicate the best adult thought on what children should read.

This list, however, is peculiarly the child's own choice. Each child in the cooperating schools filled out for each book he had read during the last year a printed ballot, giving in addition to his name and age and the name of the book the valuation he placed on it and a few lines of comment. The teacher filled in his reading grade from second to tenth as determined by a standard reading test given to all the children voting. Of the 100,000 ballots received 50,000 were on 800 books, about which there was accordingly sufficient information for them to be graded for the book list. A degree of censorship was maintained, and 100 books were dropped from the list as unsuitable or of poor literary value by a three-quarter vote of the committee of thirteen library experts.

The 700 remaining popular juvenile choices make up the list, each appearing under the average reading grade of its readers in the order of its popularity index. The compilation of figures following each book on the list also shows the number of boys reading it, the number of girls, the percentage of each who liked it and the average value they placed on it. There was found to be considerable difference in boys' and girls' taste and reading ability, so all figures are given separately. Each book is described on the graded list by a typical child's comment quoted from one of the ballots received.

The children's comments have a freshness quite unknown among grown-up critics. "Good Times on the Farm," by Ethel C. Dietz, is revealingly reviewed: "Because I live in the city and I like to read about the farm." "Reynard the Fox" is liked "because Reddy always tried to catch Peter Rabbit but always missed him." C. W. Hunt, author of "About Harriet," could surely not ask to have better things said about her than: "I like what she did on Thursday. When she was a bad girl, her mother said she would put her in a bag and cover her with paper. Don't you like it?"

What They Like.

There is a difference between adult recommendations of a book and children's estimate of the same story. Helen Bannerman's "Little Black Sambo" appears on the standard grade list as "a story invented for her two little girls by the author when in India, where black children abound and tigers are every-day affairs. Very popular." The child's verdict is even more graphic: "I liked it because the lions all turned into butter, and Little Black Sambo ate 169 pancakes in one meal."

Lang's Fairy Tales are little more than described when the adult lists them as "A Favorite Collection of Standard Fairy Tales." It is the child who soars to a passionate moral tone: "I like this book because Cinderella's sisters were sorry for what they had done."

An unusual difference of opinion comes out in the listing of Mark Twain's "Tom Sawyer." Though the book is approved by grown-ups, one young reader could not condone it. "Based on reminiscences of the author's boyhood in Missouri. Full of incident and fun," reads the grown-up summary. "I like this book, but yet I think it is one of the worst books for boys in their mature age," concludes a 13-year-old moralist. "It is so unlike real life that some small boy might get it confused with his former way of living. * * *"

An odd fault is found by a 14-year-old girl with another old favorite, "Mrs. Wiggs of the Cabbage Patch." "I don't like the story very much because it has so much slang in it that I can't understand," complains this purist. "The slang makes me nervous."

A restrained comment on Longfellow's "Evangeline" by a 14-year-old Massachusetts boy reads thus: "It doesn't seem possible that a girl would walk so many miles for her beau when now a girl wouldn't walk a mile to see him." An 11-year-old committed himself whole-heartedly regarding Altsheler's "Texan Star." "One of the best books I have ever read," he said. "I like this book because it suits my tastes. I have a wild taste."

The love of the unreal by the hardened realist is shown in a review of "The Princess on the Glass Hill." "I like it because there is no glass hill and there aren't any golden apples, and it says that there are, and I like stories about Princesses and Princes, and I like it because she was sitting in a chair on the glass hill, and if it was a real glass hill and some one was sitting on it they would slip down."

Children's taste demands the "happy ending." "Little Red Riding Hood was saved by the man and the wolf was killed," is why that popular classic is liked. Of "Three Little Kittens" it is recorded: "The interesting part is where the little kitten ran away from home and never wanted to return. But he did."

Concerning "Ab the Cave-Man" we read: "It tells how Ab jumped over the fire. He got married to Lightfoot and they had a nice time. I like the time when they had a mammoth hunt. Some of the men got killed, but they had an exciting time and a big feast." Of "Children of the Cliff" it is simply written: "I liked the part where the children were found after they had been lost."

Next to the happy ending, it seems to be "tricks" that arouse the most childish delight. "Cock, Mouse and the Little Red Hen" is reviewed: "I like it because it is so funny and the little red hen plays the trick on the fox so often." Of "Fables From Afar" an enthusiast writes: "I like the part where the fox played a trick on the dove. The other big bird told the dove that the fox could not climb a tree. The book is full of tricks." And again, of "Fairy Stories and Fables"; "Tom Thumb fell into the pudding and his mother couldn't find him. It made me laugh."

There is spirit in this synopsis of "Another Fairy Reader": "The best one is 'Mr. Vinegar and His Fortune.' I will tell you about the story. Mr. Vinegar's wife was screaming. Guess what she was yelling. She yelled, 'The door has fallen,' and it had."

Old Favorites Hold On.

The fourth-grader who wrote this one must have been in league with the publisher of "The Overall Boys in Switzerland": "I like it because the overall boys crossed the Atlantic Ocean and went into a strange country. If you would like to know more about it you will find it in the book."

Changing times have not completely altered juvenile taste in books, for old favorites still top the lists of each grade. "Papa" would recognize many of his old friends patiently waiting their turn after "The Little Pigs" and "Christmas Every Day." Such books as "Grimms's Fairy Tales," "Childs' Garden of Verses," "Peter Pan" and "Little Black Sambo" are headliners with the fourth grade. "Black Beauty," "Pinocchio," "The Little Lame Prince" and "Alice in Wonderland" endure as fifth grade choices. "Robinson Crusoe," "Heidi," "Five Little Peppers" and "The Jungle Book" are near the top of the sixth grade list. And "Tom Sawyer," "Little Women," "Hans Brinker," "Huckleberry Finn" and "Treasure Island" hold, more than any other books, the seventh grade readers.

"The Prince and the Pauper," "Wild Animals I Have Known," "Ivanhoe" ("papa" blushes a little to have thought this dull in his own youth!), "Master Skylark" and "The Three Musketeers" are top-notchers for the eighth grade. The sophisticated ninth presents a list of favorites so long in good standing that it deserves to be given in full: "Jim Davis," "Janice Meredith," "Adventures of Sherlock Holmes," "Two Years Before the Mast," "Bob, Son of Battle," "Continental Dollar," "Lorna Doone," "Mysterious Island," "Tale of Two Cities," "Ramona" and "Ben Hur."

November 22, 1925

Passing of an Epoch. No Henty books have been issued for years. Frank, that versatile hero of "Harry Castleman," whose adventures on Don Carlos's Rancho won him the devotion of boys, has long been silent. Nick Carter is gone. "Deadwood Dick" has just died. It has been a long time since "Oliver Optic" and HORATIO ALGER Jr. told of the rise of boys from virtuous poverty to equally virtuous riches. Now Mr. STRATEMEYER, whose "Rover Boys" series sold more than 5,000,000 copies, has laid down his pen. Who is to write tales of adventure for the boys of the airplane and television age?

It is probable that new formulas will have to be fused by the next boys' FROISSART. Mr. HENTY selected "Archibald Forbes," associated him with WALLACE and with the BRUCE, wove the more pleasing high-lights of Scottish history into the narrative, and there, in a lovely green buckram cover, was "For Name and Fame." The same method worked as well with innumerable other tales of historical adventure. "Castleman" put into his epics more of the flavor of the soil. "Optic" and ALGER kept uppermost the theme of the triumphs of virtue. The writers of detective and Wild West thrillers, preserving lightly the theme of sterling character, made action their handmaiden. Mr. STRATEMEYER evolved a happy combination of both.

All these are now dated. The boys of the airplane age are ready for the touch of a new and skillful hand. Fortunately, they will still turn to "Tom Sawyer" while waiting for the next instalment of something probably called "Peril in the Sky."

May 13, 1930

MERRIWELL STORIES BROUGHT UP TO DATE

Prolific Creator of Popular Boy Hero Now Busy Putting Radio and Planes Into the Books.

STILTED TALK ELIMINATED

Gilbert Patten Also Preparing Old Thrillers for Radio and Screen—He Doesn't Write So Fast Today.

Frank Merriwell, hero of a series of books for boys of which rather more than 100,000,000 copies have been sold in the last thirty-five years, soon will appear on the screen and be heard over the radio, Gilbert Patten, who wrote most of the books in the series under the pen name of Burt L. Standish, said in an interview yesterday.

Mr. Patten is writing the radio scripts and is also at work revising the paper-backed books to appear in a cloth-bound edition. He is "modernizing them, trying to make the boys talk as boys do now, and putting in some radios and airplanes for background." Many of the incidents must be brought up to date, such as one memorable fight for life on the golden dome of the World Building, which was written when that building was the high point of Manhattan.

Mr. Patten originally wrote his 208 Merriwell stories at the rate of 20,000 words weekly. Most of his work was dictated, but to dictate properly he had to walk and a pedometer showed him that he was walking about four and one-half miles each morning. He is typing out the revisions himself but with his rate greatly decreased, averaging about 1,500 words a day. So far he has revised four of the books and has two more almost ready.

In addition he writes the running story for a school and adventure strip about Frank Merriwell which appears daily in more than 200 newspapers in the United States, Canada and the Philippines.

Mr. Patten started writing Merriwell stories in 1896 and worked steadily at them until 1914. He did the work for Street & Smith, publishers, at the rate of one every two weeks, each volume containing about 70,000 words. Mr. Patten has since taken over all rights to the Merriwell stories except the paper book rights. Street & Smith are still reissuing the books, in new covers.

The Merriwell stories do not all concern Frank Merriwell. After Mr. Patten had carried this first hero around the world two or three times, through preparatory school and Yale College and it came time to make a decision on which of several heroines he would marry, Mr. Patten invented a younger brother, Dick Merriwell, to start the cycle over again. Dick was never as popular as his brother—his disposition at times being a bit surly—and finally Mr. Patten permitted a Frank Merriwell Jr. to grow up and go to Yale.

"The stories were not well written," Mr. Patten said yesterday. "They were stilted, the boys never said 'won't' or 'don't,' always 'will not' and 'do not.' But they did have action, characterization and atmosphere. I tried to keep dummy characters out of my stories, to give every one something that set him a little apart. Boys like good characterization just as much as they like action—perhaps even more."

December 7, 1932

YOUNG READERS' COMPANIONS

By ELIZABETH JANEWAY

PRODUCING books for children has become a large and profitable business—so large, indeed, that many a bookseller or librarian complains that it is almost impossible to keep up with the output. This flood of books is a striking and thought-provoking phenomenon. It is even more interesting that the main current of children's literature seems to be running counter to the general trend of books being published for adults.

One reason for the rising tide of juvenile books, I suspect, is that children are increasingly brought up not by the family, but by the community, and instruction in matters that were once thought of as private is becoming public. Manners, morals, behavior were once passed on by word of mouth. Now there are books about them. Good thing or bad thing—it's a fact, and no amount of nostalgia for family ways and family fun is going to move us back a hundred years. We are where we are. There are still storytellers, but now they are to be found in libraries, not by the family fireside. If they are not so easily available as Grandma was, they are almost certainly better storytellers, with a wider variety of tales to recount.

In addition, there are the children's books, beautiful, bright and gay, waiting to serve the function that word-of-mouth telling did in the past. How well do they do it?

At certain levels and in certain ways they do it very well indeed. There are picture books for little children, and the first reading books, that are enchanting, full of humor and fantasy and delight. Dr. Seuss and the de Brunhoffs, père et fils, who created Babar, are peers of the realm, and I would like to nominate Maurice Sendak to join them. All of them have the gift of appealing to adults and to children in just the same way: "I told you once. I told you twice, all seasons of the year are nice for eating chicken soup with rice!" A young father was reading the "Nut Shell Library" to a 3-year-old in my hearing, and all three of us burst into laughter at the same time, for the same reason. Bruno Munari's "Zoo" and his "ABC," Elsa Minarik's "Little Bear," are warm, witty and surprising. And there are many others.

When one turns to books for older children, where the text is more important than the pictures, the quality falls off. There are exceptions: a particular fine one this year is "Tyler, Tyler, Wilkin and Skee" by Robert Burch, about three boys on a Georgia farm, and as real and fresh as paint. Geoffrey Grigson's anthology, "The Cherry Tree," can stand comparison with collections for adults. Marchette Chute's "Stories From Shakespeare" seems to me better than the Lambs' "Tales From Shakespeare" that I grew up with. But when you look at the majority of books above the picture-book level, it becomes evident that these are exceptions, and that the tendency of children's books is to stick to a narrowing range of material and to sweeten their style. They are bland; they are repetitious; they are insipid.

Take an obvious example. In the books I read as a child, there were Good Guys and Bad Guys, heroes and villains. Today they have retreated to the comics, the classics (which are often abridged and bowdlerized), the fairy stories—and, of course, television. This is a remarkable change. I think it tells us something about the image that our society has of itself, and of our unconscious aims. Consciously, the disappearance of villains is owing to a generous, if misguided, impulse. It's an attempt to suppress prejudice by pretending that it doesn't exist. But things don't work that way.

I remember well a book I adored which was absolutely stuffed with prejudice—"Westward Ho!" by Charles Kingsley, who presented the Jesuit Fathers as villains, and equated the Church of Rome with evil itself. But he made the Age of Elizabeth come alive with color and excitement. Now, I am not arguing that the liveliness of his book was worth any prejudice it might instill in the reader—because, in fact, it didn't instill any prejudice in the reader. It takes a great deal more than one exciting book to bend a child's mind. I knew what his opinion was, but I also knew that that was merely his opinion. Other people, as other books I read made clear, had other opinions. Surrounded by opinionated and argumentative writers, a child is not taken in by any. What's more, he's given an opportunity to learn what opinion is worth: sometimes a lot, sometimes nothing at all. It depends—on what other people say, and on what you find out for yourself.

How does a child learn this if he is confined to books that have no opinion at all? If everyone is a "Good Guy," how do you choose between them? The set-apart world of children's books is pruned, protected and addicted to positive thinking. It has eliminated villains, but I wonder if it has not eliminated heroes too.

This pasteur-

Mrs. Janeway, novelist and critic, recently published "Angry Kate," a story in verse for very young readers.

ization of children's books is remarkably at odds with the increasing outspokenness of adult books, which are now so questioning, exploratory, eager to test rules and break them if they don't stand up, little-censored, mocking and rebellious. Never has the line between children's books and adult literature been so sharp as it is today. Once upon a time, it seems, when children were thought to be innocent, they were allowed to read and learn about wickedness and danger. But now the Freudian revolution has taken place, and society has decided that children had better be taught to be good. One sometimes gets the impression that most of the children's book trade sees its readers as potential juvenile delinquents, and is determined to prevent this by offering Little Lessons in Life Adjustment.

The trouble is that Happy People with Happy Problems make dull reading for children as well as adults. As the head of the city's biggest children's-book department remarked, "The worst reading block of all is boredom." Nor does writing about Happy Problems attract the most imaginative and creative writers. In the past, there was good writing for children of all ages—from Beatrix Potter, Lewis Carroll, Edward Lear, Frank Stockton, Kipling, E. Nesbit, John Masefield, Mark Twain, Louisa Alcott. Today, creative and original talent seems more and more to be going into fantasy and picture books. Yes, there are wonderful new books to make little children laugh. For older children there are some excellent factual books (for example, Sean Morrison's "Armor," which is superb). But the supply of new books that will tell an older child something about adult problems in the real world is very small.

This trend toward the factual, as in the various historical series, is again evidence of the increasing influence of the community in bringing up children and the decreasing role of the family. Children are offered more about history and events and less about personal relationships. Reading tends to be seen in an educational context and less as an individual occupation. Increasingly it's connected with schools, and books for older children reflect this tie instead of undertaking the larger, more difficult and more various connection with adult life in the real world. Isn't it astonishing that, two generations after Dr. Freud began to publish, books for teen-agers shun sex more firmly than did Elsie Dinsmore?

One result of this shying away from adult life is the persistent regard for the classics among children who are "real readers." A 12-year-old friend of mine is deep in Louisa May Alcott's "Eight Cousins." A 9-year-old says "Black Beauty" is the book he likes most, and a 6-year-old reports her best favorites as "Alice" and "Snow White." For children who look for entertainment and excitement, for life and reality in books, the classics are irreplaceable.

Another result of the limitation of range in children's books is that many more children look to television for entertainment and excitement, and for life and reality too. Television is attractive partly because it is not connected with school, not out to "educate," with the exception of some of the children's programs, which turn out not to be particularly popular. Most of the time, children watch exactly what adults watch. Television invites the child into the adult world — or what he takes to be the adult world — and makes him feel at home. It offers him drama, excitement, suspense. What it delivers is frequently melodrama, boredom and stereotypes, but it takes a while to find that out. And so children are going to go on looking at it.

I wish that producers of children's books would take a hint or two from television and remember what good writers (and not only of children's books) have always known. First, that it's fatal to talk down to an audience. "So many writers seem to be talking across a barrier," said the Head of the Children's Room at the Forty-second Street Library. "Of course, the children feel it." Second, that children are curious about real life, about adults and their problems. They live in the midst of them, and they need more, not fewer guides to how to deal with violence, prejudice and anger.

Of course, for those who are readers anyway the classics on high-school reading lists offer an entry to the adult world, but it comes at a fairly late date, and it will be accepted only by the few. Others will find their way to adult reading through "bridges" such as Salinger offers. But the transition is still sharp, and the more that books for young people sheer off from adult problems and confine themselves to a prettified world, the sharper it will become.

I talked recently with a librarian who had worked for a year and a half at a branch in East Harlem. "The children there wanted fairy tales," she said, "and after that, poetry. They didn't care much for factual everyday stories." Perhaps they only wanted to escape from East Harlem's streets, but I don't think so. I think they found more truth about the life they live, about anger and love and cruelty and excitement and power and chance in fairy-tales than in anything else they were offered.

November 10, 1963

CHAPTER 2

The Stage but Echoes Back the Public Voice

Lillian Russell

Courtesy The New York Public Library Picture Collection

LAST WEEK OF BARNUM'S CIRCUS

The Greatest Show on Earth Will Go to Brooklyn Next Saturday Night.

Barnum & Bailey's Greatest Show on Earth will go into camp at the end of the week, leaving New-York for Brooklyn.

The circus of a hundred shows has this season refuted the cry of "hard times," having been more prosperous than last year in this city. Fourteen times the public has been turned away at the admission wickets, and this surplus of patronage averaged 3,000 on each occasion. Once, more than 6,000 persons were turned away.

During the present week the thousand and one attractions of the show will be continued, with all the acts not hitherto presented. The last representation at the Madison Square Garden will be on Saturday night.

For the first time in the history of Barnum's Circus there will be two camps in Brooklyn. Monday to Thursday one will be at Halsey Street and Saratoga Avenue, and on Friday and Saturday at Fourth Avenue and Third Street. For each place a ground area 600 feet square is required. There are two tents, one for the menagerie, which is 300 feet long, and one for the auditorium, 550 feet long. They are so arranged that the spectators pass through the menagerie to reach the arena tent.

The great show is seen to better advantage under canvas than in a building, and one of its principal features, the Ethnological Congress, is almost hidden away at the Madison Square Garden.

There will be a street parade of the circus in Brooklyn on Monday, and a matinée as well as an evening performance. April 28 the show will go to Philadelphia.

April 17, 1894

IT'S STILL ONE A MINUTE

By MEYER BERGER

It is just fifty years since Phineas Taylor Barnum died, one hundred years since he set out to establish fame and fortune on the theory that "there's a sucker born every minute."

Fifty years after Barnum the theory remains sound and profitable. Showmen fill their tents and stadia with the old Barnum formula, only slightly varied. The chief ingredient for sucker pap is still hokum.

Neither Webster's Unabridged nor Maitland's Dictionary of Slang gives the origin of "sucker." According to Webster's, a sucker, in the colloquial sense of the word, is one sucked or bled or victimized; hence, one easily duped or gulled. "Sucker," as the showman uses it, is interchangeable with homo sapiens, mortal, or human. The sucker is Everyman.

Only two breeds seem to have any protective insulation against the sucker formula—Chinese and Down Easters. Circus men have always been baffled by this. They know through experience that it is so, but they have never analyzed it.

"Chinese and Down Easters are freaks that way," they tell you, dejectedly.

Modern showmen seldom use the term "sucker" in public. They reserve it for professional discussion. Hard-shell circus men, on the other hand, are not apt to mince it. They maintain that "sucker" has been good for a whole century, and what was good for grampa is good enough for them. They don't dress it up with whipped cream. If you won't graciously accept "sucker" they'll offer you "chump."

It was Barnum who figured out that the sucker's chief weakness was his sense of curiosity. He hired a man, a hundred years ago, to place an ordinary building brick on the sidewalk at each corner of the block bounding Barnum's New York Museum. The man carried a fifth brick in his hand.

As throngs moved past the building, Barnum's man gravely walked, on endless round, from one corner to the next, picking up a brick and replacing it with the one he carried. He grimly refused to answer questions. In less than an hour 500 men, women and urchins followed him on his aimless rounds.

At this point, following the master's orders, he walked into the museum with one brick still under his arm. Most of the crowd pressed at his heels, anxious to solve the riddle of the bricks. They paid the admission price to get in. They never found the answer to the riddle, but, having paid, they stayed to see the show.

Variations of this device seem ageless. Low-pitch workers—sidewalk fakers—use it every day on Broadway, humorously called "the world's most sophisticated street." The pitchman chalks meaningless symbols on the sidewalk, near the building line, and chants mumbo-jumbo over them.

The suckers stop. They tell themselves "this is the bunk," but their sap boils and they're hooked. If the pitchman has talent to back his come-on the sucker walks off in a daze with razor blades that won't raze, a potato peeler that won't peel or with "feelthy" art that wouldn't startle a deacon.

Ned Alvord, who has been advance agent for great circuses and road shows since the turn of the century, reaffirms the axiom that there's no sucker like a New York sucker. The sap content in Manhattan is astonishingly high. You can sell anything in New York if the cops don't break it up.

Mr. Alvord holds that the sucker crop has never been richer than in our time. Broadway has become a lane of penny arcades where men and women feverishly throw their money away for prizes that are worthless. They attend auctions and fiercely outbid one another to pay high prices for mere baubles.

Grinders—the uniformed talkers outside shabby burlesque houses—lure city folk into the theatres with the thinnest jobbery. They walk up and down with a sign that merely says "Fifty Cents" and exhort the chumps to get inside before the thirty-five-cent time limit is up. Actually there is no time limit, but when the sap runs strong the grinders pile them in.

Even the medicine man, whose art was corny when Cagliostro peddled love philtres in eighteenth-century Paris, can fill his poke in Times Square when the cops don't interfere. The other night, in Forty-fourth Street, Mr. Alvord saw a high-pitch—wagon tail—faker sell bottled "elixir" to eleven suckers at $1 a head.

"Guaranteed to make any man supreme in his own household," the agent dreamily recalled. "Probably physic and tap water. The guy had a nice pitch till the bobbies broke it up."

Barnum packed them in during the Civil War around 1863—after staging a public wedding in Grace Church for his midgets, General Tom Thumb and Mercy Lavinia Warren Bumpus. The public was tiring of midgets and the master saw the need for sucker stimulation. He hit on the romantic theme.

When Ringling Brothers and Barnum & Bailey Circus opened last week in Madison Square Garden the same device was sucker bait. Gargantua, the gorilla, and M'Toto, his prospective mate, were in adjoining cages, separated only by a few inches of

shatterproof glass. Publicity in national magazines and newspapers has whetted sucker appetites.

To hear the showmen tell it, Gargantua, 560-pound anthropoid, is that way about M'Toto, his shy 450-pound fiancée. There is great danger, though, that if Gargantua gets into the same cage with M'Toto before they're better acquainted he will tear her to pieces. You have to give them time, the spieler will explain to the suckers. Love will find a way, though only heaven knows how or when.

"Perfect," Mr. Alvord thinks. "Just perfect. The old love angle, plus the kill motif, plus suspense. Irresistible. Barnum must be smiling in showman's paradise."

BILLY ROSE, the so-called Bantam Barnum, confides that he uses the Barnum formula freely. The public is better educated in our time than it was in P. T.'s, but education is not a factor in show business. The appeal is always to basic human nature—to human curiosity, to sentiment, to color sense, to love of humor. You find these, Mr. Rose thinks, in equal quantity in the tutored and in the untutored.

Either, the Bantam Barnum says, will stop to stare into an excavation with equal gravity. Either will stop to watch a man chasing pigeons, or a man chasing his hat on a windy day. At this point Mr. Rose grows cautious.

"I will not subscribe to the belief that there's a sucker born every minute," he says. "I'll put it this way: There's a child born every minute."

IN the circus the spielers stick to the old Barnum school of florid oratory to make the suckers feel they are getting more than their money's worth. A hippopotamus isn't just a hippopotamus. It is pretty much what it was almost a century ago, "the Great Behemoth of Scripture, the Marvel of the Animal Kingdom, the Largest Amphibian Animal."

The suckers would rather have it that way.

Circus and show folk concede that when they enter an alien field they are apt to be prime suckers themselves. P. T. Barnum, they recall, plunged into bankruptcy when he ventured into real estate and clock manufacture in the early Eighteen Fifties. The fortune he had harvested from suckers was in turn taken from him.

James Gordon Bennett, whom he had antagonized, gloated over the master's entry into the sucker field. He wrote of Barnum in The Herald: "All the profits of his Fejee mermaids, all his woolly horses, Joice Heths, Tom Thumbs and monsters and impostures of all kinds * * * all swept away. It is a case eminently adapted to 'point a moral or adorn a tale.' "

Today, as in Barnum's century, the sucker still falls for the same hokum only slightly varied.

WILD WEST SHOW OPENS

Madison Square Garden Crowded with an Enthusiastic Audience.

GEN. MILES WAS PRESENT

Mayor Van Wyck and Richard Croker Also Attended—Chief Item of the Programme Battle of San Juan.

The whoop of the cowboy and the Indian, the crack of the prairie pistol, the shriek of the Cossack, the plaintive melody of the Hawaiian, and the thunder of rifles in mimic warfare all blended in one at Buffalo Bill's Wild West Show last night. Madison Square Garden was thronged. Seated in the box of honor were Major Gen. Miles, Rear Admiral Philip, Mayor Van Wyck, Richard Croker, Corporation Counsel Whalen, and a number of ladies.

Buffalo Bill has many new and interesting features in his show this year. Among them may be mentioned the representation of the battle of San Juan Hill, a number of Russian riders led by a real Russian nobleman, Prince Luika; three Filipinos, one of them a woman who rides with the stirrups around her ankles; a dozen or more of Roosevelt's Rough Riders, and John McCarthy, a man with a marvelous voice. Mr. McCarthy does the announcing and explaining from an elevated position in the rear of the Garden, and last night he talked for over two solid hours loudly enough to be plainly heard by every one, and without the aid of a megaphone.

The chief item on the programme was the representation of the battle of San Juan. The lights were turned low, giving a twilight effect, and the detachments of Rough Riders, Garcia's Cuban scouts, and infantry and cavalry came on the field, marching with a slow, weary step, the colored boys singing "There'll Be a Hot Time in the Old Town To-night." Following them were pack mules bearing cases, and some more scouts. The sentries were picketed, tents were pitched and the lights went out.

Then the sun rose with a sudden and unpoetic burst of electric light, the bugles sounded, and the troops marched away to San Juan Hill, which was built on the Fourth Avenue end of the Garden. Spaniards dotted the papier maché slopes, and looked through big glasses for the American intruders. As the first of the Cuban scouts stepped stealthily on the sawdust, the Spaniards began firing from the top of the hill. The Americans rushed in and opened fire. Three regulars rushed from somewhere with a Gatling gun, which seemed powerful enough to blow San Juan Hill itself to eternity. Finally a mad rush was made up the hill, and the Stars and Stripes were planted amid cheers from the spectators.

Annie Oakley and Johnny Baker did some dexterous shooting with rfles at clay balls, and Col. Cody took a hand at this himself, and gave an exhibition of sharpshooting while riding at full speed. Indians gave war dances, robbed mail coaches, and destroyed a settler's cabin. There was also a herd of once wild buffaloes, which Buffalo Bill and some of his cowboys punctured with paper cartridges, and some broncho riding by the cowboys and Rough Rider McGinty from Arizona, which was clever and exciting. A group of Mexicans illustrated the use of the lasso. Battery D, Fifth Regiment, United States Army, and a detachment of the Sixteenth Lancers, British Army, the Garde-Kürassiers of Kaiser Wilhelm's army, and the veterans of the Sixth United States Cavalry were seen in military exercises, athletic sports, and horesmanship. Every number was warmly applauded except the three Filipinos, whom the programme designated as "Filipino Rough Riders." They got a round of hisses, but did not seem to know the difference.

The street parade of the show took place yesterday morning. It had been postponed from the day before on account of the rain, but the cold wind yesterday was hardly less disagreeable. The half gale nearly blew some of the women riders from their saddles, and made horseback parading very uncomfortable.

The line of march was followed as laid out in the programme, being confined principally to Fifth and Fourth Avenues, between Fifty-eighth Street and Astor Place. Along the entire route there were tremendous crowds. These were composed chiefly of boys, girls, nurses, and baby carriages.

Col. Cody led the parade, seated on a massive iron gray stallion that had seen service in Puerto Rico. Following him were the cowboys, Indians, Hawaiians, and Filipinos, Cubans, Arabs, Cossacks, and Rough Riders. The parade consumed about two hours, and most of the boys who marched with it as it started followed it from street to street until it was again swallowed up in the recesses of Madison Square Garden.

March 30, 1899

LEW DOCKSTADER OPENS.

Minstrel Gives Bulletins Received by Wireless Telegraphy of the McClellan Dinner and Other Happenings.

Politics and the Democratic harmony dinner came in for a large share of Lew Dockstader's attention last night when he opened his New York season at the Victoria Theatre. As this popular minstrel sat in his flying machine and surveyed all the countries of the earth in rapid succession, he emitted various remarks about Mayor McClellan, ex-President Cleveland, Arthur Pue Gorman, and others high in the Democratic Party. With his wireless telegraph apparatus close at hand he was able to hear everything that was going on at Sherry's last night, and he gave the audience a verbal reproduction of it.

"Ah! There's our new Mayor," was one of his readings from the Marconi ticker, "making his latest promise to the people of New York; he says he won't convert the subway when it's completed into a rathskeller."

"There's our friend Grover," continued the minstrel, not aware of the ex-President's failure to arrive, "refusing some third-term sauce with a Julius-Caesar-putting-away-the-crown expression on his face.

"Now, won't you look at Andy Freedman over there in a corner sulkin' with that handkerchief to his eye. Wonder what's the matter with Andy? Oh, I see, weepin' about that ten dollars he had to give to ride through the subway last Friday.

It is needless to say that the picture of a big negro up in a flying machine, expounding the happenings of a Democratic dinner, was greeted with shouts of laughter by the crowd which filled the Victoria. But all Dockstader's attention was not given to the party at Sherry's. In his flying machine he sailed over the whole world in ten minutes and told the people across the footlights what he saw and heard.

"Look at the beautiful Philippines," he remarked, with a squint through his telescope. "Already I see Wood being promoted."

In less than a second the aerial navigator was looking down on the south end of Manhattan Island.

"What strange things do I see?" he queried. "All society down here at the Battery; there are the Astors, the Vanderbilts, the Twomblys, and look! there is dear little Harry Lehr, with his wristbag and chatelaine. There they go into the Aquarium! Funny; what are they doing there? Oh," (as he hears the ticking of his wireless telegraph apparatus.) "all going to a reception given by Mrs. Fish."

As to the rest of the minstrel show which Dockstader's company gave at the Victoria, it was an elaborate affair, abounding in rather funny dialogue, old-fashioned clog dancing, songs without number, and gorgeous scenic effects to end with.

January 5, 1904

THE CHAUTAUQUA, LIKED BY MILLIONS, IS 40 YEARS OLD

First Chautauqua Was Held on Aug. 4, 1874, for a Few Sunday School Teachers — It Is Estimated That Chautauquas This Summer in 3,000 Towns Will Cost $7,500,000 and Draw 8,000,000 Persons.

FORTY years ago next month, on Aug. 4, 1874, a group of clergymen and Sunday school teachers held the first Chautauqua meeting. This Summer Chautauquas are being held in 3,000 American cities and towns; it is estimated that by the end of the season in September 8,000,000 persons will have paid their admissions to Chautauqua tents and auditoriums, and that approximately $7,500,000 will have been disbursed as gross expenses for the holding of Chautauquas. Such is the popularity which has been attained by the Chautauqua, "the most American thing in America."

The meeting of 1874 was held at Chautauqua, N. Y., it being from this place that the subsequent Chautauquas have borrowed the name. At Chautauqua, N. Y., the Chautauqua Institution, the direct result of that assemblage of forty years ago, is carrying on many activities on an extended scale. It will hold a fortieth anniversary week, beginning Aug. 2. This week will be preceded by a musical festival week, also in honor of the anniversary.

The Chautauqua Institution has no connection with the rest of the 3,000 Chautauquas, and these, in turn, are split into groups and individual units. The two main divisions are system or circuit Chautauquas and local Chautauquas.

Independent Organizations.

There are fifteen system Chautauquas, which control circuits of towns in which Chautauquas are given, of these circuit towns there being 2,400. These system Chautauquas are independent of each other and in many instances are competitive in attempts to book towns.

In addition there are 600 local Chautauquas, these Chautauquas being owned and managed in individual towns, each being independent and having no affiliation either with the circuit Chautauqua or with the original Chautauqua, the Chautauqua Institution.

It is the circuit Chautauquas which are chiefly responsible for the large amount of advertising which the whole Chautauqua movement has obtained as a result of the appearance of Secretary of State Bryan on the platform, most of Mr. Bryan's lectures being given in the tents of circuit Chautauquas. He has, however, also spoken at local Chautauquas and has appeared—though not since being Secretary of State—at the Chautauqua Institution.

Chautauquadom as a whole is by no means pleased with the kind of advertising which has come from the discussions of Mr. Bryan's lectures. The average man on the street has been under the impression that the Secretary of State was as excellent a press agent as the Chautauqua movement could desire. But talk by a TIMES man with Chautauqua officials in New York last week produced the news that the rose of this advertising has a very distinct thorn.

The Chautauqua men say the difficulty is that the newspapers have featured to such an extent the yodlers and magicians who have chanced to be on the programmes with Mr. Bryan that a large number of people who are unfamiliar with Chautauquas have got the impression that these offer only a species of vaudeville show, whereas it is explained that the success of the Chautauqua has come largely from its informative features and its more serious side. "We are uplifters" is a saying in Chautauqua circles.

Although Mr. Bryan's Chautauquanizing has been so much commented upon, a glance at the list of men and women who have appeared upon the Chautauqua platform, or are appearing this Summer, proves that the Secretary of State is by no means the only person of spotlight prominence who has felt the call of Chautauqua.

The roster of those who have spoken at the Chautauqua Institution includes the names of Ulysses S. Grant, Rutherford B. Hayes, James A. Garfield, William McKinley, Theodore Roosevelt, William H. Taft, James Bryce, Robert M. La Follette, Charles E. Hughes, B. B. Odell, Marcus A. Hanna, Earl and Countess of Aberdeen, Henry Drummond, Lady Henry Somerset, Maud Ballington Booth, Susan B. Anthony, John B. Gough, Frances E. Willard, William James, Lew Wallace, Edward Everett Hale, Thomas Nelson Page, George W. Cable, Jacob Riis, Julia Ward Howe, Jane Addams, Charles W. Eliot, and dozens of others famous in politics, social reform, religion, education, law and literature.

Among those who have appeared in circuit or local Chautauquas during the last two or three years, or are appearing this Summer, are Vice President Marshall, Speaker Champ Clark, Joseph W. Folk, Dr. Harvey W. Wiley, Dr. Newell Dwight Hillis, ex-Gov. H. S. Hadley of Missouri, ex-Gov. Robert Glenn of North Carolina, ex-Gov. Richard Yates of Illinois, ex-Gov. E. W. Hoch of Kansas, United States Senator W. S. Kenyon of Iowa, ex-United States Senator Frank J. Cannon of Colorado, ex-Gov. Frank J. Hanly of Indiana, Judge Ben B. Lindsey of Denver, and Dean Walter T. Sumner of Chicago.

"The talent" is the technical term applied in all the Chautauquas to those who hold the platform, whether it be by lecturing, singing, or yodeling. Of this "talent" Mr. Bryan is stated to command the highest price. "And he is well worth it," said a Chautauqua manager to THE TIMES man. "Bryan certainly does deliver the goods—he draws crowds that no one else can."

Mr. Bryan is stated to receive $250 for each lecture, and a generous percentage in addition on all entrance admissions above a certain sum. Vice President Marshall is stated to get $300 per lecture, the same figure being obtained by Senator La Follette. The minimum paid to any of "the talent" in the Chautauquas is declared to be $30 a week and railroad fares.

What It Costs.

At the New York office of the Redpath Chautauqua System, one of the fifteen systems mentioned, it was estimated for THE TIMES man that the expense of a Chautauqua is $2,500 per town. It was stated that it is impossible to get definite figures for the whole United States, but that by multiplying the 3,000 Chautauqua towns by $2,500, what is believed to be a reasonable approximation is arrived at for the gross cost of the Chautauqua per season. This gives $7,500,000.

It was also explained that it is equally difficult to give definite attendance figures for the nation, but that the 8,000,000 estimate before mentioned is probably not very far out of the way. Attendances at towns of the circuit Chautauquas vary from 1,000 to 8,000 for the five or seven-day season which each town gets. Many of the local or independent Chautauqua towns have a season of from two to six weeks, with proportionately larger attendances. The Chautauqua Institution, during its sixty-day season, has an attendance of 50,000 or more. If the average for the 3,000 Chautauquas be put at 2,700—stated to be reasonable—the 8,000,000 figure results.

Chronologically, the development of the Chautauqua movement has been, first, the establishment of the Chautauqua Institution, "the daddy of them all"; second, the formation of the local, independent Chautauquas, chiefly in towns of the Middle West, these Chautauquas following the general lines of the Chautauqua Institution; third—the great development of the last ten years—the organization of the system or circuit Chautauquas.

The man who first proposed the idea which ultimately led to the foundation of the Chautauqua Institution, and thence to the nation-wide Chautauquas of today, is Bishop John H. Vincent, who in 1874 was a Methodist minister in Plainfield, N. J. His idea was, in his own words, "the establishment of a Summer camp institute for the training of Sunday school workers; a Summer institute for thorough normal drill in the interest of the great body of earnest men and women who were in 1874 Sunday school teachers and officers representing all the various church denominations of the country."

Dr. Vincent proposed to his friend the late Lewis Miller, a manufacturer of Akron, Ohio, that such an institute be held in Akron. Mr. Miller replied: "Why not take it into the woods and why not take it to Chautauqua?" Chautauqua, on Lake Chautauqua, was known to them because camp meetings had been held there.

The official record of the first meeting, held from Aug. 4 to 18, 1874, as set out by the Chautauqua Institution in its "Survey of Seasons," shows that Dr. Vincent had been making preparations for the initial assembly during almost all of the preceding year. The meetings were held for the most part in the open air, and in the evening were lighted by pine fires. Tents were used for the housing of the pioneer Chautauquans, and in externals the assemblage was in the nature of a camp meeting.

The department of entertainment was under the direction of Dr. W. W. Wythe. Fireworks, balloon ascensions, music, and displays of panoramic views relieved the heavier features of normal classes and lecture hours. Music was under charge of Prof. W. F. Sherwin.

A series of temperance meetings followed a lecture by Mrs. J. W. Willing, and the Chautauqua report states that these meetings led to a convention, held later in the year in Cleveland, at which the National Woman's Christian Temperance Union was organized.

The First Speakers.

The principal speakers at the first assembly in addition to Dr. Vincent, were the Rev. R. M. Warren, Prof. P. P. Bliss, the Rev. H. Clay Trumbull, John B. Gough, Dr. L. T. Townsend, Dr. C. H. Fowler, the Rev. J. S. Ostrander, the Rev. W. H. Perrine, the Rev. W. F. Crafts, Frank Beard, Bishop Simpson, Bishop Peck, Dr. W. X. Ninde, and Dr. Wythe.

Bishop Vincent will be one of the speakers at the anniversary celebration in August.

From these beginnings the Chautauqua Institution has expanded until today it occupies a fenced-in tract of land on the lake one mile long by one-half a mile wide, on which there are an amphitheatre seating 4,800, other large public buildings and numerous cottages. In the Chautauqua season, which lasts each year throughout July and August, there are lectures, Bible study, readings, concerts, meetings for various denominations, educational and other conferences, meetings of clubs for men, women, and children, and presentation of plays by the Chautauqua Players. There is a Summer school for six weeks of the period, with a faculty drawn from many colleges, offering courses in English, languages, mathematics, and a dozen other subjects. The Chautauqua Literary and Scientific Circle gives a four-year course of home reading, and it is stated that 600,000 men and women have taken diplomas for completing this course.

When the Chautauqua Institution had become established and known, local Chautauquas were organized on a permanent basis at many other places, the Middle West being to the front in this movement. It is estimated that at one time there were 1,500 local Chautauquas in existence. Of late years, however, the local Chautauquas have been disappearing before the onslaughts of the circuit Chautauquas, it being explained that the circuit Chautauqua, doing business on a wholesale scale, gives better "talent," offers a better performance than an independent Chautauqua, particularly in the smaller towns, can afford.

Among the places in which successful independent Chautauquas have been established are Mount Eagle, Tenn.; Winona, Ind.; Bay View and Ludington, Mich.; Ottawa and Winfield, Kan., and Lincoln, Neb.

The majority of the independent Chautauquas have built auditoriums, open at the sides, and these are usually so situated that camping in tents is possible near by, many of the persons who attend the Chautauquas thus living in the open air throughout the season.

The towns which have local Chautauquas range in size, as a rule, from 5,000 to 30,000 population. When it is decided that a town can support an independent Chautauqua, some of the business men get together and form a joint stock company to finance the enterprise. These local Chautauquas are not run for profit to the company organizers, but as a community matter. "The talent" is obtained in the open lyceum market.

Circuit Chautauquas.

The difficulties encountered by these scattered, independent Chautauquas in providing good programmes at reasonable cost led to the inauguration of the system or circuit Chautauquas. In ten years these have become of first importance as to numbers of persons reached. Each of the fifteen systems controls one or more circuits of from forty to ninety towns, averaging in population from 5,000 to 15,000. There are some places of considerable size on the circuits, including Birmingham, Ala.; Savannah, Ga.; Charleston, S. C.; Chattanooga, Tenn., and Cedar Rapids, Iowa.

Most of the circuits are arranged on a seven-day basis, one full week being the season for each town, while the entire circuit season, covering the number of towns composing the circuit, runs from twelve to sixteen weeks. Each day of the seven has its individual programme, different from that of the preceding day. Thus "the talent" playing any given circuit is playing what stage people would call "one-night stands." A lecturer or singer will stay one day in one town, then move on to the next town on the circuit, the "jumps" being short, 100 or 150 miles.

The circuit "talent" is divided into four main groups—lecturers, readers, musicians, and entertainers—while there are also organizers and directors of games for the children. There are three sessions a day, the chief programme usually being at night, when the "star" lecturer gives his talk, although at times he appears in the afternoon. "Movies" are used to illustrate some lectures.

The lecturers and readers cover a wide range of topics. A glance at the list of "talent" under the heading of "musicians" shows that the Chautauquas are getting male and female orchestras, soloists, quartets, operatic companies, glee clubs, Alpine yodlers, bands, jubilee singers, bell ringers, ladies' choirs, and numerous other kinds of melody manufacturers. Among the entertainers are magicians, jugglers, monologists, and Shakesperean players.

Ninety Per Cent. College Men.

Circuit Chautauquas are held under canvas, a large tent being pitched in some central location, usually in a park. It is stated that 90 per cent. of the tent crews, platform managers, cashiers, and field forces generally of the circuit Chautauquas are college men, most of them being undergraduates who are working their way through to their A. B.

When the circuit Chautauqua begins the opening session in any town the whole place is en fête. People pour in from the surrounding countryside. The "twenty-eight-day man" and the "nine-day man"—as the advance agents are known from the periods they precede the Chautauqua—have attended to the arousing of adequate enthusiasm. They have had the streets brightened with streamers and with what are known as awning banners; leaflets and tags and hats, blazoned with the merits of the Chautauqua, have been distributed by thousands; an automobile and band parade has been held; every one is on tiptoe for the big week.

Thus far the circuit Chautauqua has had its stronghold in the Middle West and South. But an Eastern invasion is in progress, and this Summer twenty-five towns in the northern and western parts of New York are having their Chautauqua baptism.

July 12, 1914

'OPRY HOUSE' TRAIL FAST DISAPPEARING

Old-Time Troupers Would Gladly Go Back to It if They Could.

PIONEER DAYS PROFITABLE

Mattie Keene Recalls Overland Tour of Peyton Comedy Company at $1,000 a Night.

Fast disappearing from the world of wig and buskin is a type of actor who was no less a pioneer than those trail breakers who blazed a path to Oregon, settled the Cherokee strip and transformed Oklahoma from a wilderness to a state of thriving cities and towns. Only a few of these troupers had seen Broadway in the days when they followed the rush of settlers to newly opened lands and gave their performances with the light of gas flares and candles under canvas. They traveled many a mile in stage coaches, with their scenery and props, such as they were, following in Conestoga wagons. They were the first to open the "Opry House" of the boom towns that sprang up overnight, some waxing permanently prosperous, others slowly dying.

They look back on those days, these troupers, with sighs of regret and there are times when they would gladly exchange the permanence and comforts of New York apartment house or hotel room for the tents in which they dressed when Arizona and New Mexico were territories and when, joining the rush of claim stakers into Oklahoma, they cooked their meals in the open on a camp stove. Such a company, one that will be well remembered by the settlers of the States named in the early '80s, was the Isaac Peyton Comedy Company. Its star was Mattie Keene, Peyton being her husband. So far as she knows, she is the only one left of the original troupe. She still wears, whether in street clothes or in the negro "mammy" costume she dons in "Caroline," a silver brooch fashioned from coin collected for her by a New Mexico train robber and bandit at the point of a six-shooter during a performance in Raton, New Mexico, in the days when it raised a plentifuul crop of outlaws.

Troupers Staked Out Claims.

As she rubbed brown grease paint on her face in her dressing room at the Ambassador Theatre she bewailed the passing of the day when burnt cork was considered plenty good enough for his blackface makeup. "It had to be," she said. "Only hot water will remove grease paint, and hot water was as scarce as a golf ball in the days when Guthrie, Okla., was founded, and we went with the rush to Ponca, and staked claims for ourselves before we gave our evening performance. I never shall forget the night we rode into Raton and were told by the manager of the rickety frame opera house that he didn't think it was safe to give a performance. 'Bill' Rogers—no relation to our well-known after-dinner speaker who doubles on the stage—and his band of outlaws had engaged all the seats on one side of the house and the manager feared gun-play.

"Rogers was one of those Robin Hood sort of outlaws. He robbed the express cars of money and gold and silver bullion, but believed in liquid assets and spent and bestowed freely on needy gamblers and poor saloonkeepers and dance hall proprietors what he took from the mine owners. The Sheriff, under orders to take him dead or alive, had cornered him in Raton a few days before our arrival. Rogers shot first, but instead of shooting to kill, shot the Sheriff through the hand. That made him the hero of the town. We decided to give the performance, and when the curtain went up there was Rogers and his gang, each with a brace of revolvers at his hip, on one side of the house and the townsfolk, many of them similarly armed, on the other.

"After a curtain call I interpolated in one of my songs a verse in which I gave both the Sheriff and Rogers credit for being equally brave and praised Rogers for sparing the life of his foe. Rogers arose, took a six-shooter in one hand and his hat in the other, and crossed to the other side of the house. Going to each man, he said 'dig.' 'You-all ain't got no call to flourish that six-shooter,' they told him. 'We's a-dig anyway.' The hat contained $200 in silver when he placed it on the stage. We stayed there a week, and Rogers sent flowers for the women of the company every day, but never came near us.

Receipts $1,000 a Night.

"We had twenty-eight in the Peyton company, including a band and orchestra. We always gave a street parade as soon as we hit a town. The night before the site of Guthrie, Okla., was thrown open, we waited with the others in Arkansas City, and the next day joined the rush of men and women on horseback and in all sorts of vehicles. We had a tent that would seat a thousand, and ours was the first tent up. Most of the others slept and cooked and ate on the bare ground the first day, but in three days every one had a tent with floors. We played ten nights to receipts of $1,000 a night. That's better than some Broadway houses have been doing of late.

"We made it our business to follow the rushes to the newly opened lands and pitch our tent within twenty-four hours after the settlers had established themselves. We were the first to perform in practically every one of the first 'opera houses'—they didn't have theatres then—in the towns that sprang up between the '80's and '90's in Oklahoma, Arizona and New Mexico. We played the old favorites the settlers had known 'back home'—'East Lynne,' 'Camille,' 'Frou Frou,' 'Fogg's Ferry,' 'Caprice,' 'The Old Homestead,' 'The Masterman,' 'Uncle Tom's Cabin,' and 'Ten Nights in a Barroom.' Indians were common in our audiences.

"We played Omaha and Kansas City a month at a time. They consider $3 a seat high along Broadway now. We used to get that in Tucson and other Arizona cities and towns. No seat sold for less than $2. We played the Cherokee strip and I still have in litigation a claim in Ponca which I staked out on the spot where we pitched our tent for our first performance there.

"We played under tents in Oklahoma when the wind seemed likely at any moment to bowl the canvas over and bury actors and audience under it. And cold? Our teeth would chatter so we could hardly speak our lines. I remember one night when I was playing Lady Isabel in 'East Lynne.' When the time came for Willie's death-bed scene, his teeth were clicking like castanets. He shut his eyes and was motionless, but his teeth chattered on. 'Never mind, Willie,' I said. 'I know it's cold, but just die quietly. Soon you'll be where it's warmer.'

"There wasn't a dry eye in the tent, but there were tears of laughter."

May 13, 1923

THE LADY AND THE EEL GRASS

A Musical Romance in One Act Presented at Koster & Bial's

After the athletic exhibition of the india-rubber persons who call themselves "sisters," and Picchiani at that, and some time before Charmion disrobed herself and chucked her garters at the folks in the orchestra, came "Au Bain," book by Alexandre Derolles, music by Maxime Lechamps. It was hoped, because of the excess of acrobatism in the bill at Koster & Bial's this week, that the new "turn" would not be acrobatic; but the swimming of Adele Ritchie was found to be as wonderful in its way as any other feat of physical prowess in the long programme.

Miss Ritchie appeared as Suzanne, betrothed by the testament of an elderly female relative to her cousin Anatole. She had made Anatole believe that she was old and ugly, and he had refused to marry her, thus losing his share of the old woman's fortune. Then Suzanne, it being night, undressed herself and went in swimming, while the man in the moon looked on and wept. But presently along came Anatole again, singing joyfully to himself, as Anatoles will, and naughty Suzanne was impelled (like another Eve) to make a small but serviceable garment for herself out of the eel grass. Whereupon Anatole, accoutred as he was, jumped into the water, too, and they both sang and swam and swam and sang. Finally Anatole was prevailed upon to go home, and call next day, whereupon Suzanne emerged from the wave, like Aphrodite, and the calciums spluttered and the curtain fell. The parents of many of the men and women who saw this thing last night used to go to church and reverently say their prayers every night.

April 5, 1898

TONY PASTOR'S THEATRE.

Minstrelsy was combined with vaudeville at Tony Pastor's last night, and an enjoyable entertainment resulted. In the minstrel part there was some excellent ballad singing, and with Mr. "Billy" Birch at one end, Mr. Frank Moran at the other, and the celebrated Addison Ryman in the middle of the semicircle, the fun passed briskly. Miss Jennie Valmore has become a great favorite, and she was obliged to sing her verses over and over again to satisfy an audience that left no room for more in the house. Her pretty face and becoming costumes would, perhaps, assure her success even without the songs. Mr. Pastor himself was in excellent spirits and told the ladies present how to keep their husbands at home with much felicity, while his exhibition of the manner they dance in Walhalla Hall brought down the house. Others who assisted in making the evening pleasant were Musical Dale, The Only Leon, and Geyer and Lord.

January 14, 1890

With the Men and Women of the Twice-a-Day

The Great American Vaudeville Industry ---A Sidelight on Its People--- The Plans for a Gigantic Combination and How Managers and Performers View It.

THE rumor of a new $30,000,000 vaudeville act—a regular "top-line" combination—has been giving Broadway a good deal to talk about. In the slang of the profession, it may make good or it may not. The theatrical strong family of Klaw & Erlanger, B. F. Keith, Kohl & Castle, and the rest, may succeed in hammering together a big chain of vaudeville houses from Boston to San Francisco; or, as other powerful parties in the field claim, they may be promising rather more than they can perform. Whatever happens, vaudeville people, far and wide, may be happy in feeling that their doings, their recruits, and their salaries are getting more attention than ever from a devoted public.

They are an interesting lot of people in themselves, these vaudeville folk, quite apart from their value to syndicates and combinations. There are hosts of them. Go up into one of the two big vaudeville booking agencies some morning—either at Keith's or at William Morris's, where the P. G. Williams, Hammerstein, and Proctor circuits have their headquarters. In the outer office you will find a crowd of waiting humanity, in all sizes, ages, complexions, and degrees of prosperity—but all with that indefinable air of being used to being looked at. The place looks like a big railway station. Everybody seems to have just come in from somewhere or to be just starting off for somewhere else. They lounge about, chatting, laughing, or silent, according as they are confident or doubtful of the next bookings. In one group is the smooth-shaven man you could spot anywhere on earth as the fellow who does the rapid-fire-thirteen-to-a-dozen-and-no-periods monologue in front of a row of brownstone houses, with the park in the distance. Over in the corner, with blonde hair and a faded raincoat, is the little girl who plays a cornet, dressed in smart hussar kilts and gold frogs. And so on. The big people don't come much to the office. They have their own private agents, and their booking lists are always as complete as a saint's calendar. When they do come, they "walk right in."

The rank and file of vaudeville people, who book for short periods, are encouraged to keep in touch with the office. They never know when they may be needed for fillers. Inside with a staff of clerks sits the booking man, like a train dispatcher, with his chart of theatres, acts, and dates, upon which he moves people about like so many freight cars.

For vaudeville has grown, since its humble origin in the old variety show of the Tony Pastor days, when one act had to do service over and over again, into one of the most extensive and complicated branches of the theatrical world. There are now over a hundred first-class vaudeville houses where the higher class acts are sure of continual and profitable booking, besides hundreds of smaller variety houses, with a constant demand for cheaper turns.

The evolution has been in quality as well as in quantity.

BEGINNINGS OF THE CONTINUOUS.

When B. F. Keith established his first continuous performance at his little Bijou Theatre, in Boston, in the middle 80s, and F. F. Proctor introduced the same thing in New York at his Twenty-third Street Theatre, the day of polite vaudeville dawned. Before that, variety acts had been of a rough-and-tumble, strongly flavored sort that went along with beer and sand floors. But to the continuous performance came audiences made up largely of women and children, and parlor vaudeville was soon in full swing. Plenty of people can remember when it came. It marked the first demand for the quieter, cleverer acts that have constantly attracted better and better performers from the legitimate to the variety stage.

Kitty Gordon—A New Recruit.

The continuous performance proved so profitable, and the public that had been paying 50 cents and finding its own seats, began to come so regularly and in such goodly form, that presently two performances a day, with reserved seats at $1, and a still better class of act, seemed the only way to keep up to the proper level. Since then the constant rise of vaudeville salaries and the frequent beguilement of noted stage people into the vaudeville circuits has been one of the common marvels for the man in the street.

A few nights ago F. F. Proctor, who stands for as much as anybody in the development of vaudeville in America, showed some friends an interesting old bill that he had kept in his archives. It was a variety show bill of the Olympic Theatre, dated in the early 80s. The top liners—and they were placed in little boxes side by side, so there could be no jealousy—were F. F. Proctor and Nat Goodwin. Mr. Proctor in those days, be it said, was nightly lying on his back and juggling barrels and easy chairs on his feet. Further down the bill, which was a long one, came Flo and May Irwin, Weber and Fields, and the Braatz family, the famous troupe of European jugglers. It was regarded at the time as an exceptional bill and highly expensive.

Now, the weekly cost of that "aggregation of talent," as it was probably called in the 80s, was just $1,100 per week. To-day the average weekly programme of from fifteen to eighteen acts costs from $3,000 to $5,000. The "top liner" alone often goes up to $1,500 and even $2,000. Twenty-five years ago $100 a week was big pay for a first-rate variety act, and $150 salaries were rare enough to be underlined.

To-day there is hardly an act in vaudeville, even the one that opens the bill while the audience is straggling in one at a time, that does not get at least $100; $700 and $800 salaries are the rule for families or troupes of three or four members.

SOME ENORMOUS SALARIES.

Phenomenal salaries in vaudeville are hard to quote accurately. They are usually magnified by the telling. Both manager and performer like to have the figure sound as round and as pleasant as possible, but careful inquiry only ends by amazing one at the enormous sums that actually seem to be paid. The present season furnishes examples enough.

According to reasonably reliable quotations Vesta Victoria, the English music hall singer, receives $1,000 per week; Yvette Guilbert gets $2,000; Henri de Vries, the Dutch actor, $1,750; Fred Walton, with his wooden soldier pantomime, $1,250; the Fays, $1,500. Earlier in the season Mr. Hammerstein made a contract with Williams and Walker by which they received $1,500 and a certain percentage of the box office receipts. Such a percentage is practically never allowed in vaudeville.

F. F. Proctor is said to have paid Lillian Russell $30,000 for ten performances, but

Vesta Victoria.

Yvette Guilbert.

perhaps the largest authentic offer ever made to an actor to go into vaudeville was contained in a telegram which Mr. Proctor sent to Nat Goodwin just after the failure of "Beauty and the Barge." The figure offered was $4,000.

Percy G. Williams, however, would have us believe that Vesta Tilley, who is now appearing at the Colonial, is breaking the record in the matter of vaudeville salaries. According to the story, Miss Tilley dreaded the fourteen performances a week necessary here in America and could hardly be persuaded to come. "Besides," she said, "I get off in London with two or three songs, whereas here they make me sing five or six."

"When she was here before," declares Mr. Williams, "she sang six evenings and three matinées, for which she received $2,000. I found, however, the three matinée arrangement did us a lot of harm, owing to the disappointment of people who, unwittingly, came on the off days. So I figured out that $2,000 for what she did before amounted to about $10 per minute, and I offered her that rate to appear twice daily during the present engagement. We have agreed that the time is to be reckoned from the moment she steps on the stage until the instant she finishes her last song. Curtain calls and speeches are not to be counted in. I expect this arrangement will cost me between $3,000 and $3,500 per week, which I believe is the largest salary ever paid in vaudeville up to the present time."

When one remembers that for the singer this means hardly more than driving to the theatre for an hour or an hour and a half twice a day, one understands why vaudeville has its irresistible attraction for the dramatic or musical star. "And it's not infra dig any more," one of them explained the other day. "It used to be only the worn-out, used-up stage people that went into vaudeville; now many of them take a turn at it now and then in their prime, and with their very best effort. They can count on good hours and excellent audiences." The speaker happened to be doing it just then herself, but her remark had none the less point.

But how can the vaudeville manager afford to pay these salaries, which would, of course, stagger any regular dramatic producer? The obvious answer is that he can count on two audiences a day. Also, he is supreme—the salaries he pays are final, and he has no percentage to divide with his stars. In fact, the only percentages he has to pay at all are the small ones to his booking agents.

AN EYE TO THE PROFITS.

Mr. Williams thus explains the manager's side of it: "Suppose I were managing Richard Mansfield or Sir Henry Irving, giving them 80 per cent. of the gross receipts. If we took in $12,000 one week it would be really no better, from my point of view, than $8,000 at better terms. Suppose, on the other hand, I am running vaudeville. Suppose with a certain top-line bill I take in $14,000 in a week. It makes no particular difference to me whether I pay salaries amounting to $3,000, $4,000, or $5,000. What I have to pay out doesn't increase proportionately with what I take in. My profits are not reduced by any percentage obligations."

After all, these very high salaries are exceptional. The real value of any salary to the receiver is measured to a certain extent by how much of it he has to spend. It is probably true that the general run of vaudeville people are more thrifty than their dramatic brethren. They may, as a whole, get bigger salaries—they certainly save proportionately more of their income.

There seems to be a curious bond between vaudeville and circus people in the matter of economy and simplicity. Vaudeville people look upon their daily performance as a kind of regular task. Your actor friend asks, "Where are you playing?" With the vaudeville player it is more likely to be "Where are you working?" He takes a certain quiet pride in thinking of what he does as merely the day's work, and he is very likely to tuck away a good share of the proceeds toward future comfort. As a man who has known vaudeville for many years puts it:

"They don't get their money in big chunks, but they hold on to it, and you'll find that later on it's the vaudeville people who are giving the benefits for some busted star."

A surprising number are eager to play seven days in the week for the sake of the extra money. They like to get to New York for just that reason. Of all the hundreds of actors' homes that dot certain parts of Long Island fully two-thirds are said to represent the thrift and domestic instinct of vaudeville folk. They take their profession as a matter of course, and seldom as a pose. They talk about it but little. Go into the greenroom, down at Keith's some afternoon and ten to one you'll find a couple of spangled women, who look on the stage as if they never lifted a finger for housekeeping, sewing away on socks or buttonholes while they wait their turn. Many of the men, and women, too, for that matter, are inveterate farmers with a little plot of land somewhere, to which they fly whenever they can. At this time of year their talk is likely to be far less of the Rialto than of "what are you going to raise this year?" and "isn't it time to send word to plant the peas?"

STEAL ONE ANOTHER'S THUNDER.

One bad habit these vaudeville people have. They are incorrigible stealers of one another's lines and business. If an act happens to have a clever costume or "gag" in it, ten to one some other team playing at the same theatre will borrow it. When the original proprietor springs his joke in the next town he is lucky if he doesn't find some colleague has been along ahead of him and spoiled his thunder.

There was a case in Indianapolis not long ago of a monologue comedian who originated the line "I've got money to burn, but I don't like the smell of the smoke afterward." For some reason or other he was very proud of it. When he got to St. Louis he found everybody there thoroughly familiar with his pet line. In fact, they accused him of stealing it from an act that had just gone through there. Of course he had copyright protection and all that, but by the time he got the machinery of the law in full action both acts had been taken off and everybody had forgotten all about them. No way has yet been invented to prevent one vaudeville performer from "lifting" the good points from his neighbor's turn.

You rarely hear the word "player" on the stage of a vaudeville house. Whatever you have been, or done elsewhere, in vaudeville you become a plain "performer." Just inside the stage door at the Victoria there hangs a sign, "Performers must be at the theatre one hour before their acts," and elsewhere, "Performers are not to use this exit." These signs have caused some amusement among the big theatrical stars who have recently played in the theatre. As Fred Walton remarked when he caught sight of it, "Here am I a vulgar fraction reduced to my lowest terms."

By the same token there are at Hammerstein's two star dressing rooms, side by side, just alike, and both numbered "1"—a fine preventive of faultfinding. While of course vaudeville people have their jealousies and their ambition to stand in good places on the bill, their rating is so definitely understood when they are booked that they can't fail to realize then and there just where their names are likely to be placed.

TRY OUT FOR NEW ACTS.

New acts are constantly being tried out. On certain mornings every week from the big bare stages of empty theatres you will find "funny men" cracking their best jokes and young sopranos singing the "Jewel Song" to a trio of bored managers in the dark orchestra below, who have heard every joke and every song ever sprung in vaudeville.

The past year has seen an unusual number of successful one-act plays translated bodily into vaudeville. In fact, one of the most marked advances in the vaudeville world is its growing tendency to absorb complete productions. In two cases one-act plays have been selected which it will cost from $6,000 to $10,000 merely to put on.

Vaudeville stage managers and agents bear witness to the general promptness and sobriety of vaudeville performers. "Why," said a man connected with Keith, "I only remember one case where we had to turn off a man for drunkenness, and he was a recruit from musical comedy."

There is a certain family of three—father, mother, and daughter—who have played for many years in vaudeville circles. For their sketch they receive $250 per week; out of that the father pays 10 per cent. royalty to the author of his sketch and 5 per cent. to the booking agent. Railway fares (which are never paid by the vaudeville manager, except in the case of long jumps) average $5 a week for each person. Out of the remainder this man, of course, defrays the living expenses of his family. He thinks it a very bad week indeed, however, when he doesn't have $100 to put away, and he owns a little farm up in Central New York where he and his wife and daughter spend exactly three weeks every year. But it's there for them later.

Meanwhile, the family go to small hotels and boarding houses, which are not in the least theatrical, and they could probably steer you into a dozen little cafés in New York that you never dreamed could be so good, so clean, and so cheap. This man was once David Belasco's assistant stage manager, but he finds he can make and save money on vaudeville rounds, and he does it as systematically as a man going daily to his desk.

CHANCE FOR FAMILY LIFE.

Another good thing about vaudeville from the performer's point of view is the chance it gives for family life, even on the road. In straight drama it is not often that man and wife fit into the same cast. If they do there are almost sure to be complications. If they don't quarrel with each other they quarrel together with the rest of the company. If one leaves, the other is likely to follow, and altogether the manager would infinitely rather have them cast apart in different companies. In vaudeville, on the other hand, if man and wife are in the same act, the whole thing is too small to ever develop serious complications. They are too necessary to each other. If they have separate acts they can easily get the same bookings, and year after year their names will be found together on the same bill.

Nine-tenths of the "families" billed in vaudeville are perfectly genuine. Of course, in certain foreign troupes of jugglers and acrobats there are one or two apprentices; yet acrobatic talent and vaudeville accomplishments in general are very apt to run in families, and vaudeville people are strongly inclined to marry among themselves.

Neither of the two great vaudeville booking agencies in New York, the Keith-Kohl & Castle-Orpheum circuit on the one hand, and the Morris-Williams-Hammerstein-Proctor group on the other, will admit that it wishes its colleague anything but health, long life, and prosperity.

WHAT MANAGERS CONTEND.

"We have always dealt cordially with the Keith agency," said Mr. Williams. "We have exchanged bookings and sublet acts with the greatest freedom, and I don't see why we shouldn't continue to do so.

"Frankly, I don't believe any such combine as has been reported is possible. Our vaudeville people are individually too independent to make it practicable. If there were to be any such combination, however, I should much prefer to be the man left alone on the outside of it. You see, we control the New York circuit, which is the only one cosmopolitan enough to support these very big foreign people like Vesta Tilley, De Vries, Walton, or Mme. Guilbert. The managers on the Western circuits are probably beginning to think they ought to have some of these big attractions. The rumored combine may be an effort to float a syndicate big enough to handle them. They will find, however, their audiences won't rally to things they don't understand.

"On the other hand, it may equally well be that Klaw & Erlanger are afraid that some of the smaller theatres whose bookings they control are going over to vaudeville, in which case the syndicate proposes to still retain the upper hand. Just the same, I don't believe the combine is possible."

Said "Willy" Hammerstein: "If the effect of the proposal is to raise vaudeville salaries, it won't trouble us in the least, for I believe the higher vaudeville salaries are the better. In this business high salaries keep off competition. The moment you get a scale of low salaries you have vaudeville houses opening up every three blocks; but I don't believe there will be any combine."

Mark Leuscher, F. F. Proctor's manager and booking agent, put it thus: "We are perfectly well able to look out for ourselves, and there is room for us all, anyway; but I don't believe there can be any combination."

On the other side, the Klaw & Erlanger-Keith interests, as voiced in E. F. Albee, Mr. Keith's General Manager, calmly assert that there will be a combination; that the first steps have already been taken, and that details are rapidly being worked out.

"We mean no harm to any one," said Mr. Albee, "and the whole plan is simply to secure greater efficiency of organization. But a combine there will be."

Meanwhile the vaudeville performer and his public sit tight, keep on good terms, and await results.

May 6, 1906

A Bird's Eye View of Sunday Vaudeville

With the Lid Down on Sunday Amusements, the Performers Are Obliged to Resort to Some Curious Makeshifts to Keep Within the Law.

THE lid is down on Sunday vaudeville in New York, and the police are sitting on it. The managers of the theatres go on with the shows, protesting that they are strictly observing the Sabbath. The performances are given without changes in scenery, the use of curtains, dancing, tights, acrobatic feats, stage disguises or make-up. Even programmes are hard to find. Vaudeville minus these features defies description.

A reporter dropped into a music hall on Fourteenth Street last Sunday evening to learn precisely what a Sabbath theatre concert meant.

"Glad to see you!" said the manager. "We've a show here you could give in a church. Come in and see for yourself."

The theatre was crowded. Waiters were gliding up and down the aisles with trays and glasses. The spectators looked down on the stage through a cloud of tobacco smoke. The scenery represented a drawing room, with a piano and a superabundance of tables and sofas. The orchestra wailed plaintively as a young man in street clothes leaned over the footlights and told in song how he "must say good-bye to mother now."

After the customary applause, a drop curtain was needed. It didn't come down. Instead two stage hands appeared, shifted the piano, tables, and rugs, and arranged several musical instruments in conspicuous places.

The next "turn" should have been a comedy sketch. On Sunday the dramatic part of it reminded one of "Hamlet" with the melancholy Dane left out. A haughty wife scolded her flippant husband as he dodged around the sofa, it is true, and all the old jokes were there, but the fun had the qualities of an after-dinner story told the next morning at breakfast.

"Where are the acrobats and dancers who once appeared in Sunday night shows?" asked the reporter.

"They're playing in smaller cities near New York," replied the manager.

The same story was told, with variations, at another vaudeville theatre in Fourteenth Street. There were no smoke and waiters with trays. Every seat was filled, and the spectators were enjoying themselves mildly. A drawing room scene served for a short play, a musical sketch, singers, and "monologue artists." One of the main features was a high-priced "hobo" team. The names recalled stubby black beards, red noses, bruised eyes, tattered clothes held together by ropes and dangling tin cans. The reality proved to be two modish and good-looking young men in street clothes. Their "hobo" jokes and antics seemed like a Hester Street idyl played at Sherry's.

On the Bowery they do things in a different way. The change from Union Square seemed to be as great as that experienced in a journey from Tammany Hall to the Bowery. Mingling with a holiday throng—swart Italians, Russians, sailors, and Chinamen—the reporter made his way to a Yiddish music hall. The rude theatre was crowded. Boys passed among the spectators with trays of apples, oranges, and chocolate. As the show began there were loud cries of "Hats off!" "Hats off, ladies!" "Down in front!" The first scene was a harvest field. Women garnered grain. Men stood near with scythes. They wore the dresses of old Russia and sang in Yiddish.

A man sitting beside the reporter had his word to say of Sunday shows in general.

"I'm from Brooklyn," he said, "and came over to the Bowery to have a good time. I tried to get into three theatres near Union Square. They were all crowded. Then I went to a music hall where they are acting plays in Italian. They have a fine actress there. The place was packed, and the man at the door wanted to know if I could understand Italian before he would sell me a ticket. So I came here. There are a dozen of these concert halls now, where there were only two or three a year ago."

On the west side and in Harlem the reporter found more "Grand Sunday Concerts" in progress. At one of them a short play told how a shrewish bride could bully a very meek husband. Then a woman appeared in a black dress of the baggiest sort. By this symbol the spectators knew she was a servant. The bridegroom found an excuse in her—or possibly in her dress—to pretend he was insane and scare his wife so badly that she forgot her bad temper.

In one of the Harlem theatres the inevitable drawing room scene was in reality a boudoir. There was a dressing table on one side, a piano on the other. The play would have been a "homespun" farce on week days. On Sunday it was "concert" in the strictest sense. An old man in a gingham vest was the picture of Uncle "Josh" Whitcomb. His hoary locks may have been "street clothes," but probably came from a wigmaker's. The heroine strongly suggested "Sis Hopkins," with her long apron and Maud Muller hat. Whether she appeared on the street in this garb deponent sayeth not.

Returning to the "Rialto," vaudeville was found with more odd limitations. An act had been offered there in which a man allowed an automobile to run over him. He wore tights on week days, so the people could see his muscles swell as the motor car struck him. He could not wear tights on Sundays, so he gave his performance in street clothes.

The most difficult problem was found at a performance by French players. The programme included selections from operas, classical music, a short play, and the first performance here of a French operetta. As the scene could not be changed the managers chose the most important setting. The stage represented a kitchen. There were a stove, a piano below it, and an ironing board and kitchen sink on the other side. The spectators were supposed to forget the kitchen when the piano was moved forward, and the soloists sang from "Mignon," Massenet's "Herodeade," and Hughes's "Le Légende des Capucines" against a background of pots and pans.

This was the only performance in which a programme, in the strict meaning of the term, was used. In most of the theatres the audiences were left in the dark regarding the acts to come. In the others the names of the performers appeared in a printed list, without a word of explanation. The law would not permit the regular programmes, the managers said. Even advertisements could not appear on the slips of paper. Details of the performances would make the lists playbills, and these were forbidden.

December 23, 1906

What They Used to Laugh At

By FRANK J. WILSTACH.

REDUCED to so much newspaper print for Sunday morning reading, the cross-fire patter of our so-called "sidewalk" comedians, past and present, is certainly flimsy enough stuff. But, given life by the personalities and methods of the comedians themselves, and spoken in a gay and festive music hall instead of being read over a routine breakfast table, it has been known to stir the merry chuckle and not infrequently the uproarious guffaw. Even with every allowance made, however, an inspection of what they used to laugh at in the old days is likely to be fairly disillusioning.

The comedy team, of course, is not entirely a thing of the past, although there seem to be fewer in existence today than there were not so long ago. Also, the present-day ones seem to be better, although this viewpoint is unquestionably traceable to a great familiarity with current styles of humor. The method of the comedy team remains more or less unvaried. The team is composed, in the first place, of a comedian and a "straight" man. The former asks a question, the latter answers or repeats it—and then comes the "nifty." With which consummation the straight man is struck over the head with a folded newspaper, a stuffed club, a violin, a bladder, a slapstick or an axe.

In tracking the sidewalk comedian to his lair let me begin—for reasons which will be obvious to my friends—with Bobby Clark and Paul McCullough—in other words, Clark and McCullough of the Music Box Revue. Clark and McCullough do not depend entirely upon cross-fire patter; they are expert also in other fields. But for the purposes of this inquiry let us examine this cutting from their "routine":

Clark—Who are you?

McCullough—I am a sailor.

Clark—Ever married?

McCullough—Yes, nine times.

Clark—You are no sailor; you are a wholesaler.

But to weigh the cross-fire talk of the comedy team in the scales of literature would be an incongruous proceeding. It is the team's business to make the public laugh and not to acquire bouquets of encomiums from literary critics, bookmen, highbrows and the dilettante generally. This posture of circumstance, as the late William Winter would have said, does not apply to Harrigan and Hart. It is a difficult matter, however, to lift excerpts from the sketches in which they appeared for the reason that mere cross-fire conversation was not depended upon for laughter.

Harry and John Kernell, thirty years or more ago, were a highly successful sidewalk conversation act. Here is some of their patter:

Harry—What sort of hair did Moses's dog have?

John (instead of asking "Why?")—Dog's hair.

Harry (much irritated at this)—What sort of monkeys grow on grape vines? (And giving John no chance to reply, said in the same breath)—Grayapes. Why didn't you give that away?

All the old timers—that is, those whose memories go back thirty years or more—are of the opinion that the greatest sidewalk conversationalists of the past were Hawkins and Collins,

A Shadowed Impression of Joseph Allen and George Abbott as the Cowboys of "Zander the Great."

otherwise Lew Hawkins and Ben Collins. Not only were they effective in their patter, but they could sing, dance and were highly efficient in the afterpiece of a minstrel show. None of their routine, so called, is available; but they had a catch phrase which, it appears, was immensely popular. Hawkins would tell Collins a story, or vice versa, and then one would say to the other: "That will kill Mahoney."

The cross-fire talk of the old team of Barry and Fay was of an unusually ingenuous variety. It will be recalled that Fay, after a hard night with the bottle, was annoyed by Barry's asking over and over again what he could do for him. Fay tried to drive him away and avoid a reply, but finally said in broad Irish dialect: "Oh, go out and buy me a copy of the Staats-Zeitung!"

Murray and Murphy were another famous team. Murray would say to Murphy: "Mr. Gilhooley, are you fond of fruit?"

Murphy: "I am that. Mr. Mulcahey. The last fruit I ate was a piece of cheese."

Then Gilhooley would crack a walnut on Mulcahey's head.

It wasn't so much the patter of the famous Russell Brothers—John and James—that made them so enormously popular, but rather the dancing and burlesque scenes indulged in by James. James would go up to a small aquarium, located on the side of the stage, lift it to his lips, take a drink and then shriek: "My God, Maggie, I thought I swallowed a goldfish!" People have been known to go to a hospital for repairs after seeing Jimmie Russell swallow the goldfish! He also used to produce hysterics through yelling, unexpectedly: "My God, Maggie, the cow's in the hammock!" And then again: "Good heavens, Maggie, I thought I saw a dollar!"

Thirty-odd years ago Sam Bernard and John Corrigan, the latter being the present stage carpenter of the Music Box, were doing a sidewalk act. This act usually ended in a fight. This hilarious mock trial began:

Corrigan, as an Irish cab driver: "You see this fist? I hit a man so hard with it that it sunk into him so deep that they had to get a derrick to pull it out."

Bernard, as an English tiger: "See my fist? I hit a man so hard with it that his whole family died."

Bert Williams and his partner, George Walker, managed somehow to supply themselves with unusually expert material. One of their best comedy scenes, and one which caused the most laughter, was in "In Dahomey." In the first scene of the last act, Bert Williams was incarcerated for theft. Walker visited him in jail. After Walker had been conducted to Williams by the keeper, Walker began by upbraiding Williams for having committed a theft.

"And you see, now, after you done stole, what the penalty was. A man tole you when you got in dis country what they do wit' thieves. Didn't he done tole you when if anybody stole they cuts one of his arms off, and still you go out and steal. Now you are going to suffer; you are going to have your arm cut off. Ain't you going to look nice goin' back home to your mammy with one arm and one stump? What's she goin' to think of you? What you goin' to do with one arm and one stump? How can a man make a living with a stump? Come and tell me; tell me what good is a stump?"

Whereupon Williams replied, looking at Walker sheepishly:

"I'm going to put a hook on it."

Montgomery and Stone, during their early days as a team, were acrobats more than sidewalk conversationalists. One of the old-timers recalls Fred Stone's speach when he made his first appearance in a circus concert. Here it is:

"I just removed my ulsterteena acrenanistamo and put it in the subdenilistamo, where it would be safe at a distamo."

The Rogers Brothers, Gus and Max, managed for many years with their cross-fire talk to delight the multitude. Again it was the manner, not the matter; yet they must have known the sort of thing that was wanted. Here is some of their routine:

Gus—Come along, don't wear your clothes so far away from yourself.

Max—Do I look like an Admiral?

Gus—If I told you what you look like, you would be ashamed to believe me. Put on the helmet.

Max—The hell with what?

Gus—The helmet, the hat.

Max—The hell with the hat?

Gus—That shows me you know nothing about the army.

Max—Sure I do, the Navy's the place they make Navy beans.

Gus—No, the Navy is a lot of woolen warships, made out of iron that can swim.

Really!

Thirty years ago David Warfield and Lee Harrison were the comedian and the straight man of the various musical pieces. The best remembered of their conversations was the following:

Harrison—What is the matter with you!

Warfield—A dog just hollered at me. I don't know why, I didn't done him nothing.

Harrison—You shouldn't have been frightened. Don't you know that a barking dog never bites?

Warfield—You know, and I know, but the dog don't know it.

For twenty-five years—that is, from 1886 to 1911—a popular team in vaudeville was Smith and Campbell. Campbell the comedian, Smith the straight man. They gave what was commonly known as "a patter show." Their swift, rapid-fire talk proved highly diverting to vaudeville audiences in England and America:

Campbell—You are, without a doubt, the best night-owl I ever saw.

Smith—What became of you last night?

Campbell—You shouldn't have quit me so quick.

Smith—Why not?

Campbell—After I left you I found a gold watch.

Smith—Gee whiz! that was good.

Campbell—No, that was bad.

Smith—Why?

Campbell—The man who owned it came along and I had to give it right back to him.

Smith—That was bad.

Campbell—No, that was good.

Smith—How's that?

Campbell—He gave me $10 for finding it.

Smith—That was good.

Campbell—No, that was bad.

Smith—Why?

Campbell—I blew in the ten.

Smith—That was bad.

Campbell—No, that was good.

Smith—Why so?

Campbell—I got drunk on it.

Smith—That was good.

Campbell—No, that was bad.

Smith—Why?

Campbell—I was arrested for disorderly conduct.

Smith—That was bad.

Campbell—No, that was good.

Smith—Why?

Campbell—My wife paid my fine.

Smith—That was good.

Campbell—No, that was bad.

Smith—How's that?

Campbell—I owe her ten dollars.

Smith—That is bad.

Campbell—No, that's good.

Smith—Why?

Campbell—I'll never pay her.

Smith—That's good.

Campbell—That's great.

Ward and Vokes were a famous team in their time. They dressed as tramps and called each other Percy and Harold. Ward got laugh after laugh by asking his partner: "Have another glass of Pepper whisky, Harold?" Here is some of the cross-fire talk:

Ward—Where are you now?

Vokes—I am down in the stock yards.

Ward—What are you doing there?

Vokes—Weigher, down in the stock yards.

Ward—I know, but what are you doing there?

Vokes—Weigher.

And so on and so on over and over again, till Ward would bang Vokes over the head with a stuffed club.

And then there were—and still are—Joe Weber and Lew Fields. Here follows some of their talk:

Weber (at ping-pong)—That makes me fifty love.

Fields—Fifty? There's no love after forty.

Weber—What is an octopus?

Fields—An octopus is a man who charges you $100 to tell you your eyes are no good.

Weber—No, no! An octopus is a piece of a year—Augustus, Septebus, Octopus.

Hardly profound, but still efficacious.

Some of the octogenarian vaudeville performers assert that the "Said-Mr.-Gallagher-to-Mr.-Shean" song is not new; that it had its origin with Donnelly and Gerard, who, years ago, were immensely popular in a piece called "Natural Gas." An inspection of the song, or at least as much as could be remembered by the old boys, does not reveal that it bears any marked resemblance to the one in question. The song was called "The Summer Season," and was cross-fire talk in verse.

Gerard—
Pray, how did you pass out,
In the town of old Rondout?
Did the "biz" pick up or did it take a fall?"

And Donnelly would reply—

We had to pack our grip,
And give the town the slip,
For Paddy Rooney had the other hall.

The passing of Bert Savoy of Savoy and Brennan removes one of the great teams of modern times. For memory's sake here is some of the patter:

Brennan—Is Margie married?

Savoy—No, she's a widow.

Brennan—Where did she bury her husband?

Savoy—She said his last wish was to be buried in San Francisco, but Margie buried him over in Brooklyn.

Brennan—But she should have carried out his wish.

Savoy—That's what his sister said: "If you don't, he's liable to come back and haunt you." I thought I'd die! Margie said: "We'll try him over in Brooklyn, and if he bothers me, I will send him to Frisco."

An exhaustive investigation has not disclosed the origin or the name of the first comedy team to use the wheeze:

"I live over in Brooklyn, for it has something New York hasn't got."

"What is that?"

"The other end of the Brooklyn Bridge."

Wham goes the bladder!

Profound!

July 15, 1923

A VAUDEVILLE COMPLAINT

A Former Variety Manager Laments the Passing of the One-Act Sketch

By RICHARD WARNER.

BACK in 1914 when I was stage director for Roland West, who was producing all the one-act plays for the Marcus Loew circuit, a vaudeville bill was not complete unless it had a sketch.

Today there are exactly twenty one-act plays playing over the entire Keith, Orpheum, Loew and Pantages circuits, and these twenty one-act plays that have still survived are not booked on account of the entertaining qualities which they might possess or the brilliant playwriting skil" of their authors. Rather they are booked because an actor or actress possesses a name that the public has seen elsewhere, a name that will attract business to the box office.

A good legitimate actor with a well-written one-act play has absolutely no chance to get any booking in vaudeville. The actor, in a way, has himself to blame; he has killed the goose that laid the golden egg. So often has the actor offered the booker poor material, not properly directed and poorly played, with an inferior cast, that the man who is responsible for the entertainment he places shakes with fear and trembling at the word "sketch." I am not going to blame the actor entirely for the disappearance of the sketch, but he must shoulder a 50 per cent. responsibility for its loss. The other 50 per cent. is up to the vaudeville circuits and their booking managers. They must stand the blame for the poor casts and the wretched scenic investments of the average one-act play.

First of all, a sketch without a big name is the most poorly paid act on any vaudeville bill.

Secondly, before the unknown sketch can get a showing in a regular theatre—one where the people understand English—the morale of the actors has been broken down to such an extent that the sparkle and life of the act have almost entirely disappeared. This condition has been caused by the repeated stalling methods indulged in by the powers that be.

***

By that I mean the sketch has been compelled to eke out an existence wherever it has been able to play before it is given the chance to show at a theatre where the booker would condescend to see it for a final decision. In consequence the scenery has become dilapidated, the original cast has disappeared and it would be hard to recognize it as the same one-act play that had started out for an immediate showing several weeks previously. Needless to say it is turned down as just another bad sketch that slows up the bill.

This hardship imposed on the intelligent actor with a good vaudeville vehicle is in a way due to his more successful brethren of the stage, the big Broadway actor or actress with a reputation, because the man or woman with a name that means a box-office attraction is given every opportunity to make good. The circuits do not stall them, they are given spots on the bills and the bookers come very near granting them what they ask as far as salary is concerned; but their acts hardly ever live up to their reputations. Such players are very poor vaudeville material; their scenery is inadequate, their casts poor—and in consequence they do not please. You must have more than a name in vaudeville to "get over," for it is not a matter of what you have done but what you are doing.

The booker with the one-track mind immediately comes to the conclusion that if an actor with a big reputation cannot hold his audience with a one-act play, what chance has the actor without a reputation? But he forgets what Shakespeare said, "The play's the thing." When the vaudeville circuits realize that an act should be paid in accordance with its entertainment qualities I think we will have satisfaction all around—better bills and better box-office receipts.

For example, while I was manager of Keith's Alhambra Theatre the booking office sent me a well-known "single," a woman with an international reputation. I was surprised when I found out that I was to pay her a salary of $2,500. On the same bill that week they sent me a sketch with five people in the cast, and again I was surprised when I learned what I had to pay them as a salary—$400. The famous woman "single," after singing four songs—three would have sufficed as far as the audience was concerned—walked off after her last number, and the patrons of the theatre would have been thoroughly satisfied if she had kept on walking right back to London, where she came from.

On the other hand, the unknown one-act play, with its group of unknown players, were responsible for eight to ten curtain calls at every performance. It was the one sensational act on the bill, the only turn that drew the business for the week—it was a case of mouth-to-mouth advertising. I was a mighty lucky manager that I had that one-act play to enable me to break even.

This continuous diet of music and dancing which is fed to the vaudeville public nowadays, without any variety to speak of, is one of the causes why the programs today are not giving the complete satisfaction that they did formerly. Some people will say that the motion picture gives the thrill, that it takes the place of the sketch. It does not, because it is not a living, breathing thing—it is not real. It does no more to satisfy our appetites than if when we were starving a beautiful picture of a banquet were set before us.

There is just one more thing that I would like to say: by eliminating the one-act play in vaudeville the bookers are taking the one distinguishing mark of "class" off the bills—the one spot that elevates the better vaudeville theatres and lifts them above burlesque and picture house entertainment. Another very important factor that must not be overlooked is that by doing away with the sketch we are taking brilliant minds—those of the author and legitimate actor—away from a field of endeavor that is in dire need of such mentality.

A vaudeville bill without the one-act play is like a Spring without flowers.

March 18, 1928

Madge Kennedy and W. C. Fields

'ZIEGFELD FOLLIES' HERE RESPLENDENT

Engaging Summer Show at the New Amsterdam Is Superbly Staged.

JOSEPH URBAN'S TRIUMPH

With Ina Claire, Anna Pennington, Bert Williams, and Bernard Granville Helping in the Fun.

ZIEGFELD FOLLIES OF 1915. Produced under the direction of F. Ziegfeld, Jr. Staged by Julian Mitchell and Leon Errol. Lines and lyrics by Channing Pollock, Rennold Wolf, and Gene Buck. Music by Louis Hirsch and David Stamper. Scenery painted by Joseph Urban.

THE PLAYERS.

Ina Claire,	Bernard Granville,
Mae Murray,	Bert Williams,
Anna Pennington	Leon Errol,
Kay Laurell,	W.C. Fields,
Lucile Cavanaugh,	Will West,
Justine Johnstone,	George White,
Helen Rook,	Carl Randell,
Olive Thomas,	Ed Wynn,
Lottie Vernon,	Phil Dwyer,
May Hennessey,	Melville Stewart.

"The Follies of 1915," the summertime diversion which Flo Ziegfeld and warm weather bring every year to Broadway, reached town last evening and proved to be an engaging entertainment, most sumptuously staged. Mr. Ziegfeld has fairly outdone himself. As large and as festive a representation of New York as could be crowded into the spacious New Amsterdam Theatre assembled for the ceremonies of welcome, and found there much to amuse and a great deal to delight the eye.

It would be unfortunate to lay emphasis upon the handsome trappings that have been provided for the latest addition to the city's calendar of amusements, if such emphasis gave the misleading suggestion that its only appeal were the visual appeal. But it is the notably beautiful investiture which marks the 1915 **Follies** as something apart from the common or garden variety of revue or musical comedy.

Many lovely ladies prance about the stage in the approved manner, and a goodly number of established favorites in the musical comedy world contribute their share to the entertainment, but the fact remains that the star of the new Summer show is none of these. It is Joseph Urban, the Viennese artist, who designed and painted the scenery.

It is not merely that he has used taste and a sense of color. He has used imagination, and in all the matters of decoration the latest of the Ziegfeld Follies not only surpasses the best that New York has seen in entertainments of its sort, but, in some of its scenes, equals the best that has been done in staging here this year.

All this was appreciated, apparently, and loudly applauded by those who managed to get in last night, and will doubtless be similarly received by those who had to wait for nights still to come. **From all accounts, there was a large** number of these.

Wild bids for seats could be heard in the offing, and the representatives of one ticket agency were vainly offering as much as $15 a seat for tickets to the first night of the Follies. And this price was really not so absurd as it sounded, for it turned out that there were half a dozen things in the new Ziegfeld revue that were each worth the price of admission.

Some of these might be casually mentioned. The glowing reports will not be of the music, for while this part of the program is not appreciably below the average, it is hardly the subject for rhapsodies. The fun is in the players and in the new tricks that have been devised **for them.**

You should see the motion-picture rehearsal with the movie actors—Bernard Granville, Mae Murray, Leon Errol, and all—bobbing about on the screen while Ed Wynn hoarsely directs them from out front. You should hear Ina Claire, as charming and accomplished as ever, doing a capital orchestral duet with Mr. Granville, and then coming out all alone as the novice from **Mr.** Belasco's far-off Alsatian convent. It is distinctly a mischievous little lyric that she warbles with its refrain:

"Oh, how sorry I feel
For poor Marie-Odile."

and its further account of one "who knew all about religion and whose best **friend was a pigeon" and who "took off her hood and tassel and looked just like Mrs. Castle."**

You should see Bert Williams as a West Indian apartment house hallboy. There is a good deal of fun, too, in the mean skit on the midnight cabaret, with the girls rehearsing all the new lyrics written by the chef, and more fun in the antics of W.C. Fields, an expert juggler with a sense of humor, who comes from the halls of the two-a-day.

Of course, the chief splendor is in the ensembles. There is one particularly striking one, where innumerable girls in white emerge from a background of black velvet, and another where the Rulers of the World assemble, each preceded by a comely flag bearer. You see all the men of empire from Serbia's King to America's President. Of course, there was a warm greeting last night for **Albert** of Belgium, and there was also a warm greeting of another sort for William of Germany. But the hisses were matched with applause, and everybody seemed very, very cheerful.

Channing Pollock, Rennold Wolf, and Gene Buck turned out the book and the lyrics. Between them they have made some bright contributions, but of course the book of the Follies is little more than a short story. Mr. Ziegfeld's annual entertainment is never anything beyond an amiable American hodge-podge, but this year it happens to be particularly gorgeous.

June 22, 1915

Men Behind the Plays

Florenz Ziegfeld, Jr.

HARDLY a month passes without "discovery" of Florenz Ziegfeld by some one or other. Mr. Ziegfeld, in fact, probably is the runner-up to Mr. Dooley as the most discovered man in America. The discoverer almost invariably is a self-confessed highbrow, and the burden of his argument is regularly an attempt to take the curse off the fact that his discovery is old news to the lowbrows, by finding reasons that are not common to them.

"We are a low people," his argument goes in effect, "and we have no actor equal to Soklominow, the Bulgarian, no actress as good as Massaro of Spain, no one who knows half as much about the relation of Ibsen to beaverboard as O'Brien of Belfast, and our playwrights simply do not exist. We have, however, a fellow, an artist in his way, whom I discovered at an obscure theatre—the New Amsterdam—while on a slumming tour. He should be encouraged, for he is easily first in his line, and when I was in Europe in 1919, from July 3 to July 27, I saw nothing in London, Dublin, Paris, Lyons, Beaune, Berlin, Munich, Copenhagen, Stockholm, Zurich, Vienna, Salsburg, Milan, Rome or Naples quite so good. I advise all my readers to see his production. It will be to the everlasting shame of the American theatre if this man is not encouraged. The name, I think is Ziegfeld."

When his readers get to the theatre, however, they find the seats all bought up by the pupils of the former discoverers, barring, of course, two in the fourteenth row three weeks from Thursday.

Mr. Ziegfeld, some people are regularly surprised to learn, has been doing these things—the "Follies," to wit—since 1907, and even did a few things before then. One of the things that came before the "Follies"—the very first of his enterprises, in fact—was the management of Sandow.

Florenz Ziegfeld Jr. was born in Chicago almost fifty-five years ago. His father was head of the Chicago Musical College and is today President emeritus of the institution. The young Ziegfeld, as a result of his father's position, was brought up among musical people, and, by attraction, among people of the theatre.

Florenz Ziegfeld is the Beau Brummel of theatrical managers. Only Brock Pemberton challenges him in this respect, but not even Mr. Pemberton's immaculate soft collars encircle the neck with quite the distinction that marks Mr. Ziegfeld's. Mr. Ziegfeld is quiet, self-effacing and aloof. Like some others of the managers, he is an absolute autocrat where his productions are concerned. Authors, composers, actors—none of these means anything to him if his own judgment tells him that they are wrong. He is a man whom many visit, but whom few see. Behind a magnificent desk in a gorgeously furnished room on the ninth floor of the New Amsterdam Theatre Building he

Florenz Ziegfeld Jr.

sits and passes judgment—when he is not in Palm Beach. Just at present he is in Palm Beach.

In 1893, when the World's Fair was held in Chicago, one of the attractions on the Midway was Sandow the Strong Man. The attraction failed to draw the crowds expected of it and in the midst of the cries of distress Ziegfeld had himself engaged as Sandow's manager.

A tour of the country followed a brief stay at the Coliseum, and when the country seemed to have enough of Sandow for the time, Ziegfeld sailed for Europe with him. This was in 1896.

A chanteuse calling herself Anna Held was chanteusing in Paris and not exactly setting fire to the Seine. Ziegfeld saw her and thought he detected in her possibilities for a successful career in America.

The following year "A Parlor Match," one of Charley Hoyt's farces, done by Evans and Hoey, carried a part not originally intended for the piece by the author. It was played by Anna Held, and it included her famous "Won't You Come and Play With Me?" However, she did not set fire to the Hudson, either.

Something had to be done, and Ziegfeld did it. The result was the greatest press agent story ever planted on a suspecting public in America.

Miss Held was living at the Hotel Marlborough at the time. One day, without notice to the papers, a milkman brought suit against Miss Held of the Hotel Marlborough for an unpaid milk bill of a staggering amount. The suit was brought in a Bowery court and the milkman told the Judge tearfully that he could not afford to go without payment for the milk—six large canfuls daily—that he had delivered to Miss Held.

The newspaper men covering that particular court were good cynical souls, quick to see a story when it came and just as quick to see a press agent's plant when it came. Here was obviously a story, and it is recorded that one of the more cynical of them, en route to the Marlborough expressed thanks that at last he was on a story free of the slightest suspicion of press-agentry.

When they arrived at the Marlborough they found Mr. Ziegfeld waiting for them. Why, they asked, had Miss Held ordered so much milk, and what use could she possibly have for it?

Mr. Ziegfeld registered surprise. Had they never, he asked, heard of Papeia?

Newspaper men were not so well educated in those days, and most of them, barring the inevitable liars, said no.

Mr. Ziegfeld explained. Papeia was the wife of Nero and felt that the loss of her complexion would mean the loss of his love. From an old Egyptian slave she learned that a milk bath daily would preserve this complexion—and there you are. Miss Held, two thousand years later, had heard of the story from a descendant of a friend to whom Papeia had confided her secret—and there you are, too.

So much of the story—which led to front-page publicity that immediately placed Miss Held among the most famous women of the country—is undoubtedly true and is preserved, well-documented, in the records. There is an added version, however, that may or may not be apocryphal.

According to this version, Mr. Ziegfeld did not rest with his mere lesson in history. He asked the boys point blank if they would like to see Miss Held in her milk bath. The boys, trained in a school that taught that a newspaper man must take the bitter with the sweet, said yes.

Trailed by the newspaper men like so many panthers, Ziegfeld approached the bath room, flung open the door, and there lay Miss Held completely surrounded by milk. The point of the story, it should perhaps be added, is that milk is only slightly less transparent than wood.

The boys thanked Mr. Ziegfeld and departed. It is an interesting point in connection with this whole episode that from that day, in 1897, to this, in 1923, no story dealing with milkmen's bills has ever got past a newspaper copy desk.

For about ten years after the Anna Held episode Ziegfeld was a producer of musical shows, sometimes alone and sometimes in association with others. Few of them have lived in the popular memory—none of them was an outstanding success and none of them a total failure.

In 1907 the roof of what had been Hammerstein's Olympic Theatre was rapidly becoming a white elephant on the hands of Klaw & Erlanger, who controlled the building. Ziegfeld proposed to put a Summer revue into the place.

And so, in June, 1907, the first "Follies" made its bow. Grace La Rue and Bickel and Watson among others, were in the first cast of principals and the show, which had cost $26,000 to produce, ran through the Summer.

Succeeding editions of the "Follies" came annually. They increased gradually in splendor and in cost of production. In 1911, as a result of inadequate conditions on the roof, where the seats were of the folding canvas variety and the audience semicircled three quarters of the way around the stage, the "Follies" moved to the New Amsterdam.

In June, 1914, the Midnight Frolic, an intimate extension of the parent attraction, was born on the New Amsterdam roof. It died in 1921 of acute constitutional amendments.

For two years Mr. Ziegfeld, along with Charles Dillingham, tried to breathe the spirit of life into the Century Theatre. They let it go to the Shuberts, after two expensive musical extravaganzas, with no published expressions of regret.

Among Ziegfeld's extra-"Follies" productions, "Sally," of course, must be mentioned. The play ran seventy weeks in New York, and stood out in a bad theatrical year in London. It is at the present time an overwhelming success on the road.

The present "Follies"—the name was changed to the "Ziegfeld Follies" a few years ago, because the simple name of "Follies" could not receive copyright protection—has marked a departure in the matter of the length of the shows' stays in New York. In the past the "Follies" have been brought to town in June and have stayed till late Fall and then gone their road way, regardless of any box-office demand that might still be existent.

This year, largely on account of the cost of production, which has increased to a quarter of a million dollars in sixteen years, the show has been kept in New York and will probably remain so long as its presence is financially justified. At the present time it is playing to capacity business—the receipts from week to week do not vary to the extent of $200. Nothing has been published as to whether the continuance of the present show will interfere with the production of a new edition in June.

Various theories have been expounded to account for the success of the Follies type of entertainment, and some of them probably have a certain merit. Will Rogers, when he says that the "Follies," if it does not glorify the American girl, certainly exposes her, probably came as close to the truth as any one.

The next theory will appear in the next article by the next discoverer of Florenz Ziegfeld Jr.

IN "FOLLIES" OF OLD.

A large number of actors and actresses now familiar figures in the amusement world have appeared in the "Follies" in its ten years of existence. To wit:

1907—Grace La Rue, Mlle. Dasie, Emma Carus, Bickel and Watson.

1908-Nora Bayes, Jack Norworth, Barney Bernard.

1909—Lillian Lorraine, Mae Murray, Bessie Clayton, Harry Kelly, Eva Tanguay.

1910—Fannie Brice, Bobbie North, Bert Williams, Harry Pilcer.

1911—Bessie McCoy, Elizabeth Brice, Shirley Kellogg, Leon Errol, George White, Bernard Granville, Ethel Amorita Kelly, the Dolly Sisters.

1913—Ann Pennington, Frank Tinney, Jose Collins, Martin Brown, Nat Wills.

1914—Ed Wynn.

1915—Marion Davies, Justine Johnstone, Ina Claire, Annette Kellermann.

1917—Eddie Cantor

1918—Marilynn Miller, Will Rogers.

February 11, 1923

'COHAN REVUE, 1918,' JOYFUL HODGE-PODGE

Comedy, Melodrama, Melody, and Girls in Satire on Plays and Players of Season.

BERLIN'S TUNES EFFECTIVE

Enough Dash to Bring Cohan Devotees in Droves, and Nora Bayes Supplies the Most Pep.

THE COHAN REVUE, 1918, a musical revue in two acts and sixteen scenes. Book by George M Cohan, music and lyrics by George M. Cohan and Irving Berlin. At the New Amsterdam Theatre.

Principals: Nora Bayes, Charles Winninger, Charles Dow Clark, Irving Fisher, Lila Rhodes, Frederic Santley, Sydney Jarvis, Lou Lockett, Hans Wilson, Jessica Brown, Eleanor Hanry, Phil White, Paul Nicholson, Arthur Hill, Al and Fanny Stedman, John B. Dyllyn, Bert Dunlop, Harold Tuppin, and Murry Evans.

The third of George M. Cohan's series of musical revues reached New York just in advance of the New Year last night, and was loudly welcomed by an audience of the sort which is to be found only at the first performance of a Cohan show. Like its predecessors, "The Cohan Revue 1918" takes for its subjects the plays and players of the season, and proceeds to mix them up joyfully into a Cohanese hodge-podge of comedy, melodrama, melody, and girls. On this occasion Cohan has admitted a few musical numbers by Irving Berlin, but the bulk of the piece is Cohan's.

The basic pigments this time are David Belasco and the Hindu soothsayer from "The Eyes of Youth," and upon these are laid bits of "Polly With a Past," "Tiger Rose," "Business Before Pleasure," "The King," "Chu Chin Chow," "A Tailor-Made Man," and a number of others. The show, beginning in the Belasco office with the introduction of Polly of the Follies, started somewhat slowly, hesitated here and there during the first act, struck its proper joyful stride in the second act, and was brought to a patriotic conclusion just before midnight with the new Cohan war song, "Their Hearts Are Over Here."

Although lacking in the subtleties which distinguished the other revues, and possessing no single scene equal to the famous courtroom episode of two seasons ago, the new revue has sufficient dash and cleverness to attract the Cohan following in huge droves. The generosity of Cohan in inviting contributions from Irving Berlin is proved by the fact that the Berlin numbers are in most cases superior to Cohan's, a first act finale being particularly effective. In this scene Berlin works his old trick of ragging the Mendelssohn Spring Song, and does it with infinite skill.

The most artistic work of the evening was done by Charles Winninger, who gave, with variations, the same uncanny imitation of Leo Ditrichstein which stood out in the preceding revue. Nora Bayes, who does more than any other single person to give the performance the necessary pep, gave a surprisingly good impersonation of Ina Claire, and later an equally good one of Florence Reed. Frederic Santley caught the walk and tones of Grant Mitchell perfectly, Hans Wilson was an excellent Fred Stone, and Paul E. Burns had the voice, but not the appearance, of Alexander Carr.

Among the others who contributed successfully to the evening were Lou Lockett and Jessica Brown, dancers, and the attractive Lila Rhodes. The scenery, as in the case of the previous revues, is of the sort which makes one long for a touch of Urban: the appeal of Cohan, as has frequently been said, is to the ear and not the eye. And it is only those with ears most delicately sensitized who will fail to respond to the appeal of "The Cohan Revue 1918."

January 1, 1918

CANTOR NIGHT AT FOLLIES.

Rogers Presents "Kid Boots" Star With a Watch, Gift From Ziegfeld.

"Eddie Cantor Night" was observed at the Ziegfeld Follies last night, when the performance at the New Amsterdam was given over in large part to a celebration in honor of the star of "Kid Boots," who sails for France today on the Paris.

On behalf of Florenz Ziegfeld, Will Rogers made a speech presenting a platinum watch from Mr. Ziegfeld to Mr. Cantor, with an inscription commemorating the thousandth performance of "Kid Boots." Mr. Cantor replied in characteristic phrases.

There were special numbers in honor of the occasion by George Olsen's Band, which Mr. Cantor brought to New York. Mr. Cantor was dragged from his seat in the audience and led to the stage, where he responded with several numbers.

The guests in the audience included Billie Burke, Mr. and Mrs. Horton Spurr of the "Kid Boots" company, who were married Wednesday with Mr. Cantor as best man, and Edna Leedom, who will enter the cast of the Summer edition of the Follies next week.

There was a buffet supper on the stage after the performance, with an informal "Eddie Cantor" program.

June 6, 1925

CONCERNING GEORGE WHITE AND HIS "SCANDALS"

Difficulties, Mostly Financial, of Several Earlier Productions

WITH George White's "Scandals" coining $40,000 or more at the Apollo Theatre every week with the precision and certainty of a United States mint, the young man who stands sponsor for these revels must seem to all such outsiders as ponder on the matter to be on his way to becoming a Times Square Croesus. Which he is, even with salaries and production costs being what they are, for between $18,000 and $20,000 a week is the Broadway estimate of his profit.

But it was not always so. It is only within the last three or four years that George White has achieved any sort of financial security. This is the eighth "Scandals"; they have all been more or less successful and certainly none was a failure. The reason for White's frequent insolvency obviously was not the circumstance that he went broke on his various shows; rather it may be traced to his early penchant for placing all the money within his grasp on such horses as he felt had a chance on the country's race courses, from Belmont Park to Tijuana. Sometimes he was right; just as often he was wrong. On one pony he claims to have won between $400,000 and $500,000, but he lost that and more on others.

But this is history, for since the fourth "Scandals" White has eschewed betting of all sorts, including the sure things which always promise to pay 20 to 1 or better. No longer can a friend borrow a copy of Racing Form from this dapper personage and have the k[illegible] supplemented by inside tips. For four years White has been a reformed man, and the change is certainly for the better in so far as his theatrical endeavors are concerned.

***

It was in 1919 that White came out of vaudeville with a fixed determination to break into the then charmed circle of the revue producers, in which cabal the Brothers Shubert were Supreme Inner Guard and Lord High Outer Shah and Mr. Ziegfeld the Exalted Commander of the Loyal Legion. At that time the ever unpredictable White had a bank account of $12,000 and an earning capacity in the music halls of $1,500 a week. The fact that he was worth that much to the Palaces, Orpheums and Hippodromes of the land and could go into his dance (it was not then the Black Bottom) any time he wished scene designers, costumers and other theatrical outfitters to take his notes for a considerable amount of the money involved in the production—which was about $60,000 in all.

The first performance of his 1919 revue at the Liberty Theatre was anything but a smashing success. Every detail, in fact, seemed to go wrong, and it was a discouraged though not completely disheartened young man who started early the next morning on the task of healing and doctoring the near-corpse. The entertainment responded to treatments and turned out in the end to be a rather good show which did business both here and on the road.

***

At the close of the first season White was, if anything, ahead of the game and he started upon his second presentation. While preparing this diversion, his predilection for the horses reasserted itself—he was broke off and on all during his vaudeville days because they weren't running right—with the result that when the curtain was raised on the second "Scandals" George White was again financially delinquent. Once more the production was made on credit and made successfully unless figures, against all tradition, do lie. It cost him between $75,000 and $80,000 to do this show, and although its profits were also dissipated at the race track he made preparations in the grand manner for the third number of the series, which was to be his magnum opus. This necessitated an expenditure of about twice as much money as had been lavished on the previous "Scandals." When he returned to New York after touring with his troupe, he once more engaged in his favorite relaxation, and it must be recorded, even at the risk of becoming more than a little repetitious, that the results were not only unfortunate but downright disastrous. White came back from the track that time with $600 to his name. He had lost all the money the show had made, and he still had a large pile of bills to meet. The $600 he planned to spread over a period of two weeks (he had his mother to support and other incidental expenses which made the sum no more than adequate), for in that time he confidently expected something to turn up. Something did in the form of an offer to play ten weeks of vaudeville at a salary considerably larger than he had ever received before.

While he was toying with the idea of this two-a-day engagement certain of the rumors that are always sweeping up and down Broadway were carried back to his ears. He heard faint but audible comment to the effect that he was through and that at last the hoofer would have to go back into his dance. (It was still not the Black Bottom.) These undercurrent rumors, emanating from the wise boys around town, caused him to change his mind. He would produce another "Scandals" and show them all.

Never without a certain ability at salesmanship, White went to Max Dreyfus of Harms and induced that worthy to give him $10,000 for the musical rights to any show he might do. Then White persuaded Jolson to lend him $25,000, which the Favorite Son of the United American Mammies, Ltd., did, in addition to buying in on 25 per cent. of the revue. By this time it was July, and the "Scandals" opening date customarily was in the middle of June.

***

This fourth show, seen at the Globe in 1922, was, White says, written and assembled in about two weeks' time, and during such intervals as he could escape from the frantic authors he wandered up and down Broadway signing nearly every one who was not at the moment working to appear in it. This frenzied search for talent resulted, somewhat to his astonishment, in the opening night discovery that among those employed by him were W. C. Fields, Paul Whiteman and his orchestra, Lester Allen, Pearl Regay, Winnie Lightner and others whose salary checks bore curious resemblance to the statement of the Corn Exchange Bank. White was trying to make a good showing for Jolson, who in the end was well reimbursed for his outlay. At the finish of the run White offered to let Jolson become a 25 per cent. owner in any show he might produce, but the comedian, not wanting any more worries than ordinarily fell to his lot, declined.

White by then had learned his lesson. He foreswore the turf and gambling of all sorts. Since then, he asserts by all he holds dear—the advance ticket rack in the Apollo box office, for example—that he has not bet on a race.

That was the only "Scandals" except the first, to which Sam H. Harris contributed, to be financed by money other than White's own. And since then only his capital has been invested in the revue. The following Summer he produced a negro entertainment, "Runnin' Wild," and the not inconsiderable returns he made from this comparatively nursery venture were put in, of all places, a bank. So were the returns from the fifth, sixth and seventh editions of the entertainment to which White devoted practically all his time and energies.

***

Lately, then, he has not had to go into his dance. He has not even done it for the sheer pleasure of hoofing in recent versions of what promises to become a Forty-second Street institution. He is not doing it in the current show, although it is an original dance of his which has been one of the hits of the production. And that, of course, is the Black Bottom.

George White will eagerly welcome statements from this or any other pulpit this Sunday morning which make it clear that he, and he alone, was the originator of those grotesque [illegible]rations to which the name Black Bottom has been applied. It is also one of his claims to have introduced and popularized the Charleston in "Runnin' Wild." While preparing the current "Scandals" he was looking for a dance which might follow the Charleston, then rapidly becoming passé. This dance, it seems, was done to an onbeat and off-beat rhythm. It occurred to the producer that if you could dance before the beat you would have a new rhythm—a conclusion more ingenious than it sounds. He experimented with it, and the result is the Black Bottom.

The ungainly motions of the dance, which, according to Variety, is sweeping this and other countries, are a synthetic creation on the part of White. To him belongs the glory—or the blame. And, perchance, should you wonder why the man who produces such an ornate and worldly extravaganza as the present "Scandals" should concern himself so vitally in originating a dance called the Black Bottom and take such a pride in its acceptance by all of last year's Charleston addicts and others, you must remember that this White is, first and foremost, a hoofer.

December 19, 1926

"IRENE" THE UBIQUITOUS

SOMETHING of the universality which has hitherto been the exclusive achievement of the motion picture is being enjoyed at present by the particular musical comedy success of the moment—to wit, "Irene." Twenty or twenty-five years from now, when "Irene" is revived at the Century with an all-star cast, some stress probably will be laid upon the fact that no less than fifteen companies were presenting this piece, in various corners of the world, in the year 1921. Probably by that time James Montgomery, as author and principal owner of "Irene," will be a millionaire several times over. The best available figures indicate that "Irene" has already made nearly a million dollars for him. His net income from the various companies has at various times reached $20,000 a week.

In the beginning "Irene" was owned equally by Mr. Montgomery, Carle Carleton, a motion picture promoter and Joseph Moran, part owner of the Vanderbilt Theatre. Subsequently Carleton was bought out by Montgomery, and today it is understood that the piece is owned two-thirds by Montgomery and one-third by Moran. Be that as it may, it is one of the greatest money-makers of the present theatrical generation. As is usual in such cases, "Irene" was first refused by several producers. In its original form, a musicless comedy called "Irene O'Dare," it was tried out years ago by Cohan & Harris, and was permitted to drop by the wayside after a few performances in Stamford.

The engagement at the Vanderbilt began on Nov. 18, 1919. The piece was produced at the Empire Theatre in London on April 5, 1920, and soon afterward by three additional companies in the English provinces. By this time it has been well through Scotland and Ireland. At about the same time rights were sold for the presentation of the piece in Australia, New Zealand and South Africa, and Sydney, Adelaide-Melbourne, Auckland, Capetown, Johannesburg and other cities have also been played. In May, 1920, preparations were begun for the organization of three additional companies to tour America, one of which is now in its twenty-second week in Chicago, and others, which have been heard in nearly every large city of the country east of the Mississippi and are headed farther into the West.

In June and July rights were sold for "Irene's" hearing in Sweden, India and certain parts of South America. Singapore, Bombay, Calcutta, Rio Janeiro, Buenos Aires and other cities have since had long engagements of "Irene," and in January the fifteenth production was planned for with the disposal of the rights for a presentation in Budapest.

April 24, 1921

DANCE REVOLUTION IN MUSICAL COMEDY

Adoption of Classic Principles Has Restored Choreographic Artistry in Best Types.

DANCES BECOME PICTURES

Influence of the Ballet Is Shown in Movements of Soloists and Groups in Geometrical Designs.

The first decade of the twentieth century will go down into history as producing a revolution in those forms of saltatory movement generally comprised under the term musical comedy dancing. The revolt, accomplished without propaganda or bloodletting, began simmering at the end of the war and it reached the boiling point in the season of 1924-25. Portents for the season of 1925-26 revealed in rehearsals and producers' announcements of their plans, presage an extension of the domain under the sway of those who have forsaken the rut of mediocrity.

The outstanding feature of this abandonment of the type of musical comedy dancing which ruled behind the footlights for nearly half a century is that classical technique has been the most effective weapon of the seceders. While this might seem a mere coincidence, in reality it is a return to first principles.

From 1829 to 1880 New York and the other largest "show towns" shared with Paris, London, Vienna and Milan the premières danseuses who gave to Europe the golden age of the dance in the Victorian era. Such spectacles as "The Black Crook," "The White Fawn," "Humpty Dumpty," "Bel Domino," "The Forty Thieves and Sinbad the Sailor," "Excelsior," "Antiope," "The Seven Ravens," "Dolores," "Around the World in Eighty Days" and "Matthias Sandorf" were productions of this period having ballets and such premières danseuses as Marie Taglioni, Fanny Elssler, Rita Sangalli, Marie Bonfanti, Betty Rigl, Rose Delval, Señorita Cubas, Carmencita, Mlle. Paris, Adele Boni, Mlle. de Gilbert and Mme. Cappolini were seen from coast to coast.

The Days of Mediocrity.

With the furore for the ballet there sprang up a host of gaudy and gauche imitators of the European masters of choreography who flooded the stage with tawdry, slapstick stuff which was only vulgar and depended chiefly on lines of legs encased in tights to attract audiences. Splits and high kicks superseded pirouettes and arabesques. Lottie Collins and her ta-ra-ra-boom-de-ayers set the pace and standards for musical comedy dancing. The World's Fair raised a crop of Little Egypts and "hoochie-coochers" who gave the added zest of police raids to their performances. Mabel Barrison brought Lady Godiva's ride up-to-date.

The only veritable dancing left was step dancing, exemplified by the Hengler sisters, May and Flo, and the buck and wing variety such as was exhibited by minstrels like Primrose and West and vaudeville performers like Maude Raymond.

The beginning of the change which has resulted in the restoration of dancing as an art to the musical comedy stage came with the impetus given to the ballet proper by the Russians who settled in America during and after the World War, with Isadora Duncan's revival of ancient Greek forms of poetry in motion, with the exhibitions of Far Eastern and Continental national and folk dances given by Ruth St. Denis and the continued appearance on the vaudeville stage of solo dancers and troupes in programs inclusive of all classic styles. These factors combined to educate the public, stagers and directors of musical plays and dancers themselves from principals to chorus girls. They were the forces which blazed the way for the reestablishment of dancing as the principal feature of the musical play and revue of the highest type.

The Chief Musical Comedy Steps.

The technique of the ballet or conventional classic is now being adapted by musical comedy dancers and choreographers in two ways, being applied to solo dancers by the former and group formations and ensembles by the latter. Technically musical comedy dancing embraces eccentric, step, ballet, acrobatic and jazz. Eccentric, as its name implies, may be a distortion of variation of any of the other steps except ballet done in a grotesque or unusual manner. Acrobatic explains itself, high kicks, kicking the back of the head, splits, anything gymnastic. Step dancing is also known as tap or soft shoe and includes jig, clog, and buck and wing. The principal jazz steps of the moment are the strut and the Charleston, but any step that can be used in syncopated time is a jazz step.

All these are employed in both solo and group movements. The ballet alone has a technique which forces the steps to conform to fixed and traditional molds. All the others allow full play to originality, though they have what is known as routine; that is, the repetition or linking together at certain intervals of the same steps. But the technique of the ballet—that is to say, its positions and formulas for executing pure ballet tempos—can be applied to the execution of most of the other varieties, and it is in adapting them that American dancers and choreographers have raised musical comedy dancing from vulgarity to a fine art.

The dancing of Alice Joyce last season with "The Passing Show" was a revelation to many a theatregoer of the possibilities of a combination of grace, snap and originality, accompanied by a lurking comedy, that with all its adherence to musical comedy principles was nevertheless the embodiment of precision of line, poise and clean-cut tempos in the execution of a medley of the steps that have been enumerated. To the understanding this was the fruit of daily training in the strict technique of the Russian ballet school under Tarasof.

The ballet-trained musical comedy dancer may or may not rise on her toes. She can utilize ballet technique on the half toe; that is to say, on the ball of the foot with the heel raised. Billy Tichenor pirouettes with equal facility on toe or half toe and intersperses moments of elevation founded on Tarasof combinations with buck and wing, eccentric, acrobatic and jazz movements. The recognized surpassing quality of the dancing of Queenie Smith, of Ann Pennington, of Ada Mae Weeks, of Mary Eaton and of Cecile D'Andrea, to mention a few musical comedy stars, is due to the fact that all have had initial training in the school of the ballet. The back-line chorus girl of today can dance better than the principal comediennes of a decade ago because she is getting ballet training.

New Methods of Choreographers.

If the change in the methods of individual dancers has been striking, progress in the works of choreographers and their use of classical formulas has been even more notable and more observable to the casual theatregoers. The best of them, by study or experiment, have learned that the geometric lines, architectural design and mathematical precision of ballet technique are applicable to their purposes and productive of results immeasurably superior to the methods so long followed by their predecessors. They have acquired the facility of making a dance a mural decoration, a picture in color, line and movement, which was the original purpose of the ballet.

Such dance creators as Seymour Felix and David Bennett have produced the most authentic approach to a legitimate art that musical comedy dancing has known. Bennett, with his Totem Pole Dance in "Rose Marie" and the dances of the chorus in "Betty Lee," a chorus that set a new standard for Broadway, and Felix in the group and ensemble numbers of the "Ritz Revue," "Top Hole," "Sky High" and Al Jolson's "Big Boy" exhibit their success in attaining a new understanding of classic principles. Felix has developed his skill even further in one of the new season's early productions, "The Charm School."

Felix devises his dances to be in harmony with and illustrative of the stage situation at the time the dance is introduced. Thus in "Sky High" a ballet fast spin becomes the propeller of an airplane in a finale before an imaginary air journey. The speed and pep of eccentric steps, the rhythm of buck and wing and the syncopation of jazz are contrasted with ballet attitudes and poses and leaps and turns in deliberate contrast and let down from fast to slow. While a soloist with ballet training is doing fouettes or fast turns in front, a group on the left, jazz steps. The Amer-Irish jig on the right and another group on the left jazz steps. The American kick with the foot above the head, and the English kick with the extended leg on a level with the waist, done in unison by the chorus become geometrical lines in a fixed decorative scheme.

Acrobatic cartwheels, back bends, hitch kicks and splits, ballet arabesques pirouettes and fouettes and jazz vary pace and give diversity to a constantly changing picture. No better illustration of the dance picture design could be given than that composition of Felix's in "Sky High" in which a line of the chorus at the footlights does acrobatic and jazz steps ending in a split to cover the start of an aerial split done by the back line on the shoulders of chorus men. As the back line comes to this position the front line leaps from a split into a ballet arabesque.

No better example of the diversity and range of the musical comedy choreography of today in which the leaven of the classic is working is to be seen than the dances of Gertrude Hoffman's ballet-trained performers in "Artists and Models."

September 6, 1925

'Blossom Time' Returns, Still Very Much Alive

Operetta Is Now Five Years Old and Has Been Performed More Than Five Thousand Times

BLOSSOM TIME, it seems, is five years old and still very much alive and kicking, if box office reports mean anything, which they do. This staple musical production, with the phenomenal record of a five-year run behind it, totaling upward of 5,000 performances, by as many as five road companies operating simultaneously, returns to the New York midst under the guidance of the Messrs. Shubert, tomorrow evening at Jolson's Theatre, where it has played many times before. The engagement is a limited one.

It was during the first week in February, 1921, that a first announcement heralded the approach of a new musical piece, "Blossom Time," by name. The score, it was further stated, would be by Sigmund Romberg, of "Maytime" fame, and the book and lyrics by Dorothy Donnelly.

Approximately six weeks later, all the preliminary steps having been duly taken care of "Blossom Time" made its bow, on March 21, at the Globe Theatre, Atlantic City. After skirting in the Hinterland for several weeks, so that such imperfections as were obvious could be ironed out, the piece returned to Atlantic City for a Summer run. And then, on Sept. 29, it enjoyed an astonishing premiere at the Ambassador Theatre here, where it played for two years.

One records the names, the original cast, at least, for the sake of posterity:

Mitzi..........Olga Cook
Bellabruna..........Zoe Barnett
Fritzi..........Dorothy Whitmore
Kitji..........Frances Halliday
Mrs. Kranz..........Ethel Branden
Creta..........Emmie Niclas
Baron Franz Schober..........Howard Marsh
Franz Schubert..........Bertram Peacock
Kranz..........William Danforth
Vogl..........Roy Cropper
Kupelweiser..........Paul Ker
Von Schwind..........Eugene Martinet
Binder..........Lucius Metz
Erkmann..........Perry Askam
Count Sharntoff..........Yvan Servais
Hansy..........Irving Meis
Novotny..........Robert Paton Gibbs
Rose..........Mildred Kay
Mrs. Coberg..........Erba Robeson
Waiter..........Howard A. Berman
Dancer..........Burtress Deitch
Four Guests..........Gotham City Four

Howard Marsh and Olga Cook are now playing opposite each other again after five years in "The Student Prince." Almost all the others have grown up to even higher places in the theatrical world. Since then, too, numerous changes have overcome the life and experience of almost everyone attached to the original presentation. Indeed, though obvious enough, it seems not amiss to add that they have all grown just the least bit older—five years, to wit:

Sigmund Romberg, the composer, has gone on merrily turning out new scores for such elaborate productions as "The Student Prince," "Princess Flavia," and numerous Winter Garden revues. Nor has Dorothy Donnelly stopped by the wayside to count her laurels. She, too, has occupied herself with new books and lyrics, the which includes "The Student Prince," "Hello, Lola," and other operas displaying the Shubert banner.

The original "Blossom Time" was staged by J. C. Huffman, who ranks high in these matters, and practically the same technical staff employed by the Shuberts today took part in the staging of its dances, erection of the scenery and the department of costumery. And J. J. Shubert, of course, who wields the sceptre that has waved all other Shubert musical shows into proper form, was in full charge of the entire production.

The story is divided into three acts. The scenes are laid in old Vienna. The original theme of this story was discovered in a half fictional and half biographical life of Schubert, which was published shortly after his death on Nov. 19, 1828. The material was worked over into a musical comedy by A. M. Willner and H. Reichert. Miss Donnelly then rewrote the entire Viennese book and supplied it with a new set of lyrics. The first act occurs at an outdoor restaurant in the famous Prater Park of Vienna in May, 1826. Here Schubert meets Mitzi Krans and falls in love with her. Mitzi is fascinated by his devotion and his music, but though she thinks she is in love with Schubert, she is really in love with his friend, Baron von Schober. Fortunately, he loves her, too. Schubert has not the gift to express his love, and so in the end Baron von Schober wins Mitzi from him. And that is the story of "Blossom Time."

In the course of its five years' existence "Blossom Time" has been presented upward of 5,000 performances. At various intervals there have been as many as five companies on tour, playing to every worth-while capital, town or hamlet, from Canada to the Mexican border. Every State in the Union has been visited, and generally revisited, by one of the itinerant troupes. And many farewell performances have been given, only to find "Blossom Time" reappearing there again. Indeed, the legend may be heard in local Shubert offices of travelers who, returning from the West or South, have marveled that wheresoever they went they could witness "Blossom Time" playing there.

At the moment there are three companies of "Blossom Time" playing in the West and South. The company which opens tomorrow at Jolson's Theatre is fresh from Chicago.

Wherever it has played "Blossom Time" has either broken or came close to breaking existing box office records. In New York, during the season of May, 1923, it was presented simultaneously at two theatres on the same block and only across the way from each other—the Forty-fourth and the Shubert. After two years at the Ambassador the play was moved up to Jolson's Theatre and then later to the even larger Century.

Hundreds of actors and as many stage hands, carpenters, printers, costumers and such have received employment as the result of its being. Innumerable theatrical adventures born at the same time are now almost forgotten. There were, thus, "The Monster," at the 39th Street Theatre, and the sturdier "The Cat and the Canary," at the National, and Marjorie Rambeau in "The Gold Fish," at the Shubert.

The financial reward of such a successful adventure has been great. What with sheet music for sale, graphophone rec[illegible] and other sources of royalty, the piece still yields today a veritable treasure trove. Franz Schubert might possibly and pardonably turn over in his grave a few times if he could realize a fractional percentage that would have accrued to him as the result of this work.

March 7, 1926

Musical Comedies, Today And Twenty Years Ago

By LEW FIELDS.

WHEN I look back about twenty years and recall the shows of the first decade of this century, I am amazed at the small change in the essentials of the successful musical comedy. Amusement values, on the whole, are greatly different from what they were, say in 1906. Then there were no movies, except in the crudest form. Then the radio was an uncertain means of telegraphic communication. Then the phonograph was a scratchy contrivance, not so pleasing to the ear as the old-fashioned tinkling music-box.

Each of these newer inventions has altered the attitude of the audience toward its entertainment. And there have been equally sweeping changes in what is and what is not regarded as good music. But essentially, I say, the musical comedy remains the same.

One thing has passed out of the musical comedy, one thing only, and that is the spirit of travesty. Even the term has been lost and its sister term, burlesque, has also lost its meaning in these two decades.

What I mean by travesty is what those of you who were old enough to go to the theatre before 1908 will probably associate first with the music hall which bore the names of Joe Weber and myself. Travesty did not concern itself as does a show such as "The Girl Friend," with a definite book. It began with the idea of satirizing a popular play. It might concern itself with the fads and foibles of the hour as far as the plot of that play would permit. And it required that we imitate our brothers and sisters of the non-musical theatre exactly. In other words, we had to act. Satire requires a twist in meaning. It requires a twist in thought. To fully enjoy a travesty you had to think.

The modern musical comedy audience does not want to think. It wants to be amused while it sits inertly in its seats. Travesty would, I believe, be too much for it. Not that there was no buffoonery in the old days. We could not have created one show after another without resort to low comedy. And I can recall many a time when "hokum," pure and unadulterated, was our means of rescue from the slough of a humorless interlude.

Indeed, we frequently began rehearsal with nothing more than an idea and some lines to twist into humorous gags. Willie Collier, Fay Templeton, Lillian Russell, Sam Bernard, David Warfield, Weber and myself would look upon rehearsal as the true workshop, where each put a hand to the task of creating a show. None of your labored stories, none of your absurdities in construction. Instead, everything was devoted to the turning inside out of the dark cloud of work-a-day life, with a view to revealing the silver lining in all its glory.

This spirit lingers only in name in the modern revue. The revue does pretend to travesty the play of the hour. Usually it chooses only those plays in which masked indecency is the lure and thus defeats its own purpose. For travesty should be travesty of life and not travesty of theatricalism.

I should put 1900 as the year in which the old-fashioned extravaganza was assimilated by the new musical comedy and travesty. "The Belle of New York" was a typical show of that period. It was not until 1908 that the big show came into being. "The Midnight Sons" was the first of this type. Together with supers, there were over 400 in the cast of "The Midnight Sons," a mark for the modern producer to shoot at.

Nowadays mere numbers have lost their attraction, except in operetta, where 100 voices still try to make the public believe that they are ten times better than ten voices because they make more noise. The smaller show has definitely returned. For a time it was gone. Producers felt that it had no place on the big new stages. But small theatres—the Princess first and now the Vanderbilt—have called for the intimate musical comedy. Although it would not be fair to recall the fame of the "Floradora" sextet—I believe no sextet could win such fame nowadays—a dozen girls and a dozen boys seem to satisfy the public quite as much as half a hundred.

On the other hand, the modern musical comedy has to compete against opposition quite different from that met by its ancestor of twenty years ago. The modern musical comedy is clean. It is a tribute to musical show producers that, without exception, their books have been as clean as a whistle. Yet they are vying for customers with revues in which risque sketches and scantily draped women are often the features.

I recall vividly the sensation created by Olga Nethersole when she was borne up the famous stairs in "Sapho" by her leading man. In fact, we of the Music Hall burlesqued the play in a skit called "Sapolio," in which a dumbwaiter was used to carry our heroine upstairs, our theory being that no man's arms should be permitted to touch her on our stage. The theatre in which "Sapho" played was raided and the case lingered long in the courts. Naturally, with such action taken against a fairly clean French play, the producer of 1900 and the decade following did not trifle with the possibility of his show being closed.

Audiences have become accustomed to more daring material, however. Just as the French farce, the bedroom play and others of its ilk have more or less passed away from our stage, so will the present sex play and nude revue eventually to their ways. The musical comedy, however, will never tamper with that sort of material. Its appeal is principally to the risibilities and the ear. Its audiences comprise young folks, old folks and, especially on matinée days, children.

When I visit a theatre now I am impressed with the ease with which people may be made to laugh. Long as I have been connected with the stage, it never occurred to me until recently to try to analyze the laughter of an audience—to ask myself why a certain line caused a roar and why another, intended to convulse the audience, failed in its mission. In studying not only my own show, "The Girl Friend," but others of this season, "Tiptoes," "Sunny" and several revues, notably "The Great Temptations," as well as one or two modern operettas, such as "Song of the Flame," I was interested to note that action caused much more laughter than the line. Slapstick comedy has received a great impetus from the movies. Before the time of motion pictures it was much easier to hold the attention of an audience with light comedy, persiflage and satire.

Today satire is at a discount, especially in the musical field. Omitting the drawing power of names, I believe you will find that the most successful musical comedies are those in which the book is intelligently conceived, permitting a sequence of "hokum," slapstick and light banter utterly devoid of any idea.

As for the performers themselves—why, it would hardly be fair to say that the younger folk of today are equal to those of twenty years ago—now, would it?

July 4, 1926

THE CASE OF "SHOW BOAT"

For Once a Musical Comedy Is Produced Without Tears and Torment

EMBRYONIC chiefly were the troubles which attended the production of "Show Boat." From the rise of the first curtain until the present, it has remained in virtually the same state as when it left the hands of the author and composer. This is, of course, an exception in theatrical history, and is the more remarkable considering the extensiveness of the story, the number of scenes and people concerned and the fact that the musical comedy is the re-creation of a novel, always a tricky form of stage presentation. Miraculously, the characters and scenes were just about right, the dialogue and score also. Only their length caused concern and from Washington to Pittsburgh and from Cleveland to Philadelphia there was but one problem: what must be cut out, what could be given up?

Stormy, though, were the days preceding production and the signing of final contracts. They form a tale in themselves, brightly colored, warmed with a bit of Broadway skullduggery. A summary concerning the rights to Miss Ferber's novel would be more or less as follows:

Florenz Ziegfeld invited Jerome Kern to do the score for "Betsy." He turned it down, but said, in turn, "I am sending you 'Show Boat.' It is a great title and think it would make a great show." Mr. Kern, therefore, gets the credit for being the first to discern the possibilities of the novel.

* * *

Whereupon Mr. Ziegfeld asked him to do this score and then said to him, with grammatical preciseness, "Whom should we get to write the book?" Mr. Kern replied, "I think Oscar Hammerstein 2d would be the very man." Mr. Ziegfeld said he had never seen Mr. Hammerstein and didn't know him, but if Mr. Kern recommended him, to bring him up to the office. Mr. Kern did this and plans were made for the production, the arrangement being that it would be produced about Feb. 1, 1927. On Feb. 2, 1927, Mr. Ziegfeld presented "Rio Rita," after which he became ill and abandoned his other projects for the time being.

Last March, on his return from Palm Beach, the producer announced that he had reached an understanding with Mr. Kern whereby his option on "Show Boat" had been extended until Fall and that the piece would be done at that time. This statement was disputed by Arthur Hammerstein, uncle of the librettist, who claimed that Mr. Ziegfeld's option expired on April 1, and that he had the rights from that date until Oct. 20. He inferred that his option was obtained from his nephew, who was then in Europe. Mr. Kern at the time upheld Mr. Ziegfeld, and in a few weeks the matter was adjusted amicably enough.

Then it was bruited about that Arthur Hammerstein did not want the show because the motion picture rights had been disposed of. That did not deter Mr. Ziegfeld and although he forfeited possibly $150,000 thereby, he promises to make it back several times over from his stage production.

Here are a few more revelations which may be pertinent to "Show Boat's" history:

Jerome Kern, contrary to popular belief, has not used native negro folk-songs for his score. Instead, he has absorbed the nature and mood of the South and created his own folk-song numbers.

Though writing what might be termed a modern musical comedy, Mr. Kern has tried to give every important character an individual motif according to the best operatic traditions. These motifs he uses with especial significance in the scene of St. Agatha's Convent, where the major music is a full sacred mass, reverently treated, but where an underlying orchestration is made up of all the principal motifs.

Concerning the adaptation, Mr. Hammerstein states that he found the characters so complete, as presented in the book, that his one endeavor was to adhere to their original outlines. One exception, if it can be called an exception, was in the treatment of Ravenal, whom he has presented in the best or at least the most tolerant light.

* * *

In "Show Boat" Mr. Hammerstein gives a practical demonstration of his theory of musical comedy composition. Since his graduation from Columbia in 1916 he has been writing books and lyrics for musical comedies and during this time has maintained that these should have intelligence as well as laughs and tunes. Given free rein in "Show Boat," he has relentlessly thrown aside inanities for a consistent story, sound philosophy and a definite heart interest.

What cutting has taken place has been largely due to Mr. Ziegfeld's sense of showmanship, with reducing of the playing time as the motive. An adagio dance in the Trocadero scene has gone out; the black velvet hangings and futuristic doorway have been changed to the real lobby of the Trocadero ... There is a new scene for The Natchez Daily Democrat interlude ... For several weeks Naomi Johnson doubled in "Rio Rita" and "Show Boat." She went from the Lyric to the Ziegfeld Theatre, in order to appear for a moment in the Midway Scene as a model clad in laces and pastel silks, a living duplicate of a Dresden china doll ... An important dance in the first act is now presented with an effort at complete ingenuousness as Mr. Ziegfeld feared that "selling it" would destroy the play's illusion ... The first decisive changes were extra-mural; that is, took place outside of the play and had to do with the placing of various actors' names in larger and smaller type ... Howard Marsh now wears a more sedate costume than the gray pantaloons he wore at the opening performance ... A wine colored dress that a show girl displayed in the Midway scenes is out because the producer abominated it ... And so on.

February 5, 1928

THE DANCE: ON BROADWAY

Musical Comedy's Contribution As Shown by the Astaires

THE dancing of Fred and Adele Astaire, as exhibited nightly in "Funny Face," is a subject on which might be hung a dissertation on the esthetics of dancing, incongruous though it may seem to some to associate esthetics with popular musical comedy.

We in America, though we flock to the box office month after month, are inclined to underestimate our musical comedies artistically.

The European viewpoint on them is much higher; in fact, Jacques Copeau and other eminent artists of Europe have intimated that our particular form of musical comedy is the only genuine contribution the American stage has yet made to the theatre arts. That such a view has no currency along Broadway, however, at least removes from the musical comedy world the danger of that self-consciousness which has come near to bringing annihilation upon our heretofore blithe jazz music. "Funny Face" is a type of our native product at its best, and of all the elements that conspire to give it excellence the dancing of the Astaires stands out as supreme.

In Fred Astaire we have the phenomenon of dancer who can actually "visualize" music to an extent that is not achieved once in a blue moon in our more serious dance recitals. To be sure, Mr. Astaire would flounder helplessly in Greek draperies to a Beethoven symphony, for Beethoven, and the other masters of music whose works are frequently employed by our art dancers (horrible phrase!), did not write in dance measures; hence a dance based on such works is not pure dance but rather a dramatic interpretation of the emotional content of the music.

All of this is of no moment to a sheer dancer like Fred Astaire. He gives, through feet and legs, hands and arms, head and torso, the physical actuality of the music, warp and woof. And Gershwin, though he has written better scores, provides him with rhythmic variety and some long and luscious phrases to play with. Whether his routines are his own or were devised by Bobby Connolly, who has done a good job of staging all the dances, does not matter. Almost any dancer of whatever school could spend a profitable evening at his feet and learn something new about rhythm and accuracy, accent and syncopation.

The case of his sister, Adele, is quite different, but scarcely less interesting. Style is the object with which she has concerned herself. Or more likely she has not concerned herself with it at all, for such devil-may-care freshness is free of self-consciousness above all else. At any rate she has discovered that she possesses serviceable heels; that angular lines are as provocative as curves; that a rigid spine, a rigid neck and rigid ankles are especially effective when contrasted with bent knees, supple hips and flopping arms. In short, she has developed the movements which grow naturally out of a piquant and Puckish personality, but she has developed them with such moderation and taste that they have become a legitimate style rather than personal mannerisms.

Nobody, perhaps, would be more amused than the Astaires themselves at being measured by any solemn esthetic standard, and certainly such is not the intention here. However, all the skill and artistry of the dance is not being exhibited exclusively amid chaste draperies and dim lights at Sunday evening recitals.

January 29, 1928

THE DANCE: NEW MUSICAL COMEDY TALENT

Busby Berkeley's Direction Raises the Level Of Our Stage Performances

LAST season, with the production of "A Connecticut Yankee," there hove into the light a new director of musical comedy dancing in the person of Busby Berkeley, who was acclaimed in a manner quite unusual for a newcomer. Already he is ranked with the half-dozen leading men of his craft, although he has only the meager record of two productions to back him up. In tne language of Broadway, he is generally reputed to have "got the breaks," and he probably did; but his success is more substantially based than that. It would seem, in fact, in a manner of speaking he is a man of the hour who has appeared at a time when he is needed.

With our predilection for digging into the "lively arts" and discovering fundamental esthetic principles there exemplified, it is perhaps not unnatural that the eye of scrutiny should have been trained at last upon stage dancing with a view to revealing its art aspects, if any. Of the various elements of the popular musical theatre, the music itself was the first to become the subject of evaluation by connoisseurs. No champion has yet arisen temerous enough to pronounce the musical comedy "book" an artistic item, and it is only very recently that the dancing has ceased to be on too low a level to meet the gaze of the critical. Now, however, the cognoscenti are beginning to be aware of "qualities" in stage dancing, and this not because of any lowering of the critical eyeline, but rather because of the prodigious raising of the level of the dancing.

But because of this very growth there is something of a situation to be faced. It is still in the future, but the alert dance directors are none the less aware of it. Aside from the greatly improved standards of pulchritude which obtain among the ladies of the ensemble, the two ingredients with which the dance directors have built their success are speed and novelty. In the matter of speed a limit has been reached; unless there are undreamed-of changes in the constitution of the physical universe, the human body cannot be made to move any more rapidly than it has already been trained to do for theatrical purposes. There is nothing to be hoped for along this line. As for novelty, there is, of course, no end to the capabilities of a talented mind; but nearly everything seems to have been tried, from salaciousness to prudery, and even what is known as novelty in the dance field is getting to be a bit boring.

Busby Berkeley, Who Has Brought New Ideas in Dancing Into the Realm of Musical Comedy.

Novelties Grown Stale.

Four years ago David Bennett conceived the idea of the "Totem Tom-Tom" number in "Rose-Marie," and its novelty was instantly recognized. Unfortunately, its idea is no longer novel, yet scarcely a week passes that we are not regaled with somebody's novel method of rearranging it and trying to make it pass for something new. Balieff's wooden soldiers provided a similar situation, and George White's Charleston and Black Bottom hardly require mention in this connection.

Some of the acrobatic accomplishments of the ordinary chorus girl of today would have been sufficient reason for her elevation to stardom a few years ago. But we have grown accustomed to them. Splits and cartwheels are merely routine. We look on unmoved at the feats of our most intrepid adagio dancers, and the thrills that they once would have caused are somehow not forthcoming. Surely novelty must be sought in some other channel. And that is how Busby Berkeley assumes the mantle of a kind of minor prophet, though he himself probably hasn't found it out yet.

What Berkeley actually did in "A Connecticut Yankee," and to an even greater extent in "Present Arms," was to discover a new and sound basis upon which to build for novelty. Though he has thus far relied to a certain extent upon external devices in the conventional way, he has also delved into the actual rhythmic structure of jazz to a degree that has not before been attempted, and the results he has achieved in this direction are not only novel but unwontedly artistic in their manner of utilizing to the fullest extent the actual material which author and composer have provided for him.

Here is a substantial type of novelty which depends not upon the inventiveness of one man but grows as well out of the creative work of his collaborators, as the direction of a dramatic work grows out of the work itself rather than out of the imagination of the director. If this type of novelty can be reproduced ad nauseam, as Bennett's "Totem Tom-Tom" has been, then the rank and file of dance directors are far cleverer men than they would seem to be.

Complicated Rhythms.

The first act of "Present Arms" contains complicated and subtle rhythms that many a trained musician or a trained artist-dancer would find next to impossible to perform. In many cases the dancers are required to execute contrary rhythms, and in one number they are called upon to perform simultaneously two rhythms counter to each other and also the music. A musical director who worked with Berkeley is quoted as having said that he did not dare to watch the dancing for fear he could not move his baton to the required beat of the score. In the Earl Carroll "Vanities," now in rehearsal, there are similar difficulties involved, such as counting five against four, then three against four, with a third rhythm still to be added with the arms when the other two have been mastered.

The average audience, of course, cannot be expected to grasp these subtleties, but they undeniably produce an effect even upon the most unreceptive musical consciousness. Possibly because he is afraid of this lack on the part of his audiences, Berkeley indulges in stunts. He overlays his multiple rhythms with acrobatic tricks and bits of external cleverness, so that for those who do not perceive the fine points there will still be entertainment. In these externals he is generally original and interesting, but he is also occasionally banal, as in the case of the rose garlands in "Present Arms," and he is likely to repeat himself, which is not very versatile in a man who has so far staged only two productions. Obviously, his heart is in the mazes of syncopation and not in the superficial tricks which are actually "playing down."

Time was when the chorus girl was considered a person of small intelligence, but a girl who can execute the diabolical designs of a director like Berkeley is certainly no nit-wit. Perhaps if she had more orthodox schooling she would be less willing to dare the impossible. Berkeley himself is nothing of a musician and has no technical knowledge of dancing. He first began to direct dances when as a director of dramatic stock he was occasionally called upon to stage a musical comedy bill and preferred to stage the dances himself rather than try to collaborate with some local dancing teacher.

He creates none of his dances in advance; in fact, his inspiration seems to come from having the girls in front of him on the stage ready for work. If he has to rehearse in a hall, his style is painfully cramped. His work, consequently, is marked with the freshness of improvisation and is stamped with all the qualities of theatrical effectiveness. Yet for all his lack of training in the academic sense, if there can be such a thing as "high-brow" jazz dancing, his creations cannot escape being so catalogued. The Salzburg Festival late next month is to have the opportunity of passing on some of his work. The critiques cannot fail to be interesting. Berkeley at the Salzburg Festival, and Sammy Lee with a ballet at the Metropolitan to his credit! Indeed, musical comedy dancing is not what it used to be.

J. M.

July 22, 1928

GERSHWIN'S OPERA MAKES BOSTON HIT

'Porgy and Bess,' With an Almost All-Negro Cast, Proves an Event.

SCORE MARKED BY POWER

Enthusiasm of Audience at the Plymouth Grows as Evening Advances.

Special to THE NEW YORK TIMES.

BOSTON, Sept. 30.—Both musically and theatrically, George Gershwin's and the Theatre Guild's new folk opera, "Porgy and Bess," which had its first performance at the Colonial here this evening, was an event. An audience which assembled, uncertain whether they should find a heavy operatic work or something more closely resembling musical comedy, discovered a form of entertainment which stands midway between the two. The immediate response was one of enthusiasm that grew rather than diminished as the evening progressed.

Aided by a workable libretto from Du Bose Heyward, and lyrics by Mr. Heyward and Ira Gershwin that have an idiomatic tang, the composer has put together a score which, so far as the layman can tell, is one of distinction and power. Except for the words of a few white players in an almost all-Negro cast, practically everything is sung. But the music and dances seem to spring naturally from the place and people. Many of the songs—"Summer Time," for instance or "Porgy's I Got Plenty O'Nuttin"—seem destined for immediate popularity.

In the lighting and direction, Rouben Mamoulian has done an enviable job. At the end of the performance, he, the composer and Alexander Smallens, who conducted an orchestra that approached operatic proportions, were called to the footlights.

Pattern of Play Followed.

In its outlines the opera follows the pattern of the play from which it derives, with a division into three acts and nine scenes. For backgrounds Sergei Souderikine has designed believably Charleston settings, counterparts to those of the original production. One is the courtyard of Catfish Row, surrounded by dilapidated buildings with crazily shuttered windows from which the teeming population of the Negro settlement can peep in moments of excitement, or behind which they can retire to leave the court as silent and deserted as a churchyard when white men come and danger threatens.

A second sets forth the palmetto jungle where the picnic takes place and the fugitive Crown recaptures temporarily his woman Bess. The third is in a room of the quarter, with bare walls against which gigantic human shadows tower as the mourners chant for the dead—and gather pennies for his burial—or from which echo the tumult of the hurricane and the shouts of Crown, come to reclaim his woman.

Though there have been necessary minor omissions, the story keeps to the narrative of the play. The surprising thing is that so much wealth of incident could be retained.

There is the crap game, with its racial humors and excitements; the murder of Serena's husband, the flight of Crown and the shelter which the crippled beggar Porgy alone is willing to offer the deserted Bess. There is her gradual reform under Porgy's influence. Set to music, her divorce from Crown so that she could become Porgy's, with the added "complication" in the fact that she had never been married, is still richly comic.

There is the final conflict between Crown and Porgy for possession of the woman, and the slaying of Crown by the cripple, the taking of Porgy into custody as a matter of routine to identify the body, the departure of Bess, lured away by the persistent sporting life with his "Happy Dust" and his promises of the luxuries of New York, influenced too by her belief that Porgy is lost to her forever. In the opera as in the play, Porgy returns to find her gone, and, a pathetically heroic figure, starts off in his goat cart to discover her even in that distant land.

Round this tale of primitive passions, fears and faiths clings a rich embroidery of characterizing detail to present a rounded picture of the place and its inhabitants, their joys and sorrows, their terrors and superstitions, the homely routine of their lives—the departure of the fishermen who were to perish in the storm, the crying of the wares of the honey man—jigs and lullabies as well as swift hatreds and violent deeds.

Even without a synopsis in the program, those unfamiliar with the play or novel could follow the action, so clearly do the singers enunciate. In the more conversational scenes, with the necessity for singing the dialogue, the pace is unavoidably retarded. But in the emotional moments, the music of Mr. Gershwin imparts a new and heightened intensity.

Todd Brown as Porgy, Anne Wiggins Brown as Bess, Warren Coleman as Crown, Bubbles (once of Buck and Bubbles) as Sporting Life, Ruby Elzy as Serena and the others of a large company convey the sense of characters as well as the pleasures of the music. Through them and the other elements of a polished production this is not only a fresh adventure in opera, but entertainment in its larger meaning. With their aid the guild and Mr. Gershwin have proved that opera of the American folk variety can be a cause for general rejoicing.

E. F. M.

October 1, 1935

THE PLAY

Christmas Night Adds 'Pal Joey' to the Musical Stage

PAL JOEY, a "new" musical comedy in two acts taken from John O'Hara's series of letters of the same name. Book by Mr. O'Hara. Music by Richard Rodgers. Lyrics by Lorenz Hart. Dances arranged by Robert Alton; scenery and lighting by Jo Mielziner; costumes designed by John Koenig; staged and produced by George Abbott. At the Ethel Barrymore Theatre.

Joey Evans....................Gene Kelly
Mike Spears............Robert J. Mulligan
The Kid....................Sondra Barrett
Gladys........................June Havoc
Agnes....................Diane Sinclair
Linda English..................Leila Ernst
Valerie..................Amarilla Morris
Albert Doane.................Stanley Donen
Vera Simpson...............Vivienne Segal
Escort.........................Edison Rice
Terry..........................Jane Fraser
Victor.......................Van Johnson
Ernest........................John Clarke
Stagehand....................Jerry Whyte
Max........................Averell Harris
The Tenor.......................Nelson Rae
Melba Snyder....................Jean Casto
Waiter.....................Dummy Spevlin
Ludlow Lowell..................Jack Durant
Commissioner O'Brien..........James Lane
Assistant Hotel Manager.....Cliff Dunstan

Specialty dancer: Shirley Paige.

Dancing girls: Claire Anderson, Sondra Barrett, Alice Craig, Louise de Forrest, Enez Early, Tilda Getze, Charlene Harkins, Frances Krell, Janet Lavis, June Leroy, Amarilla Morris, Olive Nicolson, Mildred Patterson, Dorothy Poplar, Diane Sinclair, Mildred Solly, Jeanne C. Trybom, Marie Vanneman.

Dancing boys: Adrian Anthony, John Benton, Milton Chisholm, Stanley Donen, Henning Irgens, Van Johnson, Howard Ledig, Michael Moore, Albert Ruiz.

By BROOKS ATKINSON

If it is possible to make an entertaining musical comedy out of an odious story, "Pal Joey" is it. The situation is put tentatively here because the ugly topic that is up for discussion stands between this theatregoer and real enjoyment of a well-staged show. Taking as his hero the frowsy night club punk familiar to readers of a series of sketches in The New Yorker, John O'Hara has written a joyless book about a sulky assignation. Under George Abbott's direction some of the best workmen on Broadway have fitted it out with smart embellishments.

Rodgers and Hart have written the score with wit and skill. Robert Alton has directed the dances inventively. Scenery out of Jo Mielziner's sketchbook and costumes off the racks of John Koenig—all very high class. Some talented performers also act a book that is considerably more dramatic than most. "Pal Joey," which was put on at the Ethel Barrymore last evening, offers everything but a good time.

* * *

Whether Joey is a punk or a heel is something worth more careful thinking than time permits. Perhaps he is only a rat infested with termites. A night club dancer and singer, promoted to master of ceremonies in a Chicago dive, he lies himself into an affair with a rich married woman and opens a gilt-edged club of his own with her money. Mr. O'Hara has drawn a pitiless portrait of his small-time braggart and also of the company he keeps; and Gene Kelly, who distinguished himself as the melancholy hoofer of "The Time of Your Life," plays the part with remarkable accuracy. His cheap and flamboyant unction, his nervous cunning, his trickiness are qualities that Mr. Kelly catches without forgetting the fright and gaudiness of a petty fakir. Mr. Kelly is also a brilliant tap dancer—"makes with the feet," as it goes in his vernacular—and his performance on both scores is triumphant. If Joey must be acted, Mr. Kelly can do it.

Gene Kelly

Count among your restricted blessings Vivienne Segal who can act with personal dignity and can sing with breeding. In a singularly sweet voice she sings some scabrous lyrics by Lorenz Hart to one of Richard Rodgers's most haunting tunes—"Bewitched, Bothered and Bewildered." June Havoc applies a broad, rangy style to some funny burlesques of night-club routines and manners. Jean Casto satirizes the strip-tease with humorous condescension. As a particularly rank racketeer Jack Durant, who is a sizable brute, contributes a few amazing and dizzy acrobatics. This department's paternal heart goes out especially to Leila Ernst who is the only uncontaminated baggage in the cast.

Occasionally "Pal Joey" absents itself a little from depravity and pokes fun at the dreariness of night club frolics, and at the close of the first act it presents an admirable dream ballet and pantomime. Joey's hopeful look into a purple future is lyrically danced by Mr. Kelly. There is a kind of wry and wistful beauty to the spinning figures of Mr. Alton's dance design. But the story of "Pal Joey" keeps harking back to the drab and mirthless world of punk's progress. Although "Pal Joey" is exp rtly done, can you draw sweet water from a foul well?

December 26, 1940

MUSIC IN THE AIR

By LEWIS NICHOLS

AFTER some time spent less happily elsewhere, the theatre came back ten days ago to the gleeful consideration of a phase it has not stressed much this season, the musical show. Once more stages in the Forties jingled to dancing that was near rockette, once more actors froze in their tracks that split second before the blackout, and once again audiences went out into the gloom of night humming tunes and on the whole pretty pleased with themselves. For ten days ago two musical shows opened on successive nights, setting forth their gaudy wares for whatever butter-and-egg men there may be left unrationed as well as for those hundreds of thousands who like musical shows anyway. In addition, one of the two gave the theatre its nicest musical play in a long, long while.

The pair were, of course, the latest edition of "Ziegfeld Follies" and the Theatre Guild's current emergence into the light, "Oklahoma!" They cannot be compared, for they are not alike, their only poin's of similarity being that both are musical, both are shown in theatres and both have superlative sets of costumes by the Miles White who these days is showing how to design them. For the "Follies" is in the tried and true tradition of Broadway, stressing girls and songs and sketches; "Oklahoma!" is quiet and easy and gay, with more subtlety than is true of most musicals, and telling its tale through excellent dancing, fresh young voices and Richard Rodgers's best score in recent years.

The "Follies"

The chances are excellent that both will be successful, although it will be for different reasons. The "Follies" knows its formula and clings to that contentedly. It has a good comic, Milton Berle, who in addition to being popular is funny — not always the same thing. He knows his audiences and like all good comedians can read them as he goes along, stressing different bits of his material from night to night and making up new conversational gags. The show also has Ilona Massey, who is one of the more beautiful flowers from the sunshine coast, and it has, but doesn't use overly much, the services of Arthur Treacher. Robert Alton has designed typical "Follies" dances, and down in the pit is an orchestra to blare forth typical "Follies" music. Big, loud and handsome, the current edition of a long line of "Follies" and Winter Garden revues is right in the groove.

"Oklahoma!" is more experimental, for on paper it never could have looked like the sure thing a new section of the "Follies" would provide. For its plot the Theatre Guild went back to one of those plays which never ran overly long but has been talked about ever since — "Green Grow the Lilacs," by Lynn Riggs. This was the tale of a cowhand, a girl and a villain, and what the play lacked in story substance it made up in color and charm. That is also true of its musical version, for the plot still is of a cowhand, a girl and a villain—although they in no sense take it seriously—and surrounding it is a delightful coloring that is gay and entertaining and which brings the players and audience together into a mood of warm attraction, which is quite rare.

Many Talents

Probably the result is due to a combination of talents. In the first place, Mr. Rodgers has been lavish with his music, and a good quorum of his tunes rank with the best there are. The play opens with "Oh, What a Beautiful Mornin,'" and before an audience can sit back to think that over, it dances along to "The Surry With the Fringe on the Top"—both numbers quite clearly destined for hit parades as soon as they are released. And there are many more; a mock-dirge called "Pore Jud"; a love song, "People Will Say"; "The Farmer and the Cowman" and the title song. To put the flutes and the violins in the place where they can give the tunes the greatest lilt is Russell Bennett, who must be the best arranger in the business and who can translate a sense of humor into a full orchestra.

Rouben Mamoulian, an old Guildsman, has come back from the Coast to direct "Oklahoma!" and has done it beautifully. In many musical shows the director, presumably trying for verisimilitude, allows the singers to sing to one another, or to the scenery or chorus; Mr. Mamoulian very simply lets them face the audience and makes no bones about it. His direction and the dances created by Agnes de Mille are perfectly blended, both having a light touch.

The main ballet of the evening is not unlike Miss de Mille's "Rodeo," which is celebrated among dance lovers, and as they do it at the St. James it obviously is completely perfect. Add such singers as Alfred Drake and Joan Roberts to sing the leading roles and such players as Howard da Silva, Celeste Holm, Betty Garde and the highly engaging Joseph Buloff, and you have a company prepared to provide one of the current theatre's most cheerfully outstanding evenings.

Of Cleanliness

One thing more. It was Max Gordon, who is not foolish in the ways of the world, who noted the other day that "Oklahoma!" may have another effect on the theatre. It boasts no double jokes but still is selling every ticket in the racks; perhaps, therefore, Broadway can get along without the jokes which a bit back led almost to the iron bars of censorship. Mr. Gordon thought that when this singular news leaks out many a composer now unhappily away from home may rush back to turn out musicals like "Show Boat" and the rest. If they do, they will find a good model in "Oklahoma!", but one also that will be quite hard to beat.

April 11, 1943

WORDS AND MUSIC

From Padua to Gotham In 'Kiss Me, Kate'

By BROOKS ATKINSON

EVERYONE agrees that "Kiss Me, Kate" is a blissfully enjoyable musical show. Cole Porter has set it to singing with the finest score that has popped out of his music-box in years. And Bella and Samuel Spewack, who settled one of the great literary problems of the century with "Boy Meets Girl" in 1935, have put together a book that is genuinely humorous without the mechanical aid of gags. Of this there is no probable possible shadow of doubt; no possible doubt whatever. The only doubt concerns the definitive quality of the best musical comedy of the season.

Does it rank with the immortal trio of "Show Boat," "Porgy and Bess" and "Oklahoma!" as some of its idolaters believe, or with "Annie Get Your Gun," which is perfection in the more modest field of book-and-song entertainment? In my opinion that is where it belongs. Although the gods are very likely enjoying it, they are not moving over to make room for it on the celestial reviewing stand.

Unlike most musical shows, which come to town after a hysterical ordeal of rewriting and applications of first aid, "Kiss Me, Kate" seems to have given no particular trouble to any of the members of its high command. The basic plan has proved to be workable, and all the workmen are skilled in their trades. The plan is to use Shakespeare's "The Taming of the Shrew" as a play within a play and thus to make wry sport of the temperament of two vain actors who are playing the leading parts. They used to be married to each other and conceivably might remarry.

Out of Shakespeare

Since their stormy relations backstage are similar to the stage relationship of the two chief characters in Shakespeare's low-comedy joint-piece, "Kiss Me, Kate" can alternate between backstage and on-stage scenes without shattering the general sardonic point of view. Backstage the two stars illustrate the validity of Shakespeare's robustious theme.

Mr. and Mrs. Spewack have had the good taste to realize that they do not have to knock themselves out trying to crack vendible musical comedy jokes on this situation. They have written their book with the relish of mature craftsmen who know how to bring characters on and offstage, how to alternate scenes without becoming monotonous and how to fill in the background gayly. From the point of view of craftsmanship as well as enjoyment, this is the best musical comedy book of the year. The story is genuinely theatrical.

If Mr. Porter's record were not so illustrious it would be easy to salute his score for "Kiss Me, Kate" as the best work of his career. There is not a mediocre song in the show; and, according to Mrs. Spewack, his best song is "We Shall Never Grow Younger," which never got as far as rehearsals. But Mr. Porter has been writing good music for a long time. In the course of about thirty years he has written songs that have become part of the musical language of our time—"Begin the Beguine," "Night and Day," "My Heart Belongs to Daddy," "In the Still of the Night," "Anything Goes" and "You're the Top," to cite some of those most familiar.

His library of scores is about as thorough a record of transient public moods as you will find in the archives—pensive, worldly and clever by turns, with the romance bitter-sweet and the impudence brassy. As his own most light-fingered lyric writer, Mr. Porter is a virtuoso performer.

Italian Milieu

The Shakespeare prank is as refreshing for him as it has been for Mr. and Mrs. Spewack. It gets him away from the hackneyed squalor of the average musical comedy book into the warm and romantic environment of Padua. "So In Love Am I" is probably the theme song of "Kiss Me, Kate"; it is soft and enchanting and gives distinction to the entire work. But there are other songs of sentiment in the score—"Wunderbar," "Were Thine That Special Face" and "I Sing of Love"; all are first rate, too.

As usual, Mr. Porter's humorous songs are lively, low and frolicsome, such as "Too Darn Hot" and "Always True to You (In My Fashion)." One of them, entitled "I Hate Men," is the perfect musical sublimation of Shakespeare's evil-tempered Kate. Probably it will never get into the juke-boxes, for it is a situation song in a drama. But apart from its vigor as a song, it is a perceptive piece of composition, and it indicates how far "Kiss Me, Kate" has managed to go toward being a homogeneous piece of theatre work.

Patricia Morison sings this hymn of hate against the male animal. From every point of view that is fortunate. For Miss Morison is an accomplished singer who can also act and, moreover, has an infectious sense of humor. Mr. Porter as well as Mr. and Mrs. Spewack probably feel very lucky to have her singing the songs as well as acting one of the two chief parts in their Shakespeare carnival. She is brilliant in it.

Actors Who Can Sing

No one is astonished to find Alfred Drake equally expert in the opposite part. He has been the top man in this field for a long time. He, too, can sing and act, and he has the intelligence of a man who can recognize the value of a new idea. Musical comedy does not have to be a stereotyped form of entertainment as long as such actors as Miss Morison and Mr. Drake are available.

In secondary parts Lisa Kirk and Harold Lang are also original and agreeable. Having startled the town last season by singing "The Gentleman Is a Dope" as though she meant it, Miss Kirk is captivating it this year as a fully accredited hoyden with a sense of humor. Before the war producers were complaining that they were unable to find performers who had voice enough to sing a piece of music that covered more than five notes.

But no longer. Every musical comes fully equipped with good singers now. Mr. Drake and Miss Morison ought to give composers as well as authors a feeling of security. In "Kiss Me, Kate" none of the performers wastes material.

January 16, 1949

THE MUSIC MASTER

'Pal Joey' Makes Three For Richard Rodgers

By BROOKS ATKINSON

NOW that a sparkling production of "Pal Joey" has set up shop at the Broadhurst Theatre, Richard Rodgers, the composer, is represented by three plays doing business every night in Forty-fourth Street. He wrote the ebullient score for "Pal Joey" in 1940 when the late Lorenz Hart was his partner in musical revelry. "South Pacific," which inhabits the Majestic next door, has been singing his music and Oscar Hammerstein 2d's lyrics to contented theatregoers since April 7, 1949. Across the street at the St. James, "The King and I" has been successfully performing a similar errand of mercy since March 29 of last year.

If anyone were reckless enough to describe Mr. Rodgers' current record as unprecedented, some qualified lexicographer would turn up with obscure facts to prove the contrary. Nothing on Broadway is ever unprecedented, including disaster. But to be composer of three memorable musical plays that are simultaneously on view is certainly very comforting and it ought to encourage Mr. Rodgers to write something else some time.

For the Record

As Broadway's most gifted composer, Mr. Rodgers seems to have been maneuvered into a position of self-defense recently. A few weeks ago at the Harvard Law School Forum he answered the charge that the musical play is driving the dramatic play out of the theatre; and in company with Mr. Hammerstein he discussed the same subject, among other things, at a luncheon of the Columbia University Alumni Federation on Dec. 27. If the charge were candidly written it would accuse Mr. Rodgers and Mr. Hammerstein specifically of conspiring to operate a monopoly in restraint of trade—an indictable offense under the Sherman Act. Look what happened to the Standard Oil Company which had to go out of business. Or did it?

No one is likely to bring such a charge for three reasons. One, there are a number of immensely enjoyable musical shows written by other hands. Two, Mr. Rodgers and Mr. Hammerstein are good eggs; they could intimidate the court with a ferocious mob of character witnesses. Three, they are genuinely gifted men. Nobody has to see their musical plays, but thousands of people would like to see them because they have so much emotional intensity.

Emotion to Music

The emotional richness of the musical play as a form is the nub of Mr. Rodgers' defense against the charge of driving the dramatic play out of business. Terrified at the prospect of facing so many learned barristers, he prepared a brief for the Harvard Law School Forum, a copy of which has been served on this department. Briefly, his argument runs as follows: The theatre is basically a "place of escape." "When the theatre is good we escape through an emotional outlet. We laugh or cry or we're stimulated to excitement." Since the number of "truly dramatic emotional plays" has been inadequate in recent years, the theatre as a whole has been fortified by the musical stage, "which is intensely emotional in drama, in romance or in laughter." "As the so-called serious play went out, the so-called serious musical play came in."

This bare summary is to some extent unfair to Mr. Rodgers' argument because it omits some important qualifications. "Good serious drama has had no trouble in finding its own public," he says. " 'A Streetcar Named Desire' had no difficulty; neither did 'Death of a Salesman,' and I firmly believe that had there been ten more of good quality they would have done equally well." He also mentions "The Moon Is Blue" as a popular comedy that is performing a valid function in the theatre. But "in the absence of a great many good dramatic plays" Mr. Rodgers does not understand why anyone should be alarmed, because the musical stage is doing such a large part of the theatre's total job.

Success Is No Crime

Since there is nothing definitely criminal about the fact that enjoyable and talented musical plays succeed at the box office, this column does not see the necessity of indicting Mr. Rodgers because he has done so well. Neither is it indicting Tennessee Williams or Arthur Miller for having written original and moving plays that have succeeded. But the reappearance of "Pal Joey" provides an opportunity to see what has happened to Mr. Rodgers' conception of the musical play in the last twelve years. Most people regard "Pal Joey" as the musical play that broke the trite formula of insipid romance. Although this assumption overlooks the originality of "Of Thee I Sing" and "Porgy and Bess," it is a tenable thesis. The pioneering of "Pal Joey" did open the way to "Oklahoma!" "Carousel," "South Pacific" and "The King and I."

For "Pal Joey" is a caustic piece of modern literature. John O'Hara's sketch of a cheap, treacherous night-club punk is mordant and penetrating; and his picture of one aspect of contemporary life is unerring and ruthless. Accepting the sardonic entertainment inherent in a malodorous environment of this sort, Mr. Rodgers has written an extraordinary score with versatility and gusto. It ranges all the way from the gaudy burlesque of "Zip" and "Happy Hunting Horn" to the dreamy melodies of "What Is a Man?" and "Bewitched. Bothered and Bewildered"; and the Lorenz Hart lyrics are neat, wry and witty. A great sense of enjoyment rushes out of the score and overwhelms the play.

Expert Coordination

Everything is expertly coordinated: the exuberant, tongue-in-cheek dance designs by Robert Alton; the pithy book direction by David Alexander; the accomplished, intimately styled singing and the droll acting of Vivienne Segal; the lyrical dancing and the baleful character acting of Harold Lang; Helen Gallagher's humorously disillusioned strutting and acting as a night-club trollop; Elaine Stritch's contemptuous travesty of a columnist; Lionel Stander's monstrous gangster acted in the grand manner. All these various skills and attitudes compose a musical ragtag and bobtail that is candid and unpretentious and that has enormous impact in the theatre.

"Pal Joey" is the epitome of Broadway and as exhilarating as though it had just been written. "South Pacific" and "The King and I" have bigger themes. Their music has greater depth and loveliness, for Mr. Rodgers has matured not only in years but in talent, and his association with Mr. Hammerstein has widened the horizon. They both accept a certain sense of responsibility about the world in which they are living. But those who recognized "Pal Joey" as a pioneer musical in 1940 were sound prophets; and now the western end of Forty-fourth Street between Seventh and Eighth Avenues has become a Rodgers music festival. It is useless for him to defend himself against the charge of being gifted. Guilty as charged.

January 13, 1952

'MY FAIR LADY'

Shaw's 'Pygmalion' Turns Into One Of The Best Musicals of the Century

By BROOKS ATKINSON

ON the day after "My Fair Lady" opened, a colleague offered a pertinent observation: In the new musical comedy, the hero and heroine never kiss.

For Alan Jay Lerner's "My Fair Lady," which is derived from "Pygmalion," reflects Shaw's lack of interest in the stage ritual of sex. It is never gooey. In fact, it departs so far from the conventions of the musical stage that the moment of greatest tension concerns the proper pronunciation of "rain," "plain" and "Spain."

Professor Higgins, the celebrated phonetician, is trying to teach Eliza Doolittle, a Covent Garden flower girl, how to speak like a lady. The moment in which she succeeds with her first word exercise is the most victorious in the comedy, and Frederick Loewe, the composer, has set one of his most joyous songs for the occasion.

But the radical revision of musical stage values in "My Fair Lady" does not deceive anyone. Shaw labeled "Pygmalion" a "romance," although he was not confining his use of the word to love. Despite its immediate preoccupation with matters of speech, "My Fair Lady" is so much a romance that most theatregoers will probably be astonished to learn that Shaw never intended Eliza Doolittle and Professor Higgins for each other. In an epilogue, which chronicles the years after the conclusion of the play, Shaw says in the Penguin edition that Eliza has sense enough to marry Freddy, who really loves her, and that they become a swanky couple with a prosperous flower shop in a railway terminal. Shaw dissociates himself from "the ragshop in which Romance keeps its stock of 'happy endings' to misfit all stories."

But these are matters on the periphery of the main event. Since "My Fair Lady" takes rank with the best musical comedies of the century, Eliza's life in an imagined future is beside the point. As a musical play, "My Fair Lady" is one of Broadway's celestial works. Although it includes the familiar elements of book, songs, dance and spectacle, it dispenses with the bromides of showmanship and stands on its own feet as a theatre creation.

Unlikely Plot

Everybody is happy to thank Shaw for the story, which provides most of the wit and knowledge and all the principal characters. It also provides something that is extraordinarily fascinating: the transfiguration of a human being. From a raucous, sniveling, ugly guttersnipe, Eliza grows into a young lady of grace and splendor. That is doubtless the most unlikely plot a popular musical comedy ever had. But it is beautiful. It gets close to the genius of creation.

Thank Shaw for the central idea. But everyone concerned with "My Fair Lady" is entitled to equivalent gratitude for the taste with which the central idea has been transformed into a polished show. Mr. Lerner has not only adapted the Shaw play without cheapening it; he has also written new scenes and lyrics that carry the story into a new and larger dimension.

In the Tottenham Court Road scenes the roistering is Mr. Lerner's. It captures the authentic spirit of that epochal dustman—Alfred P. Doolittle, the philosophical scoundrel. Although Mr. Lerner's book and lyrics are idiomatic, they are never common. He has taste as well as imagination.

Mr. Loewe is one of the most enjoyable composers in the business. As his scores for "Brigadoon" and "Paint Your Wagon" suggested, he is not self-conscious about style, but plunges into every situation with melody and enthusiasm. The music is fresh. It, too, is idiomatic without being common. Some of it, like the "Ascot Gavotte," is ironically funny, or both funny and sentimental, like "Wouldn't It Be Loverly," and some of it is romantic, like "On the Street Where You Live." But Mr. Loewe can also make evocative music out of a dramatic situation, as he does in "The Rain in Spain," which releases pent-up emotion with exultation at a climactic place in the story. According to the needs of the book, Mr. Loewe can be composer as well as song writer.

Although Moss Hart has been one of the brightest particles on Broadway for years, he has staged "My Fair Lady" without Broadway's usual devices. This is his most impeccable job. In production and performance, the accent is on elegance of style. Oliver Smith's settings are both decorative and hospitable; Cecil Beaton's costumes are gorgeous. Hanya Holm has blended the dance numbers into the story so unobtrusively that they seem like extensions of the general theme in terms of motion.

Dramatic Acting

For years there has been less and less distinction between musical comedy performing and dramatic acting. The acting in "My Fair Lady" is superb. In the low comedy part of Alfred P. Doolittle, Stanley Holloway plays his dramatic scenes adroitly and the Tottenham Court Road scenes with music-hall gusto, realizing no doubt that there is a time and place for everything. Cathleen Nesbitt brings her familiar fastidiousness of style to the part of Mrs. Higgins. And Robert Coote plays Colonel Pickering with comic subtlety.

If "My Fair Lady" has an undercurrent of real emotion and human aspiration, it is largely because Rex Harrison and Julie Andrews play the chief parts without musical comedy flamboyance. They could hardly get to the heart of the story more skillfully if they were playing "Pygmalion." Since Mr. Harrison is an experienced and gifted actor, the easy perfection of his aloof, self-centered Professor Higgins comes as no surprise. He plays the part brilliantly.

But Miss Andrews has not had such wide experience. Despite the humorous charm of her performing in "The Boy Friend" last season, the glory of her acting in "My Fair Lady" comes as a happy surprise. As a singer she has rare purity of tone. As a person she has incandescence that fills the theatre.

But the part of Eliza is neither simple nor static. It is full of impulses that are not expressed directly, and it grows with delicacy and magic during the course of the evening. In Miss Andrews' acting it is all there. She has mastered a complex part with its variety of accents, its alteration in manners and its unfolding of personality. Her performance is magnificent not only because it is personally enchanting but because it has poise, style and artistic maturity.

Although the hero and heroine never kiss in this original comedy, the romantic glow is no less affecting on that account. In taste, intelligence, skill and delight, "My Fair Lady" is the finest musical play in years.

March 25, 1956

'WEST SIDE STORY'

Moving Music Drama On Callous Theme

By **BROOKS ATKINSON**

WITH the production of "West Side Story" the musical stage recovers the maturity it had before the collapse in taste last season.

It is an organic work of art. The collaborators who put it together have fused their respective contributions into a single theatrical expression that vividly portrays the life of the streets. They are Arthur Laurents, writer, Leonard Bernstein, composer, Stephen Sondheim, lyricist, and Jerome Robbins, choreographer and director. Although the music and the dancing are the most conspicuous elements of expression, they emanate from a soundly written narrative. The whole production has the solidity of a genuine creation.

It derives from the story and character relationships of Shakespeare's "Romeo and Juliet," a lyrical, romantic tragedy set in a mythical environment. But there is nothing mythical about the environment of "West Side Story." It is New York today, and the principal characters are the tense, furtive, feral members of two hostile teen-age gangs, lost in a fantasy of hatred and revenge.

By comparison the Montagues and Capulets are romantic. Thanks to Shakespeare and his poetic tradition, they communicate in lyrical verse. In the literary context of their times they have some honor as swordsmen and gallants. In fact, Mercutio is more of a romantic hero than Romeo because he adheres to a chivalric code.

Gang Warfare

But the crafty gangs in "West Side Story" are youths of the streets whose speech is acrid and ugly and whose conduct is neurotic and savage. Although they have their tribal code of honor—loyalty, daring and silence—it is the code of hoodlums and gangsters. It is rooted in ignorance and evil; it has no relationship to anything that can be regarded as romantic or beguiling. It is part of the hideousness that lies under the scabby surface of the city.

But "West Side Story" finds bits of beauty in a wasteland of discontent. The rhapsodic avowals of "Romeo and Juliet" are full of beauty and desperation, and the equivalent situation in "West Side Story" is much the same. The Romeo is Tony, a hero in the Jets gang; the Juliet is Maria, sister of the leader of the Sharks gang, who are Puerto Ricans. They meet for the first time at a dance arranged by a social worker to relieve the tension between the gangs. It is love at first sight.

Although Mr. Laurents does not follow his model slavishly, he preserves most of the situations of the Shakespeare tragedy—the dance (equivalent to the Capulet ball), the quarreling in the streets, the futile intrusion of the law, the scuffle between the gangs and the senseless slaughter. He has also preserved the balcony scene. In "West Side Story" it takes place on the unlovely fire escape of a Puerto Rican tenement.

If the avowals of eternal devotion lack the music of Shakespeare, they do not lack rapture. For the part of Maria is played and sung by Carol Lawrence, with a girlish ardor that is sweet and touching. Larry Kert portrays Tony with a boyish fidelity and openness that are equally affecting.

Two Lovers

This is the scene when "West Side Story" pulls loose from the monotonous taciturnity of gang warfare and rises to the level of a human situation. There is something particularly poignant about Tony's and Maria's adoration because it is so much purer than the treachery and violence that swirl around it, because it is simple and honest, and also because it gives two young people a hopeless glimpse of how ecstatic and

cleansing life could be in a decent neighborhood.

Don't look for the familiar solaces of the musical stage in "West Side Story." Don't look for music that can be whistled, gay amour, ravishing costumes, stunning sets and comedy bits. The only comedy scene is staged around a sardonic song entitled "Gee, Officer Krupke." Since juvenile delinquency is a painful and baffling problem, the taste of this jeering song is open to question. It takes a light view of a frightening subject.

But the fundamental distinction of "West Side Story" is the courage with which it adheres to its artistic convictions and its unwillingness to make concessions to popular taste. The authors are playing for keeps. Mr. Bernstein's score has the shrill impetuosity of its subject. Despite the loveliness of the songs that Maria and Tony sing together and the mood of reverie in a dance number sung by Reri Grist, the score as a whole, with its biting orchestration, gives an impression of nervous drive, hostility, callousness, distrust. Mr. Bernstein is not glossing over the nature of his material.

Nor is Mr. Robbins in the ballets. In the second act there is a delicate arrangement of day-dreaming movement for a wistful song entitled "Somewhere"; it expresses the lull before the storm. But "West Side Story" begins with a grim dance movement that sets the tone for the whole production; and most of the dancing, like the music, is reckless, joyless and sinister. It portrays the tautness and malevolence of underage gorillas who are impervious to reason.

"West Side Story" would be unbearable if it were not for Tony and Maria, who never see true beauty until they exchange glances during a rowdyish dance. The contrast between the lovers and the gangs supplies perspective that makes a moving experience out of a corrosive subject. "Piteous" was the word Shakespeare used about his lovers. It is a word that still applies.

October 6, 1957

Theatre: 'Fantasticks'

Musical at Sullivan Street Playhouse

By **BROOKS ATKINSON**

HAVING won a lot of admirers with a short version of "The Fantasticks," Tom Jones has expanded it for the production that opened at the Sullivan Street Playhouse last evening.

Although it is ungrateful to say so, two acts are one too many to sustain the delightful tone of the first. After the intermission, the mood is never quite so luminous and gay.

The remark is ungrateful because the form of a masque seems original in the modern theatre. Harvey Schmidt's simple melodies with uncomplicated orchestrations are captivating and the acting is charming. Throughout the first act "The Fantasticks" is sweet and fresh in a civilized manner.

Rita Gardner

•

According to the program, it is based on Rostand's "Les Romantiques." In the form of a dainty masque, designed in modern taste by Ed Wittstein, it is a variation on a Pierrot and Columbine theme. A boy and a girl, who are neighbors, are in love as long as a wall separates them and they believe that their fathers disapprove. Actually, their fathers want them to marry. To create an irresistible romantic mood, the fathers arrange a flamboyant abduction scene in the moonlight.

Although the story is slight, the style is entrancing in Word Baker's staging. It seems like a narlequinade in the setting of a masque. The characters are figures in a legend, acted with an artlessness that is winning. As the Narrator, the Girl and the Boy, Jerry Orbach, Rita Gardner and Kenneth Nelson, respectively, sing beautifully and act with spontaneity, not forgetting that they are participating in a work of make-believe.

•

After the intermission the author substitutes sunshine for moonlight. Disillusion destroys the rapture of the introductory scene. Pierrot and Columbine have combed the stardust out of their hair. But it seems to this theatregoer that the second act loses the skimming touch of the first. As an aging ham actor, Thomas Bruce is not so funny as he is in his first appearance, and the conceits of the staging become repetitious.

Perhaps "The Fantasticks" is by nature the sort of thing that loses magic the longer it endures. Any sign of effort diminishes it. But for the space of one act it is delightful. The music, played on piano and harp, has grace and humor. All the actors are thoroughbreds.

May 4, 1960

EASY DOES IT

Imaginative Jabs Better Than Haymakers

By **HOWARD TAUBMAN**

START with Thornton Wilder in a mood of affectionate nostalgia, and make Gower Champion the generalissimo of a happy company of writers, designers and performers. How can you lose?

Well, you can, though "Hello, Dolly!" doesn't. But there is always that black abyss gaping hungrily, and either it terrifies the theater into a paralysis that precedes rigor mortis or it incites a feverish turmoil that leads to chaos.

"Hello, Dolly!" is too fresh, imaginative and buoyant to be undermined by the fears and hysteria that infest the theater. But it bears the stigmata. It makes do with a facile gag when it needn't. It tolerates vulgarities it can dispense with. It compounds comic excitement into sound and fury signifying nervous insecurity that a few dolts will miss a fairly obvious point.

As you watch this new musical comedy, so full of earthy exuberance, lavish color and freshness of imagination, you wonder why the gifted craftsmen who have created it ever strayed from the limits of good taste. So much of what they have achieved is inventive, humorous and warm. They know what they are doing, and their instincts are sound. When they go wrong, how has it happened?

The Problem

Not even the most talented are perfect. One can understand how an idea that looks delightful in the mind's eye and on paper simply does not pan out. It is easy to see how the notion of the choleric half-millionaire's chasing his employes, Cornelius and Barnaby, through tableaux vivants and a production number brimming with muses, nymphs, flowers and butterflies would seem an irresistible prospect. Through some perversity of the theater, it is merely clumsy on the stage.

Write it off as a good idea that doesn't work out. Forgive it without recrimination because risking difficult problems in the theater should be encouraged. The graveyard of musicals that died young is strewn with the remains of ventures that sought only to imitate what had succeeded elsewhere.

But what saddens one in a work so bright and vital is a resort to cheapness when it's unnecessary. The creators of "Hello, Dolly!" know the difference between good and bad taste. One can only blame a widespread malaise of show business—the uneasy state of mind that causes the theater to try too hard and to overdo.

The trouble is partly in today's inflated economics. With hundreds of thousands riding on a musical, producers, creators and performers would have to be made of steel not to press and, overstate. But the root of the difficulty is older than today's high cost of producing and lies deeper—in a distrust, I think, of the public's capacity to grasp and respond to simplicity and suggestion.

At its best, "Hello, Dolly!" like the finest musical comedies of the last two decades, is winning because it enlists and enlarges the audience's imagination. The opening, as the curtain rises without an overture, sets a charming mood with the most graceful of means.

Oliver Smith's sets with their pen-and-ink precision and airiness, Freddy Wittop's rainbow-hued costumes and Mr. Champion's patterns of stylized, airborne movement join in evoking the atmosphere of an old New York washed in wistful sentiment, yet remembered with crackling laughter. The eye is not overwhelmed; it is teased by a grouping, frozen like a Currier & Ives print, and then rejoiced by a couple strutting in an unexpected corner of the stage.

Mr. Champion has used Jerry Herman's sprightly numbers—the sentimental ones are doughy—with frequent allusiveness. For "Dancing" in three-four time he has modulated from a dancing lesson for two into arabesques of movement with partners joining and parting in dreamlike asymmetry. For "Elegance," a spoof on highflown manners, his steps are grace notes for light satire.

There is a time and place for the production numbers that fill a theater with gaudy hues and explosive high spirits. The men led by David Burns as the curmudgeonly half-millionaire erupt in "It Takes a Woman," a muscular hymn to the usefulness of a constantly toiling housewife. The male ensemble also raises the temperature in a wildly staccato "Waiters' Gallop."

With Carol Channing in scarlet gown, feathered headdress and gleaming choker to embody radiantly the earthy, opulent womanhood that was the toast of old New York, the men help to turn the title song into a communal hallelujah. They all parade around the runway that circles the pit and raise the rafters with their bursting energy.

Miss Channing

The women join the men in a colorful, effusive production number celebrating the departure of a train for New York from the Yonkers depot in "Put on Your Sunday Clothes" and in a fragrant recollection of a parade along Fourteenth Street to "Before the Parade Passes By."

All stops are out here. This is the musical theater legitimately overwhelming the ear as well as the eye. The grand effect is most exhilarating when it suits the occasion and arises out of the style of a unified conception.

These big numbers, though wonderfully theatrical, are not gimmickry. Neither is the false proscenium with its interlacing of wedding bands. Nor are the horse capering on four shapely human legs and the railroad engine spewing smoke and ashes.

Most heartwarming of all is Miss Channing as Mrs. Dolly Gallagher Levi in her bland, eager helpfulness to marry off a grouchy half-millionaire, a widowed milliner, inexperienced clerks and, of course, herself. As the widow of the beloved Ephraim Levi, who wisely believed that money should circulate like rainwater, she is particularly faithful to the fond drollery of Thornton Wilder's play "The Matchmaker." Michael Stewart's book does not traduce this motif.

When she communes with the spirit of dear, old Ephraim hovering not too far up there, "Hello, Dolly!" is like "The Matchmaker" in its grasp of quiet humor and unabashed sentiment under the tough stylized skin of broad farce.

The enchantment in such moments is proof that a musical need not knock itself out aiming haymakers all night long. "Hello Dolly!" throws some hard punches, and a few are wild and annoying, but it's the quick, easy unexpected thrusts of imagination that win the day.

January 26, 1964

LAST DAYS FOR "UNCLE TOM"

A Mainstay for Decade After Decade, the Play Has Given Way Before Modernity

THE number of "Uncle Tom's Cabin" road shows is dwindling. Before the invasion of the motion picture, they traveled the length and breadth of the land, serving multitudes as dramatic fare from childhood to old age. Many and various were the troupes that produced this play, altogether forming an institution of a less sophisticated America.

Old-time troupers tell endless tales, all strange to the modern theatre-goer's ear, of experiences with these shows. They were of two types: those that were technically called "Tom" shows and those familiarly known as "rep." The "Tom" shows stuck to their appellation. They toured the country, or their section of it, doing nothing but this play, year in and year out. Players did the same rôles for years. They were born in "Tom" shows and sometimes died in them.

The "rep" or repertory shows were themselves divided into two classes, the "house rep" shows that were quartered in theatres and the "tent rep" outfits which played under canvas. Besides these outfits, medicine shows, always a glamorous phase of the American theatre, also did "Uncle Tom's Cabin."

The répertoire of a "rep" show might include, in addition to "Uncle Tom's Cabin," such happy thrillers and "tear jerkers" as "East Lynne," "Ten Nights in a Bar Room," "The Spy," "The Black Flag," "'49," "Bertha the Sewing Machine Girl" and "Jim the Penman." Villains of extra blackness and fair, ever so fair, heroines caused, nightly, righteous hisses and equally righteous applause.

Theatre-going in those happy days was a different thing from the present scramble of box offices and agencies. Many shows charged not one, but three admissions. First, one paid a general admission. Then, inside, one could obtain a reserved seat upon payment of an additional fee. And after the performance was over one could, by a third payment, stay for the "concert."

Informality was often the rule, at least in contrast with the present-day custom in those few cities harboring the living theatre. When the queues were long, the players might assist the "front of the house" (the box office attendants) by herding into line eager children—eager to get in to see Eva and Tom and all the rest. Inside, the players "doubled," not only portraying one or more rôles but often tooting horns or playing fiddles in the band or orchestra.

The curtain lifted. The play progressed. Audiences might know as well as players what came next, but they still continued to go to see "Tom." Between acts, players in make-up and costumes went among the playgoers, vending candies and other confections.

And the show went on, until it was all over and little Eva was safe in heaven.

Players knew the lines as they knew their own names. Audiences—that is, real "Tom" audiences—knew the same lines nearly as well. Although there were only two accepted versions, one produced in England and considered the better by some, and the other produced in this country, both in 1853, changes were often made to fit conditions or a director's whim. Simon Legree might sprout a mustache of villainous black in one town and of fierce tomato red in the next. But this was all part of the show. One understood such things. It was almost a rite, this "Uncle Tom's Cabin."

Its remarkable life would put to shame "Abie's Irish Rose" and other productions that carried the years merrily and profitably on their shoulders. It has been done continuously since the Civil War period and was even more popular after the war than during it.

But the play lost its grip when America went "modern." Only a few companies now produce it. Some follow their itineraries by motor car instead of by the wagon of yesterday. Attempts to hold interest by adding to the cast have failed. When "Uncle Tom's Cabin" is produced at all, it is little changed from the way it was presented years ago.

July 12, 1931

Lionel Barrymore in "Unseeing Eyes."

ABIE

NO one remains in New York during the Summer, as is well known. No one goes to "Abie's Irish Rose," now nearing the end of its first year in New York, as is also well known. Probably it's the same people.

The history of "Abie's Irish Rose," first revealed to New York at the Fulton Theatre May 23, 1922, is indeed simple. The professional critics gave it a week or two to run, at the most. The manager of its theatre, the legend goes, was hindered in the execution of his intention to close the show only because it owed him money and his sole chance of recovery lay in continuance. Bit by bit the receipts of the show increased and a few months ago it tramped boldly and defiantly out of the cut-rate counters. It has broken stock records in Washington, Pittsburgh and other towns. Today it is the oldest show on Broadway. And only recently the press agent of a new production picked out of the abuse showered upon it the line "As Good as 'Abie's Irish Rose'" for advertising purposes.

On Wednesday last an earnest student of the drama, desiring to know exactly what made this thing tick, despite the enthusiastic slamming of it by the leaders of dramatic thought, attended a matinee performance. He made careful and copious notes of the goings-on, but he reported sadly that he left no wiser than he came.

The plot, as he understood and described it, deals with one Solomon Levy, a widower, whose only son, Abie, marries one Rosemary Murphy. To keep secret from his father the fact that the girl, otherwise acceptable in every way, is not of his faith, Abie introduces her to his father as Rosie Murphyski.

At this point THE TIMES's informant lost a good deal of what were probably important details of the plot. When he was finally brought to, he reports, he gathered that a violent struggle between the Jewish father and the Irish father-in-law over the religious disposition of the expected baby was happily ended by the birth of twins.

What makes the thing tick, thus, remains a mystery. There is no question of the fact, however, that it does tick and that it is today the undisputed leader of all New York theatrical attractions in point of length of run.

May 13, 1923

'ABIE'S IRISH ROSE' MAKES RECORD RUN

Its 1,292d Performance, One More Than "Lightnin'," Is America's Highest Score.

"Abie's Irish Rose" last night reached its twelve hundred and ninety-second performance at the Republic Theatre, thereby setting up a new long record for the American stage. The previous record was set by "Lightnin'," in 1921. "Abie's Irish Rose" opened at the Fulton Theatre on May 23, 1922.

In addition to its lengthy stay in New York, "Abie's Irish Rose" has played record engagements in a dozen other cities, and five other companies are now playing it in Detroit, St. Louis, Rochester, and in Kansas and the South.

Anne Nichols, author and producer of the play, yesterday presented the members of the casts of all the companies with anniversary gifts, which were jade bracelets for the women and diamond cuff links for the men. In all 175 gifts were thus distributed.

Last night's cast included Milton Wallace, Ida Kramer, Jack Bertin, Alfred White, Harold Shubert, Evelyn Nichols, Andrew Mack, Harry Bradley, Dorothy Pitou, Irene Antel, Elsie Nichols, Dorothy Grau and Phyllis Perugina. Of these actors Alfred White, Harry Bradley and Dorothy Grau were members of the cast that opened in the piece at the Fulton Theatre.

THE TIMES's review for May 24, 1922, said of the play in part:

"A highly sophisticated Summer audience took the little comedy very heartily, laughing uproariously at its juggling with some fundamental things in human life and at some others not so fundamental, but deeply cherished, as lifelong feelings are wont to be. * * * We hope to be present at little Rebecca Rachel and Patrick Joseph Levy's second birthday, if not their Hudson-Fulton centennial."

May 24, 1925

The Mystery of "The Bat"

THE chief mystery in the mad melodrama at the Morosco is not the identity of the Bat, which, after all, is not so very baffling to the reasonably wily theatregoer. The chief mystery is rather that involved in the strange effort on the part of the authors and producers to conceal the fact that, in this extremely popular piece, Mrs. Rinehart has, with the assistance of the ten-handed Avery Hopwood, merely written a neat dramatization of her own old $1.50 dreadful, "The Circular Staircase." To that early flier of hers into the realm of detective fiction the process of dramatization has added very little except the actual device of the arch-criminal who takes as much pride in conscientiously signing his own crimes as an artist would in signing his own etchings—a device which may have been (and doubtless was) suggested by the "Arsène Lupin" stories.

When Mrs. Humphry Ward was chided for not acknowledging the French sources of "Lady Rose's Daughter," she replied with crushing effect that she had thought them too obvious to need mentioning. No doubt a similar explanation lies behind the failure of the first musical program of "Hitchy-Koo" to say anything about the rather startling appropriation effected in its wedding song. Then, too, the discreet silence which the program of "The Half-Moon" preserves on the subject of "Our Boys," the old Byron farce of the seventies, which served as the basis for its libretto, is explicable, if not admirable.

But just why the preliminary announcements, the playbills, and the posters of "The Bat" should keep up an ostrich-like pretense that this play was not based on "The Circular Staircase" passes all understanding. Week after week the editor of the Queries and Answers column in the theatre programs has gone on solemnly assuring some memory-haunted playgoer that the piece at the Morosco had no basis in any of Mrs. Rinehart's stories. It is not known why.

When "The Bat" opened there were many among the first-nighters who shook their heads sadly over the comic extravagance of this thriller, over its fine, irresponsible mixture of storm, thefts, murders and arson, with low—nay, with sub-moron—comedy. This, they said, would never do. Some of us, however, thought then, and still think, that the dissenters quite missed the intended mood of Mrs. Rinehart's melodrama. Not real thrills, but a state of bogus, self-conscious excitement—that is her game. The mood of ghost stories told around the fire in a darkened room, hair-raising tales related in a sepulchral voice to the accompaniment of much jumpiness and all manner of half-smothered laughter, that is the mood "The Bat" invites and most cunningly achieves. It is worth noting, as part of Mrs. Rinehart's secret, that her melodramas are always cozy. Battle, murder and sudden death, these she dotes on. But they must all be enacted on something not much larger than a hearthrug—such a place, say, as the lonely, storm-bound house in "The Bat," or the quarantined home in "Seven Days," or the yacht at sea in some other yarn of hers.

It is, by the way, a curious thing about Mrs. Rinehart's hammock stories that one recalls everything about them except the titles. Indeed, it is probable that the punditical first-nighters at "The Bat" failed to mention "The Circular Staircase," not in any effort to conceal their base familiarity with such agreeable rubbish, but because they had forgotten what the plagued book was called.

November 14, 1920

HOW THEY USED TO LIVE

By BROOKS ATKINSON

ALTHOUGH Thornton Wilder's "Our Town" is set in Southern New Hampshire near Mount Monadnock, the New England aspect of his play goes deeper than that. His detached and speculative point of view conveys the New England rhythm. From Cotton Mather through the Concord cosmologists, Longfellow and Lowell to Edwin Arlington Robinson and Robert Frost, the New Englander has tuned himself to the infinite. Perhaps it is the age of the culture or the Puritan heritage, perhaps it is the somber loveliness of the landscape or the barbaric extremes of climate through the turn of the year—whatever the reason, the New Englander is aware of something mightier than his personal experience. The long point of view, which Mr. Priestley discovered in "Time and the Conways," comes naturally to him. In Santayana, who served a term of collegiate office in New England, it is refined into brooding poetry with classical models, but he puts it into words when he says: "The art of life is to keep step with the celestial orchestra that beats the measure of our career and gives the cue for our exits and entrances." What matters most is not the isolated experience of the day but the whole pattern of life from the ancient past into the depths of the future.

* * *

THAT is the genius of Mr. Wilder's very notable play. By casually dispensing with most of the formalities of the realistic theatre he has given the local doings of Grover's Corners a cosy niche in the universe. He is looking on affectionately from a distance and what he sees is a terribly poignant chapter in living and dying. Although he enfolds the play in the great amplitude of the universe in many ways, he puts the most cogent statement of it on the lips of a wondering child who is gazing at the moonlight one Spring evening; she impulsively recalls the dryly humorous address that some wag has scribbled on the envelope of a letter to a Grover's Corners girl: "Jane Crofut, The Crofut Farm, Grover's Corners, Sutton County, New Hampshire, United States of America, Continent of North America, Western Hemisphere, the Earth, the Solar System, the Universe, the Mind of God." "What do you know!" her adolescent brother exclaims incredulously, wondering what all that can possibly mean. But the theatregoer knows that Mr. Wilder simply means to offer Grover's Corners in evidence as a gentle way of life.

* * *

FROM the long point of view the ordinary things in life become infinitely pathetic. Day by day we are buoyed up by the normal bustle of our families, neighbors and friends. But the long point of view is a lonely one and the little living that people do on this spinning planet is tragically unimportant. It has been repeated so many times in so many places without plan or deliberation, and there are centuries of it ahead. Some of the simplest episodes in "Our Town" are therefore touching beyond all reason. The scene in which Dr. Gibbs patiently reproves his son for neglecting to chop firewood for his mother becomes tenderly emotional because, in its homely statement, it is a portrait of thoughtfulness and understanding. The shy, faltering scene between George and Emily when for the first time they realize they love each other is, in spite of its romantic material, overwhelmingly compassionate because of what it represents in the immutable ways of men and women. Mr. Wilder's scheme of playwriting distinguishes between what is mortal and what is immortal in the chronicle of normal living. There go all of us, not "but for the grace of God," but "by the grace of God." This is the record of the simplest things we have all been through. Grover's Corners is "Our Town"—the days and deaths of the brotherhood of man.

* * *

NOW that "Our Town" has been seen, the extraordinary form in which it is written seems to be the least important thing about it. As most theatregoers know by this time, it is produced without scenery, with the curtain always up. There is nothing on the stage except a few chairs and tables and two commonplace trellises to suggest doorways. Frank Craven, stage manager and commentator, opens the performance by setting the stage and then acting as a sort of village host by describing the play, introducing scenes and concluding them, summoning people to the stage to give vital statistics about the town and occasionally playing bits in the performance. On paper this doubtless sounds like a stunt, and almost becomes one when Mr. Craven proceeds to set the stage for a second time in the second act; the mechanical repetition results in audience self-consciousness. But Mr. Wilder's scheme, which probably derives from the Chinese and Greek theatres, is the logical way of achieving the abstraction he is after. It makes for complete theatre and intellectual candor. He is after not the fact but the essence of the fact; and a production stripped of all the realistic impedimenta of the theatre is essential to his theme. As producer and director, Jed Harris has had the imagination and daring to go through the production on those severe terms; and with remarkable artistic integrity he has used the performance to express the play without falling back on showmanship.

* * *

NOTHING is better for good actors than a stage with no scenery; it concentrates the audience's imagination on the acting and the theme. Mr. Harris has taken pains to see that the parts are in good hands. Mr. Craven, casual, almost shiftless in style, gives "Our Town" a hospitable local flavor. As fathers and mothers, Jay Fassett, Thomas W. Ross, Evelyn Varden and Helen Carew have found leisure, sweetness and good-will under the plainness of undistinguished townsfolk. As the boy and girl John Craven and Martha Scott are gloriously young and unaffected. For sheer purity of tone they give an extraordinarily rapturous performance. Although a small-town play frequently lures actors into clichés and condescensions, Mr. Harris's actors respect their parts, preserve the dignity of the human beings they represent and communicate kindliness without sentimentality.

* * *

THE people of Grover's Corners are not highly cultivated, but they have the New England instinct for knowing where they are and what matters most. "No, ma'am, there isn't much culture," the local editor replies to an inquiring member of the audience, "but maybe this is the place to tell you that we've got a lot of pleasures of a kind here: we like the sun coming up over the mountain in the morning, and we all notice a good deal about the birds. We pay a lot of attention to them. And we watch the change of the seasons: yes, everybody knows about them." Being familiar with New England, Mr. Wilder loves it, and "Our Town" probes close to the inner truth and cuts to the quick. Having something beautiful to say, Mr. Wilder has found the most vivid way to express it in the theatre.

* * *

February 13, 1938

SPEAK UP, FATHER

He Raises His Voice Continuously in the Day-Crouse-Lindsay Comedy

By BROOKS ATKINSON

ALTHOUGH every one hoped that Clarence Day's jovial sketches of his dominant parent would yield a good play, no one dared believe that it would be as funny as the period comedy Howard Lindsay and Russel Crouse have brought into the Empire. "Life With Father" is a comic inspiration. To at least one appreciative reader Father in the sketches seemed to be an isolated phenomenon. But in the play, where the whole family background is clearly defined, Father emerges as an American parent with universal qualities of vexation.

By the honest decency of their perception, Mr. Lindsay and Mr. Crouse have spared their comedy the vulgarity of the "mamma love papa?" school of fisticuffs and raised it into a humorous comment on family manners. Every father and mother will feel both guilty and pleased in the presence of this pouring of oil on the home fires, for it strikes the most intimate sort of average. "Life With Father" ought to take its place beside the popular comedies that seem to be written out of the life we have all led at home, and years from now theatregoers will be recalling it with amusement and gratitude. For it is a mature version of such folksy comedies as "The First Year" and "The Show-Off" and an ideal bit of comic theatre.

* * *

FATHER'S voice is more commanding than most male voices in the home and his mode of action is more direct. But apart from that he represents the ludicrous impossibility of ruling the roost. Father is logical from an unreasonable point of view. He plans the life of his wife and boys in terms of his own peace of mind—the dominant male always two jumps behind the scattered interests of his wife and the normal giddiness of four growing boys.

What Father wants is simple. He wants today to be as pleasant as he remembers that yesterday was. "More of the same" is his formula for the good life—breakfast at the same hour with the bacon done to the same turn of crispness, no interruptions from outside, dinner at home with every member of the family in his allotted place. As for the domestic economy, Father's requirements are equally simple. He wants to know where his money is going, and since he has in the back of his head a budget that will look after the family necessities for the next several months, he wants every item to fall neatly into place. He is a business man; running the financial department of a family is perpetual amortization as far as he is concerned. Father is a rational person.

But family life does not respond to logic. It is founded on love, which is one of the most distracting forces God ever invented, and that is the cream of the Day-Crouse-Lindsay jest. In spite of the most affectionate good-will between all the members of the family, things are always getting out of hand and disturbing the even tenor of Father's expectations. All this might be grubby satire on family life if Father's personality were not so colorful, and if the wife and boys were not so well-behaved.

But Father is a man of dignity and force who believes in direct action, and when things go wrong he bellows with impersonal rage. The whole house echoes his violence. The new maid stands paralyzed with fright, bursts into tears and falls downstairs. Mother tries to localize the tornado by closing the living-room doors. To put it tactfully, Father is one of the most communicative persons of all time. He is an extrovert. Father gives.

* * *

IN a scholarly book on "Masters of Dramatic Comedy," by Henry Ten Eyck Perry, I have just stumbled on this profound definition quoted from some other source: "The greatest comedy is rooted, not in the social order, but in the supreme human paradox that man, who lays claim to an immortal spirit, is nevertheless confined in a body and must rely upon the exercise of five imperfect senses for his perception of order, truth and beauty in his earthly pilgrimage." We do not have to promote "Life With Father" into the category of illustrious comedy in order to see that a similar inequality of balance extends to the plot of this play. Although Father is indisputably the master of his home, he is defeated on nearly every issue. Things will not fall into place according to plan. The new maid does not serve perfectly the first time she pokes her nose into the house. Clarence cannot wait until Autumn for a new suit. The doctors cannot bring mother back to health on their first visit. Visiting relatives cannot be kept out of the house. Taxes cannot be kept from rising.

There is no malice or cunning involved in Father's successive defeats. His wife and boys respect him and return his warm, though laconic, affection, and would doubtless resent any suggestion that he does not boss the home. But the ways of the world will not conform to the logical plan that Father carries around in his head, and this natural paradox redeems "Life With Father" from routine laugh-making and gives it distinction as a piece of genuine comedy writing. Things that are simple are sometimes more discerning than they have any intention of being.

So much for the literary side of "Life With Father." The theatrical side is equally convulsing. Although Mr. Lindsay has not been acting much for fifteen years and never had a part as big as this one, he plays Father in broadly humorous terms, with complete awareness of the comic spirit. The occasional vignettes of Father, with hat and cane, marching off to work are grandly comic—sober, proud and fierce. As the rattle-brained and apprehensive wife with a lovable character of her own, Dorothy Stickney gives an extraordinarily mettlesome performance.

The cast has been carefully chosen and includes some of the most ingratiating boys of the theatre, particularly John Drew Devereaux as the oldest son. For some unaccountable reason the enthusiastic first-night notice in these columns failed to say a kind word for Teresa Wright, who plays a young lady with uncommon charm as a person and willowy skill as an actress. But it would be hard to find anything in the writing or the playing of "Life With Father" that does not contribute to the frank and cheerful delight of one of the best American comedies in recent years.

November 19, 1939

TM(171-1)-23

CHAPTER 3

The Movies

Marilyn Monroe and Clark Gable in The Misfits

Courtesy United Artists

EDISON'S LATEST INVENTION

With It He Will Show Us a Railroad Wreck and the Pope Saying Mass.

The vitascope, Thomas A. Edison's perfection of the idea that caused the world to marvel when he produced the kinetoscope, has been dividing triumph with Chevalier at Koster & Bial's since Thursday night, and "the Wizard of Menlo Park" promises that before many days he will need an entire stage for the screen on which his latest invention shows life and color, with speech and the noise of movement the only things lacking.

The vitascope differs from the kinetoscope in its size and the size of its pictures; it differs in that its effects are almost the acme of realism; it differs in its possibilities, which, theatrical managers say, are boundless.

When the inventor wanted a subject for portrayal in the kinetoscope he had celebrities go to his laboratory, and there, in a dark room, they went through their performances before a camera, operated by electricity, in which was a film that was moved so swiftly that when the proof was put before the public the motion appeared continuous. The figures were minatures when they were completed.

The vitascope begins its operations in broad daylight. It shows their perfection in a darkened theatre. Sunlight is necessary for the taking of the pictures, darkness for their showing. Figures appear a trifle over life-size on the screen, which is about 20 by 12 feet. On the film in the machine each picture is about half the size of a postage stamp. Minuteness, accuracy, and electrical speed combine to achieve the results that were greeted with cheers at the first exhibition, in Koster & Bial's, Thursday night.

The machines are in the second balcony of the music hall. There are two of them—one for use in case something goes wrong with the other. Double locks keep inquisitors away, for "The Wizard" is not yet satisfied that his success has been complete, and he is afraid lest somebody should steal his first principles, and have the brain or the good fortune to beat him in the race. Bull's-eyes, only a few inches in diameter, but of strong magnifying power, throw the pictures on the screen. The film for the series now being given is 150 yards long, and the pictures go by the lens at the rate of 46 a second—2,760 per minute.

In only two of the pictures shown Thursday night were the colors brought out. The umbrella dancers seemed almost to be creatures of flesh and blood. Every movement was as natural as if living dancers were working their way toward salary day. Even blond tresses, stirred by the vigor of the performer's exercise, streamed out as naturally as if a little breeze were toying them.

In the picture from "A Milk White Flag" the actors and actresses made their entrances and exits and went through the pantomime of their parts perfectly and naturally, but it was the waves tumbling in on a beach and about a stone pier that caused the spectators to cheer and to marvel most of all. Big rollers broke on the beach foam flew high, and weakened waters poured far up the beach. Then great combers arose and pushed each other shoreward, one mounting above the other, until they seemed to fall with mighty force and all together on the shifty sand, whose yellow, receding motion could be plainly seen.

The color effects shown last week are only the beginnings of what Mr. Edison hopes to accomplish. The tinting of the pictures is one of the most delicate tasks that confronts him, for, when one considers the size of the pictures on his film, there can seem to be no exaggeration in his statement that to make a pink cheek a pin-point touch of color is all that can be used, and that the black stocking of a dancer is only one-thirty-second of an inch in length.

Charles Frohman saw the pictures Thursday night, and the remarks he made about them put into the mind of Mr. Edison another possibility.

"That settles scenery," said Mr. Frohman. "Painted trees that do not move, waves that get up a few feet and stay there, everything in scenery we simulate on our stages will have to go. When art can make us believe that we see actual living nature, the dead things of the stage must go.

"And think what can be done with this invention! For instance, Chevalier comes on the screen. The audience would get all the pantomime of his coster songs. The singing, words fitted to gestures and movements, could be done from the wings or behind the curtain. And so we could have on the stage at any time any artist, dead or alive, who ever faced Mr. Edison's invention.

"That in itself is great enough, but the possibilities of the vitascope as the successor of painted scenery are illimitable."

Mr. Edison is working hard for the absolute perfection of his machine, and at the same time is arranging for the securing of pictures the like of which, in other than inertness, the public has never seen.

He has bought, for about $5,000, two ancient, but still serviceable, locomotives and several dozen flat cars. He has built about a quarter of a mile of railroad track in a secluded spot, not far from his laboratory. In a few weeks he will start a train from each end of the track, and will run them to a crash. The engines and cars will be manned, just as trains are in active service, and all the incidents of a train wreck will be caught by machines stationed at short intervals near the track.

Machines have been sent to Rome, and in a short while the entire stage at Koster & Bial's will be occupied by a realistic representation of Pope Leo XIII. saying mass in the Sistine Chapel.

April 26, 1896

NEW YORK APPLAUDS THE TALKING PICTURE

Only Drawback Is When the Talk Falls Behind the Picture.

MUCH DEPENDS ON OPERATOR

Edison's Kinetophone Proves to be a Valuable Accession as a Vaudeville Attraction.

After Thomas A. Edison had invented the motion picture and the talking machine he dreamed of talking pictures, and the next morning he went to work again. For several years hints came from the Edison laboratory that the kinetophone was in process of development. Finally Edison spoke of his invention as a thing accomplished, and yesterday, for the first time on any stage, the "Kinetophone" was on the bill at four of the Keith Theatres, the Union Square, and the Fifth Avenue. To judge from the little gasps of astonishment and the chorus of "Ain't that something wonderful?" that could be heard on all sides the Kinetophone is a success.

The problem involved was fairly simple. Mr. Edison was looking for perfect synchronization of record and film. The difficulty was to have a record sufficiently sensitive to receive the sounds from the lips of actors who would still be free to move about in front of the camera instead of being obliged to roar into the horn of a phonograph. But the difficulties have been overcome and the kinetophone is actually in vaudeville and highly regarded there.

The first number of the exhibit was a descriptive lecture. The screen showed a man in one of those terribly stuffy, early eighties rooms that motion-picture folk seem to affect. He talked enthusiastically about the invention, and as his lips moved the words sounded from the big machine behind the screen. Gesture and speech made the thing startingly real. He broke a plate, blew a whistle, dropped a weight. The sounds were perfect. Then he brought on a pianist, violinist, and soprano, and "The Last Rose of Summer" was never listened to with more fascinated attention. Finally the scope of kinetophonic powers was further illustrated by a bugler's apoplectic efforts, and the barking of some perfect collies.

The second number was a minstrel show, with orchestra, soloists, end men, and interlocutor, large as life and quite as noisy. It brought down the respective houses but the real sensation of the day was scored quite unintentionally by the operator of the machine at the Union Square Theatre last evening. He inadvertently set his pictures some ten or twelve seconds ahead of his sounds, and the result was amazing. The interlocutor, who, by a coincidence, wore a peculiarly defiant and offended expression, would rise pompously, his lips would move, he would bow and sit down. Then his speech would float out over the audience. It would be an announcement of the next song, and before it was all spoken the singer would be on his feet with his mouth expanded in fervent but soundless song.

This diverted the audience vastly, but the outbursts of laughter would come when the singer would close his lips, smile in a contented manner, bow, and retire while his highest and best notes were still ringing clear. The audience, however, knew what had happened, and the mishap did not serve to lessen their tribute of real wonder at Edison's latest.

February 18, 1913

At Least $500,000,000 Invested in "Movies"

They Now Rank Fifth in List of Country's Big Businesses—Moving Picture Shows Attract 10,000,000 Paying Spectators Every Week

A NEW "big business" has appeared in America, and today it ranks fifth in importance among the industries of this country. First comes agriculture, second transportation, third oil, fourth steel, and then motion pictures.

From small beginnings the motion-picture industry has reached a stage of development where it is conservatively estimated that $500,000,000 is invested. That is only the investment, however. The amount of money spent annually in the motion-picture industry is far in excess of that sum.

Government experts will tell you that some 10,000,000 persons in the United States pay admission to picture houses each week. This means that one out of every ten men, women, and children in this country visits a photoplay theatre weekly. It means that more than half a billion admissions are paid annually to the box offices of motion-picture theatres.

It is difficult to think in small figures of this industry. For instance, more than 75,000 miles of film are manufactured and exhibited annually in the United States. Like a mushroom the industry has grown. It has made millionaires whose fortunes have sprung like weeds in fertile soil.

Less than ten years ago the motion-picture industry was small. In that short span it has developed from the one-reel, slapstick comedy or cheap drama to the present artistic feature production, in which stars of international repute appear. Ten years ago if a motion-picture producer spent more than $100 for 1,000 feet of film, which required fifteen minutes to be shown on a screen, he blamed himself for being extravagant. Five years ago the average sum spent in producing 1,000 feet of film was $1,000. Today there are productions, such as "The Birth of a Nation," which cost $250,000.

Just now, in the Island of Jamaica, British West Indies, William Fox is spending $1,000,000 on a production which, when complete, will be shown in such theatres as have been or are now playing "The Birth of a Nation." Incident to the taking of this feature a Moorish city has been constructed on the coast of Jamaica—a city which is the replica of a turreted, castled stronghold built by the Moors many hundreds of years ago. There has also been constructed on the coast of Jamaica a gigantic submerged photographic tank, in which a battery of cameras "shoot" the aquatic scenes which form a part of the million-dollar production. An ancient fortress in addition to the Moorish city is being built, only to be destroyed by high explosives.

There is scarcely a community of more than 1,000 inhabitants in the United States which has not a motion-picture house. The industry has brought the photoplay to the very doors of those who for years have been deprived of such amusement.

The motion-picture theatregoing public has the Federal Government to thank for the fact that there is no trust in the moving-picture business. The exhibitor buys his pictures on the open market. Competition in the production and sale of motion pictures is keen.

The restraining hand of an alert Government has been responsible for this, and with this result, the character of motion pictures has steadily improved in tone. Keen competition among the producers has brought out the best that is in them.

This happy state of affairs has not always existed, however, in the moving-picture business. In the latter part of 1908, when the money-making possibilities in the motion-picture film industry began to become quite evident, ten manufacturers of American-made films combined under a trade agreement and created one of the tightest trusts that had ever appeared among American industries. These ten manufacturers had, or believed they had, about all the patents covering the making and projecting of motion pictures. Exhibitors throughout the country soon found that in order to get film they must sign an agreement with the trust, pledging themselves to buy from it alone and to rent no other film. As the trust controlled approximately 95 per cent. of American-made film, and a large percentage of foreign-made film, it had the situation well in hand. The exhibitor was at its mercy. It was a case of buy from the trust or close his door.

At that time one dealer in motion-picture films refused to accede to the demands of the Film Trust. The fight that ensued resembled that of a bulldog yapping at the heels of an elephant. But in the end the bulldog won.

One day William Fox, President of the Greater New York Film Rental Company, went to Washington and laid a few facts before George W. Wickersham, then Attorney General. Shortly thereafter the Sherman anti-trust law was taken from its shelf, dusted off, and applied to the elephant. The Government's dissolution suit against the Film Trust was slow, as such dissolution suits must necessarily be. Many million words of testimony were taken. But the courts decided that the Government was quite right—that the Film Trust had no place in the business world of these United States. This United States Court decision was handed down on Oct. 1, 1915. Long before that, however, the Moving Picture Trust had clearly seen the handwriting on the wall, and it dissolved itself, thereby opening the field again to competition.

The ramifications of the film industry are almost limitless. Just how many hundreds of thousands of persons are engaged in it is difficult to ascertain. Many other industries have been made richer through the development of the motion-picture business. Iron and steel are used in the manufacture of projecting machines, electric light frames, and what not. The textile industry has been made richer by the money spent in costumes for motion-picture plays, and so it goes throughout the list.

A new type of actor has been developed by the movies—an actor who by voiceless expression alone must convey meaning as clearly as his brother of the legitimate stage conveys it through gesture accompanied by the spoken word. A bitter fight is now on between the actors of the legitimate stage and the actors of the screen, but it is not unusual that a star is found playing on the legitimate stage in one theatre, while down the street he or she may be seen in another production at a photoplay house on the screen.

While many thespians have entered the picture drama successfully, although untrained in picture acting, the majority of successful movie stars are men and women who have risen from obscurity to prominence in picture land.

The motion-picture industry has also developed a new type of artist, separate and quite distinct from the movie stars. This artist is the director. Five years ago the motion-picture director who received a salary of $50 weekly considered himself fortunate. Today there are directors whose annual income is equal to that of the President of the United States. David W. Griffith, Herbert Brenon, and several others are numbered among those whose work yields a revenue greater than that which the Government pays its Chief Executive. In fact, there are few large motion-picture producing companies which have not a corps of directors whose salaries range upward from $25,000 and who are under contract for several years. These contracts, ranging from one to five years, show the faith the film manufacturers have in the future of the motion-picture industry. Among the successful directors whose salaries range upward from $25,000 are Reginald Barker, Tom Ince, Mack Sennett, Allen Duan, Raoul Walsh, J. Gordon Edwards, Cecil De Mille, James Kirkwood, and Ralph Ince.

Still another product of the motion picture industry is the camera man. Five years ago the services of an expert motion picture camera man could be obtained for $25 or $35 a week. Today there are many camera men receiving salaries of from $150 to $250 a week. The development of the camera art has kept pace with the general development of the motion-picture industry.

Just now the moving-picture industry of the United States is beginning to look beyond the horizon for further fields to conquer. Several enterprising production concerns have invaded Canada. Others are preparing to open the South American field, and are arranging with European agents for the distribution of films in those countries which are now at war.

January 2, 1916

Lo, the Movies Have Achieved "Revivals"!

Who called the movie "the roughneck of the arts"? Let him stand and answer: Does a roughneck art have revivals? Does a roughneck art have "old masters"? Does a roughneck art have "vintage" pictures? Does a roughneck theatre have repertory?

On behalf of one hundred million movie fans, more or less, an answer to these questions may be set down here, in the absence of the man who thinks the movies lowbrow. Early productions of motion pictures already are being displayed on the screen. "Old masters" are being shown. In their very lifetime Charles Chaplin, comic pantomimist, and D. W. Griffith, producer, have become "old masters," so rapidly has this husky younger sister overtaken the mossbacked arts. Movies are being "revived."

Hugo Riesenfeld, managing director of the Rivoli and Rialto Theatres, has started to show a series of the first Chaplin comedies, and Mr. Griffith will soon open a theatre in New York with a repertory of the films which made him famous.

There have been reissues of photoplays since the year after the first photoplays were issued, but these cannot properly be called revivals. Frequently they have been put out in competition with a star's current productions by his or her former manager seeking to turn the player's popularity to his own account. The other fellow's advertisement of the star's name has often had

Lillian Gish
in "The White Sister."

more to do with bringing them out than any intrinsic merit of their own.

Further, many of the reissues have been intended for second-class trade. The big New York houses have not taken them. Sometimes they have been simply pirated editions. Whatever they have been, they have not been revivals, brought back by some one's faith in their enduring artistic and commercial value. The Chaplin pictures and the Griffith productions, in this sense, are revivals, and practically the first since the photoplay established itself. When "A Night in the Show," the first of the old newcomers, was put on at the Rialto two weeks ago, the box office began to have one of the busiest periods of its existence. The first Monday night was reported to be "a little off" at the "legitimate" theatres in the Broadway district, but the people were standing at the Rialto all evening.

"A Night in the Show" is an Essanay picture, made in 1915. Other Essanay productions to come are "The Bank," "Charlie's new Job," "Shanghaied," and "The Champion." Motion-picture men still speak of "The Keystone Age," 1913-14, when Keystone comedies led all the rest. Chaplin was with this company then, and appeared in "His Prehistoric Past" and "Dough and Dynamite." Both of these will be seen in the near future on the Rialto screen. Perhaps some of these pictures will go to the Rivoli, too.

Most of Chaplin's early comedies were made before his name was widely known. In the days of their production the star system had not grown to its present domination of the field, and Chaplin was simply "that funny little fellow" to thousands of those who laughed at his pantomime. It was his pantomimic ability that made his comedies so popular, for in construction and wit they were no better than hundreds of others of the horseplay, custard pie type. The others, having nothing but horseplay and custard pie, have not been and will not be revived. The Chaplin comedies are coming back because Chaplin, beginning anonymously, entered the star system because he was a star.

The Griffith pictures, too, are a testimony to that director's ability. When the now widely known "D. W." was a director at the old biograph studio, people began to talk about "the fellow who has gone movie mad." This fellow made "The Mother and the Law," "The Fall of Babylon," "The Sands of Dee," "The Avenging Conscience," "The Single Standard," and "The Escape"; and, by these productions, became the foremost producer in America. He did not follow in the paths of others, but blazed his own way. He invented or discovered the "close-up," the "fade out," the "long shot," the "cut back," and other tricks which have become elements of photoplay technique today. From his shorter works he progressed to the first real "super features. "The Birth of a Nation," "Intolerance," and "Hearts of the World" were products of his industry.

Griffith not only made enduring photoplays, but he made stars. Many an actor and actress now well known from one end of the country to the other. and even around the world, began with Griffith in obscurity and received invaluable training. Some of them are Mary Pickford, Mae Marsh, Lillian Gish, Constance Talmadge, Blanche Sweet, Dorothy Gish, Seena Owen, Robert Harron, Miriam Cooper, and Henry Walthall.

It is Griffith productions with these stars and others which will be revived here in repertory.

But the revivals do not mean that the principal figures in them are turning backward. On the contrary, Griffith, Chaplin, and the others seem to be more active than ever before. Griffith is making a series of six Artcraft pictures, three of which have been released, and his next undertaking will be the production of three photoplays for the First National Exhibitors' Circuit. Then he expects to begin work in the "Big Four" combination, consisting of Douglas Fairbanks, Charlie Chaplin, Mary Pickford, and himself. Chaplin will remain with the First National until his present contract expires, when he will join the combination.

There is one difference between screen and stage revivals that may be worth noting. When plays come back to the stage they are frequently rewritten in places and have the advantage of the latest developments in stage setting. Also, the actors may be better than those originally in the cast. But photoplays remain substantially the same. New prints are made from the old negatives, and by chemical processes some of the modern effects may be produced. Furthermore, improved methods of projection and exhibition may add something to the production. Fundamentally, however, the photoplay remains unchanged. It is the old work that is revived, practically in its entirety. There may be crudities in it, and it may have been done in a style for which the public has lost its taste. If such a film comes back, therefore, it will be solely because of the genius of an actor or director. Speaking generally, it may be said that, to a greater degree than on the stage, the productions which survive revival on the screen testify eloquently to the ability of the individuals originally identified with them.

$1,000,000 COMPANY WILL COLOR MOVIES

William Travers Jerome Tells of Process to Give Natural Tint to Films.

OPERATION IS INEXPENSIVE

Inventor Is Daniel Frost Comstock—Big Dye Men on Board of Directors.

William Travers Jerome, former District Attorney of New York County, yesterday told of the formation of a syndicate of forty-five prominent business men of this and other cities who have subscribed $1,000,000 for the development and perfection of a process of coloring motion pictures in their natural tints under a process invented by Daniel Frost Comstock, a scientist and engineer, for several years a member of the Faculty of the Massachusetts Institute of Technology.

Although Mr. Comstock has been working on the process for more than seven years and Mr. Jerome and some of his associates have been interested in it for more than two years, they have not yet shown a complete film, but will be ready for a New York public exhibition some time in October. A few hundred feet of the film have been shown privately at the Cameo Theatre here, and a private showing will be given between 5 and 6 o'clock this afternoon at the Simplex projection room in the Candler Building, 220 West Forty-second Street. Those who have seen the film are high in their praises of it.

Mr. Jerome explained that this first five reel film had been made largely as a sample, and that it was not the intention of the new company to enter the producing business. He said that it was the idea to sell the use of the patents to other moving picture companies and to color their films for them. Between fifty and sixty patents on steps of the secret process have been obtained in this country, and similar protection has been obtained in Great Britain, Canada, France, Italy and the Argentine. The same steps will be taken in all other countries as soon as possible.

Under the process devised by Mr. Comstock the negative is developed just as an ordinary film, and then is passed through additional chemical baths and processes for the fixing of the colors in tints natural to the objects shown on the films. Mr. Jerome said that the cost of treating the film in this manner was negligible, and that he expected that at least 10 per cent. of the moving picture films of the country would be colored in the future.

Special cameras are needed for the work, as in all other color processes, but the ordinary negatives are used as in the taking of black-and-white moving pictures. The completed prints are run through the ordinary projection screen, so that there is no additional cost, Mr. Jerome pointed out that the few other color processes in existence consisted of so many operations that the colors could not compete in cost with the black-and-white of the ordinary pictures.

"Those who have seen film colored in this process have been enthusiastic," said Mr. Jerome, "and they include many of the best technicians in the moving picture business, scientists, artists, college professors, theatrical men and persons who might naturally be interested in such an improvement. I have also had the film shown to small audiences, including policemen, manicurists, clerks, motormen, elevator operators and persons representative of that vast army of motion picture audiences who know far better what they like than any technician and whose opinions on this subject would be fundamentally sound. They also approved it.

"If the color process is as cheap as the black-and-white everybody will want to see pictures in color, provided, of course, that the pictures are as pleasing, or more pleasing. We think that we have already attained cheapness and perfection, and we expect that the next few months will see many improvements. According to the reports in the Treasury Department, the tickets sold in the moving picture business last year amounted to $700,000,000, and the members of this syndicate have hopes of a financial success with the process."

A corporation called Techni Color, Inc., was chartered in Delaware on Sept. 12 last, and a subsidiary is called the Techni Color Motion Picture Corporation of Maine. The Delaware corporation has 330,000 shares of no par value, but 60,000 shares are to be sold to provide funds for the construction of one factory near this city and one near Hollywood, Cal. The laboratory and development work is now being done at Boston.

Dr. Herbert T. Kalmus, a chemical engineer, and a member of the industrial engineering firm of Kalmus, Comstock & Wescott, Inc., of Boston, is the President of the new company; Mr. Jerome is the Vice President, and the Directors are William Hamlin Childs of Brooklyn, who is a Director in many dye corporations; Eversley Childs, President of the Bon Ami Company and Director in several dye corporations; N. T. Pulsifer, President of Valentine & Co.; Thomas W. Slocum of Minot, Hooper & Co., C. E. Danforth, a broker; Alfred W. Erickson of the Erickson Company, Inc., and Alfred Fritzsch of the Grinnell Company, Inc. Marcus Loew also is to be added to the directorate at a meeting on Tuesday.

Some of the others who are interested in the syndicate are Frederick H. Ecker, Vice President and Director of the Metropolitan Life Insurance Company; Horace S. Wilkinson, Chairman of the Board of the Crucible Steel Company; William L. Ward, the Republican boss in Westchester County; Henry A. Colgate, Secretary of Colgate & Co.; Austen Colgate, Second Vice President and Director of Colgate & Co.; Leroy W. Baldwin President of the Empire Trust Company of 120 Broadway; Nicholas M. Schenck, Secretary of Loew's Theatrical Enterprises; H. Hobart Porter, the consulting engineer; James C. Colgate of 36 Wall Street, and Frank Foster of the Congoleum Company.

The remaining shares are placed in a voting trust to be controlled for five years by Mr. Jerome and four other directors. This board probably also will act as a board of censorship and pass upon the scenarios of films which are to be put through the coloring process for other companies.

September 21, 1922

VETERAN PRODUCER MUSES

By JOHN FORD.

THE world that has its Seven Wonders has, too, its seven stamping grounds of civilization: the Tartar City of Pekin, the Kremlin at Moscow, the Acropolis at Athens, the Alhambra at Granada, the Campagna of Rome, the Hradschin in Prague and the Eyub Cemetery of Stambul. Within their walls or over their pavements has swept the tremendous torrent of migrations which have summed up into the history of mankind. To them tribes and peoples have brought tribute of cult and culture. From them peoples and tribes have taken tribute of wealth, material or inspirational. They have been pre-eminently the market places of the earth, rising for centuries above the level plains of the commonplaces of event. Through those long periods of their establishment no other monument of man's migratory spirit has arisen to contest their supremacy until the last decade. Then, with the World War over, there began the most remarkable hegira the world has ever witnessed. Westward and eastward the creative artistic brain power of modern civilization has been making pilgrimage to a town on the California coast of our own United States of America, until today the eighth great stamping ground of the world's restless horde is Hollywood.

If you believe this statement far-fetched, you have only to stand upon Hollywood Boulevard at almost any hour of the day or night to realize the character of this amazing invasion. English, Irish, Germans, Hungarians, Russians, Italians, South Americans, Mexicans, Chinese, Japanese, Hindus, Persians, Scandinavians, Egyptians, men and women from almost every country on the globe pass in such numbers that you soon pay no more attention to them than to native Americans. If you still believe their coming casual, you need only live through a day in the director's office of one of the motion picture studios to find that each and every one of the pilgrims has come to Hollywood out of the motive that has brought people to the other stamping grounds—the wish to barter brains for fame or fortune. Every one of them has something to sell, a play, a personality, an idea. In ten years Hollywood has become the great mental marketplace of the world.

Vast Change in Twelve Years.

The reason for its remarkable development is, of course, the growth of the motion picture industry. Written in the universal language of visual imagery, the pictures have made appeal to the creative artistic impulses of almost all peoples and to almost every class of society. No man has been too high-brow to scorn the medium of motion pictures for his idea, no man too humble to be denied the chance of success in this most modern medium of a world-old desire to tell a story. In order to understand its extent, however, one must have known Hollywood from its none too distant inception as a studio town. Only by remembering the place as the laboratory of a tentative, though never timid, project can any one realize the amazing attraction adventure still has for humanity. To those who have the steel of ambition in their minds Hollywood is a magnetic hill, pulling them up its slopes, sometimes to rewards, sometimes to failures, but always to trial.

When I came to Hollywood twelve years ago the motion picture industry was comparatively new. Colonel Selig had brought a studio out here because of his thought that a longer period of sunshine through the year would make picture-taking less of financial risk. Other producers had followed him, but the making of pictures was still a matter of hazard, both of life and money. Nearly all the pictures were either absurd comics or wild thrillers. My brother, Francis Ford, was directing one of the latter, and in it I made my last histrionic appearance.

The action of the picture demanded that I walk upon a fifty-foot trestle while the cameras ground record of my progress. No one had informed me of the plot of the story, and, when I saw an engine advancing upon me from the other side of the trestle, I turned tail and ran for life. In frantic disgust the camera men and my brother yelled to me an order to return, I went back, facing the demon locomotive. Just as it came down upon me they shouted the cry to jump. I looked down from the trestle, saw the gulch fifty feet below me—and jumped; but I had ruined the picture irretrievably, for on the verge of taking the fatal plunge I had remembered my good Catholic training and piously blessed myself. The words of brotherly counsel administered when the rushes showed my piety convinced me that I was not destined to be an actor, and so, as speedily as I could, I got a job in the Directing Department.

Constant Improvements.

If I hoped to leave hazard behind in leaping from the trestle of acting to the gulch of directing, I was speedily disillusioned. It was, however, a different kind of hazard that I found at the director's end of picture production. It was the time of real pioneering in picture making. The great trail blazer of the films,

David Wark Griffith, was swinging the axe of his frontiering, devising methods, securing effects that were to make pictures a real artistic medium as well as a stupendous industry. Those were the times when first nights meant something beyond blare and lights and noise. To those of us who were fortunate in working in Griffith's influence they meant the revelation of inspirational genius. The showing of those early pictures in the old Philharmonic Auditorium c: Los Angeles meant more to the film industry and to the making of Hollywood than all the spectacles of inauguration that Hollywood promotes in these later days and nights.

Not for a moment would I seem to imply in this statement of the value of that pioneering that the motion pictures have ended their pioneering. All art is fluid, and no phase of it more so than the development of motion pictures. Technic that is daring today will be outdated tomorrow. The quality of universality in pictures is in itself a pitfall, for the director who strives too hard to represent humanity by rubbing down the rough edges of racial and personal traits is likely to make his work drab and colorless. The picture likely to attain great and wide success must have its theme of universal appeal but its people vivid. It is my belief that it should be true to its setting—for instance, that Germany should be represented by the sons, since it is essentially a man's country, but that Ireland, being matriarchal, should be visualized as Mother Machree. This could not, perhaps, be carried on indefinitely, but it is certain that the relationship of background to character and picture development will be increasingly important in the future of the film.

Educational Idea.

The question of background has become something of a problem with American producers just now, because of the fact that nearly all the foreign outcry against American motion pictures has been inspired by the belief that it is the background of the American pictures that is luring immigration toward the United States. A current story declared that the Russian leather supply is being exhausted because of the demand of Russian peasants for leather shoes, a luxury with which most of them became acquainted through the sight of them in the pictures. Whether or not this is true, it is certainly true that the European peasant or miner or tradesman or craftsman sees on the screen pictures which show an average standard of living in the United States much higher than that of his own land, and becomes imbued with a desire to give himself and his children the advantage of such a standard. That is the political reason for the ban on American pictures in so many countries of Europe.

The Movietone.

All such bans, however, are transitory in view of the possible future of the pictures. We are only at the beginning of the use of pictures as factors in education. There is no doubt of the value of pictures in visual education nor of the effect of them upon the child mind. Tests of the receptivity of the child mind to motion pictures have shown the enormous possibilities of screen portrayal. There is no reason why history should not be taught younger children almost exclusively by this method. We should regret intensely, though, the use of visual education without the corresponding development of auditory imagery, for the pictures are just now on the threshold of one of their most important developments, the use of sound as well as of sight images.

With the same capacity for experiment in the adaptation of sound to sight that he has shown in all his work, William Fox has been working upon the use of the movietone. The synchronization of the instrument recording sound with the movement in the picture is practically perfected, but the field of its artistic possibilities is not yet furrowed. It will, I think, revolutionize the casting of films, for inevitably a different type of actor and actress will be required to vocalize the rôles. It was, you may recall, by her voice that the true princess made herself known. It will also give to motion pictures the chance to project symphonic qualities for the creation and holding of a mood, so that pictures will no longer be limited to pure and simple narrative for material.

Just as in all art, however, the simple story will always remain the most effective. Morality may be a relative term, but the producer who plans his product upon that relativity makes an artistic as well as a financial mistake. The continuation of the broad scale of production at the Fox studios through a time of near-panic in Hollywood has been no accident but the logical result of William Fox's policy of refusing to countenance filth in the pictures made in his studios. The pictures that people remember for years are not the spectacularly sensational films, but the heart-interest stories of plain people interpreting vital emotions.

Because almost every one in the world has at least one story, and because he believes that his story may win the golden prize of production, Hollywood is bound to remain the Mecca of the ambitious as long as the pictures remain the broadest medium of expression. Just as Greeks and Romans and Tartars and Moors and Cossacks and Turks and Huns have left their imprint upon the places that stand memorial to their passing, so the historian of the future, looking back upon our high-speeding, high-powered civilization, will choose as its focal point Hollywood of the hills, pointing to it as crossroads for Orient and Occident, as market square for brains and beauty, talent and genius, the ballyhoo bazaar of a whirling world. Because, however, I have lived in that Hollywood for twelve years, seeing and feeling the heartaches, the joys and the sufferings that are the lot of every mother's son of us, I shall have to tell the truth, however disillusioning it may sound, that Hollywood is, for all its Kleigs and cameras, all its parties and bootleggers, all its gayeties and extravagances, a human city. Knowing it for what it is, a town of success and failure, of aspiration and achievement, of doubt and dependency, I have come to feel that the other seven stamping grounds have been in their times no more and no less than this town of mine, not high monuments of man's accomplishment, but turbulent plazas of man's unceasing search for the something he can never find.

June 10, 1928

Jackie Coogan in "Long Live the King."

Movies That the People Want

By BENJAMIN DE CASSERES

WHO sets the national and local tastes in motion pictures—the producers or the public?

Are the producers giving the people exactly what they want, or are the producers compelling the people to take what they give them?

The answer would seem to be obvious—you cannot force anything on twenty million people every day in the year that they do not want. It is an economic law that demand is anterior to supply. The producers have nothing at stake but their pocketbooks. There isn't the slightest reason why they should have anything else at stake. They cannot raise the artistic tastes of the people (to use the current jargon of uplifters) if the people have no artistic tastes to raise.

If the moving-picture audiences of this country demanded the work of Shakespeare, Ibsen, Maeterlinck, Anatole France, Thomas Hardy or Gerhart Hauptmann on the screen the producers would give it to them. There are dozens of producers and scenario writers waiting for the people to say so. But they simply do not want the big stuff. It is humorous and hypocritical to ask the great picture companies of this country to go bankrupt out of courtesy to their highbrow critics.

How long would a newspaper, a magazine, a theatrical producer or a sporting organization—not to speak of a department store—last if it insisted on giving to the public the thing that the public has no use for?

Every newspaper writer knows that the news of the day must be told in the simplest, most concrete form. No public is ever literary, artistic or intelligent. The moving picture makes its appeal to the average newspaper reader—and those below that average. It depends for its life in a great many sections of this country on those who cannot even read the newspapers printed in their own language.

"What's the matter with the movies?" should then be changed to the question, "What's the matter with the public?" Motion pictures, like everything else in the business world, never rise above the source of their revenues.

"Give us better movies!" has been the howl of the critics of the American motion picture.

"Give us a better public and we will give you better pictures!" might well be the answer of the great picture producers.

"We stand ready," said Mr. Robert Kane, general production manager of the Famous Players, "to give the public of America the great stories, poems and epics of all times and in all languages—when they want them. We take gambling risks that no other legitimate business in the world takes. But art and reality are one thing; public taste is another."

I have lately examined thousands of exhibitors' reports from the small towns throughout the country. Their reports are psychological mirrors of the ideals and mental needs of the people. If there are any independent producers thinking of producing "Don Quixote," Ibsen's "Brand," Anatole France's "The Revolt of the Angels," Cabell's "Jurgen," or Thomas Hardy's "The Return of the Native"—producing them, I mean, as they were conceived and written, not as they might be fixed up for public consumption—I advise them to first of all spend a month in a study of these exhibitors' reports. The public are, unconsciously, in league with the censors to keep everything down to the level below which to fall is sheer idiocy. If the censors are allowed to ride the backs of our moving-picture concerns much longer, it will result in pictures for half-wits.

As a matter of fact, if the army tests are any guide, the country is made up mostly of juvenile minds and half-wits. And it is to this public, aided and abetted by the political job-holders called motion-picture censors, that the great picture industry must cater in order to live.

An exhibitor in Sheboygan, Wis., reports that one of the finest pictures ever made—a picture founded on the "Peter Ibbetsen" of George du Maurier—went flat in his town because it was a costume play. The "élite" supported it the first night. After that the general opinion was that it was a "sleepy" picture—i. e., it has some beautiful dream scenes in it. Peter Ibbetsen was played by Wally Reid, but the fans of Sheboygan want Wally cast in a "happy" rôle. They mean by this that they want to see Wally munching caramels with a flapper sweetheart in a ballroom corner or spinning with her in a Ford to lift the mortgage off her furniture.

The inhabitants of Omaha walked out on a picture because some of the guests on a ranch wore evening clothes. To see a man in a picture walk into a Fifth Avenue mansion dressed in cowboy attire and throw a Wall Street broker in a boiled evening shirt through a window arouses the Nebraskan to a frenzy of applause. But evening dress at a ranch party—à bas the effete East!

Arlington is a small town situated in the State of Washington. A big super-special hit the town—a drama of a blind man. But what do you think drew the Arlingtonians into the theatre? A scene showing a crocodile pit. This scene, when it got noised abroad from pump to pump, sold more tickets than anything else in the show, according to the exhibitor. There will be standing room only in Arlington when the great aquarium drama hits that town.

Mary Miles Minter hit Augusta, Me., some time ago in "The Heart Specialist." The show nearly went under because the female patrons hotly protested against Mary wearing French heel evening slippers while living in a harem. Augusta should read Pierre Loti. That expert on female raiment tells us that not only do the ladies of the harems now wear French heel shoes, but they bob their hair. But Maine was always strong on the Orient preserving the ancient traditions.

Gloria Swanson in one of her pictures is compelled by her director to swim the Rio Grande. When she emerged on the other side of the river she still preserved her marcel wave. The women of Portland, Ore., would not stand for this. They told the cowering exhibitor in his lobby cubbyhole that it simply could not be done. But I know it can be done—for I saw her do it. As a matter of fact, I saw Ruth somebody swim from the Battery to Norton Point some years ago, and when she emerged her bangs were dry. But how long can the "movies" withstand such Sainte-Beuvery?

Columbia City, Ind., wants Bill Hart to be more tender with children. The fans in Columbia City will not have anything to do with the logic of Bill's parts. They are trying to can Bill because he looks like himself. Smile, Bill—damn you, smile!

Bridgeport, Conn., sends in the news that the picture public there is going for "society and high life." A suppressed New York complex.

San Bernardino, Cal., wires in that they do not want any more pictures for "the grand opera class."

In Hanover, N. H., an exhibitor had his people walk out on him because the picture he showed was "for intellectuals or those with a good education." This picture, by the way, was not "Dr Caligari," but just "Peter Ibbetsen." When culture hits Hanover, we may expect the return of the dodo.

Columbus, Ga., asks for pictures based on stories like "Pigs Is Pigs," where "one can see guinea pigs or rats." That is what they call "the educational motion picture" in the South.

Texas is losing its imagination. An exhibitor writes that his audience could not imagine "a woman cowing a multitude of bad men and then killing the villain."

Waco, Texas, is also moving up a point. They don't want any more "improbable" plots down there. But what is a probable plot and what an improbable one?

In Denver, Col., the motion picture is up against the caste system. Some of the working people out there said that a certain picture was "an insult to their set" because it

"Arouses the Nebraskan to a frenzy of applause."

showed an "intermingling of the classes." I am writing these lines on the one hundred and forty-sixth anniversary of the Declaration of Independence—q. v.

When "Boomerang Bill" hit Freeland, Pa., the consensus of opinion was that a cop never urged anybody to go straight "If anything, they gave a fellow a push downward." Now, this is sound motion-picture criticism—although I once knew a New York copper who used to take the boys home from "Jack's" every Sunday morning. But evidently they don't make 'em that way in Freeland.

"Give up the society stuff!" howls Greeley, Col.

Lincoln, Ill., wires that the denizens of that town would "go through fire to see Rodolph Valentino."

Dallas, Texas, doesn't want to see any pictures with a "note of sadness in them." I never knew things were as bad as that in Dallas.

Mount Vernon, Ill., just swarms with hunchbacks. It seems everybody out there has a friend or a relative who is a hunchback. Therefore, they ask, please make no pictures that have a hunchback in them. "The Hunchback of Notre Dame" is on the Index out there.

Gilmer, Texas, wants "society pictures, where people wear flashy costumes." Naughty, naughty Gilmer! We've got your speed!

Salt Lake City, Utah, is getting sick of "murder and sudden death." It is swinging toward the Gilmer idea—"society pictures with flashy costumes."

Ardmore, Okla., wants pictures "with lots of clothes—not Western." See what comes of sudden oil wealth!

What is the future of the movies?

Ask the people of the small towns of America.

September 3, 1922

"Pictures Appeal to Dream Mind"

IT is the opinion of Allan Dwan, who has made several successful productions, that motion pictures primarily appeal to the dream mind or romantic state of people who go to see them; for that reason Mr. Dwan says that many things are done in pictures that would not happen in real life, and he further admits that directors deliberately exaggerate in their work to help along the dream mind of patrons.

"In all of us, no matter how materialistic, there is a tinge, a hope of romance," said Mr. Dwan, having called a halt on a picture he was making in the Famous-Lasky studio in Astoria. "In pictures we always try to give our lovers a beautiful background for their love scenes, because it appeals to the romantic state of the audience.

* * * * *

"In 'Lawful Larceny,' the picture I am making now, we do a thing, for the effect it produces, that would be actually impossible. We show Lew Cody in a room surrounded by a number of beautiful women. By doing this we give the impression of the character of man Cody is portraying—a philanderer, waster, a ne'er-do-well. But we must have the room empty for the action that is to take place between Cody and Miss Hope Hampton, so we fade out the women from the picture. We make them ghosts, so to speak. This is impressionism, and we convey more to the audience by this one scene than any number of sub-titles could tell them.

"Production difficulties sometimes change the entire idea of a scene. In 'Glimpses of the Moon,' for instance, we went to Florida to shoot scenes on a yacht. When we got there we could not find a suitable yacht in the Florida waters. Rather than call the trip wasted and stand a loss of several thousand dollars, we changed the scene to a house boat, which we found at Miami. However, after we had done this we found that on account of the scarcity of lighting equipment and space on the boat we could not enact the scenes on the boat. So we anchored the boat to a dock, removed the furniture to the lawn of the Palms Hotel, and gave the impression that the boat had been docked at the edge of a large estate. We played the scenes on land, with the boat in the background. On account of the tremendous investment used in making motion pictures nowadays, it is frequently necessary to do the best we can with an awkward situation, and this sometimes results in an anachronism. We strive to be correct always, but so many good things in motion pictures are born on the spur of the moment that there isn't time to create a studied effect.

"A lot of anachronisms in pictures are accidental. Nobody would put a Winchester rifle in a twelfth century scene, but if they used twelve-foot spears in that time we might make them fifteen feet long. No man living knows everything. We must rely on research and experts for much of our information. Frequently we are victimized by these experts, upon whom we depend to protect us from mistakes. We only learn from the public that we are wrong, and then it is too late to change. All we can do is to resolve not to make the same mistake again.

"If any American should wander into a European picture studio at the time a picture of American life was being made and was asked by the director what was the custom at the table of a Nebraska farmer, he would, if honest, have to say that he did not know. Only a Nebraska farmer would know.

"When we do a Parisian scene, for instance, we ask a native-born Frenchman to tell us how the people would act. But many times he is inaccurate, and then the director gets blamed for having wrong 'business' in his picture.

"Visitors who come to a motion picture studio see men at a full dress dinner party wearing pink and light blue shirts, and they are aghast. They wear shirts of this color because white is too glaring. This, however, is a technical inaccuracy that of course does not show on the screen, for the shirts look white when photographed.

"The business of a director is to hold together and direct the various forces that make a picture. If the man employed to dress the sets, the property men, the art department men, make mistakes, the fault must be placed on the department that is the cause. It is a physical impossibility for any one man to check carefully everything that goes into the making of a motion picture, especially on the scale they are now made.

"There has been a lot of criticism against screen credit. People say: 'Why should we have to read the names of the art director, the cameraman and all the others?' The object of giving these workers credit is to create in those persons responsible for the various parts of a motion picture sufficient pride in their work to make them do all they can to prevent mistakes or careless work. If a man can hide behind some one else he may have a tendency to shirk his duties.

"We use names in motion picture productions to increase circulation of our pictures and create a demand for them, just as the newspaper prints signed articles, editorials and news matter to increase circulation.

"Some inaccuracies in pictures are deliberate, but most of them, when they occur, are mistakes, and there is no director making pictures today who does not try his level best to keep these from creeping in."

Mr. Dwan is the director who is also responsible for "Robin Hood."

April 8, 1923

Thrills in Films

By LOUIS MAYER,

THE thrill is probably the one element of the silent drama that has persistently weathered the changes of the screen. When motion pictures passed the novelty stage where a policeman chasing a tramp made a successful film, a thrill injected in a plot was the screen's first step of improvement. Since then tragic, historical, mystery and sympathetic drama, and farce, dramatic and light comedy have had their periodical fling as they moved around on the cycle of time, but the thrill picture has traveled its money-making path uninterrupted.

The exact worth of a thrill in a picture defies prediction. Not until the film is released and the public has placed its price upon the thrill does the producer know the value of his climax. But it is safe to say that the box office magnetism of a real thrill begins at a figure that marks up a profit on the picture. This, of course, is based on the premise that the rest of the production is of good quality.

As a rule, a director approaches the staging of a thrill with about the same joyous feeling that one has on visiting a dentist's chair. It will be a splendid achievement when the job is done, but meanwhile much mental suffering must be gone through.

George Ade says that, while the highbrows may sniff at good old heart-touching hokum on the screen, the American public could not keep house without it. The same thing applies to the thrill as one of the ingredients of dramatic construction. It is the lifeblood and motive power of some of our greatest productions.

What would D. W. Griffith's "The Birth of a Nation" have been without the spectacular, wild-riding gathering of the clans? Many who have not seen the picture for years can still describe that epoch-making sequence in detail.

Sea Storm Thrills.

One of the most adventurous thrill-filming expeditions on record was the one launched recently by Reginald Barker in favor of "Cape Cod Folks," a screen adaptation of the old New England stage classic. To be sure of screening the utmost in realism in the swordfishing and sea storm scenes, a company was sent from Los Angeles to the Atlantic to work off the coast of Massachusetts and also at the historic Grand Banks off Newfoundland.

By sheer courage they stuck to their mission although their search for excitement brought them into the face of storms with waves running eighty feet high and made them challengers of swordfish that weighed six hundred pounds and carried swords measuring over six feet in length. Risks without number were encountered, but they passed them off without a thought. They had gone 4,000 miles to photograph the terrific storms and savage denizens of the Atlantic, and they didn't even consider personal risk among the obstacles.

In another Barker picture, called "The Eternal Struggle," the turbulent Seymour Canyon Rapids near North Vancouver was conquered by players in a canoe for a thrilling climax after the old settlers and even the Indians had refused to take a chance with the dangerous stream. Seven weeks were spent in securing enough good footage to run ten minutes on the screen. Suspended from a cable in a steel cage, directly over a waterfall, the photographer ground his camera, day after day, within a few feet of sure death.

Every business has its exalted code of loyalty, but I doubt if any industry harbors a more courageous sense of duty than that reflected in players, directors and their cameramen when it comes to filming thrills for pictures.

Standing directly in the path of a limited train one night recently Marie Prevost and Robert Ellis enacted a very dramatic scene while the engine and its tail of brilliantly lighted cars thundered down toward them and switched off on the next track just in time to avoid a tragedy. Within a few feet of the stars, and sharing in the same danger, were the director, John M. Stahl, and his battery of cameramen and assistants. If the switch hadn't worked—! But it did, and a unique and effective thrill was registered for the theatregoer.

Death Valley.

Many colorful tales are told of the incidental thrills that cropped up during Cecil B. De Mille's filming of the chariot race sequence in "The Ten Commandments." Crediting only the minor risks involved, it is safe to say that the seasoned cavalryman engaged to drive the careening war chariots in this splendid production are worthy of medal distinction for their work. The results they secured will go down in cinema history for their startling realism.

Death Valley, that arid, merciless oven that strikes terror to the hearts of even the old desert prospectors, was invaded by Von Stroheim's company in the making of "Greed," and for weeks was compelled to submit to use as a background for scenes. Death Valley's favorite allies, heat, snakes and scorpions, fought the director constantly, but he had scenes to get there and he got them, regardless of the risk and inconveniences.

In the making of the bull-fighting scenes in "Blood and Sand," Fred Niblo and Rodolph Valentino took so many chances with their lives that danger became almost a daily diet. In order to get scenes that would carry through the spirit of their arena episodes, they had to get right down in the ring with an enraged bull that would have made a worthy antagonist for a tiger.

Tom Mix has earned fame and popularity through the thrilling exploits in his pictures, and the thrills are actual thrills, not camera tricks. Hoot Gibson, Eddie Polo, Charles Hutchinson and a number of other stars of like valor have built up reputations that reach around the world on their daring and courageous feats before the camera.

Sometimes the breathless suspense of a thrill is only half told on the screen. The rest of the danger is distributed among the director, cameraman and others of the production staff. To name all of the directors and stars who have hovered on the brink of death in a sincere effort to put realism into their pictures would practically amount to calling the roster of the entire studio world. Some make a regular thing of capitalizing unusual hazards and risks for screen thrills, but nearly all the stars and directors have stared death in the face at some time or other in search of a thrill.

December 30, 1923

SAYS FILMS' SUCCESS DEPENDS ON SHOP GIRL

Dorothy Gish, Summing Up Producers' Creed, Urges More Love and Luxury Scenes.

By Wireless to THE NEW YORK TIMES.

LONDON, Sept. 26.—Dorothy Gish, who is here to make a film version of the story of Nell Gwynne, in which she will play the part of the heroine, summed up today the creed of successful American film producers in these words:

"American producers base their films on what little Mary Bush, the shop girl, wants. She asks for plenty of love, and they supply it. One producer told me of an experience he had when he was showing a picture of the French Revolution. He overheard one girl say to another that she did not want to be educated about the French Revolution and that she was fed up until the love scenes came along.

"The little servant girl and the little shop girl of America want to see pictures where 'Lady Mary' comes majestically into a room full of servants with disdain and has a tray full of bath salts brought to her in her magnificent bathroom so she may select that which pleases her for the day. Then the little servant girl murmurs 'Now ain't that fine?' That sums up the creed of the business producer. The man who puts his ideals before what he knows is really wanted will be the financial loser."

September 27, 1925

'THE BIRTH OF A NATION.'

Film Version of Dixon's "The Clansman" Presented at the Liberty.

"The Birth of a Nation," an elaborate new motion picture taken on an ambitious scale, was presented for the first time last evening at the Liberty Theatre. With the addition of much preliminary historical matter, it is a film version of some of the melodramatic and inflammatory material contained in "The Clansman," by Thomas Dixon.

A great deal might be said concerning the spirit revealed in Mr. Dixon's review of the unhappy chapter of Reconstruction and concerning the sorry service rendered by its plucking at old wounds. But of the film as a film, it may be reported simply that it is an impressive new illustration of the scope of the motion picture camera.

An extraordinarily large number of people enter into this historical pageant, and some of the scenes are most effective. The civil war battle pictures, taken in panorama, represent enormous effort and achieve a striking degree of success. One interesting scene stages a reproduction of the auditorium of Ford's Theatre in Washington, and shows on the screen the murder of Lincoln. In terms of purely pictorial value the best work is done in those stretches of the film that follow the night riding of the men of the Ku-Klux Klan, who look like a company of avenging spectral crusaders sweeping along the moonlit roads.

The "Birth of a Nation," which was prepared for the screen under the direction of D. W. Griffith, takes a full evening for its unfolding and marks the advent of the two dollar movie. That is the price set for the more advantageous seats in the rear of the Liberty's auditorium.

It was at this same theatre that the stage version of "The Clansman" had a brief run a little more than nine years ago, as Mr. Dixon himself recalled in his curtain speech last evening in the interval between the two acts. Mr. Dixon also observed that he would have allowed none but the son of a Confederate soldier to direct the film version of "The Clansman."

March 4, 1915

NEGROES OBJECT TO FILM.

Say "Birth of a Nation" Characterizes Race Improperly.

The National Association for the Advancement of Colored People is conducting a campaign against the feature picture, "The Birth of a Nation," based on Thomas Dixon's novel, "The Clansman," at the Liberty Theatre.

It was explained at the offices of the association, 70 Fifth Avenue, yesterday, that many protests had been received because of the characterization of the negro in the story. The association has the opinion of a number of prominent men who have condemned it, and today the Rev. Dr. Percy Stickney Grant and Rabbi Stephen S. Wise will preach against it, it is said.

So far the association has found no way to interfere with the film, which has been viewed by crowded houses at every projection.

March 7, 1915

BROUGHT INTO FOCUS

"THE BIRTH OF A NATION" is surely the real thing as an "all-star" production in this increasingly important year of the motion picture. When it was made in 1914 none of its players was especially prominent, as prominence is measured today, yet its revival this week and last at the Capitol Theatre brings to the same screen at the same time more than a dozen actors, actresses and directors of the present who are widely known. Some of them, of course, were not entirely unknown on the stage and screen when the picture was produced, but others had never been heard of before, and almost every member of the cast indicates the importance of "The Birth of a Nation" in his or her screen life by putting it at the head of the Motion Picture Directory list of productions in which he or she has appeared.

It is testimony, too, to D. W. Griffith's discernment that he picked so many first grade players and got so much out of them seven years ago, and it is further testimony to the value of his personal influence that several of those who came to shine so brightly under his direction have since become noticeably less luminous as "stars" under the guidance of other directors.

At the head of the cast of "The Birth of a Nation" stands Henry B. Walthall as the Little Colonel. Has he ever been so vivid in any role? But he has done good work since, though in much less significant productions. For example, he is easily remembered for his performance in Mr. Griffith's "The Great Love" (1918) and as the Lone Wolf to Thomas H. Ince's "The False Faces" (1919). He is still starring on the screen though the writer has not seen him for some time.

Miriam Cooper, the older of the Little Colonel's sisters, is now the principal player in pictures directed by her husband, R. A. Walsh, who was John Wilkes Booth in "The Birth of a Nation." Their latest productions are "Evangeline" (1919), "The Deep Purple" (1920) and "The Oath" (1921).

Mae Marsh awoke to find herself famous after the first showing of "The Birth of a Nation" and her deserved fame was increased by her performance as the mother in "The Mother and the Law" episode of Mr. Griffith's "Intolerance," but subsequently she was made a "star," her appealing wistfulness was capitalized as cuteness, her spontaneity became pep, she was set to registering stock emotions instead of repressing human feelings, and those who admired her were beginning to fear that she would soon be merely a marionette when she retired from the [illegible]en in favor of marriage and a family. Now she is about to return, it is said, and the unanimous hope is that she will truly come back.

Josephine Crowell, unfortunately miscast as the Southern mother in "The Birth of a Nation," has since established herself as a screen actress of ability in more suitable, if less pleasant, rôles, as, for instance, that of the reformatory matron in "Peppy Polly" (Dorothy Gish, 1919), and the farmer's savage wife in Mr. Griffith's "The Greatest Question" (1919). She was also among those effectively present as the designing widow in "Bunty Pulls the Strings" (1921).

Spottiswoode Aitken, the old Southerner, in "The Birth of a Nation," is still one of the fine old men of the screen, whether his assumed character is fine, as in "Reputation," not yet released, or corroded, as in Maurice Tourneur's "The White Circle" (1920).

Ralph Lewis, the party-blind politician who eggs on the negroes and carpet-baggers, has retained a definite place among screen players. Of his most recent parts, probably the best is that of the heroine's father in "Prisoners of Love" (Betty Compson, 1921), though he may be remembered for his work in "The Valley of the Giants" (Reid, 1919), "The Hoodlum" (Mary Pickford, 1919), "When the Clouds Roll By" (Fairbanks, 1919) and "Outside the Law" (Priscilla Dean, 1921).

Lillian Gish, of course, is too well known to need reference to any of the productions in which she has appeared with constantly increasing prestige. It may be significant that, until the present time, she has remained under the direction of Mr. Griffith.

Elmer Clifton, the elder son of the Northern politician, Stoneman, has become a Director on Mr. Griffith's staff. He is personally credited with many of the Dorothy Gish pictures, some of which indicate an aptitude for bright comedy on his part and others a weakness for witless slap-stick.

Robert Harron in his brief but distinctive performance as the younger Stoneman began a screen career in which one real triumph followed another, until his untimely death in September, 1920.

Wallace Reid, whose short but active part as the blacksmith in "The Birth of a Nation" would probably have led to nothing in the hands of most players, has now become a finished farceur for the discriminating and a ravishingly handsome romantic hero for the movie fans.

Mary Alden, who is tellingly expressive as the mulatto of Stoneman's fancy, even though her make-up is unnatural, has continued to do excellent pantomimic work in "The Unpardonable Sin" (1919), "Erstwhile Susan" (1919), "The Inferior Sex" (1920), "Honest Hutch" (1920), "The Witching Hour" (1921) and other pictures.

George Seigmann, the offensive mulatto Lieutenant Governor of "The Birth of a Nation," became the imposing King Cyrus in Mr. Griffith's "The Fall of Babylon" and the sinister German spy in his "Hearts of the World" and "The Great Love." He may now be seen as the arrogant (until upset) Sir Sagramore in "A Connecticut Yankee in King Arthur's Court."

Walter Long, the bad negro Gus of "The Birth of a Nation," became the equally bad and as well played "Musketeer of the Slums" in "The Mother and the Law," and since then he has been seen in many pictures, recently in "The Sea Wolf" (1920) and Marshal Neilan's "Go and Get It" (1920).

Joseph Henabery, the Abraham Lincoln, and Donald Crisp, the General Grant of "The Birth of a Nation," have turned to directing, the former having gone from Douglas Fairbanks, in "Say, Young Fellow" and "His Majesty, the American," to Roscoe Arbuckle in "The Life of the Party," "Brewster's Millions" and "The Traveling Salesman," and the latter from Bryant Washburn in "Why Smith Left Home," "It Pays to Advertise" and "Six Best Cellars" to Wanda Hawley in "Miss Hobbs" and "Held by the Enemy," with Jack Holt, Agnes Ayres and Miss Hawley heading the cast. Mr. Crisp is now in London directing for the Famous Players-Lasky British Producers, but he may again turn to acting as he did so aggressively when he vitalized Battling Burrows in "Broken Blossoms."

And finally, who is the Thomas Wilson in the minor rôle of Stoneman's servant but the famous policeman who inspires such fear in the heart of the Charlie Chaplin of "The Kid" and its predecessors?

May 8, 1921

The Real Handicap of the Moving Picture.

According to The Seattle Post-Intelligencer, the moving pictures have led many good people to wonder if the great public which finds its chief amusement there "must go on indefinitely feeding on vampire, vice, sex problem, dance hall, and gambling house plays, and wondering also what the harvest is to be." The reason why this evil influence must be greater than it could ever be when exerted through bad books is suggested: "The printed word, of course, may present vice and crime politely and get away with it, but it must be depicted in life for the pictures if depicted at all." The Post-Intelligencer might have added that the worst play cannot be as bad as a bad moving picture, for a somewhat similar reason.

Yet what is the remedy? The Post-Intelligencer says that motion picture producers are willing to produce a better class of pictures if they could get them. This is not quite what they mean. They are willing to produce better ones if they could get better ones that would be profitable. Is the trouble, then, with the public taste? In a way, but it is a little more complex than that. When a theatrical manager produces a play, he does not produce it for everybody: he produces it for a certain public, and he knows his public. But when a picture producer does the same thing, he has to produce it for everybody. His picture is released in hundreds of theatres all over the country. After people pay a dollar and a half to see it on Broadway it descends to ten-cent theatres. If it pleases only the dollar-and-a-half public, he loses money. And the biggest receipts are from spectators who can read and write, but not with pleasure.

Therefore there seems to be no hope of rescuing the movies until there shall evolve some natural precipitation of "audiences," so that pictures shall be produced, as plays are, for different kinds of publics. There are tendencies in that direction, but so slight that the makers of many of the better class of moving pictures are obliged to make some concessions to the coarser taste or lower mental development, which must be conciliated to some extent if the producer is not to have his losses for his pains.

July 10, 1917

"TARZAN OF THE APES."

Jungle Story Appears in Film Form at the Broadway.

"Tarzan of the Apes," which excited considerable interest among the readers of popular-priced fiction several years ago, was shown at the Broadway Theatre last night in film form. Being the story of a primeval man—or, rather, of a man brought up among apes and endowed with many of their abilities—it presents not a few difficulties to the movie maker. All of these have been overcome in the film at the Broadway, and apes swing realistically from bough to bough in the jungle the while lions and leopards seek their prey on the ground below.

Intertwined with the jungle story is a domestic narrative which grows tedious at times, and the expedient of the cut-back is resorted to a trifle too freely. All of this is more than compensated for, however, by the stirring scenes of the jungle. A majority of these were photographed in Brazil, and several hundred natives appear before the camera. The picture as a whole, in addition to being interesting, also has a touch of educational value. An actor named Elmo Lincoln meets the difficult requirements of the hero satisfactorily.

January 28, 1918

How Pictures Are Sold Explained by Executive

MENTION the name of Sidney Kent, Vice President and General Manager of Famous Players-Lasky Corporation, in film circles and nine times out of ten somebody will refer to him as dynamic force on the commercial side of motion pictures. He is one of the outstanding figures of the industry, a man with a keen sense of humor who can make mere black and red figures unusually interesting. He knows how to bring out the salient points of a photoplay in such an absorbing fashion that any one would want to see the subject. He expects results and he gets them, and all over the world Sidney Kent's actual words are quoted by salesmen who realize that the general manager's phrases carry conviction. There are times when the subject is far from being artistic, but Mr. Kent knows its entertainment value and whether it will appeal to the smaller communities. There is no bluff about this executive. He points out what he sees and at every convention he inspires his men to bring home the bacon.

It is not often that Mr. Kent has time to be interviewed, but the other day he managed to spare a half an hour, during which he was interrupted several times by the telephone and callers. He knew exactly what he wanted to say, where to start, and there was never the least hesitation in his convincing talk.

"We live with a picture for five years after it comes to us from the studio," said he, as he lit a cigarette. "Therefore it is not astonishing that we hear all about its merits and weaknesses from many sections of the world. It should be remembered that the sales force is largely responsible for building up an artist's career, and I might add that the spirit that planted the American flag at the North Pole is needed to sell pictures. Russia, where we deal with agents, is the only country where we are not represented.

"There is more romance about the work than one would imagine. We have what we call our Foreign Legion boys, salesmen who have been in foreign countries through revolutions and catastrophes. Some of them have been cast into jail, and two of our men had to walk eighty miles after the Japanese earthquake. The film salesman should be a diplomat, an ambassador, in disposing of productions in other lands.

Titles in Thirty-eight Languages.

"There is the shipping of prints to all countries and the titles of these films are translated into thirty-eight different languages. There are something like fifty items that accompany each print of a picture. Most of these accessories and the advertising matter have also to be printed in thirty-eight languages. They are to the picture, like the food and ammunition of a soldier, who can't live and fight with only a gun. The detail of distributing pictures is as intricate as anything of which I can think. The old system of selling is a thing of the past. Now it requires resourcefulness, and the type of man we employ is constantly improving. College men now turn their attention to the work and some big educational institutions have identified themselves with the selling of pictures. It is work that requires enthusiasm and imagination and involves long hours. Seldom, outside of the large cities, is it possible for the salesman to see his customer in the daytime. He must find his man at the theatre in the evening.

"We have forty-six domestic offices, including those in Canada, and seventy-eight foreign offices. Six hundred men are engaged in marketing our pictures all over the world. Aside from countries where one would expect we would have branches, such as England, France, Germany, Belgium, Argentina, Brazil and so forth, we also have offices and sales forces in Iceland, Finland, Turkey, Egypt and Siam.

"A peculiar psychology is required by the efficient sales mind, quite different from a salesman in any other line of business. An automobile costs the same price, plus the freight, in New York or San Francisco, but the price of a picture to an exhibitor depends on many things. A salesman without imagination may sell a picture to an exhibitor for $1,000, while one with imagination may get $3,000 for the film. What may be surprising is that the theatre owner may reap better results by paying the higher price than he would from the lesser amount, for he, too, becomes appreciative of the possibilities of the picture through the imaginative salesman's talk.

Schooling Salesmen.

"We spend months preparing for the selling of our pictures, and we insist that all salesmen must be conversant with the stories. For that reason we hold a convention and the men go to school and learn the interesting points of a picture. At these conventions some important films are screened as well as sections of unfinished pictures. The salesman must not only know the theme of a film, but he must also be familiar with the big situations of the production and its merits as a screen attraction. He is selling a series of intangible shadows, something that is there for an hour or so and then gone.

"It is perhaps the only business in which success is penalized. A theatre owner may do so well with his 500-seat house, for which he pays a nominal price for his films, that he decides to build a 2,000-seat house. But when he books a picture for the new theatre he will be asked to pay two or three times the sum he did for the same film for the smaller house. There are no fixed prices for pictures.

"The Covered Wagon" Best Seller.

"So far as productions that have made big money in recent years are concerned, 'The Covered Wagon' has the edge on 'The Ten Commandments.' 'The Covered Wagon' was a bigger financial success in America, but 'The Ten Commandments' did better business in foreign territories. Pictures of the type of 'The Covered Wagon,' like 'The Birth of a Nation,' keep going for a number of years. 'The Birth of a Nation' is by no means dead yet.

"From last August to August, 1927, we will release seventy-five pictures, which prompts me to remark that this is the only business without a season. You have to watch the dates on the exhibitors' books, for if you lose a date it is gone for good, and you have to make it up somewhere else."

Mr. Kent, in answer to a question, said that "The Grand Duchess and the Waiter," an excellent picture, had met with great success in the larger cities, but he explained that it was too sophisticated or high-brow for the smaller places. He said that his company was serving 10,000 accounts, and that 70 per cent. of the firm's income was derived from towns with a population of 15,000 or over.

"Hence," observed Mr. Kent, "30 per cent. of our business is derived from 8,800 communities, which represents the profit and more. On a big production the average profit is nowhere near 30 per cent."

Mr. Kent has been in the picture industry for eight years. He was first with the old General Film Company and then went with Famous Players, with which concern he started in the field, then worked as a branch manager, then distribution sales manager, and eventually was promoted by Adolph Zukor, President of Famous Players, to the post of general manager.

September 19, 1926

THE JEKYLL-HYDE WORK

JOHN BARRYMORE has been seen in four motion pictures in the last year and a half. The first of the four was "On the Quiet," which came to the Strand in the week of August 25, 1918; the second was "Here Comes the Bride," which was at the same theatre in the week of Feb. 2, 1919. In both of these pictures Mr. Barrymore, following the style of his previous screen work, was an out-and-out farceur. He aimed at the ludicrous—and never missed. Without doubt he was one of the screen's best comic pantomimists; and owing to the fact that he had turned from frivolous to serious work on the stage, it was thought by some that he would preserve a double identity by establishing himself permanently as a screen comedian. But his decision was otherwise. He chose to follow on the screen the same direction he had taken on the stage and his next picture, "The Test of Honor," was a serious work in which he played with a moderation and restraint that was markedly different from the merry abandon of his earlier parts. His success, however, was no less definite. Those who had feared that he would be unable to make "movie fans" take him seriously were happily surprised.

Then came "Dr. Jekyll and Mr. Hyde," which moves from the Rivoli to the Rialto this week to continue its Broadway run. Into this picture Mr. Barrymore, as Mr. Hyde, has introduced an intensity and vigor of action that make the part as different from that of Martin Wingrave in "The Test of Honor" as Richard III. is from Peter Ibbetson.

In all of his screen rôles, Mr. Barrymore has been before everything a motion-picture pantomimist. Unlike many players with stage reputations, he has come to the screen with an appreciation of the requisites for acting before the camera and the ability to suit his acting to his understanding. No actor needs fewer subtitles, or leaders, to make him intelligible. He belongs conspicuously in the relatively small class of actors in motion pictures who are really motion picture actors.

When one thinks of the dual personality of Dr. Jekyll and wonders at his moral versatility, he is struck with the even greater artistic versatility of the amazing Barrymore, at home and extraordinary in everything from farce to tragedy, on the screen as well as the stage. Jekyll's magic potion has a circumscribed and simple power compared to that by which John Barrymore is variously transformed.

THE magnificently outstanding performance of Mr. Barrymore, however, is not the only virtue in "Dr. Jekyll and Mr. Hyde." In his first review of the production, the writer neglected to mention the setting provided for Stevenson's story. The scenes seem to be faithful reproductions of their originals, with the exception of Hyde's dwelling place in Soho, which in the photoplay appears as a dingy garret, while in the story it is "furnished with luxury and good taste," and in Richard Mansfield's adaptation it had luxury without taste. The picture, in this particular, is less in keeping with the character and circumstances of Hyde than the story or the play, especially as the screen version gives Hyde a woman companion who is not unattractive to other men, and it is inconceivable that she could be induced to live with such a repellent monster as Hyde without the attraction of luxurious surroundings. The street scenes, however, and those at the homes of Dr. Jekyll and Sir Danvers Carew are consistently pleasing and realistic, without being obtrusive. Also the costuming of both the men and the women in the photoplay is in keeping with the place and period presented, and the grouping of the figures is often effective.

AS a matter of course with such acting as is done by Mr. Barrymore in such settings, the screen version of "Dr. Jekyll and Mr. Hyde" must have interest for almost any spectator, but it is the writer's persistent conviction that in adapting Stevenson's story and Mansfield's play to the screen those responsible missed open opportunities to score heavily in melodramatic effect, and lost force in departing from their originals in ways not necessitated by the technique of the screen.

In the story, for example, Hyde is the incarnation of "pure evil," and in Mansfield's play, according to William Winter, he is "a carnal monster of unqualified evil." In the story he kills Sir Danvers Carew upon what Dr. Jekyll himself considers a "pitiful provocation," and in the play he does not seem to have had any incitement except Carew's natural refusal to summon his daughter when ordered to do so. In both the story and the play Hyde commits murder because he enjoys killing. It gives him savage pleasure to destroy an innocent, defenseless man, "an aged and beautiful gentleman with white hair." But in the photoplay this point is missed entirely, except in the terrific manner in which Barrymore plays the murder scene. Carew, in the first place, is made a sort of Mephistopheles to Jekyll's Faust. He chaffs the young physician about his reputation for virtue and with satanic amusement deliberately seeks to bring about his moral downfall. And when Jeykll has fallen he turns on Carew with angry accusation and then, suddenly becoming Hyde, commits the murder. There is no sympathy for Carew and Hyde is more an agent of retributive justice than a demon relishing his act of wanton destruction. The emphasis of the murder is altered, and to the detriment of the story.

THERE may be some who consider that Mr. Barrymore has made the character of Hyde too repulsive physically. They may call attention to the fact that those who knew Hyde in Stevenson's story nowhere picture him as he appears on the screen. "He must be deformed somewhere; he gives a strong feeling of deformity, although I can't specify the point," says Enfield. He "was pale and dwarfish, he gave an impression of deformity without any nameable malformation," but all of the "points against him" could not "explain the hitherto unknown disgust, loathing and fear with which Mr. Utterson regarded him." The repulsion felt by all who came into contact with him arose from psychological rather than physical causes, and Richard Mansfield and John Barrymore, in mak-

John Barrymore

ing the character hideous to look upon, have overdone the part and broadened or flattened the subtlety of Stevenson's creation, in the opinion of some. When it is remembered, however, that the limitations of stage and screen are different from those of words, most people will probably agree than it was necessary for Mr. Mansfield and Mr. Barrymore to express in physical appearance much of what Stevenson suggested in words. They had to make Hyde horrible to the eye to make him convincing to spectators in a theatre. Mansfield's Hyde, says Mr. Winter, was a "figure shrunken, malevolent, repulsive, insolent in demeanor, horrible in facial expression * * * a loathsome image of depravity and menace." Mansfield depicted the monster "with horrible animal vigor and with intense and reckless force of infernal malignity." And the same might be said of Barrymore's impersonation.

"But Mansfield rose to a nobler height than that," Mr. Winter goes on, "for he was able in the concurrent, associate impersonation of Dr. Jekyll to interblend the angel with the demon, and thus to command a lasting victory such as his baleful image of the hellish Hyde could never have achieved. That is the reason of his success. He was distinctly individual in each of the characters." Again, the same may be said of Barrymore.

Both Mansfield and Barrymore have abandoned Stevenson's Dr. Jekyll, "a large, well-made, smooth-faced man of fifty, with something of a slyish cast perhaps, but every mark of capacity and kindness," for a younger, more beautiful Dr. Jekyll who wins the sympathy of all. In this departure they suggest something of Dorian Gray—why doesn't John Barrymore do this Oscar Wilde character?—but this is another change that seems to be an improvement for the purposes of stage and screen. John Barrymore's Jekyll, by what he is forced to do in the photoplay, is made a bit too self-consciously goody-goody, too much a movie hero, but at least, so far as the actor's impersonation of the character goes, he is interesting and human, as well as beautiful.

April 4, 1920

$1,000,000 FOR FILM RIGHTS TO 'BEN-HUR'

Erlanger, Dillingham and Ziegfeld Also Acquire Dramatic Rights From Wallace Estate.

All dramatic rights to General Lew Wallace's "Ben-Hur," which for twenty years has been one of the most successful dramatic productions in the country, have been acquired from the Wallace estate by A. L. Erlanger, Charles B. Dillingham and Florenz Ziegfeld Jr., for what is said to be a record price. Included in the transaction are the motion picture rights, for which $1,000,000 are said to have been paid. The previous high mark for film rights was $175,000, paid by David W. Griffith for "Way Down East."

"Ben-Hur" has been sent on tour every season but the present one since it was first produced. It was originally presented by Klaw & Erlanger, and it was stipulated that all rights should revert to the Wallace estate if seventy-five performances were not given each season. The break between Marc Klaw and A. L. Erlanger interfered with the presentation of the play this season—the piece was placed in rehearsal on two occasions, but was abandoned both times.

The Messrs. Erlanger, Dillingham and Ziegfeld probably will send the play on tour again next season, since it is recognized that it has far from exhausted its popularity. It was originally produced on Nov. 25, 1899, at the Broadway Theatre, and its total receipts since that time have been close to $10,000,000. More than 20,000,000 persons have seen the play.

The motion picture, when eventually it is taken, will be filmed in Jerusalem and Syria.

April 8, 1921

REVIEW

Edith M. Hull's novel, "The Sheik," which seems to have provided some kind of entertainment for numerous readers and no little amusement for the book reviewers, has followed the path of all popular fiction and may be seen on the screens of the Rivoli and Rialto Theatres this week, that is, a photoplay calling itself "The Sheik" and acknowledging Mrs. Hull's story as its parent is being offered. Again the writer must confess that he has not read the novel from which a photoplay under review has been derived. He knew he would have to see the picture sooner or later. Isn't that enough?

Anyhow, the photoplay tells the story of an unusually spiritless English girl who is abducted by an exceedingly gentle desert sheik, but will not admit that she loves him until she is captured by a really rough Arab and realizes how perfectly safe she is with her tamer admirer. Somehow, this doesn't seem to be exactly the idea of Mrs. Hull's novel as reported in the book reviews, but never mind; here's the picture tale of a nice sheik and his agreeable English girl. And you won't be offended by having a white girl marry an Arab, either, for the sheik isn't really a native of the desert at all. Oh, no; he's the son of a Spanish father and an English mother who were killed when he was a baby so the old sheik could raise him as his son. These romantic Arabian movies, you know, never have the courage of their romantics.

Agnes Ayres is the girl and Rudolph Valentino is the sheik. Both of them can make the characters they impersonate seem real in a picture, which gives any character a chance to seem real.

George Melford directed the production and, although he has given it no cinematographic quality, he has made many elaborate scenes, using the desert effectively a number of times. The only trouble in this connection is that he has used the desert too much, and especially too much in the sun. If realism was his object he has certainly accomplished it. By the time half a dozen of these glaring white desert scenes have followed each other on the screen your eyes are ready to give up. Those who go to see the picture would do well to take their amber glasses with them.

The Rivoli and Rialto programs are enlivened by one of those ingenious and amusing doll comedies periodically issued as "Funny Face" productions without credit to the person or persons who make them. The magazines at these two theatres also emphasize Armistice Week and the Washington conference with pictures of the men prominent during the war and since.

Rudolph Valentino

November 7, 1921

Great Progress Shown in New Artistic Film Presentations

THIS last week has been an exceptional tribute to the progress of motion picture producing, as several fine and costly productions have been presented at legitimate theatres. These films are of a varied nature; in fact, what is unusual in pictures, no two of them are at all similar.

Mary Pickford has accomplished wonders in her new production, "Rosita." It is probably the best picture that she has ever made, and in it she shows in every scene that she is an accomplished screen actress—no longer just the child, or the little girl, but a real actress. This picture has been produced with much unselfishness on her part, as other players are not cut down or pushed off the scene to give Mary a great opportunity. Holbrook Blinn shares the honors with her, and his acting is naturally one of the features of this photoplay. It is an amazingly beautiful film, as delicate as a piece of Dresden china. The acting throughout is of the highest order, and if there is anybody who does not like Miss Pickford's former work, or they have tired of her recent efforts, this picture will win them to her again. As we remarked in our criticism of this picture, it is one of those productions that one can see with enjoyment more than once, and the first time one sees it it is with regret that "The End" comes on the screen.

The Blond Spanish Maiden.

Ernst Lubitsch proves once more that he is a masterful director, for in every scene there is a touch of originality. Pleasing bits of "business" are incorporated in "Rosita" in so many sequences that it is impossible to mention all of them. Also, the production is thoroughly well sub-titled, without so much as a single flaw or a trivial error. There is a dash to it from the minute it starts, and Miss Pickford is very cleverly introduced, so that the spectator is interested in her before she actually appears upon the screen, as the pictured throngs are so enthusiastic about this pretty blond-haired Spanish maiden and her guitar. What a joy it is to see such a picture after the stupid stuff one has to view week after week on the screens of different theatres!

Blinn is just as good on the screen as he is on the stage. There is never a thought given to the camera, and no stupid eye-acting. Everything is done in excellent taste and with a great deal of delicacy. The story is not one of great strength, but the ensemble makes it exquisite and charming.

A Grim Production.

We have finally seen the great effort of the Universal Corporation, on which a vast amount of money obviously has been spent, and this concern is to be congratulated on the tireless efforts of the employes to make old Paris as natural as possible. The structure of Notre Dame in this production—"The Hunchback of Notre Dame"—is something to marvel at, what with the copying of the intricate sculpture on the facade and the excellent idea of the gargoyles leaning over from the towers and parapets with an apparent diabolical leer.

This is a picture of great dramatic interest with a horrible creature in the Hunchback, as portrayed by Lon Chaney. It is, of course, a lugubrious picture, as was to be expected, and no pains has been spared to bring out the evil, without too much blood. Chaney has worked hard in this part, but occasionally he makes this Hunchback too awful, by sticking out his tongue and spitting on the throngs below. It is certainly a film effort which will stay in the minds of those who see it for many a day.

Ernest Torrence is capital as Clopin, the king of beggars and assassins. The court of so-called miracles is most interesting, as one sees the wily thieves and pickpockets garbed in filthy, threadbare and patched clothes, divesting themselves of their stock-in-trade disguises. The blind man plucks off his black eye-pads, and the cripples become agile. Faces are transformed from misery to grins and temper. They are in their court to talk over the affairs of the day. Imagine later these villains, some of them companions of rats in the sewers, others who live under arches, gradually assembling for an attack on the Cathedral with flaming torches, glittering knives and sticks.

Patsy Ruth Miller, the heroine of this film, has made an able display of her talent. She is very pretty and suits the part in which she appears.

"If Winter Comes."

"If Winter Comes" is another interesting film, and one which will appeal to those who have read the book. Percy Marmont's characterization of Sabre is a fine piece of work, and the only shame is that Ann Forrest was selected to play Lady Tybar, Nona. Not in a single scene does Miss Forrest fit into the part of Hutchinson's character, and to a certain extent the miscasting of this rôle detracts from the production. The book has been faithfully adhered to, and most of the other characters were well chosen.

For farcical fun Harold Lloyd in our opinion has never done anything better than "Why Worry?" now running at the Strand. It is not only the acting of Lloyd but the contrast between himself and the wonderful giant he has chosen to support him. It is a clever film with plenty of new "business" to make people roar with laughter most of the time this production is being screened.

"Bill," or Anatole France's "Crainquebille," a beautiful little production made in France, and exhibited here in three reels, has been on at the Rialto. Hugo Riesenfeld, managing director of the Rivoli, the Rialto and the Criterion, bought the American rights to this film while he was in Paris. In doing so he has shown knowledge of a story and excellent taste. It is merely the story of a pushcart peddler, acted so well that one almost believes that the vocation of the individual on the screen is that of selling vegetables instead of acting for the movies. Wherever this little film is being exhibited, we would counsel our readers not to miss it. It is filled with pathos and subtle humor.

A Beautiful Love Story.

The most recent big opening was of "The White Sister," with Lillian Gish, which would in our humble opinion have been the great love story of the films if the ending had been brought about in a different way. It is a very long film, and will perhaps be cut, and for three-quarters of it there is a slowly moving, but intensely human love story, splendidly acted by Lillian Gish and the man who supports her. It was made in Italy and all the exteriors are beautiful and artistic, and it might be said that it is a production that helps to bring film productions into a far better light. Some persons may find the ending satisfactory, and if so it would help this picture to cut out at least part of the flood and volcano eruption scenes. It is too good a picture to have any of this part of the film put into it. The love story is so impressive that, even when writing about it, one feels that ordinary words bordering in the least upon colloquialisms should not be used, and, although there is no comedy relief, it is such a beautiful love story that it is not necessary, as the director has cleverly sought relief in contrasting scenes. We felt that it was with great regret that we had even to disagree with the ending of this film, as the first part, or even three-quarters of it, is so well told and acted. Miss Gish demonstrates that she is a remarkable actress, who even in such a story as this never once is too emotional. She is also a type, if one can be permitted to say so, who fits the character remarkably well. Even though some will be disappointed in the latter part of this story it is such a worthy and artistic effort that we heartily recommend it as an example of a very high-class production.

James Cruze, who directed "The Covered Wagon" and later "Hollywood," two outstanding successes, is also responsible for the new film version of "Ruggles of Red Gap," in which Ernest Torrence plays the rôle of Cousin Egbert. It is to be seen this week at the Rivoli, and seeing that Torrence is a player in it and that it was fashioned by James Cruze, great things are expected of it.

"The Gold Diggers" is to be presented this week at the Rialto. So popular has the Harold Lloyd production "Why Worry?" been at the Strand this week that it is being held over for another seven days.

September 9, 1923

THE SCREEN

Remarkable Spectacle.

THE TEN COMMANDMENTS, with Theodore Roberts, Charles de Roche, Estelle Taylor, Julia Faye, Terrence Moore, James Neill, Lawson Butt, Clarence Burton, Noble Johnson, in the great spectacle; in the modern story are Edyth Chapman, Richard Dix; Rod La Roque, Leatrice Joy, Nita Naldi, Robert Edeson, Charles Ogle and Agnes Ayres.

It is probable that no more wonderful spectacle has ever been put before the public in shadow-form than the greatly heralded prelude to Cecil B. DeMille's costly film, which opened last night to a brilliant and eager gathering in the George M. Cohan Theatre. It is called, and it hardly seems necessary to mention the title "The Ten Commandments." It is built in two sections, the spectacle and the melodrama. Two men might have directed this feature, as it goes from the sublime to the out-and-out movie. Not that the latter part is bad, but that almost any melodramatic picture would have fitted into the second section of this photodrama.

But the sight of the Israelites in bondage in Egypt, their slaving before the chariots, their treatment by the despots of the day, the swiftly drawn chariots and their steeds, and the great bas-reliefs of figures whose shin-bones would have made two big men. All this was obviously directed by a genius who held in his hand the cost. There are many impressive colorful scenes of the Israelites in the desert, some of them appearing better and more natural than other such effects we have witnessed on the screen.

Charles de Roche, whom we first met in a minor part of "The Spanish Jade," who recently was seen as a Hindu with Pola Negri in "The Cheat," impersonated the terrible Rameses. He was impressive, and like all the other players in this section of this picture, wore his raiment of cloth and metal as if it were comfortable.

There was the death of all the first borns of the Egyptians, and the great and so-called magnificent Rameses praying to his god throughout the night to put life into his boy's body, and no life came. His god had no power like the God of the Israelites.

Coupled with the orchestration there has been nothing on the film so utterly impressive as the thundering and belching forth of one commandment after another, and the titling and photography of this particular effect was remarkable. It was the quivering, crashing, resounding blare from the string and wind instruments that did much to assist in the desired effect. The sky clouds, and then seems to burst, and from the ball of smoke appears golden lettering with one or another of the commandments, stress being laid upon those that are considered the most important, if one may say such a thing.

The costumes in this million dollars' worth of prelude are splendidly created, and not in a single instance is there a jarring note in this regard. Theodore Roberts, who recently was seen in the character of a business man with a cigar in his mouth, gave an excellent portrayal of Moses, the Lawgiver. His make-up was faultless, and the sincerity with which he acted this part made the whole affair doubly effective. Undoubtedly it was a series of sequences that made one think, that carried a message, that was done with meticulous precision, and boomed forth so well that it would have needed an unusually perfect modern drama to stand up in comparison with it. In this spectacle, with a good photographic and scenic effect, the crossing through a water flanked path of the Red Sea was shown, and it drew applause from the packed theatre. Prior to that there was the Pillar of Fire which confused and halted the Egyptians hastening after the slaves they had released through fear of the God of the Israelites.

But—and unfortunately we have to say but—the strain on Mr. De Mille told, and as soon as he swept on to his modern drama he was back to the ordinary and certainly uninspired movie, one in which the direction at times had "business" apparently intended to appeal to the very young. Too many "inserts" were shown. In one case there was a letter which was put on the screen three different times, and from what we now remember once would have been sufficient. The cracking walls of a cathedral being constructed by the hapless man in this portion of the film are brought out so many times that it is extremely tedious, and we would also like to say that if an old mother reads her Bible it is no reason why a motion picture director should have her carrying around a volume that weighs about a hundredweight. Also, why have her pictured after death with the same huge Bible? This is a story of two sons, one bad and the other good, a woman from a leper island, and the breaking of all the Commandments by the conscienceless love making, unfaithful and plotting weakling.

At the same time it must be admitted that in this melodrama there are also some excellent and well-thought out ideas, and some eye-smiting shots. There is considerable suspense where the wife of the wicked brother ascends to the top of the scaffolding of the rickety structure, constructed with rotten cement. It is the catching of her heel on a corner that uncovers the cheap and rotten concrete, as she nearly falls. And Mr. De Mille has not forgotten to give his spectators an impression of height in the full sequence. You see the woman ascending, you see her looking down, and although a car appears insignificantly small upon the roadway this young lady can detect her husband out with another woman in an automobile.

Whatever has been done in the second instalment of this picture—which in all is said to have cost a million and one-half dollars and classed by Mr. De Mille as "the cheapest picture ever made," because of the reward in sheckels it will reap—one must say that great heights of costuming and direction have been attained in the prelude.

The actors are capable throughout, and the performance in the modern portion of Rod LaRoque, as the wicked son, was particularly commendable. Richard Dix was good as the faithful and law-abiding son.

December 22, 1923

NEW WONDER IN THE SQUARE

Electric Signmaking Achieves a New Triumph to Help a Movie.

Christmas Eve witnessed the completion of a new and artistic addition to the display of electric signs in Times Square, which are the admiration of every visitor to New York. It advertises "The Ten Commandments," the new movie showing in a theatre across the street, and from the first moment the lights were turned on evoked unstinted admiration.

The sign, one of the largest ever seen on Broadway, stretches the entire length of the Putnam Building, facing on Broadway between Forty-third and Forty-fourth Streets. The wording flashes out intermittently from a blue background, representing an Egyptian night, in which myriads of stars twinkle as the other lights grow dim. Grandiose figures, even larger than the sign containing the words, balance it on either side.

One figure represents Moses receiving the Ten Commandments. He holds a gigantic stone tablet in his arms and looks with wondering gaze on the shifting multitudes below. The multitudes stare back their wonderment. At the other end is an allegorical group composed of two men and a woman, each representing sins against which the great Hebrew law-giver has thundered through the ages.

The sign contains upward of 200 arc lights, besides many incandescent bulbs. It is the work of Norden & Co., who recently established headquarters in an office directly beneath.

December 26, 1923

The Opera Phantom

By MORDAUNT HALL.

THAT fantastic melodrama "The Phantom of the Opera," in which Lon Chaney enacts the rôle of a hideous maniac, has some magnificent scenic effects, and it also possesses an idea which is bound to appeal to legions of picture-goers. People like to be thrilled, they love to be frightened, and if you are in the mood—actually looking for excitement and not overparticular how it is served up to you—you may find that the mysterious actions of the music-mad Phantom, who dwelt in a suite of cellars under the Pâris Opéra, are just what you want.

The story is really roughly told: one does not wish to quibble over details as it is unfurled on the screen. You must not ask why the police could not track down this elusive Phantom and you should not even speculate on how the Phantom was able to teach the art of singing to a young and pretty girl from the other side of her dressing-room wall. This mysterious person also commits crimes, and yet he risks being caught when he goes to a box in the Opéra to listen to his favorite singers. He has his own idea of staving off the police. He intimidates the management, and is apparently able to accomplish remarkable and truly wonderful things, such as bringing down a chandelier on the heads of the audience, making the lights go off and on, and popping off a person or two.

The film reaches its most nebulous height when the heroine, Christine Daae, is kidnapped by the Phantom. He has a horse all ready to carry the girl on an inclined plane down to his subterranean abode. Once there, he reveals himself to be a resourceful person, for he has a gondola, which floats on what we are told is the seepage of the Seine. He has light and food in his gorgeous apartment, in one room of which there is an elaborate bed, a boat-shaped affair swung from three posts. (Years ago this bed belonged to Gaby de Lys, and it was purchased by Universal Pictures Corporation for one of the properties of this ambitious production.) In another room, wherein the Phantom himself rests, there is a bed built like a coffin, which idea rather suits his grim whims, one of which is attending the gala mask ball of the Opéra in a costume which is alluded to as "Red Death." The Phantom wears a graceful, blood-colored affair and a mask that looks like a skull.

The Phantom's Face.

The ballet dancers have all heard rumors regarding the Phantom, but they are not sure whether the descriptions are correct. He is said to have parchment skin drawn tightly over his bony countenance—and—no nose!

The first seen of the Phantom is his shadow, which is all one beholds for four reels. The outline of his face on the wall is grotesque, and at times he appears to be somewhat anxious that the spectators have plenty of opportunity to study his dark profile on the wall. When he does appear himself, one is apt to think that the fringe on his mask made the outline of his physiognomy too odd. He is so frightful of face, we are told, that he wears this mask as those who have beheld his real countenance have fled from him in terror. This mask, which he wears as he stalks behind the Opéra stage, is an abominable contraption. It has silly, fat checks, which make it look like the faec of a child. A fringe covers the Phantom's mouth and chin. It causes one to think that this facial disguise must be very uncomfortable. The Phantom ought to have appeared in a simple black mask, which would have added to the dramatic effect when finally one set eyes on his real face.

The captions describe this fiend as having a "voice like an angel," a voice which fascinated Christine, the aspiring young singer. Whatever may have been the mental condition of this Phantom, he was, at any rate, loyal to the girl he had taught to sing. It is the Phantom who threatens the management with dire consequences if Christine is not permitted to sing the rôle of Marguerite in "Faust." So Christine has the satisfaction of warbling in place of the prima donna. But the following occasion on which "Faust" is presented, the management decides that they will not bow to any threats from this Phantom! They will do as they wish! The wrath of the Phantom, following a written threat, is first expressed through having the lights flicker on and off. There is a scene showing the two managers looking very uncomfortable as they witness what is happening from the Phantom's box—No. 5. They may have anticipated that the mysterious cave-dweller would run away with the rival performer, but they did not expect that he would be able to cause the singer's note to clash with the great crystal chandelier and bring it crashing from the high ceiling to the orchestra seats far below.

The Unmasking.

The dramatic high light in this effusion is where one perceives Christine in one of the underground chambers listening to the Phantom as he, masked, plays his own organ. The girl is dumb with terror, for she had been forced to come below with the frightful being. She has heard of this Phantom, but it did not occur to her that the man with "the voice of an angel" could have any connection with this supposedly noseless monster. Though she is frightened and trembling, she cannot resist the urge of curiosity, and she creeps near to the Phantom. First she extends her hands, and it looks as if she were going to smooth his hair. Then she withdraws her hands, fearful of what might happen if she uncovered the Phantom's face. This idea may be highly exciting, but it is far from plausible, considering the nervous state of the young woman. Anyhow, Christine once more permits her fingers to steal toward the Phantom, and this time with a sudden movement of both hands she snatches off the plump-faced mask—and the Phantom's face is disclosed. He is by no means beautiful, but he is not as hideous as one anticipated. He has a nose, with long, straight nostrils. His eyes are deep, hollow and uncanny. His mouth is uncertain, with large teeth separated by dark cavities. He is pale, and his forehead is like wax and high. It is the sort of face one would not like to meet on a week-end visit to a haunted house. He is the type of man who could not have a friend in the world, but a man who, according to the story, works wonders in keeping his underground castle shipshape.

The Acting.

The athletic Norman Kerry fills the rôle of the hero. Mr. Kerry is not the person to play such a part, and he appears too self-conscious. His most annoying moments are when he endeavors to express love for the lost heroine. He struts through scene after scene, or is found posing against a pillar or a door. The posing is, of course, not his fault, as he probably was instructed to do that by Rupert Julian, who directed this subject. Far better results could have been obtained from Mary Philbin, who impersonates Christine, if one expects to live seriously in these fantastic realms. There is one period, toward the end of this production, where one perceives Miss Philbin with a smile upon her countenance, at a time one would have imagined she would have been almost unconscious and tonguetied with fright. The Phantom still is in the room, and possibly the excuse for this expression might be that it was caused by nervousness.

Mr. Chaney himself endeavors so eagerly to inject horror into this screen feature that at times he overdoes it. When this happens it is dangerous, for even those persons who may be sensitive to such a fantasy may smile instead of being awestruck.

This film is nicely presented with a prologue in which there are capable ballet dancers. The music score might be more effective, especially in the stretch where the Phantom is unmasked. However, when it comes to the selections from "Faust" one forgives almost everything, even Mr. Kerry's striding and stiffness in the hussar uniform, which incidentally never seems to belong to him.

The initial scenes in this picture are in natural colors, but they are weak and washed out. Subsequent color scenes, particularly the chapter dealing with the costume ball in the Opéra, are much more impressive, as one has a chance to study the different uniforms, the costumes of the women and, above all, the resplendent array of the Phantom as Red Death.

There is a regrettable tendency to exaggerate throughout this film. At the beginning we have a glimpse of many different nations standing on the steps of the Opéra, which is highly imaginative. It is a case of overdoing hearsay—hearsay that already has been exaggerated.

September 13, 1925

RECORD OF "BIG PARADE"

ACCORDING to statistics gathered by J. J. McCarthy's office, "The Big Parade" has now the distinction of the third longest continuous run known to the American theatre. This worthy film feature outstripped all other motion picture competitors last month and now is exceeded only by "Abie's Irish Rose" and "Lightnin'." These two dramatic productions have been shown for more continuous performances, but Mr. McCarthy believes that "The Big Parade" will step to second place before the close of the current engagement. His conclusion is that "The Big Parade" will have registered more gross business at the box office than either of its competitors before the end of this season. At the present time the box office total for the sixty-seven weeks at the Astor Theatre is a trifle under $1,300,000.

Mr. McCarthy says that not more than a score of plays were presented over 600 times in the history of the American stage since the first small productions on Cruger's Wharf 160 years ago.

"In the short space of thirty-one years," observes Mr. McCarthy, who has charge of the road showing of "The Big Parade" and the film version of "Ben-Hur," "the screen has produced no artistic and commercial success of the calibre of 'The Big Parade,' which passes its 933d performance tonight. It is a swift and interesting transition from the first exhibition of the Edison Vitascope in Koster & Bial's Music Hall in 1896 and the first feature picture in 1903, 'The Great Train Robbery,' to the production of 'The Big Parade.'

"Every big motion picture has been nationally road-showed at legitimate theatre prices since 'The Birth of a Nation,' the first of the 'two-dollar' motion pictures, which ran for more than six hundred times on Broadway. There have been many pictures shown in legitimate Broadway theatres since the first presentation of 'The Birth of a Nation,' twelve years ago, but they did not tour the country for a full theatrical season, nor did they achieve the six hundredth performance on Broadway. This is an unusual record for the screen; in twelve years each of the six recognized road-show pictures ran for more than six hundred times here and in the 160 years of New York theatricals there have been only twelve plays to pass the six hundredt' mark."

The long run records of the leading plays and road-show pictures are as follows:

	Times.
*Abie's Irish Rose	2,049
Lightnin'	1,291
†The Big Parade	933
The Bat	867
The Ten Commandments	854
The Covered Wagon	826
The First Year	760
Ben-Hur	714
Seventh Heaven	704
Peg o' My Heart	692
East Is West	680
Irene	670
A Trip to Chinatown	657
Rain	648
The Birth of a Nation	616
Adonis	603
Way Down East	602

*To Feb. 26. †To Feb. 27.

February 27, 1927

A FULL HOUSE OF FILMS

Three of a Kind and a Pair Make a Popular Winning Hand

APPARENTLY the pictures on Broadway last week are of the popular kind. This is indicated by the classifications into which they fall.

J. C. Jenkins, of The Exhibitors Herald, made a tour of theatres in Minnesota, Wisconsin and Illinois—fairly representative States—and reported in a recent issue of The Herald that the exhibitors he interviewed classified films in order of popularity as follows:

Comedy dramas.
Westerns.
Action plays.
Dramas.
Comedies.
Historical films.
War pictures.
Costume plays.

These designations may present more confusion than enlightenment to the mere spectator who may wonder, for instance, wherein an "action play" differs from any other dramatic entertainment. The only film productions devoid of action are Hollywood's indigenous "artistic flops," which achieve artiness by slow motion and soft-focus photography; but the average spectator doesn't consider these because he never sees them. They flourish in Hollywood at showings promoted by "art guilds" and art-struck individuals, and then accomplish an early and easy demise, not having much life in them to begin with.

The mere spectator may also wonder where the lines are drawn between "comedy dramas," "comedies" and "dramas," and the distinction between "historical" and "costume" plays may also bother him a bit.

"Westerns" are as easy as guessing the middle name of Francis X. Bushman. They're cowboy melodramas. But what's the difference between them and "action plays"?

It would seem that an "action play" is a melodrama without cowboys, or, to turn it around, a "Western" is an 'action play" with cowboys added, the difference being something like that between chile and chile con carne.

"Dramas," of course, are serious things, those problem-solving, cross-section-of-life studies of society as it is, ought to be, or may be made to seem—"Should a Woman Tell?" "Daughters of Divorce," "Men and Marriage" and the like. They must be contemporary, too. Otherwise they stop being "dramas" and become "costume" or "historical" plays.

Hoot, Mon!

Under the head of "comedies" are grouped the broad, slap-stick farces and burlesques of feature length, the old two-reel rough-and-tumbles grown up, you know. They do not pretend to anything dramatic. They go after loud laughs and hoots of delight.

"Comedy dramas" come between. They attempt something of a story with characters and situations, but are pointedly and plentifully gagged for laughter. They never become too serious, nor yet too broadly comic, if they stick to the prescribed plan.

It's not so easy to separate "historical" and "costume" plays, however. "Hamlet" in modern dress is "historical" without being "costume," to be sure, but that's been done only on the stage. Perhaps the distinction is merely a matter of time. A picture dealing with past people and events may be "historical" if it doesn't go back far enough to demand clothes radically different from those worn today, like "The Rough Riders," for instance. If, however, it goes back to hoop-skirts or Elizabethan ruffs it's no longer "historical" but "costume."

Herein is noticed the only instability in the classifications. A "historical" picture may become a "costume" picture in time. Stories cast in the period of the Gay Nineties, for example, with the women wearing long skirts, bustles and pompadours were "historical" once, but now they are "costume." And if wide ruffs are ever in style again Queen Elizabeth may find herself "historical," no longer "costume."

But last week's pictures are not involved in these fine distinctions. They belong up in the popular classifications. Three of them, surely, may be classed as "comedy dramas," which head the list. "Rolled Stockings" at the Paramount, "The Poor Nut" at the Strand and "The Gingham Girl" at the Capitol all offer stories and situations, but they are freely sprinkled, even showered, with comedy gags and comedians. And, it would seem, they hold their own with other films of their class. They were all well received by the fans.

There were no "Westerns" about last week, but "The Blood Ship" at the Roxy and "The Great Mail Robbery" at the Hippodrome undoubtedly belong in the "action" class. They are melodramatic thrillers of the most robust kind, and as such delighted large audiences.

Apparently these pictures indicate the trend of production for the coming year, too. Statistics compiled by Mr. Jenkins from the announcements of producing companies show that films will run very largely to the "comedy drama" class. "Action" plays listed as such are rather low in the percentage tables, but it is explained that some companies do not use this classification, although making pictures with plenty of action in them. They prefer to call them "dramas" or "comedy dramas"; also it is even conceivable that a "costume" or "historical" play may have action in it, though it must be confessed that when movie actors put on the clothes of a former day they seem unable to get away from the idea that they are part of a parade or pageant. They'd probably strut Falstaff himself.

July 24, 1927

A HOLLYWOOD FIRST NIGHT

Opening Performance in California More Dazzling Than Any Seen Here

EVEN with blazing lights and a living sign above the theatre marquee, such as was exhibited on the opening night at the Astor Theatre of "The Hollywood Revue," the film first nights in New York are but tame affairs compared with similar events in Hollywood.

At a recent opening at the Carthay Circle, where Cecil B. DeMille's initial dialogue film, "Dynamite," was the attraction, the heavens were cut by more than a dozen searchlights besides an imposing battery of other illuminating devices. Everybody who was anybody in the film world was there.

Three publicity men from the Metro-Goldwyn-Mayer studio, who know all the celebrities in the film centre, were stationed on the sidewalk in front of the long, brilliant lane that led to the portals of the theatre. As each glistening car unloaded its human cargo the names of the arrivals were passed on to an announcer at a microphone. He was broadcasting the details of the first night.

Ash blondes appeared from the expensive automobiles and they were escorted to the microphone where they invariably said:

"Good evening, everybody. I'm glad to be at the first showing of Mr. De Mille's picture."

Will Hays arrived with Cecil B. De Mille, the latter's expression betokening satisfaction with his latest pictorial venture. André de Segurola, the opera singer of old, was announced soon afterward and as is his wont on these occasions he went up to the microphone and with a circle of people in evening dress around him sang a few bars from an operatic air.

Hopeful Faces.

The most remarkable feature of this and other openings is the impressive throng of young and old persons who have no admission tickets who come to see the stars arrive. They are kept back by ropes, and some of them have brought boxes with them on which to rest. There are young men and girls in the crowd who, judging by their expressions, hope that some producer or director in passing may find their faces interesting for some forthcoming production. It has been known to happen more than once, and therefore a front line place is advantageous.

The uniformed man on the curb has duplicate tickets for the chauffeurs and the owners of cars. But well arranged as the traffic was for this particular opening, nobody could really tell whether he would have his automobile first or last. It is a matter of luck.

"Who is she?" somebody in the crowd murmured, apparently expecting the name of some screen celebrity to be announced. But this silken-clad flaxen-haired woman was only the fashion editor of a local newspaper, which fact did not interest the eager-eyed throng nearly as much as the arrival of a Dorothy Mackaill, a Lilyan Tashman, a Bebe Daniels or a Vilma Banky. The women and girls behind the ropes looked admiringly at the ermine cloaks, at the dazzling dresses and at the exquisitely coiffured heads of the dawdling actresses.

Among the faces behind the rope to the left of the entrance to the theatre was a girl who was unusually beautiful. Her hair was golden, her eyes were blue. She was slender and young. To a masculine eye it did not seem as though she had tried to intensify her beauty with cosmetics. Apparently she did not know how good-looking she was, at least not on that particular evening. The sight of other feminine faces, persons more fortunate than she in having tickets for the first night, did

not seem to arouse in her the faintest tinge of envy. Perhaps she was filled with delight at having been able to squeeze herself into the front row, but she did not betray any sign of wanting to catch the eyes of the film luminaries or those of producers. She was a healthy young person who evidently did not covet her neighbors' goods, looks or position.

The Girl in the Crowd.

No matter how many bright-eyed actresses passed, one found one's eyes returning to this girl behind the ropes, and during the busy formalities preceding the starting of the picture a smile constantly lighted her face. She beamed when Ronald Colman hastened through the crowd and she appeared to be much interested in Henry King and his charming wife. She looked with awe upon the figures of Mr. Hays and Mr. De Mille, and she laughed when other people near the microphone laughed. What a lucky person she seemed to consider herself, being there and actually seeing what thousands of others were only able to listen to over their radios.

Soon word was passed around that the show was to start. Inside the sprucely clad men and the fashionably arrayed women were buzzing conversation. The idle chatter gradually dwindled until the synchronized orchestration of the picture burst

FAIR BUT DESIGNING

Lilyan Tashman in "Bulldog Drummond."

forth and acted like an admonition against last-minute whispering.

During an intermission the foyer of the theatre was thronged and many of those present went out into the night under the canopy that led from the sidewalk to the doors. The searchlights were still signaling to the heavenly stars that there was an opening at the Carthay Circle, and, by the ropes, the throng was still waiting, some listening to the opinions of Mr. De Mille's film, others who found themselves so close to a popular actress that it seemed almost unbelievable. To the left of the entrance was the pretty Nordic maiden half smiling and showing her even white teeth.

She, this natural blonde who spurned mascaro, was still there when the men in black and white and the women in all colors of the prism slowly wended their way to the curbs, where the booted carriage caller helped the theatregoers into their conveyances.

Nobody had seen this humble but winsome face. Nobody had booked her to play in a picture, but if one could read looks, she had enjoyed the evening thoroughly. And, according to what Mr. De Mille heard about his picture, many in the audience had also passed a highly satisfactory hour or so. M. H.

September 1, 1929

HOW THE VITAPHONE ENTERS IN

ALAN CROSLAND, Warner Brothers' director, who is now filming "The Jazz Singer," starring Al Jolson in the title rôle, recently explained the details of the method by which full Vitaphone vocal numbers will be introduced for the first time into the action of a photoplay.

To begin with, it must be borne in mind that one reel of film is accompanied by just one sound record. The film can be cut, rearranged, shortened or anything desired—when not accompanied by Vitaphone—but since the record cannot be altered, once a thousand feet of film has been synchronized with a disk it must remain in precisely that form and length.

This means that if a "talking movie" throughout were being made it would be necessary to film a thousand feet at a time, synchronized with the record of the voices and used in just that form. Such is not the case with "The Jazz Singer," however. Songs will be introduced only at those points where they come in naturally and there will be no talking.

In Reel One, for instance, three songs are to be Vitaphoned in at three different points. During the other portions of the reel there will be a synchronized orchestral score.

The method which Crosland will have to employ in filming is this:

First, all those portions of the reel which do not call for singing will be filmed. Then the reel will be assembled and cut, titles and all. The singing scenes will have been carefully rehearsed and timed to the second, and in the places in the reel where these are to go, blank film of an equivalent length will be placed.

Then, in the Vitaphone studio sets will be erected side by side for all three singing scenes. In the corner will be placed the accompanying orchsetra for the picture with the projection machine to run it off, as is usual in "scoring" a picture for Vitaphone accompaniment. There will be four microphone circuits—one for each of the three sets and one for the orchestra.

When all is in readiness, the projection of the incomplete reel will start with the leader conducting the orchestra in the synchronized score which will be picked up by the first microphone. At the instant when the blank film flashes on the screen indicating the place for the first singing scene the orchestra will stop, and the microphone on the first set will be switched on while the first scene is recorded. As it comes to an end, one of the scenes previously filmed will flash on the orchestra's screen and the orchestra will resume the score. This process will be repeated for the second and third vocal numbers. All three sets must be lighted and ready, the timing must be perfect, and the players must be ready to make quick changes while the orchestra scores intervening scenes.

August 28, 1927

THOUSANDS GET IN MOVIE.

Crowd Plays for Nothing In Filming at Winter Garden.

Several thousand persons congested Broadway between Fiftieth and Fifty-first Streets from 7:30 until 11 o'clock last night playing extras gratis for Warner Brothers, motion picture producers, in filming scenes in "The Jazz Singer" at the Winter Garden. Al Jolson, stage comedian, is the star of the picture.

One of the scenes taken last night was of Jolson leaving the stage entrance to the Winter Garden. Crowds milling into the Winter Garden and then swarming out were filmed under brilliant artificial light. Warner Brothers were said to have brought a company of 100 persons from their studio in Hollywood to New York to make the scenes.

Reserves from the West Forty-seventh Street Police Station were called out to relieve traffic snarls and the general congestion on Broadway.

June 27, 1927

THE SCREEN

By MORDAUNT HALL.

AL JOLSON himself can be chatting with a friend on a Broadway corner while his image is working hard at Warners' Theatre in the Vitaphoned picturization of "The Jazz Singer." The popular entertainer can even say that he's going to hear himself, and, what's more, anybody could shut their eyes and the effect of his shadow singing would be as if Mr. Jolson had stepped on the stage. It is a marvelous result that is given in this production, for it is not merely an ordinary reproduction of the songs, but one that exudes the Jolson personality. On the opening night one almost forgot that the real Jolson was sitting in a box listening to his own songs, for it seemed as though in the darkness Mr. Jolson had crept behind the screen and was rendering the songs for his black-and-white image.

Film actors may frequently be affected by their own performances, but here was a case of a singer stirred to tears by his shadow and the reproduction of his voice. Of course, it might be argued that the rousing reception that the black-and-white Al Jolson received from the audience was enough to bring a tear or two from Jolson in the flesh. But Mr. Jolson, in witnessing the work he had done months ago before the camera and the Vitaphone, also observed on the screen a story quite like that of his own life, and the incidents may well have touched him.

Those who delight in handsome heroes may possibly discover that they are not quite satisfied with Mr. Jolson's acting on the screen. But those who are genuinely interested in a sympathetic performance will not find much to criticize adversely in Mr. Jolson's playing. The story is quite sentimental and the situations are not infrequently stressed. Nevertheless, it carries with it something that has its quota of truth, and there probably was nobody on the opening night that did not find a certain charm in the episode wherein Jolson's image renders across the footlights to his stage mother his song, "Mammy." Mr. Jolson singing without the advantage of a crowd but for a crowd has succeeded in making this one of the golden moments of the Vitaphoned production.

"The Jazz Singer," in film form, is, of course, dependent upon Mr. Jolson's work for its success, and therefore the importance of other rôles, especially that played by May McAvoy, is minimized. However, Warner Oland gives a sound portrayal of Cantor Rabinowitz and Eugenie Besserer is gentle and natural as Jack Robin's mother.

October 16, 1927

Dorothy Lee

John Boles

THE SCREEN

By MORDAUNT HALL.

A Ziegfeld Show on the Screen.

RIO RITA, with Bebe Daniels, John Boles, Don Alvarado, Dorothy Lee, Bert Wheeler, Robert Woolsey, Georges Renevant, Helen Kaiser, Tiny Sandford, Nick de Ruiz, Sam Nelson, Fred Burns, Eva Rosita and Sam Blum, based on Florenz Ziegfeld's stage production of the same name, directed by Luther Reed. At the Earl Carroll Theatre.

The singing Texas Rangers, the alluring Rio Rita, the malignant Ravenoff, the comic Lovett, the troubled Chick Bean, the graceful Carmen, the charming Dolly, the gallant and melody-loving Captain Jim Stewart and a host of dazzling chorus girls and dancers seemed to have hopped from the Ziegfeld Theatre stage to the screen of the Earl Carroll Theatre last night, when RKO Pictures Corporation launched their pretentious audible pictorial reproduction of Mr. Ziegfeld's "Rio Rita" before an unusually brilliant gathering.

This lavish production indulges but little in cinematic turns. Luther Reed, the director, has contented himself in making virtually an audible animated photographic conception of the successful Ziegfeld show. It has good comedy interludes, which provided plenty of mirth for the audience, and the tuneful melodies that were sung on the stage by J. Harold Murray as the redoubtable Captain Jim are rendered admirably by John Boles. Bebe Daniels acts the dark-eyed Rio Rita and her singing, while not up to the standard set by Ethlin Terry in the stage version, is a surprise, coming as it does from the film actress who has for the last year or so been seen only in lively pictorial comedies.

The suspense consists of: Who is the desperado, known as The Kinkajou? He blows open a bank safe within a few paces of a gay throng in a cabaret. And when it happens, the Texas Rangers fire and fire, not bothering much to aim their pistols so long as the triggers sound the alarm. Their man escapes, at least for a while (almost as long as the picture lasts), and meanwhile wads of Uncle Sam's currency seems to be filling several pockets, including those of the dry (in speech only) and alert Mr. Lovett, a lawyer who specializes in divorces, would love to be snared as a husband by a charming little ex-wife in pink, who has fallen heiress to not a nickel less than $3,000,000.

One is not always certain where one is in this picture, but it does not matter much which side of the Mexican border it is, for chorus girls appear as if by a magic wand ready to dispel the gloom of the lovers with their presence, their singing and dancing. But who is The Kinkajou, one asks, as the story proceeds. Guilt is at first fastened on Captain Jim, until one understands that he is risking life, love and freedom to apprehend the crafty bandit. Then for some time it is thought that the much-feared fellow is none other than Rita's brother, Roberto. But—in the end one learns.

Chick Bean, the alleged bigamist, happens to have a few thousand dollar notes bearing the numbers of those stolen by The Kinkajou, and the Mexican Padrone, thinking that this young man is the safe-cracker, kisses him with due respect.

This gives more than a vague idea of the seriousness with which the narrative is unfurled. Mr. Boles strikes an attitude like a valiant knight of old as he pours forth admiration for Rio Rita in captivating melody.

Rita has many gowns, each one more bewitching than the other and the cool but malevolent Ravenoff, who intrudes with a French accent from Russia into Mexico, arranges matters at his glorious dance upon the old pirate craft, so that Rita has a bridal dress, which she may wear when she consents to become his bride! It is, however, perhaps not any more fascinating than the metallic cloth gown in which Rita appears at the ball. And her lover is down in the hold (having been shot at), waiting to sing again and again of his love for her, but apparently believing that all is not well so far as Rita's brother, Roberto, is concerned.

The last half of this handsome vocalized motion picture is filmed by the Technicolor process, and although some of the scenes are not quite in focus, the effect is invariably beautiful. It is in this part that Lovett and Chick Bean are beheld turning the other cheek to each other's slaps, soft, hard, fast and slow, while sitting between those radiantly clad girls, Dolly and Mrs. Chick No. 1. The girls are singing, the orchestra is playing, when suddenly all four lose their balance and flop into the water below.

There are several impressive spectacular passages in this film, and those that are in prismatic hues are always interesting because of their loveliness.

The book of this extravaganza was written by Guy Bolton and Fred Thompson, the music by Harry Tierney and the lyrics by Joe McCarthy.

The acting is uniformly capable. Robert Woolsey is excellent as the fast-talking, deep-voiced, narrow-shouldered Lovett. Bert Wheeler does exceedingly well as Chick Bean. Georges Renevant gives a nice, easy performance as Ravenoff. Dorothy Lee is vivacious as Dolly and Helen Kaiser is attractive and competent as Mrs. Chick, No. 1.

It is an evening of good music, enjoyable fun and constant screen-fulls of striking scenes that cause one to wonder how much such a production cost.

October 7, 1929

THE OUTSTANDING PICTORIAL FEATURES OF 1933

The Blue Ribbon Films and Fifty Others Worthy of Honorable Mention

By MORDAUNT HALL.

TOWARD the end of 1932 several producers stated that in order to boost cinema box-office receipts they would be forced in future productions to supplant sophistication with hokum. Therefore the outlook was not particularly encouraging, but it so happens that in the last twelve months Hollywood has made even a greater proportion of intelligent pictures than in the previous year.

Notwithstanding the economic depression there was an increase in the number of films presented in the Broadway area, not only in the matter of American works, but also of foreign offerings. Of the 479 pictures reviewed in THE NEW YORK TIMES, more than 125 came from Russia, Italy, France, England, Sweden and other countries. Some of them, it is true, were produced under the aegis of American concerns in European countries, and others, such as several Spanish language features, were made in this country. There were, however, twenty-five more Hollywood pictures presented here than there were in 1932. Judging by the tenor of the worth-while subjects, the producers are discovering that restraint is a quality that brings shekels to their coffers. They seemed to grasp this fact when that refreshing and fine picture, "Cavalcade," was released, and recently they were somewhat astounded by the marvelous drawing power of the pictorial version of Louisa May Alcott's book, "Little Women."

To get down to the outstanding ten productions of the year without further delay, it might be said that they are even better than usual, not only from a technical viewpoint, but also from an imaginative angle and in the performances of the players. Here they are:

THE BEST TEN.

Cavalcade, with Diana Wynyard, Clive Brook and others; based on Noel Coward's Drury Lane drama and directed by Frank Lloyd under the supervision of Winfield Sheehan.

Reunion in Vienna, with Diana Wynyard, John Barrymore and Frank Morgan, an adaptation of Robert E. Sherwood's play, directed by Sidney Franklin.

Morgenrot, a German production, with Rudolf Forster, directed by Gustav Ucicky; a story of submarines in the World War.

State Fair, with Will Rogers and Janet Gaynor, adapted from Phil Stong's novel of the same title, directed by Henry King.

Dinner at Eight, with several stellar performers, including Marie Dressler, John and Lionel Barrymore; based on the stage work by George S. Kaufman and Edna Ferber, directed by George Cukor.

Berkeley Square, with Leslie Howard and Heather Angel; a version of John L. Balderston's play, directed by Frank Lloyd.

The Private Life of Henry VIII, a British production, with Charles Laughton and Binnie Barnes, directed by Alexander Korda.

Little Women, with Katharine Hepburn, Joan Bennett and Paul Lukas, adapted from Louisa May Alcott's immensely popular novel, directed by George Cukor.

The Invisible Man, with Claude Rains, based on an H. G. Wells story, directed by James Whale, from a script written by R. C. Sherriff.

His Double Life, a pictorial version of Arnold Bennett's novel, "Buried Alive," directed by Arthur Hopkins, with Roland Young and Lillian Gish in the principal rôles.

1932's List.

It may be of interest to reprint this department's 1932 list, which was:

Maedchen in Uniform.
Trouble in Paradise.
Der Raub der Mona Lisa.
Grand Hotel
Dr. Jekyll and Mr. Hyde.
The Mouthpiece.
One Hour With You.
A Bill of Divorcement.
The Doomed Battalion.
Reserved for Ladies.

FIFTY RED RIBBON FILMS.

As was done last year, we will venture to name other noteworthy examples of cinematic entertainment made in 1933:

The Island of Lost Souls.
The King's Vacation.
Whistling in the Dark.
Topaze.
She Done Him Wrong.
Our Betters.
King Kong.
Christopher Strong.
A Lady's Profession.
Forty-second Street.
From Hell to Heaven.
Gabriel Over the White House.
Bedtime Story.
The Silver Cord.
Zoo in Budapest.
The Eagle and the Hawk.
The Kiss Before the Mirror.
The Little Giant.
The Nuisance.
I Loved You Wednesday.
When Ladies Meet.
This Is America.
Mama Loves Papa.
Song of Songs.
The Stranger's Return.
Another Language.
Three-Cornered Moon.
The Power and the Glory.
Voltaire.
Paddy the Next Best Thing.
Turn Back the Clock.
The Masquerader.
Lady for a Day.
The Emperor Jones.
Thunder Over Mexico.
Doctor Bull.
I'm No Angel.
The World Changes.
The Kennel Murder Case.
The Prizefighter and the Lady.
The Mad Game.
Eskimo.
Design for Living.
Christopher Bean.
Cradle Song.
Counsellor-at-Law.
Alice in Wonderland.
Mr. Skitch.
Roman Scandals.
Queen Christina.

SOME EUROPEAN WORKS.

Among the conspicuously good foreign productions (besides "The Private Life of Henry VIII" and "Morgenrot") were:

German.

Der Hauptmann von Koepenick.
Eine Tuer Geht Auf.
Ich Will Nicht Wissen Wer Du Bist.
M.
Das Lockende Ziel.
Der Sohn der Weissen Berge.
Wiener Blut.
Quick, Koenig der Clowns.
Herthe's Erwachen.

French.

Sous la lune du Maroc.
Poil de Carotte.
Quatorze Juillet.
Mirages de Paris.

British.

Rome Express.
F. P. I.
Be Mine Tonight.
The Good Companions.

Russian.

Men and Jobs.
Pozor.
The Return of Nathan Becker.
Laughter Through Tears.

Italian.

Figaro e La Sua Gran Giornata.

Hungarian.

Piri Mindent Tud.

* * *

A Résumé of the Ten Best.

"CAVALCADE" was a magnificent contribution, so good that although it was a story of three decades of British life, beginning in 1900, it met with high favor all over the world. Miss Wynyard and Mr. Brook gave distinguished performances in the leading rôles and the staging of the varied scenes was even better than the stage work, a motion picture of a performance of which was exhibited by the producers; it had been made to guide the direction of the film. The pictorial version of "Cavalcade" evoked warm praise from the author of the play, Noel Coward.

"Reunion in Vienna" was another testimonial to Hollywood, for it reflected all the charm of the play from which it was adapted and the director, Sidney Franklin, took full advantage of the scope of the camera in his scenes.

"Morgenrot" ("Dawn"), a German picture, was a graphic story of a U-boat's activities during the World War. The direction was excellent and the acting wonderfully lifelike.

"State Fair" had the advantage of the cooperation of its author, Phil Stong. It was a wholesome and natural account of the experiences of a family at a State fair and Will Rogers and Janet Gaynor did capital work in the principal parts.

"Dinner at Eight" had the attraction of several screen luminaries in its cast. It possessed a reflection of life in many phases, including sharply humorous and tragic aspects. Besides the admirable acting of Miss Dressler, John and Lionel Barrymore, there were singularly compelling portrayals by Jean Harlow, Wallace Beery, Billie Burke and Edmund Lowe.

"Berkeley Square" was one of the most poetic features ever offered on the screen. It was a subject eminently well suited to shadow entertainment and in it Leslie Howard delivered a charming interpretation of the young American who found himself transported into the past of 150 years ago.

"The Private Life of Henry VIII," a British film, was a witty piece buffooning the much-married monarch. It was directed by Alexander Korda, who was responsible for "The Private Life of Helen of Troy," a silent production, and also of "Reserved for Ladies," one of the best films of 1932. In "The Private Life of Henry VIII" Charles Laughton gave a masterly portrayal of Henry.

"Little Women," which is still going the rounds of the theatres, attained the distinction of remaining at the huge Radio City Music Hall for three weeks, breaking all previous records. It was a remarkably tender and stirring story of the Sixties and in it Katharine Hepburn's acting excelled that of any of her previous film portrayals. Its very simplicity was gripping and its enormous success was looked forward to as a signal for the producers to make other pictures in the same wholesome, restrained manner.

"The Invisible Man," one of H. G. Wells's fantastic stories, was the best feature of the horror school. Claude Rains, who made his début in this picture, was actually beheld in it for only a half minute at the end of the narrative. Sometimes only his voice was heard and on other occasions he appeared as a terrifying object, with his face and head completely covered with bandages. It is another tale that can well boast of its originality.

"His Double Life" was a vastly amusing comedy in which Roland Young did the best work of his picture career. Another splendid portrayal in this offering was contributed by Lillian Gish. The narrative was an adaptation of Arnold Bennett's "Buried Alive," which was made into a play called "The Great Adventure." The film was well cast and Arthur Hopkins's direction was just what the strange story needed. It is a case of a famous but very timid artist whose valet dies and is buried in Westminster Abbey as the artist, while the latter assumes the name of his late valet. It was filled with genuinely humorous situations and there was not a weak moment in the film. It was an unusually well-thought-out comedy.

December 31, 1933

NOW MICKEY MOUSE ENTERS ART'S TEMPLE

He and Minnie Are Acclaimed as Classics by the Learned, but Walt Disney Creates Them With the Aid of Careful Mathematical Calculations, and Is Intent Chiefly on Earning a Living

By DOUGLAS W. CHURCHILL

HOLLYWOOD.

WALT DISNEY, the Horatio Alger hero of the cinema. . . . There is, perhaps, no more accurate way of summing up the life story of the farm youth, later newsboy, who through industry, courage and all the other Algerian virtues attained international recognition. In just two respects he differs from the hero of "Bound to Win." He has imagination and he has humor.

The world acclaims Walt Disney because he makes it laugh, and now his contribution to the gayety of nations is discovered to be art, wherefore the Art Workers Guild of London, filled with such Royal Academicians as Bernard Shaw, the Earl of Crawford and Laurence Binyon, has made him an honorary member. Yet all he has tried to do is to earn a living.

At 32 Disney is a leading producer of motion pictures. His stars, Mickey and Minnie Mouse, are the best-known shadows on the screen. The stores of the globe sell some 600 products—toys, clothes, books, clocks—bearing the cheery faces of Mickey or Minnie. And Disney takes it all very calmly.

He doesn't pose or put up a front. He has seen too much of hard struggle to be very deeply impressed by the to-do over him or by the tributes he receives in every mail. His attitude toward the public, his 175 employes and his product conflicts with every traditional attitude of the "practical" cinema.

• • •

APPARENTLY Disney has not analyzed very deeply what he is doing. Ask him why Mickey is a success and he replies, "Well, I don't know, but I guess"—and while the answer is not profound you sense that Disney is by instinct a competent craftsman who knows what he is doing but has not bothered much with theorizing.

He started by doing something he believed would entertain and he kept at it in spite of rebuffs. Cartoons were established before he entered the field in 1920. The only new idea he had was what they should be.

Until less than a year ago he worried about meeting his weekly payroll. Today, after his "Three Little Pigs" and his colored "Silly Symphonies," he contemplates spending $250,000 on a full-length feature based upon "Snow White and the Seven Dwarfs." If, after it is made, he thinks it will disappoint the public, he will destroy it. That is the one thing he is fanatical about. If quality is lacking he takes the loss immediately, knowing that he will profit in the end. And it is his own money, not that of stockholders.

Perhaps it was Disney's early life that gave him the understanding needed to appeal to world audiences. Born in Chicago, he grew up in rural Missouri among down-to-earth, middle-class people. He served as a candy-butcher on Midwest trains and saw the country and its inhabitants. He had a morning paper route in Kansas City. He worked in the postoffices there and in Chicago.

A natural mimic, he earned money in theatres by impersonating Charlie Chaplin when such turns were the menace of the hour. He tried vaudeville. Enlisted in the war, he decorated his ambulance with drawings that convinced the French that Americans were crazy. After the war he illustrated advertisements of farm products—he drew hens in nests overflowing with eggs from which hatched dollars. Then he made advertising slides for theatres, and when he had an idea for animating the subjects his employer let him take a camera home to experiment.

With a garage for a workshop he began making cartoon films which he sold to local theatres for 30 cents a foot. (To make one foot of Mickey Mouse film costs $25.) He tried cartoon fairy tales. Younger artists learning the trade helped him to make "Little Red Ridinghood," a spare-time occupation for all of them. "Ridinghood" encouraged him to quit his bread-and-butter job and form a company. They sold their films to a New York firm, which failed and took Disney's company down with it.

• • •

BY making motion pictures of children and selling cameras to parents he earned his fare to California. In 1923 he arrived in Hollywood with his drawing materials and $40. The defunct New York firm had let him take along a print of his last picture, but he found no market for it in Hollywood. After trudging about the studios, he mailed the film East. Weeks of waiting brought him a contract to make a new subject named Alice. He made sixty Alice films, then created Oswald the Rabbit, who is still in existence.

When Oswald showed a profit, Disney, then in New York, asked for money with which to improve the picture. The distributers said no, so he parted with them. On the train back to Hollywood he tried to think of a new character. He recalled a mouse that he had once trained to sit on his desk while he drew—a mouse with a personality. He decided to take it to the screen. With Mrs. Disney, who had been one of his artists, he drafted the first scenario of the new series, and when he reached Hollywood he was ready for work.

• • •

THEY called the figure "Mortimer Mouse," but that didn't seem right. Finally they thought of Mickey. His inamorata they called Minnie. Again a garage proved a haven of art, and there, Disney, with his brother Roy for business manager, and with Ubb Iwwerks for assistant artist, drew Mickey in the evenings and completed his Oswald contract in the daytime. He did not foresee any such popularity for Mickey as exists today, nor did he dream of reforming cartoon art. He was only bent on making a living.

Mickey was born in 1927, just when the movies were finding their voice and becoming the talkies. Two editions of Mickey were drawn before the Disney workers discovered that distributers were not interested in anything silent. They planned their third effort, "Steamboat Willie," for sound, and Mickey was an instant hit.

Hollywood producers now offered financing, but Disney knew that it would be perilous for his idea, for expenditures would be controlled and he would probably be embroiled in studio politics. He decided to go it alone. He began to supplement Mickey with the "Silly Symphonies" in order to provide a comparable feature for theatres prevented by competition from buying Mickey.

"Steamboat Willie" opened in the Colony Theatre, New York, in September, 1928. The first symphony, "The Skeleton Dance," was rejected as being gruesome until Disney booked it in Los Angeles and then, armed with enthusiastic press notices, went to New York and sold the idea to Roxy. It has grossed greater returns than any other picture he has made.

Such is the story of Walt Disney's start. Before he moved into his present plant—it cost $150,000—he had gone hungry, had lived with his brother in a one-room apartment in which they cooked and slept, and had managed with an office that rented for $5 a month. It was all fun, though, for it happened when he was young.

• • •

DISNEY today is little changed, his friends say, from the struggling artist of five years ago. He has a home in the Hollywood hills with a garden and a bathing pool. Swimming, ice-skating, polo and riding are his diversions. Seven of his studio associates play polo with him, but purely for recreation, unlike those actors and executives on other lots to whom the game is serious business. He mixes little in Hollywood night life, feeling that he cannot do good work if he loses sleep.

Knowing that incessant tension also is fatal to work calling for intelligence, imagination and humor, Disney tries to give his artists and writers two days a week for play. His ambition is to pay his employes well enough for them to save for old age and still enjoy living as they go along. Success is worthless, he says, if health is gone at middle age.

• • •

HE is little interested in books, but fond of sleight-of-hand tricks and mimicry. Often he regales his workers with some new trick or impersonation learned the night before. He is fond, too, of practical jokes. Thanks to the bucolic environment of his early life, his humor is elemental. Sometimes in his work it is too elemental, but those phases of it never reach the public.

At the studio he spends much of his time working on stories with his writers and artists. His office has none of the lavishness with which Hollywood executives usually surround themselves. From one wall pictures of Mickey and Minnie look down upon him at his dark oak desk. The other walls are plain.

There, when he discusses himself and his success he is almost indifferent, but when he talks of a picture or a plot he becomes animated, intense; his mimicry leaps out; he moves about impersonating the characters, making grotesque faces to stress his point. Interviewers who want to talk about his "uplift of the screen" annoy him; he doesn't want to be eulogized. Otherwise he talks freely and frankly.

What are his ideas about humor? "The proper comedy for the screen is visual," he says. "Films try to get too many laughs out of dialogue. We use pantomime, not wise-cracks. In 'Three Little Pigs' we used more talk than ever before.

"Portrayal of human sensations by inanimate objects such as steam shovels and rocking-chairs never fails to provoke laughter. Human distress exemplified by animals is sure-fire. A bird that jumps after swallowing a grasshopper is a 'natural.' Surprise is always provocative. We try to create as many laughs with gags as possible in a sequence and then give the situation a quick twist.

"Humor is something you have or haven't. We once brought in a professor to lecture the boys on the psychology of humor, but we had to give it up. None of us knew what he was talking about. We don't bother with a formula. We make the characters as human as we can so that what they do will seem logical to the audience. I play hunches and leave psychology to others."

What has made Mickey a world figure? "I don't know. Quality, perhaps. It is the thing we have striven most to put into our pictures. Abroad they feature our cartoons over the main picture. I guess the cartoon is something every one understands and likes. People may sense our endeavor to give them a quality product.

"We employ the best men we can find, and their ability shows in the pictures. I'm sorry that we can't give individual credit, but every subject is the product of a hundred minds. It is purely an organization creation. Perhaps abroad they suppose that one man does the whole thing and they are dazzled by it, which is unfortunate."

• • •

MICKEY MOUSE now speaks Spanish and French, and soon he will speak German. In the Orient and other far-away parts native titles are imposed on the action when it pays to do so; otherwise the English versions are projected without apologies, and the customers understand and like them. It is related that Douglas Fairbanks, on a world tour, won over a crowd of rebellious savage helpers by showing them a reel of Mickey. They decided that Fairbanks was their friend.

Disney is thinking much about his coming "Snow-White" venture. He says: "We will continue to follow our rule to put every cent of profit back into the business, for we believe in the future and what it will earn for us. I don't favor much commercialization. Most producers think it is better to get while the getting is good. We have not operated that way. Because we own our business we can dictate our policy.

"I am working toward longer films. We have made no profit from 'Pigs' because of the expense of making prints to supply the demand. Besides, we sold it at the black-and-white rate, which is one-third that of color. We shall profit this year, though, for we shall get a higher rental for our films.

"We have been asked to make 'Alice in Wonderland' with Mary Pickford. We have discouraged the idea, for we aren't ready for a feature yet. A feature picture will take eighteen months to make. We are now working on such a story. We will use a full symphony orchestra and fine singers. It will probably cost a quarter of a million. We've got to be sure of it before we start, because if it isn't good we will destroy it. If it is good, we shall make at least a million."

• • •

OTHER notes from the interviewer's pad: Disney believes that good films create all the publicity necessary. . . . "Pigs" went unnoticed in the first-run theatres. The neighborhood houses made it famous. . . . Most of the Disney craftsmen are in their twenties. . . . It takes eighteen months to get back the cost of a film. . . . Each story is photographed two or three times, and the sound is recorded several times, to insure perfection. . . . American theatres object to paying commensurate rentals for cartoons, although cartoons have often lured more people to the box office than feature pictures.

There has not been a censorship cut in a Disney film in four years. The last was over a cow. Since then all Disney cows have worn skirts. . . . Mickey and all other Disney characters have but three fingers and a thumb on each hand; the fourth finger gets in the way. . . . Artists often forget Mickey's tail, sometimes letting him go half a picture without it. . . . Fifteen people work in the New York office handling royalties on articles manufactured in Mickey's name. That's where the big profit is.

Previews are held for the entire Disney organization, and written criticisms are required. The wolf said "lousy." The wife of an employe questioned the word, and it was removed.

• • •

THE home life of those wonder-children of the cinema, Mickey and Minnie, is pleasant. Their mansion fronts on a wide boulevard. First are the business offices, behind which and encircling a green courtyard are offices and workrooms where writers and artists devise the antics of the pair. At one side is a sound stage. A cool, informal atmosphere prevails.

A library of fairy tales and folk music is the spring from which most ideas come. There is a staff whose sole job is to submit ideas. These are mulled over by Disney and two or three associates and are then given to the story department, which turns them into rough scripts outlining the trend of the yarn and establishing the scenes and the sequences for the action.

Every member of the editorial force has a copy of this synopsis and must return it at the end of two weeks with action and gags suggested. The story department takes the suggestions it wants. A shooting script is prepared and this is the story that will appear on the screen.

The creation of a cartoon film is purely mechanical. Two unchanging things form the foundation on which the film is built: The sixty-cycle electric impulse in the power line and the speed of film through a projection machine, which is ninety feet a minute, or twenty-four frames, or pictures, a second. The story department prepares a work sheet. The picture shall be 630 feet long, showing seven minutes on the screen, which means that 10,080 composite cartoons must be created. This total is divided into the number of feet and frames each scene will take.

The work sheet specifies the length of each shot; what Mickey is to do, and when; what he is to say; what sounds are to be heard, and what music played. The creation then passes into several channels which do not meet again until the film is finished.

• • •

THREE separate sound tracks are made, one for the dialogue, one for the noises, the third for the music, and the three are finally merged into one track. Suppose Mickey is to say "Hello." The word is spoken for him and recorded on the dialogue track. Cutters then read the recorded word in terms of frames. They find that the word takes ten frames. They mark this ten-frame space on the animator's sheet, and the artist draws his figure for those frames with the lips of Mickey speaking the word. In the end the dialogue is in its place on the first sound track and the rest of the 630-foot film is blank.

The noise men make their track in about the same way, except that their work neither governs nor is affected by the cartoonists. They know where a cow-bell is to ring, where Mickey is to be hit on the head, where a whistle will blow or a horse neigh. Their equipment is odd. A trombone is an airplane and a derby hat poked rapidly with a finger is a motorboat. A pinch of sand in the palm of the hand, worked with fingers close to the microphone is a giant eating celery.

The story department determines the tempo of the film both visually and musically. "Six time" is a beat every six frames. Each picture is drawn and recorded according to this musical beat. Through ear-phones the musicians hear a metronomic beat which keeps time with the frames of the running film, and they regulate their music by it. The three-ply sound track is completed before the cartoons are photographed, yet sound and drawing always match.

In making the cartoons the various scenes are penciled in, showing some of the action. The footage for every scene is allotted. The artists draw each scene in pencil, and this work is photographed and inspected. If it is satisfactory, the artist begins on the final draft. The backgrounds have been prepared by one artist; he has laid them out like stage sets, so that the characters can have freedom of action.

The story has been divided among four or five head animators, each of whom has his instructions in mathematical form. If it takes sixteen frames for Mickey to make one step, the animator draws numbers 1, 8 and 16, giving the extremes of the action. His assistant then draws 2 to 7 and 9 to 15 inclusive, and details and shadings are put in by apprentices.

• • •

THE drawings are made on paper 7 by 9 inches, one character to a sheet. At the bottom of each sheet are two register holes, which are standardized on all equipment in the studio, including the sheets of transparent celluloid now about to be mentioned. Girls in the tracing room place each drawing in a frame and lay a sheet of celluloid over it. They then trace in India ink on the celluloid the figure on the paper. Other girls reverse the celluloid sheet, or "cel," and make the figure opaque with gray or black paint. Only one character is placed on a sheet.

When all of the celluloid drawings for the entire footage have been finished they are sent to the camera room. Each camera is mounted above a table lighted by mercury bulbs. A frame the size of the "cels" is ready. First the background is laid down. Then a "cel" with Mickey, another with Minnie, a third with the villain and a fourth, which is blank, are slipped over the pegs, which hold them in perfect register. To the eye and the camera the picture appears to be on one sheet.

Compressed air clamps a glass pane over the drawings to remove wrinkles, the operator's hand touches the control button of the camera, a click is heard as the lens shutter blinks, a tiny bell rings, the air lifts the glass, and the photographer removes the "cels" and replaces them with the next set showing the progressive movement.

For seven minutes of screen entertainment the photographer goes through these laborious motions 10,080 times. The characters, by being placed on separate sheets, have complete freedom of movement. One figure can pass in front of or behind another without any thought on the artist's part.

So Mickey Mouse may be art, and Walt Disney may be a member of the Art Workers Guild, the only film man so honored. But he is in the business to earn a living, and his product is largely a creation of mathematics.

June 3, 1934

APOLOGY FOR GLORIA

IT may or may not have been an item for the raised eyebrow department when the news first began to be bruited about that Robert Riskin, scenarist for "Lost Horizon," had eliminated Miss Brinklow, the lady missionary, as one of the occupants of the kidnapped airplane in the James Hilton novel and substituted a certain Gloria—a pulchritudinous though cynical young woman who is neither a missionary nor a lady. This Gloria is of the "Mary, Pity Women" school of femininity. Having suffered at the hands of the male persuasion, she hates all men, coughs in a Camille-like manner and doesn't care when she dies. The salubrious air of the lamasery of Shangri La, however, rehabilitates both her lungs and her viewpoint, and she turns out to be a pretty wholesome sort after all.

Any one who wonders what young Mr. Hilton thought of the substitution, hoping for eventual tid-bits of pleasant gossip anent bickerings on the subject between the scenarist and the author, is doomed to disappointment. For this Hilton turns out to be an amenable young man, amiable almost to incredibility. There wasn't a peep out of him concerning the change, nor concerning the additional bright ideas on the part of Mr. Riskin (1) to induct Edward Everett Horton into the plane's passenger list as a paleontologist and a bit of comedy relief; and (2) to transform the Mallinson of the novel into a brother of the hero, Conway (Ronald Colman).

* * *

"After all," mildly comments Mr. Hilton, who wrote the novel in six weeks in order to pay an obstreperous landlord some back rent, "the passengers who were in the plane that was kidnapped from the Chinese city of Baskul and taken to Shangri La were a purely fortuitous group. It might just as well have been Gloria as Miss Brinklow who was crowded aboard as a last-minute rescue. The kidnapped passengers in my story were chosen for their adventure by chance. Chance might, therefore, just as well have made different selections. As a matter of fact, if I'd thought of Gloria while I was writing the book, I might have given her Miss Brinklow's seat in the airplane myself."

Could anything be a sweeter contrast to the authors who have charged Hollywood with anything from mayhem to slander because of story changes? Mr. Hilton, the arch-type of young man who would write a novel—and did—about a lamasery whose inmates practice "moderation in all things," is moderate himself—moderately tall, moderately slim, moderately shy, moderate in speech, moderate in dress.

Edward Everett Horton

Isabel Jewell

Continuing further in his peaceful attitude toward his scenarist, Mr. Riskin, and his director, Frank Capra, Mr. Hilton mildly remarked, with only a shade of a shadow of what is usually conceived as the British accent, "A novel is one thing, and a picture is another. A picture can be spoiled by being modeled either too closely on a novel, or not closely enough. The only thing an author can do is to trust the skill and judgment of his fellow-artists. And when those fellow-artists are the men who made 'It Happened One Night' and 'Mr. Deeds Goes to Town,' he doesn't have to worry. What does matter in the transmutation of a novel into a motion picture is the mood and underlying message. And these have been retained."

Ronald Colman

As for Riskin, the alchemist who transmuted the straight dun hair of Miss Brinklow to the golden curls of Gloria, played by Isabel Jewell in the picture (due Wednesday at the Globe, by the way) he nonchalantly declares that he made the change because he regarded the missionary as too much of a good thing.

"If you remember the book," he says, "Shangri La, the lamasery itself, and all its inhabitants, are steeped in an atmosphere already reverential enough, what with lamas and celebrants pad-padding all over the place, and High Lama ensconced in his holy-of-holies. To have brought in a missionary would have been to add an unnecessarily somber note to the proceedings. So we created the rôle of Gloria, quite a different kind of girl, because we wanted as colorful and varied a list of passengers on that eventual trip to Shangri La as we could gather together. There is real dramatic impact, moreover, in depicting the transforming effect of such a place of serenity and moderation on a girl like Gloria, who had been pretty much battered about, and had made a mess of things in her own world."

February 28, 1937

THAT HARDY PERENNIAL, THE SERIAL

HOLLYWOOD.

THE auditoriums of 4,000-odd American theatres presented a strange sight yesterday afternoon. In fact, they do every Saturday afternoon. More than a million youngsters, ranging in age from 5 to 17, undeterred by the line on the marquee which read "Special Kiddies' Matinee," thronged the neighborhood cinema temples to scream and shout. Garbo or Colbert or Gable may have been on the screen but the children had no time for them. They were there to see Chapter 6 of "The Mystery Rider" or "Gordon of Ghost City" or "The Adventures of Frank Merriwell." Art may come and art may go, but in the lives of young America the serial is the stable fare of the screen.

From the days of "The Perils of Pauline" and "The Diamond from the Sky," the chapter play has been a substantial, though unheralded, factor in celluloid entertainment. Politely despised by the artistically inclined of Hollywood, their title cards have carried the names of many of the industry's more famous players and directors. The serials have kept studios open in months of depression; they have saved the financial lives of thousands of exhibitors week after week. One man, Henry McRae, known in the industry as "the serial king," has made a fortune out of them. Most important, they are credited with giving generation after generation the habit of "going to the movies." When talkies came in the children were driven from the theatre; one serial, "The Indians Are Coming," was worth $20,000,000 to the industry, according to Will Hays, for it started the youngsters back to the movies.

Any one seeking a diverting afternoon can do no better than to find a neighborhood house on Saturday which advertises "Special Kiddies' Matinee." During the showing of the feature they will be unable to hear a word of dialogue uttered by the Duses of Hollywood. But when the serial flashes on, pandemonium ceases instantly. The audience hangs on every word There may be screams of delight and surprise. At exciting moments the shrieks of the customers may be ear splitting, but the bedlam in the theatre will be so synchronized with the dialogue and action on the screen that if a pin dropping in the play is a vital part of the plot, it will be heard distinctly. Both the audience and the producers know their serials.

* * *

The mature customers of today remember Pearl White, Ruth Roland, Helen Holmes and Marie Walcamp, the "big four" of early serials. They remember, too, Jack Holt, Grace Cunard, Lottie Pickford, Antonio Moreno, Anita Stewart, Kathleen Williams, Tom Santschi, Laura La Plante, Priscilla Dean, Art Acord, Ella Hall, Harry Carey and a dozen other celebrated names. They may cause embarrassment if they remember that Janet Gaynor, Irene Castle, Betty Compson, Reginald Denny, Helen Ferguson, George Brent and Doris Kenyon were one with Rin Tin Tin as stars of the chapter plays.

But if these people would rather not mention the days when they lived "on the other side of the tracks," not so with the directors. From the serial lots came John Ford of "The Informer," W. S. Van Dyke of "Thin Man" and "Rose Marie," Frank Lloyd of "Mutiny on the Bounty," Chester Franklin of "Sequoia" and Robert Z. Leonard, Alfred Green, Edward Sedgwick and John Blystone. It was a great school for the making of motion pictures. The drama was elemental, but it was drama. With the serial as a basis, the refinements could come later.

There are trends in serials as there are in all forms of the photoplay. Mysteries, Westerns and tales of the Northwest Mounted Police have lived through the years, but topical subjects and momentary heroes have their careers as well. Currently, the fantastic is desirable. But, when they were in the public eye, Gene Tunney, James J. Corbett, Red Grange and Ernie Nevers all were heroes of chapter plays. Success, for a serial producer, depends upon the ability to leap on the thing most engrossing to youth. Last year it was "Tailspin Tommy"; this year it's "Flash Gordon." Flash went to work at Universal this week.

No one seems to remember which was the first successful serial. McRae has been with Universal over twenty years, and before that he was with Colonel William Selig, and serials were a going institution when he joined the Laemmles. They reached their full flower around 1915, when the leading serial queen of the moment always was sure to defeat even Queen Mary Pickford in popularity contests. Then for eight or nine years they merely existed. McRae, who was head of Universal, believed that they would come back and always kept a serial company working even though the profits were not what they had been. But, good times or bad, they never lost money—something that cannot be said of any other form of Hollywood's art.

* * *

McRae thinks that the pictures of the Twenties were basic enough to be understandable to children and, being silent, permitted the youngsters to read their own interpretation into them. But, with the coming of sound, the young audiences fled. The industry was in a state of excitement around 1929-30 because the children were not going to the theatre. McRae believed that the time of the serial's renaissance was at hand and he threw "The Indians Are Coming" into production. Tim McCoy was the star. The plot utilized sound for the Indian language and capitalized on the sign language of the aborigines. It was a terrific success, and Hays wrote McRae that the picture was worth $20,000,000 to the industry because it brought the kiddies back.

Universal pays anywhere from $3,000 to $17,000 for picture rights to a good character. "Frank Merriwell" cost $5,000 and "Flash Gordon" cost $10,000. The stars receive from $1,000 to $5,000 a week and from six to eight weeks is the shooting schedule. Sound has added about 50 per cent to the cost and they now are budgeted at from $165,000 to $250,000 each. Their earning capacity is unlimited if released through the proper channels. There have been more million dollar profits from serials than from any other kind of picture.

Concocting the plays requires a special genius. McRae estimates he has made more than 100 of them, assisted by Ella O'Neill, who has been with him since 1914. Miss O'Neill had been a practicing attorney in Chicago and a specialist in languages. Today she copyreads every script for grammar and "morals." Generally, six to eight writers work on a plot.

There are a number of taboos not common in other films. The morals and language of hero and heroine must be watched most carefully. Neither may say "darn" and neither may smoke, drink, lie or murder, no matter what the situation. In "Flash Gordon" it was necessary for the heroine to feign affection for Voltan, the villain, in order to save Flash's life. The writers had her say that she didn't love Flash. Every member of the audience would have known she was lying, and so that wouldn't do. Finally, Miss O'Neill saved the day by having the girl say "You are a man; he is only a boy." That seemed to satisfy Voltan and the customers will regard her as pretty smart for getting out of a bad situation so cleverly.

* * *

The hero never may get revenge on the villain. He can bring him to justice, which is always good, but equally satisfying is the result if the villain falls into his own trap.

There can be no love scenes, and kisses are forbidden until the very last foot. The leads can show what they mean to each other, but that is all. It is quite a trick to pull them together close enough to be emphatic for a 5-year-old and not too obvious so as to bore a youth of 17. If love becomes too evident, the audience is apt to pull up the chairs.

Serials are made on the theory that they represent the spirit of American youth. They are the dime novels of today. Adventure is their theme, no matter what the subject-matter of the plot. And the plots must be logical within themselves. Not that the events that take place on the screen could occur—but, if they did, that is how they would happen. And each episode must be so carefully constructed that the ending forms a "pull-back," an event of sufficent import to make it necessary for the audience to return next week and to feel that life wouldn't be the same if they miss an episode. Unless that element is present, the serial has no purpose for the theatre men. And you would be surprised to learn how easily the stars get out of a menacing situation next week when all seems lost in the current episode.

The serial is a pretty virile institution to be labeled "Special Kiddies' Matinees."

D W. C.

January 26, 1936

VAMPIRES, MONSTERS HORRORS!

OFTEN, piercing the syncopation of the glittering Hollywood nights, there echoes the eldritch wail of the banshee; while outside studio doors howls the werewolf eerily, doing a stand in for the common, or timber, variety of door-step wolf. And usually, following these unearthly utterings, there is heard a steady clinking, as of good, round dollars pouring into the coffers of the cinema tycoons.

Only the other day, as a matter of fact, the shapely shade of Dracula's Daughter was glimpsed slowly materializing in the shadowy bourn just beyond Universal City, and preparing to follow in the fangprints of her cadaverous and quasi-anthropophagous pappy.

Once inside the Universal gates, she ought to feel right at home, for through those portals have passed the most hideous monsters of film history, to wit: the hunchback bell ringers, phantoms with operatic ambitions, Draculas, Frankensteih monsters of both sexes, werewolves and demented scientists who have been turning the million and one nights of the movies into one long Walpurgis Night for the past decade, and bringing back the swag for their creators.

For although it is generally conceded that superstition departed with the invention of the safety razor, horror films are still popular and profitable cinema entertainment. Frankenstein, for example, grossed almost a million dollars from its American showings alone.

Gloria Holden

And the contribution of the unearthly movies has not been to the strong box exclusively. Under the spur of having had to make ghouls and banshees measure up to their imaginary portraits, makeup, lighting, sound and camera men have all made enormous progress in their arts and sciences since the goblins first went Hollywood.

* * *

Horror films had their start in the old silent serials, notably "The Iron Claw," but the old timers were so exaggerated that they frightened only children and mental defectives. Few in those days thought of the uncanny as normal adult entertainment until Carl Laemmle Jr. began wondering whether Bram Stoker's old thriller "Dracula" might not be fun to do on the screen. But at that time Laemmle Jr. was himself a juvenile and his suggestions were not always taken seriously.

Others, however, were soon toying with the same dangerous thought. Among these were Lon Chaney and certain Teutons saturated with post-war Weltschmerz. Chaney wanted to act "Dracula" and often discussed the part with Tod Browning, who was to direct the picture ten years later. Both men believed the American public to be 90 per cent superstitious and ripe for horror films. Chaney had a full scenario and a secret makeup worked out even at that early date, but Browning held out for a talkie production.

Finally, in 1920, Chaney was able to get into action in "The Penalty," a horror opus of sorts in which he played a legless killer. Then the Germans scored with "The Cabinet of Dr. Caligari," a bona fide nightmare which S. L. Rothafel showed at the Capitol in 1921, and continued with another thriller, "The Golem." They made folks shiver and like it.

Emboldened by the success of these opera the Universal sorcerers cut loose, and in 1923 tried a feature with a central horror character. This was "The Hunchback of Notre Dame," with Chaney as a particularly knobby Quasimodo. The first persons to be horrified by this film were the producers themselves. The more they looked at Chaney clumping about his cathedral like an animated statue of arthritis, the less they felt like unleashing him upon the American public. Their fears were idle. The public reveled in it. It even outdrew the 101 Ranch Wild West Show in cow towns, and a year later Chaney, in "The Phantom of the Opera," a 100 per cent horror film, did even better.

* * *

But the real triumph of the spectral thrillers was reserved for the arrival of sound. In 1931 Carl Laemmle Jr., risen to production chief of Universal, was at last able to produce "Dracula," which had by then become a Broadway stage hit via London. No more inopportune time could have been selected, according to conservative opinion. The depression was approaching its nadir and there seemed to be quite enough horror around without any assistance from art. Furthermore, Chaney, the logical Dracula, was dead. Nevertheless, with a perverseness amounting to genius, the Laemmles made the film with Bela Lugosi, who had played the stage rôle of the vampire Count. It brought in half a million in America alone. "Frankenstein," produced a year later in still worse times, scored even more conclusively, with Boris Karloff as a brand new bugaboo. By one of life's little ironies, Lugosi, originally selected to play this synthetic ogre, disdained the part as dumb show: all makeup and no dialogue. He recommended Karloff, and thus became a Frankenstein in his own right, raising up a monster to outdo himself as the screen's pre-eminent fiend.

A triumvirate of horror: Bela (Dracula) Lugosi, be-caped and beclawed; Boris Karloff, Frankenstein's monster; and the late Lon Chaney, as The Phantom of the Opera, all delvers into the occult, the charnel and the plain horrendous, for Universal Films.

Karloff was such a sensation as the monster that he has scarcely been seen in human form since, except by his family and intimate friends. He played in "The Mummy" and "The Old Dark House," and then gave way to Claude Rains, who became the world's most self-effacing actor by playing nine reels unseen in "The Invisible Man." There followed a mass attack of hobgoblins in "The Black Cat," "The Bride of Frankenstein," "Werewolf of London," "The Raven" and "The Mystery of Edwin Drood" during 1934 and 1935. Now, with "The Invisible Ray" already released and "Dracula's Daughter" ready for her coming out party, the current film year seems fated for a bull market in lycanthropy and diabolic possession.

"Dracula's Daughter," incidentally, follows the grand tradition. Ever since "The Hunchback," each succeeding Universal horror film has had a player or director on its roster from the horror film preceding it to carry on the mystic formula. Even the director of "The Hunchback," Wallace Worsley, had previously directed "The Penalty." Chaney followed up "The Hunchback" with "The Phantom." Mary Philbin of "The Phantom" carried on in "The Man Who Laughs." Browning, Chaney's director, did "Dracula," and so on down to "Dracula's Daughter," directed by Lambert Hillyer, who did "The Invisible Ray."

* * *

Some of the best available authors, directors and players have been used in these spectral charades. Victor Hugo, Edgar Allan Poe, Mary Shelley, Dickens, J. B. Priestley, H. G. Wells, R. C. Sherriff and John Colton are among those who have written them, and Charles Laughton, Karloff, Lugosi, Rains, Zita Johan, Norman Kerry, Mary Philbin, Tully Marshall, John Boles, Colin Clive, Raymond Massey and Dudley Digges have been found on their cast lists with scores of other stage and screen celebrities. They are produced in deadly earnest. Bela Lugosi is authority for the statement that he plays his improbable Draculas and deranged chiropractors with the same high seriousness he used to give to his Romeo and Cyrano on the European stage. The studio prides itself, too, on the research in architecture, science and folklore lavished on the thrillers.

* * *

Perhaps, though, the real alchemists who turn goblins into gold are the make-up and electrical wizards at the studio, Jack Pierce and John Fulton. They work in secret and their dens are better guarded than the tower of any medieval magician. They are seen only by appointment. Pierce is the man who made Chaney's 72-pound "Hunchback" get-up, complete with rubber suit full of hunches, and he invented the Frankenstein monster out of thin air, no pictures of it existing before Karloff issued full panoplied from the mind of Jove, seven feet tall, with wooden shoes and tin head.

Fulton performs his miracles with lights and cameras. He it was who caused Claude Rains to act unseen and appal even the inhabitants of Bombay, India, where magicians are as common as boondogglers are here. His experiments advance camera art constantly. In 1933 it was necessary to retouch the film of "The Invisible Man" to get Rains out of sight. This year, Fulton made Karloff glow like a lightning bug in "The Invisible Ray" without using a bit of makeup, merely by filming him through special light filters.

Just at present Pierce's task is to perfect a makeup that will fit Gloria Holden, a newcomer to the cinema, to be "Dracula's Daughter," without blighting her dark beauty. Fulton is working with a "Rembrandt" type of light that will enable him to film the final scenes of the picture with Gloria in gray-green makeup, and five other characters in contrasting pinkish-red greasepaint. Together, they expect to make the female of the vampire species more deadly than the male when this first experiment in feminine diabolism is screened.

MUSICALS WITHOUT RHYTHM

By JANET GRAVES

HOLLYWOOD'S decision to reduce the number of musicals in future production schedules marks another turning point in the strange history of the music film. Throughout the talkie era, the quality of motion picture music has steadily risen. But, with regard to the use of that music, film makers have followed a more erratic course.

In the first tune-films, such as "Desert Song" and "Rio Rita," each musical number sneaked in apologetically on a dialogue song-cue, since the audience frequently snickered when the hero's soft words of love changed to a lyrical bellow. But gradually the more glaring absurdities were smoothed over, and we see the present-day descendants of those pioneer musical romances in the extravaganzas starring Jeanette MacDonald and Nelson Eddy. Here Hollywood has finally succeeded in gracefully recording upon film the long-beloved stage operetta, with all its quaint conventions, its rousing male choruses and ecstatic duets.

* * *

In contrast to the patent artificiality of the first operettas, the backstage realism of the "Broadway Melody" of 1929 was refreshing. In this film all music was strictly accounted for on realistic grounds, either as rehearsal or stage performance or "Listen to this little number I've just dreamed up." The same cautious plan has been followed by most tune-films, through "Forty-second Street" to the vehicles of Alice Faye, the Ritz Brothers, and the transplanted grand opera stars. This type would more accurately be designated a comedy with musical interludes, since it neatly evades the problems of blending movie and music.

The early sound cartoons had no need to fall back upon either stage conventions or backstage atmosphere. They were never afraid of music. They seized upon it eagerly, set all their creatures capering in time to lively tunes, played the harp on the old man's whiskers and the zylophone on the skeleton's ribs, translated an arpeggio into an arc of flying leaves stripped from a willow sapling. Today the world of "Snow White and the Seven Dwarfs" is dominated by music.

But the real world does not normally move to the measured rhythms of music. Those films which are photographs of real people against real backgrounds have therefore progressed more slowly than cartoons in harmonizing sight and sound. "Monte Carlo" was able to introduce its songs without embarrassment because the motions of its characters often forsook realism for the sprightly stylization of Lubitsch comedy. René Clair, working in France, brought the music film down from the glitter of the mythical kingdom to the rowdy streets of Paris, crowded with warbling butchers and bakers and artists and prancing crooks and cops.

During 1932 there was a short-lived upsurge in the freedom of imagination granted to the music film. Clair's "A Nous la Liberté" made it seem natural that blossoms on a bough should sing in childish voices. In "This Is the Night" we heard all Paris—top-hatted citizens, turning taxi-wheels and radio-beams from the Eiffel Tower—echoing one gay melody. Rouben Mamoulian's "Love Me Tonight" was a textbook of the music film. Every member of the cast sang. Songs skipped from room to room of the castle, were relayed blithely across country, grew from the sounds of awakening Paris. The whole film, picture as well as sound-track, was saturated with rhythm.

* * *

It was probably their predilection for satire and phony Continental atmosphere that cast a box office blight on the musicals of 1932. Hollywood made no distinctions. It tossed overboard, along with the whimsies of gay Paree, the whole deliberate campaign to make us believe the lovely myth of a world ruled by music. But the creation of such an illusion is still the objective of the music film, however oblique the approach has become. Though film-makers now usually feel called upon to excuse the music by making their lead characters stars of stage, radio or screen, they are inconsistent in accounting for each song. "Big Broadcast of 1938" gave us both "The Waltz Lives On," a lavishly staged production number, and "Thanks for the Memory," a reconciliation scene which simply happened to be expressed in musical terms.

The problems of the music film have always centered around that crucial moment when the player stops talking and begins to sing, or stops walking and begins to dance. The solution is in sight when a film can persuade us that singing and dancing are as normal modes of human behavior as talking and walking. For this reason, players like Fred Astaire and Bing Crosby, who seem to take to rhythmic expression spontaneously, are proving more valuable to the music film than the most gifted opera stars. Crosby's casual, conversational style of singing, requiring no elaborate introduction, slides easily into the loose structure of his amiable comedies. In a well-constructed music film, it would be difficult to find that crucial dividing line. Astaire half-strolled, half-danced through the gardens while he sang "Foggy Day" in "Damsel in Distress." The walking-the-dog sequence in "Shall We Dance?" without any definite dance-steps, was completely rhythmic.

And the music which accompanied that sequence could not be precisely classified either as a special number or as part of the humble incidental score. If film-makers would give equal attention to all the music throughout, it would be possible for the music film to achieve a musical continuity as logically integrated and smoothly flowing as the story continuity of a good dramatic film. Then the union between music and movie might be strong enough to carry the weight of even a serious theme.

June 19, 1938

MEDICOS IN THE MOVIES

THE first physician in the history of motion pictures to advocate socialized medicine will arrive here soon in the person of Dr. Manson, principal character in A. J. Cronin's story "The Citadel," which follows "Stablemates" into the Capitol Theatre. And since Dr. Manson represents the loftiest medical ideals ever attributed to a screen hero, it might be interesting here to take a backward glance at a few of the various doctors who have preceded him on the screen, on the stage and in the novel. Of these there have been hundreds, some good, some bad—specialists, routine practitioners and quacks.

One of the earliest characters to win popularity in the doctor's role belonged to medieval folklore. His name was John Faustus. He made his appearance during the Reformation, when chemistry was a new science, and he was considered to be in league with the Evil One. In 1587 Christopher Marlowe made this same character the tumultuous hero of his play "Dr. Faustus" and imbued him with a nascent spirit of reform that led him to rebel against the confines of science. About 1775 Goethe, going to folklore for his source material, wrote "Faust," greatly ennobling the doctor protagonist and making him a symbol of struggle and hope.

During the Eighteen Nineties an American adaptation of this play toured the United States with great success, thanks to the acting of a popular player.

* * *

The hero-villain propensities of Marlowe's "Dr. Faustus" were utilized by Robert Louis Stevenson in "Dr. Jekyll and Mr. Hyde," produced in 1920 as a silent movie (and in 1932 as a talkie). From this point on villainy in doctors grew exceedingly popular, especially in pictures like "The Cabinet of Dr. Caligari," "Doctor X," "The Amazing Dr. Clitterhouse" and the "Dr. Fu Manchu" series.

Ramifications in the character of the physician are as numerous as they are interesting. Balzac makes Dr. Benassis, in "The Country Doctor," beneficent and kindly and something of a progenitor of Dr. Manson in "The Citadel." Baudelaire makes the doctor an unconscious amorist who attracts women with his white apparel and scalpel. Proust makes Dr. Cottard in "Swann's Way" a medical bounder.

With the development of realism physicians talk specifically of research, formulas and laboratory methods. Emile Zola's "Doctor Pascal" is a specialist in heredity. Ibsen's doctor in "A Doll's House" is a symbol of disease and disintegration. Flaubert's doctor in "Madame Bovary" presents the first photographic description of suicide. George Bernard Shaw's doctor in "The Devil's Disciple" was a reformer. One of the most lovable doctors of the Nineties was Dr. Lavender in Margaret Deland's "The Awakening of Helena Richie."

* * *

The screen has kept pace with medical development and reform. The larger aspects of medicine were presented in "Pasteur," a dramatic study of microbe discovery, and in "Yellow Jack," which treated the particular pursuit of the yellow fever germ. The forthcoming picture, "Triumph Over Pain," by René Fulop-Miller, discusses the discovery of anesthesia and its use.

The screen has shown also the doctor's professional, economic and ethical problems in pictures like "Arrowsmith," "Dr. Monica," "Main Street" and "Of Human Bondage," and the responsibilities of the interne in "Men in White" and "Young Dr. Kildare," now on view at the Radio City Music Hall.

October 30, 1938

SWEETS SWEEPSTAKES

By THOMAS M. PRYOR

"IS popcorn here to stay?" That's the $64 question being bounced back and forth by the nation's motion-picture theatre operators at the moment. Some say yes, some say no and some say maybe. But whether popcorn stays or goes, the fact is that the sale of the crunchy stuff in movie houses has reached astronomical proportions. Exactly how much theatres are earning in "extra profits" is anybody's guess, but no one denies that the total runs into many millions and that the returns on popcorn are far out ahead of those on candy and soft drinks. The last two are, however, steadily increasing in sales volume.

Approximately 85 per cent of the nation's 16,000 movie houses, from the modest little places in the backwoods to the glittering palaces in the big cities, are keeping their customers happily stuffed with sweets. In fact, some theatre men say that they make bigger profits on such sales than they do by showing Hollywood's celluloid corn. The weekly gross in popcorn and candy sales—some theatres also offer peanuts and ice cream—ranges all the way from a modest $50 for a hole-in-the-wall theatre to several thousand dollars in larger and more ornate establishments. For instance, the Fox Theatre in St. Louis, a 5,000-seater, reportedly averages $4,000 a week on its sweet-tooth customers.

According to a spokesman for a theatre chain, who has kept close tabs on the situation, few houses gross less than $100 a week on popcorn and candy. "Multiply $100 by 16,000 theatres," he said, "and what do you get?—$1,600,000 per week. Now multiply that by fifty-two weeks. That gives you $83,200,000, a very conservative estimate," he said airily.

Profits

The lion's share of the "take" is from popcorn sales, since the return on the corn is at least 50 per cent. Candy, it is estimated, leaves a margin of from 30 to 40 per cent for the theatre and soft drinks just about the same, depending on whether a theatre serves fountain or bottle drinks. Of course, operating costs must be deducted, but there is no possible way of setting an average, since it develops that investment by theatres in display counters runs all the way from a few dollars to more than $7,000.

Out in the Midwest and along the Pacific Coast the candy displays and service counters in theatres are said to be especially lavish affairs, complete with neon tubing lights. According to reports, some of these sweet treat bars cost considerably more than $7,000. In one large circuit of Western theatres the management holds "sweet treat" intermissions. After each performance the house lights are turned up and pretty candy butchers, dressed in evening gowns, pass up and down the aisles. They don't hawk their wares, however, as the white-coated butchers used to do in nickelodeon days.

Up to about five years ago popcorn had no place in movie house operations and candy was obtainable mostly from vending machines, operated by concessionaires. Some of the enlarged candy display stands in theatre lobbies today are still operated on a commission basis. However, the trend now is to push the concessionaires out. The Fox West Coast Circuit, the Paramount Circuit and the Balaban & Katz theatre chain in Chicago are among the larger theatre circuits now running their own popcorn and candy business.

Popping Corn

Film trade journals are crammed with advertisements for corn poppers and warmers. Quite a number of houses pop their own corn right where the customers may observe the operation; other theatres take "popped" corn from jobbers and merely warm it up before serving. The popping of corn in theatres is a ticklish undertaking, since the poppers give off considerable odor and, of course, a lot of folks are sensitive to the smell of hot cottonseed oil.

Some theatre men hold popcorn will eventually drive more people out of movie houses than Hollywood's best pictures will be able to drag in. Already there are signs of revolt. Loew's houses in St. Louis have banned popcorn in recent weeks and in Kansas and Indianapolis some theatres have instituted checking services for patrons bringing packages of corn. Moreover, popcorn and candy sales are producing legal headaches for theatre owners. In Louisville a landlord has filed suit against a tenant, claiming that candy sales should be included in the "gross receipts" of the theatre in computing the rent due under the terms of the lease.

Public Service

While popcorn is decried by some theatre managers as a source of annoyance to patrons who have little or no taste for the fodder, all appear to agree that candy goes hand-in-hand with one's enjoyment of a picture. "People like to eat sweets," they argue. "By making candy available in the theatre we are adding an extra measure of enjoyment for our patrons." Anyway, the candy manufacturers are highly in favor of the idea, for it is estimated that this means of merchandising chocolates has increased the industry's sales by more than $30,000,000 annually. A representative of the Association of Manufacturers of Confectionery and Chocolate allowed that the figure didn't sound "unreasonable," though he added that he had no accurate statistics available.

The latest wrinkle in the search for "extra profits," however, has been supplied by the Century Circuit, which has opened a doughnut shoppee next to one of its theatres in Brooklyn. Next thing you know you'll be able to get anything from toothpaste to inner tubes in a movie theatre—just like in drug stores.

February 23, 1947

THE SCREEN IN REVIEW

'The Wizard of Oz,' Produced by the Wizards of Hollywood, Works Its Magic on the Capitol's Screen

THE WIZARD OF OZ, screen play by Noel Langley, Florence Ryerson and Edgar Allan Woolf; adapted from the book by L. Frank Baum; musical adaptation by Herbert Stothart; lyrics by E. Y. Harburg and music by Harold Arlen; special effects by Arnold Gillespie; directed by Victor Fleming; produced by Mervyn LeRoy for Metro-Goldwyn-Mayer. At the Capitol.

Dorothy .... Judy Garland
Professor Marvel (the Wizard) .... Frank Morgan
Hunk (the Scarecrow) .... Ray Bolger
Zeke (the Cowardly Lion) .... Bert Lahr
Hickory (Tin Woodman) .... Jack Haley
Glinda (the Good Witch) ..... Billie Burke
Miss Gulch (the Wicked Witch) .... Margaret Hamilton
Uncle Henry .... Charles Grapewin
Auntie Em .... Clara Blandick
Nikko .... Pat Walshe
With the Singer Midgets as the Munchkins.

By FRANK S. NUGENT

By courtesy of the wizards of Hollywood, "The Wizard of Oz" reached the Capitol's screen yesterday as a delightful piece of wonder-working which had the youngsters' eyes shining and brought a quietly amused gleam to the wiser ones of the oldsters. Not since Disney's "Snow White" has anything quite so fantastic succeeded half so well. A fairybook tale has been told in the fairybook style, with witches, goblins, pixies and other wondrous things drawn in the brightest colors and set cavorting to a merry little score. It is all so well-intentioned, so genial and so gay that any reviewer who would look down his nose at the fun-making should be spanked and sent off, supperless, to bed.

Having too stout an appetite to chance so dire a punishment, we shall merely mention, and not dwell upon, the circumstance that even such great wizards as those who lurk in the concrete caverns of California are often tripped in their flights of fancy by trailing vines of piano wire and outcroppings of putty noses. With the best of will and ingenuity, they cannot make a Munchkin or a Flying Monkey that will not still suggest, however vaguely, a Singer's midget in a Jack Dawn masquerade. Nor can they, without a few betraying jolts and split-screen overlappings, bring down from the sky the great soap bubble in which the Good Witch rides and roll it smoothly into place. But then, of course, how can any one tell what a Munchkin, a Flying Monkey or a witch-bearing bubble would be like and how comport themselves under such remarkable circumstances?

And the circumstances of Dorothy's trip to Oz are so remarkable, indeed, that reason cannot deal with them at all. It blinks, and it must wink, too, at the cyclone that lifted Dorothy and her little dog, Toto, right out of Kansas and deposited them, not too gently, on the conical cap of the Wicked Witch of the East who had been holding Oz's Munchkins in thrall. Dorothy was quite a heroine, but she did want to get back to Kansas and her Aunt Em; and her only hope of that, said Glinda, the Good Witch of the North, was to see the Wizard of Oz who, as every

Judy Garland

one knows, was a whiz of a Wiz if ever a Wiz there was. So Dorothy sets off for the Emerald City, hexed by the broomstick-riding sister of the late Wicked Witch and accompanied, in due time, by three of Frank Baum's most enchanting creations, the Scarecrow, the Tin Woodman and the Cowardly Lion.

• • •

Judy Garland's Dorothy is a pert and fresh-faced miss with the wonder-lit eyes of a believer in fairy tales, but the Baum fantasy is at its best when the Scarecrow, the Woodman and the Lion are on the move. The Scarecrow, with the elastic, dancing legs of Ray Bolger, joins the pilgrimage in search of brains; the Woodman, an armor-plated Jack Haley, wants a heart; the Cowardly Lion, comicalest of all, is Bert Lahr with an artistically curled mane, a threshing tail and a timid heart. As he mourns in one of his ballads, his Lion hasn't the prowess of a mow-ess; he can't sleep for brooding; he can't even count sheep because he's scared of sheep. And what he wants is courage to make him king of the forest so that even being afraid of a rhinocerus would be imposerus. Mr. Lahr's lion is fion.

There, in a few paragraphs, are most of the elements of the fantasy. We haven't time for the rest, but we must mention the talking trees that pelt the travelers with apples, the witch's sky-written warning to the Wizard, the enchanted poppy field, the magnificent humbuggery of Frank Morgan's whiz of a Wiz and the marvel of the chameleonlike "horse of another color." They are entertaining conceits all of them, presented with a naive relish for their absurdity and out of an obvious—and thoroughly natural—desire on the part of their fabricators to show what they could do. It is clear enough that Mr. Dawn, the make-up wizard, Victor Fleming, the director-wizard, Arnold Gillespie, the special effects wizard, and Mervyn LeRoy, the producing wizard, were pleased as Punches with the tricks they played. They have every reason to be.

August 18, 1939

HAIL TO A NEW AND FAREWELL TO AN OLD TARZAN

Lex Barker Strips for Action as Johnny Weissmuller Covers in New Jungle Job

By BARBARA BERCH

HOLLYWOOD.

OFFHAND, looking casually at a fellow named Lex Barker, there's nothing to distinguish him from a thousand other giants in Hollywood who stand six feet four inches, weigh two hundred pounds, wear shoulder-length hair and hang out at Schwab's Drug Store. But Barker is different—'way different—for he's a man with a steady job, and that's practically an anachronism in this sad town these days.

Barker was recently chosen to be the new Tarzan, replacing Johnny Weissmuller, who held the job for seventeen fat and fruitful years. But, as must to all men, age and flabbiness have come to Johnny, forcing the Tarzan keepers to start up a new wonder man with leaner, tighter lines. Johnny, meantime, will continue to yodel it out in the jungle in a new series titled "Jungle Jim," in which he will wear a shirt and pants and grow old less athletically.

Barker thus becomes the screen's tenth Tarzan, continuing a brawny monosyllabic tradition that started back in 1919 with a chunky character named Elmo Lincoln and has continued profitably to this day to become the longest single series of pictures in the history of the screen. There has always been a Tarzan, and as long as men are men and chimpanzees are—um—chimpanzees, there'll always be one.

Twenty-three Tarzan epics have been made since that first silent-picture muscle man started swinging through the trees. In the last fifteen years, they have turned out to be the biggest consistent money-making bonanza in the business. Charley Chan, the Hardy family and the Falcon may come and go, but Tarzan goes on forever.

Tarzan's producer, Sol Lesser, takes time out from counting the profits long enough to explain the reasons behind the series' phenomenal popularity.

"Tarzan is pure escapist entertainment," he starts, grandiosely. "He is the original superman fighting for the rights of the downtrodden and the persecuted against all villains, be they human or beast. He rules with a minimum of words—hence, he is understood by all. Rarely does Tarzan get gooey with Jane. Thus, the kids love him, and so do the old folks."

That's the producer talking, a rich and happy man. Other explanations for Tarzan's continuing success simply place him in a class with the funny papers, which are read more regularly by more people than any other published work in the world.

All the Tarzan pictures are made well—most of the late ones costing close to a million dollars—and usually they more than triple their investment before they are finished. "Tarzan and the Amazons" (1944) and "Tarzan and the Leopard Woman" (1945) are currently being double-billed again and making twice as much money this time around as they did singly in their original showings. They never date, age cannot wither them.

In our own small towns, and especially abroad, where the men

Johnny Weismuller

don't grow to quite such spectacular proportions, the Tarzans are always ready money in the bank. In Africa, for instance, they clean up. The fascinated natives watch as Tarzan, the fearless, slays lion, tiger and alligator—all with his ketchup-covered rubber dagger. Looks easy when Tarzan does it, but when they stalk up to the nearest beast breathing the same kind of fire, someone always gets hurt.

Most of the Tarzans have been real athletes. Weissmuller, of course, was an Olympic swimming champion; so was Buster Crabbe, the seventh Tarzan. Eighth Tarzan, Herman Brix (now known as Bruce Bennett), was an Olympic weight-lifting star, and Glenn Morris, interim ninth Tarzan, a decathlon winner. Frank Merrill, the fifth, and one of the silent-picture Tarzans, was originally a fireman who, after shedding his clothes for the g-string of the jungle, promptly fled the screen and went into politics.

The Tarzans are chosen for their bodies, of course—a rippling fluid arrangement of bones and flesh, instead of bar-bell biceps and power-house thighs, and also for a peculiar dead-pan facial expression which allows them to make like wild men without looking like asses.

When Metro-Goldwyn-Mayer was preparing its first try at the series in 1932, production hit a snag when a proper Tarzan couldn't be found. Finally, Weissmuller, swimming leisurely at the Hollywood Athletic Club pool, was discovered by the scenarist and the director when one of them pointed to him and said, "There—now, what we need is a guy with a blank look like that—see?" Weissmuller continued to swim—without changing his million-dollar expression—right into the juiciest job a man ever held in Hollywood.

Barker is a new type for the series. A trained actor, he was born in New York, educated at Phillips-Exeter and Princeton, and specializes in skiing instead of swimming. No one has figured out just where the giant slaloms are going to fit in with the alligator dumps and the elephant quarries, but Barker is flexible and prepared to forget everything he learned at college—the proper attitude for any neophyte Tarzan, who has to do it Dumbo-style, remember.

Other sacrifices, so far, have been fifteen pounds of excess flesh which were rolled off on the steam-tables at Terry Hunt's, and a Princeton crew-cut which he loved but gladly gave up in the interests of gold. Does he mind letting his hair grow and taking the ribbing he's getting from everyone in town?

"Are you kidding?" he booms unbelievingly. "Why, I'd let it grow down to my knees for a job like this!"

Lex Barker

Twenty-eight-year-old Barker, who put in a five-year Army stretch during the war, emerging as a major, is married and the father of two children. He appeared in summer stock and briefly on Broadway before coming to Hollywood in 1945. His movie appearances have been short and spaced, in such films as "The Farmer's Daughter," "Mr. Blandings Builds His Dream House" and the "Velvet Touch."

However, with actors dying of starvation these days, Barker was feeling the hot breath of the public soup-kitchens on his own neck just about the time the Tarzan ten-strike came up. And for the kind of money he expects to make for the next fifteen or twenty years he's willing to forget he ever met Loretta Young to flirt with any chimpanzee the producers dig up. Undoubtedly, the most violently eager of all the Tarzans!

Actually, the job does call for almost unlimited love for animals. Trained denizens of the jungle appear regularly in the series, and the great white father must be able to get along with them or hightail it back to Gower Gulch, Hollywood's no-man's land. Weissmuller took the treat-'em-rough tack with all the chimps which played Cheetah, Tarzan's best friend, socking them up a bit before each scene and usually winding up with both their hairy arms around him. None the less, he has a great collection of scars and bites on his legs and arms to show for his trouble. In his new "Jungle Jim" series, Weissmuller is chucking chimps to feature a mild little talking bird. After seventeen years, he's plain tired of wooing the ugly monsters.

Soon as Barker got the chimps to love him, the latest Tarzan picture got under way, called "Tarzan and the Fountain of Youth." The theme, of course, has brought on the best of the new Hollywood gags. "Tarzan and the fountain of youth?" the boys snicker. "Yeah, Johnny dives in—and it comes out Lex!"

January 2, 1949

Movie Crisis Laid to Video Inroads And Dwindling of Foreign Market

By THOMAS E. MULLANEY

Domestic motion picture companies have reached a turning point, the result of the convergence of a series of unfavorable developments which seem certain to lead the industry to a position of lesser importance among the nation's industries, according to financial observers.

The sharp decline in the industry's overseas markets and the expanding inroads on domestic film revenues being carved by television have combined to bring about a serious decrease in the motion-picture industry's profits. Added to these adverse factors, which are increasing incessantly, is the apparent loss of the major producers' ten-year fight to retain control of their theatre operations.

The producers themselves will admit to the seriousness of their financial situation, but none will detail it. Last week, for instance, the industry's executives received a detailed report on conditions from Eric Johnston, president of the Motion Picture Association of America, at a closed meeting. Out of this came only limited information for publication.

1947 Figure Withheld

The MPA would not divulge profit-and-loss figures for 1948, stating merely that the industry's domestic gross last year was 8.5 per cent below that in 1946, but was as good as that in 1945. No comparison was revealed for 1947. Up to the present only one major company has issued its financial statement for 1948. That was Universal Pictures Company, Inc., which reported a net deficit of $3,162,812 for the year ended on Oct. 31, contrasted with a net profit of $3,230,017 for the preceding twelve months. Restrictions on dollar remittances from foreign markets, a decline in theatre attendance and higher costs of production were blamed for the financial reversal.

Unfavorable operating reports are expected from other companies, although all are expected to show profits. Marius S. Jalet, a security analyst, has estimated the industry's income in 1948 before taxes and foreign income at $110,500,000, compared with $150,600,000 for 1947 and with $218,300,000 for 1946. He maintains that the industry's profit for 1948 could be considerably more than 24 per cent below the figure for 1947 and that it will be at least 50 per cent under the earnings in 1946.

Inroads of British Films

The declining trend is serious enough in itself, but there are two recent factors in the picture which render prospects even more ominous. One is England's determination to afford greater competition to the American industry and the other is the loss of the important income heretofore provided by the operation of theatre chains. England, of course, has always been the most important factor in the American film industry's overseas income.

The American film industry began to be deprived of its large revenues from England in 1947 when an "ad valorem" duty of 75 per cent was levied on income of imported films. Some measure of relief was obtained last July with the signing of a four-year pact with the British, whereby Hollywood studios agreed to leave in that country as "blocked sterling" all their sterling revenues from film rentals except for a basic amount of $25,000,000 and an amount equal to what British films earned here.

Loans Bolster English Films

A new restriction, however, was introduced last October when England imposed quotas on the playing time to be allowed American films on British screens. This reduced playing time of American films from over 80 per cent to 50 per cent. The latest unfavorable development occurred on Feb. 2, last, when the British Parliament approved a bill creating a national agency to lend money to the country's producers.

Loss of their theatres (which seems certain for all American companies now that Paramount has signed an anti-trust consent decree with the Department of Justice) is expected to cause a sharp reduction in the industry's income and a similarly sharp reduction in the total output of feature films, according to Mr. Jalet.

Overshadowing everything else is the uncertain influence that television will exert. It could be tremendous, and yet it could be the salvation of the domestic film industry: that is, if the motion picture companies can succeed in obtaining an interest in the television media. Film companies have not been overly anxious to take such a step yet, and some doubt exists whether they would be permitted by Government regulatory agencies to do so.

February 27, 1949

Double Feature—Movies and Moonlight

Drawing by Carl Rose

The Drive-in—"It may not represent the sophisticate's idea of a glamorous evening, but it has captured the fancy of millions."

A great new force, the movie drive-in, alters some of America's habits—and the landscape.

By MARGUERITE W. CULLMAN

MOTORING through much of the countryside of Europe, the imposing outline of a great cathedral ahead or the graceful spires of a smaller church usually are the first indication that you are approaching a town. Driving through America—and especially the Southern and Western sections—a less romantic symbol is often the avant-courier of the town to come; it is the great, blank, precise rectangle of the elevated screen, signature of the drive-in movie theatre.

The first drive-in was built near Camden, N. J., in 1933, and within a few years duplicates were scattered all over the country. These early outdoor movies rarely accommodated more than 100 cars and were likely to resemble an enclosed cow pasture, motorized. The outbreak of war pegged the growth at 160, but when building was resumed after the war more elaborate versions were built and the number leaped in 1948 to 800; in 1949 to 1,100; and by early spring of 1950 to 1,753. Now, according to latest figures, over 2,100 (more than 10 per cent of the number of conventional, enclosed moving picture houses) dot the landscapes of forty-eight states.

Statistics of a recent national survey indicate that these drive-ins show an average of accommodations for 447 cars each, and that every car contains 2.34 adults and .94 children, making a macabre total of three and a quarter people to a car. At capacity attendance that would mean an audience of 1,453 in each of the 2,100 drive-ins, or normally three million people gathering at sunset for the first show, with an equal number replacing them for the second performance, making a total of six million people a night.

NO two of these drive-ins are identical, but in general they may be said to follow a similar pattern. The amount of land involved is considerable, with a basic requirement of at least ten acres to enter for every five hundred cars. This is necessary to allow cars to enter through a toll gate, circulate in the theatre, and exit generally by a different route. The entire area must be paved, or at least finished with a hard surface. A square, or nearly square, site is considered the most desirable, with a large screen from 35x45 to 53x72 feet located catty-corner in one angle of the square.

MARGUERITE W. CULLMAN *is well known in entertainment circles as the backer of a hundred Broadway productions and as the former editor of a drama magazine.*

Ramps are laid out in a semi-circle from a point in front of the screen and are spaced about twenty-five feet apart to leave an aisle between. These ramps form a series of front-upped terraces facing the screen, so that when a car parks with its front wheels on the crest of the terrace the passengers sit back and look upward as they do in a conventional theatre.

Sound is brought to the cars parked along these ramps by a network of wires laid under the paving, with each wire terminating in a speaker post. Each post has a pair of speakers which resemble portable microphones and are equipped with separate volume control to serve the two cars on the right and left.

Although the area must be reasonably dark to show the pictures, drive-ins can't be blacked out. By putting blue and amber lights on high poles toward the back of the theatre a sort of artificial moonlight is provided, giving sufficient light so that the patron who leaves his car can see clearly where he is going.

Rest rooms and refreshment stands usually are located in a low building somewhere toward the center of the area. Here are sold, besides the usual popcorn, soft drinks and ice cream, such heartier fare as frankfurters, hamburgers and other sandwiches. As this source of revenue often provides as much as 50 per cent of the entire "take" of the drive-in, ample and attractive space is allotted. To take care of those too firmly wedded to the comfort of their own cars to get out and shop, most of the theatres have small carts which are pushed around the ramps during the show, offering easy car-side service.

The rest of the drive-in, its general décor and location, is purely individual and varies from the most modest little construction, handling no more than two hundred cars, to the most de luxe landscaped affair with ponds or lakes and accommodations for as many as 2,000 cars.

WHO fills these cars? And why do they choose this medium of entertainment?

Owners and sponsors of the drive-ins feel that in three-quarters of their patrons they have tapped a practically prehistoric strain of human—the hitherto non-movie-goer. Lest this give rise to an unwarranted optimism, let us hasten to say that this is not based upon their being lured with a superior product. On the contrary, the majority of the patrons admit that the movies are generally older and often less desirable than those offered at a more conveniently located, conventional, enclosed moving picture house. Certainly the admission price, at least for adults, is no inducement. And yet, they cheerfully will take a longer trip to see a less appealing show and pay as much or more money. The people who do this include:

Married couples with one or more young children for whom they either cannot afford or cannot secure baby sitters. It is not at all unusual to see infants asleep in the back of cars, and most of the theatres include a bottle-warming service. Two and three-year-olds sometimes are brought along in pajamas and bedded down on the back seat. Older children may be provided with an adequate supper from the refreshment stand. One genial parent can cope with a carful of neighbors' children for a special treat; there is no problem of herding them in together or securing adjacent seats.

Elderly, infirm or physically handicapped people who cannot cope with crowds, jostling, or standing on line. This is especially true of people who, owing to an accident, may be temporarily obliged to use a wheel chair, crutches or a cane.

FAMILIES who will go for an automobile ride but won't dress up after a long day's work to go into town for recreation.

People who are extremely health-conscious. Despite the fact that sitting in a car provides no more fresh air than sitting at home next to an open window, a surprising number of people look upon drive-ins as healthful, out-of-door recreation. Others, who fear to expose their children or themselves to local epidemics of flu, measles or whooping cough feel safe in the privacy of their own cars.

Whenever the subject of what attracts people to drive-ins arises, someone is sure to hint darkly of more erotic pleasures. "Passion pits with pix" is the epithet which was hurled at the drive-ins and from which owners and operators continue to smart.

Contributing to moral delinquency in the young and to traffic congestion in general are the two arguments most constantly employed against granting licenses for these theatres.

OBVIOUSLY, any time this number of cars join in a common meeting place there is bound to be a certain amount of congestion. But this is the sort of problem encountered from the Yankee Stadium in New York to the Rose Bowl in California, and in varying degrees at college stadiums all over the country. Clearly, careful planning should go into the locations of these drive-ins. But just what the intelligent approach may be remains a question on which civic leaders differ sharply.

Business Week magazine claims that drive-ins should always be located directly on a main highway; while with equal conviction and confusion, the *Motion Picture Herald* declares that they never should be located on a main highway but on a secondary road with access to it. A number of states have endeavored to meet the problem locally by writing rules governing drive-ins into their building codes in an effort to establish a standard for construction and location.

THE other phase of the anti-drive-in campaign, involving the moral issue, seems to be based upon more ephemeral material. The moral issue obviously would not touch the majority of cars which contain family groups but would seem to be confined to cars containing unchaperoned members of the younger set ranging in age from 16 to 21. This arbitrary age grouping is based upon the assumption that younger patrons either would not be allowed to drive at night or would not be allowed out unchaperoned; and that the older patrons have developed, if not a more rigid moral code, at least more reasonable facilities wherein to break it.

And now to pursue the problem: If the young man should prove aggressive and the young lady wished to repulse him, it would seem infinitely simpler to step out of the car and stroll down the ramp to a telephone booth rather than to walk or hitch-hike her way home along a lonely country road.

ON the other hand, if they were mutually amenable to the idea of romance, the drive-ins' advantages do not seem to be any better than sitting home in a darkened room to watch a television program, or lolling in a hammock on the side porch with lights out for mosquito control. It even has been rumored that some enterprising young people parked on quiet side roads long before the advent of the drive-in with its doubtful advantages of surrounding cars, artificial moonlight and solicitous wagon boys vending their Good Humors.

If the younger set actually considered the drive-ins a better short cut to the primrose path, then we should be forced to the unhappy conclusion that such a state of satiety had set in that simple sex, unless accompanied by music, sound effects and a story with a happy ending, would prove a bore.

But, despite the fact that the moral issue has become more of a joke than a threat, drive-in owners remain understandably touchy.

Refinement is pressed down firmly over any lurking carnival spirit. One well-known drive-in chain's list of instructions to their managers can scarcely be distinguished from a Boy Scout manual. They urge their managers to "watch for elderly patrons and offer to park their cars or perform other services for them * * * give free gasoline to run car heaters in cold weather * * * give the utmost in service at all times, including such little courtesies as changing tires and supplying emergency gasoline to cars which run out in the theatre."

AND now, ruggedly facing the seamier side of life, the manual of instruction says:

"One of the most important managerial tasks falling under the general heading of proper supervision is that of preventing breaches of good conduct. In this regard a special officer or night watchman should be assigned to patrol the lot after 10 P. M., looking casually into every car without disturbing the occupants. He should go from the front ramp to the back ramp and back again, never stopping, so "as to prevent any sort of misconduct."

It would take a churlish character, indeed, deliberately to misconduct himself in the face of such combined vigilance and tact.

Even in the advertisements in trade magazines we find this same determined air of piety. The enclosed theatres require over seven million chairs using eleven million yards of fabric covering to keep their patrons comfortable. Ads for these products usually depict happy young couples cuddling together in an apparent paroxysm of delight over their comfy "Push-em-back" chairs or the slippery coolness of the "Yummy-ite" upholstery which is known as "the fabric that keeps everyone sitting pretty!"

No such ads relate to drive-in products. In the first place, to the intense envy of the enclosed theatre owners, the patrons all arrive carrying their own seats, so to speak. All ads accent the refreshments or the diversions for children. If the children are not portrayed as sitting primly on their parents laps they are given a special ad showing them in a veritable paradise of swings, sandboxes, slides, seesaws, merry-go-rounds and miniature railroad trains, with an occasional live monkey village or rabbit farm thrown in. In no case does any ad ever portray twosomes, let alone handholding—the inference being that there are too many other wholesome diversions. Indeed, from the number of diversions offered to adults also—shuffleboard, quoits, concerts and dancing—one wonders how they can work in time for the movies.

At first glance, the drive-in looks like an inexpensive proposition, but this is not so. Grading, paving and equipment quickly runs to $100,000 for a 500-car theatre. Some have cost as little as $75,000 and as much as $600,000. This is a formidable sum when one considers that banks and mortgage companies take a doubtful view of advancing cash against a few acres of concrete.

UNTIL recently, drive-ins have had to be content with either the oldest or the least desirable movies on the market. But with their rapid growth and increased strength they are beginning to demand, and to get, better products. The moving-picture companies have begun to realize that drive-ins not only represent 10 per cent of their domestic market but that they are an ever-increasing potential. They are beginning to take seriously the claims of the operators who say that, far from merely cutting in on the established indoor movie trade, they are creating a new audience.

One successfully operated drive-in claims to have paid back the entire initial cost of building and equipment and started to show a clear profit all within two years.

ADMISSION price for adults is about equal for both types of houses, but as a rule the only concession the enclosed theatre can afford to make to children is a half-price charge, as a seat is no less occupied when filled by a 10-year-old. But once a car has nosed into its allotted space, it matters little whether it contains two or eight passengers—especially since only half of the drive-in's profits accrue from the admission, the rest from the concessions. An average 10-year-old, even if admitted absolutely free, generally can be depended upon to eat and drink more than his proportionate share. One drive-in owner who wisely advertised "Bring the kiddies free of charge," was confronted with a truck containing twenty-two children.

"I've brought the kiddies," the truck driver announced gravely, offering his single admission.

The owner says he didn't know whether it was a gag or a test case, but he accepted the single admission. During the show they kept the wagon boy busy. They consumed forty hot dogs, eight packages of popcorn and over fifty soft drinks. The owner says, somewhat smugly, that he came out very well on the deal.

THE enclosed theatre seems to be gravitating away from the enormous downtown "hall" or "palace" (with the attendant parking problems) to the smaller, modern-style building in decentralized locations. Conversly, the drive-in, which has no parking problem, shows a tendency to larger places with their resultant greater facilities. Indeed, they often develop to amazing and giddy heights in their fancies. One in Miami is called "a theatre in a garden" and is equipped with exotic palm trees, flowering shrubs and a hanging garden (back of the screen tower) with tropical flowers and vines.

Another in Rome, Ga., has gone all-out on the Southern plantation theme. Its thirty-five acres include carefully landscaped twin lakes flanking the entrance. The screen tower, usually an obvious, functional structure, has been thoughtfully concealed behind a white colonial facade which incorporates enough curved loggias, pavilions, white-washed brick walls and assorted Greek, Roman and Corinthian columns to keep a student of architecture busy (if not happy) for days at a time.

SOME of the drive-ins report that new heating units will prolong the time they can stay open, in some cases moving them into the all-year-round class. Twin screens within one enclosure appear so promising that the use of four is being tested for double shows or staggered performances. Experiments are also going on to develop a recessed, movable screen in a shadow box arrangement. This might make possible a late afternoon matinee with the screen set at the extreme rear of the housing and visibility limited to the center sections of the ramps. As daylight faded the screen could move forward slowly until with total darkness it reached the front of the shadow box, thus increasing its visibility until reaching total capacity.

Unless gasoline rationing should curtail this form of diversion, the drive-ins seem here to stay—and to grow. They may not represent the sophisticated urbanite's idea of a glamorous evening, but they have captured the fancy—and the steady trade—of millions.

October 1, 1950

A THEATER CLOSES

And an Era, Too, As the Paramount Goes Dark

By BOSLEY CROWTHER

FOR the present, at least, the Paramount Theater at the "crossroads of the world" in Times Square is as empty and forsaken as an old warehouse in which are stored but the shreds of memories. The 3,650-seat showplace which once rang to the shrieks and squeals of armies of bobby-soxers who all but knocked down the doors to get in to hear Frank Sinatra moan his liquefacient songs is as barren and gloomy as a cavern, as silent as a tomb. And the vast stage which has held the greatest bandsmen of an era is as dark as death.

A scribbled sign on the glass of the boxoffice reads like a weary epitaph. It says the theater is "closed until further notice." Eternity whispers in those words.

Actually the execution order for this oldest of the Broadway palaces that still has the same elaborate interior it had at the time of its opening in 1926 has not been signed and delivered to the wreckers. There's still a slim chance of a reprieve. And, at least, under any circumstances, the old showplace will enjoy one last huge feast.

There is talk in the form of mere gossip that, if the real estate firm of Webb & Knapp should not complete its present arrangement to take over the Paramount building and theater, the latter may be renovated or rebuilt as two smaller theaters. There have also been hints that, in the noodling of the notorious big noodlers at Webb & Knapp, there are thoughts of constructing a whole complex of jewel-box theaters in the Paramount's regal space.

One Last Good Night

And come what may of those grand prospects, it is certain the old house will be re-lit and restored to its former glitter for at least two appropriate happenings next month. One will be a 10-day engagement, beginning Sept. 4, of a variety stage show featuring a musical quintet from England, aptly yclept the Animals. And the other will be a charity performance on the evening of Sept. 20 for the benefit of United Cerebral Palsy of New York City, Inc., and Retarded Infants Services, Inc., by—yeah, yeah, yeah!— the Beatles themselves! So, regardless of distant bells tolling, the old place should rock at least once more.

But that sign which was placed in the boxoffice when the house went dark on Aug. 5 still betokens the grim anticipation of an inevitable doom, and the Paramount as we have known it is all but a thing of the past. For, irrevocably, it is a victim of the cultural and economic change that has been scooping the ground out from under its type of showplace for the past two decades.

The aspects of this change have been so massive and imperative over the years that no one at all sophisticated in the area of entertainment could have failed to perceive what they foretold. They included, of course, the obvious inroads which television and the steady post-war flow of population to the suburbs of big cities were making on attendance in "midtown" theaters.

But even before these major factors began to bring on the great change in the patterns of movie attendance and in the economics of the business that we have seen, the fate of the so-called movie palace, such as the Paramount, was sealed. For these giant houses, built in the 1920's, were designed to offer not only silent films but big stage shows and elaborate musical programs that would surround their audiences with sound. Live performers and the felicities of music were expected to draw the great crowds as much as did the movies and the regal and resplendent decor.

Sound

Thus the arrival of sound pictures struck the first unsuspected blow at the movie palace. They caused a subtle esthetic clash between the nature of the illusions presented on the stage and on the screen. But, more than this and as a counterpart of it, they posed the problem of what to put on those big stages that would be suitable with sound films and that attendance would support.

The history of the great movie palaces in New York and other cities in this land through the 1930's and the 1940's is too extensive to go into here. (It is colorfully recounted in a good book by Ben Hall called "The Best Available Seats.") But what it boils down to is a story of struggle to find a way to match films and stage entertainments—and still to make ends meet.

In this struggle, the Paramount Theater was remarkably successful over the years, for its management found a winning formula in the presentation on stage of singers and bands.

After the uncertain period of transition from silent films to sound and the dark years of the Great Depression, the winning formula was hit with the booking of Glen Gray's Casa Loma orchestra for Christmas week, 1935. The screen attraction that went with it was "The Bride Comes Home," with Claudette Colbert and Fred MacMurray, but the success of the engagement was clearly due to the attractiveness and popularity of the Glen Gray band.

The next 15 years were the big years—the golden age—of the Paramount. They were the years in which it magnified its image and won the sentimental attachment of many fans. While other Broadway palaces did nicely with popular singers and name bands, too, it was only when they played the Times Square theater that the fans seemed to swarm and the joint to rock.

Hot Bands

The bands of Benny Goodman and the Dorsey Brothers, Glenn Miller and Harry James were always hot attractions. The customers would dance in the aisles when these popular purveyors of swing music were performing on stage. Then came Frank Sinatra, a callow singer with an oleagenous sound, and the youngsters—the Paramount's faithful—clasped him to their hearts. Sinatra's third engagement in 1944 brought customers clamoring to the theater and lining up in the streets before dawn. Bob Hope, Bing Crosby, Dean Martin and Jerry Lewis were favorites, too.

The Paramount abandoned its policy of regular stage shows in 1952. By that time, television had taken its heavy toll. But an occasional stage show thereafter recalled the good old days. One was a coupling of Mr. Sinatra and the Dorsey Brothers' band in 1956. Another was a rock-'n'-roll program done in 1957 by Alan Freed. The boxoffice opened at four in the morning and closed at 1 A. M. the next day!

But those acts were rare exceptions, and the huge house could not make do simply with motion pictures. Like the Roxy and the Brooklyn Paramount, which have poignantly gone in the past few years, it has come to the end of the road. Other big presentation houses, the Capitol and Loew's State, have been redesigned. Only the Music Hall, which is not on Broadway, continues to prosper as a presentation house. Other theaters in the area are doing all right, but something goes with the Paramount. Is it, maybe, our youth?

August 23, 1964

Bob Hope

Bing Crosby

Dean Martin

Jerry Lewis

HOLLYWOOD FINDS GOLD ON BEACHES

Studios Compete for Stars of Teen-Age Surf Films

By PETER BART
Special to The New York Times

HOLLYWOOD, June 21—The major motion-picture studios here are following the television networks in increasing their output designed specifically for teen-agers.

Studios that once scoffed at what they called "sand and sex epics," like "Bikini Beach" or "Wild on the Beach" are competing to sign teen-age idols for their own films

"Teen-age tastes are exerting a tyranny over our industry," complains one high-ranking studio executive, who prefers to remain nameless. "It's getting so show business is just one big puberty rite."

Teen-age films cost little to make—usually a good deal less than a million dollars—and with any luck at all, their grosses are from $2 million to $3 million.

Teen-age films come into their own at this time of year when drive-in theaters are popular and teen-agers account for as much as 50 per cent of movie-theater admissions.

Though independent companies like American International or Lippert Productions have made sand-and-sex epics for a couple of years, the enthusiastic entry of the major studios is new. Indeed popular rock 'n' roll groups, formerly unable to get in to see a casting director, are being hungrily sought out.

Hence, Columbia Pictures recently signed the Righteous Brothers to make a film this summer called "Fingerpopper," while Paramount recruited Jan and Dean, popular with the surfing cult, for "Easy Come, Easy Go."

Warner Brothers, meanwhile, has signed the Dave Clark Five for "Having a Wild Weekend," and Universal will star Ricky Nelson and his wife, Kristin, in "Love and Kisses."

June 22, 1965

Movies Leaving 'Hollywood' Behind

Studio System Passe — Film Forges Ahead

By MEL GUSSOW
Special to The New York Times

LOS ANGELES — Hollywood—the old studio system—is dead, but movies as a medium have never been more alive.

Doors once locked by tradition, unions or inertia are wide open. Film students are directing features. Playwrights are writing original screenplays, and they are not being ground into studio formulas. No subject is taboo.

Modern methods of filming and editing have given moviemakers the freedom to shoot anywhere, anytime. Technical innovations, such as film cassettes, may make movies as accessible to the public as phonograph records. Studios are no longer the only places where movies are made, financed and distributed. The movie industry has fragmented into a million pieces. Power is decentralized.

The result, observes Warren Beatty, is that "there has never been a time more exciting from the point of view of what you can make on film, or from the point of view of profit."

The re-structuring has been forced on the industry by events of the recent past.

5 Studios in Red

Of Hollywood's seven surviving studios, five—M-G-M, Paramount, 20th Century-Fox, Warner Brothers and Universal — lost money in their last fiscal year. M-G-M, historically the greatest of the studios, lost $35.4-million in 1969.

More than half of the people normally employed by the studios are unemployed. Hardly anyone is filming anything—at the studios, which are selling off pieces of their property. (M-G-M has just sold all of its properties and costumes from 56 years of moviemaking.)

In their fight for survival, the studios are abandoning the notion of one centrally located, fully equipped permanent facility. It has been many years since studios produced 50 films a year, all of them on the lot.

United Artists, along with Columbia, made a profit in the last fiscal year, and it is setting the pattern. U.A. does not produce its own pictures; it distributes the work of independent producers. The surprise hit, and pace-setting picture in 1969 was "Easy Rider," produced by Peter Fonda and Dennis Hopper for less than $1-million, but distributed by Columbia.

This year almost everyone is jumping on the "Easy Rider" cycle, making low-budget movies with non-names, directed at (and often, by) young people. Beginning with Columbia's "Getting Straight," and M-G-M's "The Magic Garden of Stanley Sweetheart," both already released, the theaters will soon be filled with movies about students—M-G-M's "The Strawberry Statement" and United Artists' "The Revolutionary." Drugs, desertion, Vietnam, race, sex, ecology—no subject seems too contemporary or too controversial.

"How many years ago was 'The Moon Is Blue' denied a seal because of the word virgin?" asks the writer-producer Ernest Lehman, who is preparing to direct his first movie, "Portnoy's Complaint" at 20th Century-Fox.

Many Potential Welleces

Novelists, playwrights, critics, film editors, cameramen, photographers and actors are being given opportunities to direct—and so are film students. The industry is blooming with potential Orson Welleses, film prodigies wearing flowered shirts, beards and bell-bottoms. Many are graduates of film departments at the University of Southern California and University of California in Los Angeles, which are "raided" every year as if they were basketball teams. Some of the new filmmakers just come in off the street.

The young are adored, and the younger they are, the better. As one established director says, "The best thing you can be is 21—with no experience." Not quite. Experience does count, particularly when money is involved, but often that experience is limited to underground films or shorts.

As filmmakers get younger, so do the studio heads—not just in age, but also in life style. They read Cahiers du Cinema, talk about signing Andy Warhol and Ingmar Bergman and go to film festivals, not just to buy film but as film buffs. Informality reigns in the former dens of the moguls.

At M-G-M there is 39-year-old Herbert Solow, a highly charged former Desilu television executive. Mr. Solow, wearing a dark blue T-shirt, sitting in his dimly lit boudoir-red office, said the other day: "We're dropping the studio hierarchy bull, where everyone is a member of an echelon. I like people who think young."

At Warners there is 39-year-old John Calley, who used to be Martin Ransohoff's executive producer. The bearded Mr. Calley is down-to-earth even in his office décor—no desk, but a large square coffee table laden with film journals, celery, carrots and olives.

"When formulas break down in time of uncertainty," he says, "it's a breeding ground for young talent. Everyone is ready to listen to wilder forms and concepts. We're inclined to take enlightened gambles on young people."

The president of Fox is 35-year-old Richard Zanuck, the president of United Artists, 39-year-old David Picker, of Columbia, 40-year-old Stanley Schneider. At Paramount, 39-year-old Robert Evans is vice president in charge of production. Some studios have young executives in charge of finding new talent — Peter Bart at Paramount, Ned Tanen at Universal.

"We're out of the deal-making business and into the filmmaking business," Mr. Tanen explains. "What's going on is probably the best thing in films since sound. A shake-out!"

Not everyone agrees. Some oldtimers think it is the worst thing in films. Others are more matter-of-fact. "Tinseltown is disasterville!" exclaims Irving (Swifty) Lazar, the last of the legendary literary agents.

There are even those who think the Hollywood recession is cyclical, that the industry will come back, just as it did after the advent of sound, television and World War II. As one longtime story editor observed: "Hollywood is a little more moribund than usual."

This time, however, the illness may be fatal. For that story editor, for example, the loss of the old Hollywood means that he no longer has a platoon of assistants reading every book published and writing synopses for busy moguls. There are no synopses and there are no moguls.

Huge, outside corporations now own four of the studios (Paramount, Warner's, Universal and United. Artists)—with results not entirely favorable to either party.

Cost of Films and Their Yields

This list, composed of films first released during 1969, estimates their box-office grosses to date. The grosses are compiled from Variety's weekly chart, which estimates receipts in 24 markets.

"Butch Cassidy" and "True Grit" were re-released on bills with "The Prime of Miss Jean Brodie" and "The Sterile Cuckoo," respectively. The grosses for "Butch" and "Brodie" and "Grit" and "Cuckoo" as double bills are not listed.

The cost of each film is approximate since studios generally withhold such information.

A film must, on the average, gross two and a half times its production cost to be in the black. The ratio is somewhat reduced for such reserved-seat attractions as "Hello, Dolly!" and "Paint Your Wagon."

MOVIE	APPROX. COST	EST. GROSS Week Ending May 20
Midnight Cowboy (United Artists)	$3-million	$11,373,616
Easy Rider (Columbua)	$450,000	$9,475,059
Butch Cassidy and the Sundance Kid (Fox)	$6-million	$8,968,082
I Am Curious (Yellow) (Grove)	$180,000	$8,705,898
Goodbye, Columbus (Paramount)	$1-million	$8,230,464
Hello, Dolly! (Fox)	$20-million to $25-million	$6,497,322
Cactus Flower (Columbia)	$2-million	$5,635,920
Bob & Carol & Ted & Alice (Columbia)	$2-million	$5,533,589
True Grit (Paramount)	$4.5-million	$5,238,520
On Her Majesty's Secret Service (United Artists)	$4.5-million	$5,235,826
Paint Your Wagon (Paramount)	$14-million to $15-million	$4,742,045

The entrance of conglomerates into the movies did not consolidate the business in the hands of a few, as some might have expected.

But actors, such as Steve McQueen and Jack Lemmon, now produce films through their own companies. And Paul Newman, Sidney Poitier and Barbra Streisand have organized a filmmaking organization. Mini-major companies, like the Columbia Broadcasting System's Cinema Center, National General and A. B. C. Films, are becoming as active as the majors.

This dispersal of authority has brought in new money and new agents who know where to find it.

The trend is toward non-movie companies financing films—for profit and/or promotional purposes. The Jicarilla Apache Indians are providing financial backing for Kirk Douglas's pro-Indian "A Gunfight." Quaker Oats is supporting David Wolper's "Charlie and the Chocolate Factory."

In the past, a prime obstacle to nonstudios making movies was that Hollywood controlled distribution. "Distribution is the last great mystery with which studios held everyone at bay," one director recalls.

"Z" was turned down by every major studio before it won the first prize at the Cannes film festival. Finally, a theater owner, Donald Rugoff, released the film himself through his Cinema V distribution company. With Mr. Rugoff's individual attention and promotion, it became one of the year's big hits.

With lower budgets, salaries naturally decline, but more and more, participants in a picture are given percentages (not just the stars, but also the director, writer, and even the technicians) of potential profits. As one young studio executive exclaims, "It's marvelous! Everybody risks." And if the movie is a success, everyone profits.

The New York Times

Francis Ford Coppola, right, in the San Francisco warehouse in which he has organized American Zoetrope, talks with George Lucas, an associate who is producing "THX 1138" for Warner Brothers. American Zoetrope is a film complex with everything but sound stages.

Pilgrimage to Nerve Center

In a converted warehouse in San Francisco, 30-year-old Francis Ford Coppola, who directed "You're a Big Boy Now," has created American Zoetrope, a $500,000 super-modern film center. Zoetrope has everything anyone would need to make movies today—except sound stages.

In less than a year, Zoetrope has become the nerve center for young American filmmakers. About 10 cinéastes a day make the pilgrimage to Zoetrope. Sometimes they are hired as apprentices or stay to unspool their films at weekly movie marathons.

John Korty, who was making such films as "Crazy Quilt" in San Francisco even before Mr. Coppola, is one of the experienced directors associated with Zoetrope. Under his two-year contract with Warners, he can use the studio's facilities if he wants to. But as Mr. Korty recalls, "I told John Calley that my only interest in their lot was to use it in a movie as a movie lot."

At Zoetrope Mr. Korty is surrounded by a battery of the newest, most advanced equipment, including two Steenbeck editing tables, a German-made, multidialed invention that makes the standard Movieola film-editing machine seem as outdated as a pinhole camera; and the $12,000 Keller mixer, which can blend three sizes of film at three different speeds.

The first film off Zoetrope's Keller will be 25-year-old George Lucas's science-fiction feature "THX 1138," which Mr. Lucas first made as a short when he was a student in the U.S.C. cinema department and then revised and expanded at a cost of $750,000. Mr. Lucas, who several years ago couldn't even get a job "sweeping floors in a film department," says he wrote and directed "THX" for Warners with complete artistic freedom.

Sitting in his office at Zoetrope, with a huge blow-up of Eisenstein peeping over his shoulder, the filmmaker enthusiastically described some of the revolutions in film: the hologram, which can produce three-dimensional projections on a fixed point in space; casettes that will allow people to buy films and play them at home; more portable cameras, faster film and compact mobile production units.

"The joke here," Mr. Lucas said, "is that Mattel will come out with a complete filmmaking kit. It will be all plastic, and any 10-year-old can make a film. I look forward to the dispersal—when you don't need a place like this. I think of this as a studio."

Mr. Lucas's next film will be "an epic,"—a $1.5 million —movie about the war in Vietnam called "Apocalypse Now," written by John Milius, a college friend. He is not sure where he will film it, but it will not be in Hollywood.

"There's nothing for me there," Mr. Lucas said. "The only thing they've got that we need is money. And they're getting less and less. The most exciting thing about film is that it's just starting. Everyone in Hollywood is over 50 and creaking. They see movies as the past. We see it as the future."

May 27, 1970

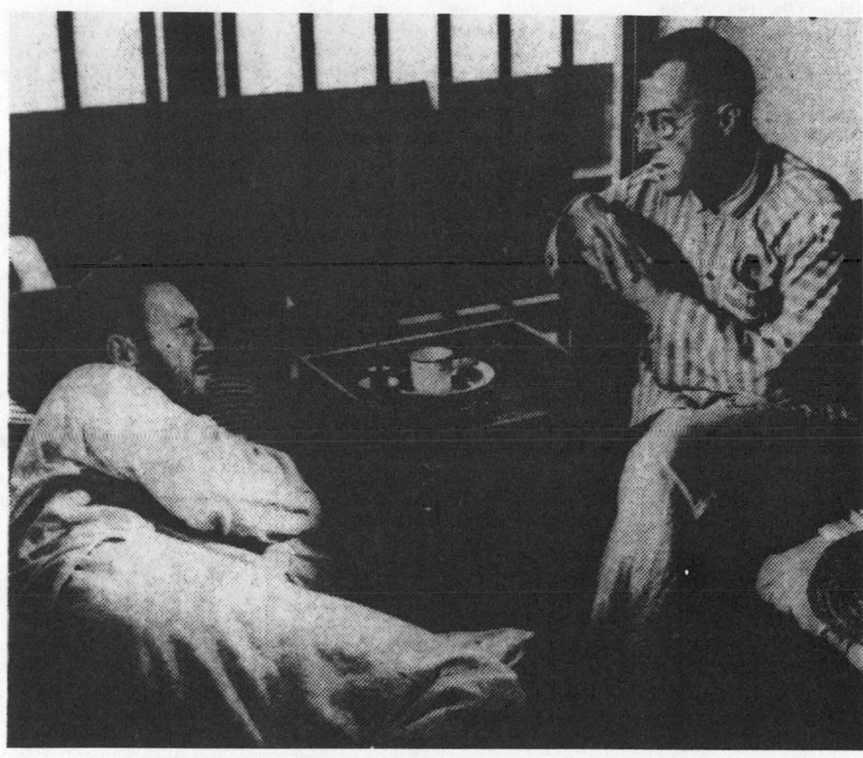

Steve McQueen, left, and Dustin Hoffman in "Papillon"

Crime In, Sex Out, in New Film Season

By PAUL GARDNER

The new movie season has no time for comedy and musicals are risky adventures, but crime continues to pay at the box office, where it joins a devilish interest in the supernatural as the year's predominant theme. A producer's ultimate achievement would be the story of a Mafioso who eliminates his victims by exorcism. Next year, perhaps.

Except for the lusty adventure "Papillon," which cost $13.5-million, most budgets will be kept down, the status of the black will be raised and the names of Liv Ullmann and Robert Redford will repeatedly ignite marquees, which hope to attract family audiences.

Hollywood will offer a sequel to "The Godfather," but until the Supreme Court clarifies its guidelines on obscenity there will be no more "Last Tango's"— in Paris or anywhere else. The X-rating (for adults only) has become a scarlet letter.

Studio chiefs echoed the sentiments of Richard Shepherd, a Warner Brothers executive, who said, "We're not interested in X-rated films. During this period of uncertainty, you just have to go on what you think is good taste. If you give it too much worry, you can end up at Menninger's Clinic." And then he laughed dryly.

So, for the time being, sex is definitely out. The new movies will expose only a smidgen of flesh, which should please slumbering wardrobe departments. Paul Newman may take off his shirt again, but Ann-Margret won't. Zealously avoiding anything that might be considered pornographic, the studio think-tanks, which seem to be operated by the computer Hal from "2001," have decided that Americans want to see movies about crime — organized and disorganized.

Malefactors on the Rise

And since "The Godfather" has earned a domestic gross of more than $75-million, and the Supreme Court is more squeamish about bodies in a bubble-bath than those in a blood-bath, the studios are preparing movies that deal with hired killers, racketeers, extortionists, the Mafia, homicide detectives fighting the Syndicate and "cops who defied the System."

Tough police detectives will be played by John Wayne in "McQ," Clint Eastwood in "Magnum Force" and Billy Dee Williams in "The Take." Anthony Quinn will be a tough gangster in "The Don Is Dead," Robert Duvall a bankrobber who declares war on "The Outfit," and Peter Boyle, a tough maverick named "Crazy Joe" who struggles against another mob in another film.

All these escapist action films will eventually reach television, which requires a dead body, a holdup or a cliff-hanging chase every 15 minutes—just before commercials and station breaks.

Black groups, which angrily protested last year against being exploited as "super-niggers" in the bedroom, private eyes in the New York jungle and groovy junkies in the gutter, will find that the studios have taken steps to give them dignity—and a lighter side. Moms Mabley uncovers political crooks in the comedy "Amazing Grace" and Cleavon Little tames a town of bigots in "Black Bart," a comic Western.

Stimulated by the success of "Rosemary's Baby" and "The Other," two horror films that investigated things that go bump in the psyche, Hollywood moves this season smack into witchery, demonic possession and spiritualism.

In "Hex," some easy riders motorcycling across the Nebraska prairie in 1919 meet two sisters who practice witchcraft. In "Don't Look Now," Julie Christie and Donald Sutherland experience a fright or two with a group of spiritualists in Italy. And in "The Exorcist," based on the best seller, a possessed child commits assorted blasphemies and hideous desecrations.

The studios find ghost stories less expensive, and more popular, than musical comedies, which can be costly catastrophes. Last season's "Man of La Mancha" suffered from rigor mortis and the Shangri-La of "Lost Horizon" was hopelessly pickled. But Lucille Ball should tickle Beekman Place in "Mame" and Mark Twain's "Huckleberry Finn" will follow his musical mate "Tom Sawyer" down the Mississippi.

The Greatest Story Ever Told, already told with rock and pop music, will be retold in "The Gospel Road" with the country music of Johnny Cash. June Carter Cash will play Mary Magdalen.

Although theater owners outside New York are reportedly boycotting Jane Fonda for her outspoken views on the war in Vietnam, one producer insisted that if she were co-starring in a film with Robert Redford there would not be any problem. Mr. Redford, who began his career in nonsense Broadway comedies, is now —in trade slang—a hot property.

This year he co-stars with Paul Newman in "The Sting."

in which they both play likable con-men (again); with Barbra Streisand in "The Way We Were," the story of a couple split apart by political issues in the late forties; and with Mia Farrow in "The Great Gatsby," a dissonant coda to the Jazz Age.

Siegel Gets Matthau

Liv Ullmann, who combines purity with sensuality, a rare juxtaposition for Beverly Hills, continues to fascinate the talent merchants who envision her as the new Ingrid Bergman—if they can ever figure out what to do with her. Miss Ullmann will be highly visible as Queen Christina of Sweden in "The Abdication," a mail-order bride in California in "Zandy's Bride" and the pioneer wife in "The New Land," a sequel to "The Emigrants."

Filmgoers who consider movie stars trivia and immerse themselves in "personal" directors will be able to choose from the works of Robert Altman, Peter Bogdanovich, Francis Ford Coppola, Blake Edwards, Mike Nichols and Don Siegel.

For "Charley Varrick," his 29th film, Mr. Siegel, who guided Clint Eastwood through "The Beguiled" and "Dirty Harry," is getting Walter Matthau to portray a dissipated bank-robber. Blake Edwards wanted his wife, Julie Andrews, for his espionage thriller, "The Tamarind Seed," and she agreed.

But Peter Bogdanovich had to accept a rejection — of sorts. He wanted to make a last Great Western with three stars — John Wayne, James Stewart and Henry Fonda—who had spent half their screen life in the saddle. But he couldn't persuade them to come together for a final roundup, so he flew to Rome where he is shooting the Henry James novella "Daisy Miller," with Cybill Shepherd as the doomed American tease.

The controversial Robert Altman will finally see his version of Raymond Chandler's "The Long Goodbye," starring Elliott Gould, released here. After hostile reviews in the provinces last spring, there were rumors that it would be re-edited, cut or possibly shelved. Instead, it will open with a new advertising campaign that prepares audiences for a satire. Originally it was sold as a straight detective story.

Keeping Costs Down

Understandably, the studios want to keep most films in the $2-million to $5-million category. Executive heads roll with big-budget failures. Francis Ford Coppola has almost completed "The Conversation," a low-budget drama with Gene Hackman about a professional wire-tapper.

Franklin Schaffner's $13.5-million budget for "Papillon" is possibly the year's biggest. "Three years ago the experts said the big movie was dead," he said. "Then word came, 'It's the property. not the stars.'" With "Papillon" he has a famous property—a best-seller dealing with an escape from Devil's Island—and two stars, Steve McQueen and Dustin Hoffman.

In any case, there will not be much to laugh about this year. Mike Nichols, so skillful at comedy, is editing "The Day of the Dolphin," a science-fiction thriller centering on a marine biologist, George C. Scott, who experiments with the built-in sonar system of the playful mammals.

Comedy will be hard to find. There is, fortunately, Woody Allen.

He may not be remarkably visual as a director, but until someone else comes along, he is the screen's constant funny boy. The shame-faced Woody, who always looks as if he were caught performing a decent act by his home-room teacher, has co-written a futuristic comedy, "Sleeper," which he will also direct. After due deliberation, he selected Woody Allen as his star.

Obviously this bespectacled Puck, who works only with himself, has discovered the key to simplicity in an implausible but always surprising business.

September 4, 1973

Swish! Thwack! Kung Fu Films Make It

Special to The New York Times

HONG KONG — The blond American girl, wearing loose-fitting pajamas, looked somewhat incongruous in the Korean street scene built on the set of the latest production of Hong Kong's Golden Harvest Film Studios.

Suddenly — swish! thwack! she clobbered a villainous-looking Oriental with a beautifully executed kick to the left ear. Everything, including the bad guy, fell into place.

Anne Winton, a 23-year-old student from Washington, was demonstrating in a new kung fu film that proficiency in unarmed combat is not solely an skill.

"We are selling to a multinational audience so it is time to have a multinational cast," Raymond Chow, president of Golden Harvest and producer of the kung fu movie "Fists of Fury," stated.

With kung fu films sudden hits in the United States and Europe, movie makers here are experimenting with new forms of martial art and new combinations of actors and actresses to keep the box-office cash registers ringing.

Kung fu films were introduced here a few years ago to provide audiences with a change from sword-play films, which had great popularity in the nineteen-sixties. The movies broke all records in Asia, grossing up to $1-million. Now they are expected to bring in $5-million to $10-million in the United States and Europe, easily offsetting an average production outlay of $200,000.

Golden Harvest's latest production is called "Taekwondo Heroes." Taekwondo is a Korean form of karate, which is a Japanese form of kung fu, which is where Chinese like to believe the martial arts began.

Jhoon Rhee, the film's star, is an American citizen from Arlington, Va., who was born in Korea 41 years ago.

Bruce Lee, a friend of Mr. Rhee's also is an American, who is the current box-office star of Golden Harvest Films.

Mr. Rhee's kung fu pupils include prominent personalities from Washington's Capitol Hill and Miss Winton. It is the first movie-making experience for both Miss Winton and Mr. Rhee, but this is not considered a drawback at Golden Harvest, where action is more important than plot and skill in martial arts more important than acting ability.

"In our early action films, we used actors who knew little about fighting," Mr. Chow said. "We had to use various camera tricks. But the audience can tell the difference. It knows a real fighter when it sees one. That's why Bruce Lee has been such a hit."

Mr. Chow intends to introduce more non-Asians into his films, including some top American stars. However, he plans to keep his movie plots simple and salutary.

"I don't believe in a complicated story line," he said. "We like to stick to the theme that good is better than evil and crime doesn't pay. Our moral standards are old-fashioned, rather like early American films."

Mr. Chow, a former reporter, joined Shaw Brothers, Asia's biggest movie organization, as a public relations man and became production manager. Three years ago, he formed his own company.

His greatest satisfaction, he said, was reading in Variety, a show business paper, during a recent visit to New York that two of his productions were the top money-makers for that week.

Heading the list was "Fists of Fury," which grossed $697,000, followed by "Deep Thrust—The Hand of Death" which grossed $459,000. In third place was "Five Fingers of Death," a production of Shaw Brothers, his former employer.

Mr. Chow recalled that he had sent copies of "Fists of Fury," which was released here as "The Big Boss," to two major studios and they "let it sit for six months." It is now being distributed by National General Pictures.

Mr. Chow is worried that the market will be flooded with kung fu films. He believes the initial curiosity of foreign audiences may be killed by too many mediocre movies.

"But I think good pictures will survive and we plan to make fewer pictures and better ones," he said.

Run Run Shaw, who with his brother Runme Shaw, controls the Shaw Brothers' organization, does not share Mr. Chow's concern. He sees an ever-expanding market for his company's product.

"Movie tastes are becoming universal and action films will always be popular," he said.

Shaw Brothers has been exporting films for screening in the Chinatowns of the United States for many years, he said, but only recently had these films been tested on a wider audience.

Shaw Brothers' current hit, "Five Fingers of Death," is four years old. Mr. Shaw considers it an experiment that has proved successful and says he has 250 films to release on the American market.

Mr. Shaw attributes part of the success of Asian action films in the United States to President Nixon's visit to China.

"The President's trip to China called attention to many things in Asia that were never noticed before by people in the United States," he said.

June 16, 1973

'Exorcist' Casts Spell on Full Houses

By LAWRENCE VAN GELDER

Movie buffs are going to the devil. No, not the way the doomsayers have been forecasting since the days Hester Prynne won an "A" rating in "The Scarlet Letter," but to drown themselves for a couple of hours in the horror and suspense of "The "Exorcist."

Like "The Godfather" and "Last Tango in Paris" before it, "The Exorcist" is drawing long lines at box offices from coast to coast and is a topic of conversation and controversy at cocktail party and hearthside alike.

"I don't think there's been anything like it in the history of the business," said Donald Rugoff, the president of Cinema 5, Ltd. He operates the four theaters in Manhattan where the film has been playing to capacity crowds that have braved 6-degree temperatures in block-girdling lines for a chance to be chilled by the doings on screen within.

Within the motion picture industry, "The Exorcist"—dealing with the demonic possession of a young girl—is regarded as a sure shot to bury "The Godfather" under an avalanche of dollars as the all-time moneymaker.

Record Take Expected

And while box-office tills fill with cash in the march toward that record, listed by Variety at some $85-million in rentals, eager audiences endure waits as much as five hours for a chance to see the Warner Bros. film, based on a best-selling novel by William Peter Blatty. For their money ($3.50 a ticket at the Cinema I theater, where "The Exorcist" opened locally the day after Christmas), filmgoers get not only the events on the screen, but also—according to all reports—the spectacle of the less hardy among them succumbing to fainting spells and bouts of vomiting.

Thomas F. McMahon, director of operations for the Cinema 5 theaters, said he had no knowledge of heart attacks brought on by "The Exorcist," but does know of blackouts and vomiting.

Mr. McMahon, who can remember when ammonia capsules were kept handy as restoratives for filmgoers overcome by the sight of Kirk Douglas, as Vincent van Gogh, cutting off his ear in "Lust for Life," said that in terms of shock, "The Exorcist" must "take the top of the class."

Mostly Young Audience

He observed, "It's like a cult. People must see it." And like other observers, Mr. McMahon noted that the audience is predominantly young, although the film has attracted viewers of all ages, including infants in tow of parents.

"In our school, it's called 'The Film,'" said Sharon Mednick, a counselor at University High School in Los Angeles. "And every other kid has a copy of the paperback."

Despite language regarded as obscene and a depiction of self-abuse, the Motion Picture Producers Association gave the film an R rating, suggesting that children under age 17 not be admitted unless accompanied by a parent.

In California, Stephanie, a 16-year-old student at Van Nuys High School, said she had no difficulty in buying a ticket, and other ticketholders were seen who could have passed for 15.

Controversy over the film—reviews have been mixed; clergymen are divided on the question of its merits as a religious experience versus its attraction as a piece of cinematic craftsmanship—satisfies William Friedkin, who directed "The Exorcist."

"It is important to me to have made a film that is controversial and provocative," said Mr. Friedkin, who directed "The French Connection," another hit.

Word-of-Mouth Hit

Word-of-mouth advertising of the film prompted the Cinema 5 organization to make it available last Friday at three more theaters in Manhattan, increasing the total number of seats available for each showing from 700 to 2,439. Last Friday, Saturday and Sunday, audiences paid out $118,123 to see it. All house records for grosses have been broken at Cinema I, the Paramount and the Paris theaters, said a Rugoff spokesman; and it is expected that when the figures are in, new records will also be established for the Beekman.

According to a Warner spokesman, the nationwide gross to date stands at $7,418,210 and "The Exorcist" will surely pass "My Fair Lady," ($34-million in rentals) as the company's greatest moneymaker.

And why all the fuss?

"Well," said Dr. David Abrahamsen, a New York psychiatrist and the author of "The Murdering Mind," "I think the exorcist is, of course, a person who is like a magician. He is trying to turn bad things into good things, like the old medicine man."

And people, with their guilt feelings and hostile aggressions, are fascinated with exorcists and magicians. "Such fascination," he said, "is, of course, unlimited, because everyone feels guilty about something or other."

What they get from "The Exorcist," he suggested, was a sense of identification, of release of catharsis in its esthetic sense.

"It might well be short-lived," he said of the film's impact.

Which probably accounts for repeat business.

January 24, 1974

Movies Are More Sci-Fi Than Ever

By VINCENT CANBY

IN John Boorman's "Zardoz," civilization in 2293 is in the control of an elitist caste known as Eternals, people who are so perfect they have forgotten what sexual desire is. The characters in Woody Allen's "Sleeper," set 200 years in the future, are neither perfect nor immortal but for a really satisfactory physical relationship they must repair to the orgasm box, which looks rather like an old-fashioned hot-water heater and is kept in the living room.

Michael Crichton's "Westworld" is all about a super Disneyland of the future, a resort community serviced by robots whose only function is to amuse the humans, which is fine until the computer breaks down and the robots suffer an epidemic of "central mechanism psychosis," meaning they start murdering the guests. A neurotic computer was responsible for much of the mayhem in Stanley Kubrick's "2001," which also hinted at the kind of dehumanized world that George Lucas foresaw in his "THX 1138," where love was outlawed.

According to "Silent Running" and "Soylent Green," the earth will soon be an overpopulated, overheated, arid desert. These two films do not predict the sort of cataclysm Woody Allen imagines in "Sleeper" (after a man named Albert Shanker gets his own nuclear warhead). Instead they see a world that is up to here in rubbish, like New York City after a five-week strike by sanitation workers.

For a society that spends so much time, money and effort pursuing pleasure as if it were happiness, we certainly are taking a gloomy view of the future in our science-fiction films. Cheer up, say these movies, everything is going to get a lot worse.

Ever since Georges Méliès' "Voyage to The Moon" (1902), sci-fi has been a standard brand of movie fiction, but never have our visions of the future been so essentially bleak as they seem to be now. It used to be that the spectacle of scientific achievement and the gadgetry involved were more or less enough to fascinate us, as in George Pal's "Destination Moon" (1950) Sci-fi was as optimistic as pessimistic. At its worst, the world of the future as shown in the old Buck Rogers serials was a place where Buck had to match his wits against those of Killer Kane. I can't remember that we worried whether or not Buck and Wilma ever made love, but if we did I'm sure it never occurred to us that they might not be capable of it *at all*. Buck and Wilma were red-blooded, all-American kids and in that day red-blooded, all-American kids didn't go all the way. Any society inhabited by them had to be pretty darn good, excepting for the few rotten apples that furnished the material for their adventures.

*

Sci-fi is clearly here to stay. Upcoming we're going to get a sequel to "Westworld" called "Futureworld." Michael Crichton's "The Terminal Man" has been completed, as has been "The Nine Lives of Fritz The Cat," which has an episode about a Martian journey and another about an American President named Kissinger who has a multi-armed secretary named Rosemary Woodstock. It will open here in late June. Saul Bass has one due called "Phase IV," about ants.

Columbia is planning to make Isaac Asimov's "Caves of Steel," with Jack Nicholson playing a human policeman whose partner is a robot, while television is supplying the sci-fi demand with "The Six Million Dollar Man," "Star Lost" and an animated version of "Star Trek."

At their most simple-minded, these sci-fi films and TV shows are excuses for fancy effects and plots that employ magic under the somewhat more sober term: advanced technology. At their best, they are less often serious predictions of things to come than sharply observed and carefully recast satires of the world and the society for whom they were created, like Samuel Butler's "Erewon."

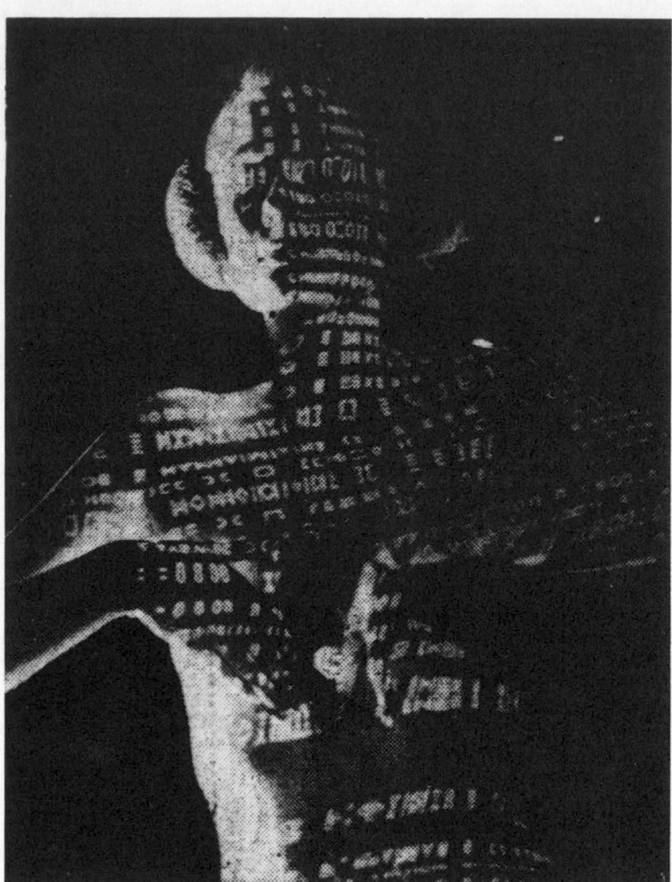

"ZARDOZ"—An eternal—and asexual—woman of the future dispenses computerized data in John Boorman's film, now at the Loew's Orpheum, Trans-Lux East and West and other houses. Sean Connery stars as a mortal but decidedly sexy brute.

If, as Michael Crichton said in a recent interview, they are basically escapist entertainments, one wonders what, specifically, the audiences want to escape from, and why.

The awful guilt implied in sci-fi post-cataclysm films would suggest extremely ambiguous feelings toward the atom. We want all the industrial and economic benefits we can get from it, but then something in the old Protestant work ethic reminds us that things easily come by aren't worth having. If we go too far, we're going to find ourselves living in a world ruled by a chimpanzee named Cornelius.

Similarly the films reflect our love-hate feelings toward technology. The more we have, the more we want, and the less we enjoy it. We demand that our shirts be returned from the laundry in individual plastic bags and then become angry when the bags clog the garbage cans. We push ahead seemingly heedless of the dangers, though we know we're not. We depend on computers more and more even though there's not one of us who hasn't had his bank account totally fouled up by one.

*

The computers of today's sci-fi are the Frankenstein monsters of yesterday's gothic fiction. We are tampering with the Unknown. If God had meant telephone bills to be on pieces of cardboard that couldn't be folded, spindled or mutilated, that would have been the way they were at the beginning.

The most peculiar theme shared by so many of these films is the vision of a society in which love/sex is either unknown or forbidden —and this in an age of permissiveness! Do we hate it that much? It would seem to be a rather obvious dramatization of the old castration fears. And if the fears are so apparent, can the wishes be far behind? Perhaps the films are intended to short-circuit fates worse than death: by picturing the disaster, we render it impotent.

Of only one thing am I sure, and that's the test that sci-fi presents for the moviemaker. Sci-fi separates the men from the boys. Stanley Kubrick's superb "2001" and "A Clockwork Orange" gave him room in which he could fully exercise his talents. "Zardoz," on the other hand, exposes John Boorman, its producer-writer-director as someone of considerably less wit, discipline and good sense than I would have thought of the man who made "Point Blank" and even "Deliverance."

*

"Zardoz" is Boorman's opportunity to create a world entirely from his imagination, which turns out to be amazingly banal and uninteresting. The film is very fancily photographed but it's been so over-costumed and over-gadgeted that it looks more like a charity ball than a movie. It presents no cohesive view of any society, ours or its, and toward the end, seems to have had no place to go.

Sean Connery, wearing fewer clothes than he should at his age, plays a kind of reverse messiah who brings the gift of death to an immortal society of the future. The screenplay seeks tone by quoting T. S. Eliot and by making some less than profound references to God's function. Ultimately it turns into a lugubrious chase movie with a lot of the extras wearing the kind of Greek tragedy masks that used to give style to college productions of Euripedes in the 1940s and 1950s.

"It's all just a joke," one character says toward the end. Boorman cannot get out from under a piece of junk that easily.

March 17, 1974

How to Make Sweet Music at the Box Office

By PAUL GARDNER

"IF Mike Nichols wants Dustin Farnum in 'The Graduate,'" said Joe Levine putting down the phone and turning to his production associates, "I let Mike have him. Now, *for the music*, he wants Simon and Schuster." The owlishly bespectacled executive smiled amiably. "I say, O.K., Mike, you can have Simon and Schuster."

Levine may be lousy at remembering names, but his willingness to trust his director made Dustin Hoffman a star seven years ago. And, with the signing of the folk-rock heroes Simon and Garfunkel, his phenomenally successful production of "The Graduate" added a new chord to movie music. Simon and Garfunkel's thematic ode, "Mrs. Robinson," a lyrical hymn to the provocative Older Woman who took a fumbling college graduate straight to bed instead of to a parsley-tasting contest at Scarborough Fair, sold more than 1,000,000 single records. The soundtrack LP was a biggie too, selling almost 2,000,000 copies.

After the sultry Mrs. Robinson came the pot-smokin' bike boys. When "Easy Rider," also in the late sixties, roared across the country with a soundtrack of rock music by every top-of-the-chart artist from Steppenwolf to Jimi Hendrix, and saved Columbia Pictures from sinking into the La Brea tar pits, Hollywood's clairvoyants saw a lucrative future of youth-oriented films—with music by teen-age idols. Studio executives, by now wearing aviator shades, beads, bell-bottoms and boots, prepared a youthquake of movies dealing with student riots, flower children and drugged hippies whose plight was set to music by popular recording names.

Today, the tiresome accent on youth has been replaced by nostalgia, gangster and supercop yarns, but studios (most of which own music publishing companies) still know the tremendous box-office value of a hit song. So they lean toward pre-recorded hits by trendy vocalists, like Bette Midler's "Friends" for "The Last of Sheila," or commissioned "original" themes from reigning favorites, like Curtis Mayfield's score for the upcoming "Claudine," or—if they're lucky—Barbra Streisand singing the title song for her own movie, "The Way We Were." Producers know that the disk jockey provides a connection between teen-age record buyers and youthful moviegoers that yields pure Hollywood gold.

"The record companies, the deejays have recently exercised a strong force behind film music," says John Green, the articulate composer-conductor and chairman of the Academy Award's music branch. In addition to the enormously popular "The Way We Were," the other songs nominated for an Oscar—to be awarded Tuesday night—are "Live and Let Die" (from the James Bond flick), "All That Love Went to Waste" (from "A Touch of Class"), "You're So Nice to Be Around" (from "Cinderella Liberty") and "Love" (from "Robin Hood").

Nowadays, before a script is completed, producers study Cashbox magazine to see who's Number One. "Their

thinking is, 'Let's get whoever sold 17-million records last year,'' sighs one publicist who's sat through many moody music sessions. When the film is completed, disk jockeys receive glossy promotion kits and private screenings. "Gee, kids, I saw a great flick last night . . . and here's your favorite . . . singing his own title song . . . " *That's* the kind of music producers want to hear.

So, Carole King sings and writes the title song for "Pocket Money." Neil Diamond is assigned "Jonathan Livingston Seagull." Bob Dylan does the music for and even appears in "Pat Garrett and Billy the Kid." John Denver, a perky new favorite, is signed to write and perform the theme for "The Bears and I," a future Walt Disney charmer. "Heck, I'm no Henry Mancini or Michel Legrand," admits the youngster with straw-colored hair, granny glasses and a double-vanilla malted grin. "I just play the guitar and write songs. I *know* I'm incapable of orchestrating an entire film. They just asked me to write something expressing the story, about a guy who's back from Vietnam, and sorta lost, who goes to an Indian village in the northwest . . ."

The use of names varies with each project: "McCabe and Mrs. Miller" featured previously recorded work by Leonard Cohen. "The Sting" offers adapted piano rags by Scott Joplin. "The Last American Hero" had an original number, "I Got a Name" (by Charles Fox and Norman Gimbel), sung by Jim Croce, who was killed last year in a plane crash. "Whether the music is original, adapted or something already recorded," says lyricist Gimbel, "the studios put a lot of value on songs. The music branches of some studios are probably more solvent than the film divisions."

*

During Hollywood's peak years, from the mid-thirties to the mid-fifties, studios had their own music departments with full orchestras and a staff of composers. Music created atmosphere and shaded personality. The sound was big and lush, the emphasis was on rich, full-bodied scores. Franz Waxman did *not* write a title song for "Rebecca," to be sung by a pop favorite, while Joan Fontaine gave the charred ruins of Manderlay one last tearful glimpse. "The giants of movie music—Max Steiner, Alfred Newman — didn't make their reputations on one song," says John Green. "They wrote entire scores—without the help of two dozen 'arrangers.'"

In the old days scores were written without an eye on Cashbox. Many films had themes but no songs at all. David Raksin's haunting music for "Laura" made the beautiful corpse a living being for the police detective (the theme was so popular that later, with words added, it became a Hit Parade song). And Bernard Herrmann's piercing violins in "Psycho" seemed to push Janet Leigh toward her bathtub death.

Then, in the fifties, Henry Mancini's jazz score for "Peter Gunn" started a new trend. Studios couldn't afford large orchestras any more and Mancini's jazz only required an 11-man group. "Also, what caught the ear was the music's sparseness," observes Mancini, who was widely imitated until the pop-rock explosion in the sixties when studios began thinking about record albums and "the young sound."

*

Usually, composers are selected by producers, who pay from $7,000 to $30,000 for a score. The composer selects the vocalist (subject to approval), who may earn $2,500 or, says one recording executive, "ask $50,000 and *get it.*" As the studios grasp hungrily for names that sell millions of records, they often find themselves hiring rock "stars" who require a suiteful of arrangers to get a score written.

"These rock composers are extremely gifted," adds John Green, "they've sold thousands of records. The studios want them. But many of them have no film background. Then, the Oscar committee discovers that maybe 16 guys helped 'arrange' the music. We now say that any person who takes a thematic entity and extends it into a dramatic score must share composing credit."

Oscar nominees in music are seldom discussed by critics who generally confine their puzzlements to the acting, directing and writing categories. This year, some critics were stunned by the omission of Alan Price, who composed and sang the music (on-screen) for "O Lucky Man!" Winner of the British equivalent of the Oscar, Price was considered by many viewers to be the real star of Lindsay Anderson's allegory, injecting the wit and surprise lacking in the screenplay. "It was a shocking omission," says Marilyn Bergman, co-lyricist with her husband Alan of "The Way We Were." Apparently, movies with potential Oscar candidates must be hits in the Hollywood - Malibu colony. "People in Los Angeles just didn't see 'O Lucky Man!'" says Mrs. Bergman. "It was that simple."

Many producers insist upon musically "book-ending" their movies—an irritating habit of having a title song over credits and again at the end. "We don't like title songs," admits Alan Bergman, "but in 'The Way We Were' it functions as a prologue and epilogue to the film." If producers aren't "book-ending," they opt for a "Clairol commercial song," heard while lovers romp through grassy glades or stroll arm-in-arm along the beach.

Occasionally, this music has nothing to do with plot or character but is just unexpectedly melodic, like "Raindrops Keep Falling on My Head," which could just as easily have been caterpillars or sunflowers plopping on the heads of Butch Cassidy, the Sundance Kid and the kid's bicycling sweetheart. "Raindrops" (by Burt Bacharach and Hal David) was criticized for being deliberately unrelated to the outlaw caper, but it sold thousands of records and helped draw crowds to the film.

John Green is optimistic about the future. "When music stops being an exploitation tool, you'll hear, once again, the kind of scores that are being reissued — and bought — by movie music collectors."

A few years ago, after the failure of "Marnie," Alfred Hitchcock was persuaded that his preferred composer, Bernard Herrmann, might be old-fashioned, that his name lacked "exploitation value." He stopped using him. But Bernard Herrmann, a name revered among European film buffs, added goose-pimples last year to Brian de Palma's "Sisters," a prickly horror story of Siamese twins.

"Everybody's looking for a new sound," Herrmann has said, "which means taking an old sound and jacking it up and amplifying it until it hurts your ears. There are no new sounds, only new ideas, and they don't come along very often."

March 31, 1974

A $17,500,000 getaway

Which Movies Made the Most Money Last Year?

Every year about this time Variety, the show business weekly, publishes a list naming each film that has earned $1,000,000 or more in the United States and Canada during the previous calendar year. The Variety figures refer to the distributor's share of box office earnings, that is, the sum that the theaters have returned to the distributor after deducting exhibition expenses. They are probably more reliable than any figures by an independent source and are indispensable to anyone interested in the state of movies, to say nothing of the state of the American Dream, which, depending on your point of view, was rather badly damaged last summer or proved its viability (if dreams can be said to be viable).

The list of 1974 money-makers, which appeared in the Jan. 8 issue, inevitably raises more questions than it answers. Can anyone really explain, for example, why "The Sting" should have made more money than any other film last year ($68,450,000). and made that sum so quickly that in 12 months' time it became the fourth biggest money-making film of all-time? It follows only "The Godfather" ($85,747,000), "The Sound of Music" ($83,891,000) and "Gone With The Wind" ($70,179,000). Only "The Exorcist" came close to "The Sting" by earning $66,300,000 in the same period. The year's third biggest money-maker earned just under $20,000,000. But why that big gap between the first two films and the ones that come next on the list?

• • •

If you think you have a reasonable answer to that question, read on.

The Variety list of 1974 hits contains the titles of a number of films you obviously have heard of and a few I'm sure you haven't. For those of you who think you have an understanding of the American public's taste, I've devised a modest test. In the following paragraphs I'm going to describe the 13 other top money-making films of the year and ask you to name the film and give some idea of the amount of money it earned. The answers will be found at the bottom of the column. For those who guess 13 out of 13 (and have not cheated by reading Variety), drop everything, you're wanted in Hollywood. For those who fail completely, don't be alarmed. You may be a movie critic.

I'll start with the film that was 15th on the Variety list, then the 14th and so on:

A $68,450,000 caper

He copped $14,100,000.

15. This is an adventure film that has a familiar story about international intrigue and treason in high places. The women in the movie are beautiful but they either are exceedingly dumb or have unreliable characters. The men prefer to pal around with each other.

14. A movie suggested by television but recalling the joys of an earlier era. Non-linear in form and as devoid of conventional narrative as a film by Robbe-Grillet. United Artists' biggest hit of the year.

13. Two guys and a girl. The guys extort a large amount of cash from a supermarket and spend the rest of the movie in a getaway car, being pursued by cops and by the movie's director who, when he isn't photographing auto smash-ups of various kinds, is photographing the chase from a helicopter. Peter Fonda is the star.

12. A Grand Motel sort of movie that gives star billing to a lot of actors who aren't, or at least haven't been for some time. Has to do with transportation. More truly representative of the Nixon years than any other film I can think of.

11. An old movie seen again. About being sincere and listening to your heart and turning the other cheek as long as you don't get too badly slapped.

10. Another old movie whose success had been an inspiration to more than one filmmaker. A high-class, elegant variation on the kind of buddy movies once played by Victor McLaglen and Edmund Lowe.

9. A movie about a loner who fights to survive in the wilderness. It's a matter of having principles and being well-armed. Virtually a one-character film.

8. You may have seen this one before too: a gangster, a married lady and a jealous husband. It's most agreeable to buffs interested in how people get from one place to another and in what they wear.

7. A sequel to No. 11. Same plot. Same actors. Same movie. Only much longer and worse.

6. A classic vision of the Old West. Fading frontiers, corruption, innocence, murder, cattle-rape.

5. The year's most successful transportation movie, and the worst, is also a sequel to an earlier film. It contains a large plug for the specific vehicle, which can virtually land itself.

4. A lesson in urban corruption given with a right-wing bias. If the system won't police itself, this man will police the system. Stars an American actor who was more or less made in Italy.

3. Two con men out to bend the system their way. One is a man of action, the other a more contemplative sort. The period is remote. Not to be confused with No. 10.

• • •

So much for the clues. Here are the answers:

15. "The Three Musketeers," $10,115,000. 14. "That's Entertainment," $10,800,000. 13. "Dirty Mary Crazy Larry," $12,068,000. 12. "Airport, 1975," $12,310,000. 11. "Billy Jack" (reissue), $13,000,000. 10. "Butch Cassidy and The Sundance Kid" (reissue), $13,820,000. 9. "Serpico," $14,100,000. 8. "The Great Gatsby," $14,200,000. 7. "The Trial of Billy Jack," $15,000,000. 6. "Blazing Saddles," $16,500,000. 5. "Herbie Rides Again," $17,500,000. 4. "Magnum Force," $18,300,000. 3, "Papillon," $19,750,000.

January 19, 1975

THE COMEDY "FILLUM" MAN

By Mack Sennett.

MAKING a motion-picture comedy is the hardest work I know of. But it's worth all the trouble it makes.

If you'll just stop to think how much there is of tragedy and trouble in life anyway, you'll agree, I believe, that anything that brings a note of joy and gladness into a person's life is well worth every bit of hard work it takes to accomplish it.

And don't for one minute get the idea that because the comedies we are making for Triangle at the Keystone studios seem to be nothing more than a series of laughing, rollicking good times they require no hard work, no painstaking thought and preparation. Every situation that causes you to laugh and that requires but a brief instant to flash on the screen has been carefully thought out in advance, has been rehearsed over and over and, finally, has been filmed, often at a really great cost.

If I have been asked once in my life I suppose I have been asked ten thousand times to give a recipe for a Keystone comedy. I simply can't do it. Every story we work out calls for a distinct and usually decidedly different treatment from every other picture we have ever made. Of course, I don't mean to say that there are not some more or less general rules for comedy work that can be laid down.

For one thing, we build up our comedies with an idea of continuing the suspense of the audience as long as we can. Then we try to surprise them by working up a climax totally different from that for which they have been looking.

The one great truth to be borne in mind by those who would make motion-picture comedies, I firmly believe, is that they must work to the great majority of movie fans rather than to the few—you must strive neither for that which is too subtle nor for that which is too broad. It is perfectly true that there are many who enjoy only the subtle joke, and it is likewise true that there are those who cannot see the point of a joke unless it is so broad that they can hit it with their eyes shut. But comedies which fall in either of these two classes are not what I call good comedies.

I am perfectly aware of the fact that each time I make the declaration I lay myself open to argument, but I really do insist that comedy is an art. The more Keystone comedies I make the more convinced I become that comedy is an art, and a high one at that. If those who are inclined to scoff at me will try their hand at directing just one of those comedies they designate as anything but art, I am pretty certain they will concede me my point.

There cannot well be any argument on the proposition that the public is steadily getting harder to please, particularly in so far as comedies are concerned. For one thing they are far better educated in what is called comedy, and the time is past and almost forgotten when you could be sure of a laugh by merely making one of your characters walk up behind another and suddenly push him down or trip him, or do any one of the scores of stunts the old slap-stick comedian was able to get away with.

To put a comedy over now you have got to have a story—a real story, filled with human interest; one that has something more than a semblance of a plot to it. And it is the difficulty of getting these good comedy stories that makes it so hard nowadays to supply the insatiable demand of the public for more and more comedies.

Comedy acting is tricky. I use the word advisedly. It is still possible for some of the film comedians to get a laugh with a fall, but they must fall funny and offhand. I can think of only four or five people in the world who can really fall in a funny way.

Generally speaking, I think men make funnier screen comedians than women. There are exceptions, of course, but, taken all in all, you can make it as a pretty positive assertion that men are funny and women are not. Certainly it is infinitely easier to do comedies with men than with women. The latter are inclined to giggle and generally destroy the value of what they are attempting to put over by being too obviously frivolous. Men, on the other hand, take their work seriously and give it the attention it really requires.

It is perfectly true that the success or failure of a picture depends to a very great extent on the director. That is true, no matter what the character of the picture, but it is most true, I think, of comedies. I don't know of any class of film work that calls for more finesse than does the comedy film. The director of the comedy picture must have the knack, or art, or ability, or whatever you may wish to call it, to work his people up to the exact pitch required for the picture, and then hold them there long enough to register before the camera. I have seen more scenes ruined by directors driving their people a point too far or by failing to drive them quite far enough than from any other cause.

During the time we have been making Keystone pictures we have had many people who have made enviable reputations for themselves in the spoken drama. A question that is put to me frequently indicates that my questioners are of the opinion that these legitimate stars are hard to handle. Nothing could be further from the truth. I have always found them more willing, if anything, to learn the tricks of the screen work than the beginner who came to us convinced he knew everything about the film business before he ever set foot in a studio.

But, just as there are all kinds of people in other lines of work, so there are all kinds in the film game, and that is one of the things that lend fascination to the work. In my experience in the moving-picture business, which extends over a considerable period of time, I have tried my hand at acting in all kinds of film plays and later at directing them, and I am quite frank to say that comedies are the hardest of all to act or to produce. And perhaps for the same reason they are by far the most interesting. At any rate, they are to me.

The film business is founded on a solid foundation, I honestly believe, and so far as comedies are concerned the public will never, I am convinced, get enough of them.

All the world loves a lover, 'tis true, but the world also has a particularly friendly feeling for the man who laughs, and as for the man who can make it laugh—well, he has earned, I like to tell myself, a little niche in the hearts of the world that money could never buy.

July 30, 1916

Above—Will Rogers in "A Texas Steer."

THE SCREEN

Will Rogers's personality penetrates through lenses and film to the screen. Rogers in motion pictures is not Rogers himself, with his chewing gum, rope, and conversation, but there is a thoroughly delightful person in a photoplay called "Almost a Husband," at the Strand this week, who will be recognized as the former star of the Midnight Frolic. For one thing, Rogers is genuine in everything he does, and genuineness counts for as much on the screen as on the stage, and, furthermore, he is by no means an insignificant actor. Cast in a part that fits him, he puts meaning into his playing, so that it is playing, and not just posing. His part in "Almost a Husband" fits him. He is the school teacher, lawyer, author, and emergency husband of Opie Read's "Old Ebenezer," from which the photoplay was derived, and the character takes on life through his impersonation. To Director Clarence G. Badger should be given credit for not forcing Rogers out of his natural rôle. He would not, for instance, seem right in protracted love scenes, and, although he becomes quite, rather than almost, a husband, there is no billing and cooing until the final fade-out, and this is beautifully brief.

Some may know, and others may not, that the story is about a New England school teacher imported into a village on the Mississippi River. He is instinctively a philanthropist, and, after saving a poor family from disaster, rescues the leading banker's daughter from an undesired suitor. At a party he goes through a mock wedding ceremony with her, and then discovers that it was valid. He gallantly offers to free the girl, but when he learns that she is safe from the villain as long as she is married to him, he as gallantly volunteers to remain her husband. The rest of the story is concerned with the unsuccessful efforts of the villain and his accomplices to get him unmarried.

The chief interest of the photoplay is in the characterization by Rogers and the performance of Peggy Wood and Herbert Standing, who play the banker and his daughter.

For once, spectators also enjoy some of the sub-titles flashed on the screen, which are surely from Rogers himself.

October 13, 1919

THE SCREEN

PAY DAY, by and with Charles Chaplin; "Trumps, Ace High"; "The Ballad of Fisher's Boarding House"; "Mark Twain"; "The Cape of Good Hope"; "Felix Makes Good"; "Odds and Ends"; "Dear Old Southland," sung by George Reardon. At the Strand.

With Charlie Chaplin at the Strand and Pola Negri at the Rivoli it can hardly be called a lustreless week for the Broadway screens.

A new Chaplin comedy, of course, is an event in the motion picture world, and all that the reviewer has to do is announce it. The rest may as well be silent so far as he is concerned, because nothing can be said about Chaplin that has not been said a dozen times already, and most people are not interested in what is said about him, anyhow. They just go to see him and laugh—and some of them understand.

It may not be entirely futile to report, however, that this new Chaplin comedy is one of his best. It is not to be ranked with "The Kid," which was a longer and more penetratingly serious venture, and it has not the significance, perhaps, of "Shoulder Arms," but it has enough pure fun, and sufficient satire, too, for any one. With or without reference to anything else, it is something to relish for its own sake.

Underlying the picture's surface buffoonery is that refreshing treatment of the commonplace by which Chaplin has so often exposed the irony of life. He shows the gods grinning at human earnestness, yet he does not join them in mocking it. He is a part of humanity, he has the feelings and the aspirations of ordinary men, he is sympathetically one of the crowd. But he sees the fatuity of it all, too, and so is one above the crowd.

For example: He is a poor workman employed in the construction of a building, and he is hopelessly married. But he sees the foreman's daughter and loves her. His love is a poem. It exalts him. She sits with her father's lunch on a platform of the scaffolding outside the unfinished building and he rides the work elevator up to adore her. Every time she notices him he shrinks from her inquiring look and signals the engineman to lower the elevator. But he comes back to worship again, and again gives the signal to descend when she looks at him. She is spreading her father's lunch and puts a round box near the elevator shaft. He comes up once more, the embodiment of true, though timid, love. He embraces her with his earnest eyes. And then he smells the limburger cheese in the box under his nose. For the last time and hurriedly he gives the signal for the elevator to descend. His love is genuine, and in expressing it there is no trace of mockery. But the cheese is strong. And the gods grin.

This is only one little incident in the picture. There are many others. For story the comedy simply takes snatches from the day of a laborer, beginning when he comes late to work and ending when his wife drives him out the next morning to go to work again, although he has just come in from a night in the back room and in the open. Such a life!

As the Chaplin comedy is short—it lasts only twenty-three minutes—Joseph Plunkett, managing director of the Strand, has filled up his program with other short subjects, and on the whole he has made an exceptionally interesting selection. There is "Trumps, Ace High," a Post Nature picture, giving another chapter of the life of that enlivening little terrier Trumps, with the rich scenic background of its predecessors, and there is also a travel-tempting Prizma color picture of Capetown and its surrounding country. "The Ballad of Fisher's Boarding House" consists of faithful and vivid illustrations of the poem, with, however, an energetically sentimental ending which surely Kipling never dreamed of. "Mark Twain," from Kineto's Great American Authors Series, shows places associated with the life of its hero and briefly picturizes his story "The Jumping Frog." A slow-motion picture of ski jumping is included in the "Odds and Ends," and "They Say," while making no particular point in itself, suggests new possibilities for caricature on the screen by the use of distorting mirrors.

April 3, 1922

CHAPLIN'S "DUTCH UNCLE"

THE name of the graying gentleman with the cockney accent in the office of United Artists was Alfred Reeves and he had been associated with Charlie Chaplin as an "uncle-sort-of-thing" since 1910. No, he had nothing to tell the newspapers on the occasion of one of his infrequent trips to town from Los Angeles, where he was guarding the Chaplin properties from hero-worshipers in Charlie's absence. Yes, he was the man who brought Charlie to America.

It was back in 1910, Mr. Reeves began auspiciously. He was in London with an English vaudeville company and there was talk in professional circles of two brothers whose talents were getting them a mild reputation in the local music halls. Their names were Sydney and Charles Chaplin. Sydney was the older and supposed to be the cleverer. When there was a part to be had Sydney usually was approached first.

But there was no denying, said Mr. Reeves, that Charlie had talent, too. A bright-eyed, rosy-cheeked boy of 20, who looked younger. He had been with the Six Lancashires troupe, clog-dancing and singing for the most part, improvising a bit of comedy now and then. He had a good speaking voice and William Gillette picked him up for several of his Sherlock Holmes melodramas in the local houses. He played Billy, the page boy.

Charlie came to America as leading comedian in the vaudeville troupe, Mr. Reeves went on, and played around the Percy G. Williams circuit in New York. That was in the Fall of 1910. The piece was a comedy called "The Wow-Wows," or "A Night in a London Secret Society." Charlie appeared as Archibald, a village busybody who was forever prying into the secrets of his friends. His curiosity irritated his friends so much that they finally decided to play a trick on him. If he were a Wow-Wow, they told him, he could be let in on all the secrets, but he would have to be initiated first.

That was the end of the first scene—Charlie announcing that he wanted to become a Wow-Wow. The second scene revealed the door of the secret initiation chamber. The audience laughed in anticipation of all the torments that awaited Archibald. The conspirators were jubilant. The climax of the torture was an electric current which was to shock Archibald into a realization of his deficiencies. In the dénouement, however, Archibald turned the tables on the Wow-Wows by fixing the current so that they received the shock instead of himself.

Charlie had two comedy parts during his connection with the Reeves troupe. One presented him as this village busybody and the other as the inebriated swell. His famous tramp character which he was later to develop at the Keystone studios had its beginnings here. The costume was never seen in its entirety until he reached the screen, but in his part of the "broken-down swell," Mr. Reeves pointed out, lay the beginnings of the idea. The big shoes, cane and baggy pants were used in his caricature of shabby English gentility.

"You know," Mr. Reeves explained, "Chaplin's costume originally was a satire-sort-of-thing on the English gentleman. The English actor, especially. All the actor needed to be dressed up was a clean collar, a shave and a cane. He could be without a bob, but he'd still consider himself all togged out with some place to go."

Charlie started making his Keystone comedies in Los Angeles in 1913 and he never deviated from the tramp character which he introduced in his first film. He made "A Dog's Life" and many other films, then "The Kid."

"Somebody told me once," went on Mr. Reeves, "that I was as English as 'arf a crown. Maybe that's why Charlie likes to have me around. I'm his Dutch uncle, sort of. When Charlie's working he likes a friendly atmosphere on the spot. I see that he isn't worried with business until he's finished.

"They say Charlie is temperamental, but he isn't, really, alongside of some stars I could mention. The thing is, he doesn't like to be bothered with certain matters while he's working."

There was a sentimental story in a paper, the Uncle-Sort-of-Thing went on, about Charlie's mustache. It said that Charlie had used the same mustache since the beginning.

"There's no sense in it at all, at all. Charlie puts on a fresh mustache every single day he's working. He twiddles a little hair with his finger and a comb, a crêpe hair or gyp, as we say in show business, and there is his famous mustache. At the end of the day he takes it off and flecks it into the air with his finger."

Charlie may like to travel, Mr. Reeves confided, but his heart is in Hollywood. He prefers America to England and is here to stay permanently.

May 17, 1931

A CHAT WITH CHAPLIN

Comedian Discusses His New Film; Pantomimes Role in Shirtsleeves

HOLLYWOOD, July 10.

CHARLIE CHAPLIN, who is by no means the easiest man to find in Hollywood, the other day sat at a table in his studio bungalow munching an apple and drinking coffee. He had just changed from his famous big shoes, tiny hat and baggy trousers to his everyday clothes, but as the sun was hot he was in his shirtsleeves. The prince of screen jesters was within a stone's throw of a reproduction of a section of the Thames embankment, erected for scenes in his forthcoming comedy, "City Lights."

He was pensive at first. He may have been thinking of sound versus silence or of new ideas for his current production. Soon, however, as he talked about incidents in his new picture, he became enthusiastic. He is virtually the last of the believers in the silent screen. The only concessions he will make to sound in his "City Lights" will be to have an incidental song, the patter of dancing feet, now and again the tones of a trombone or a cornet that are seen in the picture and the inevitable synchronized music score. He is, however, strongly averse to sound effects, as they are known. He won't have in his film any applause or even the sound of a closing door.

Some of the Scenes.

Chaplin doesn't believe that one should really hear anything if one can't hear the characters talk. He portrayed the results by shutting a door and moving his lips without making a sound. From what he said, he was even more strongly opposed to giving shadows a voice than when this present correspondent saw him last year. His friends say that he is worried as to whether his mute work will be successful, but he has no reason for anxiety. For when he expatiated upon the action of his "City Lights" it was quite evident that it was going to be just as delightful a picture as any of his others. Some of the ideas may not be quite new, but they are gilded with Chaplin's whimsy and charming pathos.

He chuckled as he outlined some of the laughable scenes and appeared quite touched over what happened to the little tramp, played by himself. It was the first time Chaplin had told the story of a picture in the making to a reporter and he enjoyed it so that he pantomimed much of the action. It was like watching Chaplin on the stage, minus his disguise. It was a performance that one would willingly have paid well to see. Two friends, who had been seated with him, silently crept away to let the master talk, not that they did not wish to listen, but that they knew that two's company and four's none.

An Attempted Suicide.

His denunciation of the talking picture was less interesting than his keen delivery and acting of the three principal characters in his picture. He demonstrated what the tramp did, what the Jekyll and Hyde inebriate did, and then what the blind heroine did. Chiefly, of course, he emphasized the actions of the tramp who encounters the intoxicated broker on the Thames embankment.

"The drunk, you see," said Chaplin, "is going to commit suicide. He has a noose around his neck and at the other end of the rope is a big stone."

The comedian imitated the way the inebriate fiddled with the rope and then told of the tramp's not being aware of what he was preparing to do. Finally the intoxicated man is ready and then the tramp grasps what is about to happen. He tries to dissuade the other from ending his life.

"He slaps his little chest," said Chaplin, "and admonishes the drunk to be a man and throw out his chest. The actions of the drunk are muddled. He, however, finally slips off the noose and listens to the tramp. Then the drunk decides that no matter what the tramp says, life isn't worth living, and in putting the noose over his own head he also gets it around the tramp's. Then when the intoxicated one stoops to pick up the stone, his own neck is freed from the rope, and when he throws the stone into the river in goes the little fellow."

A Blind Heroine.

Chaplin then told of the inebriate's efforts to rescue the tramp and of the scenes in the former's mansion. This bibulous character is, however, a peculiar specimen, for he only remembers his little friend when he is in his cups.

Chaplin then devoted a good deal of time to the sightless girl and the sympathetic tramp, who is at first unaware that the girl is blind. If this is pictured as Chaplin related it, and, of course, it will be, it should make a beautifully poetic sequence. One could shed a tear or two while listening to Chaplin tell the simple little story and one could easily chuckle when he, laughing himself, illustrated the adventures of his three principal characters.

It is a story that rather whets the interest in the picture, for the idea of having seen Chaplin himself acting it in his bungalow, as he did that day, causes one to be all the keener to see the production when it comes to the screen. But when that will be nobody knows, for Chaplin works when he will, or when the spirit moves him. He knows that when the film is finished at least half a dozen men would be ready to give him three or four million dollars for the world's rights, that is, if Chaplin considered disposing of them.

Sound and Just Noise.

He said that the success of the hitherto silent screen offerings was due, not to their art, but to the personalities in the productions. Beauty, he said, was frequently killed by the sound of the beauty's voice. Yet, he believed, the actress might have been exceptionally competent in expressing herself in pantomime.

When referring to a dialogue picture he put his fingers in his ears, saying a friend of his had done so in a theatre where a talking film was on view. Chaplin averred that the effect of hearing the voices after gazing at the scenes with stuffed ears, was frightful. He does not believe that the producers know what to do with sound; that is to say, they are not sure where the motion picture finishes and the voices, or the stage technique, begins. He declared that when he sat before a talking shadow he could never make himself believe that the shadow was speaking. It was to him artificial—the voice coming from somewhere, but, no matter how well it was synchronized, not from the image on the screen.

A Dance in "City Lights."

Chaplin, whether he is anxious or not about upholding the silent picture, is well aware that Douglas Fairbanks's production, "The Iron Mask," which has precious little talk in it, was one of Fairbanks's most successful offerings from a financial viewpoint.

In referring to sound effects, Chaplin admitted that he would do a dance in "City Lights," and that the sound of his feet would be heard. He might show a cornetist and a trombone player, and he thought that they should be heard as well as seen. A girl singing a song, he granted, would not hurt his silent production, but he considered that the producers at the present time do not know where to end their penchant for sound. There has been so much sobbing on the screen that people do not want to hear it. It is noise and never stirring!

Chaplin's strongest friends, Douglas Fairbanks and Samuel Goldwyn, who have temporarily deserted the silent picture, do not believe that it has gone for good, even though they anticipate vast improvements in the audible productions.

Harry Myers in Cast.

How far Chaplin has gone in his new comedy it is impossible to say, for with his pictures there is always a great deal made that he eventually discovers he does not want. Harry Myers was recently engaged for the part of the drunk, because a predecessor, who had started to work in the film, refused to dive into the "Thames."

Mr. Myers won his greatest distinction by his splendid acting in the Fox picturization of the "Yankee at the Court of King Arthur."

"And who is the girl?" Chaplin was asked.

"Oh," said Chaplin, "she isn't known."

He walked out through the studio grounds to the front gate, where men were busy shifting the façade of the structure to widen the street. None of the workmen appeared to recognize in the clean-shaven, dapper figure the sympathetic little comedian they had so often paid to see on the screen.

MORDAUNT HALL.

July 14, 1929

THE SCREEN

Once more the comedy captures a program. And it's Buster Keaton again, too. His latest reel of nonsense, "My Wife's Relations," appropriates first place for itself at the Rivoli this week, or at least shares the top of the bill with J. E. Williamson's stirring under-water scenic, "Wonders of the Sea," which has been moved up from the Rialto, where it played last week.

The Keaton comedy begins in a metropolitan district where the people speak so many different languages that they "misunderstand each other perfectly." There's a poor postman who has a Polish letter to deliver and holds it beside every sign on his route to see which one it matches. There's a Polish magistrate who agrees over the phone to marry a couple of his own nationality. There's an Irishwoman who speaks no Polish, and there's Buster, who, apparently, speaks neither Irish nor Polish. The Irish woman drags Buster before the magistrate to have him arrested, and the magistrate thinks they are the couple he has agreed to marry. So he marries them, and when the Irishwoman realizes what has happened she takes her accidentally acquired husband home with her.

Now, Buster, as you know, is little,

and his wife is one of a large family—a father and four or five brothers. The father isn't so large, but any one of the brothers, photographed by himself, makes a long-shot look like a close-up. And they all decide, after a careful examination of the specimen their sister has brought home, that Buster isn't even interesting—until they get the idea that he is heir to $100,000. Then he's their little Napoleon—until he tries to crowd into the foreground of a family photograph.

It's nothing but foolishness, or rather, it's free-flying, honest-to-goodness foolishness without any theatrical hokum, insincere moralizing and sham elegance loaded on to it. And it's bright and original. So it's something to enjoy, something to throw your head back and laugh at, especially in its first part, up to the point where the bride's big brothers find out that Buster isn't worth $100,000. After that it's just the usual knockabout stuff, not bad, but not importantly different from the thousands of other chase-'em-around slap-stickers. But Buster Keaton himself, who can be earnest, anxious, angry and joyful without a flicker in the fixed seriousness of his expression, must have learned how to laugh when he saw himself in the first half of the film.

The photoplay at the Rivoli is "The Impossible Mrs. Bellew." It seems designed for the special exploitation of Miss Gloria Swanson, who can wear clothes, look injured and be smart. In her present rôle she begins life as the loving and long-suffering wife of a man who lets the world think that she has been unfaithful to him so he can divorce her and marry someone else. Then, to escape scandal, she goes to a French seaside resort and dives into the gay life there. She has been the victim of terrible injustice, you see, so every one is ready to forgive her if she seeks forgetfulness in the wild, wild world of Grand Dukes, American millionaires and things—provided, of course, she doesn't go too far, which, of course, she doesn't, not with a censor board sitting in Forty-second Street and censorial parents in every movie house west of Rahway. But she can be wicked and well-dressed while the censors and the censorial parents know all the time that she loves her little son, has always been true to her husband, and will eventually marry the nice novelist who never doubts any more than the censors and the parents do, that she is a good woman.

So, it's all neatly arranged, you see. It's well photographed, too; it's settings are as elaborate and as tasteless as they should be, and its marionettes wear the clothes and make the gestures expected of them.

October 23, 1922

Buster Keaton

Harold Lloyd

Working in A LaughFactory

By HAROLD LLOYD.

BEING funny is a serious business. This remark has been made before and is likely to be made again. Since no one has ever denied it, we may safely assume that it is a fact. It is also a fact that a man must not take himself too seriously, even under the provocation of making a funny picture. That sometimes results in calamity.

For years a distinction has been made between the so-called serious drama and the comedy. This is an unfair classification. There is nothing more serious in life than the production of a comedy that attains its purpose of making people laugh. I have not the slightest doubt that more effort goes into the making of a high-grade comedy that is incorporated in the production of some of our biggest dramatic screen offerings.

Right from the start the comedy producer must of necessity accept a lot of grief that does not fall to the dramatic producer. A dramatic feature is produced from a carefully prepared script, which, in the hands of a competent director, is a detailed map of the entire picture. In our case, we never work from a script. We provide ourselves with the basic outline of a story, but the actual comedy is incorporated as we progress—as situations develop and lend themselves to "gags," by which I mean the incidental pieces of business that make the situations funny.

Various estimates have been made by scholars as to the number of basic plots possible in the drama, and the numbers range from seven to thirty-five. However that may be, it is said by those who are supposed to know that all drama, both stage and screen, must be based on one of those plots or a variation thereof. From this it may easily be seen that the producer of drama has something to fall back on. The producer of high-grade comedy has no such safety net; he can't fall back on anything. The public demands that a comedian be funny, and they do not consider him funny unless he is original. They are quick to detect any attempt on his part to work his old stuff over again, and they retaliate by refusing to laugh at his worn-out bag of tricks. When audiences refuse to laugh at a comedian he finds himself in the position of the bathing beach life saver who can't swim.

Growth of Farce.

Comedy grows no more from the things that might happen than from the things that actually do happen. The things at which we laugh the loudest are things with which we are familiar. In reading the Greek and Latin classics in our school days we frequently came upon passages which the instructor informed us represented the keen wit and humor of the author. It was well to label them, for we would never have recognized them as laugh-provoking observations. The reason for that was the fact that they dealt with people, times and conditions long since dead and gone and with which we of the present day had no possible contact.

On the other hand the spectacle of a fat man slipping on an icy sidewalk never fails to get a laugh. The same is true of a man attempting to drive a nail and mashing his finger in the process, or a man with his arms full of bundles attempting to keep his hat from blowing off. These things are funny because they have happened to all of us and probably will happen again. They are trying experiences for the individuals involved and we sympathize with them, but we laugh, nevertheless, because they are human touches.

We have found that invariably it is the little human touches which gain the biggest laughs. I might cite for example some of the situations in "Grandma's Boy." We never have screened a more effective laugh-making sequence than the one in which the boy ate the camphor balls.

Ordinarily this situation might be classified as "hokum." But the sympathy of the audience was with the boy. And when he ate the camphor balls by mistake, and yet couldn't disclose the fact to his sweetheart, it reached home and received an even bigger laugh than we anticipated.

One of the main secrets of comedy-making is getting your audience with you and having them sympathize with you. They take more interest in you. They laugh at your petty little difficulties, and the laugh is always magnified because of the sympathy they hold for your character.

The man who tries to be funny is lost. To lose one's naturalness is always to lose the sympathy of your audience.

Plots Not Difficult.

The development of a comedy, as we work, is most often along the lines of sincerity. In the instance of "Why Worry" we aimed for straight farce. We made no effort at sincerity. But in our present picture, we plan absolutely to have our story ring true, to give it the sincerity which we feel characterized "Grandma's Boy."

The least of our difficulties always is "plot" as applied to the general outline of a story. It is in the development and the treatment that we face our greatest task. We invariably find, however, that one situation leads to another—one "gag" builds up its successor. We seek always to build up every situation to the "topping off" point. A laugh sequence always is best when it builds up. The top off "gag" of any situation always must have a greater force than any other in the sequence. Sometimes the mistake is made of letting a situation fall flat through inability to furnish a top off laugh. This we always try to avoid.

Originality of "gags" is the constant bugaboo of our staff. Many ideas are suggested, but sometimes few are chosen.

There are many factors to be considered in the selection of a "gag." It must be clean; it must fit the situation, and it must have a new twist. It sometimes is impossible to furnish an entirely new gag, but when an old one is brought into play, it must be dressed in a new garb. That is quite essential.

Pages could be written on this subject. But the whole situation can be summed up in these few words:

"Make the situations funny. Preview them, and then pray for laughs.

"If you don't get the laughs, forget the prayers and go to work again."

December 16, 1923

WHO'S WHO

Enter, With Trumpets, the Brothers Marx

NOT the least extraordinary thing about the Four Marx Brothers—who, it might just as well come out now as later, are playing in "I'll Say She Is" at the Casino—is the fact that they are really brothers. This will, in fact, prove the most surprising circumstance of all to vaudeville audiences, which know that the sister acts of the two-a-day even make a hearty joke out of what the Colonel's Lady said to Judy O'Grady.

They are, then, let it be taken for granted, brothers and Leonard is the oldest. (Leonard is the Marx who plays the piano in the Napoleon scene.) Next comes Arthur, of red wig and the silent tongue, who is 35, Julius, the official wise-cracker, acknowledging 33, and Herbert, the family baby of 23.

The boys were born in New York City, on East 93d Street, and it is Julius who longs now and again for the dear old childhood days, right in the heart of the Ruppert and Ehret breweries.

Their mother, in the days before their own theatrical careers started, was known on the stage as Minnie Palmer,* and along in 1905 she decided to make up a vaudeville act composed of herself and her four sons. After much dickering with the various vaudeville managers, a price of $50 a week was secured for the entire troupe, out of which only food, clothes, rent and railroad fares had to be paid. They existed in some fashion, however, and even achieved a survival over a route that covered all of the small towns of the South.

Eighteen years ago Mrs. Marx decided to start Julius upon a theatrical career, despite his slender 15 years, and managed to place him with a small touring dramatic company. In the course of the next few years, Leonard, Arthur and Herbert were sent out to join their brother.

*Not, it should be added, the better known Minnie Palmer.

No one knows just how, but before long the vaudeville team of the Four Marx Brothers had been formed and was adding a new delight in life to two and three and four a day audiences the country over. Bit by bit the act became one of vaudeville's leading drawing cards. Thus, at the most recent zenith of their vaudeville career, the four brothers played for sixty-five consecutive weeks in vaudeville theatres in Greater New York alone. Their appearances at the Palace were so frequent that some wit, possibly in their employ, named them "The Palace Theatre Stock Company."

During all the years of their stage work the brothers have maintained a steady contact with a home life dominated by their mother. Thus, fifteen years ago the Marx lares and penates were moved to Chicago, to provide a larger opportunity for reunions between a mother and sons playing the Western vaudeville time. Five years ago, the boys having come East, the Marx demesne was established at Richmond Hill, where it exists even at the moment.

The four brothers' uncle, the brother of Mrs. Marx, is Al Shean of Gallagher and Shean, and "Yes, We Have No Bananas" is played oftener on the family victrola than any other song.

Last season, through the confidence they had inspired in James P. Beury, owner of the Walnut Street Theatre in Philadelphia, the ways and means were found for the emergence of the Four Marx Brothers from vaudeville into the wide open spaces of the musical comedy field. For almost a year now they have been smoothing their present offering out upon the ungrateful planes of the road.

A few days before their local opening, Mrs. Marx slipped and broke her ankle. On the opening night, with her ankle in a plaster cast, she was carried into her stage box and was thus enabled to be present at the Broadway triumph of her boys and their discovery in some of the public prints. They were, to be sure, not much of a surprise to vaudeville patrons, but there are four or five people in New York who rarely go to vaudeville and they all write reviews for newspapers and so the boys were discovered again. The next discovery, it is predicted, will be in the July issue of The American Mercury, to be followed by a piece in the December Vanity Fair.

June 1, 1924

HAL ROACH CARRIES ON

'Our Gang' and Laurel and Hardy Survive Despite the Double-Bill Menace

HOLLYWOOD.

THE double-feature mania which has gripped the nation has killed one of the cinema's most flourishing institutions, the slap-stick comedy factory. Most of them have given up the ghost. Hal Roach, however, has adapted himself to the times by renouncing the two-reelers for the more respected multiple-reel films. The man who once said that there is nothing as funny as a custard pie in the face still clings to his theory—with certain amendments. The pie must be composed of sterner stuff than was used ten years ago and it must be tossed a little more artfully.

The baggy trousers and the chalked face have been abandoned for the time being by the Roach players. He believes that some day public taste will demand them back. Until that time he will concern himself with eight full-length comedies a year and twelve one-[illegible]lers with "Our Gang." Charli[illegible] [illegible]hase has departed from the lot since his attempt at feature work met with public apathy; the art of Laurel and Hardy will be limited to features; Patsy Kelly has been teamed with Lyda Roberti, who has replaced the late Thelma Todd, and there will be an all-star musical each year with all the Roach comedians, including the "Gang."

* * *

The Roach lot, probably the most active single unit in town, differs from the average studio in spirit, if not in appearance. It is located in Culver City, a mile from its associate studio, MGM. Roach and his family own it outright and finance most of their own productions, which is something of a novelty in Hollywood. Normally between 600 and 700 people are employed, and one point is notable: sixty-eight of his employes have been with him fifteen years or longer. Some even date back to the old days when his studio was a converted home in downtown Los Angeles.

The oldest unit in the Roach concern is "Our Gang," which is now on its sixteenth year, with its fourth leading man, "Spanky" McFarland. Other "Gang" leaders have been Johnny Downs, featured at Paramount; Jackie Cooper, whom Roach sold to Metro for a sum in excess of $100,000, and Dickie Moore, who is featured in dramas. Mary Kornman is married and occasionally appears on the screen; Mickey Daniels is active in films; Jackie Condon is in high school; Joe Cobb is making personal appearances; Farina is in vaudeville; Jackie Davis, brother of Mrs. Harold Lloyd, is in school and "Sunshine Sammy" has his own orchestra in the East. Shirley Temple once appeared with "Our Gang," and the fact that Roach failed to recognize her genius causes no bitterness. It was just one of those things. Didn't Universal throw out Jean Harlow and didn't Warners fire Clark Gable?

Roach is using most of the "Gang" in a feature which is currently shooting "General Spanky." The cast is furbished by such troupers as Phillips Holmes, Rosina Lawrence, Ralph Morgan, Hobart Bosworth, Irving Pichel and Louise Beavers. While it is listed as a comedy-drama of rebellion, it probably will lean more toward humor than revolt. Fred Newmeyer, who has been with Roach almost throughout the studio's existence, is directing, with Gordon Douglas handling the juvenile contingent.

* * *

The children to a great extent run the lot. They have access to all the offices, and all shooting is scheduled in accord with their lives, their schooling and the play periods. Strict rules govern their conduct and that of the parent assigned to watch over them. Their salaries are determined by their public appeal. They start in at $40 a week, but Spanky, who is almost a star in his own right, receives $1,250 a week. Most of the parents put the money away against the children's later life and their schooling. The father of one boy, however, thought that his son's $500 a week entitled him to the life of a movie star, and Roach had to go to court to protect the lad's earnings from the parent.

When a child joins "Our Gang" the rules which govern him are explicitly given, and parents are called into the Roach offices for infractions. No child is frightened or coerced into doing anything he doesn't wish to do. Parents must

keep hands off during working hours. School and recreation periods must be adhered to. Every comfort must be provided child and parents on the set. No child can be scolded or spanked on the set. All disciplining must take place at home, away from the eyes of the others. All children must be treated alike; there can be no favorites as far as the crew is concerned.

Instead of ponderous conferences by executives from which, rather laboriously, the names of stars emerge on other lots, the picture crew determines the nicknames of the Roach youngsters. When they join the gang the carpenters, electricians, camera men and others are in contact with them constantly, and they give them their names. Roach believes that better results are obtained this way, for generally the titles have reason. Of the present gang the boys on the stage named "Spanky," "Buckwheat" Thomas, the successor to "Farina"; "Alfalfa" Switzer, who is very much the farm boy, and "Porky" Lee, who is as chubby as his name indicates.

* * *

In handling them Roach operates on the theory that the loss of an ice cream cone is as much a tragedy to a child as a million dollars to an adult. Therefore they are never allowed to become accustomed to false values, and the nickel cone is their standard of life and affluence. Their toys come, for the most part, from the prop shop and are implements that have been used in pictures. They have others that smack of the dime store, and they are constantly trading and making deals.

There is a complete turnover in the "Gang" personnel every three or four years. The members are replaced one at a time and each grows into his part naturally. The "movie mother menace" being so acute, Roach refuses to interview any who come to the studio. He may miss some prospects but he saves himself a great deal of grief. Parents must submit photographs. If the producer is interested, his agents look the child up, no matter in what city he lives. If he measures up even in a small way to all the things his mother claims, he is brought to Hollywood at Roach's expense and given a test. If he doesn't make the grade, other Roach agents see that mother and child are put on the train and that they don't linger in Hollywood long.

In some respects the Roach lot is a pretty strenuous place, what with so many practical jokers about. Nearly everyone is being eternally funny. The Laurel and Hardy set is the center of most of the horse play although it may break out anywhere. A newcomer went onto the parking lot where he had left his day-old car. He almost had convulsions when he saw that the side of it had been caved in. He rushed toward the machine only to find, on closer inspection, that a technician had painted the side to look as if it had been wrecked. They are such boys.

But with the studio devoted to features, the lot has taken on a more serious aspect although no one was visible who wears a beret and wants to be known as a genius. Stan Laurel may get Babe Hardy to jump into a pen of pigs just for a laugh but the making of comedies has become a more somber business. It's all right to joke when you are making pictures costing $60,000 but when they get into the $150,000 to $200,000 class, they must be treated with a degree of respect.

D. W. C.

August 30, 1936

OF THE ELYSIAN FIELDS

By IDWAL JONES

THE formula of Paramount's annual extravaganza varies not at all, whatever the year. It must have the radio motif, ninety-five diaphragm laughs from the top funny man, music-hall acts of a lunatic tinge, tunes in between and the whole hypothec must be shunted upon the screen on the eve of the vernal equinox. Which is to say the "Big Broadcast of 1938" will be upon you pretty soon now.

It was begun two years ago and was ripening up to last week. The one for 1940 is already being thought up, five of the brighter victims of schizophrenia hatching ideas for it, guided only by the stern rule that elephants are out. This seems a little harsh and anti-Winter Garden. But in last year's "Broadcast" some genius had a troop of elephants dance a polka, so completely bending Paramount's best stage floor that it is still useless, except as an Alpine set.

It will be pleasant news that the chief ingredient in this year's olio is W. C. Fields. He has triumphed over both indolence and the sacroiliac malady that plagued him a twelvemonth ago. Only Heaven and Bill's valet, whose vocabulary has been permanently enriched, knew how the great man suffered when he was making "Poppy."

* * *

The sacroiliac crisis is past. But Fields says his life has been so full of crises that he does not know what the next will be. Possibly television. He broke his neck once—running smack on a motor-bicycle into a truck—and it was weeks before he got fixed up. His first crisis came when juggling, in its larger aspects, went out. Then he went into the silent films. That was back in 1923, in a D. W. Griffith picture. Then the talkies came in and Fields was not listened to by anybody, though he offered to write, direct and act in a short subject for nothing. Then, somehow, he broke in—and also made the radio his oyster.

He has, technically, been a star for nearly fifty years, since he began juggling at the age of 9. And if a juggler in a single act is not a star, nobody is. Last week somebody had the idea of an anniversary show for him—a sort of tribute—but he roared it down, indignantly.

"What good will that do?"

* * *

It reminded him of a benefit performance got up by Minnie Maddern Fiske thirty years ago, and Fields and the entire troupe of players worked themselves up to a white heat of sacrifice until somebody asked for whose benefit it was. In the general enthusiasm that had been overlooked. Somebody had to be benefited, and the question was put up to Fields, who restored morale by announcing the check would be sent to the families of indigent bullfighters in Brazil.

Fields is packed with anecdotes at this moment, not because he is in the reminiscential stage but because he has just found three old trunks stuffed with programs, cartoons, lithos and clippings and has fetched them into his dressing-room. They remind him that he once appeared by command before King Edward at a garden party—one of those affairs with parasols, Bishops and a lot of earls in white toppers—and the other performer on the bill was Sarah Bernhardt, who recited from "L'Aiglon." Fields had on his tramp make-up, with smashed hat and a scrubby beard, and he almost spoiled his cigar-box juggling act by keeping one eye on a maharajah's mastiff that was earnestly trying to bite him.

If he were not an American, Fields thinks he would rather be a Spaniard. The Spaniards have a fanatical reverence for masters of legerdemain and cherish Agoust, Severus and Cinquevalli almost as much as they are supposed to like El Greco. Fields went to Madrid once and arrived the day the Spanish-American War broke out. It was embarrassing for him, but all went well, not because the national fondness for juggling would have forestalled a blizzard of over-ripe tomatoes but because the manager had rushed out new posters, billing him as "The Famous English Juggler Fields."

Juggling isn't what it used to be. Trick films have almost ruined the sense of mystery. Fields does a little at times, to keep his hand in, and in his dressing room, when alone, he lets a half-dozen billiard balls crawl up and down his face and neck like trained mice. In "The Big Broadcast of 1938"—there's no use keeping it secret any further—he does his golf act. With variations, of course. It wasn't in the script at first, nor for seven months; but when the script was done, the golf act was in and couldn't be dislodged, even though the story is set on a boat.

Ziegfeld once put Fields into a maritime "Follies," and insisted on a fishing turn. He got it—but on the first night it wound up with the golf act. It had to stay, although Ziegfeld insisted on putting in a girl, for he couldn't see any worth in an act without one of his girls in it. So the lady, the most beautiful of that year, walked through in ermine, leading an Afghan hound across the stage and back.

"My!" said Fields. "What a beautiful camel."

It won't do to tell what else Fields does in this film. But you might as well know that he ribs one of the strange phenomena of our times—the super-service at gas stations, the impact on the nerves induced by the swooping of trim youths in white, armed with rags and oil-cans, their faces lit by the exaltation of souls dedicated to service.

February 27, 1938

Joe E. Brown, Comedian Of Movies and Stage

Special to The New York Times

A Favorite of the Young

By PETER MILLONES

They referred to his mouth as the Great Open Space, the Grand Canyon and the Mammoth Cave, and they said that he was the only man who could not cover his mouth when he yawned.

Joe E. Brown just shrugged off the endless descriptions of his mouth and commented: "I'll open my mouth until my stomach shows if people think it's funny."

And the people thought it was funny. Almost from the start of his movie career, in 1928, until the nineteen-forties, his pictures were among the 10 biggest box-office attractions.

His mouth, from which often emerged a sirenlike howl, and his comic talents made Mr. Brown a particular favorite of the younger generation, although he never achieved the fame of Eddie Cantor with his ogling eyes or Jimmy Durante with his large nose.

Joseph Evan Brown was a stanch member of the slapstick school of humor. His early career as an acrobat in circuses taught him to fall safely. It was not unusual for him to be wearing a white suit in one of his films and to fall face down in a mud puddle.

He was forever the hapless soul—whether a soda jerk, a football player being thrown over the goal line for a last-minute touchdown, a bungling reporter, a country yokel making lemonade in a finger bowl or a rookie baseball player baffling the manager.

Mr. Brown loved baseball and developed several routines, including one of a young pitcher harried by batters, umpires and base runners. He used it on the stage, in the movies and on television.

When Mr. Brown signed a long-term contract with Warner Brothers he insisted on an unusual clause that required the company to maintain a complete baseball team for him among the employes of the studio. For a while he played with the St. Paul team. He was part owner of the Kansas City Blues from 1932 to 1935, and in 1953 he was a pregame and postgame announcer for the Yankees.

"I once had a major league job," Mr. Brown often said. "The manager wanted me to play third base. He said that if I couldn't reach the ball with my hands, I could open my mouth and catch it between my teeth. I tried it once and darn near swallowed the ball."

Big Mouth Only a Trick

Despite the popular impression, Mr. Brown's mouth was not of extraordinary size. He had a rubbery face and the apparent magnitude of his mouth was achieved by throwing back his head so that his wide-open mouth occupied the foreground of the audience's field of vision. The movie and television cameras took full advantage of this maneuver.

Mr. Brown learned the humorous possibilities of his mouth by chance. He was in a play in which he had only a few words to speak—and they were not funny. He decided he would attract attention by opening his mouth as wide as possible and holding it that way until the audience was staring at it with rapt attention, believing that he had forgotten his lines and was frozen with fear.

When he had the audience's perfect attention, he whispered his line and the audience howled. There was rarely an occasion after that that he did not seek a laugh by calling attention to the size of his mouth. His antics sometimes wore thin on adults. One critic wrote in 1938:

"Pitcher-mouthed Joe E. Brown has gone to the well once too often."

Servicemen Liked Him

But Mr. Brown's gift for pantomime, his Cheshire Cat grin and his interminable yawns endeared him to thousands of servicemen overseas during World War II. He estimated that he had traveled more than 200,000 air miles visiting battle theaters. That figure did not include the number of jeep miles, he explained, because a jeep mile was equivalent to 15 ground miles, because of the up-and-down movement of the vehicle.

His antics for the men in uniform were, in part, a work born of grief. In October, 1942, his elder son, Capt. Don Evan Brown, was killed in a crash near Palm Springs, Calif., while ferrying an Army bomber.

On Luzon, in an American advance on the town of Bambang, Mr. Brown was permitted by the commanding officer, Maj. Gen. Robert S. Beighter, to carry a carbine and to ride in the lead tank. The officer later said that the comedian had shot two of the enemy.

Mr. Brown in 1935

This made for headlines back home, but was also sharply criticized by those who pointed out that Mr. Brown was in the uniform of a noncombatant. International law forbade him to engage in any hostile action.

After the war, he appeared in films less frequently. In 1952, he filled in once a month for Milton Berle on his television show. Mr. Brown's show was titled "Circus Hour." The critics found little to applaud.

The show allowed Mr. Brown to hark back to his premovie days. He was born in Holgate, Ohio, July 28, 1892, and attended grammar school in Toledo, but ran away when he was 9 to join a circus. After much drudgery he became the junior member of the Five Marvelous Ashtons, a troupe of aerial acrobats that was one of the main attractions of the Ringling Brothers Circus.

In 1906, he formed the acrobatic team of Bell and Brown with Tommy Bell, a star acrobat, but a perfectionist. Mr. Bell frequently expressed anger when his partner turned a fraction of an inch too much, though audiences could not tell.

On one occasion, Mr. Bell tossed his partner high into the air, then uttered a low groan at Mr. Brown's imperfect movements and started walking off the stage. He was supposed to catch Mr. Brown, but didn't. Mr. Brown hit the stage and broke a leg.

"I warned you," Mr. Bell said.

A Hit in 'Listen Lester'

Mr. Brown married Kathryn McGraw in 1915. He went into burlesque in 1918. Before long, he appeared on Broadway in the hit "Listen Lester," and was soon an established star.

He appeared in "Jim Jam Jems," "Greenwich Village Follies," "Betty Lee," "Captain Jinks," and "Twinkle, Twinkle," and in the road company of "Elmer the Great." In 1928 he started his movie career in a melodrama, "Crooks Can't Win."

In the next two decades, he appeared in about 50 films. They included: "The Gladiator," "Wide Open Faces," "Riding on Air," "Sons o' Guns," "Earthworm Tractors," "Six Day Bike Rider," "Going Wild," "Sit Tight," "Alibi Ike," "The Circus Clown," "You said a Mouthful," "Chatterbox," "Pin Up Girl," and "Hollywood Canteen."

In 1959 he appeared as a millionaire in "Some Like It Hot," with Marilyn Monroe. Mr. Brown considered his most succcessful movies to be "Elmer the Great" and "Hold Everything." They involved roles in which his intimate knowledge of the circus, stage and sports aided him greatly.

Took Shakespearean Role

He also appeared as Flute in "A Midsummer Night's Dream." He contended later that he had never heard of Shakespeare. Hollywood laugh clockers reported that the best audience reaction followed his line, "I won't play any more." This was not written by Shakespeare, but was ad libbed by Mr. Brown after he was thrown into a lake.

Mr. Brown was a big hit on the campus of the University of California at Los Angeles, when his sons, Don and Joe L. were there. The senior Brown joined a fraternity, although he was nearly 50 years old. He was a sparkplug of campus activities, including pep railies and football games.

Joe L., became general manager of the Pittsburgh Pirates in 1955, which gave his father another opportunity to deal personally with the game he loved.

In 1949, Mr. Brown received an honorary degree from Bowling Green State University for his "philosophy of life epitomized in love, learn and laugh."

'Harvey' Role Won Degree

The degree followed Mr. Brown's appearance in "Harvey" as the inebriate Elwood P. Dowd. He opened the road tour of the show in Chicago and then went to the West Coast. He performed in the role more than 1,000 times.

"I'm not the comedian I once was," Mr. Brown said in 1952. "A comedian has to be slightly insulting, comedy has to be 70 per cent insults, and I'm always afraid today when I say something funny it may hurt someone. If another comic makes a crack about my mouth, I just can't insult him back."

July 7, 1973

CAVALCADE of MOVIE COMICS

By BOSLEY CROWTHER

IN the excitement attending the première of Charlie Chaplin's new film, "The Great Dictator," last week, one plain but significant detail was overlooked. Simply, it was the fact that, for the first time within memory, the most eagerly awaited picture of the year was a comedy.

Now, that remark may provoke a moment's hesitation. But the usual leafing through the records will show that, by and large, the public's anticipations heretofore have been aroused by the films with the most impressive promise. And those, for various reasons, generally have been of the sober, epic variety—for instance, a "Gone With the Wind" or an "Anthony Adverse" rather than a "Mr. Smith Goes to Washington."

Thus, the burning curiosity and impatience which "The Great Dictator" fired was a cause for academic hat-tossing. For there is no vein of American film fare which has employed more native ingenuity for a reward of less popular respect than the comic. And there is no single personality in the annals of the screen who more surely deserves elevation to an awesome eminence than Chaplin, the comedy king. Charlie has come trooping down the years at the front of the comic cavalcade, spanning the various "trends" from slapstick to modern satire.

Critics with a cultural disposition have sometimes complained that the American movie-going public doesn't take its comedy seriously enough. Yet the total effect of good, hearty comedy upon the temperaments of American movie-goers through the years probably has been more influential than that of any other type of screen fare. And ever since the "flickers" first began, a solemn concern of producers has been how to make people laugh.

As with almost everything else, fashions in screen comedy have changed steadily, and that which threw an audience into hysterical laughter a quarter of a century ago has the odd and incongruous appearance of a 1915 bonnet today. American humor generally has been of a robust and spontaneous character, so it was natural that the first important phase of screen comedy—the slapstick—tended in this direction.

Before 1912, when Mack Sennnett began directing for Keystone, humor on the screen had followed mainly the lines of short vaudeville skits—brief episodes in which such actors as John Bunny, "Happy Hooligan" and others coaxed laughs with their exaggerated gestures and farcical shenanigans. But the conjunction of Sennett and Keystone marked the beginning of the first real comic phase, for Sennett is the man who brought slapstick to flower.

THE lasting contributions of slapstick to the development of screen comedy were very great indeed. Primarily, it crystallized the famous "chase" formula which, in one way or another, has been a pattern for practically every type of comedy since. Also, it proved the value of tempo and variety. And not only did it produce such early favorites as Fatty Arbuckle, Mabel Normand, Mack Swain, Al St. John and Chester Conklin, but it started upon their careers Harold Lloyd, Buster Keaton and Charlie Chaplin.

Enough already has been written about Chaplin and the development of his style—his progression from lowest farce to the finest and most touching subtleties of humor. But more remains to be said about Lloyd and Keaton—and also about Harry Langdon and Raymond Griffith. These stars were in the van of the post-World War comedy trend, which led slowly away from the impossible exaggerations of slapstick, but still preserved the madcap and tongue-in-cheek spirit of old.

THE essential humor in the films of Chaplin, Keaton, Lloyd and lesser clowns of the day was drawn from the helpless confusions of fundamentally simple characters in a modern, mechanized civilization which seemed bent on knocking them down. Significantly, the dead-pan or frozen face was the invariable exterior they presented to the world. On the other hand, Douglas Fairbanks, whose forte was romantic comedy, represented the gay man-of-the-world who overcame all obstacles by literally o'er-leaping them.

But the chief thing about all screen comedy before the advent of sound was its frank and unpretentious make-believe, its obvious acknowledgment of fantastic trickery. When Fairbanks scaled a castle wall, or Lloyd hung breathlessly suspended from the cornice of a skyscraper, or Keaton navigated an ocean liner unassisted, or Griffith launched a battleship which forthwith sank, no one was expected to take that stuff literally. The camera was boldly used to accomplish the highly improbable, and it was in this incongruity that the charm of pre-sound comedy lay.

Unlike the stage and literature, the screen generally has not reacted to the moods of society in its humorous styles and trends. Rather, film comedy has been conditioned by technical developments and by the constant endeavor of producers to turn out something fresh and "different."

Thus, with the perfection of sound, a whole new set of conditions was presented, and comedy, along with other types of fare, underwent great changes. At first there was much confusion and experimental wallowing. Of the pre-sound favorites, Lloyd, Keaton and Fairbanks soon dropped out after trying unsuccessfully to adapt themselves to the new technique. Chaplin survived because he steadfastly refused to talk; so, too, did Stan Laurel and Oliver Hardy, a couple of lesser clowns, who are still purveying comedy in the basically slapstick vein.

HOWEVER, just as sound was coming in there also arrived in Hollywood the madcap quartet of Marx Brothers, who began in 1929, with their hilarious "The Coconuts," a comic trend which has most successfully bridged the old and new techniques. The Marxes—all except Harpo—have always talked and made sounds, but the essence of their comedy has been its crazy, grotesque inanity and reliance upon the "sight gag."

It was the lavish directorial touch of Ernst Lubitsch which started the real trend of sound comedy. Whereas Chaplin and others of the silent films had regularly indulged in suggestive and sometimes vulgar double entendres with sight gags, Lubitsch managed dialogue and action in a subtle, charming way. His sophisticated comedies, beginning with "The Love Parade" (1929), hit the top note during the early Thirties and gave the new medium a vitality and sharp wit which it very much needed to carry on.

WITH sound completely established, the range of comedy began to spread and the varieties of film fare which might reasonably be classified as such have been many in the past decade. The year 1933, for instance, offered amazing evidence of this development. In addition to the Marx Brothers in "Duck Soup," Will Rogers in "State Fair" and Marie Dressler and Wallace Beery in "Tugboat Annie," 1933 also provided Charles Laughton in "Henry the Eighth," W. C. Fields in "If I Had a Million" and "International House," John Barrymore in "Reunion in Vienna" and Mae West in "She Done Him Wrong." Fields, whose early sound pictures were some of the best the screen has ever had, followed essentially in the old fantastic clown tradition with his lampoons of pomposity.

This same year also established a universal affection for the cartoon because of Walt Disney's "Three Little Pigs." More fantasy than straight comedy, the cartoons nevertheless took over the field which had earlier been overrun by the slapsticks.

The next year brought along two of the most significant trends of comedy. Lubitsch, Miss West, Mr. Fields and the so-called "hard-boiled" comedy makers toned down their products, while coincidentally there came forward a little child to lead them. The child was Shirley Temple.

Also, there arrived Frank Capra's "It Happened One Night" and the William Powell-Myrna Loy "Thin Man," which together set the vogue for the cycle of sophisticated whimsy—a vogue which carried comedy along to its so-called "screwball" phase with such pictures as "My Man Godfrey," "Mr. Deeds Goes to Town," "The Awful Truth," "Nothing Sacred" and, more recently, "My Favorite Wife."

WITHIN the past few years, a strong new trend has been toward middle-class domestic comedies, generally developed in series, such as the Hardy, Jones and other family pictures. These have drawn their humor from the familiar difficulties of parents in raising their lively offspring. Alongside of these have come such hard-boiled comedies as "A Slight Case of Murder" and "Torrid Zone," such charming innocents as the Deanna Durbin and Bing Crosby comedies with song and, recently, the hilarious travesties on melodrama perfected with Bob Hope.

And now comes Chaplin again—the greatest comedian of them all—in a satiric farce of deep and serious implication. At a time when every one is suffering the gravest apprehensions, he is preserving the tradition of screen comedy, which has been to spoof with humor and wit the things about which most people worry. But this time he is filling a tall order. And, in certain quarters, at least, comedy now is being taken seriously.

October 20, 1940

You Name It, Woody Is Doing It

By RICHARD J. H. JOHNSTON

By his own deposition, Allen Stewart Konigsberg is an "antispecialist."

At least for the present, he intends to plunge into playwriting, acting, nightclub monology, 10-thumb piano playing and clarinet noodling under the name of Woody Allen as long as the laws allow versatile men to run rampant.

"The idea of being a specialist frightens me. They say you can't be a success unless you specialize, but it would be a crime not to exercise all and any talents one has," he said.

Mr. Allen opened to good notices Wednesday night at the Broadhurst Theater in the first play he has written and acted in, "Play It Again, Sam."

Mr. Allen was born in Brooklyn, Dec. 1, 1935. He flunked out of both City College and New York University for lack of interest while earning more than $1,000 a week as a gag writer.

He then became a nightclub comic and playwright ("Don't Drink the Water" and "Death Knocks") screen writer and actor ("Take the Money and Run" and "What's New, Pussycat?). And now, a Broadway playwright and leading man.

Having made this transition, how did Mr. Allen go about writing a play? What were his techniques?

In writing comedy, he said, everything depended on rhythm just as the delivery of comedy lines required rhythm and pacing.

"I try to establish a rhythm — whether in a 10-second gag or, as now, in a two-hour play—I have to be true to the rhythm or perish," he explained.

"Rhythm—take Jack Benny or Bob Hope—slow, beautiful pacing . . . take Henny Youngman . . . bang, bang, pause, bang, bang, pause . . . Break that rhythm and they're dead . . ." he said, snapping his fingers.

'Rhythm Interaction'

How can his relative swift rhythm be sustained for two hours as in "Play It Again, Sam"?

"Well, the pace here is a little slower, but the rhythm is there and, you've got to be true to it and in a play like this you've got the rhythmic interaction of others working with you," he explained.

"You know," he said, "if the rhythm's right, it just flows."

How can a performer who established his special tempo as a stand-up nightclub monologist take directions from a director—Joseph Hardy, in this case—for the first time on stage?

"I get along fine," Mr. Allen said. "He understands the importance and meaning of rhythm here and that's why he's great."

Mr. Hardy, for his part, observed that Mr. Allen, not a simple man, oversimplified his response to direction.

"Woody is, in fact, a dream to direct. He tries; he takes direction . . . and he has taken 95 per cent of my ideas with enthusiasm," Mr. Hardy said.

"You have to bear in mind that he is performing his own work and, in that respect, he is the best writer I have ever worked with. We have no conflicts," he added.

Mr. Hardy conjectured that there were actors who could play Mr. Allen's role, Allan Felix, successfully, but, since Woody Allen and Allan Felix are one psyche any actor replacing Mr. Allen would be playing Woody Allen. Mr. Hardy had doubts about Woody Allen's playing any other character — "at this stage of his career."

"I like acting and I discovered that the writing of this play was the hardest part of it," Mr. Allen said.

"I like acting, yes, but not enough to want to be an actor exclusively. I liked writing "Sam," but I really don't want to be a playwright, exclusively. I like applause, but I don't live for it, exclusively. I like money, but I've got money."

Serious Matter of Comedy

How could Mr. Allen, firmly tagged with the "funnyman" label, insist that he was not, at least in comedy, a specialist?

"Oh, no: Comedy is deadly serious business," he said. The chestnut that every comedian had a Hamlet performance embedded deep in his heart is "silly", he said.

"I don't differentiate between 'comedy' and 'serious' work. I resent the word 'serious' used in contrast to 'humorous.' "

The idea that most of his material is autobiographical is inaccurate, he said, explaining:

"I was not the frightened little nonparticipant as a kid, I played all sorts of games and many of them very well. I was not poor and hungry and neglected. We were substantial, lower class, well fed, housed and clothed. But a little overstatement here and there is not dishonest, I suppose, and I was not 'deprived' of a college education. What could I do with it in my profession?"

"I am a voracious reader. You have to read to survive. People who read for pleasure are wasting their time. Reading isn't fun, it's indispensable."

What kind of reading?

"Philosophy—existential—it's tough, but it has a disciplinary effect and I am trying to grow slowly. Out of this comes vocabulary, also. I never had a teacher who made the least impression on me and if you ask who are my heroes, the answer is simple and truthful: George S. Kaufman and the Marx Brothers."

"I like applause"

Ted Polumbaum for The New York Times

"I like money, but I've got money."

February 14, 1969

TOM MIX SOLILOQUIZES

Made Money, Yes, but He Doesn't Know What More From Screen

MR. TOM MIX and Penrod have much in common, both being sentimentalists and both hating dancing. Which may go a long way toward explaining—with other points being taken into consideration, of course—why the former is the screen idol of every male under the age of 13.

It is Mr. Mix who fills that aching void in the life of man when noise and heroic deeds are necessary. He has a horse, he has two guns (which he uses) and he dresses like something alien to the eighth grade, Sunday school and afternoon parties on shady lawns. He is to youthful minds the ideal, the legendary Launcelot.

It is not known how many innocent and unsuspecting old men have been rescued from the hard-hearted mortgage owers by their imaginative grandchildren fresh from an afternoon of Tom Mix. Nor is it known how many of these same grandchildren sat through several shows that afternoon. The statistics may be vague, but they are certainly high.

Then, sadly enough, at 13, the great West gives way to other things less ornate, less romantic in a daring way. Youth, in the process of growing up, changes, and Tom and Tony, the horse, are abandoned. Sometimes they are brought back, in much later years, but then it is under the ranking of literature of escape and is thus quite different.

The author of all this furore is a curious blend of varied characteristics. He knows the place he holds in the minds of the young and sincerely tries to prove himself worthy of it. Yet he has simple tastes and allows himself to be persuaded into doing things he doesn't like through his fear of being called "a stick." Under these things he highly places tennis, bridge and dancing.

He dresses like the Tom Mix of the pictures, with wide hat, knee boots, red scarf in lieu of belt and a very light-colored riding coat. When he walks about, out of respect for the Sullivan law, he leaves his guns behind, but that is the only time he may bow to convention, save in the evening, of course, when the great horseman of the plains becomes a gentleman in a dinner jacket.

He occasionally wonders just what he is getting out of it, looking backward a little, perhaps, quite as his youthful exponents look forward.

Dignity, All Is Dignity.

"I don't know," he says. "I've made some money—quite a lot of it, as a matter of fact, but I'm not sure what else. Years ago I used to live in a cow-camp, where a bed and a knife, fork and spoon were all the things I could look forward to in the evening. Now I live on what is known as a gentleman's estate. There is a big house and a lawn in front of which Barnum & Bailey could put all their tents. There are tennis courts and a swimming pool with so many different colored tiles that you feel ashamed to get in with only an ordinary bathing suit.

"I go back to this place in the evening and wander around—nothing there but dignity. Sometimes, not very often, my friends come in and we sit around talking. At others there is a series of tennis players, bridge players and professional chemists brought to analyze what we are going to eat and drink. The next day there is nothing left but cigarette butts all around the room."

When he was asked why he kept on living at the gentleman's estate, he showed his naive side.

"Well, you see," he began almost apologetically, "if I don't go on with all this, people will think that I'm just a stick. I really have to go through with it now that I started. I even have a butler at that place, and there are so many servants I sometimes don't know what to do with them all.

"The dances are the worst," he continued, reflectively. "Especially dinner dances. I go to them with a bunch of people and as soon as the soup is brought in the band starts playing. Every one gets up and starts prancing off, leaving me sitting there with some woman. I know all the excuses for not dancing, but they usually fail and I find myself up and on the floor.

"I can't dance in a corner the way the best ones do, so usually when the music stops I'm away over at the other end of the room. When we finally manage to fight our way back the soup has been taken away. The next course is put on and the same thing is repeated, so I never get anything to eat. Dancing is so silly, anyway, and I always have to keep learning new steps. As if there weren't enough now without any more."

Women, in Mr. Mix's opinion, have been ruined because "we" let them get away with too much and now can't "head them off." They go everywhere, do everything and you can't argue with them at all—even when you're right on a particular subject. The actor, for example, has "never won an argument with a woman in my life." Whether he really thinks this, or just considers woman as a potential dancing partner, is not known.

Regarding his future, he had to say:

"I'm going to keep making about the same type of picture, although not so many of them in a year as I have in the past. There is still a field for them, in my belief, and maybe I will be able to do some good for the kids."

Being the idol has its drawbacks, he said at this point, for he is known so well by the children that if ever he turns out a bad picture it will be noted as such immediately. The youngsters can spot errors quicker than their elders, he feels, and for that reason it is up to the actor to keep himself in as good physical shape as he can in order that they may not be disappointed.

"I try," he said, almost wistfully, "to make the pictures so that when a boy pays, say, 20 cents to see it, he will get 20 cents' worth, not 10. If I drop, you see, it would be like putting my hand in his pocket and stealing a dime."

And in view of his position there are certain things he must watch in the pictures themselves. For example, he cannot smoke a cigarette when the camera is looking and he dare not enter a saloon, save to get the villain. And his heroines must be the simple type—school teachers, ranchers' daughters and the like. There must be nothing in any of the films which may not be harmlessly emulated by the members of a youthful audience.

Mr. Mix tends toward considering his vaudeville engagement—especially after eight weeks of it—as somewhat "silly, like dancing." He feels foolish going out on the stage and shooting at a target, he says, and he will be rather glad when it is over and he may return to the West, even though it is to the gentleman's estate.

And Tony!

Tony, the horse, likes it even less and less, and last week was beginning to express himself about the matter quite forcibly. He feels that it is not only silly but utterly undignified to be led several times a day before a lot of people he cares nothing about. He is also distressed by the habit moving picture fans have of pulling hairs from his tail as souvenirs.

"I've owned Tony since he was born, seventeen years ago," his master said. "He is a good horse and will be for some time yet, as I have never extended him in work. He doesn't like this tour much, though, and has been getting cross about it. Several times he has tried to bite me within the last few days and once he succeeded.

"The trouble is that every one is petting him and most people don't know how. They pound instead of rubbing, forgetting that a horse's nose is just as tender as theirs. And all the children who gather around try to take a hair from his tail as something to remember him by."

As to his personal traits, the actor confessed a liking for sleep in the morning, a hatred of riveters who wake him at 8 o'clock with their incessant racket, and a profound loathing for managers and such who plant alarm clocks all over his room, setting them to go off at fifteen-minute intervals. He also expressed admiration for Mayor Walker—"a friend of some years"—and spoke admiringly of Texas Guinan as "the greatest Roman of them all."

And for self-expression, he likes to write, considering it "quite a recreation." He can't spell at all, sometimes misspelling a word in five different ways, but for the last half dozen years he has had a secretary who can. What more does he wish?

May 27, 1928

THE SCREEN IN REVIEW

Marlene Dietrich Reaches a High in Horse Opera With 'Destry Rides Again,' at the Rivoli

DESTRY RIDES AGAIN, from the novel by Max Brand; screen play by Felix Jackson, Gertrude Purcell and Henry Myers; directed by George Marshall; produced by Joe Pasternak for Universal. At the Rivoli.

Frenchy.......................Marlene Dietrich
Thomas J. Destry Jr..........James Stewart
Wash Dimsdale..........Charles Winninger
Boris Callahan...................Mischa Auer
Kent..............................Brian Donlevy
Janice Tyndall....................Irene Hervey
Lily Belle Callahan...............Una Merkel
Gyp Watson........................Allen Jenkins
Bugs Watson......................Warren Hymer
Loupgerou..........................Billy Gilbert
Hiram J. Slade..............Samuel S. Hinds
Lem Claggett.......................Tom Fadden
Jack Tyndall.......................Jack Carson
Clara...............................Lillian Yarbo
Eli Whitney Claggett............Dickie Jones
"Sister" Claggett....................Ann Todd

By FRANK S. NUGENT

Type-casting, the bane of the film industry, has rarely been more successfully pied than by Producer Joe Pasternak in his "Destry Rides Again" at the Rivoli. With a sweep of his Hungarian fist he has taken Marlene Dietrich off her high horse and placed her in a horse opera and has converted James Stewart, last seen as Washington's timid Mr. Smith, into the hard-hitting son of an old sagebrush sheriff. Such epics as Max Brand's tale of the coming of law and order to the frontier town of Bottleneck have been told often enough before. What sets this one off from its fellows, converts it into a jaunty and amusing chronicle is the novelty of finding a Dietrich and a Stewart in it and playing it as wisely as though their names were Mr. and Mrs. Hoot Gibson.

It's difficult to reconcile Miss Dietrich's Frenchy, the cabaret girl of the Bloody Gulch Saloon, with the posed and posturing Dietrich we last saw in Mr. Lubitsch's "Angel." Her "Blue Angel" comes closer to it. Once again she's hard and tough and painted to the

Marlene Dietrich

margins of the pallette. She delivers such ballads as "Little Joe the Wrangler" and "The Boys in the Back Room" with quite the proper whisky contralto effect. She cold-decks a poker sucker with complete nonchalance, tucks her earnings down her dress front and doesn't bat an eye when a cowhand murmurs "Thar's gold in them hills." (And where the Hays office was when that line sneaked through we'll never know, not that we mind it.)

The scene that really counts, though, is the cat-fight between Miss Dietrich's Frenchy and Una Merkel's outraged Mrs. Callahan. We thought the battle between Paulette Goddard and Rosalind Russell in "The Women" was an eye-opener; now we realize it was just shadow-clawing. For the real thing, with no holds barred and full access to chairs, tables, glasses, bottles, waterbuckets and as much hair as may be conveniently snatched from the opponent's scalp, we give you not "The Women," but the two women who fight it out in the Bloody Gulch over a pair of Mischa Auer's pants.

Mr. Stewart is all right, too. He usually is. Here he's Destry, son of a fighting father, who comes to Bottleneck as Charles Winninger's deputy and almost breaks that old fire-eater's heart by professing a dislike for firearms. That, naturally, sets him down as a softy, in the opinion of Brian Donlevy and the rest of the thick-necked gentry of Bottleneck. It shouldn't fool you, though; with a name like Destry and a girl like Frenchy to lend him her rabbit's foot, Mr. Stewart couldn't very well help emerging as the hero of a rather heroic occasion. And he couldn't help being Mr. Stewart, turning in an easy, likable, pleasantly humored performance.

So there it is, a bit of the old West with a good bit of the old Dietrich in it; a tightly written, capitally directed show, with perfectly grand supporting performances by Samuel S. Hinds as Bottleneck's mayor, Mr. Donlevy as the chief villain, Mr. Winninger as the shirt-tucking sheriff and Mischa Auer as a Russian cowboy. Good fun every minute of it, and another trophy for Mr. Pasternak.

November 30, 1939

Margaret Sullavan and James Stewart have roles in "The Shop Around the Corner"

THE UNMUSICAL MR. JONES

Here Is One Screen Cowhand Who Can't Sing a Note and Is Proud of It

By THOMAS BRADY

HOLLYWOOD.

BUCK JONES announced the other day that he had returned to the screen to defy the singing cowboys and save the children of the nation from the poisoned honey of Gene Autry's guitar and Tex Ritter's baritone. Since Tom Mix's death, Buck is the dean of Hollywood's cowboys, and he takes the responsibility seriously. He has just completed "Arizona Bound" at Monogram and will start "The Bad Man From Bodie" in two weeks, the two pictures constituting the beginning of a series known as The Rough Riders. No voices raised in song will vitiate the stark action of Buck's opuses, either.

He says he retired two years ago in disgust at the state of the cow-screen. He is a "hand" (by this Mr. Jones means a cowhand who earned his living on the ranges), and it wasn't consistent with his code of honor to compete with crooners. His attitude was that if the public wanted melodious treacle, he would retire to his ranch at Sonora.

Then he began thinking about the youngsters. "They used to want to grow up to be cowboys," he said. "Now they'll want to grow up to be like Gene Autry." This thought preyed on Buck's mind, and after he had wrestled with his soul for two years Monogram made him an offer, and he strapped on his six-shooter and rode down to Hollywood again.

Buck is a kindly man where horses and children are concerned, but his jaw takes on a grim line and his eyes light up with the righteous fire of a Puritan divine when he talks about the decadent musical dramas which are seducing the younger generation. "Of course," he says, "if the public still wants them, there's nothing to be done. But I think they've been overdone, now, and will disappear."

He has a bitter suspicion about songs in Westerns. "They use 'em to save money on horses and riders and ammunition," he asserted. "Why, you take Gene Autry and lean him up against a tree with his guitar and let him sing three songs and you can fill up a whole reel without spendin' any money. That's why they've overdone the singing, and that's why it's on the way out.

"In my pictures we never let up on the action. They've got as much movement as the silents. In the last one I rode a horse through a plate-glass window, and that's the sort of thing pictures need." Knowing Mr. Jones's high regard for animals, a reporter asked if the plate glass had hurt the horse. Mr. Jones hastened to explain that the window was made of cellophane, shellacked until it became brittle.

William Saal, an executive at Republic, where the burning Autry rides and sings, last week listed the five greatest screen cowboys of all time. They are Bronco Billy Anderson, William S. Hart, Tom Mix, Autry and (magnanimously enough) Charles (Buck) Jones.

Buck would hardly deny the box-office success of any of the other four. But he makes a class distinction between those who were "hands" to begin with and those who were actors or crooners first and cowboys second. Only he and Mix were genuine hands, Buck says. Bronco Bill started in vaudeville, Bill Hart as an actor and Autry as a radio entertainer. Buck explains that there is only one real hand besides himself now active on the screen. His name is Gary Cooper, and he has turned into an actor. There have been other honest-to-God cowpokes, though. The most eminent was Will Rogers. Hoot Gibson was legitimate, too. Yakima Kanutt, now a stunt man but formerly a Western actor, is as good a man as any of them, Buck thinks.

About his contemporaries Buck is doleful. He disapproves of Autry's clothes because Autry dresses like a dude. Tex Ritter has a law degree, which is certainly reprehensible. Bill Boyd, who is Paramount's Hopalong Cassidy, has earned a measure of Buck's respect because he never sings a note; but Boyd was an actor before he immortalized Hopalong. Into this category of actors-turned-cowboy fall Roy Rogers, Charles Starrett and Bill Elliott (who used to be Gordon Oliver before he became an equestrian). Buck thinks it is a dangerous sign of our synthetic times that movie actors should be encouraged to play cowboy. The most macabre incident of all, he feels, happened at MGM when Robert Taylor stepped into the boots of Billy the Kid.

What worries Buck most is the succession, now that he is the last of the movie cowhands. He doesn't want the breed to die out, for fear America's children will be led astray. Buck made his first pictures in 1919, and some of his fans are now upstanding citizens in their late thirties. Not long ago he was in Albuquerque, and a dignified gentleman approached the Jones entourage with a request to see Buck. As his introduction he presented a membership card in the Buck Jones Rangers, which organization stopped functioning long ago. Buck says with a shudder: "Where will Gene Autry's fans be twenty years from now, and what will they be like?"

He has a solution for the problem, though. He is going to institute a wide search for a genuine hand. He will comb the rodeos until he finds the right young man. Then he will introduce him to the camera gradually. A real cowhand, he says, is as shy and skittish as a colt, and at first he will have to be gentled. When he gets accustomed to Hollywood the newcomer will appear in walk-on parts in Buck's pictures. Later he will play juvenile leads. And finally, when Buck himself goes out to pasture, his successor will be ready to take up the fight against the crooners.

July 20, 1941

Town Named for Gene Autry

GENE AUTRY, Okla., Nov. 5 (UP)—Gene Autry, the singing cowboy movie star, now has a town named after him. The Carter County Commissioners, at a special session, officially approved a change in the name of Berwyn, Okla., to Gene Autry, Okla.

November 6, 1941

William S. Hart

Tom Mix

BOOTS AND SADDLES

Noting Changing Styles In Western Pictures

By LEONARD SPINRAD

THE horse opera is generally presumed to be not only the oldest but also the least changing category of motion-picture entertainment. Actually, however, styles in Westerns have undergone five distinct variations and are currently, to the accompaniment of considerable hoopla, entering a sixth.

When the first Kinetoscope Parlor was opened at 1155 Broadway, fifty-three years ago, two of the principal attractions were "Annie Oakley" and "Buffalo Bill." For a number of years thereafter famous Western heroes provided a healthy share of the subject-matter of the catch-as-catch-can keyhole productions.

In 1903 Phase 2 of the Western film was ushered in with Edwin S. Porter's historic twelve-minute production, "The Great Train Robbery." It was Mr. Porter who first used the screen to tell the story of gun fights and villains in the old West.

That story is still being told, but there have been plenty of variations, climaxed currently with what at least one commentator has described as "the burning Busch period." Mr. Niven Busch is the writing gentleman who turned out the original screen play for "Pursued." He also wrote the novel "Duel in the Sun."

Development

The new style or "burning Busch" Western, which attempts to tell an adult story of the development of characters, is based on the idea that a clash of guns is not necessarily a replacement for a clash of emotions. This is possibly an outgrowth of Phase 3 of the Western film.

In 1908 the straight crime-and-consequences technique of "The Great Train Robbery" was embellished by the presence of a popular heroic personality in the person of Broncho Billy Anderson. In the almost three decades that followed, William S. Hart, Tom Mix, Hoot Gibson and a whole legion of "mesquiteers" brought the star system to Westerns. These men always represented the forces of good. The Western film in their hands became Hollywood's modern morality play.

In the course of time—because it appealed to the youngsters—the Western acquired certain audience taboos. There was to be no kissing of leading ladies. There was to be no abuse of horseflesh. The hero was to make it clear that he did not habitually drink, even though he usually spent a good deal of his time confronting the villain in the local saloon. Even without these restrictions, which evolved in the course of time, the Western. expressed in simplest terms, a case of Good meets Evil, Good fights Evil, Good beats Evil. Evil might be represented by anything from a rustler to a man who sneered at Mix.

This concept of the movie Western continued unchallenged until about 1922, when James Cruze produced one of the classic American films, "The Covered Wagon." Now history became more important than personalities. Not even the coming of sound interrupted this phase. Indeed, it was in talking pictures that the historical Western reached its peak with productions like "Cimarron."

But sound, first presented to the public when a man opened his mouth and sang, inevitably suggested to film producers that cowboys could sing, too. The great new staple was the lyrical cowpoke who spent more time singing than shooting. Messrs. Rogers, Autry, et al, are still very much with us.

Even while "The Sons of the Pioneers" were celebrating the lyric virtues of life in the West, however, something still newer was being added to the old-time Western. When this new item was first provided, in the highly applauded Marlene Dietrich-James Stewart vehicle, "Destry Rides Again," it could have been described in a borrowed phrase as "seducto ad absurdum."

Having discovered that adults as well as small boys were entranced by the West, the movies finally got around to producing Westerns with sex. The clinch challenged the trick horse as standard equipment. Since "Destry" there has been considerable evolution of this last type of horse opera. The Hollywood producer found it advisable to utilize the undoubted charms of Barbara Stanwyck, Linda Darnell, Jennifer Jones and many other glamour girls in a setting of boots and saddles.

Bullets and Passion

Many of the films in which these beautiful ladies are appearing have been standard Westerns in the old tradition, polished to a high degree of perfection by masters like John Ford. But the central theme of "Duel in the Sun," for example, is supposed to be passion and high emotion, with gunfire providing only a noisy obbligato; and the story which is the basis of "Pursued" is an account of a man's attempt to explain the mysterious terror which comes over him in remembrance of things past.

The tendency to deviate from the previous norm can be detected even in such orthodox sagas of the great outdoors as—to cite the latest example—Warners' "Cheyenne." Dennis Morgan, the hero of "Cheyenne," at one point refuses to put up a fight because he is outnumbered. Alan Hale, the stalwart of many a screen roughhouse, portrays the most timid Sheriff ever seen in a horse opera.

Americans are sometimes inclined to pay less attention to Westerns than do foreign observers. Jean Benoit Lévy has paid public tribute to "those splendid Westerns with their headlong galloping cowboys." The cowboys are still galloping, but they are taking time out to act like human beings. And if you want to know what's happening to the non-kissing, all-pure and uncomplicated hero with a horse twice as smart as he is—well, pardner, "he went thataway."

June 8, 1947

'High Noon,' a Western of Rare Achievement, Is New Bill at the Mayfair Theatre

HIGH NOON, screen play by Carl Foreman; directed by Fred Zinnemann; produced by Stanley Kramer. A Stanley Kramer Production released by United Artists. At the Mayfair.

Will Kane .... Gary Cooper
Jonas Henderson .... Thomas Mitchell
Harvey Pell .... Lloyd Bridges
Helen Ramirez .... Katy Jurado
Amy Kane .... Grace Kelly
Percy Mettrick .... Otto Kruger
Martin Howe .... Lon Chaney
William Fuller .... Henry Morgan
Frank Miller .... Ian MacDonald
Mildred Fuller .... Eve McVeagh
Cooper .... Harry Shannon
Jack Colby .... Lee Van Cleef
James Pierce .... Bob Wilke
Ben Miller .... Sheb Woolley
Sam .... Tom London
Station Master .... Ted Stanhope
Gillis .... Larry Blake
Barber .... William Phillips

By BOSLEY CROWTHER

Every five years or so, somebody—somebody of talent and taste, with a full appreciation of legend and a strong trace of poetry in their soul—scoops up a handful of clichés from the vast lore of Western films and turns them into a thrilling and inspiring work of art in this genre. Such a rare and exciting achievement is Stanley Kramer's production, "High Noon," which was placed on exhibition at the Mayfair yesterday.

Which one of several individuals is most fully responsible for this job is a difficult matter to determine and nothing about which to quarrel. It could be Mr. Kramer, who got the picture made, and it be Scriptwriter Carl Foreman, who prepared the story for the screen. Certainly Director Fred Zinnemann had a great deal to do with it and possibly Gary Cooper, as the star, had a hand in the job. An accurate apportionment of credits is not a matter of critical concern.

What is important is that someone—or all of them together, we would say—has turned out a Western drama that is the best of its kind in several years. Familiar but far from conventional in the fabric of story and theme and marked by a sure illumination of human character, this tale of a brave and stubborn sheriff in a town full of do-nothings and cowards has the rhythm and roll of a ballad spun in pictorial terms. And, over all, it has a stunning comprehension of that thing we call courage in a man and the thorniness of being courageous in a world of bullies and poltroons.

Like most works of art, it is simple — simple in the structure of its plot and comparatively simple in the layout of its fundamental issues and morals. Plotwise, it is the story of a sheriff in a small Western town, on the day of his scheduled retirement, faced with a terrible ordeal. At 10:30 in the morning, just a few minutes after he has been wed, he learns that a dreaded desperado is arriving in town on the noon train. The bad man has got a pardon from a rap on which the sheriff sent him up, and the sheriff knows that the killer is coming back to town to get him.

Here is the first important question: shall the sheriff slip away, as his new wife and several decent citizens reasonably urge him to do, or shall he face, here and now, the crisis which he knows he can never escape? And once he has answered this question, the second and greater problem is the maintenance of his resolution as noon approaches and he finds himself alone—one man, without a single sidekick, against a killer and three attendant thugs; one man who has the courage to take on a perilous, righteous job.

Gary Cooper in "High Noon"

How Mr. Foreman has surrounded this simple and forceful tale with tremendous dramatic implications is a thing we can't glibly state in words. It is a matter of skill in movie-writing, but, more than that, it is the putting down, in terms of visually simplified images, a pattern of poetic ideas. And how Mr. Zinnemann has transmitted this pattern in pictorial terms is something which we can only urge you to go yourself to see.

One sample worth framing, however, is the brilliant assembly of shots that holds the tale in taut suspension just before the fatal hour of noon. The issues have been established, the townsfolk have fallen away and the sheriff, alone with his destiny, has sat down at his desk to wait. Over his shoulder, Mr. Zinnemann shows us a white sheet of paper on which is scrawled "last will and testament" by a slowly moving pen. Then he gives us a shot (oft repeated) of the pendulum of the clock, and then a shot looking off into the distance of the prairie down the empty railroad tracks. In quick succession, then, he shows us, the tense faces of men waiting in the church and in the local saloon, the still streets outside, the three thugs waiting at the station, the tracks again, the wife of the sheriff waiting and the face of the sheriff himself. Then, suddenly, away in the distance, there is the whistle of the train and, looking down the tracks again, he shows us a whisp of smoke from the approaching train. In a style of consummate realism, Mr. Zinnemann has done a splendid job.

And so has the cast, under his direction. Mr. Cooper is at the top of his form in a type of role that has trickled like water off his back for years. And Lloyd Bridges as a vengeful young deputy, Katy Jurado as a Mexican adventuress, Thomas Mitchell as a prudent townsman, Otto Kruger as a craven judge and Grace Kelly as the new wife of the sheriff are the best of many in key roles.

Meaningful in its implications, as well as loaded with interest and suspense, "High Noon" is a western to challenge "Stagecoach" for the all-time championship.

July 25, 1952

THE SCREEN IN REVIEW

By BOSLEY CROWTHER

With "High Noon" so lately among us, it scarcely seems possible that the screen should so soon again come up with another great Western film. Yet that is substantially what has happened in the case of George Stevens' "Shane," which made a magnificent appearance at the Music Hall yesterday. Beautifully filmed in Technicolor in the great Wyoming outdoors, under the towering peaks of the Grand Tetons, and shown on a larger screen that enhances the scenic panorama, it may truly be said to be a rich and dramatic mobile painting of the American frontier scene.

For "Shane" contains something more than beauty and the grandeur of the mountains and plains, drenched by the brilliant Western sunshine and the violent, torrential, black-browed rains. It contains a tremendous comprehension of the bitterness and passion of the fueds that existed between the new homesteaders and the cattlemen on the open range. It contains a disturbing revelation of the savagery that prevailed in the hearts of the old gun-fighters, who were simply legal killers under the frontier code. And it also contains a very wonderful understanding of the spirit of a little boy amid all the tensions and excitements and adventures of a frontier home.

As a matter of fact, it is the concept and the presence of this little boy as an innocent and fascinated observer of the brutal struggle his elders wage that permits a refreshing viewpoint on material that's not exactly new. For it's this youngster's frank enthusiasms and naive reactions that are made the solvent of all the crashing drama in A. B. Guthrie Jr.'s script. And it's his youthful face and form, contributed by the precocious young Brandon De Wilde, that Mr. Stevens as director has most creatively worked with through the film.

There is tempestuous violence in a fist-fight that a stranger and the youngster's father wage against a gang of cattlemen hoodlums in a plain-board frontier saloon, but the fight has a freshness about it because it is watched by the youngster from under a door. And there's novelty and charm in this stranger because he is hero-worshipped by the boy. Most particularly, there's eloquence and greatness in a scene of a frontier burial on a hill, but it gets its keenest punctuation when the boy wanders off to pet a colt.

The story Mr. Stevens is telling is simply that of the bold and stubborn urge of a group of modest homesteaders to hold onto their land and their homes against the threats and harassments of a cattle baron who implements his purpose with paid thugs. And it is brought to its ultimate climax when the stranger, who seeks peace on one of the farms, tackles an ugly gunfighter imported from Cheyenne to do a job on the leader of the homesteaders, the father of the boy.

This ultimate gun-fight, incidentally, makes a beautiful, almost classic scene as Mr. Stevens has staged it in the dismal and dimly lit saloon, with characters slinking in the background as the antagonists, Alan Ladd and Jack Palance, face off in frigid silence before the fatal words fly and the guns blaze. It is a scene which, added to the many that Mr. Stevens has composed in this film, gives the whole thing the quality of a fine album of paintings of the frontier.

And in many respects the characters that Mr. Stevens' actors have drawn might be considered portraits of familiar frontier types. Van Heflin as the leading homesteader is outstanding among those played by Douglas Spencer, Elisha Cook Jr., Edgar Buchanan and Leonard Strong. Mr. Ladd, though slightly swashbuckling as a gunfighter wishing to retire, does well enough by the character, and Jean Arthur is good as the homesteader's wife. Mr. Palance as the mean, imported gunman; Emile Meyer as the cattleman boss and Paul McVey as the frontier storekeeper give fine portrayals, too. But it is Master De Wilde with his bright face, his clear voice and his resolute boyish ways who steals the affections of the audience and clinches "Shane" as a most unusual film.

While the new screen on which the picture is being shown at the Music Hall is wider and higher than usual, in a ratio that slightly favors the width, the difference is barely apparent, except that some scenes appear trimmed at the bottom and the top. The greater size seems quite appropriate and unexceptional in the expanse of the Music Hall.

April 24, 1953

'The Gangsters' Picture at Weber's

"The Gangsters," the newest of the motion-picture films showing the life of the underworld, made its first appearance at Weber's Theatre yesterday, where it is scheduled to appear for some time to come. The film tells the story of how the gangsters, in spite of their lawless battles, are really more the result of bad conditions than an essentially evil nature. In the play one of the gangsters is "framed up" and executed for a murder which he did not commit. The final scene shows a reformed former gunman with the girl he loves, away from the tenements and driving a herd of cattle down a country lane.

March 3, 1914

Disgusting Motion Pictures.

To the Editor of The New York Times:

I have just returned from a moving picture production at a Broadway playhouse. It is a story concerning the gangsters of New York, and I am so filled with a spirit of horror that such a thing should be allowed in your community that I feel myself compelled to write in protest.

That such a thing as death by the electric chair should be allowed to be shown to our women and those who are growing up among us is beyond my comprehension. I am an Englishman by birth, but have lived in America for five years, and this is the first time that I have seen go unmolested such a parade of the horrifying and repellent. I can only say it is the most disgusting exhibition of the morbid that has ever met my eyes.

AN AMERICANIZED ENGLISHMAN.

New York, March 6, 1914.

March 14, 1914

The Same Films

Once upon a time they were called gangster films, and they aroused much concern among parents and educators. Now they are called G-men films, and they seem to enjoy wide approval. Where the essential difference comes in is hard to see. It is still a picture of crime and violence. The amount of gun-play is heavier than ever, with consequent results on young nerves. No higher moral is perceptible.

The old gangster stories paid formal tribute to virtue by showing that crime does not pay, and that is all the new G-men fables can boast for a lesson. Under the old dispensation the newspapers would have stories of small boys playing bandits and doing themselves serious harm. Under new conditions small boys will incur serious accidents playing Federal Secret Service agents.

May 5, 1936

DAY OF CRIME FILM IS OVER, HAYS SAYS

The Public Is Rapidly Tiring of Morbid Themes of Post-War Era, He Tells Producers.

FINDS ROMANCES GAINING

Biographical and Educational Topics Now Are Successful, Directors Are Told.

The motion picture public is rapidly tiring of films dealing with crime and gang rule and a new era of entertainment stressing romantic and educational themes is dawning, Will H. Hays, president of the Motion Picture Producers and Distributors of America, Inc., declared in his report to the board of directors at its annual meeting here yesterday.

Mr. Hays pointed out as signs of a new day in popular entertainment appeal the success of movies produced in 1930 dealing with famous epochs in American history, with themes of prison and civic reform. and with outstanding biographical subjects.

"The greatest of all censors--the American public--is beginning to vote thumbs down on the 'hard-boiled' realism in literature and on the stage which marked the post-war period," he said. "I am aware how often in the past pictures that dealt with really praiseworthy themes have proved abject and utter financial failures, but those who in 1931 are planning to invest millions in such feature productions are no longer embarking on the great unknown. The handwriting now plainly on the wall is that America is largely through with the post-war preoccupation with morbidity and crime in literature and drama. The orgy of self-revelation which marked such a large portion of modern authorship is passing. We have a new younger generation, now rising from the jazz age, that promises to support clean, high-purposed entertainment.

Sees Gangsters Debunked.

"The motion picture screen in recent months has done much to debunk the American gangster in films dealing with current conditions. Nothing could prove more forcibly the success of self-regulation in the motion-picture industry than the manner in which such subjects have been invariably treated. The insistent message flashed upon the screen has been: 'You can't get away with it.' In other films, the deadly weapon of ridicule has been trained upon the gangster and his kind--ridicule that removed from the bandit and gunman every shred of false heroism that might influence young people."

Mr. Hays submitted an analysis of the feature pictures produced in 1930. Comparisons were made not only with the previous year, but with the production of films during the past nine years.

This analysis indicated, according to the report, that in 1930 more feature pictures were produced of outstanding merit, not only from the entertainment but from the standpoint of community value, than in any previous year. On the basis of a national vote of American critics, the report asserted, the industry produced pictures of exceptional merit at the rate of at least one each week during 1930.

Educational Films at Peak.

The past year saw a new record in the production of feature films based on historical, sociological, travel and other educational themes, it was asserted. More than thirty such films were released during the year, it was said, over three times as many as the number released during 1929.

The year 1930 showed a six-to-one increase over any previous year in the production of the higher-type problem plays on the motion picture screen. Mr. Hays reported. This refers, he said, to feature films of a character usually considered outside the range of popular entertainment appeal.

The year 1930 marked an important development from a production standpoint of the movement to serve the vast child audience in the United States with pictures based upon recognized literary classics, he declared. Four productions of the Tom Sawyer type were made and released during that period. The experiment of a motion picture theatre for children was attempted, Mr. Hayes said, but failed for lack of public support.

"The true measure of achievement in motion pictures, as in any other art, is progress, not perfection," Mr. Hays concluded. "Only the professional movie baiter would deny such achievement in the industry. Nevertheless, the fact remains that no art can rest on its laurels. We shall always need constructive criticism from without. We shall always need unremitting vigilance from within.

"However, in its program of self-regulation, the success of the motion picture industry challenges comparison with any instance of industrial or social progress effected through the fiat of law, the action of political censorship or the tyranny of dictatorship."

Mr. Hays was re-elected president and Carl E. Milliken secretary of the organization at the meeting. Tiffany Productions, Inc., and RKO-Pathé Distributing Corporation were elected to membership.

March 31, 1931

WHODUNIT FIRST?

Mystery Surrounds Origin Of the Mystery Film

By LEONARD SPINRAD

ONE of the prime enigmas of the movie "whodunit" is whodunit first. You can find out from any of the standard histories of motion pictures when the first Western or the first spectacle or the first musical was produced. But the film mystery's origins are right in character—mysterious and hard to trace.

Way back in 1908, the French Eclair company instituted a series of "Nick Carter" pictures which prompted a contemporary critic to comment that: "Detective stories are perfectly suited to the cinema. With their brisk and simple plots, an absence of complex psychology, their logical development of events, their rapid jumps, their crimes, waylayings, kidnappings and chases they are fundamentally cinematographic."

The "Nick Carter" series might be regarded as the grand-daddy of screen mysteries except for the fact that, as described by the French historians Bardeche and Brasillach, it was more exactly the grand-daddy of the chapter play, the "cliffhanger."

In silent pictures, of course, the cliffhanger technique was by all odds the most effective for whodunit purposes. Even though Italian and American producers had "Sherlock Holmes" films simultaneously with France's "Nick Carter" in 1908, and despite Fox's "Tangled Lives," based on "The Woman in White," in 1917, the logical crime detection story played a definite second fiddle to such serial sagas as "The Million Dollar Mystery," "Mysteries of the Grand Hotel" and "The House of a Thousand Candles."

The work of fiction commonly regarded as the first modern mystery, with a crime detecting hero, is the aforementioned "Woman in White," the Wilkie Collins novel originally published in 1860 and now brought to the screen as a

Warner Brothers contemporary opus starring Eleanor Parker, Alexis Smith, Sydney Greenstreet and Gig Young. Up until Collins' time, the mysteries plumbed in literature leaned toward the supernatural and the terroristic.

Genesis

The mystery in silent films was largely a by-product of similar melodrama like "The Phantom of the Opera," in which the burning question was a matter of identifying the gruesome gentleman. Crime detection as we know it on the screen today did not come into its own until talking pictures enabled Philo Vance and his colleagues to discuss their theories with suitable éclat.

There have been definite cycles in mystery films since those early days. After the first vogue passed, a few stock detectives like Charlie Chan continued as hardy film perennials. The mystery story became honey for the B's. Mr. Moto and a whole homicide squad worth of other practitioners combined crime detection with violent action. But not until Dashiell Hammett came along with "The Thin Man" and "The Glass Key" did the mystery story as such have a renaissance. Such other detectives as the redoubtable Mr. Vance, Perry Mason and even Mr. Chan languished in semi-retirement, but Mr. and Mrs. Nick Charles went on and on and new kinds of celluloid mayhem prospered.

Dick Powell

Myrna Loy

William Powell

Meanwhile the mystery film had been preserved in such related forms as the psychological drama in which a probing doctor sought to detect a secret in a patient's mind. With this clinical fillip, the extra added touch of toughness provided by "The Glass Key" and the suave, debonair attitude of "The Thin Man," the mystery became a standard item.

Yet, even so, a half-dozen more years were required before the success of "The Maltese Falcon," Writer-Director John Huston's maiden two-ply effort, provided the basis for an effective combination of brutality, polished intellectual menace and hard-boiled humor. In this single highly praised film version of still another Dashiell Hammett book can be traced the various ingredients of the current pattern of films involving "private eyes," soft-voiced fat homicidal maniacs, crime with sex, psychopathic oddities et al.

Hard-Boiled School

The pattern grew more precise. Raymond Chandler's hard-boiled and much put upon investigator, Philip Marlowe, became a prize movie role for such varied talents as Humphrey Bogart, Dick Powell and Robert Montgomery. The hero's toughness was judged by what he took in the way of physical punishment, rather than by what he dished out. The influence of this esthetic approach can be noted even in an unusual thriller like "The Big Clock," which, if it does not mangle its hero physically, certainly puts him through an emotional wringer.

But perhaps the trend is changing. Humphrey Bogart is now making "Key Largo," the non-mysterious Maxwell Anderson play. Dick Powell, apparently as tough as ever, has been announced for "Rogues Regiment," which does not sound like a call for a detective. John Huston's upcoming schedule has nary a crime chaser in it. However, we still don't know, as at least thirty years of movie mysteries are rounded out by the new "Woman in White," who started the whole thing.

May 9, 1948

BOGART BALKS AT BOGEY

By HUMPHREY BOGART
HOLLYWOOD.

IT is becoming the fashion to say in Hollywood that the "take-that-you-rat" school of drama is going out, and if I am not as sanguine about this as some of the practitioners of a gentler mode of drama, it is not merely because I earn my living in this department of the workaday world. As the husband of Miss Betty Bacall, the cinema actress and heroine, and a soon-to-become-father, I could be said to have the more than casual interest in the matter possessed by any family head.

But, by virtue of producing my own films, in one of which, "Knock On Any Door" (just completed at Columbia), we have as handsome a bit of screen killing as you will find on any police blotter, I am also financially and artistically interested in the reverse side of the picture. It occurs to me then that, better than most, I am in a position to arbitrate the matter for the film people, for the writers of this sort of goose-pimple literature, and for the public, which has the wit to know what it likes, but not always, there are those who say to like what is good for it.

Personal Note

It happens that the genesis of this fascination with what happens to a gangster in a film was firmly outlined in my own early experience on the screen. Cast in "The Petrified Forest," with Leslie Howard and Bette Davis, I soon found people, who saw the picture, approaching me on the street as if I were the star of the piece. This puzzled me at first, because, naturally, I wasn't.

And then the reason occurred to me. In the picture, for most of the time I was in it, I sat on the floor of a roadside inn with a machine-gun in my lap and spoke exactly ten sides. That machine-gun was at the bottom of it all. We don't use machine-guns in committing murder today on the screen, because it has become legally unfashionable.

You may be just as dead when

you are killed by a slug, knife, maul, brass knuckle, belaying pin, poison, billie, shotgun or plain bow and arrow, but you give the impression that, like the nations which go down under cannon instead of poison gas, you have been done in somewhat more humanely, and strictly according to the code.

Pivotal Character

But to get back to that first picture. I really can't blame people for thinking I starred in it—and I say that without pride. No one felt sure just when the gun in my hand would go off, and every one found himself, willy-nilly, wanting to know who would be hit when it did, because if he looked away for a split second it might not be possible to follow the trend of the story from then on in.

That may be—and I think it is—the incidental side of the fascination for a gangster film; but there is a psychologically even more sound reason for genuine interest in this sort of film, especially among Americans. Gangsters are a more or less non-gregarious fringe of the social community who work alone and play alone (except for their molls), and rob and kill when the odds are in their favor. Up to this point they get a merely frightened acceptance of their ability to do more damage than most individuals in a given situation.

Underdog

But, the act committed, you really get down to the reason for the gangster's popularity. We don't hunt him singly, or on equal terms. We call out a horde of squad cars, the National Guard, or the entire FBI, and, after hunting him down like a rabbit, fill him so full of lead even his own mother wouldn't recognize him. Or, if we don't, for the average American the rest of the story stops moving until the gangster has, by some good fortune or some charming device on the writer's part, got away. And who in the audience, at this point, is going to say to himself, "I like those policemen?"

The young gangster, running out into the street, or up some alley, spraying the world he hates with bullets, may not be as morally acceptable as the young Crazy Horse, outwitting an American Army on the march, but, as a dramatic device, he will catch the same amount of sympathy—killer though he is.

Is there not, conversely, some merit in Samuel Grafton's argument that no first-rate novelist has ever yet written a novel about a Republican?

My friend, Louis Bromfield—who, by the bye, is a Republican, lest I be accused of taking sides here, which heaven forbid—has been a deep student of these matters for some time. He tells me that it is the man in struggle, and not the man arrived, who holds the interest of the creative novelist. It is at least worth arguing that there is a modicum of the creative novelist in all of us, and that this absorption with how men get out of difficulties, single-handed and alone if possible, but in any event get out of them, is the stuff of which we weave the warp and woof of our own better dramatic imaginings.

Cure

The cure for the gangster film then, in the light of these matters, seems eminently simple to me. In "The Maltese Falcon" we sent a single individual out against a lot of gangsters, and the result was a whole series of pictures with the lone hero against the gangsters instead of vice versa. We called him Sam Spade, but you could call him Calvin Coolidge and still get the same effect if you held to the rule. I am not in the business of pointing up morals, but even a half-hearted search might uncover one here.

Of course, I don't claim we're changing basic values. You have the cavalry for your winning money instead of the Indians; but you are going to get some killings in any event, and a lot of people are going to be very dead because of misdeeds. Personally, I'll play Sam Spade or Duke Mantee with about the same regard for the two roles. Anyone interested can call the shots.

November 28, 1948

MASTER OF SUSPENSE

Being a Self-Analysis by Alfred Hitchcock

By ALFRED HITCHCOCK
Director and Bit Player

HOLLYWOOD.

DIRECTORS of motion pictures, ever since the leather puttee era, have been permitted at least one eccentricity per capita, and my habit of appearing in my own pictures has generally been regarded as exercise of the directorial prerogative. In "Stage Fright" I have been told that my performance is quite juicy. I have been told this with a certain air of tolerance, implying that I have now achieved the maximum limits of directorial ham in the movie sandwich.

It just isn't true. There may have been a "McGuffin" in my film appearance, but not a ham. My motives have always been more devious, or, if you prefer a more devious word, sinister. I have wormed my way into my own pictures as a spy. A director should see how the other half lives. I manage that by shifting to the front side of the camera and letting my company shoot me, so I can see what it is like to be shot by my company.

Big Moment

I find that my actors are kept on their toes that way. Everyone is anxious to get his work done quickly, before I take it into my head to get in his particular scene. The technicians work gaily in anticipation of the fateful moment when I will be at their mercy. And then the moment comes. I step before the cameras. The actors call for retakes. The make-up man splashes his pet concoctions on my face; the wardrobe department tells me how to dress. The electricians and the camera man joyfully "hit" me with the lights. The still photographer tells me how to look, for his photographs.

I find myself tempted to try the same trick with some of the press people, when they come for a full-dress interview. I have a secret yen to interview them, to pose them for still pictures. I would like to focus a press camera on some photographer and ask him to "express menace and suspense, please." I would also like to write a review of some of the newspaper stories.

Purely Sinister

My purpose is, as I have indicated, purely sinister. I find that the easiest way to worry people is to turn the tables on them. Make the most innocent member of the cast the murderer; make the next-door neighbor a dangerous spy. Keep your characters stepping out of character and into the other fellow's boots.

I should like, for example, to make a thriller about the United Nations, in which the delegate of one nation is denounced by another delegate for falling asleep in the middle of an important international speech. They go to wake the sleeping delegate, only to find that he is dead, with a dagger in his back. That would be the beginning of my story—except for one thing. It is too close to unamusing reality. Which delegate will be the corpse? What tangled international threads will be caught in the skein? How do we avoid making a weighty political document instead of a suspense story?

To my way of thinking, the best suspense drama is that which weaves commonplace people in what appears to be a routine situation, until it is revealed (and fairly early in the game) as a glamorously dangerous charade. The spy stories of pre-war days fit these specifications perfectly. Today, however, there is nothing very glamorous about spying—there is only one sort of secret to be stolen and there is too much at stake for people to play charades over it.

I believe that the suspense drama is being smoked out of its old haunts. I think that we must forget about espionage and rediscover more personal sorts of menace. I think that a suspense story in the old tradition can be made today about an international crime ring, with its agents in high places, much more easily than a film about the missing papers.

The "McGuffin"

The "McGuffin"—my own term for the key element of any suspense story—has obviously got to change. It can no longer be the idea of preventing the foreign agent from stealing the papers. It can no longer be the business of breaking a code. And yet these very same elements, disguised to fit the times, must still be there.

Alfred Hitchcock

One of the ways in which the suspense drama must change is in its setting. The Orient Express, for example, has had its day as a scene for spy melodrama. I think the same may be said of narrow stairways in high towers, subways and the like. Personally, I rather lean toward Alaska as the setting for the next thriller. It is logical—as one of the last targets of international espionage—and it has the color of a frontier territory. (I could wear a beard for my own bit role.) And there is such a nice air about the title "Eskimo Spy."

But the big problem of the glamorous villain—whether, in Alaska or Times Square—remains a riddle, just one minor heritage of a brave new world in which we are becoming conditioned to suspecting our neighbors and expecting the worst.

June 4, 1950

CUMULATIVE VIOLENCE

Comment on a Tendency Noticeable in Films

By BOSLEY CROWTHER

THE report in our Hollywood column last week that the British film censors have been slapping bans on American movies that have run towards reckless violence and needless brutality probably caused some quiet rejoicing among readers of similar mind. And we cannot deny these concrete tokens of disapproval have done our own heart some sneaking good.

For, as much as we dislike the practice of official censorship, we have to agree the British watchdogs have had considerable cause for using it. Violence and senseless sadism and calculated brutality have been conspicuously present in our movies since World War II. We can't say they have been on the increase, in the past few or even several years, for these are elements that have always been present, more or less, in the body of films. But their presence within the last few years has certainly been more noticeable, maybe because we are more sensitive and alarmed by growing violence in society.

So it hasn't been too disturbing that the British have exercised a little taste in refusing to accept some more outrageous and offensive manifestations of violence in our films.

Keep Cool

However—and here's a big "however"—let's keep a couple of things in mind in talking about this matter of violence on the screen. First, it has yet to be proved that the examples of violence shown in films are the sole and singular cause of human debasement and that current critical problem, juvenile crime. Beyond any question, the exposure of violence and brutality in films—in cheap and pointless pictures, for sheer "shock effect," as the British say—does stimulate these individuals who are in a mental and emotional mood to be moved. It may propel the unstable. But it doesn't necessarily breed crime.

Second, and more important, violence and brutality in films cannot be condemned without exception. It is merely the pointless, the untrue and the willfully sensational we can fairly damn.

Some films teem with violence of this order. One opened at the Mayfair last week under the frankly inviting title of "Violent Saturday." In it, three modern bandits invade a western mining town and go about the scientific business of setting up the robbery of a bank. While they are at their preparations, some of the sleazier local characters are exposed, including an alcoholic mine owner, his bitter and faithless wife, a larcenous woman librarian and a bank manager who is a "peeping Tom."

These are repulsive people. But more reprehensible is the fact that the violence which develops has no moral purpose or point. The bandits, after handling people brutally, are luridly, sadistically killed. The last is stabbed in the back with a pitchfork in the hands of a vengeful Amish farmer. (The fact that the farmer, by his nature and religion, deeply abhors violence is the only remotely philosophical—and then defeatist—point in the film.)

Validity

There have been many other pictures, recent and past—some notorious and some obscure—that have gone in for cumulative violence with no other purpose than to thrill. But there have also been many excellent pictures in which violence has played a valid role in revealing the significant natures of individuals or the flaws in society.

Take "On the Waterfront," for instance—last year's prize-winning film and generally acknowledged contribution to an understanding—in part, at least—of the dock union strife. It was loaded with violence and brutality. Indeed, the essential point was that the gangsters who ran the stevedores' union maintained their power through brutality.

Likewise in "Bad Day at Black Rock," one of the better pictures of this year, there is a scene of a fight in a barroom that is as smashing as anything of the sort ever shown. But it is justified—indeed, it is essential—as a visualization of the moral turn that a crippled man of honorable intentions makes upon his brutish tormentors.

Here is the crux of the matter: violence must be truthful, logical and designed to convey some revelation or moral comment if it is to be commendable. This is often open to disagreement. Frankly, we thought—and still do—that "The Wild One," banned by the British, was a socially significant film. We think that "Blackboard Jungle" goes to questionable excess. But let's not stubbornly decry all violence because we disapprove sometimes or disagree.

May 15, 1955

Who's For Conspiracy?

By BOSLEY CROWTHER

PERHAPS it is the times in which we are living, perhaps it is the backlash to James Bond, perhaps it is simply because of the success of the novel, "The Spy Who Came in from the Cold." But there must be some positive reason—something more than just sheer coincidence—to account for the spate of serious movies (or pseudo-serious ones) having to do with political intrigue and conspiracy that we've been getting these past few months. Falling within the category would be films of espionage of course, and also films of brainwashing and defection, which are forms of conspiracy.

Tick off the lot. There is "Torn Curtain," Alfred Hitchcock's unfortunate attempt to wiggle behind the Iron Curtain with a questing American scientist. There are the curious "The Quiller Memorandum" and "Funeral in Berlin" and the schizoid "The Liquidator," and maybe "Fahrenheit 451." Lately there is Sidney Lumet's Hitchcock-eyed "The Deadly Affair." And now there are "The Night of the Generals" and "La Guerre Est Finie."

I ring in "The Night of the Generals" because it obviously includes an abundance of intrigue and conspiracy within its melodramatic plot. It has the intrigues of three Nazi generals evidently jockeying among themselves for military power and position in Warsaw and Paris in World War II. It also includes an ample section about the famous conspiracy of Nazi officers to assassinate Hitler along toward the end of the war—all of this in addition to its major and most formidable concern: namely, which of those three Nazi generals is the sadistic murderer of a Warsaw prostitute?

This last concern, incidentally, is so heavily overweighted in the plot and so much time is given to the sleuthing of a German major of intelligence (Omar Sharif) to find out which one it is, when all the while the film is showing us explicitly that it is the poker-faced, glazed-eyed clank-spur played demoniacally by Peter O'Toole, that the balance and suspense of the picture are lost about halfway through.

Wormy People

This is too bad because there's a great deal in "The Night of the Generals" that is very good, including an excellent performance by Donald Pleasence as one of the evil generals and another fine performance by Tom Courtenay as a sensitive German corporal, caught up, against his will, in the psychotic maneuvering of a second murder by the guilty general.

There's also a shattering sequence showing the ruthless carrying-out of a design to destroy Resistance fighters in Warsaw by the bloodthirsty Mr. O'Toole. I must add right here, however, that this sequence cannot hold a candle to the description of a comparable program of liquidating Nazi-imprisoned Jews in the Czechoslovak film, "Transport from Paradise," which came to the Bleecker Street Cinema last week. This latter film, made by Zbynek Brynych in 1963, gives a Kafkaesque image of tension in the notorious Terezin Ghetto in Czechoslovakia, and is one of the most disturbing pictures of the working of the Nazi genocide program that I have ever seen.

But to get back to "The Night of the Generals" and those films I have cited above—those films so recently upon us having to do with political intrigue and conspiracy. The interesting thing about them—or most of them, anyway—is the sense of distrust, suspicion and insidious corruption they convey. All sorts of wormy people, not just spies, are doing vicious deadly things under dark and secret circumstances. Much evil is afoot in the world, especially in middle Europe and in areas adjacent thereto.

To judge by the pointed implications and even the outright candid charges in these films, the East Germans and the Soviet Russians are the least reliable people in the world—and this is flatly supported by the attitude of those antecedent Nazi generals in World War II. Look at the treacherous behavior of the villains in "The Deadly Affair" and at the masterfully mischievous scoundrels in "The Quiller Memorandum" and "Funeral in Berlin." These are perfidious people, and middle Europeans are a lot of intriguers we'd better beware of. The times are out of joint.

I am not raising the question of whether this is accurate or not. All I am noting, with considerable astonishment, is that this is being developed with the force of propaganda in our films.

In the light of this, it is ironic and perhaps poetic justice to find that the best film —the one that makes the strongest and most affecting statement about a modern man's genuine involvement in affairs of political conspiracy —has a Communist as its hero. This film is "La Guerre Est Finie," now showing at the Beekman. It is the work of Alain Resnais.

This real, mature contemplation of the fears, the doubts and despairs of a veteran Spanish revolutionary on a brief visit into France in the present day is so far above the histrionics of those other thriller films that comparison with them is foolish. And it has a performance by Yves Montand that gives a tremendous understanding of what it means to devote one's life and sacrifice one's private pleasures to a political cause. Maybe the cause is futile. That's one of the things that worries him, too. But for him the war isn't over—and neither is the life of this film.

February 12, 1967

Bravo, Brando's 'Godfather'

By VINCENT CANBY

AFTER a very long time, in too many indifferent or half-realized movies, giving performances that were occasionally becalmed but always more interesting than the material, Marlon Brando has finally connected with a character and a film that need not embarrass America's most complex, most idiosyncratic film actor, nor those critics who have wondered, in bossy print, what ever happened to him.

The film is Francis Ford Coppola's screen version of Mario Puzo's "The Godfather," the year's first really satisfying, big commercial American film, a sort of popular-priced, Long Beach version of "Rocco and His Brothers" (even to the inclusion of an eclectic, romantic 1940ish Nino Rota score), a movie that describes a sorrowful American Dream as a slambang, sentimental gangster melodrama. It opens here Wednesday at Loew's State One and Two, the Cine, the Orpheum and the Tower East Theaters.

Brando's role is that of Don Vito Corleone, the aging Mafia chief who remains a fearsome, rudely magnificent creature even though his hair has thinned, his jowls have thickened, his belly has dropped and his walk is not always steady, like a man searching for firm footing across a swamp. The role is not big enough for Brando to dominate the film by his physical presence, but his performance sets the pitch for the entire production, which is true and flamboyant and, at unexpected moments, immensely moving. This is not only because the emotions, if surcharged, are genuine and fundamental, but also because we're watching a fine actor exercise his talent for what looks like the great joy of it, because, after all, it's there.

"The Godfather" is Coppola's fourth production as a director, but nothing in "You're A Big Boy Now," "Finian's Rainbow" or "The Rain People" (except, perhaps, some individual performances) prepares the way for this new film. Like "The Last Picture Show," "The Godfather" rediscovers the marvelous possibilities existing in the straightforward narrative movie that refuses to acknowledge it's about anything more than its plot, and whose characters are revealed entirely in terms of events. "The Godfather" moves so quickly, in such a tightly organized series of interlocking events, that the film, like its characters (who are not the sort to muse very long about their fates), doesn't have time to be introspective—to betray the excitement of the immediately felt emotion or of an explicit action by somehow commenting on it.

In this respect the film is very much like the novel, which Coppola and Puzo have adapted for the screen with extraordinary fidelity — yet the film has a life that completely eluded me in the novel. I suppose I should admit here that although "The Godfather" has sold almost as well as The Bible, I was only able to get through it by making those little 30- and 40-paragraph hops one usually reserves for perusal of the Congressional Record. The novel is a kind of first draft—an outline of characters and an inventory of happenings—that has only now been finished as a film (which, I suspect, Puzo knew would be true all along).

The difference between the first draft and the last is the difference between a fairly drab prose description of the Long Beach compound in which the Corleones live, surrounded by a high wall that is guarded by their "soldiers," and Coppola's recreation of the ugly, dark, Grand Rapids gentility in which the old don lives with his worried-looking wife, his beloved sons, their wives and their children, one of whom always seems to be crying at some distance off-screen.

The difference is also there in the film's first image, a close-up of the handsome, deeply lined old face of Bonasera, the law-abiding undertaker who, in desperation, has come to the Godfather for help after the courts have freed two men, "not Italian," who raped his daughter. The undertaker's monologue is taken directly from the book. However, as spoken almost impassively by Salvatore Corsitto, while Coppola's camera slowly pulls back to show us Brando, in heavy shadow, listening with polite impatience, the speech becomes one of the most affecting statements of an American experience I've heard in any recent fiction film. More important, the speech does not exist for its own sake, but to set out the exotic code of honor, with its terrible system of rewards and punishments, that will govern the Corleone Family wars—from New York, Las Vegas and Hollywood to Sicily—during the almost three-hour running time of the film.

"The Godfather" is definitely not "Rocco and His Brothers." Its neo-realism is not outraged. It has about it, in fact, the quality of a romantic fable whose principal characters are in some ways charmed, like Michael (Al Pacino), the don's youngest son who, though gentle-natured, Dartmouth-educated, and beloved of a sweet WASP wife, can take over the Family and lead it, through murders and massacres, to victory, with what seems to be remarkably little preparation. Within the film, Michael's Jack the Giant Killer, but it is the point of the film, as it was the novel, that the victory carries with it a life-sentence of isolation. There is, of course, something romantic even in this sentence, which is not unlike the terrible fates suffered by more pulpy heroes and heroines who gain wealth, power

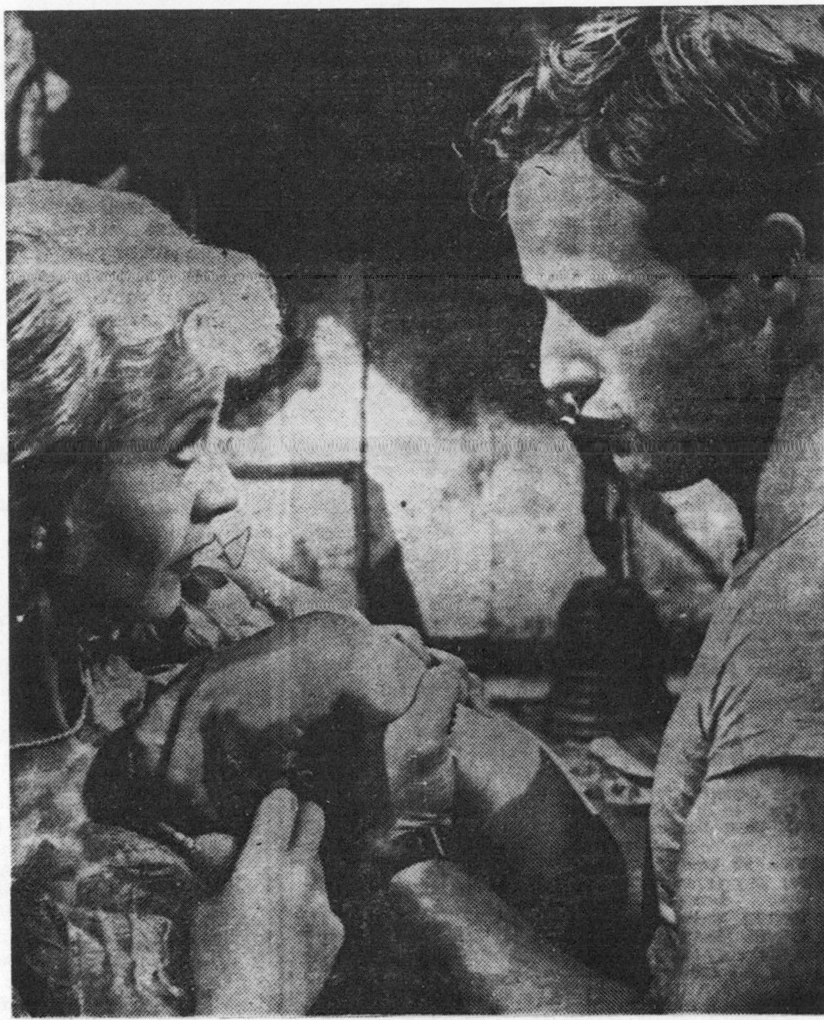

Vivien Leigh is the neurotic Blanche DuBois, Marlon Brando the brutish Stanley Kowalski in the 1951 film of Tennessee Williams's play, "A Streetcar Named Desire."

and position only to lose the kind of happiness that most poor pulp-fiction readers won't ever experience anyway.

To suggest — as I'm sure many people will — that "The Godfather" glorifies crime is to take the film both too seriously and not seriously enough. It is to deny the elation that one can experience through great storytelling, no matter what the bloody point of the story may be. It is also to confuse the movie's romanticized view of crime (to which some small part of us always responds) with a seductive view of crime, which the film does not have.

"The Godfather" does, however, honor its characters, and the coming-of-age experience that has been unique to one small group of first and second generation Americans who receive, according to the members of the Italian-American Civil Rights League, much more publicity than they have ever honorably deserved. That's a topic I'm not qualified to discuss. "The Godfather," however true or false to specific facts, is as dark and ominous a reflection of certain aspects of American life as has ever been presented in a movie designed as sheer entertainment. Now, as then, when the system doesn't work, the system will be by-passed.

March 12, 1972

Serpico, the Saint Francis Of Copdom

By VINCENT CANBY

SIDNEY LUMET'S "Serpico," the first in what threatens to be an avalanche of movies about policemen, picks up the old cop film and brings it with lights flashing and sirens blaring into the middle of the Watergate era. It is Lumet's toughest, most provocative film in years, the story of the New York City detective, Frank Serpico, who in 1970 blew the whistle on graft and corruption within the New York Police Department, leading to the Knapp Commission hearings and the biggest shake-up in the department's history.

Serpico is not a new kind of hero. The man who attempts to buck the system has been a source of fascination ever since the first Greek playwrights questioned the wit and wisdom of some of their gods.

"Serpico," however, is a new kind of cop film and its title character, beautifully played by Al Pacino, is a new kind of hero to meet pounding a beat. He's obsessed in the way that Hollywood usually sees its painters, musicians and mad doctors obsessed. The difference is that Serpico is obsessed with such things as honesty and integrity and compassion for the underdog—to such an extent that when you leave the theater, your admiration for the man may be mixed with a certain amount of suspicion: he really is a driven figure, so neurotic that you begin to feel that his obsession has less to do with a sense of justice than with toilet training. This is not to knock the man but to credit the complexity of Lumet's movie and Pacino's performance, which are, after all, based on an authorized biography (written by Peter Maas), not always the most comprehensive source material.

*

Cop movies have come a long way from "G Men" (1935), in which James Cagney, though single-minded in his pursuit of gangsters, was a more or less conventional good guy, made distinctive only by Cagney's idiosyncratic talent as an actor. It may only be a coincidence, of course, but while J. Edgar Hoover was alive, few cop films were anywhere near as much fun as gangster films. Cops were nice, clean-cut, buttoned-down and essentially blah. The gangsters gots all the psychological ticks, the hang-ups and the good lines.

"The French Connection" tried to humanize cops by showing us that they had to be as cruel and ruthless as the people they were after, and recently we've been given films to demonstrate that good cops are hamstrung by the niceties of Constitutional freedoms, as in "Dirty Harry" and "Hit."

"Serpico" does something else. It presents its hero as a sort of St. Francis of Copdom, an Establishment dropout who talks to the street people and listens to Bach, a mystic who wears love beads and sandals, who studies Spanish and takes ballet lessons. "There are five positions," Serpico explains to an appalled cop in the Bureau of Criminal Intelligence. Says the cop to Serpico: "You're being short-changed."

The movie charts Serpico's growing disgust with police corruption without enjoying the freedom to analyze it. That's the form of authorized biography. At the beginning Serpico balks at accepting free lunches at the local restaurant simply because he doesn't like the leftovers the owner palms off on the free-loading cops. Serpico wants to eat first-class.

Serpico's awareness of the extent of corruption, everything from small bribes taken to forget a traffic violation to the acceptance of thousands of dollars a month from gambling and narcotics racketeers, eventually prompts him to go to his superiors, none of whom, for various reasons, are particularly interested. The mayor, he is told, is hesitant to do anything to alienate the Police Department on the eve of what promises to be a long hot summer of possible civil unrest.

The deus ex machina of Serpico's drama is New York Times reporter David Burnham, who listened to the stories and evidence presented by Serpico and Sgt. David Durk (whose real-life role is downplayed in the film, which gives Durk the fictitious name of Bob Blair) and wrote the series of articles that led ultimately to the establishment of the Knapp Commission.

"Serpico" is essentially a thriller, one that has a number of smashing, bruising moments, as well as a few romantic ones that almost becalm the movie in midstream. These are not very interesting in themselves, although his terrible relations with the girl he loves are necessarily dramatized in an attempt to explain the depth of his mania, his obsession with doing something about the second-rateness of the world around him.

Serpico's decision to blow the whistle on other cops and on his superiors is the sort that we accept rather more easily in drama (it is the right thing to do and heroes should do the right thing) than we do in life, particularly if it's our own. It is one of the achievements of Lumet's film that we get some idea of the mental cost of that decision to Serpico, which, in turn, makes us speculate about the kind of character who could survive the ostracism and threats that followed his disclosures.

"He must be a little nuts." That's what a friend of mine said about Dr. Daniel Ellsberg. Though the friend professed to admire what Ellsberg had done, he was also worried about Ellsberg's seeming to enjoy the publicity and notoriety that came when the case of the Pentagon Papers broke.

The American public is schizoid in such matters. We want heroes but we're also frightened of them. It's easier to feel comfortable with the kind of bunglers responsible for Watergate than it is with people whose moral codes are higher and more rigid than our own. We are reassured when the Rev. Davidson falls into bed with Sadie Thompson. There must be something wrong with anyone who professes piety.

"Serpico" is about our world, not simply its police corruption but its values, which have been so diluted that when we meet someone who acts on principle we know we're in the presence of a freak.

December 16, 1973

1930's Confidence Men Are Heroes of 'Sting'

THE STING, directed by George Roy Hill; screenplay by David S. Ward; produced by Tony Bill and Michael and Julia Phillips; director of photography, Robert Surtees; editor, William Reynolds; music, Marvin Hamlisch; a Richard D. Zanuck-David Brown presentation distributed by UMNIVERSAL Pictures. Running time: 129 minutes.

Henry Gondoroff	Paul Newman
Johnny Hooker	Robert Redford
Doyle Lonnegan	Robert Shaw
Lt. William Snyder	Charles Durning
J.J. Singleton	Ray Walston
Billie	Eileen Brennan
Kid Twist	Harold Gould
Eddie Niles	John Heffernan
F.B.I. Agent Polk	Dana Elcar

By VINCENT CANBY

"The Sting," which opened yesterday at Loew's State 2 and other theaters, re-teams the director (George Roy Hill) and stars (Paul Newman and Robert Redford) of "Butch Cassidy and the Sundance Kid" in a comedy about a couple of exuberant confidence men operating in and around Chicago in 1936.

"The Sting" looks and sounds like a musical comedy from which the songs have been removed, leaving only a background score of old-fashioned, toe-tapping piano rags that as easily evoke the pre-World War I teens as the nineteen-thirties.

A lot of the other period details aren't too firmly anchored in time, but the film is so good-natured, so obviously aware of everything it's up to, even its own picturesque frauds, that I opt to go along with it. One forgives its unrelenting efforts to charm, if only because "The Sting" itself is a kind of con game, devoid of the poetic aspirations that weighed down "Butch Cassidy and the Sundance Kid."

Mr. Newman and Mr. Redford, dressed in best, fit-to-kill, snap-brim hat, thirties spendor, looking like a couple of guys in old Arrow shirt ads, are more or less reprising their roles in "Butch Cassidy."

Mr. Newman is Henry Gondoroff, the older con artist in charge of the instruction of Johnny Hooker (Mr. Redford), the bright, eager, younger man who yearns to make what the movie calls the Big Con (swindle), the way tap dancers in the movies about the twenties wanted to play the Palace.

Their quarry is a ruthless, vain, fastidious New York racketeer named Doyle Lonnegan, played by Robert Shaw in the broad manner in which the film was conceived by David S. Ward, who wrote the screenplay, and realized by Mr. Hill.

●

The director supplements the period sets and costumes with elaborate technical devices to move from one scene into another: wipes, iris-outs, images that turn like pages. Separating sequences are title cards that recall Norman Rockwell's Saturday Evening Post covers. It's all a little too much, but excess is an essential part of the film's style.

"The Sting" has a conventional narrative, with a conventional beginning, middle and end, but what one remembers are the set pieces of the sort that can make a slapped-together Broadway show so entertaining. These include a hilarious, thoroughly crooked poker game on the Twentieth Century Limited in which Henry blows his nose on his tie to the horror of Lonnegan, as well as a chase that lasts approximately two minutes, and the final swindle, the mechanics of which are still none too clear to me.

The only woman with a substantial role in the film is Eileen Brennan, who plays a madam with a heart of gold and enough time off to be able to assist the stars in the final con. "The Sting" is not the kind of film that takes its women very seriously, and the continuing popularity of these male-male co-starring teams should, I suppose, probably prompt some solemn analysis.

It is not, I suspect, a terrible perversion of the romantic movie-team concept idealized by William Powell and Myrna Loy, Clark Gable and Lana Turner but, rather, a variation on the old Dr. Gillespie-Dr. Kildare relationship, with a bit of Laurel and Hardy thrown in. It is also apparently very good box office.

December 26, 1973

Edward G. Robinson, Eddy Brophy, and Harold Huber in a quartet of which Allen Jenkins is the sour note. The film is "A Slight Case of Murder."

Three Film Stars Get $1,000,000 a Year Each

Motion Picture Business, at Pinnacle of Success, Sees No Sign of Waning Popularity—Tax Talk Stops Boasting of Profits

HE who runs and reads may have observed that the movie actors' salary contest which raged in the newspapers a year or more ago has been missing of late. New contracts have been made and new companies organized, and while there has been no diminution, in the size of salaries, no press-agent blurb about the millions paid to the World's Greatest Comedian or the Queen of the Movies has made the welkin ring.

This unwonted silence on the part of the movie makers who so recently were crying from the skyscraper tops the affluence that could pay such enormous salaries was due to a sudden and rude realization that their boasts were impressing the legislators who levy taxes, as well as the picture "fans" to whom the figures were addressed. The reaction came in the form of investigations held in various States, one of them in New York last Winter, to determine whether an industry that could afford to pay Charlie Chaplin $670,000 a year might not be capable of paying a special tax. Now a war tax that promises to devour large slices of great incomes is impending, and between the threat of it and the probings of the State tax commissions the proverbial camel would pass through the needle's eye more quickly than boastful figures through the lips of a movie magnate.

No inference is intended that an evasion of any tax is contemplated by star or producer; these new money barons have merely adopted the policy of more experienced financiers that even silence is golden when the taxmakers are at work. Having assimilated this axiom the industry has adopted an unwritten rule that salaries of six figures must be discussed exclusively with the recipients and then only in the softest words. Thus has the chief joy of the press agent—the computing of approximate salaries—and of the gentle reader—the estimating of the true figures—been removed. Consider the mental anguish of the publicity man of the new Goldwyn Pictures Corporation when he had to announce the engagement by his company of Maxine Elliott and Mary Garden, or of the feelings of the young man who is paid to get Douglas Fairbanks's name in the paper when that star recently organized his own company without one audible gloat over his Gargantuan income.

The reader who has been staggered by the size of the reputed earnings of many movie stars has doubtless wondered how nearly they approximated the truth. In the following attempt to satisfy that curiosity it must always be borne in mind that the figures given are not authentic, since with the rigid self-enforced censorship of the producers it is more difficult to arrive at facts, but they may be accepted as substantially correct. Generally speaking it may be said that while the figures of the press agents were exaggerated they were not enlarged in greater ratio than are all figures, which, as every one who has watched the estimated value of estates dwindle or has observed the divergence in printed estimates of the size of crowds knows, have a way of compounding themselves at a constantly increasing rate of acceleration. Staggering sums are paid the most popular actors and actresses in the movies when all allowances for the exuberance of press agents and figures have been made.

About a year ago Charlie Chaplin, who had become the premier screen comedian, springing from the obscurity of an inconspicuous role in an English music hall pantomimic act to worldwide popularity as a movie clown, ended his contract with Essanay, the company that developed him, and came East to sell his services to the highest bidder. His popularity was attested by the crowds that clamored for admission whenever and wherever one of his films was exhibited and by unhygienic hosts of youthful imitators in every vacant lot and alley. Immediately there was a scramble for his services, in which practically every big producing company participated. One company even sent one of its officers across the continent to accompany the actor to New York, and after his arrival he was kept a virtual captive for days while this concern's representatives labored with him.

Finally, after days of bidding, it was announced that the Mutual Film Corporation had signed a contract with the comedian, he to receive $10,000 a week for a year for his services, with a cash bonus of $150,000 for signing the contract; and a world gasped that a funny walk and a funny kick could earn so much. Mr. Chaplin was photographed accepting the bonus, smiling and looking east toward the Metropolitan Tower, and thanking President John R. Freuler with his hand on his new employer's shoulder as he gazed south. Then he boarded a special train and went west to begin earning his new salary.

The only ones who didn't gasp were the men who hired Chaplin, for they felt certain they would come out ahead. There was nothing philanthropic about their offer; on the contrary, it was based on calculations which allowed them a handsome return for their investment and daring. It is generally accepted in film circles that Mr. Chaplin's Mutual contract did call for a $10,000 weekly salary, with perhaps a percentage in the profits that would aggregate the amount of the alleged bonus, so that if this theory is true there was little discrepancy between the claim and the fact. As Mr. Freuler subsequently explained, the transaction was based on figures available from Mr. Chaplin's past record. The demand for his films was known and the possible revenue, granted that there was no appreciable diminution in his popularity, from the rental of eight new films could be computed.

The luck of Mr. Chaplin and the wide publicity it received cost the producers a lot of money which was diverted into the pockets of the players. Shortly after the announcement of Mr. Chaplin's coup Miss Pickford began to show signs of unrest. After her brief return to the speaking stage in David Belasco's production of "The Good Little Devil" Miss Pickford established herself as a great favorite in the photoplays in which the Famous Players Company starred her. She became, in fact, the most popular screen actress, and when her old contract finally expired she made a new arrangement, which is said to net her a yearly guarantee of $520,000 and a percentage of the profits from her pictures that probably swells her earnings to the million mark.

Much the same thing happened to Douglas Fairbanks. When the Triangle Film Corporation began its career with a blare of trumpets Mr. Fairbanks, an agreeable young actor unknown to the movies, was engaged for a term of years at a gradually increasing salary that averaged perhaps $2,000 a week. He achieved a great vogue upon the exhibition of his first picture, "The Lamb," and as his popularity grew so did his dissatisfaction, until he finally got a legal release from his contract and organized his own company. Under the new arrangement, which is practically the same as Miss Pickford's, it is reported that Mr. Fairbanks will receive a guarantee of $520,000 a year and a share of the profits that should bring the figure up to $1,000,000.

These form the Big Three of the movies, but they are by no means the sole recipients of huge stipends. Ever since the movies have been an important amusement factor the producers have

Douglas Fairbanks, Mary Pickford, and Charlie Chaplin, (from Left to Right,) the World's Three Most Popular Movie Stars, Whose Combined Earning Capacity Is Estimated at $3,000,000 a Year. Picture Was Taken in California.

pursued George M. Cohan, and he has as persistently fled until recently, when he surrendered. The bid that brought about his capitulation was from the Artcraft Film Corporation, the same company that controls the Pickford and Fairbanks pictures, and is alleged to have been a guarantee of $100,000 each for three pictures with a share of the profits on top of that. As it takes about six weeks to make a photoplay of this type, if this report is true Mr. Cohan will receive at least $300,000 for eighteen weeks' work.

Artcraft recently signed Elsie Ferguson under a two years' contract which is said to guarantee her forty weeks' work each year at $6,000 a week, and it is understood that if she cares to continue without rest she may do so at the same salary. If she should so elect, one does not need pencil and paper to figure that in two years Miss Ferguson can earn $624,000.

It is said that Geraldine Farrar receives $6,000 a week from the Jesse Lasky Company whenever she goes to California to pose before the camera, and even a Metropolitan Opera prima donna could not afford to overlook a little matter of $60,000 picked up in vacation time. Billie Burke is known to have received $50,000 for her first picture, and, while succeeding pictures without the element of novelty probably did not bring her so large a reward, she is still among the first twenty.

Marguerite Clark is another favorite whose weekly guarantee is in four figures and whose annual income requires six to state. Anita Stewart's salary is estimated at $2,000 a week, and Norma Talmadge, one of the younger group of stars, is credited with earning $1,000 a week and a part of the profits. Clara Kimball Young was one of the first film actresses to form her own company, and it is asserted that her gross income from her pictures is between $250,000 and $325,000 a year. Roscoe ("Fatty") Arbuckle, Mabel Normand, Mae Marsh, and Olga Petrova are other stars the demands for whose films have won them substantial salaries.

Theda Bara is one of the sphinxes of the industry and nothing authentic can be stated about her salary, but it is rumored to be out of all proportion to her value as a star. The career of Miss Bara, the first and most famous of the vampires of the screen, has been spectacular. She leaped into fame with her first picture, an adaptation of Kipling's poem about the fool who made his prayer to "a rag, a bone, and a hank of hair," and ever since her pictures have been best sellers. That first picture, "A Fool There Was," has the enviable reputation of being the only picture of its length to have earned a profit of $1,000,000.

These salaries of players who devote a part or all of their time to acting for the movies are pretty generally based on mathematical calculations; the fact that they get the money may be accepted as proof that they earn it, for the movie promoter is as shrewd a bargainer as any other man. It is the ubiquitousness of the movie that makes it the financial marvel it is, the possibility of the shadow of one person appearing in thousands of different places at one time. One hundred and fifty-five prints of Mr. Chaplin's films are distributed and shown synchronously and about eighty of Miss Pickford's. These prints work for indefinite periods until they wear out and are renewed, so that by the end of a year there are hundreds of films in circulation. Miss Bara's "A Fool There Was" is still a big seller, and some of Miss Pickford's early pictures enjoy a wide circulation today.

Film rentals are determined by two factors—the age of the film and the size of the theatre and community. Naturally, Miss Pickford's first picture, which has been seen by millions, would not be as valuable as her latest, nor could the manager of the Bijou Dream in Emporia, Kan., a town of 10,000 inhabitants, be expected to pay as much for the privilege of exhibiting it as the proprietor of the Strand, New York. The Strand and the Rialto have each paid as high as $3,500 for a week's rental of a film, and the prices scale down from this to a few dollars.

It is estimated that there are 15,000 theatres in the United States, exclusive of vaudeville and other theatres in which pictures are shown as a part of a program, devoted to movies. There have been as many as 17,000 at one time, but the tendency the last few years has been toward fewer and larger theatres. The daily attendance in these theatres is variously estimated from 12,000,000 to 17,000,000 persons. Perhaps 15,000,000 would be a fair estimate. Sometimes attendance falls off in one section, due to local causes, as it did in New York last Summer during the infantile paralysis epidemic, but these losses are quite as often offset by gains in attendance in other places. The general consensus of opinion among trade authorities seems to be that while the movies may have reached the zenith of their popularity they have not passed it. They are at least holding their own, and students of the industry believe they will continue to do so as long as the standard of excellence is increased. The standard has risen steadily, as the constant fan knows. On the other hand, it is pointed out, the movie public can never be much greater except as the world's population increases, because the world and his wife now go to see the pictures.

TWO NEW FEATURE FILMS.

Theda Bara and Douglas Fairbanks in Their Usual Roles.

Two feature pictures shown here for the first time yesterday illustrate that the movie player is bound more tightly by the accidents of personality than his brother or sister of the much more legitimate stage. The pictures were "Gold and the Woman," which again displayed Theda Bara's opulent beauty on the screen of the Academy of Music, and "The Habit of Happiness," the third of the series of Douglas Fairbanks pictures to be projected at the Knickerbocker.

Miss Bara was born to possess a certain exotic beauty, and Mr. Fairbanks a contagious smile. By chance Miss Bara was cast as a "vampire woman" in her first picture, and a "vampire woman" she has remained since, while the first close-up ever taken of the Fairbanks smile determined his future in pictures.

"Gold and the Woman," then, is only another variation of the vampire motif, and "The Habit of Happiness" a few more reels of Fairbanksian exuberance. And as laughter is more wholesome than tainted emotion, so the latter picture is superior to the former. Neither, however, is much of a picture, particularly when the talents of the two stars are considered.

The Fairbanks film starts out breezily enough and during its course there are some moments really humorous, but it ends suddenly as if the director had reached the end of his reel before the end of the story. Mr. Fairbanks plays the rôle of a poor young rich man who undertakes the task of curing a dyspeptic millionaire. In the process of making him laugh he wins his daughter and whips a band of ruffians.

Miss Bara's lot was even a less happy one. "Gold and the Woman" in the absurdities of its incidents surpasses the fantastic hallucinations of a lotos eater. One of the choicest of these is the escape of the girl from her father's home. She is the daughter of a Mexican aristocrat, and when her father's house is attacked by revolutionists she dons a suit of armor in the ancestral halls and marches out from the burning building, leaving the bandits gaping in two awe-stricken rows at this strange apparition. A newcomer in the movies who appears to good advantage in "Gold and the Woman" is Alma Hanlon.

Other new features shown yesterday and their stars were "For the Defense," with Fannie Ward, at the Strand; "The Soul Market," with Olga Petrova, at the Broadway, and "Merely Mary Ann," with Vivian Martin, at Proctor's Twenty-third.

March 13, 1916

THEDA MAKES 'EM ALL BARAS

Actress's Family Join Her in Dropping Name of Goodman.

Theda Bara, actress, and all the members of her family got permission yesterday from Supreme Court Justice Donnelly to drop the family name Goodman and call themselves Bara hereafter. In the petition of the actress she said that her family name is Theodosia Goodman, and that she took the name Bara on the stage because her maternal grandfather was Francis Bara de Coppet of Switzerland. Her father, Bernard Goodman, was born in Poland. Her birthplace was Cincinnati. She said she had made the name Bara celebrated through her own efforts and for that reason wants it as her legal name.

The members of the family who also took the name were Pauline and Bernard Bara, parents, Marque, a brother, now in the theatrical business, and Esther, a sister, 19 years old, who is about to go on the stage, and will be known as Loro Bara.

November 17, 1917

MOVIE "VAMP" EXTINCT.

Public Wants "Little Eva" Type Now, Theatre Owners Hear.

CHICAGO, June 6. — The movie "vamp," with her white face, her penciled eyebrows, green eyes and her jade earrings, is gone and will flaunt her fascinations on the silver screen no longer, motion-picture theatre owners were told at a meeting today.

What the public wants now, according to speakers, are good little girls, heroines of the little Eva type, with golden hair, blue eyes, sincerity and innocence.

"The modern picture heroine," said William J. Sweeney, "must be young and inexperienced in appearance, guileless and appealing in her actions. The public has wearied of the vampire type."

The public itself, he asserted, was voicing a demand for cleaner films and the producers were filling it.

June 7, 1922

Theda Bara

HOLLYWOOD WARNS FILM STRUCK GIRLS

Chamber of Commerce Seeks to Stop Big Influx as Jobless Cause Social Problem.

Special to The New York Times.

LOS ANGELES, Cal., Dec. 3.—Adding her voice to the warning of the Hollywood Chamber of Commerce to the movie-mad boys and girls who are swarming into the film studio city at the rate of 10,000 a month, Mary Pickford today addressed a crowd of 20,000 people who filled Pershing Square to hear her admonition.

She said she did not want to tell the young people to stay at home because the movies always need new blood, but she did think it advisable that movie aspirants be in a position to wait five years in Hollywood for movie honors and to be able to do some work while waiting, and to the girls she added: "Take mother along; you'll need her."

Now that most of the studios are closed and regular actors are idle, the authorities want to stem the tide of newcomers.

HOLLYWOOD, Cal., Dec. 3 (Associated Press).—Scores of young girls, movie-struck, are arriving here every week, most of them with no recommendations beyond flattering notices in home-town papers, according to the Hollywood Chamber of Commerce, which has started a campaign to warn young persons throughout the country of the futility of finding screen jobs, unless they are qualified and have been encouraged to apply at the studios.

The Chamber of Commerce estimates the population of Hollywood at 85,000, of whom, it states, less than 15,000 are engaged in the film industry.

The girls who drop in from the ends of the earth all are willing to become stars, but most of them are unable to find even minor parts. With their funds exhausted, many of them turn out to be a problem for social and civic workers.

The Chamber is endeavoring to spread broadcast information about how few the chances are for cinema glory and how many are the trials and privations on the path to such an ambition.

December 4, 1923

De Mille Tells How He Selects Movie Stars; Calls Personality and Work Biggest Factors

Cecil B. de Mille, motion picture producer, explaining over radio station WEAF last night how he selected film stars, asserted that there were very few stars today who were classically beautiful; and that personality, coupled with hard work, was the determining element.

He said that he had selected Gloria Swanson because of the way she leaned against a door in an early Mack Sennett comedy. She leaned like a woman in distress, he said, "with her soul expressed in the pose of her body. She was good for four or five seconds, and very, very bad for the rest of the film."

Leatrice Joy he had picked for stardom, he asserted, because of the "expressiveness of her feet."

Personality, from the point of view of a movie director, he defined as "that mystic elusive thing that shines in the eyes, that is recognized in the clothes; that you can see from in back, that you can't bottle up, that is stronger than drink."

The radio and the motion picture, he said, were "the ear and the eye of the world. They wield a more powerful influence than all the instruments of destruction ever invented. The greatest thrill a man can have is to stand behind a microphone or a camera lens."

March 4, 1926

DEFENDS SALE OF NAMES.

Head of Testimonial Firm Says Some Stars Get $5,000 for Puffs.

CHICAGO, Nov. 9 (AP).—The "testimonial game" is a legitimate advertising business and the sale of names, endorsements and pictures of movie stars, athletes and other famous individuals to advertisers is ethical, John F. Ditzell, head of Famous Names, Inc., said today in answer to an account of his company's methods by the American Medical Association in the current issue of Hygeia.

The medical association said that the company sold endorsements and specially posed pictures to advertisers at prices ranging from $200 to $275 apiece for stage and screen luminaries. Ditzell said that this scale was for local advertising. National advertising, he said, brings some stars as high as $5,000 for each endorsement.

"These stars do not endorse any patent medicines or any quack wares," he said. "Every advertising contract we make is subject to the star's approval. No star endorses any product that he or she does not use. There is no misrepresentation."

November 10, 1926

FILM STARS FOOTPRINTED.

Mary Pickford and Others Make Marks for Pavement of a Theatre.

HOLLYWOOD, April 15 (AP).—The footprints of film stars, done in concrete and signed by the makers, will become flagstones in the forecourt of Sid Grauman's new picture theatre to be opened here in May.

Mary Pickford, Douglas Fairbanks and Norma and Constance Talmadge stepped today into forms filled with soft concrete to "make their marks." Grauman plans to add footprints of others.

April 16, 1927

Mary Pickford in "Sparrows."

CLARA BOW EXPLAINS HER GAMBLING MISTAKE

She Thought $100 Chips Were 50-Cent Pieces, She Says—Will Rogers Tells His Side.

LOS ANGELES, Sept. 25 (AP).—Clara Bow, movie actress, went into details today to answer assertions that she stopped payment on checks for $13,900 after offering them in payment of gambling losses at a Nevada hotel.

The actress's statement read in part:

"While I was at Lake Tahoe, Mr. Will Rogers invited Rex Bell, my secretary, Miss Devoe and myself to dinner. I did not know the hotel was a gambling place until after we reached there. After we had dinner Mr. Rogers went to one of the gambling tables and naturally we went with him. I began to play a little at a game called 'twenty-one,' which they call there 'Black Jack.'

"They gave me 50-cent pieces to play with and I signed some checks in blank, telling the dealer to fill in the amount of the 50-cent pieces he had given me. There were four checks.

"It now seems they claim these 50-cent pieces represented what they call $100 chips and they put enough in the checks to amount to that.

"When the checks reached my bank they called me and said the checks had a slip on them asking the bank to 'wire fate of these checks.'

"This attracted the attention of my banker and I found out for the first time this gambling house claimed I had lost and owed them nearly $14,000, so I told the bank not to pay the checks."

The repudiation of the checks was called to the attention of B. P. Schulberg, Paramount studio official, by James McKay, owner of the hotel.

McKay said Will Rogers had introduced the actress at his hotel. Mr. Rogers denied introducing the actress.

"Introducing Clara Bow to anybody," he said, "is like introducing Hoover to the Senate. Clara and her boy friend, Rex Bell, film actor, were going to dinner one night and I asked them to be my guests. The hotel is not solely a gambling house. A lot of divorcees stay over there in preference to Reno.

"I saw the wives of so many of my friends from back East that it was like old home week.

"I don't gamble much. Fifty or seventy-five dollars is my limit. I don't suppose it's going to hurt my reputation much for people to know I've been in a gambling house. I couldn't have been much of a cowboy without having seen a lot of gambling. I've been to Monte Carlo, too. I went over there to see what all those old women were doing bending over those tables.

"Clara wasn't gambling much while I was there. I saw her going around making a few bets, but she didn't appear to be betting much.

"But I don't like this idea of my riding to fame on the skirts of Clara Bow."

September 26, 1930

Home Robbed, Film Dog Sleeps

Special to THE NEW YORK TIMES.

HOLLYWOOD, Calif., May 18.—Rin Tin Tin Jr., dog hero of the movies, slept calmly last night while burglars broke into the home of his master, Lee Duncan, and escaped with jewelry and clothing valued at more than five hundred dollars. In the dog's latest movie appearance he captured a whole robber band "single-handed."

May 19, 1936

Will Rogers with Shirley Temple.

CLARK GABLE NO. 1 IN NEW FILM POLL

Displaces Shirley Temple as the Most Popular Star in Trade Magazine Contest.

Clark Gable is the screen's most popular star, according to the national poll conducted annually by Boxoffice, film trade magazine, and announced yesterday. Shirley Temple, last year's leader, now is in second place, with the team of Fred Astaire and Ginger Rogers third, Robert Taylor fourth and William Powell fifth. The other favorites, in the order of their vote by independent theatre owners, motion picture editors of newspapers and civic groups, were:

Myrna Loy, Claudette Colbert, Norma Shearer, Gary Cooper, Fredric March, Jeannette MacDonald and Nelson Eddy (as a team) and Lionel Barrymore. Runners-up, after the twelve leaders, included Joan Crawford, Wallace Beery, Kay Francis, Greta Garbo, Irene Dunne and Mae West.

Last year's list of box-office favorites mentioned Miss Temple, Will Rogers, Gable, Astaire and Rogers, Joan Crawford, Miss Colbert, Dick Powell, Beery, Joe E. Brown and James Cagney.

January 4, 1937

REVIEW

Shirley Temple has been established by motion-picture exhibitors as the leading money-making star for 1936, according to the annual survey made by Motion Picture Herald, a trade publication, to determine the ten players who brought in the most money at the box office. The other nine, in the order named, are Clark Gable, the team of Fred Astaire and Ginger Rogers, Robert Taylor, Joe E. Brown, Dick Powell, Joan Crawford, Claudette Colbert, Jeanette MacDonald and Gary Cooper.

Miss Temple also led the 1935 poll, and the late Will Rogers was second, with Clark Gable, third; Fred Astaire and Ginger Rogers (as a team), fourth; Joan Crawford, fifth; Claudette Colbert, sixth; Dick Powell, seventh; Wallace Beery, eighth; Joe E. Brown, ninth, and James Cagney, tenth.

January 7, 1937

SCREEN HONOR WON BY MISS HEPBURN

She Is Voted the Outstanding Film Actress of Year at Los Angeles.

LAUGHTON FIRST OF MEN

Motion Picture Academy Also Mentions May Robson, Diana Wynyard, Muni and Howard.

Special to THE NEW YORK TIMES.

LOS ANGELES, March 16.—Katharine Hepburn, youthful Bryn Mawr graduate, who came to Hollywood after a short stage apprenticeship in New York, was voted tonight the outstanding motion picture actress of the last year and a half for her performance in "Morning Glory," an RKO Radio production. Awards, in the form of gold statuettes, were given out at the annual dinner of the Academy of Motion Picture Arts and Sciences at the Ambassador.

Miss Hepburn's outstanding performance was given in her third film appearance. Her début was made in "A Bill of Divorcement" and other pictures were "Little Women" and "Spitfire."

Miss Hepburn was not present to receive her statuette, having just completed a stage appearance in "The Lake" in New York, and gone, it was announced, on a vacation trip to England. B. B. Kahane, president of RKO-Radio, accepted the statuette for her from J. Theodore Reed, president of the academy. Runners-up were, in order, May Robson, who is 69 years old, for her performance in the Columbia picture, "Lady for a Day," and Diana Wynyard, the young English actress, for her work in "Cavalcade," produced by Fox.

Laughton First Prize Winner.

The prize for the best actor went overseas to Charles Laughton, heavy-set English thespian, for his delineation of the title rôle in "The Private Life of Henry VIII." This picture was produced in England by London Films and released here by United Artists.

Mr. Laughton has appeared in several Hollywood-made pictures, among them being "The Sign of the Cross" and "If I Had a Million." Laughton also was absent.

Runners-up to Mr. Laughton were, in order, Paul Muni, for his performance in "I Am a Fugitive From a Chain Gang," produced by Warner Brothers, and Leslie Howard, another British actor, who has appeared chiefly in the United States for the last decade, for his performance in "Berkeley Square," produced by Fox.

"Cavalcade" was not only voted the best-produced picture but was also the medium through which Frank Lloyd received first prize for directors. Its art director, William Darling, received first prize in his specialty.

Runner-up to "Cavalcade" was "Farewell to Arms," produced by Paramount, and Charles Lang, who photographed it, was chosen as the premier cinematographer of the industry. The Paramount studio was designated as having done the best sound-reproduction job.

Among the writers, Robert Lord, now an associate producer at Warner-First National studio, was adjudged the writer of the best original story, "One Way Passage," produced by Warner Brothers. The prize for the best adaptation went to Sarah Y. Mason and Victor Heerman, who collaborated on "Little Women."

The certificate of the best cartoon film was awarded to Walt Disney for "Three Little Pigs." "So This Is Harris," produced by RKO, was voted the best short comedy film, and the best novelty, accordingly to the academy vote, was "Krakatoa," made by Educational Pictures.

Certificates of merit for scientific and technical achievement were awarded to Electric Research Products, Inc., for its wide-range recording and reproducing system, and to the RCA-Victor Company for its high-fidelity recording and reproducing system.

Nearly a thousand persons, among them the most important figures in the screen industry, stars, writers, directors and executives went to the dinner dance to pay tribute to those chosen as prize winners.

Will Rogers, humorist and film comedian, as toastmaster, caused frequent outbursts of laughter with his quips.

March 17, 1934

Robert Taylor and Katharine Hepburn say the familiar "I do's" in "Undercurrent."

ROBERT TAYLOR

Hollywood's studio-sponsored star system created one of its most durable luminaries in Robert Taylor, who in 70 feature films, personalized the glamorous leading man adored by movie fans between the two World Wars.

Despite a shock of black, wavy hair, complete with an eye-catching widow's peak, a trim, 6-foot frame and classically handsome features that verged on prettiness and often overshadowed his roles, he was a painstaking professional, if unspectacular, artisan quietly dedicated to his work.

Some 32 years after he made his film debut in 1934, he confided in a rare interview that he had "no complaints." "I can't think of anything I'd rather do, or rather have done," he said. "I'm just as nervous the first day of a picture as I was at the beginning, but perhaps I calm down a little faster. I'm still like a race horse when a picture starts. I can't wait to get going."

Richard Thorpe, who directed Mr. Taylor in six films at Metro - Goldwyn - Mayer, which first signed him and where he was under contract for more than a quarter of a century, said he was a no-nonsense, untemperamental actor who efficiently and quickly learned his lines. "Bob is really a nice guy," he said, "and it comes through on screen."

Shelley Winters, with whom Mr. Taylor appeared in the 1964 film "A House Is Not a Home," was equally complimentary. "Like Ronald Colman, he was the sweetest man to work with," she said. "By that I mean he was cooperative and understanding in contrast to most leading men today, who try either to elbow you out of camera range or are off in a corner somewhere practicing 'Method' acting."

'Luckiest Guy'

Mr. Taylor's personal evaluation of his ability to maintain his star status over the years was self - effacing. "Darned if I know," he told a reporter in 1957 while he was still at M-G-M. "I've been wondering about it myself for years. I guess the most important thing is to get a good picture once in a while. Acting is the easiest job in the world and I'm the luckiest guy."

The pictures, among them some good, big and spectacular ones such as "Camille," "Quo Vadis" and "Billy the Kid," began coming his way a few years after he signed with M-G-M as a handsome, largely untried 23-year-old actor from Nebraska.

He was named Spangler Arlington Brugh by his parents, Dr. Spangler Arlington Brugh and Ruth Adelia Stanhope Brugh. He was born on Aug. 5, 1911, in Filley, Neb., a village the family left for Beatrice, Neb., where the youth received his high school education and learned to play the cello. He also was a member of the track team and won the state oratorical championship.

After his freshman year at Doane College in Crete, Neb., he followed his music teacher to Pomona College in Claremont, Calif., where he added to his academic and music studies roles in such Pomona collegiate plays as "Camille" and "The Importance of Being Earnest." An M-G-M talent scout saw his performance in the starring role of Captain Stanhope in the World War I drama "Journey's End" and signed him to a seven-year contract starting at $35 a week.

After graduation, young Brugh, whose name was changed by the studio, was farmed out to the Fox studio, where he made his movie

Robert Taylor

debut in a small supporting role in "Handy Andy," a comedy starring Will Rogers. Within three years, starting with the lead in an M-G-M "crime-does-not-pay" short subject called

"Buried Loot," Mr. Taylor appeared in 18 features, among them the 1937 "Camille," in which he played the love-smitten Armand to Greta Garbo's Camille.

'Surprisingly Good'

"Robert Taylor is surprisingly good as Armand," The New York Times critic said, "a bit on the juvenile side at times, perhaps, but certainly not guilty of the traditional sin of many Armands of the past—callowness."

Among the other films in which he appeared, and which helped boost his salary into the $5,000-a-week class, were "There's Always Tomorrow," "Society Doctor," "West Point of the Air" and the musical "Broadway Melody of 1936," in which he was the romantic lead, with Eleanor Powell and Jack Benny. However, it was his role opposite Irene Dunne in the tear-stained 1935 drama, "Magnificent Obsession," for which he had been lent to Universal Studios, that made him a top star.

He attended the President's Birthday Ball in Washington with Jean Harlow. Fans mobbed him in public places for several years thereafter and likened him to the late Rudolph Valentino as the movies' major matinee idol. His popularity was on a par with that of Clark Gable, Shirley Temple and the team of Fred Astaire and Ginger Rogers, the box-office favorites of the period.

But as a serious actor who yearned for artistry in his craft, Mr. Taylor managed eventually to escape the glamour boy classification by playing more muscular roles. These included the tough title character in the 1940 "Billy the Kid," the officer-gentleman opposite Vivien Leigh in "Waterloo Bridge," the hard-bitten prizefighter in "The Crowd Roars" and the noble killer in "Johnny Eager."

Critical opinions were varied about some of his subsequent performances. Commenting on "Her Cardboard Lover," a 1942 drawing room comedy in which he starred opposite Norma Shearer, Bosley Crowther said in The Times: "Mr. Taylor, who has finally gotten somewhere as an actor, is back . . . compelled to make the most inane remarks." A year later, in his review of "Bataan," Mr. Crowther called the Taylor portrayal of the ill-fated sergeant "believable even though he does rush about a bit too much with a dark scowl."

Flight Instructor in War

World War II put the actor's flying ability to use. An experienced amateur pilot, he was sworn in as a lieutenant in the Navy's air transport division but was deferred until he completed "Song of Russia" at M-G-M. He was then assigned to duty as a flight instructor. He also directed 17 Navy training films and did the narration for "The Fighting Lady," a documentary about an aircraft carrier. The commentary, one critic noted, was done in "a stern, self-effacing voice with no trace of the movie star."

Several years after the war, Mr. Taylor testified before a visiting House Un - American Activities subcommittee that he considered "Song of Russia" pro-Communist. The film, which was released in 1944 and in which he starred as an American conductor who falls in love with a Russian girl, was labeled "a honey of a topical musical film" by Mr. Crowther. He added, "Mr. Taylor makes a very good impression as a young American caught in Russia by love and war."

The postwar years brought roles marked by steadfast professionalism. There were serious, workmanlike stints as a secretive mental patient in "The High Wall" (1947) and as a Secret Service man in "The Bribe" (1949). And there were variations in the Western genre. In "Ambush," he played a brusque frontiersman guiding the cavalry against the Apaches, and in "Devil's Doorway" he was a Shoshone Indian Medal of Honor winner who lost his fight against encroaching white settlers.

As one of the stars, along with Deborah Kerr, Leo Genn and Peter Ustinov, who spent much of 1950 working in Italy on the $7-million remake of "Quo Vadis," Mr. Taylor played a decided second fiddle to the superspectacle of Nero's Rome. Like the other principals in this moneymaker, the actor, cast as Marcus, the Roman centurion who falls in love with the captive early Christian portrayed by Miss Kerr, was "anything but inspired," according to The Times's critic.

Following the pattern set by other film stars, Mr. Taylor also was featured in his own television series, the 1961-62 "The Detectives." As the upstanding, no - nonsense sleuth, he reminded moviegoers that he also had played a hard-fisted, venal detective in the 1954 film "Rogue Cop." He also appeared on other TV shows, including "Death Valley Days."

Offscreen, Mr. Taylor led a singularly unglamorized, scandal-free life. He married Barbara Stanwyck in May, 1939, in San Diego. They had made two films together, the 1936 "His Brother's Wife" and the 1937 "This Is My Affair." They were divorced in February, 1951, but remained friends and co-starred again in 1965 in "The Night Walker," a lightweight suspense thriller.

In May, 1954, Mr. Taylor married Ursula Thiess in Jackson, Wyo. The actress, who had been divorced from George Thiess, a German director, had been featured in several American films before their marriage but later abandoned her screen career.

The Taylors lived on a 113-acre ranch, stocked with horses, cattle and chickens, in Los Angeles's Mandeville Canyon section. There they enjoyed a quiet, bucolic retreat from the hectic schedules of films and television.

June 9, 1969

A STAR'S LIFE IS MOSTLY LETTERS

THE stream of fan mail flowing into Hollywood never runs dry. Upward of 3,000 letters each week in the year are received by the most popular screen stars.

The biggest percentage is from America, and New York and Chicago postmarks are as common as those of Gopher Prairie. Not all of the self-invited correspondents are bored housewives with nothing to do afternoons, or screen-struck boys and girls eager to get to God's country. They embrace the whole rank and file of contemporary society, and they seem to go on forever with the persistence and volubility of Tennyson's brook.

The morning studio mail is certain to receive a batch of laudatory comments on a star's latest picture, requests for money or help in getting into the movies, or for an autographed picture; in fact, most correspondents conclude by requesting a photograph. Sometimes the requests include coin or stamps to cover the postage, sometimes not. The fan mail business is a merry one for the United States Postoffice, a tough one for the army of secretaries and assistants who have to wade through the scriptorial flood.

Some of the stars take an intense personal interest in what their unknown commentators have to say. Some, like May Robson, are so conscientious that they spend a good deal of their spare time answering the more interesting or the more urgent letters, and looking over the others. These are the exceptions, however. More often the stars are content to shift everything to the backs of hirelings, except in a few extra special cases.

* * *

Some writers look on their favorite stars as Santa Claus in the flesh. Leo Carrillo, while working in "Too Hot to Handle," received a cablegram from a total stranger in Czechoslovakia complimenting the star on his fine characterizations and asking for a return remittance of $4,000 to enable the sender and his fiancée to be married. The inference seemed to be that he had to place this money on the line before she would step to the altar.

Wallace Beery received a letter from a stranger enclosing a promissory note for $1,500, a document that needed only the star's signature and a return check for that amount to complete the transaction. The writer somewhat ingenuously explained that his friends and the two local banks had refused him this loan, but that he felt sure the big-hearted Mr. Beery would prove more generous.

Demands for money are supplemented by a host of other strange and unbelievable requests. One man wrote to Clarence Brown, the director and flying expert, explaining his interest in aviation, his inability to buy a plane, and his hope that the director would ship him a second-hand one which he no longer needed. Sometimes the stars are asked to lift the family mortgage, sometimes they are merely requested to send a shawl worn in a Spanish costume scene, or a hat or dress used in some romantically outstanding picture.

* * *

For a long time after the release of "Ben-Hur" Ramon Novarro received scores of letters addressed to "Mr. Ben-Hur." Whenever a star is publicly advertised as having developed a new hobby, the promoters avidly join his fan mail group. After it became known that Robert Montgomery was an enthusiastic polo player he was the recipient of a host of air mail, special delivery and registered letters from people trying to sell him a string of ponies. Similarly with Spencer Tracy and his hunting proclivities, Alice Brady and her kennel of dogs. Promotion men for bullfrog farms, horseradish ranches and traveling whales are among the odd gentry who pursue the film players.

One of the most unusual cases of fan mail correspondence concerned Joan Crawford. For many months, she had been receiving letters filled with enthusiastic praise of her work, written in a strong masculine hand, and further distinguished by the fact that they were composed upon heavy brown glazed paper, such as butchers use for wrapping meat. Investigation disclosed that the writer was an irrigation hand working in the Imperial Valley in Southern California, and that his virile missives were written on the paper which contained his lunches.

There is a classic instance of a woman in a mid-Western city who asked Clark Gable to call her long distance at a certain hour. "My husband is beginning to lose interest and I want to show him there are other people besides him," she wrote. This letter was personally answered by the star, who explained the difficulties. Not long ago an amateur writer sent a stream of letters and telegrams to persuade William Powell to sign his latest literary creation. "I don't care for fame," the pursuing writer said. "All I want is the money and you can have the publicity."

Coast statisticians have reported that there are three feminine letter-writers to every male, and about 40 per cent of the fan mail written by men comprises marriage proposals or requests for dinner dates. Even after the published announcement of her marriage, Myrna Loy received as many as seventy-nine proposals in one week.

Some of the more artistic-minded letter writers send their messages rebus-fashion. Weird drawings or diagrams represent the names of the stars. Wallace Beery's seems to exert an unholy fascination on the horde of amateur artists. At last report he was leading the field in the number of rebus envelopes received. His first name is sometimes depicted by a sketch of a wall covered by what passes for a frontage of lace, sometimes by a wall and the ace from a pack of cards, sometimes by a "W" on an awl and an ace. His surname generally takes the form of either a berry or an effervescing stein of beer.

* * *

One of the most famous letters of this type presented what seemed to be a menacing colored diagram of the underworld, with a superimposed letter "N" and an overhanging mass of clouds. This was sent over to the Fox studios on the assumption that it belonged to some one connected with "Dante's Inferno." When the letter was opened there, however, it was found that it had been intended for Helen Hayes; the cryptic sketch on the envelope stood for hell-N-haze! So it was remailed East to the stage star.

Sometimes the amateur draftsmen try to convey their meanings by a snarling, ghoulish face. When this happens, office workers have to gamble on whether to send it to Boris Karloff, Claude Rains or Bela Lugosi. No snap judgment can be exercised on these enigmatic messages. Recently a clerk found an envelope with a collection of hieroglyphics and with a picture of Grace Moore. It was properly sent along to the lady, whose astute secretary sent it along to Lionel Barrymore. Close scrutiny showed that the "Moore" on the envelope was preceded by a very decrepit-looking lion, the letter "L" and a bunch of exceedingly lopsided berries, Q. E. D., Lion-L-berry-Moore.

July 17, 1938

WHEN MOVIE STARS MARRY

Marriage in Hollywood remains one of the film capital's most fantastic phenomena and "everybody's business."

By DOUGLAS W. CHURCHILL

HOLLYWOOD.

CLARK GABLE married Carole Lombard; Robert Taylor married Barbara Stanwyck; Tyrone Power married Annabella. And the world was agog.

Had the Messrs. Gable, Taylor and Power been department store executives or bank presidents or subway guards, and had the Misses Lombard, Stanwyck and Charpentier been home girls or secretaries or distinguished women of medicine, the alliances would have been dismissed with a few prosaic words in the public printa. But they were movie stars and so the matter was everybody's business.

Of all Hollywood phenomena marriage has been—and probably will continue to be—the most fantastic. Each of these three couples sought to remove the ritual from the carnival, and while they succeeded as far as the actual ceremonies were concerned, their wedded lives are still a part of an international circus.

THERE are those who like to think that because recent marriages have been contracted with a minimum of magnificence Hollywood has changed. They recall the pomp and glitter of the Rod La Roque-Vilma Banky union of some years ago and the Gene Raymond-Jeanette MacDonald nuptials of last season, an event that was strictly a B production by comparison, and then reason that, because the glamour children of this year sneaked off to remote spots to hum their epithalamium instead of having it played by the United States Marine Band in the Hollywood Bowl, times have changed. They have not, nor will they as long as Hollywood is Hollywood.

A standard vaudeville joke for years had the straight man saying, "Marriage is a great institution," and the comic replying, "But I don't want to live in an institution." The comedian was prophetic if he was speaking of Hollywood marriage, for here it is a public institution.

Love and marriage in Hollywood are complex states. Ordinary people who have only one another to worry about and only themselves to cope with often pursue an erratic route to tranquillity. But the poor movie stars! Their obstacles could never be surmounted by less than Olympian creatures.

CONSIDER the factors and problems that enter into the union of two children of the glamour world. Performers notoriously are egotists. Their trade makes this quality an element essential to success. First, then, is the potential clash between similar personalities, each of whom knows that the way to command respect (and consequently a substantial salary) is to display unbounded faith in one's own ability and importance.

Then there is the matter of individual careers. Being what they are, stars must be concerned with their professional life. It takes the entire energy and resourcefulness of even a dominant personality to cope with the problems that beset a career on the screen. The tension of movie-making, the fights with producers over roles, the avid thirst for success, these are things that necessitate an undivided interest in one's self. Great as may be the desire to aid whole-heartedly in solving a mate's problems, the conflict of interests and the ancient law of self-preservation restricts this activity. Being an egotist, each thinks that the other is not sufficiently concerned and friction follows.

These two factors in marriage are en famille; there are others which jeopardize happiness and over which the principals have no slightest control. They are industrial and community problems. A star must not marry beneath his or her station. Such a mating would be financially improvident. There is always the box office to think of and what the fans might say. To protect popularity and gate receipts, the caste system governs the lives and loves of the stars. A ranking celebrity may marry another star, a producer, a director or possibly a featured player; to contemplate a union with a writer, however, is to be a traitor to one's class. And so the industry sees to it that mismatings are a rarity.

IT is impossible that Hollywood means to be vicious. But whether or not the viciousness is intentional, the town undoubtedly is the most brutal community in America if not in the world. Dissemination of gossip is a greater industry than picture-making and is entered into more whole-heartedly. It is unlikely that there is a single married couple of importance in the screen colony who have not been the target of evil rumors, innocently spread. While romances remain comparatively unaffected by the chatter of the residential magpies, marriages, possibly because they are more practical and realistic, display difficulty in surviving the onslaughts of the gossips.

The columnist and the fan magazines are other disturbing influences in the relationship of famous husbands and wives. The duties of such writers, whether or not they believe they follow ethical standards, make them avenues for the dissemination of trouble. They get tips on impending divorces or marriages and feel that they cannot afford to be beaten on such delectable items. Generally they publish them without confirmation or without bothering to check the reports. Naturally, many of the rumors are without foundation, but, given substance in type, they assume the importance of fact. There are few marriages, particularly here, that can weather these public discussions.

ANOTHER threat to tranquil matrimony is the product Hollywood manufactures. Love on the screen is just as much a commercial commodity as are canned beans on a grocer's shelf. Ninety-nine per cent of American films are concerned only with the triumph of Eros. Thus, emotions which should be kept remote from business became a part of that business. Reactions that occur in more normal employment after 5 o'clock in the afternoon, when the thoughts of young America turn to courting, are discernible on the sets at 9 o'clock in the morning. It may only be play-acting, but it cannot but exert some effect, even if slight, on the participants.

Take into account, in addition to the emotional confusion, the frailties of human beings, and another hazard is contributed. Glamour boys, like glamour girls, are beautiful or have arresting personalities. Their trade on the screen is to appeal to the fundamental instincts of the customers. It is inconceivable that they can hold themselves impervious to this same appeal, working as they do in close contact with attractive members of the opposite sex, handling emotion as a potter does clay, being human and living in a community where human frailties are not only condoned but anticipated.

In spite of the seeming precariousness of Hollywood matrimony, it is enthusiastically and seriously entered into. It is improbable that any more people in Hollywood marry with the definite thought that if it doesn't work out divorce is easier than in other American metropolitan centers. Just as they believe the stories about themselves concocted by their press agents, so do they believe in the undying fervor of their love.

TO prepare a statistical report on matrimony in Hollywood would require the resources of the Social Security Board. While a tabulation of the 30,000 residents who are affiliated with the industry might present one picture which conceivably would not vary to a great extent from the tabulation describing a similar group in any other city in the country, the impression exists that in its entirety Hollywood marriage is a helter-skelter business. Hollywood has the reputation far beyond what the facts deserve.

A compilation of 474 case histories of performers, directors and executives who at the moment are gainfully employed in the art foundries discloses that 366 have been married but once and are now living with their mates. The remaining 108 have had trouble in varying degrees—a ratio of 20 per cent as compared with 16 per cent for the nation at large. Dividing these 108 further, the list reveals: 42 married and divorced; 48 married, divorced and married; 4 married, divorced, married and divorced; 6 married, divorced, married, divorced and married; 4 married, divorced, married, divorced, married and divorced; 2 married, divorced, married, divorced, married, divorced and married; 2 married, divorced, married, divorced, married, divorced, married and divorced.

The Gable, Taylor and Power weddings may be regarded as possessing a certain significance, for they are the first major unions in Hollywood that have not been shaped, in part, by the studios. The principals in all three ceremonies demanded a hands-off policy by the producers. Others in the past have demanded privacy but rarely have been accorded it. The Gable and Taylor nuptials took place in distant towns without benefit of press agents, and the Power ceremony was singularly unspectacular.

These things could not have happened a few years ago. When La Roque and Miss Banky were married, it was an industry event; to mix a few metaphors, it still is regarded as the ultima Thule in the pyrotechnics of the marriage ceremony. The studio supervised everything. Samuel Goldwyn ordered his press department to go the limit, and the boys took him at his word. Outside the church a crowd of several thousand milled and hysteria reached a new high. Women fainted. Police battled the adoring fans. All of Hollywood fought to get inside.

Love did not blossom quite as flamboyantly in 1939. Gable and Miss Lombard climbed in their car one day and drove to a small Arizona town with a lone friend. After the ceremony the friend telephoned the studio and told the publicity department what had happened. Taylor and Miss Stanwyck had hoped for secrecy in

San Diego, but they were discovered; this did not alter their plans for a quiet wedding. Power and Annabella virtually defied their studio; the producers felt that matrimony would injure the actor's career and, consequently, his box-office appeal, and efforts were made to dissuade him.

The current crop of benedicts have shown a rare determination to attend to their own affairs. They have refused to permit the studios to send photographers to their homes to make those intimate little pictures that indicate the just-folks type of romance. This differs somewhat from tradition. One studio ordered its stars back from the ceremony at Santa Barbara to have "some good art" made at the studio for the fan magazines; the couple posed in the photograph gallery most of the night and then left for their honeymoon.

HOLLYWOOD'S conception of the matrimonial bond is as fantastic as its films. America is still pretty much a land of Puritans. The people are intolerant of the carelessness with which members of the industry reputedly hold matrimony. They are shocked by the announcement of engagements and impending marriages before the principals are divorced; sometimes the news of new romances is included with the disclosures of separations. This is distasteful to a majority in the rest of the land and accounts to an appreciable degree for the criticism that is leveled at the industry.

And yet when a few friends are gathered around two glamorous stars, or when a great cathedral is filled with admiring hundreds and Hollywood hears the minister intone, "What God hath joined, let no man put asunder," eyes are damp and there are lumps in masculine throats. At the moment, marriage is just as sacred as it is at any other spot on the globe.

August 27, 1939

ROONEY TOPS STARS AS MONEY MAKER

Again Heads Poll of Theatre Exhibitors, Being Followed by Spencer Tracy and Gable

AUTRY JOINS FIRST TEN

Bette Davis and Judy Garland, Ranking Ninth and Tenth, Only Actresses Listed

Mickey Rooney

Mickey Rooney has placed first for the second consecutive year as Hollywood's biggest money making star, according to the annual survey made by the trade publication, Motion Picture Herald, among the owners of the nation's 17,000 motion picture theatres. Rooney led his closest rival, Spencer Tracy, by 4,380 points to 3,688.

The most surprising disclosure of the survey, according to the announcement, was the establishment of Gene Autry, the Western star, in fourth place in the list of the ten most popular all-around stars. Mr. Autry also heads for the fourth consecutive year the list of the leading sagebrush personalities. Autry, who entered motion pictures in 1936, thus becomes the first cowboy star to achieve that distinction since the late Will Rogers outdistanced all other rivals in 1934.

Only two feminine personalities were rated among the ten top money makers of 1940. They are Bette Davis and Judy Garland, who placed ninth and tenth, respectively. Wallace Beery, who was last on the list in 1936, returned this year in eighth place, and James Cagney rose from ninth place in 1939 to sixth this year. Clark Gable, whom The Herald refers to as "the iron man" because he is the only player who has placed among the top ten since the poll was instituted in 1932, is in third position this year, as against fourth in 1939.

Spencer Tracy is up from third in 1939 to second this year, and Bing Crosby occupies seventh place which he held back in 1934. Tyrone Power, who placed second in the 1939 list this year slipped to fifth.

Except for variations in placement the combined lists of both independent and circuit theatremen differ as to personnel in only one instance. James Stewart, who rated eleventh on the combined voting, ranks ninth with independent theatre owners.

The ten leading Western stars are, according to the number of votes received, Mr. Autry, William Boyd, Roy Rogers, George O'Brien, Charles Starrett, Johnny Mack Brown, Tex Ritter, The Mesquiteers, Smiley Burnette and Bill Elliott.

December 27, 1940

Veronica Lake, Movie Star With the Peekaboo Hair

Box-Office Favorite of 1940's Made 26 Pictures and Then Vanished From Limelight

By EDWARD HUDSON

In her movie career, which ended in the early fifties, the diminutive and sultry-looking Miss Lake—she was 5 feet 2 inches and weighed 100 pounds—became one of Hollywood's most glamorous stars, playing in 26 motion pictures.

Then her acting career went into decline, and she wound up years later working as a barmaid in the Martha Washington Hotel, 29 East 29th Street. In recent years, she had been playing summer stock and stage roles in Britain.

Miss Lake preferred to describe herself as a "sex-zombie," rather than a "sex symbol."

"That really names me properly," she told an interviewer two years ago. "I was laughing at everybody in all of my portraits. I never took that stuff seriously. I will have one of the cleanest obits of any actress. I never did cheesecake like Ann Sheridan or Betty Grable. I just used my hair."

Hazard for Rosie the Riveter

Her seductive peekaboo hair style set a fashion. So much so that during World War II a Government agency asked her not to wear it long because many women were catching their tresses in factory machinery.

Veronica Lake in the early 1940's.

Miss Lake was the daughter of a ship's master. She was born in Brooklyn on November 14, 1919, named Constance Ockelman and spent her girlhood in Lake Placid, N. Y., and Miami. She studied at McGill University as a premedical student.

Encouraged by winning third prize in a Florida beauty contest and an ambitious mother who was later to sue her daughter for nonsupport, Miss Lake moved to Hollywood. She was cast in bit parts, finally landing a leading role in "I Wanted Wings" in 1941, playing a nightclub singer.

The movie was a hit, and she was quickly cast with Joel McCrea in "Sullivan's Travels." This was followed by another hit, "This Gun for Hire," co-starring Alan Ladd, who wasn't much taller than she was. This was only the first of the "tough guy" movies they made together.

Played Witch Roles

Other films in which Miss Lake starred were "The Glass Key," "I Married a Witch," "Star-Spangled Rhythm, "So Proudly We Hail," "The Hour Before Dawn," "Bring On the Girls," "Hold That Blonde," "Out of This World," "Miss Susie Slagle's," "Isn't It Romantic," "The Sainted Sisters," "Saigon" and "Slattery's Hurricane."

She married four times. In 1940 she was married to John Detlie, a studio art director. They had a daughter, Elaine. A year after her divorce from Mr. Detlie in 1943, Miss Lake married André de Toth, a movie director. They had two children, André and Diane. The couple were divorced in 1952. Three years later she was married to Joseph A. McCarthy, a music publisher and song writer, but this marriage, too, ended in divorce, about 1960. In later years, she said she rarely saw or heard from her children.

Her fourth husband was Robert Carelton-Munro, an Englishman, to whom she was married in Fort Lauderdale, Fla., in the spring of 1972. Friends said the couple had been in the process of divorce.

Miss Lake had made her home in Ipswich, England, for some years in the late nineteen-sixties and early seventies.

In her autobiography, "Veronica," published in 1971, the movie star admitted she drank a lot in her post-fame years. Showing some sensitivity about the subject, she told an interviewer: "To each his own. At least I'm not a mainliner, and it's more fun getting high without a needle. At least you can get over the booze."

She said she would not have lived her life any differently. "How would I learn to be a person otherwise?"

July 8, 1973

THE 'FANS' GROW OLDER

A Brief Survey of That Sociological Phenomenon, the Fan Magazine

By Lillian Nadel

Before the turn of the century "a fan" was an obsolete abbreviation for fanatic. Since the advent of baseball it has crept back into usage and the movies have helped to revive it. In fact, today, the zeal of a Brooklyn Dodger fan is only matched by the loyalty of the movie fan to his favorite star. Of the purported 65,000,000 movie-goers there are 4,500,000 staunch fans. Each month this army of zealots parts with its meager dimes to learn Hollywood's most guarded secrets—"Has Nelson Eddy a scarred psyche?" "Who is the most maligned woman in Hollywood?" "Why George Raft dodges love?" "Tyrone Power's new 'blitz kiss' technique." "Eight women Clark Gable can't do without."

For the exclusive consumption of this inquisitive audience, 95 percent female—proof of the species' eternal curiosity—a score of magazines is published each month. The glamour-ridden fan magazine is an outgrowth of the glamorous film industry. For thirty years these publications have provided "a moving channel for the disposal of motion picture publicity." At the very outset they hitched their star to the star system. The two flourished simultaneously and each has since become as ineradicable as a pock on the industry.

The first fan magazine was published in 1911. J. Stuart Blackton, one of the founders of the Vitagraph, was the innocent perpetrator. The magazine, imaginatively titled "Motion Picture," still sells on the stands for a dime. With the candid purpose of making the public picture conscious it was financed by the Motion Picture Patent Company, a producing combine, of which Blackton was a member. In 1914, in Chicago, another magazine, Photoplay, came into being, and it soon led the vanguard. Originally it started as a theatre program that fell into the debt of the W.F. Hall Printing Company. James T. Quirk was engaged as editor, and to this red-headed, nimble-witted Irishman from Boston falls the title, "Father of the Fans."

The bibulous Quirk, who once sold watches through the mails on the installment plan, started folks around the country pinning pictures of movie sirens and heroes on the wall. He believed firmly in a rotogravure section and was the first to bleed portrait pictures off the page. He exploited the personality story until the intimacy of such gushing prose became the bulwalk of fan magazines. Following the Police Gazette, he featured "leg" art and started bathing beauty contests. He initiated the incendiary cover line or magazine headline. However inflammatory the title, the content of a story, with the exception of a come-on lead, was invariably fireproof. This is the formula that fan magazines pursue today. Quirk, however, also wrote indignant editorials, debunked Hollywood, and opened his columns to his readers.

Only with competition did the "fans" strive for sensationalism. In the beginning they were exceptionally intelligent and literate. The reviews were impartial and the magazines depended less on film advertising. They attempted to reach a larger, more mature audience. Among the contributors were O. O. McIntyre, Sally Benson, Adele Rogers St. John, Leonard Hall, Bob Davis, Morris Gest, Julian Johnson, story chief of Twentieth Century-Fox; Willard Huntington Wright, author of the S.S. Van Dine series; Kenneth McGowan, theatre and film producer, and Terry Ramsaye, the Boswell of the film industry.

"The composite reader," to quote from the forthcoming memoirs of Norbert Lusk, an erstwhile and surviving editor, "was not an adolescent whose intelligence had been blighted after seeing his first movie too soon after birth."

Early in their career the fan magazines may have been flippant, but interspersing such pap as "Confessions of an Anonymous Actress," there were serious, and often stinging, editorials. These articles dealt with propaganda in pictures, censorship versus regulation, the need for good screen authors and the evils of overproduction. One, in 1916, berating the movies for not recreating the American scene honestly, was precociously titled "America First!" Unfortunately this critical attitude did not last, but the slushy style of confession journalism thrived, depriving the fan magazine of its virility. The male audience declined to an infinitesimal number; the women readers increased by hordes. The fans became indispensable to the beauty parlor business.

During the lush Twenties fan magazines enjoyed a phenomenal prosperity. But with the depression advertising revenue fell off, circulation dropped from a dizzy peak and several magazines folded, while a few merged. At this time the first fan magazine was distributed through a dime chain store, starting a price war. Magazines that cost a quarter were slashed to fifteen cents; others were reduced to a dime, and some even to a nickel. Fan magazines entered a new phase, syndicated selling through chain stores. This led to the wide practice of advertising tie-ups and exclusive star endorsements for various products.

The fan magazines emerged from the depression only to face another crisis. In 1934 they were the first victimes of the determined campaign to clean up the motion pictures. To arouse an apathetic public during the lean years they had indulged in a wave of scandal-mongering. There were a succession of articles like "Janet Gaynor Ain't No Angel," "Marriage Cost Betty Davis Plenty" and "The Men in Lupe Velez's Life." These innuendoes caused the Hays office to crack down, even before the Purity Code was dusted off the shelf. The editors were summoned to the inner sanctum of Will H. Hays, and were handed an ultimatum in the form of resolutions:

(1) Interviews were to be submitted to the studios before publication, (2) a representative of the company must be present during the interview, (3) accredited writers were to be given numbered identification cards.

These cards are renewable each year, if the writer meets the quota of six stories per annum—and remeins on good behavior. Moreover, the editors signed a pledge to prohibit the publication "of false and otherwise salacious material either directly stated or implied." This "honor" system enables the Hays office to hold an admonishing finger over the "fans," and when an editor steps out of line he is called on the carpet. Still the Hays office sometimes relaxes its vigilance, and there is always some ingenious individual to squirm through the smallest loophole. Occosionally a "hot" story does appear, and in spite of an elaborate clearance system for stills, "cheesecake" pictures are often published. The Hays office objects to bosom and leg shots, but the free-lance photographers and independent press agents frequently transgress.

With all the Hays taboos the fan magazines manage to offer scoops each month. An inside story invariably points a moral—sin doesn't pay, and success only lasts if it is earned the hard way. The editors are in a constant dither to get exclusive material, although a picture is often exclusive by a hair's breadth, depending on the position of the star's head. It may be turned to the right in one publication, to the left in another.

The weekly picture magazines of recent years constitute the most serious threat to the domain of the movie publications. Although more numerous than ever before, fan magazines have become a less potent influence. They are still a force to conjure with, however, and they receive the cooperation, if not always the whole-hearted approval, of the industry. Having incubated during the last war and "matured" in the post-war period, they may burgeon again after the present conflict. As the films become more realistic, though, the fact is that the "fans" grow more escapist. Dedicated to the cult of narcissism, they are mainly preoccupied with glamour.

October 5, 1941

Judy Garland: Loneliness and Loss

By VINCENT CANBY

IN Judy Garland's engagement at the Palace Theater here not quite two years ago, there was displayed the kind of magic that has very little to do with the fun of being fooled. The voice was gone. The figure was not only slim, but vulnerably thin, and yet the performance was full of energy, transformed and shaped by her intelligence into a momentary triumph of style. It was also a somewhat nerve-racking experience, since you knew it couldn't last. It was rather like watching an extraordinary light show, and being aware that no longer was there a power source for all that electricity.

Judy Garland was that most lovable of American pheanomena, the glamorous Hollywood personality with the built-in destruct mechanism. At the time of her death, she was a 47-year-old woman who had begun as a child actress in movies and had become the star of her own adult melodrama, which, in the last couple of years, mostly played the provinces — places like Australia and the Middle West — where the notices were often bad. In between breakdowns and canceled engagements and marriages and comebacks, she talked and wrote freely about how she got that way. There were grim stories about her mother and the late Louis B. Mayer, under whose com-

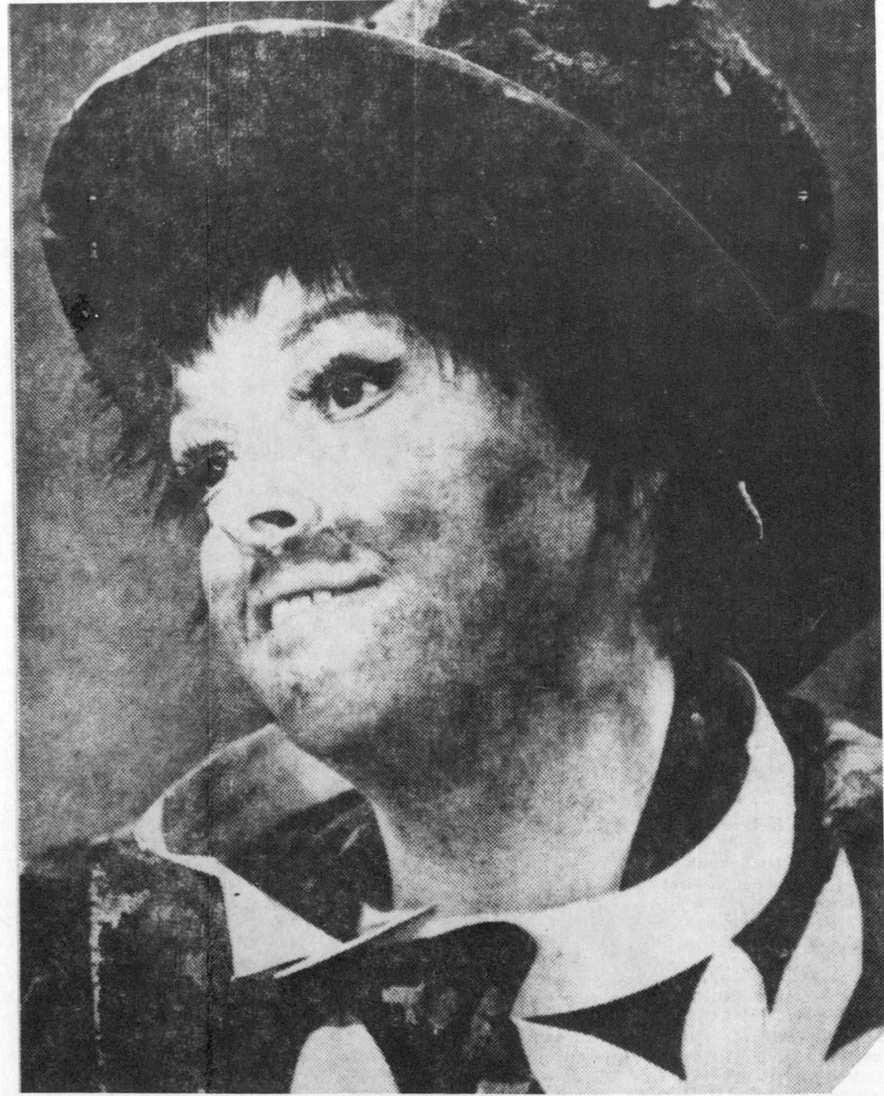

Judy Garland 1922-1969
How did she survive as long as she did?

mand she was apparently first introduced to drugs. Periodically, the men of the Internal Revenue Service, vultures in white - on - white shirts, swooped down and carried off a car or a house, and there were suits and countersuits with an ex-husband over the possession of children and a television set. Even more often than she exploited the public, by not showing up for a performance or giving a second - rate performance when she did, she was exploited by the people around her. Judy lived it, not particularly well but with elan and sometimes with rueful humor. "The teacher, I think," she said of the M-G-M studio school, "was named Ma Barker." Judy lived it and died still worrying about money, and Jacqueline Susann wrote it, as if it were a comic strip, and made a million dollars.

*

America consumes everything so fast—glass containers, automobiles, uranium, public personalities—that the only alternative to setting aside entire states as trash heaps is, perhaps, to find new uses for the things being discarded. There grew up around Judy Garland in the last years of her life a claque of admirers, most of whom seem to be men of young middle age who went through adolescence in the 1940s. Although they turned her public appearances into endurance tests for those not so committed, they undoubtedly helped keep her off the slag pile by transforming her into a totem, a symbol of their own loneliness and loss.

*

This adulation, which is really a sort of transferred narcissism, combined with the physical deterioration that set in with drinking and drugs, have obscured objective appreciation of the Garland career. It may be significant that last Sunday, when I looked through several comprehensive film books, I found only several references to Judy Garland, and then only in incidental connection with the films of Vincente Minnelli and Stanley Kramer.

Miss Garland was important to movies but, like so many star-personalities, she was a product of movies and did not often make movies important by simply inhabiting them. Her best films were the works of a few intelligent directors like Victor Fleming ("The Wizard of Oz"), Minnelli ("Meet Me in St. Louis," "The Pirate," "The Clock") and George Cukor ("A Star Is Born"). Almost all of her other films either manipulated the little plastic doll with the big voice manufactured by M-G-M ("For Me and My Gal," "Girl Crazy," "Summer Stock"), or attempted to make capital out of contrasting the Garland legend with the occasionally physically grotesque Garland ("Judgment at Nuremberg," "A Child Is Waiting"). Her last film, the otherwise undistinguished "I Could Go On Singing" (1963), directed by Ronald Neame, does contain one short scene — the only one of its kind in any of her films—that captures the nervous intensity of the real-life performer. It's hardly even a scene, just a quick shot of the star in the wings at the Palladium as she is waiting to go on stage. As the music mounts, the actress goes through a kind of intoxicating transformation from a schlump at loose emotional ends to a personality in total command of her resources, which is what Judy Garland was in her Minnelli and Cukor films and in her Palace appearances. It really didn't make much difference when finally the resources were comparatively meager. She used them with such skill and with such humorous (sometimes mocking) self-awareness that she could conquer anything and anybody, even one jaundiced man who didn't always buy the gamin pose, the sometimes consciously automated, catch-in-the-throat pathos or the "I think I'll just sit down here on the stage and talk to you" business.

*

I'll always remember her being elegant and funny in "The Pirate," singing "Be A Clown" with Gene Kelly, and tearing up the living room in "A Star Is Born" as she describes her day at the studio to a morose James Mason. I'll also remember her sitting in a not really very posh St. Moritz Hotel suite a couple of years ago, with her two youngest children, Lorna, then 14, and Joey, then 12. They seemed such sweet, wise, sad children, until suddenly Judy would recall some comparatively conventional outrage (being attacked by bugs in a tent theater), and Lorna and Joey would laugh hysterically at what was obviously an old and favorite story. A minute later Judy would mention how she really didn't like to work, that she was tired and that the doctor had told her after a hepatitis bout in 1960 that she would kill herself if she continued to perform. "I loved the idea of not working," she said, and paused, "but then I found out I couldn't afford it."

The greatest shock about her death was that there was no shock. One simply wondered how she survived as long as she did.

June 29, 1969

THE LADY FROM SWEDEN

By BOSLEY CROWTHER

PICTURE the sweetheart of a viking, freshly scrubbed with Ivory soap, eating peaches and cream from a Dresden china bowl on the first warm day of Spring atop a sea-scarred cliff and you have a fair impression of Ingrid Bergman. Such highfalutin words to describe a mere picture actress smack suspiciously of haywire, it is true, but this reporter would like to go on record that he has never met a star who compares in the slightest degree with this incredible newcomer from Sweden.

Miss Bergman, as is generally known, made her first American film last Summer when she appeared with Leslie Howard in the picture called "Intermezzo" (to which was appended the rider, "A Love Story," in case any one was in doubt). On the occasion of that visit, she was carefully kept under wraps, virtually sneaked in and out under strict "no publicity" orders and allowed to return to Sweden as anonymously as she came.

Later, reports got around of her unbelievable naïveté—how she spent her time in New York riding up and down Fifth Avenue on bus tops, eating ice-cream sundaes like a school girl and roaming the World's Fair for hours unattended. The few hard-boiled film folk who met her were completely knocked off their pins and went around drooling for months about a Scandinavian dream girl.

* * *

Well, there must have been a method behind this practically unprecedented reticence, for now Miss Bergman has returned, again under the aegis of Producer David O. Selznick, and is bound for Hollywood, where that gentleman intends to put her in a picture about—guess who! The answer is Joan of Arc. And the cloak of anonymity has been very discreetly removed.

Ingrid Bergman.

From behind it, however, has emerged a young lady whom the quidnuncs underplayed. At least they didn't circulate the bunk. For Miss Bergman is certainly as simple and genuine an article—the legendary Garbo included—as has ever been imported to these shores by the sometimes fallible film industry.

Refreshing is a word which has been badly overworked. But if—after seeing a succession of Hollywood glamour gals—you should happen upon a young lady without a detectable trace of affectation who talks about herself with frank reluctance (and you know all the time that she's good), who doesn't use a speck of make-up and has the candid smile of a kid, what other word are you going to give her?

This is really the sort Miss Bergman is. Taller than average (5 feet 8), with light brown hair, pale blue eyes, a fair complexion which radiates health and a strong, athletic figure, she is your typical Scandinavian woman—not lean and melancholy, like the young Garbo, but full of good spirits and simplicity.

And the nicest thing about her is that she obviously lacks the familiar guile. When she arrived here the other day there was some little inter-office question among Mr. Selznick's gang as to whether it should be publicized that she is married and has a little girl. This fact (considered damaging to "glamour") might conceivably have been concealed, for Miss Bergman doesn't look at all maternal nor the 24 years old that she is. But the question was early settled by her—if she ever suspected there was one—when she calmly walked off the boat with Pia (that's the tot) slung over her arm. And, while lunching with this reporter, she said as a matter of course that the next day was the nurse's day off, so she would have to stay in the hotel with Pia.

The English language is a little problem which Miss Bergman has not yet quite overcome. She speaks it well enough, but deliberately and with an inevitable accent. Naturally, she is working hard on it. During luncheon conversation, she hesitated whether to use the word "eldest" or "oldest." When told that either was correct, she popped a despairing smile and inquired, "But why must you have two?"

When asked for her impressions of Hollywood, Miss Bergman pronounced it, simply, a "lovely city," but explained she didn't get to see much of it last Summer. Apparently she was as gaga about it all—after coming from Sweden's modest studios—as any tyro might have been. The hordes of technicians, and especially make-up men, with whom she had never before had any truck, rather baffled her. She lived in a rented house, she said, but added, with a trace of wistful regret, "I had such a nice dressing room I could have lived there."

Miss Bergman has been in pictures for six years, ever since she was 18. Prior to that she had one year at dramatic academy in Stockholm, after graduating from girls' school. Her first role in Swedish pictures, she said, was a small one, playing a "young girl who falls in love with a young man." Her next one was much better.

"Already from the beginning," she said, "I have good roles." Then she added, "Playing the young girl who only falls in love—I am very glad I got through it quick."

Although "Intermezzo" presented her as a sensitive, rather wistful type, Miss Bergman said that she has played many comedy parts in Sweden, and she hopes eventually to do likewise in American films. Indeed, she says, she wants to play all sorts, even perhaps a "fallen woman"—though her ability to go that far is herewith doubted. She just hasn't the face for it.

Her husband is a doctor and teaches at the Swedish Royal Academy of Medicine. He wasn't able to come over with her, but she hopes he can make it in the Spring. His initials and hers combine to make Pia's name. That, in fact, is the only quaint touch which faintly suggests "Hollywood." (And that was probably his idea!) But you needn't worry about Miss Bergman going glamorous, because the point is—well, she's different.

January 21, 1940

PHIL HARRIS WEDS ALICE FAYE, ACTRESS

Band Leader and Film Star Go to Ensenada, Mex., From Hollywood for Ceremony

PEACE JUSTICE OFFICIATES

Miss Faye One of the Strongest Box-Office Attractions of Screen Last Year

Phil Harris

Alice Faye

HOLLYWOOD, Calif., May 12 (UP)—Alice Faye, blond film star, tonight telephoned the movie studio with which she has a contract that she and Phil Harris, band leader, were married today in Ensenada, Mexico.

The actress said she and Mr. Harris had driven to the Mexican resort early today and were married by a justice of the peace.

Although Mr. Harris had been escorting Miss Faye about Hollywood for several months, there were no indications that they intended to be married.

Miss Faye and Tony Martin, prominent singer of the movies and stage, were divorced in March, 1940. Mr. Harris was divorced about a year ago from Mrs. Marcia Harris, a non-professional.

Alice Faye, who has appeared in movies for seven years, was one of the strongest box-office attractions last year. Before she went to Hollywood she was well known as a dancer and radio singer.

Among the pictures in which Miss Faye has been featured are "The Great American Broadcast," "Tin Pan Alley," "Lillian Russell," "Little Old New York," "Hollywood Cavalcade," "Rose of Washington Square," "Alexander's Ragtime Band" and "In Old Chicago."

Mr. Harris is best known to the public because of his appearances, both on the screen and over the radio, with Jack Benny. The three movies for which he is best known are 'Melody Cruise," "Man About Town" and "Buck Benny Rides Again."

He made his reputation as a bandleader in New York when he took Rudy Vallee's place during the latter's vacation seven years ago. Miss Faye also became known on Rudy Vallee's program as a singer.

May 13, 1941

Betty Grable, Movie Pin-up of '40's

'My Legs Made Me'

By ALDEN WHITMAN

Thirty years ago, Betty Grable, a shapely, straw-blond blue-eyed film actress and singer of admittedly modest talents was the country's supreme pop culture idol. Not only did the star of lavish Technicolor musicals lure millions of moviegoers to the box office, but she also captured the fancy of American servicemen the world over. Indeed, three million photographs of Miss Grable, clad in a white bathing suit and displaying an inviting smile and curvaceous legs, were distributed in the armed forces, and G.I.'s acclaimed her as their favorite pin-up.

"People like to hear me sing, see me dance and watch my legs," Miss Grable once remarked with a directness that was refreshing in Hollywood. And she added, "My legs made me."

They achieved, in fact, a sort of immortality in 1948 when a print of them was committed to concrete in the forecourt of Grauman's Theater in Hollywood, not far from a cast of Clark Gable's ears and John Barrymore's profile.

Miss Grable was quite frank about her abilities. "My voice is just a voice," she said. "When it comes to dancing, I'm just average, maybe a little bit below."

Nonetheless, her more than

40 films, many of them for 20th Century-Fox, grossed about $100-million; and she herself earned at least $3-million in her career. At $300,000 a year, she was the highest-salaried American woman in 1946-47, according to the Treasury Department.

Some Films Listed

The money and the fame—10,000 admirers a week were said to have written fan letters to Miss Grable in her heyday—came from such pictures as "Down Argentine Way," "Moon Over Miami," "A Yank in the R.A.F.," "Song of the Islands," "Springtime in the Rockies," "Million Dollar Legs," "Mother Wore Tights," and "Coney Island." Her last film, released in 1955, was 'How to Be Very Very Popular."

Miss Grable's musicals were not long on plot. In "Coney Island," for example, she was the diamond-in-the-rough boardwalk entertainer who reached Broadway with the help of two carnival men.

Her songs bore such titles as "Miss Lulu From Louisville," "I had the Craziest Dream" and "For You, for Me, for Ever More." Cavorting with Miss Grable in her films were Don Ameche, Tyrone Power, Alice Faye, Victor Mature, Cesar Romero, John Payne, Jack Oakie and Dan Dailey, among other luminaries of the day.

Reviewers thought Miss Grable's films pleasant and buoyant. In World War II and the years that immediately followed, she could be counted on to tantalize and divert audiences, to take their minds off the grimness of armed conflict. She was, as a New York Times reviewer said, "a lot of fun."

Darryl F. Zanuck, the 20th Century-Fox producer, considered Miss Grable such a sure-fire drawing card that he pressed her to play a dramatic role. She refused, saying:

"I'm strictly a song-and-dance girl. I'm no Bette Davis nor am I out to prove anything with histrionics. I just want to make pictures that people will like."

The daughter of a frustrated actress and a bookkeeper, Ruth

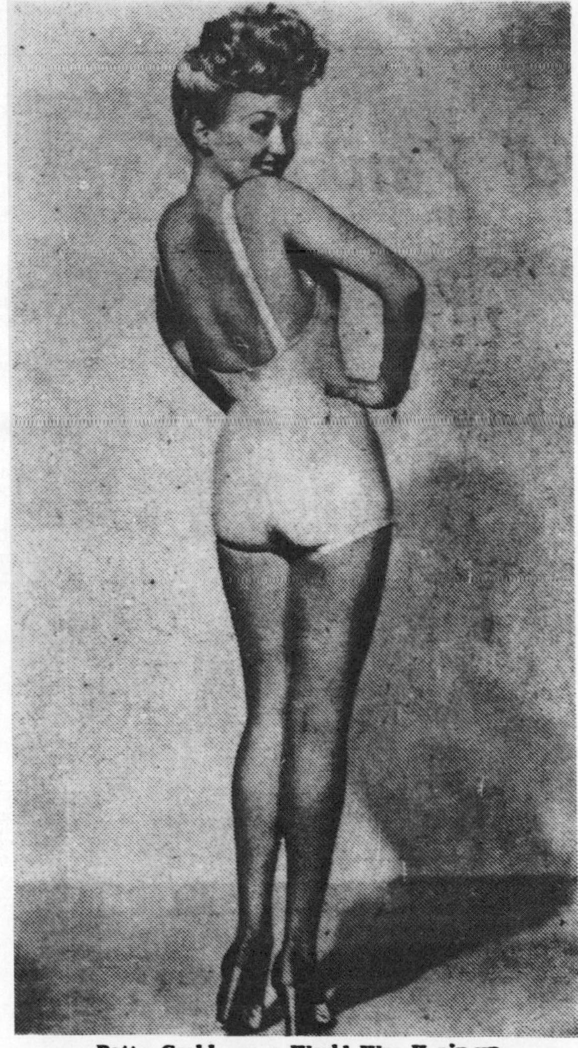

Betty Grable as a World War II pin-up

Elizabeth Grable was born Dec. 18, 1916, in South St. Louis, Mo. At her mother's urging the child studied the saxophone and various kinds of dancing. "I don't think I missed a thing except eccentric dancing," she recalled. "I dreaded every lesson."

By 1930 Miss Grable's mother had taken her to Hollywood, where she landed some bit parts on the Sam Goldwyn lot. Then there was a comic dance number in "The Gay Divorcee" in 1934 and a string of pictures starring her in Betty coed roles.

Miss Grable's catapult to stardom was a true Hollywood fairy tale. In 1939 Mr. Zanuck saw a routine cheesecake photograph of the actress in a newspaper and signed her to a contract without ado.

And when Alice Faye, then the reigning musical comedienne, fell ill, Miss Grable took her place in "Down Argentine Way." The film was a hit, and for the next dozen years she had the Midas touch.

Part of her filmic appeal was a restrained sensuousness. In "Tin Pan Alley," for instance, she danced through a harem scene, clad in a sequined bra and panties, with her legs sinuous under transparent pantaloons. The scene was comic enough to disarm the Hollywood censors.

For another thing, Miss Grable was pert and petite. She was a little over 5 feet 3 inches tall, weighed about 110 pounds and maintained a trim figure. "Girls can see me in a picture and feel I could be one of them," she once said. To men she was concededly sexy.

Married Twice

Miss Grable was the center of three highly press-agented romances. One was with Jackie Coogan, the former child movie star, to whom she was once married in 1937. The union ended in divorce two years later.

Afterward, the actress's name was linked with George Raft, who was her frequent escort. Then in 1943 she married Harry James, the trumpeter and band leader. They were divorced in 1965.

With Mr. James she raised race horses and operated two ranches and two estates. In recent years Miss Grable attempted various comebacks, but without notable success. She was often seen in television commercials for Geritol, a reputed elixir for the middle-aged.

Miss Grable leaves two daughters, children of her marriage to Mr. James. They are Mrs. Jessica Yahner of Los Angeles and Mrs. Victoria Bivens of Troy, Mich. Also surviving are five grandchildren and a sister, Mrs. Marjorie Arnold of Los Angeles.

A funeral service will be conducted tomorrow at 1 P.M. at All Saints Episcopal Church in Beverly Hills, Calif.

July 4, 1973

Personalities

POLL: Ingrid Bergman and Bing Crosby still reign as America's most popular actress and actor is the verdict of the eleventh annual "All-American Popularity" poll just completed by Boxoffice, a weekly trade journal. According to the results of the nation-wide canvass of press and radio critics, independent theatre exhibitors and members of the National Screen Council (comprised of women's clubs, civic and educational organizations), Miss Bergman is Queen for the second year, while Crosby is top man for the fourth consecutive year. Runners-up, distaff division — Claudette Colbert, Olivia de Havilland, Barbara Stanwyck, Joan Crawford, Bette Davis, Betty Grable, Greer Garson, Irene Dunne, Rita Hayworth, Margaret O'Brien and Loretta Young. Following Crosby were Clark Gable, Gary Cooper, Cary Grant, Humphrey Bogart, Dana Andrews, Gregory Peck, Spencer Tracy, Alan Ladd, Bob Hope, Fred MacMurray and James Stewart. Roy Rogers topped Gene Autry in the balloting for the most popular Western star.

November 16, 1947

'AVERAGE GUY'

Gary Cooper Reflects on Twenty Years in Films

By EZRA GOODMAN

HOLLYWOOD.

GARY COOPER, Hollywood's strong, silent man, both on and off screen, was celebrating his twentieth anniversary as a movie star by speaking freely for an interview. Cooper, who has never been noted for his loquacity, recently acquired a public relations counsel and the Hollywood press contingent has been amazed by his unaccustomed volubility.

Cooper was attired in the uniform of a Navy lieutenant. He had just come off the "Task Force" set on the Warner Brothers back lot and was resting between camera set-ups in his dressing room. "Task Force," which has to do with the history of naval aviation, is said to be Cooper's fifty-eighth starring vehicle. One of his big pictures, "Wings," made approximately two decades ago, also found him in the role of an aviator, although he played a supporting part to Richard Arlen and Buddy Rogers.

A good many changes have taken place since then, among them the screen's acquisition of a speaking voice, but Cooper, at the age of 47, is still going strong without any visible let-up. He was recently voted third in popularity in a poll of the nation's movie editors, with only Bing Crosby and Ingrid Bergman placing ahead of him. He earned $300 a week when he made "Wings." Today he commands $275,000 per picture.

Success Story

To what did Mr. Cooper attribute this success story?

"Shucks," replied the tall, lanky actor, speaking in the same patois as his screen characters, "I guess I've just been lucky. I always try to stick pretty much to the type of stuff in which people are accustomed to seeing me—typical, average-guy roles like Mr. Deeds, Sergeant York and Dr. Wassell—people from the middle of the U. S. A. Once in a while I like a good Western—gives me a chance to shoot off guns.

"My taste in art and literature is real ordinary. I don't try to pretend I know anything. I don't place myself above other people. I'm the average guy in taste and intelligence. If there's any reason for what you would call my success, that's it."

Cooper had recently returned from an arduous five-week location trip on board the naval carrier Antietam, during which director Delmar Daves and company had filmed scenes for "Task Force" along the Pacif... Coast, from San Diego to San Francisco. Cooper recalled that his first starring vehicle, "Wings," was also made largely on location, at Kelly Field in Texas. "Wings" is still remembered as the first and one of the best of the big aviation epics.

Since the days of "Wings," Cooper has appeared in an impressive line-up of pictures, ranging from "The Virginian" and "A Farewell to Arms" to "Lives of a Bengal Lancer" and "Saratoga Trunk." Cooper selects his pictures himself and he holds that actors have just as good a sense of judgment as producers and directors.

"Despite all their alleged mistakes, actors know what's good for them," Cooper said. "Most actors who have had something to say about the selection of their material have come out better. I remember when I first came to Hollywood that Gloria Swanson turned down a salary of $20,000 a week to produce her own pictures. After one or two of these, she was deader than a doornail. But actors and actresses today have a different perspective on the whole thing. They study their material, they think more and they are more hep to what goes on. There are quite a few actors who participate in producer deals now and do well."

Actor by Accident

When Cooper isn't making movies, he likes to go off on extended hunting and fishing trips. He recently purchased a thirty-acre ranch in Colorado. Cooper's predilection for the wide open spaces dates back to his formative years in Montana. He became an actor by accident.

"I had no idea of going into theatrics," he says. "I was in a play or two in high school and I sort of majored in English and debate and stuff like that. I wanted to be an artist, but after a while I dropped it cold. I'm terrible at it. I became an advertising salesman.

"I was sidetracked when I came to Hollywood and found myself working in the movies. To make ends meet, I did extra work and pony, riding jobs. On my third picture, a Tom Mix Western, I saw Mix act and was told that he got $17,500 a week. I figured I could do that kind of acting, too. People told me: 'You're an average looking guy. You don't have to be handsome or anything like that to become a success in movies.'

"I gave up the ad business and gave myself a year to try to make the grade in Hollywood. I figured that if nothing happened after a year, I'd leave town. I had a screen test made myself for $65 and circulated it around. After eleven months, I got a call from Sam Goldwyn. The part called for riding a horse. That was my first real part—in 'The Winning of Barbara Worth.'

"Then Paramount put me under contract. I've been sort of drifting along ever since."

December 19, 1948

ANOTHER DEAN HITS THE BIG LEAGUE

By HOWARD THOMPSON

JAMES DEAN is the young man who snags the acting limelight in "East of Eden," which arrived at the Astor last week. Its opening has started a lively controversy over his histrionic kinship with Marlon Brando—and his professional competence. At any rate, 25-year-old Dean, a product of an Indiana farm, Hollywood, television and Broadway, has made an impression and now owns a Warner Brothers contract.

Count his supporting chore in last season's play "The Immoralist" as having threefold significance insofar as this rapid rise is concerned. It netted him the Donaldson and Perry awards, and, indirectly, the attention of director Elia Kazan, then scouting leads for "Eden," and finally, his flourishing reputation for unvarnished individuality. In a recent chat at his agent's apartment, west of the Yorkville area, Dean gave ample evidence that he was prepared to maintain that individuality.

James Dean.

He sat quietly, awaiting the first query. The slender frame and boyish features suggested a Booth Tarkington hero. The black corduroy shirt and trousers and a penetrating neutrality of expression, magnified by large, steel spectacles, did not. Had he caught "Eden" yet?

"Sure, I saw it," came the soft, abstract reply. His verdict? "Not bad."

"No, I didn't read the novel. The way I work, I'd much rather justify myself with the adaptation rather than the source. I felt I wouldn't have any trouble—too much, anyway—with this characterization once we started because I think I understood the part. I knew, too, that if I had any problems over the boy's background, I could straighten it out with Kazan."

Background

Asked how he happened to turn to acting, Dean hoisted a jodhpur over one knee and lit a cigarette. "It was an accident, although I've been involved in some kind of theatrical function or other since I was a child—in school, music, athletics." He rose and began pacing the room. The words came slowly and carefully.

"To me, acting is the most logical way for people's neuroses to manifest themselves, in this great need we all have to express ourselves. To my way of thinking, an actor's course is set even before he's out of the cradle."

An only child of non-professionals, Dean was raised by an aunt and uncle in Fairmount,

Ind. "My father was a farmer, but he did have this remarkable adeptness with his hands," he said, flexing his own. "Whatever abilities I may have, crystallized there in high school, when I was trying to prove something to myself—that I could do it, I suppose. One of my teachers was a frustrated actress. Through her I entered and won a state oratorical dramatic contest, reciting a Dickens piece called 'The Madman.' What's it about? About this real gone cat," he chanted, "who knocks off several people. It also begins with a scream," he remembered casually. "I really woke up those judges."

"All these things," he went on, "were good discipline and experience for me. After graduation, I went to live with my father in Los Angeles—Mother had died when I was a kid—and just for the hell of it, signed up for a pre-law course at U. C. L. A. That did call for a certain knowledge of histrionics. I even joined a fraternity on the campus, but I busted a couple of guys in the nose and got myself kicked out. I wasn't happy in law, either.

"Then I tried my luck in pictures, contacted an agent, got some small parts in things like 'Has Anybody Seen My Gal?' a Korean War film, "Fixed Bayonets," and one TV play.

"I came here at the suggestion of Jimmy Whitmore, a fine actor and a good boy, a real New York boy, who wasn't too happy out at Metro." For what he learned at the Actors Studio, while edging into prominence on television and his Broadway bow. "See the Jaguar," Dean pointedly credits director Lee Strasberg, "an incredible man, a walking encyclopedia, with fantastic insight."

Would he compare the stage and screen media? "As of now, I don't consider myself as specifically belonging to either. The cinema is a very truthful medium because the camera doesn't let you get away with anything. On stage, you can even loaf a little, if you're so inclined. Technique, on the other hand, is more important. My aim, my real goal, is to achieve what I call camera-functioning on the stage.

Defense

"Not that I'm down on Hollywood. Take pictures like 'The Ox-Bow Incident,' most of the Lubitsch ones. Gadge, (Kazan) of course, is one of the best. Then there's George Stevens, the greatest of them all. I'm supposed to do 'Giant' for him. This guy was born with the movies. So real, unassuming. You'll be talking to him, thinking he missed your point, and then—bang!—he has it."

How did his Warner contract read? "Nine films over a six-year period." Story approval? "Contractually, no—emotionally, yes. They can always suspend me. Money isn't one of my worries, not that I have any.

"Don't get me wrong. I'm not one of the wise ones who try to put Hollywood down. It just happens that I fit to cadence and pace better here as far as living goes. New York is vital, above all, fertile. They're a little harder to find, maybe, but out there in Hollywood, behind all that brick and mortar, there are human beings just as sensitive to fertility. The problem for this cat—myself—is not to get lost." Dean's smile spread as far as his lenses.

March 13, 1955

VENERABLE GENTS

Age Hath Yet Its Honor and Its Toil on Present-Day Screen

By BOSLEY CROWTHER

MAYBE it is almost as brutal to refer to a gentleman's age as it is to make public comment on a lady's accumulated years. But a steady observer of the movies cannot help but note with some surprise the number of actors of unmistakable seniority who are getting lots of work in films these days—and we don't mean as cracked or creaking ancients. We mean in romantic roles.

Take James Stewart, for instance. Here is a charming gentleman who has been knocking around in movies for something like twenty years. As a matter of fact, we first recall him as Jeanette MacDonald's brother in her "Rose Marie," so he must be a few years on the far side of Jack Benny's 39, at least. Yet within the past year the screen has had him in no less than four considerable films, and in all four of them he was doing quite all right with the dames.

In "The Glenn Miller Story," he enacted an attractive and believable young man who became, through a somewhat devious courtship, the happy husband of June Allyson. You'd never have dreamed, until the end of the picture, that he had a gray hair in his head. In "Rear Window," with his gray hairs frankly showing, he had Grace Kelly fairly pawing over him. And in "The Far Country," his romantic attentions were strenuously divided between Ruth Roman and Corinne Calvet.

Now, in Paramount's enormous "Strategic Air Command," he is back as the husband of Miss Allyson and a pilot of jet bombing planes. "We don't need young kids in the Strategic Air Command," one of the generals explains. "We need old hands—experience." Well Mr. Stewart is certainly their man. Big-league ballplayer, big-time bomber pilot, big-shot romantic husband—at his age! We don't know how he does it, but it is quaint to see.

Busy Man

Or take another James, name of Cagney. This we hate to say, but we know he's on the shady side of 50—and nobody would be quicker to admit it than he. Yet here he is with four new pictures—"Run for Cover," now at the Criterion, and "Love Me or Leave Me," "Mr. Roberts and "The Eddie Foy Story" waiting to go. That is a line-up of pictures such as no other actor has.

We can't rightly say that Mr. Cagney is in his best or most personable form in this saddle-sprung "Run for Cover," which is a formula Western film. He plays a regenerated small-town sheriff who goes after the renegades, including a kid he has attempted to big-brother, when all his loud-talking deputies have turned cowards. And that is a formula they should have torn up—or at least, abandoned for a few years—after "High Noon."

However, in this minor six-gun saga, Mr. Cagney does show enough sand to set a full-bodied Viveca Lindfors doing Scandinavian nip-ups for him. To be sure, it appears that Miss Lindfors has been a little while on the vine, which is to say that she is no spectacular bargain, even in a flea-bitten town. But, at least, she's a healthy, eager woman, full of uncomplicated zeal, and Mr. Cagney makes her jitter like a schoolgirl. You've got to hand it to this old lad. And they say that in "Love Me or Leave Me," he plays the husband of Doris Day!

Watching the Fords

Perhaps it is being excessive to include in this catalogue Glenn Ford, who still looks a passable 30, even though he passed it long ago. But Mr. Ford is another Hollywood veteran who is up to his ears in jobs and is kidding somebody into believing that he's still quite a man with the girls.

He is currently in town in two pictures—in "Blackboard Jungle," at Loew's State, wherein he plays a beginning high school teacher and the husband of Ann Francis, a virtual child; and in "Interrupted Melody," at the Music Hall, wherein he is the husband of Eleanor Parker as Marjorie Lawrence.

Of the two, we must say that the latter has Mr. Ford in a more plausible role and, indeed, in one more appropriate to his customary pallid acting style. For here he is a practicing physician who, through patience, sacrifice and love, helps his famous opera-singing wife to conquer the physical and mental ravages of an attack of polio. Mr. Ford makes a good and loyal husband, and Miss Parker is pretty and skillful in the role of the young diva who actually suffered the dreaded paralysis and recovered to resume her career.

But still Mr. Ford is no chicken, and his years belie his pretended youth as a medical student in the early part of this picture. Let's face it, fellow: you're getting on.

What this propensity for older actors in romantic roles signifies is something we can't quite fathom. Not long ago, the trend seemed to be towards younger and less familiar heroes. Now, with lots of youngsters coming on, the oldsters are still picking up many of the juicier jobs. This is not marked in criticism. It is simply a phenomenon. As Lord Tennyson said in his "Ulysses": "Old age hath yet its honor and its toil."

May 8, 1955

Observer: The 'Burton-Liz' Bromide, Please

By RUSSELL BAKER

WASHINGTON, June 19— The cheap way to restore a failing superiority complex is to stop at the drugstore and buy an armful of movie magazines. Talk about misery! Nobody knows what misery is until he has had three hours on the couch with the movie magazines.

Here are the private lives of the gods, the magazines whisper. See all these beautiful successes, earning a million dollars a day and getting the royal reception from all the snootiest headwaiters, but look closely. The gods have feet of clay. All that money and all those toadying headwaiters cannot cure their miseries.

Lotus Eaters

Chewing through a sheaf of these lotus leaves convinces the reader that while his own life may be bad, it is a thundering success compared to the lives of the gods.

Take "Burton-Liz," which is movie-mag shorthand for Mr. and Mrs. Richard Burton. No movie mag is complete without its monthly "Burton-Liz" opus, usually headlined on the cover in scandal type or pictures of Mrs. Burton. Here are eleven magazines picked at random off the rack. Six display one or the other of the Burtons on the cover and all carry "Burton-Liz" material inside.

The editors use two basic techniques for making the reader feel superior to "Burton-Liz." One is a sympathetic recitation of their problems. (Read, and be thankful that *you* are not Elizabeth Taylor or Richard Burton.) This technique is used in the July edition of "Movie Stars," whose cover headline

Richard Burton

reads: "Liz cries: Why must God punish me this way?"

The other technique is outright abuse. Examples: "Has Liz become too fat to hold Burton?" "Liz: 'Burton's ruining me with liquor.'"

The first piece caddishly holds Mrs. Burton up to ridicule for putting on some weight. The second says that both Burtons drink a lot. The abusive magazines, incidentally, make the one really convincing case against the pleasures of being Elizabeth Taylor or Richard Burton: In anonymity, a person can at least take too much scotch or add an extra chin without being berated about it for the titillation of ten million readers.

This, of course, is not the intended message. The intended message is, "Read and be comforted, for even the gods run to fat and lap up the lethal booze." It is comforting to think that one's weaknesses are also common on Olympus. When the gods prove human, humans may feel godlike.

But to return to the sympathetic treatment of Mrs. Burton's problems ("Must God punish me this way?"). Earlier this year, the son of Mrs. Burton's chauffeur was killed. She went

Elizabeth Taylor

to Paris for the funeral. Returning to Dublin, her chauffeur-driven car struck and killed a pedestrian. Her father suffered a cerebral stroke, and she flew to California to be with him for a week. At about the same time, some of her jewelry was stolen.

These are the "punishments" catalogued in the cover story of "Movie Stars." They do seem like a heavy combination of misfortunes to occur in a brief time, and the reader is invited to thank his stars that he is not risking divine wrath by making a million dollars a day and carrying on in high style.

Actually, of course, examination of the fine print fails to show that Mrs. Burton ever cried, "Must God punish me this way?" But this is a small point when you are seeking comfort in the movie mag. Most of their kick comes from the cover, and the fine print is usually a letdown.

Example: "Movie Mirror's" cover asks: "Is Liz legally wed?" The answer inside: Yes. "The shocking things Burton taught Liz," promises the cover of "Who's Who in Hollywood." Inside: "He taught me to love and understand poetry; to save money."

"Liz leaves Burton twice in two weeks," announces the cover of "Motion Picture." She did indeed, the fine print reveals. Once to attend the funeral of her chauffeur's son in Paris. The second time to be with her stricken father in California.

The only exception to the rule that the fine print betrays the cover is in "Has Liz become too fat to hold Burton?" ("Screen Stars"). The writer's reply: "Burton will never stay married to someone who is fat . . . men in this day and age like women thin as fence rails." Both statements are debatable, but at least the magazine makes a show of sticking by its gun.

Misplaced Sympathy

These fine-print betrayals, however, do not dilute the comforting sensation that comes from being lapped in all this slush. The reader does not have to worry, as the gods do, if his wife attends a funeral or visits an ailing parent. Being anonymous, he feels relatively safe from direct expressions of divine anger. If he drinks and overeats, it is no more than the gods do; and if he doesn't, he feels superior to the gods.

Sensitive people may feel tempted to sympathize with the Burtons. Surely, nobody should have to sit still for all this peephole gossip. Such sympathy would probably be misplaced. "Burton-Liz" probably seem even more fantastic to them than to us.

June 20, 1965

James Cagney

Glenn Ford

Cary—From Mae to September

By GUY FLATLEY

"Do you have children?" asks the soft-spoken man with snow-white hair.

"Yes, a girl and a boy."

"*You* did it the right way," he says, returning to a shelf the third portrait he has shown me of his one and only child. She's 7 and beautiful; her papa is pushing 70 and handsome. He is also the most celebrated personality on the board of directors of Fabergé — a firm dedicated to the pursuit of happy scents—as well as a top executive of Western Airlines and a founding father of an idyllic, get-away-from-it-all-if-you-can-afford-it community that is being set up near Shannon, Ireland. And—he insists—he is a *former* movie star.

"If I had known then what I know now . . . if I had not been so utterly stupid or selfish . . . I would have had a hundred children and I would have built a ranch to keep them on."

He could easily have afforded it, since his fortune is estimated at a modest $25-million. But he never built that ranch, perhaps because he was so busy building an indelible screen image—the image of the passionate but poised lover, the man among men and, above all, the suave funnyman who was nobody's fool.

The elusive, inimitable Cary Grant style, a smoothly male style which retained its unique grace under phenomenal female pressure: from predatory Mae West purring "You can be had" to him in "She Done Him Wrong," to madcap Katharine Hepburn —and her wayward leopard —stalking him in "Bringing Up Baby," to fledgling femme fatale Rita Hayworth bedeviling him in "Only Angels Have Wings," to spunky exspouse Irene Dunne sabotaging his honeymoon with Gail Patrick in "My Favorite Wife," to naughty Ingrid Bergman nibbling his ear in "Notorious," to bebopping Shirley Temple, bent on making him her best beau in "The Bachelor and the Bobby-Soxer," to mischief-making Marilyn Monroe taking him for a joy-ride in "Monkey Business," to blue-blooded Grace Kelly burning a red-hot flame for him in "To Catch a Thief," to super-virgin Doris Day smothering him with candy kisses in "That Touch of Mink."

Culver

Cary Grant wooed Mae West in "She Done Him Wrong," 1933

"I'm retired from the movies," says Grant, "until some writer comes up with a character who is deaf and dumb and sitting in a wheel chair"

*

And it seems only yesterday that he smooched and sparred with the likes of Dietrich, Bankhead, Harlow, Lombard, Jean Arthur, Rosalind Russell, Sylvia Sidney and Myrna Loy. Yet today, this bustling, smartly dressed industrialist would prefer talking about a *new* movie, a non-Cary Grant movie. He is settled down in his Manhattan pad—a spacious suite at the Warwick, a hideaway once called home by Marion Davies—to chat about "A Touch of Class," partly because he feels the George Segal-Glenda Jackson comedy is a delicious trifle in the sophisticated but screwball tradition of such Grant goodies as "The Awful Truth," "Bringing Up Baby," "His Girl Friday," and "The Philadelphia Story," and partly because "A Touch of Class" is a Brut production, and Brut is the showbiz baby of father Fabergé.

*

If you've been reading the gossip columns lately, however, or scanning the ads on the movie pages, you probably think "A Touch of Class" was produced by Joe Levine, a not excessively timid showman who is merely functioning as the distributor of the film for Brut. "Despite what it says on the billboards, Joe Levine did *not* produce the movie," Grant says emphatically. "If anyone is responsible for 'A Touch of Class,' it is Mel Frank, the man who wrote it and directed it. I like Joe Levine, but I do believe it's a habit of his to take credit when he really shouldn't, something that applies even to 'The Graduate.'"

Be it Brut or be it Levine, "A Touch of Class" has a touch of sass about sex that would have been strictly taboo in the days when the Hays Office forced Grant to keep at least one foot on the bedroom floor. Take, for example, the scene in which cheating husband George Segal beds down in a Spanish hotel room with liberated divorcée Glenda Jackson, only to have his aching back go kaput at the crucial moment. And a few scenes later—after the frantic couple has finally succeeded in making it—Glenda gives George a not-so-gentle appraisal of his sexual performance that would have brought a blush to the cheeks of Mae West in "She Done Him Wrong."

"In the old days, we might have *liked* to be that explicit," smiles Grant, "but I'm not so sure we would have had the courage."

And who can be sure that such courageous sex will scoot by small-town censors, now that the Supreme Court has given them the power to decide what is and what is not obscene? "I'm damned if I know where I stand on the Supreme Court ruling," says Grant. "I mean, what makes one word for something obscene, and another word for the very same act *not* obscene? As for nudity and the visual depiction of sex . . . well, that's part of our anatomy, isn't it? It's the method by which we are born, so it should be thought beautiful. I just don't know what to make of it all.

*

"It does seem to me that if a man wants to see a film that reveals everything, it should be up to him. I myself have never seen a pornographic movie, except for 'Last Tango in Paris.' They had a big charity screening in Hollywood — $100, *deductible*—and everyone wore black tie. I went with a very distinguished crowd, including Norton Simon and his wife, Jennifer Jones. And I'll tell you the truth, I don't know precisely *what* I thought of 'Last Tango in Paris,' except that it did seem crude to me. I really don't know why Marlon made it."

Grant would never dream of doing a new-fangled "Tango," but he has been tempted, from time to time, to waltz back into the limelight he left in 1966, soon after "Walk, Don't Run"—a flat remake of "The More the Merrier"—caused customers to run, not walk, away from the box office. "I was asked to do the movie of 'Sleuth,' but in the end I decided it would be too much work. I mean, I've *done* all that—almost 70 times—and it's a tiresome and very strenuous business."

He was also Jack Warner's pick for the plum part of Professor Henry Higgins in "My Fair Lady." "At that time, I was considered more commercial than Rex Harrison, but the thing that stopped me from taking the role was the fact that I had seen the show on stage three times and I just didn't think anyone could do it better than Rex. Jack Warner kept pushing, though, so finally I said to him, 'Look, Rex *does* it; use him.' Actually, I always thought the movie should have been done with Julie Andrews, too, although I adore Audrey Hepburn and had a great time with her in 'Charade.' I just think that once something has been done to perfection, why interfere with success?"

*

But isn't there some role that Grant would like to bring to cinematic perfection? "I don't wish to sound ungrateful, but the truth is I have very little to do with movies any more. I seldom go to the movies. I realize that they fill an enormous gap for many people, but not for me. I am more attracted to the world of reality. I won't say that I'll *never* make another picture, because I can't look into the future. I guess you can say that I'm retired from the movies until some writer comes up with a character who is deaf and dumb and sitting in a wheel chair. At my age . . ."

"Why are you so sensitive about your age?"

"I didn't say I *was* sensitive about my age."

"I don't want to misquote you."

"Go ahead, I give you permission to misquote me. I improve in misquotation. But I'm *not* sensitive about my age. The fact is, no one is delighted about getting old, but you have no real choice but to go along with it. If one is too eager to pursue his lost youth, it becomes immediately evident."

*

Now that he has put his romantic movie past behind him and become a big business man . . .

"What makes you think I wasn't always a big business man? Do you know of any other business where a man can earn a million dollars in 10 weeks?"

"Can I ask you how much you make at Fabergé?"

"Certainly you can ask, but I won't tell you."

He'd rather tell me about the astonishingly lovely Jennifer, the daughter of his otherwise disastrous marriage to actress Dyan Cannon. Newspaper accounts of the custody dispute made for depressing reading, and it is hard to imagine that any child could survive that sort of trauma without psychological bruises.

The prison scene from "Bringing Up Baby," with Cary Grant and Katharine Hepburn.

"That's going to be all right," Grant says. "Jennifer and I level with each other. She finds it difficult to leave me, and she also finds it difficult to leave her mother. Any court that can handle that situation has to have the wisdom of Solomon. Her mother and I are trying to handle it the best we can, and I think the love we feel for Jennifer will be reflected. The press builds these things up so, using words like battling and fighting. Nobody's *fighting;* it's just that when you have a point of disagreement which you cannot resolve, you must go to the man who will arbitrate — the judge."

Miss Cannon went to the judge and told him that her husband had been physically abusive to her in front of the servants. Would Grant care to comment on his alleged breach of domestic etiquette?

"Oh, I think those things speak for themselves, don't you? So many unpleasant things come up in a divorce case."

*

One of the more unpleasant—and surprising—things pointed out by Miss Cannon in court was the fact that Grant was uncommonly keen on LSD. "My intention in taking LSD was to make myself happy. A man would be a fool to take something that *didn't* make him happy. I took it with a group of men, one of whom was Aldous Huxley. We deceived ourselves by calling it therapy, but we were truly interested in how this chemical could help humanity. I found it a very enlightening experience, but it's like alcohol in one respect: a shot of brandy can save your life, but a bottle of brandy can kill you. And that's what happened when a lot of young people started taking LSD, which is why it became necessary to make it illegal. I wouldn't dream of taking LSD now; I don't *need* it now."

Not only are illicit drugs a thing of the past, but so—apparently—is the bitterness between Grant and Miss Cannon. In fact, he just returned from personally delivering Jennifer to her mother in Canada, where she is now making a movie. But then Grant has always striven to maintain a good-neighbor policy with his former wives, from Virginia Cherrill (1933-1935) to Barbara Hutton (1942-1945) to Betsy Drake (1949-1962).

"Virginia is happily remarried," he says affectionately of Miss Cherrill, the former actress who is best remembered as the enchanting blind flower seller in Charlie Chaplin's "City Lights." "She lives in Santa Barbara now, but every once in a while she comes to Los Angeles and we have a long chat, gabbing about one thing and another. During my last divorce, Virginia called and said, 'If you need a character witness, I'll come right down there and give you one.'"

*

Nor were there ever bad feelings between Grant and Barbara Hutton. "Barbara and I talked often after the divorce. That's the way it should be, don't you think? The difficulty in going through any divorce is that the *lawyers* must do all the talking."

But of all his ex-wives, the one who has remained closest is Betsy Drake, Grant's vivacious leading lady in two slight but engaging comedies, "Every Girl Should Be Married," and "Room for One More." "I'll be talking to Betsy later today, as a matter of fact. She's applying for her doctorate in psychology at U.C.L.A. Betsy was a delightful comedienne, but I don't think that Hollywood was ever really her milieu. She wanted to help humanity, to help others help themselves."

*

Feminists might well applaud Grant's pride in his ex-wife's pursuit of a meaningful career, but they would find troublesome his assertion that the most natural thing a woman can do is to marry when young and to have children just as soon as possible. "As far as I know, most animal life behaves in that manner," Grant says. "They mate when they find they are biologically able. But *we've* thrown the world out of whack; we prevent young people from having children when they are ready, which is when a boy is about 13 and a girl achieves menstruation.

*

"In our competitive society, parents instill in children the need to *succeed.* Since they're not permitted to get jobs when they are 14, they can't support themselves or the children they might have. So what are they to do? The religions tell them that they shouldn't mate without getting married, that anyone who does is bad. But it's not that way in the South Seas; there is no need for status there, no need for the latest bellbottoms. They go to bed when the animals do, they pick leaves from the trees to protect their genital organs, they make love when the mood strikes them, and the community takes care of the children.

"You can't suppress young people. I know *I* felt the need of a girl when I was 12 or 13—I think every boy does. Yet our society sets out to divorce boys and girls. They even have bucket seats in cars now, so you can't neck in a drive-in. Just the same, I think our young people are getting it all together. Not that I think you should be making love all the time—who can do it all the time? Though I *do* try."

Does that mean that Grant has a steady girl, if that is not too old-fashioned a way of putting it?

"That does sound a bit old-fashioned, but if you mean is there one special girl that I see all the time, the answer is no. Whatever comes my way, comes my way; whatever happens, happens."

In politics, as in sex, Grant does not go steady these days. "I don't always vote on the same ticket; I vote for the man I think will do the best job. I have supported President Nixon in the past because I think he has done some wonderful things. He stopped the war in Vietnam, and he brought 550,000 men home smoothly. He has created friendship with the Russians and with the Chinese, as compared with the fiasco of the Bay of Pigs. I don't know what to think about Watergate, except that I'm sorry about it and that I think the press has blown it up out of proportion. Not that I think bugging should be excused—I wouldn't want *my* phone bugged—but bugging has been used in Washington for many years."

Without doubt, Washington is situated this side of Paradise. Does Grant ever feel an urge to pocket his $25-million and trundle off to Tahiti? "*This* is my Tahiti. I don't put a great deal of effort into my work for Fabergé. I get up in the morning, go to bed at night, and occupy myself as best I can in between. I do what I want when I want. Once, in St. Louis, I knew a fellow who ran a whorehouse, simply because it made him happy," says the trim and tanned superstar-turned-tycoon. "Well, I do what makes *me* happy."

July 22, 1973

L.S. M.F.T.

CHAPTER **4**

Radio: The Sound of Flesh and Blood

The Jack Benny Show, November 30, 1948
From the left, Jack Benny, Mary Livingstone, Don Wilson, Phil Harris, Dennis Day

Courtesy The Columbia Broadcasting Company and the Jack Benny estate

BROADCASTING TO MILLIONS

Radio Telephony's Extraordinary Growth—200,000 Stations Installed in Last Three Months

By A. LEONARD SMITH JR.

ALTHOUGH radio telephony and its phraseology, broadcasting, aerial antennae and wave lengths, are almost as common topics of conversation today as the Eighteenth Amendment, one-half of 1 per cent., and Mr. Volstead, it is extremely hard, even yet, to write in popular terms of this baby of the sciences and its extraordinarily rapid growth.

We know that great radio corporations have already established plants from which each night are sent broadcast out through the air overhead grand opera, light opera, sermons, market reports, as well as children's bedtime stories. The rendition of this ether program can be heard by any one who fastens a set of radio telephone receivers to his or her ears, or who can get within range of one of the large horns with which some of the radio receiving stations are equipped.

From estimates given by these same corporations we know that there are today approximately 700,000 American homes, schools, churches, halls and office buildings equipped as receiving stations. More than 15,000 stations have been licensed by the United States Government for transmitting wireless messages of one sort or another. Much of the popularity of the whole thing has come in the last two or three months, during which time, it is said, about 200,000 receiving sets have been installed.

Take up the headpiece of a radio receiving set and listen a minute. On a small wave length, using little power, the wireless brings you an amateur's experimental chatter as he plays with his wonderful new toy. With a thousand times the speed of any wind that ever blew it bears the recital of poetry or neighborhood gossip straight to the delighted ears of some other enthusiast, who, when the experiment is over, will, you may be sure, check up with his friend on every point. On a higher wave-length, 360 meters, in fact, come the band concerts, the grand opera arias and all the features of the professional stations' nightly program. Increase the wave length still more, and you get into the realm ruled by the crash of the wireless telegraph spark, hurling its code signals from the great Nauen station near Berlin or from the big British plant in the bleak Welsh hills near Carnarvon to Deal Beach, New Brunswick, Tuckerton or Arlington in this country.

Through it all, to a greater or less degree, runs a continuous humming or buzzing, that sometimes rattles and crackles so loud as to drown out completely whatever signals you listen for.

"What are those noises?" you ask the operator in bewilderment.

He listens a moment. "Its 'Old Man Static,'" he tells you. Then, as you look even more blank, he shrugs his shoulders. "You know as much as I do," he says.

Noises of Space.

Of course, he refers to static electricity and you are fascinated, though a trifle awestruck, to realize that you are listening to sounds that, surely, were never intended to be heard by a human being. The delicate mechanism of the radio has caught and brought to the ears of us earth dwellers the noises that roar in the space between the worlds. The sounds range from an actual whistle in the region of the Aurora Borealis to a bacon-and-egg-frying sizzle around the Gulf Stream.

Perhaps we shall go further, some day, and comprehend these sneers and chuckles of "Old Man Static." Then, it may be, we shall understand, also, some of the freaks of wireless telephony. For example, not long ago James Miller of Aberdeen, Scotland, was "on the air" one night when there came to his ears through the dark the sound of a distant voice. It seemed to have been borne in on the moonbeams. Miller adjusted his apparatus, "tuned it," to increase the strength of those faint articulations. Then his face grew tense with wonder, for he heard a man in Keyport, N. J., 3,500 miles away, calling to a brother enthusiast somewhere over there in America to "stand by" for a demonstration.

It was Hugh Robinson of Keyport, and his conversation, as well as the records of the phonograph he played for his friend in New Jersey were heard just as clearly and distinctly by the man in Scotland. The same conversation and music were heard that night by a ship 1,900 miles out in the Atlantic and by another vessel in the harbor of Tela, Honduras.

Robinson was using a small set, deriving its power from an ordinary lighting circuit. He purchased it with a guaranteed range of 100 miles. Radio men say that his achievement is just about a record. They can't explain how it happened. Perhaps the atmospheric conditions were just right—"Old Man Static" in an indulgent mood—but it happened, and that's plenty for the average layman who is unable to sit down and work out theories of air currents and "enveloping stratas" of ether.

Rapid Development

Work on the development of the radio telephone commenced at the beginning of the present century, when a number of scientists started out to make the ether a medium for the voice as it was for the Marconi spark. The job was tackled, at first, principally in college laboratories, although one or two men connected with commercial companies lent their hands and brain to the task. Put as simply as possible, the problem confronting them was to transform the thousand-feet-a-second sound waves into Hertzian waves traveling each second 186,000 miles. Then the Hertzian waves had to be geared down at the receiving end so that the vibration could be detected and comprehended by the human ear.

Radio men agree that it was the invention of the vacuum tube by Dr. Lee De Forrest that made wireless telephony possible. This instrument, familiar to all radio enthusiasts, looks not unlike a small electric light bulb. It contains a filament, also like a light bulb, around which is a grid—a spiral or finely woven screen of wire. Outside the filament and the grid, enclosing both, is a small metal cylinder known as the plate. The vacuum tube acts in triple capacity as a detector, generator and amplifier.

If it is true that the vacuum tube made wireless telephony possible, it is just as certain that it was the war that put that science on the map. Under the stress of the nation's need, the toy became the mighty machine, recompensing the universe, as it were, for the years of sickness and sorrow, devastation and death. And it has always been this way. There never was a war but it added tenfold to the store of knowledge of humanity. It was a spark struck from the stone-headed battle hammer of some pre-historic warrior that gave man the idea of kindling fire, and thus laid the foundations of our civilization.

As soon as we entered the world conflict, our Government sent word to the great electrical companies that it wanted a reliable, effective, radio telephone right away. Immediately hundreds of experts, engineers, physicians and chemists began to eat and drink and dream radio telephony. And they made the telephones according to every Government specification. Say the radio men, we were five years ahead of the enemy in this science during the years of the war.

Then came peace. The companies that had worked so hard and so loyally to help the Government found that their labors were going to bear fruit a hundredfold in the shape of a brand-new means of rapid and interesting communication. The battle ended, man was ready to begin the subjugation of the air.

Has he succeeded? You have only to go out into the night and look up at the sky. Above you in the blue, flying across the face of the moon, are the scudding ether-borne messages; neighborly gossip, "Celeste Aida," by Caruso, reproduced on the phonograph, its liquid notes transmitted far across the sea, perhaps even sounding in the land of the singer's birth. Up there in the starlight night hisses the great transatlantic wireless, dot, dash, dot dot dash, telling of the death of a King or of the marriage of a Princess. Borne on the chill winds there are also the softest of lullabies and the sweetest of thousand-year-old fairy stories told by "The Man in the Moon" to thousands of delighted, though sleepy little children snuggled close by their own firesides.

It is all there in the air above, but you may not hear it with your human ears. You must turn to the magic that has been created to serve you. You must seek the powers that science has harnessed, that eclipse with their magic the slaves of Aladdin's lamp; the powers that enable you to hear the very music of the spheres.

Cost of Equipment.

To install a wireless receiving station is not a complicated operation. One needs only the price—anywhere from $25 to $250 upward. Also, if one lives in a New York apartment, one needs the consent of one's landlord. Landlords, say the radio enthusiasts, are not apt to be susceptible to the romance of the wireless. They generally regard the aerial antennae as an eyesore and a fire menace. Of course, the eyesore business is a matter of taste and, therefore, not debatable, but, so the experts declare, there is absolutely no danger from the wires, correctly installed.

It is a bit more difficult to get a sending set, but not by any means impossible. You must be able to read a few words of the International Communication Code, enough to understand any strident telegraphic orders "to get off the air" from the big wireless at the Brooklyn Navy Yard, which does not condescend to the wave length of the telephone. You will get this command whenever there's a ship sending S. O. S. from far out at sea. Then, it's up to you as an amateur operator, to refrain from transmitting, although you may listen all you please to the hiss and crackle of the dot and dash signal as the huge naval station speeds ships and men to the rescue.

At present, no amateur may send on more than a 200 meter wave length, nor is he permitted to develop more than one kilowatt of power. He is the lowest in the scale, and if he is anywhere in their neighborhood, he can no more interrupt the 360-meter wave length broadcasting concert or the 1,000 to 25,000 meter wave length transatlantic wireless than the buzzing of a mosquito can drown out the roar of a subway express train.

Sometimes the amateur tries to get just a little more power out of his instrument. It's natural, just as it's natural for the owner of a new automobile to "give 'er a little gas." When he yields to temptation, the amateur is apt, like his brother in the motor car, to attract the heavy notice of the traffic officer of his own particular thoroughfare. In this case it is the radio inspector of the district. There is one of these inspectors in the Custom House of each of the following cities: Boston, New York, Savannah, Baltimore, New Orleans, San Francisco, Seattle, Cleveland and Chicago. He has a radio telephone and by adjusting his instruments can tell accurately whether anybody in his district is "exceeding the speed limit." The "exceeder" gets a quick call down. If he disregards it he loses his license to use the air for any other purpose than to breathe.

Some Accomplishments.

Here are a few things that this infant science has accomplished to date. Everything mentioned is a matter of record:

A man in Glenbrook, Conn., using an ordinary amateur's outfit, one kilowatt power, guaranteed range 100 miles, sent his voice and the music of a phonograph on the winds of the world 2,500 miles to British Guiana.

Sunday service has been transmitted several times by wireless to homes distant several miles from the church.

The steamship Gloucester, ninety miles off the Port of New York, talked with various stations of the Western Electric Company across the American continent, and its signals and words and music were heard in the Catalina Islands, off the coast of California.

Talks between stations in England and Holland, and in Germany and Spain have been fairly common.

Conversation has been held between the Gare du Nord in Paris and French railroad trains.

Students of Union College, Schenectady, equipped a baby carriage with a radio telephone and trundled it along a road—they declare there was a baby in it—to the tune of lullabies played several miles away.

Both the Democratic and Republican candidates for Mayor of New York used the wireless telephone last Fall to make a political speech.

A woman out in Indiana heard a sermon preached into the transmitter of a radio telephone in Newark, by her son, a clergyman of that city.

Music sent several hundred miles by wireless was so clear on a vessel at sea that a dance was held.

Of course, the question that comes into everybody's mind as he reads all this, is, "When are we going to be able to talk to Europe?" Already commercial companies have accomplished that feat, not once but many times. Several years ago, the Western Electric carried on a series of experiments from the station at Deal Beach, N. J., when it talked to Paris and to Honolulu at the same time.

However, the ordinary man, not possessing a couple of hundred foot steel towers, several thousand feet of copper wire and a hundred thousand watts or so of electric energy, can't talk to Europe over the wireless yet, unless he happens to make a freak test like that of Robinson of Keyport. Machinery hasn't been constructed that will force "Old Man Static" to "get off the wire." At that, though, there is a rumor that everybody in the radio game seems to have heard, but which hasn't been confirmed, to the effect that a certain big New York corporation has plans all completed for a great plant to be erected this year or next that will make conversations with London, Paris or Berlin just as feasible as talking to St. Louis or Chicago.

With all the things a radio telephone has done or can do or is going to do, there are some things it cannot do, and they should be listed here. In the first place, it can't give you any privacy. The world's information is yours if you have a radio telephone, and also whatever information you intrust to the air belongs to the whole world. Then, two transmitting sets of anywhere near the same power cannot operate together in the same neighborhood. The ether lanes seem to congest very easily.

Third, no means have yet been found of counteracting the effect of high buildings on the passage of the vibrations carrying wireless messages. The best receiving set in the world is helpless when it is placed low down near a skyscraper that towers between it and the sources of whatever signals it is supposed to receive. This is what has forced them to give up for the present the idea of equipping policemen with miniature radio telephones. And, lastly, there's our old friend, "Static."

Even with these handicaps, the newest science is making giant strides of progress. The men working at it are working with the very fundamental laws of nature. And not the least fascinating part of their work is the glimpse it gives them, now and then, into realms that were never before dreamed of in any man's philosophy.

February 19, 1922

Wife Leaves Radio Fan; Judge Says She's Right

BRIDGEPORT, Conn., Feb. 9.—Because he cared more for his radio set than for her was the reason given in Superior Court yesterday by Mrs. Harold K. Andrews for leaving her husband.

Andrews asked Judge Isaac Wolfe for a habeas corpus to obtain possession of his two children, whom the mother took with her when she left last August. He accused his wife of leaving him alone nights to seek pleasure.

Judge Wolfe, in refusing the habeas corpus writ, said:

"The husband was wrapped up in his radio set. A husband should remember he owes duties to his wife. Mrs. Andrews naturally had to seek pleasures elsewhere."

February 10, 1924

Ten Outstanding Events This Week

Monday, 2:30-4:30 P. M.—WEAF—Debate, "Should Coal Miners Receive Better Wages?" Ellis Searles, affirmative; B. R. Newton, negative.

3 P. M.—WJZ—American Orchestral concert.

10-11 P. M.—WEAF—Mozart String Quartet.

Wednesday, 10:03 P. M.—WOO—Cantata, "The Messiah."

Thursday, 1 A. M.—WJAZ—Concert for MacMillan Arctic Expedition.

7:30 P. M.—WJZ-WJY—Union League Club Dinner; U. S. Navy Band.

8:30 P. M.—WEAF—Letz Quartet.

9 P. M.—KSD—St. Louis Symphony Orchestra; Frieda Hempel, soprano.

Friday, 7:45 P. M.—WGY—Drama, "If I Were King."

Saturday, 8:30 P. M.—WJZ—Leiderkranz Orchestra.

March 2, 1924

BABSON SEES SOCIAL REVOLUTION AS RADIO REVIVES HOME LIFE

RADIO is rapidly changing our lives and habits as a nation," says Roger W. Babson, statistician, who sees much more than entertainment, or even education, in the millions of radio receiving sets scattered throughout America.

"The great basic law of action and reaction, which governs our social and economic worlds, is seen once more in the development of radio broadcasting and reception," he says. "Emerson called it 'the law of compensation.' Nature employs it to keep things in balance. America has always been a home-loving nation, but we may say that we have been more home loving at some times than at others.

"The coming of the automobile changed our lives. Quick and relatively easy transportation widened our horizons. We had held pretty much within a radius of five miles; suddenly our individual world is expanded to a radius of fifty miles. Our daily world has been increased tremendously, and we changed our habits of life to take advantage of our broadened horizons. Our social business and economic lives have almost had to be built all over again to meet these changes.

"The most revolutionary change came in our habits of life. Business conditions are changing constantly, new industries are coming in, old ones are fading out, the risks involved in these changes are a part of the uncertainty that every business man and every investor must assume. But when some development comes along that threatens to change our whole American life and the foundations upon which it rests, the matter should not be passed over without careful examination. The automobile did just this, for it took us out of our homes.

"I do not argue the relative advantage of the change, but the widening of our horizons, the increasing of our individual worlds to several times their previous size, naturally left the home a smaller and less important part of our lives. The country club has come and the outdoor life has made us a healthier nation, but the home has shrunk to a sort of way station where we stop momentarily to change clothes and grab a bite to eat between trips.

"Actually, we spend less than half the time at home that we used to. I am referring to those few hours between work and sleep when we live with our families and friends—where we recreate—when we should enjoy an evening's leisure surrounded by the beauty and comfort of our own homes.

"Lately we haven't had much time for this sort of thing; too busy to stop and think. Much activity with questionable progress. Some students insist that the American mind and the American home are going to pieces in this hectic age. Perhaps they are right. I do not know.

"It is certain that, as we have come to spend less time in our homes, we have spent less time and money in developing them and making them attractive. We spend every year $17 per capita for gasoline, and only $14 for furniture. At the end of the year the gasoline is gone.

"As the situation has become more serious—as congestion on highways has begun to rob motoring of its fun—nature seems to have taken a hand in the matter. Radio is developed, and as the automobile took us away from our homes the radio is bringing us back.

"Good music, education, the world's greatest speakers, entertainment par excellence in infinite variety, awaiting your command in the cabinet below the loudspeaker, are competing successfully with the movies and the boulevards. We are beginning to stay home again and a few quiet evenings with good music is assuring millions of Americans that they have been missing something that is very much worth while.

"Radio with its magic is working a social revolution. The home is growing once more, and as we value it more highly and spend more time and thought on it the American home promises to become an even finer and more beautiful institution than it has been in times past when we have been proud as a home-loving nation."

April 5, 1925

14 STATIONS REACH 12,500,000 LISTENERS

Manager of WEAF Says Radiation of Good-Will Publicity Provides Radio With Economic Structure and Improves Programs.

By J. A. HOLMAN.

THERE is a great difference in the radio program of four years ago and today.

With the advent of radio broadcasting WEAF was established as the American Telephone and Telegraph Company's experimental station for the purpose of studying the engineering and economic problems confronting the new art. Was there a demand for radio broadcasting? If so, what did the public want? How was the demand to be met from the economic point of view? Finally, how could facilities be set up to meet the demand on the part of those who had legitimate use for the new medium? These four questions were and still are the outstanding ones presenting themselves for solution.

The first question was answered immediately. The demand was overwhelming, not only from radio listeners, but from business organizations which sought to utilize the new art by installing their own broadcasting equipment. In New York alone more than 100 inquiries were received regarding the purchase of radio transmitters. This would have meant 100 broadcasting stations transmitting all kinds of programs simultaneously, with the attendant economic and engineering inefficiencies and a positive disservice to the radio audience. It was to determine how genuine was the demand by these organizations for broadcasting facilities and to carry on the general experimental work of the telephone company that WEAF was provided.

At the time that this station was started broadcasting was looked upon as a novelty. The majority of radio fans were the amateurs, the old dyed-in-the-wool fans, who, while they are still with us today, are greatly outnumbered by listeners preferring program quality to experimentation. This audience grew rapidly, for the fascination of radio telephony seized the public imagination with an overwhelming force. At first mechanical music by phonographs and player pianos sufficed. To cater to the growing audience aspiring vocalists and instrumentalists, desiring to take advantage of the new publicity medium, requested placement on the programs. For the first year or two programs were disconnected presentations of one soloist after another. While in the very earliest days of the art it was possible to secure a few of the outstanding artists, they performed only because it appealed to them as a novelty, and as a means by which they might secure other engagements.

Religious Leaders Consulted.

What were the program tendencies in these pioneering days? It was the natural development from the simple studio programs to out-of-studio events. Program managers were aided then, as now, by the radio fan's letters. While the mail was fairly heavy, it contained a smaller proportion of constructive criticism, the majority of letters being expressions of enthusiastic surprise at the new medium and its quality programs. Our station impresarios carried on extensive experiments and increased the number of program hours from fourteen per week to its present average of fifty-two. WEAF'S personnel was doubled and then tripled. Every step was taken as a result of carefully arranged experimentation.

Take the question of religion in radio as an example. The important religious bodies were consulted. From the first we felt that broadcasting activities along religious lines should be confined to such times as would not conflict with regular church services. The various denominations were consulted and invited to participate in the big radio experiment. The Greater New York Federation of Churches has presented a religious program on each Sunday afternoon and Thursday evening. The United Synagogue of America joined in the experiment and has been presenting its religious program on each Wednesday night.

Colleges Join in Experiments.

The educational problem was handled in conjunction with the outstanding educational body in the city—Columbia University. That there was a place in radio programs for serious lectures authoritatively and interestingly presented was expected, but no one anticipated the public response. When the Home Study Department of Columbia University selected as its first experimental course the series of lectures of the poetry of Robert Browning, it was felt that radio broadcasting was being given the educational acid test. The result was immediate and astounding. The university was encouraged to further efforts. Since that time, two years ago, there has been a continuous series of lectures by university authorities, discussing such subjects as history, psychology, religion, politics, economics and other major subjects. Education and radio were insolubly linked.

As may be expected, national political organizations eagerly seized upon radio's opportunities. The new medium could counteract the evils of the voter's indifference and reach the citizen and his family within the confines of his home. The real problem for the broadcasters was not to obtain the cooperation of political bodies, but rather to keep political activities from pre-empting a large share of program time that the radio audience desired. Great care has been exercised in political presentations from the earliest times. Absolute impartiality must be shown, as the radio fan has taken much interest in politics and will be the first to notice and to decry any leaning toward one party or another. Equal opportunity was offered last year to the major political parties for the broadcasting of their national conventions, with results that are known to every radio fan in the country.

Sporting Events Popular.

With the fondness of the American public for sporting events, it was not long before WEAF made experiments along these lines. The first great effort was on the occasion of the famous Princeton-Chicago football game, played in Stagg Field, Chicago, in the Fall of 1922, and relayed by specially engineered telephone circuits through WEAF to the metropolitan audience.

Now the radio audience follows every important sporting event, whether on the Atlantic or the sun-kissed fields of the Western coast, be it football, baseball, horse racing, boxing, airplaning or races by college crews or power boats.

While the many letters of the radio audience were being carefully analyzed to study program tendencies, and while the station managers were conducting independent experiments regarding program values, business organizations were not slow to step into the picture and to bring a valuable contribution to the art's development.

Advertising by Radio.

This will throw light on the third and fourth questions mentioned in the early part of this discussion. Business organizations realized what radio broadcasting meant to them. They used it to obtain "good-will publicity." It was not necessary for them to spend huge sums of money for the installation and operation of broadcasting stations, with the serious economic and engineering problems which would have resulted as indicated above. The facilities of WEAF were placed at their disposal and they quickly took advantage of the opportunity. Few fans realize to what extent these advertisers' programs have influenced the tendencies of radio programs. Professional artists were engaged. Prominent groups under trained leaders were formed. This meant better entertainment for the radio listener. Longer programs were presented which had continuity and which could be depended upon to provide the type of entertainment and the same professional artists at regular intervals, so that the radio audience would expect them and look forward to them. Programs were presented of a type that previously would have been considered impossible by radio—impossible in the sense that they assumed too high a degree of musical and general culture on the part of the radio audience. Gloomy prognostications of the failure of such programs were doomed to disappointment. The public accepted them at their real value and enthusiastically availed itself of their educational opportunities.

September 13, 1925

DOES ADVERTISING OVER THE AIR PAY?

Some Claim Good-Will Publicity in Form of Music Gains Friends for Firms Providing the Concerts

By E. H. JEWETT.

WHEN broadcasting stations first began to open their facilities to business organizations, willing to pay for the privilege of attaching their names to a portion of broadcast program, it was a matter to whisper about. It was too new to be welcome. Most practices in their early stages are the victims of prejudgment, and that judgment is usually an adverse one. Even today, when advertising over the radio is reasonably common, though far from universal, it is a subject of much agitation, though the adverse stamp upon it is not nearly so heavy as it was a year ago. This is principally due to the fact that the subject has been brought out into the open; it is no longer restricted to the whispering gallery.

About a year ago radio writers were excitedly discussing the question of who was going to pay for radio broadcasting. What a commotion that caused!

Advertising Solves Problem.

In my opinion the public should not be made to pay. I doubt very much if it would be desirable to have them pay, any more than they are now called upon to pay the cost of the newspapers and magazines they read. Advertising carries the load there, and it is my belief that advertising should carry the load in making up the expenses of broadcasting.

A considerable school of opinion has grown up. The subject has been in the open quite a while and it is still carried on agitatedly, but the trend of opinion seems to be growing toward the viewpoint that advertising must support broadcasting. When I first expressed my thought on the subject of financing broadcasting a year ago I spoke more or less in theory. Since then our company has built and opened a broadcasting station, WJR, and I have some experience to go on. I have learned that there is nothing which can supplant quality. A broadcaster seeks an audience, just as a newspaper seeks circulation. To get it you have to supply something extra good. And that something must be paid for. And the logical way to pay for it is by advertising, just as publications pay the major part of their way with advertising space they sell. They sell space, we sell time, but it comes down to the same thing.

There is no doubt that a good part of the public has had the distasteful experience of listening to extremely offensive direct advertising over the radio; so-called bargain news, solicitation for health examinations, all sorts of quackery.

Must Censor Advertising.

The protection against that sort of thing is the good sense of the public. No concern which permits such material to go forth from its station can hope to hold its audience. A good station censors its program as earnestly as a good newspaper edits its news and censors its advertising. There is no reason and no place for direct advertising at any time. The only sort of advertising over the radio that can be interesting to the public, worth while to the station and helpful to the advertiser who pays the bill, is "good-will" advertising. That portion of the program which the advertiser pays for must be on a par with that furnished by the station itself. The value to the advertiser rests in the fact that his name is identified with the program. Only that and nothing more. It is interesting to the public because it labels the entertainment. It is valuable to the station because it helps defray its expenses. It is valuable to the advertiser because it carries his name to millions. There must be this triple mutuality or it is valueless.

I venture to say folks all over the country will tune in to hear what is going to be the most interesting negro minstrelsy in the world. The entire advertising is in the label, just the name of the company or product. And that's the only kind of advertising by radio that is good, but it is, in my opinion, splendid for all concerned.

Broadcasting Is a Business.

It is all very well to look upon radio as an art and a science, the terms usually used in identifying it. But today it is more than these—it is primarily a business. Its whole organization is one of business and its growth is dependent upon this organization. You must have the sinews of nourishment to develop an art or a science, and in these days nourishment means money. Expansion, improvement, all development is dependent upon capital.

Critics of the radio art ofttimes forget this vulgar necessity, and I believe that most opposition to the use of advertising in radio broadcast is due to nonunderstanding. If the opponents will try to understand the simple truth that there is nothing to be had for nothing, the opposition will quickly cease. Because no one wants a direct public tax and every one wants the best there is. The only way to reconcile these faraway poles is to bring in advertising. Then the public can have the value it craves; the station can pay its way and the advertiser can have the publicity over the air. Everybody will be happy and there will be real progress.

Within a short time I believe broadcast stations will begin to specialize in their appeals. Up to now nearly all of them, particularly the bigger ones, have aimed at general programs. I expect them to gradually divide into types. Some will specialize on fine music, some on popular music. Some will devote themselves entirely to science, some to travel, some to agriculture, and so on.

This development will take time; it can only come gradually. But I do believe that as time goes on each station will take on a character; it will be known for its excellence in some particular regard. That is a logical development to expect and one that, in my opinion, will be very welcome to the radio public.

The strain put upon program directors today is too great. Broadcasting will have to be specialized in order to permit men to equip themselves properly for this all-important task of being a program director.

In the early days of radio the quality of material broadcast did not so much matter. For one thing its novelty excused anything it may have lacked, and, besides, reception apparatus was so inferior that one could not hear many stations anyway.

Today, however, receiving sets are so good, loud-speakers are so good, high power is so frequently employed in broadcasting that we have become just like a family. And you have to be careful to see that the family is treated right.

September 13, 1925

Audience Enables Chaliapin To Broadcast With Fervor

By Wireless to THE NEW YORK TIMES.

LONDON, Nov. 6.—Chaliapin, the Russian singer, was so daunted by the prospect of singing into a microphone instead of to a sympathetic audience that the British broadcasting station from which his powerful voice was broadcast last night provided a specially selected audience of fifty enthusiastic admirers.

Listeners-in were surprised to hear loud applause following each song and it was later explained the experiment was a great success and probably will be adopted for other notable stars. According to the experts, the audience in the broadcasting room aroused Chaliapin to dramatic fervor impossible without appreciative listeners and overcame nervousness due to singing into a mechanical appliance.

November 7, 1925

RADIO INDUSTRY CHEERED BY IMPROVEMENT IN BUSINESS

BRIGHT SPOTS AHEAD

Radio Men, Enjoying 'Small Boom,' See Reasons for It Spreading in 1936

By ORRIN E. DUNLAP Jr.

RADIO industrialists are happier than they have been since the days before their business hit rock bottom in March, 1931. At present they are enjoying what is described as "a small boom," which has all the earmarks of spreading over into 1936 as a real boom. There are no labor troubles, no strikes, no overproduction. Wage scales are in general reported to be higher than in the Blue Eagle days. Capital and labor are both benefiting from the gains.

Having swung into the final quarter of 1935, plans for 1936 are beginning to take shape. The outlook is bright. There are several reasons for optimism.

A Presidential campaign always gives impetus to the radio business. On top of that, the radio men are inclined to believe Jim Braddock and Joe Louis will confront each other under the glare of a roped arena. A championship fight always spurs the radio business; it has never failed since the memorable "battle of a century" between Jack Dempsey and Georges Carpentier at Boyle's Thirty Acres, July 2, 1921. That was the first fight broadcast. It gave the radio industry a grand push when it needed some such event to start it on the way.

Factories Are Busy.

"Right now factories are busiest since 1930," said Bond Geddes, executive vice president of the Radio Manufacturers Association. "The public is buying. There are now 50,000 factory employes, compared with a normal 40,000. Sales are 20 per cent ahead of last year and it seems safe to believe that the total number of sets sold in 1935 will cross the five-million mark.

"There are several factors responsible for the revival. Perfection of short-wave reception has done much to encourage the public to buy new all-wave outfits. Obsolete sets are another powerful factor spurring recovery. Their solid front that so long resisted the modern urge is crumbling. Increased purchasing power, especially on the farms in the South and among labor associated with building and construction, is doing much to boost radio set sales.

"The public today wants better radios, up-to-date instruments," said Mr. Geddes. "There is no better proof than in the fact that 60 per cent of the sales are console cabinets, whereas a few years ago the inexpensive midget captured 60 per cent of the business. The small sets are now generally classed as secondary or supplementary machines. However, they represent lucrative business. Young people going back to school and college usually take a radio with them and that market alone has helped the sale of the small, more portable sets. The midgets now net about 40 per cent of the business."

Auto Radio Is Booming.

Automobile sets made their appearance about five years ago. Many in the industry were skeptical that radio could "pave the highways with melody," but it has [illegible]nd, according to the statistics of [t]he Radio Manufacturers Association, it is believed 1,250,000 automotive radios will be sold in 1935. This compares with about 700,000 auto radios in 1934.

Radio and the automobile are now so definitely linked that even the most sanguine predictions have been surpassed. The idea of listening while driving has "caught," and five years of use is said to have proved that broadcasts picked up on the roads are no hazards to traffic, according to the Radio Manufacturers Association.

* * *

Building 9,000 Radios a Day.

From the factory of the Philco Radio and Television Corporation at Philadelphia come reports that the plant was never so busy; 9,000 radios are being run off the long assembly lines daily.

What is the best year you have had in radio? L. E. Gubb, president of Philco was asked.

"Nineteen thirty-five," he smilingly replied, "but we have little to complain about 1934."

"We are very optimistic," he continued. "Sales are a lot ahead of a year ago. Every single office is enjoying a boost in business. The Middle West is showing the biggest increase. The South is second. The East is normal. The all-wave sets are what turned the tide for the radio industry, sending it climbing out of the depression toward recovery. Then, too, the unit sales price has jumped materially over last year.

"Tonal quality is the first factor a purchaser of a radio looks for today; appearance is second. The way automobiles have taken on radio is a revelation. The younger generation is responsible for this branch of the industry. Youth picked up the auto-radio idea and whirled it to success. The long lines of motor radios bumping along the assembly lines every day offers proof of the activity in this field."

* * *

Phonograph Is Reviving.

IT was not long after the advent of broadcasting that sales of phonographs and records declined. Radio was blamed for "killing" the talking-machine. Today there are indications that radio through the years, by cultivating appreciation of music, and by linking its electrical mechanism with the phonograph, is reviving the music-box business.

Salesmen at the recent National Electrical and Radio Exposition in New York reported that inquiries relative to radio-phonograph machines were numerous. Prospective buyers are said to have mentioned the fact that they were again turning to the phonograph because it offers a concert uninterrupted by commercial announcements such as characterize broadcasting.

Sale of Records Increases.

Record sales are reported by RCA-Victor to be the best in four years, with classical disks leading in demand. In analyzing the cause of this renewed activity, it is pointed out that the majority of broadcasts are of the popular variety. For example, those who prefer such music as Schubert's Serenade might have to wait several days to hear it on the air, but they could pick up the hit song of a musical comedy or motion picture, possibly five times in an evening. The phonograph, however, can present the desired selection on the spur of the moment. Then, too, broadcasting by popularizing such stars of the disks as Lawrence Tibbett, John Charles Thomas and numerous others has whetted the public appetite for their recorded music.

The best years of the record business were from 1927 through 1929, and it was not until 1931 that the disk sales felt the business slump with a thud. Therefore, the merchandisers are not inclined to blame radio directly for the backsliding of the phonograph. They believe scarcity of money was the crux of the situation, and that record sales declined because they are quite generally classed as a luxury.

Now, however, with money more plentiful, the public more music conscious and the tonal quality of records far superior to those of the boom days, the phonograph is staging a comeback. Record sales so far this year are 60 per cent ahead of 1934 and sales that year were 51 per cent higher than 1933.

The October RCA-Victor schedule calls for shipment of more combination instruments than in all of 1934. Interest is highest in the larger cities, with New York leading. In September more disks were sold than in any single month during the past four years. December featuring Christmas sales is usually the top month in record sales. Merchandisers expect that the final month of 1935 will find the disk business at a peak.

There is one new radio-phonograph instrument designed to play for an hour and a half, automatically changing the disks. Assembled for use with this 22-tube machine is a record library, and it is reported that despite the comparatively high cost of the combination more than a thousand unsolicited orders are on the books.

Farmers Are Buying.

Farmers are buying radios. The majority of manufacturers report increased activity in this market. Turn-ins on new sets reveal many of the rural residents have not acquired new radios for ten years. It is believed that thousands during the depression never charged the batteries once they ran down. But now with windmill devices for automatic recharging, new low consumption tubes and improved batteries, the rural sections are casting aside the obsolete apparatus. Increased purchasing power is the real cause of revival. There are trade estimates that the farm market this year will absorb at least 700,000 new radio sets.

October 6, 1935

A TRIPLE ALLIANCE

Helen Hayes Finds Her Busy Life Divided Among Home, Theatre and Radio

HELEN HAYES, now appearing in her first regular radio series, admits that she has almost completely overcome her early inherent fear of the microphone and now looks upon broadcasting as stimulating, ever-changing and always refreshingly new. She likes radio's bustling pace, its endless variety of new situations that constantly keeps the player on the alert, offering with its swiftly changing scenery a sure tonic from boredom.

Miss Hayes is inclined to believe adaptations of stage plays cannot be done full justice on the radio, and maintains that dramatic material should be written expressly for the microphone.

"Radio of its very essence has certain limitations and the time element is perhaps the greatest of all," said Miss Hayes in explaining her viewpoint. "In order to present a full-length play on the air it must be crowded into a half hour or an hour at best, and in the pruning process the original is mercilessly butchered. I am convinced that a play should be written to meet the requirements of the microphone, just as a drama is written to answer the particular demands of the theatre.

"The serial offers the players a chance to 'get under the skin' of the characters, for unlike the changeless theatrical performance, the radio actors are encountering novel experiences and solving new problems under varying conditions from week to week."

A Matter of Geography.

Miss Hayes explained that her recent retirement from the screen was not due to any aversion on her part to motion pictures or to Hollywood, but was actuated by purely geographical reasons. The actress is very devoted to her family, and, with her home in Nyack, picture-making in Hollywood separated her for months at a time from her husband and little daughter.

"Yes, the theatre comes first with me," Miss Hayes continued, "and the theatre as it is now is largely confined to Broadway. Broadway is within easy commuting distance of Nyack and it is possible to fit radio into the scheme without either the theatre or my family being neglected.

"And so you see," Miss Hayes concluded with one of her sunniest smiles, "at last I have discovered the ideal triple alliance—home, radio and the theatre."

An Outstanding Event.

WHEN at the end of the year radio's outstanding events of 1935 pass in review, Helen Hayes as "Penelope" will be one in the front line. In the serial "The New Penny," the première of which was celebrated on the air last Tuesday night at 9:30 o'clock over WJZ, Miss Hayes revealed over eighteen stations extending as far west as Council Bluffs, Iowa, that radio drama is a fine art. This show dispels all doubt, if any exists, that drama can be wrapped in sound, electrified, flashed through space as an unseen wave and then be turned back into electricity and sound again as a living performance.

Every word registers with naturalness and sincerity. Hers a typical American voice, with no accents, inflection or touch of dialect that might disturb some sectional part of the vast audience. So perfect is her art at the microphone, so simple and natural her technique, that the scene of the drama is easily envisioned in the imagination of the listener. That is the proof of success in radio acting.

And a word must be said of "The New Penny" itself. With Edith Meiser as the playwright, the broadcasters have another artist. Miss Meiser has succeeded in writing a play that magnificently fits the voice of the character. She, too, has done much to make the play pulse with realism; what Miss Meiser has done with the pencil, in the quiet of her study, Miss Hayes has faithfully portrayed by the mere sound of her voice in the silence of the studio.

October 6, 1935

NOW THE AUDIENCE JOINS THE BROADCAST

Giggles and Applause Ride Air Channels To Those Who Sit At Receivers

By ORRIN E. DUNLAP Jr.

LAUGHS, giggles, coughs and sneezes are no longer unpardonable sins in the radio studio. Applause and realism are the order of the day. There was a time, not so many years ago, when "Silence" signs were posted throughout the sanctum of the microphone. Visitors tiptoed and so did announcers. There was something uncanny about the atmosphere. It seemed as if something terrible was about to happen. Everybody was afraid to breathe naturally lest the electrical devices amplify the inhalation to the whirl and whistle of a gale. Studio guests were warned not to applaud, no matter how much they enjoyed the show. Laughter had to be suppressed. A cough or sneeze had to be smothered. It would sound too much like thunder outside the studio and in the studio it would bother the performers.

In this early age of broadcasting it was a high privilege for a guest to enter the door of a radio studio and be permitted to sit in awe and silence while some one went on the air. Joints in the musicians' chairs and music racks were oiled daily to avert a squeak at the wrong time. Floors were heavily carpeted. Door sills were padded and the edges cushioned. The hinges were lubricated.

If a person, whether he be a guest or an ethereal star, entered the sacred court of the microphone wearing new patent-leather shoes that creaked, eyes of studio attendants sought him and quickly warned him not to exercise the footwear during the program. Once a veteran orator, but a novice in broadcasting, laid his watch on the table alongside the microphone and the ticks went on the air as a tattoo accompaniment for his words. For a long time after that announcers suggested that all timepieces be kept in pockets, so that fleeting seconds would not sound on the air like some rhythmic hammer.

Whispers were taboo. The announcer held up printed signs or wrote notes to instruct the artist to move closer to the microphone or to speak louder. There must be no background noise as the hands of the clock reached the hour when the studio was "alive." Studios were built without windows, to prevent street noises from acquiring radio wings. The theory seemed to be that the microphone was a sensitive but mute device, and therefore the atmosphere should be one of solitude except for talent. The desire for silence added to the mystery of broadcasting. It frightened many an entertainer.

* * *

MUSICIANS in general, however, found this realm of stillness ideal, in fact, just the right sort of background upon which to etch their artistry. And when they emerged with a sigh of relief from the silent dens of broadcasting they were praised for highly successful performances. The telephone outside the studio would invariably ring and a friendly voice would say, "We heard you clearly." The artist smiled. That was radio applause. It offset the dreadful quietude that veiled the handclaps all performers cherish. As time went on, violinists, pianists and songsters began to acquire reputations as radio entertainers.

So the comedian thought he would try his hand at the new art, and the politician followed suit. But the jester was embarrassed in the atmosphere of silence. He said he felt silly telling jokes to himself in a padded room. The humor fell flat. And comedians noted for their triumphs at the footlights were labeled dismal failures on the air.

Politicians found something was "dead wrong" when they talked in an acoustically perfect room. They did not seem to get their words across. Perhaps radio was no medium for a spellbinder. Possibly he should stick to the open-air rallies, where red fire glared and the crowds yelled.

One day a man wearing a brown derby approached the microphone to speak on politics.

"Where's the audience?" he asked.

"It's invisible," replied the studio attendant.

"Well, let's invite those people in from out in the corridor."

Thus Alfred E. Smith, with his flair for realism, changed the fashion. Soon an excited page boy was spreading the word.

"Do you want to hear the Governor broadcast?" he asked, and studio visitors who had come to the magic radio headquarters in hope of "seeing" a program or of catching a glimpse of some favorite entertainer flocked into the studio without a second invitation. Chairs were quickly arranged and Dr. Cadman's radio pulpit was wheeled to the centre of the floor. A large leather chair was brought in from the executive office for the Governor. But the lordly announcer occupied it, while Mr. Smith sat on a camp chair in the first row among the public until it was time to go on the air.

Radio officials were startled. All of their long-established rules were being violated. Suppose some one laughed at a humorous remark by the Governor? Some one did laugh, the entire audience applauded. The radio people wondered what was going on in the studio. They ran to the glass window and looked down on the strange scene. There they caught a view of humanized radio. Yes, radio was an avenue for politics, but it could not be successful if subdued by silence. Mr. Smith called the new brand of broadcasting rad-dio.

Comedians took heart. Possibly the Smith formula would work for them. It was so successful in small studios that the broadcasters rented theatre studios and called in a crowd.

* * *

EDDIE CANTOR in his first few broadcasts with Rubinoff's orchestra summoned a mob to applaud and laugh. But the broadcast lacked something. Cantor, the showman, said he knew what was wrong. The production man had placed him with his back to the audience, thinking it more important that the comedian see the orchestra. The next week Cantor turned his back on the orchestra and the program response, both in and out of the studio, took a big jump. He could see the audience, and take the cues that a comedian needs to hit the target of laughter.

Then along came Ed Wynn—always bashful when the microphone was mentioned.

"Well, if I go on the air I've got to have an audience," said Wynn. "If I am to get 'raspberries' I want them immediately, and not three weeks later in the mail from Sioux City."

So-oo-oo Ed Wynn is kept as close to his theatrical surroundings as possible. His radio show is staged atop the New Amsterdam Theatre, where 650 people gather on Tuesday nights. Before the performance begins the announcer makes a curtain speech inviting the guests to be natural. If they want to laugh and applaud, the noise is welcome. There is no need to choke a cough. That's all part of the show. It humanizes broadcasting. And so Wynn struck immediate success on the air because he had dodged the lucrative microphone offers until other comedians had risked their reputations by experimenting in tomb-like studios.

* * *

THE radio impresarios realized that they were confronted with two types of performers—actors from the footlights, who thrive on a visible audience, and dyed-in-the-wool radio artists, brought up and trained to act in silence. The latter dread a visible audience and are as nervous when people watch them broadcast as veterans of the stage are when confronted with a lone microphone and no one to applaud.

Amos 'n' Andy, for example, never allow any one to watch them broadcast. They say they must be alone. They fear an audience would make them unnatural. They would be embarrassed, because in imitating the various characters in their sketch they jump around and bounce up and down on their chairs. Such antics would cause laughter when not desired. Amos says he often finds it difficult not to laugh at Andy, and sometimes Andy turns his head when Amos bobs up and down on the chair to put a quiver in his voice when Brother Crawford speaks.

The Goldbergs, Sherlock Holmes and a number of other popular sketches have adhered strictly to the Amos 'n' Andy theory that they can do superior radio acting if left alone.

There are some broadcasters who argue that a studio audience is dangerous. Applause interrupts the show. The actor is likely to play for the laughs and forget the invisible audience, which should receive the most attention because it is larger. A radio director once remarked: "Actors are like little boys, they begin to show off before company." Letters from the listeners prove these ideas to be correct in many cases.

Studio applause creates a unique psychology. The joke goes over in the studio by the aid of a gesture. It falls flat on the air because the gesture was hidden and sound alone was insufficient. The radio audience begins to think the broadcaster is trying to make them out to be foolish or dumb. They may tune away to another wave that is more considerate of the invisible than the visible assemblage.

The laughter and applause, which pleases the performer, are caused to a great extent by his antics as he cavorts around the microphone. For example, Ed Wynn changes his regalia several times during the broadcast. The funny hats and coats always draw a laugh. The radio audience wonders what is so funny. They hear nothing to cause the uproar.

The performer not only revels in the applause, because it makes him feel he is "going over," but it may have a favorable psychological effect on listeners. Even those

Courtesy National Broadcasting Company.

With the Audience—The Comedian Needs Laughter and Applause.

who rate him a failure will begin to think perhaps he is right and they are wrong when the tremendous applause echoes across the housetops and over the orchards by radio.

* * *

THE studio audience is divided into two classes. One group attends the New York Philharmonic or the Philadelphia Orchestra concerts in a public auditorium and pays the price of admission while the other enters the radio turnstiles free of charge. One group is comprised of music lovers. The other is curious to see the radio "wheels go round" and to catch a glimpse of some hero of the air who has entertained them more or less as a phantom creature. And oddly enough after the character is unveiled and the imaginative picture of the broadcasting scene is destroyed by sight, the joy in listening at home may not be as pleasant.

The radio ticket demand from out of town is astounding. Those planning a trip to Manhattan Island often arrange in advance for tickets to a broadcast so they can see what they have been hearing for months at home. Twenty-five per cent of the audience at the Cantor and Vallee programs are frequently people from Pittsburgh, Detroit, Boston, Albany and other cities, with Philadelphians high on the list.

How are the tickets obtained? The listeners write to the station, to the program sponsor and to the performer. Often they are referred to their local gasoline station, bakery, grocery or delicatessen store. They serve as the radio box office.

Commuters enjoy the broadcasts for they are a short show of fifteen minutes, a half-hour or an hour. They know exactly when the performance will end so there is no worry about missing a train.

Mr. Wynn, however, has fooled the commuters in his audience. After the broadcast he makes a curtain speech. The commuter who planned on a train misses it to hear Wynn tell what he thinks about radio and its relation to the theatre. But that helps business at the ice-cream parlors, coffee counters and magazine stands where the suburbanite lingers until the next train.

Impatient, nervous souls prefer to watch a fifteen-minute or a half-hour program to a three-hour stage show or orchestral concert that holds them in an auditorium seat for two or three hours. But the invisible audience makes one complaint in regard to a Carnegie Hall concert, the Metropolitan Opera and the Academy of Music performance—coughs ruin the music. A cough is like a splash of static amid a soft passage of music. The broadcasters have received many a letter suggesting that throat lozenges be distributed to the audience to foil coughing at musicales. At a comedy broadcast the cough is not a problem. It can be buried in the laughter and applause.

Radio's visible audience is as cosmopolitan as are the unseen multitudes. In one corner of the studio may be a small family group, obviously from the country, in New York to see the sights. And next to them is a wealthy program sponsor who brings his dinner guests, resplendent in evening dress, to witness the performance.

The type of audience also varies with the program. Seth Parker, with his homely Down East philosophy, attracts chiefly elderly persons with deep religious interests. The débutantes flock to see Lanny Ross. Women of all types and ages battle for the privilege of seeing Rudy Vallee. He usually leaves by a back exit and disappoints scores of curious radio fans.

* * *

THE comedians Jack Pearl, Ed Wynn and Eddie Cantor draw the most universal audience. Every one apparently enjoys a good laugh. Those who attend the performance of Sigmund Spaeth, the Tune Detective, linger longer after the broadcast to ask questions and offer suggestions for his tune sleuthing.

Most visitors are disappointed in one particular point. They come to the studios with the preconceived notion that all the air celebrities are on a continuous parade and can be seen at all times around the corridors. Radio folk are quick to disappear, however, when the "curtain" drops.

All this humanizing of radio has given the broadcasters a new problem. The demand for tickets runs high. Seats are limited. So when the Eddie Cantor program gets a demand for 18,000 seats for one Sunday night's performance, and there are only 650 seats, the broadcasters must call upon higher mathematics and some diplomacy. Dispensing these radio tickets is no easy job.

It is free entertainment, and during a depression attendance at a broadcast featuring a line of Broadway stars such as Jack Pearl, Ed Wynn, Eddie Cantor, Fanny Brice and Rudy Vallee with his augmented cast is a popular pastime. The elevators that go up to the New Amsterdam roof take at least 4,000 persons up to the microphone to see six shows broadcast weekly. At times the crowds seeking entrance have necessitated a police call to clear the lobby.

HIGHWAY THEATRES

Auto Radios Add to Pleasure of Travel As Cars Pluck Shows From the Road

By ORRIN E. DUNLAP Jr.

MORE than 5,000,000 automobiles in the United States are reported to be radio equipped, and if a radio man goes on vacation in any one of them he is on a postman's holiday. He finds it difficult to get away from the programs and invisible people despite the off-switch science provides. It is too convenient to turn the knob when curiosity and an interest in the art of broadcasting lure the fingers to snap on the switch.

Instantly he discovers, although miles from the studios on Manhattan Island, that the same voices, songs and stories are following him. Always he is on the radio sea, with the unseen waves washing down the highways. Click the on-switch and there are the same sort of sounds that slide down the antenna into the home throughout the year. The chimes that ring off the hours are just as clear in the motor car on Triborough Bridge or rushing along the beautifully landscaped Merritt Parkway that speeds the New Yorker into New England.

As the New York broadcasters begin to fade or weaken, other stations quickly take their spots on the dial, so the show is unending and the motorist is seldom if ever out of touch with the entertainers he is leaving behind at the "mike."

* * *

BRIDGEPORT, New Haven, Hartford and Springfield stations take up the song as the waves from New York drop back while the car wheels northward on the College Highway. Springfield and Boston seem to be the "aces" for reception in the vicinity of Greenfield as the climb up the Mohawk Trail begins, offering a view into four States. But it is not long before the stentorian waves from WGY at Schenectady spread up across the Berkshires, and that station clings strongly on the dial as the car passes through Williamstown, Albany and westward across New York State on the Cherry Valley Turnpike. There are more than drums along the Mohawk these days.

It is along the rolling roadways up-State that Syracuse and Rochester send their acts across the green hills to add dependability to reception and variety to the ethereal show. Beyond Auburn, as Syracuse drops behind on the map, Buffalo broadcasts gain in strength and they hold the stage as the automobile approaches the Niagara frontier, at which point Canadian stations in Hamilton, St. Catharine's and Toronto flash across the border. They fill places on the dial left silent by the eastern seaboard stations which had their "sunsets" as the car left them beyond the horizon.

* * *

AS SOON as the automobilist travels out of range of his favorite local stations, the dial locations of which he has memorized, he finds himself groping around the tuner for the new ones of loudest caliber. It would seem that the broadcasters here, there and everywhere are missing an opportunity to win new listeners by not placing signs along the posts, rail fences or trees that might read something like this: "You are now within radio range of Schenectady. Tune in WGY, 790 kilocycles." Such informative and inviting signposts would put an end to the motorist's "blind" tuning.

Radio has made the automobile a theatre on wheels. It adds a new life to the car. Those who travel long distances alone say that broadcasts break the monotony and put an end to loneliness. They contend that radio helps to erase the danger of a lone driver dozing at the wheel after a long trip. The disembodied voices become traveling companions. The old idea that radio in an automobile was dangerous because it might lull the driver to sleep or disconcert him has long since passed. Furthermore, experience has proved that the loudspeaker, if properly operated, does not blanket the warning horns of other cars or that tuning is so complicated that it takes the operator's eyes off the road as he hunts for stations on the dial. Modern radios with push-button or "touch" automatic tuners are an added safety factor.

It was not so many years ago that many believed radio was not for the automobile because it required too much of an antenna and that noises from the ignition system would sprinkle the broadcasts with "static." Easy riding cars with improved radio circuits, sensitive tubes and amplifiers now ignore vibrations and sudden bumps. Reception is as clear as in the home, no matter the speed or roughness of the road. Antennas under the running boards scoop the programs off the concrete or macadam, while other willowy metal rods give the car an ethereal feeler that reminds one of the old buggy whips.

* * *

IT has always been recognized that broadcasts, to be popular and appealing to a multitude, must fit the surroundings and mood of the moment. A symphony may appeal one evening and a jazz band the next. And so the motorist finds the harmony of the Ink Spots Quartet or Barry McKinley's tenor cords highly entertaining when camped for the night high in the Catskills as the August moon comes over the mountain.

Radio in the automobile leads performers on to odd and picturesque stages with background so varied that they could never hope to visualize every individual setting for reception of their broadcast. Skirting the Niagara whirlpool, Margaret Speak's song is heard running along the crest of the gorge, while a few minutes later the voices of Orson Welles and the Mercury Theatre players are picked up on Goat Island amid the road of the Horseshoe and American falls, upon which powerful fingers of colored lights play across the amphitheatre from Canada. It is a bizarre setting for "Hamlet" or John Drinkwater's "Abraham Lincoln"; nevertheless, radio spreads the drama and voices of the actors across just such footlights never thought of or arranged by the showmen, who for weeks planned and rehearsed the show to fit exactly an hour.

* * *

THE motorist who enjoys band music will find the Canadian broadcasters very accommodating. They are heard playing the anthem of the United States marines, bugle calls of the regiments and Sousa's "Stars and Stripes Forever," with the friendly announcer in the Dominion adding "long may it wave" as he tells that the selection is being presented for American friends of the station who requested it.

While the traffic moves in long lines to and fro across the bridge at Niagara the motorists, awaiting inspection by the customs and immigration men, may tune in broadcasts from either Canada or the United States. The programs leap the border and follow the automobile in friendly fashion. Scattered along the dial are the programs of both nations. That so many stations in two countries close together can operate in harmony, exchanging programs and without the slightest interference, adds to the evidence of friendship that prevails between Uncle Sam and his good neighbors across the unfortified frontier.

* * *

WHEN the motorist reaches home at the end of vacation he has a bulletin-like inkling of what has taken place in the world; back home he finds the same faithful day-to-day or week-to-week entertainers still on the job and he marvels at the ease with which they followed him wherever he went.

He recalls, however, one odd effect of radio in the car. He might have been driving along at a fifty-mile clip, but after the radio was turned on the speedometer dropped to thirty miles. The pace seemed to be governed unconsciously by the beat of the music. If the station was changed and the tempo of the music increased, then the speed of the car picked up. "Smoke Gets in Your Eyes" is the sort of melody that fast drivers might safely tune in, but they should stay away from spirited martial airs and fast-tempo jazz, which seem to enliven the foot on the accelerator.

August 21, 1938

Radio Listeners in Panic, Taking War Drama as Fact

Many Flee Homes to Escape 'Gas Raid From Mars'—Phone Calls Swamp Police at Broadcast of Wells Fantasy

A wave of mass hysteria seized thousands of radio listeners throughout the nation between 8:15 and 9:30 o'clock last night when a broadcast of a dramatization of H. G. Wells's fantasy, "The War of the Worlds," led thousands to believe that an interplanetary conflict had started with invading Martians spreading wide death and destruction in New Jersey and New York.

The broadcast, which disrupted households, interrupted religious services, created traffic jams and clogged communications systems, was made by Orson Welles, who as the radio character, "The Shadow," used to give "the creeps" to countless child listeners. This time at least a score of adults required medical treatment for shock and hysteria.

In Newark, in a single block at

Heddon Terrace and Hawthorne Avenue, more than twenty families rushed out of their houses with wet handkerchiefs and towels over their faces to flee from what they believed was to be a gas raid. Some began moving household furniture.

Throughout New York families left their homes, some to flee to near-by parks. Thousands of persons called the police, newspapers and radio stations here and in other cities of the United States and Canada seeking advice on protective measures against the raids.

The program was produced by Mr. Welles and the Mercury Theatre on the Air over station WABC and the Columbia Broadcasting System's coast-to-coast network, from 8 to 9 o'clock.

The radio play, as presented, was to simulate a regular radio program with a "break-in" for the material of the play. The radio listeners, apparently, missed or did not listen to the introduction, which was: "The Columbia Broadcasting System and its affiliated stations present Orson Welles and the Mercury Theatre on the Air in 'The War of the Worlds' by H. G. Wells."

They also failed to associate the program with the newspaper listing of the program, announced as "Today: 8:00-9:00—Play: H. G. Wells's 'War of the Worlds'—WABC." They ignored three additional announcements made during the broadcast emphasizing its fictional nature

Mr. Welles opened the program with a description of the series of which it is a part. The simulated program began. A weather report was given, prosaically. An announcer remarked that the program would be continued from a hotel, with dance music. For a few moments a dance program was given in the usual manner. Then there was a "break-in" with a "flash" about a professor at an observatory noting a series of gas explosions on the planet Mars.

News bulletins and scene broadcasts followed, reporting, with the technique in which the radio had reported actual events, the landing of a "meteor" near Princeton, N. J., "killing" 1,500 persons, the discovery that the "meteor" was a "metal cylinder" containing strange creatures from Mars armed with "death rays" to open hostilities against the inhabitants of the earth.

Despite the fantastic nature of the reported "occurrences," the program, coming after the recent war scare in Europe and a period in which the radio frequently had interrupted regularly scheduled programs to report developments in the Czechoslovak situation, caused fright and panic throughout the area of the broadcast.

Telephone lines were tied up with calls from listeners or persons who had heard of the broadcasts. Many sought first to verify the reports. But large numbers, obviously in a state of terror, asked how they could follow the broadcast's advice and flee from the city, whether they would be safer in the "gas raid" in the cellar or on the roof, how they could safeguard their children, and many of the questions which had been worrying residents of London and Paris during the tense days before the Munich agreement.

So many calls came to newspapers and so many newspapers found it advisable to check on the reports despite their fantastic content that The Associated Press sent out the following at 8:48 P. M.:

"Note to Editors: Queries to newspapers from radio listeners throughout the United States tonight, regarding a reported meteor fall which killed a number of New Jerseyites, are the result of a studio dramatization. The A. P."

Similarly police teletype systems carried notices to all stationhouses, and police short-wave radio stations notified police radio cars that the event was imaginary.

Message From the Police

The New York police sent out the following:

"To all receivers: Station WABC informs us that the broadcast just concluded over that station was a dramatization of a play. No cause for alarm."

The New Jersey State Police teletyped the following:

"Note to all receivers—WABC broadcast as drama re this section being attacked by residents of Mars. Imaginary affair."

From one New York theatre a manager reported that a throng of playgoers had rushed from his theatre as a result of the broadcast. He said that the wives of two men in the audience, having heard the broadcast, called the theatre and insisted that their husbands be paged. This spread the "news" to others in the audience.

The switchboard of THE NEW YORK TIMES was overwhelmed by the calls. A total of 875 were received. One man who called from Dayton, Ohio, asked, "What time will it be the end of the world?" A caller from the suburbs said he had had a houseful of guests and all had rushed out to the yard for safety.

Warren Dean, a member of the American Legion living in Manhattan, who telephoned to verify the "reports," expressed indignation which was typical of that of many callers.

"I've heard a lot of radio programs, but I've never heard anything as rotten as that," Mr. Dean said. "It was too realistic for comfort. They broke into a dance program with a news flash. Everybody in my house was agitated by the news. It went on just like press radio news."

At 9 o'clock a woman walked into the West Forty-seventh Street police station dragging two children, all carrying extra clothing. She said she was ready to leave the city. Police persuaded her to stay.

A garbled version of the reports reached the Dixie Bus Terminal, causing officials there to prepare to change their schedule on confirmation of "news" of an accident at Princeton on their New Jersey route. Miss Dorothy Brown at the terminal sought verification, however, when the caller refused to talk with the dispatcher, explaining to her that "the world is coming to an end and I have a lot to do."

Harlem Shaken By the "News"

Harlem was shaken by the "news." Thirty men and women rushed into the West 123d Street police station and twelve into the West 135th Street station saying they had their household goods packed and were all ready to leave Harlem if the police would tell them where to go to be "evacuated." One man insisted he had heard "the President's voice" over the radio advising all citizens to leave the cities.

The parlor churches in the Negro district, congregations of the smaller sects meeting on the ground floors of brownstone houses, took the "news" in stride as less faithful parishioners rushed in with it, seeking spiritual consolation. Evening services became "end of the world" prayer meetings in some.

One man ran into the Wadsworth Avenue Police Station in Washington Heights, white with terror, shouting that enemy planes were crossing the Hudson River and asking what he should do. A man came in to the West 152d Street Station, seeking traffic directions. The broadcast became a rumor that spread through the district and many persons stood on street corners hoping for a sight of the "battle" in the skies.

In Queens the principal question asked of the switchboard operators at Police Headquarters was whether "the wave of poison gas will reach as far as Queens." Many said they were all packed up and ready to leave Queens when told to do so.

Samuel Tishman of 100 Riverside Drive was one of the multitude that fled into the street after hearing part of the program. He declared that hundreds of persons evacuated their homes fearing that the "city was being bombed."

"I came home at 9:15 P. M. just in time to receive a telephone call from my nephew who was frantic with fear. He told me the city was about to be bombed from the air and advised me to get out of the building at once. I turned on the radio and heard the broadcast which corroborated what my nephew had said, grabbed my hat and coat and a few personal belongings and ran to the elevator. When I got to the street there were hundreds of people milling around in panic. Most of us ran toward Broadway and it was not until we stopped taxi drivers who had heard the entire broadcast on their radios that we knew what it was all about. It was the most asinine stunt I ever heard of."

"I heard that broadcast and almost had a heart attack," said Louis Winkler of 1,322 Clay Avenue, the Bronx. "I didn't tune it in until the program was half over, but when I heard the names and titles of Federal, State and municipal officials and when the 'Secretary of the Interior' was introduced, I was convinced that it was the McCoy. I ran out into the street with scores of others, and found people running in all directions. The whole thing came over as a news broadcast and in my mind it was a pretty crummy thing to do."

The Telegraph Bureau switchboard at police headquarters in Manhattan, operated by thirteen men, was so swamped with calls from apprehensive citizens inquiring about the broadcast that police business was seriously interfered with.

Headquarters, unable to reach the radio station by telephone, sent a radio patrol car there to ascertain the reason for the reaction to the program. When the explanation was given, a police message was sent to all precincts in the five boroughs advising the commands of the cause.

"They're Bombing New Jersey!"

Patrolman John Morrison was on duty at the switchboard in the Bronx Police Headquarters when, as he afterward expressed it, all the lines became busy at once. Among the first who answered was a man who informed him:

"They're bombing New Jersey!"

"How do you know?" Patrolman Morrison inquired.

"I heard it on the radio," the voice at the other end of the wire replied. "Then I went to the roof and I could see the smoke from the bombs, drifting over toward New York. What shall I do?"

The patrolman calmed the caller as well as he could, then answered other inquiries from persons who wanted to know whether the reports of a bombardment were true, and if so where they should take refuge.

At Brooklyn police headquarters, eight men assigned to the monitor switchboard estimated that they had answered more than 800 inquiries from persons who had been alarmed by the broadcast. A number of these, the police said, came from motorists who had heard the program over their car radios and were alarmed both for themselves and for persons at their homes. Also, the Brooklyn police reported, a preponderance of the calls seemed to come from women.

The National Broadcasting Company reported that men stationed at the WJZ transmitting station at Bound Brook, N. J., had received dozens of calls from residents of that area. The transmitting station communicated with New York and passed the information that there was no cause for alarm to the persons who inquired later.

Meanwhile the New York telephone operators of the company found their switchboards swamped with incoming demands for information, although the NBC system had no part in the program.

Record Westchester Calls

The State, county, parkway and local police in Westchester County were swamped also with calls from terrified residents. Of the local police departments, Mount Vernon, White Plains, Mount Kisco, Yonkers and Tarrytown received most of the inquiries. At first the authorities thought they were being made the victims of a practical joke, but when the calls persisted and increased in volume they began to make inquiries. The New York Telephone Company reported that it had never handled so many calls in one hour in years in Westchester.

One man called the Mount Vernon Police Headquarters to find out "where the forty policemen were killed"; another said his brother was ill in bed listening to the broadcast and when he heard the reports he got into an automobile and "disappeared." "I'm nearly crazy!" the caller exclaimed.

Because some of the inmates took the catastrophic reports seriously as they came over the radio, some of the hospitals and the county penitentiary ordered that the radios be turned off.

Thousands of calls came in to Newark Police Headquarters. These were not only from the terror-stricken. Hundreds of physicians and nurses, believing the reports to be true, called to volunteer their services to aid the "injured." City officials also called in to make "emergency" arrangements for the population. Radio cars were stopped by the panicky throughout that city.

Jersey City police headquarters received similar calls. One woman asked Detective Timothy Grooty, on duty there, "Shall I close my windows?" A man asked, "Have the police any extra gas masks?" Many of the callers, on being assured the reports were fiction, queried again and again, uncertain in whom to believe.

Scores of persons in lower Newark Avenue, Jersey City, left their homes and stood fearfully in the street, looking with apprehension toward the sky. A radio car was dispatched there to reassure them.

The incident at Hedden Terrace and Hawthorne Avenue, in Newark, one of the most dramatic in the area, caused a tie-up in traffic for blocks around. The more than twenty families there apparently believed the "gas attack" had started, and so reported to the police. An ambulance, three radio cars and a police emergency squad of eight men were sent to the scene with full inhalator apparatus.

They found the families with wet cloths on faces contorted with hysteria. The police calmed them, halted those who were attempting to move their furniture on their cars and after a time were able to clear the traffic snarl.

At St. Michael's Hospital, High Street and Central Avenue, in the heart of the Newark industrial district, fifteen men and women were treated for shock and hysteria. In some cases it was necessary to give sedatives, and nurses and physicians sat down and talked with the more seriously affected.

While this was going on, three persons with children under treatment in the institution telephoned that they were taking them out and leaving the city, but their fears were calmed when hospital authorities explained what had happened.

A flickering of electric lights in Bergen County from about 6:15 to 6:30 last evening provided a build-up for the terror that was to ensue when the radio broadcast started.

Without going out entirely, the lights dimmed and brightened alternately and radio reception was also affected. The Public Service Gas and Electric Company was mystified by the behavior of the lights, declaring there was nothing wrong at their power plants or in their distributing system. A spokesman for the service department said a call was made to Newark and the same situation was reported. He believed, he said, that the condition was general throughout the State.

The New Jersey Bell Telephone Company reported that every central office in the State was flooded with calls for more than an hour and the company did not have time to summon emergency operators to relieve the congestion. Hardest hit was the Trenton toll office, which handled calls from all over the East.

One of the radio reports, the statement about the mobilization of 7,000 national guardsmen in New Jersey, caused the armories of the Sussex and Essex troops to be swamped with calls from officers and men seeking information about the mobilization place.

Prayers for Deliverance

In Caldwell, N. J., an excited parishioner ran into the First Baptist Church during evening services and shouted that a meteor had fallen, showering death and destruction, and that North Jersey was threatened. The Rev. Thomas Thomas, the pastor quieted the congregation and all prayed for deliverance from the "catastrophe."

East Orange police headquarters received more than 200 calls from persons who wanted to know what to do to escape the "gas." Unaware of the broadcast, the switchboard operator tried to telephone Newark, but was unable to get the call through because the switchboard at Newark headquarters was tied up. The mystery was not cleared up until a teletype explanation had been received from Trenton.

More than 100 calls were received at Maplewood police headquarters and during the excitement two families of motorists, residents of New York City, arrived at the station to inquire how they were to get back to their homes now that the Pulaski Skyway had been blown up.

The women and children were crying and it took some time for the police to convince them that the catastrophe was fictitious. Many persons who called Maplewood said their neighbors were packing their possessions and preparing to leave for the country.

In Orange, N. J., an unidentified man rushed into the lobby of the Lido Theatre, a neighborhood motion picture house, with the intention of "warning" the audience that a meteor had fallen on Raymond Boulevard, Newark, and was spreading poisonous gases. Skeptical, Al Hochberg, manager of the theatre, prevented the man from entering the auditorium of the theatre and then called the police. He was informed that the radio broadcast was responsible for the man's alarm.

Emanuel Priola, bartender of a tavern at 442 Valley Road, West Orange, closed the place, sending away six customers, in the middle of the broadcast to "rescue" his wife and two children.

"At first I thought it was a lot of Buck Rogers stuff, but when a friend telephoned me that general orders had been issued to evacuate every one from the metropolitan area I put the customers out, closed the place and started to drive home," he said.

William H. Decker of 20 Aubrey Road, Montclair, N. J., denounced the broadcast as "a disgrace" and "an outrage," which he said had frightened hundreds of residents in his community, including children. He said he knew of one woman who ran into the street with her two children and asked for the help of neighbors in saving them.

"We were sitting in the living room casually listening to the radio," he said, "when we heard reports of a meteor falling near New Brunswick and reports that gas was spreading. Then there was an announcement of the Secretary of Interior from Washington who spoke of the happening as a major disaster. It was the worst thing I ever heard over the air."

The Columbia Broadcasting System issued a statement saying that the adaptation of Mr. Wells's novel which was broadcast "followed the original closely, but to make the imaginary details more interesting to American listeners the adapter, Orson Welles, substituted an American locale for the English scenes of the story."

Pointing out that the fictional character of the broadcast had been announced four times and had been previously publicised, it continued:

"Nevertheless, the program apparently was produced with such vividness that some listeners who may have heard only fragments thought the broadcast was fact, not fiction. Hundreds of telephone calls reaching CBS stations, city authorities, newspaper offices and police headquarters in various cities testified to the mistaken belief.

"Naturally, it was neither Columbia's nor the Mercury Theatre's intention to mislead any one, and when it became evident that a part of the audience had been disturbed by the performance five announcements were read over the network later in the evening to reassure those listeners."

Expressing profound regret that his dramatic efforts should cause such consternation, Mr. Welles said: "I don't think we will choose anything like this again." He hesitated about presenting it, he disclosed, because "it was our thought that perhaps people might be bored or annoyed at hearing a tale so improbable."

October 31, 1938

FCC TO SCAN SCRIPT OF 'WAR' BROADCAST

Radio System, Expressing Its Regret at Panic, Will Curb Simulated News Items

The Federal Communications Commission requested yesterday a transcript and electric recording of the radio broadcast Sunday night which dramatized H. G. Wells's 41-year-old novel, "The War of the Worlds," and spread panic among thousands of Americans convinced that fiction in the form of tensely spoken "news" bulletins was stark fact.

Pending receipt of the script from the Columbia Broadcasting System, Frank R. McNinch, chairman of the commission, called the program "regrettable," but was silent as to the course of action the FCC might take. It was made plain that a thorough study of the text would precede any decision.

Many Listeners Incensed

Meanwhile, with large sections of the radio-listening public incensed over what they regarded as a dangerous hoax, the broadcasting system and Orson Welles, the 23-year-old star of the disputed show, joined in issuing statements of regret. The CBS, through W. B. Lewis, vice president in charge of programs, reiterated that announcements of the nature of the presentation had been made "before, after and twice during" the feature, but added:

"In order that this may not happen again the program department hereafter will not use the technique of a simulated news broadcast within a dramatization when the circumstances of the broadcast could cause immediate alarm to numbers of listeners."

Along similar lines was a statement from Neville Miller, president of the National Association of Broadcasters. It was made public in Washington, where interest in the broadcast and the probism it posed was surprisingly great. With a wide variety of conversational controversies arising from the situation, Commissioner T. A. M. Craven, New Jersey member of the body headed by Mr. McNinch, raised the question of censorship.

Mr. Craven agreed the investigation should be held, but asked "utmost caution" to avoid censorship and declared that the public "does not want a spineless radio."

Another development of the day came from H. G. Wells himself, who is in London. His local agent, Jaques Chambrun of 745 Fifth Avenue, hinted at legal trouble for the sponsors of the broadcast if a "retraction" was not forthcoming. Mr. Chambrun said:

"In the name of Mr. H. G. Wells, I granted the Columbia Broadcasting System the right to dramatize Mr. H. G. Wells's novel, 'The War of the Worlds,' for one performance over the radio. It was not explained to me that this dramatization would be made with a liberty that amounts to a complete rewriting of 'The War of the Worlds,' and renders it into an entirely different story.

"Mr. Wells and I consider that by so doing the Columbia Broadcasting System and Mr. Orson Welles have far overstepped their rights in the matter and believe that the Columbia Broadcasting System should make a full retraction. Mr. H. G. Wells personally is deeply concerned that any work of his should be used in a way, and with a totally unwarranted liberty, to cause deep distress and alarm throughout the United States."

When this point was brought up to Mr. Welles he said he had not considered the possibility of action because he had thought that the program constituted a "legitimate dramatization of a published work." Nothing regarding a step in the nature of a retraction was forthcoming from the broadcasting organization and Mr. Welles indicated he would seek legal advice if it became necessary. He expressed his admiration for the Wells "classic" and implied his appreciation for the right to make use of it in any form.

Trouble for Late Listeners

Copies of the script made available here showed clearly how persons who tuned in just after the opening of the program at 8 P. M. might have heard almost half an hour of a story that, except for its references to residents of Mars and the fantastic nature of the events described, was disconcerting to say the least—before there was any assurance that it was all in fun.

Following the preliminary announcements, listeners heard a few moments of dance music originating from a "hotel," and then an interruption in the long-familiar style of announcers rushing on the air with important news. It was at that point, undoubtedly, that fears began to spread.

Dire reports continued to flash across the country as a well-schooled troupe brought the listeners the story of a supposed meteorite crashing near Trenton, N. J., out of which hideous Martians crawled, armed with a lethal "heat-ray" and ultimately a deadly black smoke that brought all human beings to an appalling doom.

For those who tuned in late, the first announcement of the truth was delayed until the "middle break," listed on the thirty-second page of the script. The whole interruption, which comprised a five-line description of the broadcast, and system and station announcements, was scheduled to take twenty seconds. After it, there was no relapse from make-believe until the close.

The New Jersey area got the worst of the scare not only because the adapters had chosen it as the scene of the alleged catastrophe but because geographical names were taken right off the map, with Princeton, Trenton and Grovers Mill, a well-known landmark, specified.

Names of persons and institutions, on the other hand, were garbled. For what was presumably intended to suggest the American Museum of Natural History, the "National History Museum" was named. And the role taken by Mr. Welles—that of "Professor Richard Pierson, famous astronomer," of Princeton—knowingly or otherwise, inevitably brought to the minds of several persons the name of Dr. Newton L. Pierce, assistant in astronomy at that university.

Undergraduates there, incidentally, were prompt to form a "League for Interplanetary Defense," one of whose platform planks was an embargo on all "Martial"—with a capital M—music.

Although a similar levity pervaded the comments of many persons—mainly those who had not heard any of the broadcast—there could be no question that communities whose telephone service was cluttered during the peak of the fear were in no mood for joking. Such a one was Trenton, where City Manager Paul Morton sent to the FCC one of the twelve protests acknowledge later by Mr. McNinch.

Reaction Bewilders Actor

And it was plain that Mr. Welles himself, sleepless and unshaven, was concerned by the turn of events when he appeared at the CBS studios in the afternoon to issue a statement and grant an interview. His statement follows:

"Despite my deep regret over any misapprehension which our broadcast last night created among some listeners, I am even the more bewildered over this misunderstanding in the light of an analysis of the broadcast itself.

"It seems to me that there are four factors which should have in any event maintained the illusion of fiction in the broadcast.

"The first was that the broadcast was performed as if occurring in the future and as if it were then related by a survivor of a past occurrence. The date of the fanciful invasion of this planet by Martians was clearly given as 1939 and was so announced at the outset of the broadcast.

"The second element was the fact that the broadcast took place at our regular weekly Mercury Theatre period and had been so announced in all the papers. For seventeen consecutive weeks we have been broadcasting radio drama. Sixteen of these seventeen broadcasts have been fiction and have been presented as such. Only one in the series was a true story, the broadcast of 'Hell on Ice' by Commander Ellsberg, and was identified as a true story within the framework of radio drama.

"The third element was the fact that at the very outset of the broadcast and twice during its enactment listeners were told that this was a play, that it was an adaptation of an old novel by H. G. Wells. Furthermore, at the conclusion a detailed statement to this effect was made.

"The fourth factor seems to me to have been the most pertinent of all. That is the familiarity of the fable, within the American idiom, of Mars and Martians.

"For many decades 'The Man From Mars' has been almost a synonym for fantasy. In very old morgues of many newspapers there will be found a series of grotesque cartoons that ran daily, which gave this fantasy imaginary form. As a matter of fact, the fantasy as such has been used in radio programs many times. In these broadcasts, conflict between citizens of Mars and other planets has been a familiarly accepted fairy-tale. The same make-believe is familiar to newspaper readers through a comic strip that uses the same device."

Publicity Stunt Denied

Seated before a battery of newsreel cameras, Mr. Welles repeated elements of the statement in a dozen ways, then took time to deny with a weary smile that the whole thing was a "plant" to publicize the Mercury Theatre's new play, "Danton's Death," scheduled to open tomorrow night. A similar denial came subsequently from the firm of Charles Scribner's Sons, when it was pointed out that H. G. Wells's "Apropos of Dolores" had been published yesterday.

Mr. Welles, who did the adaptation himself, said that among the many telegrams he had received regarding the broadcast there were many from listeners saying "how much they liked the show."

November 1, 1938

Jingle—or Jangle

By AL GRAHAM

THE announcer tells you that the following is transcribed. A mixed quartet breaks into a snappy little ditty. You try to catch the words. They sound something like this:

Are you feeling low-low-low?
Get some Wamzi-Pamzico!
Wamzi-Pamzico is swell!
Wamzi-Pamzico rings the bell—
Ding,
Dong,
Dang!

Being a daily listener, you sense what has happened: another singing commercial has been added to the record-breaking crop already on the air.

Is there (you ask yourself) no saturation point? And what will eventually come of all this? Will it turn us into a nation of jinglers? Will we gradually go ditty-mad and start writing rhyme by the iambic (or trochaic) yard? Will America's Byrons — if any — rebel ere this doggerel has had its day?

A minor poet, recently pondering these questions, decided to do a little research. He came up with a number of facts and a poet's quota of fantasy—the jingle's past, present and future. The facts appear to be these:

JINGLE advertising was old stuff even in 1910; Sunny Jim and Phoebe Snow had long been forgotten before the first radio station was ever opened. With the dawn of network broadcasting in the Nineteen Twenties, the jingle came to life again—in the form of a theme song. As such it had a limited use until spot transcriptions came to the fore advertisingly in the middle Thirties.

Among the radio idea men haunting local stations in 1935 were (a) a certain live wire from Chicago answering to the name of Allan Kent and (b) a somewhat quieter, keen-minded British tunesmith who called himself Ginger Johnson. (His full name: Herbert Austen Croom-Johnson.) The pair met at NBC, eventually teamed up to specialize on producing musical commercials, which were slowly becoming more popular with advertisers.

The first Kent-Johnson job was a series of twenty Mother Goose parodies which sold to a bread sponsor for $600. The series was no great shakes. In fact, the boys did only moderately well until the radio world suddenly began to buzz about them late in 1939.

IN the spring of that year Edgar Kobak, then an advertising agency strategist, now executive vice president of the Blue network, encouraged the pair to try their hand at a jingle that would sell a twelve-ounce bottle of cola for a nickel. Johnson thought something could be done with an old English hunting song, "John Peel," which was in the public domain. Kent whipped up some rhymes: "nickel" and "trickle," "spot" and "lot," "too" and "you." Fitting the words to the music was a cinch; the boys claim the jingle was completed in ten minutes. You've heard it, of course:

Nickel, nickel,
too do-dee-da-da-da,

Sponsored ditties fill the air. Some folks like them, some despair.

Nickel, nickel,
too do-dee-da-da-da!
Pepsi-Cola hits the spot,
Twelve full ounces, that's a lot.
Twice as much for a nickel too,
Pepsi-Cola is the drink for you!
Nickel, nickel, nickel, nickel,
Trickle, trickle, trickle, trickle,
Nickel, nickel, nickel, nickel!'

It sold the company on first hearing, caught on quickly with the radio audience, has stayed caught on ever since. To date it has been played more than 1,000,000 times on the air, is still heard daily on some 350 stations.

By early 1940 Kent-Johnson were in demand. Up went their prices; they got $2,500 for an eight-line gasoline jingle, later received $3,000 from the same sponsor for a second ditty. A cigarette advertiser paid them $7,000 to tune up his slogan. They "lease-lent" a soap-powder song to a leading manufacturer for a $20,000 retainer. All told, they have now turned out some 250 strictly commercial jingles, sold more than 100 of them. Some have been fairly successful as sales-builders, but none has had the phenomenal and sustained results of the cola composition.

MEANWHILE, Kent-Johnson's contemporaries also prospered by the boom. Among them the better known are Phil Cook, Irene Beasley and Andy Love—all radio performers as well as jingle producers.

Specialists, however, do only a small part—possibly 15 per cent—of the country's output. Most singing commercials are concocted by advertising copywriters, but Kent insists that a sizable number are the amateur efforts of budding poets related, in some way, to a sponsor. He can produce no evidence to prove

it, but he is sure that many a jingle is the work of somebody's Aunt Tillie who once wrote "poetry" for her high school magazine. As a result, the singing commercial is now in a fair way to strangle itself, according to Kent.

For the past two years the partners (now Kent-Johnson, Inc.) have been the brains and energy behind WJZ's all-night musical show; on this they have jingled time signals, station identification, replies to fan mail, commercial plugs—everything, in fact, except the hourly news bulletins. One all-night listener says he wouldn't be surprised to hear the election returns announced in jingle form.

NO figures are available on the number of different ditties now being broadcast nationally—or even locally. But with some 900 stations airing anywhere from one to twenty or more daily, Americans are unquestionably getting an earful. Guesses at the national volume (including repeats) range from 5,000 to 50,000 daily "performances."

A local station, WNEW, told the investigating poet that it was airing some eighty singing commercials every twenty-four hours and was toying with the idea of a jingle hit parade—fifteen minutes of the things. Its program director treated the bard to a personal rendition of the following, concocted by the station and heard on scores of others the country over:

Listen, sister, listen, sister,
Though your hair is long and wavy,
And your name's not Joe or Davey,
You can take the job of any gob
By serving in the Navy!
(Clock strikes)
Time to join the Navy!

Nor was this the only jingle that was sung to the poet as he made the rounds of advertising agencies and radio stations; nearly every interview produced at least one spontaneous snatch of song from the executive being questioned. In two instances the bard had ditties crooned to him over the phone—by business men he had never met.

SO much for the facts. As to the impact of jingleering on poetry and the radio audience, the versifying investigator had some curious predictions to make.

In the first place, he maintained that the poets, by and large, have not yet heard about the fabulous prices that the jingle specialists earn. When the news gets around that an eight-line verse may be worth $20,000, such subjects as home and mother are slated to be abandoned—in favor of soap and beer. This, of course, the poets will deny; "art is long and time is fleeting," they will argue, not bothering to credit Longfellow. Nevertheless, many of them will secretly have a go at the more lucrative market—easing their consciences with the thought that perhaps Kent and Johnson's cola jingle is, after all, a contribution to American folksong.

But (warned the bard) don't expect all the highbrow poets to follow this line of reasoning.

Drawings by Jack Markow

Plenty of them are having too merry a time of it—even at 50 cents a line—to quit their present field. These are the boys who dote on being cryptic. Jingle-writing holds no lure for them. A singing commercial must needs be semi-understandable at least and it calls for the use of numerous one-syllable words. So, even if these prophets of vagueness were willing to sell their souls for $1,000 a line, it is extremely doubtful whether any of them could produce a salable jingle. Theirs is a skill confined to simpler things.

AND what does a working poet think of the jingle technically? Is it fair-to-middling verse? Do the commercial lyricists appear to know anything about the rules of rhyme and scansion?

According to this fellow, most of the jingles he has heard are not even good tripe. "The reason some have been successful as sales-getters is because they are catchy musically. A lively tune has a way of sticking in the average American's crop or subconscious or something." He admitted, however, that the words of many a jingle have been readily memorized by many a 7-year-old.

Concerning the over-all effect of the boom on the adult audience, the poet was willing to wager that nothing will come of it. "Only poets read poetry," he pointed out, "and *they* do it merely to observe how much better their own stuff is. Hence, why expect a listening audience to do anything more than buy another bottle of cola?"

"Of course, I could be wrong," he went on, after a moment's reflection. "Americans *could* take to doggerel-writing in a big way." And then, letting his fancy run wild, he guessed that unless the jingle craze subsided pretty soon people might even go further: they might eventually start talking in jingle lingo!

By way of illustration, the poet provided a typical bit of dialogue: Chap in the Bronx meets a pal in a neighborhood bar-grill, greeting him with:

"Howya, Oscar, whatcha know?
Howya think the 'lection go?"

To which Oscar poetically replies:

"Dewey's chances ain't so hot;
By the way, what time yuh got?"

And the answer:

"Time's exac'ly 'leven-ten
'Cordin' to my Pocket Ben!"

"So there you have it," concluded the fanciful fellow. "Of the people, for the people and by the people: Poesy on whole-wheat toast—including the commercial plug!"

October 29, 1944

L'AFFAIRE ALLEN

Comedy of Errors Brings Censorship to Fore

By JACK GOULD

THE best show in radio was not on the air last week. It was, of course, the almost incredible series of incidents which started last Sunday when NBC cut off Fred Allen for twenty-five seconds, continued with the silent treatment also being doled out to Bob Hope and Red Skelton, and ended with NBC blandly saying, "Oops, sorry."

After the excitement subsided it was clear that NBC had suffered a rather extreme case of "nerves." Mr. Allen's incessant ribbing of the foibles of broadcasting finally had pierced the very thin skin of the NBC program department and, in an ill-considered moment, word was sent out "to pull the plug" on the wry Fred.

Seldom has the futility and silliness of unnecessary censorship been more vividly illustrated. Out in Hollywood the comedians came to Mr. Allen's defense, Red Skelton suggesting to newspaper reporters that NBC stood for "nothing but confusion." Bob Hope rightly said that the "head censor" probably had a "cauliflower head." The deluge of criticism which NBC had to take in twenty-four hours was far worse than anything Mr. Allen, by himself could have done.

A "Beaut"

Undoubtedly NBC took the only possible course in admitting candidly and good-naturedly that it had pulled the biggest boner in many a day. But if radio had to crack under the strain of the criticism to which it has been subjected, few could have imagined that it would be on such a spectacular scale. NBC will be a long time living down l'affaire Allen, even though they finally did reverse their stand and allow any and all jokes on the air about their lapse in judgment.

As is by now generally well known, the episode started on April 13 when Mr. Allen's program ran over its allotted thirty minutes. The following week Fred submitted a joke which, while it was a long way from factual accuracy and not particularly fair to NBC, had an amusing premise. It was that there was a vice president "in charge of ends of programs." When a program ran overtime, said Fred, this veepee would save up the seconds not used and when he had accumulated a total of two weeks of surplus seconds take his vacation.

Clarence L. Menser, vice president of NBC in charge of programming, who has had to bear the brunt of Fred's sallies, declined to approve the joke for broadcast purposes. Fred tried to use it none the less, only to have his program fade into temporary silence. Hope and Skelton were treated similarly when they referred to Fred's plight.

Actually, the bizarre series of events last week reflected a situation which has been brewing for some months, if not years, and no doubt will rise again. Because, for better or worse, the popular programs on the air are subject to varying forms of censorship on a pretty regular basis and the issue is neither as black nor as white as it might seem offhand.

The first and most prevalent form of censorship is almost as old as commercial radio itself. Compared with those working in other media, comedians on the air always have been circumscribed in what they might say because of the perennial fear of broadcasters and sponsors that some substantial group of potential customers might be offended.

Symptomatic

For a comedian with an eye cocked on the contemporary scene, such as Mr. Allen in particular, this policy inevitably eliminates many good jokes and situations which otherwise are not offensive. In the main it is but symptomatic of how the principles of lively theatre are made subordinate in radio to the more conservative and restrictive dictates of the world of business.

The second form of censorship—and one where right would seem clearly on the side of NBC—is in the matter of obviously off-color gags. Several stars in the network's comedy stable have indulged in very bluish and distasteful routines which usually are more closely associated with the rowdy night club. NBC indeed would seem entitled to reject such material for consumption in the home, where persons of all ages may be listening and have no way of anticipating what is coming next out of the loudspeaker. Many of the comedians most given to complaining about censorship, in fact, have themselves been guilty of inviting that censorship.

The third form of censorship, of course, is comparatively recent and involves industry reaction to spoofing radio on the radio. Some broadcasters have been upset to see their own stations used to ridicule the medium which provides their bread and butter, and Mr. Menser's ill-fated move in the Allen case may even occasion a certain amount of approval in some broadcasting circles. But the widespread repercussions resulting from that move unquestionably will serve as an object-lesson to those who would try to suppress such barbs by inter-office memo.

If NBC showed what happened when radio took itself too seriously, it also demonstrated that radio in a crisis could laugh at itself. Possibly the latter development was the more important of the two last week.

April 27, 1947

How Comic Is Radio Comedy?

It is suffering from, among other things, monotony, undernourishment and 'repeats.'

By JACK GOULD

COMEDIANS on the radio are experiencing a new prominence which is not altogether to their liking. When the formal season on the air opened six weeks ago, they rallied to meet the competition offered by the summer's deluge of giveaway shows, hurling every available gag and witticism at the Santa Claus bogy which haunted broadcasting.

But now the comics are wondering if they have opened Pandora's box. While perhaps successful in stimulating sentiment against the giveaways, they also have heard an increasing number of audible complaints from listeners who boldly suggest that the funny boys at the microphone are responsible for their own plight.

For instance, it is asked how many more years does Fred Allen expect to take the same Sunday night stroll talking to the same familiar characters. And when will either Jack Benny or Charlie McCarthy let a week pass without a reference to the twin who waved her hair at home? Can Bob Hope think of a joke that is amusing to citizens who live on neither Hollywood Boulevard nor Vine Street?

Radio comedy, in short, finds itself on a collective spot and facing a crucial challenge: Can it overcome its repetition? Can it meet the incessant cries of its professional critics that it must develop "something new" and "something different" or, like vaudeville, slowly perish from familiarity?

Some comedians, with varying degrees of enthusiasm and success, are timidly experimenting. Mr. Hope this season has dispensed with the talents of Vera Vague and Jerry Colonna and is trying a less brash and more humble routine. Edgar Bergen has brought in the Bickerson family to bolster McCarthy and Mortimer Snerd. Jimmy Durante has a new foil in Alan Young, and Eddie Cantor has re-engaged Dinah Shore. Mr. Allen even dropped Senator Claghorn, but only for a week.

If such changes hardly represent a revolutionary innovation in broadcasting's efforts to bring laughter to the home, the trouble no doubt lies in the problems inherent in radio comedy itself.

RADIO comedy is the most difficult of all forms of humorous make-believe. It depends exclusively on the spoken word and sound effect—on the appeal to the ear. Before the microphone the comedian must do without prop, costume or gesture.

The limitation of the medium places an exacting premium on some of the most elusive and difficult talents for a performer to acquire. Foremost among these is, in comedy, a sense of timing—knowing the exact split second when to say a line or when to hold it another beat. Similarly, inflection of voice for a given line must be sure and credible, a misplaced accent playing hob with the image being created in the listener's mind.

Because his tools of interpretation are few in number, compared with those available in a visual art, the comedian's dependence on script is complete and overwhelming. He must stand or fall on its effectiveness, for he has no alternative means to compensate for its weakness. No comedian in radio can be better than his script writers.

THE radio comedian operates in the belief that the basic ingredient of the successful show on the air is in the creation of an image in the listener's mind, in establishing a character that will appeal to the listener week after week. It may be Benny's penny-pinching, McCarthy's impishness, Hope's freshness, Cantor's bumptiousness or Durante's rough-house clowning, but whatever the twist it must be preserved.

When radio comedians fly in the face of the tradition for stage and screen, where variations in humorous characterizations are a prerequisite to continuing box-office success, their reasoning is not wholly based on assumption. The storage bins of the networks are filled with scripts for shows which lacked a personality whom the audience could get to "know" by ear alone.

A current spectacular example is Milton Berle, whose brittle and extremely fast wisecracking style sounds flat and impersonal on the radio. Yet the same gags, reinforced by his visual gift for broad farce and consummate mugging, have made Mr. Berle the outstanding star on television. Whatever the medium, the comedian must have a "picture" in which he can fit. On stage or screen it can be done almost instantly with a setting. On the radio it can be done only with patience and with words.

It is in radio's inexhaustible demand for material that is found the real problem for the comedian. Broadcasting is the first of the entertainment arts which presumes that creative originality can be provided to order against an inflexible deadline every seven days, thirty-nine weeks in succession, over a winter season.

To make matters more difficult for the comedian and his writers, both are at the mercy of several sets of standards, some reasonable and some absurd, which do not prevail in other fields.

THE necessary standards involve recognition of the fact that radio plays to a different audience under different circumstances. Jokes which may be acceptable in a theatre or night

JACK GOULD, radio and television editor of The New York Times, has been covering various aspects of "show business" for the past fifteen years.

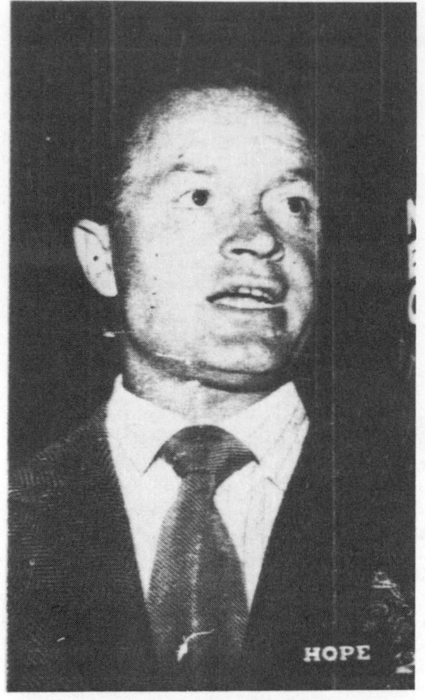

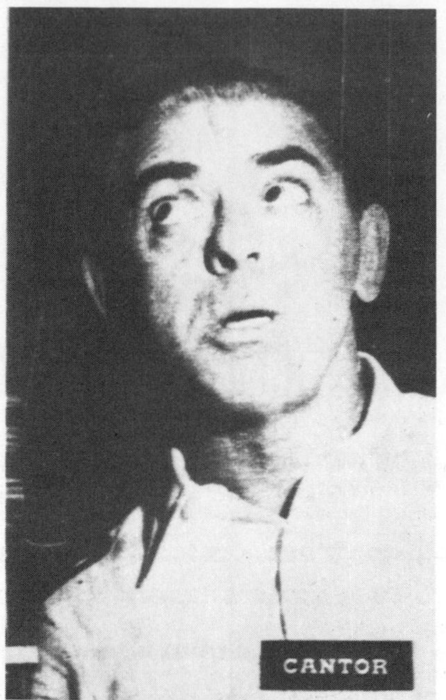

Radio has given comedians the longest "runs" in theatrical history, a "closing night" being unknown to most top air shows. Here are the debut years of these six: Hope, 1933; Benny, 1932; Cantor, 1926; Allen, 1934; Durante, 1933; Bergen, 1936.

club, where the public has an advance indication of what it will see, may arouse objection when brought without warning into the home before a mixed audience including youngsters. The blue or suggestive routine must be left out.

OF the unnecessary requirements, the most deleterious from the artist's standpoint unquestionably is the false critical criterion which prevails in radio. This is the much-publicized Hooper popularity rating. Actually, a Hooper rating merely affords a basis for comparing the relative popularity of given programs and does not presume to estimate the specific number of listeners for a show. Its purpose is purely a commercial one—to give a sponsor an idea of the "circulation" which his commercial plug on the air is enjoying.

The rating is determined not only by a comedian's personal drawing power but equally often by factors over which he has no control. These include the time of night that his show is on the air, his competition at that hour, and the comparative strength of the transmitters on the networks carrying his or other programs.

But the comedian must keep a weather eye on his rating if he is not to incur the displeasure of a sponsor who is paying heavily, and understandably expects prompt results. He cannot afford to experiment

too lavishly or ignore what probably will please most of the peope most of the time. Similarly, in line with the advertiser's desire not to offend prospective customers, he must accept a variety of taboos designed to avoid giving ammunition to some articulate pressure group.

UNDER such artistic and economic ground rules, radio comedy has come to follow a rigid formula. It divides in the main into two broad classifications: (1) the variety format employed by the majority of laugh shows; (2) the situation comedy in which there is some adherence to dramatic form.

The variety show consists usually of a stretch of straight patter featuring the star, next the introduction of the supporting members of the cast, musical interludes, and, finally, a sketch employing the services of the guest of the evening.

Generally the patter is topical in nature—a fact which is apt to find almost all shows treating on the same matter within a given week. In recent weeks the election has been the automatic peg for the routine which is intended to focus attention on the comedian's style and, if possible, also be consistent with basic characterizations.

Recently the incomparable Jimmy Durante, impresario of the non sequitur, had this sequence:

The other night I'm in the mood to take out a girl. I took my red book out—a girl or two to round up!
Startin' with the A's and proceedin' to the Z's, I made seventy calls, and how do you think I wound up?
Out of seventy calls I got 12 no-answers, 18 busy signals, 37 negatives and 13 hung up on me. But remember one thing—I waited until all the returns were in before conceding defeat!

GEORGIE BURNS and Gracie Allen are past masters at combining the topical reference with the picture of the long-suffering husband and daffy spouse:

George: Look, Gracie, you're my wife. I would only pay you if you were employed by me.

Gracie: Never mind explaining the Taft-Hartley law, just pay me.

The part of the "dope" is a widely employed device on many comedy offerings, being reduced to its barest essentials in the case of Mortimer Snerd on the Bergen program.

Bergen: I'll try once more. Now our voting system whereby everyone votes is known as universal suffrage. You can understand that, can't you?

Snerd: Sure. Everybody votes. Everybody suffers.

But for pure obviousness, Red Skelton usually is without serious competition.

O'Connor: What happened to Gallup?

Red: He slowed down to a walk.

IN the brittle exchanges that dot the airwaves, there is continued and unrelieved reliance on the use of the insult, the adult manifestation in humor of the youngster's urge to unseat a top hat with a well-directed snowball. A typical illustration was offered recently on the Jack Benny show, in an exchange between Jack and Mary Livingstone on the subject of Phil Harris.

Mary: Jack, where would Phil be going that he has to wear a tuxedo?

Jack: Well, his band has been engaged to play at the Hollywood Bowl.

Mary: But the Hollywood Bowl is closing for the season.

Jack: I know . . . they want to make sure of it. . . .

Another serviceable routine is the running gag carried over from week to week—or from year to year, in the case of the Allen-Benny feud. It may fulfill a variety of purposes: Expanding the stage ego of the star, providing a handle into an insult or affording the basis for a ludicrous comparison between the comedian and a current matinee idol. This season Bob Hope has had such a gag, thanks to Gregory Peck.

Doris Day: Yes, Bob, but a fellow as perfect as that is too much to hope for.

Hope: That's what my parents thought, but it happened.

Doris: You mean . . . ?

Hope: Yes. I have so much more than Gregory, why should I fight it?

IN theory, the advantage of the variety format is its extreme flexibility and easy adaptation to the personalities and talents of guest performers.

But in practice many of the comedians have allowed the variety format to become frozen. The tendency to repeat what was successful before has gone to such extremes that use of the device of recognition has been played out and now invites the contempt of familiarity.

The price which the comedians are paying is the insidious and slow sacrifice of the theatre's most important quality—the quality of illusion. The performers have made less and less effort to be anything but themselves and they have associated their radio characterizations more and more with the mundane matters of the world rather than with the art of make-believe. The dénouement has been epitomized in their willingness even to hawk the commercials.

By contrast, situation comedy on the radio has been less subject to critical barbs. It avoids the fragility of vaudeville and enables the performer to establish a fictional character which feeds on more than his own personality. It affords entertainment where the accent is keeping the audience relaxed and not hopped up for thirty minutes at a time.

THE durability of the situation format is perhaps best borne out in the case of "Amos 'n' Andy." Freeman Gosden and Charles Correll have fashioned fanciful yet credible characters who for a generation have been at or near the top in the ratings. Their comedy is warm and human and free of harsh brittleness, and the plots involving the immortal Kingfish are plausibly absurd. The scripts are veritable gems of sheer craftsmanship in radio, preserving at all costs the priceless ingredient of characterization.

More recently, Ozzie Nelson and Harriet Hilliard, in "The Adventures of Ozzie and Harriet," have caught the public fancy with their saga of the trials of young parents. Their program capitalizes on the mishaps, misunderstandings and confusions which can overtake any household. Its humor is not projected in the scintillating wisecrack but rather is built up slowly by leisurely asides which fit a pattern of aimability.

Harriet: Isn't this a cute lipstick . . . this is the nail polish . . . orange stick. . . eyebrow pencil.

Ozzie: Eraser?

Harriet: Could be . . . it was a real bargain . . . only $13.95. . . . They were having a clearance sale.

Ozzie: $13.95? How much was it before?

Harriet: $14.50.

THE gradual development of the situation into a strong pay-off line also is illustrated by the well-written and imaginative "Life of Riley" series, starring William Bendix. Recently, Riley and his friend, Gillis, found themselves enmeshed in a crusade against comic books and, in pursuit of their duties, were reading one of the thrillers for the kiddies:

Gillis: (wolf whistle) Who's that beautiful dame wearin' the neglijay?

Riley: She's the leader of the mob.

Gillis: What does she want with The Mouseman?

Riley: She wants the secret formula, so she's lured him to her boodwah . . . she gets him to sit down on the couch . . . then she sits down beside him. . . . Now's she's turnin' the lights down low . . . she moves closer to him . . . she's puckerin' up her lips . . .

Gillis: Turn the page! Turn the page!

(Sound Effect; Turn Page)

Riley: Well, what do you know? He picked a fine time to turn into a mouse! Trash!

BUT the basic problem which confronts the radio industry as a whole in the case of comedy is not a matter of techniques or forms but a question of the industry's own long-range lack of planning.

Radio, accepting the provinciality of Hollywood as a national norm, has shown scant regard for an increasingly mature and sophisticated taste among listeners.

Nor has radio replenished its supply of personalities which make broadcasting an attractive medium for advertisers. Instead radio has lived off the stars developed by the stage, vaudeville and screen.

If only because the imminence of television will make the need for truly experienced performers even more apparent, veteran showmen maintain that the only course ahead for broadcasting is not to abjure fresh and imaginative experimentation because of its traditional commercial timidity. Rather out of both economic and artistic necessity it must embrace and nurture new ideas and new talents and have sufficient faith in its own future to give those ideas and talents a reasonable chance to develop.

November 21, 1948

Radio Has A Future

By JACK GOULD

RADIO, once the giant of the world of broadcasting, today is the troublesome stepchild. After nine years of television, the sound medium is facing the day of economic reckoning. Reluctantly and painfully, radio is undergoing a fundamental change.

The nub of radio's crisis is a simple one: the big audiences have moved over to television and radio is being forced to adapt itself to what audience is left. The sound broadcasters who once were accustomed to the gaudiest and most costly of attire now are fighting for remnants. Their still unresolved problem is to find a pattern that will both cover them and make them look good.

But there is no serious question of radio's survival. What is uncertain is how it will survive and how much of it will survive. Actually, radio today must be evaluated two ways: (1) for what it was, and (2) for what it is. Judging radio the first way provides the key to its dilemma; judging it the second way offers the key to its future.

Radio's last golden hour was in the spring of 1949. Television still was only a relatively small speck on the electronic horizon and the nation as a whole was content merely to *hear* commercials. The structure of radio then could be likened to a vast cobweb spreading over the country.

RADIO stations affiliated with the national networks were the outlets for the glamour of Hollywood and New York. Faithfully—and profitably—they abided by the elementary law of a mass medium: give most of the people what they want most of the time. Comedians rode high, along with the lush give-aways, the mystery dramas, the plays and those insistent voices of authority, the commentators. The payoff for the networks was staggering: almost $191,000,000 for the fiscal year of 1947 alone.

If the networks were the big show, they were not the whole works. Independent outlets were thriving as well. Their stock in trade was the verbose disk jockey who played recorded popular tunes; the market for a semblance of continuous music was growing and there was enough advertising for both the network stations and the local operators.

Then came the panic: television in the fall of 1949. Almost overnight the fascinating laboratory toy of video emerged as the colossus of show business. And it struck at the vitals of the sound medium.

The radio audience swiftly grew smaller, and as it did, competition to win a share of the available listening public intensified. One development was that independent stations, which thought they had staked out a secure area of operation, discovered they had some new rivals. The big radio stations affiliated with the networks began to steal their act of relying on recorded music.

Thus, today, compared to what it once was, radio definitely has lost stature and importance. Its handicap is not only economic, but psychological. Television generates news and excitement in almost everything it does; radio is taken for granted.

JUDGING radio for itself, however, and leaving aside the undoubted fact of television's dominance and power, one can see that it isn't radio that is dying; what is marked for extinction is the old-fashioned kind of radio.

Statistics in the sound medium often are only confusing and self-serving, but one set of figures at least is highly illuminating: where do Americans today listen to the radio, and how has television changed their radio-listening habits?

In the pre-television era, something like 60 per cent of the nation's radio sets were accorded a position of honor in the living room. Today there is a record total of 111,000,000 radio receivers in working order in the United States—well over three times the number of TV sets—but only 25 per cent are to be found in the living room. The largest number to be found in any one place—26 per cent—is not in the house at all, but in the family automobile.

Inside the house radio receivers are scattered. Twenty-one per cent are in bedrooms, handy for music to read by or for hearing the news on arising or retiring, and 16 per cent are kept in the kitchen, where they can be heard at breakfast or while the housewife does her chores.

ONE conclusion that may be drawn from these figures is that a good majority of radios today are enjoyed while the listener is doing something else. Once radio pre-empted the public's attention in the home; now television does that. Radio listening has become something that accompanies another activity or is absorbed in fits and spurts.

The public, in short, is turning to radio for a different type of programming from what it expects to receive on television. It is turning to radio for music, news and other presentations directed primarily to the ear. It has found that formats which once pleased radio listeners the most, such as variety programs, are better on television, a viewpoint shared by the sponsors of such shows.

It is this

JACK GOULD has watched the inroads of television upon radio from his post as the radio-TV editor of The New York Times.

Live Concerts

News

Hi-Fi Recordings

Conversation

RADIO SPECIALTIES

new or limited use of radio which accounts for the dilemma of the networks. Radio programs which the networks are best equipped to offer are the big-star attractions, the very attractions most vulnerable to television competition. TV has also outdone radio in quiz shows, in drama, in comic hullabaloo. And the radio formats least vulnerable and most desired by the public—recorded music and news—can be offered just as well by the individual station owner who, without having to pay the network middleman, enjoys greater profit.

In the opinion of many knowledgeable broadcasters this story can have only one ending: there is not going to be enough business for four national networks in their present form. Only corporate pride is keeping some of the chains going and, if it were not for possible loss of face or for political repercussions that might affect their video interests, at least a couple would gladly call it a day.

INDICATIVE of this pessimism was a suggestion in an influential network quarter that there is just one way to restore chain radio to its economic glory. That is by revising the copyright law so that home phonograph recordings could not be played for profit by a radio station; a local broadcaster then would be forced to obtain "live" music from a network. Persuading individual stations to adopt this notion, however, would be like trying to move Radio City to the top of Everest.

Actually, the networks, though the most publicized segment of the industry, constitute only a part of the contemporary radio scene. When the whole industry is taken into consideration, it can be seen that radio not only is far from being a corpse but is very much a going business — very big business, as a matter of fact.

Between 1947 and 1954 the number of radio stations almost doubled—from 1,300 to more than 2,400. The number of frequency modulation outlets went from 48 to more than 500. In the same period, gross sales of time for the whole broadcasting industry rose more than $210,000,000—up to $769,000,000 — even though network revenues were simultaneously dropping some $30,000,000 to $40,000,000.

An industry that is doing over three-quarters of a billion dollars a year isn't a tin-cup case yet. What, then, is the future of radio? What kind of programs will it offer? What is the job radio can do and television cannot?

RADIO'S foremost task is to capitalize fully on the weaknesses of television, to exploit those areas of interest in programming which can be presented more effectively through sound than through sight. For most of radio this means leading a new way of life, just the opposite of what it has led and is still reluctant to leave behind.

In its heyday, radio never exhibited much concern for the minority audience; expediency dictated a policy of catering to the majority taste. When the television blow came, radio had no backlog of material to put in the vacuum created by the exodus of stars and popular formats.

Radio has had several years in which to lay the foundation for a new aural medium but the time has been largely wasted. Old programs have been merely sliced up in new ways — from a weekly half hour to fifteen minutes every day. Too much of radio has tried to palm off its shopworn goods by sleight of hand and then acted hurt and puzzled when the trick didn't work.

The advent of television leaves radio no alternative but to specialize and to woo those minority audiences it once scorned. The motion picture industry, which also has had its problems in the TV era, has shown that pursuit of quality can pay dividends. Radio must do the same.

Actually, some segments of radio already have made substantial progress, but they seem determined to keep it a secret. The listener who bothers to thread his way through program schedules may very easily find more fine and varied radio today than existed in the pre-TV days. But radio, wistfully hoping for the return of yesterday, acts almost ashamed of its better achievements.

UP to the present, radio has had it lucky. All it had to do was to follow obvious majority preference and let the public do its thinking. Now radio must lead public taste; this means it must think for itself.

First and foremost, radio can exploit the field of good music of all types, a field virtually ignored by TV. The ever-expanding interest in high fidelity recordings constitutes a potential audience of vast proportions for radio. Yet, with some exceptions in the larger [illegible]s, this audience is cultivated only haphazardly and irregularly, often at the most inopportune hours for most listeners.

The art of the spoken word also offers immensely fruitful possibilities. American radio never has had a dramatic series that could compare with the consistently exciting and provocative output of the Canadian Broadcasting Corporation. More recently, the National Broadcasting Company, much the most experimentally inclined of the networks, has introduced "Biographies in Sound." The installments on Ernest Hemingway and the late Gertrude Lawrence painted personality pictures in words that were infinitely more graphic than anything television could show. The know-how in radio exists; only its use is so painfully limited.

THE whole field of news is radio's oyster; television's day-by-day coverage is very superficial and often distorted by excessive concern over picture rather than news values. Yet radio's idea of turning its journalistic opportunity to maximum advantage has consisted largely of just giving the same news more often, not giving more news.

In its coverage of spot news events, radio has been especially laggard. Events of page-one importance in the press often are ignored. Radio's watchword should be: "If it's happening, you'll find it on radio."

One innovation that is a credit to many stations is the leisurely interview, discussion or conversation not subject to strict time limitations. A number of these programs often are stimulating and provocative. But here again radio acts peculiarly: you must stay up half the night to hear some of these shows.

Radio, in short, must recognize that it is a supplementary rather than a dominant branch of the broadcasting art. Its task is to concede that many persons have fallen out of the radio habit and to assume that it must build its audience anew. Radio must think in terms of what will make the public freshly conscious of radio as a medium, not remind the public of what it can no longer do in the TV age.

Radio's crying need is a sense of excitement, but this cannot be achieved until broadcasters themselves decide what their goal is to be. A medium or an industry is really no different from a human being. The trick in staying alive is to *act* alive.

Drawings by Marilyn Miller.

All-News, All-Music, All-Ghetto Radio Is a Success

The New Sound of Radio

By WILLIAM H. HONAN

RADIO station WEVD in New York City is looking for a Chinese disk jockey. Applicants should be acquainted with such personalities as Poon Sow Keng (the hottest rock 'n' roll singer today in Hong Kong), be able to report the time, news and temperature in easy-going Cantonese, and quote Confucius in the original. The resulting program may be of limited appeal—beneath the notice, one might guess, of a mass-media adman worth his double martini—and yet, it is chiefly this sort of specialization, or "fractionalization of the market," as they say in the trade, that accounts for the remarkable sonic boom reverberating from radio these days.

Right now, for example, there are more radios in the United States than people—262,700,000 at the last count. Forty-seven million sets were sold last year alone. Such profusion cannot be attributed merely to teen-agers buying transistor radios with which to annoy their parents—although that is a not inconsiderable factor. But parents are buying radios like hot cakes, too. They get them nowadays built into their tractors, hairdryers, Scotch bottles and even sunglasses. And the knobs on all these instruments are being clicked and twirled with astonishing frequency.

In fact—and this may be enough to make even Marshall McLuhan gulp with wonder—a recent Trendex survey conducted for the National Broadcasting Company found that more Americans now listen to radio in the course of an average week than watch TV. The audience for individual radio programs, of course, cannot compare with that of the most popular TV shows, but on a cumulative basis the figures indicate that 90.5 per cent of the adult population tunes in a radio sometime during the week as compared with 87 per cent who flick on television. That finding, the Trendex survey supervisor reported, "puts radio right back in the league with the other major media in terms of total audience dimensions."

THE robustness of radio is also illustrated by the fact that the giant advertisers, most notably such bellwethers as the soap and automotive companies which shifted from radio to TV in the early nineteen-fifties, have once again become substantial radio time buyers. Colgate-Palmolive, for example, which was not even listed among the top 100 radio spot advertisers as recently as 1964 was 23d on the list last year. Ford, General Motors and Chrysler were first, second and third, respectively, with a total expenditure last year of $56 million—up 17 per cent over the previous year and up 56 per cent over that of the year before.

The explanation for this renaissance of a medium which many condemned to a lingering death as recently as 10 years ago lies, to a great degree, with that sought-after Chinese disk jockey. For, once radio broadcasters began to face up to the fact that television had permanently taken their place as dispenser of general entertainment for the masses, they began experimenting with new formats and discovered that, collectively, they could recapture their old audience piecemeal by directing strong appeals to specific fractions of the population.

This discovery led to the development of all manner of limited-appeal programs, and the advancing trend is now doing away with even these one-hour or half-hour shows, since the stations themselves are beginning to take on the characteristics of a single, 24-hour program, narrowly addressed to a distinct slice of the population. Such broadcast parochialism is now revolutionizing the industry, with several stations almost every month dropping their old-style eclectic programing in preference for the new "continuous format."

Competition in a city like New York, where no fewer than 63 different AM and FM stations vie for attention, has naturally pushed specialization to an extreme, and some of the more popular formats appear to have been divided, subdivided and virtually pulled apart with tweezers in order that each station may find a niche (and presumably a distinct audience) it can call its own.

For example, WMCA, WABC, WJRZ and WOR-FM are all what the casual listener might consider standard rock 'n' roll stations, but connoisseurs are aware that WMCA tries to add a local home-town flavor by using such disk jockeys as Joe O'Brien, who has a Yonkers accent; WABC seeks to impart an all-American tone to the proceedings with disk jockeys like Herb Oscar Anderson, who is from Minnesota and full of corn and good cheer; WJRZ restricts itself exclusively to that close relative of rock 'n' roll known as country-Western music, and WOR-FM lays stress on the subdivision known as folk rock, which may include such controversial ballads (which the other

WILLIAM H. HONAN is a newspaper and magazine editor turned freelance.

Condemned to a lingering death 10 years ago because it couldn't compete with TV in a big way, radio began competing in a small way—by catering to special-interest audiences. But tall oaks from little acorns grow, right?

stations would never touch) as Phil Ochs's "I Ain't Marchin' Anymore" and Country Joe and the Fish's prickly L.B.J. put-on, "Super Bird."

EVEN in lesser cities than New York, however, format specialization has proceeded to a surprising degree. There are as many as 1,500 radio stations across the nation substantially if not exclusively devoted to country-Western music, according to the Country Music Association. And the all-talk or telephone-participation format is not only popular in New York City, where N.B.C.'s Brad Crandall and the insomniac Long John Nebel have large followings, but Philadelphians like to hear themselves gabbing over the telephone with Jack McKinney over WCAU, and nearly everybody in Salina, Kan. (pop. 43,202), listens at one time or another to Mike Cooper on KLSI to catch the latest chatter about the local school merger and to hear Cooper adding his laconic "uh-huh" to a phoned-in beef about how all the rain in June loused up the local wheat crop.

Typical of the trend is a middle-sized city like Peoria, Ill., which now has as many as six radio stations, each with its own distinctive format. WIRL, Peoria's leading outlet, is a "top-40" or predominantly rock 'n' roll station. WXCL, the local N.B.C. affiliate, is devoted to country-Western music. WMBD, the C.B.S. affiliate, is strong on conversation and plays "middle-of-the-road" music (Frank Sinatra, Peggy Lee, Vic Damone). WMBD-FM specializes in "potted-palm" fare (schmaltzy renditions of the Warsaw Concerto, and the themes from "Intermezzo" and "Gone With the Wind").

WIVC-FM has female disk jockeys — or "program hostesses," as they are known in Peoria — and plays "adult" pop, jazz and classical music. Finally, WPEO, the Mutual affiliate, having recently tried and then dropped "top-40" and "middle-of-the-road" formats, became a virtually "all-talk" station in January of this year and then in September raided WXCL's country-Western disk jockey — Cal Shrum, an old Gene Autry sidekick—and is now trying to blend the recorded yodelings of assorted farmhands-turned-vocalists with its decidedly right-leaning cast of talkers, whose ranks include Fulton Lewis 3d, the Rev. Carl McIntire and the suave pitchmen of H. L. Hunt's "Life Lines."

Such quick shifting from one format to another as practiced by WPEO is possible because the process is remarkably cheap. There is no retooling to be done, and usually disk jockeys who can handle one type of music can handle another as well. Subscriptions to the various record library services required to keep a radio station jangling with the latest tunes of whatever genre it chooses rarely run more than $300 or $400 a year. Furthermore, stations like WPEO—far from spending revenue when shifting to the seemingly expensive all-talk format—actually coin money in doing so. For every Fulton Lewis or Bill Stern whose tapes the station has to pay for, WPEO broadcasts several "Life Lines" or "20th-Century Reformation Hours" which are actually advertisements for which the station is handsomely compensated.

With specialization paying off in radio, a rise might be expected in new small stations throughout the country. Actually few new stations are being formed. As of Aug. 31, there were 4,145 AM and 1,712 FM stations—and these figures have held fairly steady for the last few years. It costs a minimum of $35,000 to start a station in a city the size of Fort Worth, Tex. — and this figure does not include promotion expenses, which are likely to be enormous.

But even that cost is not what stops people from starting new stations. The F.C.C. controls the issuance of new licenses very closely, since the

CULTURE STUFF—Left, disk-jockey Larry Josephson of WBAI, a listener-sponsored station dispensing informal, uninhibited fare for those "disfranchised by the mass media." Josephson runs a breakfast show that is "grumpy, lusty and alienated."

radio band is now almost saturated, and thus even if an entrepreneur had the $35,000 to $100,000 to spend, he would have a tough time convincing the F.C.C. that Fort Worth, say, really needs a new radio station.

So far has format specialization progressed among radio stations throughout the United States today that local affiliates of the national networks have been ignoring network programing in preference for their own locally originated material. In response to this trend, the A.B.C. radio network has recently announced that it plans to split up its piped fare into four separate subnetworks, each of which will cater to stations with distinctly different formats. There will be one subnetwork for stations with an all-talk or music-and-news format, another for "top-40" stations, one for those with more sophisticated FM formats and another for stations still using the old-style eclectic format. A.B.C.'s hope is that its subnetworks will be more congenial to highly specialized stations and will, in addition, make possible more than one A.B.C. affiliate in a given community.

ONE THING LED TO ANOTHER . . .—Above, a portable (sic) radio brightens a trans-Atlantic crossing for two passengers in 1924. Right, a portable transistor contributing to today's street scene. As our population reached the 200,000,000 mark, the number of radios in the country was put at 262,700,000.

THERE are, of course, other possible explanations besides specialization for the comeback of radio—among them the portability and convenience of the new transistor sets, the fact that car radios have become virtually standard rather than optional equipment, the development of sophisticated techniques of audience measurement to demonstrate to advertisers the large, new, out-of-home listenership, and so forth. But the basic reason for the boom is that people are listening to the radio again because it is offering them something they want to hear and cannot find elsewhere.

Of New York City's bewildering array of radio stations, three picked more or less at random — WINS, WHOM and WBAI-FM — illustrate the latest types of specialization and to whom these new formats appeal.

IN April 1965 WINS, a Westinghouse station, dramatically gave away its rock 'n' roll record library to Fordham University, kissed its disk jockeys good-by, hired 27 radio newsmen and began broadcasting news for 24 hours a day. Skeptics had said that the WINS anchor men would grow hoarse by early afternoon of the first day, and that if no worse disaster overtook the station, the babbling brook of news would simply run dry, and, on the first really slow day, WINS would be begging to get its records back from Fordham.

Neither of these eventualities came to pass. WINS provided enough anchor men so they could spell one another in half-hour shifts. And far from running out of news, a veritable geyser of gab was churned up by the station's 21 "airmen" covering New York City, by the squad of rewrite men who had access to all the major wire services and by correspondents of the Westinghouse communications network who were sending in "voice cuts" from such far-flung places as Madrid and Saigon.

As time went by, the WINS team of broadcasters developed an original and often rather exciting manner of news presentation, in which the process of news gathering is exposed to the listener in an unfolding drama. In a major news break, for example, the presentation begins with a high-pitched BEEP-BEEP-BEEP-BEEP which, according to high Westinghouse policy, may even interrupt a commercial (but never has). The beeping fades and the voice of the anchor man rises over it with: "Late word has

HIER WIRD DEUTSCH GESPROCHEN—WEVD's Jeannette van Delden conducts a variety program, "Hello, Germany," for German-speaking New Yorkers. Formerly all-Yiddish, WEVD broadcasts in 13 tongues, had its best year last year.

just been received at the WINS newsroom that President Johnson and Premier Kosygin will meet tomorrow in the college town of Glassboro, N. J. Stay tuned for further details as they are received in the WINS newsroom."

Whatever was cut into is then resumed, but pretty soon "Jim McGiffert at the editor's desk," who has been madly pawing through a stack of reference books dumped in front of him, whisks the anchor man a "sidebar" about Glassboro—where it is, its population, principal industry, etc. The next morning, Sid Davis tells about the President's helicopter chugging up off the White House lawn; there is a quick switch to Doug Edelson at the Soviet Mission in New York describing the departure of Kosygin's limousine; then reports from Rod MacLeish, Paul Parker and Jim Gordon in Glassboro shouldering their way through the crowds and finally telling of the arrival of the dignitaries the moment they appear.

So impressed by this dramaturgy was Angus McDermid, the B.B.C.'s U.N. correspondent, that he was moved to do a special feature about WINS for the B.B.C., in which he commented enthusiastically: "I found myself waiting for the next thrilling installment. It was better than many a fictional radio series I can think of."

More jaundiced listeners, however, may note that all too often the instant news in these "thrilling installments" winds up having to be retracted or modified. For example, during the emergency session of the United Nations in the wake of the six-day war in the Middle East, WINS reported that a Mohawk Airlines jet bound for Washington, D. C., had crashed near Blossburg, Pa., and that many of the 34 passengers aboard were U.N. delegates. It was a thrilling installment, all right, but it later turned out to be an example of what Elmo Ellis of WSB, Atlanta, a sharp critic of broadcasting, once characterized as "rip-snorting, inaccurate news reports." No U.N. delegates had been on the flight.

WINS spokesmen argue that the Mohawk Airlines story was an unusual case. They add with pride that WINS newsmen are not merely "rip-and-read" announcers who rip off the wire-service stories and blather them uncritically into the microphone, as do the "newsmen" at other stations they say they could name. The WINS newsmen, they say, have had analytical experience — four-fifths of them are former radio or TV station news directors—and normally they "don't jump." They did not jump on the air, for example, as did WQXR, with a rumor circulated by The Associated Press during the Newark rioting to the effect that Stokely Carmichael was leading a caravan of 33 cars into Newark. WINS newsmen were on their toes and knew Carmichael was in London at the time. And it was not a WINS man, they say, whom Newsweek pictured poking his stick microphone into the anguished face of a woman felled by a bullet on a Newark street; that, too, was "a man from another station we could name"—in this case, WMCA.

The all-news format for radio was originated not by WINS but by Gordon B. McLendon, the flamboyant Texas promoter who was also one of the first to use the "top-40" or "rock-around-the-clock" format. McLendon's station XTRA in Tijuana, Mexico, which broadcasts to Southern California, in 1961 became the first to go on an all-news bender, and was followed three years later by another McLendon property, WNUS in Chicago. (Philadelphia, Washington, Denver and St. Louis now have all-news stations, too.)

The original McLendon format, however, is substantially different from that of WINS. McLendon likens XTRA and WNUS to the weather- and time-dialing services of the telephone company, and believes that they will succeed to the degree that they strictly adhere to a "monotonous" recital of the headlines, eschewing all features and commentary. The ultimate disaster for an all-news station, McLendon once remarked, would be for its listeners to tune in expecting to hear the latest bulletins and get instead a book review.

Disagreement is voiced by Charles F. Payne, the stocky, natty-looking general manager who now presides over WINS at its chic, midtown Park Avenue headquarters. Also a Texan and, by coincidence, the manager of two McLendon stations before he joined Westinghouse, Payne explains: "It's true, of course, that we cycle the headlines every 15 minutes, do a time check every 5, weather every 7 and so forth, so when you tune in you're never far away from the bulletins. But in between we have special in-depth reports, a shopping feature, theater reviews, even editorials and sometimes a feature that continues in sections all day long — we call it a 'blitz' — on topics like the poor of New York, the overcrowded air corridors or the coming Broadway season. Furthermore, even the news bulletins are not 'monotonous.' They're changing all the time. Someone once said we're like a newspaper with 48 separate editions every day."

"The key to our format," Payne goes on, "is being informally informative. What we try to avoid is the old H. V. Kaltenborn pompousness. We want to create the image of the working newsman, the guy who's on the scene."

Although the sound of news would seem to have a universal appeal, WINS's most faithful listeners, according to a recent Politz survey, tend to be those New Yorkers with high incomes, college educations and relatively high-status jobs. Most listeners are between the ages of 25 and 64, teen-agers and senior citizens being conspicuously absent. When WINS first shifted to the all-news format, its audience, which had been accustomed to rock 'n' roll, fell off sharply. According to the latest surveys, however, the station has now more than doubled the size of its former audience—a success story which must have been read with interest across town at WCBS, which switched in August to an all-news format, too.

ANOTHER increasingly important specialization in contemporary radio is known as ethnic broadcasting, or, less euphemistically, as ghetto radio. There are now, for example, no fewer than three Negro stations broadcasting in New York City. WWRL, by far the most popular of these, anticipates that its annual revenue from advertising will rise above the $2-million mark this year, having practically quadrupled over the last four years.

WEVD, the formerly all-Yiddish station which now broadcasts in 13 different tongues, including Japanese and Norwegian, says that 1966 was "the best year ever" in its 40-year history. And The Wall Street Journal recently reported that because Pepsi-Cola was the first soft drink to advertise intensively on the local Spanish stations, Pepsi now outsells Coca-Cola two-to-one among New York's 1.5 million Spanish-speaking residents—a state of affairs that Coca-Cola is now trying to rectify by plugging away over "the Spanish Main," as the three stations between 1280 and 1480 kilocycles are known, with the jingle *"Todo va mejor con Coke"* ("Things go better with Coke").

Typical of the sound and format of ethnic broadcasting is that of WHOM, New York's foremost Spanish station, which is so hot-bloodedly Latin that it has, quite literally, blown its fuse. The program responsible for this occasional boiling over — called *"Debate Musical"* ("Musical Debate") — is the top-rated Spanish disk-jockey show in New York and is hosted by Juan Rodriguez Diaz, a deceptively placid-looking Puerto Rican. On the program, which is broadcast live every weekday afternoon at 4, Diaz spins a couple of Spanish pop records and then urges his listeners to call in and "vote" for whichever one they liked best. He can stimulate as many as a thousand calls on a good afternoon, working himself into a frenzy as the votes mount up and bawling into the microphone in Spanish:

"The vote is even! It's even! We don't want any sleepyheads here! No, you have to be *awake* to listen to *this* show! Call in! My friends! Call in! Look, if you don't call in right away, I'll fall down and break 14 ribs. I'll smash my head against the wall! If I don't get 400 calls right now, I'll break 44 ribs!"

Suddenly, the lights on all the studio telephones begin to flicker, indicating a shower of incoming calls. When this happens, Diaz puts his hands to his temples, closes his eyes and shrieks with ecstasy: *"Esto es treMENNNDO!"* WHOM's engineers, not one of whom understands Spanish, have learned to watch their volume-units meter with a hawk's eye when El Tremendo, as they call Diaz, gets lathered up and they "ride gain" on him with their volume controls like a destroyer captain in a gale. Nevertheless, on two consecutive days last summer, when Diaz was unloosing his *"Esto es treMENNNDO!"* he overloaded the station's 5,000-watt transmitter and blew out a high-voltage fuse, temporarily putting WHOM off the air.

THAT is overdoing it, perhaps, but the Latin sound and volatile temperament is all that WHOM has to sell, and the management evidently would rather err with too much than too little. "Language is our most important product," explains Ralph Costantino, WHOM's affable program director, who is himself of Italian extraction but survived the station's changeover in 1957 from Italian to Spanish broadcasting by virtue of his fluent Spanish. The dialect spoken over WHOM, he says, is Caribbean Spanish, interspersed with plenty of *ay benditos* and *Ave Marias!,* which are characteristic of the Puerto Rican and Cuban idiom one hears on East 125th Street.

So important is the sound of the Spanish language to the station's identity, in Costantino's opinion, that he has a rule of long standing that popular music, which constitutes from 65 per cent to 75 per cent of the station's programing, must be vocal rather than instrumental. Moreover, with the current unusual exception of The Monkeys and The Turtles, vocalists who sing in English are strictly *prohibido.* WHOM even snubbed Frank Sinatra's last big hit, "Strangers in the Night," and played instead Andy Russell's Spanish rendition *"Estraños en la Noche,"* which had more tropical zing.

IT is not only the disk jockeys and vocalists one hears over WHOM who radiate Latin excitement; newscasters do, too. Last summer, for example, one of WHOM's newsmen broke into a musical program almost hysterically shouting a news bulletin. Fortune Pope, the station's co-owner, who does not speak Spanish, happened to be listening and promptly called in to find out what in blazes was going on. "Has war been declared?" he asked. No, he was told, the news bulletin merely concerned a report that Che Guevara was then rumored to have been seen somewhere in Venezuela.

"Our announcers become emotionally involved in the news when they read it," says Costantino. "It isn't that they aren't professional. It's just the Latin way. You should have heard them reporting the rioting in El Barrio the last week in July. It was . . . well, pretty loud."

Baseball games and soap opera—the latter still a great favorite with Spanish-speaking audiences — round out WHOM's regular fare, and they, too, are as popular as they are tempestuous. One of the most avidly followed "soaps" carried on WHOM is called *"Collar de Lagrimas"* ("Necklace of Tears"), and seems to consist chiefly of organ music and the sound of a woman sobbing, punctuated now and then by gunfire and commercials. (It also has an enormous audience in Cuba and Fidel Castro will not permit Havana stations to broadcast it while he is making a speech.) The soaps are gradually giving way on WHOM, however, to the jiving sound of the *boogaloo* and *la nueva ola* (rock 'n' roll with a Latin beat), since the younger generation, according to the surveys, is now the dominant group in Spanish Harlem and it would rather twist and wriggle than sniffle and sigh.

So firm is the grip of the ethnic stations on their audiences that a recent Pulse survey shows the Spanish-speaking population, for example, listening to radio for an average of four hours a day, which is almost twice as much time as other Americans devote to the medium. This audience, according to surveys, is profoundly influenced by what it hears, whether commercials, news or comment.

It is particularly regrettable, then, that WHOM has an intellectual content of zero, and offers little that might be considered of genuine public service. (A notable exception among ethnic broadcasters is WLIB, the Harlem Negro station that last year won a Peabody Award — the highest honor in broadcasting—for a telephone-participation program that was believed to have served as a sort of social safety valve by permitting the frank airing of Negro grievances.) The rationale for the low level of programing by WHOM, according to Costantino, is that "most Puerto Ricans who have intellectual capacity are bilingual and thus get their stimulation from English-language sources" (which is a dodge), and that the station did in fact "give free air time to Spanish-speaking deputies of Mayor Lindsay and Cardinal Spellman to appeal for restraint during the summer rioting" (which is true enough, but surely the minimum in terms of social

ETHNIC BROADCASTING—Otherwise, and commonly, known as "ghetto radio," it is an increasingly important specialization. Here, Ed Samuels interviews a man in Harlem for WLIB, one of New York's three Negro stations.

responsibility). A strong case can be made that ethnic radio stations like WHOM, which exploit commercially the linguistic handicap of their listeners, actually serve to perpetuate that handicap, and therefore ought to be charged with providing special counterbalancing educational services.

ANOTHER highly specialized area of radio broadcasting is occupied by the 350-odd licensed noncommercial stations in the United States which are affiliated with schools, churches, municipalities and foundations. A good many of these have undergone as much format refinement as any all-news or rock-around-the-clock station on the dial. Perhaps the best known of them in New York is WNYC, the city-owned station.

Other local noncommercial stations specializing in fine music and thoughtful discussions and lectures include Columbia University's WKCR-FM, Fordham University's WFUV-FM, the Riverside Church's WRVR-FM and the Pacifica Foundation's listener-sponsored WBAI-FM, which is the left-leaning "free-speech" station that was put off the air for 52 hours in September when its transmitter was wrecked by vandalism. An articulate spokesman for WBAI is Larry Josephson, the hip disk jockey. Josephson, a rather corpulent, bearded, 28-year-old computer-programer by day, has for the last year and a half been conducting a far-out breakfast club for the station, irreverently called "In the Beginning," which is—in marked contrast to the usual fare at that hour—refreshingly grumpy, lusty and alienated.

Noncommercial stations have specialized just as have the commercial broadcasters, Josephson believes, not only because of the pressures of competition, which naturally affect them less, but in response to "the great diversity of life styles today." Back in the thirties, he says, cultural unity gave rise to relatively undiversified styles in the communication media. But today, in an era of cultural splintering, a great many people find themselves "disfranchised by the mass media" and they begin to seek new styles of experience elsewhere.

WBAI is attractive to at least some of these seekers—no one knows how many since its call letters have never appeared in a general audience survey—because it offers, according to Josephson, programs attuned to the new life styles, programs which are, in his words, "no longer sequential, but random, associative and parallel." Josephson cites as an example of such programing the breakfast club he convenes every weekday morning at 7 A.M. or whenever he gets around to arriving at the station (he is frequently late and sometimes never shows at all), and on which he is likely to say anything that pops into his head—it may be something fairly salacious or he may just indulge in a long spate of moaning and groaning.

Josephson points with admiration to his WBAI colleague, Bob Fass, the station's after-midnight disk jockey, who has lately been achieving remarkable effects by playing two records simultaneously — for example, pairing speeches by Timothy Leary and Lyndon B. Johnson about their respective visions; playing the voices of soldiers in a United States Army basic-training course along with a dog-training record, and so forth. Similar effects, Josephson says, were to be found in the dramatization of Christopher Morley's "The Trojan Horse," which juxtaposed cynicism and romanticism, and which the station broadcast, under the direction of Baird Searles, in a four-and-a-half-hour spree on Oct. 8 and 9.

WBAI, like its commercial counterparts, Josephson says, has its very own sound. "Some people say it is the sound of boredom," he begins, adding: "To some extent that's true. Some say it's aggression — a kind of postured hipness. That's true, too. Some say it's amateurishness. Some call it humaneness, or love, or naturalness. It's all of that. Naturalness, especially. For example, when we're running behind time, we say so. When we make a mistake, we admit it. We don't try to come up with our radio-broadcast *persona grata* intact. When we read news, we try to read it like human beings. I hate WINS. They read everything in the same excited monotone. It isn't human."

A few weeks ago, Josephson took over WBAI's regular book-review program for half an hour, and what he said as well as the manner in which his material was presented pretty well illustrates the WBAI "sound" he was trying to describe.

To begin with, the program, which was scheduled to follow a commentary by a spokesman for the Socialist Labor party at 7 P.M., did not start until about 7:07. Then the announcer, who introduced the program as "Books to Buy, Borrow or Burn," tripped over a word, and neglected to say who the reviewer was going to be or to give the titles of the books to be discussed. The next voice was that of a newscaster announcing the beginning of World War II on a scratchy old record.

When it was finished, an obviously "live" voice came on the air and explained that the recording was from a broadcast by Edward R. Murrow from London. The live voice went on to say in a very intimate and unradiolike tone that Murrow was "the best broadcaster ever produced by this country." Murrow had also been an intelligent and effective foe of McCarthy, the voice said, but he should not be mistaken for a true liberal because he had condoned the execution of Julius and Ethel Rosenberg.

In any case, the voice continued, Murrow was great because he came through on the human level and he made you stop and think. A collection of Murrow's broadcasts, the voice added, had been published by Alfred A. Knopf Inc., in a book called "In Search of Light," which might well be read along with "Due to Circumstances Beyond Our Control" by Fred Friendly, who, as everybody knows, resigned from C.B.S. after the network refused to permit him to drop a rerun of "I Love Lucy" in order to carry the testimony of George F. Kennan before the Senate Foreign Relations Committee. Taken together, the voice commented, the two books reveal what is good and what is bad about broadcasting in America. "This is Larry Josephson," said the voice, and stopped.

There was a long pause—a *very* long pause—and then an old recording of Murrow's voice came on again, this time saying that he had just been with the first wave of U.S. troops to arrive at a concentration camp in central Germany called Buchenwald. His voice trembled perceptibly as he said: "Now let me tell this in the first person." Murrow then described the terrible scene in short, clipped language, remarking at one point: "Men tried to lift me to their shoulders. They could not. They were too weak." And later: "When I came in, they applauded. It sounded like the handclapping of babies."

After describing several other such scenes, Murrow said fervently: "I *pray you* to believe what I have reported about Buchenwald!" He closed by adding: "If I have offended you by this rather mild account of Buchenwald, I am not sorry."

Then the first voice, that of the WBAI announcer, came on once more to say that "Books To Buy, Borrow or Burn" was over, and, tripping over a word again, he introduced the next program, which was in French.

WILL the specialized formats such as those represented by WINS, WHOM and WBAI continue to proliferate? Most radio spokesmen say yes. In fact Timebuyer, the trade magazine, recently declared that "everyone from career girls to bird watchers to traveling salesmen could well be the special province of a particular station." Others have suggested that an important area of specialization in the future will be politics—with radio stations not only backing candidates, as did WMCA in 1960 (endorsing John F. Kennedy for President), but identifying themselves as, for example, "the National Review of the air."

These notions may not be as far-fetched as they sound, what with stations like WNCN-FM in New York broadcasting programs of special interest to physicians, to which the general public is discouraged from listening, and like KADS in Los Angeles—another Gordon McLendon creation—which has become the first radio station in the country devoted exclusively to classified advertising.

Just as radio is now going through a fractionalization previously experienced by the printed media, so television will follow, industry spokesmen agree, especially once the U.H.F. stations begin to catch on. The interesting upshot of all this specialization may then be that the mass media, only recently condemned as purveyors of a bland, regularized sameness, may be counted in the near future as a vigorous force working for cultural diversity.

The level or quality of that diversity, of course, is another question, and that remains to be seen—perhaps to be overseen. ■

December 3, 1967

AMOS 'N' ANDY DO NOT DOUBT 100,000 LISTENERS ARE RIGHT

AN East-West conflict of radio listeners has resulted in a draw. Amos 'n' Andy, whose recent change in program time resulted in a threatened boycott throughout the West of the toothpaste they sponsor, will be heard twice nightly in the future.

The new arrangement becomes effective tomorrow. They will be heard from 7 to 7:15 P. M. (Eastern Standard Time), daily except Sunday, through WJZ's network. From 10:30 to 10:45 o'clock (Central Standard Time), listeners tuned to twenty stations throughout the West may hear the program repeated.

Those plans were worked out after a literal storm of protests had deluged the sponsor's offices over changing the broadcast time from 11 to 7 o'clock, Eastern Standard Time, each night. It is estimated that more than 100,000 persons have written, wired or telephoned up to the time the present decision was reached. Some of the protests carried a threat to boycott the sponsor's product.

Stations in the East which will broadcast Amos 'n' Andy on the new schedule from 7 to 7:15 include WJZ, New York; WBZ, Springfield; WBZA, Boston; WHAM, Rochester; WJR, Detroit; WRC, Washington, and KDKA, Pittsburgh.

Western stations receiving the program at 10:30 o'clock (Central Standard Time) are KYW and WMAQ, Chicago; KWK, St. Louis; WDAF and WREN, Kansas City; WTMJ, Milwaukee; KSTP, Minneapolis St. Paul; WEBC, Duluth-Superior; KVOO, Tulsa; WKY, Oklahoma City; KTHS, Hot Springs; WFAA, Dallas; KPRC, Houston; WOAI, San Antonio; KOA, Denver; KSL, Salt Lake City; KGO, San Francisco; KFI, Los Angeles; KGW, Portland; KOMO, Seattle, and KHQ, Spokane.

November 24, 1929

VERSES THAT BROADCAST CHEER WIN APPLAUSE FROM THOUSANDS

By MAJOR EDWARD BOWES.

FOR almost six years now I have stood at the microphone every Sunday night—and each week following has brought with it new food for thought, new avenues of delight and appreciation. The radio audience has taught the happy lesson that they are one and the same group that go to make up any phase of life.

First and foremost they are intelligent. They are ambitious for the better things. Hence their first demand is sincerity. Combine sincerity with a program of the finer entertainment, and the warm, enthusiastic response is almost instant with the reception. That such an audience would be friendly, indulgent, appreciative and discriminating goes without saying.

It has been my custom from the beginning to leave a philosophic thought or verse before the closing number. The subject matter of these is always designed to be helpful and encouraging to those who may be ill, in doubt, discouraged or unhappy for any reason. The mysterious medium of radio seems somehow to invest these bits of counsel with a force or an authority that they could hardly carry so effectively in any other way.

The result is that these weekly verses have been of help and support to an extent almost unbelievable. At least 95 per cent of the letters received are either asking for copies or telling of their helpful effects. A little evidence of this appreciation can easily be gained from the fact that since my first New Year's resolution reading four years ago, of Charles Hanson Towne's little poem "Around the Corner," which I repeat every New Year's, more than 100,000 requests for copies have been received.

The letters are a study, guide and inspiration in themselves: From shut-ins, travelers, the bed-ridden, old and young, entire families, the lonely and the gay. Every anniversary on the air is always another occasion of added greetings from the great "family" of listeners. We received two unique letters reporting on our fifth anniversary broadcast—one from Paris commenting on the fine reception; the other was from the captain and crew of a Peruvian submarine, cruising in the Adriatic.

September 21, 1930

MOON HANGS OVER THE MOUNTAIN AND KATE SMITH BEGINS TO CROON

She Went From the Footlights to the Microphone as "The Song Bird of the South"

KATE SMITH was posing for a photograph. Arms thrown wide, head back and her lips parted as if preparing to break into song, she faced the camera. "I'm not much good at posing for pictures, but here goes!"

Click, click.

"Did you get the entire picture on one plate?" she asked, and in that sentence she summed up her entire attitude of unconcern on the avoirdupois situation. And if Kate Smith is not sylph-like, it must not be thought that it causes her any sleepless nights. Even at her birth in Washington, D. C., twenty-two years ago, Kate Smith was plump and the ensuing years have brought her plenty of poundage. She tips the scales at 240. Furthermore, here is one young woman who has no desire to diet. She is happiest, she says, when eating rich desserts, and she likes to be happy.

Made Début in 1925.

Her professional career covers only five years, her début dating back to 1925 when she sang at a benefit in the B. F. Keith Theatre in Washington. Eddie Dowling was in the audience, heard her crooning and engaged her immediately for his show, "Honeymoon Lane." Following that she appeared in "Hit the Deck" and "Flying High."

During the run of this latter production, Kate Smith's attention was attracted to the possibilities of broadcasting. She found no difficulty in adjusting herself to this new medium and with no unnecessary conferences she stood before the microphone and sang. She seemed to catch the public fancy at once. Now she sings over the WABC network at 8:15 P. M. on Sunday; 6:15 on Monday; 7 P. M. on the next four days, and 8:30 on Saturday.

Investigation reveals the following facts regarding the personal life of Kate Smith: She has been atop the Empire State Building three times since the opening, knows most of the guards by name, and plans to repeat her visits weekly, at least. She's blonde, blue-eyed, wears no street make-up, and sings to her maid while putting on her stage make-up. She always wears solid colors—blue, white, black, but never red. Her répertoire includes concert, operatic, Irish, "blues" and Negro melodies. Her speaking voice is as hearty as any one of her songs, with the possible exception of the moment following any defeat at backgammon.

The theme song of her program, "When the Moon Comes Over the Mountain," is her most prized possession—she was co-lyricist with Howard Johnson.

Kate Smith

August 9, 1931

MERRY-GO-ROUND OF THE AIR

Bowes Celebrates Anniversary

WHEN Major Bowes led his amateur show to a nation-wide hook-up there were all sorts of estimates as to how long such a performance, competing on the air with professional talent, might endure. Today the first anniversary is celebrated.

Statistics of the amateur "wheel of fortune," as the Major calls the hour, reveal that more than 800 out of 30,000 auditioned have gone on the air, and of those who faced the microphone approximately 350 joined traveling vaudeville units.

Founded on the essential principle of human nature, Major Bowes is firm in his belief that the program "has much life left in it." As long as the audience remains part of the show interest will not lag, as he analyzes the situation, at the year-end.

"All men at heart are critics," the Major explained, "and since time immemorial they have always felt that they can run the other fellow's show better than he can. It gives them a feeling of satisfaction to believe that they may have started some one on the road to success. The listeners have an opportunity to do just that on the amateur program, where about 35,000 people cast their ballots by telephone and about 4,500 others vote by telegraph each week.

"The success of the amateur hour has been breath-taking, to say the least," the Major continued. "There were prophets who doomed it to oblivion within a few months and even the most optimistic among us never visualized the phenomenal success or the far-reaching results.

"Of course, there are bound to be some who go away disappointed," the Major pointed out, "and that is only to be expected. "We hold auditions every week for 600 tyros, knowing that we cannot provide a chance for more than fourteen to eighteen at the microphone in one broadcast. But even this wholesale elimination performs a mission of mercy in disguise, if it warns the unsuccessful candidates to abandon all hope of pursuing a profession for which they are obviously unsuited."

March 22, 1936

FURIOUSLY PROCEEDS RADIO'S GAG HUNT

It Goes on Without Intermission, for the Show Is Fleeting And After One Broadcast a Joke Is Stale and Useless

By ORRIN E. DUNLAP Jr.

RADIO comedy was born out of the depression. It thrived in the dark days, and in these days of recovery the broadcasters are thoroughly convinced that the comic man is on the air to stay. Quickly, as the storm clouds gathered in 1929, the microphone called for wags and it called for gags and it called for jokesmiths, too. And the comic man made good.

Humor did not seem to go so well on the air in the "bull market" days of Coolidge and Hoover; but when the ticker ran hours behind on the downside and things began to look black, comedy as an antidote for hysteria came to the aid of the nation's sense of humor, which had made a new low when everything else was touching new highs.

Many gloomy situations that lurked in the American atmosphere were frequently made the butt of radio jests, and as a result the people, though gripped with the fear of what might happen, suddenly realized there was humor in the situation—that it might not be so bad as imagined. More than one comedian joked about his own stock losses, and, with misery loving company, members of the unseen audience were cheered to know that they were not alone on board the leaking ship of speculation. In many an instance it was a case of "laugh, clown, laugh," and the comedian little realized at first how many long-faced listeners were beginning to laugh with him. But the fan mail was proof of the adage, "Laugh and the world laughs with you."

* * *

FOR a long time the broadcasters had frowned upon clowns. They said the comedian must face a visible audience; he would be like a fish out of water standing in a padded studio with no one to laugh at him for inspiration. The showmen insisted that the mute, cold-looking microphone would extract every laugh-provoking germ from a joke. But they were willing to try almost anything when the depression called for a change of tactics.

They beckoned jesters to the studio for auditions, and one with a happy thought invited an audience to watch him perform. He had the key that opened the ethereal gateway to the humorist. Immediately, however, he was between two fires: an invisible and a visible audience, and one far outnumbered the other. Naturally, he had to concentrate his art on the unseen multitudes, so he cleverly modified his stage technique and joked chiefly for the multitudes he could not see. On the other hand he caught his cues from the laughs in the studio and hoped that the merriment would be infectious from coast to coast.

But where was there a comic reservoir into which the sieve-like microphone could be dipped to "feed" such fluent wits as Joe Penner, Ed Wynn, Eddie Cantor, Jack Pearl, Jack Benny and the crowd of wags who flocked to the studios to jest electrically on invisible waves, while stripped of their funny antics and regalia? Here was a jocular art, demanding new skill in buffoonery. Old joke books that preserved witticisms of the ages and forgotten magazines were gobbled up from old book shops. Comic books untouched for years on library shelves suddenly found a host of readers. "Research" experts delved into the whimsies of the past, anxious to renovate and to weave the musty threads of jollity into wave lengths to tickle a new generation. And so the gagster came into his own.

The hunt for quips is intense. Trained eyes are constantly on the lookout and ears are alert for humor. The quest is a free-for-all; an ethereal treasure hunt. A fresh joke, of course, is the real prize.

There is nothing more tormenting to a radio fan than a bewhiskered pun. A song can be broadcast repeatedly and never lose its charm, but not so with a joke. The joke must be fresh. If the listener tunes in on some repartee he has heard before, no matter where, on the stage, screen or radio, he skips along the dial to another wave.

Luckily every joke can be twisted; some 1,000 times. The gagster's livelihood comes from the twisting. It is a clever technique. Modern radio has a corps of professional jokesmiths. Humorous magazines have trained many of them. The veterans, however, were schooled on Broadway. They have penned the lines for many light stage hits. But what a taskmaker is this thing called radio! One performance and the joke loses its hilarity. The theatre could use the same lines over and over during a record run and the jokesmith could rest on his laurels until it was time for a new show. No such respite is found on the radio. The show is fleeting. Every performance must be new; it must sparkle. Nothing will kill a comedian's air reputation more quickly than an ancient jest. And it is antiquated if microphoned only yesterday.

* * *

THE trick of the jokesmith's trade, of course, is to supply the comedian fresh material—the sort of stuff that fits his personality as if he had written the lines himself. The comic's job is merely to deliver the jokes with the proper punch: he puts the life into them. Comedy on the air is highly specialized. The gag writer can make or break the best of comedians, just as the comedian can make jokes fall flat or scintillate.

One noted spinner of radio humor is a mathematician. In school he reveled in arithmetic, algebra, geometry and trigonometry. Fate twisted his career just as he twists jokes that are 100 years old. Peculiarly enough, in this age of broadcasting the mathematical type of mind has prospered more than it might have if applied to engineering or chemistry. Such gag writers have made a new form of art by juggling humor and they seem to enjoy the fun.

A theory has existed for generations that there can be only seven basic forms of jokes. They are the digits of humor. What are the original seven? the inquirer asked Carroll Carroll, who has written countless comic lines that have shot through space from the tongues of popular teams, especially Burns and Allen.

"Well, I've heard of the mythical seven," smiled Mr. Carroll, "but I have never met any one who knows what they are. I suppose one is that "Anything out of place is funny.' For example, false teeth in the pocket or on a table are funnier than in the mouth. But what are the other six? I don't know."

The modern gagster thrives on the fact that there is no end of variations, repetitions and combinations of the original seven—if there is such a number. These writers bring the relationships of ancient puns down to a fine point. They switch old gags to fit modern people, events and scenes. Jests that might have made Rome laugh in the days of Caesar can be applied to events of this day, such as Roosevelt and the New Deal. Basic jokes are linked to the everyday things in life; to daily experiences of people throughout the years. But the radio showmen and the jesters agree that no program can endure on fun alone.

* * *

THE first great reservoir of humor is children. Their jokes are naturals. "Children are one of the most fertile sources of comedy," said David Freedman, one of radio's industrious gag writers. "The child takes things so seriously, very literally. And let me tell you, literal comedy is one of the giants of humor. The child is the father of the literal gag, which is born from simplicity, error, misunderstanding of actual meaning or ignorance. For example, the excited child runs to his father with the newspaper and says, 'We must hurry to the World's Fair because it is only going to last two days!' The surprised parent replies there must be some mistake, whereupon the child points to the newspaper and says, 'Look here, it says fair today and tomorrow'."

This sort of joke leads into the field of puns, double-meaning jests and rhetorical questions, which the radio jokesters can depend upon nine times out of ten for winning a big laugh. The rhetorical question, they have discovered, "hits" both visible and invisible audiences with surprise.

R. H. Hoffman.

Ed Wynn.

The radio showmen are aware that "the real gems that rock the house" are pure mistakes of childhood, and a close second are the errors of foreigners who cripple and garble the language.

One of radio's most prolific gag writers lived in a house two years, although he disliked the location. He put up with it because the landlord was a foreigner, with whom he had many arguments. One day he warned the gag writer, "I'll give you one of two choices; you can do one of two things, either get out or move." When a complaint was made about the lights in the house the landlord answered that they were all right, "they are 60-wops." Unknowingly he supplied much comedy for the coast-to-coast audience of America.

"After the literal joke and the foreigner's mistakes comes topical comedy," says Mr. Freedman. "A topical gag need be only half as funny as any other joke because it is timely. It does two things; it makes the comedian appear very clever because no one will believe he dug the joke out of an old book, and, secondly, this class of joke flatters the audience by making it think it is right up to the minute. The topical gag is one of the secrets of Will Rogers's success. He thrives on the topical joke."

The main trick in getting a big laugh out of a topical joke on the air, no matter how old the gag, is to switch it to a current event—war debts, nudism, divorce, politics, quintuplets, NRA or anything in the headlines. For example:

Friend: Where is your husband working?

Wife: He's working for the ZZZ.

Friend: How's that?

Wife: He started with the AAA and worked his way down.

* * *

NEXT in line is "outlet comedy." It is one of the backbones of radio humor. Based on daily experiences, it is called "outlet comedy" because it is an outlet for human emotions. "Kidding" about trouble seems to be a general consolation for suffering; it is a relief. Human tension is often broken by a simple gag that diverts the mind. A complete, sudden reversal of thought or a burst in the stream of emotion is like "stopping a sixty-mile-an-hour motor car on a dime." It jolts everybody. That is the psychology of outlet comedy.

Eddie Cantor and Ed Wynn, masters from the old theatrical school, bombard the radio audiences with rapid-fire gags. Then there is the "funny-situation" humor popularized by Amos 'n' Andy and the Goldbergs. They give the air a comic strip, while Will Rogers gives it a cartoon. There are the dry comedy of Tom Howard and others in his class; the dialect of Fannie Brice, of George Givot, the man from Greece; and the "nonsense" sort of humor featured by Burns and Allen, by Stoopnagle and Budd, Fred Allen and Jack Benny.

Luckily, there is a variety of humor, because one who laughs at Ed Wynn may never get a smile from Colonel Stoopnagle. And the mind that thinks Amos 'n' Andy the "grandest ever" may turn a deaf ear on the Sisters of the Skillet or Gene and Glenn. But radio apparently finds an audience for all, so the jokesmiths continue to work night and day. All have developed individual technique; no two work alike. For example, Ed Wynn chalks jokes on a blackboard and invites friends to take a look. If they fail to laugh he uses the eraser. If they "see" the joke it survives the "proving grounds."

* * *

RADIO humor, however, is not all a matter of material. The delivery counts. Every comedian can take the same joke and make it sound different to the average ear. That is another reason why there will never be a dearth of jokes. And each comedian "pitches" differently in curving humor over the home plates for a strike.

The dynamic Cantor works definitely with a "straight" man upon whom falls the job of building up the premise of the joke. Wynn, on the other hand is a monologist. The eager McNamee merely helps him build up the laugh and infect the audience with enthusiasm. Gracie Allen never must show that she thinks she is saying anything funny. To her all is serious; that's what makes her funny. Joe Penner is another "pathetic" character. He is a "male Gracie Allen," a little boy whom the children admire. Jack Pearl with his exclusive dialect builds up the joke for himself. His straight man plants the premise and Pearl, by going off at a tangent, builds up the point. The "under dog" is always the winner among successful radio comedians. They all keep that element in their formula. Sympathy is what they must win.

Stoopnagle and Budd are genuine radio comedians. The microphone found and developed them. In their nonsensical way they have a bit of the Rube Goldberg element; they feature the difficult way to do a simple thing. Phil Baker applied the stage-box stooge to the microphone. Joe Cook and Walter O'Keefe are of the smart-alec type.

* * *

IT is no easy task for the gag men to keep these clowns on the track that fits their personality; to feed lines that win sympathetic reaction.

How does the gag writer go about his work? Carroll Carroll was asked.

"First, the gag man must become well acquainted with the comedian," replied Mr. Carroll. "He must know what the comedian likes and dislikes in everyday life. He must have a thorough knowledge of how the man works. He must study his personality from all angles. From then on it is a question of creation and adaptation.

"There are no end of jokes; thousands are catalogued and filed by the comedians, by the gag men, broadcasters and advertising agencies. When first shaping the program the theme must be decided. Then the jokes that apply to the subject are collected.

"The time it takes to complete a program depends on how much interest you have in the work and what luck you encounter. The Cantor shows require a week to write, and the work does not repose in one man's hands. Often there are from two to five gag men, lyric writers and Cantor himself. The comedian must be creative to survive. The more he contributes, the more of his spirit is in the broadcast. The radio audience has an uncanny way of telling immediately whether or not a comedian is sincere or if he is merely doing a job."

August 26, 1934

PREMIERE OF A 'DESTINY' SHOW

Amateur Hour Opens Tonight on Fifty-two Stations—Major Bowes Will Ring a Gong or Crown New Performers

By ORRIN E. DUNLAP Jr.

AMATEUR performers are to be glorified in a full-hour coast-to coast "destiny" show. The curtain goes up tonight at 8 o'clock in Radio City, where Major Edward Bowes will be the major-domo. Around him at the WEAF microphone young hopefuls will rally, anxious to reveal their talents as singers and clowns, musicians and mimics, to a nation-wide audience. The prize they seek is fame. They hope the try-out will lift them out of the crowd and put them on the track leading to stardom as entertainers.

The Major, sitting in his office that looks down on Broadway, solemnly reflected on his new responsibility. He realizes what he may say or do, even a gesture or a frown, may leave a life scar on some sensitive soul who came to the studio with self-confidence, but left with it destroyed. He will banter with some so they will forget the "ordeal" and thereby relieve nervous tension. With words of cheer he will applaud those in whom he senses a spark of talent. He will ring a gong on those he believes are off key or, as he says, "round pegs in the square holes of radio."

* * *

FOR many a moon the broadcasters have been fishing in a "shallow pool," as the major describes radio's reservoir of entertainment. No matter what the catch, the "fish" is always the same from week to week. When a performer is "hooked" for a new show he is out of the water for a while but sooner or later he is usually tossed back into the pond to swim around until the bait of some new sponsor "hooks" him again. That, the Major says, is a practical view of broadcasting. But he believes it must change to progress. Radio must harbor surprises for the listener. The show must be intriguing. It cannot be if the same "fish" always swallows the bait. The amateur restocks the radio pool. The amateur brings suspense, novelty, humor, spontaneity and renewed interest. Always there is the hope that he may be the biggest "catch" on the air.

Why the Show Charms.

"The charm of the amateur show is that it pops as it goes." said Major Bowes. "Rehearsal sinks the amateur. But beneath it all is a serious purpose. The amateurs bring new blood to radio. Standard acts killed vaudeville and will raise havoc with broadcasting even sooner, because radio consumes. An act can seldom be used the second time, because the suspense is squeezed out by one broadcast.

"The amateur, of course, can be a foil for a real comedian, or the amateur can be invited to the microphone on the underlying theory of finding new talent. This sort of show must be a sincere effort to help those who have faith in themselves. Everything doesn't have to be funny on an amateur hour. Neither can the show be prepared in advance, for if it is the amateur becomes 'frozen.' It must be a pot-luck broadcast with spontaneity the keynote. What the neophyte does at the microphone unconsciously and naturally is what counts."

America Has Abundant Talent.

Based on the popularity of other amateur programs, which have brought to light the fact that America is rich with promising talent, the Major anticipates thousands of applicants to try their luck with him. The applicant for an audition must write more than "I sing," for that, of course, means nothing to those planning the broadcast. Letters will be judged by details and character. "Obviously," the Major smiled, "we couldn't invite every one who merely sings." In the auditions prior to the actual performance those who reveal some sort of talent will be chosen.

"It is easy to ring the gong on the bad ones," said the Major. "The lad who puzzles me is the middle one, who is neither good nor bad, but to leave him on the air wastes time. Yet I hate to ring the bell on him.

"I will follow my own impulse and will juggle the program as it goes to prevent it from becoming unbalanced or uninteresting. All day Sunday we will be preparing for the sixty-minute show. Hidden somewhere behind the scenes I may eavesdrop on the auditions, but I have never done that before at the WHN amateur show. My best cue is what the amateurs do or do not do when they approach the microphone. There is no blueprint; no script."

* * *

THERE are some who think the gong is cruel when it suddenly stops an amateur. But the Major reports that in his experience at WHN only two or three out of thirty feel hurt. He admits it is undebatable. He confesses he realizes that for many the broadcast is a big moment in their lives; possibly a turning point. He promises to leave no wounds. He will be as kind and as thoughtful of the amateur's feelings as possible, because the knockout gong might ring forever in some sensitive person's ears and create an inferiority complex.

"The listeners are more concerned about the gong than the performers," continued the Major. "The audience does not always understand just what is taking place at the microphone. Letters indicate they often think the gong is unkind, yet the one whom it struck out went away smiling."

A Big Telephone Problem.

The unseen audience will be invited to sit as the jury. That has given the telephone experts a real problem.

Two hundred trunk lines will handle the calls at Radio City. In addition each week a different American or Canadian city will be designated as a telephone voting centre from which the ballots will be relayed to the New York studio, where 1,300 guests will watch the show. Tonight the Chicago area will also vote by telephone. Listeners outside the two voting zones will be asked to use the mail. The winners, however, will be announced the night of the broadcast and the selection will stand unless the letters call for a radically different decision.

* * *

WHAT chance has even an experienced artist to get on the air nowadays," said Major Bowes, "no matter how much entree he or she has to the radio studio? The amateur hour opens a gateway to the microphone. I believe thousands of young people with talent are wondering 'How can I get on the air?' And they are not alone in this quandary. There are many proved entertainers trying to find an answer to the same question. The amateur hour is one answer. It offers talent a chance to perform before the public. It separates the wheat from the chaff. It encourages artistry whether it be in the form of a one-man band or a crooner. The stars of tomorrow in radio, in opera, in comedy and in music may some day look back to the day when they were 'found' in an amateur broadcast."

This amateur show is under contract for twenty-six weeks and the sponsor has an option on the Major's services as master of ceremonies for a year and a half after that time. Each Sunday night for sixty minutes about thirty amateurs will face the microphone when opportunity knocks. Who or how many will find the road to fame and fortune out of the 780 amateurs who get their chance during the first half year of the show, not even the Major has the slightest inkling. It is a free-for-all.

Station WJZ stages an "opportunity program" on Sundays at noon and WOR at 5 o'clock. Ray Perkins is master of ceremonies of a WABC newcomers revue on Sundays at 6 o'clock. Tyros are on WMCA on Mondays from 9 to 10 o'clock from a Brooklyn theatre and on Wednesdays from 11 o'clock to midnight a similar show is picked up from a Harlem theatre. Fred Allen's "Town Hall" on Wednesday night at nine o'clock at WEAF devotes about twenty minutes to microphone strangers. On Friday at 8:30 o'clock at WEVD, Sigmund Spaeth presides over an amateur hour. WNEW has "Amateur Night in Harlem" on Tuesdays at 11 o'clock, direct from the Harlem Opera House. Station WHN's renowned show continues on Tuesday nights at 7 o'clock with Jay Flippen, as master of destiny at the gong.

March 24, 1935

Charlie McCarthy Leads In Popularity Poll

CHARLIE McCARTHY, Edgar Bergen's impish dummy, led all flesh and blood radio entertainers by a wide margin for popularity honors among listeners, at the opening of the New Year, according to the latest program survey reports received by the broadcasters. His nearest rival is Bing Crosby, whom Charlie leads by eleven points. Crosby jumped from fourth to second place, which he held in the race last November. Major Bowes and his amateurs now occupy third spot in the balloting.

Among the hour shows the Monday night "Radio Theatre" is reported as fourth; Vallee's Varieties, fifth; Fred Allen, sixth; Hollywood Hotel, seventh; Kate Smith's show, eighth; the Sunday night 9 o'clock WABC symphony concerts, ninth, and the Thursday night WEAF broadcasts from Hollywood, featuring film stars, tenth.

The popularity poll of the half-hour programs indicates that Jack Benny maintains the lead over his nearest rival, Eddie Cantor by ten points; Burns and Allen are third, Al Jolson fourth, and "The First Nighter," fifth.

First place in the quarter hour shows is held by Amos 'n' Andy, with Lowell Thomas a close second.

January 9, 1938

STUMPING THE EXPERTS

"INFORMATION, PLEASE" is one of the more recent additions to the rapidly growing list of broadcast quizzes. To qualify for wattage and a place on the wave lengths, again the quiz is presented with a novel twist to make it different from other programs in the riddle category.

The formula specifies that a board of experts, led by Clifton Fadiman as master of ceremonies, be lined up at WJZ's studio on Tuesday nights at 8:30 o'clock to answer questions submitted by listeners and by several guests in the studio. The trick is to stump the experts. If the board fails to attain a certain percentage of accuracy a cash register rings and the person who submitted the "sticker" interrogations wins $5. Incidentally, the bell rang four times during last week's broadcast.

First, the program smacks of the professional; it is presented with showmanship intensified in listener interest by the fact that well-known persons, for instance, Marc Connelly, playwright; Franklin P. Adams, columnist; John Kieran, sports writer, and others, comprise the board. The unseen audience always revels in watching people "on the spot" before the microphone. It is the same element that makes for success of the amateur hour, but in this case the "amateurs" are "experts" and the gong that signifies error is the cash register.

The fact that membership in the board changes from time to time adds renewed interest, otherwise this type of program runs the danger of becoming another link in radio routine and the listener shifts along the dial in quest of something new and more entertaining. As long as the "guest stars" change, the program maintains freshness.

Another element in the popularity of this class of broadcast is that it invites listener participation. Not only are the wise men answering, but members of the radio audience subject themselves to the same test; they may find themselves smarter or less informed than the experts. For the listener there is a double-barreled "kick"; he can submit questions to puzzle the experts, and hear them read on the air along with his name.

Furthermore, the quiz is educational as well as entertaining. Any broadcast that informally brings the unseen audience close to the studio for a game or matching of wits goes a long way in winning attention. Then, too, this is no "background" or "atmosphere" program; to enjoy it the listener must give undivided attention. He cannot be reading, playing bridge or visiting with friends. The quiz is a concentration program; it exercises the mind.

Here is a broadcast which brings out the fact that all voices are not radio voices. The average person who steps out of the studio audience to ask a question is generally difficult to understand. Mindful of this fact, those invited to serve on the faculty of experts are made to pass a voice test in audition, and Mr. Fadiman, who has a lively radio voice, puts the questions naturally and informally, embellished by a bit of humor which cuts the formal broadcasting stiffness. His tactics make it seem to the listener as if the program were being played by the family and friends in the parlor.

The main keynote of success, however, is that the listener has an opportunity to see what the experts know, what simple questions they miss and what complex ones they may answer correctly. The expert becomes a mirror for the listener, who at the end of the half hour is delighted if he finds himself with a higher score than those in the seats of the mighty around the microphone.—O. E. D.

June 19, 1938

BREAKING A SPELL

Charlie McCarthy Gets a Sunday Half Hour —Shuffling of Shows Is Foreseen

By ORRIN E. DUNLAP JR.

RADIO'S witching hour is to be split in two. Much to the delight of many a broadcast performer, including veterans of stage and screen, the ten-year stranglehold on the clock Sundays from 8 to 9 o'clock is to be broken. Effective Jan. 7, Edgar Bergen and Charlie McCarthy will headline a thirty-minute variety show opening at 8 o'clock.

When they sign off at 8:30, the curtain will go up on "One Man's Family," a serial of the "Life with Father" type, which will move out of its current Thursday night spot. Despite the six-year success of the family on the air, songsters, bands and clowns are reported to be confident they can compete with young McCarthy out of the way. Their hope springs from what seems to be a rule in broadcasting that there is always an audience for music irrespective of the dramatic sketch or speech on opposite wavelengths.

Don Ameche and Dorothy Lamour will be among the missing. The Armbruster orchestra, Donald Dickson, baritone, and weekly guest artists will, however, be part of the new deal.

Ever since Maurice Chevalier took to the air in 1931 on Sunday evenings to "receive one of the largest sums ever paid to an individual for a similar series of broadcasts," the hour from 8 to 9 o'clock has been generally considered as offering a large audience. The marvel of it is that an individual star could win so many ears and do it so effectively as to frighten even the seasoned Broadway stars away from the microphones of competing stations. Chevalier did it; so did Cantor, Bowes and McCarthy.

The proof of their success and evidence of the program's ups and downs is found on the radio popularity chart. It is based upon the number estimated to be listening as revealed by telephone calls in key cities, believed to represent a cross-section of the unseen audience.

* * *

WHY has 8 to 9 on Sunday become known as the witching hour? The day of rest is about ended. Supper is over, at least in the thickly populated East. The family in city and on farm is envisaged sitting around in a receptive mood to be entertained. The theory seems to be more fact than fancy. Few hours on the air, if any, have been so defiant in competition, so dominated by one personality.

Behind the scenes the showmen in planning the hour, like coaches on the football bench, have been hawk-like in sensing the right time to shift or change the plays and players. They have been fortunate, too, in having the right player pop up just at the opportune time. Skillfully the headliners have been manipulated. At the first indication of waning popularity the show was changed, although not always with the same public response.

After Chevalier's run, Eddie Cantor was the star. He captured the hour and built a stronghold around it. No one was anxious to enter the ethereal lists on other wavelengths to compete with Cantor. Timeliness had something to do with it and so did Cantor's lively personality. He appealed to the populace. He stepped up to the microphone on Sunday evening just when the depression caused no end of people to relish a comedian. He joked about Wall Street and falling prices; he sang that potatoes and tomatoes were cheaper. Tunefully he told the country, "Now's the Time to Fall in Love." That was in 1932!

Cantor's songs and jests pushed the hour's popularity chart to a new peak. When he went off the air for vacation or for a trip to Hollywood, the comic theme was continued with George Jessel, Harry Richman, Georgie Price, Bert Lahr and Jimmy Durante enrolled to hold the fort, but never did the curve go on high until Cantor reappeared. He hit the pinnacle in the Winter of '32, according to the chart, then again the next Winter, but not quite so high.

Finally, the curtain dropped on the jesters and an Opera Guild, offering operas in English, was substituted. The sands of popularity in the hour glass ran low. But fate was kind. A new luminary was in the ethereal heavens. Major Bowes was attracting widespread attention with his local amateur hour. Summoned to recapture the Sunday evening audience, he marched his amateurs from WHN to Radio City. Within a few weeks the performance of the Major and the neophytes became the most talked-about and popular broadcast from coast to coast. Bowes as an experienced showman fortified with just the right idea for radio at the moment sent the popularity chart up to a peak which looked like a tracing of Mount Everest. The top was scaled in the Winter of 1935.

* * *

THEN came the day when the major shifted sponsors; he went over to Thursday nights and boarded a new network. Again the popularity curve of Sunday's "witching hour" slumped badly. The "Good Will Court" and a show of California origin called "So You Want to Be an Actor" failed to save the day. For a while it looked

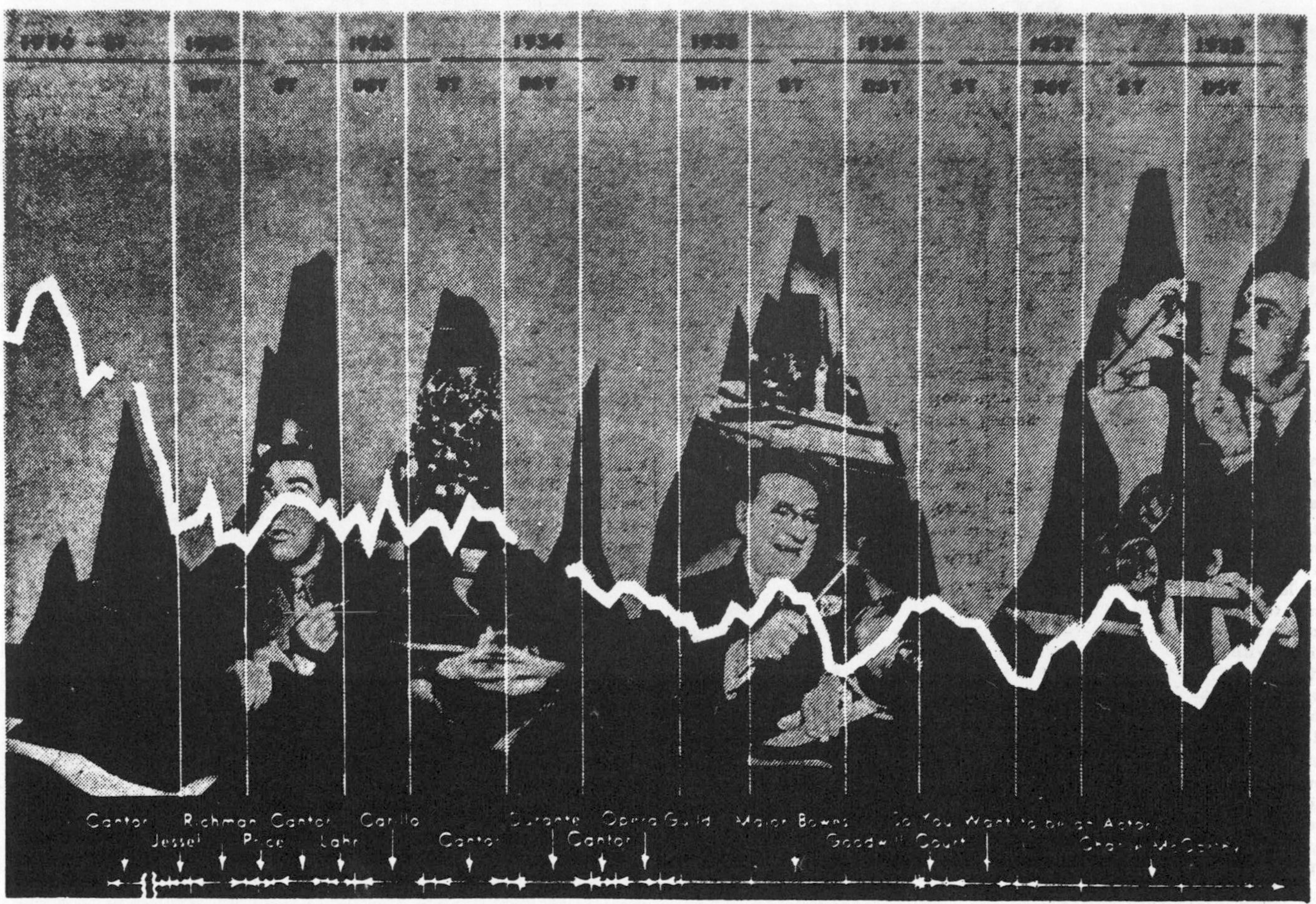

Advertising and Selling

That the ups and downs of a radio show's popularity depend to a great extent upon its performers is revealed by this nine-year chart of WEAF's Sunday night program from 8 to 9 o'clock. The peaks reached by Eddie Cantor, Major Bowes and Charlie McCarthy are vividly revealed by listener polls. The white line traces the rising and falling popularity of Amos 'n' Andy across the same period of years.

glum for the hour. Listeners were envisaged as disorganized, running all along the dial in search of Sunday evening entertainment. How could they again be corralled inside the network, as Cantor and Bowes had done?

It seems that in all the world there was some one who did want to become an actor. He had been trying for quite some time in vaudeville; he was ready for the big moment. Edgar Bergen, fresh from triumphs on the Vallee varieties, had been "discovered." He had with him a dummy named Charlie McCarthy. Here was the man of the hour.

By the end of 1937 Charlie as a national hero had the chart rushing upward and by the opening of 1938 hit a new peak, surpassing that of Cantor and Bowes, and, according to the 1939 records, he has topped his own 1938 pinnacle.

Charlie became the whole show; the brightest star by far in the variety performance. And now he is to headline a condensed version of the show, which if successful the broadcasters believe may establish a vogue for half-hour programs, sounding the end of costly hour-long broadcasts, which it is admitted require considerable variety to keep them sparkling.

* * *

CHARLIE in the half-hour class runs into competition with Jack Benny in measuring his popularity rating. Benny is top-notch in the thirty-minute class.

It is believed, however, that Charlie will set a fast pace. It will not be difficult to listen to Bergen in a half-hour show. His task will be easier. Up to now he has had to pull the audience along and hold it for an hour. To hear Charlie perform, the audience had to listen to others, too, or else run the chance of missing the headline act. Veteran performers have confessed that it was a waste of time to attempt competition with Charlie McCarthy. As one old-timer of the stage put it, "Any one who tried to run opposite Charlie would be a blockhead, too." Such has been the evaluation of Mr. Bergen's impish companion. Now, at least, he has relinquished half of the hour in which other performers may go down the wavelengths without meeting him.

SPINNING ENDLESS YARNS

Serials on Family Life, Triangles and Romance, Saturate the Air —A Script Writer Helps to Explain the Flood

By ORRIN E. DUNLAP Jr.

THE American air in the daytime is saturated with family troubles, joys and sorrows. Educators are heard to protest that there are too many throbbing serials; too many trivial triangles of love and romance. Parents and teachers complain that radio from morn to night is out of balance. They want more music and news.

Only recently 600 Westchester clubwomen unanimously voted to urge the broadcasters to electrify fewer love dramas, described as an "insult to intelligent women," and concentrate on more programs dealing with home making and child training. Also mothers want fewer contests as bait, fewer calls flashed to children urging them to send in box tops or wrappers.

But there must be some reason or method in the madness of it all. Radio in the United States is said to be built upon the public wishes. The broadcasters assert that they cater to the listeners; that they give them what they want. Their letters are the applause and criticism that form the yardstick of public taste. In fact, listeners are told that through their approval or disapproval they have the power to hold programs on the air or push them off. Ask a radio showman why so many sentimental serials are broadcast and he answers, "Because the public likes them; listeners are engrossed."

* * *

WHERE do these endless serials come from? Ask Elaine Sterne Carrington, who writes two of them, "Pepper Young's Family" and "When a Girl Marries," both heard five times a week and calling for 20,000 words. They trip out of everyday life. They are not based on the imagination, but upon the simple events and experiences of life.

How do you account for the popularity of the daytime serial? Mrs. Carrington was asked.

"A great number of people, especially women at home in city and on farm, are lonely," she replied. "To them the people in the serials become real people who talk to them. They become wrapped up in their ups and downs; their troubles become real and become theirs too. Before they know it they find themselves living along with the radio family. They rejoice and sorrow with them. They find their problems are the same as those of the people who dwell on the wavelengths, and when their problems are solved the listeners' may fade too. Radio becomes a mental uplift, also a mirror of life to them; they are made more a part of the world, and each day they keep a rendezvous with these unseen neighbors who come along to visit and to interrupt time which otherwise would be humdrum and empty."

* * *

"LISTENERS are child-like in their belief of the radio story," continued Mrs. Carrington. "They become part of it. They are pulling for the character to come out on top."

How can you write two serials without mixing the stories, and where do you get the ideas? the interviewer asked.

"The trick, if it may be called a trick," she replied, "is to let the listener hear his or her own problem solved. They learn without being taught; unconsciously they learn without being lectured through a cut-and-dried script. Dialogue is the keynote. On the radio as in the theatre, the basic ideas plus good dialogue is everything.

"My suggestion to those who want to write for radio is to look around their own home and into their own lives for the things they know and understand best. It is from such stuff that serials are made. But radio time is fleeting; and the ever-hungry microphone consumes one page of dialogue in a minute. A 15-minute story calls for twelve pages.

"It is important to remember that the story must be one that tugs at the heart, for this is the element that brings the listener back day after day. The situation must be one which they experienced. It's the common things in life and simplicity that are the driving force of the serial.

"The secret of writing two shows at once without conflict of characters and plots is to completely shut the door on the one group as soon as their tale of the week is finished."

* * *

AMERICAN families seem to have five "big" problems in common, Mrs. Carrington observes, based upon the mail she receives from all parts of the country. She lists them as follows:

Should the 16 or 17 year old boy or girl be permitted to use the family automobile?

Should children be given an allowance or be paid for chores such as cutting the grass, shoveling snow or milking the cow?

Should youngsters be given a latchkey or should the family sit up and wait for Johnny to come home? (This question pertaining more to boys.)

How late should the 16 or 17 year old Mary stay out in the evening?

Why cannot a boy decide for himself whether he is to go to college or go to work. For example, if a young man wants to be an airplane pilot why should his parents insist that he follow in his father's footsteps in the grocery store?

Following the formula "write about something you know," Mrs. Carrington works three weeks ahead of the broadcasting schedule. She completes the episodes for the ensuing week on Thursday nights. Until Monday she forgets radio.

* * *

IN planning for the broadcasts, first she lays out the yarn's general scheme or the direction it will follow for a year. This is broken down into a monthly synopsis and a day to day outline. Then it is time to put the words into the characters' mouths.

"Monday morning I start to dictate about 10 o'clock and I keep at it until midnight," explained Mrs. Carrington. "I do take time out, and have an occasional nap. I may cover two or three episodes a day. When five are finished they are typed and overhauled by numerous corrections. It's all sort of a seance. While dictating I see the whole affair acted; the lines spoken. Interruptions are disastrous."

* * *

IN no category of broadcasting is so much repetition tolerated as in the serials. A number of sketches are broadcast on both the morning and afternoon air, and one New York station devotes two hours nightly in repeating from recordings sketches heard earlier in the day on the networks.

No end of characters created by radio are traveling down the wave lengths. On and on they go from morning until night, running from family to family, from the O'Neills to Billy and Betty, and from "Stepmother" to "Big Sister" or "Manhattan Mother," from Lorenzo Jones to Young Widder Brown.

The "theatres" in which these actors fall to earth to stalk the home stage are envisaged as the kitchen, where the audience may be cooking, ironing or dishwashing; or the listener may be waxing the floors, making the beds, rocking the cradle, sweeping the carpets, washing the windows, or the baby. The daytime audience is visualized as made up of busy people. Nevertheless, the cry is heard from city clubwomen that daytime radio is dull, blunt and all one-sided.

A survey of daytime radio programs is being planned by the Women's National Radio Committee, according to a decision reached during the past week, "to determine whether daytime broadcasts actually interest home women and shut-ins, for whom they are particularly designed."

"Members of our listening groups have complained at the monotony of being obliged either to listen to one 'talkie' or serial after another, or else turn off the radio," said Mrs. Samuel Kubie, who will serve as chairman of the Daytime Programs Committee. "They also contend that many of the daytime programs are an affront to the intelligence of the home-woman who has a wide range of interests.

"While these complaints have prompted the survey, we are starting it without preconceived prejudices. The women who have written to us may represent a minority of the daytime audience. On the other hand, however, although a volume of fan mail has in all probability been responsible for continuance of some of these programs which have been on the air for several years, does writing in for leaflets or information and premiums really constitute approval of the program itself! That is what we want to find out."

February 11, 1940

RADIO 'LOVE' HELD VITAL TO PROFITS

Broadcasting Officials Tell Clubwomen 'Tripe' Pays for Worth-While Programs

Special to THE NEW YORK TIMES.

MOUNT VERNON, N. Y., March 15—"Dripping" love dramas and the crackling of gangster guns on the air waves were defended today as good business, if not culture, by broadcasting company officials as a symposium here before representatives of Westchester women's clubs who are conducting an "I'm Not Listening" boycott of radio programs they find objectionable.

"We are in the broadcasting business to make money and dripping dramas pay for the worthwhile programs that don't pay their way," Donald S. Shaw, executive vice president of station WMCA, told the thirty-five club presidents and committee chairmen at a luncheon at the Studio Club Restaurant.

He said that it might be a "sad commentary," but it was a fact that a leading soap company had found through surveys that the radio public listens to serial stores and "they sell soap—and plenty of soap."

Listeners Like to Be Teased

Radio listeners like to be teased; that is why there are so many serials of the "Did Jenny really break her left leg?—Tune in tomorrow afternoon and find out" type, according to Mr. Shaw. He added that radio had never offended to such an extent as some of the comic magazines.

Mrs. Charles H. Phelps Jr. of Bronxville complained that the radio hours from 5 P. M. to 8 P. M. had become "hideous" with sordid adventure and "cheap wisecracks that belong in the gutter." Her 9-year-old son, Mrs. Phelps said, had become, through the radio, altogether too familiar with "gun-toting gangsters, gun molls, the Big Boss and his henchmen, the inside of prisons and the hot seat." He knows, she added, "how to cover up a trail to escape the bulls, how to cut telephone lines, how to hide license plate numbers, so that he can scram successfully."

She recommended as a substitute for gangland theatrics the dramatization of historical events dealing with romantic but actual heroes, even that stories from the Bible be sandwiched between Charlie McCarthy and "flashes in staccato fashion on the latest tidbits from Hollywood" on Sunday evenings.

Sees Educational Advance

A. L. Simon, publicity director of Station WHN, advised the women to be patient. He said radio was in its infancy, but, bad as some of its programs might be, it already had advanced education.

"To women not so culturally fortunate as you club ladies, radio is a boon," he said.

Leslie Evan Roberts, a WMCA vice president, asserted that there was "as much tripe to be found in literature and on the stage as on the radio." It was his opinion that the majority of listeners either did not understand or were bored by the higher type of program, and as long as they demand serials they will get them.

Mrs. Everett L. Barnard, chairman of the "I'm Not Listening" committee, reported that the movement had spread to thirty-nine States.

March 16, 1940

PEOPLE SEEM TO LIKE IT

WITHIN the studio the dress rehearsal, as usual, left the cast vibrating with nervous tension. The author, sitting in the control room, could hardly be described as a bronze of serenity. The second hand ticked around relentlessly, however, until the appointed moment and the curtain went up on the opening scene of one of the longest-running dramas on record.

The date was March 29, 1932, the drama was "One Man's Family," and the curtain not only went up—it stayed up for what is now almost ten years.

"One Man's Family" is only one of several NBC dramatic offerings which admiring audiences have kept on the air for an uncommonly long time despite change of broadcasting time and sponsor's heart. Considered with "Vic and Sade," "Betty and Bob," "Ma Perkins," "The Story of Mary Marlin," "The O'Neills" and Irene Rich's plays, all seven, eight and nine years old, the record-run legitimate shows, "Abie's Irish Rose" and "Tobacco Road," were subway-door dramas—open and shut.

Patriarch

The oldest of the lot, "One Man's Family," was born on Station KGO, San Francisco, on the aforementioned lucky date. The story locale was, and still is, San Francisco, although the program now originates from Hollywood. A quick local success led to an NBC network debut on May 17, 1933, and it has been doing beautifully ever since, thank you. The story, as you must know by now, centers in the Barbour clan—not small to begin with and well propagated since—and has for its underlying theme the clash between conservative parents and their liberal-minded offspring.

The author of "One Man's Family," Carleton E. Morse, although married, has no children of his own. Much of the juvenile psychology which the program expounds from week to week comes, the author confesses, from a young brother-in-law who makes his home with Mr. M. When two of his characters took their honeymoon on the China Clipper, however, they were reliving in fiction Mr. Morse's experience on the clipper's first round-trip several weeks earlier. J. Anthony Smythe, who plays Father Barbour, has no inspiration to point to—he's a confirmed bachelor.

In addition to Mr. Smythe, the large cast includes Minetta Ellen, Michael Raffetto, Bernice Berwin, Barton Yarborough, Kathleen Wilson, Page Gilman, Winifred Wolfe and Barbara Jo Allen. There hasn't been a change in the original cast, except for additions from time to time and the fact that the pre-broadcast tenseness of 1932 is gone. Some time ago, when Michael Raffetto was taken quite ill, Mr. Morse, instead of casting a substitute, wrote him out of the script for six months.

Trophy Room

Besides its faithful following, "One Man's Family" has been singled out for official awards more often than almost any other program on the air. Its trophy room boasts the Radio Stars award for distinguished service to radio, a San Francisco Press Club award and the Women's Press Club award for several years running.

But the most remarkable chapter in its career came some time ago when a broadcast of "One Man's Family" was introduced as an alibi in a Chicago court. A boy, accused of robbery, pleaded innocent and said that he was at home listening to the program at the time of the crime. He was questioned minutely on the details of the script, his answers were compared to an actual copy of the program; on the basis of complete accuracy, he was acquitted. Sounds like something out of a daytime serial.

December 28, 1941

RADIO'S PERENNIAL FAMILY: 'THE BARBOURS'

By VAL ADAMS

CARLTON E. MORSE, writer of the "One Man's Family" radio series on NBC, arises in his suite at the St. Moritz hotel every morning at 5:30 o'clock, cooks his own breakfast of steak and fried potatoes (sliced very thin) and then sits down to a stint of script writing. In a way, he operates like a one-man family himself.

Morse is a man who leans toward placidity in a business famed for its addiction to nervous disorders. That's one reason he gets up at 5:30 A. M. He prefers to write two and a half hours before the whole world breaks loose upon him.

"If you know NBC," Morse comments, "people are climbing all over one another. Phones ringing. People rushing in and out all day. I like to get my writing done before the hubbub starts." Morse's normal bedtime is 9 P. M. or earlier. "If we have guests at home," he says, "I'll try to stay awake after nine."

The creator of the 17-year-old program, who also produces and directs the series, just arrived in New York from Hollywood to put radio's Barbour family into television. Since April, 1932, radio listeners have imagined themselves a neighbors of the Barbours who live in Sea Cliff, a section of San Francisco. When the television series begins on NBC Monday, Aug. 1, at 9:30 P. M., viewers will be able to see the Golden Gate bridge through the Barbours' living room window. The radio show is broadcast on Monday nights at 8.

When "One Man's Family" went on the air, there were Father and Mother Barbour and five children ranging in age from 14 to 28. Possibly to simplify matters, Morse cast the show with actors and actresses whose real life ages correspond with their radio characterizations. Today, four of the Barbour children have been married—some of them more than once—and there are thirteen grandchildren, one adopted.

The seven performers who started on the program are still there. Actress Minetta Ellen, who plays the role of Fanny Barbour, now a grandmother, has grown to the age of seventy-eight in real life. Father Barbour is played by J. Anthony Smythe. Actor Page Gilman, who plays the youngest of the Barbour children, Jack, went into the Army during the war so Morce had the performer's radio counterpart do the same thing. Wherever the actor moved during the war, his radio characterization went right along in the script of "One Man's Family."

Morse joined NBC's production staff in San Francisco in 1929 as a producer and writer. He thought radio might be steadier than some of the newspapers which had been folding underneath him up and down the West Coast. After three years of writing such radio plays as "Chinatown Squad," "Dead Men Walk" and "The Game Called Murder" he got fed up with mysteries and turned to thoughts of the simple life. Morse was inspired by two things—a love of John Galsworthy's "Forsyte Saga" and nostalgia for the family life of his boyhood when he was the oldest of six children. He submitted a few scripts to NBC under the title "One Man's Family." The network told him to go ahead but to write the story so it could be ended in six months.

Tempest

"One Man's Family" had its première as a local program only on KGO, San Francisco. Shortly afterward it was expanded to a regional network and finally it went "transcontinental," as Morse expressed it, sometimes using the abbreviation "TC." The program's first national sponsor was Kentucky Winners cigarettes, an event which aroused listener protest over a tobacco firm being tied up with a family program. After nine weeks, the network asked and received a release from the contract with the sponsor. As a sequel, the cigarette incident created so much fuss over "One Man's Family" that Standard Brands picked up an interest in the show which led to a continuing sponsorship of nearly fifteen years.

Standard Brands dropped out of the picture only a few months ago, leaving the program sustaining, and Morse had to cope with rumors that the series was about to leave the air. He announced on the program that the sponsor was leaving and that it would be comforting to have listeners write and tell how they had appreciated knowing the Barbour family down through the years. Rumors of the program's passing seemed to fade overnight when listeners wrote of their sadness, should the program fold, and many sent financial aid.

The artists on the program are frequently amazed at the parallels between their real lives and their roles on the air. One actress, no longer in the cast, began having trouble with her husband in private life. Later a similar difficulty turned up for her in the show.

On another occasion, an actress kept secret the fact that she and her husband were awaiting the stork. During a studio rehearsal at NBC, she picked up a script and discovered she was going to have a baby on the air at about the same time she expected one in real life.

Down through the years, Morse has kept "One Man's Family" going with only a minimum of plot. He intentionally stays away from the soap opera type of story and lets the characters motivate themselves as they would in an average family. While the five Barbour children still live, there have been a few deaths and divorces among the mixture of relatives, one grandchild dying at the age of three. When Morse was asked if he wrote in such incidents merely to create sympathy, he answered: "Well, those things happen in a lot of families."

The 48-year-old writer and producer of "One Man's Family" has been married for nearly twenty-one years and he brought along his wife, Patricia, to New York. Her waking hour every morning is not as early as his and frequently Morse will leave a note at her bedside when he goes to the studio.

Before leaving Hollywood, Morse and his cast recorded sixteen radio shows in advance so they could devote all their time to television in New York. He also has a second television show which will start on Friday at 9 P. M. It is entitled "Mixed Doubles" and already has been seen on the West Coast.

"One Man's Family" on TV will start with Jack Barbour's wife giving birth to triplets. Morse wants to get the show off with a bang.

July 24, 1949

HE TALKS ALL NIGHT

ON the theory, perhaps, that people who sit up all night are not likely to be awake between 6:30 A. M. and 7:45 A. M., which is the time when Arthur Godfrey holds forth on WABC six days a week, the Columbia Broadcasting System recently had a bright idea.

At least once a week, the Columbia Broadcasting System decided, the stay-up-all-nights in this vicinity really ought to have a chance to hear Mr. Godfrey. And so it was arranged, and so he comes over from Washington (whence he usually broadcasts) and sits in a studio here and talks and sings and plays records from 1 A. M. to 6:15 A. M. every Saturday. He then draws a long breath and goes on to his early morning stint at the aforementioned 6:30.

This Mr. Godfrey is quite a fellow, as witness a few random notes on his life and methods, collected (the notes) from hither and yon:

He is heavy-set, red-haired, freckle-faced, and about 38 years old. He likes to sing, and he takes singing lessons, but he refers to his voice as "pure barreltone." In fact, he spends a good deal of time kidding himself, describing his program as "The Drip Hour" and himself as a fugitive from a faucet.

While the Bosses Sleep

"People have been writing in wondering why CBS pays me," he said one morning. "Frankly, they don't know what goes on, on this show. I'll prove it to you. Any Columbia officials listening?" he asked. He then paused and delivered a strident Bronx cheer.

Among other things, he is—for the purposes of his program—a philosopher, poem-reader and meteorologist. That is to say, he discusses life, recites bad poetry, and submits frequent weather reports to his listeners, all between records. And he does a lot of recruiting for the Navy.

The Godfrey interest in the Navy began when he enlisted at 16 and served a four-year hitch, re-enlisting later in the Coast Guard after an interval as a short-order cook in a Manhattan diner, master of ceremonies in a Chicago hot spot, salesman of cemetery lots in Detroit and vaudeville actor in Los Angeles.

But getting back to the radio. While still in the service he got involved in an amateur air show in Baltimore and wound up as "Red Godfrey, the Warbling Banjoist," sponsored by a birdseed firm. But the real milestone was a four-month convalescence spent in a hospital in 1933 after an automobile accident. Mr. Godfrey, who had become an announcer, got a chance to listen to the radio. He didn't particularly like what he heard.

The boys were too stilted, he thought. When he got out of there he would do something about it. He did.

In January, 1934, he launched the Sun Dial program on WJSV, Washington, and he has been there ever since. It was about four months ago that he started his duties for WABC, "piping in" the show from the capital.

Other Godfreyana: He lives on a 150-acre farm at Vienna, Va.; does most of the farm work himself, is married and has a son, sails three boats and flies a plane and gets up at about 5 A. M. to make the trip to Washington, sixteen miles away. Just the same, he likes his work.

December 7, 1941

THE IMMORTAL RANGER

Earle H. Graser was killed in an automobile wreck early Tuesday morning, but the rumor that the Lone Ranger is dead is unfounded. It was a man who died—a man with a silver voice, a modest, pleasant personality, several college degrees and, it was said, an ambition to act Hamlet. His death, like the deaths he tried to prevent in his radio campaign for safety, was pitifully unnecessary. But he didn't take the Lone Ranger with him. The Lone Ranger doesn't die, and Silver, his horse, will never get broken-winded.

The Lone Ranger, under that name, came into being in this generation for a radio public, but under various names he has been alive for many centuries. He was Ulysses, William Tell and Robin Hood; he was Richard the Lion-Hearted, the Black Prince and du Guesclin; he was Kit Carson, Daniel Boone and Davy Crockett; he was honest, truthful and brave—and so he remains.

He got into dangers that would paralyze an ordinary man, but if there was an injustice to be righted, a wrong to be prevented, he liked danger. In the simple hearts of children, and possibly of adults who were willing to take a vacation from what unhappily has to be printed nowadays on the first pages of newspapers, he was as real as the policeman on the corner. He still is, and his trusty steed waits to carry him on his errands across the face of the wondrous West, where the air is crystal and virtue never lacks for its reward. Listen! There is a beating of hoofs as, in the nick of time, he swings into action. Ride, Tonto, ride, Lone Ranger. Hi-yo Silver!

April 10, 1941

THE 'MIKE' DEMANDS TOP ACTING

By LANFRANCO RASPONI

DIVORCES on the air every Friday night have taught more acting tricks to Joan Blondell, star of the series "I Want a Divorce" on the WOR network, than nine years of screen career. It is she who says so. During a recent visit to New York the actress discussed over the breakfast table the various phases of her first important radio assignment.

"These twenty-two weeks on the air have been stimulating," she said in her frank, direct way, "for I have had to stand on my own feet again. You forget all about real acting in pictures. You have to concentrate for one minute and then you have perhaps a couple of hours' rest. You have no worries about timing or anything else, for the directors, the camera men do it all for you. But on the radio you have got to be alert; you have to prepare as well as execute whatever evolutions the script calls for."

One Way to Get in Radio

Miss Blondell explained that the show "I Want a Divorce" has been on the air a long time. When the sponsors were looking around for a "name" to play the different heroines, they happened to think of her, for she had made a picture by that name. And though she hesitated to accept their offer, she followed the advice of her husband, Dick Powell, a radio veteran, and started a new career before the microphone.

"Many of the plays are somewhat corny," she went on, "and deal with Sallies, Marys and Pollies who get into terrific jams. One week I have to be a rascal and the following one a little martyr. But the important thing is that I am always getting myself into trouble. The drama develops during the first fifteen minutes. Then the wedding march prepares for another fifteen minutes in which everything is cleaned up, and just before the commercial I am on the right path again.

"One week," she recalled, "I married a man who had a grown-up son who hated the sight of me. In the midst of this situation a flood swept the town and we all had to swim out of the house. I had to breathe so heavily into the microphone, to give the impression of drowning, that I had hardly any strength left when the show came to an end. But my mother, who listens in regularly, remarked that I would develop into a tragedian some day."

Intermission Note

In the midst of the interview a powerful voice in the next room began singing the baritone aria from "The Barber of Seville."

"Oh, that's Dick," she laughed, "in the bathroom. He has operatic ambitions."

According to Miss Blondell, acting for the radio is much more closely associated with the stage than with the screen.

In Hollywood, she said, good-looking people often make a success with hardly any acting ability. Stars are made overnight. "But that very rarely happens on Broadway or on the air," she observed. "In radio it is all a question of sustained feeling. You never can let down, for the climax approaches at great speed, and you have got to work up to it.

"On the screen when you start a picture you probably shoot the ending the first day and the beginning the last day. You have to wait around until certain sets are built or certain actors are free from other commitments. You have been up since 5:30 o'clock in the morning and you are deaf from the noise you have been hearing on the set all day."

Guest Appearances Were Few

Her radio experience, until she started the present series, had been limited to a few guest appearances prepared by many rehearsals.

"The first few times," she confessed, "the mere fact of reading made me nervous. It almost seemed as if I could read only a word at a time. But after more performances and listening to recordings made of the show I began to feel my way around. Of course, when you first see yourself on the screen or hear yourself on the air, you wonder whether it can be really you. Then you begin thinking about yourself in a sort of objective manner, almost as if you were somebody else."

One of the things that have pleased Miss Blondell the most is the fact that her radio sponsors have given her the opportunity to play roles in radio she has never had a chance to play in Hollywood. In motion pictures, she thinks, it is practically impossible to get away from the type of part you were assigned to at the start of your career.

"I have been in at least seventy-five pictures," she said. "At one point I made thirty-two pictures in twenty-seven months. And yet I have always been cast as the same type of girl. They started me out as a gold digger and for what seemed centuries I was given only gold-digging parts. And yet if at the time I had been asked what gold-digging consisted of, I dare say I should not have given the right answer. Now at last I am a free lance and it feels good."

"It is strange," she said, "but I am not really terribly ambitious any more. After having cracked the same jokes in different gowns for nine years, I find them just a little stale. The startling performance I had hoped to give some day seems to matter less now and I content myself with being adequate. I would love to go back to the stage, but mountains of scripts won't help me. It is one alone and a good one that I need. Still, this radio episode in my life has encouraged me somewhat and when this series ends, I am very keen to start on a new one."

March 30, 1941

These amiable folk are, of course, Fibber McGee and Molly, who will be back at "Wistful Vista" this Tuesday at 9:30 P. M. on WEAF.

LISTENING AT RANDOM

By R. W. STEWART

TUESDAY night is a good night on the air for comedy. For ninety racing minutes beginning at half-past 9, Fibber McGee and Molly, Bob Hope and Uncle Walter's Dog House pass before WEAF's microphone at half-hour intervals, each selling a different kind of humor. Their pooled material for one evening would be virtually enough to stock up a Broadway musical comedy.

While the style of Fibber and Molly is not so spectacular as that of Hope and Uncle Walter, who emphasize satire or gags, its effectiveness and popularity does not suffer in the comparison. As radio's "Jiggs and Maggie," they have entertained listeners from coast to coast for the last six years with the turbulent family life they portray in their comic strip of the air. Moreover, their favor in radio is based strictly on their radio performances. Since they entered the field about fourteen years ago they have not indulged in any personal appearance or motion picture ventures, which are generally regarded as efficient means for developing an audience.

The Jordans, Jim and Marion, as they are known in private life, follow a policy of situation humor, instead of relying on fast-breaking jokes. They project their characterizations along broad lines, mainly touching those situations that actually occur in the lives of everyday folks. A clever change of pace in situations adds freshness to the comedy series.

Like most radio headliners today, Fibber and Molly have trod the boards. Both are troupers of the old school, having gone through the vaudeville mill of one-night stands and sleeper jumps. According to the latest listener surveys, they have been building up strong selling points at the counter of public approval.

March 2, 1941

THE SHADOW OF LAMONT CRANSTON

Wherein the Deeds of a Microphone Merriwell Are Recounted

By GEORGE A. MOONEY

LAMONT CRANSTON, radio's rich, handsome and well-dressed man-about-town, continues as popular with the thrill-loving set as he was ten years years ago. Still in his thirties, Cranston, who has been described as a "combination of Lucius Beebe and the Thin Man," is a New Yorker, educated at the best schools, widely traveled and a student of the occult sciences. While in India he learned the secrets of thought projection, the rope trick, suspended animation and escape from bores. He vanishes into thin air.

The character known as "The Shadow," heard each Sunday afternoon over WOR, seldom meets bores these days, but he does encounter thieves and fiends aplenty. The vanishing stunt is invaluable then—in fact, it would be a dull script without it. But the life of a microphone Merriwell, even with such a trick at his command, is no easy existence. There is no time for the social whirl when you must crusade against crime and be forever rushing to the aid of a friend like Margot Lane.

Mischief and Margot

Margot, who has owned to being 26, is attractive, intelligent, well educated and generally shows pretty good sense. But somehow, nine times out of ten, wherever she goes, there is certain to be some kind of monster, mechanical man or plain crackpot lurking in the vicinity. If it isn't one thing it's another.

There was an occasion when she got mixed up with a mad scientist and in no time at all he was preparing to exchange her vocal chords for those of a cat. The Shadow saved her from that with only two minutes to spare and they, of course, had been reserved for the sponsor's sales talk.

Another time there was a homicidal maniac who was doing a very successful business with poisonous spiders encased in gelatinous pellets. He would secretly deposit one on the person of his victim and after body heat melted the substance the spider was free to take a bite, and that was that. In Margot's case the clever fellow was less subtle and had just decided to dispense with the gelatin when the ubiquitous Mr. Cranston arrived to go into his "shadow" act with the usual effect. The poor fiend lost his wits completely and died a horrible death.

Justice Catches Up

The Shadow's enemies and Margot's tormentors invariably die hard. Death by the kiss of a jackdaw with a cyanide-tipped beak; a midget with lethal instincts extinguished by becoming a meal for a hungry Great Dane; and the crushing of a criminal by the gorilla he had trained to kill, are a few Horrible Examples.

"But The Shadow himself never kills anybody," said Bill Johnstone, the young radio actor who for the past three years has made that worthy and Lamont Cranston articulate. "The Shadow," he went on, "was originally the voice of conscience and it was through the fear which he aroused in the minds of criminals that they exposed their own villainy or destroyed themselves.

"Ten years ago, when the show was first presented, The Shadow was only a sound effect, a nasty, snarly voice that would burst in with a blood-curdling laugh, and sneer, 'The Shadow knows.' Now the part has been expanded into that of a dual personality—Cranston, the educated, society man, and The Shadow, the name he affects when employing his unusual talents in a good cause."

Johnstone, Scotch born, has been in radio work for the last eight years and entered show business fifteen years ago carrying a spear in a Theatre Guild production. Orson Welles was his predecessor in the part of The Shadow and Johnstone takes his job quite seriously.

A Popular Role

I've had great satisfaction in the work," he explained, "because it seems that everybody who has ever listened to the radio has heard of The Shadow. Recently I had a part in a radio show put on from a Brooklyn high school. I was introduced as 'The Shadow' and it was like a scene in a movie when a box is opened and a baby's head appears. Everybody said 'Ah!'

"When I first took over The Shadow, the part still had a lot of crude, scary stuff and he was a very stupid person. I've tried to make him intelligent and real. We have had thousands of letters from kids and it's pretty plain that he's got to be somebody they can respect and admire."

As he spoke, Margot, The Shadow's "friend and companion," as she is described in the scripts, nodded assent. Margot, nee Marjorie Anderson, was born in Spokane, Wash., and attended Miss Finch's school here. After three years as a social worker and a sojourn abroad, she entered radio work in 1932, becoming Margot in 1939. She shares Johnstone's belief in the social responsibility of the characters they portray.

Metamorphosis

"At first Margot was a stupid stooge," she explained, "but now she has some ideas of her own. As I see her, she is intelligent, educated and with a good sense of humor. She is very much interested in this fellow Cranston and is always ready to be a sort of guinea pig and take a chance, if it will help him. She is genuine, sincere and the kind of girl I like."

That the characters of Margot and Cranston have been so volatile over the course of the years is not surprising in view of their origins. At least fifty authors, including the renowned "Ellery Queen," have written scripts for the show, each providing his own version of the couple's personalities. The kids—and their elders—quick to discover any discrepancies of character, wouldn't stand for it. While the scripts are still written by various authors, two special writers are now employed to adapt scripts and keep the characters "in character."

In character or out, however, Lamont Cranston and Margot Lane, while their radio lives continue, seem destined to share a harrowing existence. But whatever happens, "The Shadow knows!"

February 2, 1941

THE PRECOCIOUS QUIZ KIDS

Radio and the Movies Are Attracted by Their Talent

By LANFRANCO RASPONI

FROM a group of child prodigies it is allowable to expect temperament, bad manners, egotism and a few other none-too-pleasant manifestations. However, the Quiz Kids, who are heard every Wednesday night over WJZ's network, did not follow the expected formula during their short visit in New York from Chicago.

Interviewed during a long, tiring day at the Paramount studios on Long Island where they were making their motion picture debut in a short, they proved to be excellent sports. Responding to directors and camera men like old troupers, they gave no sign of boredom and behaved as well as little Lord Fauntleroy.

Seated in tall armchairs with glaring lights before them, they answered impromptu and unrehearsed the same types of questions asked of them during the broadcasts. While four poetical quotations, for instance, were recognized immediately, a sketch of the claws of an owl brought no response from any of them.

An 8-Year-Old "Veteran"

Eight-year-old Gerard Darrow's proudest possession is a record of twenty appearances since the radio program started last June. Although two children are dropped out each time—those with the lowest proportion of correct answers to questions—tenacious Gerard has tagged right along. He was forced out a couple of times, but thousands of fans' letters made it clear that without him the show suffered.

His chin scratched and bruised, he explained during the interview that he had fallen off a bicycle Santa Claus had brought him for Christmas. Denying that he was in any way nervous on this rather important occasion, he skipped about the set incessantly.

"I like any sort of question," he said, his hands fidgeting restlessly, "but I am at my best with anything that has to do with nature. I collect birds' nests, feathers, butterflies and insects. My ambition is to become a professor of ornithology some day."

Though Gerard has not yet taken history or geography at school, where he is in the fourth grade, he knows the names of hundreds of cities and rivers and mountains and quite a few historical dates. Asked to state his 1941 resolution, he replied: "Tolerance." When told that Mrs. Franklin D. Roosevelt was going to receive the Quiz Kids in Washington on their return journey to Chicago, he said only, "Will it be fun?"

Dressing for Movies

During the broadcasts, the children wear caps and gowns, but it was decided that for the movie they should wear their everyday school clothes. Make-up was excluded, too, as not pertaining to the character of the performance.

The two girls, Cynthia Cline, 15, and Joan Bishop, 13, both hope to become singers. Joan, who appeared in 1938 as piano soloist of Mozart's D Minor Concerto with the Chicago Symphony, goes to a private school and plays the piano five or six hours a day.

Plump and good-natured, Joan said she considered this experience as "a stepping stone to greater achievements."

"This quiz is very amusing," she went on, "until you realize that you don't know something which you ought to know. Then you get sort of cross at yourself. But it is not exactly thrilling. The thrill I want is to sing a big role in opera with a large audience present. I was picked out for this program and given several appearances because I have done pretty well with my piano and also because I spend a great deal of time reading."

An Ambitious Ambition

Cynthia's story was much the same, except that her ambition includes photography, dancing, composing and writing poems. Her favorite pastime is to play the Lily Pons records and accompany them with the flute she is now learning to play.

"When I play the Mad Scene of 'Lucia'," she added, "I can't resist putting down the flute and just singing along with Lily. When I am answering questions on the air or attending to my music at home, I am never conscious that there might be people listening in on me. The public does not worry me one bit."

Van Dyke Tiers, 13, was the only one in the group to be accompanied by his father, the others all being in charge of either mothers or aunts. H. W. Tiers, proud of being the 67-year-old parent of an intelligent son, insisted on helping out Van with the interview.

"My real interest is chemistry," Van said, his little eyes glued on his father, "and I already have my own lab at home. I don't think I would like to become an actor for I feel it would become a bore after a while."

Boys Rated Higher

That boys on the whole have proved brighter than girls on the program was the opinion of Louis Cowan, originator and producer. Often with an older girl and a younger brother appearing the same evening, the boy would come out on top. To explain it, Mr. Cowan says that boys have perhaps fewer interests than girls, but are apt to develop one of them very thoroughly.

"The main difficulty we have to face," he said, "is to persuade the public that these kids haven't really the faintest idea what they are going to be asked. Our process of elimination is extremely careful, and before we put a child on the air we try out his degree of culture in every possible way."

While 11-year-old Richard Williams expressed a particular inclination for geography and enthusiastically emphasized his desire to become a combustion engineer, Mary Clare McHugh rolled her beautiful light-blue eyes and made the ungrateful job of stand-in seem a graceful one.

"I was made to come along," she sighed, philosophically, "just in case one of my five colleagues should fall sick or something. They are all in very good health, alas! and so I have nothing to do. Of course I am a little disappointed, but life, I am told, is a series of disappointments."

January 12, 1941

DR. WATSON SPEAKS UP

By LANFRANCO RASPONI

RADIO cars, G-men, fingerprinting and the whole bag of tricks with which streamlined sleuths are equipped have definitely dated Sherlock Holmes and Dr. Watson, but their exploits still enthrall that most modern of all publics—the radio audience. Basil Rathbone and Nigel Bruce, beginning their Sunday broadcasts last week, found that the characters, whose adventures kept our grandfathers awake, are now especially satisfying to the unseen listeners.

During a brief stay in New York between broadcasts, Nigel Bruce expressed the opinion that old-fashioned stories are a great tonic in these days of stress. The war with all its untold horrors, he feels, ceases to exist for the people who listen in on the air to the problems involving Scotland Yard detectives of long ago. The London of the Nineties with its rolling cobblestones and its open landaus can be re-created in imagination almost as if the reality of bombing planes were yet to be experienced.

"We all strive to keep the period intact," Mr. Bruce said, "and Edith Meyser, who writes the scripts, doesn't even change the name of a village or of a person. It is not easy to condense some of the long stories into a half-an-hour version without leaving out some important passages, and yet she seems to be able to do it. Our plays appeal to the old who remember with fondness and envy the good old days and to the young who never knew them and wish they had."

The numerous Sherlock Holmes clubs all over the country keep in constant touch with Mr. Rathbone and Mr. Bruce, and if even a small detail in a story is left out a flood of raging protests usually follows.

A Long Friendship

"The friendship which unites Watson and Holmes," Mr. Bruce continued, "is just as real between Basil and myself. We have known each other for over twenty years, ever since we played in London together, and we are devoted pals. Our wives happen to be most congenial, too."

Mr. Bruce is glad that his broadcasts don't take place before an audience, for he finds it difficult to concentrate on a few people in a theatre and on millions of listeners over the waves at the same time. Radio technique is to him a matter of extremely clear diction and of timing the different tones in proportion to the distances from the microphone.

"One can't just rush to the mike," he explained, "and read. The characterization is just as important as on the stage and, although one's face is not made up, it is sort of a mental make-up. As Watson I must become rather slow, stupid, affectionate, misguided and doing the wrong thing most of the time."

Although Conan Doyle wrote his 130 stories roughly between 1894 and 1912, Mr. Bruce thinks he managed to keep his two main characters always coherent. Throughout the series Holmes very rarely shows his feelings, while Watson does so and much too much.

A Popular Character

"There is no real evolution in their minds," the actor observed, "but I think it is a great tribute to these two imaginary persons that after fifty-five years they still should be so alive and create such interest. As you probably know, Conan Doyle killed Sherlock Holmes off, but the disappointment of the readers was such that he had to bring him back by popular demand.

"Acting is a complicated medium," Mr. Bruce declared, "which demands most of all the sinking of the artist into the role he is portraying. I have always considered myself a comedian and since comedies date quicker than any other form of entertainment, most of the plays I have appeared in have been contemporary. However, I have had some experience with Shakespeare and I must confess I have no great love for the bird!

"His clowns are the most awful bores," he asserted, "for actors to play. I would die rather than go through Falstaff or Tobias again. While I would be a fool not to realize that some of Shakespeare's passages are about the most magnificent that have ever been written, I cannot bring myself to find his fun really merry.

"Having been all my life on the stage," he said, "and having made some thirty-five motion pictures in Hollywood, I have come to the conclusion that many of the movie actors are not really actors. Some, of course, are magnificent. Emil Jannings, Jean Gabin, Spencer Tracy are among the finest I have ever seen, but most movie actors would be flops on the stage. For radio a great subtlety is needed to do away with the immediate vision of the action."

In Hollywood, Mr. Bruce said, he recently finished "Reuter's Dispatch," with Edna Best and Edward G. Robinson, and "Hudson Bay," with Paul Muni, in which he takes the part of Prince Ruprecht. He has also been busy appearing in Noel Coward's "Tonight at Eight Thirty" on the West Coast for the British war relief.

"But I am glad to go back to old Watson," he smiled sadly, "and to the old London where I first gained success and fame. When so much we love is being destroyed, it is comforting to go back to it, even if it has to be re-created by the unreal world of acting."

October 6, 1940

A CRITICAL VOTE FOR VARIETY

Kate Smith Stands Pat on A Winning Combination

By R. W. STEWART

ALTHOUGH the majority of radio's showmen agree that variety is an effective means of producing a successful, interest-provoking broadcast, there is a dissenting school of thought which holds that it defeats its purpose by too often resulting in a potpourri of disjointed features without rhyme or reason. For the affirmative side, however, there is no better argument than Kate Smith's Friday night variety show, which recently opened on WABC's hookup for the 1940-41 term. Weaving song, drama and comedy into a clever pattern, Miss Smith presents an entertaining hour on the air between 8 and 9 o'clock.

Recognizing a winning combination, in the new edition of her program she is standing pat, more or less, on the format of last season's series. While her voice has spelled her fortune, she is too shrewd to believe that this alone can carry a sixty-minute spot. So, in addition to enlisting the regular services of a comedian, an orchestra and a chorus, she also invites actors and well-known personalities to the shows to complete her broadcasting scheme, which provides for dramas and interviews. Nevertheless, it is Miss Smith's singing which binds the program into a cohesive production.

A Switch in Comedy

Switching from the low comedy of Abbott and Costello, who, incidentally, made their radio debut on the Smith show, the program now features humor in dialect with Willie Howard as the funny man. Even though one performance does not provide too accurate a gauge for criticism, the fact remains that Willie definitely was not at his funniest for the opening broadcast. He has his work cut out for him. If he lives up to his stage reputation his part in the show should become one of the highlights.

For the dramatic portion of the première Dean Jagger, Mary Astor and Tyrone Power played excerpts from their roles in "Brigham Young—Frontiersman." Their competent portrayal indicated that the film folk are becoming educated, or at least accustomed, to the microphone and its technique. Top performance laurels, however, belong to Joan Banks, a product of radio, who assisted in the sketch. Thoroughly trained in transmitting every emotion, every nuance, to the listeners by voice alone, she plays to the "mike" as though it were a living audience. She is not a reader. But glancing at the script from time to time in action, she physically acts out her part.

Musically the broadcast is well equipped, with the Kate Smith Singers under the direction of Ted Straeter, Jack Miller's band, the Mullins Sisters and the Smart Set rounding out the cast. Summing up, the Smith show must be put down as preferred entertainment.

Bob Hope Returns

A mad merriment marks the swift pace of Bob Hope's program.

His return to the air last week for the third consecutive season makes Tuesday night a brighter spot on WEAF's schedule. Possessing a style wholly independent of trick costumes or miming, his comedy is especially effective for the "mike."

Taking up where he left off last Spring, few flat spots creep into the Hope show for, by nimble ad libbing, he often has stepped into the breach when a gag misfired. The scripts indicate careful preparation in selecting jokes fitted to his delivery and a sense of timeliness that keeps the show fresh. For instance, on the opening show conscription and politics were targets for humorous barbs.

With the exception of Judy Garland, the cast of the show is intact. And to followers of the show her absence will be felt, for the girl with the big voice was very much a part of the program; she played her part well. She takes to the microphone naturally and naturalness is the difference between a good and bad radio performance. Gloria Jean was called up as guest on the opening program for the Garland spot, but her work was unseasoned and unappealing.

Jerry Colonna was back with his pithy, abrupt comedy. His participation in the broadcast is one of the things that makes it worth-while listening. Jerry is enough of a comedian and a personality to have his own program.

The Ennis band and Six Hits and a Miss provide the music and, with Brenda and Cobina, the "unglamor" girls, complete the cast of a racy show that makes the thirty minutes tick off like so many seconds.

September 29, 1940

'MR. D. A.'S' BOSS TAKES THE STAND

By EDWARD JENKS

RADIO being a young industry barely 21 years old, it's not surprising that Ed Byron, who has spent fifteen of his thirty-six years in it, knows the business inside out. Mr. Byron has been announcer, sound-effects man, engineer, actor, writer, director and producer. He's done everything, in fact, but sing on the air. Altogether he has written or produced over 1,500 shows.

No wonder, then, that "Mr. District Attorney," of which he is director, producer and co-author, is doing fine. Experts have figured that when it goes on Wednesdays at 9:30 P. M. on WEAF, 24.7 per cent of the nation's radio sets are tuned to it—this despite the fact that "Mr. District Attorney" is produced on what is regarded in radio circles as a remarkably small budget.

Mr. Byron attributes its popularity in part to its ring of authenticity, which he spares no pains to achieve. While the plots are fictitious, the basic ideas often are suggested by newspaper stories. Points of law and medicine are carefully checked. When a big bad racketeer gets plugged, Mr. Byron consults a doctor to make sure the racketeer's voice under such conditions has the right sound.

"Another thing that contributes to a good show is close teamwork between director, engineer and cast," Mr. Byron believes. He breaks with tradition by doing all his direction from the stage. He finds it builds an esprit de corps impossible to achieve when a glass partition separates the director in the control room from his cast on the stage. Stage direction helps in other ways, too.

There was the time an actor was stopped dead by a word in the script. Simply couldn't get it out, and the show was on the air. Mr. Byron just nudged the actor's elbow. That broke the spell. "But suppose I'd been in the control room?" he asks. Once, during a tense scene, an actor turned the page of his script. But the next page wasn't there. Mr. Byron was, though, with a page from his own script.

He explains to his engineer and sound-effects man the effects he wants, then leaves it to them to produce. "The engineer is the last man to have control over the program before it goes on the air, and he can make or break a show." So one of Mr. Byron's cardinal principles is that a good director must have a good engineer, put confidence in him and let him do his job without interference.

Mr. D. A. for President

"Mr. District Attorney" is a kind of 1942 Sherlock Holmes. It has shared honors with Mr. Thomas E. Dewey in glorifying the District Attorney. Mr. Dewey himself, as a matter of fact, owes something to the show, for it is reported that three votes were cast for him at the 1940 Republican National Convention by people who thought he was the radio District Attorney.

Mr. Byron also reports that the part of the D. A. has wrought changes in the man who plays it. "When Jay Jostyn (the D. A.) started on the show," he recounts, "he was the typical Broadway actor with the checked suit, loud tie, wrist watch turned in, and the flashy ring. But you should see him now! He's wearing quiet business suits and ties, his wrist watch is turned around, and his ring's quite modest.

"The D. A.'s children have felt the influence, too. They used to tear around the studio and get into all sorts of mischief. But the other day when they came in they just shook hands quietly with the cast and departed. You see, there's a District Attorney tradition to live up to now."

The war has opened up new fields of story material, Mr. Byron finds. "For a time the networks were chary about letting writers portray Germans and Japs as villains. Espionage themes were frowned on. But now these restrictions are being lifted." This suits Mr. Byron, who has long wanted to use plots which would show the nature of the enemy. "Besides," he adds, "if radio characters don't get into war work soon, listeners will demand to know why they haven't joined the Marines."

Hearing Is Believing

"Mr. District Attorney" is one of the few top radio programs which do not have a studio audience. "Radio," its director says, "is aimed at a listening, not a seeing, audience. Its charm depends on an illusion. That illusion is spoiled for the listener who calls up the picture, when he hears a galloping horse, of a sound-effects man beating his chest with a couple of rubber cups."

Another illusion may be shattered when a listener discovers that the lovely voiced heroine is not, in real life, all he had been led to believe. But on this score Mr. Byron can speak with detachment. His actors look their parts, and the winsome "Miss Miller" of the D. A.'s office is a real-life charmer.

Mr. Byron recognizes, however, the value of the studio audience to the comedy or quiz program. In the first the audience provides laughs and helps timing, while in the second audience participation is the basis of the show.

"Radio has developed only one unique form of entertainment," he finds. "Music and drama were ready-made for radio, but the quiz show, with audience participation, is radio's unique contribution to entertainment." He is qualified to speak with authority on the subject, for among the many shows he has written or originated is "What's My Name?" second oldest quiz show.

Too many people are going into radio today without enough knowledge of the medium, Mr. Byron thinks. "To be a successful radio writer and producer, you must bring to the work a varied background supplemented by vicarious experience gained through wide reading."

On his shelves are well-thumbed copies of "Middletown" and "Middletown in Transition," which he regards as basic reading. Another important book, he says, is Gustave LeBon's "Psychology of Crowds." "LeBon wrote his book in 1895, before any one was thinking of radio, but he wrote as though with radio in mind. And if you think a radio audience isn't a crowd, remember Orson Welles's Martian broadcast."

May 10, 1942

HAVE A CIGAR, HENRY

By EDWARD JENKS

THE lighted sign outside NBC's studio 8-G said "Rehearsal" in plain red letters, and the page boy insisted his orders were to let no one in. "Besides," he added, "your appointment is with Ezra Stone, and he hasn't come in yet." A reporter was waiting in the lobby for Mr. Stone — now Sergeant Stone of the United States Army—when a stocky young man got off the elevator. He smoked a cigar and wore an old suit. At the reception desk he made some telephone calls. His voice was pitched low, but it carried clear across the lobby. This husky young chap was Ezra Stone, known to listeners as Henry Aldrich, Thursday night Penrod.

Mr. Stone went on into the studio where the cast was rehearsing for its 186th performance. "About that cigar," he was asked, "if listeners knew that in private life Henry Aldrich smoked cigars, wouldn't they kick?" Mr. Stone imagined not, "Henry Aldrich being the boy he is."

Is he known as Henry Aldrich in the Army? Well, when he appears on Army camp stages the men have been known to stop the shows dead, calling "Henreee!"

The Henry Aldrich program is popular in the Army. The drama is among those shortwaved to armed forces overseas. The British like it, too; the Bermuda Base Command recently voting it their favorite program. Here at home last week it won an award from the Women's National Radio Committee as the best radio drama. Not many shows can please an audience so varied.

In the Army Mr. Stone is assigned to the work of organizing camp entertainment activities. Seventy-five per cent of the camps in his area, comprising New York, New Jersey and Delaware, now have their own entertainment programs, Mr. Stone reports. He makes frequent appearances on Army camp stages, and estimates he has played to over 200,000 men since entering the Army.

By arrangement with Army authorities, he visits the NBC studios for a brisk two days a week in the interests of the "Aldrich Family." An hour and a half of rehearsal on Wednesday is followed by three hours Thursday morning, two more in the afternoon and a final hour and a half in the evening. At 9 (over WEAF) comes the first broadcast and at midnight a repeat.

Mr. Stone started acting at 8. Now, at 23, he has fifteen years of stage life behind him. His first Broadway appearance was in "O Evening Star," an ill-fated star as it happens, for it soon folded, leaving Mr. Stone unabashed. He subsequently appeared in several plays successful on Broadway, including "Three Men on a Horse," "Brother Rat" and "What a Life," in the last of which he created the part of Henry Aldrich.

Fast Start

In 1940 he made his film debut in "Those Were the Days," and in the same year acted in the stage play, "Horse Fever." His first radio appearance was made at 10, at which tender age he took part in a children's program over a Philadelphia station.

As a youngster, Ezra Stone had a lisp, which had something to do with his becoming an actor. As he explains it, "A friend of the family was the actor, Maurice Sloane. He was called in to give me elocution lessons. I hated doing the lessons and preferred to listen to Sloane. He stimulated my imagination."

"However, elocution lessons don't make actors," he adds. The boy persuaded his parents to put him through the American Academy of Dramatic Arts in preference to Yale University.

"A conductor doesn't make music by standing up and waving a stick. He needs an orchestra. That goes for acting, too. The orchestra is more than actors. It includes the author, sound men, engineers and, in films, the camera men. They must all work together. Sometimes the actor carries the ball, sometimes the sound man or the camera man.

"Radio tends to minimize the actor's contribution, spreading the responsibility for the total effect to the sound man and engineer. Radio often makes actors careless, too. Too many of them read scripts without moving a muscle. But in radio, as on the stage, actors must act."

Although Mr. Stone has been eminently successful as an actor, he finds production still more to his liking. In that field he has had more experience at 23 than many much older. In pre-Army days he managed George Abbott's office in New York while that producer was out on the Coast. As George Abbott's assistant casting director he has scoured the country for dramatic talent, discovering on one such trip a talented but inexperienced youngster named Maureen Cannon, who emerged in the cast of the musical show, "Best Foot Forward."

May 24, 1942

SCRAM, CINDERELLA

By RICHARD MATCH

"LOOK—up in the sky!" "It's a bird!" "It's a plane!" "It's Superman!" These magic syllables are "Once upon a time——," 1942 style. They introduce the time-hallowed fairy tale as the modern American youngster knows it and wants to know it.

Every day, as suppertime draws near, Young America, aged 7 to 14, rushes for home, hearth and radio to absorb his or her daily hour of modern children's "literature." Young ears listen avidly as the heroic Captain Midnight and five or six other modern Jack-the-Giant-Killers spend fifteen minutes ranging a 1942 Never-Never Land.

The old fantastic two-headed giant has been replaced by master spies and supercriminals. The fair damsel in distress is now a stolen airplane design. And a twin-motored monoplane takes Jack farther and faster than seven-league boots ever did. None of that hard-to-believe, old-fashioned fairy tale stuff for the modern kid. Fantastic romanticism has been replaced by fantastic "realism."

The daily adventure serial has been a juvenile best-seller in radio since way back—eleven or twelve years ago—when the earliest of the genre, "Little Orphan Annie," first trod the ethereal boards over a local Chicago station. But getting the little ones to ask mother for this or that sponsored product isn't easy. The standard lure is a "secret" club: the Tom Mix Straight Shooters, the Mandrake Magicians' Club, Captain Midnight's Secret Squadron. Secret "high signs" and simple codes are devised, membership cards and "Slide-O-Matic Decoders" are exchanged for boxtops.

Then the announcer solemnly intones a "tease line":

"Well, there seems to be no hope. Can Mandrake, single-handed and unarmed, cope with Captain X and the crew of the submarine?" It hardly seems likely that he can. But come Monday, he can and does—before a large and appreciative audience.

No Flowers, Please

Adventure serials are not generally long-lived. Most of the efforts of the years now repose in the thankless oblivion of office files. Gone, perhaps forever, are "Dick Tracy," "Omar the Mystic," "Flash Gordon," "Buck Rogers in the Twenty-fifth Century," "Og, Son of Fire," "Terry and the Pirates," and numerous others. There are few to mourn.

Jack Armstrong, venerable prototype of the "All-American Boy," started out about ten years ago as the athletic hero of a small-town high school. After some years Hudson High's football team was forgotten and Jack began to range the world in an amphibian plane. Now he spends most of his time in Madagascar, India and Polynesia, dodging fanatical Hindu sects and Japanese troops.

You can see that "Jack Armstrong, the All-American Boy," has a distinctive flavor of its own. All adventure serials have. But strangely, when you've heard one, you've heard 'em all. They're twin brothers in different uniforms. Their common formula is physical danger encountered on a hunt—for an enemy base, for a treasure, for a missing "defense plan." Subtle characterizations are avoided. The hero, man or boy, is a simple, modest fellow, all courage, all virtue. His opponent, very often a "master criminal," bent on control of the world or the destruction of the United States, is the epitome of evil and low trickery.

Immediately after Pearl Harbor the adventure serial went to war in a big way. One epic, "Hop Harrigan," features the exploits of an Army flier currently chasing Nazis in the Caribbean. Today's typical villain is the agent of an enemy power, who steals the plans of the new airplane and hides out in a jungle villa.

Evidently the modern kid likes it. His modern mother doesn't. Clubwomen and parent-teacher associations call for educational programs, fiercely condemn radio's late afternoon chatter of tommy guns, and perennially pin medals on "Let's Pretend," a dramatization of authentic fairy tales.

But radio stands firm. One can hardly expect radio's juvenile serials to be keyed anywhere near the child prodigy level when all indications are that children like what they're getting now. Of course, as the modern mothers point out, the children might like educational programs too. But, for better or worse, the adventure serial is a sure thing.

November 1, 1942

Are Soap Operas Only Suds?

Twenty million women listen to the serials daily and in them find a world of dreams. Is the effect good or bad?

By John K. Hutchens

ALONG Radio Row, all unsuspected by people who merely listen to the radio, an old discussion is raising its disputatious head. It's those fifteen-minute daytime serials again, or soap operas, so-called because they first wept their way into radio's higher brackets under the sponsorship of cleansing products companies. From time to time since circa 1930, when the serials began to flourish, Radio Row has been hearing arguments about them—about, chiefly, their effect on the millions of women who listen to one or more serials a day, Monday through Friday, at some time between 9 A. M. and 6 P. M. Now, however, the argument is really steaming.

In a series of indignant pamphlets a New York psychiatrist has recently belabored the serials as neurotic and a liability to the national psychology in wartime. To this charge an investigating committee of three physicians appointed by a network has replied indirectly that the serials are more beneficial than otherwise. In the trade magazines radio executives have been airing their views, sometimes a little testily, and arguing about trends. While the argument steams, the soap operas go right on making money.

Indeed, they are virtually an industry within the industry, two of the four major networks — the National Broadcasting Company and the Columbia Broadcasting System — receiving an estimated combined income of around $30,000,000 annually from the sale of air time for the five-a-week dramas, far more revenue than any other one type of program brings in. Thirty-odd serials are heard each week in New York on the network stations, and an undetermined number of others are produced on local stations throughout the country.

A few authors who created and now write—or supervise the writing of—their own shows have made fortunes (or should have, if they saved their money), and other people earn a respectable living as directors, dialogue writers, announcers and organists. Under the radio actors union scale of $21 for each fifteen-minute performance, plus added fees for rehearsals and repeat broadcasts, actors making three or four appearances weekly on each of several serials may draw down salaries of $300 to $500 weekly—actors whose names their public seldom knows. Clearly, this is quite a business.

Like most successful mass-production businesses, it is conducted along very businesslike lines. The majority of the shows are created, written and produced by advertising agencies and delivered to the broadcasters. (A single such agency, Blackett-Sample-Hummert, produces no less than eleven daytime serials, grinding them out at the rate of six million words a year with a staff of dialogue writers and script editors—and with no apologies.) The weekly production cost of the average fifteen-minute daytime serial is $2,000, exclusive of the radio time cost, which comes to about $9,000 for a network hook-up of, say, sixty stations.

IS the soap opera worth this outlay? Obviously it is, in terms of the audience reached and the results achieved. Of the ten leading weekday, daytime programs, nine are serials, according to the ratings of the Cooperative Analysis of Broadcasting. At any given moment during the day 2,000,000 women are listening to a soap opera.

Its most ardent defenders will grant that the soap opera does not contribute to the world's enduring literature. It is what it is, a piece of storytelling for wide popular consumption. In narrative form it is a first cousin to the never-ending newspaper comic strip; in tone and content, a counterpart of the pulp magazine story. Its principal theme is trouble. Almost no one in a soap opera is happy for very long at a time. The prevailing sound effect is the barely repressed sob.

SINCE the men and women in the soap opera business know what they are doing, you may be sure there are plausible reasons for the theme. Trouble is more apt to be dramatic than merely pleasant existence. Again, as in the theatre, it is easier to write and act than is comedy. Finally, most people enjoy hearing about other people's troubles, if only for the compensating satisfaction it gives them in knowing that they are not alone in misfortune.

Not all the "soaps" are so dolorous, and not all of them are produced as by a machine. Among the more cheerful items in the field are "Vic and Sade," "Pepper Young's Family" and "The Goldbergs," which tell of normal happy family life, and "Snow Village," a genial character study set in a New England town. Sandra Michael's "Against the Storm," now off the air, won the Peabody Award last year as radio's finest drama; it was remarkable for its literate writing, excellent characterization and sensitive concern with political and cultural problems. But these are notable exceptions to the soap opera's accepted, gold-line formula.

That formula, as any one can discover in a single day of lachrymose listening, is simple and almost inevitable. A character, usually a weak one, is manoeuvred into trouble. The problem is to get him (or her) out of it before submerging him (or her) in more of the same. Frequently the bout involves the Eternal Triangle, and, considering the feminine audience to which the serial is addressed, it goes almost without saying that the trouble-maker is usually a man.

Within these specifications, there is a deal of shrewd craftsmanship in the preparation of the "soaps," just as there was in the stage's old ten-twenty-thirty melodramas and the Pearl White movie serials. As a rule Friday's chapter is designed to leave the listener in a fair lather of excited anticipation over the week-end while awaiting Monday's developments. For the soap operas move in sequences each of which is a little story with a plot and climax of its own, and the dénouement is naturally timed for the point at which it will provide the longest suspense.

The first desideratum is a good "story line," which is charted six or eight months in advance, then broken down into small segments. Should the story line be ill-received, it can be changed with reasonable speed, because the script writer works only two or three weeks ahead of the performance and sometimes less than that. Since the commercials, the "lead-in" and the "lead-out" absorb five minutes of the fifteen-minute program, you might think offhand that he does not write a great deal of story. You would be mistaken. By the end of a year he will have turned out the equivalent of twenty full-length stage plays.

It is like no other writing, in or out of radio. Whereas most radio programs are presented for the individual listener, but are just as effective when heard by small groups in the living room, the serial is as private as a diary. It invites its listeners singly and vicariously to project their secret hopes and disappointments.

Of all the odd factors in the soap-opera industry, the audience is the most mysterious. As you hear trouble march by quarter hours through the morning and afternoon, you sometimes wonder what a listener on Mars would think of the American housewife and her environment.

On the assumption that a nation's civilization is reflected by the type of program which outnumbers all others, the baffled fellow on Mars would certainly conclude that the United States is a very strange place and scarcely a happy one; that its population includes a great many more women than men, and that the latter are slightly balmy, in the romantic sense, when they are not actually trying to put over something dubious on a fine, lovely sample of American womanhood.

As he went on listening, he might begin to feel pretty sorry, and with good reason, for that housewife who is the soap-opera public. The commercials alone would give him to understand that she has a hard life, most of which she spends in the kitchen, either washing dishes with soap that makes her hands red, rough and uninviting, or cooking with materials from which she had better change at once to the ones advertised on the program she is listening to, if she values her health and that of her family. The nature and setting of the stories would suggest that she is married, belongs in the modest income bracket, is 30 to 40 years old, and leads a not very interesting life, probably in a small town.

Molly Goldberg (Gertrude Berg), author and heroine of "The Goldbergs," and her daughter Rosalie (Roslyn Silver).

In some of these deductions the Martian listener would be right. Almost every one agrees that the soap opera is addressed to the great middle class, in particular to the woman who does her own housework. Almost every one agrees, too, that there are easily discernible reasons for her interest in the serials.

It is the opinion of Dr. Paul Lazarsfeld, director of the Office of Radio Research, Columbia University, expressed in a talk before a group of radio executives, that women apparently "get two gratifications out of listening: first, there is an escape, a day-dreaming, which carries them away from their daily lives; second — almost the reverse — women use the stories as a source of guidance in their private lives. About 40 per cent of the listeners say that the serials helped them to solve their own problems; they give concrete and detailed instances in which they dealt with people more successfully because they had listened to these programs."

Queried by the Women's Institute of Audience Reactions, women in several categories (housewife, employed, etc.) who said they liked serials gave as the reasons that "the serials (1) make work seem lighter; (2) provide guidance, helpful philosophy, inspiration; (3) supplant reading, saving time and eyes; (4) provide pleasant escape and take one's mind off personal troubles; (5) create pleasant anticipation and suspense; (6) satisfy a natural appetite for entertainment, particularly dramatic entertainment; (7) help dispel loneliness."

But precisely at this point the controversy about daytime serials begins. If 20,000,000 American women listen to two or three serials daily, as Dr. Lazarsfeld estimates, there are those who think the potential effect debilitating. They view with alarm a stupendous amount of wishful thinking, self-pity (through identification with characters whose misfortunes resemble one's own), phony philosophy and neurotic egoism.

Speaking for this school of thought is Dr. Louis Berg, psychiatrist and author, formerly physician to the New York Department of Health at Welfare Island. Having studied forty episodes of each of eight serials, he found that "the constant listener to the programs studied can become as morbidly fond of his fantasy world as the user of opium of the pipe that brings momentary surcease with drugged dreams." The "state of anxiety" they create is the "very same over-anxiety which is the end of all enemy propaganda, for it lays the groundwork for civilian panic in emergencies and saps the productive energies of the afflicted individuals in all their essential efforts," Dr. Berg opines.

But Dr. Lazarsfeld, reviewing the charge that "serials make women less responsible citizens and that they lead them into emotional difficulties," finds no corroboration as yet for that gloomy theory. On the contrary, he maintains that while "the average daytime serial listener has somewhat less formal education than the woman who does not listen," the two groups participate equally in church and club activities and civilian defense work, have the same interest in radio news programs and politics, and show the same taste in films, books and magazines.

Similarly, a committee of three physicians, appointed by the National Broadcasting Company to study the problem of morale on network broadcasts, was happy to report that "since the tendency of all the dramas studied is toward the solutions that are generally accepted as ethical in our social existence, the effect of the dramas tends toward helpfulness."

Outside the debate is the Office of War Information, which is less interested in art than in reaching a big audience and which is making significant use of the serials as a vehicle for its messages to housewives. Its "allocation plugs," or special bulletins on rationing, fuel, etc., have been broadcast regularly and with great success. Written and produced especially for the OWI, special versions of the leading serials have been offered outside their regular schedule times on the networks and in recorded form on local stations. And in this wartime use to which the serials have been put, some observers think they see the beginning of a trend.

That is to say, in a few soap operas characters who used to moan and passively accept their dismal fate are now on the aggressive side; a greater theme has come along to take their minds off their personal troubles. The change of tone has not gone to any startling lengths as yet, but still there has been a change. It is not to be overlooked, the soothsayers point out, that Dr. Joyce Jordan has gone to work in a war plant and that Stella Dallas, that sad, brave lady, has entered a munitions factory.

How far the industry will dare to go with this approach, and whether it will continue after the war, is anybody's guess. Until the war it was a rare serial that even hinted at social forces operating in this world. Now the serial listeners, who have earned millions for the industry by feeding on personal woes, are getting a little taste of something else. It would be sensational news if they kept on liking it.

March 28, 1943

VISIT TO THE SHRINE

Notes on an Evening Among Mr. Sinatra's Admirers at the Saturday 'Hit Parade'

By JOHN K. HUTCHENS

ONCE it was the Hammerstein Theatre, which Arthur Hammerstein built in memory of his father, the great Oscar, but now it is CBS Radio Theatre No. 3, at Broadway and Fifty-third Street, and on Saturday nights it is another kind of shrine. For an hour before the "Hit Parade" goes on the air, at 9 P. M., over WABC-Columbia, the sidewalk in front of it is crowded with boys and girls, but mostly girls, and their average age, you would guess, is 16. The lucky ones who have tickets to the broadcast, who will actually see him, are buzzing with anticipatory excitement. The others have not entirely given up hope. "Got a ticket for the broadcast?" they ask wistfully, as if it were not impossible that a bit of manna might descend from heaven, even at this late hour.

Inside the theatre, at 8:30, the orchestra is full and late arrivals are being routed to the balcony. The younger worshipers are not altogether happy about this, because it means that they will be just that much farther from their hero, but then they seem to realize that merely by being there at all they are among Fortune's elect. At 8:40, looking over the house from the sixth row, you can't see an empty seat among the 1,200 in the theatre. There is a considerable sprinkling of middle-aged folk, some of them with children, and there are quite a few service men, but chiefly there are the 16-year-old girls.

In fact, two of them are sitting right behind you. One, who says very little, has an intense, excited look about her, as if she doubted whether she could really live through the next few minutes until the great man appeared. The other, who seems to be named Dolores, is more voluble. She knows all his songs by heart, and she is going through them in a kind of chant. She applied two months ago for the ticket which brought her here. Thank God, she hasn't got a busted leg or something else that might have kept her away, she says.

The Build-Up

It is now 8:45 and time for the studio audience "warm-up." The master of ceremonies, Ken Delmar, a young man with an amiable smile and a jocular delivery, appears from the wings at the left of the stage and starts right off with a quip.

"I'm not Frank Sinatra," he says, which gets a laugh, but not from Dolores, who did not come here to listen to jokes.

"Frank is a regular guy," Mr. Delmar says a little later. "And he has a tremendous amount of charm." The applause is prolonged, although Dolores says something to indicate that Mr. Delmar is guilty of understatement.

There follows a series of introductions—the gentlemen who do those tobacco auctioneer commercials; Lyn Murray's Hit Paraders, a choral group; Bea Wain, the feminine soloist, very fetching in a black lace gown; Mark Warnow and his orchestra; and even the boys in the control booth—and then, at 8:59, green lights on either side of the stage flash "stand by." At 9, on the second, red lights flash "on the air," the orchestra goes into an opening theme, and the hero walks on stage from the left.

He is a solemn, pleasant-looking young man of medium height, who looks as if he were both very tired and suffering slightly from malnutrition. He wears a brown checked tweed coat, tweed trousers of another color, a diamond ring on the little finger of his right hand, and he could use a haircut. Never looking at the audience, he toys nervously with the music stand and the microphone while Mr. Delmar is introducing his first number, an item called "Paper Doll." He goes into the song, and, despite Mr. Delmar's plea that applause be reserved until the end of the number, a squeal from the audience blots out a couple of words.

"Shut up, you dopes," says Dolores to the noisy ones.

Quiet, Please

The applause and the squealing at the end of the song are prodigious, although he has done nothing whatever to encourage it. He simply walks away, yielding the microphone to Miss Wain. At 9:17 he is back to sing "I Hear You Cried Last Night," and it occurs to you that even from the sixth row you hear him less well than over the radio because a good part of the time he seems merely to be breathing into the microphone. At 9:26 he re-enters to render "If You Please," but there is no prefatory applause. You gather that there would be something profane about it. Miss Wain sings "Sunday, Monday or Always," and the choral group gives out with "Pistol Packin' Mama," and there is some resentment among the customers because he is especially identified with the first of these two ballads.

But they forgive that when, at 9:38 he comes out to sing "People Will Say We're in Love." The forty-five-minute show is almost over now, and this time the audience does break in with the applause and the squealing in the middle of the number, although Mr. Delmar is frantically trying to shush them. They pay no attention to Mr. Delmar, but they heed the upraised hand of Mr. Sinatra as he confides the final lyrics to the microphone. Then he goes to another microphone for the sign-off song and a few words to the effect that he hopes everybody will be listening again next week. Then, like a business man who has concluded a deal without fanfare, he walks across the stage, his job done.

Dolores, her eyes slightly glazed, watches him depart.

"Good night, Frankie," she sighs. "Good night, gorgeous."

At the stage door on Fifty-third Street, a few minutes later, his public is waiting, but in vain. A man with a cold eye and an unsympathetic voice sticks his head out of the door and tells them, "Frank's gone. There's no use waiting. Beat it." They shuffle away reluctantly, and you notice that someone has written in chalk on the stage door: "Boo to Dick Haymes. Boo to Barry Wood." Mr. Haymes and Mr. Wood are also singers.

November 7, 1943

OZZIE AND HARRIET

Radio Version of Nelson Family Life Born of Fact and Fiction

By DOROTHY O'LEARY

HOLLYWOOD.

WHEN Oswald Nelson, a knickered grammar school sprout, submitted a story on lion hunting in the African veldt, hi composition teacher suggested that Master Nelson's writing would improve if it were limited, fact or fiction, to subjects on which he had first-hand knowledge.

Some twenty years later Ozzie Nelson, who has a bird dog memory, parlayed that advice into a lucrative radio series which provides him, his wife Harriet Hilliard and their sons David and Rickey, with a goodly slice of worldly goods. The show, as listeners to CBS's Sunday stanzas of "The Adventures of Ozzie and Harriet" are well aware, is based on the home life of the Nelsons.

Naturally, there must be some fictional license; no real family provides thirty-nine solid comedy shows a season, as needed for this series now ending its third year. But the basic structure is actual.

Ozzie and Harriet portray a happy young couple, parents of two boys with the same names and ages as their own children. As the series progresses the boys are growing. "That makes the writing easier because we know the sort of things David and Rickey say and do in real life," says Ozzie. "Besides, Skeezix grew up in the funnies and no one objected."

The Children

Many people, including the boys' young friends, ask if David and Rickey portray themselves on the air. They don't. Tommy Bernard and Henry Blair, both 14, have the respective roles. David is 10 but Rickey is only 6 and too young to

FAMILY-STYLE SITUATION COMEDY

Ozzie Nelson and Harriet Hilliard and their sons, David (left) and Ricky.

read lines well. Besides, the Nelsons want them to have childhood and schooling uncluttered by acting. If ultimately they want to act, they will meet no parental objection; Harriet labels entertainment a "happy business."

Although Ozzie has three writers who work with him on individual scripts, on a stagger system to avoid going stale, and all cooperate on story line ideas, he does final rewriting himself. To check authenticity of the children's dialogue, to avoid cute or overly precocious lines, he often reads scripts to his sons, asking if they understand and would say things that way. They're brutally honest.

The boys also regularly hear the programs, but Ozzie and Harriet have instilled in them a detached attitude toward show business and their radio counterparts. They think the boys in the air show are like them, but not themselves.

Incidents in the Nelson household frequently have been incorporated in the radio series. For example, one Thanksgiving the Nelsons had finished their own dinner when Ozzie's mother telephoned and asked where they were, she was expecting them for a holiday repast. They managed to eat it. Last November they used the experience, with an extra dinner added, for their Thanksgiving program.

"Because ours is a family story we try to keep our situations believable, but as a comedy series it demands some exaggeration, so we stay within what I call 'farce believability,'" explains Ozzie. "If seven-eighths of the story is plausible and only the end is hypoed, the audience will stay with it."

Ozzie, who was born in Jersey City forty years ago, organized his first orchestra while a student at Rutgers University. Though later receiving a degree from the New Jersey Law School, he decided to continue in the world of entertainment and before long his band had engagements at the major roadhouses and hotels in the New York area.

It was in 1933 that Harriet Hilliard, whom Ozzie first noticed in a film "short," joined the Nelson ensemble as featured vocalist. Born in Des Moines, she had played with Ken Murray and Bert Lahr on the vaudeville boards and later had a solo dance act. She became Mrs. Nelson in 1935.

March 30, 1947

ONE THING AND ANOTHER

By SIDNEY LOHMAN

THIS week marks the return to standard time by the nation. And this week, too, will find a full complement of the fall season's radio entertainers —with the exception of a very few latecomers—back at the microphone.

Here, then, is a list of the more prominent new and returning programs to be heard, in the next seven days:

Today—Hollywood Star Preview, with Ronald Colman and Vanessa Brown, as guests. NBC, 6:30 P. M.

"Adventures of Sherlock Holmes," with a new detective in the person of John Stanley and a new Dr. Watson, played by Al Shirley. WOR, 7 P. M.

"Christopher Wells," adventure series with Myron McCormick in the title role. CBS, 10 P. M.

Monday—Lowell Thomas makes his first broadcast as a CBS commentator at 6:45 while Ray Henle, Felix Morley and Ned Brooks make their debut at the same time on NBC.

Edward R. Murrow, who recently resigned as CBS vice president and director of public affairs, starts his new series of news summaries and analyses at 7:45 P. M.

Paul Whiteman presents a group of talented young entertainers in a half hour variety show called "On Stage, America." WJZ, 8 P. M.

Tuesday—Amos 'n' Andy return to NBC at 9 P. M.

Wednesday—"Vox Pop," featuring Parks Johnson and Warren Hull, becomes a WJZ feature at 8:30 P. M.

"Duffy's Tavern" opens its door on NBC at 9 P. M. Back again will be Ed Gardner, as "Archie," with Eddie Green, Charlie Cantor and the other regulars.

Abbott and Costello begin their new cooperatively sponsored venture on WJZ at 9 P. M.

Jack Paar, summer fill-in for Jack Benny, branches out on his own at 9:30 P. M. on WJZ.

Bing Crosby entertains Gary Cooper as his first guest of the season on WJZ at 10 P. M.

Jimmy Durante plays host to Greer Garson of the movies. Also on the program are Peggy Lee, Arthur Treacher and Tom Harmon. NBC, 10:30 P. M.

Thursday—Al Jolson begins his new program, NBC, 9 P. M.

Bob Hawk, with his questions and prizes, becomes an NBC regular at 10 P. M.

Friday—Spike Jones and his City Slickers and the songs of Dorothy Shay start on CBS at 10:30 P. M.

Saturday—Judy Canova resumes on NBC at 9:30 P. M.

Kay Kyser and his College of Musical Knowledge open a new session on NBC at 10 P. M.

DISCUSSION: The New York Times Youth Forum, with Dorothy Gordon as moderator, will return to WQXR for the fall season on Saturday from 10:30 to 11 A. M.

This year the panels will be extended to include the senior high school age group which will alternate with junior high school students. All programs will originate from Times Hall.

The initial broadcast will present senior high school students from five Greater New York public high schools and one parochial high school in a discussion of "Can the Marshall Plan Assure World Peace?" James B. Reston, diplomatic correspondent of THE NEW YORK TIMES, will be guest.

September 28, 1947

CHAPTER 5

Television Invades the Livingroom

Milton Berle

Courtesy The National Broadcasting Company, Inc.

SARNOFF DISCLOSES PLANS FOR NATION-WIDE TELEVISION

RADIO-VISION ERA IS DAWNING

Television Looms as Mighty Force, Says Sarnoff—He Predicts Influence It Will Have on Home, Stage and Screen

By DAVID SARNOFF, President, Radio Corporation of America.

WHERE is television? When will it be ready for the home? What form will it assume? How about the necessary television transmitting stations? What are its likely effects upon the established radio and motion picture industries? These are pertinent questions, frequently asked. The answers are of peculiar significance to Hollywood, yet thinking men and women of all the world likewise are evincing keen interest.

Any discussion of this subject should be prefaced with the general statement that television, or the transmission of images by radio, still is in the laboratory stage. True, rapid progress is being made. The sweep of events during 1930 and the first months of 1931 has been substantial. One year ago, television was a subject of engineering conversation and a topic for technical dispute. It now has progressed beyond that point. Today, transmission of sight by radio is a matter of accomplishment, not of speculation.

It must be understood, however, that the present sporadic activities in this direction cannot be classed as a practical service. They are purely experimental, but as such deserve encouragement and merit public interest.

The present status of television might be likened to the condition of radio in the immediate pre-broadcasting era, when amateurs were beginning to hear faint sounds through the air. Voices and music were passing through space in those early days of radio; comparably, there are actually some images passing through the air today.

Ready for Public in 1932.

The next stage—and I should anticipate its realization by the end of next year—should find television comparable to the earphone stage of radio. At this point, the public may well be invited to share in its further unfolding.

By that time, television should attain the same degree of development as did radio sound broadcasting in the early period of the crystal set. This does not mean that the actual physical structure of the first television receiver will be similar in any way to the crystal receiver. The similarity will lie in the class and condition of the service. The visions which first come through the air to the public will be of the same embryonic quality as the first faint sounds which sent mother hurrying to the earphone of the boy's crystal set in the attic.

When television reaches this stage rapid strides may be expected, comparable perhaps with the growth and development of broadcasting of sound. The progress to follow should make possible the projection of moving images on a screen on the wall. Reception of sight by radio then will be comparable to the loudspeaker stage of sound reception.

The Radio Corporation of America is conducting its present experimental developments in television through a large research staff in the RCA-Victor plant at Camden, N. J. When television emerges from this experimental stage it will be handled as a service by the National Broadcasting Company. Before television reaches the practical stage of service it is necessary that several experimental stations for the transmission of sight by radio be established.

Two Stations for New York.

The Radio Corporation of America contemplates building several such stations by the end of next year. One will be on the top of the new fifty-story RCA Building at 570 Lexington Avenue, New York. Another will be on a still higher building in New York. These sites have been chosen because height is an important technical factor in the successful transmission of sight by radio. These two stations probably will be located in such manner as to serve New York and its vicinity.

A third station will be located on the Pacific Coast. Additional experimental stations may be located in other sections of the country.

Through the operation of these experimental stations we expect to obtain exact information and practical field experience which are required before definite plans can be developed for a television service of nation-wide scope.

New Sets Are Expected.

The effect of television upon the present established radio industry will be beneficial. There will be no interference between the broadcasting of sound and of sight. These services will supplement each other and complete the impression upon the human mind by reaching it through both the ear and the eye. Television broadcasting stations will operate on wave lengths different from those now used for the broadcasting of sound. An entirely different receiver will be necessary. Radio sets now used for sound reception are not equipped to receive television.

In the practical sense of the term, television must develop to the stage where broadcasting stations will be able to broadcast regularly visual objects in the studio, or scenes occurring at other places through remote control; where reception devices shall be developed that will make these objects and scenes clearly discernible in millions of homes; where such devices can be built upon a principle that will eliminate rotary scanning disks, delicate hand controls and other movable parts; and where research has made possible the utilization of wave lengths for sight transmission that will not interfere with the use of the already overcrowded channels in space.

The Radio Corporation of America is pursuing the foregoing development aggressively in its laboratories and will not attempt to market television equipment commercially this year, as it is concentrating its efforts upon the primary technical developments to be completed before undertaking the manufacture and sale of television sets on a commercial basis.

A Tonic for the Arts.

The motion picture industry need experience no alarm over the impending advent of television. Transmission of sight by radio will benefit not only the radio industry; it also will prove a welcome stimulant, a pleasant tonic to all the entertainment arts. There will be no conflict between television in the home and motion pictures in the theatre. Each is a separate and distinct service. Television in the home will not displace the motion picture in the theatre.

Man is a gregarious creature. Granting that we can develop 26,000,000 potential theatres in the homes of America, public theatres will continue to operate because people will go there in response to the instinct for group emotions and to see artists in the flesh. These are human demands which television in the home cannot satisfy.

Television, when it arrives as a factor in the field of entertainment, will give new wings to the talents of creative and interpretive genius, and will furnish a new and greater outlet for artistic expression. All this will stimulate and further advance the art of motion-picture production.

No Limit to Audience.

The potential audience of television in its ultimate development may reasonably be expected to be limited only by the population of the earth itself.

The instantaneous projection through space of light images produced directly from objects in the studio or the scene brought to the studio by remote control involves many problems. Special types of distribution networks, new forms of stagecraft and a development of studio equipment and technique will be required. With these must come a new and greater service of broadcasting, both of sight and sound. A new world of educational and cultural opportunities will be opened to the home. New forms of artistry will be encouraged and developed. Variety and more variety will be the demand of the day. The ear might be content with the oft-repeated song; the eye would be impatient with the twice-repeated scene. The service will demand, therefore, a constant succession of personalities, a vast array of talent, a tremendous store of material, a great variety of scene and background.

Homes Become Art Galleries.

There is little in the field of cultural education that cannot be visioned for the home through the new facilities of electrical communication. Assume sufficient progress in the television art and every home equipped for radio reception may at certain times become an art gallery. The great works of painting and sculpture in the art galleries of Europe and America lie buried there, in so far as the vast majority of the earth's population is concerned. Television, advanced to the stage when color as well as shadow may be faithfully transmitted, would bring these treasures vividly to the home. Conceive the exhibition of such works of art in the home, accompanied by comments and explanations by the proper authorities. Just as sound broadcasting has brought a new sense of musical appreciation to millions of people, so may television open a new era of art appreciation.

But even more appealing to the individual is the hope that television may, at least in a measure, enable man to keep pace with his thoughts. The human being has been created with a mind that can encompass the whole world within the fraction of a second; yet, his physical senses lag woefully behind. With his feet, he can walk only a limited distance. With his hands, he can touch only what is within reach. His eyes can see at a limited range, and his ears are useful at a short distance only.

When television has fulfilled its ultimate destiny, man's sense of physical limitation will be swept away, and his boundaries of sight and hearing will be the limits of the earth itself. With this may come a new horizon, a new philosophy, a new sense of freedom, and greatest of all, perhaps, a finer and broader understanding between all the peoples of the world.

May 31, 1931

Radio News

By JACK GOULD

The "Amateur Hour," presented at 7 o'clock Sunday nights over WABD and the DuMont Network, has scored the highest rating in the first popularity poll of television programs to be conducted by C. E. Hooper, Inc., it was announced yesterday.

The figure for the "Amateur Hour" was put at 46.8. It was said to be the highest Hooper rating since the 46.9 registered in 1936 by the original Major Edward Bowes amateur hour, on which the present production is patterned.

Runners-up to the "Amateur Hour" in the Hooper television analysis were not announced, the survey organization explaining that more complete reports would be forthcoming at a later date.

March 5, 1948

Family Life, 1948 A. T. (After Television)

By JACK GOULD

Privacy goes out the window when the video party enters through the door.

THE American household is on the threshold of a revolution. The wife scarcely knows where the kitchen is, let alone her place in it. Junior scorns the late-afternoon sunlight for the glamour of the darkened living room. Father's briefcase lies unopened in the foyer.

The reason is television. If the art of video carries a boundless promise, it also has brought an upheaval in pantry and environs. Today's pioneer owner of a set is not only a looker and a listener. He also is a boniface. Yesterday it was the game of charades which intrigued the avant garde; now it is the television party.

Superficially, video may seem no more sinister than mah jongg or gin rummy, a trifling example, as it were, of paralysis in the parlor. Indeed television's host of experts have maintained a meaningful silence on the impending crisis. However, it is no longer possible to conceal that our way of life since Lincoln and Jackson is more than just in danger. It has gone.

The television party comes upon a family gradually, relentlessly. The first step leading to a cathode carnival comes when Mr. Jones, the one who is to be kept up with, puts foot inside the television store. Whether he favors a table model or a console has no bearing on his imminent fate. Once he makes a deposit on a screen of his own, he opens his home to the world.

JACK GOULD, radio editor of The Times, has closely followed the development of video, not overlooking its complex sociological implications.

The world is not long in coming in, three or four at a time. The first crew to arrive is the covey of specialists assigned to convoy a television set to its ultimate resting place in the unsuspecting domicile. Wire is strewn over roof and out of window. Favorite chairs are moved to one side, books and magazines are swept off the one strong table, lamps are shifted to new spots where there are no wall outlets.

Mrs. Jones of course can only sit grimly by, as the electron demands sacrifice of the hours spent in arrangement of the furniture. In a facile lingo of their own, having to do with weird matters of ohms, microfarads and millivolts, the service men explain it is necessary. Daddy's den must become an amphitheatre.

BEFORE leaving, the men make sure no Jones will have to live alone. Upon the rooftop they put an assortment of fishing poles, the social booby-trap of the atomic age, to let neighbors know that here is a house with wherewithal and video. The television party is on.

The television party runs in two shifts, starting in late afternoon and lasting through to whatever bedtime is chosen by DuMont or NBC. Electronic festivities in the home begin with the arrival of the younger set, eager for the movie marathon embodied in "Howdy Doody," "Small Fry Club," CBS "Scrapbook," and the offerings of the two-fisted if balding Tim McCoy.

CHILDREN'S hours on television admittedly are an insidious narcotic for the parent. With the tots fanned out on the floor in front of the receiver, a strange if wonderful quiet seems at hand. The adolescent bedlam which customarily heralds the approach of the final meal of the day is sublimely absent. A cocktail can be had with nothing worse than a distant echo of video's Uncle Dons. The weary feet of the household's distaff division can be put up for a merciful few minutes before another bout with the dishpan. Marconi's cup truly runneth over.

The dream of years, alas, soon starts to walk. As word passes along the moppet grapevine, alien mamas decide there is no use in merely leaving off the offspring and then making a second trip later to pick them up. It is simpler to stay with the video hostess, who soon finds that her cocktail shaker, once adequate for a tolerable amount of company, is no better than a thimble. Like radio and television, the hen party goes on a five-a-week basis. So does the supply of olives.

Thereafter the kinescope confusion

Drawing by Carl Rose.

Television party—"No more is the family's evening tainted with such an archaic pursuit as one person talking to another, once known as conversation."

mounts in the home. The head of the house makes an appearance to find dinner assuming an increasing likeness to a GI menu. Sliced spam becomes a fixed staple, if only because it can be served without regard to an orthodox hour for the evening's vitamins. A simple salad, i.e., a few greens doused in chain-store dressing, is also offered as though it were a substitute for something to eat. But hot coffee? In the video house it long since has boiled away.

The repast is served with all the éclat to be found in a one-arm cafeteria. Even if one would, one cannot dawdle over the spam. In the three and one-half minutes between dinner and the start of the CBS schedule there are things to be done. The children must be sent to bed, bathless just this once, of course. The dishes must be washed. The living room must be tidied up. Company is coming for the second shift.

THE requirements for the successful television party are many. The first essential is that the participants rid themselves of all the outworn notions for the informal get-together. Here, in brief, are the accepted rules of behavior for the video guest:

(1) Do not sit too close to the receiver; it makes the picture look fuzzy.

(2) Resign yourself to the fact that you will not grab one of the really comfortable chairs in any house.

(3) Don't fuss or squirm if you saw the motion picture ten years ago.

(4) When seeing a prizefight, keep cool when the host says he can make the picture clearer and brings in a jumpy, black-and-white crazy quilt, just as the announcer says Joe Louis knocked down Jersey Joe Walcott.

(5) Under no circumstances rub your eyes, clean your glasses or just go to sleep. You're seeing history in the making, man.

(6) Never suggest that you saw a better television receiver at somebody else's house.

(7) Don't ever fail to ask the host if there is not a better program on another station. Tuning the television receiver is the host's crowning glory, the Common Man's link with the atomic age.

(8) Don't talk. Ben Grauer is the Voice of Authority.

THE rules for the host are no less stringent. Their text follows:

(1) Upon installation of the television receiver the fireplace must be sealed off. The heart-warming glow of hickory logs can only prove distracting. One flicker in a home is enough.

(2) All deliveries of milk must be discontinued upon the first peep of light in the cathode tube. Even the refined refrigerator cannot accommodate both bovine juice and soda pop for the first shift and soda for the second.

(3) In the case of televised prizefights, the host will display both patience and fortitude when a guest, who has not read a sports page since the days of Walter Camp, asserts categorically the fight will end by a technical k. o. in the fifth round.

(4) Greater patience yet will be shown when, upon the third roll-call of states at a political convention, the guest maintains, "Isn't it interesting?"

(5) The host will be on his guard against the neighbors who bring their own refreshments. It takes them longer to drink up.

(6) When your "guests" bring their guests, do not call the Homicide Bureau. The pioneer always was a sturdy chap.

(7) When longing for the good old days, sympathize with the laymen still pursuing a grand slam or an inside straight. The odds are against them, too.

(8) For all the tribulations of his present lot, the television set owner should appreciate his temporary role as a social arbiter. Once the crystal set owner was important; today he is but a decimal point in a Hooper rating.

With both factions adhering to the platform of the television party, success is assured. The family's evening is not tainted with such an archaic pursuit as one person talking to another, a practice, it may be recalled, which once was known as conversation. The Kinsey report, the Berlin blockade, "Mister Roberts," the price of a Pontiac and the state of the weather no longer are allowed to heat the passions at the hearth.

Instead, a mute tranquillity has overtaken the American home. Who can argue the matter of the Lord & Taylor bill in the company of strangers? Who has the courage to read a book in a room full of wrestling fans? Not the proud owner of a new television set. He has a choice of programs and a new purpose in life: the off-and-on switch.

WHAT YOU SEE ON TELEVISION: A CRITICAL SURVEY AND REVIEW

The Manifold Artistic and Economic Problems of the Medium Make Many Extensive Innovations Improbable in Near Future

By JACK GOULD

TELEVISION today offers a growing variety of programs running from mid-morning until late at night. The shows in the daytime hours mostly follow the pattern of radio—women's features and popular musical offerings. In the afternoon there are the ball games and presentations for children. The major attractions which best exemplify the progress of television programming in the past year come on after 6 o'clock at night.

All programs fall into two broad classifications: those originating outside the studio and those originating inside. Outside, the most effective programs are those which take the viewer to the scene of an event, such as a Presidential address or a sports contest. Inside, the most successful shows are the drama productions and the up-to-date comedy offerings.

Here, in brief, is a critical summary of representative types of shows under the main program classifications:

Drama: The two best shows in this category now are "Studio One," seen twice a month, and the "Ford Television Theatre," seen once a month. Each runs a full hour, has an excellent cast and is not afraid to experiment. "Studio One" on May 1 will repeat its modern-dress production of "Julius Caesar," widely regarded as the best television drama yet shown. There are a number of half-hour drama programs, exemplified in the "Kraft Theatre" and "Chevrolet on Broadway," but they usually reflect the problems inherent in limited running time and limited budgets.

Variety: The hour-long show of Milton Berle is undisputed leader in this field, the comedian's quick wit and flair for slapstick being ideally suited to the medium. Mr. Berle also appreciates the need for visual pace: He and others in the show make many costume changes. The runner-up in this category probably is Arthur Godfrey, who pursues an erratic course in television via two programs. His leisurely style, which makes for relaxed radio listening, is sometimes very effective in TV but can be trying after viewing for a few weeks. "Toast of the Town," another hour variety show, suffers from the listless job of Ed Sullivan as master of ceremonies.

"The Broadway Revue," seen simultaneously on two networks every week, is one of television's more ambitious efforts to date. With the services of Sid Caesar, Mary McCarty, Imogene Coca and the dancing Champions, it frequently lives up to its title, but at other moments bogs down in noticeable repetition.

Situation Comedy: The program built around a basic situation has not come too quickly to television, perhaps because it is among the most difficult to do. Gertrude Berg, author of "The Goldbergs," has transferred her popular radio serial to TV with great success, chiefly because her characters, devoid of any artifice, seem genuine. Paul and Grace Hartman, the dancing comedy pair of the Broadway theatre, have tried to portray a whacky couple in suburbia but have been handicapped by rather severe script trouble.

Mystery: What might be expected to be a favorite—the mystery show—thus far has had scant representation. The one major example, "Suspense," has proved that it is going to be much harder on television than it is on the radio to keep an audience from guessing the solution.

Children's Programs: A program which probably could be done only on television—"Kukla, Fran and Ollie"—has assumed leadership in this important classification. "Kukla" and "Ollie" are two puppets; "Fran" is Fran Allison, singer and actress. Miss Allison and the two puppets engage in spirited high jinks which also have satiric overtones to divert the adult. Another favorite is "Howdy Doody," a marionette who "talks" to Bob Smith. His antics, however, are not as amusing as they once were. One unique innovation is the television "baby sitter." She is Pat Meikle, who tells stories and draws pictures for pre-school youngsters.

There are also any number of Western films especially addressed to the children. Television has brought new fame to William Boyd for his "characterization" of Hopalong Cassidy.

Feature Films: Like Westerns, other films presented on television are still old in years, except for a few importations from England which are of more recent vintage. Made for projection on the larger theatre screen, they include many feet of long shots, where the action is lost to the TV viewer.

Imogene Coca and Sid Caesar resume their comic ways Saturday evening from 9 to 10:30 o'clock over Channel 4 (N.B.C.).

Interviews and Discussions: The success of these programs depends largely on the personality of the participants and on the personal interest of the individual viewer in the subject under discussion. "The Court of Current Issues," using the format of a courtroom trial, is usually one of the more provocative. Other lively half-hours are "Meet the Press," on which reporters interview persons in the news, and "Meet Your Congress," on which members of the House and Senate debate the issues of the hour. The television version of "People's Platform" has suffered somewhat from preoccupation with visual effects rather than with what its guests have had to say.

News: The presentation of straight news, as contrasted to the pick-up of an event as it happens, has not been too successful on television. The difficulty is that comparatively few spot news events lend themselves to immediate pictorial treatment. If only because he recognizes this limitation, the reports of Doug Edwards are probably most effective, but his program would be done equally well on the radio.

Musical Programs: The number of popular musical shows have increased substantially, the most lavish being the new Fred Waring offering, which opened only last week. Kyle MacDonnell, one of television's first new stars, continues to command a loyal audience, thanks to her videogenic qualities and a pleasing mezzo-soprano voice. Perry Como's "Supper Club" also is an unhurried show and makes for easy looking. For the swing enthusiast, there are a couple of jam sessions.

On the classical side, not too much has been done as yet. The Jacques Fray "Music Room," while uneven, frequently offers young artists of very promising talent.

Opera: Opera on television has not been plentiful. Far and away the most effective single production was the televising of Gian-Carlo Menotti's "The Medium," both its intimacy and simplicity suggesting that it might have been especially conceived for television. As a precedent-setting experiment, the Metropolitan Opera's "Otello" was an event of the early season. An attempt to do an English version of "La Boheme," on the theory that it would have a wider appeal to a mass audience, proved only awkward.

The Dance: The limited range of the video camera thus far has restricted use of dance forms dependent upon extensive movement. The first major attempt to devise dance interpretations especially for television was launched last week with Michael Kidd in a ballet version of "Robinson Crusoe."

Women's Programs: For the most part these make the assumption that some housewives at least will not have much time for looking. Essentially, the majority are straight radio shows done before cameras. If only because it features a trained newspaper woman who knows how to ask questions, Dorothy Doan's "Vanity Fair" show is among the best.

Sports: As a ready-made attraction whose outcome is never certain, the sports contest continues as a major television staple. Now the attention is on baseball. Unfortunately, many sports announcers, brought up on radio, insist on talking too much, forgetting that the viewer can see a great deal for himself. Bob Stanton, who has worked on most of the major prize fights, is one of the few who does not intrude unnecessarily.

Programming Problems

For all the advances which it has made in programming in the last year, television continues to be beset by many production problems peculiar to the new medium itself. How they will be resolved will be an important factor in deciding the type of future offerings.

The primary problem is one of economics. The cost of a television show is most sharply reflected in the personnel and time needed for its preparation. In radio, for example, an hour-long dramatic show can be produced with sixteen persons; in television, a total of forty is needed. In radio, the rehearsal of an hour-long dramatic show usually takes about eight hours; in television, it takes forty hours or more.

Television, in short, starts with all the basic expenses of radio and then must add the costs of a visual medium: camera men and their equipment, lighting crews, stagehands, scenery designers, make-up specialists, wardrobe women, costumers, choreographers, and so forth.

These economic factors necessarily play an important part in determining what can be shown on the air. A good example is to be found in the case of films especially made for television. Producers already have found that for the present at least it is not possible to take full advantage of the wider range of action which is common to the motion picture. To take the time to do the extra "shooting" or to build the necessary settings would make the total cost prohibitive for a sponsor.

The primary artistic problem of television is centered on what always has been a first consideration of any entertainment form—obtaining talent and script material. The difference in the case of television is that this need is infinitely more acute.

Already there is a noticeable degree of repetition in many programs. Particularly in vaudeville shows the same acts may pop up on a half dozen shows and then disappear from the scene. In this respect, television poses a question of the greatest import to the whole entertainment world: How long and how often can an artist appear in person before wearing out his welcome?

The answer, if there is one, is related directly to the matter of the availability of script material and its quality. With only a half dozen dramatic programs on the air, a shortage of plays which can be revived already has been felt, with the need for comedy material being even more pressing.

Plans for the Future

The combined economic and artistic problems of television explain why program directors are not expansive about the shows that may be expected in the immediate future. They expect an increase soon in the number of different types of shows presented, but revolutionary improvements, they believe, will come gradually.

Thus far only two major Hollywood stars—Jack Benny and Eddie Cantor—have made plans for doing shows next fall. Both are of the opinion that two shows a month will be the maximum that they can do well, an arrangement which also has its attractions for the sponsor who has to meet the bill. An every-other-week schedule of operations, in fact, may become increasingly common among television programs.

April 24, 1949

TIME FOR A HALT

Radio and TV Carnage Defies All Reason

By JACK GOULD

IF radio and television aren't careful, somebody's going to call the cops. In their desperation to find inexpensive fillers for their summer schedules the two media have exceeded the bounds of reasonable interest in murder, mayhem and assorted felonies. Both the kilocycles and the channels are fairly dripping with crime and it is time that a halt was called.

Last week the broadcasting industry's admiration for the violent way of life reached the inevitable denouement. The National Broadcasting Company put a sordid mystery show right in the middle of its delightful Saturday morning schedule for children. The youngsters at home who had just finished hearing a recording of "Jack and the Beanstalk" were regaled with a lurid tale about a two-timing wife and her husband who was beaten to death with a beer bottle.

Actually, it may be doubted if even the television and radio broadcasters themselves realize to what extent they have been gripped by the fad for shooting it out in front of microphone and camera. The figures are both startling and shocking.

Taking into account any form of show embodying violence or the threat of violence, including both adult and children's offerings, there was available on the radio last week a total of more than eighty-five separate time periods at which a listener could tune in a show of this type. This total, incidentally, involved only the four major network affiliates.

In television the situation was just as bad. On the seven stations in the New York area the listener had his pick of more than seventy-five periods during the week when he could find a taste of life outside the law, the figure including both "live" and film shows. If anything, this total is low because some programs, although ostensibly dedicated to wholesome drama, often incorporate in some degree the theme of homicide.

No matter how many novels may be written by disgrunted emigres from Radio Row, broadcasters are not stupid men and they know full well that they are playing with fire. The volume of protests against the orgy of crime on the air has deluged many a desk in Washington, and Wayne Coy, chairman of the Federal Communications Commission, months ago issued a warning.

The crime shows are justified by the broadcasters primarily on the grounds of expediency and economic necessity. But there is something fundamentally askew when an industry which constantly prates about its freedom is incapable of enforcing two of the most essential conditions for continued enjoyment of that freedom: moderation and self-control.

No person either expects or wants a blanket ban on mystery shows; their appeal is as old and durable as literature itself. And the broadcasters have a thoroughly valid point when they note that other forms of entertainment—magazines, books and the movies—rely heavily on the crime story.

But they err seriously if they think the problem of crime shows on the air can be told in terms of quantity alone. Rather more serious, as a matter of fact, is the quality of such programs after they have been put through the rewriting mill and tailored to fit the needs of two arts which always are in a hurry.

The majority of crime shows are presented within a span of thirty minutes and this time often is reduced further by the minutes consumed by the commercials. Although a program series may derive its basic source material from outstanding fiction writers, what is euphemistically known in broadcasting as the "adaptation" generally squeezes out of an original work much of whatever distinction it may have had.

There is not time in broadcasting for extended characterization or detailed description of setting. The writer's job is to "hop up" the narrative so that it captures the audience's eye or ear in the shortest possible time and holds the attention of that organ until the Hooper rating is tabulated.

In practice this means that the major emphasis must be put on the so-called "action." The exposition, the climax and the resolution fall all over each other, with the delights of genuine suspense, characterization and the understated phrase sacrificed to the demands of the stop-watch. It's scant wonder that many a viewer feels he has heard or seen every mystery show before; he probably has.

Ultimately, of course, broadcasting's current preoccupation with crime probably will be tempered by the public itself, just as the worst of the give-away fad finally ran its course. But as with the mania for prize contests, very likely this will not come about until radio and television needlessly have incurred another batch of black eyes. If radio and television suffer many more of the same, the public may be justified in coming to the conclusion that the broadcasting industry is incapable of seeing where it is going.

July 16, 1950

GUEST RELATIONS IS BIG BUSINESS

By VAL ADAMS

The Networks Distribute More Than 8,000,000 Tickets Each Year

THE biggest ticket business in New York is conducted by the television and radio networks. Last year N. B. C. and C. B. S., the chains distributing the bulk of tickets, issued some 8,000,000 complimentary tickets to their various television and radio broadcasts. All networks have ticket staffs who do nothing but answer requests from viewers and listeners who are eager to be inside studios or to pick up a few prizes.

Nine out of ten people visiting here prefer to see a television rather than a radio show, judging from the ticket requests received from forty-eight states and foreign points as distant as East Africa. Included among the video shows most sought out are those of Arthur Godfrey, Milton Berle, Jackie Gleason, Ed Sullivan, Sid Caesar-Imogene Coca and the "Howdy Doody" and "Your Hit Parade" programs. The big productions get the biggest play, the hour-long extravaganzas offering comedy and variety are most in demand.

Star Attraction

The star attraction at C. B. S. is Mr. Godfrey, who has three different series of programs. The biggest visitor demand is placed upon his daily morning show, two-thirds of which is presented both by television and radio and the final half hour by radio only. Last January alone C. B. S. received 55,000 ticket requests for the show. The studio accommodates only 250 persons at a sitting.

Each morning at 8:30, when the C. B. S. ticket bureau opens at 57 East Fifty-second Street, people line up and plead for Godfrey tickets, offering cash bribes or telling fantastic tales as to why they must be admitted to the show. They ignore a sign that says, "Tickets for Arthur Godfrey must be written for six months in advance." They are unmindful that some mail requests received last June are just now being filled.

Some C. B. S. personnel suspect that Mr. Godfrey's warm and friendly personality is not the sole factor in drawing crowds each morning. The word has spread that a goodly amount of loot is available, consisting of samples of sponsors' products and a free lunch during the broadcast. The latter features crackers and other food passed around the studio. Milk, tea and orange juice also are served. A visitor leaves the broadcast with a loaded shopping bag on which is written, "I've just come from the Arthur Godfrey show."

The "Howdy Doody" children's program on N. B. C. is a major problem for TV ticket dispensers. The demand is so heavy for a studio holding only forty children in the "peanut gallery" daily that the network accepts no more requests, although they continue to come in at the rate of 1,000 weekly.

Peter M. Tintle, manager of N. B. C. guest relations, is not sure what name holds the record on the waiting list for "Howdy Doody" tickets, but reported:

"According to one woman who wrote in, she has a 3-year-old child who has been waiting five years to get into the peanut gallery."

Mr. Tintle believes that young children themselves do not create the great demand for "Howdy Doody" tickets as much as their parents do.

"The parents want to see them on television," he said, "but a lot of the kids don't know what it's all about when they come here. Some start crying and yelling. No wonder Bob Smith (conductor of the program) doesn't want to move to a bigger studio as the network has considered from time to time."

It is not uncommon for networks to receive ticket requests from people in England, France, Italy, New Zealand and Australia who are planning to visit here. Interestingly enough, most of these requests are for quiz programs. "I guess it's because of the old fable of how money grows on trees in this country," said Mr. Tintle.

Recently C. B. S. received a letter from a woman in Uganda, British East Africa, asking for two tickets to a morning quiz program for a March date. In return for the tickets, she said, if anyone at C. B. S. was interested she would swap information on the "non-political aspects of East Africa."

Oddity

One odd fact in the distribution of broadcast tickets is that a radio show, identical with and using the same cast as its television counterpart, will not draw a studio audience as well as the other. "What's My Line?" — a simple panel show—is high on the list of TV ticket-seekers, according to Laurette Banks, manager of the C. B. S. ticket bureau, and fills all 691 theatre seats on Sundays at 10:30 P. M. But on Wednesdays at 8 P. M., a more convenient hour, the same John Daly and company on radio draw only an average of 230 guests into a studio that seats 300. The radio version of "Howdy Doody" also is in far less demand than the video edition.

There is no decline, however, in ticket requests for Toscanini concerts broadcast by N. B. C. radio. Another 5,000 arrive each week, although the network announces on the air that it can accept no more requests this season. Carnegie Hall, where the broadcast originates, seats 2,760.

A man recently wrote from Minneapolis asking for one Toscanini ticket on March 14, saying that he would fly here specially for the broadcast. When the network informed him by mail that the ticket would be forthcoming, he telephoned New York to confirm the letter and said he would make his plane reservation immediately.

A woman in Rome wrote that she would arrange her trip to New York around whatever date she might be granted two Toscanini tickets.

Complications

Right now the ticket bureaus are making plans for Easter week, the heaviest season of the year, when schools are closed and thousands of visitors come to town. How they'll cope with the demands remains to be seen.

"Television makes the distribution far more complicated than radio ever did," said Mr. Tintle. "In radio a show had only one sponsor — and remember we turn over from 70 per cent upward of all tickets to a sponsor, if he wants to distribute them himself. But a television show may have six different sponsors and we have to deal not only with them but their advertising agencies as well. And television shows have larger casts than radio shows, all of whose members want tickets. It's a great problem."

March 1, 1953

TV NETWORKS PASS RADIO IN TIME SALES

They Increased 41% for 1952 —Total Broadcast Revenues for Video $324,200,000

Special to THE NEW YORK TIMES.

WASHINGTON, July 31—Last year, for the first time, television network time sales surpassed those of radio networks, the Federal Communications Commission revealed today in a report containing financial data on the operations of the television broadcast industry. The agency reported that TV network time sales totaled $137,700,000 last year, compared with $102,100,000 network time sales of the four nation-wide radio networks.

The TV time sales, it was added, represented a gain of 41 per cent compared with 1951. The total time sales for the four nation-wide radio networks in 1952 were off $12,000,000 compared with the preceding year.

The report showed that total broadcast revenues of the TV industry in 1952 were $324,200,000 or 38 per cent above those of the preceding year. Total broadcast revenues, it was explained, comprise the sale of time, talent and program material to advertisers. Broadcast income, before Federal taxes, was reported at $55,000,000 or 33 per cent above the 1951 level.

Networks (including fifteen owned and operated TV stations) reported TV revenues of $180,200,000, expenses of $170,300,000, and income, before Federal taxes, of $9,900,000.

Ninety-three TV stations (excluding the fifteen network establishments) which were in operation before Sept. 30, 1948, when the F. C. C. "froze" the granting of further licenses, reported total broadcast revenues of $143,400,000, or an average of $1,541,825 a station in 1952. The average station's income before taxes was $492,351.

Fourteen other TV stations, licensed after April 14, 1952, when the "freeze" was lifted, reported aggregate revenues of $600,000, expenses of $800,000 and a loss of $200,000. Of the fourteen new TV stations, only three were in commercial operation more than two months in 1952.

Of the 108 stations, including network stations in operation before the "freeze," ninety-four reported profitable operation during last year. Of the ninety-four, seventeen reported profits, before Federal taxes, of $1,000,000 or more.

The report said that the average TV station's revenues of $1,541,825 in 1952 were made up as follows: Network time sales, $387,252; non-network time sales to national and local advertisers (after commissions), $941,604; and sales and commissions on talent and program material, $212,969.

New York's seven TV stations, the report showed, had aggregate station revenues of $26,800,000, expenses of $20,800,000 and income, before Federal taxes, of $6,000,000.

August 1, 1953

A Clinical Analysis of TV

An observer offers a not wholly laudatory view of the medium: it has evolved faster than expected, with results both awesome and awful to behold.

By GILBERT SELDES

WHEN H. G. Wells was in New York on his last visit I asked him what television could do in "the race between education and catastrophe," and to my dismay he answered that it would be useless if not actively damaging. "You'll have nothing but parades," he said; "an endless newsreel of parades and sports."

He was wrong. So were many others. To strike a trial balance as TV approaches its tenth year of commercial operation, it might be helpful to recall what people hoped and feared and expected when it began.

A few months after my talk with Wells, Paul Kesten, then the executive vice president of C. B. S. for whom I was working, took me to lunch to explain the facts of life. Kesten is one of the few authentic geniuses of the business world and he interprets figures the way a virtuoso interprets "The Devil's Trill." Before my dazzled eyes he set the *proof* that no matter how many TV sets were sold, no matter how much you charged the sponsor, television could *never* pay its way.

Other predictions were that television would put an end to reading but would reunite the family (without conversation) around the 21-inch hearth, that it would make adult education popular, that it would be the decisive factor in the choice of Presidential candidates.

ALL things are possible, if not likely, and these forecasts may yet prove sound. Already taking its place beside Mr. Hoover's prediction (in the Twenties) that the American people would not stand for commercials on the air is the wishful thought that TV commercials would be less aggressive because the sponsor's product would be visible. The strangest prediction of all is one in which the entire industry took part—that television wouldn't be more than a chemical "trace" in the broadcasting business for a long time to come.

Regardless of what the various managements wanted, they had a rough calendar at the back of their minds which allotted about two years after the war to regular AM radio (replacement of obsolete equipment, production of programs held up by the war); then Frequency Modulation would come in and occupy us for a decade, during which the apparatus and the techniques of television would be developed; and then TV, launched in black and white in the mid-Fifties, would hold us for another ten years, so that about 1965 the country would be ready for gorgeous color.

This is really the essential fact about television: It is ten years ahead of itself. A combination of economic pressures and technical advances resulted in the appearance of reasonably priced sets with a fairly clear and steady picture soon after the war ended, and the installation of large screens in cafes and roadhouses gave the business a sort of final push. The result was that the entire country became aware of television through cartoons and jokes about it even before Milton Berle arrived in 1948. Since then it has been an obsession with the American people. Even the eggheads and intellectuals (probably subversives every one of them) and the snobs who boast of never having seen a TV show are concerned with what television can do to them, to their fellowmen, to the economy, to the nation.

WHAT has it done?

It has knocked off Ibsen's "A Doll's House" in 22½ minutes and it has also done stage-length versions of Shakespeare with intelligence and skill. It turned "Author Meets the Critics" into a brawl and back into civilized discussion. It has presented and still presents over a hundred separate acts of criminal violence a week, many of them seen by children, and at various times it presents serious studies in the cause of crime. In collaboration with colleges and universities, the commercial networks have carried studies in archaeology, in the dramatic arts and in history, and have had brilliant and popular educators on the air, yet the TV stereotypes of the teacher, of the man of science, of the educated woman, are almost all ridiculous or disagreeable.

For a time it seemed as if the Comic Spirit were to be incarnated in Berle and that our

Some "triumphs of a medium"—The Durante show (left) and "Ethel and Albert."

GILBERT SELDES is a pioneer in TV program production, and the author of the books, "The Seven Lively Arts" and "The Great Audience."

last view of Fred Allen would be with a pig in his arms (this is called a "sight gag" and when you've seen one you know how appropriate the name is). It has urged children to eat a "superatomic" bread and presented a thirty-minute filmed advertisement for a scalp treatment (which was shown every night for weeks, and was more popular than many programs), and it has also let us see productions from which the sponsors have voluntarily omitted their commercials. It has exploited the depths of human misery and mocked at native ignorance while it has collected hundreds of millions to alleviate suffering and has made great men and women known to millions, presenting their thoughts and their emotions simply and effectively.

IT has brought advertising into the great ritual of democracy so that only the actual ceremony of the Presidential Inauguration is now unsponsored and, at great expense to themselves, the two less prosperous networks carried the Army-McCarthy hearings. It has been a godsend to the half-talented, promoting them into "personalities," and it has degraded or failed to use finer talents; it put over Liberace after the Continental and sent Victor Borge back to the theatre. It has the vigor of youth and is as pestiferous as a precocious child; it is a monster and a Medici.

THE most honorable accomplishments of television have been in the hour-long play and in the handling of actuality.

The various dramatic series resemble one another, particularly in being uneven in quality from week to week, but rarely falling below a reasonably high level. The productions of Fred Coe have a special interest because he has surrounded himself with a group of writers who have actually created a style of drama which is neither theatre nor movie and definitely is television. It took the movies twenty years to escape from the wrong style—photographing a stage play—and almost as long again to create in cinematic terms.

Among the dramatists in the Coe group, Horton Foote, N. Richard Nash, and Paddy Chayefsky have reworked their TV plays for the theatre or for the movies, but their plays were originally shaped for production in a studio to be seen by two or three people at home. They and Robert Alan Aurthur, Sumner Locke Elliott, Tad Mosel and David Shaw, who complete the group, concentrate on character, letting plot rise out of the hopes and fears and habits of human beings without over-projection, with intensity and passion. Their predilection for the "downbeat" or sad ending got Mr. Coe into trouble last season, but these writers are still writing the kind of TV plays which have their special quality.

In the area of straight communications, television reached a surprising maturity when the Kefauver Committee hearings were transmitted and the standards of TV reporting were established (by the directors and crews of the independent station WPIX). Not for a single moment were the cameras used to dramatize or to comment; dispassionate separation of fact from editorial opinion was not an abstract ideal, but a fact. The industry can be proud of having arrived at this point so early in its career.

Vastly to its credit also is the demonstration, led by Edward R. Murrow, of the value of courage on the air. His controversy with Senator McCarthy also demonstrated the emptiness of the old formula, "equal time to reply," because in television the time may be mathematically equal, but without equal money and skill, as well as the prestige of the program on which the attack is made, the reply cannot be effective.

The right to use television for controversies in which individuals are attacked and the right of stations and networks to editorialize about broadcasting or about other public issues are being discussed by the managers of the industry and it is a hopeful sign that Frank Stanton, the head of C. B. S. and Gen. David Sarnoff, of R. C. A.-N. B. C., are not at all agreed on some fundamental principles—the clash of opinion is all to the good.

NOT quite so good is the industry's habit of making decisions affecting the public without inviting public discussion. Motor car manufacturers and makers of candy bars do this, but they are not required by law to operate in the public interest and the broadcasters are. More and more citizens, wondering what television may be doing to them, finding the managers of the business not responsive to anything but boycotts, organized phone calls and other pressures, turn to their Congressmen and now television finds itself on the defensive, facing investigations and threats.

Most of these arise from that part of the program schedule usually held as the industry's worst — its endless stream of crime shows, many of them available to children, bringing even lower the average, uninspiring to begin with, of programs for the young. Their standard is negative: "So long as no one can prove that harm comes from a program we have the right to show it."

Proof is lacking that crime shows contribute to juvenile delinquency, but television at this point has been lumped with the horror "comic" books and is sharing the odium they have deserved. The outcry against the networks has been going on for years and during this time the number of crime programs has steadily increased. The impression becomes strong that broadcasters are indifferent to unorganized complaints and this is matched by the broadcasters' confidence in the indifference of a great majority of their listener-viewers. It is not a good foundation for mutual respect and helpfulness.

BEYOND the actual or potential damage done by any single type of program, more serious in the long run is what television does by filling so much of the air with the innocuous, the merely acceptable. I am thinking of dozens of half-hour series, all alike, all imitating one of two or three originals which in turn begin to imitate their followers, as "I Love Lucy" did, with all its individual cock-a-doodle-do lost and with Lucille Ball, a superlative comedienne, not using nine-tenths of her talents. And if they are not comedy programs outright, they are "situations" and you can't tell one from another because the star of one may be a lady orthodontist and of the other a boy veterinarian. In the end they all do the same thing: there's a mix-up, see, and just before the middle commercial he (she) gets mad (drunk) and in comes . . .

NO one believes in these things any more. They are produced without conviction and received with a kind of low-order apathy, and, anyhow, if someone got really tired of them he could turn to spelling bees and parlor games and exhibitions of personalities, all pleasant, most of them amusing, the people on them retreating farther and farther behind the masks of themselves, so that when a personality suddenly remembers that it belongs to a human being and something with bite or tang is spoken on the air seven people protest and the man's fired.

The willing suspension of all real wanting, the readiness to take whatever is given, is the consequence of routine schedules (which are, I think, inevitable) and routine thinking (not inevitable) which brings too many programs to a single level—not only of intelligence and education but also of emotional maturity. They all are looking for the same responses—a quick laugh, a quick jolt. A vast "so what" suffuses the atmosphere and people turn away from exceptional single shows to follow the favorites where they can see the same things being done this week as they saw last week. Giving the people what they want has degenerated into giving them what they are ready to accept for nothing without protest—and without passion.

INTO focus floats Jimmy Durante, the great spirit of comedy of our time—and others: there are Burns and Allen, as good in television as they've ever been, and the most underrated, the shrewdest comedy of American domestic manners, "Ethel and Albert"; there is Benny, whom the screen hasn't intimidated; there are "Kukla, Fran and Ollie," now held down to the quarter-hours which are just right for them; there is "Omnibus," which fumbles at times but is still an act of faith; there is even a newcomer named George Gobel who has freshness and wit; there are special programs — opera commissioned for television and great events.

You begin to list these special people, these triumphs of a medium of communication and entertainment which only began to open its eyes in 1945, and it seems ungrateful to pick faults. But without criticism television may go further than it has—against its own best direction.

BY 1950 critics were complaining that the new season's new programs were copies of all the others. This year a program called "Medic" duplicates the style (as artificial as blank verse) of "Dragnet," as if childbirth in which a mother must be sacrificed to save a child is somehow the same thing as tracking down a firebug. Next year we shall have, in clipped tones, after three bars of a hymn: "My name is Arthur Dimmesdale. (Pause) I'm a minister. (Pause) Working out of Boston, mostly. (Pause) Tuesday afternoon—routine check on Hester Prynne—charged with being an A-girl. (Pause) Not wearing her letter. . . ."

It is ungrateful to bring up such things, but the lack of pungent characters, of variety, of the excitement of discovery, all trace back to the principle of playing safe by imitating whatever has been successful. This is the cyclical method of Hollywood, which did more than television to keep people away from the movie houses. The complaints of the critics become almost as routine as the programs against which they protest. Them, as Durante says, them's the conditions that prevail.

IT is a fair guess that within a few years some form of pay-TV will arrive, perhaps in the home, perhaps in theatres, using new movies and specially produced plays, bringing exclusive events in sport. Ten cents each from one-tenth of all the TV set owners in the country will provide a stupendous budget for production, and if the FCC allots any frequencies to this type of transmission they will be side by side with another kind of competition: the educational stations.

Between them these two may siphon off so large a segment of the audience that the commercial broadcasters who now have everything their own way will have to compete, not with one another, which fatally leads downward in the search for common denominators, but with new concepts of "the public interest."

Then, perhaps, we shall have a truly democratic television service, in which the wants of the majority are neither neglected nor basely exploited, while the legitimate wants of all substantial minorities are satisfied without snobbishness or pedantry.

November 28, 1954

TV TRANSFORMING U. S. SOCIAL SCENE; CHALLENGES FILMS

Its Impact on Leisure, Politics, Reading, Culture Unparalleled Since Advent of the Auto

MOVIE TRADE OFF 20-40%

But 'Good' Pictures Still Draw Crowds—Inflation a Factor —Hollywood Weighs Plans

By JACK GOULD

Television, in commercial use for only a little more than five years, is influencing the social and economic habits of the nation to a degree unparalleled since the advent of the automobile.

The now familiar dipole aerial perched on the rooftop symbolizes a fundamental change in national behavior: The home has become a new center of interest for the most gregarious people on earth.

Reports by correspondents of THE NEW YORK TIMES in more than 100 cities, towns and villages over the country show that the impact of pictures sent into the living room is being felt in almost every phase of endeavor.

The ability of television to conquer time and distance together, permitting millions of persons to see and hear the same person simultaneously, is having its effect on the way the public passes its leisure time, how it feels and acts about politics and government, how much it reads, how it rears its children and how it charts its cultural future. The country never has experienced anything quite like it.

Inflation Plays a Role

The rise of television also has put the spotlight on corollary factors that are contributing to a shifting pattern of preferences in diversion. The inflationary spiral, especially the high cost of food, is working to the advantage of television as almost every community, even those without TV, reports a major decline in spending for "luxury" items.

The immediate consequence is increased activity, ranging from frantic self-appraisal to costly promotional outlay, among those who are competing for a share of the individual's budget of time and money. And the catalyst in the new era of intensified competition is society's powerful unknown: The continuous free show available upon the flicking of the switch of a television set.

What happens when the screen lights up in the home and the public curtails its spending is demonstrated graphically in the case of motion pictures.

Attendance at theatres has dropped 20 to 40 per cent since the introduction of television, according to reports from THE TIMES correspondents. Many film distributors believe the national decline is roughly 35 per cent.

In contrast, representative cities that do not have television report business is holding up well and attribute at most a 10 per cent decline to the higher cost of living.

There have been theatre closings—seventy in Eastern Pennsylvania, 134 in Southern California, sixty-one in Massachusetts, sixty-four in the Chicago area and at least fifty-five in metropolitan New York. The New York Film Board of Trade said that in the last six weeks there had been perhaps thirty closings, some only for varying periods in the warm-weather season.

Many cities reported film houses going on part-time schedules to a far greater extent than in any other summer.

But any assumption that the film industry faces extinction is contradicted by numerous other considerations.

Many of the theatres that were closed were outmoded buildings in distressed neighborhoods and could be considered normal business casualties. In addition, there have been many new houses that, in some cases at least, actually have added to the total seating capacity in a community.

Especially significant, however, is the number of drive-in theatres, where customers can avoid parking charges, baby-sitter fees and traffic congestion, and can dress as they please. These have increased by 800 in the last year, bringing the total to about 3,000. And almost all report a booming trade.

Quality Films Stressed

Exhibitors in every part of the country emphasized that pictures of quality or those boasting a fresh personality were doing a good business and were immune to TV's inroads. "The Great Caruso," "Born Yesterday" and "All About Eve" were among those repeatedly cited.

In pleading with Hollywood for an improved product, exhibitors lost much of the hesitancy that had marked their answers on the status of business at the box-office. Here are some sample observations:

Washington: "You can't charge for mediocrity any more when everybody can get it at home for nothing."

San Francisco: "Quality counts. That's the story."

New Orleans: "The good picture still packs 'em in."

Richmond: "Before the war movie-going was a habit. Now people come when they really want to see a picture."

The plight of the theatre owners is borne out by specific reports of TIMES correspondents. TV was mentioned invariably as a contributory cause, but living costs and picture quality also received strong emphasis.

TV's Effect on Theatres

Here are representative reports from cities having television stations:

City	Effect on Box-office Since TV
EAST	
Boston (2 stations)	25-40% off
Providence (1)	25-40% off
New Haven (1)	10-40% off
New York (7)	10% on Broadway, 20-40% in neighborhood
Philadelphia (3)	"Definite inroads"; "bad"
Wilmington (1)	"Slump in business"
Baltimore (3)	"Off sharply"
Washington (4)	"Definite drop"
Syracuse (2)	50% off
Schenectady (1)	"TV unquestionably hurt"
Binghamton (1)	"Badly hurt"
Utica (1)	30% off
Rochester (1)	"Drop in attendance"
Buffalo (1)	"Hit hard"
Pittsburgh (1)	15% off
Lancaster (1)	"At least 25%"
Johnstown (1)	"Big drop"
MIDWEST	
Cleveland (3)	25-35% off
Columbus (3)	"Noticeable drop"
Detroit (3)	18-25% off
Grand Rapids (1)	12-20% off
Lansing (1)	20-40% off
Milwaukee (1)	"Poor attendance"
Minneapolis-St. Paul (2)	20% off
Chicago (4)	20-40% off
Kansas City (1)	15% off
St. Louis (1)	"Definite effect, cutting attendance
SOUTH	
Richmond (1)	"Downward trend"
Atlanta (2)	"Operators blame TV"
Birmingham (2)	"Badly hurt"

Jacksonville(1)	5% off
New Orleans (1)	"Not noticeable—only one station"
Memphis (1)	10-20% off
Nashville (1)	"Decline in attendance"
	SOUTHWEST
Houston (1)	"Slight crimp"
San Antonio(2)	"Very definitely cut"
Fort Worth (1)	"Fallen off sharply"
Oklahoma City (1)	"Effects uncertain"
	WEST
Los Angeles (7)	25-40% off
San Francisco (3)	5-10% off
San Diego (1)	40% off
Seattle (1)	15-20% off
Salt Lake City (2)	"Sluggish box office"
Phoenix (1)	"Not much effect"
Albuquerque (1)	"No sustained cut"

Business in the suburbs outside the major cities reflected the general trend, except in the case of drive-ins. Population shifts—new housing developments having a preponderance of young families with no teen-agers to baby-sit—and parking facilities were factors. In the New York area, Stamford, Conn., reported a decline running up to 50 per cent; Passaic-Clifton, N. J., 25 per cent; Patchogue, L. I., 20 per cent; Peekskill, N. Y., 25 per cent, and Englewood, N. J., 10 to 25 per cent.

Non-Video Areas Report

By contrast with returns from cities with television, the box-office situation in non-video cities varies substantially. For example:

City	Box-office Business
Portland, Me.	"Attendance o. k."
Portland, Ore.	"Same as last year—some cases perhaps off 10 per cent"
Austin, Tex.	"Same as year ago"
Fargo, N. D.	"Business down slightly, but still good"
Denver	"Slightly higher"
Little Rock	"Virtually no change"

That the American public is feeling the "squeeze" between rising costs and rising taxes likewise is borne out in reports from local theatre owners and business men:

Oklahoma City: "An occasional sirloin steak for the whole family is a hell of a lot more entertainment than it used to be."

Newark: "We're in some kind of a recession; people haven't got the money."

Seattle: "It costs about $5 for a couple to attend a movie. Two 94-cent tickets with all the taxes, parking expense, cup of coffee or dish of ice cream and then the baby-sitter."

Memphis: "The people are fearful; they don't know what's going to happen."

Chicago: "A lot of people are still paying for the hard goods bought during the rush after the start of the Korean war."

Isolated and highly tentative reports — from Erie, Pa.; New Brunswick, N. J.; Miami, Syracuse, White Plains, N. Y., and Dallas—give the first hints that veteran video viewers are beginning to resume the movie-going habit after a steady dose of TV. Business shows signs of leveling off, it is reported, and in some instances there is a slight upward trend at the box office.

"The housewife sooner or later is going to get fed up staying in the house day and night," remarked one exhibitor in Westchester County.

But the average theatre owner across the country has his fingers crossed and many correspondents reported persistent rumors that more closings could be expected. Granting that inflation is an important influence adversely affecting attendance, it was noted that many persons now were looking at television as a replacement for "movie night." That is what is new.

Hollywood's Big Problem

If the local theatre is acutely aware of television, the capital of the film industry, Hollywood, thinks of little else at the moment. Though a variety of causes are responsible, the gross revenues of the eight major film companies have declined from $952,000,000 in 1947 to $861,000,000 in 1950. Retrenchment is the order of the day on the West Coast.

In 1947 the average craft union employment in the Hollywood film industry was 18,400 persons and the average monthly payroll was $7,000,000.. By 1950, the average employment was down to 13,600 and the payroll to $5,600,000, but some of the slack has been taken up in production of films for video. Reductions in executive personnel as well as among actors, writers and directors appear inevitable, it was noted, and there will be further economies in production schedules. All indications, however, point to maintenance of the volume of picture output.

Production of films especially for television is a growing business in Hollywood, and seems certain to increase. According to one source, film footage for TV was being produced in May at a rate of 988 hours a year, compared with 855 hours of feature films for theatre showing.

Hollywood's difficulty is that it isn't geared to what the television sponsor can pay for a film. In this connection several of the smaller companies — Republic, Monogram and Lippert—have made arrangements to release their backlog of films by agreeing to make a new musical sound track that will benefit the American Federation of Musicians. Other producers have hesitated to release their old films lest they offend their primary customers, the theatre exhibitors.

Of increasing importance to both Hollywood and its exhibitors is theatre television, whereby video images are projected directly on the large-size screen. The recent box-office success in theatre television's pick-up of the Joe Louis-Lee Savold fight, which the home TV audience did not see as it happened, has stimulated interest. By fall perhaps more than 100 houses will have theatre TV equipment and will be in a position to outbid an advertising sponsor on home video.

Theatre TV, in turn, has led to a consideration of subscription television for the home, a system under which the viewer would have to pay if he wished to view "unscrambled" pictures. Paramount Pictures has invested in one coin-operated device and, with some reluctance, other producers have co-operated with the Zenith Radio Corporation's box-office method known as "Phonevision." In New York later this year there may be further tests of another method called "Skiatron."

Speculation on "Marriage"

A matter for major speculation has been the possibility of "a marriage" between TV and Hollywood. While many deals have been rumored periodically, the only concrete development has been the contemplated merger of the American Broadcasting Company with United Paramount Theatres, which is a theatre chain and is not to be confused with the producing concern, Paramount Pictures, Inc.

But overshadowing all other considerations in the relationship between television and the motion-picture world is the fact that television is still only in its relatively early stages of development.

Today 107 stations are operating in sixty-three cities, within range of roughly 62 per cent of the country's population. Of the sixty-three cities, however, only twenty-four have between two and seven stations, and a choice of TV programs generally has been a prerequisite for the medium to exercise its full impact on competitive media. The remaining thirty-nine TV cities have only one station each.

For the last two years there has been a "freeze" on the construction of new television stations, which to some extent has provided the film industry with a chance to catch its breath. But the plans of the Federal Communications Commission envisage ultimately perhaps 2,000 stations serving several hundred communities.

Military priorities and many other factors may affect TV's expansion, but the motion picture business none the less has reason to worry. Television's major strides still lie ahead.

Waiting Across 1,500 Miles

Milton Buhr of Saskatoon, Sask., in the western part of Canada, has a 100-foot television aerial in his backyard and a modern set. His only trouble so far is that he hasn't seen a program; the nearest station is 1,500 miles away.

"I'm going to be ready," he explained.

Reaffirming of "Progress"

Twenty-five years ago Volmer Dahlstrand, president of the Milwaukee Federation of Musicians, complained to a theatre owner about the movies hurting the employment of pit orchestras.

"This is progress," replied the operator, curtly.

A few weeks ago the two men met and the theatre owner complained about television hurting his business.

"That's progress," replied Mr. Dahlstrand happily.

As One Medium to Another

In Kansas City, Mo., movie houses are plugging their pictures on television while knocking the medium in their advertising statements.

A typical "ad" will describe the picture to be shown and close with this sort of announcement:

"Only the giant motion picture screen can present the true grandeur and magnificence of . . . etc."

June 24, 1951

VIEWS OF A 'PROFESSIONAL MEDDLER'

By PAUL GARDNER

"TELEVISION'S talk shows are the ultimate form of decadence," observed Gore Vidal the other day. "We have reached the point where we gladly sit and let the machine talk to us. The talkathon has replaced the dance marathon. The question is, can Zsa Zsa Gabor talk for 24 hours? Should prizes be awarded to the person who asks the most interminably inane question?"

Mr. Vidal, whose epigrammatic conversations have enlivened "Open End" and "The Les Crane Show," two late-evening talkathons for viewers indulging in the New Wave decadence, was feeling particularly philosophical. He had just agreed to appear on a preview of Channel 11's projected "Hot Line" and serve as a political commentator during the Republican and Democratic conventions.

Political Assignment

His political assignment will not begin for two weeks,

but "Hot Line," with Dorothy Kilgallen, David Susskind and the Reverend William Sloane Coffin of Yale University answering questions phoned in by viewers, was on Tuesday night.

Unlike most national talkers who eagerly accept invitations to gather at TV's round-table and then flounder helplessly through a series of incomplete sentences expressing incomplete thoughts, Vidal, stylishly, confidently and usually accurately, comments on just about everything under the sun—plus some topics that are not.

On "Hot Line," Vidal went from topless bathing suits to the question of nudity ("It is, a question of esthetics—for the people watching"), to J. Edgar Hoover, integration, Georges Sand and the California primary.

Alarming Candor

Describing himself as a professional meddler, Vidal's candor was alarming enough to unnerve the entire industry. "I appear on TV to sell books [his current best-seller is "Julian"] and stir people up. It's very satisfying if you can get in one little stab that will start a chain-reaction. Of course, television has made everyone aware of the great American personality cult and can be dangerous."

Gore Vidal
Politics of the Absurd

The day before "Hot Line" went on the air, the playwright, critic and novelist read in his morning newspaper that he would be host. "That came as a surprise, not exactly pleasant. It is inhibiting to host because discretion is necessary. I do not approve of planned spontaneous conversations. They are a mistake. And, if a television conversation starts off badly, well, down it goes."

A writer with the viewpoint of Nathanael West would be needed, he continued, to capture TV's decadence. "During the golden years of television drama, I thought, 'At last, the audience is writing the plays.' Now we have creeping audiencism: they are running the talk shows.

"These programs take on dark aspects since they are made successful by people who feel compelled to conduct telephone calls with panelists after midnight."

As a commentator for the Westinghouse Broadcasting Company, Vidal will be heard here on WINS. "Whatever it is I'm doing, I'll be doing it twice a day. At first I was going to write about the conventions in an article, 'Politics of the Absurd.' With Goldwater as a candidate and Johnson as a leader of the liberal coalition, they should be gloriously funny."

He decided, however, that his new novel and a film project would not permit the time required for a magazine piece, so accepted the WINS offer. Vidal, familiar with political stratagem, was an unsuccessful Democratic candidate for Congress and a delegate in 1960 to the Democratic convention.

"I do welcome Goldwater as a candidate. Having a rather simple man doing the things simple people do—and then saying what he does in print—is useful. There is a lot of conservatism today. In fact, people are so conservative that they don't like to change Presidents. Change reminds them of death."

Partisan Politics

It has been unusual for a station or network to employ as a political commentator anyone publicly associated with partisan politics. But this year A.B.C. will use former President Dwight D. Eisenhower at the GOP convention and Senators Hubert Humphrey and Sam Ervin at the Democratic convention.

Although Vidal will not be on a major network, his opinions will be stirring up listeners in eight cities and should provide a pleasant breather from the incessant droning of typical long-winded experts who take themselves seriously.

"Just so I don't black out in the middle of a terribly important sentence," Vidal added. "I don't want to be saying, 'I'm going to make two points' and then suddenly forget what point two is or was. I want to be—how is it put—oh yes—provocative, yet anodine."

June 28, 1964

Color TV Is Growing Faster Than Other Consumer Fields

By GENE SMITH

To the Chinese, this is the year of the snake. To the television industry, it is the year of the peacock.

By yearend the peacock is expected to be seen in color regularly on some 5 million television screens across the nation. There is no longer any question about it: 1965 is the year that color television finally arrived.

Perhaps its present status was best described by Fred J. Borch, president of the General Electric Company, at the annual meeting on April 28: "Color television is the most rapidly growing segment of the consumer goods market."

Industry observers attach great significance to that statement from the head of one of the leading electronics companies, particularly since G.E. had dragged its feet in the 12-year evolutionary struggle of color television.

Many also believe that it was more than coincidence that the Radio Corporation of America, the color pioneer, announced just two days later a shortage of color picture tubes had developed.

Mr. Borch had told his annual meeting that G.E. had gone into pilot production on April 5 of an "improved version of the 'shadow-mask' type, which is standard in the industry but is of a simpler design that can lead to less costly tube installation and service."

This means that most of the major radio-television set makers are either in some stage of color picture tube production or have announced plans to get into the business.

Those actually turning out picture tubes, in addition to R.C.A., are:

Sylvania Electric Products, Inc., a wholly owned subsidiary of the General Telephone and Electronics Corporation, the National Video Corporation of Chicago and the Zenith Radio Corporation and its subsidiary, the Rauland Corporation. Admiral Corporation, the Philco Corporation subsidiary of Ford Motor Company, and G.E. expect to begin production this year.

2.2 Million Units

Industry statistics have placed color picture tube production for this year at about 2.2 million units. R.C.A. said last week that it would produce 1.5 million of that total, with "the vast majority" of the 21-inch round tube type. National

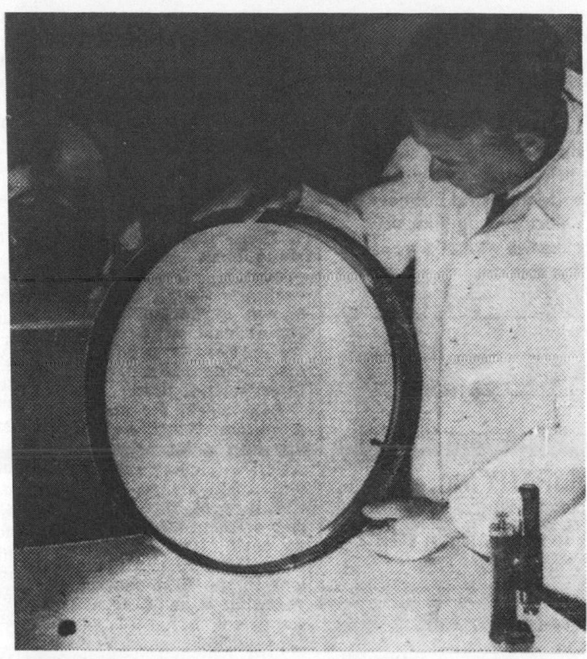

Above: Engineer inspects new phosphor dot screen at Sylvania unit in Seneca Falls, N. Y. Screens improve color.

Video is shipping the new 25-inch rectangular tubes as is R.C.A., which is also in pilot production of a 19-inch rectangular version.

Just about all manufacturers now indicate that they are experimenting with various size color sets. Industry rumors indicate that the new G.E. tubes may be in 10-,12-or 14-inch sizes but the company would only acknowledge that "A variety of screen sizes" have been tested.

The obvious objective of smaller screens would be to bring about lower costs. David Sarnoff, chairman of R.C.A., said in an interview last week that his company has reduced its lowest nationally advertised price for color sets from $495 to $379.95 in the last two years.

"We look for a continuation of this pricing pattern, but on a gradual basis, since we see no major technological breakthroughs on the horizon that could bring about extreme cost reduction," Mr. Sarnoff added.

Successful smaller screen sets could hasten price cuts, but the main stumbling block seems to be in the shortage of picture tubes. William E. Davidson, general manager of G.E.'s tele**vision receiver department, acknowledged that his company's pilot operation is only at "a learning stage" at present, with actual output to be determined after monthly checks through August.**

Over - all, industry figures show that the average color television set sells at retail for $525, while the black-and-white average retail price is $150. The fact that monochrome sets are so low has been due in large measure over the last several years to the emergence of small-screen sets.

Mr. Sarnoff would neither confirm nor deny that R.C.A. had any plans for small sets at this time: "We're looking into all practical sizes from the smallest to the largest. No part of the color spectrum is being overlooked, but no one can tell which size the public will like best without actually selling them."

The color television industry stands today at just about the same spot that black-and-white did in the early 1950's—set production is rising so fast that tube shortages are developing; prices have come down and major technological changes could bring about big cuts; and at the same time programing is expanding.

Last Wednesday, for example, Columbia Broadcasting System, which has been the color laggard, and American Broadcasting Company announced that approximately one-third of their nighttime programs next fall would be in color.

The National Broadcasting Company, the R.C.A. subsidiary and programing pioneer, has announced that 96 per cent of its network evening schedule will be in color starting next September. All but two of its nighttime programs will be colorcast, while daytime schedules will amount to 30 hours a week of color. This will result in more than 3,000 hours of color a year on that network alone.

Potential Termed High

According to latest industry tallies, some 150 of the nation's 670 television stations on the air are equipped to originate color film or slides, while only 51 have facilities and equipment for "live" programing of their own. However, more than 90 per cent of all the stations are now capable of transmitting network-originated color shows. This is more than adequate to provide the better color programs to the overwhelming majority of potential television viewers.

At the same time the lack of color cameras provides yet another boom for equipment makers. Again, R.C.A. is in the lead in this phase. Its broadcast and communications products division reported last week that it now has orders for more than $15 million of new live and film cameras. It expects to ship about 225 live and film color cameras this year.

At the conclusion of the recent National Association of Broadcasters annual convention, Marconi Company, Ltd., a subsidiary of English Electric Company, Ltd., announced that it planned to offer a competitive color camera in time for next year's meeting. The British company is a strong factor in the industry, having sold 267 of a total 850 Mark IV black-and-white cameras in this country.

Color cameras provide business for tube makers since the latest models use four pick-up tubes against only one for monochrome cameras. Each of the tubes pick up the primary television colors—red, green and blue—while the fourth picks up the "luminance," or black-and-white signal. Technical developments and improvements in the camera side of the industry also provide new markets for makers of various components.

Picture Tube Developments

The same is true for the picture tube itself. About a year ago, Sylvania announced its discovery that by using certain rare earths, namely europium and yttrium, not only was color reception improved but also black-and-white pictures showed far greater contrast. This lack of contrast had been one of the deterrents to color set sales so long as color programing remained inactive.

A Sylvania spokesman said last week that since the introduction of the brighter rare earth tubes "demand has far exceeded supply."

In order to meet such demand, Sylvania plans to double the present output of its picture tubes through "an extensive expansion" of color tube manufacturing facilities at Seneca Falls, N. Y. The company manufactures at present 21-inch round and 25-inch and 19-inch rectangular tubes. All tubes use the rare earths.

The company agrees with industry estimates of 1965 color set production of about 2.2 million and expects 1966 output to reach 2.8 million, rising to 4.7 million by 1970. Being more optimistic, R.C.A. has revised upwards its projection for industry sales this year to 2.33 million.

A spokesman said: "At the sales rate of the last four weeks, nearly 2.6 million sets could be sold this year if there were enough tubes. Industry sales are running 84 per cent ahead of the same period of last year."

He added, quite happily: "Our share of the market is now exactly double that of our nearest competitor, according to a national survey of consumer buying preferences. We expect 25 per cent of the television sets sold in this country will be color—double that of last year." The earlier estimate was 23 per cent.

Mr. Sarnoff added: "The most important figure is the fact that total dollar volume of color set sales at the retail level will exceed the total of black-and-white sales for the first time this year."

Television Digest also appears more optimistic than Sylvania with predicted 1966 industry sales of 2.87 million rising to 5 million in 1970.

The color television boom is also helping the producers and compounders of rare earths, such as the Michigan Chemical Corporation and the Molybdenum Corporation of America. The entire domestic industry shipped less than 2,500 tons of these rare earth oxides in 1963, according to Government figures. Now they are expected to at least double that output this year.

Molybdenum, for example, is increasing the development of its deposit at Mountain Pass, Calif., from 1.5 million pounds of all types in 1963 to nearly 3 million pounds in 1964 and perhaps 10 million pounds in 1965.

Sylvania reported that its chemical and metallurgical division at Towanda, Pa., which supplies all rare earth phosphors for the parent company, sells europium to other tube makers and foresees no shortages.

And so the color television business has become firmly established this year. Mr. Sarnoff has predicted that the industry's billion-dollar annual volume would triple within the next five years. Even some of the giants of the industry are returning.

William M. Day, general manager of Westinghouse Electric Corporation's television-radio division at Metuchen, N. J., said last Friday:

"Westinghouse is re-entering the color television production field. This reflects our confidence, along with everybody else, in the future of color. The boom is really on in color."

TV's Quiet Revolution: Censors Giving In

Once-Taboo Topics Are Common in Today's Fare

By ROBERT E. DALLOS

Jack and Jill went up the hill
Ostensibly for water
Now Jack is proud to show the crowd
His wife and baby daughter.
Rowan and Martin's Laugh-In

Los Angeles is known as the swingingest city in the world. There was a headline in the paper today about a wife-swapping scandal in the valley. They had to close down the entire high school.
Johnny Carson on the Tonight Show

Little boy walking down the street, crying his eyes out. Old man walks up to him and asks him why he's crying. Little boy says: "I'm crying cause I can't do what the big boys do." Old man sits down with little boy, starts crying too.
Smothers Brothers Comedy Hour

These lines from recent television programs would not have passed the censors a few years back. Today such risqué material is common fare, illustrating the growing permissiveness of the medium.

Satirical gibes at the Johnson Administration and its Vietnam policy have been more pointed—indeed more cruel—than any in television history prior to the President's withdrawal as a candidate for re-election.

Every day, viewers hear a barrage of double-entendre gags, view hip swaying, undulating girls and listen to attacks on the American Establishment. Dramas and soap operas often deal graphically with such once-taboo subjects as illegitimacy, adultery and premarital relations. Talk shows now openly discuss homosexuality, free love, suicide, suburban sex life and the problems of transvestites.

To be sure, not all taboos are going by the board. Some material still is outlawed. Some films, though they have been boxoffice successes, continue to be out of bounds. "Who's Afraid of Virginia Woolf" and "A Man and a Woman" are two such films. And movies that are bought are often cut. Advertising pressures remain but they appear to be diminishing. Indeed, commercials for some products are becoming increasingly sexy.

Network officials and independent broadcasters, assessing in recent interviews TV's trend toward permissiveness, generally agree that the movement primarily is a reflection of the changing moral values of American society. They have also encouraged the publicity the trend has nurtured.

"If TV is more permissive, it is because the audience — indeed the whole society is going along," Robert D. Kasmire, vice president for corporate informtion of the National Broadcasting Company, says. "Girls are wearing miniskirts, universities and colleges are more permissive. It is the whole attitude toward sex. We try to keep up with social changes."

"We are doing today what we would not have done in the past," he added. "The philosophy here used to be: 'Boys, don't do anything that will get you into trouble.' We once had a hypersensitivity toward audience complaint.

"When we got a letter of protest, we calculated it represented the feelings of thousands of viewers. Now we consider a complaint as the viewpoint of a single person. There are always some people who see a phallic symbol in the test pattern."

'World Is a Madhouse'

William H. Tankersley, vice president of program practices of the Columbia Broadcasting System, points to a stack of protest letters on his desk and says:

"As you can see from this mail, we no longer shut our eyes or shut off the facts. The world is a madhouse. TV gives some voice to what is going on in the world."

Another reason for the frankness, some network officials contend, is the daily television news program film of the Vietnam war.

"Sure TV is getting more adult and open about touchy subjects," says Daniel Melnick, who with David Susskind puts on many discussion programs about subjects once considered out of the question. "But which is more frank: a blue joke, a suggestive movie or TV films of Marines fighting the Vietcong? It's hard to become emotionally involved with a risqué joke when you watch a South Vietnamese general shoot a defenseless Vietcong in the head."

It is difficult to determine when the trend began.

"The process is subtle and it is indiscernible as it occurs," says Mr. Kasmire. "You actually can't see it if you compare this season with the last season. But if you stand back and compare the current season with three seasons ago, it stands out.

"No one ever sat down here at N.B.C. and said, 'Golly, this year we've got to be more permissive.' It's a natural process. Each year we do things we wouldn't have dared a year earlier."

C.B.S.'s Mr. Tankersley believes the pace has accelerated this season more than ever.

He notes that his network has twice this season shown "The Apartment," a film in which Jack Lemmon's bachelor apartment is used for a series of assignations.

The film, he says, was purchased by C.B.S. three years ago. Had it been shown then instead of during the current season "we would have edited out much more than we did when we finally showed it. We would have taken out all of the explicit sex business," he says.

Associated Press

Johnny Carson with Judy Brown, a model on whose back he wrote a check to see if it would be cashed. Some of his nightly quips are "blipped" from tape before air time.

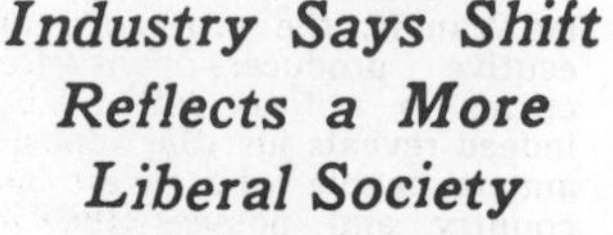

Industry Says Shift Reflects a More Liberal Society

More Franker Films

Motion pictures like "The Apartment" and "Never on Sunday," which N.B.C showed in an almost uncut version recently ("we would never have considered it five years ago") are an overriding factor in TV's uninhibitedness toward matters relating to sex.

"Feature-length films dealing with the lives of prostitutes and extramarital relationships or that are quite explicit in the bedroom carry with them a sort of built-in rationale for broadcasters," Mr. Kasmire says. "Since they are not produced for TV but have been in wide circulation, they have already stood the test of acceptability with the public, which can make a choice whether to watch it on TV or not."

Thus there is no public clamor when, in addition to such movies, TV producers inject sex into some of their own programing.

TV specials in recent months have been the source of considerable frankness. "Dear Friends," on C.B.S., a melodrama about four couples who found misery in marriage, was rather blunt in its treatment of adultery. During a scuffle that takes place between two affluent Manhattan families, the audience learns that one of the wives has been sleeping with her husband's friend.

The changing economics of the industry has also helped break down many of the medium's former attitudes. Until a few years ago, single sponsorship of an entire program was the norm. But high production costs have resulted in participation sponsorship by groups of advertisers, none of whom have a say in program production and can influence content as once was the case.

"Pressure from advertisers has practically disappeared," one network spokesman who declined to be identified commented. "By the same token, they are off the hook. Today, when a customer writes to a sponsor and complains about instances of bad taste in a program, he can answer by saying that he had nothing to do with the production."

When Milton Berle recently did a skit on the American Broadcasting Company's "Hollywood Palace" entitled "And a Messenger Was Sent," the network received several hundred letters complaining to a reference to "the prince of teach."

The writers felt this was an attack on President Johnson.

Keyed to Irreverence

"This piece evolved not out of any lack of respect," Nicholas Vanoff, the program's executive producers answered critics in a form letter, "but indeed reveals just the opposite among people who revere our country and possess the inherent humor so vital to us as a nation. We cannot express too strongly our dismay at having offended you. We hold our God-given gift of laughter very dear and regret having used yours poorly through misinterpretation."

Of the regular weekly network series, two of the newer ones, "The Smothers Brothers Comedy Hour" on C.B.S. and "Rowan and Martin's Laugh-In" on N.B.C. have been franker, industry observers say, than any other television show. And, although it was always possible that the occasional suggestive crack might have passed network censors, these two shows — presented in prime evening hours — are keyed to irreverence and "blue" material.

Network officials agree that neither program would have been considered a few seasons ago, possibly even last year.

On Monday nights this season, millions of viewers have tuned to Rowan and Martin to see how "far" they will go.

One of the most popular regular routines on the program is a satirical news show. Here are some recent examples:

News item: Curators of the London Art Museum announced today they are still awaiting further development on the long-overdue bust of Twiggy. When contacted in London, Twiggy said, "Me, too."

The planned parenthood society today announced some of the wonderful things they won't be doing next year.

Woman to Priest: Do you think there will ever be a union of clergymen? Priest: Why not, we're all white-collar workers.

My daughter says that now that the Supreme Court has outlawed prayers in school, the convent's just not the same.

It is much the same on the Smothers Brothers program, which recently had a skit in which a man's zipper was open in a restaurant. His woman companion across the table tried to tell him about it in a subtle way but he didn't take the hint. She finally blurted it out and in zipping his fly, he got the table cloth caught, dragging it across the restaurant.

With the increased amount of dissent in this country over national issues, jokes about President Johnson and the Government have also become more frequent, outspoken and biting. By the time Mr. Johnson announced that he was not a candidate for re-election they had reached the stage of cruelness.

Carl Watson, director of broadcast standards at N.B.C., whose office has to pass on all questionable material, noted recently that there was much kidding on radio of President Franklin D. Roosevelt and his family and of President Harry S. Truman.

But in recent months, the jokes about the President and the Administration have become quite cruel, he said.

"The current liberalization extends beyond humor," Mr. Watson observed. "'It has developed from true satire to the sighting of opposition to the Administration's position. True satire makes foolishness without making fun of an individual. We are tending now to make fun of an individual—Mr. Johnson."

Mr. Tankersley, C.B.S.'s head of program practices, said: "We are greatly concerned about this recent disrespect to and about the President. We have given a great deal of thought to it. But if we err, we are on the side of freedom. We are creating new courses. At least until it's clearly abused."

Perhaps the greatest amount of permissiveness shows up on the talk programs. Mr. Susskind has a weekly 40-station syndicated program, seen locally on WNEW-TV, which has given a platform to everything from homosexuals ("Homosexuality, sickness or perversion?") and unmarried couples who live together to persons who expound sexual exercises ("Sexercises-for sex cripples").

On the nightly program of his WNEW-TV colleague, Alan Burke, a bearded provocateur who elicits candor from his guests, subjects have ranged from "sexual life in suburbia today" and "four-letter words" to the problems of obtaining an abortion. Recently Mr. Burke played host to a nun turned go-go dancer at a discothèque and a transvestite.

But though long-standing barriers have come down considerably, there are still some taboos. N.B.C. recently censored a skit from the Rowan and Martin program in which a girl asks a young man if "the Queen Mary has barnacles on her bottom." The answer: "I don't know, you'll have to ask King George."

And Johnny Carson's ad lib quips on the "Tonight" show keep N.B.C.'s censors on the jump. The program, which is taped only a few hours before it is televised, always has a censor in attendance. Occasionally Mr. Carson's lines are "blipped."

Recently, for example, Criswell, a self-styled clairvoyant, predicted that before long there would be a federally sponsored semen bank to which all American males would be required to contribute.

When Bob Newhart, a guest, jestingly got up and said he had heard enough and was leaving, Mr. Carson asked him if he intended to "make a night deposit."

The few words were edited out. But the next morning N.B.C. received letters charging censorship.

April 29, 1968

Prime-Time Programing Is a Show in Itself

By TOM BUCKLEY

At 8 o'clock tonight, barring catastrophe, 45-million of the 66.2-million households in the continental United States that enjoy the blessing of television (only 2.1-million do not) will be watching it.

At an average of two persons a household, the accepted figure in the industry, that comes to 90-million viewers. It is an average-size audience for an average midweek early evening during the cold-weather months.

What is a bit unusual is that 94 per cent of the viewers—4 per cent above average—will be watching one or another of the three national networks as opposed to independent local stations.

They will be chuckling at the one-liners of "Maude" on the Columbia Broadcasting System, sharing the adventures of the young Los Angeles patrolmen on "Adam-12" on the stations of the National Broadcasting Company, or immersing themselves in nineteen-fifties nostalgia with the American Broadcasting Company's comedy "Happy Days."

It is unlikely that very many will be wondering why it is these three series that are competing for their attention at that hour on that night or why they have cut the audiences for the independent stations in their areas in half.

But the answers, in terms of jeopardy, conflict and intrigue, with many millions of dollars at stake, have all the ingredients of a successful series in itself.

Commercial Warfare

Programing, the making of such decisions, is a form of commercial warfare that goes on seven days a week, year after year, without truce or quarter. It is waged most savagely during the prime-time evenings hours, of which tonight at 8 is typical.

The objective is to win as large a share of the audience as possible, since its size largely determines the price that advertisers will pay to show their commercials.

"What you have to keep in mind is that the audience for television is relatively inelastic," Bill Behanna, an executive of the A. C. Nielsen Company, said the other day. "That is, the number of people watching television on a Tuesday night in March won't change much as a proportion of total sets from week to week or even from year to year.

"That makes television and, of course, to some extent radio, different from the other entertainment media. You can have five hits on Broadway at the same time or five or six big movies, as we do right now, and they don't hurt each other. In fact, they help, since they get people back in the habit of going out. But with television, you can only increase your audience at the expense of the competition."

The Nielsen company is the pre-eminent television rating service. Since 1950, the Nielsen sample of 1,200 households which for the past decade has been comprising 1,800 sets, has provided the industry with basic data on what the country is watching.

Decision Days

A program's rating — the percentage of all television sets on which it is being seen, extrapolated from the sample —and its share of the viewing audience are almost always the most important factors in determining whether the show remains on the air.

Occasionally, a series will do so poorly—except against the strongest competition a 17 rating and a 28 share are generally regarded as the minimums for bare survival —that it will be summarily canceled.

Ordinarily, though, these decisions are made twice a year. In November and December the networks decide on the basis of the fall ratings which runts will be culled for what they call "the Second Season," beginning after Jan. 1. This month in meetings on both coasts, the fall line-ups are being worked out, contracts are being signed and cancellation notices being sent.

During these sessions, network executives, knowing that their jobs are, as always, hostage to their success, try to arrange their stock of programs not only to form harmonious units, but also to provide the strongest competition to what they believe the competitors will be offering.

"I'd be very surprised if there will be any changes for us on Tuesday night next season," Martin Starger, a senior programing executive at the American Broadcasting Company, said recently. "'Happy Days' has given us a whole new mood that night."

A.B.C., which throughout television history has been the weak-sister network, with fewer affiliated stations, less income and less access to talent, had moved into second place behind C.B.S. in total prime-time viewing for the first four weeks of the second season, and on Tuesday nights it was in the lead.

"Tuesday has been very strong for us for several years," Mr. Starger said. "We had 'Mod Squad,' 'Movie of the Week' and 'Marcus Welby, M.D.' But when the Federal Communications Commission reduced network prime-time programing from three-and-a-half to three hours at the beginning of the 1972-73 season, to try to stimulate local programing, we had to move 'Mod Squad,' which was an hour show, to Thursday nights. It was opposite the 'Flip Wilson Show' on N.B.C. and didn't do well, so we canceled.

"On Tuesdays we replaced 'Mod Squad' with 'Temperature's Rising,' a situation comedy with a hospital background," he continued. "The ratings were disappointing, but we had faith in the show. Over the summer we changed the concept, made it more of a black comedy, and replaced James Whitmore with Paul Lynde, and sent it out again, as 'The New Temperature's Rising.' It was better, but still not good enough, so for the second season we canceled it and brought out 'Happy Days.'"

Counterprograming Stressed

This choice, he said, was an example of what television people call counterprograming. That is, it was markedly different in subject matter from its competition and was likely to appeal strongly to teen-agers, who would be seeing what was purported to be a nineteen-fifties version of themselves, and to adults under 40, who would fondly recall their own adolescent years.

The network also had decided that "Happy Days" would provide a strong "lead-in" to the rest of the evening schedule. Since viewers, by and large, prefer to stay with the same channel, networks make a special effort to place a strong program at the beginning of prime time, which runs from 8 to 11 P.M.

Since such strategies don't always work, there was probably a certain amount of astonishment mingled with the delight at A.B.C. when, in the first three weeks of the second season, "Happy Days" edged out "Maude," which had dominated the time segment since its debut during the 1972-1973 season, in the Nielsen shares.

Rating news, good or bad, travels fast these days. Neilsen's printed standings of Tuesday's shows are in the shaking hands of network and advertising executives by the following Thursday morning.

In the tripolar world of prime-time television, the second and third-place networks always gang up on the leader. Thus, N.B.C. had also made a second-season scheduling change that it hoped would improve its position against "Maude."

Programing Strategies

"We decided simply to switch 'Adam-12,' which had been leading on Wednesday night at 8, and 'Chase,' which was doing poorly against 'Maude,'" said Marvin Antonowsky, who was hired away from A.B.C. six months ago as a programing strategist.

"It didn't make any sense to have 'Chase' where it was," he continued. "It was an hour show opposite two 30-minute shows that were followed by an hour show, 'Hawaii Five-O,' on C.B.S. and an hour-and-a-half movie on A.B.C. What it meant was that 'The Magician,' which followed 'Chase,' was being hurt because it couldn't get switchovers from the other networks. Now that we've got three half-hours in direct competition we're in better shape on Tuesdays."

"Adam-12," a standard model Los Angeles Police Department drama produced by Jack Webb, the old "Dragnet" star, which had been the top show in its time slot on Wednesday, slipped to third in its new position, but achieved a respectable 28 to 29 share, while "Happy Days" and "Maude" were getting about 33 each.

"The way we saw it was that 'Maude' was a false hit," Mr. Antonowsky said. "It had been obvious from the start that it was no 'All in the Family' or 'Sanford and Son'"—both of which are also produced by Norman Lear and Bud Yorkin, the hottest team in television—"but it was simply that it hadn't had any respectable opposition."

However, N.B.C. turned out to be a net loser on the switch, since "Chase" lost more share points on Wednesday night than "Adam-12" gained on Tuesday. Wouldn't it have been wiser, a visitor asked Mr. Antonowsky, simply to concede the Tuesday time slot and keep "Adam-12" where it was.

"You can't figure that way," he replied, "'Chase' would have been lucky to get a 20 share against 'Maude' and 'Happy Days.' Besides, in this business, if you're willing to settle for No. 2 you usually end up No. 3. If you settle for No. 3 you're nowhere."

Class Fares Poorly

N.B.C.'s slide in prime-time, although it was offset to some extent by its continued dominance of the profitable early morning and late night markets with the "Today" and "Tonight" shows, had led to rumors in the trade press that dismissals of the executives who had failed to come up with hit shows were imminent.

Mr. Antonowsky, who had been hired too recently to be vulnerable, took note of the fact that the network may have suffered because of its long-standing dedication to public-service programing and specials of artistic merit.

"We did Clifford Odets's 'Country Girl' with Jason Robards and we got a 14 share. All that does is to make a hit out of your competition."

For years, critics of the networks' dependence on the ratings have been suggesting that the reason prestige productions generally do so poorly against the paltriest assembly-line series is that the Nielsen sample does not provide an accurate reflection of the viewing public.

The fact is that it probably is too accurate, mirroring the tastes of a nation in which, according to current data, 51 per cent of households have incomes of less than $10,000 a year and only 27 per cent of household heads have as much as a year of college.

Although C.B.S. was comfortably holding its over-all lead in prime-time viewing, there was an air of tension at "Black Rock," its forbidding black granite headquarters on the Avenue of the Americas.

"It calls itself the comedy network," said a longtime observer of the industry, "but I've never seen anyone laugh there."

Pitch to 'Adults'

"We sell to adults in prime time, not to children," snapped Fred Silverman, the programing chief, dismissing the success of "Happy Days."

Prime-time leadership is a matter of prestige, but, more importantly, it is a matter of economics. A 30-second commercial on "All in the Family," the top-rated show on television, can bring as much as $60,000, double the price for the same spot on a lesser show, based simply on a cost-per-thousand viewers.

With four minutes of commercial time, three for the network and one for the local station, available in each 30-minute prime-time segment, and the cost of an installment of "Family" about $120,000, it is obvious that there are very substantial profit opportunities in having a hit, and substantial economic penalties for failure, and that is what commercial television is all about.

March 5, 1974

Poll Finds Films Regaining Popularity

Although watching television remains the country's most popular evening pastime, going to the movies or theater, listening to the radio and staying home with the family have shown marked increases in popularity, according to the Gallup Poll.

Nearly half of all persons interviewed in the latest survey —46 per cent—said that watching television was their favorite way of spending an evening. However, the popularity of television has not increased since a 1966 survey when the same proportion named it as their favorite pastime.

On the other hand, movies, theater and radio have regained some of their former appeal, while the percentage who said that being with the family at home was their favorite way of spending an evening doubled from 5 to 10 since the 1966 survey.

The Gallup announcement said that the preference for being with the family tended "to confirm the observation of some social scientists that the trend toward dissolution of the family unit may be abating."

Reading Led '38 List

By way of comparison, reading was the highest on the 1938 list, followed by the movies, theater and dancing. Each of these pasttimes fell off sharply in the next survey in 1960. By that year, television dominated the list, with 28 per cent. It next reached its high point of 46 per cent in 1966 and has remained there since.

Next in popularity in the 1960 survey was engaging in family activities, named by 17 per cent. However, this dropped sharply in the 1966 survey—to 5 per cent—but has now reached the present 10 per cent.

The latest findings were based on a total of 1,562 adults, 18 and older, interviewed in person in more than 300 localities during the periods Feb. 8 to 11 and Feb. 15 to 18.

Following are percentages in the recent poll, based on the same question asked in each of the previous surveys—"What is your favorite way of spending an evening?"

Watching Television	46
Reading	14
Dining Out	12
Staying at Home with Family: Engaging in Family Activities At Home	10
Movies/Theater	9
Resting/Relaxing	8
Visiting Friends	8
Entertaining Friends	8
Playing Cards/Scrabble/ Crossword Puzzles/Games	8
Participating in Sports	5
Listening to Radio/Records	5
Dancing	4
Sewing	3
Working in Home Workshop/ Home Repair	3
Club or Church Meetings	3
Other Responses	9
Total	155

(Note: The total adds to more than 100 per cent because of multiple responses.)

The following table compares favorite pastimes in 1938 with those recorded in 1960, 1966 and 1974:

	1938	1960	1966	1974
Reading	21	10	15	14
Movies/ Theater	17	6	5	9
Watching Television	—	28	46	46
Dancing	12	3	2	4
Radio	9	X	2	5
Playing Cards	9	6	5	8
Staying at Home With Family	7	17	5	10
Visiting Friends	4	10	5	8

X Less than 1 per cent.

March 7, 1974

The Killing Has to Stop

By MARYA MANNES

ON the top floors of their giant gray and black monoliths, the yawns of the network heads are barely stifled. They are shorthand for "Here we go again, boys," as they look at the headline: "New Senate Hearings on TV Violence Begin."

Back to the same old song: corrupting the kids, crime on the streets, etc., etc. Don't those old vote-suckers ever learn? Every year they collect a basket of letters from citizen's groups and dear old ladies and quotes from dumb psychiatrists or high-minded writers blaming us for the state of the nation. But no proof—just hot air and moral outrage.

And anyway, don't they know we're putting on a lot more "Waltons"-type shows next fall? Family love and morality in the good old times?

*

Well, way back in the good old nostalgic fifties, neither broadcasters nor Senators may have read a piece that appeared in the now-defunct Reporter magazine. The article was called "Trigger Mortis."

It concerned a fairly close future—the seventies, in fact —in which doctors observed a strange phenomenon in the hands of newborn babies. The fingers were curled, as usual, but now the second finger of the right hand was higher than the others and crooked in the position of holding a revolver.

After a great deal of argument and endless seminars, the prevailing conclusion was that the cause of this slight crippling was both genetic and psychological: the heritage of young parents who had watched television shows in which the gun was the dominant factor for 20 years.

*

Public alarm was so great, the article continued, that the usually passive Federal Communications Commission was forced to act. The result, after long Congressional delay, was a bill forbidding the use of guns in entertainment programs or series (as opposed to news films or war pictures) unless the full results of this use were shown in close-up and, preferably, living color.

This bill — bitterly fought by the networks—had three interesting results. One was that scriptwriters were forced to find other solutions than killing for exciting viewers and resolving plots; a second was the passage, two years later, of a very strict gun-control law; the third was that the intimate view of exploding brains and gushing wounds (now mandatory if the results of shooting were involved) so repelled and shocked the public that the broadcasters had to abandon this "out" altogether.

The writer of that fantasy (and this piece) was a cock-eyed optimist, as any regular TV viewer can see.

Now Trigger Mortis is more prevalent, more violent than ever. Babies' fingers may not display that common defect, but in the crime serials—whether "Mannix" or "Cannon" or "Hawaii Five-O," or "Barnaby Jones," or "Streets of San Francisco," or "Hawkins," or "Kojak," or "Shaft" or the separate "crime-dramas" that appear if not weekly, then often—in all of these the men may plot but the gun decides.

In this favorite national "entertainment," the private eyes, the investigators, the detectives, the cops (whether fat, lean, kindly, homey, young and tough or old and shrewd) are of course the "good men," the lawmen,

Marya Mannes is an author and critic.

who kill for justice. But they kill as fast and remorselessly as the bad men, and the shoot-outs blur in a relentless montage of sleek black cars gunning at 80 (will they still be doing that?) on endless freeways, of crouching and running figures and the crumpled bodies of the bad men in handsome homes or dirty back alleys.

*

O.K., there are fists and knives and karate and Kung Fu, too. Yet they are all part of a screen violence which absolves the audience from real horror by being sanitized. A little blood, sure, but not enough for gagging. A knife sticking out of a back: unpleasant, but the guy was asking for it. A punch in the jaw—but no teeth falling out of the man's mouth, spitting blood.

Only the severed head of the horse in bed with the Godfather's foe sickened some viewers. They weren't used to horse's heads, especially in bed. But apparently the TV audience could now take with equanimity and/or excitement the brains of Mafia enemies fragmented by bullets and splattered on pavements. Public fascination with this continuous ferocity made $90-million for "The Godfather" producers, and the Family lovable people.

There seems, then, no end to two overwhelming appetites of Americans—sex and violence. The two overlap, of course, in that violence in sex is now as popular as sex in violence. Few movies or crime shows, in fact, can do without both.

Why? If we are not born with crippled fingers, we must as a people suffer some other grave deformity. If smoking—another huge public appetite—could be at least temporarily diminished after researchers found it could and very often did cause cancer of the lungs, then somebody had better come up fast with the specific nature of our new mutation and the steps now urgently needed to arrest and prevent it.

It seems in any case unarguable that there is a clear connection between the daily diet of violence on the screen and the tidal wave of senseless killing on our streets and in our hallways and rooms and parks. Only very recently there were two cases in which boys poured gasoline over a girl and a man and set them on fire—after seeing this technique on TV that same week.

Black or white, poor or solvent, unschooled or educated, the killers have had for 10 to 20 years a steady diet of human slaughter on television to feed on. Every one of them has access to that prime scepter of power and hate, a gun. Every one of them has learned by looking that, without a gun, you are no one.

Oh sure, they kill with knives, too, or pipes, or razors. But the gun is surer and quicker.

O.K., so the cop usually gets the "bad guy" in the end. All the more reason to get the cop and the "good guy" (read "helpless, with cash") first.

"The accused showed no remorse," we often read of a convicted killer in court. Why should he, when massive processes of desensitizing have numbed in so many any sense of guilt, let alone humanity?

It is not enough for the sociologists to go on saying that poverty and discrimination and urban blight are the real and only triggers of violence, or for the broadcasters and moviemakers to repeat their litany of "reflecting reality" or "We only give the people what they want." "What they want" is the operative phrase. And if they can indeed point to the vast majority of crime-show viewers of TV and movies who commit no murders, they must also—if they are honest — shoulder a hefty share of blame for a climate in which men killing each other (for whatever reason) is the climax and solution of the human story, whether of revenge or greed or just blind hate. What crime shows tacitly proclaim is that there is no plot exciting enough to hold an audience without the commission of murder.

It is a terrible admission. It has had a terrible effect. And if the makers of movie films and TV shows continue to put ratings and profits above the mental and spiritual good of the public, they can count themselves among those who mug and murder the American conscience.

Maybe there were some clues in that old fantasy-piece towards a way to stop them from doing it.

Maybe. . . .

April 14, 1974

What a Crazy Brain!

OBSERVER

By Russell Baker

We are sitting in front of the TV set, the brain and me, the way we do sometimes in the evening, and the brain is complaining again. You know what a brain is like. Always complaining.

"Why have we got to watch TV again tonight?" it asks, only naturally, being a brain, it doesn't ask it in plain English like that, which, I admit, would make me sore if it did. I mean, a brain isn't earning its keep if it can't ask a foolish question in words of five syllables.

Anyhow, I give the same answer I always give when the same question is always asked. We are watching television, I explain, because it is easier than doing the crossword puzzle and more fun than standing on the corner eating a piece of cheese.

In that case, the brain says, I'm going to start thinking about why I never see Andy Granatelli any more. I miss Old Andy, says the brain; and I want to know why we never see him come out of his house at the Arctic Circle at 3 o'clock on a winter morning any more and start up his car on the very first twist of the key because he has had an STP treatment, and drive off into the Northern Lights.

What a crazy brain! Leave it to me to wind up with a brain that's an Andy Granatelli freak.

Anyhow, down goes the beer. One, two, three—who keeps count when they're watching TV?—and there is no action at all coming from up there between the ears. Nothing.

Cops with terrific Southern California suntans are cleaning up homicides on all channels, and Johnny Cash is singing about not using gasoline, and women with voices like crow beaks on a tin roof are going on about the laundry and sink grease and so on.

I lock into an old Bogart in which Bogie, as "Gloves" Donohue, the gangster with a heart of gold who loves his mother (Jane Darwell), is going to clean up a pack of Nazi spy rats led by Peter Lorre.

"Did you see that?" asks the brain.

It is awake again. It is a nuisance because in a minute Bogart is going to do one of my favorite scenes, one in which he refuses to eat the cheese cake Phil Silvers brings him and tells Phil never again to serve him any cheese cake but Miller's cheese cake.

"But why?" the brain is saying. "Why would a family of three ever want to dry their hair in just seven minutes?"

Bogie is telling Silvers to bring him some coffee and cheese cake.

"Wake up!" says the brain. "You know Bogart is going to refuse to eat the cheese cake because it isn't Miller's. What you ought to be thinking about is that family of three's hair."

What a pity, that brain! "Didn't you see that last commercial in which the husband, wife and child have their heads soaked with a bucket of water and then get their hair dry in exactly seven minutes?"

"With a terrific brand new electric hair dryer which I can't afford to be without," I reply. "Sure I saw it."

Jane Darwell—I remember when she used to be Shirley Temple's mother; and now, Bogart's—Jane Darwell is leaning out a Warner Brothers window smiling the way a successful gangster's mother ought to smile, and I missed the key lines in the cheese cake scene. "The trouble with the world today," I say, "is there are too many brains in the world."

"Don't be a baby," says the brain. "You know very well that in the next scene Peter Lorre is going to throw old Miller down the steps and shoot him. Let's think about drying hair."

"And there'll never be any more Miller's cheese cake for Bogie," I say.

"Bogie is dead," says the brain. "Hair is alive. This machine is trying to sell you another machine that will dry the fully soaked heads of you, your wife and one child in exactly seven minutes."

"Yes," I say, "the machines are always thinking of me."

"But is there any situation," asks the brain, "in which all three of you could not possibly appear in public seven minutes after washing your hair unless that hair was perfectly dry?"

Lorre has shot Miller during all this, and I have missed it.

"Just for that, Mister Brain," I say, "you get another fast beer to the *compos mentis plexus.*" With which, in fact, I then flatten the brain for the knockout. It has been quiet up there ever since. A respectful kind of quiet.

Still, the question won't go away. Why would we have to get the whole family's hair dry in seven minutes? Maybe if we were going to be rounded up by Bogie for Nazi espionage, and it was very cold outside on the way to the paddy wagon, and we didn't want to go to jail with dirty hair, and yet we didn't want to risk catching cold on the way to the paddy wagon . . .

What a crazy brain!

December 15, 1973

Why Are College Kids in a Lather Over TV Soap Operas?

By FERGUS M. BORDEWICH

It's a gray afternoon in the Flatbush section of Brooklyn. The time is 1 P.M. A television set glowing dully across the room is tuned to "All My Children," a serial tale of frustrated love among constantly distraught young adults.

On the screen, Phil, a tall, dark-haired, athletically built Vietnam veteran in his mid-20's, stands nervously in a phone booth and at the other end of the line is Tara, a tall, striking brunette in her mid-20's, whose relationship with Phil to date has included elopement, illegitimate childbirth and wartime separation among other no less emotional cataclysms. *What does he want from her now? She thought he was gone from her life forever!*

A gasp rises from the audience.

The *audience? Is this gathering, perhaps, a group of middle-aged housewives who have assembled for tea and vicarious sympathy?*

Scarcely. The scene is the TV lounge at Brooklyn College. More than a hundred young faces—white, black, male, female — are staring fixedly at the television screen. All the chairs are filled. As still more students pack into the room, they squat on the floor or lean against the walls. And now, there's standing room only. Just as the climax of the half-hour episode approaches, two late-comers bang open the lounge doors and start noisily across the room.

"Hey, shut up!" bawls a male voice. "This is heavy stuff!"

There is nothing unique about this scene in Flatbush. The situation is much the same in Columbia University dormitories and New York University's Loeb Student Center, in fraternity and sorority houses from Boston to Madison to Berkeley, in Ivy League college lounges and student apartments throughout the metropolitan New York area alike. A clutch of Lehman College co-eds rush from classes to their shared Bronx flat to catch the latest installment of "One Life To Live"; a band of Queens College underclassmen try—unsuccessfully—to switch the school's closed-circuit TV station to pull in the "soaps"; a Wheaton, Ill., graduate boasts that her most adroit accomplishment over the past four years was never to schedule an afternoon class while "All My Children" was on the air.

Although soap opera aficionados would seem to be a minority among college students, there are nonetheless thousands of young people around the country who daily put aside their Sartre, Machiavelli and Freud —not to mention such obsolete writers as Fanon and Debray—to watching the moiling passions of middle-class America as portrayed on daytime TV. What is it about these slow-moving melodramas with their elasticized emotions that today's college students find so engrossing?

Dov Stern, business manager of Lehman College's student newspaper, "Meridian," offers one possible explanation: today's students are going through a process of "internalization, putting more emphasis on developing themselves" than on the idealistic causes of past years. Soap operas, he suggests, teach people something about themselves by portraying "life as it is" or at least by providing living characters that young viewers can easily identify with, as they would with similar characters in a novel. "It's just easier to go home and watch TV than to get 'involved,'" he says.

But that's not the whole story. For the fact is that in recent years the subject matter of daytime TV has changed and become much more relevant to the interests

Fergus M. Bordewich is a free-lance writer based in New York.

of young viewers. Into the world of frazzled passions and leaden drama, which could grip chiefly the bored housewife (homebound women still comprise the largest proportion of afternoon viewers), contemporary issues have been injected. The "generation gap," abortion, obscenity, narcotics and political protest are now commonly discussed and dealt with on the soap operas of TV.

From its inception in January, 1970, "All My Children" has consistently employed topical material. "It was a kind of 'first,'" explains Lewis Antine, an American history graduate student at New York's City University. "It was a sense of your *stuff* being on TV for the first time, like 'Hey, they're talking about us on Mom's show! How will they handle it?'"

In the wake of the success of "All My Children," (right from the start, the show has enjoyed healthy Nielsen ratings) even such hoary serials as "Love of Life," "The Guiding Light" and "Search for Tomorrow" have begun to toy with "relevant" social subjects. At least one new entry this season, "The Young and the Restless," revolves almost entirely around young people's problems.

•

In general, most regular campus serial-watchers are underclassmen, having picked up the habit while in high school. And, though some co-eds might be less than flattered by the assertation by Brooklyn College biology senior Ian Newmark that "most females in our society still hover toward the romantic, and the soap operas spoon-feed them vicarious thrills," noticeably more females than males on college campuses are seemingly addicted to the "soaps."

Some students claim they watch the soaps for a dose of "realism," others for a taste of "unreality"; some say they find them thrilling and exotic, while still others see in the soap opera an emotional blueprint of their own home life. Jeff Loesser, a Queens College senior majoring in communications, believes that young viewers prefer to "concentrate on somebody else's problems instead of their own — problems you know are going to be a lot bigger and worse than your own."

Sherma Smith agrees. An education major in her third year at Brooklyn College, she has rarely missed an installment of "All My Children" in its four turgid years. "Although the show isn't realistic," she says, "it does make life seem more exciting and romantic."

And, as Lewis Antine at CUNY points out, "A soap opera moves *awesomely* slow, as slow as life itself. A day in real life is a day in the soap opera, not like an evening show where everything is compressed into an hour or two. The soaps set up an unresolved situation and you spend a month waiting and waiting and waiting for them to resolve it. It's addicting."

Indeed, many students admit that once they have become hooked on a given TV serial they find it virtually impossible to kick the habit. For example, Susie Monaco, a sophomore at Barnard College, concedes that she has been watching "General Hospital" at least once a month for years; when asked, however, what interested her in the program, she replied, "Nothing. It's terrible."

Bud Kloss, producer of "All My Children," by far the most popular serial among college students, receives loads of letters and petitions from student groups around the country requesting that the serial's story line be developed in one or another way. The program's creator, Agnes Nixon, also receives quantities of similar correspondence; in addition, a year ago this past spring she received a visit from a delegation of seniors from Duke University in Durham, N. C. A student spokesman for the delegation of "All My Children" fans told her: "The show is one of the few constants in our lives."

A long-time professional writer for television, Mrs. Nixon lives with her husband and their four children (three girls and a boy, all in their late teens or early 20s) in Bryn Mawr, Pa., a community which, according to Mrs. Nixon, is the prototype of the serial's "Pine Valley." She graduated from Northwestern University (in the same class with such future Hollywood notables as Charlton Heston and Cloris Leachman) and has had at least one of her shows aired every day for the past 19 years. She created "Children" essentially for herself, she says, and draws its material from the daily events she sees around her in Bryn Mawr.

"I used to think," Mrs. Nixon says, "that one reason for the show's popularity was that old people would be interested in young people's romances, but it turns out that young people are just as interested in the older characters in the series as in the young ones."

•

Marc Frons, a Brooklyn College sophomore and soaps fan, suggests that the TV serials are not only the heirs to the pulp magazines of earlier times and the 19th-century serialized fiction of writers like Bulwer-Lytton, but also the cousins, in their sweep of time and emotion if not their depth, of Balzac, Dostoevsky and Proust. Soap-opera time flows with expansive slowness, and human affairs are (at least theoretically) explored as slowly as they are in real life; at best, perhaps, the soaps manage to portray life in all its true banality rather than attempting to squeeze art from what is inherently a pretty bland affair.

"After all," as one Columbia art history graduate student — female — observes, "life itself is a soap opera anyway." ■

October 20, 1974

TELEVISION REVIEW

Milton Berle Appears on Star Theatre—CBS Offers 'Toast of the Town'

By JACK GOULD

MILTON BERLE, who was never a very funny man on radio, has proved a capital clown for television. As master of ceremonies for the past few weeks on the Texaco Star Theatre (8:00 Tuesday nights over the NBC video chain), the nimble-witted child of the Rialto has displayed all the ad lib accoutrements of the great presiding officers of the Palace Theatre days. Register Mr. B. as television's first real smash!

What Mr. Berle has offered before the cameras has been as different from the usual run of vaudeville as the Palace was from Loew's State. On stage for almost the full hour and working with every turn, the comedian has endowed the Tuesday night bill with the cohesion and individuality which only a great personality and greater presence can bring.

The quality of real informality, which always has eluded radio, is Mr. Berle's major attribute and television has proved ideally suited to capitalize on it. From the moment he walks on the apron Mr. Berle makes the looking listener feel a partner to the evening's high-jinks and nonsense. With the effortless ease that comes to one who has been through the arduous schooling of a lifetime before live audiences, he establishes that indefinable liaison between player and audience. It is theatre as it should be.

Cheering Note

As is no secret by now, Mr. Berle's specialty is the patter delivered with lightning speed. Its contents include the situation item, the straight wisecrack and the barbed insult. But always it is said with tongue in cheek, Mr. Berle knowing, as so many purely radio comedians do not, that a line should not be hit too hard. His reliance is on a sense of timing and impromptu verve that is second nature for the trouper reared far away from such demoralizing gadgets as a radio microphone or a Hollywood camera. Mr. Berle is of the show business.

The increasing maturity of Mr. Berle's art was, perhaps, best demonstrated in the likable accord which he established with the other acts on the bill. His wonderful bit of business with the incomparable Bert Wheeler and his blackface routine with Harry Richman brought back nostalgic memories which through the sheer force of personality of all three acquired a 1948 newness and pace.

Indeed, the Texaco Star Theatre should cheer many a Broadwayite. More than any other video show to date it has proved that the real performer, as opposed to the radio automaton, is going to have a new lease on life, thanks to television. The priceless ingredient of spontaneity, which is the heart of the world of make-believe, at long last is coming to Radio City. Let the hucksters make way for the show-folk!

"Toast of the Town"

Not to be outdone by its senior rival, WCBS-TV also is presenting an hour-long variety show under the title of "Toast of the Town" (9:30 P. M. Sundays). In terms of lavishness and expense, it is on a par with "Texaco Star Theatre" but suffers badly if the comparison is extended to such matters as routining and general professional know-how.

For a variety revue, where a dominant personality is so helpful in tying up the loose ends, the choice of Ed Sullivan as master of ceremonies seems ill-advised. Since he is a newspaper man there is no reason to expect him to be an actor, but his extreme matter-of-factness, plus his predilection for introducing his friends in the audience, does not add up to very sparkling entertainment. In such a key spot an experienced and versatile person must be in charge if the whole show is to acquire a distinctiveness and fluidity of its own.

As it works out, "The Toast of the Town" bears more resemblance to a radio program than to a live stage show. Last week it presented an impressive roster of acts—the Ink Spots, Peter Lind Hayes, a singing patrolman; Nan Wynn, Raye and Naldi, Paul Winchell and a troupe of dancers. All displayed a high degree of competence, but the main honors were taken by Mr. Winchell, whose gift for ventriloquism should rapidly win him a steady video spot and give Edgar Bergen a few anxious moments.

Effective though the acts were individually, their order of presentation was far from happy and most of them ran too long. The closing production number built around the introduction of Irving Berlin also could have enjoyed more sparkle and originality.

CBS has all necessary ingredients for a successful program of variety. Once it appreciates more fully the need for knowing hands to guide the proceedings—both on stage and off—it, too, should have an enjoyable hit.

July 4, 1948

JACK BENNY CONSIDERS HIS FUTURE

The CBS Comedian Talks Of TV, Radio and Other Matters

By ARTHUR ALTSCHUL

JACK BENNY, who has made a decent living on radio for seventeen years as the amiable tightwad, doesn't give the impression of being a bit disturbed about television. He already is convinced that he will succeed in the new medium as in the old, but is in the process of working out the changes in his radio format which he thinks will be required. In any event, he wants to start in television in the fall.

"This is going to give me the chance of picking up where I left off twenty years ago at the Palace Theatre," is the way Benny put it when he was in town the other day. He was sitting in an armchair in his Sherry-Netherland Hotel suite puffing on the familiar cigar.

A vaudeville type show is what Benny sees as his basic formula in television. Within that flexible framework he will use most of the characters—his wife Mary, Rochester, Don Wilson, Dennis Day, Phil Harris—who over the years have become permanent fixtures in the 7 P. M. Sunday night show.

'Business'

Benny figures, however, that his most important asset will be to continue the same "business" which has been the trademark of his radio show—that carefully worked out formula of the badgered and heckled Benny fighting back against jibes and practical jokes with the combined personality of a scornful self-confidence and an overstuffed ego. Benny the musician will still be drawing that scratchy bow over the violin strings.

Just how he will adapt himself to television is, at the moment, the comic's main concern, as it is of CBS, which, of course, recently put out a million or two dollars to lure him from the NBC fold. The purpose of Mr. Benny's present visit is to discuss with CBS officials the various problems involved.

At his hotel, Benny was up by 8 o'clock every morning last week during his stay in town. He hurriedly explained, however, that this was not a result of worrying.

"You know, no matter what time I get to bed at night, I wake up at 8 in the morning," he said. "It's a pain in the neck." That was Benny's way of getting the conversational ball rolling. It was 10 A. M., but he had already finished breakfast and was more than half way through his first cigar of the morning.

"Have one," he proffered. "That'll make one fewer I smoke." Conspicuously placed against one wall in his hotel living room was a large television set. Mr. Benny acknowledged that he had been watching a few of the shows which are not seen on the West Coast.

Benny noted that most people who have just bought a set tend to use it whether the programs are good or bad. But soon, he stressed, the day will come when they will begin shopping around for the better programs the way they do now on radio.

"After all, watching a bad show can get to be like watching a dull fight—you can just sit there so long," he said.

Debut

His own television debut several weeks ago—at the KTTV dedication program in Los Angeles—was nothing short of terrific, Benny declared modestly. In defense of his statement, Benny explained that even his wife, Mary Livingstone, thought that it was good—praise which he had not expected.

One problem which Benny said that he had encountered in the rehearsals for the show was in keeping the director from switching the camera from one player to another and from changing from long shots to close-ups and then back to long shots. In many cases, he said, the camera let on that it knew the joke and much of the humor was lost. The fault, he said, was corrected before air time.

Benny's principal concern over television at the moment is whether he will be able to put on his shows from the West Coast. If he has to fly to New York to do the program, one show a month will be his maximum. "Don't forget, I still like my golf," he explained. If the shows can be done on kinescope film and shipped East for later presentation, Benny sees the possibility of perhaps two shows a month.

Benny's radio show tonight was recorded before he left the West Coast, the first time since he's had his own Sunday night show that the performance hasn't been put out on the air "live." He concedes that the delay prevented his script writers from making any overly topical allusions. But thinking ahead to the time when all his television shows may be put on film, Benny tended to discount the importance of live performances.

"If the show is good, the audience will like it," the Waukegan wit with the high Hooperating declared. "That's all there is to that."

The comedian said that he did not believe he would switch completely from radio to television before the coaxial cable is laid across the country to allow simultaneous, nation-wide telecasts. That is not expected for a year or two. When the cable is ready, he doubted if he could do both radio and video.

"You can't go on forever doing ninety things at once," he said.

April 10, 1949

THE GIRL FRIEND OF KUKLA AND OLLIE

Fran Allison Finds Life With a Dragon Can Have Its Own Unique Rewards

FRAN ALLISON, a tall, slender ex-schoolteacher from Iowa, is responsible for the middle word in what is probably television's most enigmatic program title: "Kukla, Fran and Ollie." She is, of course, the lady who acts as mother, sister and girl friend to a dragon, which is Ollie, and to a worrying, elfinish figure, which is Kukla.

But Miss Allison is the last one to be dismayed by her unusual assignment. For upward of a year and a half now she has been spending a half hour or more a day chatting with the puppet figures born in the fertile imagination of Burr Tillstrom. As is true of Edgar Bergen's regard for Charlie McCarthy, today Miss Allison thinks of Ollie and Kukla as distinctive personalities who in more ways than one have influenced her career.

Miss Allison talked last week of her life with dragons, dolls and rabbits while enjoying a brief visit to New York. Her program, of course, originates in Chicago, where friends are substituting for her. If on television she appears as a diminutive blonde, in real life Miss Allison is on the lanky side and has attractive steel-gray hair. In conversation she is endowed with a quiet animation which makes for interest yet is not wearing, a faculty which in large measure explains her knack for sustaining spontaneously on the screen her dialogue with Ollie and Kukla.

No Rehearsal

"Except for the music, we don't have any rehearsal for the show," she said. "There's never a word spoken which has been learned in advance. When we start, we never know exactly how it'll turn out. It keeps the surprise.

"Burr and I may talk over in a general way the tack Ollie is going to take, but it is not all worked out. Then on the air you say exactly the same thing you would say if it happened for the first time off the air. This perhaps is what makes it real."

Miss Allison said that at one time she and Mr. Tillstrom decided they should be very business-like and show up at the studio in mid-afternoon (the program itself goes on the air at 7 P. M., Monday through Friday on NBC).

"I guess that lasted about three or four weeks," she recalled. "Now we came into the studio just in time for music rehearsal."

Miss Allison met Mr. Tillstrom in Chicago during the war while both were working on Red Cross and war bond shows. It was on Oct. 13, 1947, that they first started doing an hour-long show on the pioneer video outlet, WBKB. That program employed films, records and other specialized pitches for the younger generation. Later it was decided to cut down the time to the present half-hour and to concentrate on the affairs of the assorted characters in Mr. Tillstrom's "Kuklapolitan Players."

Genealogy

It is Mr. Tillstrom who not only manipulates all the puppets, which includes such worthies as Fletcher Rabbit, Madame Oglepuss and Cecil Bill in addition to Ollie and Kukla, but also does all the voices. It is he, too, who conceives the basic story line from day to day.

Ollie, the dragon rascal who is always in and out of trouble, is a lineal descendant of an earlier Tillstrom puppet act, "Sir George and the Dragon." Kukla received his name from a Russian ballerina to whom Mr. Tillstrom showed the doll-like figure.

Miss Allison has her own ideas as to the origin of the two characters.

"Burr is Kukla," she said, succinctly.

As for Ollie?

"Ollie is what we'd all like to be some time if we didn't think we'd get whacked for it," Miss Allison explained.

In addition to Miss Allison and Mr. Tillstrom, the show has three other important personages working behind the scenes. They are Beulah Zachary, the producer; Louis Gomavitz, who does the staging, and Jack Fascinato, the pianist.

Miss Allison came to television via a circuitous route. She was born in La Porte City, Iowa, and studied music and education at Coe College in Cedar Rapids. In the theatrical tradition, she is not wont to volunteer the number of her years, though her appearance certainly belies the need for adoption of such strategy.

Her teaching career was passed in a rural schoolhouse outside Schleswig, Iowa, which, she believes, then had a population of 700 persons or so. She operated under some degree of handicap in the predominantly German community.

"Some of the children didn't speak English and I didn't speak German," she said.

Deciding that a teacher's life left something to be desired financially, Miss Allison in 1934 descended on a radio station in Waterloo, where she won a job as a singer. It was there that her big break came by chance.

An announcer, perhaps a little weary of the sameness of his job spied Miss Allison in the studio, and, without further ado, announced on the air: "Why, here's Aunt Fanny; step up to the mike and speak to the folks." Knowing the rural idiom, Miss Allison met the challenge with several minutes of small town gossip.

Her next step was Chicago, where her characterization of "Aunt Fanny" was to become a mainstay on Don McNeill's "Breakfast Club," even though she does not receive air credit for playing the part. Some listeners still find it a bit of a shock to learn that it the same Miss Allison who essays two such dissimilar roles.

Miss Allison, who in private life is the wife of Archie Levington, a Chicago representative for the Leeds Music Publishing Corporation, is taking very calmly her present success. She admits to a number of offers for various video projects, but she is looking each one over with considerable care. She wants to make sure none would upset her present relationship with Ollie and Kukla.

May 29, 1949

RE: MR. ALLEN (STEVE)

Gentleman of the Owl-Like Solemnity Eases Along With Ad Libs

By JOHN HORN

PROFESSIONAL funnymen are apt to be quite serious fellows. No exception is Steve Allen, a young man with deadpan mien and rugged television schedule. The comedian, whose tortoise-shell eyeglasses give him an owl-like solemnity, is before the C. B. S. television cameras for forty-five minutes a day at 12:45 P. M., Monday through Friday, on the "Steve Allen Show," and an hour at 10 P. M. Saturdays on "Songs for Sale."

If there were lines to memorize on these stanzas, Steve Allen (no relation to Fred) would be a dead duck instead of a live owl, hooting with faint derision at the world about him. The hoots, incidentally, are frequently directed at himself, a subject he considers ideally sporting game when he's out sharpshooting.

Situations

"No one, not even Thomas Babington Macauley," says Allen, "could memorize my lines for a week, week after week. They must be delivered ad lib, for which I am grateful. I think there are more genuine good laughs in funny happenings, and spontaneous comments on them, than in prepared gags. Ready-to-laugh gags, carefully prepared offstage to be delivered carefully onstage, hit me the way warmed-over food does. I may eat the food, but I wish I had been there when it was originally brought to a state of cooking perfection."

Situations are what Allen looks for, situations with a slight touch of incongruity. Several weeks ago, with a camera stationed outside the studio, Allen opened his afternoon show by arriving in a taxicab and working his way to the stage with a hand microphone, interviewing members of the audience. He had read off a list of ingredients printed on a box of candy; with a rising sense of horror he gradually intoned: "lecithin, benzoate of soda, citric acid, pectin, invertase."

He has gone outside the studio to chat with a man selling bananas, naturally buying and eating one. Recently, he wound up his afternoon program by getting his entire audience to play "Follow the Leader." He led the audience out into the street, where he left it. Ducking back into the empty auditorium, he signed off while playing poker with the boys in the orchestra.

Once a situation is established, Allen ad libs his way through it. "I say what comes naturally," he says. "I don't strive for a gag line. If it comes, all right. But if it doesn't, the situation and comment on it are enough."

The casual, dry wit—"The night I first substituted for Arthur Godfrey, I didn't know anything about making tea"—comes from Allen's contention that "humor is a serious thing—it blossoms best in an atmosphere that is relaxed and unhurried."

Allen's serious approach also is reflected in other ways. Interested in the problem of cerebral palsy, he has utilized comedy to achieve a worthy end. He organized, and is promoting, an All-Star Comedy Softball Game, Broadway vs. Hollywood, at the Polo Grounds next Thursday night. He is a pianist of more than casual grace, and is a songwriter with such credits as "Let's Go to Church Next Sunday Morning," which sold more than 300,000 copies; "Cotton Candy," and "An Old Piano Plays the Blues." Moreover, he is author of a book of poems, entitled "Windfall."

New Yorker

Allen, born in New York City on Dec. 26, 1921, is the son of Belle Montrose, a vaudeville comedienne, and Billy Allen, singer and straight man. Traveling extensively, he attended sixteen schools in many states. Before the Army called, he had entered radio via stations in Chicago and Phoenix, Ariz.

After his discharge, he went to Los Angeles, where he built up a local radio following and changed gradually from disk jockey to raconteur and humorist. He came East for his own television show last December. Since then, an ever-increasing audience has come to agree with Groucho Marx about the youngster with the facility to ad lib songs as well as lines before company.

"Steve," said Groucho, "is the best Allen since Fred."

September 2, 1951

NOT ON TV: THE ED SULLIVAN STORY

Some Notes on Smiles, Showmanship and Critics

By VAL ADAMS

NOW that Ed Sullivan's "Toast of the Town" television show is all wrapped up in presenting stories of famous people in the theatre, this is probably as opportune a time as any to present the Ed Sullivan story.

It was on June 20, 1948, that the Broadway newspaper columnist made his first chilling appearance over the Columbia Broadcasting System network. He has had many battles with television critics, network executives and others in an effort to win personal acceptance, although the show itself had a good popularity rating from the start. His own story may not be the artistic success of the theatre elite whom he has profiled on his program, but he has finally cornered the fame and high income chased desperately since his youth.

As master of ceremonies for a variety show, Mr. Sullivan got off to rapid recognition in television because of a frozen face and the stiffness of the Washington Monument. He had labored for years as master of ceremonies for all kinds of events from a firemen's ball to the opening of a new airport, but this background aided him none in the new element. His face muscles were as dormant as human understanding of another man's problems.

Mr. Sullivan still is no bubble of champagne, but he has learned to smile now and then when his head is turned away from the camera during conversation with a person on the show. "I've tried every way I know to smile into a camera, but I can't do it," he explains.

Budget

In the early months of "Toast of the Town," before it had obtained a sponsor, Mr. Sullivan was shocked—and infuriated—to learn that C. B. S. was peddling the show to prospective advertisers "with or without Ed Sullivan." This was a concession being made to sponsors who, C. B. S. feared, might have read some of the critiques published on the master of ceremonies. The network dispelled his anger, however, by explaining that the optional offer had been originated with a single executive and had not been approved by a full policy-making body meeting at a long table.

When his show began, C. B. S. gave Mr. Sullivan a budget of $500 weekly to hire talent, consisting of six or seven acts. According to records at the network the talent costs on the première performance were as follows:

Dean Martin and Jerry Lewis, $200; Eugene List, pianist, $75; Monica Lewis, singer, $50; Kathryn Lee, dancer, $50; Ruby Goldstein, boxing referee, $75, and a singing fireman, $25. A man who planted celebrities in the audience, seating them within camera range, also was paid $25.

Today the program spends $15,000 a week for acts. It has paid up to $7,500 to a single performer for one appearance. In addition to the cost of acts, Mr. Sullivan receives $2,500 weekly, fifty weeks in the year, by terms of a five-year contract with C. B. S., which eventually will pay him $3,000 a week.

"For the first year of the show's run I didn't get paid," says Mr. Sullivan. "All the money went for acts."

"Toast of the Town" made its debut before a talent union was organized to set minimum wage scales for TV performers. Because the Ink Spots were offered and accepted $100 for an appearance on the show in those days, Lena Horne, $125, and Sam Levenson, $100, charges were made that Mr. Sullivan was using the power of his Broadway column to induce performers to appear on his show. He denied all accusations.

Ed Sullivan

A Broadway press agent, who has known the columnist for many years, sums up the situation this way:

"Ed is a great guy for paying off in his column, and the talent knew that in the early days of his television show. He can always give them a mention in his column without referring to his show. Having a column and a show is like two legs. One helps the other."

Mr. Sullivan himself does not believe that a columnist has any advantage over others in television.

"Other columnists and writers have given shows on television but lost out," he comments. "If a newspaper connection or by-line meant anything, they'd all still be in business."

Probably some of the most scathing—and long—letters ever received by television critics have come from Mr. Sullivan. Even though a newspaper man, no one is quicker to dash off a complaining letter to the editor.

"Some of the criticism used to tear my guts out," comments the columnist. "Here I was working for nothing, trying to get somewhere. When they kicked me around as a performer, that was justifiable. But nobody can tell me how to routine a vaudeville show. As for acts, I'm familiar with more show business acts than anybody else around. The original panning I got bit into me very deeply."

Today Mr. Sullivan believes that his chief talent lies in directions other than that of a performer.

"I am the best damned showman in television," he says. "People who work on the show think so too. I really believe, immodestly, that I am a better showman and have better taste than most and have a better 'feel' as to what the public wants because of my newspaper experience. And I know quicker than anybody else on Sunday nights whether we have done a good performance or not."

Sports Enthusiast

Mr. Sullivan, the showman, was born forty-nine years ago in New York but grew up in suburban Port Chester. As a youngster he was fascinated by sports—today he's a golf enthusiast—and show business. His own ideas about staging vaudeville shows first came to him as a youth while watching matinee performances at the Palace Theatre.

In 1920 he joined The New York Evening Mail as a sports writer, later moving to The Graphic. The Graphic made Mr. Sullivan a Broadway columnist, a three-dot job he considered contemptible for a writer, although he later changed his attitude. In 1932 he switched to The Daily News, which now syndicates his column to other papers.

On The Graphic sports staff he originated annual sports award dinners and has been staging assorted banquets, benefits and vaudeville shows ever since. He has tried his hand in radio, movies, where he wrote several flops, and musical revues on Broadway. Nothing paid off like television.

On television Mr. Sullivan keeps his fences in good repair. He loves to introduce celebrities, who also love to be introduced. At one time he wrote scores of letters to prominent people and government leaders, inviting them to be introduced on his show. Some accepted, some declined. One high city official who did accept asked to be introduced before 8:15. He had tickets that evening for "Guys and Dolls."

March 23, 1952

THE BISHOP LOOKS AT TELEVISION

By VAL ADAMS

Fulton J. Sheen Has Some Comments to Make About Performing for Video

THE Most Rev. Fulton J. Sheen, Auxiliary Bishop of the Archdiocese of New York, says that he is not at all concerned in competing for a television audience with N. B. C.'s Milton Berle on Tuesdays at 8 P. M. Bishop Sheen's inspirational chalk talks, presented by the DuMont network under the title "Life Is Worth Living," began two months ago on three stations and now are carried by seventeen.

"I went on television to help my sponsor, the good Lord," says the clergyman. "The success of the program proves that the American people like to be given reasons for things. Some shows give points of view without reasons. But under the surface every modern person is deeply yearning for the Infinite. The modern mind is starving and this program offers it bread. I'm just trying to satisfy the decent aspirations in people."

"Life Is Worth Living" is presented from the stage of the Adelphi Theatre on West Fifty-fourth Street. The clergyman speaks in a setting, representing a study, especially designed for the program by Jo Mielziner. Clad in the vestments of his office, he moves around at will, never sitting, and makes frequent use of the blackboard on one side of the stage to illustrate his comments.

While the clergyman's viewpoints reflect the doctrine of the Roman Catholic Church, he has generalized so far in a philosophical vein rather than emphasizing pure religious teachings. He has no doubt that the Protestant and Jewish faiths are included in his audience.

"To be successful, there must always be a common denominator between any television program and its audience," explains Bishop Sheen. "In my discussions I have started out with such topics as anxiety, fear, hate and other traits that have been experienced by everyone. In trying to explain these things, I've been talking only about the natural order. I haven't gotten into the liturgy yet. What I'm doing is just appealing to reason."

No Script

Bishop Sheen's program is uniquely staged. Like the dawn, it sort of comes up at the appointed hour seemingly without much effort on anyone's part. There is no script, no cue cards from which the speaker could read, no frantic director wildly waving his hands and no prompted applause from the studio audience. The latter responds voluntarily at the clergyman's whimsical comments.

There is never a camera rehearsal before the program begins. The camera man is strictly on his own in anticipating Bishop Sheen's movement about the stage. Three cameras are at hand, but the director prefers to use only one so as not to detract from the talk by switching back and forth from one camera to the other.

Bishop Sheen spends up to one hour and a half preparing his talk by a series of bare outlines, consisting of one-word ideas or notations. After jotting down the initial outline, he throws it away, repeating the process several times until the talk is clear in his mind. He times his message from the back—never the front—deciding upon his last statement and then building toward it.

Penetrating

Once on the air the clergyman never is given a cue by the director. A clock at the base of the camera advises him when his half-hour is up. So far he has never run over or under.

With his deep-set eyes staring directly into the camera, Bishop Sheen appears to be penetrating into the living rooms where his program is viewed. This, in fact, is what he thinks about as he speaks.

"I have in mind a home that I may be entering," he says. "The family is sitting in the living room and I'm there talking to them. My blackboard on the stage is a piece of paper. I imagine the program as just a tête-à-tête with people in their own home. I don't visualize masses of people. If I did, I would be much more energetic in speaking."

By interspersing his serious talks with witticisms, Bishop Sheen does not feel that he is being theatrical. He insists that the amusing asides just naturally creep into his discussion and are not planned.

"I've always been inclined to strike a light note here and there in serious subjects," says the clergyman. He recalls it was common practice for him to do so during the twenty-four years he was on the faculty at the Catholic University of America in Washington, before becoming a Bishop.

Bishop Sheen has been conducting radio programs since 1927, when he began a series on WLWL, the former Paulist Fathers station on West Fifty-ninth Street. In 1930 he initiated the Catholic Hour on N. B. C., which still continues. He finds at least one outstanding difference in television.

Sincerity

"Television is more fair to the audience than radio," he says. "In radio one can use a manuscript and even a ghost writer. But television judges the sincerity of the speaker. Sincerity is vital to anyone appearing on television. That's why advertising has fallen so flat. The advertising copy used on television was meant to be read, not spoken. No one speaks in real life as do the announcers in television commercials. One announcer removes a cigarette from a package and remarks that it has been tried by a thousand doctors. This smacks of insincerity and it's so artificial. Now if I happened to be a cigarette smoker, I wouldn't try to sell you my brand with that kind of language. You know, I would like nothing better than to write some of those television commercials. I would humanize them."

On the general subject of television, Bishop Sheen is not disposed toward issuing opinions as to how television should be operated or whether it is serving as a good or bad influence for the viewing public. He does believe, however, that the public "is a good censor itself" in selecting the good from the bad.

"All programs are trying to make good," he says, "and so am I."

April 6, 1952

NEW MILTON BERLE

By JACK GOULD

LAST week's return of Milton Berle to television was an extraordinary experience in theatre-going. Out in full view before an audience of millions a major star tried to make over his entire personality and adopt a new style of performing. The experiment was as intriguing psychologically as it was disappointing theatrically.

Mr. Berle is a man with a problem. Four years ago he was probably entitled to the billing of "Mr. Television"; he undoubtedly did as much as any one man to stimulate the sale of sets. Last year he dropped from the top ratings and got caught in a steady shower of brickbats, most of them deserved.

Some analysis of what happened in the intervening years is helpful in throwing light on the rather astonishing occurrence of last Tuesday night on N. B. C. When he started on TV, Mr. B. was really an engaging guy. Not alone did he bring a sense of big-time show business to a medium floundering around in mediocrity, but he did it with a certain amount of warmth and charm.

Brash and Brittle

The original television Berle was actually a new Berle of sorts. As an oldtimer on the night-club circuit, his brashness and brittleness were familiar commodities in the entertainment world, but when he came to the cameras he tempered them with a measure of humility and humaneness. He was often very funny.

But in the last couple of years Mr. Berle apparently had difficulty in coping with success. A coarseness crept into his turn. There was indeed almost an attitude of outward belligerence and antagonism if the audience didn't warm to his monologic sallies. His intrusion into other acts became a mere nuisance. Whistling through his teeth, using grotesque make-up and dressing up as a woman proved the high points of his art.

If over the summer Mr. Berle concluded that 1952 was the year for his change, his audience hardly could have anticipated the drastic reform that materialized. Gone was the whole Berle of old; not just the less attractive parts.

In place of Berle there was a road company Jack Benny threading his way through Mr. Benny's perennial opening show of the season: getting ready for the first program. Berle was just a pathetic and unhappy straight man for sixty minutes without anything to do beyond participation in a limp take-off on "Dragnet", a maudlin number with two children and a brief duet with Martha Raye.

Switch

Recasting Mr. Berle as a patsy rather than a headstrong star is, of course, the obvious "switch" for what ailed the comedian's program a year ago. But both Mr. Berle and more particularly, his large stable of writers, headed by Goodman Ace, err if they think such a transition can be accomplished by just pulling a switch.

Mr. Berle as yet simply doesn't have the delicacy of timing which enables Mr. Benny to inject real amusement into the role of the fall guy. His style is naturally broad and loud whereas Jack's is meticulously disciplined and soft. But more to the point, the initial Berle program seemed lacking in purpose, direction, style and wit.

Actually, Mr. Berle may be taking a too harsh view of his plight. If he is to be at his best and take advantage of his long experience in show business, he should distinguish a little more carefully between his theatrical assets and debits.

There was nothing ever vitally wrong in past years with the format itself of Mr. Berle's opening monologue, wherein he established an intimacy and union with his audience. The drawback was almost wholly in his material, which was repetitious and dull, and in his lack of self-effacement and naturalness. If those needs can be met, there is no reason why Mr. Berle can't go back to his introductory sequence in which he is much more comfortable.

By the same token, it was hardly necessary to place Mr. Berle in isolation. The complaint of the last two years was that he tended to be on stage continuously and chisel in on the other acts. All that Mr. Berle still needs to do is not to outwear his welcome and just be a little more modest.

The new Berle program does have some significant improvements. Getting away from the vaudeville staging technique and using strictly video methods does lend greater visual contrast, though the use of subdued lighting was overdone. Dropping the elaborate announcements of each guest also is welcome.

In doing the informal and intimate type of show, however, it would be well for Mr. Berle and Mr. Ace to recognize some of its hazards. Last week there was an obvious reliance on one idea—a deflated Berle—and on the techniques of production. But the most vital ingredients are still the basic personality of the star and what the star has to do.

If these elements are restored with tact and feeling, Mr. Berle could fool a lot of his critics yet. Even at this stage he is entitled to credit. It is not every player who will try to mend his ways in Macy's window.

September 21, 1952

ABOUT 'I LOVE LUCY'

Hard Work and Four Days Make a Half-Hour Show

By FLORENCE CROWTHER

HOLLYWOOD.

EVEN the voluble, volatile Desi Arnaz is somewhat awe-struck when he discusses the ratings of "I Love Lucy," the weekly TV romp starring Desi and his wife, Lucille Ball, seen Monday nights at 9 o'clock on the C. B. S. network. According to the Nielsen poll, television's exposure-meters, "I Love Lucy" is viewed by 10,753,000 families, or—computed at the rate of three and a fraction persons per family—more than 30,000,000 individuals each week.

"That's a lot of people," Desi says in rumba tones, flashing a smile, but returning quickly to the serious again. "It's a beeg audience and it wouldn't pay to make even a small mistake."

To keep that many people happy and to keep a lid on possible errors, actual production work on the show uses between fifty and seventy-five people, including the cast and Desi's orchestra. They work fairly constantly from Tuesday morning until late Friday night when the complete half-hour production has been filmed from start to finish before an invited audience in the 300-seat Desilu Playhouse, Las Palmas Avenue and Santa Monica Boulevard, Hollywood.

With a budget of between $21,500 and $27,000 weekly, the producer, Jess Oppenheimer, and his writers, Bob Carroll and Madelyn Pugh, all of whom have worked together for four years, can be generous in using actors, costumes and music, and in moving the action beyond the four basic sets, bedroom, living room, kitchen and night club, which sit next to each other like segments of a pie on the huge stage.

Rehearsal

With the show on paper, the cast, which regularly includes two Broadway ex-patriates, Vivian Vance and William Frawley, goes through a stage rehearsal every Tuesday and Wednesday, from ten in the morning until six at night. On Thursday, the cameras are rolled on and rehearsal continues from noon until six. At seven, there is a "dry run" (no film) while the three camera men, headed by Karl Freund, sit in the front row and discuss angles with the men in the control booth. From eight until ten, the entire production staff—Oppenheimer, Freund, the director, Marc Daniels, the prop man and the assistant director—

Lucille Ball

has a fine-tooth comb session. They work over the show from beginning to end, scene by scene.

On Friday, the camera men are in at nine in the morning, blocking out their lines on the floor; the lighting men are in too, using stand-ins to mark cue sheets and to criss-cross the floors for the regular players. At 2 in the afternoon, Lucille and Desi and the full company go through the show completely several times, including the dress rehearsal.

At 8 o'clock an atmosphere combining Chautauqua and summer theatre takes over. The audience files in and is seated on a rising tier of bleachers dotted with multi-colored cushions. As in radio, the audience is supposed to work a bit for free admission. Assistant directors give them their cues for laughter, cheers, groans or applause. Desi grabs a microphone, introduces the entire company, including the grips (stagehands), Kenny Morgan, his personal business manager and brother-in-law; the writers who are always seated in the top row of the bleachers, and occasionally his mother and Lucille's mother, who are also seated in the top row of the bleachers.

Custard Pies

The constraint in the use of plot, which starts with Lucille Ball, airy, svelte, undaunted and undeniably chic, and winds up with Lucille falling on her face, groaning as the custard pies fly through the air, probably stems from an early and decisive event in the star's career. Having quit New York for a try at Hollywood, Lucille doggedly sat at home for quite a while waiting for a picture call. One day—partly in disgust, partly in search of morale—she went to the hairdresser and ordered the works, massage, facial, mud pack, hair-do. Naturally, at the peak moment, with her hair still in curlers, she received a hurry call from a studio, chorus girl wanted.

"They couldn't do that to me," she says, "so I went as I was, hair up in pins, traces of mud clinging to my ears. Of course, the director, or assistant director, or assistant assistant director, thought I was pretty fresh, but he had to admit I looked different from all the rest of the blondes lined up on the stage. He hired me."

The Desilu Playhouse, the name hardly needs parsing, was installed at a cost of $25,000 and has a false front to make it look like a summer theatre. It is on one of the two sound stages which Desi and Lucille rent from the General Service Studios, an independent production outfit. It also affords them a bungalow, complete with kitchen and their wardrobe, to provide living quarters during the four-day concentration period. The rest of their time Desi and Lucille spend on their boat moored at Balboa, California, on the Pacific Ocean, or their five-acre ranch in Chatsworth in the San Fernando Valley. In this latter haven, Desi pursues his other hobby, rebuilding and redecorating his home almost as assiduously as he reworks the program.

September 28, 1952

'OZZIE AND HARRIET'

Life With the Nelsons Is Now on Video

By **THOMAS M. PRYOR**
HOLLYWOOD.

"THE Adventures of Ozzie and Harriet," a radio standby since Oct. 8, 1944, based on a humorous, homespun treatment of the Nelson family home life, this year has turned to television over the facilities of the American Broadcasting Company. The tribulations of the Nelsons, mother and father, and the escapades of David and Ricky, older and younger sons, respectively, are shown each Friday night from 8 to 8:30 o'clock over Channel 7 and sixty-one other stations across the country.

The success of the Nelsons is unique, for their program is to all intents and purposes a family affair from the actual writing of the household contretemps which impel the comedy to the actual staging of the show. Ozzie, the good natured, somewhat childishly naive breadwinner, is in fact the guiding spirit of the program. He helps to develop and write the scripts in collaboration with his younger brother, Donald, and two other writers, Ben Gershman and William Davenport. Ozzie also edits the scripts and directs the programs.

Putting the half-hour show on film is a process which requires two days before the cameras every week. The average "below the line" cost—that is, not counting story cost and performers salaries—came to $14,000 on each of the first six programs completed. But Ozzie is catching on fast to the tricks of directing movies. Because he has on hand a backlog of three or four ready-to-film scripts, he can cut expenses by filming scenes for two or more future shows when the action calls for the same camera set-up.

Time-Saver

For instance, the other day Harriet was coming down the stairs of the Nelson home to answer the telephone. The scene was made and she immediately changed into a different dress and repeated the stair scene which would be used in another story to be made two weeks later. The maneuver saved time (which means money in a movie studio) because the camera was in the right position.

But Mr. Nelson, the director, doesn't stint on film. He will shoot a scene over and over until it comes off the way he wants it. Even then, if Mrs. Nelson, their sons or the camera man makes a suggestion which he believes will improve the shot he orders a retake. "The knack," he says, speaking with the assurance of a man who knows where he is going all of the time, "is not to get rattled and cost-conscious when you're having trouble. We take our time and do it the best way we know how. Of course, being so close to the writing of the scripts, and being fortunate to be ahead on them, it is easy for me to double up and take advantage of a similar scene in the next story by swinging into it as long as the camera set-up and the lights are right. We are lucky in this respect because we don't change the set every time as other shows do, and Harriet and the boys know how to respond almost by instinct."

Harriet Hilliard

The pattern of the TV show is the same as that the Nelsons use on radio, and that in turn is inspired to large degree by incidents they or their friends have experienced in real home life. The difference is that the program exploits the humor which underlies a good deal of family life, so that "The Adventures of Ozzie and Harriet" is not so much a reflection of typical family life as it is a representation of the genial atmosphere most families strive for but which few achieve due to various stresses and strains.

Ambitions

The boys, David, 16, and Ricky, 12, haven't yet lost their fascination for the movie camera, and when not acting, or attending school sessions on the set, they are constantly pumping the camera man and technicians for information about the mysteries of film-making. David, a junior at Hollywood High School, plans to study law (as his father did before breaking into show business as a bandleader), but he also wants to become a TV producer. Ricky's long-range ambitions remain to be defined, but meanwhile he is getting a big kick out of being able to ride the camera dolly. In any event, the boys will have no immediate financial worries, for their weekly salaries go into a trust fund which becomes payable when they reach the age of 21.

Mr. and Mrs. Nelson started out by making all the television scenes involving the boys on Saturdays so as not to conflict with attendance at school—Ricky is in the eighth grade at Bancroft Junior High in Hollywood—but they since decided to switch filming to Mondays and Wednesdays and to hire a private tutor for those days. David plays football with the school team on Fridays and his parents soon discovered that rest would be better for him—and them—than work the next day.

The boys have been working with their parents four years now and Mrs. Nelson—she was Harriet Hilliard and the vocalist with Ozzie's band when they married in 1935—says neither has ever shown any signs of being impressed with his importance. Mr. and Mrs. Nelson just wouldn't stand for that kind of conduct, for they are themselves in private life as much like "the people next door" as the characters they portray.

November 23, 1952

A Peep at Mr. Peepers —and Wally Cox

The shy teacher and the new TV star are deceptively alike— but there's a $1,500-a-week quality that's different.

By HARRY GILROY

AT 7:30 this evening you may tune your television set to NBC and spend a satisfying half hour enjoying the misfortunes of Wally Cox. There on your screen will appear this nice, decent little epitome of ineffectuality in the role of Robinson Peepers, the science teacher in the junior high school who tries his best to discharge adult responsibilities, but is handicapped by being as mild as a rabbit and as shy as a weeping willow. He will arouse in you, if you are anywhere past the age of 12, a protective instinct. But just before you reach out your kindly superior hand to pat him on the head it might be instructive to consider that for making you feel that way Wally Cox gets $1,500 a week, while you had to pay for the TV set on which he is appearing.

Wallace Maynard Cox, born in Detroit 28 years ago, came to New York at the age of 12 with his mother, a mystery story writer, who was separated from his father, an advertising agency copywriter. Mixed up slightly by this kind of youth, he went into the Army via the draft and received another shock — the Army didn't want him because he was more susceptible to heatstroke than the average male. An aptitude test then produced the disquieting verdict that he wasn't up to anything serious like conquering the business world and indicated that he should specialize in the arts and crafts. He studied at New York University, became a silversmith and earned $40 a week. There seemed to be little surprise among his friends that he was not making more.

BUT then he began to delight social assemblages with a monologue about an unfortunate Army private. Getting up his nerve, he went to the Village Vanguard, a nightclub, and there five years ago for the first time he received pay for having people laugh at him, something they had always done whether he was trying to be funny or not. There followed other nightclub engagements, some TV bits which turned out increasingly well, and so last summer Fred Coe, an NBC producer, and David Swift, writer, concocted the story of Mr. Peepers which seemed to fit Cox better than his own clothes. The show went off the air, for lack of a sponsor, at the end of the summer—and NBC received 15,000 protests. The Reynolds Metals Company appeared as sponsor, the show began again in October, and its rating under the Nielsen system of evaluating audience response went up like a rocket. Beginning last summer at 9, it has reached 35.5 — "and any show that does above 30 is doing all right," in the words of Producer Coe.

A visit with this young man who makes such a success out of failure indicated he *is* the character he plays and then again he *isn't*. "If I wasn't the Peepers you see on the screen, in some measure, I couldn't play him," said Cox, pondering this question at one point in the day. "On the other hand, if I was—I wouldn't have the sense to play him."

MEDITATING further in the char-

Wally Cox, as Mr. Peepers, the science teacher, launches into one of his bumbling lectures.

HARRY GILROY of The Times Magazine, who often writes about actors, describes himself as a veteran critic of dramatic rehearsals.

acteristic Peeperish fashion, Cox said: "This Peepers doesn't have reactions where other people would. He doesn't react spontaneously, only after thoughtful consideration—and most people find that to be a very funny way to behave. The normal man watching me as Mr. Peepers is going to say — 'Isn't he weird? *I* know what to do with that girl, and *he* doesn't.' Then every woman wants to baby this fellow. The fact is that (a) I used to be like that and (b) people thought it funny. Well, I didn't stop people from laughing then, and I certainly don't want to now."

The rehearsal was in one of the Malin Studios at 225 West Forty-sixth Street, a cheerless but brightly lighted room about sixty feet long. Cox and the people who work on the show with him entered this room shortly before 11 A. M., and the star promptly said: "How're we doing for air in here?" and opened a window, a more decisive reaction than Mr. Peepers could ever make to such a condition. Then he hung his blue topcoat and brown hat in a closet, put the coat of his brown-and-white checked suit on a chair and rolled up the sleeves of his cocoa-with-milk shirt. The label on the lining of his suit showed it was from the popular-priced section of a men's suit chain; Cox took out a penknife and cut the suspender buttons off the trousers, relying on his belt. It appeared he was stepping out with a new suit—but frugally.

As the rehearsal went on under the direction of Hal Keith, a far more muscular man than Wally and looking more the entertainer in a blue-and-red silk shirt that hung outside his gray slacks, it was hard at first to see that Cox wasn't Peepers. He obediently sat at a table with four other actors and the script secretary, read lines as requested, fumbled a little over changes in the script. When Marion Lorne — who plays Mrs. Gurney, another teacher—was having even more trouble than Cox in following script changes, Cox announced seriously: "There are going to be counting classes after rehearsal. Anyone who cares to sign up may do so at this point." This mild witticism, which threw the whole company into a fit of laughter, seemed to acquire humor from its unexpectedness, the pedantic quality of its delivery and the expression of gratified surprise with which Cox received the others' amusement.

The actors found the script a source of ironic merriment, somewhat further in the proceedings, when it specified after a funny line: "TAKE." Cox said that reminded him of a friend who worked on a show with a big, aggressive sort of director. "Now you go out there in the center of the stage and do a 'take,'" ordered the director. "I don't do 'takes,'" said the actor. "There are lots of actors who don't do 'takes,'" conceded the director, "but they are actors who don't work."

When Cox finished the story Anthony Randall—who acts a third teacher—asked: "And who was the actor who told you that happened to him?"

"Come to think of it," said Cox in his most baffled Peepers fashion, "it was you."

It was well along in the afternoon rehearsal before Cox finally showed how he uses the prerogatives of a star when he came to a sequence where someone cracks him three times on the head with sharp knuckles, and Mr. Peepers makes a comment to the effect that it is not only hard on the head "but your knuckles will get swollen."

While the rest of the company was chuckling over the way he read the lines, Cox said: "I know what's wrong with that, it's untrue."

Keith pleaded for retention of the line about the knuckles because it would get a laugh. "It's not funny," said Cox. "It's the old psychology of the gag writer. Let's drop that bit."

One thing about his success that he finds amusing, Cox said, is that the number of people who show condescension toward him has gone diving toward zero since his $1,500-a-week salary was published. "It used to be that I was a poor heathen by the standards of their religion," he said. "Now my salary makes me one of the gods."

Even after he became a nightclub entertainer, Cox said, there would be some spectators who would hoot derisively at him for the character he portrayed. "You know the kind of thing—they'd yell, 'Go get your hair cut,' or some such crushing witticism," he said. "Of course anyone like that is basically insecure himself." This brought up the report that Cox has undergone psychoanalysis for four years. On the basis of his present success, it was suggested, he did not need psychoanalysis. "But if I hadn't had it all that time," he said, "I might now *be* the character I was close to being instead of *playing* the character."

January 11, 1953

No Question About Quiz Shows

Their smash popularity on TV attests to our unquenchable thirst for the knowledge that we already know all the answers.

By MILTON BRACKER

No jackpot of $9,573, no mink coat and no all-expense trip to Europe will hang on the answer; but if the frenetic quizmasters who are bringing between forty and fifty different programs to the television screens these days would like a really tough question for their contestants, here it is:

Why is a quiz show?

Whether it involves audience participation, a professional panel of experts, or a combination; whether the queries involve background knowledge, current news or the most fantastic trivia, it is plainly part of an American phenomenon — a consistent, comfortable and curious preoccupation with facts.

Radio discovered this in the early Thirties and has exploited the discovery ever since. "Information Please," on the air from 1938 to 1948, became a national institution. Fred Allen, who had often spoofed at quiz shows, was himself historically defeated by one ("Stop the Music") which a rival network put opposite him in 1948. It is a sign of the times that Mr. Allen is scheduled to appear on a modified TV quiz show called "Judge for Yourself" beginning Aug. 18.

Oddly enough, "Information Please" was on TV for thirteen weeks last year —and flopped. The sheer expertness of men like Franklin P. Adams and John Kieran was insufficient to make the show a hit on live video—although it had actually made successful film shorts from 1939 to 1942. There is no absolute explanation for the failure of the old favorite to take hold in the new medium. But it would appear that the sine qua non of a successful TV quiz in 1953 is light entertainment. If the entertainment involves the spreading of a little worth-while information, all to the good. But most televiewers apparently prefer generally easy questions, wrapped up in comic or surprise situations by interesting personalities, to hard questions which elicit brilliant answers but a limited kind of fun.

Quizzes are on the air all year

MILTON BRACKER, a *Times* reporter for twenty-three years, has played Q & A games with news sources in some forty countries.

round but they really come into their own in summer. With the big variety stars on vacation, replacement programs are in order. Quiz shows are relatively easy to put together. In TV trade jargon, the cost-per-thousand-listeners-per-commercial minute is relatively low. And the chances for what is called "informal sponsor identification" —gratuitous plugs for the product—are relatively good.

OBVIOUSLY, everything is relative in television. For even on these "cheap" shows, $200 may hang lightly on the knowledge that Matthew B. Ridgway was the NATO commander recently recalled for an Army post in Washington. (The Vermont woman who had a chance to garner that $200 became an obvious victim of mike fright, could only say with quivering lips that it was "on the tip of my tongue"—and got nothing.) On the same program, a New Jersey boy earned $390 for knowing that the man associated with "Bring 'Em Back Alive" was Frank Buck. And on another show, a Navy nurse won $1,000 in prizes for saying "Treasure Island" to the query, "If you were sailing with Long John Silver, what would be your destination?"

The summer schedules of four networks list quiz shows during the morning, afternoon and night. Some are on once a fortnight, some six times a week. Some are on more than one network, some separately on TV and radio. In more than a score of audience-participation programs ("Break the Bank," "The Big Payoff," "Two for the Money,") a professional questioner works with amateur contestants. In nearly as many panel shows ("What's My Line?", "Who Said That?", "Down You Go"), professional experts try to figure out something that has been submitted by an amateur. Hybrids like "It's News to Me" and "I'll Buy That" combine features of both the other types.

IF the success of the quiz shows is thought of as a nation-wide jigsaw puzzle, the home audience supplies by far the most pieces. Why do millions react so favorably to the questions and answers?

Television professionals and everyday psychologists agree that the American fondness for competitive games is at the root of it. Every quiz is a game; every viewer is a player, even though he doesn't participate physically. The viewer identifies most readily with the amateur contestant trying to answer the professional question. The viewer both sympathizes with the participant —and likes to feel that of course he himself can answer the question more quickly.

If the question has been submitted by an amateur to stump an expert, the home viewer is likely to side with the questioner—except that, above all, he wants to feel that he could answer the question before the expert could. One viewer who beat a professional sports columnist to the answer, "Rawlings to Kelly to Frisch," as the play that ended the 1921 world series, will be comforted by the recollection for the rest of his life.

THE oldest truth in quiz business is that the viewer can get the answer more readily at home than if he were up there, hemmed in with equipment, strangers and his own fears. So like the theoretical horseplayer, with his infallible system, the viewer gets no cash but has the soothing feeling that he could have cleaned up. At the same time—tieless, shoeless and as relaxed as he likes—he can miss an answer with impunity. He gets credit for what he knows without suffering for what he doesn't. In a double sense, he can't lose.

And apart from his comfortable role in the timeless drama of Q and A, the home viewer also identifies with the amateur contestant in another "conflict"—that between the individual wage-earner and the vast, impersonal "corporation" with all the money to give away. The more money the average viewer sees given away, the better he likes it. It costs him nothing. As for a sponsor who happens to have a TV set, he has a good idea of his maximum, all-deductible risk anyway, so he is not likely to be upset by a know-it-all on his own program.

Most home viewers think at least vaguely of being on a quiz sometime themselves, or of seeing one in the studio. Waiting lists for tickets to some shows reach the tens of thousands. Those who get them stand amiably in line for two hours to get a better seat. In some cases, those in the second balcony see only a spot movie version of the show, projected above the stage. Nevertheless, they cheer, groan, prompt and disapprove audibly if a question strikes them as unfair.

By a show of hands, from two-thirds to three-quarters of studio fans these days are out-of-towners. They come because they have always watched the show at home. Many of them want to "try to get on." But a poll at three recent shows suggested that most had come more for fun than for prizes—or information. A cop from Seattle put it this way: "There's just nothing more interesting to watch," he said, adding in sly afterthought, "especially the way the money builds up."

STUDDING every studio quiz audience are the "steady customers" or "regulars." These are usually women over 35, as well known to one another as to the page-boys who handle the seating.

In many cases, some form of loneliness is behind the addiction of the regulars. They are able to lose themselves in the crowded excitement of the quiz. They include suppressed exhibitionists; the kind of person who as a child never had a kindly audience. Others are frankly prize-crazy. They know the partiality of some quizmasters to Texans, to twins, to honeymooners or to small towns with curious names. They identify themselves aggressively; the south Bronx has been known to produce a deep Southern accent. Although not every successful applicant has relied on the working of blind chance to get on a quiz, most producers resist both the inevitable special pleading—by friends, relatives and press agents—and the wiles of the old-time regulars.

THAT is one reason why studio fans picked in a pre-show "warm-up" are carefully screened before actually being selected. Often there is a twenty-four hour lag, so that those who are called up front one night never really go on until the following night. Anyone who raises a hand, gets the quizmaster's recognition and identifies himself interestingly, is likely to be called up. But there are always more persons called than can possibly be used—and this fact is impressed upon the crowd.

The quizmaster's aides seek quietly to establish, both from filled-out cards and in personal chats, that the aspirant is honest, reasonably intelligent, unlikely to be overly extrovert or eccentric—and of a background that provides a nice balance with the others chosen. About half of all contestants are selected in advance by mail. Here again, further screening is provided by staff researchers who check on promising applicants by telephone.

The fans seem to have a kind of appetite—an acquizitive instinct, as one wag put it—although not necessarily for money or gifts. The loot motive is strong but not always primary. A West Point cadet remarked, "I just wanted to show a fellow in my class I wouldn't clam up." An Iowa housewife said, "They do give nice things away—but when I was up there, all I could think of was how silly I'd look if I didn't know the answer." A New Yorker admitted it was the ham in him: "I always wanted to be some kind of actor, so why shouldn't I act like I know all the answers?"

All contestants suffer from a certain amount of tension but many of them get over it rapidly. By virtue of the trend to more "popular" questions in recent years, the paradox has arisen whereby a person who fancies himself an "intellectual" may face the mike with more of an inferiority complex than someone who eats popcorn at movies and puts nickels in jukeboxes. A viewer who knows the meaning of initials like UNICEF, the boundaries of Afghanistan, and the name of the man assassinated at Bogotá on April 9, 1948, may well despair at the uselessness of such knowledge in the face of the questions that win big money these days. As a two-time winner of the Pulitzer Prize put it, "Einstein would be a flop on a TV quiz."

A CLASSIC recent example involved Corp. Martin Diamant, a young veteran of Ko-

WHY QUIZ SHOWS ARE POPULAR

We love to compete vicariously . . .

All that money looks so good . . .

Complacency if you answer right . . .

Drawings by Roy Doty.

And impunity if you answer wrong.

rea, wearing crutches and a cast, who appeared on "Break the Bank" on Dec. 14, 1951. The bank had reached $11,840. ("It goes to show what happened to the $64 question under inflation," remarked a carryover from the early radio quizzes.) Anyway, with that fortune at stake and the final question coming up, Corporal Diamant might have wished he had gone further in school than through Samuel J. Tilden High. But the poser involved a fact no Ph. D. could have learned in any university or from any book. It was:

What was the title of a recent movie, starring Frank Lovejoy, which was based on the life of a man named Matt Cvetic?

"'I Was a Communist for the F. B. I.,'" the soldier replied.

"He passed out right on the stage," recalled the winner's mother. It developed that the boy had actually seen the film in a sniper-proof tunnel in Korea before going into action.

BUT the possibility of such a windfall—what Fred Allen calls the "appeal to greed"—does not necessarily attract the largest audience. Fifty dollars is the limit paid to anyone whose occupation stumps the panel on "What's My Line?" Yet this show has one of the highest ratings on the air. A hit quiz is a complex variable, compounded of fun, excitement, suspense, challenge and humor, or occasionally, as in "Strike It Rich," pathos spelled with a b.

The professional participants, or panelists, have reasons of their own for loving the shows. The job is easy—it requires very little beyond getting one's self selected in the first place. There is virtually no preparation, study or rehearsal.

THEN there is the pay—not dependent on fickle luck, but earned with clockwork regularity. A panelist on one morning quiz is Vanessa Brown—who attributes a trip to Europe, her meeting with her husband, and the contact which led to her present role on Broadway, to her previous work on panels. Once a Quiz Kid, she now gets more for her, time in five TV half-hours a week than in eight performances of "The Seven Year Itch."

Quizmasters are an even more specialized category of people atilt with the psychology of quiz shows. Men like Groucho Marx ("But can you tell me who's *buried* in Grant's Tomb?"), Herb Shriner, Bert Parks, Al Capp, Mike Wallace strive to keep the tone of the Q and A within the prescribed framework of the program.

Accordingly, they vary considerably in style. In "You Bet Your Life," Groucho is less reluctant than most to make jokes at his contestants' expense. But the show is on film, which permits editing. Psychologically, according to one educator, Groucho knows that a viewer enjoys feeling that Groucho can make a bigger fool of the participant than he could of the viewer.

Quizmasters whose performances are "live" are supersensitive to their contestants' feelings. A wrong answer on the first of a series of build-up questions will often be baldly prompted into a right one. Many of the quizmasters evince little or no interest in the "information" aspect of the show. The questions are selected by others, and simply handed to the quizzer on typed cards. When a quizmaster flubs an answer it's because he had no idea of the answer himself, and simply misread it.

Still, the programs are reasonably foolproof. The only drawback, according to Mr. Shriner, who refuses to step out of the character of a gently spoofing Hoosier, is that if anyone wins money on a show, "your relatives see you win it, and they have it all spent before you get home." Less insistent on a gag, Mr. Wallace sums up the craze this way: "You can't go wrong—it's as simple as that."

BUT is it? Or is there a deeper relationship between the quizzes and the American mind? Do we like all parlor games or particularly those that involve information-swapping? Do we crave knowledge or merely facts?

Professor Irving Lorge, executive officer of the Institute of Psychological Research at Teachers College, says that the programs permit an "ego involvement in which the viewer is protected against his own inferiority feeling." A person is unlikely to "stay with" a program, Professor Lorge believes, if he doesn't have "better than an even chance" of competing successfully with the answerers on the screen. Awareness of this fact is what has impelled producers to lower the question level, the psychologist continued.

Professor Lorge doubted that the desire to gain information had much to do with the success of the programs. In this connection, Margaret Halsey wrote in "The Folks at Home" that it is not quite accurate to say that Americans like "the facts." There is a certain kind of fact we like, she said, "the isolated fact."

IN other words, the *title* of the movie that won $11,840 for a veteran of Korea undoubtedly meant more to every one who experienced that program than the issues raised by the film, or, for that matter, the forces that had sent the soldier to Korea and brought him back on crutches. Knowing that Jefferson and John Adams died on the same July 4 meant far more to a recent quiz group than the ideas of either man. And so on.

Thus the quiz show puts a premium on facts, but only as entertainment. Americans who support the shows enjoy accumulating bits and pieces of information. They like games and they like to test themselves—and a quiz show is just a game with a test in it. What's more, by virtue of the general easing of the questions, those tested are rarely found wanting.

July 26, 1953

Television in Review: Celebrity Time

Murrow Puts Camera Into Their Homes in 'Person to Person'

Leopold Stokowski and Roy Campanella Are the First Subjects

By JACK GOULD

IF names make news, people make television programs. Fresh proof of the adage is afforded by Edward R. Murrow's new program, "Person to Person," which is being presented at 10:30 P. M. Fridays over C. B. S. By the simple process of taking the cameras into the homes of different personages, the presentation offers interesting TV.

"Person to Person" is a kissin' cousin of the N. B. C. network's series of conversations with elder leaders in many fields. But where that series is done on film and has been mostly interested in an individual's general philosophy of life, "Person to Person" is done on a "live" basis and offers a brief glimpse of how people live, as well as what they think.

Technically, the new Murrow show is tricky, albeit not too intrusively so. All the bulky equipment for a "live" pick-up is set directly in the homes of the persons to be interviewed. Mr. Murrow is seated in a studio and looks at a large screen, framed as a window, on which he sees the persons to whom he talks over a distance of some miles.

Edward R. Murrow

The camera serves as Mr. Murrow's eyes, just as it does the viewer's.

•

For the première Mr. Murrow visited two homes. The first was that of Roy Campanella, the Brooklyn catcher, in the St. Albans section of Queens. The second was that of Leopold Stokowski, the orchestra conductor, and his wife, Mrs. Gloria Vanderbilt Stokowski, in Gracie Square.

The program opened in the living room of Mr. Campanella's home, and then switched to his trophy room in the basement. There, Roy casually displayed some of the awards he had won, talked about an ill-fated fishing trip, explained how many hours of sleep a star catcher needed (eight hours), mentioned his household routine and discussed the world series (the program was on the day he had hit the home run that won the third game).

The visit lasted only fifteen minutes, but at the program's conclusion a viewer did have a feeling that he had come to know Mr. Campanella. The catcher's warm personality and wonderful smile came over very vividly on the screen. And his casual chitchat with Mr. Murrow brought out the human being behind the celebrity.

The visit to the Stokowski home made for excellent contrast after the stop at Mr. Campanella's house. The celebrated couple explained that one end of their living room was reserved for Mrs. Stokowski's art, the other for Mr. Stokowski's music. Mrs. Stokowski showed several of her paintings and explained how they had evolved spontaneously from her inner emotions.

Mr. Stokowski played a few bars at the piano, expressed his preference for "long hair" in both his wife's coiffure and music, showed his somewhat disorganized studio and dutifully carried around a microphone. If the cameraman and Mr. Murrow slighted the maestro a trifle, they can hardly be blamed. Mrs. Stokowski is strikingly videogenic.

•

"Person to Person," however, will have to find ways of overcoming the stiffness and formality that were noticeable during the visit with Mr. and Mrs. Stokowski. The motivation behind the show should be a casual call, not a state visit.

In the advance announcements of "Person to Person" it was said that the program would concentrate on famous personalities. This Friday the cameras will be taken to the homes of Valentina, the fashion designer, and Col. Earl "Red" Blaik, West Point football coach.

Television already is too celebrity-conscious. "Person to Person" will be missing a real bet for fascinating viewing if it does not, at least occasionally, give some time to individuals who are not household names. The unsung doctor, teacher, chorus girl, construction worker, storekeeper and Wall Street clerk also could make absorbing interviews.

Up to now, such persons usually have been seen only as Exhibit A on quiz shows; television could introduce no greater novelty than to show them as they really are.

October 7, 1953

THE 'SWEETEST MUSIC' MAN ON TV

By VAL ADAMS

GUY LOMBARDO has started a personal crusade against the theory that all dance bands are better heard than seen on television. The leader of the Royal Canadians thinks his own musicians' clean-cut appearance enhances an appreciation of Lombardo lullabies each Friday at 7 P. M. over Channel 4.

"I resent people saying they don't want to look at a dance band on television," says Guy, who has played swoon tunes in the same style for more than thirty years. "They've been looking at the wrong band all these years. I agree that the majority of bands and musicians should not been seen on television. Some musicians drive you crazy with their wild hair and brown shoes with tuxedos. And when you put four lights before them, they put on dark glasses.

"But we built our band from the standpoint of appearance. People want to see us as well as hear us play, and the proof of the pudding is the way they turn out for our concert tours."

All Lombardo musicians wear carnations in their lapels and make-up on their faces for the television show.

"You couldn't put make-up on most musicians even if you chained them," he says. "But our boys did demand the extra $12 for putting on make-up, which the union contract calls for."

Selling Sound

The telecast of the Lombardo band amounts to no more than simple coverage of a scheduled event outside a studio. It originates during the regular dinner hour in the Hotel Roosevelt Grill, where the band plays nightly for dining and dancing patrons. The show probably marks the first time that a television sponsor ever bought a dance band in its own habitat.

"We're a dance band, period," says Guy. "Sound is the thing we're supposed to sell—not trick camera shots inside a piano and under a drum. Nine-tenths of the television shows still pay no attention to the sound of the music. When I did my first television show several years ago they told me I had to use boom mikes—none on the floor that could be seen. Ridiculous! You can't hear the music unless mikes are placed among the instrumentalists. On this show we use three.

"On Friday nights we play just like we do on any other night. but the audience at home has a chance to look in. There are no gimmicks. When I introduce the twin pianos I say this is Fred Kreitzer and Buddy Brennan with their version of 'Humoresque.' What more can you say about two piano players?"

Home viewers notice an unusual naturalness about the setting and appearances of the musicians and customers seen on the Lombardo show. Most appear unmindful of the TV camera and rarely does a Grill patron wave.

No Waving

"Before we go on the air I ask the customers not to wave at the camera with the red light," explains Guy, "because that's the one that will be feeding the picture out on the air. The catch is that none of the cameras have red lights. We removed them so the customers wouldn't know which of three cameras was operating. It's also a good thing for the boys in the band. Without a red light they don't turn on that television look."

One of the few minor concessions the Royal Canadians made for television was a rearrangement of the pianos and a switch to blue shirts, which are now worn on non-TV nights also. The show brought back Carmen Lombardo—Guy's brother who plays the lead saxophone and flute—as a vocalist. He quit singing several years ago, surfeited by the spoofing of his wavering tonal quality. But Guy begged him to try again on the ground that his singing was a trade mark of the band.

Lombardo's firm determination to do nothing on television but be natural and play dance music was formed several years ago after an unhappy experience with a TV show called "Cavalcade of Bands." Against his will, he was saddled with girl singers, sight acts and a script on his first two appearances. On the third performance he threw away the script just as the show went on the air, and followed through in his normal style. He decided that would be the only way thereafter.

Although Guy's current program, televised only in the New York area, has been on the air less than three months, he is amazed at some things that have resulted from it.

"My record sales in New York are up 40 per cent," he says, "and there's no doubt at all that television has done it. Business at the Roosevelt Grill is up at least 20 per cent, although we had a big business before television. In the old days radio was a great help in building a band, but radio never had the wallop for putting over a band that television has. TV provides better sound, since it's high fidelity. People get a kick out of seeing the vocalists and instrumentalists."

As to why he thinks his music —billed as "the sweetest music this side of heaven"—is still successful, Lombardo says:

"It's very easy to get away from the thing that made you successful, but the important thing is to keep on doing what people tell you they like. Don't get out of character. Don't fool the public."

January 24, 1954

FRIDAY'S MAN SMITH

Ben Alexander Talks About His Role as Jack Webb's Partner in 'Dragnet'

By VAL ADAMS

ACTOR BEN ALEXANDER doesn't care much for acting, isn't especially happy about his role on "Dragnet" and doesn't like the way he looks on camera, but otherwise he is well adjusted.

On "Dragnet" he's the big fellow with the round face, Detective Frank Smith, the partner of Detective Joe Friday, played by Jack Webb, the star and director of the show. He was hired for the job, he thinks, because "I look like 90 per cent of the cops in Los Angeles," the locale in which the stories from local police files occur.

"Being an actor is not the dearest thing to my heart," says the 42-year-old Alexander, who made his Hollywood movie debut at the age of 4. "I'm really a business man. I've got some gas stations and a motel in Hollywood. I own a boat and I have a home on Telegraph Hill in San Francisco. Being Frank Smith—I just play big, fat Frank—is not the greatest joy in the world, but it's pretty wonderful being part of something where the finished product goes over big with a lot of people."

"Dragnet," the "finished product that goes over big," is presented by N. B. C.-TV on Thursdays at 9 P. M. and N. B. C. radio on Tuesdays at 9 P. M. The TV version is filmed at such rapid pace that rarely are the actors and production crew free of tension. According to Alexander, the technique used is totally different from any other show filmed for television.

Shooting Schedule

"We shoot two half-hour films each week," he says. "We work six days a week from 8:30 in the morning until about 8 at night. Jack and I never memorize any of our lines. We can't because we're always working on six pictures at once. We read our lines from a teleprompter. No one will believe this, but let me tell you how this guy Webb works.

"On Monday morning he walks on to the set and says, 'Okay, what's this story about?' Somebody tells him it's called 'The Grandma,' a story that was done on the radio version of the show three years ago. Hurriedly he reads the first page of the script and says we'll do a long shot here, another long long shot there and everything else in close up. We start shooting immediately. The show is never rehearsed."

This does not mean, adds Alexander, that Webb is not concerned with turning out the best performance possible. Frequently an actor's reading of a line of dialogue is filmed over and over again until Webb feels that just the right inflection has been recorded. Alexander estimates that two-thirds of the film exposed in shooting "Dragnet" never gets beyond the cutting-room floor.

Only one camera is used in filming. Any viewer familiar with "Dragnet" knows that it leans heavily on close-ups, with the camera seemingly darting from one individual to another, all speaking short sentences or phrases. But the average viewer would never suspect just how these sequences are filmed. Alexander tells it this way:

Filming Close-Ups

"Let's say that Jack and I are sitting at a table questioning a suspect. First we put the camera on Jack and he looks at the script moving up on the teleprompter. When a line comes up with his name on it, he reads it for the sound track. For cueing purposes, somebody off-stage reads the other lines. Jack will do every close-up he's got in the scene at one sitting. Then I do all of mine and the actor playing the suspect does his. Later a film editor takes the three different reels of film, cuts them up and puts the pieces together in proper order.

"Jack's idea is to tell a story with people's faces," adds Ben. "When you say something on 'Dragnet,' everybody knows what you say. It's got impact. Viewers seem to remember practically every line on the show."

Alexander insists that Webb makes no effort to have all the actors read their lines in a monotone. He says that they don't—it just seems that way.

"The monotony in the playing that people talk about is not deliberate," he says. "The editing and cutting makes it sound monotonous. Webb has never asked any actor to talk in a particular style. I've noticed that very few motion picture actors 'dig' the the show. Some of them, when they're first hired, come out with their lips drawn and talk in a monotone. Webb tells them it's not done that way."

Various people, including Alexander, write scripts for "Dragnet." Many a crime writer finds it frustrating until he catches on to the peculiar style of merely solving a murder instead of creating one.

January 17, 1954

Imogene Coca and Sid Caesar

Television in Review: Ave Caesar

Comic's Long Alliance With Imogene Coca Is Nearing Finale

By JACK GOULD

THE break-up of television's pioneer comedy team of Sid Caesar and Imogene Coca does not come as surprising news. Sooner or later the split was inevitable, both for the two stars and their producer, Max Liebman. The trio's program, "Your Show of Shows," simply had run its course.

It seems hard to realize that it was only three or four years ago that Sid and Imogene were the mainstay of Saturday night television. Their show was so far above the average run in adult wit and satire that their competition was practically nonexistent. Amid the plethora of vaudeville at that time, theirs was a review of style and discernment.

•

What happened? Mr. Caesar and Miss Coca have not lost their technique or artistry. Their performances individually may be just as good as they were four years ago. The difference is that millions of persons now know "Your Show of Shows" backward and forward. Within its framework there is hardly anything that Mr. Caesar and Miss Coca can do that seems fresh and bright. It is not a case of a viewer not liking the show; he has just seen it before, not once but many times. Meanwhile, there are other programs now to watch on Saturday night—Jackie Gleason, Herb Shriner, et al.

Concurrent with the toll taken by the audience's familiarity with the program were unseen economic influences at work. Both Mr. Caesar and Miss Coca had step-up clauses in their contracts, and at the moment he is receiving $25,000 a week, and she, $10,000. Such a large fixed overhead, especially for a show that had passed its peak, is simply too rich for TV's blood. Success of the stars on television in part was responsible for their show's undoing.

Where Mr. Liebman may have erred—and admittedly this is the questionable wisdom of hindsight—was in not seeing the handwriting on the wall at least a season ago, perhaps two. Unlike Milton Berle, who did take the needed step before it was too late, Mr. Liebman was hesitant to tinker with a going success. His few gestures in the direction of breathing new life into the program were halfhearted and not very imaginative. In due course, "Your Show of Shows" became a task, not exciting theatre.

After Providing Many Happy Hours, Team Bows to Inevitable

Mr. Liebman's concurrence in the decision for everyone to embark on new and different assignments next season speaks well, however, for his basic sense of showmanship. To close a show is never easy.

The troubles besetting Mr. Caesar and Miss Coca are by no means unique. Virtually all television comedy has been undergoing a change for some time. Many showmen now are convinced that the situation format is the only solution for the clown who appears week after week.

A strong story line can ease the burden on a star and give him things to do and say beyond his fixed routines. The so-called "stand up" comedian, who appears alone and gives off with funny sayings and a song, is now a gentleman in search of characterization. Both Mr. Caesar and Miss Coca are slated for situation shows next fall.

•

If everyone does situation comedy, sooner or later there also is bound to be a reaction against this type of programming. Formats in TV, undoubtedly, will go through a succession of cycles. Therein lies the fundamental difference between television and radio, a difference many sponsors are only beginning to grasp. In radio a program could rock along for a decade without substantial alteration; in television the only certainty is the need for change.

When Jimmy Durante started on TV several seasons ago, he wisely observed: "The audience can only hate us if we keep doing the same thing." The decision of Miss Coca, Mr. Caesar and Mr. Liebman to break up bears him out. There is already a new inter t and sense of anticipation in how each will fare next season. The excitement, in short, is back. Meantime, a viewer will want to thank all three for the many happy hours they have provided in the past and wish them well in their new endeavors.

March 1, 1954

BOB SMITH: IDOL OF THE PEANUT GALLERY SET

By VAL ADAMS

DAY in and day out for six and a half years Buffalo Bob Smith has faced a television studio audience of fifty wildly cheering youngsters, most between the ages of 3 and 5. Sitting in the "peanut gallery" of N. B. C.'s "Howdy Doody" program for children, they scream with delight at the antics of 36-year-old Buffalo Bob, who conducts the show. When he first walks into the studio, their lusty lungs pour out an ovation that well might cause Liberace, out of professional jealousy, to crawl into his candelabra and hide.

These high-decibel surroundings would shatter the equilibrium of the average adult or parent, but not Buffalo Bob, the father of two boys. He insists that he enjoys every moment of his show. He denies that his exuberance in front of the "peanut gallery" is just an act.

"I love kids," he said last week. "Kids never get on my nerves."

In this connection it should be pointed out that Buffalo Bob, unlike the average parent, is paid $2,000 a week to entertain children for only thirty minutes a day.

"He can afford to like kids," commented one of Smith's associates.

Different

Buffalo Bob said that he isn't disturbed even when children in the "peanut gallery" try to outshout him and talk when he is talking. Although this makes Mr. Smith markedly different from the usual parent, he told a story to emphasize his point.

Recently Buffalo Bob, who wears a pioneer suit on the show, led into a commercial by asking how many in the vibrating "peanut gallery" had eaten vegetables for dinner the night before. Hands shot up and the studio thundered with shouts of "I had peas!" or "I had carrots!"

"They screamed through the whole commercial," explained Mr. Smith with a laugh, relishing an appreciation for childish enthusiasm. "The funny thing was that while I told the kids to put margerine on their vegetables, one boy kept yanking my arm and yelling in my ear, 'Hey, Buffalo Bob! We had soup last night, not vegetables.' I thought I would burst out laughing before I finished the commercial."

Certainly the average parent could not sustain the patience of Buffalo Bob in these small fry versions of the Army-McCarthy hearings. On the other hand, the average parent doesn't have a sponsor watching to see that the sales pitch is put over in a friendly manner.

Cast

It is unlikely that any adult, with the possible exception of Buffalo Bob, will ever comprehend the "Howdy Doody" program, presented from 5:30 to 6 P. M. on Mondays through Fridays. It is aimed directly at the 2-to-8-year-old age group and anyone who is 9 or over may be puzzled at the proceedings.

As for the cast, "Howdy Doody" is a freckled face puppet whose goofy voice is supplied by Mr. Smith, off camera. Another key puppet character is Flubadub, a strange animal. Clarabell the clown is a human, but makes only one sound, which resembles a honking horn.

"Some people say our show is silly," said Buffalo Bob, "but they forget that we are playing for 3 and 4 and 5 year olds. Did you ever watch them play? Pretty silly, isn't it? If some college professor wants to come out and say that our show is moronic, I'm not going to argue with him."

Despite the adverse comments, Buffalo Bob believes his show is partly educational for children.

"We do constructive things," he said. "We talk about safety and good manners and encourage the kids to go to their place of worship on Sunday. And the show is an emotional outlet for children. They like to see Clarabell chase me with a seltzer bottle because it's something they'd like to do."

But as one would suspect, "Howdy Doody" was not conceived as purely a public service. Buffalo Bob, in fact, has turned his pal "Howdy" into one of the hardest-working pitchmen in television. They frequently discuss a sponsor's product and encourage the children to influence their parents to purchase it.

Buffalo Bob, who was born and reared in Buffalo, N. Y., came here in 1946 as a disk jockey for radio Station WNBC. Finding the work not as profitable as he had hoped, he later encountered television and "Howdy Doody."

"I would still love to do an adult show," he said with a sigh, "but I would never give up 'Howdy Doody'."

At the prevailing prices, that's the understatement of the week.

May 30, 1954

TV: Life of a General

Clark Passes in Review on Edwards' Show

By JACK GOULD

RALPH EDWARDS, presiding jumping-jack of "This Is Your Life," at times can be thoroughly trying with his forced enthusiasm and excitement, but it must be conceded he also comes up periodically with television of genuine human interest. He did on Wednesday evening over the National Broadcasting Company network when his guest was Gen. Mark W. Clark.

In the public's eye the general heretofore has seemed the proverbial military figure—stern, unbending and rather distant and cold. "This Is Your Life" illustrated how misleading inadequate knowledge of a man can be. Before the cameras the general and his family were an immensely likable group of individuals.

The general's face was a fascinating study in itself: lean, tranquil and rugged. As acquaintances of both his childhood and Army years were brought into the studio by Mr. Edwards, the general once or twice had difficulty controlling his emotions. But his obvious pleasure and surprise in seeing old friends, the twinkle in his eye and his soft smile provided a revealing insight into the man.

The New York Times Studio

Gen. Mark W. Clark

•

When Mr. Edwards gets around to recalling the marriage of one of his guests, the going on "This Is Your Life" frequently becomes sticky. But in the case of General and Mrs. Clark it was the program's most warmly humorous moment.

Mrs. Clark, a vivacious and charming woman, said they had met on a blind date. "He was a complete bust," she laughed.

General Clark noted that on the date Mrs. Clark had the misfortune to sit down on a bee. "We got to know each other better," he said.

Mr. Edwards did an unusually thorough job in rounding up persons who have played a part in the general's career—the English commander of the submarine that took him on his daring trip to Africa before the start of the Allied invasion in World War II; the enlisted man in the front lines for whom the general took the trouble to find a proper pair of boots, a classmate at West Point, and many others.

•

A few viewers still might wish, however, that Mr. Edwards could learn to curb his energetic ways. Both for his guest of honor and for his audience it can be embarrassing to see him superimpose his own extreme melodramatic touches on a situation that usually is sufficiently dramatic in itself.

Mr. Edwards especially should be careful that he does not inadvertently leave the impression that he is gloating over the revelation of some deeply personal moment in a guest's life. His is a difficult chalk-line to walk but sometimes he is forgetful of the virtue of restraint.

The middle commercial on "This Is Your Life" continues to be a problem. Breaking into the story of an individual's private life to make a pitch for cosmetics can be jarring and in dubious taste.

Perhaps Mr. Edwards would be well advised not to switch so swiftly and casually from ecstatic praise of his guest to ecstatic praise of his sponsor. Instead he could state simply that there would be a pause for the commercial. In this instance non-integrated advertising would be the most intelligent advertising.

April 29, 1955

GODFREY CONFIRMS DISMISSING LA ROSA

'Fired' Singer and Bleyer, Citing Their Outside Activities—But He 'Loves' Them Both

Arthur Godfrey confirmed yesterday that he had "fired" Julius La Rosa and Archie Bleyer from his radio and television shows because of their outside business activities, although he "loved" them both. He also referred to a growing morale problem among his cast members and said that he had warned them three weeks ago, "Do better or I'll drop you."

During a press conference in his office at 49 East Fifty-second Street, the C. B. S. star said that Mr. La Rosa, a singer, had become uncooperative in rehearsals and lost his "humility." He added that "the straw that broke the camel's back" was the contract that the singer signed last week with the General Artists Corporation, a talent agency.

"One thing I will not have is interference by outside agents," Mr. Godfrey explained. "My kids don't need outside help. The best brains in the world are right here in my organization."

'Julie's Swan Song'

Without advance warning, the star fired the singer on the air last Monday morning by announcing at the end of the show, "That was Julie's swan song." Mr. Godfrey said he planned it that way "so everybody would know what had happened."

On the same day Mr. Godfrey called in Mr. Bleyer, his orchestra conductor, to ask if he had been in Chicago during his vacation making a record with Don McNeill. The conductor, the majority stockholder in the Cadence Records and Publications Company, confirmed the report, Mr. Godfrey said.

"I just fired Julie and it was like tearing my eyeballs out, and I guess you're next," Mr. Godfrey quoted himself as telling Mr. Bleyer. "McNeill on A. B. C. is in competition with us. Archie is an outstanding gentleman, but he used my show just to get money and make records. But I told him he could have one of the night time shows and he picked 'Talent Scouts' on Monday night. He can have the job as long as I can stand him. I love that guy. There is a possibility we could resume our relationship on both night time shows."

No Comment on Statement

The other show is "Arthur Godfrey and His Friends," televised on Wednesday evenings.

Neilther the singer nor the conductor had any comment on Mr. Godfrey's version of what had happened.

Mr. Godfrey recalled that some cast members had not been taking the proper interest in the "institute classes" he had arranged—such things as tap dancing and ballet lessons to overcome their awkwardness. He accused Mr. La Rosa and the Mariners, a quartet, of skipping classes.

Mr. Godfrey complained about the troubles that arise from the fees his cast members—some of them very young—receive.

"There are no real artists on my show," he said. "The only one with a really good voice is Marion Marlowe. The others are just so-so voices, some good and some not so good, but a lovable personality is more important. Kids go from nothing to $500 a week on my show just on union scale alone. Oh, the trouble I had with Lu Ann Simms, one of the singers."

But on his television program from 8 to 9 o'clock last night, Mr. Godfrey seemed unusually cordial to his whole company. Among those he singled out for commendation were the Mariners and Miss Simms.

He became affectionate in introducing the McQuire Sisters, a singing team, and placed his arms around them. With obvious significance of developments this week, and possibly earlier ones, he told the audience:

"Im sure you have noticed through the years that those who are the great ones stay with me."

October 22, 1953

SANDWICHING IN MORE WESTERNS ON TV

By OSCAR GODBOUT

HOLLYWOOD.

TELEVISION is engaged in in the second opening of the West. When asked last week to comment on evidence pointing to a trend in Western film series, Alan Livingston replied:

"Trend? It's an avalanche." The head of programing for the National Broadcasting Company's Pacific division added. "We've made a decision to put on an hour-length Western film series next fall and very well might have an additional two new thirty-minute Western shows."

Buckle on your six guns, viewers, for the horsy set of the Hollywood TV film coalition appears to be in the saddle this season. Next fall will tell the story. Plans for twenty-one series garbed in Western dress of one sort or another have been initiated by eight producers in the last 100 days. The total number of sagebrush sagas announced in the last twelve months is better than two dozen.

Plans

Behind the trend is the fact that Westerns appear to have a better chance for network success. In the fall of 1955 the American Broadcasting Company started "Wyatt Earp" and "Cheyenne"; N. B. C. brought forth "Frontier" and "Fury," and the Columbia Broadcasting System introduced "Gunsmoke." With the exception of "Frontier," all have prospered. This past season saw "Broken Arrow" and "The Zane Grey Theatre" added to the list.

Currently there are offered on network time eleven horse operas. N. B. C. has "Roy Rogers" and "Cowboy Theatre;" A. B. C. "Broken Arrow," "Wyatt Earp," "Rin Rin Tin" and the hardiest perennial, "The Lone Ranger." C. B. S. also has the "Lone Ranger," along with "The Zane Grey Theatre," "Gunsmoke," "Wild Bill Hickok" and "Tales of the Texas Rangers." The flood of old Western feature films shown on local stations is more grist for the mill.

"Oaters"

In addition to the hour-long "oater," as the genre is termed by the trade, N. B. C. has on tap "Union Pacific" and "Pony Express." (It is jumping the gun with "Wells Fargo" March 18.) Warner Brothers has four hour-length projects which may go to A. B. C.-TV. They are "The Oklahoma Kid," "Trouble Smith," "The Texan" and "The Gambler." The Columbia Broadcasting System is involved with "Without Incident," "Have Gun, Will Travel," "Cavalry Patrol" and "Lone Woman." C. B. S., incidentally, is trying an interesting method of pilot film productions with two of these, of which more later.

Screen Gems has a pair titled "The Man From Texas" and "Daniel Boone," Desilu Productions is represented with "The Last Marshal," while Revue Productions is keeping its franchise with "The Sixshooter." T. C. F.-TV has put "Man Without a Gun" into its production hopper and Walt Disney is preparing "Zorro" for A. B. C.

While the above are period pieces of the "head-'em-off-at-Eagle-Pass" variety, there are also a pair of contemporary variations on the chaparral theme, A filmed musical program titled "Western Ranch Party" is under way at Screen Gems and C. B. S.-TV is tinkering with "Guestward Ho," a situation comedy built around a New Mexico guest ranch.

If the trend develops substantially it may be that TV Westerns will come to be the programing staple they once were with theatrical films. Some may not consider this a particularly exciting turn of events, but, generally speaking, Westerns made for prime-time showing seem to be more amply endowed with quality than their theatrical counterparts.

March 3, 1957

New Season

The Columbia Broadcasting System would appear to have a winner in its new Western film series entitled "Gunsmoke," derived from the radio show of the same name. It's done in the taut, understated style associated with "High Noon" and should quickly prove a Saturday night fixture (10 P. M.)

On the opening show, Paul Richards gave an uncommonly good performance as a psychopathic killer, and James Arness, who will appear each week as the United States marshal, looked appropriately rugged and noble.

George Gobel, who had things pretty much his own way last season at 10 o'clock on Saturdays over N. B. C., may have his hands full this year in the ratings.

September 13, 1955

Raymond Burr

Durable Sleuth

Perry Mason, the durable sleuth created by Erle Stanley Gardner, began one of his more formidable assignments Saturday evening: to catch Perry Como in the popularity ratings. Even with a head start in time—he begins at 7:30 P. M. on Channel 2, a half hour before the singer starts on Channel 4—the resourceful counselor may have his problems.

In its translation to the TV medium the mystery series is faithful to the taut and compact Gardner style of presentation. It also has an advantage in its hour-long format—the extra time does permit more attention to detail, particularly in the courtroom. But beyond that the première was not so long on distinction as to suggest serious competition for Mr. Como.

The initial story was "The Case of the Restless Redhead," an account of a young lady framed on a variety of raps and then dutifully liberated by Mr. Mason. Raymond Burr is playing Mr. Mason very straightforwardly. The lawyer-investigator, as a matter of fact, seemed a wholesome resident of suburbia on his way up the executive ladder. The volatile Mason of the printed page was not very evident.

Mason's secretary, played by Barbara Hale, only fetched coffee and sandwiches for her boss on TV; in her own right, of course, she is a shrewd member of the Mason investigative corps, not merely a stereotyped decorative doll.

On Saturday night "Perry Mason" was a competent if unexceptional pot-boiler.

September 23, 1957

OLD MOVIES ON TV PERIL HOLLYWOOD

Secret Report Says Rise in Home Viewing Threatens Life of Whole Industry

By BOSLEY CROWTHER

Financial failure looms for most of the nation's movie theatres and film makers if the trend of public interest in old movies on television continues to rise.

Since last September, old movies have come to command close to one-quarter of the total of the nation's television-viewing time. The public is spending four times as many hours a week looking at old movies on television as it is in attending new ones in theatres.

The direct consequence of this development, which began noticeably with the influx of top-quality old pictures on free television last fall, has been a 7,000,000 drop in average weekly movie attendance in the final quarter of last year, compared with the same period in 1956.

Loss Is $50,000,000

In money, this has meant a loss of some $50,000,000 in net theatre grosses in that time. This decline is traceable to the growing popularity of the old films.

These are the salient findings in a secret report on movie-going and television viewing, prepared for the Theatre Owners of America by Sindlinger & Co., business analysts, of Ridley Park, Pa.

It was this report, based on a continuing survey of markets in all forty-eight states, that was presented at a closed meeting of theatre owners and heads of all the movie craft guilds in Hollywood Jan. 17. Those who attended refused to disclose what was discussed, but it was noticeable that they came away in a state of grave concern.

Impact Is Analyzed

Requests by newsmen for copies of the report have since been refused by officers of the theatre owners' group on the ground that its release might be "depressing." However, a copy has been made available to this newspaper by a person well-placed in the industry who feels that its contents, while alarming, should be known to the public and especially to the whole film industry.

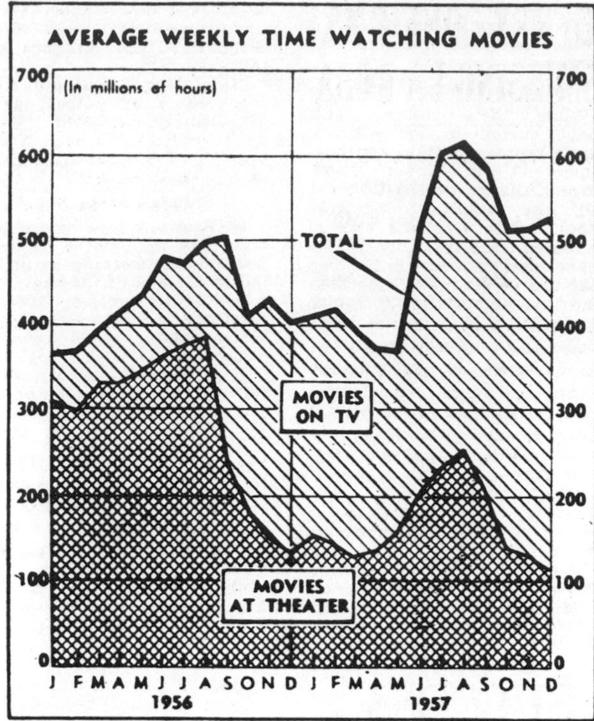

The New York Times Jan. 27, 1958

Comparison of home TV and theatre movie viewings.

The cause for alarm is contained in the final summary of the analysis. It holds that, if the post-1948 Hollywood product is released to television broadcasters as the pre-1948 product has been, it "would be a death blow to theatres and to production."

In the last week, the Screen Actors Guild, the Writers Guild of America, West, and the Screen Directors Guild have served notice separately on Republic Pictures of "cancellation of contract." Republic recently released its post-1948 pictures to the National Broadcasting Company without first negotiating with the guilds for additional payment of the talent participation in those pictures, according to the guilds. Existing contracts with the company require such negotiation, it was said.

Beginning with a review of the impact of television on movie attendance, the Sindlinger report discloses that in the twelve months from October, 1954, through September, 1955, the nation's theatres including drive-ins had their best twelve months, on a consolidated basis, since 1948. This, it says, was because:

¶The bigger movie stars had stayed off television.

¶Only a few old movies were being shown on the late television shows.

¶The public recognized that the local theatre and the local television station were competing for its time and attention.

Changes Are Noted

However, with the beginning of the so-called "courtship of movies and TV" in 1955, signaled by the showing of film clips and film company programs on the air, significant changes began to appear. Theatre attendance was off 17 per cent to 20 per cent in areas where the public had an opportunity to view such programs as "Warner Brothers Presents," "M-G-M Parade," "The Twentieth Century-Fox Hour," "Disneyland" and the Ed Sullivan guest - artist show. In areas where the public could not watch these programs, attendance was up 3 to 7 per cent over the comparable period of the previous year.

"Thus, during the movie-TV courtship, TV was the winner," the report says.

Then, with the "wedding of movies and television," which the report holds began in October of last year on the general release of pre-1948 products from most of the major studios, the changes in audience behavior became most noticeable.

Average weekly attendance was off from 13.5 per cent to 17.5 per cent in the last six months of the year, where it had been up from 2.1 per cent to 6.2 per cent in the first six months, as against the same periods in 1956. Simultaneously, the public's viewing time devoted to old movies on television

rose from 86.5 million hours a week pre-September to 426.2 million hours a week in December.

Rise in Interest Seen

While the public's "talk about" current motion pictures, which represents potential customers in the Sindlinger system, did not change perceptibly last fall, the simultaneous "talk about" old movies on television increased precipitously. This change was reflected in the fact that the percentage of persons who thought about going to movies but didn't rose from 64.6 in the last quarter of 1956 to 76.5 in the last quarter of 1957.

Putting a dollar value on this percentage of "lost admissions," the Sindlinger report holds that it amounts to a potential $10,000,000 a week.

The report recognized that "some first-runs, many with higher admissions, did break house records" during the past Christmas week, "and some of the new product did well." Certain producers, indeed, have indicated a rise in their film rentals in the past few months.

But the report continued that "the over-all holiday attendance decline this year came from the Midwest, from small towns and from big city neighborhood theatres that didn't have the new product."

In estimating the total amount received by all the major film production companies (excepting Paramount) for their backlogs of films as against the calculated loses suffered by the fall-off in theatre attendance, the report concludes that the production companies took a net loss of $5,300,000 on the transactions last year.

If the national level of theatre gross for the next nine months follows the trend of the past six months, according to the report, theatres and production will be down about 17 per cent. This would mean that theatres will have a $200,000,000 annual loss in net gross and production will have an annual loss of $73,000,000 in film rental.

This, the report concludes, could be disasterous to the industry.

January 27, 1958

SUCCESS STORY

From Edward to Edd, Or How Kookie Paid Off

HOLLYWOOD.

THE young man said he sometimes thought about revisiting the pawnshop where, just a few years ago, he left his high-fidelity set and electric razor to help finance his quest for fame as an actor. Now he has the money to redeem the pawn ticket. In fact, he has just purchased a home here with good acoustics for his new hi-fi by knowing how to comb his wavy blond hair and talk in a curious jargon as a parking attendant on the American Broadcasting Company television series "77 Sunset Strip."

Success has made Edward (Kookie) Byrnes reluctant to enter a pawnshop on business. "I would be recognized," he says, "and how would I explain what I wanted with the stuff. Anyhow, hock shops bring back unhappy memories."

In the roller-coaster world built on teen-age acclaim, popularity can strike so quickly that it is easy for a 25-year-old actor to recall his past. Moreover, Kookie is as realistic as the Manhattan sidewalks on which he has spent most of his life. With his New York accent, his easy grin and his hoofer's bouncy walk, he sometimes suggests a younger edition of the most famous of Hollywood realists, James Cagney.

Talent

Kookie, for example, has no illusions about his talents. He knows that he is no great singer despite the sales of more than a million copies of his first record, "Kookie, Kookie (Lend Me Your Comb)." He also knows that in spite of star billing in a new movie, "Yellowstone Kelly," he is no more competent to try a Broadway play than he is to offer advice to the lovelorn teen-agers who send him mail by the carton.

"I don't want to try any plays," he said. "I am not the arty type of actor. I would rather make a name in motion pictures and television."

The saga of Kookie, as he told it the other day at the Warner Brothers Studios, is, in a sense, the substitution of courage for ability; of stubbornness for training; of personality for artistry. Kookie's rise is almost symbolic of how easily television can upset the rules of show business.

Kookie first felt the urge toward acting after finishing high school in New York and trying such jobs as driving an ambulance, roofing, salesman in a flower shop. "I used to be a great movie fan," was his only explanation of the urge that drove him to badger a friend into getting him a nonpaying job with an obscure summer stock company in Connecticut. That was in 1956.

Parts

"Then, believe it or not," he said, "I started to get acting parts in the company. Some of them were pretty big."

Whereupon Edward Byrnes began making the rounds in New York. "I went from door to door. I tried Broadway; I tried television. I tried everything. Every once in a while I would get a walk-on in television. They would tell me I was no good because I had a New York accent or because I had no experience or because nobody knew me."

After a year of "getting nowhere," he got into his car and drove to Hollywood. He exaggerated his experience to enlist the assistance of agents. He tried for anything in movies or television. He drew the line at only one thing—working in a nonentertainment job.

A short time later, the refugee New Yorker was down to his last nickel and had pawned everything of value. Hunger was almost constant.

Finally he was accepted by a small acting company that performed here in a tiny theatre. He was paid $22.50 a week. He boarded with a family for $8 a week and lived mainly on hamburgers and hot dogs.

Break

His great opportunity came unexpectedly when he was cast as a hired killer in what was to have been a ninety-minute movie for Warners. When it was finished it was decided to do the movie as a ninety-minute television show instead. From this came the series known as "77 Sunset Strip." Kookie was switched from killer to parking-lot attendant after his first appearance.

KOOKIE—Edward Byrnes, tenant of "77 Sunset Strip."

As the new Edward Byrnes developed, his first name underwent a change from Edward to Edd. "I just dreamed it up one day," he said. "Edward is too formal and there are lots of Eddies."

Kookie has no intention of taking acting courses.

"I am not studying. Why should I?" he asks. "I get all my experience in front of the camera. You get in front of a camera every day and you've got to learn."

And as long as the teen-age mail keeps pouring in, Kookie will not want for cameras.

MURRAY SCHUMACH.

August 30, 1959

MAN BEHIND CAPTAIN KANGAROO

By RICHARD F. SHEPARD

THE seven stages of man as reflected on the home screen might be "Captain Kangaroo," "Superman," "Walt Disney Presents," Dick Clark's rock 'n' roll, the adult Western, the discussion show and, for the twilight years perhaps, wrestling. For the self-conscious, a disclaimer: this depicts the theoretical viewer who, as everyone knows, exists only in such statistical abstracts as Kinsey reports and rating surveys.

But, nonetheless, in the beginning there is "Captain Kangaroo." This Columbia Broadcasting System telecast has been hailed by authorities, both on television and on children, as an excellent way to introduce toddlers to the medium when they are still knee-high to the volume control. Although there are excellent shows for toddlers on local stations and some on networks over the week-end, the Captain is the sole survivor of his class to be shown on a network basis six days a week.

The captain is the creation of a thoughtful father of three named Bob Keeshan, whose children (ranging from 4 to 8) have become used to the schizophrenic situation that brings their father to their receiver as a genial 60-year-old host and, later in person, back home to Babylon, L. I., as a 32-year-old commuter.

Look

Mr. Keeshan appreciates the advantages of being able to leave his TV personality, consisting of a baggy uniform, shaggy mustache and gray thatch, in the make-up room at the studio. It makes for a more normal existence both for himself and his family.

In a recent interview, he scouted some of the reasons that have made parents write letters ranking in vehemence with Emile Zola's "J'Accuse" when his program has been threatened with nullification over the past four years. The children's show of any sort leads a tenuous existence and it is only now that "Captain Kangaroo" seems to have found a sound financial footing with the acquisition of a big sponsor starting in October.

It was noted that many shows try to get to the family pocketbook through the children in a most obnoxious fashion, by arousing envy or cupidity in young bosoms.

"We will probably make some mistakes, but we will iron them out," said Mr. Keeshan. "We can't make a 'hard sell,' because none of us on the show are characters of that type."

Indeed, "Captain Kangaroo" is a quiet sort of program in contrast to some other presentations that rely on screams, gunshots and practical jokes to keep the children quiet.

"It's one of the tragedies of bringing up children today that gentleness is associated with weakness," observed Mr. Keeshan. "We try to place in the person of Captain Kangaroo a gentleness. I suppose there's room for noisy shows too."

When adults watch a show such as "Gunsmoke," he said, they know that such methods don't really settle problems; there is a yardstick for adults to gauge their entertainment by that children don't have.

"But then, lots of people, even TV producers who have their own children at home, say, 'Look at fairy tales. They're full of violence,'" the performer continued. "I say that violence on television is different. Fairy tales were read at home by a parent who could comfort and explain. But on TV, there is a literal reality with no one to temper it as at home."

When Mr. Keeshan inaugurated his program four years ago he had certain ideas that time has not changed. He thought that children were intelligent beings who craved knowledge that could be gained by an entertaining approach. "Captain Kangaroo" is not a show, according to his philosophy, it is a visit.

"We can teach anything within reason," he said. "We've done programs on the inventions of Leonardo Da Vinci and Alexander Graham Bell, on submarines and the St. Lawrence Seaway—all this for children between 3 and 8.

"We may try something new soon," he went on. "During the year I have been appearing before audiences between the ages of 3 and 8 or 9 with symphony orchestras in various parts of the country.

"The executives at C. B. S.—and the network has done a lot in keeping the program on the air with an unmatched public service attitude—have asked us to design two, three or four such shows for possible use on Sunday afternoons," Mr. Keeshan explained. "There's been a great interest. After an hour, children are introduced, not formally, to a symphony orchestra."

Career

The performer started out classically in TV, as a page boy at the National Broadcasting Company. He was then a pre-law student at Fordham and had little idea of becoming an actor. But he was assigned to carry props on the "Howdy Doody" show.

Bob Keeshan.

Soon, he sported a clown's costume and became an integral part of the show. After five years, he left to work out his own project. He accomplished this on "Tinker's Workshop" on an American Broadcasting Company station. He eventually left Tinker and became Captain Kangaroo on C. B. S.

A possible future in adult television?

"Not for me," he said emphatically. "I think a lot that we use could be used in adult programs. They are often guided so much out of fear of a boring moment or two. But, just as actors are afraid of child audiences, because they're so honest, I would be scared stiff of going before the big folks."

August 30, 1959

FIFTH ANNIVERSARY FOR 'WELKISM'

By MURRAY SCHUMACH

HOLLYWOOD.

WELKISM is not yet a part of any musical dictionary but the music of Lawrence Welk, which will begin its sixth consecutive year on network television this month, has become as much a part of American patterns of popular music as progressive jazz, rock 'n' roll or Leonard Bernstein's mixture of classical and jazz music in Broadway musicals.

In his five years on American Broadcasting Company TV—an anniversary to be observed on his show this week—Mr. Welk's resistance to musical innovation has been admired stolidly by between 20,000,000 and 30,000,000 persons each Saturday evening. His forty-eight record albums and 600 single records have brought the cautious Welk style into millions of homes on a more permanent basis than his 250 Saturday night programs.

Mail

His mail from video admirers has averaged better than 3,000 pieces a week. Life in the balanced Welk world has been so smooth he still has the sponsor he signed with five years ago.

The man who went from self-taught accordionist on a North Dakota farm to musical mogul, with a home in the expensive Brentwood suburb of Hollywood, explained here the other day how one man's musical corn can be another's champagne. As befits a successful business man in his middle years, Mr. Welk was dressed soberly, spoke calm-

Lawrence Welk.

ly and was tolerant of those who find little excitement in his approach to music.

"We cater to the masses," he began. Mr. Welk, who looks upon his forty-four-piece orchestra with a paternal eye, is fond of using the first person plural. "We cater to the people who want a melody as it was originally written. Our audiences want songs that tell a story. We do not want any song with questionable moral standards. We always remember that our show is going into homes where children also watch us."

In selecting songs to please this audience, Mr. Welk does not bother with trade-paper reports of the latest hits. He used to. But he has decided that the favorites of the moment are too ephemeral to hold an audience that seeks what he considers fundamentals in music. Mr. Welk favors the established composition of Irving Berlin, Victor Herbert, Vincent Youmans, Rodgers and Hammerstein. Some of Cole Porter's pieces pass the Welk muster, but he is likely to turn a tin ear to "I've Come to Wive It Wealthily in Padua." "Songs like 'A Pretty Girl Is Like a Melody,'" Mr. Welk believes, "still have a lot to them."

Arranging

Contrary to some theories that Mr. Welk must do his own arrangements, he claims he has an annual budget of $50,000 for arrangements, with a staff of six or seven arrangers. He has had, he says, as many as eighteen men puttering with notes and orchestrations, to give them what he considers the proper bubbly effect that he calls "champagne music."

Mr. Welk is aware that, among pop musicians, he does not evoke unanimous enthusiasm.

"One time I hired an arranger," he said. "He was a good man. Knew his business. He started to give me an arrangement that was not for me. I explained to him what we did on our show. He said: 'If I have to write that kind of stuff, I would rather not write music'."

Mr. Welk feels badly about losing members of the show. He talks of them as though they were somehow related to his actual family of a wife, two daughters, one son and two grandchildren.

In arranging this family atmosphere, Mr. Welk begins planning his show about four weeks in advance, and actually working on it two weeks before he goes on from the Aragon Ballroom in Santa Monica, Calif. He figures a show for about twenty-two or twenty-three songs, with at least one polka, one waltz, one accordion solo and a half-dozen pieces with full orchestra, to include two or three in his champagne style.

In addition to Mr. Welk's office staff, which varies from ten to twelve persons, the American Broadcasting Company supplies between seventy and eighty persons to stage the show under his producer, Ed Sobel; his director, Jim Hobson, and his musical supervisor, George Cates.

"We have to be very careful about what we do," Mr. Welk pointed out. "Our audience is very fussy."

June 12, 1960

SIDEWALK 'SOCIOLOGY'

Allen Funt's 'Candid Camera' Relies On Human Reactions and Luck

By BERNARD STENGREN

SIMPLE ideas, and the spontaneous reactions they evoke in unsuspecting customers and passers-by when they are deviously and often risibly compounded, provide a livelihood for Allen Funt and a full-time staff of eighteen.

And, adds the keeper of the "Candid Camera," the response from those who watch the taped episodes on the Columbia Broadcasting System television network is sometimes almost as interesting as the reactions of the subjects of the episodes.

Mr. Funt, who has been hiding microphones and cameras in unlikely places since 1947, has been accused of "making people look silly," of baiting and badgering his subjects and of "unscrupulous tactics."

The reaction of the husky, 45-year old personality ranges from mild amusement at the first two of these accusations to scorn at the charge that he is unscrupulous.

The basic premise of "Candid Camera"—and of the "Candid Microphone" radio shows that preceded it—is that "people are able to laugh at themselves," he maintains.

"Pretty nearly everybody is able to do that," Mr. Funt adds. "It's when a viewer can't picture himself in the same situation that we get protests from those who didn't think the show was funny."

Mr. Funt, who regards himself as something of a sidewalk sociologist, conceded that a few years ago there was some merit in the "baiting" charge.

In this connection he recalls "the barber-shop incident" ruefully. The simple idea in this case was that some barbers try to sell all sorts of "extras" while they are cutting hair.

Barber

Taking the part of such a barber, Mr. Funt suggested, persisted, and finally insisted that the customer get a sunlamp treatment, scalp massage, tonic, and the like.

The man sat so quietly that the "barber" was completely unprepared when he leaped from the chair and began chasing Mr. Funt around the shop.

Whether that incident was responsible or not he will not say, but now in "Candid Camera" episodes no subject is provoked into doing something—"We depend on the idea, the subject, and the important element of luck to carry the ball.

What the husky ex-soldier chooses to call luck played a decisive role in "The Talking Mail Box," his own all-time favorite of the television series that was seen last season on the Garry Moore Show. Starting Oct. 9, the series will run for a full half hour Sundays at 10 P. M. on C. B. S.-TV immediately after the "Jack Benny Show."

In "The Talking Mail Box" episode the simple idea was that a person mailing a letter would be nonplussed if the mail box seemed to strike up a conversation with him.

One man was speechless for a moment, but then began holding a conversation with the mail box—which of course had a speaker and microphone concealed in it with a distant camera trained on the scene.

Then another passer-by happened on the scene, and the man told him that the mail box "talked." The newcomer scoffed and the first man offered to prove his point by asking the mail box to demonstrate. Mr. Funt, at a concealed microphone, said nothing.

In filming "Candid Camera" episodes, about 9,000 feet of film are shot to get the 450 feet needed for the five-minute spot that appeared last season. Each one of the persons photographed is asked to sign a release and given a dollar or more to bind the contract.

When the editing is done, those persons who appear in scenes that will be televised are paid an additional fee, based on the length of time they will appear and other factors. The average has been about $50.

The original idea for the show occurred to Mr. Funt when, in the Army, he was assigned to a service club to help G. I.'s make those phonograph records of their voices to be sent home.

Many of the soldiers, who chatted while preparations were made to cut the record, got "mike fright" when they saw the pointed finger that meant they were "on the air."

Mr. Funt found the pre-recording chatter so carefree and natural that he began recording before giving the signal. From this stemmed the idea that the spontaneous reaction of people to unexpected situations would have a wide audience appeal.

July 3, 1960

ANIMATED, YES—FRANTIC, NO

By MURRAY SCHUMACH

HOLLYWOOD.

THOSE who would seek out the lair of that great avenger of injustice, "The Purple Pumpernickel," will have to come to Hollywood. For it is here that Huckleberry Hound puts on such disguises as member of the French Foreign Legion, American fireman, London bobby, international veterinarian trying to extract a lion's aching tooth.

Since this hero's voice is always the same soothing Tennessee mountain talk, and his speeches are forever those of the same amiable mongrel, an estimated 16,000,000 Americans are satisfied to look for him eagerly on some 200 television stations on the half-hour program known as "Huckleberry Hound." It appears Thursdays at 6:30 P. M. on New York's Channel 11.

Domicile

The true home of Huckleberry Hound, however, is in a maze of corridors of three loosely connected buildings here, where Charlie Chaplin once made silent films. Huddled over drawing boards, the artists of William Hanna and Joseph Barberra put the good humor into Hucklberry's rubbery face; flatten the pork-pie hat on Yogi Bear's head; adjust the tie on Boo-Boo, the bear cub; plant the pompous smirk on Jinx, the cat, and the mischief in the eyes of his tormentors, Dixie and Pixie, the mice.

Though all these characters are but cartoons, their cereal-selling sponsors of nearly three years obviously find them more alive than most performers of the Westerns, private eyes, situation comedies and panel shows that fill most of television.

The atmosphere of the Huckleberry Hound residence is appropriately zany. Since all offices are cluttered, with doors either wide open or nonexistant, it is difficult to tell which are the offices of the bosses. Grown men will be down on their knees as though in a dice game. Actually they are examining a series of comic-strip panels known as a storyboard.

Messrs. Barberra and Hanna are proud of the informality of their enterprise and resent the word "factory" to describe their incessant output of television cartoons by the 150 employes who do, in addition to "Huckleberry Hound," "Ruff N Ready," "Quick Draw McGraw" and "The Flintstones," which will make its debut this fall.

"We have no time clocks here," said Mr. Barberra. "We have no closed doors and nobody makes appointments. They come in when they want and they leave when they want. All they make is money—and cartoons."

Transfer

Mr. Barberra vows that this Bohemian atmosphere will not change when, in the near future, the Huckleberry Hound workshop moves into a new air-conditioned building, with its own dining room and kitchen. He and Mr. Hanna did a twenty-year stretch in a movie factory called Metro-Goldwyn-Mayer, where they created a world-famous cartoon about a cat and a mouse called "Tom and Jerry."

Mr. Barberra, who wrote the first twenty-six installments of "Huckleberry Hound," recalls that when he first proposed the introduction of this character, one serious objection was raised. One of the sponsor's representatives was afraid that the name of the hero was a bit too long for a television screen.

The present author of the scripts is Warren Foster, a mild-mannered man, who worked on Bugs Bunny cartoons for twenty years and has a fondness for his creatures that transcends their employment record.

Huckleberry Hound.

"I think of Huck as human," he said. "He is a sort of Tennessee-type guy who never gets mad no matter how much he is outraged. He is the fall-guy, and a large part of his humor is the way he shrugs off his misfortunes. To Huck nobody is really bad."

Yogi Bear, the incurable filcher of picnic baskets from visitors to Jellystone Park poses two problems.

Since he is "bright in a stupid sort of way," his adventures must show ingenuity as well as blunders. Second, there is the problem of what to do about the morality of thievery. "So we let him get his picnic basket—and then we get him punished."

Feline

Mr. Foster is happy about the philosophical quality of the mice, Dixie and Pixie, toward the cat, Mr. Jinx. "The mice make allowances for the occasional attacks on them by Jinx. They understand he is not evil. He is just a cat and he can't help being himself. They are not disillusioned each time the cat's thin veneer of civilization cracks. The important thing in these stories is to keep out the rough stuff and mayhem."

One rule is applied to all the creations of the "Huckleberry Hound" series: all animals must have something around the neck—a tie, a collar, a scarf. This is not for good manners or cuteness, but because the neck camouflage makes it unnecessary to worry about whether the neck of a particular character looks the same each time it is drawn.

The motto of the House of Huckleberry is that children can understand a great deal more than adults realize. No script is "written down" to the child's level. The show is not afraid to use puns. Thus, when Yogi Bear was punished for stealing a witch's broom and riding around on it, stealing picnic lunches, he said:

"They lowered the broom on me."

Some connoisseurs of cartoon shorts think Huckleberry Hound and his friends have done the business a good turn.

"Disney's trend was more and more toward beautiful art," says Mr. Foster. "Huck and the others have restored cartoons to caricature and fun."

August 28, 1960

TV: Animated Cartoon

By JACK GOULD

ONE of the innovations announced for the current season was a half-hour situation comedy to be done in the format, of the animated cartoon. With so many sponsors making witty use of drawings — indeed some of the commercials have been more amusing than many of the shows—the prospect of such an entertainment series was both enticing and overdue.

Last night the event finally came to pass; "The Flintstones," conceived by the young men who won assorted prizes for "Huckleberry Hound," made its debut at 8:30 on Channel 7. Regrettably, the verdict cannot be pleasant; the show was an inked disaster.

•

The producers, William Hanna and Joseph Barbera, have concocted two married couples, the Flintstones and the Rubbles, and put them down in the town of Bedrock. The masculine figures are notably unattractive, coarse and gruff, and the women nondescript. The speaking voices assigned to the four characters are similarly not very tasteful.

Where it was presumed a Stone Age perspective would be applied to civilization's contemporary foibles, the thirty-minute cartoon turned out to be an extremely heavy-handed and labored effort. The humor was of the boff-and-sock genre, nothing light or subtle. The story was about how the men wanted to go to a bowling alley and the women to the opera; much of the action merely suggested the Three Stooges' capering on an easel.

The cartoon was accompanied by intrusive canned laughter to alert the home audience to the appropriate moments for reaction. The injection of such a mundane touch played complete hob with any sense of illusion or make-believe. So did the commercials in which the cartoon characters served as pitchmen for vitamins.

October 1, 1960

RAYMOND BURR: CLEAN CASES ONLY

He Chases Truth, Never Ambulances, In Role Of Perry Mason

A COUPLE of seasons ago Perry Mason did lose a case. This untoward event so startled his faithful courtroom viewers that his record as television's most notable defense counsel has been without blemish since. It is always possible, of course, that the accused will be guilty and the poor prosecutor who always gets the short end of the story will win one again in the future, but the odds are on the side of law, order, innocence and Raymond Burr (his name really isn't Perry Mason). The glass slipper can be counted upon to fit on Saturday night until Sept. 27 when he moves to Thursdays at 8 P. M.

Erle Stanley Gardner's famous detective-type of lawyer has changed a great deal on television. In at least one respect the transition from the movie Perry Mason to the TV Perry Mason reflects the way in which the most mass of mass media treats a Cinderella story. When Warren Williams played the criminal lawyer in the Nineteen Thirties, he was cunning, wily, indefatigable, clever, charming and so resourceful that he would be willing to step up to, if not overstep, the limits of the law for the sake of his client. As portrayed for the home audiences, by Raymond Burr, he is genial, soft-spoken, polite, patient, still clever, and dedicated to his clients in an ethical but not tricky way.

New Look

Della Street, too, has undergone a new look on television. In the books, which were often called "The Case of the . . .," Perry's secretary was usually more provocative and jealous of his beautiful clients, and there was a hint that if only Perry was not so darn wrapped up in his cases that they would have more time for extra-professional relations. Not so on the home screen, where Barbara Hale, while as attractive as any movie Della Street, plays the indispensable, faithful, intelligent Girl Friday, with only a hint of mint.

The changes in characterization, according to the in-life affable Raymond Burr, are a reflection of the changing times. "We've been on the air for five years," he said the other day, "and it took less than two seasons before all the original Erle Stanley Gardner stories were exhausted. He is a prolific writer, but the need for a weekly story used up more than sixty originals. Now the stories are contributed, but Mr. Gardner approves every line. The conception of the character on television is his."

The range of the programs enables "Perry Mason" to get away from murder. In a recent story, "The Case of the Promoter's Pillbox," Perry defended a young pharmacist who charged that his idea for a television show was stolen by a corrupt producer. The law drama that follows "Perry Mason" on C. B. S. on Saturday night, "The Defenders," handles more serious themes. E. G. Marshall, the lawyer in Reginald Rose's courtroom series, takes a legally more sophisticated view. In a recent story on "The Defenders" called "The Accident," the drama concerned the death of a child after an automobile accident when his parents, because of their religious beliefs, denied him surgery and a blood transfusion. Raymond Burr is an admirer of both E. G. Marshall and "The Defenders" on TV's court calendar.

Ambivalence

"There is Raymond Burr and there is Perry Mason," Mr. Burr said, his familiar blue-eyed stare giving him a convincing look of wisdom. "When I'm Perry Mason, I try to be true to the character and the story. When I'm Raymond Burr, I try to be true to myself."

Still, the imaginary world of the Prince Charming of the TV courtroom has encroached, in a most constructive way, on Mr. Burr's private activities. In the past year he has averaged a speech a week before civic organizations. When the series first began there was some criticism from lawyers who felt that this wasn't really the way it was, but nowadays many of his most avid viewers are members of the legal profession who recognize that "Perry Mason" is a drama and that Raymond Burr has given them a good name. He frequently speaks before lawyer groups. Few people know the name of the head of the bar association in their city but nearly everyone knows Raymond Burr as Perry Mason.

When May 1 was designated "Law Day, U. S. A." by Presidential proclamation, Burr stood up at the end of the broadcast and urged his viewers to share his own interest in legal processes. He asked them to rededicate themselves to the "inalienable right of all citizens to life, liberty and the pursuit of happiness, to equal protection by our laws and equal justice by our courts." Another of his related interests is accident prevention. He has played a strong role in the safety campaign of Greater Cleveland to cut its accident rate in half through public education, and he hopes that the success here will spread around the country.

Walking in Manhattan recently, he was stopped every few feet by shouts of "Hiya, Perry" or loudly whispered remarks, "There's Perry Mason." Passersby, recognizing his strong features, envisioned him not as the old villain he often portrayed in the movies but as Raymond Burr, their heroic defense counsel, Perry Mason, Esq.

HERBERT MITGANG.

August 5, 1962

Critic at Large

Cartoon Flintstones Possess Freshness Rarely Found in Acted TV Comedy

By BROOKS ATKINSON

SINCE Actors-Equity has co-existed with animated cartoons through most of its history it has taken no official action against "The Flintstones," now in its fourth season on American Broadcasting Company television.

But the comedians' section of Equity might consider a suit on grounds of unfair competition. No actor could duplicate the exuberant frenzy of Fred Flintstone, the Stone Age extrovert whose combination of bullheadedness and blundering—both in an excessive degree—is the weekly topic of a remarkably fresh cartoon. "Barney, you know I never have any trouble sleeping," he once gloomily observed to his pint-size buddy. "It's when I am awake that my troubles begin." Fred is a rugged individualist with a feeble brainbone.

•

If the cartoon elements could be scientifically analyzed, they would probably emerge as a version of the familiar big-man, little-man comedy—Mutt and Jeff, Bert and Harry Piel, etc. But William Hanna and Joseph Barbera, who invented the characters in 1960, lifted their cartoon out of mediocrity by setting it in the Stone Age. It is pure fantasy in the genre of "Alice In Wonderland." Although the Flintstones, and their next-door neighbors, the Rubbles, lead modern lives with modern equipment, they are Stone Age people who have domesticated Stone Age animals and birds to perform the household chores.

As a crane operator in the Rock Head and Quarry Construction Company, situated in Bedrock, Fred drives a patient dinosaur. The current introduction to the program pictures Fred sliding joyously down the back of the dinosaur when the whistle blows and yelling "ya-ba-da-badoo," which is his theme cry. The family pet in the home cave is a young dinosaur that obeys Fred's "Down, boy" literally by knocking Fred down and smothering him with kisses.

A starved buzzard under the sink is the garbage disposal, and an elephant's trunk is the kitchen faucet; a lizard with sharp teeth is the can opener; a mastodon with an evil look is the vacuum cleaner; a bitter crow with a sharp beak is the needle on the hi-fi set; a pterodactyl with gnashing teeth and a mean disposition is the lawn mower.

During the last season "The Flintstones" lost some of its original enthusiasm for the fantastic setting. It has become increasingly preoccupied with domestic affairs, like the birth of a bland, self-contained daughter, Pebbles, to Fred and Wilma. (Isn't Pebbles rather large for her age?) But the original genius of the cartoon was the comic ingenuity with which it played variations on the incongruous, inventive and humorous background of the Stone Age.

The traditional business of cartoons is to explore the battle between the sexes. After losing one round to Wilma recently, Fred said: "Why doesn't someone invent something but women for us to marry?" Both Wilma Flintstone and Betty Rubble are more sophisticated than their husbands and take appropriate action in defense of their prerogatives when necessary. There is nothing mean about any of them. But an ominous drop of sentimentality intruded on domestic dissonance the other day. After Fred had worn himself out trying to look after the baby and the house simultaneously, Wilma said: "Fred, you are the dearest bungler in the world." This expression of mawkish affection in a cartoon is wholly untraditional.

•

A sentimental cartoon is a contradiction in terms. It is getting close to the stuff that human beings act. On the drawing board, Fred and Barney are outside human scale. Everything they do is excessive. In their Stone Age model T they bounce through a grotesque landscape with superhuman speed and agility. At the meetings of the Order of Water Buffaloes they luxuriate with superhuman gusto. Thanks to the raciness of the cartoon medium, they are worth a hundred of the standard comedies, and they make actors look inept and anxious.

October 4, 1963

The G.A.P. Loves the 'Hillbillies'

Folks who look down their noses at TV's No. 1 show have it all wrong, this feller sez. In truth, it mocks pretension—a spectacle the Great American Public has always enjoyed.

By ARNOLD HANO

THE taste of the Great American Public—hereinafter G.A.P.—has often been a source of dismay, especially to a small, self-appointed culture cult that becomes especially pained when G.A.P.'s taste differs markedly from its own. Fads such as "The Music Goes 'Round and 'Round," hula hoops, Liberace, Ma and Pa Kettle, pegged pants, Hopalong Cassidy, Davy Crockett, the Twist and Liz Taylor arouse more than irritation in this high- and middle-brow cabal. The cult would really love to do something about it all—like quick, cheap burial. Each to his own taste (the cult says it in the original French, of course), but only if you can throw a picket line around the building where some of these eaches go forth to scratch.

One of the greatest sources of current dismay is a weekly half-hour television show called "The Beverly Hillbillies." It deals with a mountain clan which finds oil below its Ozark cabin and moves to Beverly Hills on a 1921 flatbed truck, laden with jugs of corn likker, $25,000,000, and a set of simple mores that remain unsullied, though tested weekly, by the wealthy city slickers of modern-day L.A.

Please do not get me wrong. I'm no "Hillbillies" lover. The show bores me. If I can think of a worse, cornier joke than "Do you know Shaw's Pygmalion?" "I don't even know Shaw, let alone his pig," it is: "Do you like Kipling?" "I don't know—I ain' never kippled." Both appeared in the same episode of "The Beverly Hillbillies."

THE Clampett clan is such that just by knowing their names—Jed, Granny, Elly May and Jethro—any student of comic strips could describe them. But the show is surely no national disaster, nor is it necessary for us to follow David Susskind's advice and write our Congressman (Susskind is alarmed that imitators may spring up and Hillbilly us to death).

The show premiered on Sept. 26, 1962, and if the producers were counting on the G.A.P.'s wanting to escape from the outside world into something safer and more comfortable, they could not have picked a better date. There had just been church burnings in Georgia. An 18-year-old East German had been shot and left to die while trying to scale the Berlin Wall. State troopers had again prevented James H. Meredith from entering the University of Mississippi campus. There was talk that the Russians were to finance a "fishing" port in Cuba. We were giving missiles to Israel. No progress was reported at the Geneva disarmament talks.

Within five weeks, "The Beverly Hillbillies" had become the most popular program on television. It has remained unvaryingly No. 1 well into its second season. Nielson estimates that over 36 million people watch it.

Adverse criticism greeted the program's debut, and continues. The show has been variously labeled—and these are verbatim quotes—an esthetic regression, mindless, stupid, a striking demonstration of cultural Neanderthalism, a shopworn formula of stock characters and hoary jokes, a home-brewed mash of malapropisms, clichés and vintage gags. Time magazine took offense at the show's addiction to puns, and accordingly headed its review; "The pone is the lowest form of humor." U.P.I.'s Rick Du Brow said: "The series aimed low and hit its target." Richard Warren Lewis, in The Saturday Evening Post, compared "The Hillbillies" with a Mickey Spillane best-seller in that both were "deliberately concocted for mass tastelessness."

TO these critics, the show was proof that television did indeed cling to the assumption that the G.A.P. has the intelligence and taste of a 12-year-old.

ARNOLD HANO lives near California's "Hillbilly" city and thus knows exactly what Jed, Jethro, Granny and the rest are up against.

Elly May, Jed, Granny, Jethro—Does the Clampett clan pack a message?

There is more than criticism in these comments; there is righteous indignation, outrage, the bellows of wounded men. For if the critics are correct in seeing the show as aimed at a feeble-witted audience, then the show's smashing success proves how huge this feeble-witted audience truly is.

Gone is the cult's momentary exultations arising from the turnstiles clicking at Lincoln Center. Gone is the cheerful belief that with President Kennedy, Newton Minow and Leonard Bernstein—pardon, *Lenny* Bernstein—at the helm, a mass cultural awakening had taken, and is taking, place. Thirty-six million people! How could they do this to us?

The cult is more frightened than it need be—by the above statistics, for one thing. Slightly over half of all television sets that are turned on at 9 o'clock on Wednesday evenings are turned to "The Hillbillies." Which means that nearly half aren't. Millions of other sets aren't turned on at all. We have more television receivers in this country than bathtubs—please don't lose me here, cultists, and go out agitating for more tubs—and 16 or 17 million of these receivers tuned to one particular program is still nothing more than a sizable minority. Seventy-five million people watched the first Kennedy-Nixon debate. Over sixty million saw Glenn's orbit. Perhaps people *are* going to those concerts.

More important, the squeals that the show is a cultural esthetic regression may be uncalled for. I have laid before you the body of adverse criticism leveled at the show. There has been some praise, and not just fan-magazine praise. Robert Lewis Shayon, in The Saturday Review of Jan. 5, 1963, saw in the program a contribution to social criticism. The show's value lay in what Shayon calls "its unendurable challenge to our money-oriented value system."

I am dubious about "unendurable." Surely there are some of us who welcome a challenge to a system of values that has proved itself so hollow. The culture cult exalts the masses. Shayon—here — underestimates them. But it is the notion that "The Hillbillies" is a contribution to social criticism that is intriguing.

It is easy to pass off the show as pure escape. Its creator and script writer, Paul Henning, says: "Our only message is — have fun." Yet members of the cast see the show as something more. Buddy Ebsen —the patriarch Jed — notes that the Clampett family took a piece of tanned hide in the truck with them when they came to Beverly Hills, although they were worth $25,000,000.

"These people used to sit out on the front porch back home and tap the soles back on their shoes. It is the way they always did it. Why change because they're rich? This is an almost novel idea today. We live in a throw-away economy. But must we?" (Ebsen is type-cast. Nothing in recent years offended him so much as President Kennedy's speech at Yale suggesting that a planned deficit was a good thing. Ebsen was shocked and ashamed; his sense of thrift had been violated.)

Donna Douglas — the nubile Elly May — thinks that whatever it is that the Clampetts have, "it is better, less frothy than the artificial, showy things of their Beverly Hills neighbors."

Irene Ryan — the irascible Granny—thinks the show represents one of the last folk traditions in America, the lives and culture of hill people.

Max Baer — the big, good-natured, stupid Jethro—points out the emphasis on family life, on respect for the family elders, on obedience to parental authority.

There is more, of course. People have always been fascinated by the phenomenon of one culture smacked up against another. It is "Alice in Wonderland," H. G. Wells's "When the Sleeper Wakes," "The Wizard of Oz." And, of course, there is the empathy one feels for the underdog. Each week we root for the Hillbillies to kick the whey out of their snooty neighbors, which leads me to believe further that to some of us—perhaps most — the challenge is not unendurable at all. We welcome it.

And more. You prowl the set of "The Hillbillies," and the third-floor executive suite of C.B.S.'s Hollywood offices, and people will tell you the show is a link with Charlie Chase, Chaplin, Harold Lloyd.

Robert F. Lewine, C.B.S. vice president in charge of programs on the West Coast, thinks it "may be the forerunner of a low comedy, away from the middle-class kitchen comedy we've had so much of —'Father Knows Best,' Danny Thomas, and the rest. We may be moving back to a more elementary American comedy —the slapstick of Buster Keaton, W. C. Fields, the appeal of the banana peel in the street."

Perhaps the most erudite member of "The Hillbillies" staff is the show's director, former Shakespearean actor Richard Whorf. Whorf lists all the conventional reasons the show is a hit: "You can turn on our show and you know that no one will be killed, no one will have a brain tumor. We will offend no group. No one will cry in earnest." He adds: "When an entertainer strives to educate he's in trouble."

Then Whorf goes beyond the notion that the show's roots lie with Chaplin, Lloyd and the comedians of the early days of movies. It reminds Whorf of the old Toby shows that have played the Mississippi River towns since Mark Twain's day, and still exist in hamlets of the hill country of Virginia, Kentucky and Tennessee. Toby — Whorf recalls — was an English country bumpkin, a rube outfitted in red wig, red nose, straw hat and straw suitcase, invariably waylaid on the road by a city slicker, over whom he was finally triumphant. "The picture of the hayseed triumphant is part of our tradition."

But these are only words. You cannot expect the company men to knock the product. We are at last thrown back on the show itself for further evidence that the culture boys are perhaps missing a bet. David Boroff, in an attack on "The Hillbillies" in The New Leader of Feb. 18, 1963, calls the program "a mélange of slapstick, bucolic *schmalz,* and backwoods exoticism. It is L'il Abner in Beverly Hills, but without Al Capp's corrosive point of view."

Still, consider. In an early "Hillbillies" episode — Oct. 31, 1962 — Granny returns to the Clampetts' 32-room mansion in a typically feisty mood.

"I been all through these 'Beverly Hills' and let me tell you it ain' easy! You got t' climb fences an' walls, jump over hedges, git aroun' them cement ponds, where they's usually a bunch o' half-nekkid people smearin' theirselves with oil, an' yellin' at you to git out! This place is full o' the laziest, greasiest, unfriendliest mess o' people I ever laid eyes on!"

On the same show, a Clampett eats a piece of wax fruit and complains of its lack of taste. Jed suggests maybe the fruit isn't supposed to be eaten.

Granny: "That's the trouble with this mis'uble place, y' ain't *s'posed* t' do nothin'! Ain't s'posed t' keep cows er pigs er chickens . . . ain't s'posed t' plow up th' ground an' plant corn er rye er 'falfa . . . ain't s'posed t' fire up th' still an' make a little moonshine whiskey! Answer me this—what *kin* y' do in Beverly Hills?"

And Jed answers: "Well—we kin talk t' our friends on th' telephone." Which, it turns out, they cannot do, because they have no friends in Beverly Hills.

Later — all in the same episode, mind you — Granny

sits in her hickory rocker at the edge of the swimming pool and fishes. She hooks something, and draws up a plastic toy fish, deflated. Granny looks at, this strange species and says:

"There's Beverly Hills fer you! All flashy an' show on th' outside, but nothin' inside where it counts."

The irreverence takes other forms. Granny drinks her corn likker and *enjoys* it. Elly May is given a ball gown—and promptly plays ball in it. With the boys. These people are natural. They are vulgar without being dirty. The son of a Beverly Hills banker comes calling on Elly May.

Sonny: "Is Elly May ready?"

Granny: "She shore is! She's been ready since she was 14!"

And a debutante sees the muscular Jethro.

Deb: "Permit me to present myself to you."

Jethro: "Well, thanks, but I don' think Uncle Jed'll let me keep y'."

In one episode we see Granny getting ready to fix a meal: a bowl of toad soup to begin with, then possum stew, grits n' jowls, cornpone, pickled crawdads, whatever they are. Immediately we swoop into the home of a typically snooty Beverly Hills family. It's still breakfast time there — they're having caviar and champagne.

PERHAPS all this is not corrosive enough, but it is a twitting of shallowness and of pretentiousness. A contemporary English playwright, Norman Frederick Simpson, says more or less the same thing: "I don't think life is excruciatingly funny. People traveling every day on the tube and doing things which are a means to an end, but become ends in themselves, like buying cars to get about on weekends and spending every weekend cleaning them."

This is the target of the Beverly Hillbillies. They wash the truck when it's dirty (if they wash it at all). A striptease dancer says to Elly May: "Your dad's got 25,000,000 bucks. Why do you wanna work at all?"

November 17, 1963

SULLIVAN'S SHOWMANSHIP: SINGERS TO SIMIANS

By MICHAEL J. BANDLER

WHEN Ed Sullivan's weekly potpourri of glee clubs, Broadway original casts, native dancers, acrobats, jugglers, comedians and animals takes over a TV studio on Sunday evenings, both breathing and loitering spaces are at a premium.

The backstage area at Sullivan's midtown studio is only 25 feet long, and performers must await their turns in upstairs dressing rooms, in downstairs men's room, on staircases (where the 95-man West Point Glee Club lined up) or, in the case of monkeys, dogs, bears, tigers and elephants, in trucks parked outside. Thirty-six singers and dancers from the cast of "The Girl Who Came to Supper" recently bided their time in their *own* dressing rooms in the Broadway Theater.

However, week after week for the last 15 and a half years, Sullivan has presented "live" the most unusual agglomerations of talent with a minimum of backstage confusion. When two elephants appeared several months ago, they simply were led out of

Larry Fried from Pix

Ed Sullivan, host, checks the off-camera cue card before announcing the next act.

IN THE WINGS AT THE ED SULLIVAN SHOW

The Sunday night variety program goes on amidst turmoil and confusion, working puppets, tigers and people, with only an occasional hitch. Below, some of the performers on last week's show wait for their turn before the camera.

Carmel Quinn and dancers relax before their entrance. The Irish singer was one of the headliners on the show's salute to St. Patrick.

Technicians watch the Dave Clark Five performing.

Pat O'Brien, right, waits quietly backstage before opening his bag of Irish humor for TV audience.

their truck, through a sliding door in the loading area on the street, and onto the stage.

Although the show is normally presented without hitches, the columnist-host can't forget the time he booked a bear months in advance, sight unseen. "When she arrived to perform," Sullivan recalls, "we discovered she was pregnant."

Backstage consensus is that elephants follow the script exactly, seals make too much noise, and multiple acts, such as one combination of ponies, poodles, Afghan hounds and monkeys, are potential troublemakers.

Bob Precht, producer, said that tigers present a timing problem. "Because of their temperament they must be permitted to complete their act or they will become enraged." A tiger act, therefore, may run well over the allotted time.

Sullivan calls the May 19, 1957 appearance of the Clyde Beatty tigers "the roughest act I've ever featured." On that occasion, one beast chased the veteran trainer from the caged area. An assistant to the producer remembers freezing as 900 pounds of tiger meat hurtled against the bars inches from where he was standing in the wings.

Sullivan's weekly assortment of men and beasts is the longest-running weekly live variety show of television, and at present is the only in-person entertainment hour on the video tubes.

Why does Sullivan insist on live television, with the possibility of a muffed line, a missed cue or a major embarrassment ever staring him in the face?

"You can't pretend to be spontaneous," he explained last week. "A taped program lacks a certain earthiness ... a light will go out, something will be said wrong; that's okay. I'd rather have something go wrong and let the people know that the show is live than to correct and polish a tape."

He recalled the night that Frankie Laine appeared in a ranch setting with a horse in the background. "The beast was not housebroken, and unfortunately for Frankie, we couldn't get the animal out of camera range in time. To top it off, the song Frankie was introducing was 'I Believe'!"

One of the host's pet peeves is the whining comedian or manager "who comes into my dressing room and says, 'You gave me five minutes and I need seven.' That's rougher than any animal act." He also cannot tolerate backstage chatter during airtime, which is sometimes difficult to control, especially when thirty-odd people—stagehands, performers, managers, wardrobe mistresses, guards, photographers—all crowd into the tiny space.

But of all the confusing moments in the annals of the show, few stand out like the arrival of Augspurg's Jungle Wonders last fall. Midway through the monkeys' prepared antics, one went berserk and began a paw-fight with a bigger simian. On and on the brawl raged, much to the delight of the unknowing audience. When it was over, the jungle "terrors" had succeeded in using up the time of the next act as well.

As the bewildered trainer left the stage, he muttered, "I've been looking for a good ending to that act for 15 years!"

March 22, 1964

TV: Evening Soap Opera on A.B.C.

'Peyton Place' Returns in Cleaner Version

By JACK GOULD

ALLISON, Constance, Betty, Mike Rossi, Rodney, Catherine and Leslie, seven frustrations with but a single thought, ushered in a new television era last night, soap opera in the evening.

The celebrated residents of "Peyton Place" came to the home screen under the nervous auspices of the American Broadcasting Company, which is serializing their expectations and subsequent anxieties at 9:30 P.M. Tuesdays and Thursdays. If all goes well the network may add Wednesdays.

The sanitized derivation from the late Grace Metalious's novel will undoubtedly be greeted with understandable dismay by some viewers, who will wonder where TV will descend next. If so, it will just go to show that they don't know what's been going on. By the present, if little publicized, standards of daytime soap opera, "Peyton Place" is highly conventional.

•

In purchasing the rights to "Peyton Place," the A.B.C. network acquired at one effortless stroke the basic need of a soap—a setting of dark unpleasantness that is the approved milieu for upstairs brinkmanship.

But where Paul Monash, the executive producer of the TV serial, encountered instant difficulties was in the awesome task of exposition. Since he paid for all the liaisons he apparently felt he had to use them. Two by two everybody goes up to the volcano's edge only to be left there while Mr. Monash trudges back to the waiting queue and brings on the next couple. For evening wear, a soap should unroll its passions more leisurely, not on a Yo-yo. The premiere was almost a satire of soaps.

It would be nice to think that "Peyton Place" will perish of its own opening night boredom, and conceivably it could. But the odds are not encouraging. The program has nowhere to go in coming weeks but toward

Premiere of Serial Is Almost a Satire

more contemplated consideration of the individual dilemmas of the distraught New Englanders. Then will come the soap opera's hypnotic appeal of sharing in intimate close-up the ordeal of others coping with temptation and surrender. There is no greater box office than life on the verge.

In its introductory sequence, "Peyton Place" was fairly skillful in creating the reckless mood of ominous restlessness designed to last until the next installment. What remains to be seen is whether the viewer will sit on his cliff from Thursday night until the following Tuesday, which is a long time to wait, and see whether the protagonists did or didn't.

As Allison, Mia Farrow is notably effective in suggesting the hesitant girl on the threshold of womanhood. Dorothy Malone, playing Constance, was impressive as the mother with her residue of unspent affection. Distaff viewers may have an entirely different opinion, but most of the TV men in "Peyton Place" have the dullness that goes with one-track minds. The settings and camera work were first-class.

•

The disquieting aspect of the evening presentation of "Peyton Place," of course, is to introduce the youthful nighttime audience to all the Metalious sordidness, to make a household attraction of love and romance bereft of the slightest redeeming trace of beauty, to dwell on a community that never knows the exhilaration of wholesome laughter. It is hard to down the thought that something else could have been chosen to fill an hour of nighttime TV.

But it might be well to note that it was the book publishing industry that first unloosed the blight of "Peyton Place" and that untold millions of adults obtained copies of the book in fine stores and libraries so they could cluck their disapproval with personal authority. If self-appointed censors scream out against A.B.C., it would be interesting to learn if they looked only at their picture tubes or also in their mirrors.

September 16, 1964

Ponderosa Gold Under A Painted Sky

By JOANNE STANG

HOLLYWOOD.

IF you've just gotten off the Freeway and are looking for the Ponderosa, pardner, don't look among the tall trees. The Ponderosa is over on the Paramount lot, bounded on the south by those pink and pistachio Hollywood bungalows, and on the north by the Hollywood Cemetery. You don't have to be a woodsman to find the "Bonanza" cast either, just follow the gaggle of ladies to where Lorne Greene, Dan Blocker, Michael Landon and Pernell Roberts are riding in front of the hand-painted sky. And that dust—stirred up by the horses' hooves and filtering down from the rafters—that dust, pardner, is 14-karat gold.

In its sixth year on television "Bonanza" is a popular phenomenon. Consistently at or near the top of all the rating polls, it is watched by an estimated quarter billion viewers around the world each week, supports a small army of writers, directors and technicians, and has made many people immensely wealthy, notably its cast. All of this has emanated from a formula contrived from one father figure (Greene), one large comic (Dan Blocker), a "deep" son (Roberts)—presumably for all the intellectuals watching the show—and one juvenile (Landon), a man who has five children of his own at home, the oldest 16, but who—on television—is still asking, "Pa, can I have the horse tonight?"

•

Why this particular combination should be so persuasive is something nobody has quite figured out, and the pervading philosophy is "why bother?" The show is so firmly entrenched with the public that every year hordes of people appear in Virginia City seeking the Cartwright family burial plot. The Queen of England is reputed to be a fan. During the summer school vacation, the "Bonanza" set is a tourist attraction second only to Disneyland. With all this going for them "Bonanza" principals are apt to heed that famous nautical admonition "don't make waves," but some changes are already in the works, principally the departure of Pernell Roberts.

Roberts, a man with a faintly maniacal smile, whose conversation is peppered with interesting Elizabethan allusions, looks at you sincerely and says, "I feel I am an aristocrat in my field of endeavor. My being part of 'Bonanza' was like Isaac Stern sitting in with Lawrence Welk." Roberts complained for several seasons that the "Bonanza" scripts had the intrigue of an elementary reader. He scored NBC on their "lack of imagination" in shying away from more controversial stories, and accused them of "perpetuating banality and contributing to the dehumanization of the industry." There may be some merit in these observations, but it is vitiated by the fact that Roberts arrived to deliver them on a motorcycle—wearing helmet

DAN BLOCKER
There's virtually no change in the characterizations

and goggles—and sounded more pompous than any network vice-president stereotype.

Not signing for another "Bonanza" stretch may cost Roberts in excess of a million dollars a year, but he claims it will be worth it not to have to be "a cowboy in pancake make-up on a show where the horses face the only real challenge as actors." Producer David Dortort is regretfully writing him out of next season's shows—physically, at least. From time to time the scripts will mention that he is "traveling" or "studying abroad." Killing him off is out, according to Dortort, "because the 'Bonanza' audiences are so loyal they would expect the whole family to go into mourning," casting a pall over the old corral.

Strictly speaking, "Bonanza" is not just a television program any more, but rather a minor industry, and as such it inspires a peculiar reverence in its staff. "Bonanza" scripts are handled and referred to as

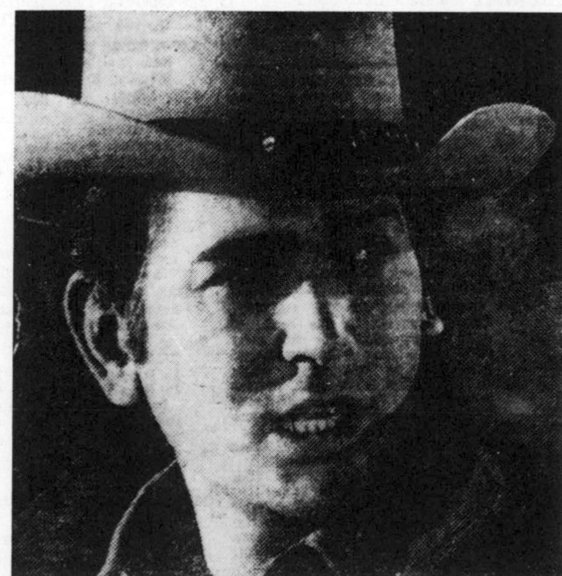

Photographs by Paul W. Bailey

MICHAEL LANDON
Pa, can I have the horse tonight?

though they were fragments of the Dead Sea Scrolls. Publicists flutter around the stars like details of nervous duennas, and all facets of the show are spoken of strictly in the superlative. Dortort, who may be more attuned to reality, says merely that he believes the show is successful because of its ingredients: "good humor, drama, wholesome fun, and a sense of the great American West."

Greene, Blocker and Landon remain, apparently perfectly contented. If subjects like contracts and residuals are mentioned, they are honest enough to take on the unabashedly gleeful expressions of men who have discovered it isn't raining rain at all, it's raining stocks and bonds. When big, booming Lorne Greene sits down to lunch, phrases like "a million and a half" and "4,000 acres near Bakersfield" waft away from the table. Greene, a Canadian who was the voice of the CBC during World War II and who often appeared in the Shakespeare productions at Stratford, Ont., travels an average of 26,000 miles a month doing public appearances, mostly on weekends. He has built a replica of the Ponderosa on the edge of a golf course in Arizona, which he calls a "swinging, beautiful house," but only got to sleep in it twice last year.

•

Greene, Blocker and Landon have the ingratiating characteristic of apparently wanting to share their good fortune. Striding through a group of children, or chatting with the visitors who fringe the set every day, they exude a "Shucks, we're just folks, too" kind of warmth which sounds and feels genuine, and anyway apparently satisfies the customers. They work at a fairly brutal pace, either on the set or in Oregon, Nevada, the High Sierras or Ventura County, Calif., where the outdoor shots are filmed.

A big problem is keeping the characters fresh. Blocker, who once taught in the Sonora (Texas) High School, says, "There's virtually no change in the characterizations, week to week. They're all so defined, and there's so much sameness, that it would be easy just to coast. But we all try to keep the lines from sounding stale—to think up bits to keep them fresh." Greene admits this is tricky. "It takes discipline not to retreat to the same reactions every time. After all, how many ways can you give a boy advice?" Landon, an athletic former U.S.C. javelin-thrower who does most of his own stunts and fighting on "Bonanza," summed up the general attitude with, "Sure, the work is hard, and sometimes it's difficult to bring anything new to the scripts, but for all of us the Ponderosa is kind of a golden land. A 'Bonanza' is something that happens to an actor once in a lifetime—if he's fantastically lucky—and I'd be a stupid fool not to enjoy it."

May 30, 1965

Dr. Kildare

Richard Chamberlain is in the title role and Raymond Massey plays Dr. Leonard Gillespie. Produced by Norman Felton. 8:30 to 9 P.M., Mondays and Tuesdays, on N.B.C.

The evening serial appears on its way to becoming one of the reigning formats of TV. Dr. Kildare, who had worked one hour a week, is now on a split shift, 30 minutes on Monday and 30 on Tuesday. Moreover, each story of the vicissitudes at Blair Hospital will run at least four installments to make sure that the viewer does not precipitously kick the habit of caring.

Kildare is being toughened up for his revised schedule of ward duty. In his inaugural confrontation with a difficult senior surgeon (James Mason), Mr. Chamberlain has been positively surly, not merely the bland young resident. Mr. Massey's portrayal remains fixed, the Abe Lincoln of the American Medical Association. The dialogue is making more mention of a possible Mrs. Kildare and a pretty nurse is slated to have a stronger continuing role. If the injections of B-12 drama vitamins help Kildare, look for a deluge of continuing stories in nighttime TV. It may not be long before the critics will look back on the middle 1960's as Jim Aubrey's golden years.

September 15, 1965

TV Review

N.B.C. Offers 'Ironside,' With Raymond Burr

By JACK GOULD

A TELEVISION spin-off from the motion picture "Ironside" was introduced at 8:30 last night on Channel 4 with Raymond Burr playing the role of the detective in a wheelchair. The hour was a tepid whodunit of very modest interest over the network of the National Broadcasting Company.

After Mr. Burr's many TV years as the defense counsel of the "Perry Mason" series, the viewer may require a moment or two to adjust to the actor's character switch to the side of the law. But the change imposes no major difficulties: Mr. Burr afoot or on wheels is very much the same man, the predictable investigative genius who finds the decisive clues that others miss.

Mr. Burr's maiden assignment was to unravel a robbery at a race track, and with the help of an ultraviolet light he learned where the loot had been hidden. In dialogue and plot the outing was completely conventional and the element of characterization distressingly automated. Except for the van that enables the chair-bound detective to enjoy a degree of mobility, the hour-long film was devoid of discernible innovation and "Ironside" was merely another routine chase seeking to capitalize on Mr. Burr's prominence as the star.

•

The actor's substantial personal following could wish that he had been confronted by a greater challenge of wits and a genuinely different environment because last night any distinction between his interpretation of Mason and Ironside was difficult to uncover. On TV, however, type casting seems to be the sure path to profit so any quarrel on that score undoubtedly is entirely academic. But where "Perry Mason" had the dramatic virtue of a courtroom confrontation, "Ironside" is but one of video's endless assortment of stereotyped pursuits.

September 15, 1967

'With Only Five Seconds to Live . . .'

By BURT PRELUTSKY

HOLLYWOOD.

EVERY television series gets up a book known as a writer's guide. Its contents include sections on all its characters, its format, its standing sets, as well as answers to many varied questions about the show.

On the first page of the "Star Trek" guide, Producer Gene Roddenberry poses the following challenge to potential script writers: "Can you fine the major 'Star Trek' format error in the following 'teaser' from a story outline?

"The scene is the bridge of the U.S. (United States Spaceship) Enterprise. Capt. Kirk [William Shatner] is at his command position, his lovely but highly efficient female Yeoman at his side. Suddenly and without provocation, our Starship is attacked by an alien space vessel. We try to warn the alien vessel off, but it ignores us and begins loosening bolts of photon energy-plasma at us.

"The alien vessel's attack begins to weaken our deflectors. Mr. Spock [Leonard Nimoy] reports to Capt. Kirk that the next enemy bolt will probably break through and destroy the Enterprise. At this moment we look up to see that final energy-plasma bolt heading for us. There may be only four or five seconds of life left. Kirk puts his arms about his lovely Yeoman, comforting and embracing her as they wait for what seems certain death.

FADE OUT.

"Please check one:

"[ ] *Inaccurate terminology.* The Enterprise is more correctly an international vessel, the *United* Spaceship Enterprise.

"[ ] *Scientifically incorrect.* Energy-plasma bolts could not be photon in nature.

"[ ] *Unbelievable.* The Captain would not hug pretty Yeoman on the bridge of his vessel.

"[ ] *Concept weak.* This whole story opening reeks too much of 'Space Pirates' or similar bad science fiction.

"No, we're not joking. The preceding page was a very real and important test of your approach to science fiction. Here's why.

"[ ] *Inaccurate terminology.* Wrong, if you checked this. Sure, the term "United States Spaceshp" was incorrect, but it could have been fixed with a pencil slash. Although we do want directors, writers and actors to use proper terminology, this error was certainly far from being the major 'Star Trek' format error.

"[ ] *Scientifically inaccurate.* Wrong again; beware if you checked this one. Although we do want to be scientifically accurate, we've found that selection of this item usually indicates a preoccupation with space and gadgetry over people and story.

"[ ] *Concept weak.* Wrong again. It is, in fact, much like the opening of one of our best episodes of last year. 'Aliens,' 'enemy vessels,' 'sudden attack' and such things can range from 'Buck Rogers' to classical literature, all depending on how it is handled (witness H. G. Wells' novels, Forester's sea stories, and so on).

"Understanding the right answer to this is basic to understanding the 'Star Trek' format. This was the correct answer:

"[ ] *Unbelievable.* Why the correct answer? Simply because we've learned during a full season of making visual science fiction that believability of characters, their actions and reactions, is our greatest

Frank Carroll

Spacemen Leonard Nimoy and William Shatner of "Star Trek."
The hippies think they're psychedelic

need and is the most important angle factor."

In other words, the captain would *not* start hugging his lovely Yeoman when total destruction of his spaceship seemed imminent. Not Capt. Kirk!

Science fiction has been notably unsuccessful on TV. The fact that "Star Trek" has made it into a second season, on NBC Fridays at 8:30, makes it an exception. Its success must be attributed to creator-producer Roddenberry and his insistence on the credibility factor. For this reason, he urges his writers not to get too wrapped up in the wonder of it all. "People aren't going to stop eating or sleeping or getting dressed in a few hundred years. We're trying to imagine, based on what we know today, what they'll most likely be eating or wearing or thinking."

On Stage 9, at Desilu, I spoke to the two stars, William Shatner and Leonard Nimoy.

*

Canadian-born Shatner, who portrays the captain of a 400-man spaceship on a mission hundreds of years in the future, is about 35 and wears a hair piece. I asked him to compare the current season to the first. "Our scripts are better. Our shows are more finely tuned. Last year there were too many problems still to be solved. How do you make what's essentially a military adventure the basis for a sympathetic story?"

Shatner is a rare species, hardly the type you expect to find starring in a TV series. No one discovered him parking cars on the Strip and he's not the nephew of an agent, and he can count to 20 without taking off his shoes. He's a trained actor with such credits as the Stratford, Ont., Shakespeare Festival, "Tamburlaine" and "A Shot in the Dark" on Broadway; TV guest appearances and various movie roles.

I wondered why he had gotten tied down to a TV series, which, while better than most, is still no earth shaker, and makes few demands on Shatner's acting abilities. "To tell you the truth, I'd turned down a good number of TV series, including 'Dr. Kildare' and 'The Defenders,' because at the time the thinking was that anyone associated with a series would become too identified with one character. But then people coming off TV series were beginning to make it in movies, so I made a couple of pilots that didn't sell and one, "For the People," that did. We shot it in New York and it was pretty good. But we went on opposite 'Bonanza' and lasted just 13 weeks. The day after we were canceled Gene Roddenberry called and asked me to see a pilot of 'Star Trek.' He had already shot it and NBC had liked it, but they wanted it done with a different cast."

Shatner would naturally like to see the show run for at least three seasons, so that it could go into syndication. After that? "I'm hopeful to go on to movies and the stage. I played Broadway and made movies, but I wasn't going far enough fast enough. I was in a category a lot of young actors are in—I played leading roles. But in a recent Photoplay poll, I was one of the top 10 favorites—because of 'Star Trek.' And I haven't made a movie in over two years!"

He feels "Star Trek" appeals to a widely varied audience. "It has action-adventure, with lots of fights and villains, so the kids like it. On another level we deal with a philosophical concept—that what's alien isn't necessarily evil—so we reach their parents. Many of our episodes deal with scientific concepts, so our program entertains the technicians and space scientists. And with the hippies we have a far-out show. *They* think we're psychedelic."

Nimoy, who plays Spock, the pointy-eared science officer on the spaceship, agrees with Shatner about the wide appeal of the show, and attributes it, as Roddenberry does, to its credibility. "I taught acting classes out here for five years before all this started. Most of my acting has been in television, and I find 'Star Trek' a notch above TV in general. If you're an actor, offered a running part on a TV series, the enticements are great. Most actors, therefore, have to rationalize their roles. But in my case I have an interesting character to work with."

To the question what makes Mr. Spock so appealing from an actor's point of view, he answered, "Obviously he's not a cliché; he's not a re-vamp of any other character—he's not a sheriff or a deputy or a lawyer or the guy next door—he's not even human!"

The man who dreamed up the show, Roddenberry, is a former poet, former airlines pilot, and former Los Angeles cop. "I always wanted to be a poet, but when I got married and started to raise a family, I realized it was impossible on what a poet earns. So, after the war, I went to work for the airlines. Then in 1948 I decided to get into TV writing. I came to Hollywood. Unfortunately, I got out here before television did. So I joined the police department. I was on it for five years and it was great experience; you get a look at life, at real emotions." He finally broke into TV by selling a script, naturally, to "Dragnet."

The fact that "Star Trek" is the most successful science fiction show to have emerged on TV (discounting "Twilight Zone" which was essentially supernatural) is a good sign. In a genre that generally goes overboard on BEM's (bug-eyed monsters, as they're known in the trade) and weirdo sound effects, "Star Trek" has stressed scientific honesty. And it has a suggestion of a theme. "The point we'd like to bring home," says Roddenberry, "is that we—on earth—have the choice of living together or dying together." He'll attempt to stress this point by introducing before long a Russian character as a crewman aboard the ship.

Expressing admiration for Roddenberry and his concept of "Star Trek," actor Nimoy nevertheless quipped, "But let's keep in mind that anyone who's been a cop can't be *all* good."

October 15, 1967

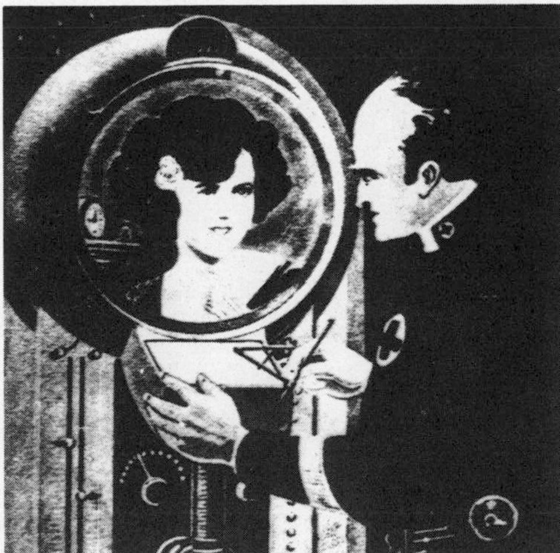

SEEN FROM AFAR—For romantic and other reasons, a form of TV was conjured up as long ago as 1911.

'Young Cops With a Soul'

By JUDY STONE

LOS ANGELES.

IN Chicago at the Democratic Convention, a very scruffy hippie carefully photographed a reporter from The London Observer. Later the reporter, to his surprise, observed the hippie flash a badge in a leather wallet at a policeman. The hippie was, of course, a cop.

It could have been a scene right out of ABC's new TV series, "The Mod Squad." But television's "young cops with a soul," as the publicity fellows neatly put it, won't be making their debut until this Tuesday at 7:30, in a special 90-minute introduction on ABC-TV. Thereafter, "The Mod Squad" will revert to the traditional one-hour segment.

Little else will be traditional, the network implied in a full-page, self-congratulatory ad announcing the series, which proclaimed that ABC is "not afraid to change, to be a little different, to be *unconventional*" (ABC's italics.) "The police don't understand the now generation and the now generation doesn't dig the fuzz. The solution — find some swinging young people who live the beat scene, get them to work for the cops."

*

The idea provokes cynical laughter among the "now generation," but the series may not, if a sneak preview of one upcoming segment is any indication. In it, the three young members of the Los Angeles police department's mod squad are assigned the job of tracking down the murderer of a popular high-school history teacher. To do this the three infiltrate the school.

The Negro member of the squad, Lincoln Hayes, supposedly recruited by the police after being picked up during the Watts riots, becomes the substitute replacing the murdered teacher. The second character, Pete Cochran, a wealthy rebel who had been arrested in a stolen car, gets a job as gym teacher. The third, Julie Barnes, a runaway teen-ager who had been booked for vagrancy, poses as a new student. In the process of solving the crime, the show deftly sketches some current social tensions as it depicts the relationship between a black teacher and his students, and the students' suspicion of the police. There is even criticism of the way in which Civil War history is taught in our schools today.

All three of the actors in "The Mod Squad" have definite feelings about the show — and their roles. Clarence Williams III, who plays Lincoln Hayes, says: "If people think of us as finks, the show won't come across. And I don't think I'd like to be in a show that gave that idea."

*

For Michael Cole, 24, an inarticulate Wisconsin drifter who purposely incorporates his own misgivings about himself into the part of Pete Cochran, "nothing was ever with any longevity" until now. Personally he feels unrelated to the police, is "very concerned" about the human beings he has to deal with in the series. The show is a "blessing" to him: "For the first time in my life, I've put myself into perspective. I feel the settledness within my soul."

Ted Shepherd

Clarence Williams III is an undercover agent for the Los Angeles police in "The Mod Squad," the ABC series which will have its premiere Tuesday at 7:30.
"I'm doing TV, not the second act of 'Hamlet'"

Blonde Peggy Lipton, 21, who plays Julie, comes from the security of an upper middle-class home in Lawrence, Long Island. She has never "disobligated" herself from society, but she said stanchly there were certain things she would never do in front of a camera, like "bust someone for smoking grass or hit anybody over the head with a billy club."

Clarence Williams, whose acting and personality dominate the squad, attended the Food Trades Vocational High School in Harlem, and got hooked by the acting bug at the YMCA. Later he made a hit on Broadway with his brilliant performance in "Slow Dance on the Killing Ground." He finds it a drag to be asked how he feels about playing an undercover agent. With his gold-rimmed glasses, he looks studious and intense; the sense of bottled-up passion is there even when he speaks quietly, considering each phrase, but then some questions uncork him and a torrent of words pours out, his voice rises, and you feel as if the pent-up vitality and frustration of all black youth in the country have suddenly engulfed you.

"I'm in an awkward position," he said at his attractive A-frame house in a sheltered grove in Laurel Canyon. "My whole thing now is thank God we're getting some black faces on the tube. Some reporters asked me if I didn't think Negroes were being overemphasized on TV. I said, 'No, years ago when I watched Caucasians on TV, I didn't think *they* were overemphasized.'" When he haunted movie houses as a youngster, he didn't dream of being an actor "because I never saw any black people on the screen."

*

About 25 per cent of the actors on "The Mod Squad" series are Negroes, estimates Aaron Spelling, the executive producer and partner in Thomas/Spelling Productions. "I try to keep away from Negro secretaries with one line to speak. A lot of producers in this town are using

Negroes because it's the 'in thing.' Just to say 'Let's use a Negro cop so they won't get mad at us' doesn't mean anything. I think we must present them as intelligent people with the terrible needs they have. We have one episode, 'When Smitty Comes Marching Home' with Louis Gossett, that shows a Negro war hero coming home from Vietnam and he's not accepted. He left here a second-class citizen and comes home a third-class citizen. Two months ago, we needed Negroes for some crowd scenes, but we couldn't find them in the Screen Extras' Guild. Not enough people had the $150 initiation fee. We paid the fee for one girl and called up a lot of studios and worked out a deal so that Negro extras can work and pay off the fee on a weekly basis."

"If you're interviewing a white actor," Williams said, "you can talk about McLuhan or the wasteland on TV, but when you interview a black actor, the material is secondary. Of course, if it's derogatory or negative, who needs it? I'd love to be doing the life stories of black men like Charles Drew, who organized blood banks, or Jan Matzeliger, whose invention of the lasting machine revolutionized the shoe industry. These would be groovy specials—like those on Pasteur or Zola — but we're not doing that. Lincoln Hayes is trying to make it, he's trying to adjust in this world, but the odds are against him."

"Linc's also trying to make a contribution," Williams's wife, actress Gloria Foster, added. She wears a natural hairdo like her husband, her round face glows with a spontaneous warmth that complements her husband's own, and they obviously share enormous pride in each other. Miss Foster won an Obie for her performance in "In White America," and she had the title roles in "Yerma" and "Medea" in New York. In Hollywood, she has been cast in three upcoming segments of ABC-TV's "The Outcasts."

"Lincoln Hayes blew a lot of opportunities," her husband continued, "and the system blew more of them for him. He was involved in the Watts riots. But once he goes to work for the police, technically, you could use a term for him like undercover agent, I guess.

"If you're asking whether I have reservations about the police," Williams said, "yes. In most cases, it's justified. There are reservations, too, about black police; some people think they're part of the power structure that is oppressing them.

"But I don't care what the stereotype may be. Basically, I'm trying to derive some entertainment out of 'The Mod Squad' and maybe along the way something will be said, like in 'South Pacific,' a beautiful entertainment. I know a little about the streets. I used to write numbers. I've seen police take bribes. I do know that a lot of officers love to get these jobs in the ghetto because they can shake people down. I know what's going on, but that has nothing to do with a TV show. I'm not appearing on the show each and every week to seduce people into believing in their police departments. I'm not a social expert. I'm not trying to elongate this poison.

"I'm doing TV, for God's sake, not the second or third act of 'Hamlet.' 'Mod Squad' is an entertainment, an illusion. If you want to, we can talk about the incredible crimes perpetrated by the police and the crimes perpetrated by the people. If you want to talk about crime and police protection, there are millions tied up with the narcotics business and those clowns never go to jail, but some kid with long hair and dirty feet gets 90 days for vagrancy and loitering because he doesn't move when they say 'Move on.' You can see kids busted for breaking windows and running off with TV sets and you could put the profits they get from it in an ashtray.

"No one—in politics or the movies — is really interested in coming to grips with the things that *are* tearing us apart. They're just shoring up the dam before it breaks and we're all flooded."

September 22, 1968

'MARCUS WELBY, M.D.'

The American Broadcasting Company joined the medical trend on television with the premiere last night of "Marcus Welby, M.D." at 10 P.M.

The winning veteran Robert Young played the physician who had to cope with the unavoidable agony of comforting an unmarried school teacher who had terminal brain cancer and also introducing his younger colleague, played by James Brolin, to the reality that a doctor's relationship extends to intensely human terms.

In the course of "Marcus Welby, M.D.," the author of last night's installment, Jerry DeBono, had some sensitive words on the departure of one from those a person loves, in this instance, the teacher's class, and there was the satisfaction in knowing that loveliness of spirit is a worthwhile heritage by which to be remembered.

With the popularity of medical shows, "Marcus Welby, M.D." no doubt will join "Medical Center" as a success. In the premiere, Susan Clark, playing the teacher, was effective in making the point that the best preparation for death is to live life to the fullest.

September 24, 1969

Still Hotter Than a Pistol. Why?

By ROBERT LASSON

NETWORK television is a relentless, remorseless program-swilling beast that gorges on pilots and spits ulcers. The numbers tell the story, and when the numbers are wrong, the attendants are trained to push the "Abort" button. That's how it's been ever since advertisers learned to count. Selling The Product is the name of the game. To paraphrase the Media Maven, the show is the sideshow.

In this milieu, where the only tradition is transition, a prime-time network show that lasts five years is amazing. One that lasts 10 is phenomenal. Right now, "Gunsmoke's" Marshal Matt Dillon is riding into his 15th year—long enough to put saddle sores on King Kong.

When a TV show has this kind of staying power, an assumption must be made: the reasons for its popularity lie in areas that cannot be fully explained, either by its creators (or they'd have 10 "Gunsmokes" on the air) or by its fans. As for the latter, we can further assume that a deep psychological affinity has evolved between the viewer and the viewed—the characters, the situations, and other elements. These affinities, I maintain, are beyond verbalization because they are not even held in the conscious mind. So the man who tells us that he's been watching "Gunsmoke" for years "because I like adult Westerns" is telling us nothing.

*

All right, what *are* we talking about? We're talking about a show called "Gunsmoke," which started out 18 years ago as a radio program. Three years later, on Sept. 10, 1955, it went on as a half-hour TV series and instantly made stars—rich stars — of its four principals, James Arness, Amanda Blake, Milburn Stone and Dennis Weaver. In 1960, the show was extended to an hour. It has thus far played 233 30-minute and 283 60-minute shows—an astronomical total of 516 original scripts.

So much for the packaging. How about the contents? First, we have the "Gunsmoke" regulars, the program's "family": Dillon himself, strong and resolute, a righteous man, slow to anger and not vindictive; tough, bittersweet Kitty (Amanda Blake) of the Long Branch Saloon. (Is she really making it with the Marshal off camera? Only her writers know. She obviously doesn't stand a chance on camera because the hero must be alone and unburdened. This, of course, also keeps the options open for the 12 million women who tune in every week.) Then there's Milburn Stone as Doc Adams, stubborn, feisty, irritable, but dependable as sunrise, and a charming derelict of a deputy, first called Chester when played by Dennis Weaver, now dubbed Festus and acted by Ken Curtis. Put them all in a row and you have what country folk call "good people" — people you'd be proud to have for friends in real life. So we have, first, an appealing cast of characters with whom we live through some adventure each week.

*

But the people are more important than the adventure, for if raw plot were everything, "Mission: Impossible" would be the most-copied show on the air. "The Forsyte Saga," which currently is keeping American viewers glued to their sets after a highly successful run on the BBC, proves that there's nothing more compulsively watchable than sympathetic people (yes, even Soames Forsyte) caught up in an utterly believable experience.

*

"Gunsmoke's" executive producer John Mantley recognizes this. "I tell writers to forget plots and bring us scripts with strong character conflicts," Mantley says. "I tell them not to worry about setting the story in Dodge City or fitting the narrative to our particular characters. That we can do, if the vital first element is there. Sometimes a story emerges from a simple idea. We had a script once that wasn't going anywhere. I suggested an adaptation of the theme of Sydney Carton in Dickens's 'Tale of Two Cities.' Out of that, we developed a character named Charley Moon and the story of a rogue who in the end gave up his life for people he liked.

"Other times, a story grows from a character that a writer is eager to develop. One writer, Preston Wood, came in one day and said, 'I want to do a story about a middle-aged, ailing con man who wants to accomplish two things before he goes. First, he wants to pull off the perfect con. Second, he wants to have the biggest funeral the West ever saw.' I told him to develop the idea. The result was an episode called 'Danny,' starring Jack Albertson, who gave, in my opinion, the finest performance of his career—and I'm not forgetting 'The Subject Was Roses.'"

How does Mantley, who has been involved with "Gunsmoke" for six years, explain the show's amazing appeal? "First, the characters were, right from the start, so marvelously conceived and so beautifully cast. Look at this lineup: you have the lawman, who holds the power of life and death—with a gun. You have the doctor, who also holds the power of life and death—with science. For relief, you have a likable derelict, a town drunk. And, finally, you have a seasoned woman of the world who is also the mother of all men. Now you take these people and you put them in deep conflict rich with problems. That's 'Gunsmoke.'"

*

So, number one, we have a show with the strongest emphasis on character-in-conflict, the very basis of drama. What else?

In this era of endemic revolution, when even the family, society's basic cell, is infirm, when liberal churchmen argue "my-God-is-deader-than-your-God," *homo vidensis* does not wish to be reminded that he is nothing more than 175 pounds of dying protein. Something in him remembers other times, other places, when man—or, more pointedly, *a* man—could act on his environment, when he could face a problem and solve it. There would be risk involved, to be sure, but life without risk is salesmanship.

All right, you ask, how about "The Invaders," "The Fugitive," that "Run For Your Life" fellow and the rest of them—didn't they all face risks, too? And I answer: what *about* them? Where are they? They have all crossed the Styx into the shady land of re-runs and UHF. They didn't last.

Why? (1) Not one of these characters could sustain a series indefinitely. (2) They had no family to play against. (3) Every episode took place in a different locale—which did not jazz up viewer interest, as might be expected, but vitiated it.

"Gunsmoke" is more than a show, more than an idea. "Gunsmoke" is also a place, a place with dimension, a past, and a population. When you turn the set on, you're going some place. Some place that's as remote as Camelot, yet an ever-never land that can be more real than the one you see outside your window. Mythic, if I may borrow a word that keeps falling out of Partisan Review.

So when Jim Arness rides furiously by in that opening credit, friends, that's not Marshal Matt Dillon. It's Odysseus and Theseus and Siegfried. On Mondays, at 7:30 P.M. on CBS, you can support your local myth.

January 11, 1970

The Message Sounds Like 'Hate Thy Neighbor'

By STEPHANIE HARRINGTON

CBS's new half-hour gift to Tuesday nights, "All in the Family," is kind of like wishing for a little more frankness in political dialogue and getting your wish in the form of Spiro Agnew. A working-class family situation series with a message, "All in the Family" is vulgar and silly. And after the disgust-at-first-shock wears off, the vaudeville clinkers passed off as humor are totally predictable, both in themselves and as means of conveying the show's moral: All prejudice—racial, class, sophisticated against unsophisticated and vice versa—is bad.

In describing the means used to get this message across, it is impossible to employ any adjective that could possibly get into the same thesaurus with words like nuance or subtlety or dimension. And Carroll O'Connor as the "hero" (or anti-hero), Archie Bunker, plays to the camera as if he were on a vaudeville stage instead of a set that is supposed to be someone's living room. For the home viewer, that little conceit is destroyed anyway by the laughter of

the studio audience, which also makes painfully offensive lines that, if not milked for laughs they don't deserve, might at least have some shock value in terms of making people face their prejudices.

Archie is a paunchy, middle-sized, slightly more than middle-aged, white, working-class type. His victimized wife Edith, acted by Jean Stapleton, whom he repeatedly, and with great imaginative thrust, refers to as a "dingbat," is alternately insulted by him or patronized or ignored. Her only revenge is to get off some of the best lines of the show (which isn't conceding much). Living with tnem is their 18-year-old daughter, who looks like a 6-year-old Shirley Temple in a blonde wig and black leather mini. Her mental life consists of affirming whatever her husband says, and she should have women's lib out after CBS in full cry. Her husband, a reasonably socially concerned student with moderately long hair, is the principal antagonist to Archie (he is evidently of Polish-American background since Archie refers to him as a "Polack").

•

Archie, we can assume, is not Polish. Nor is he a "Spic," a "Spade" or a "Yid," the epithets he uses with some satisfaction to refer to those groups. (He might, however, be Irish since he never uses the word "Mick.") The joke —and the message—cf the first episode were sprung on us when the neighborhood handyman, a young black engineering student, in the course of being patronized by Archie, who insists he is not a racist, turns the tables. In put-on-Whitey Uncle Tomese, the young man asks Archie if he is Jewish, noting that he uses the word *"tuchas"* and talks with his hands. Everyone takes up the joke while Archie helplessly sputters his denial. Which just goes to show Archie (and us) that bigotry can boomerang.

We are also supposed to get the message that if we have categorized Archie as a bigot just because he calls people names, then we are victims of our own bigotry. Archie, after all, is moved by the corny sentiment of a verse on a not-quite-Hallmark anniversary card. And that is supposed to prove that behind the gruff exterior is a warm, sympathetic, perhaps even potentially brotherly human being just aching to be recognized. But the characterization gives us no reason to believe this. Archie does not come across as a sympathetic character who victimizes others because he himself is a victim. For 30 minutes Archie is *nothing but* bigoted about others and unrelievedly rotten to his family. And because the show is so one-dimensional, because its characters are caricatures, it cannot even claim the shock value of being courageously,

Carroll O'Connor stars as the bigoted Archie Bunker in CBS's new Tuesday series,"All in the Family."

By making the expression of hostility more commonplace, do we really exorcise it? Or do we, in fact, make it more acceptable?

uncompromisingly, true to life. In an attempt to discredit stereotyping, it resorts to stereotypes. In its sledge-hammer determination to tell it like it is, it over-tells, and, instead of being the breakthrough in courage it was meant to be, it over-kills itself.

*

But beyond the question of success is the question of intent. "All in the Family" is a logical extension of the kind of tell-it-like-it-is "confrontation" television in which hostile blacks, on discussion programs or documentaries, shout their long-simmering resentment at whites with a minimum of euphemisms, and whites come back with their gripes. (Indeed, had "All in the Family" succeeded, it would have been gutsier, much more shocking and much more effective than these confrontation-dialogues, which themselves quickly become predictable and stagey.) The question raised by both these attempts, or pseudo-attempts, at dramatic, consciousness-raising honesty is: Just what social purpose is being served? By making the expression of hostility more commonplace, do we really exorcise it? Or do we, in fact, make it more acceptable?

The first episode of "The Smith Family," ABC's new (and I quote the release) "family drama about the home life of a policeman," indicates that it, too, is meant to present things in the perspective of a social type not very well-beloved by the young and the liberal (although the policeman's point of view has been featured before in "Dragnet" and more recently in series like "NYPD" and "Adam 12"). But this is a policeman series with a difference—it stars Henry Fonda as Detective Chad (Chad?) Smith.

On the opening program Smith is caught in a moral dilemma. At the request of a friend he arrests her daughter on a charge of possession of marijuana. To his surprise, he finds his own daughter on the premises at the time. He is morally compelled to take her in, too. But her friends are convinced that she finked to her father and they ostracize her. Everything turns out all right, in the end, of course, regardless of how open-mouthed gee-whiz, corny and full of motivational holes the denouement must be to achieve this happy ending. But we do get the point: Fuzz are people, too.

It's a point worth making, but worth making convincingly. Everything on "The Smith Family" is just too pretty, too right, too according to hack formula. There is nothing in the first installment of "The Smith Family" to explain why an actor of Henry Fonda's caliber would be in it. Except maybe to rescue the Fonda image from Jane and Peter?

*

To turn from social significance to entertainment, the new "Pearl Bailey Show," Saturdays on ABC, is certainly more of an "event" than either of the foregoing, but what new under the sun can you say about variety shows or Pearl Bailey? The show was at its best in its simply musical moments. Most moving of all was a vocal jam session with Pearl and Louis Armstrong. There is not much television that bears repeating, but I would watch the show again to recapture that moment. Just music and feeling and no gimmicks.

Indeed the trouble with variety shows is the variety.

January 24, 1970

What's a TV star?

Someone who is beautiful and sexy, but not threatening

Why 30 million are mad about Mary

By Tracy Johnston

HOLLYWOOD. "What's a TV star?"

"It's someone who has the acceptance of a mass audience," says Perry Lafferty, vice president of programing for C.B.S. in Hollywood. "It's as simple as that. Mary has what we call star quality."

"Can you explain exactly what that is?"

"If I could, we would have a billion dollars and beat out the other networks. It's something that makes more than 30 million people turn on their TV sets Saturday night at 9 to 'The Mary Tyler Moore Show.' "

"Do you think Mary is that exceptional?"

"Well, she's the well-scrubbed, all-American girl that everyone likes. I think it's her vulnerability that makes her particularly appealing. Little girl lost. Also, she's beautiful and all that without being threatening."

"Is being sexy threatening?"

"A sexy woman, or sexy sex, or whatever you want to call it, is not acceptable on TV. It raises all the id-like elements inside people and they don't know how to deal with it. The wife looks at her husband; the husband doesn't know how he's supposed to react. It's too confusing for them."

Tracy Johnston is a freelance who is based in California.

Lou Grant (actor Ed Asner) eyes Ted Baxter (played by Ted Knight) in a scene from the MTM show.

"Wouldn't you put Marilyn Monroe on TV if you had the chance?"

"Not in a weekly TV series. Don't forget that the TV audience is different from the film audience. It won't take change in the characters. In film, people are expected to grow because of external pressures. But the TV audience wants to know what to expect, and when you try something different it upsets them. 'The Beverly Hillbillies' is a classic case. After a couple of years the writers felt the show was getting a bit monotonous so they had the family buy a motion-picture studio. The ratings dropped instantly. It took us a few weeks to get them out of the situation, but when we did, the ratings went back up immediately."

"So you don't think the audience will respond to a show that is just plain good, with good writing, good acting and so forth?"

"A show never succeeds on TV just because it's good. One-half of all the TV sets in America aren't turned on to 'The Waltons' just because the show is good. It has to be something else... to fulfill some kind of deep-seated need."

"Do you think the feminist movement, then, has anything to do with making Mary so acceptable?"

"No."

"Did it bother you that the critics found her too goody-goody when the show was first aired?"

"Not at all. Fortunately, TV critics don't have anything at all to do with ratings."

On one level, as the network executive well knows, TV is an art form without vision and without visionary men or women, a medium whose most complex ideology is based on numbers. It has produced, as a mere appendage, the largest selling magazine in the world (TV Guide) and has made a lot of people millionaires and a few million Americans either more passive or perhaps more violent. Although both Mary Tyler Moore and her husband, Grant Tinker (a former N.B.C. executive), say that television entertainment shows exist so that programs like the news and "60 Minutes" can be produced, Vice President Gerald Ford says, "Carol Burnett and Archie Bunker have just as legitimate a claim to the attention of the American people as do Lord [Kenneth] Clark and Alistair Cooke." And most of America agrees with him. The news is not put on in prime time simply because not enough people are interested in it (just over 16 million for Walter Cronkite).

Nevertheless, a sizable number of sophisticates have strong personal feelings about "The Mary Tyler Moore Show" and join the Saturday night audience along with the rest of the 30 million across the nation. Daniel Menaker wrote in The New York Times: "Mary is so In, actually, that it has become especially fashionable to drift into the den at a party—or even go home—at 9 on Saturday night because you 'simply must not miss' her program." The New Yorker recently ran a cartoon depicting a man in front of the tube, drooling over Mary. A TV news broadcaster in San Francisco says, "Every person I know involved in TV news watches the show. Every newsroom has its Ted Baxter anchorman, a boss like Lou and a woman like Mary. There is a tacit understanding that we will not date her, but we sure all do hope she will remain single."

A woman sociology professor at the University of California says she watches the show when she's alone Saturday night, "and therefore morose. Her show is the only one I can stand then; it's not offensive from a feminist point of view and I appreciate the friendship between Mary and Rhoda. And if I'm stoned, it's the only show that doesn't make me feel like committing suicide."

Four years ago, Grant Tinker, then a vice president of Twentieth Century Fox, asked TV writers Jim Brooks and Allan Burns to design the show that C.B.S. had offered Mary. They attended a meeting of C.B.S. big shots in New York where they explained their plan: Mary was to be divorced, working at a nondescript job, and involved in all the difficulties of starting over again.

"Well, we sat there," says Allan, "in a room full of divorced New York Jews with mustaches and heard them say that there are four things Americans don't like: New Yorkers, divorced people, men with mustaches and Jews. It was strongly hinted that if we insisted on having Mary divorced, the show would go on at 1 in the morning. At that point Jim and I really did want to quit the show. I mean Mary couldn't be married, since she was still coupled with Dick Van Dyke in the eyes of the public, and we insisted on having her over 30 so we could make her a real adult. And it was already the year of the widow — remember Doris Day and Julia? We just didn't want to have to kill another man off to get Mary on the air.

"Finally, it occurred to our male-chauvinist minds that a girl could be 30, unmarried and have a past involving men. [It was suggested, in Mary's first show, that she had lived with a medical student before coming to Minneapolis.] Then we hit upon the idea of the newsroom, and we liked it immediately because it wasn't one of those TV jobs where the people never work. We went around to lots of newsrooms all over Los Angeles and researched the characters. In every one we found a Ted, a Lou and a Murray."

Ted Baxter is TV station WJM's anchorman: dumb, insensitive, egotistical, and paid more than anyone else simply because he has silver hair and a deep voice. Murray Slaughter is the news writer for WJM, who detests Ted for mangling his copy and being paid so much money while doing so. "There were Murrays in all the newsrooms," says Allan, "muttering under their breath when the anchorman breezed through the studio, wafting cologne after him." Lou Grant (played by former dramatic actor Ed Asner) is the producer of WJM News, which seems to be a rather rinky-dink operation. He is a hard-drinking, gruff ex-newspaperman who has a heart of gold. "Even Walter Cronkite," says Allan, "told us that his managing editor was just like Lou."

Rhoda (played by Valerie Harper, formerly of "Second City") was created as a direct contrast to Mary: a New Yorker, Jewish, aggressive and open. "Our idea," says Allan, "was to have Mary and Rhoda immediately hate each other and gradually realize the things they have in common. Actually, their friendship somehow grew quicker than we had planned."

In January, 1971, a half season after the MTM show debuted, "All in the Family" hit middle-American living rooms unaccompanied by any irate calls on the special phone lines C.B.S. had installed to tell the public it wasn't serious. It was a breakthrough for television. Now most of those hands reaching out in the darkness on Saturday night turn the dial to C.B.S. at 8 and start with Archie Bunker's jokes about impotency and menopause, go on to "M*A*S*H" one-liners (such as "We're having an orgy, come one, come all") and wind up with Rhoda and Mary discussing children's books on sex: "I was given those books as a kid," says Rhoda, "and I got very confused. I kept thinking I would have to swim up the Columbia River."

Besides loosening up, the characters on the MTM show have all changed over the years—not enough to upset the audience, but enough to make the supporting roles more real than any others on TV. Lou Grant separated from his TV wife this year. Mary's landlady (played by Academy Award winner Cloris Leachman) discovered first that her brother was gay and then found her husband having an affair with station WJM's sugar-coated bitch, "The Happy Homemaker." (This was no "I Love Lucy" misunderstanding, but a real affair where the two spent the night "in an all-night body shop having the car fender repaired.")

Mary Richards (the character played by Mary Tyler Moore) has gotten more assertive while still managing to have something for everyone. Men, whose taste in women runs from Tammy Wynette to Gloria Steinem, think she would make the perfect girlfriend. Women like the fact that she's the star without being a sex queen or a loser (she may be the only female TV comic actress who hasn't had to be a dope or unattractive). Mothers think she's an ideal daughter despite the fact that she spent the night out, presumably with a man, and takes the pill. She may, in fact, be the most well-liked character in America.

"It's comfortable for people to think that there is someone like her in America," says Allan Burns.

"Well, I can't think about that," says the real Mary Tyler Moore. "It would drive me bananas. I do the show for my friends and colleagues."

"The real Mary Tyler Moore is a bit more relaxed, I'm happy to report," adds her husband.

Rhoda has also changed character over the years. Originally, her forte was fat jokes ("I don't know why I bother to eat this candy, I might as well apply it directly to my hips") but one summer Valerie Harper returned from a Florida vacation thin and beautiful. Somehow, the TV audience managed to survive this and went on to like her so much that Rhoda will have her own show next fall.

"Since we just can't replace Rhoda," says Mary Tyler Moore, "we're looking for a man. But they're hard to find, as they are in real life."

"So you don't have a commitment to playing a happy single woman," I ask.

"No, because the character doesn't. If we find a man and it doesn't work out—the audience doesn't like him or something—he could move to Chicago. But I don't see anything wrong with her getting married. It's interesting, isn't it, that we're saying there's nothing wrong with getting married these days?"

Although talking to the network executive about the MTM characters is like talking to a broker about the stock market, and Mary herself tends to simply praise them and let it go at that, talking to the producers of the show about these characters is like talking about their best friends.

"I have a thing about calling up people at 3 in the morning, when it's rough," says Brooks. "And you know I really feel I could call up either Lou or Rhoda."

"I would call up Rhoda," says Allan Burns, "just because it would be more fun. You know, I have found myself on the stage when we're filming absolutely loving Rhoda, not in a sexual way but just as a person that I really adore. I don't know where my affection for Valerie Harper leaves off and my affection for Rhoda starts."

Treva Silverman, a Bennington graduate and the only woman to hold the position of senior story consultant in TV, says, "I just love to write lines for Ted. It's a real catharsis. I mean, every man with an overblown ego that I meet on the street or in bed goes into Ted."

"Oddly enough," says Allan, "there's an enormous affection for Ted, even though he's not too bright and all that, because he gets the screams. People like him because they know they're going to laugh when he comes on. There's that anticipation that's like a release when it comes."

Treva, Jim and Allan (producer Ed Weinberger was on vacation when I talked to them) all seem to agree about one thing; they don't want the MTM show to resemble the dream world they grew up believing in as kids.

Jim Brooks says: "Really the only issue that I care about is that we don't recreate the old Ozzie and Harriet myth of an ideal family and an ideal world."

"I am really aware of the fact that TV and movies gave me the idea that you were supposed to be perfect," says Treva. "I spent hours on the analyst's couch just because Doris Day wouldn't sleep with

Rock Hudson. It was supposed to be the perfect ending, but for me it was money out of my pocket.

"Jim and Allan and I agree on most important things. None of us would ever write in a gratuitous putdown just because it was funny or satirize something that was pathetic. The characters have a lot of affection for each other and we don't want to destroy that."

Norman Lear, who produces and writes the only other TV comedy shows worth talking about, is not as sentimental as the MTM crew. A gentle, though outspoken man who hung around Hollywood for years before coming up with "All in the Family" and credit for lifting TV out of its morass of meaninglessness, sees conflict as the central aspect of comedy. When I mention that life seems to be a constant fight in most of his shows, he replies, "That's my constant observation about life."

While Jim Brooks and Allan Burns talk about George Gobel, Phil Silvers, Sid Caesar and Jackie Gleason as their models and Treva Silverman mentions Benchley and Thurber, Lear talks about Lenny Bruce. "Meaningful allusions to sex, politics, religions—all of that began with Lenny Bruce. Anybody who ever saw him was influenced by him. By the end I couldn't laugh at him as much because he was sad. But in terms of breakthrough and where a lot of things started, I think history will show that an awful lot began with Lenny Bruce."

The main difference between Lear's shows and the MTM show, of course, is that the latter doesn't attempt to take on any issues nor does it want to satirize anyone where it might really hurt.

"Norman Lear takes on issues tremendously well," says Jim Brooks; "why should we? The issue we care about is people being honest in relating with each other."

"We did an issue show once," says Allan, "and it was terrible. It was about anti-Semitism."

"We were against it, in case you couldn't figure it out," adds Jim.

"We like to sneak things in," Allan says, "but when it's no big deal. In a soft-pedaled, low-key way I think we may have done some good things for women."

"But that's a trap," Jim interrupts. "If you're going to write about a woman now, there is only one way to write: she has to be in touch with the world we live in. If you get too caught up with the message, it's anti-writing."

For Mary, Allan says, they try to write good "attitude lines": "She's funny when she's in a situation where she is vulnerable, tired, angry, surprised—she can play those attitudes with a very funny slant. And she surprises us. We don't write the attitudes into the script; sometimes she just comes up with completely offbeat responses."

"The 'Mary Tyler Moore Show' is the kind of show that keeps a vice president of programing in business," says Perry Lafferty. "It has no problems whatsoever. The ratings are just perfect, staying generally in the top 10 or 15, and we have practically no complaints about the show." One is reminded of other cultural entities millions of Americans will accept with "practically no complaints"—The Reader's Digest, Norman Rockwell, Muzak, Hallmark Cards, McDonald's hamburgers—and the MTM show seems a mass cultural event of a certain significance.

Mary Tyler Moore speaks in complete sentences and never lets them trail off into "you know's" or "sort of's." She never wanders off the question an interviewer asks, nor tries to charm him with not-for-print anecdotes; in fact she is so attentive during an interview it is almost disconcerting. Although she has charm (star quality, perhaps), she plays it down; no reporter has been to her home in Malibu or accompanied her in the Rolls-Royce for a day of errands.

"There are certain things about me that I will never tell to anyone because I am a very private person," she says. "But basically what you see is who I am. I'm independent, I do like to be liked, I do look for the good side of life and people, I'm positive, I'm disciplined. I like my life in order, and I'm neat as a pin."

"She is a very gutsy lady," says Grant Tinker, who is now president of MTM Enterprises Inc. "She is single-minded and has an amazing ability to concentrate. She is ambitious, but for her talent, not necessarily for power or control over the show."

"Mary is brilliant," says Treva. "A person has to be to respond so appropriately to everything as she does. Comedy really is a form of perception. Mary is quiet about it, but she knows everything that's going on around her."

When Mary talks about herself, the words "discipline," "responsibility," "contained," "control" and "neatness" come up insistently, as if she's warning reporters that there's no use in prying. If she didn't have that incredibly expressive face and body and wasn't so energetic and vibrant looking (she's in bed by 10:30 and up at 7) one might label her uptight. Typical Mary statements are:

"I don't share my innermost feelings with my friends." "Ballet is like an old friend, classic and unchanging. I like to work on things like getting my leg just another inch higher. In fact I fault myself that I don't take jazz classes because they require so much self-expression." "I love order and discipline—God, I sound like a Nazi, don't I?" "Some people say I err on the side of being too thin, but I'm afraid that if I once overeat, I won't be able to stop." "I would love to really be able to be a buffoon like Carol Burnett, but I'm not that way. I'm more constrained."

Other than her career, Mary has her charity work: The Cleveland Amory Fund for Animals and Los Ranchos Amigos, a hospital for bedridden children. She is learning how to direct a three-camera TV show, which will make her the only female director in the trade, and she is hunting for a house in Beverly Hills to buy and decorate.

"There is no aspect of my life at the moment that isn't quite satisfactory," she says.

But things weren't always so satisfactory. After working five years in the Dick Van Dyke show, she made some "awful" films for Universal and played the lead in a Broadway version of "Breakfast at Tiffany's" that folded during the previews. She also had a miscarriage and learned during that time that she had diabetes. In Los Angeles she saw an analyst for a year, "which was the most boring year of my life," she says. "I went to him because I was scared. I thought, if I'm not going to be an actress, what or who am I? I wasn't a hostess, a gardener, a great cook or a full-time mother. But he never said anything. Luckily the TV show came along and I didn't have to worry about it."

As a child Mary says she was "kind of quiet, a loner, and concentrating solely on dancing. From the time I was 4 years old I knew what I wanted to be, only then I thought it was a dancer." Her childhood she describes as "relatively happy" although she attended strict Catholic schools and lived off and on with her aunt and proper English grandmother at various times when she and her parents "weren't communicating." She married at 17 a man who was 27. One wonders if she was ever a giggly, awkward adolescent. "Getting married," she says, "was the only way I could get out of the house legally, since I didn't want to go to college." The marriage ended after 6 years. "We didn't grow together," she says. "I obviously didn't know what I wanted when I was 17. I'm sad if I made my husband unhappy by leaving, but life is too short not to live it fully."

"Do you regret those years?"

"I can't regret them," she replies, "I have Richie."

Richie is her 17-year-old son, who has now gone to live with his father and stepmother in Fresno, Calif. He has no interest in show business, Mary says, but emphasizes that they have a "very, very" close relationship.

Three weeks before I saw Mary in Studio City, a reporter from Esquire magazine had been around, she said. "He said he liked the show and wanted to do a story, but after awhile he said to me, 'You know, I think everyone is trying to protect you, that there's something about you that isn't like your image.' Then one day he just left, without canceling his appointments or anything."

"Basically, we're dull people," says Grant Tinker, over lunch in a low-lit show-biz restaurant where everyone knows his name. "But I raised the red flag about that guy from Esquire; weird people want to find something weird, even if it's not there."

"Another woman reporter," Mary said, "recently called me aside and in a very confidential tone said, 'Tell me, Mary . . . tell me that you aren't Wonderbread.'"

"Wonderbread" seems a poor epithet for Mary. Certainly someone who knew what she wanted to be at the age of 4, who has rejected a strict Catholic upbringing, who got out of a marriage because she felt "trapped," and who has trained herself to be a dancer, has more substance than Wonderbread. Like Mary Richards, her character, she seems to have the energy, the sheer will power to remain the "all-American girl" as the C.B.S. execs put it, and to create happy endings.

She is a high-school sweetheart who hasn't gone sour; an intelligent, highly polished, well-engineered product of the American dream that hasn't faded. She is a Republican; she wears tight T-shirts with rhinestones; the only subject that makes her angry during our several hours of conversation is Dennis Hopper's slaughtering of a sheep for a movie. America is still home for her; she has no desire to travel. Somehow Mary Tyler Moore has fended off the sixties, without turning her mind or her life to mush.

The one drama in her life now—her separation from Grant Tinker, to whom she was married for 11 years—reads like a script from out of the fifties:

"I had heard rumors," says Treva Silverman, "and when Grant didn't show up in the control room that Friday night for the filming, we knew. The tension was just awful, but Mary was wonderful on the stage. I don't know how she did it."

"Grant moved out of their house in Malibu Nov. 30," says Dan Jenkins, Mary's P.R. man. "I'll never forget that date. That afternoon Mary had to entertain some British journalists. One of them leaned over to her at the end of lunch and said, 'Tell me, Mary, how is it that you have such a *marvelous* marriage?' Well, Mary gave all the right answers, but when she got up to leave I could see her put her hand to her mouth, kind of choking back a sob."

It must have been difficult, in real life, to make the ending happy, but somehow Mary managed to do it. During two tense months of separation she threw herself into her work and wrote furiously into a diary at night. Then she and Grant began "dating." Now they spend most of their time together and talk happily about what a good idea it is for couples to separate and reassess how much they love each other. They both insist that they have grown, individually, from the experience and will be happier for it, no matter what happens in the end. Mary breezes into Grant's office after work, smiling, charming. He greets her, calm, decisive, confident. Their show is a comedy, and the most important rule applies: The ending must be happy.

To her interviewer Mary smiles her broad, familiar smile and remarks, "Couldn't you just slap my face for being so positive and optimistic?" ■

April 7, 1974

Why My Sons Watch 'The Waltons'

By ALJEAN HARMETZ

SAFETY is what is stressed. Outside, it is dark and cold. There are bears on the mountain, and the night is full of howling. Inside the house, there is light and warmth and coffee on the stove—a blue enamel coffeepot grasped with the edges of a faded cotton apron.

My sons wrap themselves in blankets and lie motionless on the bedroom floor—in a suburban house with two toasters and an electric can opener, 40 years away from the television family.

It is their desire that we watch "The Waltons" ritualistically each Thursday night. They stumbled upon the program last September in the week of freedom they are given at the start of each television season to explore. It is a week of carnival and excess, a week without parental time limits and censorship. That they should have returned from their riot of violence with such zeal for "The Waltons" surprised me. It may also have surprised CBS.

In the last national Neilsen ratings, "The Waltons" was in 22d place, with a 32 per cent share of the audience during its 8 P.M. Thursday time period. "The most we realistically expected," says Fred Silverman, CBS vice president in charge of programing, "was to reach about a quarter of the audience. We thought 'The Waltons' would be a good counter-program to 'Flip Wilson' and 'Mod Squad.' The basic appeal of those two shows is urban. We hoped 'The Waltons' would have a big appeal in rural areas and small towns. We knew 'Flip Wilson' would be No. 1, but we thought 'The Waltons' might make a good race against 'Mod Squad'

Tony Esparza

Kami Cotler as Elizabeth, the youngest of "The Waltons," shares a secret with the family cow
Why do children watch "The Waltons"? The word they use most often is "real"

for second place, that it might even be neck-and-neck."

"The Waltons"—a gentle, low-keyed story of seven children growing up poor during the Depression—has demolished "Mod Squad." It has also had larger effects. The UCLA film library has asked to be the depository of all Walton memorabilia because the show "has no equal on network television." The Chamber of Commerce in Richmond, Virginia, has had over 100 requests from tourists for directions to the imaginary town of Walton's Mountain. Three hundred and forty-six elementary schools use "The Waltons" for class lessons — something that started and grew spontaneously without the connivance of the show's producer, Lee Rich.

*

"The Waltons" has also brought to CBS and the show's producers nearly 1,500 letters each week—an amount that far exceeds that of any other CBS show including the national champion, "All in the Family." The letters come not from rural areas but from large cities. Many of the letters are written by college professors. Almost all the letters thank the men responsible for the "honesty" and "love" implicit in the program.

My sons put it differently. "That's what I like about this program," said my 11-year-old, pointing to the television set a few weeks ago. After finding a wagon of trespassing gypsies, two Walton children were running to get the sheriff. "They're never stupid enough to try to handle everything themselves."

Both my sons, interviewed separately, used virtually the same words. "Everybody's not perfect," said the younger boy. "They are real people with real feelings," said the 11-year-old. "'The Waltons' isn't like 'The Brady Bunch' where everything always turns out right, and everybody is so moral. Everybody is always perfect on all those other series."

There was a tendency on some of the early programs for ends to be tied too neatly. One occasionally had to swallow hard to choke down the sentiment of lessons learned, sinfulness melted by the warmth of the Walton family, acts of contrition and forgiveness. But, even so, I continued to watch because the reality of the characters transcended the sticky endings.

"There's never been a Mary Ellen-type child on television," says my 11-year-old of the 13-year-old Walton daughter who should never have been born a girl to such a sexually demarcated family. Sticking pins into the pages of an atlas and daydreaming great fantasies of Afghanistan and revenge on her prissy younger sister, defiantly raising bullfrogs and "sassing back" and smoking behind the barn, Mary Ellen Walton is continually stifled by the boundaries of the feminine role in this particular family.

An injustice collector with her dress unwrinkled and her ribbons always tied, the younger Erin Walton dotes on the same role—outdoing her mother in finding specks of dust and neatly breaking eggs. They are joined each Thursday night by a humorless, narrow-minded grandmother whose sharp tongue can never totally repress her more humanistic husband; by a mother who has reduced her potentialities to fit her role, losing a little width and gaining a little depth in the process. Time and place allow the men — grandfather, father, and a 17-year-old brother—to be broader than the women, less frightened by liquor and strangers and new ideas.

Perhaps out of a confidence born of no longer having to seek an audience, the melodrama and moralizing that marred some of the early programs have diminished. In recent weeks the stories have been painfully simple—although the resonances have not.

A 64-year-old bachelor uncle—a bank accountant—comes to visit because he has been laid off during the bank holiday. Born in mountains such as these, he is now too urban to fish without self-consciousness. Against the wishes of the Walton mother and grandmother, he is introduced to a coquettish old lady they consider a scarlet woman because she has been married four times and divorced twice. Each old person fills the emptiness of the other. They lived happily together, a postscript tells us, until they died within months of each other in 1953.

John-Boy, the 17-year-old eldest son, falls in love. He manages to take the girl for a hike up the mountain without taking his six younger brothers and sisters along—a moment of triumph and guilt. He plays a love song on a borrowed dulcimer. The dulcimer is borrowed because the year is 1933 or 1934 and there is no money for dulcimers during the Depression. Promises are made. They will never be kept. When the girl leaves Walton's Mountain, she gives John-Boy a dulcimer—the finest dulicimer ever carved by the local craftsman—as "a going-away present." "But I'm not going anywhere," he says. The sentence starts in bewilderment. Before John-Boy has finished saying it, he knows the truth. No words are used to hammer feelings down. No more is said because no more needs to be said.

Network television has, for the most part, equated success with violence: The gun, the knife, the whispered threat, the brutal beating in the dark, the demolishing of witness by lawyer, of husband by wife, of child by parent; the sharp scalpel of the surgeon amputating a leg; the verbal violence of most situation comedy; the heroic captain fighting the monsters of undersea or outer space; the fires and car wrecks and broken bodies and intensive care wards and sirens that form the paraphernalia of disaster. Yet the children watching "The Waltons" outnumber those watching "Mod Squad" three to one, and even teen-agers prefer "The Waltons" by a ratio of 3 to 2.

There are moments of violence in "The Waltons." A drunken man accidentally sets a barn on fire. Another drunken man deliberately burns down the schoolhouse to destroy the evil things that are taught there. A child is beaten. Another child's father is killed in a senseless accident. But the violence comes out of character and is not a substitute for it. It is never a lollipop stuck into the mouth of the viewer to divert his attention from joyless artificiality.

*

Children like to watch children, but some random samplings of West Los Angeles elementary school classes suggest that the success of "The Waltons" among children is more than that. The word they use most often is "real." The word that comes next is "old-fashioned." They find in the show, I think, a safety similar to the safety of which John-Boy writes on his lined tablet late at night—an ordered world wide enough to encompass both Erin and Mary Ellen Walton, narrow enough to close out the dark and frightening things that roam the mountain.

The adults who write of "honesty" and "love" are wistful, I think, for relationships that no longer exist in this idealized form—if, indeed, they ever did. For the children of the 1960s—each of whom was born in the year of some assassination—it is different. "The Waltons" does not abuse the spirit. And the children know it.

February 25, 1973

TV May Be Giving Sex a Bad Name

By DANIEL MENAKER

TELEVISION programs managed to steer clear of the bedroom for a remarkably long time, considering the sexual atmosphere that was thickening around the rest of American popular culture during the sixties. The clean apron that Mom Anderson wore on "Father Knows Best" covered up sexuality on TV until January of 1971, when the Bud Yorkin-Norman Lear "All in the Family" made its debut and opened a Pandora's box of taboo topics. CBS reportedly formed early contingency plans to cancel the show if the viewing public reacted too negatively to Archie Bunker's bigotry. But when the controversy — and there was a lot of it—died down, the network found itself with a monstrous hit on its hands, and Lear and Yorkin steadily broadened their exploration of subjects never treated on television before.

*

"All in the Family" and its Lear/Yorkin progeny —

"Maude" and "Sanford and Son,"—as well as other regularly scheduled comedies and dramas, became bolder and bolder. But the idea of increased TV permissiveness did not spring full-grown from the brows of Lear and Yorkin. It was a symptom, an idea whose time would have come even if Lear and Yorkin had been dentists instead of producers. Television executives were, on the one hand, ready to adjust to a climate that had already changed, largely as a result of the acceptance given to sexual explicitness in theatrical movies. Furthermore, the networks were eager to capture younger viewers for their advertisers, because the young-adult market had so much buying power. In other words, TV's new frankness should be seen not only as the product of a laudable spirit of experimentation but also as a response to economic realities. Sex pays, and the TV people want a piece of the action.

*

This season, television writers and producers have given the tendency toward permissiveness its full head. So far, we have witnessed a lesbian psychiatrist defending her right and competence to treat an adolescent girl's emotional problems, on "Medical Center"; a love affair between an over-30 high-school teacher and one of her students, on one "Owen Marshall," and a teacher accused of molesting a student, on another; a story line involving rape, homosexuality and bisexuality, on the premiere of James Stewart's "Hawkins"; frank cohabitation, in an episode of "The Streets of San Francisco"; a hand on a fanny ("Lotsa Luck"); a man, even if ever so briefly, on a woman ("Diana"); and a tough, disturbing show about prostitution and a high-toned black pimp ("Police Story"). The list could go on and on, but the most convincing and symbolic piece of evidence of the change in television morality was the revelation that Ozzie Nelson, in his new show, "Ozzie's Girls," has taken out a subscription to Playboy! If Ricky or David had brought that trash into the Nelson household in the fifties, all heck would have broken loose.

Two of the three network presidents—Robert Wood of CBS and Herbert Schlosser of NBC — have recently made speeches defending their commitment to more "mature" fare on the home screen against objections from conservative viewers. "Part of our being fully responsible to our public," Mr. Wood said, "is to make sure that we do not allow a small, vocal and, at times, highly organized minority to determine what can be seen on your television set." From Mr. Schlosser: "Programing decisions based on fear of controversy, fear of misunderstanding, or fear of pressure are not in the public interest."

These noble words represent a new fighting spirit that has perhaps been encouraged by the decline in autocratic power of the Nixon Administration. Indeed, the networks have delivered some unusually adult programing from time to time. Ingmar Bergman's teleplay, "The Lie," aired on CBS last April, was one of the shows that Wood had in mind when he spoke out. It was not uniformly good drama, but it was a damn good try, and it included a startlingly explicit love scene between Shirley Knight and her lover. They were under the sheets, admittedly, but they were also definitely naked.

And this fall several delicate subjects have been handled with intelligence on the tube—every now and then. "Mary Tyler Moore," still my favorite show, does a consistently fine job in this respect. In one episode, Mary and Rhoda reminisced about the trials of female puberty. "Gee, Mare," Rhoda said, "remember when your mother told you that something wonderful was about to happen to you—once a month." What made this line and the rest of the conversation work was the fact that it was integrated with the rest of story: Mary and Rhoda were going back to New York for the marriage of Rhoda's younger sister, so the topics of parents and growing up seemed perfectly natural.

And I recall a particularly outstanding segment of "The Waltons" in which the advent of a zealous hell-fire preacher in the Walton household led to sexual tension between Ma and Pa. The preacher's stern moralism had caused arguments between the husband and wife, implicitly to the point where they were no longer having sex. The reconciliation begins with Ma and Pa lying in bed in frigid silence. Finally, they start talking. Pa eventually says, "I can't stand this trouble between us any longer," and they embrace warmly. The scene was acted and directed with restraint and compassion. It was comprehensible on a general psychological level as well as on a sexual level. And, once again, it was integrated with the rest of the plot, which concerned rigid morality, abstinence, and indulgence. Incidentally, the double bed has only recently been discovered by television. Until a year or so ago, married couples were either not shown sleeping with each other or slept in twin beds.

For the most part, however, the new permissiveness hasn't worked very well on a day-to-day basis. The chief result of relaxed strictures in sitcoms has been a ceaseless flow of puerile, gratuitous sex-and-bathroom humor. For example, much of the first episode of "Lotsa Luck," Dom DeLuise's new show, concerned the efforts of Dom and his relatives to free his sister Olive from the clutches of a toilet in which she had somehow got her foot stuck. What a scream.

In prime-time drama, the sexual situation has grown very complicated. "Marcus Welby" and "Owen Marshall" and "Medical Center" have taken on a glut of adult themes—impotence, adultery, promiscuity, venereal disease, and so forth—but the producers apparently still feel compelled to exalt traditional values. Thus, in an early-fall installment of "Marcus Welby," a husband who is impotent with his wife turns to a younger woman; his adultery not only threatens his marriage but also antagonizes his doctor (Welby) and precipitates severe asthma attacks in his daughter.

*

During the course of the show, Welby delivers a couple of long monologues explaining the male climacteric in reasonably clinical terms. But the outcome of the plot is "straight," old-fashioned, and optimistic. The writers still need to wrap up the realistic content with soothing platitudes. The result is a pretty schizzy viewing experience, in which large gobbets of modern psychology float around somewhat aimlessly in a generally bland moral pabulum. The shows are trying to be simultaneously objective and admonitory. As is the case with comedy, TV drama is facing the dilemma of blending new, raw material into old formulas.

The fact that it is mainly bilge which now flows through the newly opened moral floodgates on television is a particularly lamentable development insofar as it undercuts what might otherwise be progress toward genuine acceptance of greater sophistication and freedom of expression. In the Oct. 13 issue of TV Guide, Neil Hickey reported that 31 per cent of the participants in a nationwide poll thought that TV strikes "just about the right balance" in its moral tone, but 40 per cent felt that "television is more frank and open than it should be."

*

I wonder how many of those people in the 40 per cent plurality who found TV too frank might have responded more positively if what they had been seeing in the way of frankness was also tasteful and meaningful. Perhaps not too many. Perhaps what those people really want is a return to "Father Knows Best" and an un-Hefnerized Ozzie Nelson. But as matters stand right now, I can't blame them for being offended. I'm offended, too. Because the new permissiveness on TV is, paradoxically, giving sex a bad name.

Daniel Menaker is on the editorial staff of The New Yorker and reviews movies for WBAI-FM.

The Quick Redd Foxx Jumps Into a New Kettle of Fish

By PAUL GARDNER

LOS ANGELES

SO, *what's the story?*

When John Sanford reached puberty, he displayed his moxie. In American folk-hero tradition, he ran away from home with his two best chums. Home had been St. Louis, Milwaukee, Chicago. The country, sporting a long face, was rousing itself from the Depression; V-mail, rationing and air-raid blackouts were still a few years away.

For young Sanford, the bright lights of Broadway beckoned. With washtubs and catgut string, he and his friends had already formed their own tramp band and had been performing on the sidewalks of Chicago. But his friends, too, heard the beat-beat-beat of Manhattan's distant drum. It was time to bid good-by to Cook County. Beautiful tomatoes and juicy steaks and drinks with fizz lay ahead.

The lads were penniless; they scrambled aboard a freight train for a bumpy, windowless ride into New York. The next morning, when the train puffed into the freight yard, they jumped. Sanford's companions were caught and hauled off to jail for 30 days. But Sanford ran like the dickens. Friendless, alone—a Charlie Chaplin figure—he found a job washing dishes in a New Jersey diner. The town was Secaucus. *Organ music.*

*

NBC, Burbank: "Hey, lemme see that!" Redd Foxx reached across a rehearsal table and grabbed a magazine left by a fleet-footed messenger. He picked it up and stared at the cover. What he saw was a picture of Redd Foxx. He grinned wickedly at himself. Then he threw his head back and laughed. "Y'know, I been waiting 25 years to make the cover of Jet!" Proudly he tapped the magazine. "In the black community, this is the Bible."

In a few hours, at 8 P.M. that Friday evening, to be exact, his first series "Sanford and Son," would have its premiere. "Sanford" was adapted from the BBC favorite, "Steptoe and Son," just as "All In The Family" is a BBC export with a Brooklyn accent, which suggests the networks are discovering a felicitous operation — the Series Transplant.

Even "Steptoe's" alliterative title smoothly underwent a slight sea change: At a story conference, Redd Foxx simply divulged to his cohorts that his *real* name was John Sanford. Exit Steptoe, enter Sanford. In show business, some problems are ridiculously easy to solve.

The show's adapters, Bud Yorkin and Norman Lear, had already made Archie Bunker of "All In The Family" an acceptably cheeky hardhat. But nobody could say for sure, least of all Foxx, how the Nielsen ratings would now react to a middle-aged black comedian playing a sassy junkman in a crummy section of Los Angeles. The dandy reviews—and ratings—were still to come, and Foxx was trying to keep his cool. "Y'know the guys, my friends in the black community told me they're gonna be at home tonight watching, just like it's a Joe Louis fight. Means a lot to them. And me too."

The show certainly seemed a good mid-season replacement bet, an antidote to the Rinso-White world of TV's Norman Rockwell families, so prettily removed from reality amid hurricane lamps and tons of maple furniture. It was not the "who dat?" slapstick of Sapphire and Kingfish on "Amos 'n' Andy." And it was definitely not "Julia," with Diahann Carroll sashaying around in $2,000 originals like a black Loretta Young.

*

Sanford and his son, Lamont, are funkily mature men, "failures" so far, from a low-income minority. The son dreams of a better life, away from home; his father wants to keep him there. The son would like to teach his father some niceties—how to choose a cocktail, appreciate a reserved seat movie, order dinner in a Chinese restaurant; his Pop would just as soon stay home in his easy chair with a six-pack and watch television. They frazzle each other's nerves, but there is always affection.

Co-starring with Foxx is Demond Wilson, a young black actor and former (child) tap dancer, who acted in the New York Shakespeare Festival's production of "Jazznite" last spring. Wilson plays the nearly 30-year-old son, who calls himself a collector of fine objects instead of a junk dealer, to Foxx's warmly irascible father, a man who doesn't doll up his profession with fancy words. On the British version, the two leads were cockney. The old man was portrayed as a mean, selfish near-illiterate who would not hesitate to rip off an antique for his junk store, and some 27 million British viewers loved him. His character was softened for America. Foxx sees the role as "a little bit of a Jewish mother."

"This is not a black 'All in the Family,'" stresses Aaron Ruben, "Sanford's" producer. "The only similarity may be some kind of breakthrough, away from the safe antiseptic series where you're convinced the houses don't even have bathrooms."

Ruben, who wrote for Burns and Allen and for Fred Allen and also created "Gomer Pyle," has been adapting most of the British scripts with improvisations from Redd Foxx himself. "Our theme is the father-and-son relationship—the generation gap. The humor transcends color. Norman Lear, who wrote 'All in the Family,' is from Massachusetts. He has a Jewish background. Should only a hardhat from Long Island, or Brooklyn, write Archie dialogue?"

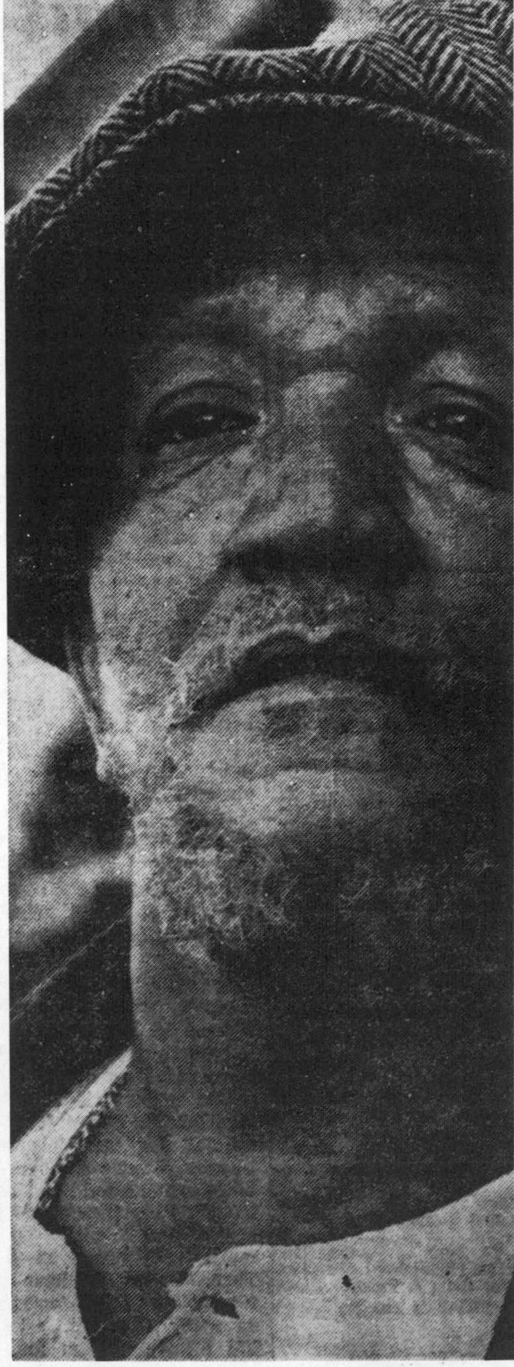

Fred A. Sabine

Redd Foxx

Redd Foxx sneaked a last glimpse of himself on the cover of Jet and was then led, for some publicity photos, across the Flip Wilson set, grinning and nodding at the studio audience, to Flip's dressing room, where Flip was being combed, dusted, dressed and booted, and taking none of the ministrations seriously.

"Hey, Redd, what're you doing in *here?*"

"They want pictures of us."

"What'll we do?" Flip asked, making faces at the mirror.

"Aw . . . let's have a drink." Redd poured some Scotch into paper cups. "Flip, y'think this is *bad publicity?*"

A rascal, that Redd Foxx. He's a teetotaler, almost. What does he do to make himself feel better? Spotted popping something into his mouth, he laughed *"peppermints.* Man, I had chili and onions for lunch."

With the peppermint roll and a cup of coffee, he explained, "I'm a Sagittarian, see, I can't be fenced in. I been living in Las Vegas, greatest city in the world. I look out my window for 100 miles. In Vegas, there's nothin' to do but gamble, drink or have sex. I have two of 'em."

*

The story (conclusion): When John Sanford left Secaucus, he rejoined his mates on the sidewalks of New York. On good days, the little tramp band collected $40. No top-hatted producer appeared waving bags of gold, but they did win a spot—and second prize—on the Major Bowes radio show. No turning back now.

Then, World War II broke up the troupe and Sanford took odd jobs, as a short-order cook, a bus boy; he pushed racks of dresses in the garment industry. And he began working alone as a comedian. When he had no dough, he slept on a roof in Harlem under a blanket of newspapers. When he had classy bookings, like the 125th Street Apollo, there was steak.

After the war, he teamed up with another comedian, Slappy White, and they played together for five years. But in 1951 he was in East Los Angeles, sleeping in a truck. He'd come to California on a hope, for the Big Break. Sooner or later, doesn't everybody get rich in California?

Back in the forties, he'd selected a new name for himself, one with some marquee zap. John Sanford was black, but not very, very black. His friends called him Red (one "d"), they said he was foxy, too. Foxy was forties slang. Like some mashers were said to be wolves. His new moniker, Redd Foxx, wasn't quite enough to impress the people who order cement mixers to start turning at Grauman's Chinese, but his titillating material got him a record contract.

It would take another 20 years before he hit it big—two shows a night at the Las Vegas Hilton and a part in the movie "Cotton Comes to Harlem." It was his portrayal of a crafty junkdealer in the film that led to his getting the TV series. His one indulgence: a St. Bernard weighing 260 mother-lovin' pounds. Redd Foxx feeds *it* steak left on plates at the Las Vegas Hilton.

*

NBC Burbank: "What is black dialogue?" asks Demond Wilson. "They want black writers on the series, but one sent in a script filled with, 'Hey, baby, you dig the jive?' That's not dialogue. That's argot. You don't ask, 'Is the director black, is the writer black?' but, 'Is this guy a pro?' Last year 'Barefoot in the Park,' with a black cast, was a cop-out; the characters weren't recognizable.

"Any situation Redd and I aren't comfortable with, we tell 'em. If anything, black militants might resent that we're showing this much of ourselves. I mean, we aren't caricatured. We aren't glamorized. We're poor but we're trying to get along, which is the way it is for most blacks. It's honest and I can say that 'cause I'm from Harlem; I know."

Foxx told the producers to just let him talk naturally. He'd already balked at roles with a super-dialect. "I'm not gonna eat watermelon on TV. I don't at home."

Home is now an acre in Las Vegas but he may be forced soon to secure another domicile in Beverly Hills. At 49, Redd Foxx is ready to enjoy the good California life at last. His three personal mementos, acquired over the years, include a wife and daughter and a medallion of friendship from Elvis Presley. To the medallion, he has added three diamonds.

February 6, 1972

Still Serious About Series Comedies

"M*A*S*H" could be a major innovation for television. Or it could slip quietly into the category of "Hogan's Heros."

The first episode, written by Mr. Gelbart and directed by Gene Reynolds, who is producing the series also, met the demands of this issue with surprising effectiveness Brightly paced, it introduced its stable of wacky combat surgeons in a plot to raise money to send a Korean houseboy-martini mixer to medical school ("America has sent thousands of boys to Korea; the least we can do is send one Korean boy to America").

For television, the editing was refreshingly brisk and the humor unusually adult. Tomorrow evening, however, in the second episode, written by Burt Styler and directed by Michael O'Herlihy, the pacing and the comedy show distinct signs of slackening. Revolving around the routines of a Korean black-marketeer, the story degenerates into standard situation-comedy skits.

September 23, 1972

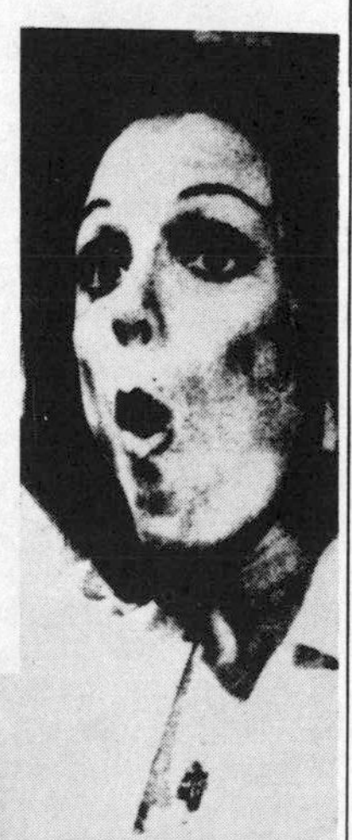

Living the single life on three new TV shows are Clifton Davis, far left, on "That's My Mama" (Mama is Theresa Merritt); Freddie Prinze, left, a young Chicano on "Chico and the Man" (Jack Albertson is the Man) and Valerie Harper, above, starring as "Rhoda."

CHAPTER 6

Music Makes the World Go Round

Elvis Presley

Courtesy RCA

HERBERT'S TOYLAND MUSIC.

Among the various elements that are contributing to the success of "Babes in Toyland," the new musical extravaganza at the Majestic Theatre, the music must not be left out of account. It might almost have been left out of account in "The Wizard of Oz." The new production appears to be repeating the success of that ingenious piece, if the public interest shown during the first week is a correct indication, and while it lacks some of the most striking excellences that constituted "The Wizard's" magic, it is a long advance upon it in respect of the music. It is an advance, too, upon much heard in New York recently in the shape of musical comedies, musical burlesques, and all the other things that have come in to take the place of comic operas, bewailed by old fogies with memories a dozen or more years long. What Mr. Victor Herbert has written is clearly the work of a musician of fancy and skill, showing in much of it a certain distinctive charm. He is not one who is willing to adopt the well-worn rhythms, the staled melodic ginger, and the noisy orchestral commonplaces of the Broadway school of composers, who have been exchanging the dregs of ideas with each other for some years. He has done something that has a breath of fresh air in it. The score of "Babes in Toyland" is not a masterpiece of musical art; in fact, as an extravaganza and not, by intention, in the least an operetta, its music must necessarily hold a subordinate place, but it is of a kind to give genuine pleasure for its own sake.

Mr. Herbert's vein of infectious melody crops out frequently. "Babes in Toyland" is distinctively tuneful. The opening chorus, "Don't Cry, Bo Peep," taps the vein immediately. Its tune is communicative, and there is a captivating swing in its rhythmic movement. So it is in the refrain of the gypsy song, "Floretta," sung by Alan to help carry out his disguise; here the familiar characteristics of gypsy melody and rhythm are amusingly burlesqued with a touch of mock tragedy, only to be quite wiped out the next moment in the ingratiating lilt of the chorus—one of the most taking moments, musically, in the whole piece. The Widow Piper's sumptuous and attractive children seated on the garden wall sing their artless arithmetical chorus, "Put Down Six and Carry Two," to a very pretty little ditty—the tune can be heard in the orchestra, at least, if not in the girlish squeals of the ingenuous young calculators. The "Christmas Fair Waltz," at the beginning of the second act, has the right sort of swing, and so has Bo Peep's song, "Maybe the Moon Will Help You Out," with its dance, in the third act.

Besides these things, which fix themselves at once in the ears of the audience, there is the usual allotment of more serious songs of a sentimental sort—songs that the company is unusually well-equipped to do justice to. Mr. Herbert has done a capital thing, falling back upon his rights as an Irishman, in the Irish ballad, "Barney O'Flynn," given to Contrary Mary. Miss Amy Ricard sings it admirably, and, indeed, her fresh, light voice and good understanding of what singing is, her neat and graceful style, all removed from the conventional methods of the comic opera stage, are among the pleasantest features of the production. Miss Bessie Wynn has a sentimental song, "An Old-Fashioned Rose," that Tom Tom sings at the beginning of the third act for no especially apparent reason except that the time has come for such a song, and does it well, as she does the song "Toyland," with the male chorus in the second act. Miss Frances Marie has the most elaborate of these productions, relating the legend of the Toymaker's castle, in the scene representing that imposing structure. She has obviously been given this chance for a special purpose, for she has nothing else to do, but while she does not seem altogether at home in her surroundings, she does it in a really artistic manner.

The singing is, indeed, chiefly confined to the women of the company, for Mr. Norris, whose representation of Alan is very clean-cut and crisp in its humor, can hardly be called a singer by any stretch of the imagination. Nor can the athletic and energetic Mr. Charles Guyer, in his part of Grumio. Mr. Norris gains very effective results, however, from the song "Rock a-bye Baby," in which that well-known air is presented as it would be sung by a nursemaid in the park at the approach of a policeman, as it would be performed by two highly distinguished brass band conductors, and as it would sound if the coon-song manufacturers took it in hand—a clever idea cleverly worked out. Neither he nor Miss Ricard tries to do much singing in the inevitable topical song "Before and After." The chorus of women's voices is of rather unusual excellence for this sort of a performance, and has a remarkably sweet and pure sound, being much better than that of the men, which is kept in the background of both sight and hearing.

It is a pleasure to hear the orchestra so discreetly treated as it is by Mr. Herbert, with delicacy and color and variety of expression. His instrumentation has many pretty touches; and those who care for such things will notice the skill of his harmonization and how the effectiveness of even his most obviously popular melodies is enhanced by it. He has had a good opportunity for descriptive and characteristic music, and has used it intelligently; the gruesomeness of the Spider's Forest is illustrated all through the scene by the darkling accompaniment of the orchestra; there is even a "bear motive" for the charming mother and her cub; of course the storm at sea and the crash of the wicked toymaker's castle are vigorously depicted in orchestra tone. The dream music for the two children in the fearsome forest and the "Toy Soldiers' March and Military Ball" are both subjects that have been better done by greater men than Mr. Herbert, working on similar lines. But his version of the former has charm and grace, and of the latter is not without apt and characteristic humorous expression. The music of "Babes in Toyland," in fact, is an attractive and really important feature of the performance.

October 18, 1903

BERLIN SINGS SONG IN A LONDON CLUB

Appears With Wife at Sophie Tucker's Farewell in Glare of Movie Flashlights.

HE RESENTS AFFRONT HERE

'A Nightmare of Lies,' He Says, Telling How One Reporter Made Ellin Cry.

Special Cable to THE NEW YORK TIMES.

LONDON, Jan. 17.—Mr. and Mrs. Irving Berlin emerged from their hiding place in a Carlton Hotel suite early today and stepped directly into the limelight at a farewell party at the Kit Cat Club to Sophie Tucker, the American vaudeville star, who has been such a success here.

Not only that, but Berlin, at Miss Tucker's request, sang "Remember." He sang on the dancing floor in the full glare of the movie lights, in a voice which was scarcely audible even in the hush, which greeted his unexpected appearance.

In the meanwhile his wife stood on a table by the side of Sir William Wiseman, former Chief Adviser on American Affairs to the British Delegation in Paris, and listened.

One London critic declared it was the finest sing song and the greatest smoking concert London has known for some time and that it proved that the American conquest of the English stage is practically complete.

"For nearly two weeks," said Mr. Berlin afterwards in an interview, "I have had to protect my wife from insults too bitter for me to speak of. We have lived in a nightmare of lies. When we were going to board a train one reporter was so insulting that my poor wife burst out crying. Then a Chicago newspaper printed in large type 'Berlin's bride in tears regrets step.' If you see an interview printed except this one it will be lies."

LONDON, Jan. 17 (AP).—What happened at the Kit-Kat Club when the Berlins came was related afterward by some of those present.

It seems that Berlin's barrier against receiving missives was broken at midnight on Saturday when he received an urgent message from Miss Tucker, who begged Irving to come and share in her farewell. Berlin was unable to resist. He and his bride came out of the hotel, hailed a taxi and drove to the Kit-Kat Club.

There Mr. and Mrs. Berlin found a brilliant gathering of actors, actresses, singers and society personages, few of whom knew the couple or noticed their entry. Mrs. Berlin wore a simple pink evening gown.

After the bride and bridegroom had sat together a while watching and listening, Miss Tucker mounted the rostrum and said:

"I will now ask Irving Berlin to play some of his melodies for us."

All eyes were immediately turned upon the couple. Berlin, looking shy and uneasy, left the side of his wife and went to the piano. Instead of playing, however, he decided to sing, and it is said, that this was the first time he had sung here in public.

"Not for any other artist would I have risked it," Berlin said to a Daily Express representative. He then went on to tell of the close professional connection between Miss Tucker and himself.

January 18, 1926

CROONERS IN SPOTLIGHT AS YEAR NEARS AN END

Radio History Will Record 1931 a Good One for Many Soft-Voiced Songsters—Some Deplore Their Invasion

By RICHARD B. O'BRIEN

THE mushroom growth of the radio crooner has been nothing short of phenomenal. There can be little doubt that 1931 will go down in broadcasting records as a "boom" year for crooners. Even a falling stock market has not been able to check their meteoric rise or curb their princely salaries. Turn the dial to the right or the left and you hear the crooner's plaintive voice. The listener may take them or leave them but he cannot elude them in the vicarious dial wanderings.

It all began only a few years ago when a soft-voiced, mild mannered young man named Rudy Vallee—or was it Will Osborne?—introduced this new style of troubadouring. Gone was the strident wail of the saxophone, the shrill cry of the clarinet. The wild jargon called jazz blended into a hushed, melodic, rhythmic type of music in slower tempo and softer cadences. Simultaneously with the soft-tongued orchestra, the crooner appeared, his voice pitched to harmonize with the caressing notes of the muted harmonies.

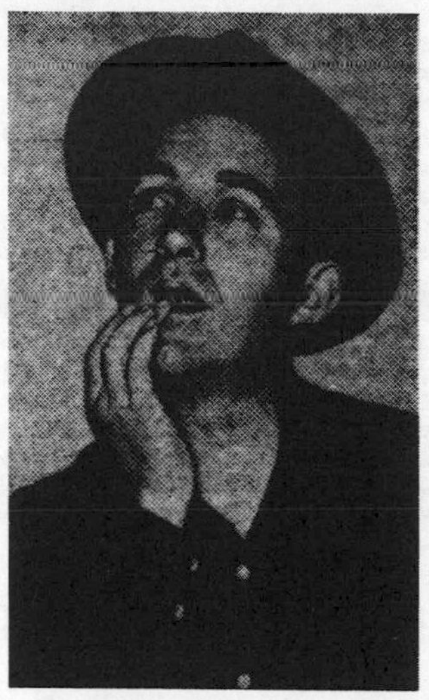

Bing Crosby thoughtfully watches a rehearsal of his Thursday night show which is on the air from 9 to 10 on WEAF.

Among the Romeos of Song.

While Rudy Vallee, among the radio crooners, still wears the royal purple, he no longer holds undisputed sway in the realm of radio songsters. The past year has seen their ranks swell tremendously. "A Vagabond Lover," the Vallee theme song, has given way to "Wabash Moon" and "As Time Goes By." Kate Smith, Morton Downey, Bing Crosby, Russ Columbo, Singing Sam, Ruth Etting, Frances Williams—these are but a few of the names that twinkle brightest in electric lights and occupy the studio spotlight. Theirs are the names affixed to the biggest contracts. And they do not all care to be called "crooners." Morton Downey prefers to be designated as the "radio minstrel boy," while Russ Columbo rejoices in being tagged successively "The Vocal Valentino" and "The Romeo of Song."

Any consideration of the niche that this type of singer occupies in the radio and entertainment world depends largely upon one's individual viewpoint, musical standards and personal taste. Frances Alda, former leading soprano of the Metropolitan Opera, who has since been won over to the microphone, once remarked that she enjoyed the musical mood exemplified by Rudy Vallee, adding that such a style of singing "fills a distinct place in any entertainment world where the tastes are as cosmopolitan and diversified as those of the American radio audience."

A Megaphone Helps.

Erich Kleiber, the Viennese maestro, who last year made his American début as conductor of the New York Philharmonic-Symphony, expressed his admiration for the modern jazz music heard on the radio today, and while he confessed that he thought it was being overdone, nevertheless, he was of the opinion that it "represented a cross-section of American life and was therefore decidedly worth while." Mr. Kleiber was equally decisive in his attitude toward the classics, deprecating the broadcasting of too many symphonies and operatic works.

On the other hand, John McCormack deplores the invasion of the crooner. He charges that the current style of radio singers is tending to warp the musical tastes of the nation and offend those who still look upon music as one of the arts.

"All you need today is a cardboard megaphone and a little nerve and then to stand near a microphone and 'fake' a thing they call singing." Mr. McCormack is quoted as saying in a Boston paper, when he returned from Europe.

The Irish tenor fears for the future of the vocal art in America. He remarked recently that since the country had gone radio mad every one wants to be a crooner, and there is little demand for the serious operatic singer.

"Whereas a generation ago," said Dennis McSweeney, McCormack's manager, "any singer endowed with talent aspired to be a Tetrazzini or a Caruso, now our young singers are fired with an ambition to be a Kate Smith or a Russ Columbo. A few thousand devotees of this type of singing are permitted to set the musical standards of the day by writing fan letters to the broadcasters applauding the efforts of the crooners, while the real music lovers refrain from engaging in such a naive pastime."

The Vallee Rebuttal.

Here is what Rudy Vallee had to say of McCormack's criticism of the crooner in a recent interview in Radio Dial:

"It always seems foolish to me to try to criticize the public for liking a thing. We of the soft-crooning radio type of singer are giving the people what they want. The American public as a whole does not care for full-throated, operatic singing. And why should it? Down through the ages it has been the simple song which has lived and continues to touch the heart of humanity. And so it is with singing."

But whatever one may think of the "personality" singer, there is no disputing his tremendous popularity. Julius F. Seebach, director of program operations for the Columbia Broadcasting System, was asked for an explanation of the popular favor that this type of singer now enjoys.

Personality a Big Factor.

"It is not easy to analyze the elements that make for the success of the radio crooner," said Mr. Seebach, "but it is certain that the element of personality enters very largely and most definitely into creating his popular appeal. The public is fickle and is quick to embrace something new and different. This appeal the crooner undoubtedly possesses to an extraordinary extent. His superior in vocal equipment and technique, who is lacking in "voice personality," to use a much abused term, may leave an audience cold. Emotional appeal is a very definite requisite for any entertainer reaching such a wide public as the radio singer.

"It seems to me that the success of the current favorites is due to their ability to take a song and make it their own. Kate Smith, Morton Downey and Bing Crosby each sings 'I Surrender Dear' and puts his individual stamp upon the song. Each sings it differently, but to the complete satisfaction of the audience. Each one projects his own personality into the mute device known as the microphone. Each has the power to exert an emotional appeal upon the listener."

December 6, 1931

SONGS THAT THE LEGION SANG

By OLIN DOWNES

WE were not present when the virile representatives of the American Legion fired pistols in Macy's department store. No one assaulted us with a squirt gun. The cannon, the crackers, the whistles, yells, ditties and marches sounded fiercely, but at a merciful distance outside the office doors. Though why the door of this department had to be passed by a posse playing upon whee-jees, with a bass drummer and a leader interpreting Chopin's Funeral March upon a fife is incomprehensible. Perhaps it was intended as a ceremony for the Unknown Musician and a preview of the hereafter of a music reporter.

The reunion of the American Legion in New York had memories for those who embarked from these ports to make the world safe for piracy, and for those who watched them go. One of the most stirring of the parades was the procession of sons of the war veterans, a whole new generation sprung up since 1918, and marching with a magnificent snap to music that had been heard "over there." And, of course, the occasion revived the American songs of the World War.

That war generated much music and verse. An army always sings; modern warfare found the song as efficacious as ever to promote morale. It would be hard to make detailed classification of the variety of American songs, composed here or invented on the spot for the occasion. There were fighting songs, marching songs, mother songs, ribald ditties—prime favorites—and travesties fitted to famous tunes expressive of heroic sentiment.

* * *

The many unprintable adventures and recommendations of "Mademoiselle From Armentières" gave vast satisfaction through the length and breadth of the line. It was probably the lively rhythm of the song and the Rabelaisian jocosities of the verses that commended it. "Madelon" was of the same genre.

One of the best songs was certainly George Cohan's "Over There," a racy exhilarating tune, like so many of the songs that Cohan produced, music and verse, and imbued with the spirit of his day. The appeal of the song was in the energy and simplicity of its idea. The motive had irresistible dramatic suggestion, and the rhythmical pounding of emphasis on the words of the last line, "And we won't come back till it's over, over there," says something, when sung by he-men, that isn't forgotten. It is of such simple and real stuff that a war-song is made.

Cohan companioned this song with "Good-bye, Broadway, Hello France," which was of a less dramatic and a gayer sort. It made a fine marching song, and so, as it proved, did "Keep the Home Fires Burning." Geoffrey O'Hara's "K-K-K-Katy" went over big, and had many textual variations, such as "C-C-C-Cootie."

* * *

The favorite sentimental song was the "Long, Long Trail," and sentimental airs were much liked. The mother song, dwelling upon the significance of each of the letters, "M-O-T-H-E-R" was often intoned—sometimes, it is to be feared, with the effect enhanced by beverages, as when, on a certain occasion back of the lines, it was performed very earnestly in half a dozen dialects, by Americans, Canadians, British, Irish and Scotch. Then an Irish sergeant reached forward and crashed a beer-bottle upon the head of an Englishman who happened to be within range. A perfectly grand free-for-all ensued.

There were all sorts of comic songs, and topical ones, such as "I've Got My Captain Working for Me Now." The English liked "Over There" almost as much as they did "Tipperary." The Canadian song of Captain Gitz-Rice, "Keep Your Head Down, Fritzie Boy," composed after the Battle of Ypres in 1915, came somewhat belatedly to the fore. Here and now, down in the street as we write, sounds one of the grand old-timers that has served for so many occasions great and small, "Hail, Hail, the Gang's All Here."

Well over a hundred songs went into the repertory of the soldiers, aside from the far greater variety furnished by the Y. M. C. A. entertainments. But this must be said, when you come right down to it: nothing invented during wartime surpassed or equaled such magnificent creations of the American past as Dan Emmett's "Dixie" and the best of the marches of John Philip Sousa.

* * *

Individuals will vote differently for favorite airs. For this writer nothing America has produced in the line of a popular song has equaled for characteristic andoriginal expression the wild, laughing, debonair &Dixie'' of our old American minstrel. For this is one of the most glorious and reckless tunes in the world. It has the laughter of haughty young men, and something of the skirl of a bagpipe, and the unmistakable accent of the free-born. It would illustrate well the subtle distinction drawn by the psychologist who said that an Englishman entered a house as if he owned it and an American as if he didn't care who owned it. What a miracle is this glorious tune, and what must it have meant to our men overseas!

* * *

And you shall rank only a little lower Mr. Sousa. In certain of his strains he struck an incomparably popular and vital note. He said the national thing in a certain way that no one else achieved, and that could only be said of this nation. What other country since the Eighties has put such powder into its marches? It is true that all sorts of things enter into a Sousa march. There is national braggadocio of the imperialistic era: Uncle Sam in his striped hat, goatee and trousers, out to lick the world, by gum. The introductory flourish of "The Stars and Stripes" always makes us think of that. But what follows says something else again, and says the brave and gallant thing with a lift that would put heart into a sheep and fire housewives to deeds of derring-do. And there's the tune of the trio, the serene, long-sustained, deep-breathing melody that John Philip once told us had come to him as he was sailing homeward to America and, looking up from the boat deck, saw the flag of the United States streaming nobly against a turbulent sky.

* * *

But we are not here to apostrophise the literature of American national song or provide notes upon the many marches of Sousa. This question is apropos: How do the songs that the American soldiers sang in the World War impress us today? How many of them will stand, after the occasion that produced them has passed, as living music? Will any of them rank with the earlier compositions to which reference has been made?

It is hardly likely that they will. Nothing evolved in the last war period matches the great national songs of earlier days. The reason for this may be the pure accident that no genius appeared, as a Rouget de Lisle, to compose a "Marseillaise," greatest of all war-songs, in the passage of a night. And there may be another reason which often has operated in music. This is, that music, which comes, in its greatest manifestations, from a source so deep in the individual as to rest in the subconscious, appears often in history to have been the latest of all the arts to mirror the emotions or experiences through which a nation has passed. This, at least, is a theory supported by the evidence of the "romantic" school of composition of the nineteenth century, which evolved after results of revolution in thought and society had manifested themselves in literature and other arts; and by the birth of music drama, and the modernism of Monteverdi, constituting one of the last of the fruits of the dying Renaissance.

Did the war last long enough for it to engrave itself upon the profoundest consciousness of our people? Probably it did not, save for those who knew the ultimates of sacrifice and suffering at the front. Their majority, sweeping triumphantly forward, was not to know a single crushing reverse, or the despair of others, to whom defeat and annihilation must have appeared at certain times inevitable.

* * *

Our war songs, sometimes melancholy in a sentimental way and, once or twice, in the verses, tragic and grimly realistic, are as a class the songs of those who knew neither fear nor hate, and to whom, with all its horrors and catastrophes, the journey overseas meant a gallant and honorable adventure. They are football songs. They would go splendidly during a game. They are expressions of buoyant, confident youth, of the irrepressible spirit of a young and singularly fortunate nation, which began in an adversity that our forefathers knew and that we do not know and cannot wholly comprehend. The boys overseas had the stuff in them, and showed it immortally, to endure any hardship, take any position, and fight with invincible energy and the generosity of those who have not yet had bitterness wedged into their very souls. How young and glorious in their spirit they were, and how young, untwisted by cruelty or terror, they remain! It's in the songs. We can be thankful that their spirit did not alter, and has not changed.

September 26, 1937

'39 GONE, BUT THE MELODY LINGERS ON THE AIR—

TWO songs, "Deep Purple" and "Over the Rainbow," are likely to go into the musical records as the topnotch melodies of 1939, according to the year's statistics of the "Hit Parade," broadcast Saturday nights through 100 stations. Both were played seven times as the No. 1 song of as many weeks. "Beer Barrel Polka" was broadcast sixteen times on the program but never reached the favorite spot as No. 1.

The songs selected for the program are based on phonograph record sales, requests to band leaders, sale of sheet music in all parts of the country and the number of times the music is broadcast after 6 P. M.

The statisticians point out that "My Reverie" was in first place only once in 1939, but established a record of eight consecutive weeks as No. 1 song, because it was the favorite for the last seven weeks of 1938.

Listed as No. 1 for five times each were "Jeepers Creepers" and "South of the Border"; four times, "And the Angels Sing," "Wishing," "Stairway to the Stars" and "Moon Love"; three times, "Scatterbrain"; twice, "Heaven Can Wait," "Our Love" and "You Must Have Been a Beautiful Baby"; once, "My Reverie," "Day In-Day Out" and "Blue Orchids."

January 14, 1940

The First Ten Since 1900

These songs have stood the harsh test of time.

By SIGMUND SPAETH

TIN PAN ALLEY works every day at its job of creating popular songs. While it is always interested in a quick turnover, a constant parade of machine-made hits, the actual hope of every music publisher is to find an occasional song that will maintain its popularity through the years and eventually establish a kind of permanence justifying the industry's crowning adjective, "standard."

There have been many such songs in the present century—enough to make it exceedingly difficult to name the "first ten." But such arbitrary decisions are a customary part of American life, so why shrink from an obvious duty? If the results provoke some controversy (and perhaps some readers too), so much the better. Let's take the "ten most popular songs of the century" in chronological order, with a brief consideration of their backgrounds and at least an attempt to find out what they have in common and the reasons for their human appeal.

Naturally the term "popularity" is relative at best. Certainly the quality cannot be measured merely by the sale of sheet-music and records or by the total of public performances, including radio. A truly popular song is one of which practically everybody can recall the tune and at least some of the words. The surest test is to ask a crowd to sing, without song-sheets or slides or other aids to memory. The songs that ring out most clearly and spontaneously are the true leaders. Such songs of course must have sold millions of copies and as many or even more phonograph records, representing a variety of interpretations, and they must also be heard frequently in public, on the air, and in private amateur performance.

SIGMUND SPAETH, writer and lecturer on music, is best known as radio's "tune detective." His twenty-third book, "A History of Popular Music in America," was published last autumn.

***Only two of the following ten songs* fail to pass the test of community singing and these two have compensating qualities which cannot be overlooked. There is only one "production number" in the list, meaning a song first heard in a musical show. There are no real "novelties"—a term applied to almost anything nonsensical, from "Yes, We Have No Bananas" to "Open the Door, Richard." There are no "rhythm numbers" or tunes intended for dancing rather than singing. Most of the songs selected would be called "ballads" by Tin Pan Alley, not because they necessarily tell a story, but because they are basically sentimental. America likes a musical joke, but not too often. Our songwriters still sing of love, and they always will. So the list logically begins with a song about a girl—one of the most famous in modern history.**

SWEET ADELINE

THAT classic of close harmony was published in 1903, but Harry Armstrong actually composed the music in 1896 when he was working in a Boston jewelry store and doing a little boxing and piano-playing on the side. He called it "Down Home in Old New England" and organized a barber-shop quartet to sing it. It didn't set the world afire.

***A few years later* Armstrong came to New York and met a postal clerk named Richard Gerard Husch, who gave him a new lyric called *"You're the Flower of My Heart, Sweet Rosalie."* It had the appeal *of a girl's name* but the final syllable did not invite sustained harmony and still there was no conflagration. Then the name of Adelina Patti on a billboard suggested the right answer. The Quaker City Four tried out "Sweet Adeline" at Hammerstein's Victoria Theatre (now the Rialto) and it made an immediate hit.**

***Since then it has become, among popular songs, the most famous tribute to the feminine ideal.* But why does it live? Well, *for one thing, it is the best example of the "echo" effect in barber-shop harmony,* with a solo or unison phrase regu**larly followed by a series of chords on the same words. The trick occurs in "How Dry I Am" and other old favorites which likewise share with "Sweet Adeline" the four-note melodic pattern of the Westminster Chime. On the other hand, it is completely useless as a dance number and thus it has what any publisher today would consider a fatal handicap. It is never sung in strict time and its improvisational quality seems actually to add to its appeal. Anybody can pick up the tune immediately and its almost inevitable harmonies seem to give the illusion of creative power to its singers, men and women alike.

Harry Armstrong, the composer, now approaching 70, is still active on Broadway as booking agent and perpetual guest of honor. He likes nothing better than to sing the comparatively unfamiliar verse of his song, then lead his audience in the sure-fire chorus. Richard Gerard (who dropped the Husch when he became a professional song writer) died last year at 72.

SCHOOL DAYS

WORDS of "School Days," a 1907 publication, were written by Will D. Cobb and the music by Gus Edwards, who is remembered for other outstanding hits that include "Tammany," "In My Merry Oldsmobile" (which has achieved the immortality of a singing commercial), "Sunbonnet Sue" and "By the Light of the Silvery Moon." The two men had collaborated on such hits as "I Can't Tell Why I Love You But I Do," "Good-Bye, Little Girl, Good-Bye," and the song made famous by the French accent of Anna Held, "I Just Can't Make My Eyes Behave."

"School Days" outstripped all these, both in immediate success and in vitality through the years. Words and music are simple and direct: the tune is a gay little waltz, easily learned and remembered; the text fits every note perfectly. It is hard to imagine a group of average people today who are unable or unwilling to sing it. Historically, it supplied a theme for that group of "Schoolboys and Girls" including Eddie Cantor, George Jessel and Walter Winchell, whom Gus Edwards introduced to the professional stage as infant prodigies.

Will Cobb, whose name is little known to the millions who have sung his words, died in 1930; Edwards, just over three years ago.

SHINE ON, HARVEST MOON

THE one production number on our list, "Shine On, Harvest Moon," was written by Nora Bayes and her husband Jack Norworth for the Ziegfeld Follies of 1908. It was revived in 1931 by Ruth Etting in another Follies production and more recently it has supplied the title and musical theme or a motion picture supposedly portraying the public and private life of the Bayes-Norworth vaudeville team. Its first-year sale of over a million copies has been repeated many times and people will sing this favorite almost everywhere with a minimum of urging, for it is a home song as well as a show tune. Its words and music contain far more than the average of originality and humor.

Nora Bayes died in 1928; Jack Norworth recently has been running a novelty shop in California and appearing occasionally in benefit shows.

LET ME CALL YOU SWEETHEART

IN the year 1910 two of the most popular songs of all time appeared, along with other million-copy hits. Both of those two are waltzes. They suggest the taste of the Naive Nineties rather than that of our century, but everyday human beings still sing them with enthusiasm.

Of all the candidates for a place among the first ten, "Let Me Call You Sweetheart" probably can put forward the best claims. The words were written by Beth Slater Whitson and the music by Leo Friedman, who had collaborated a year earlier on a hit of almost equal proportions—"Meet Me

Tonight in Dreamland." The total sales of the two songs have perhaps exceeded ten million copies.

"Let Me Call You Sweetheart" is unquestionably the best bet for starting any mixed group on a successful community sing. It harmonizes easily; the range of melody is only a half-tone beyond an octave, and the words apply comfortably to either sex. The tune follows a logical pattern, starting on its lowest note and reaching a climax near the close with the simple, direct statement, "I'm in love with you."

DOWN BY THE OLD MILL STREAM

SUNG almost automatically in the course of any program that starts with "Let Me Call You Sweetheart," "Down by the Old Mill Stream," of the same year, was written by the legendary Tell Taylor, who lies buried in his native Findley, Ohio, where a park is named for the waterway that presumably inspired the song.

Its appeal lies not only in its waltz melody but also in the romantic nostalgia of its words and in other properties both usual and unusual. It is essentially a boy-meets-girl song, liked equally by men and women, though the point of view is definitely masculine. It is a perpetual favorite among harmonizers, who often interpret it with dramatic gestures as well as vigorous chords. (The climax of specific action comes when they count out the girl's age—sixteen—on their fingers.)

I WANT A GIRL

THE long title of this song, which appeared in 1911, is "I Want a Girl Just Like the Girl that Married Dear Old Dad." The music was the work of Harry von Tilzer, whose list of hits is so impressive that it is hard to choose one above the others, particularly since those others include "Wait Till the Sun Shines, Nellie."

"I Want a Girl," for which Will Dillon, still living in Ithaca, wrote the lyric, is a solid standby among the devotees of barber-shop harmony, and its unquestionably masculine point of view does not seem to interfere with enthusiastic acceptance by mixed groups. The dependable factors of a logical pattern of melody, a limited vocal range (one octave), easily remembered words and music and a simple direct message of human interest work once more with undeniable effect.

SAINT LOUIS BLUES

ON the basis of frequent performance and a great variety of recordings, William C. Handy's "Saint Louis Blues," published in 1914, must have its place on our list. It is widely known instrumentally as well as vocally and it represents the final, comprehensive expression of a form that is deeply rooted in the folk-music of America. Its Negro composer, still living and working in New York, explains the tango rhythm of the main strain by observing that the Tangana was originally an African jungle dance, taken to Spain by the Moors and brought to Cuba (where it became the Habanera) by slaves.

SMILES

LEE S. ROBERTS, a salesman of player-piano records, wrote down a tune on the back of a cigarette package, for which J. Will Callahan supplies the words, and "Smiles" appeared in the last year of the first World War. In less than a twelve-month it had sold nearly two million copies and it is still heard wherever people sing together.

There is something of the old moralizing spirit in "Smiles"; its popularity may be compared with that of Kipling's "If," sacred to innumerable dens and business offices. The creators of "Smiles" managed to combine the "cheerio" school of uplifting verse with a final punch-line of personal affection.

STAR DUST

AN instrumental hit in 1929, "Star Dust" four years later began a new life as a song when Mitchell Parish added an imaginative text to the highly individual melody of Hoagy Carmichael. While not for community singing, though millions know its strikingly original tune, "Star Dust" has been the most recorded song of the century. It appears in countless arrangements.

GOD BLESS AMERICA

OUR list ends almost automatically with a song published only ten years ago and by no means a typical product of Tin Pan Alley. It expresses a love of country rather than of any individual and it is not intended for dancing, although ideal for a community sing ending patriotically.

As a matter of history, that stirring march song "God Bless America" was written in 1917 but remained unpublished for more than two decades until Kate Smith had introduced it on the air.

Since then it has become a sort of unofficial national anthem, sung by millions of school children and millions of adults as well.

Irving Berlin, the composer, who is definitely our most popular song-writer, could not possibly be omitted from the "first ten," and might actually have contributed several of his many hits to the list. The selection of "God Bless America" may be challenged by the champions of "Always," "Blue Skies," "Easter Parade," "White Christmas" and other Berlin favorites. Obviously there are plenty of songs worthy of mention for such a roll of honor, but space and editorial judgment have placed the limit at ten.

• • •

WHAT, then, constitutes a popular song? Look back over our ten and we see that, with the possible exception of "Star Dust" and "Saint Louis Blues" the common denominator is simplicity. The tunes are of limited range, easy to sing and perfectly fitted to direct, intelligible words. There is no artificial cleverness, no double meaning. The lyrics are full of homely American words and phrases. Apparently it is just straightforward, unaffected songwriting that the people want and will cherish, as they cherished Stephen Foster in the past.

March 20, 1949

Premiere

Nat (King) Cole, who starts his own show on television tomorrow night over the National Broadcasting Company network is determined to make it a simple presentation. The popular singer, noted for his soothing vocal style, talked about the format of his program here the other day.

"So many shows these days are big productions," he said. "They're trying to be different and they seem to stumble over themselves. I think something simple might be a good idea—for me, anyway."

Backed by a vocal group and a rhythm section, Mr. Cole will play the piano and sing some of the numbers that he has popularized, including "Nature Boy," which he has selected as his theme song. "If I can get the same sort of spontaneity and the same sort of reaction that I do in a night club, I'll be happy," he said.

Reported to be the first Negro entertainer to be signed as the star of a network TV show, Mr. Cole said that he found the assignment most gratifying:

"Negroes have been exposed to many single appearances but have not been given a chance to do a regular show before now," he said. "I've been waging a personal campaign, aiming at a show of this kind. I hit a few snags here and there but I didn't give up the fight. It could be a turning point so that Negroes may be featured regularly on television."

The Cole show will begin as a sustaining program. Its star is confident that it soon will attract a sponsor.

November 4, 1956

MUSIC

A Concert of Jazz.

By OLIN DOWNES.

A concert of popular American music was given yesterday afternoon in Aeolian Hall by Paul Whiteman and his orchestra of the Palais Royal. The stage setting was unconventional as the program. Pianos in various stages of deshabille stood about, amid a litter of every imaginable contraption of wind and percussion instruments. Two Chinese mandarins, surmounting pillars, looked down upon a scene that would have curdled the blood of a Stokowski or a Mengelberg. The golden sheen of brass instruments of lesser and greater dimensions was caught up by a gleaming gong and carried out by bright patches of an Oriental back-drop. There were also lying or hanging about frying pans, large tin utensils and a speaking trumpet, later stuck into the end of a trombone—and what a silky, silkily tone came from that accommodating instrument! This singular assemblage of things was more than once, in some strange way, to combine to evoke uncommon and fascinating sonorities.

There were verbal as well as programmatic explanations. The concert was referred to as "educational," to show the development of this type of music. Thus the "Livery Stable Blues" was introduced apologetically as an example of the depraved past from which modern jazz has risen. The apology is herewith indignantly rejected, for this is a gorgeous piece of impudence, much better in its unbuttoned jocosity and Rabelaisian laughter than other and more polite compositions that came later.

The pianist gathered about him some five fellow-performers. The man with the clarinet wore a battered top hat that had ostensibly seen better days. Sometimes he wore it, and sometimes played into it. The man with the trombone played it as is, but also, on occasion, picked up a bath tub or something of the kind from the floor and blew into that. The instruments made odd, unseemly, bushman sounds. The instrumentalists rocked about. Jests permissible in musical terms but otherwise not printable were passed between these friends of music. The laughter of the music and its interpreters was tornadic. It was—should be blush to say it?—a phase of America. It reminded the writer of some one's remark that an Englishman entered a place as if he were its master, whereas an American entered as if he didn't care who in blazes the master might be. Something like that was in this music.

There were later remarkably beautiful examples of scoring for a few instruments; scoring of singular economy, balance, color and effectiveness; music at times vulgar, cheap, in poor taste, elsewhere of irresistible swing and insouciance and recklessness and life; music played as only such players as these may play it. They have a technic of their own. They play with an abandon equalled only by that race of born musicians—the American negro, who has surely contributed fundamentally to this art which can neither be frowned nor sneered away. They did not play like an army going through ordered manoeuvres, but like the melomaniacs they are, bitten by rhythms that would have twiddled the toes of St. Anthony. They beat time with their feet—lese majeste in a symphony orchestra. They fidgeted uncomfortably when for a moment they had to stop playing. And there were the incredible gyrations of that virtuoso and imp of the perverse, Ross Gorman. And then there was Mr. Whiteman. He does not conduct. He trembles, wabbles, quivers—a piece of jazz jelly, conducting the orchestra with the back of the trouser of the right leg, and the face of a mandarin the while.

There was an ovation for Victor Herbert, that master of instrumentation, when his four "Serenades" composed for this occasion were played, and Mr. Herbert acknowledged the applause from the gallery. Then stepped upon the stage, sheepishly, a lank and dark young man—George Gershwin. He was to play the piano part in the first public performance of his "Rhapsody in Blue" for piano and orchestra. This composition shows extraordinary talent, just as it also shows a young composer with aims that go far beyond those of his ilk, struggling with a form of which he is far from being master. It is important to bear both these facts in mind in estimating the composition. Often Mr. Gershwin's purpose is defeated by technical immaturity, but in spite of that technical immaturity, a lack of knowledge of how to write effectively for piano alone or in combination with orchestra, an unconscious attempt to rhapsodize in the manner of Franz Liszt, a naiveté which at times stresses something unimportant while something of value and effectiveness goes by so quickly that it is lost—in spite of all this he has expressed himself in a significant, and on the whole, highly original manner.

His first theme alone, with its caprice, humor and exotic outline, would show a talent to be reckoned with. It starts with an outrageous cadenza of the clarinet. It has subsidiary phrases, logically growing out of it, and integral to the thought. The original phrase and subsidiaries are often ingeniously metamorphosed by devices of rhythm and instrumentation. There is an Oriental twist to the whole business that is not hackneyed or superficial. And—what is important—this is no mere dance-tune set for piano and other instruments. It is an idea, or several ideas correlated and combined, in varying and well contrasted rhythms that immediately intrigue the hearer. This, in essence, is fresh and new, and full of future promise.

The second theme, with a lovely sentimental line, is more after the manner of some of Mr. Gershwin's colleagues. Tuttis are too long, cadenzas are too long, the peroration at the end loses a large measure of wildness and magnificence it could easily have if it were more broadly prepared, and, for all that, the audience was stirred, and many a hardened concertgoer excited with the sensation of a new talent finding its voice, and likely to say something personally and racially important to the world. A talent and an idiom, also rich in possibilities for that generally exhausted and outworn form of the classic piano concerto.

Mr. Gershwin's rhapsody also stands out as counter-acting, quite unconsciously, a weakness of the program, that is, a tendency to sameness of rhythm and sentiment in the music. When a program consists almost entirely of modern dance music, that is naturally a danger, since American dances of today do not boast great variety of step or character; but it should be possible for Mr. Whiteman to remedy this in a second program, which he will give later in the season. There was tumultuous applause for Mr. Gershwin's composition. There was realization of the irresistible vitality and genuineness of much of the music heard on this occasion, as opposed to the pitiful sterility of the average production of the "serious" American composer. The audience packed a house that could have been sold out twice over.

February 13, 1924

SAD, RAUCOUS BLUES CHARM WORLD ANEW

Their Music, as Old as the Hills, Is Working a Weeping, Sweeping Jazz Revolution

By HOLLISTER NOBLE

BLUES, raucous blues! Blatant, tender, sardonic, sentimental, poignant or pathetic, this musical medium of modern life has attained the proportions of a phenomenon worth attention. Battles over jazz continue to rage. Ernest Newman, noted English music critic, pronounces jazz "dead from the neck up." Enthusiasts point to its vitality from the waist down. German bands are beseeching Government legislation to bar American jazz bands, which are over-running the Fatherland. Native musicians here lay their troubles to a queer ingredient of popular music called the "blues."

Blues in the original form are vanishing, but their influence has wrought a revolution in jazz and the moans of sad horns and the wails of demoniac saxophones have caught the country's ear until the intelligentsia debate their worth; sponsors of the blues produce erudite anthologies, and sober psychologists ponder the social significance. While they do so, the blues sweep and weep over the world. Zulus in Africa are reported to have retreated before the menacing strains of "The Memphis Itch." A war tribe in the Congo was delighted with the "Rockpile Blues." Park Avenue débutantes, the rural élite of Jackson's Corners, Harlem "creepers," and Birmingham belles languish to the melancholy moans of this blue-tinted jazz.

Whence come these sad strains, and why? The growth and appeal of the blues, with their influence discernible in all jazz today, seems too universal to be dismissed as a temporary triumph of cheap music. By all the signs of the times the blues have brought about the true sophistication of jazz. Jazz, until a few years ago, was blatant, direct, often blind in its outbursts of barbaric rhythms. Today, thanks to the blues, orchestration, scoring and musical content have greatly improved. The blues seem to be a form of healthy repentance, perhaps leading jazz, despite Mr. Newman's forebodings, to higher and better things.

The blues attained early popularity, for in them the public found its beloved broken-hearted clown. Wailing minor thirds and shrieking glissandos, with ghastly grins hinting at secret sorrows and employing glycerine tears, guarantee pleasantly to twang the heartstrings of night club patrons and Main Street Lotharios.

Just as negro spirituals were products of higher forms of human sufferings, so the blues first expressed the tragedies, often trivial, of illiterate negroes, bar-room pianists, stevedores, street-walkers, porters and barber-shop habitués. Convicts, construction gangs, track-walkers and river men contributed their individual **blues to the great mass of social songs. The negro blues were poignant and usually built on genuine sorrows. Self-pity was a popular ingredient, as expressed in**

Po' boy 'long way from home
Got no where to lay my weary head

or "Got de blues but too damn mean to cry."

Other laments were more desperate. There were dire threats of "Gwine take morphine an' die" and "Gwine lay my head on de railroad track."

The iniquitous boll weevil of Southern cotton fields inspired many mournful blues and this term was often applied to hard-boiled railroad conductors who watched the "rods" and side-door Pullmans for non-pay-

ing passengers. A black cat's bone, so valuable in love, was celebrated in many a negro song. The blues were seldom symbols of pure despair. In them there was often a bit of philosophy; were always touches of personality, melancholy exuberance, sly humor—occasionally a touch of beauty near to tears. For the blues, which often captured some spark of the spirituals, first sprang from friendless wanderers, jailed transgressors, lonely souls and forsaken lovers. There were pleas for "Jes' one more chance"; for more pay, more food—and, always, less work. "Learn me to let all women alone" was the fervent plea of one early blues.

Handy Daddy of the Blues

In the jargon of the blues, W. C. Handy, colored musician, born in Alabama, is their own true "Daddy." Since the publication of his "Memphis Blues" and "St. Louis Blues" his authority has been unquestioned. He has recorded scores of blues tunes. Genuine "blues" tunes have been notoriously hard to capture. They changed with localities and shifted with the seasons. Mr. Handy in collaboration with Abbe Niles has recently issued an anthology. The blues were born of work songs, slow drags, pats, stomps, love plaints and all the great mass of social songs evolved by the negro in the varied phases of his life in turpentine camps, on the levees, or in the stokeholds of "river fliers." Some negroes recall blues in existence forty years ago. But 1910 marks the first general acceptance of the term. At that date, like a prophetic rash on the gay face of popular music, there wailed forth a series of "Weary" blues and "Worried" blues and "Blue Monday" blues, all cast in a direct simple mold admirable for projecting one's troubles in a loud lament.

Suddenly a nostalgia for travel seized upon the blues writers. Every vine-covered cottage below the Mason-Dixon Line became the goal for innumerable songsters. Foreign visitors must have thought the second great exodus was under way. Every one born north of the Ohio seemed to long for Dixie, batter cakes, gin rickeys and mammy. The blues of Texas song writers sobbed for Michigan; Michigan minstrels cried for Alabam'; rock-ribbed New Englanders longed for "deah ol' Georgiah."

The blues underwent a series of amusing developments. George Gershwin's "I've Got the You Don't Know the Half of It, Dearie, Blues," loosed the tongues of a thousand babbling title writers. Music counters were flooded with lengthy labels such as "Gee, But-I-Wish-I-Had-Known-You-the-Winter-Before-Last-Blues," or "Now-I-Come-to-Think-of-What-You-Told-Me-Not-to-Think-of-Blues."

There was the "Dontcha Remember" epoch; the "Gee, I Want to Be There" era; the "Take Me Back to Alabamy" age and the hot-blooded tunes from the East (Side), which have frightened all genuine sheiks into permanent retirement. More recently we have had the anatomical blues dealing with Red Hot Mamas, Ice Cold Sweeties, Hot Lips, Flat Feet, Blue-Gummed Blues, Broken Rib Blues and Luke-Warm Luke. Jazz and her raucous handmaidens have laid rude hands on every country for material. As a blues character "Mama" seems to have had the hardest time of all. There are blues entitled "Blue Mama's Suicide Wail," "Mama's Prison Yard Blues" and "Mamma's Deathbed Shout."

It is interesting to note the metamorphosis of the blues. Poignant with grief against a background of blasted hopes, they first appeared; but when the real blues and the sad secular songs of the blacks fell into the hands of white arrangers and composers, much of their sincerity and depth of grief vanished. The blues of Tin Pan Alley that moan today through the Main Streets of 10,000 towns have effloresced into far subtler forms and strike far different notes than the poignant strains of the old negro blues. But though the old blues lost much of their emotional power, the white man's prosperity, allied with the rush and turmoil of a new age, has transformed the blues into a valuable leaven of jazz which may yet lift the latter form to a position of dignity.

With white people the grief of the blues has degenerated into sentimentalizing. In a certain sense the blues mark the sophisticated decadence of jazz. The unbuttoned gayety and blare of "Alexander's Ragtime Band" and "The Dark Town Strutters Ball" have become tinged with the pale cast of afterthought. Memory, reflection, vague regrets and other features of the "I-Wish-I-Were, I-Want-to-Be, O, Don't-You-Remember" school are all characteristic of the blues. Once jazz was its own blind, blatant self; but now out of its whirring wheels come, thanks to the blues, wild glissandos, minor thirds, malicious discords; Neapolitan sixths and the moans of saxophones that mirror the mixed emotions of the modern age.

Musical Mirror of the Masses

For the blues provide a long-sought musical medium wherein to mirror the fleeting melancholies and light sorrows of today's masses. The blues reflect admirably the social psychosis of the present age. They sing the sadness of satiety, their hoarse joy is torn with discontent. They shout skepticism, nostalgia, humor, exuberance and all the tinselled brilliance of a Coney Island crowd. They are the blues of after-dinner contentment of blasé youngsters, of well-fed loungers, of temporary solitude, flickering flirtations and the amorous aspirations of drug store dandies.

Jerome Kern's "Left All Alone Again Blues" is filled with the doubtful sorrows of a forsaken spouse. Only Clara Smith, billed as the world's greatest moaner, or one of her talented sisters, could have imparted conviction to this song. The wife's heartfelt sentiments sound a bit specious. Behind their smoke-screen sighs, all the forsaken lovers of the modern blues seem to be thumbing the leaves of the telephone directory. Years of solitude faced the dark singer of the old-time blues. But today's solitude is a few hours of mild melancholy, a sigh over last night's party, skepticism over tomorrow's blind date, nostalgia over today's duties.

A wife yearns for her husband, who has gone to town for eight hours. A hundred thousand belles of Main Street, surfeited with the dapper youth of the town, sit in dimly lighted ice cream parlors and long for the strong sweep of desert love. Partings, daily adventures, light sorrows, infidelities of friendship and affection, lugubrious humor—all are merged on a vague, misty, emotional plane marking the aura of the blues.

Humor marks the musical notation of many of these songs. "Tempo di weary" directs one composer over the opening bars. "Tempo di sadness, tempo disappointo, tempo di low down," sigh other directions. Sophisticated, subtle, endless in their efflorescence of conflicting moods and moments, the modern blues mock the stars and wail for the moon, ringing the changes of variable temperaments whirled along a jazz-strewn highway vibrating with the rush and roar of contemporary life. There is often an amusing conflict of qualities, true and false, in the blues. They toast a tawdry beauty that is close to crocodile tears. There is a catch in their grief-stricken cry that often turns into a hiccough. For the white man's blues are a luxury; their sorrows are shallow and their griefs groundless. Their loudest laments are often filled with unconscious irony.

It is these new complexities of the blues that promise to deliver jazz from the monotonous shackles of foxtrot rhythms. George Gershwin's "Rhapsody in Blue" has become the historical example to which jazz and blues reformers point with pride.

To date the blues as developed in commercial music centres have retained a semblance of genuine grief and emotion. The sentiment of the words is excessively naïve and pretentiously sincere. But the music belies the sentiment. Listen to the sardonic groans, the ironic moans, the cries and haunting minors of a good "blues" specimen. Doubt and pessimism, long since present in the music of the blues, are already

"The Rattling Sticks of a Good Blues Drummer Keep Harlem Echoes Sounding Until Dawn."

A Study in Blues.

Saxophones Still Play the Leading Part.

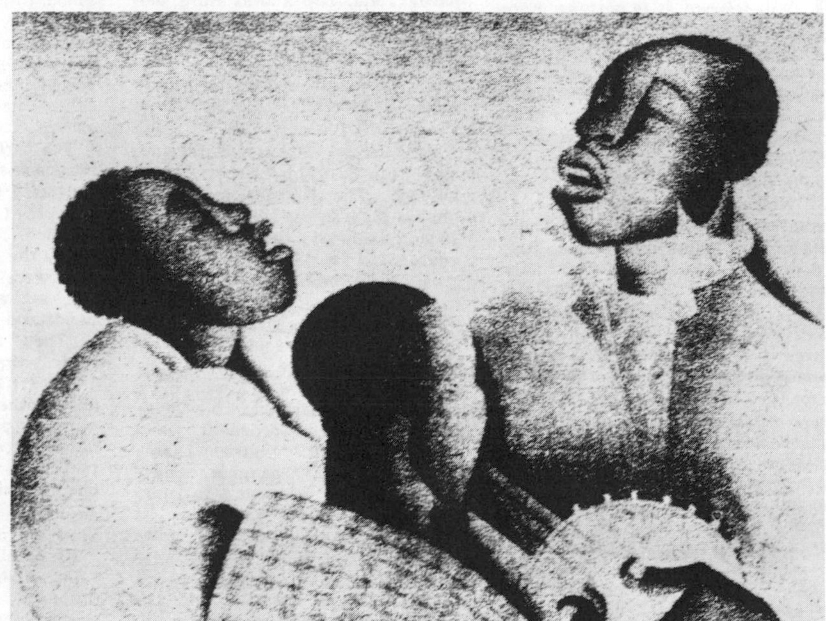

"Any Trio Can Improvise a Blues Guaranteed to Produce a Soporific Melancholy."

The Drawings on This Page Are by Covarrubias and Appear in "Blues."

Edited by W. C. Handy and Published by Albert and Charles Boni.

creeping into the words. The lonely damsel, according to the latest blues, may be longing for "you-hoo"; but that absurd tell-tale shriek on the saxophone makes you suspect that she already has half a dozen good telephone numbers revolving in her pretty little head. No matter how yearningly the dephlogisticated tenor with belladonna in his eyes wails to the top box, he has no intention of returning to his vine-covered cottage in Alabam.

In John Alden Carpenter's ballet, "Skyscrapers," given at the Metropolitan Opera House last season, there was a brief but striking illustration of this growth. A group of sorrowing blacks begin with a simple, primitive dirge, which develops into a slow, rhythmic lament. The lament rises to the poignant heights of the spirituals; then subtleties of rhythm and accent creep in; the tempi accelerate; the whole movement is suddenly captured by irresistible rhythms and bursts into the utter abandon of jazz, shot through with the minor moans of a mild "blues." In their present form many blues are mild musical hangovers, following the first exuberant outbursts of ragtime and jazz.

Staid inhabitants of intellectual towers and dwellers in the more rarefied realms of musical esthetics may shudder at the boisterous bellows and discordant groans. But to the victims in the din and dust of the marketplace, here is a flexible medium of expression through which, in the popular manner of the masses, may be expressed in infinite variety the tremendous spectacle of a sprawling continent. This lusty concoction of contemporary music, a blend of ragtime, jazz and the blues, reflects with blaring color and barbaric fidelity the gay, absurd and giddy world of Broadway belles, flivver courtships, straphangers, success slogans, tabloids, chewing-gum customers, Hollywood philosophies, Main Street solitudes and all the more trivial trials and tribulations to which America's amazing population is heir.

September 26, 1926

Duke Ellington and His Band to Invade World's Fair Hall of Music

IT seems pretty definite now that jazz, which many folks have never conceded to be more than an unfortunate fad, is ordained for an existence that will endure at least until the World of Tomorrow. For Duke Ellington and his orchestra have been booked for an appearance at the World's Fair Hall of Music on Saturday night, June 3. Jitterbugs (if there are still some about) can stay home, for the Duke will be giving a concert to be attended by the ears alone.

The Duke returned last week from a tour of Europe in which he played twenty-eight concerts in as many evenings, in France, Holland, Denmark, Norway and Sweden. His program, which probably will be given at the Fair, traced the "authentic musical history of the Negro from Africa to Harlem."

May 14, 1939

MEMORIAL CONCERT HONORS BESSIE SMITH

A concert in memory of Bessie Smith, celebrated Negro blues singer, was presented by the Friends of Jazz last night at Town Hall for the benefit of the United Negro and Allied Veterans of America. Many noted jazz players and singers, some of whom appeared with Miss Smith in clubs and on records, took part in the program, which was given under the direction of Bernard Katz.

Participants included Mme. Ernestine B. Washington, Gospel singer; Coot Grant, Wesley "Sox" Williams, Eve Taylor, Irene Williams and Ruby Smith, blues singers; and Bessie's Blue Boys, a jazz band composed of James P. Johnson, piano; Albert Nicholas, clarinet; Max Kaminsky, cornet; Jimmy Archey, trombone; "Pop" Foster, bass, and Warren "Baby" Dodds, drums.

Featured among the artists was Fredi Washington, actress, who, in a script by Peter Martin, narrated important episodes in Miss Smith's career and gave an account of the historical development of the blues, which was illustrated by solos and ensembles by the artists mentioned. The program also included the first public showing of Miss Smith's only sound film, "The St. Louis Blues."

Irene Williams, daughter of Clarence Williams and Eva Taylor, made her debut as a blues singer at this concert, at which many of the offerings consisted of compositions made popular by Miss Smith, including some by Coot Grant and Wesley "Sox" Williams, the latter of whom shared the keyboard honors of the evening with James P. Johnson, pianist-composer.

January 2, 1948

BOP: SKEE, RE OR BE, 'IT'S STILL GOT TO SWING'

By CARTER HARMAN

IT is called "bop." Its exponents will tell you it is nothing more than a liberated style of playing jazz. Its semicontrolled frenzy, however, epitomizes a strong new tendency toward popular music for listening—rather than dancing—and thus deserves a closer look this morning.

The young men—and they are all young—who make this music have few illusions about it. There is plenty of bad mixed with a little good, they will tell you. They know "it's still got to swing," and one of the more serious arrangers went so far as to say, "How fractured you can sound isn't necessarily good music."

Woody Herman, whose band is "bop-influenced," has developed a neat description of the new style. The old jazz used "long flowery sentences," he says, while "bop is in short, terse phrases."

Nonsense Phrases

The name probably derives from scat-singing, the nonsense phrases of Cab Calloway's heyday such as "skee-bop." From there the transition was easy to "re-bop" and "be-bop," which the music was called a year or so ago when it moved into the spotlight in the persons of Thelonius Monk, Dizzy Gillespie and Charlie Parker. Now, although the singers use the same syllables for their frenetic choruses, the public has become intimate enough with the style to address it familiarly as bop.

To get more technical (if you would rather not, skip these three paragraphs) bop makes more "advanced" use of harmonic materials including dissonance. It is moving away from atonality, its exponents claim, although one would hate to have to determine the key from the last chord.

Melodically, the music develops more like Stravinsky than Tchaikovsky. The brasses and saxophones play flying melodies of virtuoso complexity in unison, and the augmented fourth (once known as "the devil's interval") is strongly in evidence.

There is freer use of uneven meters than one could hear two years ago in dance music, for the younger performers are more flexible with rhythms. They delve into the hitherto sacrilegious waltz time and even five-four bars—changes which arrangers believe would "throw a curve" to older players. Rhythms are "more legitimate" than formerly, as eighth notes are now played as written—evenly instead of "dotted."

The flashing brass sounds, the weird turns of phrase, the extended rhythmic patterns and breathless tempos which result have been largely responsible for taking swing bands out of the ballrooms and putting them on concert stages. The young crowd, while it is more than willing to listen, seems to have forgotten how to dance fast tempos.

One result is a new kind of night club, notably the Royal Roost (with a roped-off section labeled "Metropolitan Bopera House" where, for a small fee, a crowd gathers in the Goetterdaemmerung gloom to bend an ear without having to buy drinks) and the brand-new Clique Club. In these spots there is no dance floor, no "lavish" review, just tables and the shattering blasts of twenty-odd musicians.

The performers are a dedicated lot, constantly alert to their deficiencies. One of them heard a distinguished rhythm section which sounded "pretty ungroovey." It seems the piano man and the bass man were together, but the drummer sat all the way across the bandstand.

"They didn't even like each other," the listener complained.

Nor are they reticent about criticizing other factions, although, as a rule, progressives back each other. After confiding his discontent with a competitor recently one of them said, "I won't mention any names, but the initials are Stan Kenton."

Mr. Kenton's "progressive jazz," while not bop, makes equal use of the modern concert idiom. He has been sticking by his principles for about seven years, and believes so strongly that his music should be heard and not danced-to that he is disbanding his outfit after his present engagement at the Paramount Theatre.

He says he will devote his time to establishing "Halls of Jazz" around the country, where bands such as his, Boyd Raeburn's and the bopists' can give listeners "musical treatments" a la symphony concerts.

No Improvement

Ray McKinley's fine band has had poor luck with the "progressive kick."

"Play that stuff in a ballroom and get ready to duck," he remarked ruefully. Music is supposed to be an improvement over nature, he added, but "some of the sounds you hear are close to nature's rawest."

The new jazz may be credited safely to its arrangers. Mr. Gillespie was one of Mr. Herman's arrangers, a few years back, following his stretch with the Calloway band. In point of fact the arrangers are composers, for most of the bop pieces are "originals" with names such as "Elevation," "Euphoria" and "Robbins' Nest" (a tribute to Fred Robbins, the disk jockey, who has done much for bop).

The style has influenced nearly every band in the land. Some, like Duke Ellington, have come to it in their own creative development. Even the ones which are most reluctant to leave the styles which have made them famous insert little surrealistic figures among the traditional "licks."

But it is the strictly bop outfits such as Charlie Ventura's and Gillespie's and the dedicated singers, Ella Fitzgerald, Mel Torme and Billy Eckstine, that are making the news and getting the fan mail from radio performances.

December 5, 1948

ELLINGTON BAND IS TOPS

Down Beat Poll Shows Duke's Troupe Is Most Popular

CHICAGO, Dec. 25 (AP)—Be-Boppers to the contrary, Duke Ellington's band has been voted the most popular in the country in the annual poll by Down Beat, the music magazine.

Ellington's band has won several previous Down Beat polls, but a new accolade came to the Duke this year. He was named favorite soloist, a category in which a musician is chosen regardless of instrument.

Spike Jones came through again as king of corn. Guy Lombardo and Vaughn Monroe were second and third corniest, respectively.

Bob Crosby beat his brother, Bing, by three places in the male vocalist division. Bing and his hottest competitor of a season or so ago, Frank Sinatra, weren't even in the money. Sinatra placed fourth and Bing sixth.

December 26, 1948

Hot Renaissance of Dixieland Jazz

By MILT GABLER

The two-beat stuff of New Orleans vintage has drowned out bebop, and nobody seems sorry.

ANY Friday night down at Central Plaza or the Stuyvesant Casino, two elderly meeting halls on lower Second Avenue, America's only genuine contribution to the arts—Dixieland music—may be heard in steam-heated revival by some of the finest hot musicians around. These Friday night affairs or "bashes," as they are known to initiates (whose numbers have increased greatly in the past year or so), are only the most immediate manifestation of the folk idiom's nation-wide renaissance.

More disk jockeys are playing more Dixieland records than ever before in the history of jazz. It has invaded night clubs with dance floors and floor shows where once it was confined to night clubs without either, and it has made bright the gilt on such New York shrines as Nick's and Eddie Condon's. Song writers, music publishers and recording companies have discovered once more that there is a profit in Dixieland and it is no coincidence that the revival of Dixieland went arm and leg with the revival of the Charleston. The style of music and that peculiarly frenetic kind of dancing belonged to each other in the Twenties.

YOU don't have to be a cultist to like Dixieland, nor do you have to make learned comparisons between it and Bach fugues (although the similarities are legitimately there). But it helps to know what Dixieland is all about. Some years ago, a jazz critic, in talking about jam sessions, came up with a definition that covered the ground handsomely. He spoke of it as "an informal gathering of temperamentally congenial jazz musicians who play unrehearsed and unscored music for their own enjoyment." The definition is a little romantic in spots but "unrehearsed and unscored music" is the hallmark of Dixieland.

It is music played by a small band consisting, classically, of trumpet, trombone, clarinet, guitar, drums, piano and bass. Sometimes a saxophone is included. In the old days in New Orleans, when the jazz bands played impartially for parades, funerals and routes of one kind or another, a tuba took the place of the bass and piano, and a banjo the place of the guitar.

A Dixieland band will take a standard thirty-two-bar tune (a lot of the old jazz classics were not thirty-two bars long), play it through ensemble, sticking pretty much to the tune as written, and then improvise on the theme, never losing it, always creating on the basic song. There will be improvised solos by the trumpet, clarinet and trombone (with the rest of the band backing each of them up without any written arrangement), and, finally, a furious "rideout" with the whole band in perfect harmony for the finish. It is music that could not be played by a big band, because it would be impossible for a band with, say, four trumpets, four trombones, three clarinets and so forth, to improvise—the result would sound like a cat fight.

NOW, added to the freedom of the lead instruments—the trumpet, clarinet and trombone—is the music's two-beat rhythm, so-called because of the accent on the second and fourth beats of the bar. There are a lot of bands that play Dixieland with equal accents on all four beats, but this is only a variation, a mannerism popularized in Chicago in the late Twenties.

To appreciate the style, you must first know what is going on. How can you tell what a Dixieland band is doing to a tune that you are unfamiliar with in the first place? To feel really funny inside and thrill all over, you've got to be able to follow the tune, and you can't do it if you don't know it. That's why other kinds of music are more successful commercially: the soloist plays a song you know and therefore it's easier to understand. He has a smooth, arranged background and good rhythm accompaniment and he plays pretty.

In these days of the Dixieland revival the music-makers are taking just such popular tunes and playing them in righteous style. Today, it is "Music, Music, Music," or "If I Knew You Were Comin' I'd've Baked a Cake." A year ago it was a rejuvenation of "Twelfth Street Rag," by Pee Wee Hunt, and a little before that Bing Crosby doing "MacNamara's Band" in Dixieland style. If you go back through the years you will find that Dixieland never quite died. It was just very, very sick.

THERE are at least three reasons for the current passion for Dixieland. The first is nostalgic: it is of a piece with such dances as the Charleston, with tight hats for women (and short hair), and the comeback of the ukulele. The second is that Dixieland is primarily

MILT GABLER, recording company executive and music shop president, has been instrumental in keeping hot music from cooling off.

happy, melodic music. The thing that preceded the current revival—bebop—was surrealist, discordant, hard to listen to, and wild. People just closed their ears to it. And the third reason is that the music business has realized that the only way to make any style of music popular is to use it on songs that people like. Without the hit songs that have come along recently, Dixieland might still be in bad shape.

Dixieland was born in New Orleans some years before the turn of the century. It was created by Negroes in that city and by the Creoles and taken up by other men who heard it played and caught fire from it. Have you ever tried to relax while some fine Dixieland horns were blowing? It's impossible, and your heart wears your collar as soon as the first note gets past your eardrums. Picture three good men: to hear any one of them individually is enough to make you melt; but three all at once, and each of them going his own righteous way—that's better than any straight music you ever heard. It is like hearing the work of three composers, all with the same spirit, all in the same groove, writing and playing at the same instant, playing new thoughts simultaneously and weaving them all together without getting in each other's way. That was the kind of music born in New Orleans.

Its instrumentation was similar to that of the old military bands that used to play for dances. In fact, many of the exciting old Dixieland tunes were based on marches, notably, "High Society," "Panama," "Original Dixieland One-Step" and "That's A Plenty." The music moved up the Mississippi River to Chicago and Memphis, with the migration of such great musicians as King Oliver, Louis Armstrong and Jelly Roll Morton, and it flourished mightily in the Twenties. But by 1933 it was as much out of the picture as a record without a hole. Nobody knows exactly why.

THE crooners and groaners took over. Symphonic dance orchestras and sweet popular bands were all the public wanted—they were easier to listen to. Rudy Vallee, Bing Crosby, Russ Columbo, the Boswell Sisters were the vocalists. The orchestras were led by Guy Lombardo, Paul Whiteman, George Olsen, Isham Jones and Ben Bernie. Jazz musicians played sweet, joined large orchestras, gave up music for more lucrative occupations or gave up. And

ENSEMBLE—The front line of a Dixieland band "rides on down," every man improvising as he goes: Muggsy Spanier, cornet; Ernie Caceres, clarinet; Freddie Ohms, trombone.

then along came swing music. Swing was really an advanced form of Dixieland in that it used its basic rhythms. Where it differed was that it could be played by a big band because everything but a few solo parts was tightly arranged. Thus, the effect of a free-riding hot solo could be achieved by, let us say, the clarinet, while at the same time the remaining reeds, trombones and trumpets followed a written score and played a disciplined choir behind the lead instrument. It was a type of music that called for talented arrangers and the most expert musicianship. Benny Goodman became the "King of Swing." He was followed by the Dorsey Brothers, Glenn Miller, Artie Shaw and dozens of others. The nation went dance-band crazy. The Paramount Theatre in New York became the home of name bands and the kids danced in the aisles and were called jitterbugs.

The real thing, Dixieland, thrived with swing. First, there was a spot off Times Square called the Tap Room, run by a Dixieland stalwart, Adrian Rollini, which featured the colorful trumpeter, Wingy Manone. Then, Fifty-second Street was born—the Onyx Club, the Famous Door across the street, the Hickory House.

After that came the public jam sessions at Carnegie Hall, Town Hall and elsewhere. Books were written about the real American music. Record shops like the Commodore Music Shop in New York and the Jazz Man Record Shop in Los Angeles pioneered and made true Dixieland recordings, trying to recreate the old bands. Soon other cities and night clubs emulated the New York spots. By the time the Forties rolled around, Dixieland was enjoying a steady two-beat pulse. By the end of World War II, it was in bad shape again. Its current popularity represents its second revival in thirty years.

Dixieland enthusiasts never give up. It's like being a member of an exclusive society. You hear something, the next one doesn't and you want everyone to hear and enjoy the same music you do. You tell another man the story and you win one battle. Now, there are two of you—it's better with two, you can talk to somebody who understands. You play records together; you hear the musicians in person, and you go out looking for new converts. Soon there are four of you, then eight and then a Hot Club.

The two-beat music-lovers are people of all kinds and descriptions and they comprise an intelligent cross-section of the great American public. Every sector of the music business is catering to them.

Radio stations across the land feature Dixieland programs today. Ted Husing, the ex-sports announcer turned disk jockey, pushes Dixieland consistently and with excellent taste. Single-handed, he has created more followers for the style than any other radio man around. Frank Bull, in Hollywood, has been spinning Dixieland for over a dozen years—but his mail is ten times greater now than it was then. Teaming up with Gene Norman, another record spinner, the two packed the Hollywood Bowl for a Dixieland concert. The affair was a huge success. One radio network even presents a live weekly jazz concert from the fount — New Orleans.

And, finally, the young musicians are learning Dixieland. There was an interval when none but the oldtimers could handle it. Louis Armstrong, Eddie Condon, Max Kaminsky, George Brunis, Wild Bill Davi-

"12th Street Rag," copyright, 1914, by Euday L. Bowman; copyright, 1942, by Shapiro, Bernstein & Co.; "Who Threw the Overalls in Mistress Murphy's Chowder?" copyright 1928, by Shapiro, Bernstein & Co., Inc.

VOCALS—King Louis Armstrong (above, left) and Hot Lips Page put down their horns and sing.

SOLO—Clarinetist Edmund Hall takes off on several unpredictable hot choruses.

son, Miff Mole, Kid Ory and Bobby Hackett, to name just a few of the best, are still around, but there are youngsters playing Dixieland these days, like Bob Wilber and his Wildcats, the Firehouse Five Plus Two, Turk Murphy's Bay City Stompers.

THE trend toward authenticity in jazz is so marked these days that Decca, for example, has recorded an authentic New Orleans funeral march with Louis Armstrong and the fine band he took to Europe. That may sound strange, but the same band that played dirges on the way to the cemetery in New Orleans fifty years ago played marches and jazz on the way back. Many other companies are reissuing the jazz classics, the masters of which grew dusty in storerooms years ago, and, even more significantly, they are recording new Dixieland efforts.

There is, of course, a difference now. In order to be truly popular, the Dixieland form must be used with a popular song of hit caliber. It is realized that it will be acceptable to the public only if the song itself is a hit. But it is also true that Dixieland music lovers are more numerous now than they ever were and for a good reason: it is good music, a true art form. It will never die.

September 24, 1950

SINGER'S PARTY

Ella Fitzgerald the Star Of Her Own Evening

By HOWARD TAUBMAN

THEY gave a party for Ella Fitzgerald twelve days ago. The occasion was her nineteenth anniversary in show business, an odd number to honor, but how are you going to fence in a press agent with tidy round numbers? In any case, Miss Fitzgerald rates a party any time anybody wants to get one up for her.

The shindig took place in the gloomily lit cavern on Fifty-first Street and Broadway known as Basin Street, where, by a strange coincidence, Miss Fitzgerald was opening an engagement. A lot of famous people were there, representatives of the theatre, the radio, television, the record industry and Tin Pan Alley, and along about midnight the management seemed to be having difficulty finding a table for a party headed by Audrey Hepburn and Mel Ferrer. That's the kind of shindig it was.

Maybe Some Jazz

Well, a sampler of serious music does not get around to the popular centers very often, and it seemed good for this one's education to join the Basin Street party. It would be nice to hear Ella Fitzgerald again, and maybe there would be some worthwhile jazz.

There must be something about working in an environment like this that gets under the skin of some jazz players. The second band, which was heard first, behaved as if it were going to knock itself out with its opening number. The writhing and grimacing that went with the playing seemed to an innocent observer more exhausting than the work of blowing or pounding on instruments.

It is said of some long-hair pianists and violinists, whose faces reflect the emotions of the music they happen to be playing, that they cannot help it if they suffer. Clearly there are jazz players who suffer as they play, too.

No Soft Sounds

In the case of this band, however, there was one thing it did not do—play softly. That seems to be a cardinal sin in a place like Basin Street. Or was it that these poor fellows, in a secondary position on the program, were determined to make a big impression by hardly ever descending below a fortissimo?

It turned out that the next band, whose standing was evidently higher, was afflicted by the same fears. It is true that it allowed itself a few

VETERAN SINGER

The New York Times (by Larry Morris)

Ella Fitzgerald appearing at Basin Street, where her 19th anniversary in show business has just been celebrated.

phrases where the instruments were granted a chance to sing, but for the most part everything was made to sound loud, insistent and high-pressure.

This gave a stranger to these haunts cause to wonder. Here was a good band, led by Louis Bellson, a fine drummer, with two gifted trumpeters, Charlie Shavers and Roy Eldridge, as soloists. Both Shavers and Eldridge took turns in the forefront with the band, and it was clear that each was a virtuoso. Shavers' tone was the cleaner and more lyrical, while Eldridge's had a bit of a smear that gave it an effect of amusing "dirtiness." But, heavens to Betsy, these boys seldom gave one a chance to relax.

For their wind-up they got together in a kind of duet with the others giving them rhythmic support. The basic idea was delightful. It was like a trumpeter's competition. But the emphasis was on who could play higher, louder and faster. They seemed to shy away from lyricism as if it were a commodity that would contaminate the place.

Now this observer admittedly does not get around to the night spots as a regular thing, and he assumes that there are resorts where a jazz musician may play with relaxed feeling and that there are audiences for jazz of this sort. Not square jazz, you understand, but lyrical, imaginative music.

But it was difficult to keep one's perspective, especially when Bellson took the center of the stage and played an endless solo for percussion. Granted that Bellson is a first-rate technician. But are the percussion really solo instruments? And how much can the human ear endure, especially in a low-ceilinged room where the reverberations become more overwhelming than a dentist's drill?

Simple Style

One was about to conclude that ears made tender by sweet sounds in Carnegie Hall were not meant for this sort of thing when Ella Fitzgerald took over. Sanity seemed to be restored. It became clear again that sheer insistence and noise were not necessarily the hallmarks of quality or success. For Miss Fitzgerald was simple and unaffected. Of course, she has know-how as an entertainer, but her personality is warm and she is not afraid of emotion.

She stood there on the stage with a great natural dignity as important folks made a great do about her. She wept a little, and that was disarming, too. Then they played a recording of her first smash number, "A'Tisket A'Tasket," and without affectation she went up to the mike and joined herself in the song. It was a touching moment, and for once, one did not need ear plugs.

June 6, 1954

NEWPORT ROCKED BY JAZZ FESTIVAL

7,000 Pack Casino for First Concert as Staid Resort Turns Its Back on Past

TOP MUSICIANS ON HAND

Audience 'Sent' by Dixieland, Swing and Progressive Styles of Performers

By HOWARD TAUBMAN

Special to The New York Times.

NEWPORT, R. I., July 18—This town, which has been described as one of "the last resorts," gave itself a shot in the arm this week-end with an infusion of one of the liveliest arts.

It started a jazz festival, and it hopes this will become an annual event that will help to recapture some of Newport's former luster.

In years gone by, the families bearing famous American names made Newport a dominant social center in the summer. Their stately palaces still front the sea, but Newport's glamour no longer is what it has been. Led by Mr. and Mrs. Louis Lorrillard, one of the gold karat names, Newport now has chosen to align itself for the future with a vigorous, youthful, democratic art.

The festival got off to a thumping beginning last night. More than 7,000 persons—men and women, young and old, formally and informally dressed—poured into the staid Casino for the first concert. The most optimistic hopes of the management were for 5,000. As a result there were not enough chairs to go around.

People stood all over the outdoor arena where tennis matches normally are played. Some sat on the ground, and a few wild young 'uns took posts on the roof of a two-story building. On this precarious perch several of the lads stood and dipped and swayed when the music pulse grew so warm that there was no remaining still.

Influx Chokes Town

The festival brought such an influx of visitors into the narrow, quiet streets of Newport that at concert time the town was choked. Hotels and restaurants were hard pressed to accommodate the trade, and last night's concert began forty-five minutes late and skipped the intermission. This morning a veteran summer resident remarked: "It was like old times. We haven't had anything like it in years."

You can bet Newport never has had anything quite like it. In the good old days there were band concerts and brilliant dances with large bands providing conventional music. This week-end the bandstand set up on the Casino grounds jumped to all manner of jazz style—Dixieland, swing, progressive.

And a Newport audience reacted like jazz aficionados the nation over—with pounding of feet, beating of hands, rocking of bodies and ecstatic cries of "go, go, go." They were not all Newporters, to be sure, since many in the audience came from considerable distances. But Newporters who belong to a more decorous tradition were there: they sat and listened and watched, and perhaps smiled.

Typical of the variety and ambition of this undertaking was last night's gathering of performers. To start with there was an exhibition of old-time jazz by Eddie Condon and several different groups. Then Lee Wiley sang, and Condon and all his men came back for a brief jam session.

Crowd Is 'Really Sent'

Then the Modern Jazz Quartet, a new group, was given a chance at the limelight. It was followed by Dizzy Gillespie's Quintet and Oscar Peterson's Trio, which really sent the crowd. Lee Konitz' Trio was followed by the faithful work of Gerry Mulligan's Quarter. And then Ella Fitzgerald came on to sing and steal the show.

This afternoon there was a forum on the theme, "The Place of Jazz in American Culture." And for tonight's wind-up, there were listed some of last night's performers as well as such figures as George Shearing, Bill Harris, Errol Garner, Gene Krupa, Lennie Tristano and the singer, Billie Holiday.

There are some bugs in this festival. The loudspeaker system was disconcerting. And in the open, without a low-ceilinged room filled with smoke, there seemed to be a loss of intimacy. But the big turn-out should encourage Newport to feel that its alliance with jazz places it on the side of the future.

July 19, 1954

SONG STORY TOLD BY BILLIE HOLIDAY

Excerpts of Autobiography Read at Carnegie Hall Give Meaning to Recital

Billie Holiday told her story at Carnegie Hall Saturday night. She told it in both song and prose.

The songs were those that have been most closely associated with her during her twenty-year career. The prose dealt largely with her offstage background—her tawdry beginnings in Baltimore and Harlem, her battles with Jim Crow, narcotics and the law (she has not been allowed to appear in a New York night club for ten years.)

Excerpts from her autobiography, "Lady Sings the Blues," were skillfully edited and read with appreciative insight by Gilbert Millstein.

Mr. Millstein's readings were interspersed with Miss Holiday's songs, providing a setting that made many of them more meaningful than they usually have been even for one who has been listening to her since she first approached them freshly and adventurously.

Feeling of Wonder

She still manages to convey that feeling of wonder that, along with her rough, throaty croon and her expressive dips, lifts and dolorously twisted notes, are the essential ingredients of her highly personal style.

In the course of her career, her control of these mannerisms has often been erratic but at Carnegie Hall she revealed a talent that has matured soundly. She sang with assurance, with warmth and with a wonderfully expressive artistry.

She recalled the hard-bitten, rollicking style of her early days with "I Cried for You," "Miss Brown to You" and "Them There Eyes." She evoked a deep and moving mood with "I Cover the Waterfront" and her most widely known number, "Strange Fruit."

She was accompanied by a notable group of jazz musicians, at least two of whom—Buck Clayton and Roy Eldridge, both trumpet men—were heard with her on some of her earliest records.

Other Accompanists

Miss Holiday's other accompanists were Coleman Hawkins and Al Cohn, saxophonists; Kenny Burrell, guitarist; Carl Drinkered, pianist; Carson Smith, bassist, and Chico Hamilton, drummer.

Miss Holiday was preceded on the program by the Chico Hamilton Quintet, a group that hovers between jazz and a romanticized form of impressionism. The Quintet includes, besides Mr. Hamilton and his bassist, Mr. Smith, a 'cellist; Fred Katz, a guitarist; John Pisano, and Paul Horn, who plays flute, clarinet and tenor saxophone.

These latter three, who contribute the most toward coloring the work of the group as a whole, all lean toward a "legitimate" rather than a jazz style and it follows that they work together to the best purpose on those pieces that are the least in the jazz idiom.

J. S. W.

November 12, 1956

W.C. Handy, Composer, Is Dead; Author of 'St. Louis Blues,' 84

Son of Ex-Slaves Made Popular a Form of Music Like a 'Darky's Sorrow Song'—Started With 'Memphis Blues' in 1910

W. C. Handy, composer of the jazz classic "St. Louis Blues," died before dawn yesterday at the age of 84. He had been in Sydenham Hospital in Harlem since Sunday with acute bronchial pneumonia.

Mr. Handy suffered a stroke three years ago. Since then he had been able to travel only in a wheelchair. With the exception of a few special occasions, he had been confined to his home at 19 Chester Drive, Yonkers.

At his bedside when Mr. Handy died were his wife, Mrs. Irma Louise Logan Handy, whom he married three years ago; two sons, William C. Handy Jr. and Wyer Handy; a daughter, Mrs. Katherine Lewis; a brother, Charles, and a grandson, William C. Handy 3d.

Mr. and Mrs. Handy had planned to fly to St. Louis on April 7 for the opening of the Paramount film "St. Louis Blues," a fictionalized biography of the composer, and featuring, of course, many of his blues songs. The film will open also in New York and other major cities on the same date.

In announcing Mr. Handy's death, radio stations throughout the country played "St. Louis Blues," "Memphis Blues," "Beale Street Blues" and other of his songs in tribute to him throughout the day.

Honored at Party Here

Mr. Handy's last public appearance was on Nov. 17, 1957, at a birthday party for him in the Waldorf-Astoria Hotel. More than 800 actors, musicians and public personalities gathered in the Grand Ballroom to hail the "father of the blues."

President Eisenhower, Vice President Richard M. Nixon and Governor Harriman were among the notables who sent telegrams of congratulations. Mayor Wagner proclaimed "W. C. Handy Week" in New York.

William Christopher Handy, son of emancipated slaves, rose from an Alabama log cabin to a Westchester mansion by capturing in song the melancholia of all loneliness and the sadness of his race.

Yet the composer of more than sixty other melodies, was outwardly cheerful, despite blindness during his later years.

Moon-faced and benign, with the deep chest of the trumpet player, the chunky composer was a bit of a philosopher. One day, in his eighties, he told school children how, in his youth, he had slept on cobblestones and Mississippi levees "and heard the roustabouts singing on the steamboats and it hung in my ears." He patted his trumpet and said:

"Life is something like this trumpet. If you don't put anything in it you don't get anything out. And that's the truth."

By then most of his friends were dead and, though the music for "I hate to see that

The New York Times

W. C. Handy, the "father of the blues"

evenin' sun go down" was still in most jazz repertoires, his blues style, so popular for thirty years, seemed to have yielded to new jazz fads.

This did not disturb Mr. Handy's good cheer.

"The Negroes," he said, "invented jazz, and the white folks made an industry out of it."

In a sense politics started the "blues" in 1910. In that year Mr. Handy wrote a campaign song for Edward H. Crump that helped the "Boss" to become Mayor of Memphis. The song became more widely known than the Mayor after it was recorded in 1917 as "Memphis Blues," which described "that melancholy strain, that ever-haunting strain is like a darky's sorrow song."

Mr. Handy was born on Nov. 16, 1873, in Florence, Ala. His father and grandfather were Methodist preachers, pastors of the first Negro church in that community.

Describing his early childhood in his autobiography published in 1941 under the title "Father of the Blues," Mr. Handy recalled that his upbringing was rather more strict than that of most of his white contemporaries.

"With all their differences," he wrote, "most of my forebears had one thing in common: if they had any musical talent, it remained buried. My mother admitted a fondness for the guitar, but she could not play it because the church put a taboo on such instruments."

When a small boy, Mr. Handy saved enough money to buy a guitar of his own, but his father ordered him to trade it for a dictionary.

At 15 he graduated into a minstrel show from his school singing class, only to return home when the traveling show ran out of money.

His second venture from home, with 20 cents in his pocket, had as its goal the World's Fair in Chicago in 1893. The years following found him alternately employed, penniless, hungry and cold, and in St. Louis he reached his nadir.

"I have tried to forget that first sojourn in St. Louis," he once said. But he must never quite have obliterated it all from his memory, for out of the experience grew "St. Louis Blues." Written in 1914, it set the pattern for hundreds of blues songs.

Upon that melancholy composition a whole new school of popular music writing was based. From its simple, sobbing lyric of frustration grew scores of songs that later were to become the "torch numbers."

Organized Minstrels

Mr. Handy's break into the theatre occurred at the turn of the century. Before that he had eked out his musical education at the Negro Agricultural and Mechanical College near Huntsville, Ala. From this time on he was increasingly successful in organizing orchestras and minstrels and in arranging the popular tunes of the day for minstrel performance.

In 1898 Mr. Handy married his boyhood sweetheart, Elizabeth V. Price. They had six children. She died in 1937. In 1954, when he was 80 years old, Mr. Handy married his secretary.

President and treasurer of the Handy Brothers Music Company, Mr. Handy was a member of the American Federation of Musicians and the American Society of Composers, Authors and Publishers. He also belonged to the Negro Actors Guild.

Mr. Handy had been totally blind since he fell from a subway station platform in 1943 and suffered a skull fracture. He had lost his sight after World War I, but had partially regained it.

In later years, his works had been performed at the Stadium Concerts here. He was in the audience a few years ago when Louis Armstrong wound up a world tour there by playing "St. Louis Blues."

March 29, 1958

The Beat Heard 'Round the World

Jazz, says a well-known music man, is an American export with an international appeal, making friends wherever it goes.

By DAVE BRUBECK

BETWEEN 5:30 P. M. on Feb. 8, at the Royal Festival Hall in London, and midnight of May 10, in the Khayyam Theatre in Baghdad, four American jazz musicians—Paul Desmond (alto saxophone), Joe Morello (drums), Eugene Wright (bass) and myself (piano) — traveled better than halfway around the world and played above seventy concerts in Great Britain, Germany, Holland, Belgium, Sweden, Denmark, Poland, Turkey, India, Ceylon, Pakistan, Afghanistan, Iran and Iraq. I give the itinerary in this much detail for the most relevant of reasons: it is illustrative of both fact and symbol, the one hardly less tangible than the other.

The fact is that jazz, our single native art form, is welcomed — not simply accepted — without reservation throughout the world and is felt to be the most authentic example of American culture. It would be fatuous of me to pretend to correlate its importance with the billions of dollars we have spent in restoring nations ravaged by war and in raising the living standards of underdeveloped countries, or the day-to-day spadework of statesmen and diplomats. But there is no mistaking its effect: it arouses a kinship among peoples; it affords them flashes of recognition of common origins, because of its basic relationship to folk idioms; and the forthrightness and directness of its appeal are grasped alike by the naive and the sophisticated. More of it is being heard abroad today than ever before. Even more heartening to me is the knowledge that occasionally, as was the case with the major portion of our tour, it is being sent overseas under official auspices. From Warsaw to Baghdad, we were financed by President Eisenhower's Special International Program for Cultural Presentations, as administered by the American National Theatre and Academy.

TO me the symbol is uncomplicated. It is one of unity and of uninhibited, if sometimes wordless, communication, but I think it has to be examined on two levels, sociologically as well as musically. In the first place, the range of language, culture and race between London and Baghdad is wide, so very wide. But there are three white men in our quartet and Gene Wright is a Negro. A number of other bands that have toured foreign countries come to mind. There have been white instrumentalists in all of Louis Armstrong's bands, and in those of Dizzy Gillespie

DAVE BRUBECK is a piano player, jazz band leader and important influence in modern jazz.

and Lionel Hampton; there have been Negroes in those of Benny Goodman and Stan Kenton, to say nothing of Norman Granz' big troupe, "Jazz at the Philharmonic."

Jazz is color blind. When a German or a Pole or an Iraqi or an Indian sees American white men and colored in perfect creative accord, when he finds out that they travel together, eat together, live together and think pretty much alike, socially and musically, a lot of the bad taste of Little Rock is apt to be washed from his mouth. Obviously, a similar effect is produced by the best of our serious music, our theatre and our literature, but I am concerned here specifically with jazz.

THE United States assumes the most moral role of all internationally. A greater demand is placed on us for human decency than on any other country, and while the sight and sound of a mixed band improvising on "Love Walked In," for example, is not to be compared with a summit conference in Geneva, Washington or Moscow, it is not to be ignored. Louis symbolizes even more than he understands. He is in life what you find more frequently in fiction—the uneducated American Negro who, through his genius, has overcome all possible obstacles and who is loved universally. Love walks in, all right, when Louis plays.

So much for the social aspects of jazz. I am convinced—though it may be no more than the prejudice of the jazz musician—that the effect of jazz on people is more profound than our serious music or art or literature, for the reason that it is being created at the very moment it is played before an audience. The one element common to all religions, we are told, is the act of creation. For man to be creative is to be godlike. Now, the form and notes of a symphony are fixed; pictures have already been painted; books already written. The conductor of a symphony orchestra must, in my opinion, be a genius to transcend these things and bring an element of creativity to what he is doing. The viewer has to bring a previously existing knowledge and sympathy to a picture. So must the reader.

BUT jazz is another matter. Musically, by its very nature, it is the most creative, the freest and most democratic form of expression I know. What is the essence of jazz? It is music freely created before listeners (watchers, too) by a group of instrumentalists, each of whom is afforded a maximum of individual expression in a democratically agreed-on framework of rhythms, harmonies and melodies. It is music wherein the instrumentalist may take a theme or a melody and do with it what he chooses, sometimes for as many choruses as he pleases, remembering only the discipline of agreeing harmonically and rhythmically with his fellow-musicians. And experience, incidentally, has repeatedly taught me that improvisation in the music of any country soon begins to sound like American jazz—whether it is in the West, where melody and harmony have reached so high a state of development, or in the East, where rhythms are predominant.

Furthermore, jazz is music whose sources are world-wide—African, European, Asian, American—and therefore may be understood almost instantly, whether by a provincial group of Indians 500 miles inland from Bombay or a cosmopolitan audience in West Berlin. Shall I be even more basic? I remember something the philosopher Gerald Heard once told me. The first thing a man is aware of, he said, is the steady rhythm of his mother's heartbeat and the last thing he hears before he dies is his own. Rhythm is the common bond of all humanity; it is also the most pronounced and readily understood ingredient of jazz.

I will make one or two more generalizations about jazz and then I will attempt to prove the truth of them. I don't like to use the word "propaganda" in connection with it, although it is the easiest one to explain its value. Maybe it is and maybe it isn't "America's secret weapon," as a New York Times correspondent once said in describing Louis Armstrong's effect in Europe. But I do know this—and I believe it to be more than coincidence—generally, wherever there was dictatorship in Europe, jazz was outlawed. And whenever freedom returned to those countries, the playing of jazz invariably accompanied it.

I have not forgotten that during the second World War a large part of the French underground made good military use of jazz. Some of its agents had been jazz fans. A lot of underground fighters who were record collectors communicated with each other in a code made up of the serial numbers of records they liked. The serial numbers, of course, identified different songs. Strung together, the titles became messages. The part jazz played in helping win the war was small, but the significant thing is that it *did* play a part.

EVERYWHERE we went—in the free nations, in dictatorships, in undeveloped countries—the unifying influence of our kind of music was brought home to us. Audiences didn't break up auditoriums as they have for Louis and the police didn't have to turn fire hoses on anybody (we play a more intellectual kind of jazz, I guess) but I remember sharply, for example, our arrival in Cracow. We got off the train at 5 o'clock in the morning in a snowstorm and there in the station was a little Polish jazz band—clarinet, trumpet and trombone—swinging "Yankee Doodle!"

We played fourteen concerts in seven cities in Poland. Somewhere along the line I had a talk with a man—I will identify neither the man nor the city nor even the place in which we talked,—but he said this to me: "Dave, I must agree with you that Poland is the most misunderstood country in the world. We realize we have to be misunderstood. This is the pitiful part of it. If Russia realized how pro-Western we are, we would lose whatever freedom we have. We want freedom as much as you do." He went on to say how much jazz had become the symbol of freedom in Poland, particularly through the broadcasts of the Voice of America, and he wound up by telling me, "Your very presence indicates that we have more freedom now than we had two years ago."

IN another Polish city, we were shown a letter written to the country's only jazz publication. It was sent by Czechoslovak fans. "If you will send us tickets to today's performance," the Czechs wrote, "we will cross the border and enter Poland at the risk of our lives." Nobody wanted them to take any chances, so we just mailed them some programs, handbills and autographed pictures.

If the word "freedom" recurs and recurs here, it is because it was in the mouths of everybody we had anything to do with. Toward the end of our Polish stand, we were given a dinner by about thirty artists, writers, musicians and students. It was held quite openly. Two years ago, I was told, even a meeting of this group would have had to be held in secret, with the members drifting in by ones and twos. But what struck me most about that dinner—apart from the Polish hams and vodka, the soups and pastries, all of which I know cost these people at least a week's wages—was the toast one of them offered in English. "Now that you have been with us this long," one man said, "perhaps you will take back with you the knowledge that we Poles love freedom as much as you Americans."

I was moved nearly to tears by something that happened at our last concert in Poland. This was in Poznan. On the train trip to Poznan from Lodz, I wrote a song I thought might be a nice tribute to our last Polish audience. I called it *"Dziekuje,"* which is Polish for "thank you." I knew, of course, the reverence in which Chopin is held in Poland, so I put in a sort of Chopinesque introduction for it. We rehearsed it before the concert and gave it as our final encore.

There was a moment of silence when we had finished, the only silence we had experienced in Poland, and I wondered whether I had offended them by presuming a variation on Chopin. Then people burst into applause. A youngster who had taped the concert made us take his tapes and would accept nothing in return. It need not be pointed out how difficult it is to come by a tape-recorder and tapes in Poland. A Polish Government worker said to me backstage, "Why don't the artists rule the world?" There were tears in his eyes and he almost made me weep.

IN one way or another, in one place or another, the things I have been setting down about jazz and its influence were exemplified anew. In Madras, I asked John Wiggin, who heads up the United States Information Service there, whether he really thought we were doing any good. "In all of Russia," he said, "there's no one who can come here and play the drums like Joe Morello. You reach people on a personal level. It's that simple."

In Bombay, I tried to play piano behind Abdul Jaffar Khan, a nationally known performer on the sitar, the Hindu guitar. His influence made me play in a different way. Although Hindu scales, melodies and harmonies are so different, we *understood* each other and I feel that in a few more meetings we would have been playing jazz together. The folk origins of music aren't too far apart anywhere in the world.

At the airport in Istanbul, a Turkish band consisting of a bass player and two trumpets serenaded us with our own arrangement of "Tea for Two." In Ankara, we invited three Turks (bass, French horn and drums) and an Italian (guitar) up on stage to play with us and we jammed fifteen choruses of "All the Things You Are." That was no accident. The night before, we'd drifted around to a nightclub where the Turks, the Italian and a refugee Hungarian piano player sat in with us and proved what they could do. We invited them because we liked them and because they were good musicians and if what we did had any political significance, that's fine, but it was secondary.

THE editor of an anti-Western magazine sat next to my wife during one of our two concerts in Ankara and she noticed he seemed pretty agitated all during the performance. We found out later why. "For the first time in my life," he told me backstage, "you have made me forget that I am a Moslem and that you are Christians."

I am not a little proud of the fact also that one of the Ankara performances was heard by Cevat Menduk Altar, Turkey's General Director of Fine Arts. I was told by Patricia Randles, assistant cultural officer of the U. S. I. S. in Ankara, that she had "been here fifteen months and this is the first time I've been able to get him to attend any United States function." (Two days after the band got back to New York, we read that Miss Randles had been killed in an automobile accident in Ankara.) Altar, I learned afterward, is a friend of Hindemith and an expert on Chopin, and he had lectured on the latter in Poland.

What made Altar a jazz fan was nothing more mysterious than the circumstance that his two daughters were enthusiasts. And that brings me around to what I suppose I can call the coda of this piece. The understanding that comes out of jazz begins with the musician. It doesn't make much difference whether a man plays traditional style, or Dixieland, or bop, cool, modern or progressive, and it doesn't matter much what he thinks he is playing, as long as that ensemble understanding exists among the players. That's the first circle.

The second circle is that of the fans who have bought tickets to a performance. Somewhere in a set of program notes I wrote is this sentence: "I think of an audience as a co-creator, the fifth instrument to our quartet. How an audience chooses to play its part is determined anew each time musicians and listeners gather together." The third circle consists of those people who read the reviews of our jazz concerts and are prompted to come either to the next one or to one staged by another group. And the fourth circle is that of people who, all charged up by the third, finally become members of the second themselves.

LET me take one more chorus. In Kabul, I was met by an ex-policeman from Berkeley, Calif., Al Riedel, who is helping organize Afghanistan's forces. He pointed to this huge mountain around Kabul and at its top a wall. "For 5,000 years," he said, "people have been fighting over that wall—Tamerlane, Genghis Khan, Alexander the Great, the Indians, the English, who knows who. If a small fraction of what they spent had gone into education instead of defense, that wall would have come down long ago. At best, defense is a temporary thing."

That night, lying awake in my hotel room, I heard three or four nomads—shepherds—passing under my window, playing their flutes. The music they made was the same they had made for 5,000 years. And the music had survived. How many of the things that were fought for over the wall on that mountain have?

June 15, 1958

Jazz Makes It Up the River

The long voyage from New Orleans barrelhouse to public respectability ends in a triumph.

By GILBERT MILLSTEIN

ALTHOUGH the art of jazz has only lately been certified by, among others, the State Department and ministers of several faiths, and has arrived no closer than a scrabbling handhold to a comfortable definition, the fact is that more of it is being played and written by more musicians and listened to by more people with more catholic tastes than at any time since the sainted Charles (Buddy) Bolden is reputed to have shouted, "Let's call the children home," stuck his cornet out of the window of a New Orleans dance hall and blown loud enough to be heard ten miles away.

"You can't hold it in your hand or encompass it," the pianist Thelonious Monk remarked on a recent night, immediately subsequent to his choice in an international critics' poll as the

JELLY ROLL MORTON, pianist and composer, bragged he "invented jazz." He does hold high rank.

outstanding performer of the year on his instrument. "It's something to enjoy. I never tried to think of a definition. I never had time to think of it. *Listen*, that's all, *listen, listen, listen!* You supposed to know jazz when you hear it. You can't talk it. What do you do when someone gives you some-

GILBERT MILLSTEIN, of The Times Magazine, is a "moldy fig" bred in the years when Dixieland jazz was thought to be "far out."

BIX BEIDERBECKE — Only a handful knew in his lifetime (he died in 1931) of the refinements he made in Dixieland.

thing? You feel glad about it; you take it." Monk's adjuration, like Bolden's before him, has been obeyed; it is there, but no one has said, beyond cavil, what it is.

AMONG the anti-romantic proofs that jazz has finally stopped coming up the river from New Orleans, obscured in the mists of nostalgia, are these: the sales of jazz records of all kinds are at an all-time high. The number of night clubs devoted exclusively to jazz has grown markedly in the past three years, while those committed to standard entertainment have declined. The music has become a regular fixture on radio and a reasonably regular, if not always expertly produced, fixture on several television programs, one of which, the Art Ford show on Thursday nights, is permitted to run for an hour and a half.

The jazz concert, an occasional promotion in the past, has become an enormously profitable and institutionalized business. Not until the early Fifties was the interdict placed on jazz by major concert halls lifted. (Exceptions were made for such men as Benny Goodman and Duke Ellington.) This was largely the work of a persistent promoter named Norman Granz, who began touring his "Jazz at the Philharmonic" troupe in 1945. In the colleges, jazz, once the coteric possession of a few fraternity brothers, is now the province of entire student bodies as a result of the campus tours pioneered by Dave Brubeck in 1950 and taken up later by the revered Louis Armstrong and the astringent Modern Jazz Quartet.

LESTER YOUNG—A giant figure in early Basie bands and Kansas City style, "Prez" is revered as well by the moderns.

An accompanying manifestation has been the growth of the jazz festival. The first of these, according to the critic and historian, Leonard Feather, was held in Wilkes-Barre, Pa., in February, 1951. Since then they have proliferated: Newport, Randalls Island, Stratford, Ont., Great South Bay, French Lick, Ind., and Monterey, Calif. As pointed out recently, by Nat Hentoff, another expert, the number of books on jazz published in the past five years is greater than the total output of the preceding quarter century, and Down Beat, the Good Book of the jazz fan, has doubled in circulation in the past year. A stunningly final evidence of the recognition the music has achieved may be seen in the decision of S. Hurok, an impresario of the classical all his life, to take on his first jazz client, Errol Garner, the pianist.

BUNK JOHNSON—An early New Orleans jazzman, rediscovered in 1938, he had a vogue until his death in 1949.

THERE are a good many reasons—some cultural, some economic and sociological, some seemingly contradictory, a few bordering on the mystic—why jazz has reached its present eminence, an elevation not quite so likely to be abandoned in a hurry as it has been several times in the sixty or so years of its recognizable existence. For one thing, it has achieved respectability—in a manner having little or nothing to do with the music. From its beginnings jazz was associated—correctly, often as not—with sporting houses, sporting women, whisky, disorder and more latterly, narcotics. Its practitioners were seen—hazily—as artists *manqués*, a picturesque lot with great talents, souls, lusts, hangovers and neuroses, and they were ticketed for the sort of destruction Zola unfortunately was born too early to write about. They were also barefooted, unable to read music, or both, and gave their finest performances, only after hours in illegal saloons. Sometimes this was true.

CHARLIE PARKER—A founder, with Dizzy Gillespie and others, of the modern movement, he set new standards for jazz.

THE portrait was fine for coterie types, sentimentalists, historians and the writers of bad naturalistic novels, but repellent to the general public. Today, while the level of morality among jazz musicians is no higher than it is in the lay population, it is possible to find a heavy percentage of instrumentalists married for long periods to one woman (and having children), who read music (and may even, like Dave Brubeck, have studied with Milhaud), wearing shoes (and Brooks Brothers suits), playing openly in bosky dells and giving many indications of staving off physical and psychic rot for decades.

As Gunther Schuller, a composer and instrumentalist of both jazz and "serious" music re-

STAN KENTON — He and Woody Herman broke ground in employing the big band as a medium for modern jazz.

LENNIE TRISTANO, pianist and jazz iconoclast, has had a profound influence on many of the moderns.

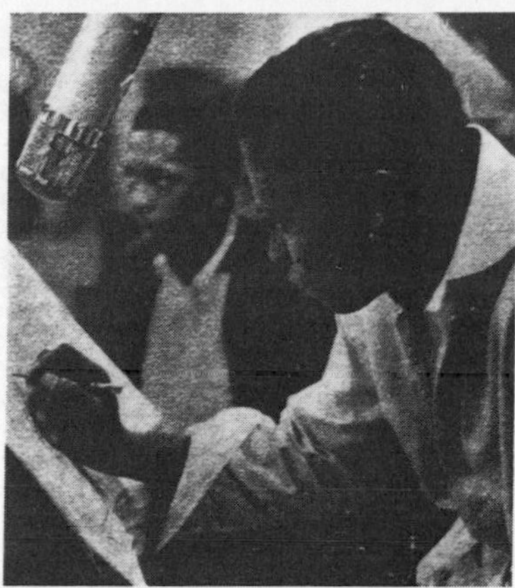

MILES DAVIS—At 32, he is probably the best known of the modern trumpeters and studied at the Juilliard School.

BESSIE SMITH, "Empress of the Blues," was, many think, the greatest jazz singer the world has known.

marked not long ago, "These people are much more organized as people, and they gave others the assurance that they could behave like normal, everyday, decent citizens—they showed up on time for a job; they knew what they were doing, and they weren't drunk." Having read of jazz's glamorously disheveled past, audiences were thus in the highly titillating position of being able to approve jazz's sanitary modern morals and, at the same time, savor its steamy antecedents. The imaginative could equate Mahogany Hall with Carnegie Hall, and, if the musician's soul were rent, it at least burst its seams in the corridors of the Juilliard School of Music.

THE standard intellectuals—not the jazz cabalists, talkers of hip language and wearers of beards, berets and dark glasses—whose gauges of respectability are more apt to be bookish, were, at long last, drawn to jazz as its academic qualifications rose to suit their tastes. Once they had decked jazz in ivy and scholarship (the Brubeck album, "Jazz Goes to College," is, incidentally, one of many bearing roughly similar titles), the intellectuals then discovered it offered them something classical music did not.

Classical music is fixed in form; one symphony orchestra's or one performer's interpretation differs from another's, but the notes are forever the same and the market has lately been glutted with different, if not too much differing, renditions of the serious warhorses. But jazz, being an improvisational music, must renew itself constantly and its freshness appealed to the academics.

ANOTHER factor is what the saxophonist, Paul Desmond, calls the "indescribable worsening" of popular music in the last decade, coupled with the spread of rock 'n' roll (which, it is true, has its origins in jazz, but which bears it as much resemblance as a city dump does a vinaigrette), and the growth of a glutinous kind of mood music made portentous by the use of such devices as the echo chamber. The relatively mature listener—not particularly a classicist—was, respectively, alienated, irritated or bored. There were others to whom the swing bands of the late Thirties represented, whether they were aware of it or not, a smooth, satisfying wedding of popular music to jazz, but these bands were no longer in existence. For them, as for a generation of college students, the void appears to have been filled with the sound of jazz.

The element of fashion is present in the usual disingenuous way, in this instance with a small sprinkling of irony. The Europeans have, by and large, been serious students of American jazz for well over twenty-five years and, with the exception of a few *avant-gardists* in this country, were well ahead of America in recognizing it as an art form. This became known here shortly after the end of the Second World War and hot music was taken up with the same avidity reserved for Italian shoes and British sports cars.

In his "The Story of Jazz" Marshall Stearns has taken note of the "protest-music" appeal theory of jazz as laid down by several psychiatrists. Summarized, the proposition runs this way: the music has such flagrantly disreputable associations that "it takes real courage and * * * rebellious spirit to identify oneself with it." On the one hand, the rebel can defy society with complete safety—he has only to listen—and, on the other, make cause with a small band of like-minded rebels. One hot musician, unaware of the ground broken by the psychiatrists, remarked, half in earnest, one night to a friend, "People wonder why we get paid relatively well. Man, we take people's chances for them." Nat Hentoff has put it still another way: "In an era of compulsive conformity we want something that connotes freedom; we can always shut it off when the boss comes to dinner."

NOT the least important aspect of the music's current popularity is linked to changes in attitude toward the Negro. In its earliest days jazz was widely regarded as an exclusively Negro music. Even when this was found not to be the case, the Negro musician was permitted to play only with Negroes and the Negro audience was rigidly segregated, excepting only in the freemasonry of dives. Negro and mixed orchestras were barred from hotels. Until only a relatively few years ago some intellectuals compounded the crime by condescending to jazz as something "inherent" in the Negro personality (like shiftlessness, good humor, the ability to dance and to take a punch in the head, although not in the belly), and they also made a foolish distinction between what they termed "white jazz" and "Negro jazz." The reversal of these conditions and states of mind, while it has yet to constitute an idyll, is gradually increasing, with "all deliberate speed."

The most obvious reasons are economic and technological. Where audiences are concerned, the nearly uninterrupted rise in the standard of living since the beginning of the last war has been reflected in an increase in leisure and of money to spend it on. Some of it has been spent on jazz. In terms of the musicians, the process is a little more complicated. Artistic reasons apart, they were, in a sense, forced into playing the jazz for which they had yearned unrequited previously. A great many talented jazz musicians played in the big bands of the late Thirties. The draft broke up most of these bands; the 20 per cent Federal entertainment tax drove almost all the rest out of the hotels, motion-picture presentation houses and some night clubs.

For the most part, jazz is played by small groups. Small bands cost less to hire than large ones and these were hired by night club owners whose interest in art may be termed, at its highest, peripheral. Few musicians will concede it, but the iron of economics has also, admittedly to a small extent, even helped to change jazz from a dancing music into a listening music. There is no 20 per cent tax in clubs where there is no dancing. There are also more tables if the owner has a dance floor he can cover with them.

TECHNOLOGICALLY, the long-playing record had two effects. In the first place, it enabled the jazz musician to free himself of the straitjacket imposed by those which revolved at seventy-eight revolutions per minute and limited a performance to three minutes or less. An uninhibited jazz performance is apt to last anywhere from five to twenty minutes or more, depending on the number of choruses the players are moved to take. Thus, the conditions under which jazz is at its best were met on long-playing records. Furthermore, it became possible to reissue on one record large numbers of much older and still cherished short selections. The over-all cost was smaller and the general gained easy access to the collector's caviar.

The reasons jazz has gained the acceptance it has are easily come by, by comparison with attempts to define what it is. Very likely, the classic utterance on the subject (as beautifully succinct as Carlyle's injunction to Margaret Fuller, upon hearing that she had accepted the universe: "By God, she had better!") was made by the late Fats Waller who was called upon for a definition. "Ma'am," he replied, "if you don't know by now, don't mess with it."

In a chapter of his "The Encyclopedia of Jazz," Leonard Feather reminded his readers: "It must be borne in mind that no two musicians at any time in jazz history have ever agreed completely on a definition, and that even when they find an area of agreement their opinions are bound to change as time goes by." And he added, "Where jazz begins and popular music ends is another question that I would hesitate to answer * * *."

NEVERTHELESS, Feather and other students have suppressed their misgivings and managed to work out formulas which may not be all-embracing but have the virtue of being readily understandable. To take just two examples, jazz is the following to (a) Feather and (b) Stearns:

(a) "The music we recognize today as jazz is a synthesis drawn originally from six principal sources: rhythms from West Africa; harmonic structure from European classical music; melodic and harmonic qualities from nineteenth-century American folk music; religious music; work songs and minstrel shows."

(b) "Jazz: a semi-improvisational American music distinguished by an immediacy of communication, an expressiveness characteristic of the free use of the human voice, and a complex flowing rhythm; it is the result of a three hundred years' blending in the United States of the European and West African musical traditions, and its predominant components are European harmony, Euro-African melody and African rhythm."

It is possible to identify the *kinds* of jazz that are played and the periods in which they began—the experts speak of Traditional or New Orleans, Dixieland or Chicago, Kansas City, Swing, Bop, Progressive and Modern; Ragtime, Blues and Boogie-woogie—but from there on the definitions show an annoying tendency to grow highly technical and disputatious where they are not hedged about with splinters of qualification and fragments of interpretation. Opinion is no longer unanimous, for example, that the music even originated in New Orleans, some scholars contending that it simply had its greatest impact there. One critic stated positively that ragtime is not jazz, nor is jazz ragtime, and was set upon by the others. Most of the attempts to make clear to the layman what a musician means when he says his music "swings" have ended in frustration, and, today, there is a fine, noisy controversy raging over where jazz is going and whether it is proper to call a lot of what is being played jazz.

UP to this time, improvisation on a theme by a soloist has been considered an absolute essential in jazz. However, a school of thought has come into being among some musicians, composers and commentators, the essence of which is that it is possible to have written music that can honorably be called jazz. The other day, at the conclusion of a heated argument along these lines among three modernists and a "moldy fig"—traditionalists are known as moldy figs—the fig cried out in pain, "This is the end of jazz as we know it."

The substance of the argument was relayed to Gunther Schuller and to Orrin Keepnews, the latter a former jazz critic and a founder of Riverside Records. Schuller's comment was that "jazz is a folk music in the process of becoming an art music. It may be absorbed into the stream of classical music as has happened before with folk music. But jazz is so strong a folk music, it may withstand absorption and form a third stream. The musicians aren't concerned with labeling it, just with playing it. Someone will label it later." Keepnews was a little more jazzy. "This music," he said, "is no innocent little maiden to be seduced by the big, bad stranger from Symphony Hall."

August 24, 1958

Coltrane's 'Sheets of Sound'

By JOHN S. WILSON

FOR all their theoretical sense of freedom, jazz musicians have a tendency to be surprisingly hidebound. As a rule, they find their mode of expression quite early in their careers. After that, polish may be added to their playing but, basically, the adventure is over and they remain on whatever track they started on.

There have been a few jazzmen who were disinclined to be hemmed in in this fashion. Coleman Hawkins and Red Norvo moved out of the Swing Era into the be-bop period with enough curiosity about the then "new thing" to feel at home with the boppers. Their basic styles, however, were not changed to any great extent by whatever they absorbed from these new influences, primarily because they were already working from unusually broad and sturdy foundations. Duke Ellington, who could never be pigeonholed in any period or style, has gone on evolving in his own independent way.

*

John Coltrane, who died on July 17 at the age of 40, was much like Ellington in this respect. His career was a process of constant development. Yet, unlike Ellington, he was affected by the jazz trends of his time and had a strong and influential role in shaping them.

After a preparatory decade in which he played with numerous small groups, mostly rhythm and blues bands, Coltrane joined Miles Davis's group in 1955. During this same time, he moved out of

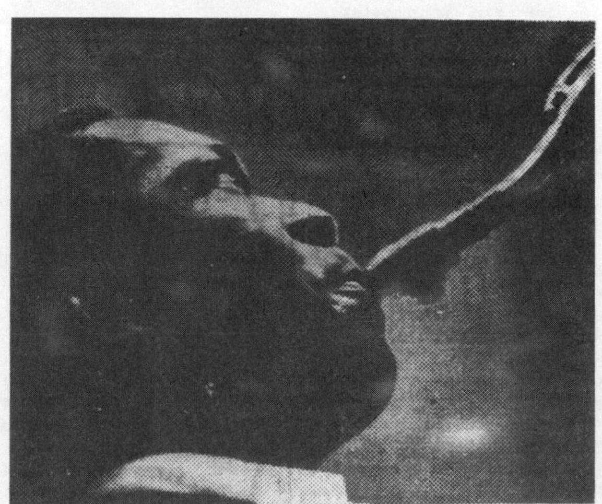

Chuck Stewart

The late John Coltrane
He was disinclined to be hemmed in

an early absorption in the work of Charlie Parker by switching from alto saxophone to tenor. From the time he joined Davis until his death, the saxophonist was engaged in an extended series of explorations while he worked as a sideman with Davis and Thelonius Monk and, since 1960, as leader of his own group.

He created solos in which he ran rapidly through the entire scale of each chord, creating what Ira Gitler, a jazz critic, called "sheets of sound." He picked up the soprano saxophone, an instrument that only Sidney Bechet had used successfully in jazz and, through the tone he produced on the soprano, found a means of expressing his growing interest in Indian music.

He was affected by Miles Davis's interest in "modal jazz" and by the music of Ornette Coleman and Eric Dolphy. He became involved in the free expression of the current avant-gardists. At one of his last recording sessions, he played flute in a flute-and-piccolo duet with Pharoah Sanders.

"Since 1959," Joe Goldberg wrote of Coltrane in "Jazz Masters of the Fifties," "he has run through several musical ideas so rapidly that a given Coltrane record may be obsolete before its release; it will almost surely be out of date before reviews of it are published."

The record of Coltrane most recently released at the time of his death, **Kulu Se Mama** (Impulse 9106; stereo 9106) happens to be an unusually good summation of what the saxophonist was doing in the past few years. This, it should be noted, is not the product of his last recording sessions. They will be represented by **Expressions** (Impulse 9120; stereo 9120), which is due for release at the end of August.

*

"Kulu Se Mama," dates back more than a year to the period when McCoy Tyner was Coltrane's pianist, and Elvin Jones his drummer.

The disk is made up of three selections. The title piece, "Kulu Se Mama," which takes up an entire side, is built on a ritual poem by Julian Lewis who sings it in a chant-like manner in an Afro-Creole dialect. Around and over this, Coltrane and a seven-piece group (which includes three drummers) build a free flowing instrumental performance that, with its coaxing, singing saxophones weaving and entwining through the rolling, insistent percussion, creates an almost hypnotic spell.

Musically, the style is much like that used by Coltrane in his free form work, "Ascension," a 30-minute performance which occupies both sides of Impulse 95, a recording released last year. But where "Ascension" is a roaring, barreling assault on the listener, "Kulu Se Mama" invites and seduces so that when the saxophones or bass clarinet begin to sing on the raw edges of their tones, they convey a sense of intensity without rousing an accompanying sense of confusion.

The remaining two selections expose two contrasting sides of Coltrane as a saxophonist. "Vigil," a drum and saxophone duet with Elvin Jones, is a remarkable tour de force in which both men dive directly into powerful, full-bodied, unrelenting virtuoso performances that are sustained for almost ten minutes with no resort to sidepaths, gimmickry or time-fillers.

The forthcoming Coltrane disk on Impulse, "Expressions," contains, in addition to the flute-piccolo duet, three selections by his last group with his wife, Alice Coltrane on piano, Jimmy Garrison, bass, and Richard Ali, drums. One piece, "Offering," is a remarkable statement by any standards — an extended saxophone solo that progresses with inevitable logic from a strong, stately opening to torrents of furious, driving sound (the "sheets of sound" a decade later), and a return — drained and exhausted — to a variation of the opening level. "Offering" is an exploration of all the resources of a saxophone set out in an utterly awesome performance.

*

Coltrane's ability to make viable use of all those strange nooks and crannies of the saxophone that are so attractive to the current jazz avant-garde set him apart from the bulk of the avant-gardists. He had arrived at his way of using those devices through the discipline of long and probing experience. Because of this, he was able to provide young, less experienced experimentalists with some sense of direction which might guide them in threading their way through what has often seemed to be a rambling, disorganized maze. Not the least of the losses resulting from Coltrane's death will be the guidance and example he brought to this currently chaotic area of jazz.

August 13, 1967

Jersey Jazz Buff Is Host to Beiderbecke Memorial

By JOHN S. WILSON
Special to The New York Times

LONG VALLEY, N. J., May 24 — The sounds of 45 jazz musicians celebrating the memory of Bix Beiderbecke, the jazz cornetist who died in 1931 at the age of 28, echoed yesterday through the normal weekend drowsiness of this village at the foot of Schooley's Mountain, 18 miles west of Morristown

The occasion was the sixth annual Bix Beiderbecke Memorial Stomp, held each year on the back lawn of the home of E. William Donahoe, a Beiderbecke enthusiast who keeps his kitchen clock permanently stopped at 9:30, the time when Mr. Beiderbecke died on Aug. 6, 1931, in Queens.

Mr. Donahoe, an executive of Automatic Data Processing, Inc., of Clifton, originated the observance six years ago and pays all its expenses. Those include the bill for enough beer and hamburgers to satisfy more than 200 musicians and guests from 4 P.M. until midnight.

The musicians, playing in groups of seven or eight, performed on a platform set against Mr. Donahoe's garage, on the side of which were a large portrait of Mr. Beiderbecke and a red banner that proclaimed, "Bix Lives." The audience sat in lawn chairs or wandered around greeting old friends who come to this affair every year. As darkness settled in, flares were lighted on either side of the bandstand, and the farther reaches of the grounds were lighted up by bonfires.

The music. which went on continuously as one group gave way to another, focused on the general repertory of traditional jazz with only occasional direct references to Mr. Beiderbecke. "Singing the Blues," a celebrated Beiderbecke solo, was performed with a great sense of style by Larry Weiss, a cornetist, while Billy Barnes, playing flugelhorn, led a group through an exceptionally easy, relaxed treatment of "Louisiana," a favorite Beiderbecke recording.

The musicians, representing such groups as the Southampton Dixie, Racing and Clambake Society, the Red Onion Jazz Band, Chuck Slate's Traditional Jazz Band, the Upper Greenwood Lake Footwarmers, the Buffalo Disaster Band, the Orange Valley Washboard Ramblers and the Original Washington Monument Dixieland Jazz Band, held to a remarkably high and consistent level of performance no matter how they were shuffled on the bandstand.

Their rapport was particularly impressive when they all assembled as a marching band on Mr. Donahoe's front lawn and marched twice around the house to the lusty strains of "Bourbon Street Parade," in which Mr. Donahoe made his one musical contribution of the day on washboard.

May 25, 1970

Scholars, Get Busy on Scott Joplin!

By HAROLD C. SCHONBERG

THIS is the story of Scott Joplin and me, and of a few weeks of adventure with his music.

It started just after the new year, when I played Joshua Rifkin's recording of eight of Joplin's piano rags (Nonesuch 71248). I was enchanted. The music had a lovely swing, and as one rag succeeded another, it was clear that Joplin had a style very much his own. Melody succeeded melody, and even though Joplin was working in a rather circumscribed form, every rag sounded different. And the music not only had an elegance of its own, in such a work as "Euphonic Sounds" it had a good deal of delicate color and harmonic imagination. This was not just any man's music. The syncopations—and ragtime is based on syncopation—were as idiomatically applied as the rubatos in a Chopin mazurka. Joplin was a real composer.

Rifkin, whose playing was relaxed and smooth, also wrote the notes to his record. From them I learned that Joplin was a black composer (1868-1917), born in Texarkana, active in the Midwest, who ended his career in New York. He was a pianist and cornetist, but primarily he wrote music, and his "Maple Leaf Rag" of 1899 made him famous. He also composed two operas, one of which has disappeared. The other, "Treemonisha," is thus the first known opera ever composed by a black. Joplin himself published the piano score. There seems to have been one semiprivate performance of the work. Nobody was interested in a ragtime opera about black people and their aspirations.

*

The Joplin tunes on Rifkin's record refused to go out of my head, and I kept hearing them over and over. A few days after playing the record, I was telling some of the music staff of The Times about my "discovery." That was on Jan. 6. "Did you know," Ted Strongin asked, "that there is going to be a concert of ragtime music at the Free Music Store this Friday?" I didn't know, and I immediately called Dan Kavanaugh of WBAI, the station that sponsors the Free Music Store concerts. Sure, said Kavanaugh. Three pianists and others are going to participate. Come along.

Friday night found me at the Free Music Store, in Martinson Hall on the third floor of the New York Shakespeare Festival Public Theater on Lafayette Street. The place was crowded with young people, sprawled all over the floor (there are no seats in Martinson Hall). Feeling terribly ancient, I listened to Bill Bolcom, Rifkin and Dan Paget play rags, who announced each piece to the kids as they went along, adding whatever commentary they thought fit. There also were two young guitarists, David Laibman and Rick Schoenberg (no relation, as far as I know), trying out a series of rags on two guitars.

The music held up fine, and it was interesting to hear the same pieces—"Maple Leaf Rag," say—played by two different pianists. Paget was much faster than Rifkin in the "Maple Leaf." I can't say which interpretation was better (though the sheet music insists that the tempo in ragtime music should never be fast): both had their points. The pianists also played rags by other composers, including Joseph Lamb, Clarence Woods and James Scott. None of those composers were in Joplin's class.

During the concert, I had a few words with Rifkin. He is a young man, Juilliard trained, who teaches at Brandeis and also is an avant-garde composer. He said that the music was by no means easy. "It's as exposed as Mozart, and you can't afford to make a technical or rhythmic mistake." He said that nearly all ragtime music was out of print, including the once-famous 100 Ragtime Classics selected by Max Morath. A volume named 34 Ragtime Jazz Classics, published by the Edwin H. Morris Co., is, however, available. Rifkin, a true child of his time, was worried about the Morris collection. "I suspect," he said, "that some of the editions are corrupt."

Ragtime composer Scott Joplin

That floored me, though on reflection I don't see why it should have.

*

The following Monday morning found me at the Music Library in Lincoln Center, talking to Richard Jackson, head of the Americana collection.

"Joplin is in the air," Jackson said. "Did you know that Mrs. Lawrence is working on a two-volume edition of all Joplin music?" Vera Brodsky Lawrence, a former concert pianist, is the lady who was largely responsible last year for the five-volume reprint of Gottschalk piano music, published by Arno Press. "I have a folder on Joplin," Jackson continued. He brought it out. "And here's what we have of his printed music."

There wasn't much. Very little work has been done on Scott Joplin, and that is surprising, considering that ragtime was the predecessor of jazz. Scholars are going to have to get busy on Joplin, and among the things they will be investigating is the influence of Louis Moreau Gottschalk on Joplin. Gottschalk's nationalistic music, including his use of Negro elements, was still extremely popular in Joplin's day. Gottschalk was more sophisticated, and much of his piano writing is for virtuosos, but as one listens to Joplin's music it is clear that he must have known such works as "Bamboula" and "Le Bananier."

In Jackson's folder were odd pieces of information about Joplin. He composed 504 piano pieces, including marches, waltzes and cakewalks as well as ragtime. He published, in 1908, a little book of instruction on the secrets of playing ragtime. The first time the word "ragtime" was used on a sheet of music was in 1893, in a work by Fred Stone named "Ma Ragtime Baby." In 1896 came "The

Harlem Rag" by Tom Turpin. Joplin's first published work, in 1898, was "The Original Rags," a medley. His "Maple Leaf Rag" in 1899, swept the country. Over a million copies of the sheet music were sold. Ragtime was on its way, and until the end of World War I was the popular musical rage of America.

That afternoon, after finishing at the library and thanking Jackson, I phoned Mrs. Lawrence. She said that she was preparing reprint editions of out of print and unavailable, historical American music under a Rockefeller Foundation grant. The Joplin volumes, she thinks, will be ready by September of this year and will be brought out by a major publisher.

"You have no idea of the interest in Joplin," Mrs. Lawrence said. "Once word began getting around that I was preparing an edition, material started coming in. People even sent first editions. I got one from, will you believe it, Vienna. Did you know there was a recording by Knocky Parker of all the piano rags? I'll let you borrow it; it's hard to locate. Have you seen a score of 'Treemonisha'?" I hadn't. "I'll lend it to you, and also the Blesh book."

Mrs. Lawrence was as good as her word. I spent the next two days listening to the records (Audiophile 71/72), reading "They All Played Ragtime" by Rudi Blesh and Harriet Janis, and going through "Treemonisha." The Blesh-Janis book is the authoritative study of ragtime, and naturally its central character is Joplin. Informative and well written, it is in its third edition and can be purchased as a paperback (Oak Publications, New York).

*

As for "Treemonisha," I studied it with mixed feelings. Could it be staged today? It is largely in ragtime, with some adulterations in the late romantic style. Some of the music is beautiful, and the slow drag that ends the opera is a knockout. But the libretto! If the Delius "Koanga," which recently had its American premiere in Washington, was condemned as creeping Uncle Tomism by the black critic Carman Moore, what would he do with "Treemonisha," an opera about the triumph of education over superstition? There is nothing about race prejudice in "Treemonisha," and its solution to the ills of the black man is, merely, education. This may be an idealistic conjecture, or it even may be true (though whites need also to be educated as well), but the libretto is pretty bad.

However, it should be taken as the period piece it is. And it is an opera composed by a black, with black characters only, expressed in music that reflects the black heritage. It will have to be orchestrated. Joplin's orchestral sketches are no longer around. Perhaps a concert version would arouse enough interest for a full-scale production.

I had a subsequent talk with Mrs. Lawrence, who firmly believes that "Treemonisha" is so beautiful, and of such historical importance, that it has to be produced. Then I asked Mrs. Lawrence if Joplin's piano music was really that hard. The figurations, after all, looked as though they lay in the hand, and none of the music I had examined was of a virtuoso nature.

"Just wait," Mrs. Lawrence said grimly. "Just wait until you try it."

January 24, 1970

Armstrong Was Root Source of Jazz

By JOHN S. WILSON

An Appraisal

Louis Armstrong was more than a great jazz virtuoso. He was the root source that moved jazz onto the path along which it has developed for more than 45 years. Through the sheer power of his musical imagination and personality, he reshaped the relatively limited urban folk music in which he grew up, opening up the possibilities that have made it part of a global culture.

When young Louis Armstrong left his home in New Orleans to join King Oliver's Creole Jazz Band in Chicago in 1922, jazz was still a music of ensemble improvisation.

But this form was being shaken up in the active jazz world that Mr. Armstrong found in Chicago. Soloists were breaking through the ensemble pattern. It was Mr. Armstrong who gave the solo stature by showing such steadily developing virtuosity in the series of records made by his Hot Five and Hot Seven that his solos soon became the focal point of the recordings.

"Cornet Chop Suey," "Potato Head Blues" and, in deeper and more deliberate fashion, "West End Blues" and "Tight Like That" contained jazz solos of such compelling brilliance that the emphasis in a jazz performance was changed from the ensemble to the soloist.

And it was Mr. Armstrong, too, who provided the spark that made the big jazz band viable. His presence in Fletcher Henderson's orchestra in 1924 changed a dance band that was not unlike other dance bands of the period into a jazz band, the first of its kind.

Because he made these essential contributions to the development of jazz in the 1920's when jazz—the real thing as opposed to the popularly accepted "jazz" of such bandleaders as Paul Whiteman—was still largely an underground music, most of Mr. Armstrong's career was, in a sense, an anticlimax.

But, fortunately, he had a second string to his bow as a singer and entertainer and through this, in his latter years, he reaped the fame and rewards that too often have eluded the influential creators in jazz. To gain these, he became known to a generation or two primarily for his toothy grin and his singing of pop ballads. But that was just a surface. Underneath bubbled that same spirit and expressiveness that had made possible the jazz that musicians were playing 30 and 40 years ago, the jazz they are playing today and whatever they may play tomorrow. Wherever they are, they're playing Louis's music.

July 7, 1971

PROFESSOR BENNY

Benny Goodman, his cla[illegible] sheet of swing music—the occasion being [illegible] announcement tha jazz band conductor [illegible] on a series of music lectures for New York school children.

May 23, 1931

GOODMAN IS HEARD IN 'SWING' CONCERT

Carnegie Hall Crowded for Orchestra's Rendition of 'New Kind of Music'

'JAM SESSION' A FEATURE

Soloists Join in Collective Improvisation — Virtuosity of Players Much Admired

By OLIN DOWNES

The writer of these lines, whose principal occupation it is to report performances of symphony and opera, is much interested in jazz and other forms of American popular music. He thinks, as Debussy put it, that there is only one music, which may exist in a dance, a folk-song, a waltz or a symphony, and is often to be encountered in undignified places. He therefore hurried with much curiosity and anticipation to the concert given last night in Carnegie Hall by Bennie Goodman and his famous "swing" orchestra.

He went expecting a new, original, and elemental kind of music; one that we had been told marks a novel and original form of expression. This is not the sort of thing that Paul Whiteman triumphed in introducing to the polite musical world some fourteen years ago in this city. In those fourteen years a great deal of water flowed under the bridge. In the interim the pioneer, Whiteman has been practically canonized by the younger generation, and relegated to last by the Goodmans, Dorseys, Duke Ellingtons and such of the present. In a word, jazz has given way to "swing." "Swing" is that subtle creative something, the je ne sais quoi in popular music, which has superseded the older product and gained a greater power of popular appeal, according to its special proponents, than jazz ever exerted.

Leader Warmly Welcomed

It may therefore be imagined with what a thumping of the heart the present scribe got into his seat, in good time before the concert began, to hear the very first notes of Goodman's orchestra. It may be said immediately that he was enormously impressed, though not in the precise way he expected. When Mr. Goodman entered he received a real Toscanini send-off from the excited throng. It took some minutes to establish quiet. There was quivering excitement in the air, an almost electrical effect, and much laughter. The audience broke out before the music stopped, in crashing applause and special salvos as one or another of the heroes of the orchestra rose in his place to give his special and ornate contribution to the occasion.

That is almost the sum of it. We went to discover a new, original, thrilling music. We stayed to watch a social and physical phenomenon. For the great gathering was almost off its head with joy. The "hotter" the pace, the louder the blasts, the better it went. Sometimes shouts threatened to vanquish the orchestra.

This form of sound is a curious reduction, almost disintegration of music into its component elements. There is hardly an attempt at beauty of tone, and certainly none at construction of melody. A few fragments of well-known popular tunes suffice for a sort of rough material, subject to variation by the players. They do such feats of rhythm and dexterity as occur to them on the tune's basis. The tone of the brass instruments, almost continually overblown, is hard, shrill and noisy. The other instruments add what they can to swell the racket.

What Rhythm Can Do

But why claim that this is new? These are effects and devices as old as the hills to any one who has listened in the last fifteen years to jazz music. They are merely carried to extremes. It is very interesting to see what rhythm can do. It can get an audience wild, and it did. But it did not seem to be able to generate music.

Attend a Negro camp meeting. The people shout and become possessed by rhythm. This invariably produces music. Song is thrown off as a sort of grand ferment of the tumult. The playing last night, if noise, speed and syncopation, all very old devices, are heat, was "hot" as it could be, but nothing came of it all, and in the long run it was decidedly monotonous.

Nor is Mr. Goodman, when he plays his clarinet, anything like as original as other players of the same instrument and the same sort of thing that we have heard. Nor did we hear a single player, in the course of a solid hour of music, invent one original or interesting musical phrase, over the persistent basic rhythm. Not that they lacked technical accomplishment and amazing mastery of their medium. Musically, they let us down.

Much was expected of the "jam session." A "jam session" is improvisation, free for all members of the band, over a basic rhythm, and the devil take the hindmost. Such a form is a special test of the players' invention. No doubt a "jam session" can be dull as ditch-water one night and inspired at the very next meeting. Last night's "jam session" seemed to last a good ten minutes, and though soloist after soloist of the band tried in turn to contribute something original to the ensemble, little or nothing of the sort materialized.

If this is the ideal presentment of "swing" we must own to a cruel disillusion. We may be a hopeless old-timer, sunk in the joys of Whiteman jazz, unable to appreciate the starker, modern product. But we greatly fear we are right, and venture the prediction that "swing" of this kind will quickly be a thing of the past. Some say that it doesn't pretend to be music, but to be "something else." That is perhaps true. If so, rhythms that carry music with them will supplant it.

It is to be recorded that last night's audience remained applauding and cheering till a late hour. It is to be added, so far as one observer's reaction is concerned, that "swing" is a bore, long before an evening has ended.

January 17, 1938

GOOD-WILL SET TO MUSIC

By JOSEPH J. RYAN

DANCING America's growing movement for more rhumbas, more congas, more tangos, is a tribute to the perseverance of Xavier Cugat, whose name has become synonymous with the undulating rhythms of Latin America.

The sagacious Mr. Cugat, however, envisions more in his music than entertainment. With Uncle Sam emphasizing a "good-neighbor" policy between the Americas, he considers his tuneful crusade here a bridge to hemispheric unity. In support of his point, he recalls that it was not so long ago that the popular conception here of Latin Americans was a Hollywood-inspired composite of gauchos, guitar players and coffee growers. He feels that the growing understanding of the music of our Latin-American cousins has done much to dispel these musical comedy impressions.

Traditionalist

While other band leaders have stressed Latin-American rhythms from time to time, Mr. Cugat has steadily and hopefully abided by the colorful dance ditties of Old Spain, Old Mexico and South America in the face of competition both "sweet" and "swing." He is responsible, perhaps more than any other orchestra leader, for the popularity of Latin melodies in this country.

His reward has been a growing army of followers. The younger generation is particularly enthusiastic, according to a recent poll conducted in seventy-two American colleges. His orchestra swept the votes of fifty-three of the schools, while his nearest competitor could muster but eleven.

In South America, where the seductive Latin cadences are the rule rather than the exception, the rhumba-wise population voted him the winner in another popularity contest with 59,000 votes. He won out over several other native bands.

While Mr. Cugat does not confine himself exclusively to Latin tunes, he does adhere strictly to the Latin motif. Songs of the day are treated in the off-beat measures of the Spanish popular school. In this manner he programs his broadcasts over WEAF's hook-up Thursdays at 7:30 P.M.

First a Fiddler

Although Mr. Cugat's reputation has been built largely by radio, he achieved some fame as a concert violinist, and thanks for his present tunes should be given, oddly enough, to the music critics. In commenting on his virtuosity twelve years ago, the critics described it with less than the extravagant praise his Latin temperament required. This lukewarm reception of his work as a violinist—the career he first pursued—determined him to forsake the concert stage. He said he could not appreciate practicing almost all his waking hours for "the thankless returns of the concert stage."

He expressed only half sorrow about this decision, pointing to his financial success, growing popularity and comparative leisure as no small substitute. The move eventually led to his resolve to popularize his native Spanish tunes—he was born in Barcelona—although a fling into newspaper cartooning separated the two.

The strain of playing on the concert stage was explained by Mr. Cugat as beyond ordinary comprehension. He added:

"Why, if you were to discontinue playing for two months, it would take a full year to regain your touch."

Recalling Fritz Kreisler's accident, he said: "I don't believe Mr. Kreisler will be able to regain his former perfection in less than a year, though the fact will be apparent only to keen students of the art."

A Pioneer, Too

Early in his career as a violinist Mr. Cugat had the distinction of being the first to fiddle for radio. Describing the event, he said: "I was greatly impressed. We were all crowded into a little room, nothing like the present elaborate studios, awaiting our turn to play. Presently, Major Andrew White, who officiated, called me and I stepped up to a strange metal contraption and played my selection. It was hard to conceive of the music actually traveling many miles through the air and being picked up by the few pioneer listeners of those days."

Mr. Cugat gave the date of his first trial at the microphone as Dec. 28, 1921, over Station WDY, Camden, N.J.

Having fiddled since he was old enough to hold a violin—about five years old—and having studied under eminent masters in this country, Germany, France and Spain, his career immediately preceding the concert stage was spent with the great tenor Enrico Caruso, who was on concert tour in this country. Shortly afterward he played as soloist with the Los Angeles Philharmonic Orchestra.

Caruso liked to sketch caricatures of the people he met, and young Cugat, in hero-worshiping mimicry, began drawing pictures, too. This hobby was a windfall when, stranded in San Francisco after having cut abruptly his concert career, he had to abandon music temporarily and turn to drawing.

Music Wins Out

His talent sufficiently impressed the editors of The Los Angeles Times, who gave him a berth on the staff. However, this means of livelihood was unsatisfactory, for (1) he was not especially equipped to draw "on order" and (2) music was too strongly engendered in his make-up for him to remain out of this field indefinitely.

Today Mr. Cugat enjoys an enviable position in contemporary music. His persevering endeavor has borne the fruits of success.

July 20, 1941

HAL KEMP, ORCHESTRA LEADER

Bandsman Known Here and in Europe for Modern Style Injured in Coast Crash

WON KEITH PRIZE IN YOUTH

Duke of Windsor Often Heard Him Play in London—Had Appeared on the Screen

James Hal Kemp, a lanky Southerner known as "Ole Cunnel Kemp" among his bandsmen, was one of the most popular dance-band leaders in the country. He played over the radio, from the stage, in hotels from coast to coast, and in cabarets in Europe before the war. He had also appeared with his orchestra in motion pictures.

Starting his orchestra just as a hobby while attending the University of North Carolina, he was soon in London on a trip given as a prize in a nation-wide college band contest sponsored by B. F. Keith, the showman. During an engagement at London's Cafe de Paris, Mr. Kemp moved in society circles and met a young man who remarked that he would like to drop in at the cafe with his brother.

"Fine, bring the whole family," Mr. Kemp replied. He learned later that the young man was Prince George, the Duke of Kent. His band was a favorite of the Duke of Windsor, then Prince of Wales, who often visited London clubs where Mr. Kemp was playing and once substituted at the drums in Mr. Kemp's band.

Hoped to Enter Railroading

Back at the university young Kemp continued his studies with the idea that music was still just a hobby and that railroading would be a real career. His father was an official of the Southern Railroad and the orchestra leader had considered himself a railroad man since his earliest days.

But tunes were in his head and in his feet. His prize trip to London had already won him recognition and so many offers of professional engagements in this country that he decided to forget railroading. His popularity carried him to Paris, where he played at Les Ambassadeurs, but in 1930 the French unions insisted upon a ban on foreign orchestras and he was obliged to leave.

He appeared for several seasons at Manhattan hotels and in Miami and with Kay Thompson and the Rythm Girls appeared weekly over

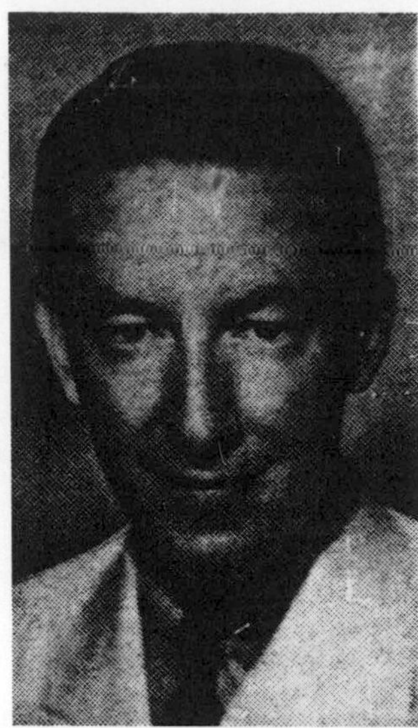

HAL KEMP

the radio stations of the Columbia Broadcasting System. His ultra-modern style ranged from the cacophony, dear to jitterbugs, to soft sophisticated harmonies.

Friends said he had a secret aspiration to become a symphony conductor. He had been studying symphony music daily for three years and was welcomed by symphony conductors throughout the nation, who permitted him to study their styles at rehearsals. He had plans to enter the guest-conducting field immediately.

Encouraged Kay Kyser

A close friend of Kay Kyser, Mr. Kemp was credited by Kyser with encouraging him to take up dance orchestra work and Kyser organized the campus band which succeeded Kemp's at the University of North Carolina.

Mr. Kemp was born at Marion, Ala., in 1905, and while still a child his family moved "no'th" to Charlotte, N. C. A the age of 6 he was an able pianist and at 12 he could also play the cornet and clarinet. He formed his first band while still in high school.

In 1932 he married Bessie Slaughter of Dallas, Texas. They were divorced in 1938. The next year he married Martha Stephenson, debutante daughter of Mrs. Paul Forester of this city and of James Wallace Stephenson of Birmingham, Ala. A daughter was born to them last July.

After turning his hobby into a career, Mr. Kemp turned back to his earlier idea for a career and made it a hobby. In his home in Forest Hills, Queens, and later at a large estate he bought in Morris County, N. J., he maintained a miniature railroad system, building his own rolling stock.

December 22, 1940

He Kills Them With Hot or Sweet

A portrait of Harry James the trumpeter. And a talk with him in which he explains and defends the hepcats and jitterbugs who flock to hear him.

By S. J. Woolf

THE Pied Piper of Gotham has been in town lately and New York youngsters, like those of Hamelin town centuries ago, have flocked after him. For hours they stood in long lines outside the Paramount Theatre waiting for a chance to hear the brazen notes, at times staccato and shrill, then coaxing and seductive, which tall, thin, loose-jointed Harry James toots from his shiny trumpet. They were noisy, they pushed policemen around, they crashed shop windows; a strange mass hysteria seemed to have laid its spell on them. Across Times Square the war bulletins were posted, but war meant nothing to these youngsters. They were there to see Harry James.

"His music sends tingles down my spine," said a girl of 14 made up like a young woman of 20. "When he goes hot I have to come up for breath," said a boy not much older. "I like his sweet numbers," another girl explained, "they make me feel mushy." "So do I," her neighbor piped up; "they remind me of a night last Summer." A dark youth in pork-pie hat, long tan coat and baggy trousers gathered at the ankles volunteered, "I wants to wiggle and shout the way my grandmother does in church. That trumpet gives me religion."

In the theatre the sense of anticipation made itself felt. These youngsters had not come to see American tanks in an African desert. They were interested in jive, not in jeeps, and when the stage with Harry James and his music makers on it slowly rose in the darkness a long pent up "Ah," followed by handclapping and shouts, drowned out the blare of brass. The spotlight fell on the leader of the band. Some of the audience leaned forward in their seats, their bodies swaying to the rhythm of the music. Others stood up and yelled "Get hot" and "Get sweet" in hysterical tones. The music went on. A few, more daring than the rest, shrieking "He's in the groove," began to dance in the aisles until the ushers pushed them back into their seats.

There was a barbaric note of frenzy. There was a feeling of savagery unleashed as the strings and brass, reinforced by

"Youth must have its swing."

Drawn from life by S. J. Woolf

the monotonous beat of the drum, called forth echoes of the pursuing tom-tom in "The Emperor Jones." Outside was the Gay White Way, streamlined and up to date. Here was something primitive.

THE witch doctor who is able to unleash this outburst of pent-up ecstasy seems strangely out of the picture. At his work he wears a light, loose-fitting coat which is typical of Broadway. No pointed conical hat conceals his well-oiled, naturally wavy hair. The large ring on the third finger of his right hand which sparkles as he plays hides no magic powder. There is no air of necromancy about him; he is as easy and nonchalant as the chap who sits at the table next to you at Lindy's.

As he lays his trumpet down on the white piano and turns to his band, which is still playing, he snaps his fingers, moves his elbows and keeps time with the heels of his tan shoes. He reflects Tin Pan Alley rather than the sorcery of sound. The pandemonium in the audience does not seem to register. The piece is finished and he walks over to the microphone and announces the next number—a song or some comic patter. His tone is confidential.

Psychologists may discuss the phenomenon and its import; historians may make comparisons between his followers and the chanting children who, early in the thirteenth century, marched out of European cities hoping to snatch the Holy Land from the infidel; parallels may be drawn between the dancing of the jitterbugs today and the dancing of medieval youth of Germany and Italy who kept it up until they dropped from exhaustion. But to Harry James, tooting the trumpet is just "show business"—business in which, so far as he is concerned, music plays the principal part. In speaking of that music he says: "It has to sound hard to kill 'em."

I saw James the other day in his dressing room, just after he had "killed them" with "The Two o'Clock Jump" and other tunes. His coat was off, worsted slippers had supplanted his tan shoes and he lolled in an easy chair. Coats and neckties belonging to the members of his band dangled from hooks above a small couch. His trumpet rested in a red velvet case in one corner of the room; and on a make-up shelf, surrounded by packages of cigarettes, stood photographs of his two children.

Harry James

HE has the same easy-going way with him off the stage as on. The only time I noticed any tenseness about him was when I asked him to pose with his trumpet. He grabbed it tightly with his left hand and, all the time I was drawing, the fingers of his right hand kept moving up and down on the three brass keys.

James attributes his popularity to the phonograph and radio. "People heard our tunes and then they wanted to see us in person. We sold over two and a half million records of 'You Made Me Love You' and 'I Don't Want to Walk Without You,' and when that number of people hear something that hits them they want to see the band and the guy who leads it. The same thing goes for the radio. We play three times a week. This gave us more of a following.

"In order to hold it, we have to be on our toes all the time. New tunes are not enough. The public wants other novelty. Band leaders must be like automobile manufacturers before the war. They must be bringing out new models all the time. We have to vary our programs, playing sweet numbers and jump numbers, and we have to play them in different ways. Trick arrangements which I outline, vocal choruses and stuff like that hold the interest.

"The one thing that we must always keep is the pulsing rhythm. It's the beat that gets under their skin and keeps them going."

I ASKED why his music appealed particularly to the young people. He looked at the pictures of his own children and said: "Rhythm comes natural to every one. And when kids hear it they respond to it. But they have not got all their feelings under control. They are not ashamed of showing that they are happy or sad. Most of them are full of emotions that are ready to burst out. They have to get rid of these overflowing feelings, and listening to music gives them a good healthy outlet.

"When I was a boy down in Texas a bunch of us used to go to the theatre every Saturday morning. The organist played the songs that we knew and the crowd of us would join in singing. That was the way we let off steam. It was a good thing for all of us and, take it from me, many a boy was kept straight by singing those songs.

"Let me tell you a true story. One night last Summer up at the Stadium a couple of kids heard Tchaikovsky's 'Romeo and Juliet' for the first time. They looked at each other and one said, 'Gee, what a swipe from "Our Love."' Those kids had been introduced to classical music by swing. And that's something that a lot of people don't realize.

"Swing," he went on "has made thousands of boys and girls music-conscious. There is more to their enthusiasm than throwing fits on dance floors. They want good music played outside a concert hall, played in a new way, and in a place where they don't have to sit still.

"Some of our most popular numbers are by the great classical composers. Take our arrangements of 'Flight of the Bumble Bee' or of 'The Afternoon of a Faun.' The kids go crazy over them. In order to give them their proper rendering I added a string section to our band and, believe me, many people thought I was going nuts when I hired those long-underwear boys. But it is not only the kids who like our stuff. Kreisler himself approved a record we made of our arrangement of his 'Caprice Viennois.'

"The longer I am in this business the most certain I am that young music lovers like the same kind of pieces that the older ones do. More than that, I have noticed, even in the short time I have been playing, that their taste is constantly improving. So, for that matter, is mine.

"Swing was my musical appetizer. It made me hungry for music. It was on a phonograph that I first heard Stravinsky, Ravel and Debussy. They hit me so hard that I introduced dancing arrangements of some of their works. They went over big. People don't give swing credit for a lot that it is doing. It is growing up and in doing so it is popularizing fine music. Many a swing fan has become a concert-goer. Swing is developing the tasté of jitterbugs and hepcats who once were satisfied with the output of Tin Pan Alley."

Notwithstanding his success in the theatre, James prefers playing in hotels and on the radio. Although he has been in show business all his life (his mother continued her trapeze act up to a month before he was born), the five or six daily stage appearances he has to make get on his nerves. He does not have time to practice or to attend ball games. Baseball is his pet hobby and the chances are that one of the reasons he organized his own band was so that he would always have enough men with him to start a ball game. One of the first things he does when he strikes a town is to look for an empty lot where they can play.

HE says that when he retires he hopes to be able to build a house right on the first-base line and "pay seventeen other guys enough to hang around and play ball when I feel like it." Between innings, however, he will continue to practice and to listen to records of his favorite composers.

However, even if he ever builds that dream house the chances are that he will not stay in it long. His entire life has been a series of circus parades, and the sawdust ring and the smell of tanbark still hold a fascination for him. His father and mother were both circus people. The elder James was the bandmaster of the Mighty Haag Circus, whose drummers beat a tattoo when Mrs. James made her daring leap into an outstretched net.

Harry, whose middle name is Haag, was born in Albany, Ga., twenty-six years ago. At the time the circus was playing a two-week stand in that town. Harry grew up amid the trumpetings of elephants, which may have played a small part in shaping his career. By the time he was 4 years old he was a human pretzel billed as the youngest contortionist under canvas. An illness at 6 straightened him out and his father taught him to play the "hot" drum in the band. Within a couple of years the older man left the Mighty Haag Circus to join the Christy Brothers amazing aggregation of animals and athletes, and by this time young Harry was blowing his own trumpet. At 15 he was the leader of the second circus band.

IT was then that his parents decided to settle down in Beaumont, Texas, the Winter quarters of the circus. Harry settled down too and went to high school. By this time he was pretty well fed up on marches and began looking around for other kinds of compositions. He won a State contest for trumpet-playing and began to "sit in" in local orchestras. Finally Ben Pollack, who had a big name band in the Southwest, offered him a job. It was then he wrote his first song. It was called "Peckin'," and while it started a dance craze deep in the heart of Texas, it brought few dollars and little fame to Harry.

However, a record of it in which Harry played a trumpet solo was heard by Benny Goodman and the swing king sent for the young Texas troubadour. For two years Harry tooted for Goodman and then, with his leader's blessings, started out on his own. That was four years ago and since then Harry James has been on the up and up. A friend remarked, "Harry did not join the circus—he made the circus join the band."

He has never forgotten the lessons he learned in the pad room under the big top. The snap of the ringmaster's whip is re-echoed by the snap of his fingers as he directs his jaunty musicians to play sweet or hot. Like the man on the flying trapeze, he goes through the air—be that air "Sonate Moderne" or "Flatbush Flannigan"—with the greatest of ease. He looks out at his audiences and compares the youngsters to whom he now gives five and jam with those whom he once heard shouting and applauding as they gaped at the acrobats twirling high above. He sees little difference between them in feeling.

For, says he, "Youth must have its swing."

May 16, 1943

Making Catnip for the Hepcats

Being the leader of a name band is big business, and war problems, including manpower, bear down hard. But the war has swelled the market for hot and sweet.

By John Desmond

LEADERS of the eight or nine name dance bands, who can throw a cordon of jitterbugging youths around any big city theatre on a half hour's notice, are not complaining aloud these days, but privately they admit that "government competition" is having a lot to do with their ability to get it hot or sweet to suit the mood of the hepcats.

The competition comes principally from the War Manpower Commission and the Office of Defense Transportation, and with manpower growing short and travel time long, the name-band leaders are beginning to wonder if they will be able to cash in fully on the million-dollar bonanza into which the hepcats and the war have swelled the business of producing jazz notes.

The ace leaders—Harry James, Benny Goodman, Tommy and Jimmy Dorsey, Kay Kyser, Sammy Kaye, Xavier Cugat, Duke Ellington, Horace Heidt—can have more film contracts, theatre bookings and other lucrative engagements than they know what to do with, and the competition among them for contracts has virtually ceased. But competition for manpower is different. The Selective Service Act has been draining off trombonists, clarinetists, saxophonists and trumpeters—along with bricklayers, waiters and messengers—and since replacements must be found largely among the young musicians who have the energy and the desire to play jazz, they are hard to come by. Moreover, even holding one's own draft-exempt men has become a major problem, especially in recent months, owing to "raiding" among the top leaders and the evolution of the radio station house band.

RAIDING is the very much frowned on but almost universal practice of offering a featured player in a competitor's

band more money than he is getting. It has had the effect of raising the salaries of instrumentalists sharply since the war, and as manpower shortages become even more pressing, wages continue to spira' and the band leaders' headaches to swell.

But even this raiding can be combated, while the relatively new development of the radio house band leaves the leader with few defensive weapons. In the last two years the best instrumentalists in the business, tired of bouncing through the night in a crowded day coach while clinging tenaciously to a bass horn, have been gravitating to the radio stations in increasing numbers. They quit the bands principally to get away from the grueling eight-shows-a-day schedule on the theatre circuit, but they soon found that by free-lancing on commercial programs they could boost their incomes to well over the best pay in the name-band outfits. One featured instrumentalist appears on as many as ten or twelve commercials a week on the Blue Network at $60 a program.

To combat the manpower drain, the leaders have been combing the highways and byways of music, grabbing promising musicians from bands in lower income brackets, granting auditions to youngsters in their middle 'teens who wouldn't have a chance of hitting the big time for years in normal days, and bidding here and there for a competitor's instrumentalist. These practices aren't new to the band leader. He has followed them ever since he organized his band. In fact, it is the only way a musician who thinks he has the talent to organize his own orchestra can make his start and maintain his reputation when he gets one.

In peacetime a leader on his way up recruited the best group of musicians his funds could command and trained them to play in his style and to interpret his arrangements so as to give the band a distinctive stamp. Generally the recruits were trained and experienced men who had started in small hotels, won the attention of more successful bands and finally became masters of their instruments. Occasionally, however, the leader would run across a talented youngster with no experience in orchestra playing. Such men are easy to mold to the leader's style of playing and often have proved outstanding.

Today, the top leaders spend as much time listening to other bands as they do directing their own. And their musicians frequently act as scouts, visiting the dance places in every town they hit and seeking out instrumentalists who might be just the material the leader needs.

To hold the men they have, the leaders have been doing everything in their power to satisfy them and to ease the strain of the exacting schedules. In this they have one great advantage arising from the fact that no musician plays in a name band today unless he wants to. Band playing in the big time is one business that a man has to like before he will put up with it. Most of the players are so sold on it that they spend their spare time lipping their instruments. Furthermore, many of the straight jazz men hate the "long-haired" stuff and are not candidates for radio house bands—which must play both popular and classical music—either because they are unable to play, or won't play, the classics.

In some ways the orchestra leader's problems today are not greatly different from those he faced seven or eight years ago when he was just beginning to experience the hard knocks of the business. But they have been intensified by the war at a time when most of the leaders had begun to enjoy the fruits of their long struggle to get to the top.

Although jazz was an increasingly marketable commodity in the years that followed its introduction by the Dixieland Jazz Band in the early Twenties, the name band of today—one that can draw $10,000 a week and up for a theatre engagement—is a purely post-depression phenomenon.

It all started back in 1935 when New York's Paramount Theatre, which couldn't seem to draw enough patronage to keep the marbled lobby and upholstered seats from gathering dust, booked Glen Gray's Casa Loma Orchestra for a two-week Christmas engagement, just as an experiment.

On the day that Gray opened, the management rubbed its eyes as the swing addicts of the middle Thirties put on the first of the shows that have been a Times Square perennial ever since. In Chicago, Philadelphia, Cleveland, St. Louis, Los Angeles and half a hundred other cities, theatre managements began adding help and casting around for bands to put them to work. Show-wise Broadwayites shook their heads and said: "There ain't that many jitterbugs. It's a flash in the pan. It'll be over in four months." The Paramount's managing director, Robert Weitman, laughs at that. The Paramount has never been without a band since that Christmas in 1935 and it hasn't had a losing week since.

But while all the theatre had to do to cut its share of the name-band patronage was to sign up the bands, ambitious young leaders fought long and expensive battles for the names that would pack them in. Some—like Benny Goodman—came along fast and were playing the Paramount a year later at double the money Gray received. Others, like the Dorseys, Harry James and Cugat, had hard pulls. Most others never hit the crest and got rid of their own money and as much of their friends' money as they could legally lay their hands on in the attempt.

A lot of capital was spent—sometimes as much as $50,000—before a band had sufficient fame to demand ceiling wages from a theatre manager. And since most of the band leaders who reached the top started with nothing more than their instruments, a good sound knowledge of music and a lot of ambition, they had to find backers.

Once his orchestra was reasonably well financed, the leader tried to book one of the big hotels that are noted for their famous bands. Such engagements pay only the union scale or slightly more, except under special conditions, and the leader's receipts were often less than his musical payroll, to say nothing of his outlay for arrangers, secretaries, managers, production men and operational expenses. However, these "spot" bookings were and are extremely valuable, since they have "outs" over the air and give the leader a chance to get his name noised about among radio sponsors, and record manufacturers who, until the Petrillo ban went into effect, contributed a large part of an orchestra's profits.

SUCH a hotel booking in the middle Nineteen Thirties got a leader enough of a following to permit his manager to arrange a road trip that might cover as much as 80.000 miles in a single year, playing high school dances, college proms, out-of-the-way resorts and small theatres. How grueling those road tours could be —they are out of the question today because of transportation restrictions—only an orchestra leader and his musicians know. Jimmy Dorsey's band back in 1938 played ninety-three one-nighters in a row. Toward the end of the run, the musicians were so frayed that there was very little of the Jimmy Dorsey style left, save the name and the blazers. Jimmy had years of that grind before he clicked with a recording of "The Breeze and I" in late 1939 and moved into the select Class A bracket.

Every other top

Xavier Cugat

leader had his share of the same fare. Harry James, with a $4,500 loan from his former boss Benny Goodman, and a national reputation as a trumpet player, took two years to get to the top. Cugat spent nine years on modest hotel and theatre bookings before he put Latin-American music into the big time. Kyser, Shaw, Kaye, Tommy Dorsey and the others at the top all did their stint in the hinterlands before they came up with a record that earned them top billing at a movie palace.

ONCE at the top the leaders, all of whom are virtuosi at their instruments, must maintain their instrumental superiority while directing a dozen or so overworked, temperamental musicians, looking after the business end of organizations that have weekly payrolls of $5,000 and wrestling with manpower and transportation problems that grow increasingly worse as each day passes.

The theatre bookings which opened the door to the million-dollar band continues to be an orchestra leader's greatest source of income, but at the same time they are the most troublesome. Since the twenty-four-hour, three-shift day became the norm in war-busy America, theatres have been scheduling as many as eight shows a day, starting at 8 A. M. and running through until 2 the next morning. The orchestra men can't stray far from the theatre, since their appearances are spaced only two hours apart, and most of them use the between-show hours to catch up on the sleep they didn't get on the day coaches en route.

Radio engagements are exacting, too. They require intensive rehearsals, two before each broadcast, and the rehearsals often last as long as three or four hours at a stretch before the leader is satisfied that his band is getting the most out of an arrangement. In routine rehearsals such perfection isn't demanded, since the leader can improve the interpretation in later public playings, but over the air the leader's reputation rests on a single rendition. Making films is the band's easiest chore, but unfortunately from the musicians' point of view motion pictures don't pay enough in the few weeks that it takes to make them to keep the leader and his boys in the manner to which they are accustomed for the remainder of the year.

GROUSE as they may at the rigors of their life, the depredations of the draft and the inconveniences of travel, both top leaders and musicians are hoping they can go on living that way for some time to come. The musicians are earning anywhere from $150 to $500 a week and the yearly income of the leaders runs into six figures. Even with the draft and day coaches, the piper is getting well paid for his tunes and he wants to keep it that way—at least until the peace brings a new generation of swing fans with perhaps a flair for North African or Indonesian melodies.

June 20, 1943

Hello, Everybody: Lopez, 70, Speaking

'The Piano Kid' Plays On at Taft Hotel

By JOHN S. WILSON

On Nov. 27, 1921, Vincent Lopez got his bandsmen together at the Pennsylvania Hotel, where they played every night in the Grill, and herded them with their instruments to the Hudson Tube station one block away. They boarded a train, rode to the end of the line in Newark where they were driven to a factory of the Westinghouse Company. There they hauled their instruments up a narrow, rickety stairway to reach an old cloakroom which served as the studio of radio station WJZ.

In this unlikely hideaway, the Lopez band played for what proved to be a history-making hour and a half—it was the first live broadcast ever made by a popular dance orchestra.

The 43d Anniversary

A few weeks later, the Lopez band took part in another precedent-setting event. It broadcast directly from the Pennsylvania Grill the first of the remote dance band broadcasts that were to dominate the late night air waves all through the

Editta Sherman

Vincent Lopez

1930's and into the 1940's until disk jockeys and, later, talkers replaced them.

Tonight on the 43d anniversary of his first pioneering live broadcast, Mr. Lopez will step up to a microphone in the Grill Room of the Taft Hotel, where the Lopez band has been playing for the last 24 years, and, using the same greeting that he first spoke on the air in 1921 "Hello, everybody: Lopez speaking" he will start one of the three network remotes the band broadcasts every week. The man who

He Led the First Radio Show for Band in '21

started it all is now one of the very few band-leaders who can still be heard regularly on remotes and the Taft Grill is one of the equally few hotel rooms where the atmosphere of the great days of the name bands is still carried on.

The Grill is a large, low-ceiling room that seats more than 600. The dance floor is spacious but Mr. Lopez's band, which plays every night from 6 to 9:30 and on Saturday from 12:30 to 2:30, keeps it filled. The dancers are a bit older than those who once stepped out in the Cafe Rouge of the Pennsylvania, the Blue Room of the Lincoln or the Astor Roof but neither their skill nor their pleasure seems to have diminished.

Mr. Lopez, who was known as the Piano Kid when he first became a bandleader in 1916 at the Pekin Restaurant at Broadway and 47th Street, appears as little changed by the passing years as the atmosphere he conjures up in the Taft Grill. His black hair, once slicked straight back, is now trimmed to a close-cropped crewcut. Standing in front of his band as it mixes tunes that go back to his days as a great society favorite at the Casa Lopez and the St. Regis with such current hits as "Do Wah Diddy Diddy," he is a trim and genial blend of maestro and host.

Mr. Lopez was born in Brooklyn 70 years ago. His father, a music teacher, kept him practicing the piano three hours a day during the school year. By the time he reached his teens and his father wanted him to enter the priesthood, Mr. Lopez had decided that his natural affinity was for the piano. Even when his parents enrolled him in business school, Mr. Lopez still pounded the keyboard; a rival pianist at Clayton's, a Brooklyn saloon, was Jimmy Durante.

Watches the Stars

Mr. Lopez's interests are strongly rooted in the present and, even more, in the future. Since 1941 he has been an ardent student of numerology.

He has deduced that the years between 1963 and 1971 will be a great period for American music and that out of it may come what he would consider the first completely American music.

"It's already beginning," the bandleader asserted. "The accentuated rhythm of rock 'n' roll is the foundation. Now we're getting all kinds of crazy beats. It's still floundering but it will unfold. We'll begin to see this new music in 1966. I don't know what it will actually be like. I have the intuitive power to sense what is happening but I can't tell what the format will be."

November 27, 1964

Miller's Magic Still Remains

Glenn Miller: "The prime favorite of courting couples in those innocent years just before World War II"

By JOHN LISSNER

"Maj. Glenn Miller, director of the United States Air Force Band, is missing on a flight from England to Paris, it was announced today. No trace of the plane has been found."

The New York Times
Dec. 25, 1944

I WAS one of millions of Miller - mesmerized kids, home from school for the holidays, who must have stared bleakly at that Christmas morning news. It was Christmas Day, 1944, and it was not yet peace on earth to men of good will. A few weeks earlier, the British, Canadians and G's had taken Aachen from the Germans, and had made several breakthroughs on the Rhine. But on December 15, Von Luettwitz's Second Panzer Division, in a swift and savage counterattack, caught the Allies by surprise, and in seven days had driven the Americans back to Bastogne.

It was also on December 15 that Major Alton Glenn Miller, full of great plans for a six-week European tour for his splendid AAF orchestra, set off for Paris to make some advance preparations. He flew in what appears to have been an uncharted plane, all AAF transport planes having been grounded because of the foul weather. It has been reported that the pilot had not received clearance for the flight. Thus there was the Major, the pilot, and another AAF officer in their small plane, trying to make it across the Channel in pea soup weather, spotted only by radar, fair game for friend as well as foe. Neither the plane, nor any of its three occupants were ever heard from again.

Three days later, at the height of the Battle of the Bulge, the Glenn Miller band arrived in France. So hard-pressed were the Allies that the Miller musicians were fully prepared to trade instruments for guns, but that proved unnecessary as the Americans soon rolled the Germans back. Now ready to bring the sounds of home to those battle-weary troops, the Miller band soon discovered that, without its missing leader, the going got tougher. Authority was now split three ways. Miller's close friend and business associate, Don Haynes, assumed administrative duties, arranger Jerry Gray conducted the large orchestra, and drummer Ray McKinley led the dance band unit. Though they performed heroically, staying on through July, 1945, entertaining an estimated 600,000 GI's, without Glenn it was never quite the same.

*

Yet hopes were high when the war ended. The men were reassembled in civvies by Haynes, acting for Glenn's widow, Mrs. Helen Miller. Haynes became business manager of the orchestra while the star saxophonist of the pre-war orchestra, Tex Beneke, was named leader. "The Glenn Miller Band With Tex Beneke," organized in 1946, did well enough in its first year. But the affable, easy-going Beneke, a very talented musician, lacked Miller's leadership qualities. He was also at loggerheads with Haynes, who wanted to play it safe. Haynes wanted the Miller band to play just the way it had always been playing. Beneke felt that a new world required new sounds, and had Miller been here, he would certainly have tried new things. By 1947, with the band business turning sour, the Beneke-Miller band started to disintegrate. What was needed was an authoritative, forceful leader who was also a skilled musician and creative innovator—and that man was gone, lost over the Channel.

*

George Simon, in his "The Big Bands," calls Glenn Miller the "compleat leader." And he was just that. He was a man of artistic creativity, great imagination, and a first rate administrator and strict disciplinarian. Back in 1937, Miller had taken a bunch of green 17, 18, 19, and 20-year-old kid musicians like Beneke and Hal McIntyre, and whipped them into such perfect shape that by the spring of 1939 he had a superb dance unit, one that had the spit and polish of the best of the swing bands, and was soon to command a greater audience than any of them.

Of all those glorious, glamorous name bands, none ever held the public in its grip the way Glenn Miller's did. During its brief period of dominance, the Miller aggregation outstripped them all in popularity — even Benny Goodman's. It was a remarkable achievement, for Glenn Miller's band appealed not only to the jitterbugs but, in some degree, to all tastes.

The reason for this unprecedented mass support and contagious appeal was the neat balance of instrumental and vocal effects. The jazz solos were brief and tasty; the section work razor-sharp, and the ensembles impeccably rehearsed. A Down Beat reporter once quoted a Miller sideman as saying, "We not only rehearse arrangements, we rehearse every bar a thousand times until he's satisfied."

Miller expected the same kind of perfection and discipline from his singers, and brooked no lapses. (He sacked the popular Ray Eberle one night because of the singer's lateness for a rehearsal.) Indeed, it was through Eberle, and his other vocalists — Kay Starr, Marion Hutton, Dorothy Claire, Paula Kelly, and the Modernaires that Glenn Miller reached the public that his highly successful instrumentals had not quite won over.

*

The Miller band has something to offer everyone. It was an organization of many moods, great contrasts, and great excitement. A new RCA release. **Glen Miller, A Memorial 1944-1969** (VPM 6019) reflects those contrasts and that excitement. Though this "new" collection reassembles 30 of Miller's most familiar and already-available classics, it's good to hear them in natural monaural high fidelity. RCA has not souped up the original sound with "electrically reprocessed stereo." Even if you have the 78's (they're probably beat and scratchy as hell by now), or earlier long-playing reissues of "In The Mood," "Little Brown Jug," "String of Pearls," etc., the superior sonics of this memorial album recommend it.

Considering the age of the original Bluebird and Victor recordings, RCA's engineers have done a remarkable job. Along with the bright sonics, there are the Miller band's cohesive drive and spirit. Rhythm numbers like "Chattanooga Choo Choo," American Patrol," "Anvil Chorus," "Pennsylvania Six-Five Thousand," "Elmer's Tune," and "Juke Box Saturday Night" have a jaunty joy and incredible esprit de corps. Smooth ballads like "Moonlight Serenade," "Stardust," "Skylark," "Perfidia,' "At Last," "Danny Boy," "My Prayer," "Sunrise Serenade," "Serenade in Blue," and "That Old Black Magic" come through with amazing clarity and brilliance.

Unquestionably, the Miller band was the master of the romantic song, the prime favorite of courting couples in those innocent years just before World War II. There was never a band anywhere that had such a romantic effect on its listeners. Playing those old records, one who has listened or danced to that band can still feel the potency of its music, lingering across the rush of the years. Whether you were at the Meadowbrook Ballroom, the Glen Island Casino, or the Cafe Rouge of the Pennsylvania Hotel, dancing with some dreamy-eyed girl, or whether you were like myself a 14-year-old kid, listening late at night to one of the band's radio remotes, or waiting to hear Art Ford spin the latest Miller release on the "Milkman's Matinee," you may be stabbed with the memory of an old refrain or stirred to tap your toes to some catchy riff.

But Glenn Miller's music is much more than nostalgia. Its memory and magic remains because it is great music. The Miller sounds are still fresh, still inviting. Put on Glenn's "Serenade in Blue" and listen to Bobby Hackett's soft, sweet cornet soaring over the rich, full-bodied ensemble . . . ah, play it again, Glenn.

January 11, 1970

SIGHTLESS MUSICIAN SOUNDS OFF IN COURT

The beat-beat-beat of drums and the howl of a timberwolf shattered the otherwise sober atmosphere of the Supreme Court yesterday as a blind man offered a musical backdrop to his $100,000 damage suit charging misuse of his art.

Thomas Louis Hardin, 38 years old, a sightless street musician and peddler, who told the court he uses the name of "Moon Dog" for professional reasons, has brought a suit against Allan Freed, a disk jockey. "Moon Dog" says that Mr. Freed, on his radio broadcasts, has been calling himself the "King of the Moon Doggers" and has been playing "Snake Time" music and other tunes allegedly composed by Mr. Hardin without the complainant's permission.

Justice Carroll G. Walter listened to the complaint of "Moon Dog," who appeared in court in a wrap that resembled a monk's habit, then reluctantly agreed to listen further to "Moon Dog Symphony" and "Howl of the Timberwolf," compositions that the blind man said he had written.

As the musical mélange of jungle sounds, plus harmonies that sounded like melodies from a Chinese mambo and clattering chopsticks, poured from a portable phonograph and echoed through the chambers, Justice Walter buried his face behind a handkerchief. He called for an intermission and then scheduled another court session for 10 A. M. today.

November 24, 1954

U. S. Film Causes Rioting

LONDON, Sept. 4 (UP)—Theatre managers called for police protection today to keep teenage audiences from rioting during showings of an American "rock 'n' roll" movie. Seven zoot-suited "Teddy boys" were fined for rioting in one theatre during a performance of the film "Rock Around the Clock." They said the music "sent them up the wall."

September 5, 1956

ELVIS PRESLEY

Lack of Responsibility Is Shown by TV In Exploiting Teen-Agers

By JACK GOULD

TELEVISION broadcasters cannot be asked to solve life's problems. But they can be expected to display adult leadership and responsibility in areas where they do have some significant influence. This they have hardly done in the case of Elvis Presley, entertainer and phenomenon.

Last Sunday on the Ed Sullivan show Mr. Presley made another of his appearances and attracted a record audience. In some ways it was perhaps the most unpleasant of his recent three performances.

Mr. Presley initially disturbed adult viewers—and instantly became a martyr in the eyes of his teen-age following—for his strip-tease behavior on last spring's Milton Berle program. Then with Steve Allen he was much more sedate. On the Sullivan program he injected movements of the tongue and indulged in wordless singing that were singularly distasteful.

At least some parents are puzzled or confused by Presley's almost hypnotic power; others are concerned; perhaps most are a shade disgusted and content to permit the Presley fad to play itself out.

Neither criticism of Presley nor of the teen-agers who admire him is particularly to the point. Presley has fallen into a fortune with a routine that in one form or another has always existed on the fringe of show business; in his gyrating figure and suggestive gestures the teen-agers have found something that for the moment seems exciting or important.

Void

Quite possibly Presley just happened to move in where society has failed the teen-ager. Certainly, modern youngsters have been subjected to a great deal of censure and perhaps too little understanding. Greater in their numbers than ever before, they may have found in Presley a rallying point, a nationally prominent figure who seems to be on their side. And, just as surely, there are limitless teen-agers who cannot put up with the boy, either vocally or calisthenically.

Family counselors have wisely noted that ours is still a culture in a stage of frantic and tense transition. With even 16-year-olds capable of commanding $20 or $30 a week in their spare time, with access to automobiles at an early age, with communications media of all kinds exposing them to new thoughts very early in life, theirs indeed is a high degree of independence. Inevitably it has been accompanied by a lessening of parental control.

Small wonder, therefore, that the teen-ager is susceptible to overstimulation from the outside. He is at the age when an awareness of sex is both thoroughly natural and normal, when latent rebellion is to be expected. But what is new and a little discouraging is the willingness and indeed eagerness of reputable business men to exploit those critical factors beyond all reasonable grounds.

Television surely is not the only culprit. Exposé magazines, which once were more or less bootleg items, are now carried openly on the best newsstands. The music-publishing business—as Variety most courageously has pointed out—has all but disgraced itself with some of the "rock 'n' roll" songs it has issued. Some of the finest recording companies have been willing to go right along with the trend, too.

Distinctive

Of all these businesses, however, television is in a unique position. First and foremost, it has access directly to the home and its wares are free. Second, the broadcasters are not only addressing themselves to the teen-agers but, much more importantly, also to the lower age groups. When Presley executes his bumps and grinds, it must be remembered by the Columbia Broadcasting System that even the 12-year-old's curiosity may be overstimulated. It is on this score that the adult viewer has every right to expect sympathetic understanding and cooperation from a broadcaster.

A perennial weakness in the executive echelons of the networks is their opportunistic rationalization of television's function. The industry lives fundamentally by the code of giving the public what it wants. This is not the place to argue the artistic foolishness of such a standard; in the case of situation comedies and other escapist diversions it is relatively unimportant.

But when this code is applied to teen-agers just becoming conscious of life's processes, not only is it manifestly without validity but it also is perilous. Catering to the interests of the younger generation is one of television's main jobs; because those interests do not always coincide with parental tastes should not deter the broadcasters. But selfish exploitation and commercialized overstimulation of youth's physical impulses is certainly a gross national disservice.

Sensible

The issue is not one of censorship, which solves nothing; it is one of common sense. It is no impingement on the medium's artistic freedom to ask the broadcaster merely to exercise good sense and display responsibility. It is no blue-nosed suppression of the proper way of depicting life in the theatre to expect stage manners somewhat above the level of the carnival sideshow.

In the long run, perhaps Presley will do everyone a favor by pointing up the need for earlier sex education so that neither his successors nor TV can capitalize on the idea that his type of routine is somehow highly tempting yet forbidden fruit. But that takes time, and meanwhile the broadcasters at least can employ a measure of mature and helpful thoughtfulness in not contributing further to the exploitation of the teen-ager.

With congested schools, early dating, the appeals of the car, military service, acceptance by the right crowd, sex and the normal parental pressures, the teen-ager has all the problems he needs.

Mercenary

To resort to the world's oldest theatrical come-on just to make a fast buck from such a sensitive individual is cheap and tawdry stuff. At least Presley is honest in what he is doing. That the teen-ager sometimes finds it difficult to feel respect for the moralizing older generation may of itself be an encouraging sign of his intelligence. If the profiteering hypocrite is above reproach and Presley isn't, today's youngsters might well ask what God do adults worship.

September 16, 1956

FAD ALSO ROCKS CASH REGISTERS

Sales Jump in Many Fields —Records, Clothing, Films and TV Feel Impact

By ALEXANDER R. HAMMER

The rock 'n' roll fad is increasing sales for many segments of American business.

Such diverse fields as phonograph records, clothing, motion pictures, emblem-making, television commercials and dance studios are increasing their volume as a result of the craze.

Rock 'n' roll has made its biggest impact on the music industry. Many record companies are operating on a three-shift basis to fill orders for this type of record. R. C. A.-Victor last year sold 13,500,000 records and 2,750,000 albums of rock 'n' roll's No. 1 singer, Elvis Presley.

Retailers of soft goods last year sold more than $20,000,000 worth of Presley products. Such items as pre-teen and teen-sized jackets, skirts, T-shirts, jeans, hats, nylon scarves, charm bracelets, sneakers and nylon stretch bobby sox, all bearing the Presley insignia, are big sellers in the nation's stores.

Chain, drug and novelty stores now feature lipsticks in autographed cases bearing color names for such Presley hit tunes as Hound Dog orange, Love You fuchsia, and Heartbreak pink.

70,000 Dungarees

One large manufacturer of dungarees has sold more than 70,000-odd pairs of black twill jeans with emerald green stitching for the nation's youths.

Rock 'n' roll motion pictures also have been doing well at the cashier's booth. Columbia Pictures Corporation rang up profits of $3,000,000 on the film, "Rock Around the Clock," which cost only $350,000 to make.

Alan Freed, whose rock 'n' roll stage show opened at the Paramount Theatre in Times Square yesterday, broke the house record set by the Brooklyn Paramount Theatre with the show he put on there last Easter week. The gross for ten days was $204,000. Mr. Freed has appeared at the Brooklyn Paramount five times, including an eight-day stretch last Christmas, when the theatre grossed about $180,000.

Like most devotees of fads, the rock 'n' roll cult is emblem conscious. John Atkinson, director of sales of Lion Bros. Company, Inc., of Baltimore, a large maker of emblems, said that his company was turning out 47,000 emblems a month for teen-age rock 'n' roll clubs.

Alan Freed, star of show

The premium and box-top people, who ordinarily capitalize on every craze from Davy Crockett to space men, have been slow to take up the fad. Gordon C. Bowen, president of the Premium Advertising Association of America, explains that "since parents by and large disapprove of rock 'n' roll, many advertisers are reluctant to appeal to young people with premiums which may antagonize the parents."

On the other hand, major advertisers like Coca-Cola and Schaefer beer have used rock 'n' roll music for singing commercials with good results, and a growing number of radio and television commercials are rocking now.

One advertiser that has it both way is the Ralston Purina Company of St. Louis, maker of cereals and mixed animal and poultry feeds. A recent commercial on its television program had the announcer satirize rock 'n' roll, singing:

Who-ho-ho-ho
Rock that rock
And roll that roll
Get that Ralston in the bowl.

The popularity of rock 'n' roll also has affected the earnings of dance studios. Arthur Murray, president of the Arthur Murray Schools of Dancing, said yesterday that the craze had led to an influx of teen-age pupils that had raised total registrations 10 per cent. He said the trend had started last summer but had hit its stride in the late fall.

Some rug manufacturers have benefited from the fad. Edward Fields, president of E. Fields, Inc., rug maker, observed that rock 'n' roll had brought about a good increase in area (small) rug sales. He attributed this increase to the fact that parents of the gyrating youngsters preferred to buy this type of rug because it was easy to remove for dancing.

February 23, 1957

Why They Rock 'n' Roll —And Should They?

By GERTRUDE SAMUELS

Come on over, baby,
Whole lotta shakin' goin' on,
Come on over, baby,
An' baby you can't go wrong.
Ain't nobody fakin',
*Whole lotta shakin' goin' on.**

"ROCKING" the song as though in a life and death struggle with an invisible antagonist was a tall, thin, flaccid youth who pulled his stringy, blond hair over his eyes and down to his chin. He shook his torso about as the beat of the band seemingly goaded him on. Screams from thousands of young throats billowed toward him. In the pandemonium, youngsters flailed the air with their arms, jumped from their seats, beckoned madly, lovingly, to the tortured figure onstage.

The song could scarcely be heard over the footlights. No matter. The kids knew the words. They shrilled them with the singer—and kept up their approving, uninhibited screams. The singer finished off at the piano. The applause and yells all but raised the roof. Then a Negro quartet raced onstage, adjusted the microphones, and a new tune brought on a new cascade of screams and energetic handwaves.

This was the teen-age bedlam at the Paramount Theatre in New York where in recent days Alan Freed emceed a rock 'n' roll show. Now the spectacle is moving on to the national scene, to Philadelphia, Washington, Cleveland, Chicago, Detroit, Los Angeles.

What is this thing called rock 'n' roll? What is it that makes teen-agers —mostly children between the ages of 12 and 16—throw off their inhibitions as though at a revivalist meeting? What—who—is responsible for these sorties? And is this generation of teen-agers going to hell?

For some understanding of the rock 'n' roll behavior which has aroused a great deal of controversy, at least in adult circles, one must go to the sources.

* * *

AN important source, of course, is the music itself. Technically, rock 'n' roll derives from the blues. But rock 'n' roll is an extension of what was known as Rhythm and Blues, a music of the Thirties and Forties that aimed primarily at the Negro market; that music emphasized the second and fourth beats of each measure. Rock 'n' roll exploits this same heavy beat—by

*©1956 by Marlyn-Copar, New York

GERTRUDE SAMUELS, a staff writer for The Times Magazine and a parent, has long studied trends in music and adolescent behavior. She took the pictures with this article.

making it heavier, lustier and transforming it into what has become known as The Big Beat. It is a tense, monotonous beat that often gives rock 'n' roll music a jungle-like persistence.

In his Encyclopedia Yearbook of Jazz, Leonard Feather comments that "rock 'n' roll bears the same relationship to jazz as wrestling bears to boxing." Freed claims to have invented the term "rock 'n' roll" back in 1951 for a radio show in Cleveland because "of the rocking beat of the music."

Of the top sixty best-selling records in 1957, forty were rock 'n' roll tunes, the biggest seller being Elvis Presley's "All Shook Up" which sold 2,450,000 across the country.

Another rich field for research is found among the children themselves. They come from all economic classes and neighborhoods, sometimes lone-wolfing it, but mostly with their pals, dates, clubs and gangs. Outside the theatre they seem to become one class —rocking the neighborhood with wild and emotional behavior as they break through the wooden police barriers to improve their positions in line or fight toward the box office and their heroes inside.

Like young teen-agers generally, they tend to keep the sexes segregated; girls are mostly with girls; boys with boys. Their clothes and manners bespeak a kind of conformism: so many of the girls wear a sort of uniform—tight, revealing sweaters with colorful kerchiefs, skin-tight toreador pants, white woolen socks and loafers; so many of the boys conform to a pattern —leather or sports jackets, blue jeans, loafers and cigarettes.

Physically, it would seem as though the children feared to look different from one another, or lacked confidence in individuality. Indeed, many admit to this cheerfully: "All the kids have this jacket," said one boy, "and I don't want to be different."

Inside the theatre, the emotional conformism is even more obvious. A scream of approval or delight starts—mostly a girl's scream—and everyone starts screaming. An arm shoots up fifth row center, and instantly all arms appear to be flung up and bodies leap

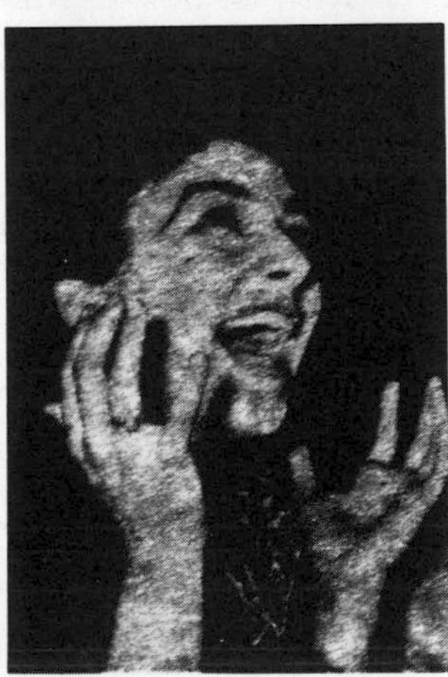

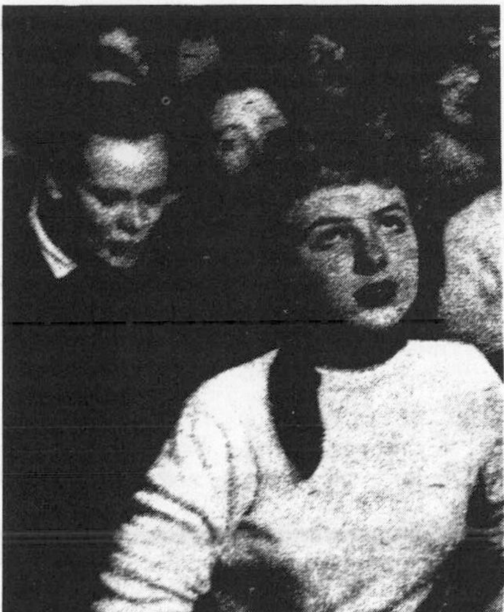

GOAL ATTAINED—After a long wait, these boys and girls have found seats to hear

up or start swaying crazily. Anyone can touch off the stampede of screaming youngsters who always rush the stage after a show is over. Sometimes, they fling themselves onstage, as did one member of a Brownsville gang who jumped on, zip gun and all, "as though he was Superman," and was firmly ejected.

How do the teen-agers feel about rock 'n' roll?

A black-haired, starry-eyed beauty of 15, emerging from the theatre looks as though she had returned from outer space.

"It's just instinct, that's all," murmured Roseann Chasen of Norfolk, Va., visiting in New York. "I come to hear it because I can sing and scream here. Because it's not like at home where your parents are watching TV and you can't. Here you can scream all you like. And the stars wave to you, and don't act like they don't care whether you're there or not."

Roseann had about fifteen favorite tunes, "but the best are 'Teardrops,' 'At The Hop,' and 'Great Balls of Fire.'"

"He was rocking the house with that 'Great Balls of Fire,'" she said, "did you hear it, when the kids went crazy? It was just instinct with him, that's all," she added dreamily as she went off to join her girl friends. She didn't sound as though she could raise her voice to a scream.

KENNY PUNCERELLI, 16-year-old from Englewood, and his two pals, Bob Brennan of Tenafly and Wayne Whalen of Hillsdale, N. J., tried to find words to describe their favorite, Jo-Ann Campbell, the diminutive singer in a shimmering green dress whom no one could have heard over the footlights because of the screams.

"Just say she's the greatest. It's the beat. It's different from any other beat," Kenny said, talking almost with a beat. "It's the rhythm. It's easy to listen to."

"It's the beat," the others confirmed knowingly.

Three 15-year-old girls from Queens, one with braces on her teeth, another in pin curls, the third smoking ("gee, I wouldn't want my mother to know I was smoking,") had saved their money for the show. Every day they listen to the rock 'n' roll show over Channel 7 "because it's music we can understand."

"And here we can look at the actors and wave to them," one caroled. "They're cute, they're young, and we don't have to do the housework."

The Lords, who called themselves a "sports gang" from Flower Park and Melrose in the Bronx, had been waiting for hours in the queue, lost their place when they went to buy lunches, and failed to persuade a policeman that they deserved their old position in line

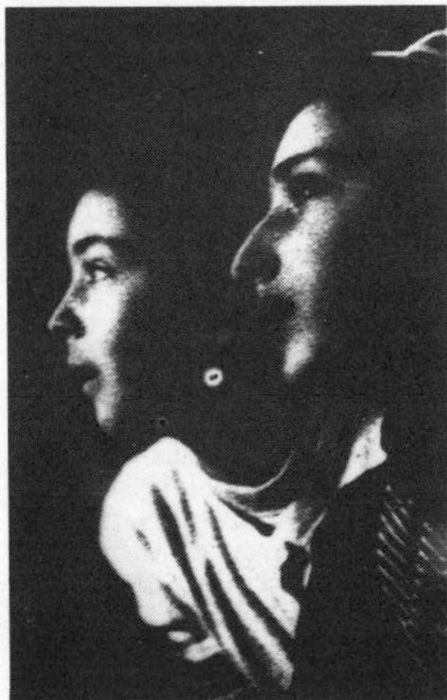

RAPT—At a rock 'n' roll show.

when they returned. The red-jacketed 15- and 16-year-olds moved to the back to start waiting anew. Why?

"Because it's great music." * * * "It makes you feel good." * * * "We like to go crazy." * * * "It hops us up. It's different from the records when you can see them and be with them." Some of the boys play instruments. Two were planning college careers (one to be an engineer, another a veterinarian).

VIVIAN STOKER, 16, and Jerilyn O'Neill, 16, juniors at the Villa Maria Academy in the Bronx, had sat through three shows with Vivian's mother. Both girls "like classical music, too" and have Beethoven, Mozart and Chopin records as well as rock 'n' roll.

"The main thing about this music," said brown-haired Vivian, "is that it's lively—it's not dead. It makes you want to dance. With a waltz you have to be in a good

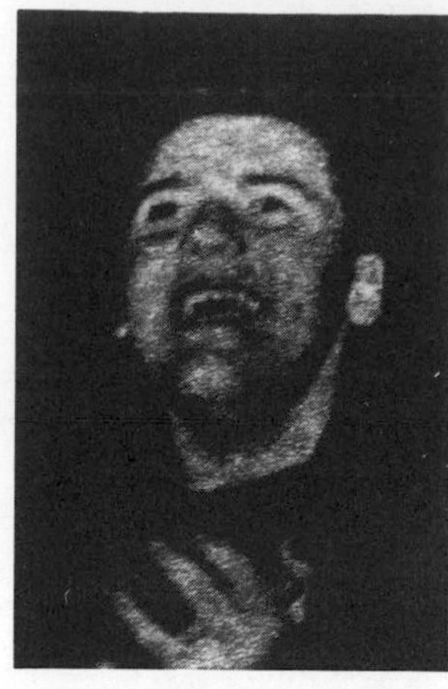

mood to dance to it. But with rock 'n' roll, no matter what your mood is, it gets you."

Did they think the effect of the music, the lyrics, the physical contortions of the actors, was making delinquents?

"SOME of the kids say that Presley affects them," Jerilyn put in. "My girl friend says he sends chills up her spine. But I think the majority of the girls just like the beat. It's new."

And Mrs. Stoker added: "I like it. The girls have their record collections and keep their minds occupied. They just enjoy it all."

Eddie Cook, 14, and Frankie Mielke, 13, of Queens, attend the same parochial school. Eddie wore a religious medal on a chain around his neck. Said Eddie: "I don't like this symphony stuff that my father puts on the radio. My mother doesn't mind rock 'n' roll though."

Frankie said: "In my house, they don't mind it as long as they're not around." And Eddie adds reflectively: "If there wasn't this music, we might be getting into trouble — you know, there'd be nothing to do at night."

* * *

IN show business circles there has been bitter controversy about the worth and effects of rock 'n' roll.

Frank Sinatra, a veteran showman, was quoted in a Paris magazine recently as follows: "Rock 'n' roll smells phony and false. It is sung, played and written for the most part by cretinous goons and by means of its almost imbecilic reiteration, and sly, lewd, in plain fact, dirty lyrics * * * it manages to be the martial music of every sideburned delinquent on the face of the earth."

Between shows at the Paramount the other day, Alan Freed replied to Sinatra and other critics.

"I was shocked when I read what Frank said. He has no business knocking show business. It's been good to him. As for charging that this music is 'dirty' and making delinquents of children, I think I'm helping to combat juvenile delinquency. If my kids are home at night listening to my radio program, and get interested enough to go out and buy records and have a collection to listen to and dance to, I think I'm fighting delinquency.

"This music," he went on, "comes from the levees and the plantations. It's simple to dance to, and to clap your hands to, and the kids know the words to every song. That's why they come. This is an audience-participation kind of music. They come in and pay to sing louder than the performers.

"And it's natural that kids should look for excitement and thrills. Well, I'd rather that they find it in the theatre than in street gangs. I say that if kids have any interest in any kind of music, thank God for it. Because if they have the interest, they can find themselves in it. And as they grow up, they broaden out and come to enjoy all kinds of music."

* * *

WHAT does it all prove? One on-the-scene observer, Robert Shapiro, manager of the Paramount Theatre, pointed out that back in the Thirties Bing Crosby, Benny Goodman and Glen Miller were idolized by the young jazz fans. With the advent of Frank Sinatra, Shapiro recalled, teen-agers "swooned, moved and screamed with his every gesture—and now the daughters of those teen-agers are here."

"The young people of all generations," Shapiro said, "are only looking for a chance to express their enthusiasm."

A. D. Buchmueller, a psychiatric social worker and the executive director of the Child Study Association, a national organization working in the field of child development and parent education, said:

"Kids, just like adults, get caught up in a mass kind of hysteria, which is contagious. Some get hurt by it, physically and emotionally.

"But it is not helpful, and may even be harmful, for adults to take a strong and condemning attitude and action toward adolescents in their rock 'n' roll behavior. This behavior is part of their individual as well as collective or group rebellion against the strictness of adult society.

"This doesn't mean that I approve of rock 'n' roll. I don't. I think there are many other kinds of music, more beautiful and culturally more valuable, that they might be hearing. And also the suggestiveness of a sexual nature in crude and open exhibitionism, used by some singers, is to be deplored.

"THE charge that rock 'n' roll may be an outlet for impulsive behavior or sexual aggression by the youngsters may be true. But this has not been proven by any thorough studies. The charges are mostly hunches that people have been having. The rock 'n' roll behavior seems faddish, as was the behavior for other generations that liked the Charleston, the black bottom, jitterbugging. I don't think it does a bit of good to outlaw it. It will pass, just as the other vogues did."

Finally, Judge Hilda Schwartz, who regularly presides in Adolescents' Court and has made many studies of youth problems, had this to say:

"Rock 'n' roll does not produce juvenile delinquents. The causes of delinquency and youth crime are far more complex and varied. But for the disturbed, hostile and insecure

youth, the stimulation of the frenzied, abandoned music certainly can't be considered a therapy.

"However, only a tiny proportion of youngsters lining

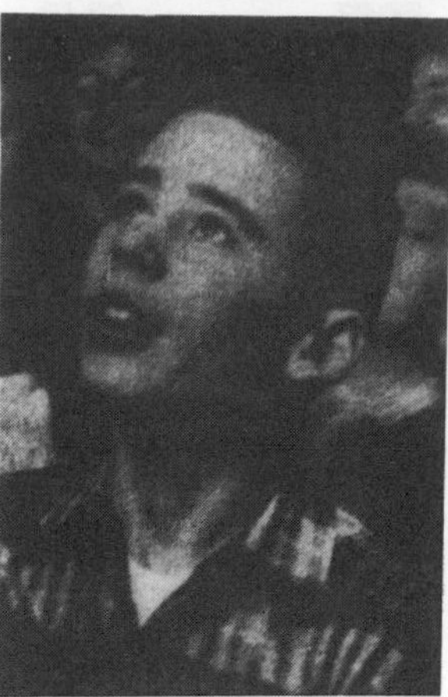

up around the theatre are hostile and insecure. The vast majority are wholesome boys and girls following an adolescent fad as only adolescents can.

"But what a pity that this tremendous hero worship, this yearning for something and someone to look up to, this outpouring of energy and love should have been concentrated on a fad that can only be a passing interest. It is our fault. We haven't stirred the children with something to live by, to worship, to put their hopes in. They haven't the inspiration because we ourselves haven't put a high value on courage and liberty and working for others. Perhaps we have taken the glamour out of the good life — and, because they're young, they're looking for excitement and outlets."

* * *

ENTHUSIASM, hysteria, misguided hero worship? On one thing all experts agree: rock 'n' roll will surely be with us for a while longer. For apprehensive adults who think nothing as alarming as The Big Beat has ever existed, there may be comfort in a college joke of some years back. An Englishman, watching some contorting American dancers in fascination and disbelief, turned to his friend, murmuring, "I say, old boy, they get married afterwards, don't they?"

And that was in the foxtrot and shimmy days, long before rock 'n' roll appeared, amid commotion, on the scene.

How No-Talent Singers Get 'Talent'

Some of today's 'pop' record stars need little or no singing ability to be successful. They are the creation of the recording engineer's ingenuity.

By JOHN S. WILSON

LAST fall a recording company executive was sitting in front of his television set watching a private eye series called "77 Sunset Strip" when he was struck with a sudden loathing for one of the characters—a young, jive-talking parking lot attendant named Kookie who looked like a teen-ager's idea of a rock 'n' roll singer.

"I was offended that there should be someone who looked like that and talked like that," George Avakian, who produces pop disks for Warner Brothers Records, recalled recently. "But in the same instant I was struck by an obvious inspiration—he should make rock 'n' roll records. I was sure that kids would like his talk and his looks, especially a way he had of looking out of the corner of his eye. And—the real clincher for his popularity with kids—parents would loathe him."

The fact that there was no evidence that Edward Byrnes, who played Kookie, could sing a single note did not dampen Avakian's enthusiasm in the slightest. He was quite aware that singing ability is one of the least essential qualifications for success as a pop singer today. Recording techniques have become so ingenious that almost anyone can seem to be a singer. A small, flat voice can be souped up by emphasizing the low frequencies and piping the result through an echo chamber. A slight speeding up of the recording tape can bring a brighter, happier sound to a naturally drab singer or clean the weariness out of a tired voice. Wrong notes can be snipped out of the tape and replaced by notes taken from other parts of the tape.

THIS last process—splicing—once enabled comedian Jerry Lewis to sing a completely breathless record called "Busybody." Lewis made several takes of the song, breathing in a different place on each take. In the final editing, all the breathing spaces were cut out, leaving an exhausting listening experience.

The move toward the synthetic singer has been progressing slowly ever since Whispering Jack Smith found that the microphone eliminated the need for real vocal projection early in the Nineteen Twenties. But not until the past few years has the gadgetry of electronics and tape taken a dominant role in the creation of pop recordings. The gadgetry dam really burst after Elvis Presley's recorded voice was so doctored up with echoes that he sounded as though he were going to shake apart. Since then "sounds" have often taken precedence over music.

JOHN S. WILSON listens to pop recordings in line of duty as jazz critic for The Times.

In today's highly competitive bedlam of pop recordings, the bulk of the disks are propped up by some form of gimmick or engineering acrobatics, although it is still possible for "singing" singers—Perry Como, Frank Sinatra, Patti Page, Nat "King" Cole or such more recent arrivals as Pat Boone and Johnny Mathis—to produce consistently successful disks without resorting to non-musical crutches. In fact, it is to the advantage of these singers to avoid trickery because the individual sound of their singing is a potent element in selling their records.

Yet a successful popular singer today may actually be nothing more than the product of a recording engineer's creative ingenuity. Last Christmas' inescapable popular hit recording, "The Chipmunk Song," was ostensibly sung in shrill, piping voices by three English-speaking chipmunks named Simon, Theodore and Alvin. Their voices were all produced by one man, Ross Bagdasarian, who wrote the song. He recorded each voice on separate tapes which were later played at double speed and blended by a process called overdubbing.

If three nonexistent chipmunks could make a hit record, there was no reason for Avakian to hesitate about using a live TV actor who seemed to have teenage appeal. But even Avakian was not prepared for Byrnes' monumental lack of talent as a singer. When the actor reluctantly submitted to an audition, it was found that he not only could not carry a tune (a failing so common among potential pop singers that it is almost taken for granted) but he had no sense of pitch, practically no range and his grasp of rhythm was so uncertain that his accompanist was unable to stay in line with him.

This seemed to be more than even the most skillful recording techniques could rectify. But meanwhile Byrnes' popularity with teen-agers was building week by week and his potential value as a record star was increasing. Some means had to be found to get him on a record.

The solution hit upon was to have a girl do the singing while Byrnes interjected an occasional spoken line. The girl, Connie Stevens, was written into the TV script so there would be an excuse to have her on the record. Tying in even more closely with Byrnes' booming popularity on TV, a song was created for him which stressed the name of the character he played and his compulsive habit of combing his hair—"Kookie, Kookie (Lend Me Your Comb)." By the time the recording was made, Byrnes had been taking singing lessons for several weeks and it was daringly decided to let him sing six bars so that the record would not be dominated by Miss Stevens.

SIX months after Avakian had first flinched at the sight and sound of Kookie, Edward Byrnes' record was released. Three weeks later it had leaped to first place in Variety's weekly compilation of the nation's most popular recordings.

Byrnes' success in a medium for which he would appear to have no talent stems from one of the odder aspects of a very odd business. Although a singer's popularity is measured today by his record sales, the crucial elements in his appeal are visual and non-recordable—his appearance and personality. When non-singing television and movie stars with teenage appeal, such as Byrnes, Tab Hunter and Tony Perkins, attempt to transfer their appeal to disks, their limitations as singers have been no handicap.

Television or movie reputations can simplify the process of creating a recording star but they are not essential. During the past year an unknown teen-ager with no noticeable talent has climbed a remarkable route to popularity.

TWO years ago 14-year-old Fabian Forte was observed sitting on the front steps of his South Philadelphia home by Bob Marcucci, head of a small record company. To Marcucci, he looked a bit like Elvis Presley or Ricky Nelson but with the down-to-earth quality of the boy next door. With nothing more than this visual impression to go on and despite young Forte's insistence that he could not sing, Marcucci began calling regularly at his home to urge him to try. ("Ma, that crazy guy's here again," Fabian called out to the kitchen one night. "He still wants to teach me how to sing.")

Fabian eventually tried out his vocal wings by singing along with a Ricky Nelson record. The demonstration proved that the boy was right—he was no singer. Marcucci sent him to a voice teacher. The teacher sent him back, advising, "Don't waste your money." A second teacher made the same suggestion. When Marcucci took the boy to a third teacher, he beat the teacher to the punch.

"Don't tell me not to waste my money," he said. "Just work on the kid for a few months and try to teach him to sing a little."

The teacher managed to open up Fabian's voice slightly, although he was not able to inculcate any sense of pitch. Nevertheless Marcucci decided that his find was ready to be recorded. His first disk, on which he was billed simply as "Fabian," was an excellent example of what the music trade knows as a "bomb"—a complete failure. But when Fabian made personal appearances to promote his record, teen-agers responded to him excitedly. Appearances on Dick Clark's TV show made him known, visually, to a wider audience.

Drawing by Doug Anderson.

AUTOMATED SINGER—*In the Age of Electronics, a performer's voice may be secondary.*

SINCE February, 1958, Fabian has spent every school holiday (he is still in high school) and every week-end appearing before teen-age audiences. His second record, with his picture emblazoned on the sleeve, sold a respectable quarter of a million copies. His most recent effort, "Turn Me Loose," reached the top ten in the popularity charts. He was seen on the Perry Como show in April, with Ed Sullivan in May, returns to the Sullivan show tonight, and starts his first film for Twentieth Century-Fox in July.

Fabian's singing has improved since he made his first record but it is his physical attraction rather than his voice which has carried him upward so fast. Part of this attraction may lie in the fact that he is the opposite of the stereotyped conception of the rock 'n' roll singer. He does not wiggle. He simply stands up and tries to sing and, in the view of one of his fans, "projects a kind of joy of living." He dresses neatly but informally and he is well-mannered.

"Gee!" exclaimed a startled camera man on the Como show. "He called me 'sir!'"

A CAREFULLY created performer such as Fabian is still a rarity in pop music. More typical are singers or groups, as obviously untalented as Fabian was when Marcucci found him, who flash across the pop music charts with a single meteoric success and then disappear.

"Usually they are a group of kids who hang around a street corner together," a recording supervisor has explained. "They can't really sing but they work up one song and bring it to a record company. If we like it, we try to think which of the people we have under contract could use it. Usually it's not suitable for any of them. The only ones who can do it are these kids, so we record them. But then it's good-by because they can't come up with a follow-up."

Performances by these amateurs give recording engineers an opportunity to call up all the ingenuity and trickery at their command, although almost every pop recording made today, even by well established talent, carries some evidence of the use of echo chambers, tape reverberation, equalizing, speeding, over-dubbing or splicing.

A singer's voice is now piped through an echo chamber—a room with solid walls, a solid ceiling and a high reflecting surface—almost as a matter of course to give it a big, resonant sound. Ten years ago, when echo was a new toy, makeshift echo chambers were used. Two early echo advocates, engineer Bob Fine and recording director Mitch Miller, sent Frankie Laine's "Mule Train" cascading up and down a circular stairwell to give it echo, and they piped Vic Damone's "Ave Maria" through a bathroom.

A variant of the echo chamber, tape reverberation (or "tape reverb") gave Elvis Presley's early records their distinctive, frantic, jangling sound. Unlike an echo chamber, which sustains a sound, "tape reverb" repeats it like a very rapid echo. This is a common device on rock 'n' roll recordings because it is a simple method of covering up a paucity of instruments or poor voices.

IT is even possible for engineers and recording directors completely to rearrange a recording after the performers have left the studio. The sequence of choruses can be shifted, certain instruments or voices can be given more prominent roles, others can be deleted entirely.

Two hit recordings by the Coasters, a vocal group — "Charlie Brown" and "Yakety Yak" — were created in this fashion. Tom Dowd, chief engineer for Atlantic Records, recorded the original performances on eight channels, producing eight different tapes. Then he mixed these tapes in whatever proportions or sequence he desired, first putting down the lead voice and harmony, then adding the bass voice, next running in a guitar, implementing that with a second guitar, then a saxophone —slowly building and shaping the final record as though he were working with colors or clay instead of sounds.

BECAUSE so many pop disks are a product of the recording engineer's skill, it is often impossible for a singer to reproduce his hit recordings in personal appearances. This is one reason why lip synchronization, or "lip synch," is so prevalent on television, particularly on shows which feature pop recording stars. In lip synching, a vocalist mouths the words of a song while his recording is being played. This guarantees that the TV performances will sound exactly like the record.

But lip synching has its dangers. A young singer named Johnny Sardo recently prepared for his appearance on the Alan Freed show by painstakingly rehearsing his lip synchronization with his new record. As he stepped confidently before the cameras, prepared to synch, he froze in horror when he heard the first bars of music: They were playing the other side of his record.

Although the use of non-singers and engineering tricks in an effort to create hit records does not seem to disturb those who produce the records ("Pop music is in such a low state now that it can't be injured by non-musical performers," George Avakian has declared), others are less complacent. Alan Drake, a comedian, recently withdrew from a scheduled appearance on a bill which included Fabian because he felt that he would have nothing to offer the kind of audience that would be attracted by the recording star.

APPEAL—Often the charm of a record star is visual, not musical.

"A GIFTED singer takes literally years of painstaking work to become a polished entertainer," said Drake, "while someone like Fabian comes along with a gimmick in place of true talent and is immediately foisted on the public for purely monetary gain, offering nothing in the way of constructive entertainment in return. I feel it is an insult to the public to pass these wonderless wonders off as artists and I refuse to have any part of Fabian or his ilk."

However, these "wonders" are not "wonderless" to the teen-agers and sub-teen-agers who provide the bulk of the support for pop recordings. As long as teen-age taste is catered to, singers who reflect an immature concept of excitement and glamour are likely to remain in favor. Talent will not be a drawback. But, thanks to echo, tape reverb, over-dubbing and splicing, neither will lack of talent.

June 21, 1959

The Beatles Will Make the Scene Here Again, but the Scene Has Changed

By ROBERT SHELTON

John, Paul, George and Ringo are bringing it all back home.

That means the Beatles are returning to the United States. They will arrive Friday to begin a third concert tour of the country from which they have gleaned much of their musical inspiration and probably half their earnings.

John Lennon, Paul McCartney George Harrison and Ringo Starr will perform Sunday night for their largest live audience, about 55,600 persons, at Shea Stadium in Flushing, Queens.

They will then whirl through 11 concerts by the end of the month in the San Francisco Cow Palace, the Hollywood Bowl, the Astrodome in Houston, the Maple Leaf Gardens in Toronto and at ballfields in Chicago and Minneapolis and stadiums in Atlanta, Portland, Ore., and San Diego, Calif.

In less than two years, the Beatles have inspired an upheaval in pop music, mores, fashion, hair styles and manners. They have helped conquer a growing number of adults with their charm, irreverent wit and musical skill. They have, in this country, provided marching songs for the teen-age revolution.

New Culture Heroes

They have helped raise to the level of culture heroes such figures as Murray (the K) Kaufman, a disk jockey, and Phil Spector, a young record producer. The Beatles have brought rock 'n' roll, which many have tried to dismiss as ephemeral since its start in 1954, to its third and greatest fever pitch of popularity.

It is estimated that more than 100 million single recordings and more than 25 million LP disks of the Beatles have been sold throughout the world. There have also been Beatle fan magazines, wigs and bubble gum.

However, some reports from Europe indicate that all is not box-office triumph for them. There were 150 policemen on call at the Rome Airport last spring, but only four docile Beatle fans turned out. Concerts in Vienna were canceled this week for lack of advance sale. Britain's record-popularity lists have been yielding increasingly since spring to the American invasion, with hits by Elvis Presley, the Byrds, Bob Dylan, Joan Baez and the Everly Brothers.

Certainly, the promoter of the Shea Stadium concert, Sid Bernstein, has had no cause for concern, despite his guarantee to the Beatles of $100,000 for part of one evening's work. Mr. Bernstein reported that 50 per cent of the tickets had been sold before they were printed.

The slight popularity decline for the Beatles has been caused by the strong competition of such groups as the Rolling Stones, the Dave Clark Five, Herman's Hermits, the Animals and Wayne Fontana and the Mindbenders. They and others have done well with recordings and in concerts.

The music of the Beatles is a form of American music that ricocheted to Europe, became infused with the group's personality and has since bounced back here. Mostly, the "Liverpool sound" is a buoyant, urgent, infectiouly rhythmic series of cadences, with some unsettlingly exciting harmonies (in open fourths and fifths), a bedrock blues beat and an aura of youth, channeled sexuality and exuberance. Often there is a wistful, plaintive quality to their slower ballads.

The Beatles were influenced, while working in the Cavern in Liverpool, by contact, directly or through recordings brought by American seamen from the Gulf Coast, with American rhythm and blues, rock 'n' roll or rockabilly interpreters, such as Mr. Presley, Little Richard, the Everlys or Buddy Holly and the Crickets. From this, with a dash of the British folk-jazz called "skiffle," the Beatles style emerged. Mr. Lennon and Mr. McCartney have written about 100 songs for their group.

More is happening in rock 'n' roll than those who do not appreciate it might suspect. Perhaps most encouraging is the emergence of more meaningful lyrics, long a point of attack for hostile critics.

Although not yet reflected in Beatles records, there are more and more "message songs" in rock 'n' roll. A new recording by the British group the Animals is a cameo describing social entrapment and hope for release from the tedium of meaningless work:

In this dirty old part of the city
Where the sun refuse to shine
People tell me it ain't no use in tryin'.
My little girl, you're so young and pretty and one thing I know is true
You're gonna die before your time is due.
See my daddy in bed a-dyin', see his hair turnin' gray,
He's been workin' and slavin' his life away,
I know, he's been workin'—yeah, Everyday
Slavin' his life away. He's been workin', workin', work—work.
We gotta get out of this place
If it's the last thing we ever do.
We gotta get out of this place, girl; there's a better life for me and you . . .

The song is by Barry Mann and Cynthia Weil, a New York husband-and-wife team. They have also composed "Uptown," which finds solace in a tenement life, and "It's Gonna Be Fine," which stresses patience and hope in a problematic situation.

Also part of the trend of meaningful rock 'n' roll lyrics is "The Eve of Destruction" by P.F. Sloan, a 19-year-old West Coast writer. The song was recorded two weeks ago by Barry McGuire, formerly of the New Christy Minstrels:

The Eastern world
It is explodin',
Violence flarin'
And bullets loadin'.
You're old enough to kill
But not for votin'.

Don't you understand
What I'm tryin' to say,
Can't you see the fear
That I'm feelin' today?

Marches alone
Can't bring integration
When human respect is disintegratin'.
This whole crazy world is just too frustratin'

Other songs recorded in recent weeks by Bob Dylan, the Byrds, Sonny and Cher, Jackie De Shannon, the Rolling Stones and Jody Miller examine conformity, the nature of freedom, teen-age clothes, brotherhood, recording executives and the right to wear long hair.

There is no clear-cut name for this trend, although "folk rock" or "folk pop" are frequent. Essentially, the trend is toward a marriage of the vitality and popularity of rock 'n' roll with the folk movement's general concern for saying something about reality and injustice.

Recording the Sound

The British invasion has helped re-invigorate American musical thinking and activity. There are now many categories of rock 'n' roll, from the "Spector sound," to the "Chicago sound" and the "Rebelation sound" of the Lake Charles area in Lousiana. But knowledgeable persons in pop music think the strongest element of American rock 'n' roll now, musically and financially, is the "Detroit sound."

The leading recordings of Detroit pop music are issued by the Motown Record Corporation on Motown, Tamla, Gordy, V.I.P. and Soul labels. Motown is operated by Barry Gordy Jr., whose six-year rise to musical success antedates the Beatles. At the age of 35, Mr. Gordy, a former assembly-line worker, has a roster of nearly 200 Negro performers and is considered by one authority to be the greatest producer of single pop disks in the world.

Essentially, the "English sound" is a white derivation of Negro music, while the "Detroit sound" is Negro pop music and rhythm and blues. It is refined out of the church choirs and ghetto bars where many of its stars, such as the Supremes, Marvin Gaye, the Miracles, Smokey Robinson, the Temptations and Martha and the Vandellas learned their music.

One technical definition of the "Detroit sound" is that it uses a muffled double drumbeat with tambourine and a large brass section. A less technical definition was offered by the Supremes, who are appearing at the Copacabana. The three girls defined the sound as "rats, roaches, guts, struggle and love."

Whatever the school of rock 'n' roll, the groups continue to proliferate, often with outlandish names to attract attention. There are the Guilloteens, Georgie-Porgie and the Cry Babies, the Rotten Kids, the Detergents, Little Caesar and the Consuls, the Turtles, the Leaves and the Bees. Sam the Sham and the Pharaohs wear Bedouin costumes, and the Great Scots wear kilts.

Few spokesmen for pop music would predict what the outlook for rock 'n' roll is. Tastes are fickle, and trends change mercurially. But the British popularity of American rock 'n' roll and folk music has not reached its peak. Although folk purists regard "folk rock" as opportunism now, it can be only to the good that rock 'n' roll lyrics are moving away from banality. In whatever form, rock 'n' roll appears to be with us for a long time.

And promoters here are still scrambling about for a group that could become the American Beatles.

But, as their coming tour will undoubtedly prove, and as Queen Elizabeth II indicated when she named them members of the Most Excellent Order of the British Empire, there are only four Beatles.

August 11, 1965

The Big, Happy, Beating Heart Of the Detroit Sound

By RICHARD R. LINGEMAN

DETROIT.

AT night as I stand on the other side of East Jefferson Street in Detroit, the Ford Auditorium, a long, low, blue-granite-faced building with a vertical latticed metal front, suddenly looks to my wondering eyes like a gigantic hi-fi amplifier. A hallucination, no doubt, caused by my having spent two days at Motown Records, the big happy beating heart of the Detroit sound.

Those who think of "Detroit sound" as referring to the din of the auto assembly line intermingled with the muted wail of manufacturers announcing price increases on their 1967 models may be surprised to learn that in the pop record business the Detroit sound means the kind of music made by Motown Records, a relatively small company which sells more singles than any other company in the country.

What is more, Motown is a Negro-owned business, with mostly Negro performers and composers, whose musical style stems from what is called rhythm-and-blues music—in the past, a trade euphemism for a kind of music performed by Negroes and sold mainly to a Negro market. Due in great degree to the popularity of a Motown singing group called the Supremes, Motown's records have attained national, as opposed to racial, best-sellerdom; and the company has become sort of the compact giant of rock 'n' roll, standing in relation to the real giants as George Romney's Rambler once did to the Big Three.

Why am I going to the Ford Auditorium? Why, damn it, man, I am going to the Soul Show, starring Jackie "Moms" Mabley and also a rhythm-and-blues group called Smokey Robinson and the Miracles, which happens to be the very first of many such groups formed by Motown and has been with the company ever since it was founded in the late fifties by a young Negro auto worker and part-time song writer named Berry Gordy Jr.

A word about "soul," a vogue word among Negroes having had a number of transmogrifications these days. Soul can mean a mild manifesting of race pride and social solidarity —"our thing"—a shared emotional bond of unity and good feeling. In the early sixties there was a "soul music" movement among Negro jazz musicians, most of them conservatory-trained, advocating a return to the roots of Negro music for inspiration, a return to field hand chants, work songs, funky blues and gospel rhythms in what was a rejection of sophistication in favor of strong feeling. Some even felt compelled to eat "soul food"—deep South and ghetto dishes like ham hocks and collard greens, pigs' feet, pigs' knuckles and chitterlings.

A fraternal term, "soul brother," has had recent ominous manifestations, as in the Watts riots when Negro businessmen chalked it on their stores so the antiwhite rioters would pass them by. It also operates as a commercial thing, as when New York's WWRL calls itself "soul brother radio" and gives its predominantly Negro audience a steady diet

RICHARD R. LINGEMAN is executive editor of the magazine Monocle. He is now working on a social history of the domestic front during World War II.

of rhythm-and-blues music, an elemental, emotional kind of popular music with a strong, pounding beat, right down to an R & B version of the Pepsi singing commercial.

Now, in the pop music field, "soul" has entered the vocabulary as a loose description of the kind of music made by invariably Negro performers, many of whom record for Motown—performers such as James Brown, Otis Redding, and the Supremes, who are Motown's star vocal group and probably the leading girls' vocal group in the world, based on their record sales and international appeal.

INSIDE the austerely appointed auditorium, the Soul Show opens with a white Southern comic named Dick Davey, who is a sort of hip Bob Burns telling reverse Dick Gregory jokes slanted at the 90 per cent Negro audience. He tells of doing a show in Harlem ("They was real polite to me in Harlem. Kept calling me 'Mr. Charley' all the time.") and draws applause when he says he asked a colored dancer why she was enjoying herself so much and she replied: "Honey" (infectious laugh), "if you could be colored five minutes you'd never want to be white again."

Next come the Miracles, four catlike young men attired in bright red shirts with flowing sleeves. Robinson does the solo, singing in a near-falsetto voice, and the other three back him while performing intricate, whirling figures of choreography. The choreography is a great crowd pleaser in its own right, bringing frequent cheers, and has something of the unintentional camp quality that those Negro shows at the old Kit Kat in the Village had—as though they had been choreographed by George Raft in the thirties and never changed since. At one point, a buttery Pearl Bailey voice wafts down from the balcony: "When you get done singing, Smoke, you come on up here."

"Moms" Mabley closes the show with some wry jokes about crime in the streets — to borrow Mr. Goldwater's phrase — encountered while walking down "Saint Ann-twine" (St. Antoine) street in Detroit, and tells of the poor beggar who came up to her and said in a pitiful voice: "Moms, Moms, I ain't got any money. I ain't got any friends. I ain't got any warm clothes. I ain't got nuthin' "—her voice shifts into menace—*" 'cept this gun!"* She closes with a pitch for brotherhood to the tune of "Together":

If we do the right thing together
We'll bring peace together
No more black and white
Only wrong and right

—and so on. Such is the current state of soul, baby.

THE offices of Motown (for Motor Town) Records are in a cluster of seven neat, middle-class brick bungalows with porches and green lawns, spaced among a funeral home, doctor's office and private residences on both sides of a wide tree-lined boulevard in a middle-class, integrated residential section of Detroit. On a fine autumn day knots of producers, song writers, performers stand around, shooting the breeze. A group of colored school kids arrives and casually circulates among the groups, collecting autographs from their favorites. Only one of the Motown buildings jars the tranquility of the scene. It is painted a glaring white and bears a big sign: HITSVILLE, USA.

Berry Gordy and his company have been a mecca for Detroit's rock and roll talent, the majority of whom are Negro youngsters who grew up in the Detroit slums, ever since he founded the company on a song ("Way Over There") which he wrote and which the Miracles recorded and which became Motown's first hit, plus $700 borrowed from his family's credit union. The Motown complex now houses four separate companies: Jobete, a highly successful musical publishing company; International Talent Management Incorporated; Hitsville, USA, which owns Motown's recording studios; and the Motown Record Corporation, which issues singles and L.P.'s under a variety of labels, including Gordy, Tamla, Motown, VIP and Soul. In addition, the company has a burgeoning foreign business conducted by indigenous licensees and international distributors. The international flavor—symbolized by the globes on display in Motown offices—reflects the global scope of American teenage music today.

Though Motown is a predominantly Negro corporation, one sees a healthy sprinkling of white faces in every department and it is integrated at all levels of management. At the same time, it is still very much a family firm; there are presently 10 Gordys and in-laws now employed at Motown in a variety of positions. Gordy's sister, Esther, wife of a Michigan legislator and active in civic affairs, is vice president in charge of management and wields authority second only to Gordy in the company's affairs.

Motown began as one of a number of small R & B record companies which sprang up in Detroit during the fifties, partly in response to a demand for such music by Negro-oriented radio stations, which were also born at about the same time to serve Detroit's large (now over 500,000) Negro population. "On nearly every block in some neighborhoods," says Peter Gzowski of The Toronto Daily Star, a close observer of the Detroit musical scene, "there seems to be at least one small record firm, sign over door, Cadillac in driveway. Motown is the first of these firms to break into the big time."

The extent to which Motown has broken into the big time was, the week I was there, obvious for all to see: in the sales surveys that week, the company had three of its single records in the top five position. Such a near-monopoly was unprecedented even for Motown, which has been, for the past two years, the leading vender of single 45 r.p.m. records in the nation. When one asks Motown's controller, Edward Pollak, about the firm's income, he declines to answer on the grounds of the 16th (income tax) Amendment, but the company will probably gross about $15-million this year, according to other sources.

SUCH success is reflective of a growing demand for R & B music among teen agers who, of course, make up the bulk of single-record buyers. R & B music, once known as "race music," used to be considered music primarily for a Negro market (record-trade publications still maintain separate R & B charts, measuring air play by Negro-oriented radio stations and sales in predominantly Negro outlets). And since the strictly R & B market is limited, the name of the game is to score what the record industry calls a "pop breakout," i.e., a song played by pop "top 40" disc jockeys, and achieve ranking on the pop charts, which reflect sales in the broader mass market.

Motown's performers and com-

MR. MOTOWN—Berry Gordy (left) meeting with some of his record producers. A song will be recorded 20 or 30 times—or more—until the "Motown sound" is perfected.

posers, under the generalship of Berry Gordy Jr. have come up with a style of music that embodies a consistent "breakout" formula, yet which still does well on the R & B charts. Lately, other R & B artists in other cities—Memphis, Chicago, New York—are more frequently "breaking pop." As Dave Finkle, an editor of Record World magazine, explains, "This is due in great measure to the sound of Tamla-Motown, which created a wide market so that R & B broke across the racial barriers."

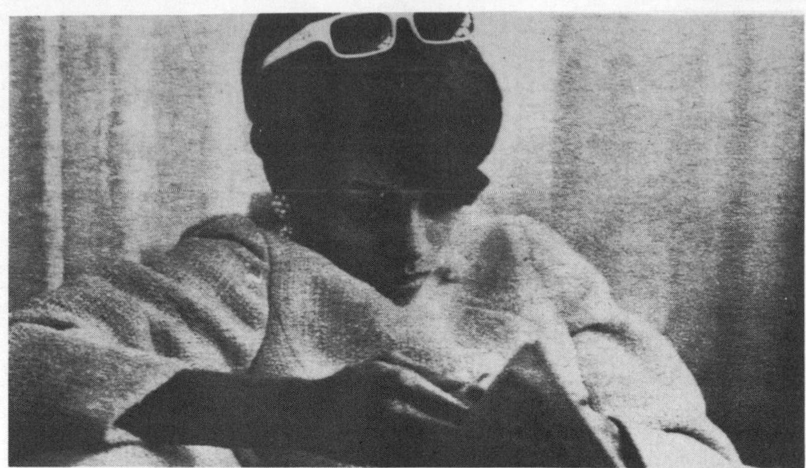

THE SUPREMES—Diana Ross is the lead singer,

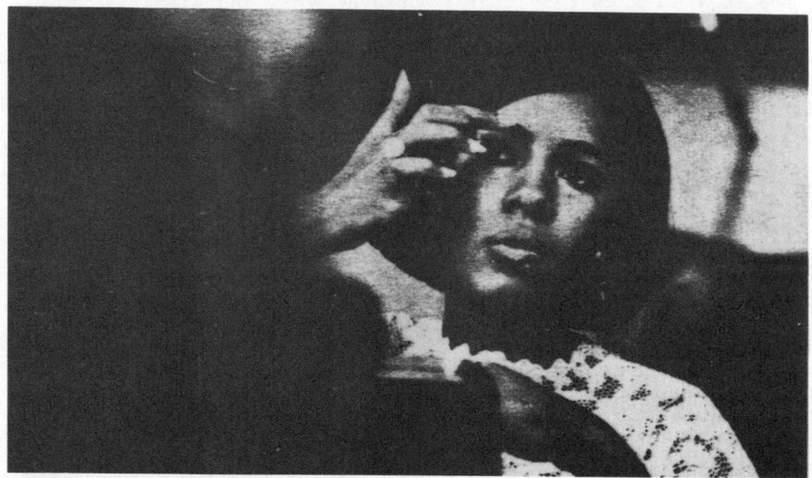

with the harmony provided by Mary Wilson and the

third member of the popular trio, Florence Ballard.

MUCH of the credit for the spreading of the Motown gospel belongs to three herald angels known collectively as the Supremes, and individually as Diana Ross, Mary Wilson and Florence Ballard. "The Supremes were our big breakthrough," says Motown record promotion man Larry Maxwell, whose job it is to stimulate air play and sales of Motown records. "A few years ago we couldn't make a WABC pick [that is, be selected for air play]," Maxwell recalls, "because they'd say, 'That's a blues sound.' Used to be you had 'good' music or popular music and you had 'race' music. Then you had rock and roll and you had rhythm and blues. Now Motown's bridged the gap between pop and R & B." Translated, that means that R & B was once not generally considered a pop sound, hence, no pop air play and no pop charts; now it is a pop sound, and the deejays will play it.

Of course, ever since Elvis Presley began twitching his hips, R & B has been a major influence on teen-age music. Elvis is supposed to have developed his singing style by imitating a Negro R & B performer named Arthur Crudup. The pop music that came to be known as rockabilly, a mixture of country music and R & B, has been called a "whitened" R & B. In other words, mass audiences would accept R & B only when filtered through white performers—including, recently, British performers, most of whom borrowed from Negro R & B performers.

In today's pop sound mix, the heavy reliance on electronic distortions has helped considerably to make the sources of pop music extremely eclectic. A long-time student of pop music, WMCA disc jockey Joe O'Brien, thinks R & B no longer has much meaning as either a term of classification or ethnic orientation. "These boundaries no longer mean a damn thing," he says. "You have whites out in Wasp areas buying just as much Negro music as they do white. Sometimes we play Motown records on WMCA before they do on WWRL. In today's pop music, any imaginative musician will use any style or sound. There is no longer even a straight 'white sound.' Everything is fair game—Latin, folk, country and Western, Viennese, schmaltz—you name it. Anything can be used because there's no longer a right way to make a record. Whatever works, works."

Today's pop record is a palimpsest of noninstrumental sounds; even an old hand such as O'Brien, who plays the stuff for four hours every morning, confesses that he can no longer identify the instruments used because of the use of such sound techniques as reverb, overdub and feedback. The biggest influences on contemporary pop music, O'Brien says, are Latin groups (such as the Joe Cuba Sextette), the Motown sound, and folk music (not traditional folk, but contemporary folk by such groups as the Mamas and the Papas and the Lovin' Spoonful, who, of course, write their own folk songs.) In such a climate the novelty and variety of R & B performers seem to be finding a hospitable teen-age ear.

Thanks to the Supremes and other Motown artists such as Stevie Wonder, Marvin Gaye, the Temptations, the Four Tops, and Martha and the Vandellas, as well as three of the hottest composers in the pop market, none of them over 25, named Brian Holland, Lamont Dozier and Eddie Holland (known in the record world as Holland-Dozier-Holland, or simply HDH—names with the solid ring of Merrill Lynch, Pierce, Fenner & Smith in the financial world), plus a number of other composers and producers of energy and talent, Motown has come to stand for a distinctive kind of R & B. It is so distinctive that it is known the world over as the Motown sound or the Detroit sound.

Roughly, that sound may be described as a sophisticated, slicked-up, unique R & B sound that is an amalgam of gospel harmonies, a blues beat, symphonic effects, electronic gimmickry and a "sweet" kind of rock 'n' roll. The lyrics usually convey a sort of inspirational message or hymn the yearnings of adolescent love in a direct and energetic manner that avoids soppiness. The lyrics of "You Can't Hurry Love" may be taken as an example:

I need love, love to ease my mind
I need to find, find someone to call mine
But mama said you can't hurry love
No, you just have to wait
She said love don't come easy
It's a game of give and take . . .

Brian Holland, Lamont Dozier, Eddie Holland ©1966 Jobete Music Co., Inc.

Gordy describes the music simply as, "a happy sound, a big happy beat with a good strong bass. Tambourines gave it a gospel flavor," he says, "but it doesn't have so much of that now."

GORDY—husky, taut, a Napoleonic head, shy engaging grin—is sitting at the desk in his paneled, darkened office. With a turntable at his side and big speakers concealed in the walls, he monitors records, deciding whether they should be released. Much of his time nowadays, he says not too happily, is spent in meetings and reading countless memos, or else traveling with his artists on tours (he had just returned from the Far East with the Supremes). But he still listens to all the company's records at one stage or another.

An assistant brings in the newest Supremes and Miracles records, and Gordy places the Supremes on the turntable, cocks his head, and turns up the volume to about 100 decibels. He sends back the Supremes, saying it needs more work, commenting: "It's O.K., but not really the one." Gordy calls my attention to the "Bach counterpoint" in the lead-in to the Miracles and suggests that the title be changed from "Come Around Here, You're the One I Need" to, simply, "You're the One I Need."

"Most people think all rock 'n' roll sounds the same," Gordy says, "but that's not true. You have to be a creative artist to decide what people will like." To prove his point, he sends for the three current Motown hits and plays a little of each, pointing out the differences and analyzing each record in a terse esthetic which is encompassed in a few words such as "strong," "good rhythm" and "that song has a philosophy."

The Supremes' "You Can't Hurry Love," No. 1 that week, has that "good rhythm," and it is obvious from the fondness with which he says it that this is the heart of the matter. Lyrics are important, he indicates, praising the "philosophy" in the Temptations' "Beauty Is Only Skin Deep":

So in love, sad as I can be
'Cause a pretty face got the best of me
Suddenly you came into my life and gave it meaning and delight
Now good looks I've learned to do without
'Cause I know now it's love that really counts
'Cause beauty's only skin deep . . .

Eddie Holland, Norman Whitfield. ©1966, Jobete Music Co., Inc.

But most important is the sound and the successful merger of rhythm and melody. And, of course, each record must have a quality of novelty that will catch the listener's ear.

Without overpraising the musical values of the records (Motown's critics accuse its song writers of writing sounds rather than songs), one agrees with Gordy that each one *is* different and clever, distinctively styled and lathed to a shining chromium perfection. Perfection is another of Gordy's talisman words, and I am told that Motown will record a song 20 or 30 times and then "if it still isn't right, we'll record it 15 more times."

"A Supremes record will sell 500,000 almost automatically," Gordy says. "Kids buy their records without even listening to them. We are putting something into their homes sight unseen so we want it to be good."

Watching Gordy in the mastering room, where the producers are editing a final tape of a Supremes record, you sense, as he helps them solve a cutting problem by clapping and stomping out the beat himself ("That's strong. Fine. Right there."), that he has that big, happy Motown beat throbbing inside him like a coiled, twanging string. He frequently hums a little bluesy tune under his breath—wooo-wooo-wooo-wooo. *There's* the Motown sound, on a little tape recorder playing inside Berry Gordy Jr.'s head. Bim-bimbimbimbim. Wooo-ooo-ooo-ooo. What more can one say?

BUT don't get the impression that Motown is a sort of hit-hazardous operation. Berry Gordy Jr., the one-time auto worker, has built himself something of a pop assembly line. He has attracted a lot of young raw talent and created an organization capable of nurturing and polishing that talent until they become smooth, well-drilled performers who are capable of holding a night club audience, as well as catching a teen-ager's ear for a couple of minutes.

There is at Motown, for example, something called an artists' development department, whose function is to take rock and roll kids and convert them into a viable night club act. This "finishing school," as it is known among the Motown performers, employs a galaxy of veteran showmen to train the kids to make the break from the sound studio to a live performance on stage. As one faculty member says: "Rock 'n' roll shows us the plum. Our job is to bring it in here and can it."

Canning it involves teaching that intricate Motown choreography and blocking, as well as broadening the repertoire so the businessman at the Copa will hear something like "There's No Business Like Show Business" as well as "Baby, Baby I Need You" with his $7.50 steak. Portly, genial Maurice King, an experienced bandleader, either conducts the night club orchestra himself or else selects the conductor and musicians—who play Motown arrangements, of course. Gordy insists on keeping the Motown style, King says, even in the case of standards. There is also a charm school in which girl performers are taught how to sit, how to hold a fork, how to walk, how to speak. "They learn how to behave both on stage *and* off," says Mrs. Ardenia Johnston, the smiling, maternal lady who teaches them, with something of a school marm's glint in her eye. "I just can't tell you what Motown has meant to these kids," Mrs. Johnston says. "Some of them would have ended up juvenile delinquents if they hadn't had this opportunity."

ONE of Motown's most charming and accomplished finished products is the group known as the Supremes. Since their first big-selling record, "Where Did Our Love Go?" in the summer of 1964, the three girls, still in their early 20's, have amassed a continuous string of top-10 hits (including six gold, or million-selling, records), won a worldwide popularity among teen-agers and appeared with great success on television and in night clubs.

Chic in their dazzling array of gowns (the girls call them "uniforms"), most of which are selected for them by Mrs. Harvey Fuqua of Motown's special projects department, the group is full of youthful exuberance and gives off a charming naiveté. They were praised by reviewer Robert Shelton as "unusually vibrant, exultant vocalists who soar with seemingly endless energy."

Diana Ross, the lead singer, has been compared often to Eartha Kitt, but she has a flexible, sweeter style of her own that can shift gears from a gospel fervor into a romantic ballad. Florence Ballard and Mary Wilson are posted in the background, adding a vibrant, close harmony, delicately tapping their tambourines against their hips, or chiming in with jokes from time to time. The Supremes have a hard, driving quality, too, deriving both from sheer energy and an intense competitiveness; though they will boost other Motown performers with company-girl correctness, they also will give their all to outstrip them when playing on the same bill.

Such was the case at a Forest Hills Stadium concert last August. The Temptations' flashy and well-choreographed act had drawn three encores and the singing of Stevie Wonder, the little, 15-year-old blind blues singer, had drawn enthusiastic ovations. It was a simple matter of pride to the Supremes to close the bill with the greatest applause of all and, as witnesses present will attest, they went out and gave the performances of their lives. Or, as Diana put it, "We got out there and worked like hell. I wasn't really nervous until I heard that crowd screaming. It was a big shock. The audience was so far away, you couldn't see them, and I worried about that. I wanted to see everyone. I was soaking wet when we finished."

IT is sometimes said about the Supremes that they have a "white sound." Diana rejects the description. "The white sound means the commercial sound," she explains a little hotly, as if to say, "This is our sound, baby, not theirs." She gives credit to British pop groups for making R & B more palatable to American audiences, but adds: "They copied a Negro sound and sang a popular version of R & B."

The girls, who grew up in Detroit's slum ghetto, have been singing together since they were about 14. They gravitated to Motown and Gordy after high school ("Everybody was talking about him," says Diana); he started them dubbing in background on records and christened them the Supremes. They began to record, while learning as much as they could from other groups. "The Temptations would teach them harmony to get them off their backs," Gordy recalls.

For a time, they were at the bottom of the Motown pecking order and were known as "the girls." (Now another, newer, group is known as "the girls.") Success began coming their way after they were placed in the hands of Holland-Dozier-Holland, who wrote their first hit, "Where Did Our Love Go?", and just about all their subsequent ones; the producing team of Brian Holland and Lamont Dozier gave their records a style and identity they had

QUINTET—The Temptations, like other Motown ensembles, have a flashy and carefully choreographed act. Above, they wind up a rehearsal with an exuberant flourish.

NEWCOMER—Chris Clark, a recent addition to the Motown stable, practices her repertoire. Most performers are Negroes, but the company is well-integrated at the management level.

previously lacked, emphasizing Diana's voice in the solos, with Mary and Florence contributing in the harmony.

OFFSTAGE, the Supremes are friendly, rather ordinary girls with a bouncing sense of humor; their conversation is studded with little in-jokes about one another based on what someone had written about them. Diana seems a trifle more mature than the others, displaying an earnest, serious manner and a cool professionalism. She is almost achingly thin (size 5) with fine, large eyes set in a feline face and she speaks in a hoarse June Allyson voice. Mary is small and nicely proportioned, demure in a tan suit and frilly blouse. In conjunction with the others she tends to fade into the background, which is deceptive because she has a distinctively droll sense of humor; when she smiles, her eyes crinkle into two horizontal crescents. Florence is earthier. She is usually known as "the quiet one," but she can be outspoken in an abrupt, flaunting way if the spirit moves her.

Gordy speaks about them in a bemused, detached manner. "We had some trouble with them at first. You must be very strict with the young artists. That instills discipline. But once they have a No. 1 record they tend to get more independent. They start spending their money extravagantly." In the case of the Supremes, in their first flush of success they bought new homes with lots of expensive furniture and moved in their families.

"After a year, they saw their mistakes and came to appreciate our handling of their affairs," Gordy observes. The Supremes' money, as is the case with many Motown artists, is invested for them in a variety of business interests, stocks and bonds. Though their yearly income nowadays is in five figures—record royalties are divided equally—they have been put on an allowance of $50 a week. "If I'd been strict when they had their first hit, it would have been bad," Gordy says. "They were growing up, demanding to live their own lives, so I loosened up on them. Now they're more sensible, and they seek and appreciate advice." His brow furrows as he adds: "I don't know what the next phase will be." Then, hopefully: "But now they're less mixed up, more relaxed about their love lives. They take more interest in learning about the world. It's amazing how they've educated themselves in their traveling."

I sense that keeping happy these volatile, ambitious girls who account for a sizable percentage of Motown's record sales is one of Gordy's important executive functions. Anyhow, he spends a lot of time with them on the road. "Every company has trouble with its artists," he says. "It's always the little things that blow up. If the little things can be cleared up before they get big, trouble can be prevented."

November 27, 1966

200,000 ATTEND COAST ROCK FETE

Free Concert Causes Huge Jam Near San Francisco

By ROBERT A. WRIGHT
Special to The New York Times

TRACY, Calif., Dec. 6—Thousands of fans of the Rolling Stones rock group converged on the hillsides around the Altamont Speedway here today, turning pastures into parking lots and campsites

The Rolling Stones, the Grateful Dead, the Jefferson Airplane and other rock groups were giving a concert, and it was free.

Some 5,000 youths arrived last night and camped as near the hastily built stage as possible. By 10 A.M. the population of these fields mounted to an estimated 200,000. Traffic on Route 580 from San Francisco was backed up for 20 miles.

Until yesterday, the racetrack had scheduled a motorcycle race. Then, because of a disagreement between the Rolling Stones and the management of Sears Point Racetrack in Sonoma County, the concert was suddenly shifted here. It had originally been scheduled for Golden Gate Park in San Francisco.

'Follow Them'

Nobody knew exactly where the new site was.

Eager fans turned off the highway into an impromptu parking lot eight miles away and began walking. Highway patrolmen, asked directions, advised simply, "Follow them, they know."

Until midday the only music heard came from portable radios and a rock group that performed from a motorized, sound-equipped truck in a meadow far from the stage in the center of the crowd.

At 11 oclock a bright blue and yellow striped hot air balloon ascended from the bandstand and hovered over the crowd. This produced some cheers from the audience. Otherwise even the sound of the crowd's conversation was dissipated in the country air.

People seemed content to talk, picnic and pass marijuana cigarettes. Six helicopters, shuttling in and out performers, provided most of the noise.

The show began at 1 o'clock, as scheduled. The Rolling Stones arrived by helicopter about 2:30 and were the last to perform.

Toilet facilities were few, and a long walk from the crowd. Fans were prepared for a picnic, and many brought food and their children with them.

The crowd, considering its size, was well behaved. The police made few arrests. A total of 75 Oakland policemen and hired security guards seemed to enter into the spirit of the affair.

"We had to talk to a couple of guys walking around up there nude," a police sergeant said. "But we're trying to hold down arrests so we don't blow the whole show."

Dr. Richard Fine of a group of volunteer doctors from the San Francisco chapter of the Medical Committee for Human Rights, said his emergency medical tent had no severe injuries to treat.

"We had about 30 bad trips [drug-induced traumas] and eight or 10 lacerations, only one from a fight."

The Rollings Stones conceived of the free concert, they let it be known, as a means of expressing their thanks to fans for a very successful American tour. Before returning to Britain they would entertain without charge and turn any revenues from film or recording rights over to charity, they said. Other rock groups rallied around.

Future Events Possible

John Ellsworth Jaymes, president of Young American Enterprises, Inc., promoter of the Rollings Stones nationwide tour, said: "It's a Christmas and Hanukkah gift from the Stones and other groups to American youth."

Dick Carter, owner of the speedway, said, "I'm handing over the speedway at no cost, just for the publicity and to prove I'm a good guy. Of course, if it works out, I'll probably be presenting my own paid rock concerts there in the future."

The sudden shift in plans produced a logistics problem Mr. Jaymes called "staggering."

Cargo helicopters spent yesterday afternoon transporting some 33,000 pounds of equipment, including sound paraphernalia and lumber for the stage. Some 100 private guards and a working crew of more than 300 were rerouted here.

A spokesman for the Rolling Stones said the reason for the disagreement with the Sears Point management was that the company wanted distribution rights for a film to be made of the event.

December 7, 1969

'A Joyful Confirmation That Good Things <u>Can</u> Happen Here'

By PATRICK LYDON

BETHEL, N. Y.

IT ALL happened up at the farm and everything happened. Half a million kids—hippies, rock people, and even straights — ran up to the farm for a long weekend of rock 'n' roll music mixed with mud, no sleep, rain, drugs, more mud, and even more smiles. Too many people came to the Woodstock Festival but they came high and they only got higher.

It started on Route 17, hip cars passing bread to the cycle riders and waving "V" signs everywhere. Bethel townspeople gazed in awe at the streams of hippies, but they murmured "Peace" to the visitors, offered free water, and returned smiles. Everyone arrived to find the whole show was free. As the weekend went on, the miracles kept coming — the kindness of the scattered police, the "food-drop" by an Army helicopter, and flowers from the sky. Yet faith makes miracles and it was the astonishing peace and joy of the youthful masses that brought happy results.

Before it became the greatest hippie demonstration of unity, the music was the focus of the festival. Friday was the folk night but the playing was plagued by rain and delays. Every artist was received with warmth because they all played well and because the listeners were glad of any music. Joan Baez closed the evening in the rain, but she roused the masses to join her in "We Shall Overcome."

Saturday brought continued rain, some despair, and greater crowds. The roads toward the site were jammed with cars — cars full of sleepers. Fields and forests of motley tents stretched on every side. As the morning wore on, the weather cleared and good energy seemed to come with the sun. The music started not long after one o'clock and slowly built in intensity and excellence. Once again the crowd gave every group a standing ovation. Saturday's closing series of the Grateful Dead, Creedence Clearwater Revival, Janis Joplin, Sly and the Family Stone, The Who and the Jefferson Airplane must be one of the great shows of rock 'n' roll history. Sly had the whole audience chanting "Higher" and raising "V" signs with their fingers. Pete Townshend of The Who had it spellbound with his dynamic finale. The Who brought in the dawn. The Airplane did not finish until after eight o'clock in the morning—over eighteen hours after the day's start.

The Sunday show was meant to start at 1 o'clock and most people slept on the field before the stage. In the easy atmosphere of timeless togetherness, waits didn't seem long. The show didn't begin until shortly before 3 and the cruel rain stopped it not long after 4. The site had dried slowly since Saturday morning, but it was quickly mud again. The rain came down hard for an hour but spirits held out bravely. A large part of the crowd took up tonic cans and banged them together, danced and chanted at the sky — "Sun's Comin'". By the time the sun was ready to come back, it had nearly set and the music was on again. The intensity of Saturday night was never recaptured, the rain and sleepless hours had drained off some enthusiasm, and drugs were running out. But each group played hard and well — the bands all seemed genuinely thrilled to be there. The long night ended with the humor of Sha-Na-Na and a disappointing set by Jimi Hendrix's new band. Even then, at 10 o'clock on Monday morning, there was universal good heart.

The music on stage was only a part of the weekend's activity. The art exhibit of painting and sculpture was rather small but interesting. Followers of Meher Baba, the Avatar, sat nude on a suspended rock testifying their faith. The Grateful Dead gave two independent concerts at the nearby Hog Farm. Despite the bad weather, hundreds of people went swimming.

Although it was consistently excellent, the music will not be what participants remember best. It was natural that a huge crowd should arrive in good spirits, laughing, getting together in the music that brought them, but that their good vibrations never broke was extraordinary. As the announcer on stage praised the crowd, and as the bands registered their excitement at playing for such a gathering, the crowd felt an increasing sense of good in itself. The free food given by the people of the Hog Farm held body and soul together, the Red Cross Station took care of those who were ill, and a special tent treated those who were on bum acid trips.

There was the joy of confirmation, the delight in accenting what others could give. Hippies had never been quite so successful together, never before had they so impressed the world that watched. The strength of the crowd seemed strongest in the hard rain on Sunday afternoon. To the banging of the cans, dancing hippies gave all of themselves. Instead of despairing at the discomfort of rain and mud, the crowd rejoiced in its power to resist the weather. One boy stood covered with mud, ornamented with refuse he found in it, yet overjoyed that he could make happiness for others.

Out of the mud came dancers, out of electrical failure came music, out of hunger came generosity. What began as a symbolic protest against American society ended as a joyful confirmation that good things *can* happen here, that Army men can raise a "V" sign, that country people can welcome city hippies. One of Hendrix's last numbers was "The Star Spangled Banner." Yes, most everything happened up on the farm.

August 24, 1969

Jane Phillips.

COUNTRY STYLIST

Connie B. Gay Discusses Lucrative Formula

By McCANDLISH PHILLIPS

ANYONE who has ever, in the democracy of war, shared barracks with a knot of fiddle-scraping wahoos from the swamp country will probably not be an instant admirer of Connie B. Gay, packager of a morning cowboy jamboree called "The Jimmy Dean Show."

Mr. Gay is the cultural shepherd of that considerable portion of the American public whose appetite for country music cannot be gratified in any merely twenty-four-hour day.

He is, by self-admission, a) just a homebody, b) the largest individual promoter of country music in the nation, and c) pretty nearly tone deaf—a concatenation of circumstances that the average music lover will probably consider altogether reasonable.

Successive mouthfuls of spaghetti stood between Mr. Gay and lucidity the other day as he searched his mind for a definition of country music.

His first resort was to vehicular metaphor: "If hillbilly music is a Model T and pop music is a Cadillac, then country music would come along about Oldsmobile," he said.

Definition

Somebody asked what that would make Mozart, and Mr. Gay ventured into the philology of the thing: "Can't can't be can't in hillbilly music—it's cain't," he said. "But can't can be can't in country music."

A nice distinction, all hands agreed, but something short of definitive. The ungracious imputation that "country music" is a motivational-research euphemism for hillbilly music drove him deeper into his resources:

"Hillbilly music was banjos, guitars, fiddles," he said with a deprecatory wave of the hand. "We've added a sweet touch to it and taken out the twang. You don't get the raucous plink, plank, plunk of a couple of decades ago."

Mr. Gay explained that country music is not really a kind of music; it is a style, a way of playing.

The one quality indispensable to a country music performer is "down homeliness"—an amalgam of simple virtues of the kind that your sweet old Grandmother used to praise.

"The Jimmy Dean Show" is a case in point. Young Dean affects the standard hillbilly get-up—ill-fitting trousers, flannel shirt and neckerchief—and occasionally slips into melancholy reflections on the last round-up, but mostly he wears an easy flippancy and has the grace of taking himself not too seriously.

Like Como, Godfrey, Gobel and Ernie Ford, Dean is of the Just-Folks, or Don't-Mind-Me, school of television presentation. He soft-tongues his way through his show with a hasteless good humor that makes it hard to decide whether he is merely tolerable or actually engaging.

Engaging

Mr. Gay, a man of easy-going Southern courtliness and charm, is indisputably engaging. He may be the largest can of corn to have hit New York in years, but it's honest corn and there is no savor of Madison Avenue about the man.

Not long ago, when he told some of the local sharpies that he was "from a little place called Lizard Lick, North Carolina," they screwed up their faces in pain and said, "What is this Lizard Lick bit, anyway?"

It was no "bit." Lizard Lick is a farm community eighteen miles east of Raleigh and Mr. Gay was authentically reared there.

He now owns twenty-two television shows in Washington —a much-blessed city—a chain of three country-music radio stations, an automobile sales agency and assorted real estate. He does about a $1,000,000-a-year traffic in country music.

During the busy season he keeps about eighty musicians and singers under contract and

Connie B. Gay

rents them out on a per diem basis to everything from supermarket openings to television shows.

Mr. Gay's rise in the country music field was swift and uninterruptedly profitable. While serving as the "Voice of Agriculture" on the National Farm and Home Hour for the Department of Agriculture during World War II, he noticed that music with a rural flavor drew consistently more mail than other kinds. When the war was over, he withdrew from Government service and sold a local radio station into giving him half an hour in the morning to play country music.

"Pretty soon I went from half an hour to an hour," he says. "Then from an hour to two hours and from two hours to three hours. We were sponsored to the gills. We had them standing in line.

"I had the first country music air show in the nation. I rented an air circus—planes doing stunts and all that, men walking on the wings and all—and I put my country music artists on the ground. They'd fly a bit up there and we'd play a while down here. Twenty-five thousand people paid a dollar to see it.

"A little later I decided to go into Constitution Hall on a one-night gamble. Well, it was such a smash that we stayed there for twenty-seven weeks with a $6 top and filled the place most of the time."

This explosive success fits right in with Mr. Gay's assessment of the business merits of country music.

"In a radio station, country music given any degree of reasonable exposure will become the tail that wags the dog," he says.

"You can start with thirty minutes a day in the average city and pretty soon it spreads. It becomes a monster that you can't get away from."

Mr. Gay credits Selective Service with having done a great deal for country music. As he sees it, the draft "took a little country boy from Georgia and put him in Paris and it took a lad from New York and moved him down to Georgia and that was it.

"It's like bread. All the lad from New York ever had was store-bought bread. He never had any home-baked hot biscuits. But some little Georgia girl takes him home to mother for hot biscuits and pretty soon he gets so he likes them."

Mr. Gay eyed an urban roll suspiciously. "Now this darn bread here * * *," he began, leaving the thought unsaid.

Presumably, the Georgia boy wins Paris to country music and the New York lad, fatally infected, brings it home to the city.

Mr. Gay declares, with all evident sincerity, that he regulates his empire "according to the Golden Rule and Jeffersonian principles of democracy."

There is a "Ninety Day Salary Re-evaluation Plan" in effect at his radio stations, whereby the employes gather round the books every third month and vote themselves salary boosts in line with the profits.

He will not inflict on his audience a sponsor he thinks is peddling shoddy. Not a few manufacturers of rejuvenation juice—a product that seems to have a special appeal to country music fans—have gone away wondering what this Golden Rule bit is, anyway.

September 8, 1957

DURABLE FORMULA FOR 'GRAND OLE OPRY'

By ROBERT SHELTON

NASHVILLE, Tenn.

AFTER thirty-five years of broadcasting, the grand old dinosaur of American radio, "Grand Ole Opry," is as boisterously alive as ever. The show began on Nashville's Station WSM on Nov. 28, 1925, and aside from time off for a few Fireside Chats by the late President Franklin D. Roosevelt, has an uninterrupted record of Saturday nights that span a whole era.

A night at the "Opry" is a concoction of corn, color, confusion and country culture. From 3,000 to 4,000 paying guests throng the cavernous Ryman Auditorium here for the four and one-half hour show each week in a mood that combines a visit to a shrine and a barn dance.

The "Opry" went off the National Broadcasting Company network last year after being on it since 1939. But New Yorkers will have two opportunities to see stars of the "Opry" this week. At Carnegie Hall on Wednesday night ten acts from the show will appear at a benefit for the Musicians Aid Society. On Saturday, at the Ethical Culture Auditorium, two of the "Opry" stalwarts, Lester Flatt and Earl Scruggs, will give a pair of concerts.

Guests

Watching the program in its native habitat is seeing a spectacle in the American grain. Only part of the show is provided by the nearly 200 musicians milling about the stage. The rest is by the audience. A total of more than 6,000,000 persons have traveled from forty-one states just to see the proceedings. Babies are dandled on knees, camera flashbulbs pop as favored stars amble to the microphone, popcorn is crunched and soda pop swilled. Announcers and program officials continually try to whip the audience into applause, but the listeners know what they like and will often miss their cues and clap only when the spirit moves them.

Onstage, huge back-drops tout the products of such sponsors as makers of evaporated milk, flour and corn meal, starch, salt and rat eradicators. The procession of stars begins. Old-timers like Sam and Kirk McGee and the Fruitjar Drinkers look, and sound, like tintypes from the Nineteen Twenties. A strikingly handsome singer, Jim Reeves, wears a red tuxedo jacket you would never find in a mail-order catalogue. A corral of cowboy types — Ernest Tubb, Hank Locklin, Bill Anderson, Cowboy Copas or Hawkshaw Hawkins—outsplendor each other with mother-of-pearl guitars, fancy boots, big Stetson hats and jackets studded with sequins and even rhinestones. It is a dazzling hubbub.

"New York advertising people don't believe it when they see it," says Ott Devine, the "Opry" manager. "They just don't understand the informality. When we start producing it, we kill it."

Impact

There seems to be no danger of the show's being killed, or even of dying a natural death. On WSM alone, a listening audience of about 2,500,000 hear the show weekly and half-hour transcriptions are played weekly on the 200 outlets of the Keystone Broadcasting System in the South and Midwest, adding another million listeners. The roster of performers on the "Opry" is so long—fifty acts, with fifteen more on a waiting list—that for twelve years WSM has been putting on an overflow show, a studio "Friday Night Opry."

It is doubtful that any radio show has had such an impact on the city from which it emanates, nor such a powerful role in the development of an industry. In large part because of the vortex provided by the "Opry," Nashville has become the center of the country-music business. Song-writing, publishing, recording and the myriad tours in which "Opry" stars make 3,000 yearly personal appearances bring about $35,000,000 a year into the city—the figure is that of Tennessee's Governor, Buford Ellington.

The names of notables who have started or appeared on the "Opry" would fill a book. Roy Acuff, Gov. Jimmie Davis of Louisiana, Dinah Shore, Pat Boone, Hank Williams, Uncle Dave Macon are just a few. An obscure chap named Elvis Presley appeared as a bass player before anyone knew or cared who he was.

Mixture

The sort of music made on the "Grand Ole Opry" is not easy to characterize, for it runs from good to bad, mixed the slick with the sincere, the commercial with the traditional. It is a composite of more than a half-dozen styles of country and western music. Lovers of old-time folk music feel that the "Opry" musical quality has declined over the years. The critics point to the addition of snare drums to give teen-agers a beat to dance to, the extensive use of electric instruments, the singing commercials and the commitment to hit-song policies.

The old-timers and traditionalists would not trade a bit of the informal good spirits that still pervade the show. However, some of them feel that much has been lost since the days of George D. Hay, who called himself the Solemn Old Judge, who directed the "Opry" for more than two decades. Judge Hay fought to retain the grass-roots folk flavor of the show.

It was Judge Hay who started the "National Barn Dance" on WLS in Chicago, then came to Nashville to begin the WSM "Barn Dance" in 1925 by introducing an 80-year-old fiddler named Uncle Jimmy Thompson. Two years later, the show was on the air directly after Dr. Walter Damrosch's "Music Appreciation Hour." Judge Hay remarked one Saturday night, "For the past hour we have been listening to music taken largely from grand opera, but from now on we will present 'The Grand Ole Opry.'"

The title stuck, and so has the amazingly durable institution it describes.

November 26, 1961

Glen Campbell Leads List Of Country Music Awards

NASHVILLE, Oct. 20 (UPI)—Glen Campbell, who sings his own "uptown" version of country music, was chosen the country music entertainer of the year and the best male vocalist at the annual Country Music Awards banquet Friday. Mr. Campbell, who starred this summer in a weekly hour-long color TV show over the Columbia Broadcasting System's network, was cited for "By the Time I Get to Phoenix" and "Gentle on My Mind."

Glen Campbell

Chosen as the best single record of the year was "Harper Valley P.T.A.," a song about a miniskirted mother who "socks it" to a hypocritical school group, recorded by Jeannie C. Riley.

The best album award went to Johnny Cash. The album, recorded before a live audience at a California prison, was titled "Johnny Cash at Folsom Prison."

Bob Wills was named to the country music hall of fame.

October 21, 1968

'Ain't Nothin' Too Weird for Me'

By MICHAEL LYDON

AMARILLO, Tex.

BACKSTAGE at the Amarillo, Texas, Civic Auditorium, a fresh kid with glasses held out a plastic cup of coffee.

"Here's ya coffee, Mr. Cash. You want cream and sugar? It's real strong."

"That's O.K.," said Johnny Cash. He took a big gulp and coughed like hell.

"I told ya it was strong," said the kid.

"That's O.K.," said Johnny, scowling. He was getting over the flu, his throat was a mess, he had to sing for two thousand smug Amarillans in their brand new auditorium, and this *kid* was trifling with him. "Oh, hell," said Johnny, his voice rising to a shout. The kid scurried away.

Handsome Johnny Cash, as fans call him, is too big to be trifled with ("biggest man I know," says his wife, June Carter, batting her false eyelashes): 6 feet 2 and 250 pounds, with ploughboy shoulders, massive arms, and a crude heaviness in his gut. But he's strange too. His brown eyes stare out of his wasted yet fleshily powerful face, with its scars and mashed-over nose. "Ain't nothin' too weird for me," he says. "People call me wild. Not really though, I'm not. I guess I've never been normal, not what you'd call Establishment. I'm country."

*

Country is right. Even while resplendent in his stage costume of white turtleneck, black frock coat, diplomat-striped pants, and patent leather boots, he'd still be known by folks back home as Ray Cash's boy, raised with five other kids on a 20-acre cotton farm near Dyess, Arkansas.

Cash has been riding high on the wave of new interest in country music. His 1968 album, "Johnny Cash at Folsom Prison," helped start the wave, and now seemingly every rock group is going to Nashville to record. Tonight at 8 on Channel 13, Johnny will be the subject of "Cash!", a 90-minute color documentary produced for Public Broadcast Laboratory by Arthur Barron, whose film "Birth and Death" was a PBL success earlier this season. In addition, Cash has just been signed by ABC-TV for a summer variety hour to be called "The Johnny Cash Show." Hard as it may be for urban listeners to believe, in recent years Cash has been among Columbia's top four best-selling artists.

*

But country music, sometimes known as country and western, Grand Ole Opry, or the Nashville Sound, is more than music; it is a myth on a grand scale. William Jennings Bryan used to tell the crowds that if the country were ruined, the cities would die, but level the cities and the country would live on. C&W, even though much of its audience is only rural in spirit, has that assumption built in. Mother still means mom in country music; dogs, the seasons, trains, Jesus, sweethearts, preachers, mules, and home sweet home still matter. So do sheriffs, prisons, and doin' time. Johnny Cash is fully at home in the music and the myth.

New rock fans may dig him, but to him they're "hippuhs," a breed out of his ken. Bob Dylan is a close friend—Cash gave Dylan his most valuable guitar as a present—and they are now musical partners: a few weeks ago in Nashville they wrote a song together, called "Wanted Man," and recorded some duets which Dylan may include on his next album. Cash is excited about his new audiences and their business, but he doesn't really give a hot damn what city folks think of him. "Gonna ride that Orange Blossom Special," he sings, "and lose these New York Blues."

*

It was as a country boy that Cash took his show to California's Folsom Prison a year ago, singing to the country boys inside. "I felt I was bringing 'em a message from home," he says, "A prison audience is the most exciting in the world. The men are with you, feeding you, every second. Maybe because they need you so bad." He had played prisons many times before, but this time the concert in the prison's huge dining hall was recorded by Columbia engineers. "Folsom Prison" was the result, his best and best-selling record. Late in February, Cash recorded another live show at San Quentin which may soon be released as a second prison LP; included is a bitter song about San Quentin he wrote for the occasion.

From the introductory "Hello, I'm Johnny Cash" and his own "Folsom Prison Blues" ("I know I had it coming, I know I can't be free, But those people keep on moving, And that's what tortures me"), Cash is singing with the convicts — "all brothers of mine," he wrote in the eloquent liner notes. The prisoners whoop when he sings "I shot that bad bitch down" in "Cocaine Blues" and when he shouts "this ain't the movies, so forget about me!" in "Twenty Five Minutes to Go," and they crack up when he slips in the "mean bastards, ain't they," about the guards. At the end, one prisoner comes forward to give him a present from all of them, a made-in-Folsom-Prison striped cap and jacket. "Make you one of the in crowd while you're out," the convict yelps in a split-second of bravado.

"It was some afternoon," said Johnny. The West Texas plains, hot and flat and brown, went slipping by Cash's mobile home bus as he talked. It was a sleepy day during a recent tour; Carl Perkins, the fine country rock guitarist who wrote "Blue Suede Shoes," was studying his Norman Vincent Peale; Fluke Holland, Johnny's drummer, was passing the time of day with bass player Marshall Grant as he drove; and June was eating a plum.

"I gave them a stiff shot of realism, singing about the things they talk about, the outside, shooting, trials, families, escaping, girl friends, and coming to the end. They knew it was for them. Just them and me."

"Why, those pore babies were listening to John so hard you could *feel* it," said June, who has a Holly-Golightly-returned-home mixture of parodied and real Southern charm.

"You can't be in prison without being a prisoner," said Johnny. "They had guards all around with riot guns. Before and after the show, we were kept in the kitchen. None of the boys were allowed to talk to us. One kid broke regulations. A guard stepped between us, but I said it was O.K. so the guard let him have one question. 'You know so 'n' so back in Arkansas?' 'Never heard the name,' I said. 'He said he knew you,' the kid said, and the guard pushed him back. He broke the rules just trying to make an old country boy connection.

"I kept thinking I could have been down there listening with the prisoners," John went on. "Only been in jail twice, and just overnight, but you don't need much to see what it's like. Both times it was for pills, dexedrine. Second time I woke up in a Georgia jail not knowing how I got there. Could've ended up on a chain gang, but the jailer was a fan of mine and he let me go. I was real hung up on those pills. I put pore ole June through hell with 'em. For years I was down to skin and bone, never sleeping, never eating. But that's all over now, isn't it, June?"

"It sure is, John."

"Come here, honey, and give your man a kiss." June did, and the boys cheered.

*

That night was Lubbock. "We played here so many times, I know everybody in the audience by their first names," said June. The mother of Waylon Jennings, a young country star, came by the bus. A fluttery creature, Mrs. Jennings said Waylon's new record was doin' fine, and that she just wished Johnny could meet her youngest, Phil. "John and June, he's *always* at that *guitar*, crazier about it than Waylon was. Ah'll lose another son to country music, Ah swear."

The Lubbock crowd—half town, half ranch — was up for the Johnny Cash Spectacular. Carl Perkins came on first to break the ice, then the Carter Family — Mother Maybelle, "Mother of Country Music and sole survivor of the Original Carter Family," and her daughters Helen, Anita, and June—did old favorites like "Wildwood Flower." Mother Maybelle's autoharp sang as it has for 40 years. June threw in a little comedy ("Just 'cause this is an all girl act," she deadpanned, "don't go thinkin' it's a girlie show. This is as sexy as we're gonna get"). After intermission it was Johnny.

On he ran, rebel yells cutting up from the crowd. He picked up his guitar and, standing on his toes, started "Hey Porter," with Marshall, Fluke, and Carl laying down the unique "boomchicka" (its onomatopoetic name) rhythm. Spotlights outlined his wavy hair and made his eyes deep shadows. He *was* Handsome Johnny, mean, nonchalant sexuality with the force if not flamboyance of Elvis's old style. He just stood and sang, but with his heavy, hooded eyes and hooded voice, one saw this easy moving man, one-quarter Cherokee, like an outlaw cowboy, his power held gracefully but menacingly in check. The women watched him silently; the men shouted, waved their hats, and stomped their boots. For both, Johnny was everything they could want and more.

When he came off, a tough babe with silver-sculpted hair grabbed him by the arm. "Hey, Johnny, remember me, that night in El Paso in '58?" Johnny didn't. She drew him into a dressing room. When they came out a minute later, he was blushing. "He remembers now," she crowed, "Wild wasn't it?" "It was wild," he said with a slow laugh.

*

"Folsom Prison," Johnny said the next day as we drove to El Paso, wasn't all that special. Ever since his albums on the legendary Sun label in the mid-fifties, he has made each one around a theme. He did "Ride This Train," a song-story narrative of American history, an album of Indian songs called "Bitter Tears," and a two-record collection of "Songs of the Real West." "The new one is the one I'm really proud of—'Johnny Cash the Holy Land.' When June and I were in Israel last spring, I went around to all the holy places and taped my impressions right on the spot, and then we did songs to match when I got back. That record means a lot to me."

"Send a copy to mah uncle," said Marshall. "His lifelong prayer as a preacher is to walk where Jesus walked. He'll feel it from what you done."

"Marshall, I'm havin' Columbia send copies to preachers all over."

"Billy Graham too," said Fluke.

"Billy Graham too," said Johnny. He isn't a religious sort of man, but he doesn't drink, watches his language in front of ladies, and knows in his bones that the debt owed to preachers as men of God must be paid. Tough as he may be, Handsome Johnny has a morbid fear of snakes, can't even stand to touch a picture of one, and sometimes when flying gets so scared he can hardly breathe. So considering that it's a commercial proposition too, it doesn't do any harm to keep on the right side of preachers.

*

But life has been good to him. He made his success early and has been able to hang on to it. He's got his quarter-million-dollar house set into a cliff above a Tennessee lake near Nashville. The woman he's loved for years is now his wife and, at 36, after 13 years of touring, he still has it in him to keep going. He's not going to be like Jimmy Rodgers, the Singing Brakeman, who smoked cigarettes to the day he died because he thought the nicotine killed the germs. Johnny has quit smoking, is off the pills for good, and is watching himself. It hasn't always been easy, but he's making it now.

Marshall started singing in the front seat, doing a broad imitation of Jimmy Rodgers.

"I got those mean old Tuheee, Buheee, Buhloos."

"Yo ho ho ho," Johnny chimed in in falsetto.

"Those mean old Tuheee, Buheee, Buhlooos," they all sang, cracking up and slapping their thighs.

"Mah pore silly babies," said June.

March 16, 1969

Radio Tuning In to the Country Styles

By JOHN S. WILSON

Country music, once generally dismissed as the doleful maunderings of illiterate hillbillies, is attracting an ever-widening audience and has spread from its base in the South-Central states to become a programing staple on a majority of the nation's radio stations.

It is now heard on 56 per cent of the stations in the United States, putting it ahead of even the seemingly ubiquitous rock music, which is heard on only 40 per cent.

But, in the process of gaining a new audience, country music itself is changing. It is splitting into what are, in effect, two kinds of music—a commercial branch and a traditional branch—much as jazz, during the Swing Era of the nineteen-thirties, found a mass audience for its popular, big-band aspects while basic, hard-core, small-group jazz went its own way in relative obscurity.

The sudden spurt of interest in country music took place during the same period when rock was becoming established. Since 1961, when there were 81 radio stations playing country music exclusively, the number of all-country music stations has shot up to more than 700. This is in addition to the 1,300 stations that play some country music.

Big stations that play country music are found in every section, with one notable exception—New York City.

Until a few weeks ago WJRZ in Hackensack, N. J., had been supplying the New York area with country music for more than five years. But it has now changed its music policy to rock and its call letters to WWDJ.

Some of the Outlets

Country music pours out of KLAC in Los Angeles, WBOX in Dallas, WIL in St. Louis, WJJD in Chicago, WDEE in Detroit, WAME in Cleveland, WSHO in New Orleans, WPLO in Atlanta, WEEP in Pittsburgh, WWVA in Wheeling, W. Va., WRCP in Philadelphia and WCOP in Boston.

On television, despite the disappearance of the Johnny Cash show and "Hee-Haw" from the networks, there are 21 syndicated shows headed by country-music performers, some of which—the Porter Waggoner show and the Bill Anderson show, for example, —are seen on more than 100 stations.

And on records and tapes, country music, with 16 per cent of the nation's sales, is second only to rock.

All of this has grown out of centuries-old Scottish, Irish and English songs that were brought to the hills of Tennessee, Virginia, Kentucky and the Carolinas by early settlers. The songs were blended with Negro musical influences (the blues, the guitar) and took on religious and inspirational coloration.

Over the years this melding process produced a body of hoe-downs, sacred songs, "heart" songs and "event" songs, the last report of some dramatic or shocking event (much as "The Death of Floyd Collins") closely related to the broadside ballad of England.

When the pioneer recording men began taking their portable equipment into the hill country in the nineteen-twenties, their recordings of such "event songs" often brought the first news of what had happened to the isolated mountain people.

These early records first made this music available to more than a relative handful of listeners, but it was radio that began to pull country music followers together into a mass audience during the Twenties.

Barn-dance programs went out into the hill country from WSB, Atlanta; KDKA, Pittsburgh; WLS, Chicago; WWVA, Wheeling; WLW, Cincinnati, and, most notably, WSM, Nashville, where the barn-dance program that became "The Grand Ole Opry" was kicked off in 1925 by an 80-year-old fiddler called Uncle Jimmy Thompson, who said he could "fiddle the bugs off a sweet 'tater vine." He had a repertory of 1,000 tunes.

As the following of the "Opry" grew in the late Twenties and the Thirties, it became the keystone in the spread of country music. This was supplemented by the recordings made between 1927 and 1933 by Jimmie Rodgers, "the Singing Brakeman," who is now identified as "the father of country music."

He was the first big country-music star, and he influenced a generation of young country singers who later rose to stardom — among them Gene Autrey, Ernest Tubb and even two Canadian singers, Hank Snow and Wilf Carter, who was known as "Montana Slim."

Much of the appeal of country music was—and still is—the directness, the simplicity, the down-to-earth quality of its lyrics. "Reality" is the word that invariably comes up in any discussion of country-music lyrics.

Gloomy Reality

"Pop music of the Thirties and Forties always lacked a sense of reality," says Brad McCuen, president of the Country Music Foundation. "It was 'Stairway to the Stars,' 'Paradise'—that sort of thing. But country music dealt with human emotions, often the gloomy side of reality—'Seven Years With the Wrong Woman,' 'Walking the Floor Over You.'"

The dolefulness that pervades much of country music was, according to the late Frank Walker, one of the early recording men in the country field, a very natural thing.

"Life in the country, particularly in the early days, was a lonesome life," he once said. "Farmers would often talk to themselves and to the horses and stock, and the sound of the railroad train, that lonesome whistle, had a powerful emotional impact."

Country music was concentrated largely in the South-Central states until World War II when non-Southerners (and upper-class Southerners who had looked down their noses at this music) found themselves in Army barracks scattered around the South where, if they turned on the radio, country music inevitably came out. They began to develop a taste for its simple melodies and lively novelties, and they carried this interest back home with them.

During the Fifties, the relationship between country music and what had traditionally been called "popular music" became ever closer. Such popular singers as Perry Como, Jo Stafford, Eddie Fisher and Rosemary Clooney were singing country hits, while a new breed of country singers with scarcely a vestige of twang in their voices began to appear in the persons of Eddy Arnold, Jim Reeves and Jim Ed Brown.

Meanwhile, Nashville was growing into the second largest recording center in the nation and the musical side of country music was becoming more sophisticated.

"The traditional simplicity of the words and the message is still there," says Harry Jenkins, a vice president of RCA Records who is in charge of that company's country music output. "Good still prevails over evil. But the way it has become integrated with the music content has become more sophisticated and more listenable to a greater part of the listening audience."

The steady flow of blue-collar workers from Southern rural areas to Northern metropolitan centers has contributed to the geographical spread of country music.

"You find this happening in most big northern cities," Mr. McCuen declared, "but there's a particularly interesting parallel in Chicago to the blues singer there who for years have been singing Negro blues and southern Negro songs to black migrants from Mississippi."

There is only one nightclub in the city that regularly offers country music —Henry's, in the Bay Ridge section of Brooklyn. And only a single hour a week of country music is broadcast by a New York radio station—a program from 8 to 9 P.M. on WBAI on Saturdays, conducted by Bill Vernon and Frank Mare. They concentrate on bluegrass and old-time music rather than what Mr. Vernon describes as "modern country."

The influence of country music has spread to such rock groups as the Byrds, Sea Train, Poco and the Band, and the interrelationship of the two has been emphasized by recording sessions held in Nashville by such rock figures as Ringo Starr and Bob Dylan.

A Rogers Revival

That the interest in country music may soon take on deeper, more probing characteristics is indicated by a revival of interest in Jimmie Rodgers among college students, a revival that has grown to such proportions that RCA Victor is planning a 10-LP reissue series of all of Mr. Rodgers's recordings, paralleling a similar 10-record series of Bessie Smith's blues recordings now being released by Columbia.

This may also emphasize the split in the country-music audience, already suggested by the differentiation between blue-grass and old-time music on one hand and "modern country" on the other.

"There are country artists who will stay country," says Mr. McCuen, "singers who are now legends—Hank Snow, Ernest Tubb—old timers who haven't changed with the times. The people who buy their records are now in their late 40's, 50's and 60's. But there are others who are moving with the times—Ray Price or Lynn Anderson, for example—whose records are bought by people in their 20's, 30's and 40's, people who once might have put pop music down but are not so liable to do that any more."

Some Doubts

The future of country music as an industry seems to be on the upswing. But there are those who have grave doubts about the future of the music itself.

"It is altogether probable that for many years the term 'country' will be affixed to a particular form of American music," wrote Bill C. Malone in his book, "Country Music, U.S.A.," but he adds that "the designation itself will become meaningless."

"The meaning will vanish primarily because the 'country' itself is disappearing. No one will ever again sound like the performers of the early period. If one would preserve the rural musical styles, he must also preserve the culture that gave rise to them, a society characterized by cultural isolation, racism, poverty, ignorance and religious fundamentalism.

"As country music becomes a mammoth industry, it will attempt to obtain larger profits by marketing a product that a host of consumers will buy. The performers, still for the most part Southerners not far removed from rural backgrounds, will remain immersed in the characteristic American drive for respectability and success.

"In this urbanized middle-class quest there will be little room for a pure rural heritage. Every change, every modification, every surrender to the 'popular' audience, and even the destruction of country music itself, will be rationalized under the general heading of 'progress.'"

July 19, 1971

A CIVIC TROUBADOUR

By ROBERT SHELTON

NEW YORK'S nearest equivalent to a municipal troubadour, Oscar Brand, has sung more tunes in his thirteen years on WNYC than that radio station has watts. But he keeps returning to just one theme—folk music is vital and exciting and you must listen to some.

This singleness of purpose has turned Brand, the guitarist-singer who squires the half-hour "Folk Song Festival" on Sundays at 6 P. M., into one of radio's most genial fanatics. He has been willing to serve his 8,500,000 employers on the city-owned station without a penny's wages since December, 1945, all in the interest of popularizing a musical form he believes to be a healthy antidote to much of Tin Pan Alley's conjured emotion and banality.

Format

The "Folk Song Festival" is a mélange of Brand's own singing, guest interviews and performances and occasional recordings. During his tenure, Brand has played host to nearly every well-known singer in the field—Burl Ives, Harry Belafonte, Josh White, Leadbelly, Richard Dyer-Bennet, Jean Ritchie, Marais and Miranda—often before they had attained prominence.

The show, despite the capital of sophistication from which it emanates, is about as urbane as a barn dance. Scriptless and impromptu, Brand's formula is often mixed as he goes along. About one-fourth of the shows are taped so that Brand can be off on his frequent concert tours. But even when taped and edited the show carries the flavor of an unrehearsed song-swapping session, the folksiness of a cracker-barrel convocation.

On the air Brand groups music from all over the world into programs, say, of election songs, army ballads, in celebration of the French Bastille Day, the Scottish St. Andrew's Day, or around any of the myriad subjects handed down through a folk-song legacy of hundreds of years. The United States Information Service has found the show to be a representative enough segment of Americana to transcribe and rebroadcast overseas.

Recording

On a recent Wednesday evening, Brand was taping parts of two shows. His companion group for the last year, the Shanty Boys, were clustered around the tape-recorder's mike. The Shanty Boys are Roger Sprung, banjoist; Mike Cohen, guitarist, and Lionel Kilberg, who plays the Brownie bass, a hybrid born of the union of a washtub and a bass. Brand, lean and tall, wearing a bright tie that matched nothing he was wearing but his perpetual crescent-moon smile, waved his chin at the trio and all four started singing the show's theme song, "New York Girls Won't You Come Out Tonight."

When the song ended, Brand ducked into an adjoining alcove so cluttered with tapes, records, books and memorabilia it makes the Fibber McGee counterpart look like a barracks on inspection day. Brand listened to the tape and yelled out from his closet-control booth, "Fine, now let's do that old Irish ballad, 'The Bard of Armagh.'" There was a thirty-second pause while one member of the Shanty Boys took a refresher course on the lyric of the song from which the "Streets of Laredo" comes.

The next day in his Greenwich Village apartment, hunched alone over the tape recorder, Brand spliced, edited and improvised continuity to put together a show.

Brand learned to sing in Winnipeg, Man., where he was born thirty-eight years ago, by listening to player-piano rolls when he was a child. His family moved to Minnesota, and then he spent several youthful years on farms in New Jersey before attending Brooklyn College. Brand considers "Folk Song Festival" his favorite broadcasting venture, even though he's had others that paid, dating back to an early association with Norman Corwin. Brand was the music director of a "Camera 3" series, has appeared on "Today" and is writing and directing his forty-fifth documentary film for Evinrude Motors.

Opinion

"Folk Song Festival" is regarded by most of the old hands in the folk field as an institution, with all the blessings and shortcomings such a status earns. While some feel the programing is sketchy and haphazard, others stress that the show has filled a void and has served a valuable function as the city's oldest continuing program to be devoted solely to folk music.

Speaking loudly for the affirmative was Seymour N. Siegel, WNYC's chief, who congratulated Brand on the show's thirteenth birthday show Dec. 7. "Folk songs go further than entertainment," he said. "They help stimulate inter-group understanding." To do his tuneful bit to show New Yorkers from many backgrounds how similar are their varying traditions is a labor of love for Oscar Brand. He looks forward to what he hopes will be his next thirteen years on the municipal radio station.

February 1, 1959

FROM THE BITTER END

Bikel Broadcasts Taped On Bleecker Street

By JOAN BARTHEL

EVEN for Greenwich Village, where the colorful is commonplace, Bleecker Street is exceptional. In 1954 Gian-Carlo Menotti chose the sounds of that street as the basis for an opera score. If he had waited a while, he could have blended another Bleecker Street element into his music — the sound of a radio program originating from a coffee house.

The coffee house is The Bitter End, an establishment so far out that the customer who orders espresso is considered square. (The menu says so.)

The radio program is a medley of folk music, poetry reading and casual commentary conducted by Theodore Bikel, a man of many talents and no pretensions. Although he lately has been a Broadway leading man and consistently portrays principal television and motion picture roles, he is still at ease on Bleecker Street, and the coffee house crowd, not always receptive to such conspicuous success, accepts him so wholeheartedly as leader that he is able to call his program "Theodore Bikel at Home."

On a recent Sunday evening when the program was scheduled to be taped, The Bitter End was jammed with patrons assorted enough to make a sociologist's head spin. There were girls in black tights and shaggy sweaters, others in expensive little knit dresses. Bearded young men shared tables with uptown types in suits and ties. Shortly after 11 P. M. Mr. Bikel stepped onto the tiny stage.

Start

"Good evening," he said. "This is Theodore Bikel at Home. Where we are at the moment is called The Bitter End, a haven for people who like folk music."

A murmured comment came from the side of the stage where a technician presided over taping equipment, and he turned toward the voice. "What do you mean, are we on the air?" he demanded. "Don't ask me; *you're* the producer."

The audience laughed appreciatively, but became suddenly silent when he put his foot on the rung of a battered wooden stool and strummed his guitar. His first song was in Russian, one of twenty languages in his repertoire (Zulu is another).

If the atmosphere earlier had been casual, it soon became downright folksy. Mr. Bikel took off his coat, loosened his tie and introduced the Tarriers, a folk-music quartet. Two of them are Negroes, and they preceded their first song with a satirical introduction.

"The four of us were driving through Arkansas, about ten miles south of Little Rock. We were driving *fast*. It was a balmy summer evening; the air was heavy with the scent of magnolia . . . honeysuckle . . . tar and feathers. . . ." The Tarriers sang several numbers, including one billed as "an aria from Handel's 'Messiah' as orchestrated for banjo."

The roof-raising high point of the program came when all present joined in "a love song to the United States of America."

"This land is your land, this land is my land/From California to the New York island. From the redwood forests to the Gulfstream waters/This land was made for you and me."*

As the final notes died away, Mr. Bikel stepped forward and said softly that he would say a few words about freedom. He mentioned regretfully that "sometimes loyalty is believed to be demonstrable by signature only," an oblique reference to some folk-singing colleagues involved in a highly publicized loyalty oath controversy.

"To them," he said, "and to all the audience: Don't succumb to the false values that will use the word 'freedom' in order to rob you of it. Good night. This is Theodore Bikel at Home."

After a ten-minute intermission "to clear out the smoke," a second program was recorded. Usually two or three tapes are made during one Sunday night session, for Mr. Bikel's work takes him out of town so often that weekly tapings are impossible. (Sometimes on a trip he tapes the program in other cities.) Dates of tapings at The Bitter End do not follow any regular schedule, but prior announcement usually appears in The Village Voice, and somehow the word gets around among the cognoscenti.

At the end of the evening, Fred Weintraub, who owns the place, called out good nights as the customers poured into Bleecker Street. The young proprietor's enthusiasm for his work is immense, perhaps because he reached The Bitter End last year by way of Scarsdale and Madison Avenue; he speaks of his trading an advertising agency for a coffee house in the relieved tones of a prodigal who has at last gone straight.

A taping session at The Bitter End is not a spectator sport, and unadventurous souls can hear "Theodore Bikel at Home" each Tuesday at 10:45 P. M. on WBAI-FM. But those who hear it only on the radio are missing half the fun.

*Words and music by Woody Guthrie; copyright 1956 Ludlow Music, Inc.; used by permission.

May 20, 1962

JOAN BAEZ SINGS AT FOREST HILLS

14,700 Hear Her and Bob Dylan in Folk Concert

Joan Baez unwrapped several surprises Saturday night for a capacity audience of 14,700 at the Forest Hills Music Festival at the Tennis Stadium in Queens.

With dignified modesty the soprano folk singer devoted more than half of her program to new songs by Bob Dylan, sung either by herself or by the young minstrel-poet in an unannounced appearance.

"Bobby Dylan says what a lot of people my age feel, but cannot say," Miss Baez declared.

Her enthusiasm was contagious. The audience was as reluctant to let him leave as it was to let Miss Baez go.

She has never seemed quite so relaxed and warm in a performance. She used the occasion to taunt the television show "Hootenanny" for what it uses and for whom it excludes. To heated applause, she said: "I will appear on that program if they will let Pete Seeger on that program."

Musically and vocally, Miss Baez gave the sort of impeccable concert her listeners have come to expect. Her ability to probe beneath the surface of traditional material and extract meaning was masterful.

In addition to many of her recorded favorites, there were songs new to her repertory. Her unaccompanied "Black Girl," her free-form spiritual "A City Called Heaven" and her defiant "Oh, Freedom" were done with such depth that these familiar songs seemed as if they had not been fully understood before.

As for Mr. Dylan's songs, Miss Baez first offered "With God on My Side," a scorching antiwar statement, and "That's All Right," a lilting, but sardonic, love song.

Mr. Dylan took the stage alone for "Only a Pawn in Their Game," a musically inventive explanation of how white Southerners are also victimized by segregation. His long, symbolic "A Hard Rain's a'Gonna Fall," which many regard as a masterpiece, won tumultuous applause.

Together the two singers, who have joined forces a half-dozen times since last month's Newport Folk Festival, sang Mr. Dylan's "Blowin' in the Wind," the comic "Troubled" and the lyric "Fare Thee Well."

Miss Baez's ability to hold and move an audience by herself is widely known. To have her so closely align herself with Mr. Dylan's charismatic poetry resulted in an unforgettable evening.

ROBERT SHELTON.

August 19, 1963

Peter, Paul and Mary Fill Carnegie

The folk-song concert season, which, within recent memory, used to begin in some drafty loft behind a union hall off Fourth Avenue, began last night, as it has for the last several years since the folk revival has been enjoying its moments of elegance, status and attendance, at Carnegie Hall.

Peter, Paul and Mary were the performers. The hall was filled to the rafters.

The trio stands at the very top of its profession, as regards audience acceptance, record sales and being generally regarded as pace-setters, trend-makers, hit-producers and all that.

What was surprising about this concert is that while many another pop-folk group has droned its way out of popularity by remaining static and formula-trapped, Peter, Paul and Mary remain definitely in motion.

Some of that motion is regressive while some decidedly takes them forward. The regression is a serious set of concessions to the Beatles-Animals-Rolling Stones-Dave Clark syndrome of rock 'n' roll.

These concessions were subtle. The group's able and facile musical director, Milt Okun, may have suggested only minuscule changes, but somehow every gospel song—from "Come and Go With Me" to "Jesus Met the Woman"—seemed to lurch with added syncopation, relentlessly pounded the beat, triggered the tempo and generally tried, subtly, of course, to whip up the kiddies with effects similar to those the Beatles and their imitators use.

So much for the negative. There were many surprises on the plus side. Mary Travers sang with considerably greater control and nuance than she showed at the trio's Carnegie Hall concert a year ago. Her solo on "The Water Was Wide," in a finely placed, confortable range, was one of the evening's most touching believable moments.

The concerted work on the Ewan McColl-Peggy Seeger topical song, "Springhill Mine," was nothing short of a triumph. Beginning with an unaccompanied madrigal-like introduction, the ballad built in tension and suspense, and frankly imbued the song with more sense of epic drama than one had ever believed it contained.

This moment of artistry almost redeemed the trio's murder of the once-simple, once-tender "The Cuckoo," a crime that ought to be reported to the Society for Prevention of Cruelty to Animals.

So it went. A trio in motion, not with consistency, but unlike dozens of other folk groups that have frittered away their staying power with a formula. As long as Peter, Paul and Mary keep moving, even if not always forward, they'll be worth paying attention to.

ROBERT SHELTON.

September 19, 1964

Pop Singers and Song Writers Racing Down Bob Dylan's Road

Musician's 'Sound' Inspires a Variety of Entertainers in 'Folk Rock' Idiom

By ROBERT SHELTON

If imitation is the sincerest form of flattery, then Bob Dylan must be one of the most flattered performers in American popular music today.

The singer and song-writer, who will appear tomorrow night at the Forest Hills Music Festival in Queens, has fostered a trend that music circles call "the Dylan sound."

At least three groups and one individual who consciously style their singing after Mr. Dylan are listed high on popularity charts of recordings. Sonny and Cher, the Byrds, the Turtles and Donovan all have a strong Dylanesque quality in their recordings.

Many others, from the Beatles to Johnny Cash to the song-writing team of Barry Mann and Cynthia Weil, have publicly acknowledged their debt to Mr. Dylan. And John Lennon has even recorded a song in the Dylan mode.

In a telephone interview, Mr. Dylan, the often enigmatic folk performer, parried questions about his new imitators and the controversy over his fusion of folk music with rock 'n' roll, called "folk rock."

Bob Dylan

'Missing Something'

"It's all music; no more, no less," the 24-year-old musician from Hibbing, Minn., said. "I know in my own mind what I'm doing. If anyone has imagination, he'll know what I'm doing. If they can't understand my songs they're missing something. If they can't understand green clocks, wet chairs, purple lamps or hostile statues, they're missings something, too."

Many pop-music insiders regard Mr. Dylan as the most influential American performer to emerge since the rise of Elvis Presley 10 years ago. Some think he is on the brink of superstardom.

Mr. Dylan is a wiry, sharp-featured, sunken-eyed youth who affects a somewhat bizarre image. His hair has grown so long since he became interested in "folk rock" that the Beatles look clean-cut by comparison. After leaving Hibbing, he studied briefly at the University of Minnesota but flunked out of the science class, he says, "for refusing to watch a rabbit die."

He went on the road, playing at a carnival and elsewhere, until he got off the subway in Greenwich Village in the spring of 1961.

Since Mr. Dylan was discovered at Gerde's Folk City in September of that year, he has evolved through several composing and performing approaches. Each time he has changed he has brought an increasingly larger segment of the pop and folk music world with him.

The tousle-haired musician, who has written more than 100 songs, expressed a driving need to create and perform new material. "I get very bored with my old songs," he said. "I can't sing 'With God on My Side' for 15 years. What I write is much more concise now than before. It's not deceiving."

When Mr. Dylan first appeared in New York he was strongly under the influence of Woody Guthrie, the Oklahoma ballad-maker. By the spring of 1963, with the popularity of his antidiscrimination protest, "Blowin' in the Wind," he became nationally known. His "Times They Are a' Changin' " was considered a credo for the discontented protesting collegians, for whom he became a spokesman.

Personal Expression

About a year ago he veered toward more personal expression with "Mr. Tambourine Man," a current hit. Last spring he introduced "folk rock" with "Subterranean Homesick Blues" and the currently popular "Like a Rolling Stone."

Some of Mr. Dylan's lyrics are obviously "camp" fantasies, while others are poetically profound. Many are sufficiently elliptical to spur squadrons of interpreters.

Mr. Dylan refused to explain this avant-garde direction. "I have no idea what I'll be doing at Forest Hills Saturday," he said. "I'll have some electricity [electrically amplified instruments] and a new song or a couple of three or four new songs. Time goes by very fast up there onstage. I think of what not to do rather than what to do."

August 27, 1965

Judy Collins: 'Life Is Groovy, Not War and Hypocrisy'

By JOAN BARTHEL

"INSIGHT" is both the wrong and the right word to use. Wrong because it is an umbrella word that can be stretched to cover feelings and responses as well as thoughts and meanings, right because it is the word that lingers, both in Judy Collins's conversation and in the course of an outsider's attempt to understand, illuminate and convey. Inevitably, however, one man's—or woman's—insight is another's question.

Although Judy Collins, who is appearing this week at the Newport Festival and gives a concert on July 21 at Central Park's Wollman Skating Rink, plays the guitar, wears sandals and has long, straight hair, she is not a folk singer. "A very bad label. I'm a contemporary singer, period." She is a member of the group centered loosely on tax rebel and radical headmistress, Joan Baez, at the latter's school (the Institute for the Study of Nonviolence) in Big Sur, but she is also a favorite of such a blue-ribbon-respectable as the director of the Metropolitan Museum, Thomas Hoving. She is familiar to the solid Nielsenites who watch "The Smothers Brothers" and to the beads-and-bell-wearers at the springtime be-in in Central Park. She is pro-LSD (two trips of her own) and anti-war.

In her belief that music is not an end but a means to communication, Judy Collins is a part of what might as well be called the new music. Stripped of pretentious explanation and painfully clever phrases, the new music is personal and communicative, what happened "when rock 'n' roll and folk music—exemplified by the Beatles and Bob Dylan — began to cross streams. But I don't know what kind of definition is possible, or even necessary. The Monterey Festival had all kinds of music, mostly electric, but they also had Ravi Shankar, and how do you fit him in? One of the influences on the new music is the Eastern idea of accepting your life, accepting change; if you can do this, you can be happy.

"The music is an expression of what's happening now. There's so much more understanding than there was a generation ago in this country. The be-in here was just overwhelming; a completely beautiful, open experience, so friendly and so warm. At Monterey, the cops all had flowers on their motorcycles and the police chief was so pleased with everything that he wore a wig to work Monday morning. There's just no other answer than to love and to get together and to be open; there's just no other choice, and part of this is being reflected in the music."

*

The talk and the outlook is clearly hippy, and although her breezy, spacious apartment (3 baths) on West 79th Street is something other than the crammed communal quarters of Haight-Ashbury, a similarly casual disregard for slick-magazine standards for middle-class neatness is reflected in the living room jumble of limp curtains, overflowing ash trays, withered flowers, no-longer-edible fruit, and a fat candle stub solidified in a waxen purple puddle. Moving around the room with a long-legged stride, she gathered up one of her cats, Presbyterian Jam ("sensuous, but with built-in standards"), curled up in a leather sling chair and talked about music, which meant talking about what's happening.

"The flower people and the new music and people like Martin Luther King and Staughton Lynd are all intricately woven together by their coincidence in the same generation. These are all parts of the same puzzle, and the puzzle is an answer to the double standard. People are concerned and disturbed over what Martin Luther King has said, but what he said is, 'I will not accept a double standard in my life; I will not accept that it is wrong to kill in the civil rights movement and all right to kill on another level.' It is no longer possible for young people to say, 'I'll go talk about love, and sing, and I'll also go fight,' and I think that within the next few years, there will be an attempt to get things straighter, to get things a lot clearer about personal integrity and personal decisions. You start with one person being able to think something through and trying to figure out where he stands.

"There's so much mass everything today — mass propaganda, mass communications—that a kid of 18 is in a terrible spot when he gets out of high school and has to decide maybe whether he'll go into the Marines or the Navy. What does he know? Who is he? What can he possibly think that will have any real bearing on the kind of training he'll be put through? A delicate, changing mind subjected to that kind of thing doesn't have a big chance unless he's lucky enough to go to Joan's school, or unless the hippies get to him first.

"The hippies and the young followers of the music are the ones who are extending themselves into more understanding, because they understand that personal isolation is not the answer, and that it's life that is groovy, not killing and war and hypocrisy and the double standard. And acid is tremendously important to all this. It's becoming too available as far as I'm concerned, because not enough is known about it, but it has everything to do with the way people are thinking because it makes so clear the ridiculous, aimless, time-wasting nonsense people go through in this society. It might be just as time-wasting to sit around and dig the sun and sand, but at least it's not as destructive as going across the ocean to destroy a buddy. I think LSD has great potential for saving the world."

She carried the antiwar message across the Pacific two months ago, when she went with Woody Guthrie's son Arlo and Joan Baez's sister, dancer Mimi Farina, on a concert tour of Japan, where Baez had had translation troubles. "We got someone we knew to do our press conferences and radio and TV appearances, because Arlo is a conscientious objector. We didn't find hostility, and it wasn't so much shock at Arlo's long hair and our involvement in social change, as a great curiosity. Everybody wants to know. Among students the desire for peace was greatest, but then, that's natural.

*

"Every place I go I talk to kids to see what they're doing and what they're thinking about, and I would say that in this country 70 per cent of the college students are apathetic and depressed about their lives, because they feel it won't make any difference what they say. But there are some places that swing, like Austin, Texas — amazing Austin—where there was a be-in around the tower where the man shot all those people, and 4,000 students expressed themselves in colored chalk on the sidewalk. And Duke University has a very active bunch of kids. The lefties and the righties all work together; they overthrew the student government, and they're involved in organizing the textile mill workers. They have short, clipped hair — no longhaired ones—and they're a bunch of the most completely straight people you'd ever want to meet." A wide smile. "You can't even tell who the hippies are anymore."

*

The light touch, and a non-handwringing posture over many admittedly handwringing situations, both in her own background and in the world she sees around her, seem to differentiate Collins from other musical dissenters. "I don't think protest music, as such, has a place anymore, because it has the sense of lecture instead of the sense of life." She brushes aside a magazine's linking one of her album titles, "A Maid of Constant Sorrow," to her own life because of her father's blindness, her bouts of polio and tubercular pleurisy, her divorce four years ago and the subsequent loss of her son in a custody fight, with a minimizing "Everybody has problems."

What Collins wants to say seems to be, at the close of conversation, both inconclusive and unsettling.

Inconclusive because it is rambling and obscure. "I'd like everybody to try to save the trees and the grass and everything; conservation is very important. You may well ask what I am doing in New York City. I have no idea. I travel a lot." Later, "I'm not in analysis at this point because I'm unhappy. I'm there because I'm there."

Bob Greene

Judy Collins sings of the "contemporary" scene
"You can't tell who the hippies are anymore"

BLESS UNCLE SPIKE AND AUNTIE SALLY... AND BLESS "DADDY"... AND ALL OUR MEN OUT THERE....

... WHOSE COURAGE MAKES IT POSSIBLE FOR MILLIONS O' US KIDS TO GROW UP HERE IN DECENCY AND PEACE...

CHRISTMAS EVE! BACK HOME, SHE'LL BE SAYING HER PRAYERS...

FROM HEROD TO HITLER AND HIROHITO! BUT THE PRAYERS OF THE LITTLE ANNIES ARE GREATER THAN ALL THE HERODS OF ALL TIME!

CHAPTER 7

The Funny Papers

"Little Orphan Annie"

"Comic Sections" Condemned.

To the Editor of The New York Times:

After reading the striking article in today's TIMES—"The Sargasso Sea of Passions"—which contains much food for thought, I sat turning it over in my mind. I suddenly remembered what I had seen in the small store where I bought the paper—great armloads of "Comic Sections"; gayly colored pictures full of vulgarity, even indecency, waiting for the eyes of the children and the youths of today.

I had a strong desire to voice a protest against this poisoning of the mind of childhood and adolescence. What can be expected of a boy or girl brought up on a diet of "Comic Sections"? Is not this the source of that great Sargasso Sea of criminal mementos which the writer in THE TIMES so feelingly portrays? I am the mother of a boy of 16, and I am firmly of the opinion that until this flood of indecent trash is stopped—prohibited by law, if necessary—all efforts to inculcate reverence, nobility of soul and a taste for good literature are absolutely useless. Parents should refuse to purchase papers pandering to this depraved taste. This matter is fully as important as is the drug habit. Here is the fountain-head of that frivolity, that utter lack of serious purpose, which is deplored on every hand.

FLORENCE VAN CLEVE.

New York, Dec. 9, 1923.

December 13, 1923

Against the "Comic Section."

To the Editor of The New York Times:

Allow me as an Argentine editor to compliment you upon the insertion of the letter of Mrs. Florence Van Clev in respect of the use (and I would add abuse) of the so-called comic sections of the majority of the newspapers of this country.

Unfortunately, this kind of "feature" work is ever increasing in volume as also in inanity, and in some of the "manufactured" newspapers I have been able to see as many as ten distinct sets of drawings in which the theme is invariably the disparagement of man by his daughters and wives, conveying to the mind of the readers that the head of the family, and the backbone of the nation, is a subject fit only to be ridiculed. Daughters mocking their fathers and wives chastising their better halves hardly uphold the idea of family authority, without which family life surely perishes. Nothing sinks deeper into the simple mind than the repetition of these scenes dished up in a manner suited to their low mentality.

Surely, the press organization of the United States of America, headed by men of brains, should see that, following the material greatness conquered by the country, evolution must bring about a spiritual predominance equal in power, which is being killed in the bud by just such foolish, inane and at times immoral sections as the "feature" service, which should be labeled "For illiterates only."

ALEJANDRO HOCH.

New York, Dec. 13, 1923

December 21, 1923

A CREATOR OF PUBLIC TASTE.

The free-silver campaign was just dawning, and the "mauve decade" was in its final lustrum when RICHARD F. OUTCAULT, an illustrator in The World office, made an adventure in comic drawing which began an epoch that seems far from ending thirty-three years thereafter. He fashioned what we now know as a "comic strip," though its humor was contained in one rectangle, and the title was "Hogan's Alley." In this imaginary purlieu an ancestor of FONTAINE FOX'S "Mickey McGuire" tossed dead cats and brickbats about, and later—in The New York Journal—this terrible infant became "The Yellow Kid." The light literature, song and drama of America, and the talk of children, felt that influence for ten years.

"The Yellow Kid" had his own rough day, and then from Mr. OUTCAULT'S brush a better-born descendant came, the immortal "Buster Brown." With his dog, "Tige," namesake of a million pets of American boys for a generation, he was an entertaining feature of The New York Herald and had a popularity not before known in the world of comic art. He did not live in an alley, as did the Yellow Kid; he played his pranks amid gentle surroundings to the consternation of his pretty mother and the delight of countless surreptitious imitators throughout the United States. Clothes were named for him; children were proudly called "Buster"; indeed, one yet survives on the motion picture screen. Almost until the great war came to Europe, and comedy became adult and grim, to be succeeded by the definite "wise-cracking" variety, "Buster Brown" and "Tige" were the favorite Sunday reading in many American homes.

They died before their creator did, but the journalistic enterprise they and their gamin predecessor instituted has become one of the leading outputs of American newspaper workers. Syndicates have spread these characters for simultaneous publication all over the country, and even in some parts of Europe they are to be seen with strange languages ballooning from their mouths. To few men has there been vouchsafed the inventive genius to father an enduring public taste.

September 27, 1928

Rudolph Dirks Created Katzenjammer Kids

Rudolph Dirks with his cartoon characters

Mr. Dirks in early 1950's

Young Cartoonist Invented Bad Boys in 1897—Was Also a Painter in Oil

Rudolph Dirks, the cartoonist who originated the "Katzenjammer Kids" comic strip, died Saturday night at his home at 257 West 86th Street. His age was 91.

Mr. Dirks created the mischievous Katzenjammer brothers, Hans and Fritz, in 1897, when he was 20 years old, at the suggestion of an editor for the Hearst papers. He had kept up their antics ever since—continuing through two World Wars and several revolutions in public taste.

"In an age that regards delinquents as more sinned against than sinning, Dirks's mixed-up kids have never been better understood," Time magazine said some time ago. "Child psychologists and teachers these days deplore their influence; children love them."

Bad Boys Are Ageless

Although they never grow up, the impish roly-poly boys with jug ears and bristling hair are considered to be the oldest inhabitants of United States comic pages.

When Mr. Dirks moved from the Hearst to the Pulitzer papers in 1912, the strip had to be renamed, because the Hearst organization won title to the name "Katzenjammer Kids."

For 15 years Mr. Dirks collaborated with his son, John, who said yesterday he would carry on the comic strip. It is syndicated by United Features to about 100 papers, including The New York Knickerbocker.

Mr. Dirks was a tall, gray-haired man who resembled Carl Sandburg. He was born in Heide, Germany, on Feb. 26, 1877, the son of John Henry and Margaret Buenz Dirks. At the age of 7 he went with his family to Chicago. His father was a wood carver.

Spanish War Veteran

Entirely self-taught, Rudolph Dirks did some commercial art in his teens and at 17 came to New York and sold cartoons to Judge and the old Life magazine. He served as a corporal in the Spanish-American War.

Hans and Fritz arose out of the circulation war between Joseph Pulitzer and William Randolph Hearst. In 1896 Mr. Pulitzer's New York Sunday World started a colored cartoon, whose star, a slangy infant in a yellow nightgown, won fame as "The Yellow Kid." He was promptly snatched by Mr. Hearst for The Sunday Journal's eight-page color supplement.

A year later The Journal got Mr. Dirks to model a cartoon after the "Max and Moritz" drawings of Wilhelm Busch, the noted German cartoonist.

Mr. Dirks pioneered in developing a plot with a series of consecutive panels and enclosing all his dialogue in balloons. His diabolical Kids, named Katzenjammer (German slang for hangover) caught on and soon gathered their supporting cast: the sorely tried Mama; Der Inspector, a white-bearded truant officer, and Der Captain, a seafaring martinet, Mama's star boarder and the chief victim of the kids' pranks.

When Mr. Dirks took his diabolical duo to The World he called them "Hans and Fritz." Because of the anti-German sentiment in World War I, he changed the name to "the Captain and the Kids."

Son His Chief Assistant

In recent years Mr. Dirks let his son, John, do most of the work on the comic strip and spent much of his time painting landscapes and marines in oils. He had been a member of the Ash Can School of artists early in the century and more recently painted in post-impressionist style.

With Walt Kuhn, Yasuo Kuniyoshi and others, he helped form the artists' colony in Ogunquit, Me., in the nineteen-twenties. He gave a one-man show at the age of 89 at the Ogunquit Art Association.

Surviving are his widow, the former Helen Marie Walsh; his son, John, who, besides working on the cartoon, sculptures metal fountains, a daughter, Barbara Dirks of San Francisco, who is Western head of the Experiment in International Living, and a sister, Mrs. Labert St. Clair of Washington.

A private funeral service was held yesterday.

April 22, 1968

ANDY GUMP FINDS IT EASY STEP FROM CARTOON STRIP TO RADIO

LOOKING through the roster of families listed on radio program schedules, the Gumps come familiarly to view. And a turn of the radio dial will bring the voice of Andy Gump calling "Oh, Min!" But before Andy and his Min and little Chester had a radio audition it was Himan Brown who paved the way for the Gumps' venture into the broadcasting milieu.

The family created by Sidney Smith for the cartoon strip had been living in rebus for many a long year before Mr. Brown came along with his flair for radio drama. Mr. Brown, being in a sense like a reporter with a nose for news, sees in family life of any sort a potential subject for the air waves. It was while musing over the cartoon strip one day that he pictured Andy yelling his "Oh, Min!" through the microphone. No sooner had this thought occurred than he made a trip to Chicago to get in touch with Mr. Smith.

The Gumps Were Willing.

Yes, it was all right, said the cartoonist; Mr. Brown could go ahead with his idea. Nor had the Gumps, themselves, any objections. They soon found themselves inside of a studio at WABC. But it was not so easy as all that. For Mr. Smith, who had given them life by virtue of India ink and his skill, had also given Andy a sawed-off chin. And here is what Mr. Brown was up against.

"The most important thing in radio sketches is the casting," said Mr. Brown. "Those acting the principals must not only be able to represent true characterizations of their parts but must also 'look' their parts. By that I mean their manner of speech must enable the listener to 'see' almost exactly what the characters look like, for that is necessary in radio, since the listeners cannot view them in person.

The Chin Was a Problem.

"Now with the Gumps, the actor taking the part of Andy had not only to typify the boisterous and braggart husband but had also to give the unseen audience some conception of the cartoon-strip—Andy with a sawed-off chin. Strangely enough, I had no difficulty in casting such a person. Nor had I any difficulty in casting Min, an amiable and indulgent woman; Chester, an average American boy, or Tilda, the maid."

Soon the Gumps were ready to go ahead with their family intimacies and tribulations. The ideas that form the basis of their broadcast are almost wholly divorced from those making up the cartoon-strip. And where the strip takes about four or five square little blocks to tell a story, the radio script takes about twelve typewritten pages. Nor has Sidney Smith anything at all to do with the writing of the broadcast; this is done by men responsible to Mr. Brown, who directs and otherwise supervises the program, as well as several other dramatic serials current on the air.

For a cross-section view of family life, wherein the American scene is painted with all the varied colors that go to make up that elusive thing called human nature, the radio offers perhaps the greatest medium, according to Mr. Brown, who has been writing and directing programs for the past seven years. There is no personality, no incident or emotional circumstance that doesn't find itself mirrored in one of the many families that live on the air waves, he said.

When Family Life Differs.

But family life as it is commonly known and family life as it is lived on the air have many things that are not in common.

"In family programs," Mr. Brown pointed out, "radio has found a wide field for the development of the drama. It is a type of drama that has found much favor with the public in the past few years because of its varied appeal; for, within the scope of the family life that is depicted, matter that might interest adults as well as juveniles can be found. Furthermore, it is a brand of drama that, because of the fact that it goes into a great many homes, must be kept morally clean." And to illustrate this point Mr. Brown tells of the time the word "lynch" had to be blue-penciled to read "hang."

January 6, 1935

Fontaine Fox, Cartoonist, Creator of 'Toonerville Trolley'

His Rickety Car Rolled on for 40 Years Through More Than 200 Newspapers

GREENWICH, Conn. Aug. 9

As the creator of "Toonerville Folks," Fontaine Fox added a host of characters to the American pictorial and fictional legend. In his Toonerville Trolley, he brought immortality to the otherwise dying tradition of a personalized public-conveyance service.

His cartoons appeared in the form a square panel, the figures in which have been described as having local character while being still true everywhere.

The children Mr. Fox drew were given children's words to speak, and, while not from the farms, they were not urban either. They lived in some kind of commuting circle, where an occasional train or trolley made a creaking visit.

The cartoons, it has been said, made it appear that the reader was looking down on the characters from a three-story window. Mr. Fox's figures were small, and he used a lot of them.

The Toonerville Trolley

Among the characters he made famous were the trolley Skipper, the Terrible Tempered Mr. Bang, Aunt Eppie Hogg, the Powerful Katrinka, Suitcase Simpson and the Toonerville Cop. And, of course, there was Mickey (Himself) McGuire, terror of the Scorpions' Club, who added to his fame in the movies.

Another Mickey McGuire

Mickey McGuire became so well-known as a little tough guy that a child actor named Joe Yule Jr. changed his name to Mickey McGuire when he began in Hollywood. He abandoned the name, however, and became Mickey Rooney after Mr. Fox proved in court that he owned a copyright on the character.

So realistic was his creation of the rickety trolley line that two communities — Louisville, Ky., and Pelham Manor, N. Y.—laid claim to its origin. Actually both were correct.

In his home town of Louisville, Mr. Fox rode the Brook Street line—then establishing a reputation for lackadaisical service. He lampooned it in cartoons for The Louisville Herald. Some years later, he visited a friend in Pelham Manor.

The accommodating Pelham Manor trolley motorman, seeing that Mr. Fox was a stranger, stopped his trolley to show him the friend's house. Mr. Fox then hit upon his idea for the Toonerville Trolley, incorporating the best—and worst—characteristics of the two ramshackle lines.

Associated Press

Fontaine Fox as he appeared on a golf course in 1955.

Most of the inhabitants of Toonerville, however, were born in his home town. In the Terrible Tempered Mr. Bang, Mr. Fox said, Louisville friends recognized his father. He added that the Powerful Katrinka was a combination of two of his family's cooks, one immensely strong and the other immensely stupid.

Mickey (Himself) McGuire was a very real personality in Mr. Fox's boyhood days, he declared. The Little Scorpions were his own bunch, while Mickey's gang came from across the railroad tracks.

Fontaine Talbot Fox Jr. was the son of Fontaine and Mary Pitkin Fox. Upon graduation from high school, he worked briefly as a reporter for The Herald and then attended Indiana University.

While there, he was also supposed to provide the newspaper with a cartoon a day for $12 a week. This caused a certain amount of indifference to his studies.

Then he discovered he also had to stay up and put the cartoons on a train that left for Louisville at 1:10 A.M. This was because the cartoons were too large to put into first-class mail boxes, and he said that he did not dare to leave them on top of mail boxes because the local youngsters did not have the proper awe of the United States mails.

This exacting schedule of cartoons and studies and the financial burden that his schooling was to his family led him to drop out after two years.

In 1906, Mr. Fox returned to The Herald as a cartoonist for two years and then switched to The Louisville Times. From 1910 to 1915, he drew cartoons about boys for The Chicago Post.

When his work attracted the attention of the Wheeler Syndicate in New York, Mr. Fox began creating his Toonerville characters. From 1920 to 1955 his cartoons were alternately distributed by the McNaught and Bell Syndicates.

Residents of Westchester County formed a strong sentimental attachment to the Toonerville Trolley. When its Pelham Manor prototype was replaced by a bus in 1937, 1,000 persons describing themselves as pallbearers turned out to watch its last run. The same incident occurred in 1950 when the extension line into New Rochelle was replaced.

Trolley Into Bus

Mr. Fox drew his final panel in February, 1955. Two years before that, with trolleys vanishing from the American scene, Mr. Fox drew his rickety trolley shattered in a wrenching accident. He then showed the parts salvaged for a new Toonerville Bus.

But three months before he retired, he put the trolley back on the tracks, ready for its final trip. It was said that Mr. Fox had earned about $2 million from his cartoons.

Mr. Fox was the author of several books, including "Fontaine Fox's Funny Folks," "Fontaine Fox's Cartoons" and "The Toonerville Trolley." He also wrote a series of humorous articles on his escape from the European war zone in 1939 for The New York Sun, in which his cartoons appeared for many years.

In World War II, he was a member of the Division of Pictorial Publicity.

Mr. Fox was a member of the New York Coffee House, The Players, West Side Tennis Club, Blind Brook and North Hempstead Golf Clubs, the Authors League of America and the Society of Illustrators.

An accomplished golfer, Mr. Fox frequently placed well in the winter championship of the Artists and Writers Golf Association. He won the title in 1934.

August 10, 1964

Harold Gray, Creator in 1924 Of 'Little Orphan Annie'

Comic-Strip Artist Depicted Wide-Eyed, Ageless Child in Violent Situations

Special to The New York Times

LA JOLLA, Calif., May 9 — For almost 44 years Harold Lincoln Gray's "Little Orphan Annie" was compulsive fare for millions of newspaper readers. Annie, 12 or 13 years old, with heavy legs and with eyes drawn merely as large circles, was one of the best-known characters in popular folk culture.

She was engaged in enough villainy to have matured any flesh-and-blood child, she never aged; nor did she lose her courage and determination and the simplistic moral values with which her creator had endowed her.

Annie's frequent co-protagonist was Daddy Warbucks, a bald multibillionaire and political conservative who had some mysterious helpers, Asp, who wore a tuxedo, and Punjab, who was identified by his turban.

They always came to Annie's rescue or to Daddy Warbucks's in moments of direst peril. Annie herself was invariably accompanied by her dog, Sandy, whose contribution to the multiple homicides and recurring violence of the comic strip was "Arf!" and sometimes "Arf! Arf!"

"Little Orphan Annie" made its bow in The New York Daily News Aug. 5, 1924, and it first appeared in color, in The Sunday News the following Nov. 2. The lost child (she never did find her parents), with forever-blond hair and the same red dress, was the joint idea of Mr. Gray and the late Joseph Medill Patterson, editor of The News.

Mr. Gray was working on The Chicago Tribune, helping Sidney Smith draw "The Gumps." Mr. Patterson wanted a new strip for his fledgling morning tabloid.

"Make it for grownup people, not for kids," he urged Mr. Gray. "Kids don't buy papers. Their parents do."

Mr. Gray found the model for Annie in a Chicago street urchin, who was wise beyond her innocent years. "I talked to this little kid, and liked her right away," he recalled a few years ago. "She had commonsense, knew how to take care of herself. She had to. Her name was Annie.

"At the time some 40 strips were using boys as the main characters; only three were using girls. I chose Annie for mine, and made her an orphan so she'd have no family, no tangling alliances, but freedom to go where she pleased."

Ogled the Swells

In the initial years Annie was a pathetic child with a black shawl, who often pressed her nose against a windowpane and ogled the life of the swells indoors. In addition to the faithful Sandy, Annie had a doll named Emily Marie, to whom she confided her miseries.

More grim than comic, "Little Orphan Annie" took on a detectable conservative coloration in the nineteen-thirties, and also went in heavily for violence.

Once described as "a Republican to his toenails," Mr. Gray contrived episodes in which he made clear his diehard opposition to gasoline rationing, income taxes, the welfare state, Madison Avenue, his version of Communism and "left-wingers"

Little Orphan Annie and Sandy, he of the "Arf!"

Harold Gray, creator of "Little Orphan Annie."

—an epithet he habitually applied to all Democrats.

"God deliver me from a reformer," Mr. Gray told an interviewer in 1951. "I dislike preaching, and missionaries of any kind. I don't mean religious missionaries exclusively. They are bad enough. Worse, in my opinion, are communistic evangelists, or evangelists of democracy, or the capitalistic system."

Episode Evoked Protests

The adventures of Annie and her companions dismayed some newspaper editors. An episode in 1956 that seemed to glorify hoodlumism evoked so many protests that 30 papers suspended the strip, and there were other suspensions from time to time.

Defending the high crime rate in "Little Orphan Annie" Mr. Gray said four years ago:

"Sweetness and light—who the hell wants it? What's news in the newspaper? Murder, rape and arson. That's what stories are made of.

"Annie is tougher than hell, with a heart of gold and a fast left, who can take care of herself because she has to. She's controversial, there's no question about that. But I keep her on the side of motherhood, honesty and decency."

For her part, Annie kept Mr. Gray in opulent circumstances, earning him more than $5-million. He often said he had to work hard for his money, toiling from 11 A.M. to 11 P.M. to keep paying his taxes. With what he felt the Government left him, Mr. Gray bought a $750,000 Georgian mansion set on four acres on Sasco Hill in Southport, Conn. He sold it in the nineteen-fifties and moved into a 10-room house nearby on 22 acres. He also maintained a home on the West Coast.

Mr. Gray worked at home in a book-lined study. In recent years Robert Leffingwell, his cousin, did the lettering and put in some of the background in the strips.

"I'm no artist," Mr. Gray once said. "I've never gone to any art school. But I know what I want and do the best I can. Bob does the dirty work."

Was a Farm Boy

Mr. Gray was a farm boy. He was born in Kankakee, Ill., Jan. 20, 1894, the son of Ira and Estella Rosencrans Gray. After graduating from Purdue in 1917 and serving a hitch in the Army in World War I, he became a newspaper artist.

Once "Little Orphan Annie" had become established, he moved East. In his life in New York and Connecticut, he was rarely gregarious and never made speeches. He liked to motor about the United States in his Lincoln, following, he once said, "the long brown road leading wherever you chose." He went abroad only once.

Mr. Gray's strip was handled by The Chicago Tribune-New York News Syndicate here. At his death it was appearing in 400 newspapers in the United States, Canada and foreign countries.

Like most comic strip artists, Mr. Gray was ahead of publication, and the syndicate said yesterday that strips bearing his signature would be distributed into late July. The strip will continue, the syndicate said, but a new artist has not yet been chosen.

May 10, 1968

MICKEY MOUSE AND THE COMIC SPIRIT

The Art of Making Laughter in One of Its Modern American Manifestations—The Comic Strip as an Art Medium

By ELISABETH LUTHER CARY.

LAUGHTER has been the subject of much theory, conjecture, philosophy, physiology, but Henri Bergson's simplification, long since demoded, seems to get closest of any to the tricky comic spirit. We laugh because we are amused and we are never amused except by what is human. That is his first point. A landscape may be beautiful, sublime, insignificant or ugly, it is never laughable. We may laugh at an animal, but only because we surprise in it some human attitude or expression. Which brings us forward to the present moment and to Mickey Mouse.

Again Bergson, with a surely incontestable comment. Perhaps, he says, we should go back to the plays that amused us as children for the preliminary sketch of what amuses us as adults. Too often we fail to recognize that which still remains of the infantile in the greater part of our pleasures. Ah, wise Bergson! You may have failed to impress your generation with the body of your philosophy, but how often your comments make sense! Again Mickey Mouse to your support.

A boy in his teens watching the antics of a pair of little mice because they gave him childish delight and a few years later a Mickey and Minnie renewing the boyhood of thousands of adults in the most sophisticated cities of the world. They should be cherished as an authentic source of restorative laughter, especially because in the current exhibition of Walter Disney's drawings at the Kennedy Galleries there seems to be a slight drop in the buoyancy of his inspiration as he moves away from his little friends of the Hole and Cheese toward fantasies more suggestive of Sindbad the Sailor or Gulliver's Travels.

* * *

THE history of caricature and cartoon, with the later introduction of the "comic strip," is not a long affair in America. Americans have been slow to discover the various uses of humor, although if presented to them in a familiar form their appreciation hardly could be exceeded. Tom Sawyer and Huckleberry Finn promptly became idols of the nation, yet at the crest of their popularity it would have seemed to this very nation something akin to sacrilege to place the adventures of Mark Twain's young heroes upon the formal throne of mural decoration, as Mr. Brinley lately has done for a public that has no stones to throw at his cheerful audacity. There hardly could be a better proof that we are reconciled to humor in high places. We long had but a little art with our humor in low places, if we can bring ourselves so invidiously to characterize the funny pages of the daily or weekly press. The earliest political and social cartoons were seldom dominated by an idea of paying as great respect to their "art" as to their message. To the majority of their public that would have been indeed a "funny" idea, worthy only of contempt. The moral sentiment, the serious conviction and sufficient point to the work to make these clear were all that was asked, although in a short time considerably more was given, and the public unconsciously leaned heavily upon the more that was given for its understanding of the messages.

As we have moved further and further away from Nast and his immediate followers we have found ourselves walking between the steadily increasing ranks of two opposite classes of artists, those who see their greatest opportunity in the serious cartoon to which they give their best in art, a best that may be measured by looking through any considerable collection of the World War cartoons; and others, who strive only to excite laughter. The comic strip was born and grew to obesity with sad results in the spread of visual vulgarity. The repetition of crude jokes and exaggerated types that missed their intention through a curiously unerring preference for insignificant over significant features were so prominent that the word art had to be thrown out in referring to the strip in its inferior forms. Yet in this medium a few flowers of art could early be discovered, and even in the stereotyped style of the hacks avid gossips could find coarse but credible digs at foibles of humanity usually screened from publicity by good breeding or good humor or a decent lack of interest. The lack of interest proved an uncertain element even in persons who would shudder at the thought of peering through strange windows and the comic strip prospered in its worst as in its best aspect.

Its best aspect is clean, droll and gay, with as much art in its making as we get in the run of work honored by exhibition in public galleries. Nothing could be more reassuring as to the ultimate preference for this best aspect than the fact that the adventures of Mickey Mouse are daily chronicled in the comic strips of sixty European newspapers, and as animated cartoons are playing to delighted crowds made up of all sorts and conditions of men, women and children. Another fact in this connection is also reassuring where reassurance was much needed. Art at a high level is no longer pushed snobbishly aside because of its popularity. Mr. Disney has been invited by the College Art Association to lend his original drawings to form a circuit exhibition for the leading museums and colleges throughout the United States. Down goes the ivory tower at last under the impact of what has been accurately described as "the embodiment of a new art, an art in motion and an art in rhythm, the keynote of a new epoch in the history of aesthetics."

* * *

LET joy be unconfined" is not only the subject of one of the Mickey Mouse drawings, it is the keynote of all. That is why the writer on "caricature" in the eleventh edition of the Encyclopaedia Britannica would have had nothing to do with them. Of certain forms of graphic humor he writes, "some have no other object than to amuse, and therefore do not call for serious notice." We have got far beyond that attitude of mind. It seems quite necessary to give these drawings at least this much of the kind of serious notice which breaks out among historians of art; to confess, that is, to a restored confidence in the health of a generation able to laugh spontaneously and repeatedly at Mickey's gay and innocent design for laughter. Among our many recognized symptoms of disease it is a triumphant sign of a good constitution. And the royalty of a republic has spoken when ten thousand theatre audiences say with one voice, "We are amused."

May 7, 1933

Influence of 'Funnies' On Children Deplored

To the Editor of The New York Times:

The letter of Jacques W. Redway on sloppy speech published in The Times last Sunday is one which might well be addressed to the newspapers of the country—or at least those which publish "funnies" for children.

Following are a few excerpts from a single strip of so-called entertainment for youngsters:

"Snubby runned away!"

"I ain't sawn him in two whole days!"

"Didja tell the police?"

"Is Snubby got enemies?"

"Cert'ny I done all them things!"

"Twice as many too * * *"

W. H. Charlton.

Smithtown Branch, N. Y., Jan. 20, 1938.

January 23, 1938

HUMOR CALLED AN AID TO MORALE IN SERVICES

Coast Guard Publication Officers Hold Conference Here

There are many phases of morale and all officers do not see eye to eye on the solution of the problem but all agree that every little bit helps to build it, Rear Admiral L. C. Farwell of the Coast Guard declared yesterday before a conference of Coast Guard service publication editors in the Hotel Astor. More than fifty editors and officials attended the session, which was styled as a "clinic" for camp newspapers and their problems.

Lieut. W. C. Dunning (jg), USCGR, told the men that humor against themselves was a real morale builder. Lieutenant Dunning explained that when an unpleasant thing or situation is taken out into the light of publicity and made to look funny the seriousness of the matter is deleted and the humor helps it to pass over. The lieutenant also advised the editors to leave the heroes to the public press, keeping the service papers devoted to the "little guys."

Master Sgt. Joe McCarthy, editor of Yank, told of new ideas for the Army's paper. He asserted that the service publications are building confidence for the men in the ranks, that they are willing to write to the paper of their gripes and problems where they would hesitate to discuss these matters with their own officers.

Milton Caniff, creator of the comic strip, "Terry and the Pirates" and "The Male Call," which appears widely in Army papers, advised on comic-strip and art work. He explained methods of putting across gags or jokes and also listed many "don'ts" for the Coast Guardsmen to avoid in their own strips.

January 23, 1944

'ARTHUR' IN TRIPLICATE

Hollywood.

The Arthurian legends received attention from three sources in the film industry last week. The United Artists cartoon producing firm of Harman-Ising disclosed that work has begun on a feature-length cartoon to be called "King Arthur and the Knights of the Round Table," for which Hugh Harman and Robert Edmunds have written a scenario. Eagle Lion announced the purchase of screen rights to the newspaper comic strip, "Prince Valiant," which involves characters from the Arthurian cycle. And Douglas Fairbanks Jr., who is now producing independently for Universal-International, announced that he will go to England next year to produce and play Sir Lancelot in "The Knights of the Round Table," a photoplay which Clemence Dane is writing in London. Fairbanks had previously been interested in a similar venture at Paramount, which was abandoned before the war.—T. F. B.

November 24, 1946

COMING:

Al Capp's cartoon strip "Li'l Abner" is in the process of adaptation for a weekly half-hour radio series tentatively slated for introduction this fall. Particulars as to time and network are still unsettled.

Details otherwise, according to Mr. Capp, are that the radio version of the hillbilly saga will parallel but not duplicate the published cartoon strip. "Li'l Abner's" portrayer will act in a supervisory capacity for the broadcasts, and he is currently busy examining scripts submitted for the series.

The cartoonist also disclosed that a television film series to be known as "The Al Capp Show" is being prepared. He said that the video programs would take the format of "drawing and fun," and would include appearances by "maddeningly beautiful models."

September 12, 1948

Walt Kelly

'Cartoonist of Year'

Walt Kelly, creator of the comic strip, "Pogo," has been chosen "cartoonist of the year" in a poll of 300 members of the National Cartoonist Society. Mr. Kelly will receive the sixth annual Billy DeBeck award, a cigarette case with the "Barney Google" comic strip characters drawn by the late cartoonist engraved on it, at the society's annual dinner at the Pierre Hotel tomorrow night.

April 22, 1952

A VIDEO SATIRIST

Al Capp Dissects Life In His Own Fashion

By BERNARD KALB

AL CAPP, a veteran comic-stripper known to millions as the man behind "Li'l Abner," turned up on WNBT this summer as a "verbal essayist"—a satirist with some pointed comments on the current scene.

He did fine. On his first show he blew to smithereens several beliefs long cherished by the rest of us, did some sketches in a looseleaf book nine feet high and filled the screen with his face—a folksy; I-know-you-from-some- face.

Since July 13 he has been appearing every Sunday at 12:15 P. M. with dissertations like "How to Win the Next War Without Anyone Getting Hurt" and "How to Predict Exactly How Long Elizabeth Taylor and Michael Wilding Will Remain Married."

Capp's is no new face to the television audience—far from it.

"I used to be inevitable on TV a few years back," Capp reminisced the other day. "I turned up on dozens of panels. All you have to do is be alive, and you're spectacular." Still, a panel wasn't exactly the kind of TV showcase for Capp's satire of the American scene, so he went blithely along, doing his strip, lecturing and getting himself compared to Voltaire and Twain.

Reasons

He'd often spun the dial on the TV set at home, Capp said, but he'd never found the sort of program that pleased him. "This," he said, in a reference to his own show, "is the kind I would have liked somebody to do for me. A sort of variety show of ideas. My feeling is that a humorist—a serious humorist—is like a man with a flashlight; he's got to throw it around to expose lunacy. Well, no one was doing it," he added, "so I am. I simply must. That's the only reason I'm doing it, too—not for any respectable reason, like dough."

Capp stuck loyally to the essay form through the early shows. He was the only man on the program.

Yet he felt a little claustrophobic and, a couple of Sundays ago, he broke loose. "I had seen a kinescope of the show one afternoon," Capp recalled. "I almost went out of my mind. 'I want to be delivered from that face,' I said. So now I bring in a couple of friends, Chandler Cowles and Lenore Lonergan, to help illustrate a point."

There is no chance, however, of any of Dogpatch's barefooted celebrities turning up on the TV show. "The strip's the strip," Capp notes, pithily, "and TV is TV."

However, something that looks like a blood relative of the Schmoo will become a permanent fixture. It's called the Schmooth. Statements are put into a Schmooth, like money in a till, and the Schmooth evaluates them. Once, Capp submitted "If you elect me I promise to lower your taxes and strengthen your defenses." The Schmooth said it added up to: "NOTHING."

Capp, who is 42, has a wife and three children, spends his weekdays in Boston, close to a lucrative bottle of India ink, and his week-ends in New York, close to the Waldorf-Astoria Towers, where he usually checks in Friday nights, for a final once-over of the week's ideas. Capp was in fine fettle one recent Saturday night. He was curled like a banana over a typewriter stuffed with a script, part of which had to do with modern art. "That comes under the heading, 'How I Can Break Every Rule of Decency on Television and Get Away With It,'" Capp said, and he thought it would be just as well to talk about that as anything else to demonstrate how the show was written.

Audience of One

"Picasso is an enormous fraud," he began, as he riffled through a book of Picasso reproductions. "His women look like chopped liver. If that's art then this is a poem," he added, holding aloft a sheet of paper on which he had just raced a pencil back and forth.

"Anyway," Capp went on, "I'll show the Picassos to the audience, then I'll draw"—he etched each word carefully in mid-air—"a birdseye view of Rita Hayworth in a bathtub—without any water in it." Capp paused. "In terms of modern art, of course." In terms of modern art, it developed a few pencil strokes later, Miss Hayworth was a rectangular blur of arms and legs soaking in knobs and tile.

Capp writes the show singlehandedly, but he uses Bob Condon, a script writer, as a preview audience of one, and Condon smiles, winces, grimaces, roars, pounds the floor, shakes his head, or nods. "I've got to watch out for the word 'horrible,'" Condon confessed later. "If you don't watch Al, he'll put in twenty 'horribles.'"

Sunday morning at 11:30 all the Capp people assembled in N. B. C.'s Studio 3A. It resembled a cave, with baby spots hanging from the ceiling like incandescent stalactites. The show began at 12:15, and it went off smoothly, except that Miss Lonergan fluffed a word, "pugilistic." The Picasso bit went fine. Capp himself was feeling wonderful, and what especially pleased him was that the show had not gotten a single guffaw from the audience. "This isn't that sort of program," said Capp. "All we can do is generate a spirit of friendliness." Suddenly, as though a thought had just struck him, Capp drew a deep breath. "You know," he muttered, "if this show doesn't win a Peabody Award, we may survive."

August 31, 1952

Seriously, They're Funny

THE POGO SUNDAY BOOK. By Walt Kelly. 132 pp. AL CAPP'S BALD IGGLE. By Al Capp. Unpaged. New York: Simon & Schuster. $1 each. WANTED: DENNIS THE MENACE. By Hank Ketcham. 64 pp. New York: Henry Holt & Co. $1.

By DAVID DEMPSEY

A THEORY, prevalent for some time now, holds that the comics are no longer funny; that they are political satire, social commentary, mythology or pure adventure, so that to be caught laughing at them is a breach of faith. But if this is true it hardly explains the success of the two outstanding practitioners of the comic strip art: Al Capp (creator of Li'l Abner, the Schmoo and, more recently, the Bald Iggle) and Walt Kelly (father of Pogo, the possum of the Okeefenokee swamp), both of whom have endeared themselves to a vast book-buying (in addition to newspaper-reading) public simply by being absurdly and ridiculously funny.

Capp, it is true, has a "message," although he never lets it take over his humor, which, like Kelly's, is directed at the proprieties of civilization. Both men rely heavily on word play and the primitive disorganization of the English language, and in Kelly's case the human comedy is filtered through the animal kingdom so that what you get is the sort of behavior you would expect from people if they were as smart as possums and alligators.

"The Pogo Sunday Book" is Kelly's tenth since 1951, and the question here, I suppose, is what makes Pogo stick? In five years, Pogo has racked up sales of 1,625,000 copies, 80 per cent of them to college students, according to the Simon & Schuster sales department. Kelly's book contains a good deal of dialogue such as "I be DOG-NABBED, I do b'leeve Pogo is SCUTTLEBUTTERED off to MexiMAco." Obviously, this kind of possum talk takes some getting used to, but once you manage it the story line comes through in a remarkably heady and whimsical fashion—and you realize, with considerable admiration, that Kelly in this book, unlike some of his previous volumes, is not really trying to say much of anything—he is simply restoring comic-strip art to the position of nonsocial, apolitical, unmythological and self-contained humor which it abdicated some years ago.

If Capp's Bald Iggle lacks the behavioristic non sequiturs of Pogo, it is a good deal more devastating and points a moral so close to home as to make outright laughter slightly uncomfortable. The idea is a stunning one—the Iggle symbolizes something that we have become more and more conditioned to avoid: the truth. It is not "pure" humor, and the fact is that you have to have awareness to appreciate Capp. "Pure" humor or not, the reception of the two Capp books prior to "Bald Iggle" was impressive. They topped a half-million.

If Pogo and the Iggle are college fare, the third cartoon offering of the season, "Wanted: Dennis the Menace" should stir up quite a fuss at the Choate School and Exeter. This is the fourth trip out for Dennis (sales have exceeded 350,000 copies altogether) and I turned the current volume over to my 10-year-old son (Antioch '64), who reported as follows: "Dennis is a kid about 4 years old who not only gets in trouble but does stupid things like locking himself up in the car, peeling bananas, etc. I liked the jokes but they wouldn't be as good without the pictures. The book was very funny."

No hidden meanings, politics or folkways in this appraisal, and I'm inclined to buy it.

Mr. Dempsey is a free-lance critic and short-story writer.

Illustration from "Wanted: Dennis the Menace."

"It's Jimmie's brother. I traded my turtle for him."

June 24, 1956

Washington

Daddy Warbucks Finds the Answer

By JAMES RESTON

WASHINGTON, May 10—All the news in the papers is not bad. On the front pages the course of the cold war may be running against the United States, but in what used to be called "the funnies" we are winning every day.

No account of the defense of the free world is complete without some reference to the exploits of Daddy Warbucks in Little Orphan Annie, "Fat Stuff" and "Lava Lava" in Smilin' Jack, Macloud, Ovlov and Hot Shot, who are defending the Arctic frontier in Terry and the Pirates, and Winnie Winkle, who is in Iran. Somehow, in the confusion over John Foster Dulles, we have overlooked the much more successful adventures of Daddy Warbucks. Just this week he leaned on his cane and watched an intercontinental ballistic missile break up in harmless fireworks before it could reach its target.

"It hit our new electronic umbrella," he explained to Annie. "Like a racing car doing 200 hitting a stone wall: nothing can get through that." Readers of The Times will be reassured by Annie's reaction.

"Wow," she said, "am I happy to know that!"

Naturally, the trend of the funny-paper war does not always favor the brave and the true. For example, Smilin' Jack is now in deep trouble. He has penetrated Soviet territory all right and discovered Nikita Khrushchev's great secret. This is "Operation Hexenhammer," which can deluge New York with rain (very much like last week), and otherwise visit cyclonic destruction on Omaha or anywhere else in the United States.

Precisely what Winnie Winkle, Birdie and Bruce Bailey are doing in Iran is not clear to this newspaper. The last time we saw Winnie, her only interest was love. But now she is deeply involved in saving the oil resources of the Middle East, presumably for the forces of freedom, and it is not at all clear what will happen if she does not find Bill Wright, or what she proposes to do with him when she does.

Page Allen Dulles

If the Soviets want evidence that the United States Air Force is flying over their territory, and infiltrating their nirvana with capitalistic spies, they need look no further than this week's installments of Buz Sawyer.

It is highly unlikely that Al Capp will tolerate this soft of thing for long. In the funnies the old American virtues still prevail. Washington may deplore the loss of the initiative, the lack of boldness, the delinquency of youth, and the complexities of the world and space, but Tiny Yokum and Moonbeam, though now behind bars in a zoo on Pincus Number Seven, will make their way somehow back home.

In the process, however, Jack has been captured with Lava Lava and Fat Stuff, and the outlook is grim. For example, The Times is informed that tomorrow Fat Stuff will be installed in a Soviet sputnik.

The "Wise Guys and Dolls" in Li'l Abner are also in difficulty. They are engaged in an interplanetary tussle, in which they can stupefy the enemy with a harmless spray gun, but this week, in a temporary setback, Tiny Yokum and Moonbeam McSwine were captured and carried off in a flying saucer to another planet.

Commander Sawyer flew to Libya this week. He is in the process of being taught Russian with a Bulgarian accent, and if he doesn't show up as a waiter in the Kremlin by the end of the month, there will be great disappointment all over this Republic.

As an instrument of propaganda in the cold war (second-generation division), the cartoon is, on the whole, following the popular line. The Soviet soldiers are vicious and wicked, and their objective, of course, is to capture and communize the world.

Trouble in Paradise

One subversive note, however, is creeping in. As is well known, the Soviet women are all supposed to look like weight-lifters. As Adlai E. Stevenson recently noted, Moscow invented the chemise and exported it to this country as a means of stirring up dissatisfaction among American men.

The cartoonists, however, are making them look attractive, and even permitting our heroes to fall in love with them. This fellow George Wunder, for example, who draws Terry and the Pirates, is doing a grand job in the Arctic. Last week he saved the nation by rolling a vast Soviet patrol sled into an icy ravine, but this week his Captain Macloud has started making goo-goo eyes at Ovlov, the captured Soviet spy.

Otherwise, the cartoonists are doing all right, and official Washington is providing them with new ammunition every day. The Congress was told this week, for example, that our explorers in outer space must be prepared to meet up with one and two dimensional people, and Major Gen. William M. Creasy, chief United States Army chemical officer, said he would like to have a weapon that would immobilize an enemy without killing or maiming him.

This, of course, is precisely what Tiny Yokum is using in Li'l Abner tomorrow—a spray gun loaded with "mule stupefier"—but whether the general got the idea from Al Capp, or vice versa, is not known.

May 11, 1958

It's Easy to Say It in Pictures

By WALT KELLY

THE first couch of psychiatry in the human school must have been held by some prehistoric dawdler on a mud bank. There, stick in hand, he traced the wanderings of his mind in the perishable slop. Freudian fears; his wife was spared a measure of gloomy companionship, and he saved a cool twenty-five feet of whatever passed for wampum in the dawn of history.

Today, the tracer of errant thought, the cartoonist, works on a presumably cleaner, smoother, less fleeting surface. Otherwise he is the same shaggy-brained, barefooted freehand thinker. For it is most likely true that the steady and proper pursuit of the cartoonist is the Idea. He may be beset by Notions in the night or waylaid by Facts in the day, but neither these nor sleet nor storm of life stay him from his appointed rounds.

A Notion, to him, is but the glimpse of an Idea, a flash of fur in the underbrush of his brain. A Fact, respect it though he may, represents to him a stone monument set up by some worshiper of strange gods and he would rather go around it, over it or through it than be stopped by it.

Mentally, the primitive dawdler must have been comforted and soothed by shedding his thoughts in the mud. In original innocence, the present doodler does the same. An idea occurs to the holder of the crayon or the stick, and he puts what he can of it on a receptive surface. Such an act relieves him. But he finds himself trapped when a parent or some other relative catches sight of the result and decides that little Sam is an artist.

Thenceforth he no longer works merely for psychiatric relief. He is lulled and chivied into the conviction that he is more or less a genius. "Our Harry can draw Abraham Lincoln," cracks the voice of doom. (Who can't?) Whereupon the child tries for Harding. He finally runs out of Presidents and begins to search for other ideas.

THE Idea, that *rara avis* of the human intellect, is seen nowhere less frequently than in the highlands of the cartoonist's mind. But the draftsman has some advantages over other hunters of the elusive. For one thing, he should be nimble enough to leap upon the Idea when he sees it, if, of course, he is awake enough to recognize it. Having leaped, he is forced, willy-nilly, to do something with his quarry. Too often this consists of beating it with a pencil and rendering it dead, distorted and meaningless on a piece of paper that could have been put to some utilitarian purpose. But sometimes he captures the thought for the rest of us to admire in its captivity.

Probably never does the cartoonist produce the complete and handsome conception that snorted and roared, danced and dashed from peak to peak

Mr. Kelly, a former political cartoonist, produces the comic strip, Pogo.

inside his head somewhat like Rex, King of the Wild Horses, or Pepper Martin in 1931. Sometimes he brings the Idea back twitching slightly, so we know it was once alive. With infinite care he may rebuild it so that it can sit up and groan at us through the sterile bars of technique. But it is not the same animal and the cartoonist knows it. He takes to drink, or worse, he golfs.

Most of the time the cartoonist, knowing he is a heavy-handed husbandman, does not trust himself alone to resuscitate the Idea to a semblance of self-reliant life. He then gets the help of those antibiotics in the field of ideas: Words.

Now Words are all right. There is nothing basically wrong with Words. They are perverted pictures and more to be pitied than blamed. Words have the same relationship to the picture as the modern Maypole dance has to the original bacchanal. Few cartoonists use them without letting them go to their heads. The cartoonist who bolsters his drawing with Words is often carried away, much like a young and inexperienced drinker. Almost anybody who touches Words will press just one more upon the unsteady Idea until neither one nor the other knows who is at the wheel.

IN a discussion of this kind, at least one individual always picks his prim way to the platform to announce that the Chinese said that one picture was worth ten thousand words. Herblock says that Alan Barth, editorial writer for The Washington Post, claims that this is a misinterpretation from the original Mandarin. The Real, or Original, Mandarin said no such thing, according to Barth. He said that one word was worth ten thousand pictures, says the writer, and even more. Mr. Barth explains that this has something to do with the International Date Line, which precedes a good deal of overseas copy.

Another, and possibly better, explanation of the Chinese theory is that the Chinese were talking about Chinese words. In that linguistic area, the use of pictograms to form words has been carried pretty far. One Chinese alphabet has more than three thousand characters in it or enough to populate a minor De Mille epic not counting horses.

The Idea when captured alone, alive and in its primitive state, comes out best as a single picture. Words merely confuse the issue. They are flimsy devices to express the complexities of our disorganized minds. It is here that we find the allegory of the Tower of Babel meaningful and that **we perceive the breakdown of all human communication: language.**

It is not because I resent having been told, as a cartoonist, that I did not spell "Antarctic" correctly in a cartoon (it seems there is no hyphen) that I advise the human race to return to the simple drawing without words as a means of communication. I do so because, for one thing, a captionless cartoon means the same thing in Russia as it does in the United States.

Furthermore, there cannot be more than a half dozen clearly thought-out ideas by anybody in all the world, give or take a few hundred. And it is hard to see why all of us are continuing to pervert the work of the original mud scribbler. He meant no harm when he did it. He probably only wanted to say that he had killed a wart hog, or he planned to kill a wart hog, or he had had an erstwhile friend who had resembled a wart hog.

November 30, 1958

Six for Kicks

Here are six new collections of cartoons selected from the full fall crop for their witty gags and lively line. An example from each appears in the adjoining columns.

THE PICK OF PUNCH. 1958. Edited by Nicolas Bentley. E. P. Dutton & Co. $4.95.

THE BROCKBANK OMNIBUS. By Russell Brockbank. G. P. Putnam's Sons. $3.95.

THE HALF-NAKED KNIGHT. By Andre Francois. Alfred A. Knopf. $3.95.

BEWARE OF THE DOG. By Giovannetti. The Macmillan Company. $3.50.

THE NEW YORKER ALBUM OF SPORTS AND GAMES. Harper & Bros. $5.

SLIGHTLY OUT OF ORDER. Best Cartoons From the Continent. Edited by Ralph E. Shikes. The Viking Press. $3.50.

From "The Brockbank Omnibus."

From "Beware of the Dog."
"You're not paid to think, lieutenant."

BENEFITS ARE NOTED IN COMIC BOOK CODE

The five-year self-imposed code for comic books has benefited both readers and publishers, John L. Goldwater, president of the Comics Magazine Association of America, said yesterday.

Since the association was formed and the self-regulating code for comic books adopted, both quality and circulation have risen, Mr. Goldwater told the annual meeting of the association at the Hotel Biltmore.

He reported that circulation had risen to 600,000,000 copies annually, an increase of 150,000,000 over circulation immediately before the code was adopted.

The code set up regulations for controlling horror, crime, violence and indecency, for which many comics had been censured.

April 15, 1959

From "The New Yorker Album of Sports and Games."

"Mebbe 'tis, mebbe 'tisn't. Your name Spalding?"

From "Slightly Out of Order."

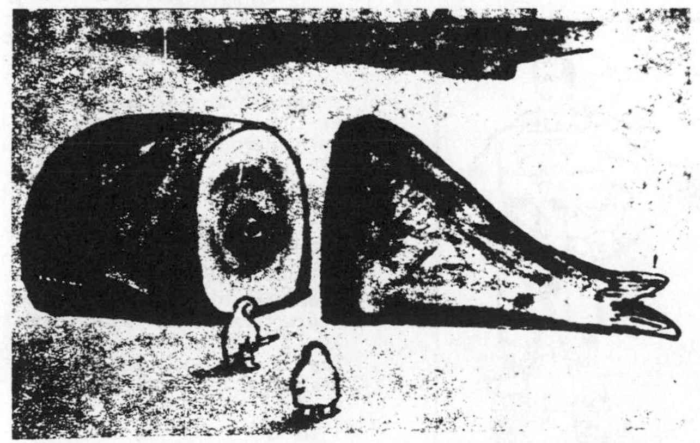

From "The Half-Naked Knight."

"Now what?"

From "The Pick of Punch."

Tokyo Newspaper Drops 'Pogo' Because of Khrushchev-Like Pig

Soviet Embassy Protested—Editor Says Caricature Is in 'Bad Taste'

TOKYO, May 20 (AP) — A Japanese newspaper announced today it was temporarily eliminating the American comic strip "Pogo" because the Soviet embassy had pointed out that a "Russian" talking pig in the strip's current episode bore a striking resemblance to Premier Khrushchev.

Kimpei Shiba, editor of the English-language Evening News said the Embassy had not requested that the strip, which is by Walt Kelly, be dropped. The decision to discontinue the series until the current sequence ends, Mr. Shiba said, was made because of the newspaper's policy not to use caricatures of heads of state "if they are in bad taste."

Panel from the comic strip that has been discontinued by a Tokyo newspaper.

"I want that made very clear," he said. "We would not remove anything just because the Soviet embassy said so.

"It could have been Khrushchev and it could have been someone else. As for myself, Pogo is one of the cartoons I do not understand."

He said Vyacheslav N. Bounine, the Soviet Embassy's first secretary, approached the newspaper last week and pointed out the similarity between the caricature and Premier Khrushchev. After a study, Mr. Shiba said, he wrote the Soviet official there is "now no doubt in our minds that the figure of the hog is Khrushchev. We consider it in bad taste."

The hog speaks in mock-Cyrillic characters.

Another animal in the sequence is a bearded goat resembling Fidel Castro whose conversation is dotted with Spanish phrases. But Mr. Shiba said no one from the Cuban Embassy had protested and he did not know if the artist were referring to Premier Castro "unless somebody tells me."

Kelly 'Understands' Move

Mr. Kelly, at his home in New York, said he was not angry about the cancellation.

"I'm just glad they read it as far as they have," he said. "But I understand their position, they are so near Vladivostok."

He said he did not think the cartoon was in bad taste but he declined to specify if the hog represented Premier Khrushchev or the goat represented Premier Castro.

"I haven't identified them in the strip and I won't go any further than the strip goes," he said. "But maybe some people's conscience bothers them.

"We look around the world to see what's funny background material, and I think this fits into a comic strip."

Toronto Drops Sequence

TORONTO, May 20 (AP)—The Globe and Mail has eliminated the "Pogo" sequence on the pig from its comic page. A box announced: "Pogo will be back when Walt Kelly returns to the Okefenokee folk."

May 21, 1962

Superman Faces New Hurdles

By PETER BART

It was just a year ago that some rather surprising news was announced to the world about a venerable American institution. The announcement said that Superman had gone public.

Now Superman, as any tot can testify, is a man among men capable of formidable deeds, but peddling stock was not considered one of them. Thus, having permitted a year of grace to elapse, it seemed appropriate to drop in on the great man to see how he was taking to his new role.

Superman, it developed, emanates from a crowded, bustling suite of offices high above Lexington Avenue in the East Fifties. His principal mentors over the last two decades have been Jacob S. Liebowitz, the solemn, gray-haired president of National Periodical Publications, Inc., publisher of Superman and other comics, and Mort Weisinger, a portly, balding writer who edits the magazines.

Hero Brought Prosperity

Seated in a small, modern office adorned by contemporary paintings, both Mr. Liebowitz and Mr. Weisinger allowed at the outset that they had a healthy respect for their comic book hero. Superman, they noted, had come through some trying times in the comic book industry. And, where other comic strip heroes had fallen by the wayside, Superman not only has continued to thrive but has forged his publishing house into a prosperous, publicly owned concern.

The comic book industry as a whole, it was noted, has narrowed considerably in recent years. Today comic books sell at a rate of about 350,000,000 a year compared with 800,000,000 a year a decade ago. Where once more than 50 comics publishers prospered, today there are less than a dozen publishing houses of any magnitude. Among them: Dell Publishing Co., Inc.; Archie Comic Publications, Inc., and Harvey Publications, Inc.

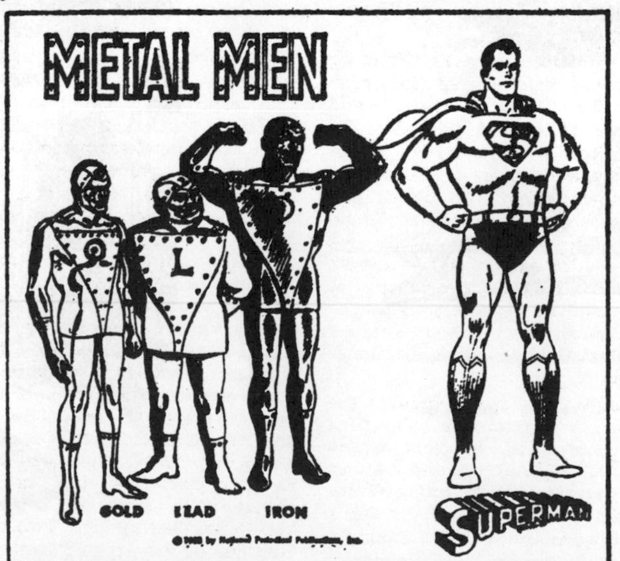

Superman, the first prodigy of National Periodical Publications, Inc., will shortly be followed by the metal men.

Moreover, the comics industry once a major advertising medium for reaching the teen-age and younger market, today has lost much of its revenue to rival media. Even National Periodical, Superman's publisher, presently derives only about $176,000 a year from advertising, compared with nearly $1,000,000 a decade or so ago.

Television has been the principal cause of the industry's problem. "The kids became accustomed to seeing their comic characters on television," notes Mr. Liebowitz. "Unfortunately, the comic book action often seemed a bit pale by comparison."

In the early days of television, some comics publishers tried to meet this new competition by making their own product a bit racier. Their efforts resulted in the short but incredible era of the horror comics. Amiable newsstand denizens like Nutsy Squirrel and Atomic Bunny suddenly gave way to a hair-raising assortment of ghouls and monsters that terrorized both the youthful readers and their parents.

The horror-comics boom ended abruptly with passage in many states of legislation restricting the sale of comics books. And the comics industry itself responded in 1954 with a stringent code aimed at eliminating the offensive magazines.

The code provided, among other things, that "good shall in all cases triumph over evil," and that "females shall be drawn realistically without exaggeration of any physical qualities."

A Bitter Pill

The parents liked the code but it proved a bitter pill for the comics publishers. Within three years of the code's enactment, 24 of the 29 original subscribing members were out of business.

Through all of the industry's trials and tribulations, however, Superman continued to fly his own course. Today, according to Mr. Liebowitz, Superman and and the other comic book characters published by National Periodical (The Flash, Superboy, Lois Lane, Batman, etc.) account for about 30 per cent of total comic book industry sales.

National Periodical itself derives about 60 per cent of its $36,000,000 annual sales from its comic books, with the remainder coming from the distribution of about 55 magazines and paperbacks published by other companies.

National Periodical makes no effort to conceal its reverence for its comic hero. In its annual report the place normally reserved for a picture of the president is given over to a drawing of Superman, hands on hips, his cape, as always, swirling in the breeze. Many of the company's other comic books derive from Superman's coterie of friends—Jimmy Olsen, Lois Lane, Superboy and others.

Surprising Hold

Superman's continued hold on his readers is perhaps surprising in this era of real-life space men. According to Mr. Weisinger, Superman's editor, however, the advent of the space age has only whetted the appetites of youngsters for more of Superman's daring deeds.

"The kids still love this sort of stuff," Mr. Weisinger affirms. "But in putting together the book we have to bear in mind that the kids today are much more sophisticated than they were twenty years ago. There are a lot of things they just won't accept nowadays."

Hundreds of readers wrote in some time ago, for example, when Superman grabbed Lois Lane and took her on a fast ride into space. The children, it seemed, felt that Miss Lane would be destroyed by friction, the Van Allen radiation belt and similar hazards. As a result of these complaints, Superman has since draped his girl friend in a space suit for such voyages.

Still other literal-minded youngsters not long ago protested when Superman gave Lois Lane a blood transfusion. Since Superman's skin is well known to be impenetrable, they said, how could he donate his blood? Mr. Weisinger told the readers that Superman could puncture his own skin with his super-powerful fingernails.

These questions were of minor difficulty in contrast to the lengthy dissertations sent in by a group of students at the Massachusetts Institute of Technology who regularly monitor Superman's accomplishments. The students have protested, from time to time, that some of Superman's mortal friends have taken liberties with the laws of physics.

An even sterner challenge emanated some years ago from a commission established by the French Chamber of Deputies which looked into Superman and other comics figures imported from the United States. After a brief review, the commission ruled Superman "unacceptable" on the ground that it was absurd to depict a character capable of propelling itself through space.

Rejected by France

On appeal, the commission agreed to accept Superman if its creators agreed to affix jet boosters to his belt and thus, presumably, give him an aura of reality. Nothing doing, said Mr. Liebowitz, and Superman remains persona non grata in France.

Although Superman looks the same as he did when he made his debut 24 years ago, his friends have changed a bit. Lois Lane, following a series of emphatic protests from girl readers, has modernized her hair-do along Jackie Kennedy lines.

Jimmy Olsen, the 18-year old newsboy and cub reporter, has put on three years and now is a reporter. But Clark Kent has stayed the same—he still needs only to shed his suit and spectacles to transform himself into the full-fledged hero capable of taking on villains from outer or inner space.

Says Mr. Weisinger: "In a sense Superman commands greater believability now than he did two decdes ago. Now our audience consists to a large degree of the children of former readers. The old folks now and then peek over the shoulders of their kids, and get a nostalgic twinge. I think the parents help us sell the magazine."

September 23, 1962

'Krazy Kat' Has Something to Tell Us

THE FUNNIES: An American Idiom. Edited by David Manning White and Robert H. Abel. Illustrated. 304 pp. New York: The Free Press of Glencoe. $7.50.

By STEPHEN BECKER

THIS book is the editors' tentative answer to the question, "What do the comic strips tell us about American culture?" The answer is tentative, because some of the conclusions contradict others (which the editors point out), because the word "culture" is used ambiguously (we learn more about manners, morals and social goals than about books or music or art; "society" might have been a better word) and because a few of the selections add interest to the book without addressing themselves to the question (e.g., a poem, a vignette by Heywood Broun and Al Capp's fine piece on Charlie Chaplin).

The editors—David Manning White, who co-edited the encyclopedic "Mass Culture," and Robert H. Abel, a columnist for The Realist magazine — range widely, which is a polite way of saying that the book is a grab-bag. "The Funnies" is no less interesting for that, but the reader entranced by Gilbert Seldes' classic evocation of "Krazy Kat" is likely to be far less enthusiastic about reports of statistical research, and vice-versa.

Seven sections indicate the diversity of approach. The first is a survey of the field, which the editors felt obliged to call an "overview" — a mongrel intruder, an ugly substitute for a good word and a choice example of what jargon tells us about American culture. Of the five essays in this section, Reuel Denny's "The Revolt Against Naturalism in the Funnies" is the most cogent and thoughtful. "Dissent" follows, with a sharp regret at the decline of humor (not borne out, incidentally, by the later statistical reports), a brief and devastating critique of artistic values in comic strips (just, as far as it goes, but no cartoonist has ever claimed to be working in the fine arts; only the fans do that) and an examination of Little Orphan Annie's maverick political economy.

The next section, called "The Highest Praise," neutralizes these attacks with two of the best essays in the book: Seldes and the late Robert Warshow on "Krazy Kat." The poem and Broun's piece compose, rather sketchily, a separate section, "Myth and Metaphor." Two discussions of kid strips "Smitty," "Peanuts," etc.. follow.

SECTION VI is "The Research ers Report" and comprises five investigations of what goes on in the funnies and why from 80 to 100 million people enjoy them enough to read them daily, complete with tables, footnotes, graphs and the occasionally dizzying paraphernalia of pollsters and statisticians. The reports should not deter the reader: they are fascinating. A tendency to giggle at their unconscious humor must be sternly suppressed; to the newspaper industry, to syndicates and to some cartoonists there is nothing funny in a table headed "Rank Order of Major Goals Sought by Different Occupational Groups" (among comic strip characters) or "The Expression of Hostility in Interpersonal Relations, by Type of Strip and Type of Hostility."

A detailed investigation of a sequence on mental health in "Rex Morgan, M.D." and its effect on readers' attitudes, points up the influence of the funnies: people take them seriously, it seems, and have accepted the true-to-life comic

Mr. Becker, a novelist, biographer and translator, is the author of "Comic Art in America."

From "The Funnies."
A "Krazy Kat" comic strip of 1935, drawn by George Herriman.

artist as a sound and honest fellow with an occasional message of importance.

Section VII, consisting of essays by Al Capp, Allen Saunders ("Mary Worth," "Steve Roper") and our Voltaire of the Marshes, Walt Kelly, raises a dismaying cultural question: why are comic artists usually better writers than the people who write about them? (Even the few quotes in the introduction from a 1958 article by Milton Caniff, creator of "Terry and the Pirates" and "Steve Canyon," reveal a forceful and stylish prose.) This last section crowns the work, perhaps because the artists themselves are less concerned with the broad and troublesome matter of their influence and motivations, and prefer to concentrate on the work at hand.

There are sufficient provocations throughout to keep the reader alert: minor jabs like a misplaced "whom" or the lamented Colonel McCormick's name misspelled; or a major surprise like the statement (qualified several pages on by its author) that "there seems to be no problem of racial relations in the world of the comic strips. Only one Negro was identified in the population," on which basis it may be argued that there is no problem at the University of Mississippi either. But that is perhaps balanced by the arresting information that in the comic strips "men lose strength as well as height after marriage."

The bibliography is astonishingly thorough, and a boon to students. It may even justify the overpricing; $7.50 is too much for a 300-page book with a couple of dozen line-cuts. This is not the editors' fault, of course — but the publishers ought to know better. They may have been confused by the mixed nature of the book. In part it is an anthology for specialists, in part a smorgasbord for enthusiasts. Either way it says a good deal about us and the funnies, and says it well.

June 23, 1963

Old Comic Books Soar in Value

Dime Paperbacks of 1940's Are Now Collector Items

Old 10-cent comic books that tidy parents either threw away or sold by the hundred weight to the junk dealer are now being sold, individually, for prices ranging from $2 to $25.

The old comics, especially those published in the early nineteen-forties, are now considered collector's item and fans of Captain Marvel and Superman are finding them at Louis Cohen's backdate magazine store on the Avenue of the Americas between 43d and 44th Streets.

Mr. Cohen, 42 years old, the owner of Jay Bee Magazine Stores, Inc., says that customers for the old comics include "kooks," nostalgic men in their 20's and 30's, pop artists studying the techniques of early cartoonists and colleges and universities studying the "social attitudes" of the times that are reflected in them.

According to Mr. Cohen, even some of the cartoonists who originally created the comics visit his store occasionally to purchase their own works. They study them for story content for adaptation to today's society. "Their ideas run dry," Mr. Cohen said.

Many of the comics in stock are still being published but Mr.

Cohen looks at them with disdain. "The old comics are like fine wine; they get better with age," he said, then added:

"The techniques of the artists mature as society changes. The attitude of the artist changes and it reflects in his work."

The most popular comics in the store are old issues of Superman, Captain Marvel, Batman and Robin and comics published during World War II when many of the cartoon heroes "went to war." The price for many of the books in this category is $7.50.

Their covers show the "dirty Japs and Jerries" being "demolished" by such heroes as Spy Smasher, Air Boy and the currently popular Joe Palooka.

December 6, 1964

CARTOONISTS' HONOR SCHULZ FOR 2D TIME

The National Cartoonists Society last night named Charles Schulz, creator of "Peanuts," the outstanding cartoonist of 1964.

Mr. Schulz won the award in 1955. This was the first time in the society's 20-year-history that a cartoonist has won the award twice.

The award was announced at the society's dinner at the Plaza Hotel. The halcyon days of pre-World War I were recalled as the society honored a brother and sister who had inspired the cartoon strip "Buster Brown."

Richard F. Outcault Jr. accepted for his sister, Mrs. Mary Jane Outcault Pershing, scrolls in which they were cited "for being their father's inspiration in the birth of Buster Brown."

April 21, 1965

You're a Good Man, Charlie Schulz

By BARNABY CONRAD

"CARTOONING is a *fairly* sort of a proposition," said Charlie Brown's creator recently. "You have to be fairly intelligent—if you were really intelligent you'd be doing something else; you have to draw fairly well—if you drew really well you'd be a painter; you have to write fairly well—if you wrote really well you'd be writing books. It's great for a fairly person like me."

For an only *fairly* person, Charles (Sparky) Schulz bids fair to becoming the most successful newspaper cartoonist of all time. "Peanuts," which appears in some 900 newspapers in the U.S. and Canada, plus 100 abroad, has endeared the characters of Charlie, Lucy, Linus, Schroeder and Snoopy to an estimated 90 million readers. Records, films, advertisements, sweatshirts, dolls, books, cocktail napkins and other "Peanuts" paraphernalia have capitalized on the craze to make it a $20-million-a-year industry. The statistics of the triumphs of the strip and its various offshoots are so staggering that its millions of fans—and even its creator—are wondering how the original quality and simplicity of the product can be maintained. As I was interviewing him in his studio—an unexpectedly over-

CHARLES SCHULZ — "He bids fair to becoming the most famous newspaper cartoonist of all time."

BARNABY CONRAD is a frequent contributor to magazines who lives in San Francisco.

decorated and plush office—near Sebastopol, Calif. (an hour north of San Francisco), the telephone interrupted constantly: A Hollywood producer wanted to talk about a big "Peanuts" musical movie; a caller wanted to know something about the London opening of the hit play "You're a Good Man, Charlie Brown," (now running Off Broadway in New York), another wanted information on his new paperback, "The Unsinkable Charlie Brown." And then there were all the calls from people who wanted him to paint posters for charities, make personal appearances or donate money to this or that cause. Each time Schulz—who, with his crew cut and serious boyishness looks like every freshman's senior adviser—hung up the phone with a sigh. It was not a sigh of exasperation, but rather regret—regret that he was not always able to do the many things that people demand of him.

"I usually get between 400 and 500 letters a week and for years I've managed to answer all of them personally, but I don't know." He leafed through some of the letters. "Most of them are so nice and their requests are so polite and worthwhile—a drawing for a crippled kid, a poster for a special high-school dance. 'Just do a quick sketch of Snoopy,' they ask; 'it'll only take five minutes.' And they're right—it *would* only take five minutes. But they think their letter is the only one on my desk. The five minutes have to be multiplied by hundreds." He looked mournfully at the heap of mail. "Thousands. They forget that I not only have to do some drawing, I occasionally have to do some thinking."

HE looked out of his studio window and studied a clump of trees beyond an artificial pond. "It's hard to convince people when you're just staring out of the window that you're doing your hardest work of the day. In fact, many times when I'm just sitting here thinking and therefore working like heck I hear the door open and I quickly grab the pen and a piece of paper and start drawing something so that people won't think I'm just goofing off and anxious to have a little chat. But I like visitors when I'm drawing. It gets lonely up here all day, not like an office or a dentist or somebody who has company around him all the time." Schulz has been termed a recluse but he says: "Oh, we go to San Francisco about once a month, see friends, go to a play. But we aren't nightclubbers or cocktail types. Neither of us drink, never have, just isn't part of our life and our friends just have to accept us like that."

He picked up some more letters. "Lots of people write in ideas. Some are good, but I don't seem to be able to use other people's suggestions. Here's a pretty good one—'Why not make Snoopy pretend he's a Grand Prix racing driver?' Now that's not a bad idea, and I guess it would work. But first of all, I didn't think of it, and secondly I'd be imitating myself—sort of copying the Snoopy and the Red Baron business. It's always dangerous to copy yourself. Al Capp had a great success with the Schmoos, so then he had to try to repeat with the Kigmies and it wasn't as good. The Red Baron was a good idea but let's not imitate it. My son says he gave me the idea for that—he was working on a World War I model and claims he suggested the Red Baron business, but I don't remember. People think I'm a World War I nut and send me these"—he gestured at shelves of flying books.

I asked him about the hit record "Snoopy and the Red Baron," based on the dog's flights of fancy and aerial encounters with The Red Baron, the king of World War I skies. "I based the Baron on Richthofen because he's sort of the Beethoven of flying. Incidentally, I never heard about this record by the Royal Guardsmen until a friend said, 'Great song you wrote.' I checked with my lawyer the next day and we put a stop to that right away. Or rather we threatened to put a stop until we were included in the success. I understand they've sold two and a half million copies of it already. (Schulz gets a varying percentage of two other hit records as well—Vince Guaraldi's "Jazz Impressions of Charlie Brown" and "Charlie Brown's Christmas," put out by Fantasy Records.)

"Speaking of records, have you heard this?" He picked up the album of "You're a Good Man, Charlie Brown," and played the overture. "I'd like to see the show, but haven't really had time. Maybe next month we'll get to New York, but first I'm taking my wife and four of our five kids and four kids of friends of ours to Sun Valley for our first real vacation in two years. I hear it's a good show—love the music."

CHARLIE BROWN—"Sure he's wishy-washy but I like him. I didn't mean to give him a failure face in the beginning—I just wanted him to have an anonymous bland round face while the others had more character in theirs."

SNOOPY—"He has his origins in Spike, my dog that I had when I was a kid. White with black spots. He was the wildest and the smartest dog I've ever encountered. Smart? Why, he had a vocabulary of at least 50 words . . ."

LUCY—"Little girls of that age are smarter than little boys and she knows it better than most little girls. But she's not as smart as she thinks she is. Beneath the surface there's something tender. But perhaps if you scratched deeper you'd find she's even worse than she seems."

SCHROEDER—"I thought it was funny to give a big pompous name like that to a little kid. Named him after a caddy I met in 1941. Schroeder's a dedicated artist, but he's a real boy, not a snob, a good catcher on the team."

The Off Broadway play, made up of prose taken from "Peanuts" strips, opened on March 7 at Theater 80 St. Marks. In his ecstatic review Walter Kerr wrote: "They [the people of 'Peanuts'] have marched clean off that page of pure white light . . . and into forthright, fuming, explosively funny conversation without losing a drop of the ink that made their life-lines so human."

WHEN Schulz talks he is every bit as modest and unassuming as one could want the progenitor of "Peanuts" to be, yet there is a pride of profession in his voice. "Hollywood wants to make a movie of the play and I guess some day we'll do something. There was a nice fellow up here recently who produced 'To Kill a Mockingbird,' and we talked pleasantly. But the moment they start talking about 'their writers' I kind of get chills. I want it to be my words in everything I do. Just as I guess I'm the only cartoonist who doesn't have a helper to do the Sunday strip or fill in backgrounds and stuff. I even do my own lettering. I've thought of it—hiring someone to help. Sometimes I think it would be nice. But then—what would be the point? I don't do this for the money"—he gestured at his big drafting table with several half-inked-in strips on it. "People think I do, but I don't. I do it because I love to draw.

"The things I like to do best are drawing cartoons and hitting golf balls. Now if I hire someone to do my work for me what fun would I

LINUS—"He's the brightest, most promising, practical. But then there's that blanket. All my kids had their blankets, but only one sucked his thumb."

get? It'd be like getting someone to hit the golf ball for me. But maybe I'll have to." He glanced balefully at his secretary as she brought in a new stack of mail. "Life magazine said I was a multimillionaire—heck, no cartoonist can become a millionaire—but that's what the magazine said and now I'm getting requests for money from all over the world."

Whether or not he is in the millionaire bracket yet, Schulz lives like one. On his 28-acre estate, Coffee Grounds (on Coffee Lane), he has two elegant houses besides his big studio. Then there are stables, a cat, dog and horse per child, a tennis court, a baseball diamond and a four-hole golf course. He is an excellent golfer, 5 handicap, and shoots consistently in the 70's. The highlight of his year is the coveted invitation to the Crosby golf tournament in Monterey. He tries to play golf once a week, but as his success mounts and the work load increases he has to forgo more and more games.

SCHULZ begins his day at 9:30 by walking the quarter mile from his sprawling one-level house across the lawns of his golf holes, past the big swimming pool to his studio. With a secretary in the outer office and a plush living room before you arrive at the place where he actually draws, it could very well be the office of a successful real-estate broker or a pre-need cemetery-lot salesman.

Clinically neat and organized, Schulz sits at the drawing board and begins by playing around on a scratch pad with a pencil, doodling situations and ideas. He tries to conceive of the week's work as a whole; six separate days' drawings which will somehow make a unity. When he has the ideas fairly well set in his mind he takes a 28-inch illustration board, which has the margins of the four panels printed on it already, and inks in the dialogue. When he has all six days' strips "dialogued in," he begins to draw the figures and the action, preferring to draw directly with the pen with a minimum of penciled guidelines.

One day's strip takes him about an hour to draw. The Sunday page takes the whole day. He is required by the syndicate to be five weeks ahead on the daily and eleven weeks ahead on the Sunday. When I called on him he was just finishing up the strips for the week of May 8 to May 13, the theme being "Be Kind to Animals Week." (In one sequence, Snoopy is holding a sign with that legend on it, and as Lucy goes by he shuts his eyes and puckers up for a kiss. "Not on your life!" bellows the dear girl, bowling the dog and his sign over backward. Another day ends with Snoopy's saying: "This was a good week—I didn't get kicked.")

Right now Schulz is also busy preparing an hour-and-a-half film, plus another TV special. (He writes every word, and supervised the animation of the other three TV specials.)

The books are a further drain on his time. Since the first one, called plain "Peanuts," Holt has published some 4,493,000 copies, and they are all in print. After Holt has had a year or two to sell a "Peanuts" book at $1, the rights are turned over to Fawcett, which takes the Holt volume, splits it in two, and sells each copy for 40 cents. To date Fawcett has sold 12 titles to the tune of 10 million copies. But the publishing doesn't end there. A few years ago an enterprising San Francisco woman named Connie Boucher persuaded Schulz to do a book for her Determined Productions company. It turned out to be "Happiness Is a Warm Puppy," and it was on The New York Times best-seller list for 45 weeks in 1962 and 1963. This was followed by more "Happiness Is—" books, plus a Peanuts Date Book, totaling around three million copies in all. In 1965 the John Knox Press published "The Gospel According to Peanuts," being the theological thoughts extracted from the strip, which has been that firm's best seller of all time at more than 635,000 copies.

Which brings one to another consuming interest of Charles Schulz: religion. A member of a Scripture-oriented Protestant nondenominational organization called the Church of God, he keeps 12 Bibles, plus a set of the dozen volumes of the Interpreters' Bible, in his studio. On Sundays he teaches Sunday School in Sebastopol ("to adults only—I could never teach other people's children"). A pushover for charities and organizations designed to help people, he recently consented to accept the chairmanship of the National Aid to the Visually Handicapped and set about organizing a huge golf tourney, to be known as the "Charlie Brown-Lucy Tournament," the proceeds of which will go to the aid of partly blind children. He brooded for weeks over a request to do a poster for Aid for Retarded Children, tried dozens of ideas, and finally had to give up. "There was simply no way to do it without the danger of seeming to mock them."

SO this is the hectic world that was created by Charlie Brown/Schulz (he confesses that they are one and the same person). How did it come about and how did it snowball into these proportions?

Charles Monroe Schulz, as every good "Peanuts" aficionado knows, was born 44 years ago in Minneapolis, Minn. When he was two days old, he was nicknamed "Sparky" by his family for Barney Google's horse Sparkplug, and is still called that by his family and friends. From almost the beginning he wanted to become a cartoonist, thinking it among the noblest of the artistic professions.

"It's a great art," he says now. "I'm convinced it's much harder and more important than illustration. Look at that"—he points to a framed original cartoon page of "Krazy Kat" by George Herriman—"that's art. It was done around 1912 and its humor is every bit as fresh today as then."

Sparky's early life was very Charlie Brownish. "People read a lot into the strip, and I guess what people see in it, that's what's in it. But actually the strip is just about all the dumb things I did when I was little."

In fine Charlie Brown fashion he was the goat on the baseball field, once losing a game 40 to nothing, and even his drawings were turned down by the high school yearbook. In the Army he was similarly unsuccessful. After being trained as a machine gunner, he discovered he had forgotten to load his weapon the one and only time he was confronted by members of the enemy forces.

"It was the last week of the war and we were going along a road in Southern Germany in a halftrack and somebody said, 'Hey—look over there, there's somebody in that hole over there in the field, shoot him.' So I swung the gun around—50-caliber—pressed the butterfly trigger, and nothing happened. Before I could load he came out with his hands up and I was sure glad I hadn't been able to shoot him."

After the war he got a job lettering a comic magazine, then taught in a Minneapolis art school of the "Draw-me-and-win-a-scholarship" mail-order variety. A fellow instructor was named Charlie Brown, and later unwittingly lent his name to posterity. Another had a pretty blue-eyed sister named Joyce Halverson, and Schulz married her. In 1948 he sold his first cartoon, to The Saturday Evening Post. Then he did a weekly cartoon for The St. Paul Pioneer Press called "Li'l Folks." Within a year it was dropped. After many rejections from other syndicates, it was picked up by United Features in Manhattan. Over Schulz's protests it was renamed "Peanuts." To this day he is still indignant.

"What an ugly word it is," he says disgustedly. "Say it: *Peanuts!* I can't stand to even write it. And it's a terrible title. Now 'Peppermint Patty' is a good title for a strip. I introduced a character named that into the strip to keep someone else from using it. Funny, people don't tell you how to draw or write but EVERYBODY's an expert on titles."

The first month Schulz made $90 with his newly titled strip. A few months later it was up to $1,000 a month. Now, 17 years later, it is close to $1,000 a day.

"Funny," Sparky muses, "I never set out to do a cartoon about kids. I just wanted to be a good cartoonist, like, say, Herriman or my boyhood

©1939, King Features Syndicate, Inc.

PRE-CHARLIE—"I just wanted to be a good cartoonist," says Schulz, "like, say, Herriman." Above, a sequence of panels from Herriman's "Krazy Kat."

idol, Roy Crane, who draws 'Buz Sawyer'—a fine cartoonist. I always dreamed of some day coming up with some permanent idea or phrase that would pass into the language, like Snuffy Smith's 'bodacious' or some of Al Capp's gimmicks. I guess maybe 'Good grief' has made it. And perhaps the Great Pumpkin. And the 'Happiness Is . . .' title.

"There are a lot of good cartoonists around. I read all of 'em. Capp, Caniff, 'Miss Peach.' It pleases me that my children seem to like 'Peanuts' as well as any of the others. They know all the books by heart and have favorite strips on their walls and play the records. It's all very gratifying."

When asked about Snoopy, who is my family's favorite character in the strip, he said, "Snoopy's not a real dog, of course — he's an image of what people would like a dog to be. But he has his origins in Spike, my dog that I had when I was a kid. White with black spots. He was the wildest and smartest dog I've ever encountered. Smart? Why, he had a vocabulary of at least 50 words. I mean it. I'd tell him to go down to the basement and bring up a potato and he'd do it. I used to chip tennis balls at him and he'd catch and retrieve 'em." Schulz's sensitive face clouds at the memory. "Had him for years before he died."

MANY psychiatrists who charge a good deal more than Lucy van Pelt's 5-cent consultation fee have tried to analyze the special appeal of "Peanuts." My pedestrian conclusion is that Charles Schulz feels the loss of his dog Spike today as deeply as—or more deeply than—he did a quarter of a century ago, just as he feels the loss of his childhood. Happily for the readers, he is able to translate this long memory and deep feeling into words and pictures. It seems to be universal, either because we had a childhood like that, or wish we had. There's a little Charlie Brown in all of us males and, Lord knows, we've all known, and maybe even married, a Lucy van Pelt, a girl who shouts: "I don't want any downs—I just want ups and ups and ups." Certainly there's been *someone* in each one of our lives ready and eager to pull away the football just as we're about to kick it.

So very often the strip touches chords that remind us of things and homely events we thought we had forgotten. As the catalogue for the recent Whitney exhibition of Andrew Wyeth (Schulz's favorite painter, along with Picasso) stated: "But art arises in the human spirit beyond the reach of words from the levels of deepest memories. We are creatures who need the near and the familiar as well as the exotic."

Emerson wrote in 1838: "A man must have aunts and cousins, must buy carrots and turnips, must have barn and woodshed, must go to market and to the blacksmith's shop, must saunter and sleep and be inferior and silly."

ANOTHER factor in the strip's popularity with all ages is his sublime handling of how far the fantasy should go. For example, Snoopy's dog house is always shown in profile; we never see it three-quarters view or actually go inside it. We just accept the fact when it is said that Snoopy has a Wyeth and a Van Gogh and a pool table in there, but if we actually saw inside and discovered an unbelievable dog house we would cease to believe in Snoopy as a dog and his relationship with the children. Another all-important factor in Schulz's astonishingly good batting average is his unfailing sense of what is subtly funny.

"I get letters all the time," he told me, "from optometrists saying, 'How come you're always talking about ophthalmologists'—Linus wore glasses, you know—'why not give us a break?' It's hard to tell them that ophthalmology is somehow funny and the word optometry just isn't. Like Beethoven. My favorite composer is Brahms—I could listen to him all day—but Brahms isn't a funny word. Beethoven is, so I gave him to Schroeder. Like names: Linus is a good name. I borrowed that from a friend, Linus Maurer. Funny, the other night I was trying to think of a good last name for Pigpen—he hasn't got one—and I fell asleep and I dreamed of a new character named José Peterson. That's a good name, isn't it? But I only put him in the strip for a week—he was a baseball player — but he just didn't belong, so out he went, along with some others I've gotten rid of. My strip is not like the kind that depends on variety or new characters. I've got pretty much the same characters and basic idea that I had 17 years ago. I want to keep the strip simple. I like it, for example, when Charlie Brown watches the first leaf of fall float down and then walks over and just says, 'Did you have a good summer?' That's the kind of strip that gives me pleasure to do.

"I liked one I did that I got from one of my children — the only idea I've ever gotten right from something they did or said. We were at the dinner table and Amy was talking away on a real talking streak and finally I said, 'Can't you *please* be quiet?' and she was silent for a moment and then picked up a slice of bread and began to butter it, saying, 'Am I buttering too loud for you?'

"I gave the line to Charlie Brown after Lucy yelled at him. And I like the violent action ones, kids getting bowled over and such things that cartoons were born to do. Too many of these new strips are not cartoons—they're imitations of films, and the movies can do it so much better, beat them at their own game. But I like the quiet ones too. I like it when Linus says, simply: 'Sucking your thumb without a blanket is like eating a cone without ice cream.' I like it when Charlie Brown gets all excited about a big spelling bee and then goes out on the first word because they say, 'Spell "maze,"' and, being the good baseball fan he is, he spells it 'Mays.' I like to keep it all simple. For instance, it seems to me that Snoopy's been getting pretty fantastical lately. I think I'll simplify him, let him just be a dog for a while.

"Incidentally, Snoopy wasn't in the most popular strip I ever did, the one I've had the most mail on. That was the one where the kids are looking at the clouds and Linus says, 'See that one cloud over there? It sort of looks like the profile of Thomas Eakins, the famous portrait painter. And that other group over there—that looks as though it could be a map of British Honduras. And then do you see that large group of clouds up there? I see the stoning of Stephen. Over to the side I can see the figure of the apostle Paul standing.' Then Lucy says, "That's very good, Linus. It shows you have quite a good imagination. What do you see in the clouds, Charlie Brown?' And Charlie says, 'Well, I was going to say I saw a ducky and a horsey, but I've changed my mind.' "

The phone rang and he talked for a while. When he hung up he said, "That was something about having a helicopter be attacked by the Red Baron. Over Chicago. They've got a real German World War I plane. Publicity stunt of some kind." He shook his head incredulously, and a little sheepishly, at the world he had created. "Where's it all going to end?"

Where, indeed, is it all going to end? Last Thursday I came home from work, hungry for dinner, to find the entire kitchen given over to the making of a two-foot birthday cake for my daughter. It was in the shape and color of Snoopy. Like any other red-blooded male of this generation, I could only look straight out of the panel at the reader and say, "Good grief!" ■

SCHULZ AT WORK—One day's strip takes him about an hour to draw; the Sunday page, all day.

HOME GROUND—A section of the roadway that Charles Schulz walks each morning to his studio.

Returning From the 25th Century...

Above, the well-remembered logotype. Right, there was also snappy dialogue.

Below, a splashdown of some 40 years ago. Today, "she" would be a frogman.

Chelsea House-National Newspaper Syndicate

By McCANDLISH PHILLIPS

Buck Rogers, for nearly 40 years a syndicated wanderer in space, is flying again because a City College professor and a Manhattan publisher judged his grounding to be premature.

Rogers was forced into retirement, a casualty of the space age, when science caught up with the comic strip he appeared in and it was killed in July, 1967.

Now, however, a chronicle of his adventures has been presented in book form, "The Collected Works of Buck Rogers in the 25th Century," published recently by Chelsea House and distributed by Random House at $12.50.

The bulk of the 376-page, 11- by 14-inch volume is given over to 12 complete episodes of the strip, which had originally appeared in newspapers between 1929 and 1949.

The episodes include "The Mongols" (1929), "Martians Invade Jupiter" (1942), and two episodes in Sunday supplement color: "Martians Invade Earth" (1939), and "Battle on the Moon"(1948).

A striking thing about the strip is that some of its aerospace inventions are remarkably similar to those in use today, both in principle and design.

"What was the world like then?" Ray Bradbury, the science fiction writer, asks in an introduction to the book, speaking of 1929. "It was a world without even so much as one small rocket, or the promise of one. . . . The first streamlined trains were merely in blueprint stage (and passengers) departed the color of milk, arrived the color of soot. . . . Radio? The merest infant. . . . So, for all intents and purposes, compared to 1968, I was raised, all of the Twenties boys were raised, in the last steams of Steamboat America, in the last go-round of the fringed surreys, milk-trucks, and ice-wagons drawn by summer-lazy horses."

Into that world Phil Nowlan and Dick Calkins, writer and illustrator, respectively, brought rocket ships trailing blazing plumes of fire, and speed sleds and atomic disintegrator guns and weightless flight and inertron, described as "a synthetic element of great reverse weight which falls away from the center of the Earth instead of toward it, and which counterbalances all but a few pounds of the wearer's weight."

"The enemy of every boy is gravity," Mr. Bradbury writes, "and here in the first few days of Buck Rogers that incredible stuff 'inertron' plucks us off our feet and hurls us through the sky, free at last."

"And with a cat's-hair crystal radio in one pocket and our Lon Chaney vampire-teeth in the other, beaten down by dull reality, dying for romance, we waded out into the sea of space and happily drowned," Mr. Bradbury fondly recalls.

Buck Rogers, he says, was his "first, huge mania."

Delighted with the eloquence of Mr. Bradbury's tribute, the publishers invited the science-fiction writer to wade out into the ozone and come to New York for interviews and were a bit taken aback to discover that "our moon man won't take a plane ride."

The book, Harold Steinberg, a founder of Chelsea House, said, is "half camp and half Americana." A perusal suggests that it is hokum, but Mr. Steinberg is no ordinary bookseller. He is the man who found a way of selling Sears, Roebuck catalogues to Sears, Roebuck. Chelsea House published the first of the turn-of-the-century mail order catalogues as a collector's item in 1968. They sold so well (140,000 copies, it is said) that Sears, Roebuck began buying copies, advertising them in its catalogues and selling them by mail.

On splashdown day of the United States' first moonshot, Mr. Steinberg saw Rick Yager, who drew Buck Rogers for many years, on a television news show. The experience sparked the idea for the book.

Mr. Steinberg asked Fred Israel, a City College professor who had thought up the Sears, Roebuck catalogue reprint, to call Robert C. Dille, president and editor of the National Newspaper Syndicate and son of John Flint Dille, the man who originated Buck Rogers.

"Anybody that can move an 1897 Sears, Roebuck catalogue can move Buck Rogers," Mr. Dille concluded. Given the job of selecting the best of Buck Rogers for the book, he read through 38 years of Rogers strips in 8 days.

"I got blurry," Mr. Dille said in a telephone interview. "Just kept steadily at it, did nothing else, started at 9:30 A.M. and read to 2 A.M."

Mr. Dille was extremely reluctant to say what the effect of reading 38 years of Buck Rogers had been on him, but at length he said that he found things in it that "give great hope for mankind" along with "other things that take you to ultimate despair."

He found "the parallelisms" between the strip's fantasies and the present realities "frightening." He regarded the Red Mongols who were destroying much of North America as a sad indication of "a prevalent view that there is something sinister about the Orient," but, again, the parallels between conjecture and history struck him.

But the similarities were a result of something better than pure guesswork, Mr. Dille said.

"There wasn't a month in my father's life when he wasn't on the quadrangle of the University of Chicago. He was constantly in touch with scientists and with educational and industrial leaders, men of unusually curious natures. As soon as he said he was associated with Buck Rogers, a guy would start pouring out his ideas of what the future was going to be like," and some of it showed up in the strip.

Buck Rogers began on Jan. 6, 1929, in 47 newspapers. The strip appeared in 287 papers at its high point in 1934, was translated into 18 foreign languages for use in more than 40 countries and ran in more than 450 newspapers altogether. Its distribution had dwindled to 28 papers in the United States when it was killed on July 8, 1967.

December 2, 1969

'Terry' of the Comics Is Facing Taps at 38

By LAWRENCE VAN GELDER

Lieut. Col. Terry Lee. Born, Oct. 19, 1934. Scheduled to die, Feb. 25, 1973.

Perhaps another victim of the war in Vietnam, perhaps a casualty of shifting tastes, Terry Lee has been handed his discharge from the army of heroes whose adventures enthrall devotees of the comic strips.

After Feb. 25, having disrupted a plot by an aerial acrobatic team from Latin America to smuggle narcotics into the United States, Terry Lee—and all the cast of "Terry and the Pirates"—will be no more.

"When I learned about this," said Milton Caniff, who created the strip and abandoned it to begin Steve Canyon in 1947, "I felt as if my children—long since departed—were going to be executed."

A Vanishing Audience

Terry, which once enjoyed an audience estimated at more than 30 million in more than 300 newspapers, was relegated from the drawing board to the chopping block after George Wunder, who succeeded Mr. Caniff, decided to resign.

"It still had quite a few fans," said Arthur Laro, the president and editor of The Chicago Tribune-New York News Syndicate, which distributes Terry. But, he acknowledged, the number of newspapers carrying "Terry

Left: Part of the "Terry and the Pirates" strip created by Milton Caniff in 1934. Above: part of strip's last adventure, with Terry piloting a jet, done by George Wunder.

and the Pirates" has been declining for some time, although, he said, more than 100 still feature it.

"We had a debate whether to continue the strip or not," Mr. Laro said. "After talking with several artists, we decided not to go ahead with it."

The Daily News, which carried Terry in New York City, sent him packing in mid-adventure on Feb. 3. The action prompted about 25 letters and postcards and a "substantially" higher number of telephone calls, a spokesman for The Daily News said.

'Smilin' Jack' Downed

Several years ago, The Daily News also dropped another adventure-flying strip, "Smilin' Jack." Mr. Laro said "Smilin' Jack" was still being syndicated, but would end a 40-year run on April 1 because Zack Mosley, its creator, was retiring.

Mr. Mosley, like Mr. Wunder and Mr. Caniff, is i nhis 60's.

Mr. Wunder confessed to mixed reactions about ending his association with "Terry and the Pirates" after 26 years. "It's a strip I've enjoyed doing," he said, "but on the other hand it has been, oh, a chore. The sheer mechanics of producing that much work week in and week out ties you down."

Asked if he knew of anything to account for the decline in popularity of a strip whose Dragon Lady, Big Stoop, Hot-Shot Charlie, Burma, Pat Ryan and Flip Corkin once captivated such fans as the Duke of Windsor, Margaret Truman and John Steinbeck, Mr. Wunder replied:

"I really don't, other than the fact that taste in strips seems to be changing. People just don't seem to follow continuity strips any more the way they used to. They get an average of three to four complete stories a night off the boob tube. There's no reason why they should hang around anywhere from 8 to 12 weeks to find out just how one story came out.

The war in Vietnam, he said, had a lot to do with the end of Terry, even though the hero was never a participant. He pointed out that the basic premise of Terry, who took up flying at the outbreak of World War II, was that of the fighter pilot, a breed that once had the image of square-jawed young men on a new frontier. The image, he said, has changed to that of droppers of napalm on women and children.

Dragon Lady

Tastes in 1934 were somewhat different. On a summer day, Mr. Caniff, who was working for The Associated Press Feature Service here and had created a strip called "Dicky Dare," answered a summons to the office of Capt. Joseph Patterson, publisher of The Daily News, who offered him a chance to do a new comic strip.

Captain Patterson suggested the Orient — a last outpost of adventure — as the locale, a youngster to attract a juvenile following, a handsome hero to create love interest and someone zany to provide comedy.

During the next three days and nights, Mr. Caniff, who had never been to the Orient, prepared a sample. The youngster, 12 years old, was named Tommy Tucker. The hero was Pat Ryan. The comic figure was named George Webster Confucius. And Pat and Tommy were in China to find a secret mine.

Mr. Caniff called the strip "Tommy Tucker." Captain Patterson liked everything, but the name. So Mr. Caniff prepared a list of new names, and the publisher circled "Terry" and wrote next to it, "and the Pirates."

The strip bred not only avid fans, but also a radio program and even a television show.

Mr. Caniff, whose Steve Canyon is running in 638 papers, said he had written to Mr. Wunder to compliment him on his work.

Mr. Caniff said he had no plans to quit. "Oh, heavens no," he said, "not as long as you can make a buck."

Suggested Reading

General Works

Cantor, Norman F., and M. S. Werthman. *History of Popular Culture.* New York, Macmillan, 1968. Pb.

Gans, Herbert. *Popular Culture and High Culture.* New York, Basic Books, 1974.

Nye, Russel B., *The Unembarrassed Muse.* New York, Dial Press, 1970.

Rosenberg, Bernard, and David Manning White. *Mass Culture: The Popular Arts in America.* New York, The Free Press, 1967. Pb.

Mass Culture Revisited. New York, Van Nostrand, Reinhold, 1971. Pb.

White, David Manning, ed. Popular Culture in America: 1800-1925. A reprint series of 27 titles. New York, Arno Press, 1974.

Popular Literature

Hackett, Alice P. *Seventy Years of Best Sellers.* New York, Bowker, 1967.

Hart, James D. *The Popular Book.* New York, Oxford, 1950.

Haycroft, Howard, *The Art of the Mystery Story.* New York, Simon and Schuster, 1966.

Murder for Pleasure. New York, Appleton-Century, 1941.

Madden, David, ed. *Tough Guy Writers of the Thirties.* Carbondale, Ill., Southern Illinois Univ. Press, 1968.

Moscowitz, Sam. *Explorers of the Infinite.* Westport, Ct., Hyperion, 1974. Pb.

Seekers of Tomorrow. Westport, Ct. Hyperion, 1974. Pb.

Mott, Frank Luther. *Golden Multitudes.* New York, Macmillan, 1947.

Nolan, William F. *Dashiell Hammett: A Casebook.* Santa Barbara, Calif., McNally and Loftin, 1969.

Watson, Colin. *Snobbery with Violence: Crime Stories and Their Audience.* New York, St. Martins, 1972.

The Stage

Green, Stanley. *The World of Musical Comedy.* 2nd rev. ed. Cranberry, N. J., A. S. Barnes, 1973.

Toll, Robert C. *Blacking Up: The Minstrel Show in Nineteenth-Century America.* New York, Oxford, 1974.

Wilson, Garff B. *Three Hundred Years of American Drama and Theatre.* Englewood Cliffs, N.J., Prentice-Hall, Inc., 1973.

The Screen

Adler, Renata. *Year in the Dark.* New York, Random House, 1970.

Crist, Judith. *The Private Eye, the Cowboy, and the Very Naked Girl.* Chicago, Holt, Rinehart and Winston, 1968.

Gabree, J. *Gangsters from Little Caesar to the Godfather.* Pb: Elmhurst, N.Y., Pyramid, 1973.

Garfield, Brian. *The Complete Guide to Western Films.* New York, McKay, 1975.

Powdermaker, Hortense. *Hollywood the Dream Factory.* Boston, Little Brown, 1950. Pb.

Rosenberg, Bernard, and Harry Silverstein. *Real Tinsel: The Story of Hollywood Told by the Men and Women Who Lived It.* New York, Macmillan, 1970.

Seldes, Gilbert. *The Public Arts.* New York, Simon and Schuster, 1957. Pb.

The Great Audience. New York, Viking, 1950

White, David Manning, and Richard Averson. *The Celluloid Weapon and Social Comment in American Films.* Boston, Beacon Press, 1973.

Radio and Television

Bogart, Leo. *The Age of Television: A Study of Viewing Habits and the Impact of TV on American Life.* 3rd ed. New York, Frederick C. Ungar, 1970.

Buxton, Frank, and Bill Owen. *The Big Broadcast: 1920-1950.* Rev. ed. (original title, *Radio's Golden Age*) New York, Viking, 1972. Pb, Avon.

Harmon, Jim. *The Great Radio Heroes.* Garden City, N.Y., Doubleday, 1967.

Higby, Mary Jane. *Tune In Tomorrow.* New York, 1968.

Lichty, Lawrence W., and Malachi C. Topping. *American Broadcasting: A Source Book on the History of Radio and Television.* New York, Hastings, 1974.

McLuhan, Marshall. *Understanding Media.* New York, Macmillan, 1964.

Sterling, Christopher H., *et al.*, eds. "*History of Broadcasting: Radio to Television.*" 32 books; reprint. New York, Arno, 1972.

White, David Manning, and Richardson Averson. *Sight and Sound and Society.* Boston, Beacon Press, 1968.

Music

Ewen, David. *Great Men of American Popular Song.* Rev ed. New York, Prentice Hall, 1972.

Panorama of American Popular Music. New York, Prentice Hall, 1957.

Nanry, Charles, ed. *American Music: From Storyville to Woodstock.* Rutgers, J.J., Transaction, 1972. Pb.

Atkins, Chet, and Bill Neely. *Country Gentlemen.* New ed. Chicago, Regnery, 1974.

Garland, Phyl, *Sound of Soul.* Chicago, Regnery, 1969. Pb.

Mattfield, Julius. *Variety Music Cavalcade: Musical-Historical Review,* 1620-1961. Englewood Cliffs, N.J., Prentice Hall, 1966.

Sander, Ellen. *Trips: Rock Life in the Sixties.* New York, Scribner, 1973.

Wilder, Alex. *American Popular Song: The Great Innovators, 1900-1950.*

The Comics

Couperie, Pierre, and Maurice Horn. *A History of the Comic Strip.* New York, Crown, 1968. Pb.

Robinson, Jerry. *The Comics.* New York, Putnam, 1974.

White, David Manning, and Robert Abel. *The Funnies: An American Idiom.* New York, Free Press, 1963.

Index